MATTHIAS

st date

Revolutionary Empire

by the same author

RUSSIA DISCOVERED: NINETEENTH-CENTURY
FICTION FROM PUSHKIN TO CHEKHOV

THE PEOPLE'S WAR

Revolutionary Empire

The Rise of the English-Speaking Empires from the Fifteenth Century to the 1780s

ANGUS CALDER

JONATHAN CAPE

THIRTY BEDFORD SQUARE LONDON

First published 1981
© Angus Calder 1981

Jonathan Cape Ltd, 30 Bedford Square, London WC1

British Library Cataloguing in Publication Data
Calder, Angus
Revolutionary empire.
1. Great Britain – Colonies
I. Title
909'.09'7521   DA18
ISBN 0-224-01452-8

PRINTED IN THE UNITED STATES OF AMERICA

For David Rubadiri and Ngugi Wa Thiong'o

We carry in our worlds that flourish
Our worlds that have failed ...

CHRISTOPHER OKIGBO

Contents

Illustrations

MAPS

Preface

For kind permission to reproduce illustrations, I wish to thank the following: the Warden and Fellows of All Souls College, Oxford, 27; American Antiquarian Society, 14; Ashmolean Museum, Oxford, 3; Royal Hospital of Saint Bartholomew's, 10; Boston Athenaeum, 68; British Library, 6, 8, 9, 19; Anne S. K. Brown Military Collection, Brown University Library, 64, 65; City Museum and Art Gallery, Hanley, Stoke-on-Trent, 40; Colonial Williamsburg Foundation, 62; Cyfartha Castle Museum and Art Gallery, Merthyr Tydfil, 80; Dyrham Park, the National Trust, 21; Edinburgh University Library, 1, 13, 31; Mary Evans Picture Library, 32, 34, 51; the Director of the India Office Library and Records, 12, 23, 43, 53, 55, 56; Kungliga Biblioteket, 11; Library Company of Philadelphia, 24; Library of Congress, 26, 67; Mansell Collection, 50; Massachusetts Historical Society, 60; Merseyside County Museums, p. 625; Mrs Elizabeth Murray, 46; National Gallery of Canada, Ottawa, 45 (gift of the Duke of Westminster, 1918), 63; National Library of Ireland, 52; Trustees of the National Library of Scotland, 20, 30, 41, 48, 58, 73, 77; National Maritime Museum, London, 5, 7, 33, 36, 71, on loan from M.O.D. Navy: 76, 79; National Museum of Wales, 78; National Portrait Gallery, London, 4, 17, 18, 28, 29, 37, 38, 49, 54, 69, 70, 72; New York Public Library (I. N. Phelps Stokes Collection of American Historical Prints), 35; Pilgrim Society, Plymouth, Massachusetts, 15; Private Collections, 66, 82; Public Archives of Canada, Ottawa (neg. no. C–2001), 81; St Louis Art Museum, 42; Science Museum, London, 74, 75; Scottish National Portrait Gallery, 16, 22, 47; Trustees of Sir John Soane's Museum, 44; Stichting Johan Maurits van Nassau, 25; Tate Gallery, London, 2; Victoria and Albert Museum, Crown Copyright, 57; Yale University Art Gallery, 39 (bequest of Eugene Phelps Edwards, 1938), 59 (bequest of Edith Malvina K. Wetmore), 61 (gift of Roger Sherman White, B.A. 1859, M.A., L.L.B. 1862, Jan. 1918). For the map on p. 126 I would like to acknowledge reference made to 'Tudor Plantations' by K. W. Nicholls in *A New History of Ireland III*, ed. T. W. Moody, F. X. Martin and F. J. Byrne, © Oxford University Press on behalf of the Editors and Contributors.

I am also indebted to Michael Yeats for permission to reproduce extracts from 'Nineteen Hundred and Nineteen' and 'Meditations in Time of Civil War' by W. B. Yeats.

Any writer who takes eight years to complete a book must have conversations with so many people who give him tips or set his thoughts off on new tracks that proper acknowledgment will be impossible. These are the thanks I remember to give.

My debts to published historians, dead or alive, are partly acknowledged in my references and bibliography; yet sometimes a book cited only once or twice here will have given me days of instruction.

To my family and friends, this is the place to apologise for all those occasions when I have been with O Leary in the grave and oddly reluctant to come out.

The Scottish Arts Council gave my wife Jenni the money for her own researches which enabled us both to visit the U.S.A. and Canada, and gave me the grant which permitted me to go to Malta, where Daniel Massa and Nora Zammit provided kind help. The British Council, prompted by James Stewart, sent me on a tour to Kenya and Mauritius, and the Inter-University Council, likewise prompted by Adrian Roscoe, provided me with a month in Malawi, where J. B. Webster and his colleagues in the History Department of Chancellor College were also most hospitable.

To the staff of the National Library of Scotland I owe vast gratitude for excellent service. The Librarian of Edinburgh University kindly allowed an outsider invaluable borrowing facilities. The Sterling and Beinecke Libraries at Yale University, the Royal Commonwealth Society Library and the Library of the University of Malta have also given me accommodation, with results which will, I hope, appear in the sequel to this volume.

I owe great debts to George Shepperson, Ian Duffield and Christopher Fyfe who, amongst other kindnesses, have invited me year after year to participate in seminars in Edinburgh University's Department of History and Centre for African Studies.

For stimulating talk, useful references, loan or gift of books and articles, and on occasion criticism or reassurance, I am grateful more than some probably realise to Robert Anderson, Tom Barron, Jack Bumstead, Nigel Calder, Henry Cowper, Cairns Craig, Harry Dickinson, Ian Donnachie, Owen Dudley Edwards, Paul Edwards, Nuruddin Farah, Neal Fraser, Henry Frendo, Chris Harvie, Fay Jacobson, Arnold Kettle, Victor Kiernan, Kenneth King, Bernth Lindfors, Tom Lowenstein, Charlie Myles, Kole Omotoso, Nick Phillipson, Kenneth Richards, John Riddy, Lord Ritchie-Calder, George and Zara Steiner, Dennis Walder and Phil Wigley. Duncan and Susan Rice, and Robin Winks were most helpful when I was lucky enough to work at Yale. Anthony Thwaite, Claire Tomalin and Liz Thomas, as literary editors of the *New Statesman*, indulged me with books I wanted to read for review.

And I should not forget to thank those Open University students who studied 'the Age of Revolutions' with me, with results which appear in the title as well as in the detail of this book.

I am most affectionately grateful to Liz Austin for her long labours to produce a fair typescript, unaided until near the end. I also called on the help of Mrs Sheila Somerville and Mrs S. Campbell.

Very special thanks must go to people who agreed to undertake the horrid task of reading draft MS. Alan Day, David Daiches and Gary Dickson were kind enough to comment on large chunks. Reid Mitchell commented on the whole book in proof.

Michael Sissons, as my agent, has skilfully made this long operation possible. I could not have worked on without the unfailing patience and sympathy of David Machin at Jonathan Cape, nor finalised the book without the warm help of his successor, Liz Calder, and of Jill Sutcliffe, and the very careful labours of Jane Hill. Valerie Buckingham helped find illustrations.

To Alastair Niven, I owe more encouragement and support than he will have guessed or have chosen to remember. Graham Martin, though extremely busy with other things, found time to read the whole book in final draft, and picked out scores of infelicities and confusions. Paul Addison, throughout, has been a confidant and energiser without whom my whitened bones must have littered the trail. And my deepest thanks to Jenni Calder.

A.C.

Introduction

I

Nairobi, 1968. Very recently arrived to lecture in literature at the then 'University College', now University, I am sitting on the veranda of the Norfolk Hotel, the oldest building in town, with David Rubadiri, old friend and fellow student at Cambridge. He introduces me to Reuben, a serious Kenyan in a dark suit. A carriage, which children love to swarm over, stands in the centre of the veranda. As if to teach a lesson to a tyro, Reuben tells me about such carriages. Horses did not pull them. Once a famous gallant imperialist, white settler, beat, Reuben says (I have never checked this story) to death the African who was pulling his carriage, for not going fast enough. From this veranda, where Lord Delamere stood and shot elephants in the earliest days of white occupation, Tom Mboya, not long before independence, was kicked by outraged whites for his intrusion.

Dublin, 1973. The taxi-driver, Irishly talkative to perfection, points out the 1916 bullet holes preserved in the colonnade of the post office as he drives us up O Connell Street. There was trouble in Dublin last night – he blames it on Ulstermen and, searching for explanations, begins to talk about Wolfe Tone. But he is soon remarking that he was born in Manchester and did his National Service in the British Army in Cyprus; he is happiest to discuss the latest performances of the England soccer team. British currency is cheerfully accepted here. Though the post boxes are painted green, most still bear the initials VR or EVIIR or GVR. The centre of Dublin is being transformed. A new Liberty Hall in glass and concrete, headquarters of the Transport and General Workers Union, towers over Gandon's great Customs House. Georgian streets are gashed with building sites. Expensive suburban housing advances boldly into the glens of Wicklow from which O Tooles and O Byrnes once came down to harry the Pale. Yet many things remind us of 'underdevelopment'. The little general shops, like East African *dukas*, stock a mélange of cheap necessities, bananas and cakes, fading magazines. Small boys serve in bars. Women with babes in arms and dirty faces beg on the O Connell Bridge.

Mauritius, 1975. On tour for the British Council, I sit perusing my notes one morning in the delicious courtyard of a hotel, under whispering palms. An extremely small, very depressed looking woman, descended from slaves brought from East Africa to serve French painters, is slowly, one would say grudgingly, at work watering the lawn. She is almost certainly ill with malnutrition. The people here, Asian, Creole, are mostly small. The lush green of sugar which still ripples over the island seems inexpressibly mournful and sinister.

Malta, 1978. Another overcrowded small island, but somehow cheering. Farmers who still speak the unique Maltese language still work in the amazing little fields handmade down the centuries by carrying earth from here and there to mask bare stone. Yet Valletta, thanks to the Knights of St John and the British Navy, is a large proletarian city, on an island about one-seventh the size of Skye. Henry Frendo, a brilliant young Maltese historian, seems to see what I mean when I suggest that what has happened here is overdevelopment. At another time he remarks, with a combination of glee and anger, that on Gozo there is a ramshackle, flea-bitten pub which still bears the name 'Glory of England'. It's true. I see it myself.

North-eastern U.S.A., 1978. Traffic speeds on a six-lane turnpike through dense Connecticut woods. John Davenport's New Haven and Roger Williams's Providence are dominated by knots and loops of highway. Almost everywhere that Puritan pioneers settled, the insignia of suburbia glare: Howard Johnson's restaurants and Colonel Sanders's Kentucky Fried Chicken Houses, unvarying in their Disney-like design, as are McDonald's hamburger diners and Arthur Treacher's hygienic 'fish 'n' chip' shops. Each mighty shopping plaza seems the same. Yet escaping from the industrial wastelands of northern New Jersey, not far south, in that very state, there are fertile agreeable farmlands where Swedes (or more properly Finns?) were the first white farmers. The Jamestown peninsula in Virginia, deserted by planters as the tobacco weed marched inland, is still, though a playground for tourists, capable of evoking the mystery sensed by John Smith and his quarrelsome comrades, who woke at morning to the songs and cries of unknown birds in thick woods of unusually tall trees, to glimpse the flicker and poise of strange butterflies and the scamper of squirrels (grey, not red like the English ones), to endure by noon and later an unfamiliar, stifling summer heat by hazy blue water. And up through the very beautiful, rolling Piedmont, one reaches Monticello, middle-class man's loveliest monument, commanding its airy prospects of farmland and blue hills, where, stretching out on the grass, one can only exclaim, 'You lucky *bastard*, Jefferson.' There proves to be so much space in America, even in the north-east. How, with these rich-looking, near-empty vistas, can the world, one asks oneself, have a food problem? In the Pennsylvania lowlands, rather like Yorkshire, one still sees pubs named the Eagle and the Lion. But this vastness is nothing at all like home, really.

West Lothian, 1980. Home, at the moment, is this unique territory – a landscape, like Malta's, manmade, perpetually moving, where 'Beaker people' had forts before the Romans built the Antonine Wall, the feuding lairds reared their bristling castles, improving landlords drained bogs to provide rich fields, the canal, then the railway came, dug for by cursing Irish navvies, and 'Paraffin' Young's enterprise set shale miners to work heaping up manmade hills which, now that the industry is dead, are moments of time transfixed, russet and beautiful. The majestic Forth Road Bridge has now joined the chunky and legendary Rail Bridge. History crowds into a not-large space between wind-swept hills and grey sea, and makes, under Arthur's Seat, the severe splendour of Edinburgh's New Town, that heavenly city of the Scottish Enlightenment.

All this, one might say with pride, is the work of the hands and brains of Scots, their achievement in bitter winds, driving rain, an unkind environment. But that wouldn't be the whole truth. The history which explains what we see around us shows that Scotland acquired such wealth as its people have had very largely from trading, soldiering and investing overseas, from leeching upon the labour of Caribbean and Virginian slaves, Red Indian fur-hunters, Australian shepherds and shearers, Zulu gold-miners, and Asian peasants. Scots were spurred to effort not only by the dynamic of their grim Calvinist religion, fighting a stone-hearted God in a land of stone, but by jealousy of England's prosperity, of the wealth which colonies, sugar plantations, eastern 'factories', were bringing to England.

We need history then, at very least, so that we don't misunderstand what we see around us.

II

How can one write the history of the English-speaking peoples and their empires?

Not long ago, I found myself being beckoned towards a Chinese restaurant in downtown New Haven by the legend (as it must have been, in both senses), 'Our Chef Specialises in Mandarin, Cantonese and American food'. I felt a certain sympathy with his gymnastics.

One cannot, based on Scotland and striving to cover so much else, be at home, for instance, with the immense literature produced by native historians of America where, it would seem, no township of a thousand souls was too obscure to have its very own class struggle, and where 'democracy' is defined with such theological rigorousness and purism that one will horrify advanced minds if one mildly insinuates that, since the concept found its first comfortable home in the U.S.A., factors involved in the early colonial settlement may have foreshadowed it rather strongly. Nor can one keep abreast of the exciting torrent of work on slavery in the New World and in Africa, and on African history more generally which, properly understood and more widely known, should transform the treatment of all human history. Other historiographical schools — Anglo-Indian, Canadian, Australasian — have had and have very distinctive strengths and failings which can make it hard to find matching studies as one seeks to compare one area with another. Current Irish historians, honourably, are often so preoccupied with disarming murderous myths that they run the risk of blunting Cromwell's sword; meanwhile the notorious Scottish landlords of the 'Clearances' are locally execrated for doing precisely what Irish landlords of the same period are blamed for not having done, and few Scots have noted that their 'cleared' compatriots tended to thrive mightily in colonies where Irishmen fleeing from famine found menial jobs and slum conditions. And Englishmen, with that niceness of theirs, continue to write as if their own section of the home islands constituted the whole, apologising from time to time for their incapacity to cope with Scottish, Irish, and Welsh history.

So I may plead, in respect of my vast ignorance and my native failure to understand what it feels like to be a Virginian, a New Zealander, Bengali or Yoruba, that somebody, somewhere, had to try to put together the diverse 'stories' of the areas overrun and governed by English-speakers (together with many Gaels and not a few Welsh-speakers). These stories continually intersect, interact, determine each other, under conditions created or exposed by the 'expansion' of Europe from the fifteenth century onwards. If I can reveal or suggest more strongly than hitherto some of these links, interactions, dialectics, then my brokerage will not have been useless.

But granted that synthesis may, for a blink of time, clutch a few strands valuably together, how should and can one make readers 'feel' these links, those stories? Should one be telling stories at all?

In his masterly book, *The Ordeal of Thomas Hutchinson*, Bernard Bailyn argues, following Herbert Butterfield, that there are three stages in the interpretation of history. Firstly we have the 'heroic' accounts, written near to the events themselves, still, in effect, part of the events, emphasising overwhelmingly the significance of individuals. The 'whig' account follows from a safe distance. Individuality diminishes as the events take their places as links in a long chain of events and as the historian tries to show how the future, our present, was implicit in the past. Thirdly, we have 'tragic' history such as Bailyn wishes his memorable biography of Hutchinson to provide. The historian can now be neutral. 'He has no stake in the outcome. He can now embrace the whole of the event, see it from all sides. What impresses him most are the latent limitations within which everyone involved was obliged to act; the inescapable boundaries of action; the blindness of the actors — in a word, the tragedy of the event.'[1]

Yes, without people, without a vivid sense of men and women pitched against forces which they hope to control or evade but cannot master, history lacks its deepest significance. I have given a number of individuals, in these pages, relatively detailed attention. Most of these persons happen to be very famous. This does not mean that I believe for a moment that 'great men' and 'great women' act in history with autonomous force — I would insist, on the contrary, that their 'greatness' is a creation of trends and events. But neither am I a vulgar determinist. On the frontier of consciousness, *now*, we are free to make choices which influence events, as were King Oedipus, Hamlet, Ralegh, Hutchinson, Livingstone, Lenin. Only when choices have been made do they become 'inevitable', so that our history is partly like a coral reef raised on the corpses of millions of private choices.

The choices of people who are not famous also mattered. But since I am writing in this book about hierarchical, deferential societies, I am inclined to plead that my method is veridical. Describing pre-industrial rural England in *The Rainbow*, D. H. Lawrence writes of the women of the village, 'The lady of the Hall was the living dream of their lives, her life was the epic which inspired their lives.'[2] And we, many of us rejecting 'deference', carry the myth-making habit forward in our creation of Churchills, Kenyattas and Kennedys. Through their conspiracy to create the myths of Drake and Strafford and Pitt, their agreement during and after the lives of such men to invest them with the status of representative heroes and demons, ordinary people participate in the tragic life of this volume. Events in America in the 1770s were 'revolutionary' because they hoisted obscure middle-class provincials suddenly into such heroic and representative roles; while the British middle classes, willy-nilly, thrust past 'deference', in that other, 'industrial' revolution.

But deference, inequality, are not dead, and this points us towards a fallacy in Bernard Bailyn's position. One must, even now, take sides for or against Thomas Hutchinson. What happened in Boston in the 1770s, counter to that man's 'tragic' efforts, was a necessary condition for the later experiment of 'democracy'. If we become 'neutral' we are in effect avoiding our own freedom to choose *now*, and resorting to undignified, and, one must add, anti-tragic fatalism.

III

Another master, Lawrence Stone, remarks acidly and with evident justice, ' ... The main thing which distinguishes the narrative from the analytical historian is that the former works within a framework of models and assumptions of which he is not always fully conscious, while the latter is aware of what he is doing and says so explicitly.'[3]

Rather, one might say, as any 'modernist' novel is an 'anti-novel' engaged in perpetual criticism of the narrative act which the reader expects from writers of fiction. I once thought of trying to produce, in this book, a historiographical counterpart to the fiction of Virginia Woolf.

Large-scale historical narrative has fallen out of fashion – not, it would seem, with the general reading public, which likewise continues on the whole to prefer fiction written, still, within the conventions of nineteenth-century 'realism', but, most emphatically, with serious historians. One reason relates to the morphology of all artistic genres. Euripides, had he merely imitated Sophocles, could have said nothing fresh, made no new impression. The intellectual children and grandchildren of Sir Walter Scott, historians as well as novelists, have, definitively, been there before us. Able men, some of them much more than able, wrote imposing narratives through the nineteenth and early twentieth centuries. Scott stamped his pattern on Scotland, Macaulay on England, Lecky on Ireland, while Bancroft and Parkman, and their counterparts in other ex-colonies, asserted similar kinds of authority. The best works of the school have not wholly fictitious fire and colour. It would be distasteful for an ambitious man to attempt to repeat what is well done already. Students can always be referred (if not with sneers, with cautions) to serried ranks of volumes bespeaking the industry of our recent forebears. Now the brilliant monograph, the discursive essay, the epigrammatic survey of several centuries, or the 'overdue' trail-blazing biography, are the routes to fame for a new historian.

A graver reason for our mistrust of narrative relates to the collapse of nine-teenth-century liberalism, whether in its nationalist or internationalist variants, as a code for serious people. Yeats wrote in 'Nineteen Hundred and Nineteen' as revolution swept across war-wrecked Europe,

> We pieced our thoughts into philosophy,
> And planned to bring the world under a rule,
> Who are but weasels fighting in a hole.

Like nineteenth-century domestic novelists, narrative historians required a satisfactory conclusion. Justice was done at last. All the pain was worthwhile. A typical 'whig' narrator would draw from the past explanations for our own present comfort, enlightenment and general rightness:

> O what fine thought we had because we thought
> That the worst rogues and rascals had died out ...[4]

But the Battle of the Somme, like Leopold's Congo, mocked all virtuous national destinies, mingling several in the mud. Dachau, Dresden, Hiroshima have ground home the message — stories which promise happy endings, wrongs righted, are lying. Where the brooding Pole, Conrad, the watchful Yankee, James, had begun to lead before the nineteenth century ended, other clever people have followed, including historians. Ladies in hats read romances; bright students are into Faulkner and Pynchon.

Sound men now believe that history is bogus. They swipe off its tricorn or top hat and pull down its breeches or trousers. Forget the little epics of school textbooks, the tales passed from grandfather to grandchild, the well-loved original 'sources' like Bradford's *On Plimouth Plantation* or Horace Walpole's letters. Shakespeare misleads us. Scott is a faker. What were alive were statistics and analyses. As I have heard Eugene Genovese observe, it should soon be pos-sible to prove econometrically that the American Civil War never happened. Unless we can calculate the median size of a New England colonial family, Governor Bradford can tell us nothing of import.

Such positivism, in correct doses, is healthy. Like so many prescriptions for health it is, taken too far, life-denying. (One remembers the story of the man who has reached 100 years being asked by a local newspaper reporter to what he attributes his longevity. 'I've never touched alcohol, never smoked,' he says, 'and never had anything to do with women.' Smashing wine-glasses, feminine giggles, are heard above. 'What's *that?*' inquires the anxious reporter. 'Oh, that's just my father, having another party.')

Man lives by stories as well as by bread. He fits his own childhood, his mating, his aspirations, into narrative structures, irresponsibly failing to question the 'models' he is using. Man, to adapt George Steiner, is not only a 'language animal', but also a 'narrative animal'. My own maternal grandfather, a hoary sceptic in the tradition of independent-minded Scottish Calvinism, nurtured my boyish curiosity with such remarks as 'Gladstone was a blackguard ... David Livingstone, *he* was a blackguard.' But if I had asked him to explain why the received heroic tales so lacked truth for him, he would have had to tell me stories. While Namierism has fooled many sages into believing that eighteenth-century Britons were unembarrassed by ideas and ideals except in so far as these barely masked their naked, rude and quantifiable appetites, while psephologists and allied tradesmen try to persuade us that graphs of public opinion are some-how what politics are about, uninstructed persons of all ages and classes, and both sexes (and even these same severe thinkers, when they switch on their television sets after a hard day's Gradgrinding and myth-bashing) inanely insist on believing that life has heroes and villains, epics and tragedies, and that these will proceed on a *Star Trek* into outer space with humankind, when it goes there.

IV

But we see in Ulster and in South Africa how much harm an Orangeist, Sinn Fein or Afrikaner historical mythology can abet. Both the English and the Scots have false views of their separate and related histories which promote intellectual crassness and psychological confusion. Can a more truthful and useful story be told, digesting some of the insights of recent 'analysts'? One must hope that there are better ways of correcting racialist fallacies than televising *Roots*, with its endearingly unselfconscious deployment of antique melodramatic stereotypes and narrative patterns, its sturdily unexamined model of *Homo Americanus (Niger)* hitting, at last, the trail west. New lies may do as much harm as old lies. To say that Livingstone *was* a blackguard, and no more than a blackguard, won't do.

Perhaps a truer sense of what life has been like, of the contradictory forces moving the past's countless tragedies into our own hopefully tragic lifetimes, will save no lives from pogroms; but then, neither will scholarly monographs. To explain how capitalism and statecraft have denatured the world in ways more vivid than those of the theorist will not in itself halt brutalism; nor will the most immaculate theory.

We had fed the heart on fantasies,
The heart's grown brutal from the fare;

> More substance in our enmities
> Than in our love; O honey-bees,
> Come build in the empty house of the stare.[5]

The hope may be held that, if bad narratives have palpably helped to inculcate maiming fallacies, better narrative might start to make a difference. It is a slim hope; but why write otherwise?

So this story is not just about men. It is an essential feature of the capitalism which emerged in Europe and has spread from there over the last few hundred years, that it gives commodities a life of their own while turning human labour, and even the human person, into commodities. If my tale is anything like an epic, its main characters are called 'Spices', 'Tobacco', 'Sugar', 'Tea', 'Cotton'. Sugar links Africa and the New World in a sinister pattern to which another commodity, Man, is also essential. Slave-grown Cotton fuels Lancashire's 'industrial revolution' in which all workers, like slaves, become 'Hands'. Meanwhile Spices and Calico have taken Britons to India where, in the age of Tea they seize the chance to begin to capture what will prove to be Cotton's indispensable market in the age of consummated Steam.

In 1971, I began work towards a history of the British Empire from Tudor times to the present day, in one volume. After a year in which I failed to emerge from the Middle Ages I began to see that I had not foreseen the problems. In 1977, my patient publishers agreed that I would write a narrative ending in the 1860s, and then proceed to write a different kind of book about the last hundred years or so of empire. After the full fascination of Canadian and Australasian history had dawned on me, I realised that to abandon the infant U.S.A. in 1783 would be stultifying. The U.S.A. was the main sphere of British emigration. Its evolving 'democracy' had very obvious repercussions in Britain and the 'white' colonies, while Lancashire's textile industry depended on slave labour in the U.S. South.

The sequel to this book, *Empire and Democracy*, will end with the U.S.A.'s arrival at full independence, as a major military, industrial, and imperial power; at the point where Zeus really can challenge Chronos. After that, I would like to write a book about the latter years of the British Empire only. From 1865, narrative of the kind which I am attempting here would prove impossible unless, as writers commonly do, one were to leave out numerous interesting territories: Fiji, Somalia and Scotland, for instance. Analysis, by themes, will have to suffice.

But, till Appomattox, I am essaying a narrative of the years and processes which transformed Britain from a cluster of warring kingdoms and chiefdoms to international pre-eminence and which raised a new empire, latently mightier yet, on lands in North America purchased or seized from Amerindians. Each chapter aims to convey as much as possible of the experience, trials, tragedy, opportunities of one or at most two generations. The generation, as Scott and

Turgenev knew, and as some historians forget, is the natural unit of historical self-consciousness.

The problems involved in trying to bring so many stories into a single continuum will be obvious to any American, Canadian or Australian historian who has tried to digest the histories of a number of more or less diverse colonies, provinces, states into one narrative flow. Region by region or theme by theme, life would be easier. But the quiddity of the epoch would be lost. Correspondences, like contrasts, between different areas could only be stated, not amply displayed.

This narrative covers the days in which Western man was weaned from an 'oral' understanding of the past through ballads and folktales by the generalisation of literacy, and in which the projection of stories about the past was, in a sense, perfected by historians with the help of novelists. It is a story about people who believed that stories – those found in the Bible and the ancient classics, later those provided by up-to-date works of fiction and of reconstructive scholarship – captured the truth about life past and present. By the 1860s, the bewildering savagery of industrial society and of mechanised warfare, the increasing complexity and dominance of capitalist enterprise, the growing weight of the State, the new conditions of mass politics, are all helping to push commentators on life down towards the analysis of underlying causes. The consciousness of highly intelligent people ceases to move forward frankly and easily telling stories about themselves, about life. They become aware of the subconscious and notice that, like their books, they have been lying. While Samuel Smiles is writing his *Self Help* (1859), a tissue of uplifting stories about good men, theologians have begun to undermine faith in the veracity of the West's basic narrative, the Bible. My own narrative will end, not with justice done, but with triumph in tension with tragedy. Thanks to the empire-making process, at least the preconditions of 'democracy' will be present wherever white people outnumber black and brown in the English-speaking empires. In the age of Carlyle, Smiles and Dickens, of Abraham Lincoln and Walt Whitman, 'independent' labouring men are arriving in positions of esteem and even influence, and stories at last are being written in which working men, as workers, figure heroically. White labour at last is valued. The exploitation of black and brown labour and its rationalisation in racialism are both proceeding from strength to strength. David Livingstone roams the 'Heart of Darkness'.

Prologue: The World is the World's World

dalla man destra mi lasciai Sibilia,
dall'altra già m'avea lasciata Setta.
'O frati,' dissi 'che per cento milia
perigli siete giunti all'occidente
a questa tanto picciola vigilia
de' nostri sensi ch'è del rimanente,
non vogliate negar l'esperienza
di retro al sol, del mondo sanza gente.
Considerate la vostra semenza:
fatti non foste a viver come bruti,
ma per seguir virtute e canoscenza.'
Li miei compagni fec'io si aguti,
con questa orazion picciola, al camino,
che a pena poscia li avrei ritenuti ...

On my right hand I left Seville, on the other had already left Ceuta.
'O brothers,' I said, 'who through a hundred thousand perils have
reached the west, to this so brief vigil of the senses that remains to us
choose not to deny experience, in the sun's track, of the unpeopled
world. Take thought of the seed from which you spring. You were
not born to live as brutes, but to follow virtue and knowledge.' My
companions I made so eager for the road with these brief words that
I then could hardly have held them back ...

Ulysses, speaking in DANTE's *Inferno*, c. 1314[1]

I

In the third year of the Yungo-Lo reign period, an emperor of the Brilliant
dynasty sent forth the Three-Jewel Eunuch on a mission to the Western Oceans,
bearing vast amounts of gold and other treasures, with nearly forty thousand
men in sixty-two ships. The exploits of this Admiral, Chêng Ho, were 'such as
no eunuch before him, from the days of old, had equalled.' Beginning in 1405,
on this and six later expeditions, the great junks ranged from Borneo as far as
Zanzibar, from the Red Sea to the Ryukyu Islands of the Pacific. Before they

left on the expedition of 1432, the last, and perhaps the most dazzling of all, sailors erected a stele in gratitude to a Taoist goddess. 'We have traversed more than one hundred thousand *li* of immense water spaces, and have beheld in the ocean huge waves like mountains rising sky-high. We have set eyes on barbarian regions far away hidden in a blue transparency of light vapours while our sails, loftily unfurled like clouds, day and night continued their course with starry speed, breasting the savage waves as if we were treading a public thoroughfare.'[2]

Everywhere, the Chinese chronicler tells us, 'they made known the proclamations of the Son of Heaven, and spread abroad the knowledge of his majesty and virtue. They bestowed gifts upon the kings and rulers, and those who refused submission they overawed by the show of armed might. Every country became obedient to the imperial commands, and when Chêng Ho turned homewards, sent envoys in his train to offer tribute.'[3] Yet, or so this eighteenth-century writer relates, the Eunuch's men had to fight only three times in seven expeditions. The goods they carried, we can be sure, were welcome in every port — silks, porcelains, other unmatched products of China. And they were, we are told, tolerant of the customs of others. In Mecca, where Chêng Ho's father, a Muslim, had once been on pilgrimage, 'they conversed in the tongue of the Prophet and recalled the mosques of Yunnan, in India they presented offerings to Hindu temples, and venerated the traces of the Buddha in Ceylon.'[4] They were systematic and they were curious. From the East African coast, they brought back giraffes to entertain the Son of Heaven, their emperor.

With power like his, he could afford tolerance. Chêng Ho's 250 long-distance 'treasure ships' were drawn from a navy of 3,800, and had cannon. The largest of them would carry over 1,000 men. There was nothing anywhere to match these nine-masted products of a fertile and ancient tradition in technology which had been the first to produce the crossbow and the magnetic compass, gunpowder and cast iron, printing, stern-post rudders, paper and porcelain. Though the pugnacious Vietnamese to the south were at this very time successful in ejecting the Brilliant intruders who had occupied their country, wherever the Three-Jewel Eunuch sailed it was credited that Ming China was the greatest power on earth; as, indeed, it was.

The Ming dynasty, established in the mid-fourteenth century, would endure until the mid-seventeenth, providing 'one of the great eras of orderly government and social stability in human history' for a population greatly exceeding Europe's. The Ming political system would survive without much change until 1912.[5] An élite of officials selected by an empire-wide system of competitive examination, and supported by a much wider class of educated men, the so-called 'scholar gentry', most of them landholders, but not a hereditary nobility, governed great masses who provided compulsory labour services, paid their taxes, and fed the poets.

The Emperors were seen as representatives of all mankind before heaven, rulers of the central area of the world. People from smaller nations who wished to trade with China must pay formal tribute. After Chêng Ho's tours, foreigners flocked to Peking for this purpose. But as the fifteenth century wore on, the trouble and expense of receiving tribute missions as guests of state came to seem greater than the benefits of trade. What was the need, asked the scholar-bureaucrats, for an intercourse which brought nothing but superfluous exotic luxuries? Meanwhile, the threat of the Oirats grew behind the Great Wall, on China's north-west frontier. The Brilliant Emperors sent no more expeditions. The navy was permitted to run down. By 1500 it was a capital offence against imperial regulations to build a sea-going junk with more than two masts. The ocean was left to those who might want it.

Far to the west, in the ruins of the extinct Empire of Rum (which the Son of Heaven might as late as 1618 imagine to be paying tribute to him, when a stray foreign trader pretended to be its ambassador so as to gain facilities) there were barbarian peoples prepared to use the sea in order to reach the fabulous land of China, of Cathay, about which a travelling merchant from Venice, Marco Polo, had written at the end of the thirteenth century. Those who read his book, or the spurious tales of 'Sir John Mandeville', learnt of wonders of wealth and craft which Europe had never equalled. The Chinese, 'Mandeville' averred, sur-passed 'all the nations of the world in sublety of wit'. Their ruler, the Great Caan, he said, ate at a table made of gold and precious stones: 'For sickerly under the firmament is not so great a lord ne so rich, ne not so mighty as is the Great Caan of Tartary. Not Prester John, that is emperor of India the less and the more, ne the sultan of Babylon, ne the emperor of Persia, ne none other may be made comparison of til him.'[6]

As that roster of Asian potentates suggests, the wealth of the East dazzled Europeans and humbled them. Not for four centuries would Europe's traders be able to find much market for European goods there. As late as the 1790s, when Britain's navy dominated all the world's oceans, her ambassador would be snubbed and sent away with contumely when he tried to convince the Chinese Emperor that it would be worth his while to admit the merchants of the world's first industrialised nation more freely. Yet in little more than another century after that, the Chinese Empire would be in final ruin, and European powers would govern directly 85 per cent of the world's surface while dictating terms to almost all the rest. Only Japan would retain full independence, and that at the price of imitating Europe.

Many factors involved in this have been very imperfectly studied. We still know far too little about such things as fluctuations in climate and the dynamics of population growth, we are still too clumsy at comparing social systems of East, West and South, to explain neatly how this immense lurch of the world's political and economic balance can have occurred. But it is clear that Europe could not have surged outwards without the help of borrowings from Chinese technology. And it is also clear that the lure of Cathay was a crucial incentive.

In Marco Polo's day Mongols had ruled in Peking and Mongols had controlled the whole overland trade route from there to the Black Sea. Their tolerance had permitted Polo, and other Europeans, to penetrate Cathay by land. By the fifteenth century this was impossible. To sail directly to the East, to make contact with Prester John, who was supposed to be a Christian potentate, and beyond him to trade with Cathay and 'Cipango' (Japan), formed a group of motives, among others, for seafarers sent out by Prince Henry 'the Navigator' from the petty barbarian realm of Portugal. In 1434, the year after the great Ming voyages ceased, Gil Eannes, one of Henry's captains, doubled Cape Bojador, south of the Canary Islands, which, with its furious waves and currents, its shallows, its fogs, its unhelpful winds, had marked for Europeans a limit beyond which they had not dared to venture, in that realm of peril and hope where Dante had imagined dauntless Ulysses foundering suddenly on his last voyage. By 1488 the Portuguese, pressing south, had discovered what certain Chinese had already gathered – that Africa ended in a triangular tip, which Bartolomeu Dias rounded to enter the Indian Ocean.

In 1493, a Genoese adventurer serving the Spanish Crown, Cristóbal Colón ('Columbus') returned from a sea voyage by which he believed he had found a direct route to Cipango and Cathay. What he had in fact found, neither Chinese, nor Europeans, had known of.

II

The inhabitants of Cipango, not in fact vastly wealthy, bothered the Brilliant Emperors with their piracies at sea. One had written to their ruler in 1380, 'You stupid Eastern barbarians! ... You are haughty and disloyal; you permit your subjects to do evil.' Two years later the Japanese had replied: 'Heaven and Earth are vast; they are not monopolised by one ruler ... The world is the world's world; it does not belong to a single person.'[7]

At the time of Columbus's voyage no one – in East or West – had an inkling of all the worlds that there were in the world. It would happen that those who revealed the world to its peoples were Europeans who (like apes) had thin lips and copious body hair, rather than Africans who had little body hair, or Mongolian-type peoples, with rather more. Yet a visitor from another planet able to survey the earth in 1493 would not have discerned with ease any elements of superiority in European culture, even if China had been left out of the comparison.

The ruins of Rome would not have proved much; the largest temple in the world lay abandoned in a jungle in Indo-China. And if he had seen the stone cities built by the Incas in the Andes, the buildings of Florence, let alone Lisbon, might not have stirred him to wonder. The Koreans had been the first people to put to extensive use the method of printing from movable type. The bronze sculptures of Benin in West Africa could stand comparison with Donatello's.

Were Europeans most effervescent as traders? The Javanese merchant patricians who ruled Malacca, dominating narrow straits, creamed great wealth from the growing intercourse between India and ports east. The Sultan of Gujerat, lord of ports and textile workers, rivalled in his power the grandest monarchs of India's interior.

And Christianity would have seemed less vital, even less vitalising, than Islam, which was spreading down trade routes from the Middle East, making rapid headway in Indonesia and drawing to Mecca the spectacular pilgrimage of Askya Muhammad after he usurped the rule of the powerful West African empire of Songhay in 1496. The Hausa kingdom of Kano on the fringe of his was a centre of resort for Islamic scholars from far away, and on the Swahili coast of East Africa educated Muslim ruling classes dwelt in cool stone houses and ate off Chinese porcelain in a pretty chain of trading cities. Muslims, Turks, had captured the ancient Christian capital of Constantinople in 1453, and had then swept the Balkans from coast to coast. In the 1490s they defeated Christendom's best fleet, that of Venice, and ravaged the island city's mainland territory.

Europe was 'smaller and poorer' in the fifteenth century than it had been in the thirteenth.[8] Then, population had expanded beyond natural resources. The climate had changed for the worse early in the fourteenth century and decades of undernourishment had assisted the work of the bubonic plague, the 'Black Death', which had swept the continent from 1348, killing a quarter or a third of its people. The plague remained a regular visitant. Its victims stank horribly. Black buboes sprouted in their groins and armpits. Men were still helpless in the face of this and most other diseases. The expectation of life at birth and indeed into a person's teens was no more than thirty. The peasant lived with his beasts in a sooty hut. Illiteracy was still general. Pleasures and punishments were barbaric. The Church burnt witches and heretics at the stake. The miracle plays which expressed popular religion imitated these burnings, using, to achieve realism, dummies stuffed with animal bones and entrails. Even England, a country unusually centralised, had suffered a long series of civil wars. In the 1490s, invasion ravaged Italy, famine confronted Germany, outbreaks of plague in France emptied whole towns whose inhabitants fled to the forests and wastes and starved there, and Europe in general endured what was thought to be the first assault of syphilis. In an age when kings were as credulous as their crudest subjects, 'rumours and portents multiplied: monstrous births, rains of milk and blood, stains in the sky.'[9] Scholarly men expected the end of the world very shortly. Art and literature expressed the dominant morbid pessimism. 'Do not call me highness,' said John II, King of Portugal, towards his death in 1495, 'Do not call me highness, for I am only a sack of earth and worms.'[10] Confronted with these violent, demoralised idol-worshippers — one church in Germany contained no fewer than 17,443 holy relics, which were supposed to have the power of helping a person reduce his stay in purgatory by as much as two million years[11] — many Victorian explorers would have concluded rapidly that they needed to be governed in their own interests by the enlightened products of the British public school.

Yet, it was Europe which would produce such arrogant explorers. Geography is one partial explanation. Europe, V. G. Kiernan points out, 'was a big peninsula jutting out from Asia, broken up and nearly surrounded by seas. It had no huge cavernous interior like Asia's or Africa's, and always in one way or another looked outwards.'[12] The seas, and the great river Rhine, facilitated trade in the products of areas as different in their climates and resources as Sweden was (and is) from Italy. The first countries to 'expand' overseas, Portugal and Spain, peered over a narrow strait to Africa and found themselves on an easy route to America. There was in Europe a unique balance, tension, interaction between feudal lords dominating the countryside and, on the other hand, towns, independent or largely self-governing. Both lords and townspeople cherished privileges which gave them some power of self-assertion against kings, and which ensured scope for expansionist individuals.

'Imperialism' was not of course a fifteenth-century invention, nor even a European one. The Ming rulers governed a real 'empire', with numerous peoples gathered in one system. In every continent except Australia, rulers had managed at one time or another to subordinate collections of numerous separate peoples or states. Europeans had behind them the example of Imperial Rome, which fascinated them perpetually – the so-called 'Holy Roman Emperor', chief over a medley of German and Italian states, remained a political fact for a thousand years, until the early nineteenth century. In medieval Europe we can see developing two interrelated prototypes of the modern version of imperialism.

Land, it was understood, could be grabbed from infidels and the status of the raptors as overlords, exploiting the people as serfs or slaves, could be sanctified by the Pope and by feudal legality. In Iberia, led by the legendary Cid, Christians began in the eleventh century to wrest land from Muslims, who had left them only a small enclave. The German 'drive to the East' from the twelfth to the fourteenth centuries was a crusade against pagan Slavs. But a 'regular body of entrepreneurs' fanned the colonising fever.[13] Forests and swamps were claimed for agriculture; the Wendish Slavs in the way were massacred, forcibly transplanted, enserfed, while around the Baltic German traders established that chain of posts which became the cities of the Hanseatic League. The landlust of noblemen married with the goldlust of merchants. By the sixteenth century, furthermore, the demand for Baltic grain from Western European towns was such that German 'junkers' ruling non-German peasants found it profitable to tie them to the land – to create, in effect, plantations with coerced serf labour. This coincided with the emergence of slave plantations beyond Europe. The rise of cities in Western Europe would very largely depend on both these developments, while the German and Polish towns in the East went into decline.[14] What has been called 'the development of underdevelopment' had begun.

Stadluft macht frei, said the Germans: 'Town air makes free.' Freedom attracted runaway serfs from the countryside. Towns jealously asserted their liberty against feudal overlords: Judith the tyrant-slayer, in Donatello's sculpture, stood before the Palazzo Vecchio in Florence. Yet the freedom of Florentine 'freemen' stemmed from the degradation of others. They owned many slaves. Merchant patricians exploited the labour of craftsmen. Like other towns, Florence bled the areas where its food and its raw materials were produced. In the relation of the Italian city-state to the countryside (*contado*) which it controlled around itself, we can see a prototype of the transactions between the 'imperial', metropolitan country and its 'underdeveloped' colonies. Towns which raised tariff walls to protect their own industries from competition and which fought each other with arms as well as competing in trade anticipated the quarrelsome mercantilist powers of the eighteenth century.

Italians had gone everywhere in Europe, as merchants, technical experts, tax farmers, entrepreneurs and moneylenders. They had developed a most significant trade in slaves. The word comes from 'Slav'; Italians went to the Black Sea where Tatars sold them captives from the Slav lands they dominated. In Venice alone 10,000 slaves were sold between 1414 and 1423. Even quite lowly people in Italy commonly used them as servants. Domestic slavery was a worldwide fact, but Italians, following ancient Roman precedents, worked up an idea which seems to be peculiar to Europeans, the island plantation tilled by slaves. In Cyprus, Italians running such plantations grew sugar cane with the labour of imported people who, by 1300, included some black Africans.[15]

So this idea developed simultaneously with the 'commercial revolution' achieved by the Italians; along, that is, with such things as marine insurance, double entry book-keeping, bills of exchange, cheques, and banks with far flung foreign branches. Lombard Street is still there in the City of London to remind us that Italians opened up England, then an important, rather backward wool-producing area, exchanging the products of the Mediterranean and the East for native raw and manufactured materials. They brought new tastes, new 'needs', new perspectives and new methods. In the winter, carriers came from Westmorland, one of the lesser centres of English textile manufacture (Grasmere then had twenty fulling mills), transporting cheap but durable cloth made from the wool of hardy fell sheep, for sale direct to the great Italian galleys which called in at Southampton. They jogged back to their own rocky valleys taking casks of alum and woad for dyeing, but also luxuries — oranges, nuts and wines.[16] The lives of Westmorland people were now involved with what happened thousands of miles away: in Cairo, for instance, where Venetian merchants haggled with the Sultan of Egypt over his imposts on the trade in 'spices', a general term for Eastern produce.

In remote Indonesian islands, the Moluccas and Bandas, and nowhere else in the world as far as was known, nutmegs and cloves grew. The tide of spices began there and flowed towards Europe gathering in silks and rhubarb, gems, cotton and dyestuffs, drugs, perfumes and unguents, all the drowsy syrups of the

East, besides cloves, nutmegs and cinnamon to mask the taste of that humdrum or rotten food which even the richest in Europe ate. Pepper was the most valuable product of all, a near essential. To preserve meat for the winter with salt alone would have meant so much soaking later when the time came to eat it that it would have been tasteless. With pepper mixed in, less salt could be used.[17] The spice trade was the richest and most risky open to Europeans. A merchant, it was said, could ship six cargoes, lose five, and still make a profit when the sixth was sold. On the spice trade Venice had risen to glory, so that in Columbus's day that small city-state seemed the mightiest power in Europe.

'Nations' in the modern sense did not exist. Nowhere in Europe did political boundaries coincide with 'racial' or even 'linguistic' ones. Maritime explorers, like artists, went where the pay was best, undeterred by any sense of disloyalty. Europe consisted of 'realms', claimed by kings, dukes and cities. These claimants were insatiably competitive. Monarchs envied, as well as feared, the despotic Ottoman sultans with their superb armies. The realms of Europe were not by contrast impressive. 'Italy' was still only a geographical and 'Germany' a racial expression; the areas concerned were divided among many small states. The realm of the king of 'France' was the most populous; that of the king of 'England' was probably the most unified, except for the smaller kingdom of 'Portugal'. While kings sought to extend their power at the expense of their own subjects, they also thought freely in terms of extending their realms beyond natural frontiers. Kings of 'England' had until recently ruled much of 'France'. The digestion of new territories in other continents presented no conceptual problems. And the wealth of the spice trade, if it could be tapped, would formidably increase a monarch's resources.

Once the kings of Portugal and Spain began to aggrandise themselves through expansion, rivalry within Europe ensured the backing of other monarchs for overseas exploits. Growth in the power of kings, transforming itself later into that of 'states', would accompany the extension of European scope. But some subjects from the outset were prepared to go further and meddle with more than rulers had the imagination to propose or, sometimes, the interest to endorse. The Catholic Church, with its missionary ambitions, would keep up its own momentum overseas. Some men of the landowning strata felt short of land or had none and sought lordships over savages. Some merchants hoped for rich hauls from risky overseas enterprises. When conditions in Europe were so dismal for so many, no enterprise would lack sailors to face death in tiny ships, or soldiers to fight in little conquering armies. Power, for kings; profit, for merchants; opportunity, for all classes — these were strong enough pulls to explain the initial European impetus. Europe was poor. Life was brutish and generally brief there. Hazards in tropical climates would hardly deter all its people. Comfort, security, scope in Europe itself came in the aftermath of expansion and, as we shall see, chiefly because of it.

The 'industrial revolution' which expansion would help to promote was still four hundred years in the future when America was discovered. Then, Europe remained, in one expert's words, 'a technically backward region whose chief advantage was its ability to adapt and improve its borrowings from more advanced societies.'[18] Leonardo da Vinci's remarkable ideas found no application in his own day. The clumsy wooden machines in use were too inefficient to encourage much further invention, granted labour was so cheap.

Nevertheless, conquistadors, merchants and kings had two large advantages over all the non-European peoples at whose expense the expansion took place. One was conceptual. The discovery by fifteenth-century artists of ways of representing space in a painting through the rules of perspective was a step towards reconstructing and imagining it from a map.[19] And the backward-looking obsession of the Renaissance with ancient texts had at least encouraged geographical speculation through the rediscovery of the classical mapmaker Ptolemy. A second advantage owed nothing to learned argument. This was in sailing ships.

The fifteenth century had seen a marriage between the carvel-built Mediterranean ship, with its triangular lateen sail, and the tough, buoyant, clinker-built, tubby 'cog' of the North, able to fight its way up to Iceland and back on a regular run through heavy winds and seas, though its square sails gave it less manoeuvrability. Extra masts were added, and a range of hybrid, adaptable ships came into existence, so that Spanish and Portuguese seamen, who lived at the point where the two traditions converged, were able to make immense voyages in ships which were built for the everyday trade of Western Europe.

Such ships mounted cannon. These had been used on land and sea in Europe and Asia for a long time, but in quality and quantity, Europe, thanks to its incessant warfare, was establishing a lead over other areas, and its rulers were now mounting the unreliable weapons of the day in such numbers upon their ships that the old sort of naval battle decided by boarding parties of soldiers was on its way to becoming obsolete. And Europeans had borrowed from Arabs (who had themselves borrowed from further east) enough techniques to make navigation possible in deep water under clouds and storm. They had the sternpost rudder, they had the magnetic compass, and they had 'Arabic' numerals, Hindu in origin, which made calculations of angle and distance more feasible. Accurate measurement of longitude was impossible till the eighteenth century, but using an astrolabe or simple quadrant a seaman could establish a fairly accurate latitude by taking polar altitudes. In 1484 John II of Portugal established a commission to find a more universally useful method of settling latitude by solar declination. Drawing on the work of a Jewish astronomer, these experts produced a manual, the first such thing in European history, which meant that literate seamen, where they existed, could work out a position from that of the sun. By 1500, navigation methods were known which lasted, refined but not essentially changed, until the 1920s.

Apart from the bluster and drive engendered by a sense of inferiority, Europeans had other psychological factors working for them. Educated men knew about Ancient Rome and were not embarrassed by any scientific understanding of history. The exploits of Caesar, they fancied, were of a kind which they themselves could repeat. And the illiterates in the expedition could share with their betters assurance that as Christians they were, and must in the long run prove, superior. This conviction had been sharpened by the long struggle against Islam, the only other religion to match Christianity in fanaticism and missionary zeal. When Pope Pius II coined the adjective 'European' in the 1450s it was, ominously, equated with 'Christian'.[20] Amongst the fuels which drove expansion forward, the vivid, hungry desire to put the Turks in their place and give Christian Europe its rightful position had real importance. Men acting in their own material interests generally need to believe that they are fighting for something transcending themselves, if they are to press daringly forward into contention. And in those days people believed without question in the torments of hell and the raptures of paradise. Turkish power straddled the spice routes. Muslim traders flocked in eastern ports. The new-found lands to the west were full of pagans. To help to transform these depressing circumstances might assist one's fortune in that after-life which pressed so closely even on young men in days of casual slaughters and treacherous diet and inefficacious medicine.

Yet the quest for an earthly, material paradise also beckoned nobleman and commoner. Millenarian longings had frequently flamed out in the revolts of urban craftsmen, the fury of peasant insurrection. Joachim of Fiore, in the twelfth century, had prophesied a Third Age of the world in which all men would live in voluntary poverty, in joy and love and freedom, without pope or emperor or private property. His vision haunted Europe. Those who set out to sail for Cathay remembered also stories of islands of bliss to the west. By 1502, Columbus, who had started the transmutation of these islands from hopeful legend into hapless fact, was thinking of himself as the Joachite messiah, bringing in that Third Age 'of the spirit'.[21] The belief that in new worlds life could be just and free, and that some magic found there might revolutionise even Europe, would help to draw poor and wealthy alike overseas up to our own century.

III

For the nobility of Iberia, crusading against Moors had become a traditional way of life. In 1415, the Portuguese captured Ceuta, in North Africa, a Moorish town where, according to a chronicler, the soldiers were astonished, 'for our poor houses look like pigsties in comparison with these.'[22] Ceuta was a terminal point in the trans-Saharan gold trade from West Africa. Backward, aggressive Portugal was one of the few European countries which did not then have a gold coinage. The captains sent out thereafter by Prince Henry the Navigator, a member of the Portuguese royal house, were looking for the origin of the gold which flowed to the Moors. They found other sources of profit as they explored down the coast. In 1441, direct shipment of slaves began. Seven years later the prototype *feitoria* ('factory' in the old sense of the word) was set up at Arguim, below Cape Blanco, and this was able to draw much trade in gold and ivory from the Moors. Before Prince Henry died in 1460, the mint in Lisbon was issuing gold coinage, and his ships had probed as far south as Sierra Leone.

Two types of imperialising activity followed. The 'factory' was a base for trade. The overseas colony also fostered commerce, but in addition gave the chance of a new life. Prince Henry, from the 1420s, had put colonists on the unoccupied island of Madeira and the first boy and girl born there were named Adam and Eve. Madeira, with its vineyards and sugar plantations, proved very profitable, as did the Azores, also empty, which Henry peopled a little later. A 'fashion for islands', in J. H. Parry's phrase, was set which lasted for several centuries.[23] In the 1470s, Spain fought Portugal in the first modern colonial war, over possession of the Canary Islands. Spain got the Canaries and their stone-age inhabitants, the Guanches, were extinguished.

A few years later the Portuguese encountered a great unknown kingdom, far more populous than their own, south of where the river Congo discoloured the sea for many miles with its mud-laden waters. This was the land of the Mani-kongo, the 'blacksmith king'. A scenario developed which would often be played out again. The king saw the religion of his clever visitors as a new source of power for himself, and he was baptised. But the Portuguese would not give their Christian ally ships of his own when he asked for them, and the price of their spiritual and technical assistance was slaves. Before long, even members of the royal family were being kidnapped, and the nearby island of São Thomé, populated with black slaves under white settlers, was thriving by the second quarter of the sixteenth century on the production of that lush and sinister crop, the sugar cane.

Meanwhile, Vasco Da Gama had opened up direct trade between Portugal and India. When he arrived at Calicut in 1498 the zamorin, ruler of that important town, was disgusted with the gifts which Da Gama presented to him, and his courtiers laughed at the hoods and washbasins, hats and honey the white men brought. The trade of the East could not be peacefully entered. The Portuguese turned to their cannon for help. In 1510 the famous viceroy Albuquerque grabbed Goa and, so he claimed, put all Muslims in sight to the sword, or burned them alive in their mosques. By 1515 he had also seized two of the great entrepôts of the Indian Ocean trade, Malacca and, in the Persian Gulf, Ormuz.

The Portuguese never monopolised the whole trade of the Indian Ocean. Venice continued to thrive on spices which reached Europe by other routes than Da Gama's. Off China, the Ming coastguard fleets beat the Portuguese twice in the early 1520s. But what the Portuguese managed was very remarkable. With ships largely crewed by Asians and black Africans, a few scant parcels of white men, scattered in fortified posts from East Africa to the Moluccas, were able to domineer in Indian Ocean trade for most of the sixteenth century. And besides maintaining their bases in West Africa, the Portuguese started the permanent settlement of Brazil. Beneath all later empires, a Portuguese substratum showed, even where they had not ruled directly. They spread new crops and techniques wherever they went. Their pioneering presence brought with it a new trade language which influenced pidgins used later by all Europeans. The word 'sabby', for instance, or something like it, is found in the pidgins of Africans and of Chinese, of Caribbean and of Pacific islanders.[24]

The Portuguese voyages, R. H. Tawney observes, were 'as practical in their motive as the steam engine.'[25] Their impetus, backed by Italian and German merchants, was primarily commercial. Christian fervour, and hunger for land and spoils, gave a different coloration to Spanish expansion. The pattern is almost too neat: only a few months after the Spanish monarchs, Ferdinand of Aragon and Isabella of Castile, entered Granada, completing the reconquest of Iberia from the Moors, Columbus sailed in quest for Cathay. The momentum of the crusade seems to carry itself on at once to new continents.

Hundreds of years of war against Islam had given the people of Spain's arid central plateau a characteristic noble rapacity. In between battles, soldiers accustomed to live by plunder had scorned to go back to agriculture. To conquer land, to loot it, and then to live as lord over native serfs became the ideal of a large class of men, mostly poorish *hidalgos* ('sons of someone', petty nobility), who were ready to justify their behaviour by reference to a militant Christianity and to an exalted code of chivalry. It was convenient for such people that Columbus found, not the rich trade of the East for which his own Genoese background prompted him to look, but land, occupied by apparently tractable pagans: islands, in the first instance, more Canaries.

He did not 'discover' America, whatever that means; amongst Europeans, Norsemen had certainly settled briefly in Newfoundland early in the eleventh century.[26] But he did initiate the rape of the Caribbean. Returning to Hispaniola in 1493 with 1,200 colonists, he was soon hunting the natives with savage dogs. Indians, however, seemed to prefer death to working for Spaniards, and the conquerors, with their *hidalgo* pride, would not work themselves. The need for a third kind of person was soon very clear, and in 1510 the Spanish Crown began to license the importation of Africans. 1515 saw the first shipment of slave-grown sugar from the New World. The Indians, no more used to European diseases than they were to white concepts of slavery, were dying out with catastrophic rapidity, and loss of labour was one factor driving some Spanish colonists from the islands to the mainland, from which in 1513, at the Isthmus of Panama, an adventurer named Balboa saw the 'South Sea', the Pacific.

Then Hernán Cortés gave Europeans a new and potent myth. The daring white man with only a little band penetrates a vast pagan empire and by his coolness, his cleverness and his courage, swiftly and finally masters the whole. Less than two and a half years after he had set out from Cuba in 1519 with six hundred companions, Cortés had made himself effective ruler of Mexico, on the ruins of the great city of Teotihuacan and of the Aztec empire which had built it. Thirteen muskets and sixteen horses had been sufficient against opponents who were still using stone-age weapons. The example which Cortés set Europe resounds through the whole subsequent history of imperialism. In the first instance his deeds inspired Francisco de Pizarro, with a still smaller force, to conquer the even more impressive Andean empire of the Incas, and Spaniards rapidly took over the more accessible parts of eastern South America.

For Spain, also, Fernao Magalhaes (Magellan) had sailed in 1519 to drive through the straits which bear his name into that sea which he called Pacific. His men went for three months and twenty days without fresh food: they ate hides from the rigging, sawdust and rats: then, after their landfall, Magellan was killed in the Philippines. But one of his captains completed, in 1522, the first circumnavigation of the globe. He brought back spices, along with fifteen survivors.

'West' had now become 'East'. This created confusion in international law. The Treaty of Tordesillas (1494) had divided the world into a Spanish half, west of an imaginary line drawn 370 leagues beyond a point in the Azores, and a Portuguese half, which included Africa and Asia as well as Brazil. The two powers now fought in the Moluccas. A new line of demarcation, east of the islands, was arranged in 1529. Spanish conquest of the Philippines followed in the 1560s, and a commerce in silk with China opened up from Manila, whither Spanish argosies sailed from Mexico. European trade routes now girdled the world.

IV

This spate of discovery and conquest brought intellectual revolution. Contrary to the cherished tale, every literate man in Europe knew in Columbus's day that the world was round. But no one had thought that there might be a continent to the west between Europe and Asia. Since Columbus died believing that he had pioneered a direct route to Cathay, it is not unfair that the continent came to be called after an Italian businessman, Amerigo Vespucci, whose travels there convinced him that this was a 'New World' for which neither Christian doctrine nor geographical theory had allowed. He publicised his views in 1504 and three years later a German, Waldseemüller, drew a map showing the new lands as separate from either Europe or Asia and giving them the name 'America'.[27]

Most Europeans, even literate ones, were slow to react to the discovery of the New World or to its implications. But the Englishman, Thomas More, who set his imaginary communist Utopia in the new lands in his book of 1516, exemplified the imaginative impact on advanced and speculative minds. America wasn't in the Bible. The Romans had known nothing of it. To come to terms with it intellectually, 'it would be necessary to reject ideas accepted for many centuries, to conceive the structure of the universe and the nature of its reality in a new and different way, to work out a different kind of relationship between man and his Creator, and to develop a new idea of man's place in the world.'[28] It would be absurd to suggest that the discoveries by themselves could be held to explain the large changes in European consciousness which took place in the sixteenth century. But the new theology of Luther and Calvin, with its unintentional invitations to scepticism and individualism, came after the voyages in point of time; so did the new cosmology of Copernicus, Kepler and Galileo. Amerigo Vespucci himself prefigured the spirit of Baconian science when he wrote to his patron in 1500, 'Rationally, let it be said in a whisper, experience is certainly worth more than theory.'[29] A new audacity, and a fresh empiricism, started to march together. In the sixteenth century Europe began to draw ahead in technology; by the seventeenth, Europe had achieved a clear lead.

The effects of invasion on America may be measurable: the population of central Mexico seems to have fallen from about 11 million when Cortés first arrived to 2½ million by the end of the century.[30] The European impact on Africa would be epitomised in the traditions of a people living in what is now Angola – 'One day the white man arrived in ships with wings, which shone in the sun like knives. They fought hard battles with the Ngola and spat fire at him ... They brought us maize and cassava, knives and hoes, groundnuts and tobacco. From that time until our day the Whites brought us nothing but wars and miseries.'[31]

The material effects on Europe itself were less dramatic. New fisheries across the Atlantic were valuable, as was the new commerce with colonists. New sources of bullion were not at first very important. Then in 1545 there was a silver strike at Potosí in Peru, and from the 1560s mines were successfully exploited. They solved the longstanding problem of how Europe could pay for luxury imports from Asia. For centuries New World bullion would be essential to the far trade with India and China. Though it did not cause the startling rise of prices which had important results in sixteenth-century Europe, it certainly helped to sustain them at higher and higher levels.

But the chief 'economic' effect was surely a psychological one. European men of business were learning to scheme grandly. The long-distance trades demanded finance on a new scale with their costly ships, large crews and great risks. The Portuguese and Spaniards themselves lacked the required capital and experience. In 1503 the Portuguese King made Antwerp the depot for the Eastern trade. This port became the major centre of banking and finance in Europe. German and Italian financiers sucked most of the proceeds of empire away from Portugal.

Peruvian silver helped the Spanish Crown to overawe Europe, and its pikemen and arquebusiers dominated the continent's wars until well into the seventeenth century. The bullying attitudes developed towards Indians in America quickly came to bear on the Spanish people themselves. The possession of the Indies encouraged Spanish kings 'more and more to ignore unwelcome advice from the *Cortes*, from the nobility and from public opinion generally, in Castile; and public opinion grudgingly acquiesced in the growth of absolutist practices born of successful imperialism. Bureaucratic absolutism spread, as it were by contagion, from the Indies to Castile, where it was naturally more directly felt, more burdensome, less tempered by distance and procrastination.'[32] And further: Philip II of Spain wrote in 1570 to the governor of Milan, one of his possessions, 'These Italians, although they are not Indians, have to be treated as such, so that they will understand that we are in charge of them and not they in charge of us.'[33]

Spain was envied; Spain was feared; kings wished to imitate and to challenge Spain. From the outset the spheres of Iberian conquest drew ventures from other countries, with or without diplomatic support from their rulers. The world was no longer the world's world in European eyes. Growingly, it seemed open to all Europeans. When a Spaniard taxed King Francis I with his interventions in America, the French ruler drily remarked 'That the sun shone for him as for others, and he would like very much to see Adam's will to learn how he divided up the world.'[34]

V

The French were early poachers in Brazil. It was under the French King's patronage that a Florentine, Verazzano, in 1524, first sailed the North American coastline from the Carolinas to Newfoundland, and it was Jacques Cartier from France, perhaps the most brilliant of all sixteenth-century explorers, who made three voyages to Canada without losing a ship, penetrated far up the St Lawrence, and helped to found an abortive colony there in 1540.

But the English could claim to be first discoverers of North America. From at least the 1480s, merchants of Bristol had been sending out ships to search for land in the Atlantic, and it was from this port that a citizen of Venice named by the English (after much indecision) 'John Cabot' proposed to sail west in search of spices. On 5 March 1496, King Henry VII of England granted to 'John Gabote' letters patent giving him 'full and free authoritie, leave, and power, to sayle to all partes, countreys, and seas, of the East, of the West, and of the North, under our banners and ensignes, with five ships ... and as many mariners or men as they will have with them in the saide ships, upon their own proper costes and charges, to seeke out, discover, and finde, whatsoever iles, countreyes, regions or provinces of the heathen and infidelles, whatsoever they bee, and in what part of the world soever they bee, whiche before this time have beene unknowen to all Christians.' Cabot might govern these lands as the King's lieutenant, monopolise their produce, and pay the Crown 'the fifth part of the Capitall gaine so gotten'.[35]

This was an example of the combination of private initiative with royal support which characterised the discoveries of the period, including those of Columbus. Cabot, at his own 'costes and charges', could raise only one ship, the *Matthew*, with a crew of eighteen. He sailed about May 20, 1497, and within five weeks or so arrived in Newfoundland. By August 9 he was back in London to claim his 'New Isle'. The King gave him £10 for his discovery at once, and a few months later an annuity of £20 was settled on his 'welbiloved John Calbot'. Calbot, Gabote or Cabot bought new clothes and swaggered around London in gay silken apparel. In February 1498, Henry issued him new letters patent to go back to his island, though Cabot bragged that his real intention was to reach Cipango, where he thought all the spices and jewels in the world had their origin, and to set up a 'factory' there. Of 'Kaboto's' five ships, Henry gave one, stocked by London merchants. The men of Bristol provided the others with 'coarse cloth, Caps, Laces, points and other trifles', deemed suitable for trade with pagans. One ship put into an Irish port in distress. Four sailed on and were lost. As a contemporary noted, Cabot had found 'new lands nowhere but on the very bottom of ocean'.[36]

A Portuguese, Gaspar Corte Real, reached Newfoundland in 1500, but he too was lost on his second expedition. A disappointed rival, João Fernandes, an Azorean, formed a syndicate with other Azoreans and men of Bristol which was given letters patent by Henry in 1501. They brought the King presents of birds and wildcats from the New-found Island, and also three Indians, but no important results. Then English exploration lagged. French seamen moved in to fish for New World cod, and drove off the Portuguese colony briefly established on Cape Breton Island in the early 1520s. Of the very few English New World voyages known to us from this period, the most memorable was Richard Hore's of 1536. A leather merchant of London, Hore chartered two ships to catch cod and to give a trip to certain sightseers, including some thirty cheerful young gentlemen of London. One ship was lost at sea. The other anchored in New-foundland. Supplies ran out. Depressed by a diet of 'raw herbes and rootes in the fields and deserts', the passengers began to eat each other. The captain denounced this practice, whereupon the culprits agreed to do it more fairly, casting lots as to who should provide the next meal. The survivors eventually pirated a French vessel, and sailed home, past 'mighty Ilands of yce'.[37]

BOOK ONE:
1530—1660

Apparently, while sovereigns of the realm were struggling to pacify the tribal Celts, and the Puritan colonists in North America were wrestling with the Red Indian for his soul and his lands, all frontier antagonists looked more or less alike. Whether Irishmen or Pequots, Scots or Iroquois, they were enemies, they were ignorant, and they were animal-like.

MARGARET T. HODGEN[1]

The Dragon that our seas did raise his crest
And brought back heaps of gold unto his nest,
Unto his foes more terrible than thunder,
Glory of his age, after-ages' wonder,
Excelling all those that excelled before —
It's feared we shall have none such any more —
Effecting all, he sole did undertake,
Valiant, just, wise, mild, honest, godly Drake.
This man when I was little I did meet
As he was walking up Totnes' long street.
He asked me whose I was. I answered him.
He asked me if his good friend were within.
A fair red orange in his hand he had;
He gave it me, whereof I was right glad,
Takes and kissed me, and prays, 'God bless my boy',
Which I record with comfort to this day ...

ROBERT HAYMAN, 'Of the Great and Famous ... Sir
Francis Drake, and of My Little-Little Self', 1628;
written in Newfoundland, where Hayman was
governor of a plantation[2]

Cromwell the First

Send thy summons east and west for the Gael from the field of Leinster; drive the Saxons westward over the high sea, that Alba may suffer no division ... The roots from which they grow, destroy them; over great is their increase; so that after thee no Saxon be left in life, nor Saxon woman to be mentioned.

Bard inciting the Earl of Argyll into battle
against the English at Flodden, 1513[1]

I

The modern imagination finds it hard to recapture the British Isles as they were around 1530. Where snug farmers collect their profits today, the countryside was commonly still untamed and beasts and birds and fish swarmed with a freedom unthinkable now. Wolves were not yet extinct. Even the people who lived in the most settled areas would seem to their descendants crude, ignorant and poverty-stricken.

Two kingdoms claimed all the isles between them. The monarch in England, a man of recent Welsh origins, was also titular ruler of Wales and of Ireland, and he had his eye on the realm of his weaker neighbour in Edinburgh, who called himself King of Scots. Both courts spoke English, and so did most of the subjects whom the kings were actually able to control in any way. But the dialects used in different areas were still often mutually almost incomprehensible; from a little before this time we have Caxton's famous story of the housewife in Kent who, to a request for eggs, replied that she knew no French, and who only understood when asked for 'eyren'. Cornish was still spoken in the far south-west, Welsh generally in Wales, and forms of Gaelic, closely allied to each other, throughout Highland Scotland, Ireland and the Isle of Man. Man had its own 'king' until 1504, when the Earl of Derby, who held the title, agreed to become merely 'Lord of Man'. But he and his descendants effectively ruled the island until the late eighteenth century.[2]

Nor was such virtual independence exceptional. A Campbell Earl of Argyll, or, in south-western Ireland, a Geraldine Earl of Desmond, was in most respects a hereditary king in his own right, and undercover diplomacy would recognise him as such. In Scotland the king was commonly not even manifest first among his peers. In Ireland, royal power stopped short a few miles outside Dublin. Even in England, in times of weak kingship, as during the Wars of the Roses, the tribalism of the periphery could spread its infection towards the centre in anarchy and rebellion.

Race-consciousness did exist among Celts, and was fostered by their poets, but there was no question that they might unite against English-speakers. Sea divided Wales and Cornwall, where Brythonic languages were spoken. Though the narrower North Channel did not prevent constant intercourse between Gaels in Scotland and Ireland who shared a Goidelic tongue and, in great part, a common culture, there were many petty chiefs divided by mutual jealousies and English-speaking rulers would always find allies among them. Institutions within the Gaelic lands reflected varying dates and durations of two great transmarine interventions. Vikings from Scandinavia had much affected the Hebrides and Man, but had made rather less impact on Ireland, while Normans had spread over most but not all of the British Isles after 1066.

The Anglo-Saxon footsoldiers of England had been the first to succumb to mounted Normans wearing mail coats and characteristic conical helmets. The Normans eventually adopted the English language, but only after making an almost clean sweep of the old Anglo-Saxon ruling class and bringing in feudal institutions previously absent. South Wales was rapidly overrun, and Pembroke became and remained a 'little England', but elsewhere the Welsh tribes rallied to regain much lost ground, and eventually a fringe of Anglo-Norman lord-ships to east and south girdled with moated castles a zone still basically Celtic.

In Scotland and Ireland also, Normanisation was left incomplete. By the eleventh century four distinct racial groups had come to give allegiance to the King of Scots: the Scots themselves in the west; the Picts to the north; the Welsh-speaking Strathclyde Britons in the south-west, and the Angles of the Lothians. King David I in the first half of the twelfth century brought Normans and feudalism together into his sparsely settled realm. In the Lowlands the graft caught so effectively that to the present day feudalism remains quaintly entrenched in Scottish law. Some Norman lords, in parts of the Highlands, adapted themselves and their feudal institutions to the role of Celtic clan chief-tainship. But the north and west remained Gaelic-speaking; a deep divide was beginning within the kingdom.

The Irish, by contrast, had long shared a common culture and language, but their 'High Kings' had rarely had much authority. A chance for Norman incursion arose from the struggle of Dermot MacMurrough, King of Leinster, against his titular overlord, the High King. He did a deal with Richard Fitzgilbert de Clare, Earl of Pembroke, later nicknamed 'Strongbow' by historians. 'Strongbow' was promised Dermot's daughter in marriage and succession to rule in Leinster. In 1170, he accordingly brought over from Wales archers, and some mounted Norman knights. Dermot soon died, and as king in his own right, Strongbow submitted to Henry II of England. Though Henry had forbidden the expedition, he had in his pocket a grant of hereditary possession of Ireland which the Pope, concerned to bring the island more effectively into his own sphere of power, had made him in the 1150s. So, by the standards of the day it was not mere lawless thuggery when Henry, like so many rulers after him, legalised the results brought about by freebooting on the frontier. He came over himself in 1171, confirmed Strongbow and other Normans in the lands which Dermot had granted them, took submission from numerous native chiefs, and left a viceroy behind him. He had secured, without fighting, a claim to the island which the Irish Church conceded was just. And the flow of aliens into Ireland about this time was no crude military occupation, 'but a part of that great movement of peasant colonisation which dominates so much of the economic history of Europe from the eleventh to the fourteenth century, arising out of what can only have been a spontaneous growth of population and slackening as that growth slackens ... '[3] Land-hungry English and Welsh peasants came to outnumber the natives in many parts, but there was plenty of room for everybody. The Irish had no urban traditions, and generally left the towns to the English-speakers. As the Middle Ages wore on, the Anglo-Norman lords were gaelicised and Irish chieftains commonly borrowed some English ways. Only Ulster, never finally brought under Norman overlords, stayed more or less untouched.

Celtic Wales meanwhile part-anglicised itself. Llewellyn the Great (1196–1240) managed to overcome the country's chronic disunity and ruled something which looked like a kingdom in North and Central Wales. Llewellyn the Last (1255–82) was recognised as *de facto* independent by the English Crown at the Treaty of Montgomery in 1267 and 'the first, and indeed the only legally acknowledged, native prince of Wales entered on a brief ten year experiment in the control of a miniature feudal state.'[4] Much Anglo-Norman thinking had been brought into Welsh law and the Llewellyns had introduced the paraphernalia of feudal kingship. But the last Llewellyn's dabblings in English politics brought the power of Edward I against him and by 1284, with the native upstart dead, the alien king was able to symbolise English power with four royal castles at Conway, Carnarvon, Criccieth and Harlech, under which boroughs grew up peopled by English settlers. Many prominent Welshmen had resented Llewellyn and were happy to serve the greater Crown.

The Anglo-Saxons had driven the native Celts into the hilly regions of north and west, leaving Ireland untouched (as indeed the Romans had done). The Anglo-Normans pushed further and brought with them not only the evolving English language, which gradually became a mark of boasted social and racial superiority, but also the seeds of what became capitalism. The contrast between Celt and Saxon began to crystallise as one between grain growers and people chiefly, though not solely, pastoralists. A feudal system of landholding involving inheritance by the eldest son eschewed the view that land belonged to the clan or surname or tribe as a whole and that inheritance was partible; above all the town, as it grew and its influence spread, infiltrated alien ideas, English speech, and the influence of the European trading system, into areas which became, by comparison with its own values and standards, backward. Native leaders took note and aspired. 'Without buying and selling I can in no way live', wrote the O Toole chieftain from Ireland to Richard II in 1395. ' ... I would that you send me your letters patent so that for the future I may enjoy free buying and selling in your fairs and towns.'[5]

II

Yet England itself in the early sixteenth century was a 'backward' country, so remote from the consciousness of educated Europeans that the Portuguese poet Camoens, as late as 1572, could refer to it as a 'great northern kingdom of perpetual snow'.[6] The greatness was no more obvious than the snow. England's three million people were much outnumbered by the nineteen million of France. Only 8 or 9 per cent of them lived in towns, as compared to 15 per cent in Spain. England could not match either rival. Its people, like those of underdeveloped lands later, were notorious elsewhere for their 'laziness', and for the same reasons: they were underemployed. Most of them still lived in smoky, dark, stinking and cramped little dwellings made of timber and mud, dressed in skins or clothes made of leather or canvas or sackcloth, and ate black bread from wooden trenchers. Most households were still economically almost self-sufficient. Sorcery and witchcraft probably had as much influence as Christianity, and that growingly rational urban culture which had sprung up in Italy, Flanders and Germany had made as yet little impact on England. In 1500 there were seventy-three towns in Italy with printing presses while in England there were only four.[7] In Professor Hoskins's words, England was 'still a colonial economy, with too few people to civilise the whole landscape ... ' It was 'a green and quiet agricultural country in which miles of deep forest alternated with thousand-acre "fields" of barley, beans or wheat, or with variegated heaths and bleak moors, and little pasture closes.' Sheep outnumbered men by perhaps three to one, bearing the famous wool which had attracted Italian buyers so greatly, but which was now exported in the form of English-made cloth.[8]

That cloth, however, was mainly distributed by German merchants from the Hanse towns which, in the fifteenth century, had shut the English out of direct trade with their markets in the Baltic. English naval forces had failed against these competitors, and it was one signal of the ambitions of Henry VIII that he was building up a navy which reached a total of eighty-five ships; his father had found only three when he had seized power in 1485.[9]

Where England was in advance of the rest of Europe was in its precocious achievement of something approaching 'national unity'. No doubt its island position had helped. In the Middle Ages, England had built up traditions of strong royal authority which were to hand as Edward IV and his Tudor successors sought to repair and strengthen the powers of the Crown after a long phase of civil war. The centralisation of the economy assisted the concentration of authority. London, with its population reaching 200,000 or more by 1600, far outstripped all other towns in size and significance. It was not only the seat of the king, it was also clearly the commercial capital, and with cultural dominance added, it achieved triple hegemony unique in Europe. In some years in the 1540s nearly nine-tenths of England's exports of cloth went through it.[10] And as a great market for food, it became a magnet by which first the South Midlands, Kent and East Anglia, then ultimately the rest of the country, were drawn into agriculture conducted for profit.

And the oligarchies which ran the smaller towns, so far from resisting centralisation, favoured the growth of royal power. In England, almost uniquely, townsmen had come to form 'an essential part of the machinery of royal government'.[11] They had their representatives in the House of Commons, which from 1376 had elected its own Speaker. The Tudors, driving towards absolute monarchy, relied on the support of substantial middling people, urban and rural, who provided the 'justices of the peace' enforcing the law in each locality. But if the growing economic weight of such people could strengthen the royal power, it could also, as time would show, counteract it.

At a time when noblemen on the Continent were tending to emphasise their separate status, and had won immunity from taxation, in England the ranks of the peerage were thin, and were kept so; the broader body of knights and squires below was taxed, and merged into the shifting and amorphous class of 'gentlemen', who were themselves often hard to distinguish from merchant groups on the one hand and from substantial yeomen on the other. Whereas in France the Crown ruled in 1560 that any nobleman who engaged in trade would thereby lose his caste privileges,[12] in England such behaviour was commonplace and accepted among 'gentlemen'. Prosperous peasant farmers by thrift and polite behaviour could win recognition as 'gentry'. In England, as nowhere else, 'blue blood was purchaseable'.[13] Anyone who could afford to keep up the part of a 'gentleman' was a 'gentleman'.

While serfdom was still the typical condition of ordinary people elsewhere in Europe, England (and Scotland) had moved away from it. Villeinage had begun to wither in England from the fourteenth century onwards; the Black Death, which made labour an item in shorter supply than land, had assisted the shift from customary tenures involving unpaid service towards leasehold and copyhold, and in effect to contractual relationships between master and man. So in the 1530s when a Leicestershire landlord tried to extort by force the goods of a wealthy grazier by declaring that he was his bondman, he was unsuccessful, and the upstart plebeian continued his rise. In theory there were still some serfs in England in the late sixteenth century, but in practice a writer in 1577 was justified in the claim that 'As for slaves and bondmen we have none; nay such is the privilege of our country by the especial grace of God and bounty of our princes, that if any come hither from other realms, so soon as they set foot on land they become so free of condition as their masters ... '[14]

Yet the spread over the English countryside of men pushing with a sharp eye for profit towards the gratifications of upward social mobility bore very hard, very often, on the less lucky 'free' people around them. In Henry VIII's day the encloser, the man who put up hedges and fences where there had been open fields and common lands, was generally and violently hated. While small hedged fields were traditional in some parts of the country, in much of it, above all in the Midlands, enclosure was felt as a tyrannical outrage. Villagers practising open field agriculture were used to working together, agreeing on crop rotations, sharing the common pasture. 'They toiled side by side in the fields, and they walked together from field to village, from farm to heath, morning, afternoon, and evening. They all depended on common resources for their fuel, for bedding, and fodder for their stock, and by pooling so many of the necessities of livelihood they were disciplined from early youth to submit to the rules and the customs of their community. After enclosure, when every man could fence his own piece of territory and warn his neighbours off, the discipline of sharing things fairly with one's neighbours was relaxed, and every household became an island unto itself. This', concludes Joan Thirsk, 'was the great revolution in men's lives, greater than all the economic changes following enclosure.'[15]

An Ibo tribesman in Chinua Achebe's twentieth-century novel, referring to the white colonialist, says, 'He has put a knife on the things that held us together and we have fallen apart.'[16] He might have been echoing the thoughts of an English peasant of four hundred years before, in one of the Midlands areas where a man who could get his hands on the scant supply of common grazing could drive his neighbours into poverty and wage labour and where one-sixth of the villages and hamlets in Leicestershire disappeared between about 1450 and 1600,[17] as large privately-owned pastures were created with an eye to markets in meat, cheese, butter, and wool. Speaking of wool, Sir Thomas More wrote in 1516 that 'a few greedy people have converted one of England's greatest natural advantages into a national disaster ... you create thieves, and then punish them for stealing.'[18]

Enclosure did not go far in those early days — as late as 1700, half of England's arable land would still be under open field. But already thousands of vagabonds roamed the roads: dispossessed by enclosers; or cast away as a result of the break-up of great bands of retainers previously kept by feudal magnates but now demolished by royal policy and by the price rise; or thrown into joblessness by slumps in the textile trade. These were the 'poor naked wretches' King Lear would see on his night of storm and revelation. They were desperate, and dangerous. A spokesman for four thousand Suffolk men up in arms in the 1520s said the name of the rebellion's leader was 'Poverty' and explained, 'The clothmakers have put all these people and a farre greater nomber from worke.'[19]

Because of the relative weakness of English towns, clothmaking had been able to escape into the countryside, away from guild regulations which kept up the price of labour. The 'clothmakers' — the merchants who co-ordinated the numerous different processes and gave work to country people in their cottages – dominated many rural areas. The Cotswolds produced a famous heavy broadcloth much in demand in Central Europe, and there were also markets abroad for cheaper, lighter cloths – 'Kerseys' from various southern and eastern counties and from the West Riding of Yorkshire, 'Kendals' from Westmorland, and Welsh 'frieze'. The scale of demand abroad made possible an extended division of labour, and the cloth industry, in England as elsewhere, was the forcing house for 'capitalist' techniques. The English industry had advantages over its rivals on the Continent. It commanded its own local supplies of the best wool in Europe, and, unlike its competitors in Italy and Flanders, it could exploit cheap rustic labour.

The great price rise forced by mounting population dominated European history at this time. In England the general level soared five-fold between 1530 and 1640, ferociously depressing the living standards of poor people but favouring, in such a fluid social structure, middling men – lesser landlords, farmers, yeomen – at the expense of major landlords, including the Crown. Rents, on which great men depended, lagged behind the price of foodstuffs, which lesser men, steering their agriculture towards the market, could now offer. ' … Where they pay after the old rent,' noted a contemporary, 'they sell after the new; that is, they pay for their land good cheap, and sell all things growing thereof dear.'[20] Families claiming 'gentility' multiplied rapidly; but along with 'gentility' now commonly went a thrifty, individualistic outlook. Merchant patricians who married their daughters into the 'gentry', bought land, and took an interest in the direct exploitation of the rural poor, were increasingly meshed with 'gentlemen' who represented towns in Parliament, sent their sons into commerce, exploited mines or timber on their estates, and developed interests in shipping and foreign trade. As capitalism emerged in England, it was not simply a product of town life. The shrewd landlord, the rich plebeian grazier, the rural 'clothmaker' and the merchant-oligarch all acted in ways which helped to set England on the long road to world-wide commercial dominance. The land-hunger which fuelled the expansion of Spain, and the commercial drive which informed the growth of Portugal's empire would be married in England, as they could have been nowhere else, to produce the world's first industrial revolution and, beside it and through it, the largest of all territorial empires.

As that expansionist, capitalist ethos developed, civilised and prosperous Englishmen were clarifying their loathing for the vagabonds of their own country, for the customs of the most backward parts of England, and for the dirty, cowkeeping Celts on its fringes.

III

The turbulence of the Celtic fringe made it a constant threat to the security of English kings, and a standing temptation until the nineteenth century for foreign enemies anxious to meddle or invade, as for pretenders seeking support. The arrival of the Tudors, and its aftermath, illustrate such factors vividly.

A Welshman from Anglesey, Owen ap Maredudd ap Tudor, had wedded, or anyway bedded, the widow of Henry V, and one of their children had married a woman who gave him a claim to the throne. Owen's grandson Henry spent twelve years in exile in the Celtic land of Brittany and became the focus of hope among the Welsh poets, who hailed him as the 'Black Bull of Anglesey'. When he landed in Pembrokeshire in 1485 to assert his claim, the greatest Welsh and Anglo-Welsh magnates threw in their lot with him. The 'Red Dragon of Cadwaladr' (emblem of the last Celtic king to rule all south Britain) flew over his army when he defeated Richard III at Bosworth. The new Henry VII named his son and heir Arthur, after the greatest of Celtic heroes.

But when pretenders rose against Henry, they too looked to the Celtic fringe. Garret More Fitzgerald, Earl of Kildare, the virtual ruler of Ireland by appointment of the Yorkist kings, gave open support to Lambert Simnel, who was crowned 'Edward VI' in Dublin in 1487. Then, after his pardon for this offence, Kildare failed to prevent the Anglo-Irish from offering a welcome to the next claimant, Perkin Warbeck. Warbeck moved on to Scotland, and King James IV agreed to help him. A Scottish army crossed the Border, and burned and looted in its favourite fashion. This in turn provoked a rebellion in Cornwall, where the inhabitants resented being taxed in respect of a fight so far away to the north of them. The Cornish peninsula was still Celtic in its place names and in its superstitions. The English language had made little headway in the parts west of Truro where the 1497 rising started under the leadership of a blacksmith, Michael Joseph. It attracted the minor gentry, though more substantial landlords of Norman stock held aloof. The Cornishmen, said to be 15,000 strong, were defeated only at Blackheath, near London. And then Warbeck himself arrived in Cornwall a few weeks later and raised a fresh brief rebellion there.[21]

England north of the Trent, down to the eighteenth century, also presented dangers. The easier lands were commonly cultivated in the Midland–English way, but up in the hills tribalism survived. The people of Redesdale in Northumberland claimed rights of common pasture in the fells not in respect of their landholdings but in respect of their surnames, 'for that they are descended of such a surname or race of men to whom such a summering belongeth.' They still harked back to their origins in a single family, and accordingly practised partible inheritance, a custom radically opposed to the primogeniture which held sway in the south, and one which had implications for law and order. Younger sons, instead of moving away, stayed in the valleys, overcrowding them and lending their arms to the favourite sport of cattle raiding. The shifting of the cattle to the fells in spring was a common ritual, planned like a military operation, with straggling strictly forbidden, and no one without good excuse allowed to stay behind.[22]

The outlaws come frae Liddesdale
They herry Redesdale far and near;
The rich man's gelding it maun gang,
They canna pass the puir man's mear.[23]

In adjacent parts of Scotland English-speaking tribalism likewise prevailed, and the most notorious surnames clustered in Liddesdale – Armstrongs and Elliotts, Bells, Nixons and Crosers. The whole area north and south of the Border can be seen as 'a single economic and social unit', where national feeling meant little or nothing.[24] In summer beasts were driven to high pastures; in winter the main occupation was reiving. The Liddesdale men raided deep into Durham and Yorkshire and also as far as Edinburgh in the north. The Border reiver, astride the nimble little horse which was his most precious possession, was a permanent recruit in warfare against anyone not of his own surname. A contemporary reported such men to be 'Scottishe when they will, and English at their pleasure.' When James IV was defeated and killed at Flodden in 1513, after invading England in support of the French King, the 'Scottish' borderers in his army stood aloof from the battle, then pillaged the Scottish dead.[25] But it was the existence of a frontier, creating problems of jurisdiction, and the wars of royal armies across the Border, which had fostered the lawlessness of the area. Under the weak Crown of Scotland, large Border landowners like Kerr of Cessford or Lord Maxwell wielded power outside feudal law as chiefs of their own surnames, and pursued continuous blood feuds among themselves. Lesser men who quarrelled with them were forced into outlawry with their surnames. They robbed the 'poor man's mare', drove off the rich man's cattle, levied 'blackmail' (protection money), and fought each other in vicious vendettas; the ballad of 'Parcy Reed' describes how one Redesdale man was betrayed by three false ('English') Halls into the hands of his ('Scottish') Croser enemies, who 'hacket off his hands and feet'.[26] The minstrels devising out of ceaseless violence the richest body of folk poetry in the language 'praised their chieftains', in Walter Scott's words, 'for the very exploits, against which the laws of the country denounced a capital doom.'[27] Such conditions affected, taking both sides of the Border together, something over 150,000 people.[28]

In England, the 'North Country' was aberrant. In Scotland, feuding and clannishness were normal. Scotland was both politically and economically 'backward' compared to its southern neighbour, chiefly for the good reason which Scots have often remembered, but have sometimes decided to forget, that the country is intrinsically poorer. The King of Scots' half million or so subjects were scattered in scant fertile tracts among the moorland, mountains and rough pasture which formed the vast majority of his territory. One English pound was worth four Scots pounds in 1560, twelve in 1601.

Londoners, to judge from Elizabethan plays, seem to have found it hard or impossible to distinguish between the speech of a Scot and that of an English north-countryman.[29] Why Gaelic should have been replaced by the English language over most of Lowland Scotland in the Middle Ages is a mysterious question about a firm fact. By the sixteenth century, the Lowlands, decisively part of Catholic, feudal Christendom, had much in common with England. But across the language boundary, Gael and Sassenach in Scotland still had one thing in common, their violence. 'When contemporaries wrote about the Highlands, the one thing they did not stress as being different from the Lowlands was the clan system,' T. C. Smout observes. 'Highland society was based on kinship modified by feudalism, Lowland society on feudalism tempered by kinship. Both systems were aristocratic, unconscious of class, designed for war.'[30] A Spanish ambassador wrote at the end of the fifteenth century, 'They spend all their time in wars, and when there is no war they fight with one another.'[31]

English-speaking Scots founded a fairly strong sense of separate identity on the independence precariously established by Robert Bruce at Bannockburn in 1314, before and after periods of English dominance. The Stewart line of kings initiated in 1371 commanded the loyalties of most Scots for over three hundred years, and of some for a half century more. But from the mid-fifteenth century, no fewer than seven successive Stewart monarchs inherited as children (or babies) through the deaths, usually violent, of their parents. With minority and regency more common than not, the great feudal magnates became virtual kings in their own areas. The Crown was for long phases the plaything of overweening men. Civil war and commotion became habitual.

Whether in Lowlands or Highlands, landlords were still war leaders whose attitude to their tenants was governed, and softened, by the belief that having plenty of men to follow you mattered much more than exacting maximum rents. Serfdom had long since disappeared, and the country had never known a peasant revolt. The humblest Scot could assuage his poverty and insecurity with fierce pride in his kinship to the great man of his name, or in the fidelity with which, freely, he followed a chosen leader in feud or war. ' ... The hail people', a six-teenth-century cleric noted, 'nocht onlie the Nobilitie because thay fecht upon thair awne purse, enioy a gret freedome and libertie; quhairof cumis that undiscrete consuetude, undiscrete maneris, that pride, and bosting of thair nobilitie, quhilkes ... al obiectes to us.'[32] Or in more up-to-date, if not plainer, English, we might say that the Scots already showed a proto-democratic tendency to think that no man was worse than another. 'I am Little Jock Elliott — who dares meddle with me?' one Border reiver is said to have exclaimed as he stabbed the great nobleman who was trying to dispose of him.

The big man, chief we may as well say, leased out land to kinsmen and followers who became his feudal vassals and were legally obliged to follow him in war. Besides his own people, others would look to him in the prevailing anarchy, and these he could fasten to himself by 'bonds of manrent'. They gave armed service in return for protection. Three different kinds of tie — kinship, feudalism and manrent – therefore co-existed, sometimes reinforcing each other, sometimes cutting across each other. The Crown, in the early sixteenth century, was making only slow headway in asserting its power against barons who had come to control the sheriffdoms. Within the barony itself, a lord dealt out his own justice in his own courts and in many areas there were heritable 'regalities' where great men could legally exercise almost all the rights of a king. Some of this would survive till the mid-eighteenth century. Meanwhile feuds raged for generations and sometimes involved pitched battles between hundreds of armed men. In the typically pithy words of James VI and I they banged it out bravely, 'he and all his kinne against him and all his.'[33]

Gaelic chiefs north and west of the 'Highland Line' commonly held their land by irreproachable feudal tenures, and their junior relatives were from the point of view of parchment legality simply principal tenants, while parchment bonds of manrent might legitimise the adoption into the clan of outsiders. However – and here a distinction can be seen from the Lowlands – within Gaelic culture the faith that the clan really were all one family was vital, and even such formerly Norman or Flemish lords as the Grants and Frasers of the Eastern Highlands had been able to build up a sense of clan identity based on the myth of a common parentage. Kinship, conceived in this way, could obliterate feudal loyalty, hence an episode in 1562 when the chief of Mackintosh raised his people to fight for Queen Mary while certain Mackintoshes, tenants of Gordon lords, were summoned to fight against her. Mackintosh, so the story goes, waylaid his errant clansmen, and brought them all over to the Queen. Certain chiefs were legally speaking landless, their followers all the tenants of others.

The chief's main function in the eyes of Highlanders was to lead his people into battle, and his power was both paternal and absolute. The Gaelic custom, whereby he would place his child with foster parents so that the boy grew up in a special relationship with one family of vassals, helped to bind lesser families with his own. His leading followers, *duine uasails*, were generally kinsmen of his own, who held lands from him at easy rents until he chose to replace them with closer kin. He had power to shift his people about at will or even, if it suited himself, to move them all to a new district. Nevertheless, the idea grew deep roots that the glen which it occupied belonged to the clan, as a clan, to all its members together.

Highlanders already liked tartan garments. Tartan plaids were used in the Lowlands as well. But a Sassenach wore his plaid over breeches. The poorer Highlanders went bare-legged, and their way of life struck Lowlanders as primitive. The hunting of red deer for food was still a common recourse. Transhumance, as in the Borders, was generally practised, with cattle taken about midsummer up to mountainside 'shielings'. Highlanders traded their beasts for Lowland corn, and the two economies were complementary. But the Church barely affected Highland life. The area had no towns, no centres of trade and 'civil' behaviour. Its people favoured instead the most uncivil custom of raiding into the Lowlands, where their wild and frequent descents were greatly feared. In the sixteenth century pressure of population was mounting on the scraps of fertile soil in the mountains and isles. The chiefs of the stronger clans had now divided most of the land between them, and no one could expand except at his neighbour's detriment. Macleods, for instance, occupied Gairloch, to which Mackenzies had legal right, and the two clans fought for a century over it.[34]

The greatest of all Highland chiefships had been that of the Lord of the Isles, head of Clan Donald, whose Gaelic–Norse dynasty had emerged in the mid-fourteenth century, thereafter habitually claiming sovereign independence. The Scottish Crown had fought back and in 1493 the Lord was deprived of his title and his estates. 'It is no joy without Clan Donald,' a bard lamented, ' ... the best race in the round world ... the gentlest among ladies ... hawks of Islay for valour ... it is no joy without Clan Donald.'[35]

Clan Donald itself fell apart as the lesser Macdonald chiefs emerged as individual powers. The Crown began deliberately to advance the scope of the Campbells at their expense. The Campbell Earl of Argyll—his Gaelic title was MacChailean Mor, 'son of great Colin' — was made Lieutenant of the Isles. His clan had before that begun the long career of expansion which makes its name the mostly widely hated in Scottish lore. The Earls of Argyll used the King's favour, and their uncommonly sharp grasp of laws which other chiefs found it hard to master, to secure Campbell domination over a great swathe of territory. In Edinburgh they were civil subjects, on their own lands absolute rulers by Gaelic tradition, ready on occasion to intrigue with England or in Ulster for their own purposes.

Their position was almost like that of the Earls of Kildare in Ireland, where the area under effective control by the Crown had contracted to a small slab around Dublin, 'the Pale'. Beyond it, where 'English' settlers could still be distinguished amid the Gaels who had flowed back around them, they had to pay tribute, 'blackrent', to Irish chiefs, or were found in rebellious league with them. Such nobles of settler descent as the Geraldine Earls of Desmond in the south-west employed, like the Gaelic leaders, clans of Scots 'gallowglasses', mail-clad Hebrideans armed with ferocious axes who settled on the island permanently. Faced with the impossible cost of anything like direct rule, Yorkist kings had exalted the other great Geraldine house, that of Kildare, to the status of virtual 'High Kingship'. In so far as Ireland was ruled, which was not very far, from 1477 onwards, it was governed by the Earl of Kildare, except for a couple of years when Henry VII sent Sir Edward Poynings across to replace him. Ireland had its own parliament, though this now represented only the Leinster counties and a few towns. Poynings extracted from it his famous law. No parliament in Ireland was from now on to pass any Bill which had not been approved by the King beforehand. Henry's wish to restore the Crown to its former powers was made clear in various other morsels of legislation, but actuality was starkly acknowledged when the parliament laid down that a double ditch should be made around the Pale to keep out marauders.

In Munster the heirs of Norman conquistadors lived by a mixture of English and Gaelic laws and customs, with the latter in practice gaining ground. In Connacht and Westmeath other 'Anglo-Normans' like the Burkes, originally 'de Burgos', were indistinguishable from their Irish neighbours. In Ulster, O Neills and O Donnells went on their purely Gaelic way. Though the Butlers of Tipperary and Kilkenny emerged in Tudor times as fairly steady friends of the English Crown, the Brehon judges of ancient tradition administered Irish law for the Earls of Ormond, and their followers went into battle with the war cry 'Butler Aboo'. The *file*, hereditary poet, whose person was sacred and whose curses were thought lethal, was as ready to flatter a Butler or a Fitzgerald (or indeed a chief in Perthshire when his travel took him there) as he was to pour praises on a pure-bred McCarthy or an O Brien of ancient Gaelic stock.

The Irish chiefs ruled what the English called 'nations', but their lands had no fixed boundaries and they measured their greatness in men, not territories. An official report by an Englishman in 1515 reckoned there were over ninety independent powers in Ireland, two-thirds of them found among 'the King's Irish enemies', the others Anglo-Norman in origin.[36] In practice, however, most of these were loosely subject to the great chiefs whose names have been mentioned, and whose degree of power at any one time was expressed through their capacity, or lack of it, to quarter soldiers and other followers on their vassals. By contrast with Gaelic Scotland, chiefship was passed on by primogeniture only among the Anglo-Normans. Lesser chiefs were appointed by great chiefs. The latter themselves emerged by election and struggle from within the clan's ruling *derbfine*, a group composed of all those descended from one ancestor inside four generations. Anyone whose great grandfather had been a chief was theoretically eligible, and since virtual polygamy obtained, with marriage in church exception rather than rule, while Gaelic law generously refused to distinguish bastards from legitimate children, it was commonplace for a chief to have two or three score real or putative grandsons. The succession struggles resulting were often ferocious, before the chief at last was inaugurated with rituals handed down from a distant pre-Christian past, on some primeval sacred stone, when one vassal might place a white rod in his hands and another put a shoe upon his foot.

The land was owned by the ruling clan as a whole and was freshly shared out at intervals, sometimes annually. The cultivators beneath them were mere tenants at will, wholly dependant. (It should be stressed that the peasantry in more anglicised areas were equally oppressed; Irish tenants almost everywhere were the most vulnerable rural class in Western Europe.) Chieftains and poets alike despised the common people — 'mere churls and labouring men, not one of whom knows his own grandfather.' Poets, like those other guardians of tradition, the brehons, the annalists and the physicians, formed a hereditary caste, parasitic on the rulers. Though marriage of priests was in theory forbidden, the

Irish clergy was also hereditary; and at least two early-sixteenth-century bishops led their clans in conflict as chiefs of their names.[37] The Irishman of the ruling classes, carrying his javelin overarm, riding without stirrups, was more picturesque than useful in battle, and the hard work was done by mercenary septs of gallowglasses and by the ordinary able-bodied freemen fighting on foot, the 'kerns'. There was plenty of it. In the Gaelic *Annals of the Four Masters*, the entry for 1533, a relatively moderate one in respect of slaughters, records only two deaths by natural causes. The rest is wholly given over to such mayhem as this:

> MacDermot of Moylurg ... was treacherously slain by the sons of Owen, son of Teige MacDermot; and Owen, the son of Teige, assumed the Lordship after him.
>
> O Molloy ... Lord of Fircall, was treacherously slain on the Green of Lann-Ealla by his own brother, Cucogry, and Art, his brother's son; and his brother, Cahir, was styled O Molloy ...
>
> The castle of Sligo was taken by Teige Oge, the son of Teige Oge, son of Hugh O Conor, by means of a nocturnal assault, the warders of the castle having betrayed it and surrendered it to them.
>
> The castle of Ard-na-riagh was likewise taken at night by the sons of Thomas Burke, from the sons of O Dowda.
>
> A great depredation was committed by O Donnell upon O Hara Boy, between the two rivers, because the latter had been disobedient to him.[38]

And so on. It was as much conventional praise for the annalist to report of a dead chief that he had made many predatory excursions through Ireland as to say that the same man had been freehanded in hospitality. Rustling was not a crime, but a kind of sport.

Wealth was measured in small black cattle. Chiefs had hundreds or thousands. Transhumance was general in Ireland, and in Ulster, uniquely, herds wandered from place to place throughout the summer. Cultivation was of lesser concern, and such methods as ploughing with a share fastened by willow twigs to the tails of four or so horses struck English outsiders as disgustingly primitive. Scotland, compared to England, was backward enough in trade and used very little money, but Ireland was more uncommercial still, though there was some business done through small ports on its southern and eastern coasts. Irish culture was not static; for centuries it had been changing slowly under influence from England. The problem would be that England had changed far faster.

Wales, by contrast, had managed, if not to catch up, at least to follow the richer country quite closely. Because the Welsh themselves willingly adapted, some distinctiveness would be allowed to survive—here is a major reason for one of the strangest facts in history, that such a small country still contains many Welsh-language speakers and has a real sense of peculiar identity. In Ireland and in the Scottish Highlands, only the extirpation of a whole culture would ultimately suffice to make matters agreeable to English-speakers; and

Ulster first of all and above all would pay the full price of obstinate tribalism.

The Welsh were breaking away, far enough, from the Celtic idea that the clan owned its land in common. ' ... Small peasant proprietors whose rights in the soil derived from clan status were still the most prominent element in Welsh rural society.'[39] But one factor involved in the outburst of peasant discontent which from 1400 for a few years had established Owen Glyn Dŵr as an independent prince, crowned before the envoys of foreign nations, had been the disintegration of kinship and the rise of a kulak class. Then, producing a massive turnover of land, Glyn Dŵr's revolt had itself helped clear the way for a Welsh gentry. By the mid-sixteenth century, a basic division between landed and landless men was established and the Welsh social structure, though not identical, was compatible with the English.[40] And of course the Tudors themselves were sympathetic. 'The Welsh,' the Venetian Ambassador reported, as Henry VII showered rewards on those compatriots who had supported him, 'may now be said to have recovered their former independence ... '[41]

But their land of about a quarter-million people had no obvious centre of its own; the highland hump athwart the country prevented it. English towns, Shrewsbury and Oswestry, gave the country its economic direction by providing a market for cloth and cattle. Wales was chronically lawless and disordered. The near-independent 'Marcher lordships' which survived on its border made possible customs evasions which ate into royal revenues, and provided a haven for criminals fleeing royal jurisdiction. When magnates committed crimes, juries feared to convict them, and if such a man were fined he would extort the money as a forced 'gift' from the poor. In 1529, Rhys ap Gruffyd, a major landowner, burst into the Sessions House at Carmarthen with forty armed supporters, hoping to overawe justice into releasing one of his followers. When he was disarmed and detained his wife rode in with 140 men in an unsuccessful attempt to rescue him. Rhys, with friends in high places, was acquitted, but two years later he was beheaded for plotting to murder the King and make himself Prince of Wales. Yet Wales was no more, if no less, vexatious, than England's northern borderlands, and 'the heart of the problem was thought [by administrators] to lie in the English marcher lordships rather than in the Welsh tribal system'.[42]

The ideal for such administrators, and for the well-to-do English-speakers who shared their values, would have been two islands where men grew corn and drank beer and did these things in a settled way in seemly parishes and shires. Such people were easy to tax and easy to control. But cattle-culture as Celts and others practised it was nomadic, or semi-nomadic. 'Wherever transhumance is or has been practised', a geographer, Estyn Evans, remarks, ' ... it has provided opportunities for escape from authority and served as a means of preserving and transmitting ancient traditions.'[43] What could one do with people following improper customs like those of the Scottish and Irish Gaels, who would seethe an animal's flesh in its own hide and consume blood tapped direct

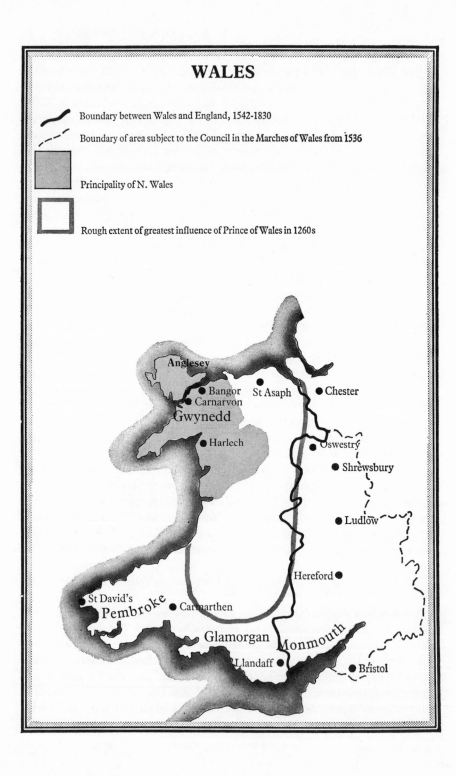

WALES

Boundary between Wales and England, 1542-1830

Boundary of area subject to the Council in the Marches of Wales from 1536

Principality of N. Wales

Rough extent of greatest influence of Prince of Wales in 1260s

Anglesey

Bangor
Carnarvon
Gwynedd

St Asaph

Chester

Harlech

Oswestry

Shrewsbury

Ludlow

Hereford

St David's
Pembroke
Carmarthen

Glamorgan
Monmouth

Llandaff

Bristol

from living cattle? Customs in the other sense did not yield much to the Crown in such beastly areas. The revenues of all ports on the west coast, taken together with those on the east north of Aberdeen, accounted for well under 10 per cent of the King's customs in Scotland in 1542.[44] Up to the reign of Edward I, Ireland, through feudal dues and other revenues, had brought much profit to English kings; now, if it were to be so useful again, it would have to be reconquered at great expense.

The Celtic lands and the Borders between them account for an overweening proportion of the surviving folk traditions of Britain which children are asked to love and admire today. But sixteenth-century English-speakers associated such lore with the weakness of the Church, that cardinal instrument of centralisation, and with the tribal character of the areas which preserved it. The bagpipe which Scottish Gaels were now using to urge their forces into battle had not yet acquired pleasant associations for Sassenachs – nor had the great ballads of the Borders. Oral tradition prevails where few people can write or read. 'Certainly,' Sir Philip Sidney wrote about 1580, 'I must confesse my own barbarousness. I never heard the olde song of Percy and Duglas that I found not my heart mooued more then with a Trumpet; and yet is it sung but by some blinde Crouder, with no rougher voyce then rude stile ... '[45] Another Tudor witness gave an account of the social role of the Irish poets which explains why even Sidney, a great poet himself, was dubious about 'barbarous' balladry: 'Their first practice is, if they see any young man descended from the septs of Os and Macs, who has half a dozen men about him, they will make him a rime wherein they will commend his fathers and his ancestors, numbering how many heads they have cut off, how many towns they have burned, and how many virgins they have deflowered, how many notable murders they have done, and in the end they will compare him to Hannibal or Scipio or Hercules, or some other famous person; wherewithal the poor fool runs mad and thinks indeed it is so.' Thus incited, the young chief would prove his manhood by gathering a 'rabble of rakehells' to attack villages, burn and pillage, then drive off all the livestock.[46] Poets would be a prime and constant target for men who sought to extend the authority of English monarchy. (The Scots kings seem to have been less worried by them.) In Wales as well as in Ireland, the bard seemed an obvious enemy of the state, to be banned on principle, hanged whenever chance offered.

The English-speaking official who wanted his own royal master to have a monopoly of bullying and exaction naturally led the chorus denouncing the high-handed behaviour of Marcher magnates, Highland clan chiefs and Irish chiefs. There is no doubt that the last sort in particular, aiming to live wholly off his vassals as he travelled about, could be as oppressive in many cases as even a Tudor monarch. It is also clear enough that the periphery bristled with private armies at a time when aristocratic thuggery was receding in England – the last dwelling there to be called a castle was built in the second decade of the sixteenth century, and even then its castellations were purely ornamental.[47] But Tudor, and

Stewart, crown servants who sought royal monopoly of violence backed the use of great violence towards this end. As they succeeded, the idea gained sway that murdering Gaels, or foreigners, or Red Indians, as part of a royal army or with royal approval, was patriotic, heroic, and just, whereas to defend yourself and your way of life against the advancing forces of English-speaking empire showed human nature at its worst and most bestial. Historians tend to identify this view with moral progress; the habit of flattering power has not been confined to the Irish annalist caste.

As the middle- and upper-class English-speakers asserted themselves against the Celts around them, they developed notions of racial superiority which would easily be adapted to justify the enslavement of Africans and the conquest of the Indian subcontinent, and which many people of Celtic descent would come to share. Non-English, non-commercialised cultures were manifestly so wicked and silly that to liberate people from them must be in their best interest.

Even in the Middle Ages ineffectual cultural laws had been introduced in Ireland, by 1366, and in Wales, after Glyn Dŵr's revolt. Settlers were ordered not to marry Gaels, use Gaelic surnames, speak Gaelic or ride in the Irish fashion. The Welsh were not to acquire land in towns, carry arms or assemble without special permission. Henry VII, of course, gave the Welsh equality before the law with Englishmen. Even so their concern with livestock rather than cultivation aroused deep suspicion among English observers, one of whom wrote around 1540 that they 'did study more to pasturage then tylling, as favorers of their consuete idilness'.[48] All pastoralists were thought 'idle'. By the early sixteenth century we find a Lowland Scots writer deploring the aversion of Highlanders to 'honest industry'.[49] As Gaelic-speakers, they came to be sorted in Lowland minds into two sorts of inferior person – poor 'wild Irish' and prosperous 'Civil Irish'. 'There be also many of the Campbells that be English', reported a cleric, himself a Campbell, early in the seventeenth century, meaning that the remainder spoke Gaelic.[50] To be 'Irish' whether in Scotland or Ireland seemed increasingly stubborn and wicked as the century wore on. Philip Sidney would accuse the Gaels of choosing 'rather all filthiness than any law.'[51] Gaelic dress in Ireland seemed as uncouth and sinister as the characteristic 'glib' of hair worn over their faces by old men. Men and women had distinctive long fringed mantles, and these would excite Sidney's fellow poet Edmund Spenser into frenzies of prurient aversion worthy of a betrousered Victorian missionary in the Dark Continent. After complaining that outlaws used the mantle as a tent and bed, that rebels used it as a shield and thieves hid their loot in it and masked themselves with it, Spenser declaimed that for a wandering loose woman it was 'half a wardrobe; for in summer you shall find her arrayed commonly but in her smock and mantle, to be more ready for her light services; in winter, and in her travail, it is her cloak and safeguard, and also a coverlet for her lewd exercise; ... yea, and when her bastard is born it serves instead of swaddling-clouts.'[52]

Spenser was a devout Protestant. His contempt for the Irish was reinforced by esteem for his own religion and loathing of theirs. The one thing needful to crown the sense of superiority enjoyed by English-speakers within the British Isles was the possession of two national reformed Churches. The 'Tudor revolution in government' in England, and its feebler counterpart in Scotland, came to involve the establishment of Protestantism as well as the conquest of the British barbarians.

IV

Sir Walter Ralegh would write of the 'bluff' King Henry VIII who ruled England from 1509 to 1547: ' ... If all the pictures and patterns of a merciless prince were lost in the world, they might all again be painted to the life, out of the story of this King.'[53] Yet the continuing infatuation of English people with the disagreeable Tudor dynasty has some real basis; they consolidated the English nation-state and English patriotism, making religion one of their main means of doing so. Aiming (it can be argued) at complete despotism, Henry VIII unwittingly forwarded the creation of the English middle classes and their world-changing self-confidence.

The 'Tudor revolution in government' meant that great landed noblemen lost power both to the Crown and to the gentry and merchants represented in the House of Commons. Its presiding proponent was Thomas Cromwell, son of a tradesman, trained in business and law, who was Henry's chief minister in the 1530s, and became Earl of Essex before his royal master lopped off his head. He had learnt in Italy, land of Machiavelli, 'to think in terms of function and efficiency, to disregard hidebound traditions and all-embracing philosophical systems', and, in short, to break out of medieval ways of thinking.[54] His great work was the 'Reformation' which ended the Pope's authority in England. The events of 1529–33 promoted patriotic self-awareness, which Henry could share with his middling subjects. They added urgency to the drive towards unification of the island, which would make it harder for the Pope and the Catholic powers of Europe to undo the nationalisation of the Church of England. Protestant doctrines as yet interested few people. What was approved of was Henry VIII's attack on the opulence and corruption of a Church which represented an intrusion of alien authority. 'The English', an Italian visitor had reported around 1500, 'are great lovers of themselves ... they think that there are no other men than themselves, and no other world but England; and whenever they see a handsome foreigner they say that "he looks like an Englishman," and that "it is a great pity that he should not be an Englishman".'[55]

Cromwell wrote the preamble to an Act of 1533 which provided that appeals in spiritual causes should no longer go to Rome but be finally settled in England: 'This realm of England is an Empire ... governed by one Supreme Head and King ... '[56] The word 'empire', till the nineteenth century, did not imply expansion or colonies, it simply suggested that England was self-governing, equal in independence to the Holy Roman Empire on the Continent. No foreign ruler could claim any authority. England was, in modern parlance, a sovereign national state. The ideas behind the preamble can be traced to those of Marsiglio of Padua who in the fourteenth century had argued in ways which made him the forerunner of the Protestant view of the State in the sixteenth century, of the democratic theory of the nineteenth, and of the State-worship of the twentieth. The Church should have no worldly power. The State derived its comprehensive authority from the whole people of the country, who had the ultimate right to decide its constitutional forms. A corollary was that the king should rule effectively everywhere, overriding local magnates. Certain of Henry VIII's subjects could still legally claim special rights and immunities, within 'palatinates' like Durham and Lancaster, 'liberties' like Ripon and Richmond (all these four, it will be observed, in the North), and more widely wherever a lord had the right to hold his own courts. In an Act of 1536, Cromwell ended this, extending the operation of royal justice and the system of 'shires' over all England. What happened in Wales and Ireland, we shall see. It was typical of the new policy of consolidation that representatives of the town of Calais, which was all that remained in the English King's hands of the wide territories his predecessors had ruled in France, should sit in the House of Commons after 1536. Cromwell shared with his royal master a still more radical vision, of the whole British Isles united under one king.

Church revenues were diverted to the Crown. The monasteries and convents were dissolved and their far flung lands became crown property. In a generation or two, these were mostly disposed of for the sake of ready money and the middling class of gentry acquired with them a vital stake in the Reformation. Over the next hundred years, knights and lesser gentry trebled in numbers while overall population scarcely doubled. 'By 1600, gentlemen, new and old, occupied a far greater proportion of the land of England than in 1530 – to the disadvantage of Crown, Church, aristocracy and peasantry alike.'[57] In other ways also the Reformation launched tendencies ultimately fatal to royal power. Cromwell encouraged translations of the Bible and ordered the book to be placed, in English, in all churches. By 1545 Henry himself was complaining that 'the most precious jewel, the Word of God, is disputed, rhymed, sung and jangled in every ale-house and tavern.' In the Bible, men read stories of bad kings and bold, just prophets and of the military exploits of a chosen people. 'Without it', A. G. Dickens justly remarks, 'we can hardly imagine English constitutionalism or English imperial expansion.'[58]

Literacy became for the godly a matter of elementary self-respect. Disputing Old Testament texts helped to develop intellectual self-reliance. Craftsmen and seamen learnt to read, and could pick up new skills and new vision. Protestant religious ideas fostered individualism, and they bear a relationship which must seem crucial, though it is elusive and much-debated, to Britain's precocious progress in trade and industry. Calvinism, which became dominant as the sixteenth century wore on, was an activist creed, seeking 'the sanctification of the world by strife and labour'.[59] The existence in England of a faith distinct from that still held in Spain, the great imperial, colonising power, would foster a spirit of crusade, aligned with envy and emulation, and would, as in Holland, help to fuel struggle through trade and with arms on the high seas and in the New World.

Surviving Catholicism in England became identified with old-fashioned sections of society. This was true as early as 1536-7 when an idealist, Robert Aske, led the revolt in the North known as the Pilgrimage of Grace. Peasant rebels who called for the return of papal power feared that new landlords replacing the former monks would interfere with customary tenures generous by southern standards, while northern nobility and gentry had been offended by Cromwell's extension of central control. The series of outbreaks was swiftly beaten down, a spate of summary executions followed, and Cromwell had a pretext to reduce the influence of the great northern magnates. The process was not completed till exiles and confiscations followed a later northern rising in 1569, but Cromwell's strong new Council of the North, a permanent body dominated by royal officials, would survive to preside over that consummation.

It was the counterpart of a Council in the Marches of Wales which had been set up at the start of the century. Cromwell made president of this body, in 1533, Rowland Lee, Bishop of Coventry and Lichfield, 'stowte of nature, readie witted, roughe in speeche, not affable to anye of the walshrie, an extreme severe ponisher of offences.' A contemporary claimed that Lee hanged 5,000 men in nine years of office; he was especially glad to string up those of high birth. He also built up an exemplary spy service.[60] But the Reformation meant that more was needed. The legal changes which it involved could only be carried through in Wales constitutionally if the country was unified with England.

Hence the 'Act of Union' passed through the English Parliament in 1536. It argued that Henry VIII was rightful King of Wales, yet in that country 'dyvers rightes usages laws and customes be farre discrepant frome the lawes and customes of this Realme.' Furthermore, 'by cause that the people of the same dominion have and do daily use a speche nothing like ne consonaunt to the naturall mother tonge used within this Realme' — that is, they wilfully spoke 'unnatural' Welsh — 'some rude and ignorant people' had 'made distinccion and diversitie betwene the Kinges Subiectes of this Realme and hys subiectes of the said dominion and Principalitie of Wales'. Hence Wales must now be 'for ever' incorporated, united and annexed to England. While people born in Wales would have all the rights and privileges of Englishmen, English law would now obtain in Wales, specifically in matters of inheritance — 'division or particion' of an estate, that Celtic aberration, was forbidden. The Marcher lordships were digested into five new Welsh shires — Brecon, Monmouth, Radnor, Denbigh and Montgomery — and certain English counties. Welsh shires would now have representatives in the Commons, but there had been no Welsh members in the parliament passing the Union.[61] However, the bards were silent. There was no outcry in Wales against the Act. Little was really changed. More or less the same people remained in charge of the country, while English criminal law and, largely, the English common law, had been used and welcomed in Wales for a long time.

But a further Act of 1542 did fix boundaries for Wales, a unit of twelve counties, from which Monmouth, despite its Welshness, was detached for legal purposes. The division was rough and ready – Welsh was spoken in parts of Herefordshire until the nineteenth century – and the Council for Wales had authority over wide, not exactly defined, tracts of the English borderland. But by the 1550s the Council had established its permanent bureaucratic presence, and the fact that it was not abolished till 1688 gave Wales a token of distinct existence over a long and formative period.

Rowland Lee had doubted whether the Welsh could govern themselves under English law – where, he asked Cromwell, were the men of substance needed to make J.P.s? 'There be very fewe Welshemen in Wales above Brecknock that may dispende ten pounde lande and, to say truthe, their discretion (is) lesse than their landes.'[62] And because the country was so poor, the property qualification for J.P.s was waived. But the Welsh gentry were men with rising self-confidence, very happy to exploit the uncertainty about land tenures arising with the enforcement of primogeniture and other English laws. Welsh squires looked out for English wives and English squires married Welsh heiresses. It became common for Welsh gentry to send sons to England for schooling. One expressed the hope that the boy he was packing off to London would learn to speak English 'without any corruption from his mother tongue, which doth commonly infect men of our countre, that they cannot speak English but that they are discovered by their vitious pronunciation or idiotisms.'[63]

English laws against retainers had little effect yet. Herberts still feuded with Vaughans, though each clan would produce a great English poet in the next century. But gradually litigation began to supplant riot, with hereditary enemies taking each other to law rather than staging fights through the town or even in churches. While Wales still depended heavily on the cattle trade with England for what little cash the country could muster, other fields were now explored. Some gentry developed mines. The ports of South Wales began to thrive a little. New tastes for comforts, even for fopperies came in as commerce tied Wales securely to England.

The Welsh, with few exceptions, remained indifferent to the Reformation, tolerating what changes it brought but not yet (not for two hundred years) displaying much vivid interest in Protestantism. However, the Reformation was crucial for the preservation of the Welsh tongue. Fearing popish contamination, Parliament in 1562 enacted that the Bible should be translated into the language which most Welsh people still spoke. Though the job was not properly done till 1588, this meant that a force which helped to destroy Cornish and which would greatly limit the literary uses of the Lowland Scots dialect – the influence of God's word in English – did not have scope in Wales. And the gentry, besides retaining a famous infatuation with their family pedigrees, still patronised bards, and wrote poems in Welsh themselves. Many gave attention to Welsh antiquities, and this was encouraged at the highest level. The Tudors were not ashamed to be Welsh. Certain patriotic themes, the alleged purity of the Celtic Church, for instance, were very useful for propaganda purposes. David Powel, compiler of a history of Wales (1584), acknowledged the help of no less a person than Lord Burghley, the Queen's chief minister, whose own grandfather had been Welsh, and, though he made some complaints about medieval Norman and English oppressions, he concluded 'there was never anie thing so beneficiall to the common people of Wales, as the uniting of that countrie to the crowne and kingdome of England ... '[64]

The notion that 'Britain' owed its name to one 'Brutus' or 'Brut', great grandson of that legendary Trojan Aeneas who had founded Rome, seat of Empire, was one to which Welsh intellectuals clung fondly. They liked the concept of Britain itself, and while they saw themselves as the true 'Britons', they were ready in charity to style the English 'Britons' also, 'usurpers and mere possessors' though they might be.[65] The expression, 'Brytish Impire' seems to have been first used by a Welsh scientist, John Dee, in 1577.[66] Dee was an early proponent of overseas expansion. Of that, Ireland would be the prime laboratory.

V

From the purely legal point of view, Ireland was a fief where some vassals had become unruly, and where chieftains without feudal status had usurped land from other vassals. But to English-speakers settled within the Pale, Ireland was a colonial country, with a native problem, confronted with which men were, in modern parlance, doves or hawks. In the early sixteenth century a dove-like view preponderated. The gentry of the Pale and the merchants of the isolated towns beyond it were men of property who wanted a strong administration to protect their position. Ideally, they would like to see the Gaelic chieftainships destroyed, the feudal powers of gaelicised Anglo-Norman magnates curbed, and the whole country brought under the system of law and order which now existed only within the Pale. A smallish garrison from England would be needed – but not more settlers, or even officials; the Palesmen themselves, so they thought, could enforce English custom and law. This view of matters, expressed in successive schemes for reform throughout the century, appealed to English chief governors and statesmen because 'reformacion' seemed cheaper than thorough-going conquest and colonisation.[67]

In 1515, bitter complaints came from the Palesmen to King Henry. The 9th Earl of Kildare, Garret Oge, had succeeded his father smoothly as ruler in 1513, but now his subjects denounced this barbaric potentate, moving about with a

c

great troop of kerns and gallowglasses and extorting entertainment from the people, while the Palesmen themselves were having to pay blackrent to the Irish. Henry for a while continued Kildare in office and even increased his powers. Then, why it is not clear, royal policy changed. Henry summoned Kildare to England and detained him, and sent out the Earl of Surrey as lieutenant, with a sizeable army but with plans to bring Ireland peacefully under royal control by 'politique driftes, and amiable persuasions ... '

Surrey became the first Tudor Englishman to be transmogrified into a hawk by the Irish Heart of Darkness. At first he did pretty well, conducting vigorous campaigns on the borders of the Pale, striking agreements with great Ulster chieftains and taking a force of nearly 2,000 with him on progress through the south-east. But then the Irish damp, the insects, the diarrhoea, the uncouth language, began to invade his doings and his mind. He could hardly find healthy quarters for his soldiers; three of his servants died; no place in the country was safe; he feared for his wife and children. He was short of money and supplies. As he came to a standstill, he was asked to cut down on his English troops and to maintain himself out of the barely-existent Irish revenue. The King told him he could not afford to send reinforcements, and pay £16,000 or £17,000 a year, just to defend the Pale's four shires. But Surrey was soon asking for far more than that – 6,000 men for an unspecified number of years. These would need to be financed and fed from England. English settlers would be required to set the Irish to work on the land, and castles and towns would have to be built as the armies went along. 'After my poor opinion,' Surrey announced, 'this land shall never be brought to good order and due subjection, but only by conquest ... '[68]

Henry, deciding that he could not afford to maintain a viceroyalty on Surrey's scale, now turned to Kildare's rival, Sir Piers Butler, virtual Earl of Ormond, and made him ruler. But Kildare was the only available magnate who could maintain a retinue large enough to produce respect. Henry soon had to restore him. Meanwhile, the danger that Ireland might be the backdoor for foreign invasion increased as Henry's divorce and Reformation went ahead. Kildare turned a blind eye while the Earl of Desmond intrigued with the King of France and with the Emperor Charles V, and in 1534 he himself was summoned to England under suspicion of treason and imprisoned in the Tower. Enraged by a rumour that he was dead, his son, 'Silken Thomas', refused to act in his place and led his people against the Crown. There was no way round it; another army had to be sent from England. Sir Thomas Skeffyngton, a tough new English viceroy, led the force which captured the Kildare seat at Maynooth in 1535. Kildare had died. His son and several leading kinsmen were shortly executed. The great noble house was temporarily smashed.

Ireland from now on was to be governed by a bureaucracy in Dublin, where a permanent Council was set up resembling those in Wales and in the North. Royal policy had quite swift successes. By Henry VIII's death, direct Dublin rule was fairly effective over half the island. Ireland had its own 'Reformation

Parliament' in 1536-7, which seems to have recognised the authority of King over Church willingly enough. The religious houses were dissolved, and over the years their property gradually came under lay owners who included some Gaelic chieftains as well as many intruding Englishmen. But the lag between legal Reformation and thorough conquest of Ireland helped ensure that the Irish could never be absorbed into an English polity as the Welsh and the Scots would be. The Catholic religion maintained, strengthened, and reformed itself among the people and would become identified with resistance to Tudor rule.

Henry was advised by the Dublin Council to call himself 'King' (rather than 'Lord') of Ireland to dissipate the 'foolish opinions' of the Irish that the Pope was their real overlord, and in 1541 a new Irish Parliament thrust this title upon him, so committing the English Crown to extending its authority all over the island. Through confiscations of estates held by traitors and by religious houses, the King, on paper, owned vastly increased territories, but, except in the south-east, he could not get rents from them, and where his lands were subject to raids by the natives, he could not find Anglo-Irish or English tenants to live on them. 'By 1547 great areas were described as "waste" or leased to Irish tenants.'[69] Hence it was a great object to persuade the Irish to recognise Henry as their landlord and to pay him enough rent, as he put it, to 'defend the State there; and after, as the country shall grow into a further civility, so our profits to be increased.'[70] The new policy of 'surrender and regrant' for the first time embraced the Gaels within the protection of English law; they could now hold their lands in a precise legal manner and have access to the King's courts. The Gaelic lord who acknowledged royal authority would be granted the territory which he currently possessed, and would hold it henceforward from the Crown, to which he was bound to give military aid. The Palesmen, who hotly favoured this policy, believed that with the Gaels so pacified, they themselves need no longer pay for or quarter the Viceroy's unpopular standing army. Throughout 1541 the Viceroy, now St Leger, took submissions.

The parliament of 1541 actually included some four or five Gaelic chiefs. Ulick Burke became Earl of Clanricard, Murrough O Brien was named Earl of Thomond and Con Bacach O Neill accepted the fateful title of Earl of Tyrone. Lesser chiefs became barons. A Gaelic poet was furious: 'Shame on you, o men of the Gaeil, not one of you has life in him, the foreigners are sharing your lands among themselves, you are like a phantom host ... Shame on the grey foreign gun, shame on the golden chain ... shameful the denial of Mary's son.'[71] The gold chain was a symbolically apt present from the King to O Neill when he went to London for his earldom and the descendant of a long line of Irish kings knelt before the English throne.

St Leger seems to have been a creditable colonial administrator, able to get on with Irish lords while actively strengthening the Crown. For generations, O Tooles had harried the Pale from their base in the Wicklow Mountains. They were a small clan of virtually landless men, at odds with the great house of

Kildare and with no recourse save raiding and levying blackmail. Turlough O Toole proposed a deal to St Leger. He would forego his plundering and wear English dress in return for the grant of the district of Fercullen. St Leger thought this fair enough and lent him £20 to travel to England. O Toole became the King's tenant by knight's service.[72] This episode exposes factors always at work in England's favour. There were always weak or disadvantaged clans ready to back the Crown against stronger rivals, while Gaelic political ideals could give no basis for Irish unity.

The petty Border surnames had much in common with the O Tooles. James V of Scotland had begun to imitate Henry VIII as strong new-style king. The Borders soon attracted his interest. The English had ravaged the land in a brief war in 1523 – making robbery once again seem a far safer occupation than cultivation. In the summer of 1530, James with a strong force invaded Liddesdale to confront Johnnie Armstrong, most famous of all reivers, and chief of his surname. A great ballad tells, with much dubious picturesque detail, how the two men met:

> When Johnnie cam before the King,
> Wi' a' his men sae brave to see,
> The King he movit his bonnet to him;
> He ween'd he was a King as weel as he.[73]

Johnnie was strung up, and numerous others with him, but the Armstrongs, and the Border, remained unsubdued.

In 1540, James made a voyage round the Hebrides, taking several chiefs as hostages and gaoling them when the trip was over. That year, the whole group of Isles was formally re-annexed to the Scottish Crown. But the old Macdonald power had one last kick left in it, delivered when Henry VIII in his last years made a prolonged and notably ruthless attempt to subjugate Scotland itself. James's mother had been Henry's sister, through a marriage designed to pave a way for eventual union of the two Crowns. But the threat of Scottish–French alliance, and Henry's own ambitions, made him impatient. James died, tradition says of a broken heart, after his army was routed by smaller English forces at Solway Moss in 1542. In July 1543, Henry forced a treaty upon the Scots. Peace was to be cemented by the marriage of James's infant daughter, Mary, now Queen, to Henry's son the Prince of Wales. The Scots, with a pro-French party in control, would not accept this. The 'Rough Wooing' which followed was terrible. In 1544 English forces sacked and burned Edinburgh and ravaged the whole of southern Scotland. The French helped the Scots rally; the Wooing was repeated. Meanwhile the chiefs of the Hebrides had rallied to Donald Dubh, Black Donald, grandson of the last Lord of the Isles, on his escape after forty years in prison. Henry VIII offered Donald money for his allegiance, and Scottish and Irish Gaels combined in an unsuccessful invasion, starting from Ulster. It was 'the last occasion upon which the whole of the Hebridean clans were ever united in a common purpose';[74] and it was against Scotland that they united. When Donald, the last generally recognised Lord of the Isles, died in Ireland, Henry VIII paid for his funeral.

Still the Scots would not submit. The results were momentous for England. Combined with Henry's futile war against France, they permanently weakened the English Crown. By the time the expensive fighting was over, most of the monastery lands had been sold, and the mercenary army which any king needed to enforce absolute rule had been disbanded for lack of funds. Hereafter, at the first hint of war, the English state would have to ask Parliament for money. The Commons had purse-power. They could assert themselves, enlarge their own role and keep taxation low, while the Crown became weaker at home than its foreign rivals, with only a tiny personal bodyguard and whatever armed support its subjects would give it. Cromwell the First had achieved unification; but his successors could not impose centralisation. Protestant squires supported the Crown against magnates and foreign enemies; in return they were left to rule their own roosts.

Henry's death in 1547 left his young son and successor Edward VI under the Protection of the Duke of Somerset, who went north with the largest army yet and routed the Scots again at Pinkie. Fighting went on till the English withdrew in 1549. Queen Mary was shipped to France, where she married the King's son, while her French mother, Mary of Guise, became Regent in Scotland.

Meanwhile, Somerset took the Reformation further. A new Prayer Book, in English, not Latin, combined with a proclamation from London which ordered removal of images from churches, provoked the final risings of Cornwall, an area proud of its Celtic saints. Cornish men joined forces with some in Devon and demanded a return to the old religion. ' ... We Cornish men (whereof certain of us understand no English) utterly refuse this new English.' After they had besieged Exeter for a month, the rebels were savagely suppressed. Devon families whose names would figure famously in subsequent overseas exploration and expansion were amongst the rebels' opponents; the episode may have helped fan the blazing anti-Catholicism of Grenvilles, Raleghs and Drakes.[75]

The bitter aftermath of Henry VIII's rule served in other ways to create powerful anti-papist groups, in Scotland as well as in England, and to identify most of the larger British island with the Protestant cause in the coming century of religious wars. The Lowland Scots, under the rule of Mary of Guise and her French clique, began to associate Protestantism with patriotic self-respect. The death of young King Edward brought in his sad sister Mary, determined to restore the old Catholic Church. She was too late. The gentry, grasping their former Church lands, were not going to give them up. Mary could only proceed with outside help, and her marriage to Philip II of Spain involved the virtual absorption of England into the Hapsburg Empire, provoking bitter patriotic resentment. The heresy trials which the Queen opened in 1555 brought nearly three hundred people to the stake. The stench of burnt flesh gave many of her subjects a loathing of popery, and of 'Spanish cruelty', which they transmitted in published writings and popular lore down to the nineteenth century. Even when Philip drew England into war with her traditional enemy, France, in 1557, this was unpopular. The French next year overran Calais in a week, and with it the last extant trophy of those pretensions to rule on the Continent which the English Crown would soon drop. Spain, on the sea, not France, on the land, was coming to seem the true national foe.

And events were in train which would help diminish the old enmity between England and Scotland. Amongst the distinguished body of hundreds of leading English Protestants driven into exile by Mary's persecution mingled the looming Scot, John Knox. They flocked back when Mary died at the end of 1558. While Queen Elizabeth, succeeding her sister, made a new, non-Catholic religious settlement with a parliament dominated by Puritans and by the influence of the returned exiles, Knox went on north to inflame the struggle against the French regency which dissident lords had already launched under the banner of Protestantism. In the spring of 1559, he broached popular revolution, unleashing a mob in Perth which sacked the town's religious houses. Elizabeth sent ships and troops north. (The French were claiming her own throne for the young Scottish Queen, Mary.) With this help, the 'Faithful Congregation of Christ Jesus in Scotland' were able to win. The Treaty of Edinburgh in July replaced the traditional Scottish alliance with France by a cordial new understanding with England.

The red-haired young woman who was to rule England till 1603 needs less introduction to readers of that country's language than any other figure in history. She was, we all know, clever and vain, personally tolerant in matters of religion, brave and yet extremely cautious and often dilatory, proudly imperious and absurdly fickle: the paragon of her sex, a pattern for all princes, an ornament to her nation; and so forth. What is less commonly grasped is that she was a dedicated conservative in an epoch of racing social change. Like Burghley, her chief minister for all but the last few years of her reign, she would have preferred a stable society rooted in the soil and governed through an accepted social hierarchy. ' ... Even foreigners accustomed to the style of Habsburg and Valois were amazed at the elaborate formalism of the Elizabethan Court.'[76] The image – one is tempted to call it the 'icon' – of the Virgin Queen, as painters and poets designed it for her, was soundly calculated to create a focus of national faith, a bond of English unity, glittering, pure, untouchable, far beyond criticism, so as to hold together a society cracking and creaking under intense and novel economic and intellectual strains. We find it all, if we care to look for it, in the amazing plays of her greatest subject, Shakespeare. Divinity hedges the king – but men are beginning to notice with anger that a dog's obeyed in office. War and lechery, treachery and corruption are staples of public life in an age of dissolving feudalism and mounting cynicism. The medieval world order is tumbling, and against its fall conservatives chant 'degree,

degree' — take but degree away, take away the unthinking respect accorded by commoner to aristocrat, subject to monarch, and hark what discord follows. Yet, 'say to the court', writes a great courtier, Ralegh, 'say to the court it glows and shines like rotten wood.' No one typifies better than Ralegh the spate of energies, idealistic and predatory, military and commercial, intellectual and solidly material which pushed England towards overseas expansion while its own backlands were still incompletely conquered.

The Age of Ralegh

heisa, heisa
vorsa, vorsa
wow, wow
one long draft
one long draft
more might, more might
young blood, young blood
more mude, more mude
false flesh, false flesh
lie aback, lie aback
long swack, long swack
that, that, that, that
there, there, there, there
yellow hair, yellow hair
hips bare, hips bare
tell 'em all, tell 'em all
gallowsbirds all, gallowsbirds all
great and small, great and small
one an' all, one an' all
heist all, heist all

English sea chantey, c. 1550[1]

I

Elizabeth's England was peaceful, compared to most of Europe, and many of its middling people prospered. Their affluence and confidence promoted a wave of new building; comfortable houses for all social groups, in town and country, except the poorest and largest class. The first distinctively English style emerged, mixing elements borrowed from the European Renaissance with Perpendicular Gothic notions. The most fecund age of English music had a domestic base in the brick mansions of the mighty, while domesticity, with a desire for privacy informed the planning of the black and white timbered houses of lesser people, yeomen, even in some cases husbandmen. The Englishman's home was coming to be his castle – but a castle which thanks to a novel plenty of cheap glass was graced with those most unwarlike features, glass windows. Privacy, music and light; comfort and social harmony; even after Elizabeth's reign had ended in misery and confusion, Shakespeare would look back on it as a time when every man had eaten in safety what he had planted, and had sung 'the merry songs of peace to all his neighbours'.[2] And though this was old-man's nostalgia, or propaganda, a minority had indeed done very well.

England had perhaps 3 million people in 1530, over 4 million in 1600.[3] Mouths to feed increased faster than food. Those who had surplus produce to sell prospered. As the line of human settlement surged forward into moorlands and heathlands and woodlands, capitalistic attitudes came with it, helping to tame the backlands. Cornwall, favoured with nature by many harbours from which exports could be made to London and the Continent, was civilised swiftly away from Celtdom by a mania for agricultural advance. 'Everyone seemed anxious to improve the yield of his land by enclosure, consolidation and the use of fertilisers. Sand, seaweed, marl, lime, soap ashes, paring and burning, all helped to increase the harvest.' By the seventeenth century the Cornish language was fast dying.[4]

Through mines in Cornwall, England was Europe's largest producer of tin, a most important export. And in other remote and hilly areas, coal-mining helped to bring wild men into the economic mainstream. (For instance, numerous collieries started in Derbyshire during Elizabeth's reign.) The island was running short of timber, and landlords exploiting mines on their estates so responded to the demand for fuel that England was far and away the biggest producer of coal. By the end of the century, Tyneside was shipping out about 165,000 tons per year, and exports had more than quadrupled within five decades.[5] The manufacture of window glass was one of the industries now beginning to base themselves on coal. Meanwhile, prices of goods in England, though soaring, lagged behind those in Europe, and this fostered the export trade in cloth.

Yet the Queen died £400,000 in debt. Administration was getting more expensive. Muskets and cannon were dearer than bows and arrows. Ships for the navy cost more. Royal revenue increased far more slowly than prices. England was lightly taxed, and getting used to the idea it should be. The Englishman, encastled in his home, rejoiced that no standing army was needed as he sang merry songs of internal peace. England's bureaucracy was small compared to that of France or Spain. The gentry and merchants left by default to govern the country liked it that way. Power was redistributed steadily from the Crown to those gentry who were cashing in on the price rise. The Queen's stinginess became part of her legend, but though she doubled or trebled the Crown's income, she could not raise the money needed to take full control of England. In fact, her peddling of licences and offices for cash helped in itself to weaken her position. Half the ordinary state revenue came from customs. But customs officials who bought their jobs and were then paid next to nothing were of course willing to connive, for a consideration, at massive evasions. The Crown's attempts to increase its revenues with new duties and tariffs merely fostered the first great age of English smuggling, and the addiction of coastal gentry to piracy. In the south-west and Wales, landlords financed pirates to hijack Spanish wines or Newfoundland fish. The town fathers of tiny Welsh ports acquired luxuries like ginger and ivory which they could otherwise hardly have afforded. Officials themselves dealt most amicably with pirates. All these people were by their own lights perfectly loyal (as, no doubt, was the Suffolk landlord who sold English captives as slaves in Algiers) but defrauding the Queen was a part of their way of life.[6] As the State captured the backlands, the gentry and merchants captured the State. 'Merchants', noted a writer of 1559, 'have grown so cunning in the trade of corrupting ... that since the [first year of] Henry VIII there could never be won any good law or order which touched their liberty or state, but they stayed it, either in the Commons, or higher House of Parliament, or else by the prince himself.'[7]

But the Queen did have patronage, and it helped her power. Noblemen clustered at court, looking for pickings. Elizabeth could balance their factions against each other, buy the loyalty of all factions, and exploit in the interests of her own influence the vines of clientage which went with them. Each land-owning family struggled for its own ends, along with the other families with which it intermarried, and kinship mattered immensely, not least to the Devon network of Gilberts, Raleghs and Grenvilles. The difference from Scotland was that such groupings were horizontal; landowners commanded less and less personal, let alone 'family' loyalty from their social inferiors. A sense of kinship did not spill across classes, and feudal attitudes were weakening.

There was after all no way in which their feudal superior, the Queen, could hold back the thrust of such gentry, allying themselves with merchants in trade and industry and colonisation, pushing change through in the countryside, challenging royal authority in Parliament on the rare occasions when she would let it meet and, since they were, as J.P.s, in charge of law enforcement, making statutes they didn't like inoperative. By the end of the century there was, thanks to enclosure, a virtually continuous belt of grassland in Northants and Leicester-shire where sheep and cattle grazed over what had been arable lands. The Queen and Burghley would have preferred it to stay under corn. They did not like the spread of capitalist attitudes. They did not like the cloth industry which those sheep served. While their attitude to the poor was paternal, that of gentry and merchant J.P.s raised the possibility of proletarian revolt.

Serfdom was dead and the ownership of land was increasingly seen as 'a source of wealth rather than as the basis of political function or social degree.'[8] So land-lords had less and less scruple about evicting their tenants. While the growth of population was depriving labour of its scarcity value, the price rise relentlessly inflated the cost of necessaries for the poor. 'The mass of the population was forced down to a diet of black bread', and a wage freeze was 'enforced by the whole power of the state and the ruling class.' A vicious spiral was in motion. Low wages stimulated the growth of the cloth industry. The clothing boom encouraged enclosure for pasture, and so encouraged eviction which in turn replenished the pool of workless which kept wages down – until one of the main arguments for colonisation would be that it permitted the export of desperate, unemployed poor, who could be seen dying of starvation in the streets of London.[9]

Meanwhile, to stave off revolt, the 'poor law' was developed until at the end of the sixteenth century it assumed much the form it would hold until the nineteenth. It had no counterpart in Europe. It reflected the localisation of power in England. It was the duty of the parish, under control of the J.P.s, to provide for the helpless, the aged and the sick out of a compulsory rate levied upon householders, and to provide work for those who were genuinely unemployed. An Act of 1531 had laid down that deliberate idlers should be whipped; one of 1547 had provided that any able-bodied person adjudged a vagabond should be branded and made a slave for two years to the man who brought him forward, who was encouraged to treat him harshly. If he ran away, his servitude would become permanent. This astonishing law was repealed after three years because it was too extreme to be useful, but its spirit was representative of the hatred of vagabonds which was revealed in Tudor legislation. The poor law was 'in origin purely a matter of police regulation', but it had the side-effect of permitting the payment of low wages, since the parish had to subsidise families of wage-earners who would otherwise starve.[10] Keep people still, stop them moving about, the government thought; keep them under our thumbs, added the local rulers of town and countryside.

Yet the spirit of the Elizabethan Poor Law was never really like that of the cruel legislation brought in to succeed it in the 1830s. Nineteenth-century men were conscious of being capitalists, economists, individualists. Elizabethans were not; the coal-mines they worked, still small and scattered, served mostly local markets; cloth was made in workers' homes; the idea of subsistence still dominated agriculture; men still saw themselves and the world in religious terms. A very great part of what was most vital and forward-pointing in Elizabeth's England – whether in poetry, commerce or even privateering – was informed by a deeply-felt 'puritanism'. The word is elusive, and hence controversial. But one might argue that as in Victoria's day even 'tories' were 'liberals' in so far as they were at all attuned to the dominant motions of the age, so in Elizabeth's virtually all Protestant spirituality was more or less 'Puritan'. Though Archbishop Whitgift persecuted the more extreme 'Puritans' who wanted to do without bishops and strove for a Presbyterian or Congregational system, he was himself a strict Calvinist.[11]

Despite – or because of – their terrifying belief that each man's fate was predestined, Calvinists devoted intense spiritual energy to the everyday tasks of the world. The Middle Ages had locked both learning and spirituality up in a celibate clergy; now both must be released into lay lives. Acting well meant hard work, constant self-scrutiny, and fierce zeal against papists. Along with such effort came a proud independence of thought and spirit. 'In Italy in 1518',

Lionel Trilling remarks, 'one could speak plain to sovereign power only if one possessed a trained perfection of grace and charm. In England a century later the only requirement for speaking plain was a man's conviction that he had the Word to speak.'[12] What plain speech implied for the future was shown in Parliament. 'Sweet indeed is the name of liberty,' Peter Wentworth cried there in 1576, objecting to the Queen's interference in its affairs. 'Certain it is,' he added, ' ... that none is without fault: no, not our noble queen.' For this he spent four weeks in the Tower of London.[13]

Puritanism in its anti-Establishment form failed to capture the Anglican Church, but it won a large section of the gentry. Calvinism was a difficult doctrine, radically hostile to superstitions which still mattered to most people, and it flourished where literacy was found — in the ports, the market towns, the centres of the cloth industry in East Anglia and the south-west; in fact, in the areas and among the classes most concerned with overseas trade and expansion. Some important courtiers, led by Sir Francis Walsingham, sought an anti-Catholic foreign policy. Conservatives, led by Burghley and the Earl of Sussex, favoured the traditional understanding with Spain. The tide was set against them. To support Calvinists in France and in the Netherlands who opposed lawful monarchs with radical new political theories had alarmingly subversive resonances, while to thumb noses at Spain, the greatest power in Europe, suggested more zeal, or greed, than common sense. Nevertheless, Elizabeth's England did both those things.

II

Calvinism was winning in Lowland Scotland. Simply as a way of organising spiritual care for the people, when the whole Catholic Church structure had degenerated, a semi-democratic congregationalism now emerged as the practical solution. Elected kirk sessions supervised ministers chosen by congregations, and since Mary Queen of Scots was not Protestant, a General Assembly of the Church was needed to act as supreme authority in her stead. After 1572 bishops were appointed, with Knox's approval, but the extremist Calvinist party led by Andrew Melville launched later in that decade a long struggle against the Crown over their existence. Meanwhile, under Knox's lead, the reformed Church had aimed at nothing less than the disciplining of the whole people. It was not until the seventeenth century that much of the way was travelled towards realising Knox's noble project of a school in every parish, but the reformation was already helping to form a dour, hard-driving, self-disciplined, self-punishing, disputatious, pedantic Lowland Scottish character. The rift between Lowlands and Highlands was greatly widened. The Reformation made little impact in Gaelic-speaking areas, which remained part Catholic, largely, in effect, pagan: in any case, quite outside the pan-European movement which took a lead from Calvin's Geneva.

In France, perhaps half the aristocracy went over to Protestantism, and three and a half decades of civil war followed. The psalm-singing Huguenot troops fought against forces rallied by a reviving Roman Catholicism, which clarified itself at the Council of Trent in the early 1560s. Philip II of Spain stood forth clearly as Rome's secular champion. With France in turmoil, its power in eclipse, Spain dominated the battlefields and diplomacy of Europe. Philip worked late into the night on papers and despatches, governing with obsessive attention to detail a personal empire which included much of Italy and the whole of the Netherlands. In 1580 Philip successfully enforced a claim to the crown of the other Iberian power, and the Portuguese empire joined Spain's under his rule. His struggle against the Turks in the Mediterranean was far from decided by his half-brother's naval victory at the colossal battle of Lepanto in 1571. Philip's vast forces were paid for by taxation which growingly crippled the Spanish economy and, above all, by annual remittance of silver from the New World. The flow turned into a flood in the 1580s. By 1600, Spain was drawing an average of 40 million ducats of silver a year from America, of which the Crown alone received 13 million. Such wealth and power were at the Pope's service. Philip said, 'I would rather lose the Low Countries than reign over them if they ceased to be Catholic.'[14] His Spaniards were wonderfully brave fighters, and their pride in their faith helped them to be so.

But Protestant Europe, confronting Spain's arrogant might, developed that myth of 'Spanish cruelty' which was to fire its own soldiers, sailors and privateers for two centuries. William of Orange, leader of Dutch revolt against Spain, crystallised it in his *Apology* of 1580. The Spanish priest Las Casas had published a fiercely critical account of his countrymen's behaviour towards Indians in the New World, which had been translated into several European languages. William used Spain's destruction of '20 million Indians' as proof of innate Castilian cruelty, alongside Philip's murder of his son and heir and his expulsion of some 150,000 Christianised Moors from Spain.

This 'black legend' had important psychological functions. The supposed viciousness of the Spaniards made ruthless and cynical procedures against them seem justifiable. And since the Indians of America were enduring a hellish rule, to forestall the Spaniards in New World lands which they had not yet occupied, even to oust them from territories which they possessed, could be projected as acts of Christian kindness and justice. Of course, to strike at the sources of that silver which paid Philip's armies was to aid Protestant resistance everywhere. Many English, remembering Mary's burnings, were very willing to cast her husband as dragon for St George to slay.

Yet there were important English commercial interests involved in trade with Spain. Some manufacturers used Spanish wool, others exported their wares to Iberia. Antwerp, focus of England's overseas trade, was in Philip II's territory. And England was a weak little country when Elizabeth came to the throne; in the early years of her reign she badly needed support, which Philip, for his part, was prepared to give her. Her heir, if she went, was Mary Queen of Scots, who returned to her throne from France in 1560 and made an uneasy peace with her Protestant subjects. While Parliament in England clamoured that Elizabeth must marry, to have offspring and to avert a Franco–Scottish, Catholic succession, Philip also had no wish to see England controlled by his rival France.

Elizabeth did not marry. Mary's son James, born in 1566, would not in the end miss his English heritage, despite the fatuous conduct of his mother. She connived in the murder of her husband, married one of his assassins and was duly driven out of her kingdom in 1568. Within five years, her supporters in Scotland were mopped up, and a succession of Protestant, Anglophile regents ruled on behalf of her son. They had Elizabeth's friendship, and she did not embarrass them by returning her rival across the Border. She kept Mary in prison in England, where she became a focus of plotting and Catholic subversion. In this, Spain began to take a hand.

The English alliance with Spain was crumbling from the mid-1560s. An outbreak of Calvinist rioting in the Netherlands provoked unwise repression from Philip's viceroy there, the Duke of Alba, and these troubles hastened the weakening of England's trading link with Antwerp. The English cloth trade was already shifting away to North German ports as Antwerp itself fell into slow decline. The war of Dutch independence would see Antwerp's ruin. Elizabeth had no sympathy for rebels, but she did not stop her own subjects from helping their co-religionists, nor did she bar the swarms of refugees who fled from Alba's terror and brought great gifts to England – Flemish clothworkers took their skills to East Anglia, refugee merchants settled in London and traded on a large scale with their now scattered relatives in Germany, Italy and Sweden. And when in 1568 a fine shipment of bullion, despatched by Philip's Genoese bankers for the payment of Alba's troops, was driven into English waters, Elizabeth confiscated it and borrowed the money from the Italians herself. Alba embargoed all trade with England and seized English goods, and commerce with Flanders was interrupted for five years.

The Spanish ambassador was involved in the plot in Mary's favour which produced the 'Northern Rising' of 1569. The Earls of Northumberland and Westmorland said mass in Durham Cathedral, tore up the English Prayer Book and set off south with feudal hosts. Their main motivation was resentment at the Crown's behaviour towards them. The easy defeat of their army 'really ended feudalism in the North.'[15] Pius V had prepared the bull *Regnans in Excelsis*, intending it to coincide with the rising. It was published in February 1570, too late to help the northern Earls. But its call to all faithful sons of the Church to help oust the heretic Queen from her throne, and its absolving of all her subjects from allegiance to Elizabeth came as a great encouragement to a fresh wave of rebels in Gaelic Ireland.

III

The English were getting uncomfortably active there, and a new kind of Englishman had begun to arrive; a Puritanical sort, commercially minded, very impatient indeed with the wretched natives who were wasting their island's fine resources. Though Edmund Spenser came as a colonist only in the 1580s, his attitude may be taken as representative. 'And sure,' he would write, 'it is yet a most beautiful and sweet country as any is under heaven, being stored throughout with many goodly rivers, replenished with all sorts of fish most abundantly, sprinkled with many very sweet islands and goodly lakes, like little inland seas, that will carry even ships upon their waters; adorned with goodly woods, even fit for building of houses and ships, so commodiously, as that, if some princes in the world had them, they would soon hope to be lords of all the seas, and ere long of all the world. Also full of very good ports and havens opening upon England, as inviting us to come unto them, to see what excellent commodities that country can afford.'[16]

A vision of manifest destiny was beginning to gleam for such men. England was running out of wood. The timbers of Ireland could carry Englishmen further west. The lords of the seas might be lords of the whole world. Humphrey Gilbert, Grenville and Ralegh, with numerous less-known pioneers, had their first experience of expansion and colonisation in Ireland. Even Drake played a significant part there. Ireland was for these West Countrymen the first stop on routes to Virginia and the North West Passage. Such men hated Catholic Spain, yet, by that paradox of attraction of opposites which is so familiar to historians, they were ready to imitate Spanish methods, to treat Gaels much as Spaniards had treated Indians, and even, out of arrogance and their fear, to produce very passable replicas of the 'Spanish cruelty' which they denounced.

The 1540s had seen the first extension of the narrow Pale for centuries. Laois and Offaly lay to the west of it, under control of the O Connor and the O More. In 1546 they were goaded into revolt. Their lands were confiscated, and, after sufficient slaughter, two forts were built there. Under the Earl of Sussex, Lord Deputy from 1556, resettlement of the area began. It was 'shired' as Queen's County and King's County and divided into townships, manors and baronies which were dealt out to some eighty or more grantees: Palesmen, officials, soldiers and natives. Besides paying an annual rent to the Crown, tenants were obliged to maintain a quota of armed men and to help keep up the county's fortress. They were not to bring in wild men from the unshired lands as armed retainers, nor to intermarry with such people. The O Connor chief and the O More were both assigned land, on condition that they adopt the English style of dress and teach their children English. The wild men who followed them were not appeased and constantly harried the new counties and the rest of the Pale from the wastelands where they found a home. 'The spoilers of the Pale', wrote the Lord Deputy in 1572, 'are named Rory Oge with the O'Mores ...

Fiach MacHugh ... with the O'Connors ... the manner of their coming is by daylight with bagpipes, by night with torchlight.'[17]

Not that the Palesmen themselves were model subjects. Sussex, still viceroy under Elizabeth, brought her Church settlement into Irish law in 1560 but even within the Pale illegal celebrations of mass continued.[18] Outside it, of course, there was no question of enforcing Anglican conformity. This does not mean that the Gaels were good Catholics. Their behaviour would have shocked Pius V as much as John Knox, as can be judged from the story of Shane O Neill.

The affairs of Elizabethan Ulster are hard to understand. Gaelic custom survived almost untouched. The area's politics, intricate in themselves, were tangled with those of the Hebrides and of Gaelic Scotland in general. When Con O Neill accepted the earldom of Tyrone from Henry VIII, his son Matthew had become his 'legal heir'. But this intrusion of primogeniture struck helplessly against the traditional concept of elected chiefship. While English officials saw Matthew as heir-apparent, to Con's second son Shane he was simply a poorly qualified rival. Tough, clever and arrogant, Shane was able at Con's death in 1559 to seize full power. The people recognised him as O Neill, and the earldom of Tyrone became a meaningless title. Shane was now, and wished to remain, a king by Irish right. Matthew was killed by Shane's men and his eldest son Brian was murdered by Turlough Luineach, another rival claimant. Matthew's second son, Hugh, a 9-year-old boy, was rescued by the English and crossed the water to spend eight years as the ward of Sir Henry Sidney, which meant that the most dedicated of Tudor colonial governors helped to bring up a prototype of all nationalist rebels.

Shane asserted authority over a circle of satellite chiefs – MacMahon, Magennis, Maguire, O Hanlon, O Cahan. From 1561, furthermore, he was effective overlord also of Tyrconnell, the land to the west of his occupied by the O Donnell, traditional rival of the O Neill power. He seized Calvagh O Donnell and poached his wife from him. This lady was a Maclean of Hebridean family, and widow of a Campbell Earl of Argyll.

There were plenty of other 'Scottish' Gaels in Ulster. The Mull of Kintyre, south-western tip of Scotland, could always be seen from Antrim on a clear day, only twenty miles across the water, and the annual incursions of 'Redshanks' into Ireland was a perpetual problem for the Dublin government. Hebridean chiefs brought their men across in galleys in summer to fight as mercenaries in Irish wars. Furthermore, the Macdonalds had a hereditary claim to an area known as the Glens, and a sizeable number of them were now based there and were challenging for possession of another tract, the Rout. The name of Somhairle Buidhe ('Sorley Boy') Macdonald figures constantly in the intrigues of Elizabeth's day – a most resilient and most lucky chieflet who eventually handed on a fine haul of land to his sons, and whose descendants became Earls of Antrim.

Sussex wanted to smash Shane's power and flush out the Macdonalds. Elizabeth favoured a cheaper policy. Let Shane be recognised as legitimate heir. To Sussex's outrage, she invited the dread O Neill to visit her in England. With their long curled hair, saffron-coloured shirts, long sleeves, short coats and heavy mantles, Shane's bodyguard created a stir among the sophisticates of the city rather as if a Red Indian *cacique* had arrived. Shane, in that fawning Irish fashion which would always disgust the English, confessed to rebellion with howls and sobs, did homage on his knees, and signed a submission. But thereafter he proved a smooth enough diplomat, and made a deal with the Queen whereby he would have the rule of O Cahan's country and the greater part of Antrim, as well as Tyrone, in return for his loyalty and for driving out the Macdonalds.

But Shane did not understand his share of the bargain. He thought that Elizabeth had given him authority to rule all Ulster. He was soon raiding O Donnell's country again, and when a new foray by Sussex against him failed in 1563, Shane was left very much in command. All the government could do was accept the position and give him a free pardon. Sussex had regular forces of under a thousand men, and Shane had five times that number of horse and foot — perhaps the most impressive force yet mustered by a Gaelic chief. In October 1565, when Sir Henry Sidney came out as the new Deputy, Shane was deep in intrigues — dealing with Archibald, Earl of Argyll, the greatest power in Highland Scotland, and going so far as to ask Mary Queen of Scots to recognise him as her subject.[19] And with Desmond at war with Ormond, and the Gaels of the Midlands striving to overthrow the Laois-Offaly settlement, it looked as if the English might be swept utterly out of Ireland.

Sidney, aged 36, was a cultured man, father of one poet, patron of others. He was also a most experienced frontier official, who from 1565 to 1571 and again from 1575 to 1580 combined the Deputyship in Ireland with his longer-standing post as Lord President in Wales. In sharp contrast with Sussex, he belonged to the aggressive anti-papist faction led at court by Leicester. He filled senior civil and military posts in Ireland with supporters of this faction and he favoured 'forward' policies — further forward, in fact, than the Queen was always prepared to go. Sussex had aimed at 'reformation', not conquest. Sidney had less patience. When he marched against Shane, two Irish victims of the O Neill's ambition, the O Donnell and the Maguire, went with him, but he aimed to establish a base on Lough Foyle as a permanent restraint on Ulster chiefs of all descriptions. He made no attempt to bring Shane to a decisive battle. Instead he adopted tactics which his successors would take to the point of near-genocide. He set off in September with his own horses well fed after the summer, but in time to burn the crops of the Gaels before they were harvested. Meanwhile a force he had sent round by sea penetrated Lough Foyle. Sidney met it and garrisoned there a place called Derry, with 600 foot and 50 horse. Then he marched into Tyrconnell, setting up Calvagh O Donnell as ruler again, then he proceeded southward through Sligo into Munster. His whole great march round the Gaelic periphery cost him only three men, he boasted, and those through sickness.

But the domination of Ireland would need more resources than the Queen was yet willing to grant. The Derry garrison lost heart and sailed away next spring when an accidental fire rased their camp. The Gaels had their own story about that. Gunpowder had been stored in a church and St Columba, enraged by this desecration, had taken the form of a huge wolf which had galloped out of the wood and spewed sparks into a powder barrel. In any case, though Sidney and his successors would be very well aware of the site's strategic value, the English would not encamp again at Derry for thirty-three years.[20]

However, the O Donnells now beat down Shane. When he came at them with his thousands, their new chief, Hugh, rallied his few hundred and butchered Shane's army in a surprise attack as it lay, fuddled with drink, by the banks of the aptly named Swilly. While Shane's supporters submitted to Sidney, he himself—this was June, 1567—fled to the Macdonald camp in Antrim. The Macdonalds received him pleasantly. Much wine and whiskey were swallowed. Then they paid an old score and hacked Shane to pieces.

Traditional clan violence disposed of Shane and when shortly before his death he replied defiantly to Elizabeth's overtures, his language was that of traditional chieftainship: 'My ancestors were kings of Ulster, Ulster was theirs and shall be mine. And for O Donnell, he shall never come into his country, if I can keep him out of it, nor Bagenall into the Newry nor the Earl of Kildare into Dundrum or Lecale. They are mine; with this sword I will keep them. This is my answer.'[21]

Yet the same Shane had opened negotiations with the King of France and had employed the new dialect of militant Catholicism. The English were heretics. Let Ireland be joined to the French Crown. Such an appeal to Catholic Europe on the basis of common faith emphasised how urgent it was for the English Crown to tame Ireland. After Shane's death the drunken but shrewd Turlough Luineach succeeded him as O Neill and, while he mixed petty insubordination with ever-ready submission, Ulster remained deceptively quiet for three decades. But Sidney pushed ahead with his sharp new ideas.

In Ireland as in Wales, he displayed himself as a dedicated anti-feudalist. 'Sidney's encouragement of Flemish craftsmen to settle at Swords and his introduction of a number of commercial and industrial monopolies showed that his objective was to encourage the exploitation of Irish resources in the interests of English businessmen ... ' Still more significant was his development of the idea of establishing new colonies of Englishmen through the private enterprise of individuals or syndicates of grantees. Sidney had visited Spain as a diplomat, and the charters now given to speculators in Irish lands were reminiscent of grants awarded by Spanish kings to conquistadors. They introduced a new idea into English settlement in Ireland, expressing the 'conscious aim' of turning the native Irish into a permanently inferior and exploited labour force, dependent on settlers like slaves on masters.[22]

Here was an attractive outlet for restless scions of landowning families. A younger son like Humphrey Gilbert could hope to become a great landed magnate, on this green and fertile frontier which teemed with cattle and fish, and where even the people, cowed, might be made useful. English gentry, especially Devonshire gentry, pressed forward to realise projects for colonies in Munster and in Ulster. Sidney interested in his Ulster project Lionel Duckett, one of London's great merchants, who had recently helped to finance one John Hawkins in a pioneering triangular trading voyage taking in Guinea and the Caribbean. Other City men were attracted by the prospect of ripping down Ireland's rich woods and wresting from traders from Iberia the potentially valuable commerce of Munster's harbours. 'In thus bringing about an amalgam of merchant and gentry interests, Sidney', Nicholas Canny observes, 'was anticipating the coalition that backed the development of English enterprise and empire during the later sixteenth century.'[23]

His newfangled outlook would provoke spasms of élitist, reactionary rebellion by Norman-descended aristocrats who still saw themselves as a cut above mere Gaels, but whose antics would involve many of the latter in death or ruin. The strongest Norman prop of English rule, 'Black Tom' Butler, tenth Earl of Ormond (1532-1614) was aligned with the anti-expansionist faction in Elizabeth's court and had an especially good understanding with the Queen herself, so that when Sidney at first sided against him in his private war with the Earl of Desmond, Elizabeth called her viceroy sharply to heel and it was a triumph for Black Tom when his enemy was arrested and put in the Tower. Yet Sidney's policies still did not spare Black Tom's people. The Deputy and his council in Dublin upheld the claim of an English adventurer, Sir Peter Carew, whose ancestors had included certain Norman invaders of Ireland, to lands held by Ormond's brother Edmund. Then Carew announced his claim to part of the old kingdom of Cork, rousing the fears of Desmond's people and of the MacCarthies. Sidney's conviction was that the methods which, since Rowland Lee's day, had pacified Wales would work equally well in Ireland; his policy was to set up Lee-style 'Presidencies', backed with troops, to rule under him in Munster and Connacht. These must hack at the power of all local magnates. When, in mid-1568, James Fitzmaurice, Desmond's cousin and rival, pursuing the star of private ambition, in effect usurped the Earl's lands and power and launched open revolt in the south-west, the MacCarthy More joined him and so for a time did Ormond's brothers.

New English settlements had recently sprung up round Cork. Fitzmaurice ravaged them. Humphrey Gilbert commanded the English force which did much more than retort in kind, rejoicing, like others of his adventurous sort, heartily in the coming of a rebellion which gave a chance to seize lands and destroy Gaels. He slaughtered Irish women because he thought, without women to feed them, the menfolk must perish from famine. 'His manner', an observer reported, 'was that the heads of all those ... which were killed in the day should be cut off from their bodies and brought to the place where he encamped at night, and should there be laid on the ground by each side of the way leading into his own tent, so that none should come into his tent for any cause but commonly he must pass through a lane of heads, which he used *ad terrorem*, the dead feeling nothing the more pains thereby. And yet did it bring great terror to the people when they saw the heads of their dead fathers, brothers, children, kinsfolk, and friends lie on the ground before their faces.'[24] For such zeal, Gilbert was knighted by the Lord Deputy.

Meanwhile Fitton, the President of Connacht, had offended powerful local magnates. O Brien, Earl of Thomond, came out in revolt and other chiefs followed, and though they were soon quelled, by the spring of 1571 Fitzmaurice had recovered and taken the offensive again. Next year he swept through Connacht and effectively destroyed the hated Presidency.

The mercenaries he relied on left as their contracts expired, and early in 1573, learning that he would be given mercy, Fitzmaurice submitted. The Queen was anxious for reconciliation, and gave Desmond back his freedom. But privately, both men were unforgiving. Fitzmaurice in particular was a new kind of Irish leader. His personal ambitions, insistent though they were, were legitimated by a menacing new combination of Catholic idealism and pan-Irish patriotism. In 1570, when he and his council had appealed to Spain for help, asking that Don John of Austria, Philip's half-brother, should become King of Ireland, they had shown a significant and novel awareness of how Irish disunity played into English hands. 'Because we have not a king and are divided among ourselves the English attack and rob us daily, and we suffer grievously as a result.'[25]

After a tour of Connacht in 1576 Sidney boasted to the Privy Council at home of the number of Irish 'varlets' he had killed there, in time of peace, with scant respect for the laws which the English were claiming to introduce. 'Down they go in every corner, and down they shall go, God willing, if her Majesty will countenance me and your Lordships will comfort me and such as I shall set a-work.' Hundreds of 'masterless men' who might have enlisted in private armies were hanged in an appalling reign of terror. Sidney did not care to acquire the least understanding of what Irish law and custom amounted to. 'Surely,' he wrote on another occasion, 'there was never people that lived in more misery than they do, nor as it should seem of worse minds, for matrimony amongst them is no more regarded in effect than conjunction between un-reasonable beasts, perjury, robbery and murder counted allowable, finally, I cannot find that they make any conscience of sin, and doubtless I doubt whether they christen their children or no, for neither find I place where it should be done, nor any person able to instruct them in the rules of a Christian, or if they were taught I see no grace in them to follow it, and when they die I cannot see they make any account of the world to come.'[26]

An English Jesuit priest posted to Limerick a few years earlier had written in a remarkably similar vein, severe as missionaries usually are amongst a 'backward' people.[27] Yet the movement of Counter-Reformation which he represented would in the end succeed in making the Irish only too Christian, and Fitzmaurice precociously showed himself aware of how religion might overarch Ireland's chronic divisions. The Protestant arrogance of Sidneys and Gilberts and Fittons would continue to foster self-conscious Catholic zeal along with a simpler drive for revenge and repossession. As England expanded her power in five continents during the next three and a half centuries, her own neighbour island would sulk and snap at her heels, unreconciled and irreconcilable.

The Norman-descended aristocrats who had risen were now mostly thoroughly cowed. But Fitzmaurice formed a new conspiracy called 'The Catholic League' and set off in 1575 to enlist help in Catholic Europe.

IV

One man who would distinguish himself in war as a virtually insane anti-Catholic was Richard Grenville, a Cornish landowner, whose household was massacred and whose colony near Cork was swept away by Fitzmaurice's rebels in the late 1560s. Another man whose defiance of Spain would make him a legend was associated with the other large Irish colonising scheme: Captain Francis Drake.

In 1571 Sir Thomas Smith, one of Elizabeth's leading councillors, launched, with much publicity, a programme for colonising part of Ulster, the Ards. Smith was an enthusiast for the ancient Romans, but found a model closer to him in time for the colonial aristocracy which he intended to set up: the Spanish conquest of Mexico and Peru. The Gaels would be forbidden, on pain of death, to wear English clothes — mark the contrast with King's and Queen's Counties only a few years earlier. Smith proposed that the Irish would have no legal rights and would be permitted to learn no skilled trades and to buy no land. They would become a servile labour force. To younger sons of the gentry – 'our law, which giveth all to the elder brother, furthereth much my purpose', Smith wrote – were offered holdings of which the smallest would be three hundred acres. They must, of course, take up the Puritan's Burden. 'To inhabit and reform so barbarous a nation ... were both a godly and commendable deed, and a sufficient work for our age ... I judged surely, that God did make apt and prepare this nation for such a purpose.'[28] But Smith's bastard son, also Thomas, arrived in the Ards in 1572 with only a hundred men, ran into fierce opposition and then was killed by his own servants.

Meanwhile Walter Devereux, Earl of Essex, had come up with a still more ambitious plan. In May 1573 he proposed to the Queen that he should be given the whole of Antrim in fee, including the areas where the Scottish Macdonalds had intruded. The Queen agreed and in 1573 a great expedition set forth, half paid for by Essex himself, half by the Queen. Every 'gentleman adventurer' was to be given 400 acres for each horseman he maintained and 200 for each footman, at the rent of 2d. per acre.

Fiasco followed. The local Gaels would not be brought to decisive battle; Essex was short of stores; his 'adventurers' mostly forsook him and went home. It was the act of a desperate man when he sent three frigates under Captain Drake to Rathlin Island, a Macdonald stronghold where his men treacherously slaughtered everyone there, several hundred Scottish Gaels – old people, women and children included. Next month Essex resigned his grant. He soon died in Dublin of that miserable dysentery which plagued the English in Ireland, a Sassenach's Grave. 'Sorley Boy' Macdonald went in and destroyed his fort at Carrickfergus.[29]

Yet this disaster did not deter further hopes of colonies, soon given scope by the forfeiture in the south-west which followed a fresh round of rebellions. Fitzmaurice, after two fruitless years in France, had been warmly welcomed in Rome by the Pope. Gregory XIII gave him troops. Though the main body were diverted on the way to fight for the King of Portugal in Morocco, Fitzmaurice had a few score with him when he landed at Dingle Bay in July 1579, and a distinguished English priest, Dr Sanders, landed with him as papal commissary. This was a crusade, but the Irish in Connacht saw Fitzmaurice as merely a raiding clan enemy. In the words of the annalist, ' ... They proceeded to plunder the country as they passed along. The country began to assemble to oppose them; and, first of all, the sons of William Burke, son of Edmond, namely, Theobald and Ulick; and Theobald dispatched messengers to Tuath-Aesa-Greine, summoning Mac-I-Brien Ara, to come and banish the traitor from the country. Mac-I-Brien sent a body of gallowglasses and soldiers to Theobald. These then went in pursuit of those heroic bands, and overtook James, who had halted in a dense and solitary wood to await their approach. A battle was fought between both forces, in which James was shot with a ball in the hollow of the chest, which caused his death.'[30]

Desmond's south-west remained rebellious. Relations with Spain were worsening, and the acting viceroy, Pelham, marched into Munster in 1580 determined to make it, in his own words, 'as bare a country as ever Spaniard set foot in'. To systematic devastation was added great slaughter. 'It was not wonderful,' wrote the Irish annalist, 'that they should kill men fit for action, but they killed blind and feeble men, women, boys, and girls, sick persons, idiots, and old people.'[31]

The rebels were forced back into the woods. But when they seemed beaten, revolt suddenly flamed out in Leinster, where Viscount Baltinglass, an ardent Catholic, and Fiach McHugh O Byrne rose in August. A new and inexperienced Deputy, Lord Grey of Wilton, came, and over 2,000 fresh troops from England with him. In the deep, boggy, heavily-wooded gorge of Glenmalure, the Leinster rebels defeated Grey's raw men and this encouraged new risings elsewhere. Then, in September, a papal fleet debouched some seven hundred soldiers, mostly Italians, in the south-western harbour of Smerwick. The officers were Spanish. Their banner was that of the Counter-Reformation. They were checked and encircled at once by zealous Protestant Englishmen.

Besieged in Smerwick, the papists craved a parley. Grey refused to offer them any conditions of surrender. They yielded nevertheless; there was nothing else they could do. Irish tradition would say that they were promised their lives. They laid down their arms. Grey had no hesitation. 'Then put I in certain bands, who straight fell to execution. There were six hundred slain.'[32] The cold-blooded massacre was neatly conducted, according to Grey's orders, by Captain Mackworth, and Captain Walter Ralegh.

Desmond had done nothing to help the papal forces. Other rebels had moved too late. Next year, Baltinglass fled the country. Yet the agonies were drawn out. Elizabeth, making one of her false economies, insisted on the discharge of more than three thousand troops. Desmond regained some ground and Grey, now almost universally disliked by English as well as by Gaels, was recalled in July 1582. Black Tom Ormond was given the chance to subdue his own hereditary foe, and he cut down Desmond's clansmen and supporters until he was sick of bloodshed. In November 1583, the last Earl of Desmond, now a half-crippled fugitive in the woods, was captured and killed by some Gaels, O Moriarties, whose beasts he had stolen. Vacillating and foolish in his lifetime, Desmond became part of Irish legend. His ghost on a phantom horse shod with silver rode in the night near Limerick, and people in Kerry centuries later still heard, in the West wind off the Atlantic, the howl of the Desmond gallowglasses in battle.[33] What had happened at Smerwick would not be forgotten either. Nor would the manner in which the Munster rebellion had been put down, with what one prominent Englishman did deplore as 'inhuman cruelty'.[34]

The greater part of the old Norman-Irish aristocracy of Munster had been destroyed or had destroyed itself in the fifteen years between 1568 and 1583. Over 500,000 acres were forfeited to the Crown. A large-scale colonisation plan was inevitable, since only if the land were populated could it become profitable to the Queen. Under the plans which emerged in 1585 twenty-four 'seignories' of 4,000 to 12,000 acres of arable land were to be given to 'undertakers' who would have the trouble of gathering gentlemen, freeholders and tenant farmers, along with craftsmen, shopkeepers, servants and labourers. No Irish must be allowed in the 'plantation'. The undertakers would pay no rent for a while, and thereafter only a modest one. This attractive scheme was publicised widely in England, with circulars sent to J.P.s and with leading officials packed off on tours to extol the project. Success was urgently needed. 'If Munster were left almost bare or allowed to fill up again with Irish people, then Spain might find too easy a backdoor into England.'[35]

Relations between Spain and England withered. In 1572, perhaps to conciliate Philip, Elizabeth had expelled the corsairs from the Low Countries who had been using English ports as bases. Ironically, the outcome had been the first strides towards Dutch independence. The 'sea-beggars', alighting at Brill, had found they could sweep over the northern Netherlands with the help of Calvinists in the towns there. In July the Estates of the Province of Holland had recognised the rebel William of Orange as their Stadtholder. Then, in August, Protestant Europe had been horrified by the news that the Catholic Guise faction had butchered two or three thousand Huguenots treacherously in Paris, in the 'Massacre of St Bartholomew'. Grey's counter-slaughter at Smerwick can be put down to fear as well as cold-bloodedness; no papist could be trusted, alive.

Elizabeth was not a timorous woman, nor a dogmatic one. She had no wish to bear the expense of fighting Spain, and would not incinerate Catholics for their faith. But English priests were now slipping back to their homeland from the Continent, to minister to the small minority which was all that remained of English Catholicism. Such men were sent by a Pope who denied her queenship and when they were caught Elizabeth had them executed as traitors. Meanwhile, the great general Parma began to swing the balance in the Low Countries back in Spain's favour and Elizabeth was ineluctably drawn into support for his Protestant adversaries, rebels though they might be.

Events in Scotland were ominous, too. The Earl of Lennox, who won control there in 1579–80, was in touch with the Duc de Guise and his militant Catholic League. An attack on England was discussed. But Protestant nobles abducted the boy-king James in the 'Ruthven raid' of 1582. Lennox was driven into exile and in 1586 the 'Treaty of Berwick' cemented an alliance between England and Scotland. While Elizabeth would not explicitly concede that James was her heir, she agreed to respect his rights, without defining what they were, and he was given a small annual subsidy, which turned out to be the price of his mother's head; there was one plot too many in Mary's favour and she was executed in 1587.

V

The balance of power was slowly swinging from Mediterranean Europe towards the north-west of the continent. England was catching up technically with her more advanced rivals. Cast-iron gun manufacture came to England only around the beginning of the sixteenth century. Henry VIII's war needs had energised production in the Weald, and by 1585 English cannon were in great demand elsewhere in Europe. Elizabeth's people had an edge in the weapons of naval warfare.[36]

But woollen cloth remained far and away the most important English export. Historians tell us about little else when they discuss trade. English exports had grown rapidly in the late fifteenth century, then progress had slackened. London had continued rapid expansion, but this had been at the expense of such ports as Bristol and Southampton. An intensive trade between London and one continental market, Antwerp, had been substituted, in effect, for scattered trade involving many English and foreign ports. Foreigners commonly took two-fifths or half of the cloth from London to Antwerp; the English share of the trade was monopolised by the misnamed company of 'Merchant Adventurers' established under Henry VII. In the short run, this concentration of trade in the hands of a small, very un-'adventurous', group which did no more than shovel cloth across from the mouth of the Thames to that of the Rhine (while Bristol, facing America, dropped in importance) inhibited English involvement in overseas expansion. In the long run, however, the sheaving of merchant capital in London would be to England's advantage in the distant trades where great capital was a necessity.

The trade in cloth to Antwerp reached its apogee in the late 1540s, after a debasement of the English currency. Then the government stepped in to restore the value of sterling and the Merchant Adventurers' exports slumped. This shock jolted the City of London so hard that it began at last to look for alternative markets. Quite a spate of far voyages was the result. ' ... The fifteen-fifties were to form a most crucial decade in the history not only of English exploration but also of English foreign commerce.'[37]

The most dramatic sign of the new outlook was the floating in 1552-3 of a company to pioneer a North-East Passage to Cathay. There was, of course, no feasible passage, but an important trade with Muscovite Russia resulted from the search. English cloth and metal wares could be exchanged there for fish-oil, potash, hemp and flax and ropes, and for almost a century England eclipsed all other European countries in commerce with that backward and semi-Asiatic land. The first recorded commercial voyage to Morocco dates from 1551. The trade with the Moors (cloth for sugar and, later, saltpetre) was swiftly established as a recognised and important line of business and from 1553 onwards, ships chartered by London merchants began to visit the coast of Guinea for slaves and gold dust, 'elephants' teeth' and pepper.

Meanwhile, English merchants gradually came to control more and more of their own island's trade. The Venetians ceased to pay regular visits to London after 1533 and were last seen at Southampton in 1587. The Hanseatic merchants, who had held a privileged position in London, exempt from English law, lost it temporarily in 1552 and never regained it in full. Their London headquarters, the 'Steelyard', finally closed in 1598. In the late sixteenth century, England ceased to be a semi-'colonial' country on the periphery of European trade. London was no longer a satellite of Antwerp. The Muscovy Company founded in 1555 was playing in Russia much the same role as the Venetians had recently played in England.

The risks of the Russia trade through icy seas were enormous. The Muscovy Company was organised on the novel 'joint stock' basis. This major new device in the capitalist development of England was also employed from now on in some industrial enterprises. Merchants and others pooled their capital under a single management, and the pickings of courtiers and savings of landowners could be mobilised for trades and industries in which such people might play little or no direct part. The Guinea Company, also founded in 1555, likewise began with joint stock. But individuals and small partnerships still dominated the scene, and as soon as their distant trades were well established, both the Muscovy and Levant Companies reverted to a 'Regulated' basis. The 'Regulated Company', corresponding to the guilds which still monopolised town industry, had a long history behind it and a long one ahead of it. Groups of individual merchants, banded together, each paying a fee as in the 'Merchant Adventurers', had from the Crown the right to monopolise trade in a certain commodity or a certain area. While regulation made it easier for the Crown to tap merchants' profits – they paid heavily for their privileges – it also gave trading interests access to the ears of government.

Elizabeth and her ministers invested from time to time in overseas voyages. The royal palace at Westminster was only a mile or so up the Thames from the City of London. The English government had much more to do with merchants than the French or the Spanish. It would be wrong to suppose that Elizabeth and her chief ministers had any consistent, positive commercial policy. Far from it; Burghley in 1564 actually argued in favour of reducing exports. Fear of social disorder, of the 'unbalancing of the hierarchy of degree by excessive commercial wealth', made many high-placed Elizabethans deeply suspicious of trade and industry. But the government was short of money. The Crown was always open to bribery by pressure groups, and it was growingly forced into dependence on the goodwill of the chief cloth exporters, who could make it loans. Hence the wavering, opportunistic behaviour of Elizabeth and her ministers when it came to questions of trade and overseas expansion.[38] The Crown was not strong enough to push enterprise forward, or to stand in the way, and Ivan the Terrible, Tsar of Muscovy, had a point when he wrote to Elizabeth in 1570, ' ... Wee had thought that you had been ruler over your lande ... but now wee perceive that there be other men that doe rule, and not men but bowers [i.e. peasants] and merchaunts ... '[39]

Like the trade with Muscovy, the Baltic trade was coming to have the acute strategic importance for the state which both would maintain till the days of sailing ships ended. Cold northern forests provided 'naval stores' of pitch and rope and timber, and as the Antwerp entrepôt failed, English merchants strove to increase direct access to them. The Eastland Company was chartered in 1579, to regulate operations in the Baltic. Antwerp, through its control of Portugal's East Indies wares and its links with the Mediterranean, had also provided the luxuries which the wealthy in England swilled and savoured and smeared on themselves. Here was a rich bait to lure merchants further afield. ' ... The best opportunities for securing more than routine gains from trade', Ralph Davis observes, 'were usually to be found in importing.'[40] Huge profits could be made on wines and sugar and 'spices' — and most English imports at this time were, in fact, luxuries. In the third quarter of the sixteenth century, voyages to Morocco and Africa, and more famously to the Caribbean, were motivated by the quest for exotica, as were the very dangerous expeditions in search of a North Eastern or a North Western Passage to Cathay.

The daring enterprises of Hawkins and Drake, Frobisher, Gilbert and Ralegh brought at best only windfalls of profit or loot. While their psychological impact was decisive, and their ultimate follow-through confirmed a new direction in world history, their immediate impact on the economy was insignificant compared to that of the little-sung English invasion of Mediterranean commerce from the 1570s. The Christian victory at Lepanto checked Turkish dominance in the Mediterranean yet created a power-vacuum in which opportunists jostled for decades. With Venice flagging and Antwerp in decline, the Dutch moved in as carriers of Baltic corn and North Sea fish direct to the Mediterranean. The English had a far smaller share of that trade, but, thanks to Cornwall, they could meet the strategic need for tin, which was essential for casting bronze cannon. For the sake of their tin, the Turkish sultan gave privileges to English traders and on the basis of these the Levant Company was formed in 1581. Through it, English cloth found a large vent. These were the early days of the 'New Draperies' — in some manufacturing areas, notably East Anglia, the classic heavy English broadcloth gave way from the 1560s to lighter and cheaper worsted and semi-worsted products, suitable for a trade with warmer countries.

Meanwhile, unregulated interlopers surged in the Levant Company's wake. English ships muscled into the Mediterranean carrying trades, transporting goods and even, in one case, troops for the Venetians themselves, and making themselves notorious for their readiness to freight Christian slaves for the infidels of the North African coast. Philip II, in 1585, moved to exclude all English ships from his dominions and failed, abjectly. They were too useful. Their ships were too fast. The great Elizabethan voyages into Arctic seas and through the Pacific should be set against a background of regular, thriving, aggressive trade to Constantinople and Leghorn, Smyrna, Aleppo, Algiers, bringing experience to seamen and giving confidence to merchants.

VI

There could be no more captivating topic than the long sea-voyages of Elizabeth's day, which found their vast and ramshackle literary monument in Richard Hakluyt's *Principal Navigations, Voyages, Traffiques & Discoveries of the English Nation*. No astronaut will seem so brave as the mariners who steered through icebergs and spent months afloat on tropical seas in ships which were tiny by modern standards. Martin Frobisher first searched for the North West Passage in a bark of no more than 30 tons. Drake's *Golden Hind*, in which he sailed round the world, was between 100 and 150 tons.[41]

Such ships had keels of oak, decks of pine, spars of spruce. The parts under water were covered with black tar or pitch as protection against weed and barnacles, while topsides and deck were caulked with a mixture of pitch and hemp. Hemp gave the rigging, flax gave the sails. All the materials mentioned were as vital to maritime trade as diesel oil to road haulage today. To get or to safeguard supplies, it was worthwhile to fight wars or to found colonies. And as Europe's maritime expansion continued, the agriculture of whole regions would be diverted towards the supply of food for ships. Sixteenth-century ships carried dried codfish for fast days; pickled beef and pork, the notorious hardtack biscuit which always bred mould and maggots on a long voyage; butter and cheese, honey and oil, vinegar, beer and wine to help the monotonous diet slip down somehow. While officers slept in bunks in the steerage, seamen still dossed down on the main deck, though hammocks – first seen by Columbus in the Bahamas in 1492 – were coming into use in English ships before the end of the sixteenth century. Mariners seem to have worn the same set of clothes – coarse serge gowns, loose trousers – day in day out and year in year out. They reeked. Their ships would soon reek as ballast and bilges were fouled with urine and vomit and scraps of stale food. Ducking, keel-hauling and other savage punishments met indiscipline. Sailors, while they survived them, were formed by the conditions in which they laboured. An early-seventeenth-century writer sketched the typical seaman: 'His familiarity with death and danger, hath armed him with a kind of dissolute security against any encounter. The sea cannot roar more abroad, than hee within, fire him but with liquor ... Hee makes small or no choice of his pallet; he can sleepe as well on a Sacke of Pumice as a pillow of doune ... He cannot speake low, the Sea talks so loud.'[42]

Little record survives of voyages made by Englishmen to far continents before the second half of the sixteenth century, but we do know that in 1530 a Plymouth merchant, William Hawkins, sent ships to the Guinea Coast and thence to Brazil, trespassing on the Portuguese monopoly. Hawkins seems to have carried on this trade for a while without interference from Lisbon, and to have been followed into it by Southampton merchants. In sticky heat, they somehow traded English woollens and even, it seems, English nightcaps (nineteen dozen such went in a ship sailing for Hawkins in 1540) for the coarse malagueta pepper which gave the 'Grain Coast' of Africa its title, and for the Brazil-wood which bestowed a more familiar name on the opposite coast, and which was used in its turn to dye cloth.[43]

The Africa trade seems to have lapsed till it was revived by London merchants in 1553. The French were already busily interloping in Guinea, and the three ships commanded by Thomas Wyndham, a Norfolk gentleman, initiated an 'era of triple rivalry'.[44] English merchants interviewed the King of Benin in his 'great huge hall' and he gladly offered them 'four score tunne of pepper.' But it took a month to gather this precious cargo, and meanwhile, down at the coast, the chronicler tells us, 'our men partly having no rule of themselves, but eating without measure of the fruits of the countrey, and drinking the wine of the Palme trees that droppeth in the night from the cut of the branches of the same, and in such extreme heate running continually into the water ... were thereby brought into swellings and agues: insomuch that the later time of the yeere coming on, caused them to die sometimes three & sometimes 4 or 5 in a day.' Wyndham himself died, and those of his men who survived sailed precipitately home, leaving merchants and pepper up country at Benin. 'And of sevenscore men came home to Plimmouth scarcely forty, and of them many died.' But the two ships which got back were laden with a valuable cargo.[45]

Elizabeth showed some favour to the Guinea traders, and for a few years the English outpaced the French as interlopers in West Africa. But the profits to be had from exchanging basins and beads, linen and knives, woollens, kettles, brass rings and such like nicknacks, for the ivory, pepper and gold offered by peoples along the West African coast came to seem insufficient as Englishmen saw the growing trade in slaves driven by the Portuguese between Africa and America. John Hawkins, son of the pioneering William, born in 1532, had carried on with his elder brother, another William, the family's thriving trade after his father's death. He had voyaged often to the Canaries and learnt much from the Spaniards there about conditions across the Atlantic. Well-educated, and notably suave and courtly, he had ambitions which took aim beyond Plymouth and visions far broader than those of the average merchant. About 1560 he pulled out of the family business. The £10,000 he got as his share of the capital made him a man of some wealth. He shortly moved to London, and formed a syndicate there of merchants and royal officials. Their plan was to win from the Spanish Crown a share in the West Indian slave trade.

Such a scheme was not rash or implausible at that time. Hawkins had been a loyal subject of Philip II when the latter had been King of England. Their nations were at peace, while decades of struggle between the Hapsburgs and France for predominance in Europe had brought French corsairs flocking into the Caribbean, where they had more than once despoiled the great treasure fleets and ravaged coastal towns. The sale of African slaves to the Spanish planters was conducted under the *asiento* system where the Crown sold licences to merchants and financiers who in return for their money received monopoly rights and huge returns. Most of these contractors were non-Castilian — Portuguese, Genoese, Germans, Flemings, Italians. Why should not Hawkins win permission to trade in the Caribbean, in return for assisting the Spaniards to keep down French corsairs and contraband traders?

He sailed from Plymouth with four ships in October 1562. Between Cape Verde and Sierra Leone he procured slaves, probably four hundred or so. Some he captured on shore himself, some he bought from the Portuguese. Despite the Spanish ban on foreign traders, he was able to dispose of these very profitably in Hispaniola, taking pearls, gold, hides and sugar in return. He sent two ships to trade in Spain itself, and he was so confident that his proceedings would prove acceptable that he was surprised when these were confiscated. Despite this setback, he brought back to England three ships with enough aboard to show a remarkable profit.

The Queen herself was attracted. For the next and much grander expedition planned by the syndicate, she lent a (barely seaworthy) naval vessel, the *Jesus of Lubeck*, and Hawkins's fleet flew the Royal Standard. Perhaps the Spaniards would welcome its help; the French had recently founded a colony in Florida. It sailed in October 1564, it obtained its cargo of Africans after a good deal of fighting and, helped, so one Calvinistic gentleman with it suggested, by 'the Almightie God, who never suffereth his elect to perish', arrived to sell them on the Spanish Main.[46] Though the colonists had now been specifically forbidden to trade with him, they could not resist the human wares he brought. Again there were handsome profits, and soon after his return the College of Arms, on the recommendation of Burghley and Leicester, both shareholders in his enterprise, granted Hawkins coat armour with, as its crest, a demi-Moor proper bound with a cord: a black slave.

But the Spaniards now showed they could deal with the French themselves. In 1565 they massacred almost all the French settlers in Florida. Colonial officials who had connived at Hawkins's trading were sharply brought to heel. Hawkins pressed ahead with plans for a third voyage but faced with Spanish displeasure the Queen withdrew her open favour and the expedition, commanded by one Captain Lovell, was baulked from trading on the Spanish Main and and to leave slaves at one place without payment. Even so, Hawkins pushed on, had he led the fourth voyage himself, in 1567.

Quite why Elizabeth let him go is not evident. Spanish views were now clear. There would be no deal, no concession. Yet Hawkins sailed with two of the Queen's ships, one of them the dilapidated *Jesus*. His fleet numbered six and he took over four hundred men; this was his most imposing venture yet. Francis Drake, a distant relation of Hawkins, sailed under him. Drake was a fiercely zealous Protestant, whose farming father had fled from the south-western 'Prayer Book Rebellion' of 1549 and had later served as a chaplain in the naval dockyard at Chatham. He was also a natural man of action, decisive, self-confident, daring, an obvious leader. The Caribbean would help to make him a mythical hero even before he died.

The profits of the Portuguese Crown had fallen. In 1569, English inroads would at last produce threats of war. Hawkins found that he needed to fight Portuguese as well as Africans and could only obtain slaves with difficulty. He had to force trade on the Spanish Main town of Rio de la Hacha. Yet elsewhere commerce still went ahead without unpleasantness, and all might have ended well as before if the *Jesus* had not started to fall apart. Hawkins, rather than let the Queen's ship sink, felt compelled to put into a Mexican port, San Juan de Ulua, where the annual treasure fleet from Seville was shortly expected, convoyed by two ships of war. When it came, Hawkins took possession of a battery on an island commanding the harbour's entrance and told the Spaniards they could come in only if they gave him strict pledges. Hostages were to be exchanged. Hawkins was to be permitted to refit and revictual, on proper payment, and meanwhile to hold the battery. The Spaniards agreed, and were let in. But they had no intention of keeping their word to a Protestant interloper.

A Spanish attack partly misfired. Hawkins's guns sank one warship and burnt the other, but he had to abandon the *Jesus*. He had only two ships left. Drake escaped home in one, deserting his leader. Hawkins and those with him suffered horribly on a small vessel overcrowded and undervictualled. Half or more of the crew successfully begged Hawkins to set them ashore on the Mexican coast. Most of these surrendered to the Spaniards and many subsequently suffered the lashes and galley service awarded by Old or New Spain's Inquisition to heretics. Most of those who stayed with Hawkins died at sea. Out of 200 leaving San Juan only 15 survived, with their captain, to enter Plymouth Sound.[47] Hawkins forgave Drake. He never forgave the Spaniards. The story of Spanish treachery at San Juan now took its place in the Protestant Black Legend.

Though one of the Queen's ships was involved, general confrontation with Spain did not result. Over the years since Columbus's discoveries, the 'doctrine of the two spheres' had evolved. It prevailed for centuries. Conflict in the New World, 'beyond the line', over territory or trade, would not necessarily be taken as cause for war in Europe. The doctrine had been made explicit at the Treaty of Cateau-Cambresis in 1559 when it was orally agreed that Spaniards had the right to throw any Frenchmen they caught in the Indies 'into the sea' without contravening the agreement between the two Crowns in Europe.

Hawkins's interloping was not the only cause, or the main one, of breach with Spain in 1569–72. His voyages made him a very rich man, but while a few other venturers followed him into the trade in human beings, English involvement soon lapsed, along with most English commerce with West Africa. Meanwhile, in 1569, a court ruled, in a case involving a slave brought from Russia, 'that England was too Pure an Air for Slaves to breathe in.'[48] But Hawkins had shown others the way to the Caribbean, and English ships flocked there from now on, imitating French and Dutch interlopers in piracy and contraband trade. The 1570s would see a wholly novel range and momentum in English overseas doings. The age of the 'sea dogs' had begun.

VII

Few men could yet love the sea. Its risks were fairly depicted, after all, in the procession of wrecks and disasters through Shakespeare's plays. In a poem dedicated to his friend Ralegh, 'the Shepherd of the Ocean', Edmund Spenser revelled in execration of it:

Thousand wyld beasts with deep mouthes gaping direfule
Therin stil wait poor passengers to teare.
Who life doth loath, and longs death to behold,
Before he die, alreadie dead with feare,
And yet would live with heart halfe stonie cold,
Let him to sea, and he shall see it there.
And yet as ghastly dreadfull, as it seemes,
Bold men presuming life for gaine to sell,
Dare tempt that gulf, and in those wandring stremes
Seek waies unknowne, waies leading down to hell.[49]

Yet Spenser, as we have seen, was an expansionist. Was it just 'gain' which tempted voyagers and projectors? Mainly, but not solely. Frank though they frequently were about the rewards for which they hoped, the groups of men who now fostered expeditions and colonies were ridden by other motives besides greed.

Sheer curiosity counted. In a famous passage, the younger and greater Richard Hakluyt described how as a schoolboy he visited his elder cousin of the same name, a Gentleman of the Middle Temple, and 'found lying open upon his boord certeine bookes of Cosmographie, with an universall Mappe: he seeing me somewhat curious in the view thereof, began to instruct my ignorance ... He pointed with his wand to all the knowen Seas, Gulfs, Bayes, Straights, Capes, Rivers, Empires, Kingdomes, Dukedomes, and Territories of ech part, with declaration also of their speciall commodities, & particular wants, which by the benefit of traffike, & entercourse of merchants, are plentifully supplied. From the Mappe he brought me to the Bible, and turning to the 107 Psalme, directed mee to the 23 & 24 verses, where I read, that they which go downe to the sea in ships, and occupy by the great waters, they see the works of the Lord, and his woonders in the deepe ...' The boy vowed, in his 'high and rare delight', to follow the study of geography, and at Oxford University immersed himself in every printed or written account of voyages and discoveries he could find, in ancient or modern languages.[50] Part scientist, part economist, part propagandist, he was the natural successor-apparent to Dr John Dee, mathematician, cosmographer, astrologer and magician, who argued that conquests made by King Arthur gave Queen Elizabeth a claim to various isles in the Atlantic and that she had a right to America on the basis of the purported colonising exploits of a twelfth-century Welsh prince named Madoc. A scientist of European reputation, Dee, with his theories regarding North East and North West Passages, had an important influence on the group at court which looked towards the New World.[51]

As the 1570s wore on, that group grew less and less disposed to hide its interest in activities which violated Spain's claims. Hostility to Spain in itself seems to have been the prime motive for the ardently anti-papist minister,

1 (*above*) An Elizabethan artist's picture (1581) of 'Wild Irish' attacking the Pale

2 (*left*) Captain Thomas Lee, dressed for soldiering in Ireland, by Gheeraerts (1594)

3 (*above*) Dr John Dee, magician and geographer

AN° · DÑI · 1571 ·
ÆTATIS · SVÆ ·
· 29 ·
Sir Richard Granville, killed
in a sea-fight near the Azores,
1591

4 An unknown artist captures superbly the pride and violence of Sir Richard Grenville (1571)

Sir Francis Walsingham, who with other 'great' men – the Earl of Leicester, the Sidneys, father and son – formed an expansionist faction. 'Mercantilist' ideas, clarified notably by Hakluyt, of how trade and colonisation might promote national grandeur, also played a significant part. But so did the craving for individual profit, which at this time was most likely to come from piracy and the rich plunder it might bring home. Great men patronised pirates. The voyages in which they invested, aimed at exploration or colonisation, commonly collapsed into treasure-hunting: a search for precious ores, or sheer robbery on the high seas. Just as little fishermen down in Devon when war began smartly supplied pilchards and butter to the enemy, so the high-minded, anti-papist Sidneys, owning an iron-works, were involved in the illegal trade selling precious English cannon to Spain.[52]

Even Ralegh, epitome, it would seem, of all that was worst in his age as well as all that was best, combined the ideals of a poet and the vision of a statesman with, on occasion, the ethics of a pickpocket. As he rose to 'greatness' in Elizabeth's court he formed the natural link between the aggressive faction there and the gentry, merchants and seafarers of his native south-west. To adapt phrases from Hakluyt, these startling adventurers bore 'fame-thirsty and gold-thirsty mindes'. They sought for reputation and profit on that grandiose scale which would make 'all perils and misadventures seeme tolerable unto them'.[53] They moved on from petty piracies in the Channel and blood-spattered projects for colonies in Ireland to immense ventures which brought them all the fame they had wanted, and they hitched their self-seeking so wholly to their religion and to their sense of Englishness that generation upon dazzled generation after them would hardly notice their insatiable pecuniary avidity. As one scholar puts it, they were men 'for whom Protestantism, patriotism and plunder became virtually synonymous'.[54]

As Drake was the paragon of Devon sailors, and as that sagacious slaver Hawkins rose from the Plymouth merchant community, so Sir Humphrey Gilbert and his cousin Sir Richard Grenville stand out among the seafaring gentry. They were quarrelsome, violent people. Grenville had killed a man in a brawl by the time he was twenty, running his sword six inches into him in a London street. In the Azores, terrified locals would tell stories of how when Grenville was there he could, after a few drinks, take wine-glasses between his teeth 'and crash them in pieces and swallow them down, so that often times the blood ran out of his mouth without any harm at all unto him.' While clearly untrue, the story is well found: it recaptures for us the style of reckless bluster with which Grenville faced at home or abroad anything in the shape of a papist. He owed his knighthood to his services as Sheriff of Cornwall, where he made notable headway in putting down Roman Catholicism. He enslaved a score of Spanish sailors whom he brought home on one of his prizes, making them 'carry stone on their backs all day for some building operations of his, and chaining them up all night.' He somehow combined prodigal fury in action

D

with a very passable head for business. He owned a ship jointly with John Hawkins's brother William, one with a fine record of privateering, and he also owned, as was possible then, the town of Bideford, which he made into a prosperous port.[55] As will be seen from this, he did not begin with nothing. He was fiercely proud of his ancient lineage, and it was dynastic ambitions, not pennilessness, which took him to Ireland; he aimed that his elder son should inherit his West Country estate and that his younger son should have patrimony in Munster.

The 'younger son' factor in English expansion is famous. Humphrey Gilbert was, precisely, a younger son whose elder brother had taken the main share of the family's extensive property. There is an ominous ring to a contemporary's verdict that 'His natuer is as good as eny gentleman in England as sone as he is owt of his stormes.'[56] His cruelty in Ireland matched his vindictiveness in other contexts. He was vain, boastful, an overreacher. Yet, he could write, somewhat. Amongst all the projects he spawned aimed at his own enrichment, there was a single disinterested one, for a technological university. Like Grenville, he took musicians on his voyages, men who could play while the captain ate his dinner in state — Christopher Marlowe's monstrous world-conqueror *Tamburlaine*, aptly the favourite hero of Elizabethan theatregoers, had, we remember, a huge love of beauty. And what was a younger son of spirit to do? The great feudal households where such men had sought advancement were broken up; the monasteries which had provided a living for prospectless gentlefolk had been swept away (and there was a more than symbolic point in the fact that Grenville, 'gran hereje y perseguidor de catolicos', as the Spaniards dubbed him, lived in one ruined Cistercian abbey by Cork and converted the church of another, in Devon, into a mansion, which Drake bought from him.) Gilbert gambled his life at sea. Like Grenville, he lost it with a consummate sense of heroic style.

The patriotism of both men was married to the Renaissance cult of 'vertue', a militant ideal most remote from Victorian 'virtue'. ' ... Give me leave without offence,' wrote Gilbert, 'always to live and die in this mind, That he is not worthie to live at all, that for feare, or daunger of death, shunneth his countrey service, and his owne honour, seeing death is inevitable, and the fame of vertue immortall.'[57] As the public in England responded to the remarkable show staged for them by their seafarers, a belief grew up that these were great days to live in, that the English God was showing marked favour to his beloved people, that the deeds of the ancients were being matched, that to be 'mere English', as Elizabeth phrased it, was a fine thing indeed. Above all, Francis Drake gave his countrymen pride.

VIII

In the 1560s, the Spaniards evolved a system for gathering in New World treasure which they maintained for a century and a half. In May each year one treasure fleet, the *flota*, left Seville for Vera Cruz in Mexico. In August a second fleet, the *galeones*, sailed for Nombre de Dios on the Isthmus of Panama. After the crossing of five or six weeks, it unloaded its European wares and retreated to Cartagena on the Main for the winter. In the spring, it went back to the Isthmus to pick up the silver consignments from Peru which had been brought by ships up the Pacific coast, then painfully carried by porters or mules through the jungles. The *galeones* would sail thence to Havana in Cuba for a rendezvous with the returning Mexican *flota*, and the combined fleet would return home in a heavily guarded convoy, bearing the sinews of war for Philip II's campaigns. The main streams of this great and cumbersome movement were fed by legions of ships moving along the coast. While Protestant pirates could only rarely succeed in their attempts on the *flota*, even the minor hauls from little ships and from stragglers could make a seaman wealthy.

Drake, though lenient and generous to Spanish prisoners, was a hard Protestant, and this must help to explain the daring with which he sought not only golden scraps but a whole meal. After his dubious part at San Juan de Ulua, he returned before long in the swarm which preyed on the Caribbean, and learnt of the *cimarrones* ('cimaroons'), black slaves who had escaped and formed guerrilla bands in the unmapped backlands of the Isthmus along with the Indian women they took to bed. The Spaniards, chronically short of men in the vast lands they claimed, could not put them down. In 1572, Drake arrived in the Isthmus with plans to seize the main stream of Peruvian silver on the last stage of its long journey into the holds of the *galeones*.

A surprise attack on Nombre de Dios in July captured the town (as large as Plymouth) but failed to extract treasure. Drake remained on the Isthmus, allied with some 'cimaroons', and, in January 1573, tried out a different plan. With twenty whites and about as many blacks he marched to ambush a Spanish mule train. He took about £40,000, which he shared with some French Huguenot corsairs who had joined him.

Spain seemed weak in the Isthmus, a slender neck of land which linked the trade of two oceans, and in 1576 a Plymouth man, John Oxenham, formerly Drake's lieutenant, tried to seize it with no more than fifty men. After depredations still more successful than Drake's, his band was destroyed by the Spaniards and he himself was eventually hanged in Peru. But Drake was prepared for an even grander gamble; from a tree in the Isthmus he had seen the Pacific, and while Oxenham was being questioned in Lima on the colonial schemes of the English, Drake, most amazingly, was raiding on the Peruvian coast.

So far as we know, no English ship had yet reached the Far East or even India. Englishmen were all the more likely to credit the idea, encouraged by a misreading of Marco Polo, that there were rich lands to the south-east of Asia. For two generations, the best maps had shown a conjectural continent in the South Pacific, trending from the southern tip of South America north-west to

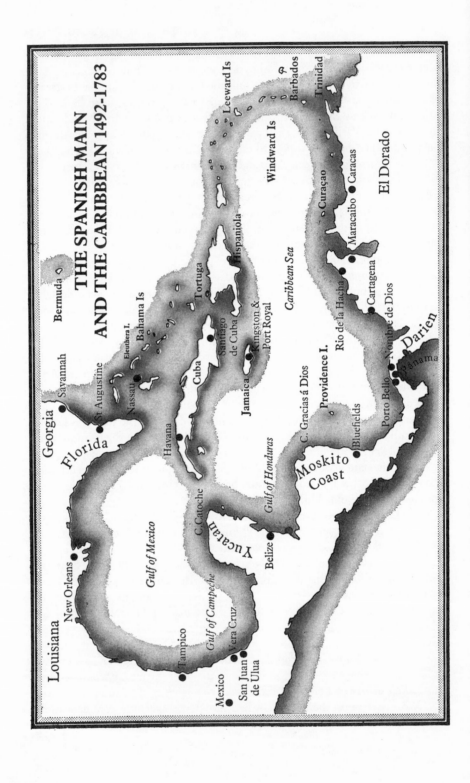

THE SPANISH MAIN
AND THE CARIBBEAN 1492-1783

Louisiana

New Orleans

Georgia

Savannah

St Augustine

Florida

Bermuda

Nassau

Eleuthera I.

Bahama Is

Tortuga

Hispaniola

Leeward Is

Barbados

Trinidad

Cuba

Havana

Santiago
de Cuba

Kingston &
Port Royal

Windward Is

Curaçao

Maracaibo

Caracas

El Dorado

C. Catoche

Jamaica

Caribbean Sea

Rio de la Hacha

Cartagena

Nombre de Dios

Darien

Yucatan

Gulf of Honduras

C. Gracias á Dios

Providence I.

Bluefields

Porto Bello

Panama

Belize

Moskito
Coast

Gulf of Mexico

Tampico

Gulf of Campeche

Vera Cruz

Mexico

San Juan
de Ulua

the tropics. The existence of this great southern continent would not be dis-
proved finally for two hundred years, and credulity was stiffened by the news,
leaking in through an English merchant resident in Mexico, that a Spaniard
named Mendaña was claiming to have discovered it. (What he had found, in
1567, were only the Solomon Islands, so called because his ecstatic imagination
made them the land of Ophir, linked with the king of that name in the Bible.)
For Englishmen, the hankering for direct contact with China, expressed at this
time in the search for a North West Passage over America, could mingle with
hopes of the discovery, along the south-west route which Magellan had
pioneered, of lands as rich as those now exploited by Spain and Portugal.

In any case, lavishly laden Spanish vessels now sailed the Pacific. The spices
of the Moluccas were an old prize for seafarers. The West Country gentry and
merchants who joined with Richard Grenville in 1574, petitioning the Queen
for permission to undertake 'The discovery, traffic and enjoying for the Queen's
Majesty and her subjects, of all or any lands, islands and countries southward
beyond the equinoctial or where the Pole Antarctic hath any elevation above
the horizon', however misty their geographical concepts, no doubt reckoned
that if discovery failed, piracy would still bring them good profit.

But their supporting arguments began to develop the ideas of 'mercantilist'
imperialism. Portugal, Spain and France had each got 'one part of the new
found world' and 'now the fourth to the south is by God's providence left for
England.' The litany of objects for the adventure would be re-echoed down to
the nineteenth century. 'Enlarging the bounds of Christian religion' piously
headed the list. Home industry and commerce would be advanced by 'the
beneficial utterance of the commodities of England' – primarily by the sale of
English cloth, since *Terra Australis* was supposed to lie chiefly in temperate
latitudes. 'The increase and maintenance of seamen' in the interests of English
striking power at sea was an argument which would hold immense weight so
long as the Royal Navy relied in wartime on men who had sailed on merchant
ships during peace. Any far trade could be promoted or justified on the grounds
that it increased the number of mariners and gave them experience of difficult
conditions, and the concept of a 'nursery of seamen' would retain its mystique
into the days of Nelson. 'The relief of the people at home' was an objective
which would have a still longer life: while rich new trades might increase
employment in industry, emigration could bring opportunity to the unemployed. And the whine of international jealousy would always be heard.
Grenville and his colleagues sought 'the abating of the prices of spices and such
commodities that we now have at the Portugals and Spaniards hands', and 'The
increase of the quantity of gold and silver that shall be brought out of Spain
itself into England when the commodities coming out of Spain becoming this
way cheaper.' Tortuously expressed, this was the mercantilist case that it was
vital for the nation to corner as much bullion as possible.[58]

Grenville's project was later amplified to include the notion of finding the western outlet of the North West Passage by sailing up the Pacific coast of America, a sensible-looking plan when no one, except their skin-clad inhabitants, knew of Alaska or of the Rocky Mountains. The Queen blew hot and cold. Grenville was needed for military service, first in Ireland, then in Cornwall. And when the plan was accepted in 1577, a sailor was preferred to a soldier for its execution. A powerful syndicate of courtiers and officials, including Leicester and Walsingham, hijacked the scheme from Grenville's West Country group, and employed Drake, out of a job since the failure of Essex's project for colonisation in Ulster.

The Queen gave a ship. Though she still hoped to keep peace with Spain, she seems to have seen no harm in taking the chance of direct personal profit from an expedition which she could disavow if need be. Drake had an excellent record as a gold-grabber, and she may have known that his real intention would be to prey on the Spaniards on the undefended Pacific coast. In the event, the lofty aim of Southern Empire was tossed overboard. Drake made no attempt to locate *Terra Australis*, and only a perfunctory search for the North West Passage. Other things being equal he might perhaps have done more, but sixteenth-century seafaring was at the mercy of hostile weather, and of the appetites of the crew.

As it was, sailors who had enlisted, so they thought, for a voyage to the Levant (this was the screen put up to deceive the Spaniards) grew restive on the initial, Atlantic stage of Drake's expedition, which left near the end of 1577 with four ships, a pinnace and about 160 men. There was serious trouble. Drake, an ebullient little plebeian, struggled for power with Thomas Doughty, the leading gentleman present. He won, and at Port St Julian, just short of Magellan's Straits, had Doughty beheaded after a kangaroo court had found him guilty of incitement to mutiny, and of witchcraft practised against the expedition. If the second accusation reminds us of how archaic some ways of thought of the 'sea-dogs' were, what followed shows Drake in a much more modern light. Soon after, one Sunday, Drake deposed the chaplain and preached his men a sermon himself. There were numerous gentlemen with him. He denounced their class consciousness and aversion to toil. ' ... My masters, I must have it left, for I must have the gentleman to haul and draw with the mariner and the mariner with the gentleman.' It was a remarkable moment, displaying precociously how nationalism, imperialism and democracy would, in Britain, advance pretty steadily together until by our own century there had arisen the concept of a democratic, secular state where Britons 'hauled' together, defying all foreigners. 'There is no doubt,' K. R. Andrews observes, that Drake's 'sympathies lay with the sailors whose background he shared.'[59]

The rest is familiar. Drake sailed through the Straits, then, in bad weather, lost his two companions. In the lone vessel which he renamed the *Golden Hind*, he harried the coasts of Chile and Peru, where no one expected him, taking one prize above all which filled his own ship with silver. (Altogether the expedition seems to have pirated some twenty-five or thirty vessels, besides various robberies on land.) By June 1579, having left his pursuers far behind, he was refitting at an anchorage in California. Drake seems to have got on well with Red Indians, as with 'cimaroons'. He called the country Nova Albion, 'New Britain', seeing some resemblance between its white cliffs and those of Kent, and claimed it for Elizabeth after receiving, as he thought, due obeisance from the inhabitants. This annexation had no practical sequel, nor did the 'treaty' which Drake later made in the Moluccas, where, finding the Sultan of Ternate on bad terms with the Portuguese, he (perhaps) arrived at an understanding with him that he would sell spices exclusively to England, before sailing on with several tons of cloves. When he arrived at Plymouth again in September 1580, after nearly three years at sea, he had matched Magellan's crewmen and circled the globe.

The Queen was pleased. She took all the bullion Drake had brought home and put it safely in the Tower. The other shareholders were amply contented with a 100 per cent return on their investment. Drake was knighted. Foreigners were impressed. Englishmen passed word of the voyage round with excitement. An appetite for great deeds was whetted.

IX

Meanwhile, others were no less brave, but not so lucky. There had been an upsurge of interest in the North West Passage. The Muscovy Company claimed a monopoly of all northern exploration, but its lack of fresh enterprise irked some ambitious spirits. In 1566, in between spells of fighting in Ireland, Humphrey Gilbert found time to write a *Discourse of a Discoverie for a New Passage to Cataia*. He had petitioned the Queen for a monopoly of trade through the putative 'Strait of Anian' which, like other informed people, including John Dee, he supposed to begin in the Atlantic somewhere between 60° and 70° N. and to trend south-westwards towards 40° or 50° N. Proponents of the rival North East Passage claimed that a unicorn's horn had been found on the coast of Tartary and that it could only have come with the tides through their favoured outlet, 'there being no Unicorne in any parte of Asia, saving in India, and Cataia': nonsense, Gilbert retorted, there were 'great plentie' of beasts like unicorns in Lapland. He proposed a trading base on the Pacific in the region of the Sierra Nevada (known from the Spaniards) and colonies along the Strait into which could be decanted 'suche needie people of our Countrie, which now trouble the common welth, and through want here at home, are inforced to commit outragious offences, whereby they are dayly consumed with the Gallowes.'[60]

Nothing came of this proposal, but in 1575 the Muscovy Company's monopoly was at last breached, on the Queen's orders. The schemers now were Michael Lok, a former Levant merchant, and his nautical ally Martin Frobisher, a tough unlettered Yorkshireman who had somehow survived his first long voyage with Wyndham to West Africa when still a boy, and a subsequent career which had mingled successful piracies with two stretches in gaol. Frobisher sailed in 1576 with three tiny ships. He found a long bay in Baffin Land. He came back with word that he had discovered the Strait, with an Eskimo aboard whom he claimed was a Tartar, and with a sample of black ore, probably iron pyrites, which one expert only, the others not being so rash, was now prepared to say contained gold.

Mania set in. Besides Elizabeth, great courtiers, big merchants, rushed to subscribe to the 'Company of Cathay' which was now founded with Lok as its governor and Frobisher as its admiral. Sailing north again, Frobisher wasted no time on exploration; he loaded 200 tons of ore and dashed for home. Still no one could actually extract any gold from it, yet even so the Queen increased her stake in the next expedition which left in 1578 with no fewer than fifteen ships, by far the most expensive speculation of its kind in the whole Tudor period. Fog, which made Frobisher lose his way, did ensure a contribution this time to geographical knowledge. He followed the strait later named after Hudson for 200 miles and was sure that this was the true passage. But when he got home, with yet more worthless ore, he found that faith, so rashly sustained, had collapsed, and with it the Company of Cathay. Lok went to a debtors' prison, while Frobisher returned to his piracy (though Fate had up her sleeve for him later distinguished service against Spain, a knighthood, and a gentleman's estate.)

What he and his men had seen, apart from fool's gold, was not encouraging. 'Nothing fit or profitable for the use of man', as one of them put it, grew in the bald tracts inhabited by dangerous Eskimos, who would provide little market for English goods, contented as they were with 'raw flesh and warme blood to satisfie their greedy panches, which is their only glory.' Gnats, fogs and 'horrible snow' (in July) made the dreariness consummately disgusting.[61] Yet somewhere beyond were the riches of the East; in this faith the quest was resumed in the mid-1580s, under a new company, short of funds, which was led by Humphrey Gilbert's brother Adrian. John Davis of Dartmouth, the greatest scientific navigator of his times, voyaged three times in 1585-7 and in his last attempt reached the record latitude of 72° between Baffin Land and Greenland and saw open sea ahead to the West before hard winds drove him back. There, if he could have followed it, lay the true North West Passage, through Lancaster Sound, but it would never have a commercial use, and now search for it was suspended for another generation.

Humphrey Gilbert himself had been even less lucky, though he earned himself a secure place in the hagiography of three nations (Britain, Canada and the U.S.A.) by being the first Englishman to work on the colonisation of North America. The rather sketchy interest which he had shown in colonies in his *Cataia* discourse was deepened by his involvement in the attempted settlement of Ireland. He saw a prospect of more wealth than he could acquire through his speculations in mining and alchemy at home, more status than he could find as M.P. for Plymouth, more of both than were offered him by his office as Receiver-general for certain fines. Besides, instinct and training made him a warrior; he fought for the Protestant cause in the Low Countries. In 1577, he offered the Queen a fine plan for attacking Spain in the New World. He would seize the papist fishing fleets off Newfoundland under pretext of a patent to colonise. Then he would waylay the Spanish treasure fleet. Then he would grab Santo Domingo and Cuba.[62]

Nothing at first sight came of this. But Elizabeth liked this dashing, if cruel, adventurer, who had been for a while a member of her household when he was a youth and she was still a princess. In June 1578 she 'granted him letters patent of such wide scope as to deserve the title of the first English colonial charter.'[63] He was empowered to found a colony anywhere between Labrador and Florida, along that North American coastline which England still claimed by virtue of Cabot's 'discovery'. He was given viceregal powers over his vast domain. Though this may have been a subterfuge, masking a real intention of piracy, it did provide adequate legal basis for a genuine colony.

Gilbert brought into the scheme his two brothers, Sir John and Adrian and also both of his Ralegh half-brothers, Carew and Walter, but his main co-adventurer was Henry Knollys, son of the treasurer of the Queen's household. Characteristically, Gilbert quarrelled with him and Knollys sailed off with three of their ten ships to be a pirate in European waters. After Gilbert left with the rest, bad weather scattered the fleet and the random robberies which followed, combined with those of Knollys, were too much even by Tudor standards. Gilbert was held back by the Privy Council when he wanted to try again the next year, and was sent to serve at sea against the Irish rebels.

However, Gilbert later resumed the struggle to make something of his patent. A novel basis for action was now advanced, prophetic of what would follow in North America. Might not the New World provide a haven for dissidents in religion? Gilbert, surprisingly, turned for support to the English Catholic community. An Act of 1581 put them under severer penalties than before, and it was likely that patriotic papists would prefer to live in America, still under English rule, than flee to Europe or face ruin from the fines of £20 a month per household now demanded at home. Elizabeth, however, insisted that recusant emigrants must pay up all fines overdue in full, and the Spanish Ambassador, on his side, mobilised the priests against the scheme, which he saw as a cunning device (perhaps it was) for counteracting the growth of Catholicism by exporting the people who would support papist missionary work.

Yet Gilbert could still go beyond the Catholic gentry whose interest was thus damped down to appeal to the land hunger of Protestants of his own class. Men sought wealth and freedom in land. Land in England was now very dear, 'and much land was in any case not profitable owing to cumbersome tenurial arrangements and the heavy burdens placed on land held by feudal tenures from the crown.' Now Gilbert offered the bait of 'vast' estates, and aristocratic lordship over them.[64] He had land at a low price, in stupefying profusion. Over nine months, in 1582–3, he assigned eight and a half million acres (and seven whole islands off the coast) to Catholics alone, while Sir Philip Sidney, the poet, acquired an individual stake of three million acres.[65]

But there would be land for poor people, too; for anyone who brought with him seed and tools to the value of forty-three shillings. Gilbert was the first Englishman to attempt a New World Utopia. He would govern with the help of counsellors chosen by the consent of the people, and the landowners under him, maintaining armed men, would also be expected to help support scholars. One thinks for a moment of Cecil Rhodes. The colony would have virtual independence, though the laws would follow those of England. Gilbert would in effect be a philosopher-king.[66]

Friends and relations were called on for help – Walter Ralegh had risen at court and contributed heavily. The merchants of Southampton bought a monopoly of the colony's commerce. But the money which Gilbert could mobilise came to pitifully little, and he would never have planted his colony securely.

Elizabeth asked Gilbert not to sail. She knew him to be a man 'of not good happ by sea'. But he insisted and left, perilously late in the season, on 11 June 1583. He had five ships, and some 260 men, including masons and carpenters to erect buildings and metallurgists in case there seemed to be gold or silver.[67] The largest ship turned back after only two days. The rest reached Newfoundland in August.

According to an account of five years before, there had then been only fifty English boats exploiting the nearby prodigious shoals of cod which, salted and dried, found such a ready market in Europe. There had been as many Portuguese, twice as many Spanish ships, and three times as many French. But on 5 August 1583, at the summer settlement of St John's, Gilbert formally took possession of the island, laying down that public worship must be according to the Church of England and that anyone insulting the Queen was to lose his ship and his ears. A fortnight's merry feasting followed.[68]

Gilbert left again, on August 20, with three ships, of which the 120-ton *Delight* was the largest. He intended to reach the mainland and work his way southwards prospecting for a suitable spot for a colony. He himself commanded his tiny pinnace, the 10-ton *Squirrel*. Edward Haies, the gentleman-captain of the 40-ton *Golden Hind*, wrote a haunting account of what followed. The night of August 28 was 'faire and pleasant, yet not without token of storm to ensue, and most part of this Wednesday night, like the Swanne that singeth before her death, they in the Admirall, or Delight continued in sounding of Trumpets, with Drummes, and Fifes: also winding the Cornets, Haughtboyes: and in the end of their jolitie, left with the battell and ringing of doleful knells.' After this music had died away, the helmsmen heard 'strange voyces' in the air. Next day, there were rain and thick fog. The *Delight* struck shoal, and most of its hundred men drowned in sight of their comrades on the other ships. Gilbert shortly agreed with Haies that they must head for England. As they set off home they saw a 'sea-monster', which looked like a lion, roared like one, and 'passed along turning his head to and fro, yawning and gaping wide, with ougly demonstration of long teeth, and glaring eies'. The cheerful Gilbert took it for a good omen, 'rejoycing that he was to warre against such an enemie, if it were the devill.' This spirit of almost rapturous fatalism, which seems characteristic of the Elizabethan personality, gave way to the time's equally typical peevishness. A couple of days later Gilbert came aboard the *Hind* and caroused with Haies, 'lamenting greatly the losse of his great ship, more of the men, but most of all of his bookes and notes, and what els I know not ... ', and beating his cabin boy in drunken fury. Haies reckoned that what hurt Gilbert hardest was some ore brought from Newfoundland which he had hoped contained silver and which had also gone down with the *Delight*.

Yet he left in good spirits, insisting on going back to his own absurdly small pinnace. On Monday 9 September, in foul weather and huge seas north of the Azores, the *Squirrel* nearly sank, 'yet at that time recovered: and giving foorth signes of joy, the Generall sitting abaft with a booke in his hand, cried out unto us in the *Hind* (so oft as we did approch within hearing) We are as neere to heaven by sea as by land.' He was quoting from Thomas More's *Utopia*, with its account of an ideal society in the New World. Haies thought the man was a fool, and deduced that he sailed in the *Squirrel* to prove to the world he was not afraid of the sea. Noble aspirations were mixed with rankling avarice and with terror of the world's contempt. So Shakespeare would make Othello and Anthony go. About midnight, the *Squirrel*'s lights suddenly vanished. The ship was 'devoured and swallowed up of the Sea.'[69]

Ralegh, perhaps as unpleasant, certainly still more remarkable, now took over his dead half-brother's role.

X

In the early 1580s, Ralegh, who had long hung about Court, at last attracted the Queen's full notice. He had made his mark in Ireland, partly at the massacre at Smerwick. The Queen liked fine men about her. She was much taken, we are told, with Ralegh's 'elocution', though 'notwithstanding his so great Mastership in Style and his conversation with the learnedst and politest persons, yet he spake broad Devonshire to his dyeing day.'[70] He was tall, with an ivory complexion, wavy black hair, a high forehead, a brooding manner. His sudden conquest of the Queen brought him jealousy and enemies. Elizabeth gave him those prime favours which all her courtiers sought, economic monopolies. A patent for granting licences to sell wines was the foundation of his fortunes, followed by other profitable concessions to do with the sale of woollen cloth. In 1585, he was made Warden of the Stannaries, controlling the tin mines of Cornwall; Lord Lieutenant of that county; and also Vice-Admiral of both Cornwall and Devon. He was not one to hide his wealth; he matched the pearls in his hatband, the jewels on his fingers, with an arrogance which made many detest him. 'Damnable proud' was the verdict handed down to the biographer Aubrey in the next century.[71]

Yet he was popular with the Devon sailors, and with the common people wherever his offices put him over them. He spoke up in Parliament for the poorest taxpayers, and he earned the devotion of children. Contradictions dominated his personality and his position. The most intelligent man at Elizabeth's court, he was kept out of positions of crucial responsibility. The most far-sighted projector of his time, he directed only one clearly successful great stroke of action, the capture and sack of Cadiz in 1596. A serious patriot, he nevertheless sold wood from his Irish estates to the Spaniards in wartime.[72] His greed was remarkable even by Elizabethan standards, and we must accept his enemies' taunt that 'Raw Lie' was on occasions a great liar. Also, his self-love was prodigious. He hated having anyone else above him. He wrote to Leicester from Ireland, 'I have spent some time here under the Deputy, in such poore place and charge, as, were it not for that I knew him to be on(e) of yours, I would disdayn it as miche as to keap sheepe.'[73] He resented dependence on others and sought wealth to make himself free. 'Poverty is a shame amongst men,' he wrote, in the *Instructions to his Son* which were published after his death, 'an imprisonment of the mind, a vexation of every worthy spirit.'[74] His letters to those above him, like the poetry he addressed to the Queen, radiate a species of arrogant sycophancy — look, here it is, he seems to be saying, you want this flattery, here it is.

He saw through the mystique of queenship and kingship and did not disguise it. The artifice of political life disgusted him. He was very touchy about being called a play actor, yet one of his most famous poems expressed the idea that life itself was no more than 'a play of passion':

> Our graves that hide us from the searching Sun,
> Are like drawne curtaynes when the play is done,
> Thus march we playing to our latest rest,
> Onely we dye in earnest, that's no jest.[75]

The voice of Ralegh's poetry rises sombre and thunderous over his period's prattle of lyrical conventionalities, presenting, in accents of self-transcendent self-pity, the general yet deeply personal truth that time steals all joys, from the past only sorrow stays.

While his ambition pressed him to high politics, he despised the court and mistrusted action, and a contrary urge drove him to the solitude of scientific experiment, and to the company of a group of daring and controversial intellectuals. He was extremely learned. The friend and coadjutor of Drake was also the intimate of leading poets. The friend of Spenser and Jonson was also abreast with the most advanced scientific thought of his time. He had for mentor Thomas Hariot, greatest of Tudor scientists, one of the founders of algebra, first observer of Halley's comet and a precocious thinker in the mathematics of navigation. Ralegh himself experimented, in shipbuilding as well as in chemistry, and was 'a pioneer in naval medicine, dietetics, and hygiene.'[76] Like other advanced thinkers, he took a Faustian interest in the possibilities of magic. Inevitably he was accused of atheism, and certainly, like Hariot, he tended towards what was later known as deism. He asked sceptical questions about the existence of the soul. And in practical matters also his mind cut through the pieties of his age. 'Machiavel' was another smear-word against him, and his contemporaries must have found his grasp of certain real-political themes as distasteful and unnerving as other facets of his diamond intelligence.

Despite his own monopolies, he argued for freer trade. He admired the maritime drive and the commercial ruthlessness of the Dutch, and yet, rightly, he feared them as dangerous competitors. Above all, he grasped the importance of sea-power. 'Whosoever commands the sea, commands the trade', he wrote; 'whosoever commands the trade of the world, commands the riches of the world, and consequently the world itself.'[77] Through him the Elizabethan mind met America, and the future.

In March 1584 he applied for, and was granted, his dead half-brother Humphrey's rights in America, saving the power to exercise a monopoly over the Newfoundland fishery. Then he sent out two ships, under Philip Amadas and Arthur Barlow, to search for a site for a colony in the area north of the Spaniards' tenuous settlement in Florida. In July they landed on Hatteras, an island forming part of the Carolina Outer Banks, and took possession of the area in the Queen's name. They exchanged presents with mild and curious Indians, and were hospitably entertained on Roanoke, another island between the reef and the shore. They arrived home in September, bringing two Indians with them, and reported, like so many such explorers before and after, that they had seen an earthly paradise. They ignored the fact that they had found no good harbour. They vastly overestimated the fertility of the soil. They spoke rapturously of huge, high cedar trees, laden grape-vines, great flocks of birds, herds of deer, a handsome people, and of 'their country corn', maize, 'very white, faire, and well-tasted', grown with prodigious ease.[78]

Even before they came back with their fine-seeming news, Ralegh had enlisted the services of Richard Hakluyt for a propaganda exercise designed to attract funds for a colony. Though Gilbert and Grenville had anticipated sketchily much of what he had to say, Hakluyt's *Discourse of Western Planting*, presented to the Queen in October, deserves its reputation as the first manifesto of English imperialism. Colonisation was extolled as the best escape from a doleful economic prospect, as a panacea for almost all ills, and as a fine way to do down Spain. Hakluyt could imagine profitable colonies everywhere from Newfoundland to South America, the Spaniards ousted from the New World and crippled in Europe. 'Mercantilism' was adumbrated. With colonies in America, England would have safe sources of supply of naval stores and Mediterranean dainties, and could soar into full economic independence, selling its manufactures to colonists and to Indians in return for raw materials. English traders need no more confront the Inquisition in Spain, impositions in France, Danish exactions in the Baltic or the rising competition of Holland.

Convicts who would otherwise stuff English gaols could be sent to the New World to fell timber for shipmasts and make tar and cordage, or to work in the rich mines, or to plant sugar. A rapturous page is packed with mouth-watering visions of the commodities of America and the work which they will provide. English vagabonds will dress vines in Virginia, hew marble to make 'noble buildinges there', sow dyes and gather honey, whale, and engage them-selves in 'dryinge, sortinge and packinge of fethers whereof may be had there marvelous great quantitie.' And so on. Paupers too infirm to brave the Atlantic can be employed at home 'makinge of a thousande triflinge thinges' to trade with the Indians, whose demand for the 'coursest and basest' English (and Welsh, and Irish) cloth would revive 'decayed townes'. Prophetically, Hakluyt saw that if England could only find more work for its people, it could support as many mouths as France and Spain together; this would indeed come to pass in the nineteenth century, and with it Hakluyt's vision of an island workshop drawing in raw materials and using its skills on them to make goods for export.

And, besides malefactors, what glowing prospects the New World would offer to other sorts of people. Astronomers would be needed there, and historio-graphers. Ruined men could regain fortune and status. Puritan preachers could save the souls of the Indians, 'those poore people which have sitten so long in darkenes', rather than subverting the state at home. The realm was 'swarminge at this day with valiant youthes rustinge and hurtfull by lacke of employment', who could be used in colony-making. And it would not be hard. 'Philippe', Hakluyt observed, 'rather governeth in the west Indies by opinion, then by mighte ... ' A few Spaniards were engrossing a vast area by bluff. The Indians could be stirred against them. Hakluyt gloated that Philip would soon be humbled, 'a laughinge stocke for all the worlde ... ' But England must strike fast, or be a day late for the fair. The French were already active, and would, if not forestalled, rob England of the fruits of North America which, Hakluyt insisted, she claimed by the right of prior discovery.[79]

Ralegh was ready to act. Besides sharing Hakluyt's anti-Spanish afflatus, he aimed to gain such pre-eminence through America, where he could be sole lord of vast territories, as his rivals had denied him in England. But, could he pay for the enterprise? He was ready to risk a great deal of his own money but he had other business concerns, notably in Ireland. He raised backing from

Walsingham, Grenville, London merchants and others. The Queen would lend him a Royal Navy vessel for his expedition's flagship. But she would spare him no more government backing.

His experiment would show that a steady stream of capital was needed in the early days of a colony when there might be little or no immediate return. Ralegh, however, thought that 'Virginia' must pay its way as it went along. He and his backers saw plunder at sea as the answer. Even before his expedition sailed, Ralegh was sending out ships to raise funds by 'privateering', and he aimed that his colony should provide a base for raids in the West Indies and on the Spanish treasure fleet. Piracy and the colonial project were inextricably mixed. Prizes should pay for a base which would ensure bigger prizes.[80] By contrast with Gilbert's scheme, there would be no grants of land, and the settlers would work together as paid servants of the investors under the commander – a soldier – appointed by Ralegh.

Ralegh's first name for the area which he proposed to colonise was 'Wingandacon', based on a misunderstanding arising when some of his people had asked Indians what the country was called and they had answered with something like that set of syllables, meaning perhaps, 'you wear fine clothes' or perhaps, 'those are fine trees'.[81] But then the Queen agreed that the land might be named 'Virginia' in honour of herself and her singular chastity, and she knighted Ralegh in return for the compliment. The first English expedition actually to form an American colony left Plymouth on 9 April, 1585, in five ships and two pinnaces, with Grenville, Ralegh's cousin, in command.

XI

On the way, Grenville picked off such prizes as offered and gathered livestock, cuttings, seeds and roots for the colonists in the Spanish West Indian islands. Late in June he was trying to bring his flagship into a harbour in what we now know as the Carolina Outer Banks when it was grounded, with great loss of needed supplies. Amadas and Barlow had opted for an area which could in fact provide no useful base for attacking Spain. The Banks, formed by a long series of narrow islands, were shoal-infested and very dangerous to shipping. Furthermore, the mainland beyond them was swampy and impossible to cultivate except along the edges of rivers and sounds; this section of what became North Carolina has never afforded a prosperous agriculture.

However, Grenville and his men explored Pamlico Sound, lying behind the Banks. They soon ran into trouble with Indians. Barlow had described the Algonquian-speaking people here as 'most gentle, loving, and faithfull, void of all guile, and treason, and such as lived after the manner of the golden age'.[82] But Grenville, predictably, was soon bullying them. The first quarrel was picked by the English. A village was burnt and its corn destroyed. The Indians had stone tomahawks, no metal weapons at all, their tribes were petty, their villages

hey were many and the white men were few. The offer of violence
well as arrogant.

the colony was settled on, Roanoke, a large island between Pamlico
Albemarle Sound, where the Indians were friendly, and invited
settlement; there was the disposition to regard white men as supernatural
visitors, soon to evaporate in face of their conduct. A fort was built, Grenville
departed towards the end of August and captured a rich Spanish prize on the
way home. With that help, the Queen was rewarded, and Ralegh's credit stayed
high.

Ralph Lane was left in charge at Roanoke, an experienced soldier who had
recently served in Ireland and whose greed for Munster land had lost him the
goodwill of his superiors there. Now he was a virtual dictator, advised by an
informal council of fifteen gentlemen. He had no real grasp of the commercial
and agricultural questions on which the future of his colony would depend.
With the Indians, his one idea was force. In this respect, he fell far short of two
of the men with him, John White and Thomas Hariot, who worked together
to evoke the region in words and pictures. White drew and coloured wonderfully lifelike pictures of Indians and their dwellings, of birds and beasts. Hariot,
sent by Ralegh as scientific expert in residence, wrote a *Briefe and True Report*
which became known all over Europe as one of the most authoritative accounts
of American conditions, and he took the trouble to learn the language of the
Indians whom he studied so respectfully, whereas, he aggrievedly pointed out,
some of the gentlemen present 'had little or no care for any other thing than to
pamper their bellies' once it transpired that gold and silver were not be had
at once.[83]

Altogether, there were just over a hundred colonists, including several
Irishmen brought by Lane from Kerry. The bulk of the rank and file were
probably ex-soldiers, who had no skill at feeding themselves. The party
revealed that puzzling incapacity to capture the fish swarming around them
which was characteristic of Europeans in the New World. What seems to have
happened, here and in later colonies, was that men landed in malarial country
after an exhausting sea voyage were impressed by the fact that the Indians would
at first shower gifts of food upon them, and became convinced that their lack
of zest for work need not produce starvation so long as they had trinkets to trade
with and arms with which to assert themselves.

Though Lane prevailed upon the Indians to sow some ground for his men
and to clear more for them to plant themselves, native resentment was bound
to build up as the feckless white men clamoured for food. Lane chased hither
and thither in search of some great thing to make all rich. An early explorer,
mistaking Pamlico Sound for the Pacific, had spread the idea that the highway
to Cathay might be only a step from the coast where the English had now
settled. Lane did find Chesapeake Sound and see what is now called Virginia.
He realised that with its deep water anchorage, this would be a far better site

for a colony, but was distracted by Indian tales which made copper sound like gold and suggested to him that the Pacific was close, into an exploration up the Roanoke River on the mainland. And meanwhile the Roanoke chief *(werowance)* Wingina, had turned against the intruders. Allying with Indians on the mainland, he withdrew there with his people and ordered that no food should be sold to Lane's men. Hearing of Indian plans for attack, Lane himself struck and murdered Wingina. By now it was June 1586. After only a year, the colony was close to extinction. Lane and his men were short of supplies and expecting a native counter-attack. Then into view sailed Drake as their saviour.

The colonists had left in April 1585 just as real war with Spain boiled up. In May, Philip II had seized all the English ships in Iberian ports. The valuable Iberian trade had acted as a brake on English aggression. Now the clamour of England's merchants trading with Spain abetted the noise of the war party. The merchants demanded and got from the Queen permission to strike back against Spanish shipping. In August the Queen allied with the Dutch rebels. Eighteen years of open struggle with Spain began, the golden age of the privateers, and the ruin of the English Crown, which had somehow to fight on four fronts. The realm had to be defended against invasion. Expeditionary forces had to be sent to the help of allies in the Netherlands and France. Ireland, the half-closed back door, would prove the biggest front of all, and nearly a fatal one. And there was the struggle with Spain at sea which engaged the zest of merchants and plunderers. While Spain's own economy had started to weaken, England's, like that of the amazing Dutch rebels, had been growing stronger. The war was not merely one between Protestant North and Catholic Spain; two rising trading powers confronted a muscle-bound empire which barred the way to their further expansion.

But Elizabeth's own aims were modest. Her realm must be kept safe, and the enemy must be pressed hard enough to bring him to terms; to go further would merely raise the new danger of an overweening France. This was not a duel, there were four hands in the game, and England's was weakest. Providing soldiers for Europe, and then for Ireland as well, left the Queen no cash to spare. So, while she was glad of the windfall profits it sometimes brought, she had no hankering for offensive war at sea. She left that to her subjects, to avid gentry and eager merchants ready to wage a guerrilla campaign in the Atlantic on their own initiative and to bring her into their joint stock on occasion. Such men and their friends among high officials, the bellicose party devoted to deep-water schemes, certainly kept in part of their minds Hakluyt's idea of trans-ocean strikes which would sever Philip's sustaining transfusion of treasure and open his New World possessions to English trade, but they never clarified an overall strategy. They hunted for short-term profits and schemed for *ad hoc* objectives. The sea war was dominated by privateers while the Royal Navy played a lesser role, under a Lord High Admiral, Lord Howard of Effingham, who was himself a promoter of privateering (and was to boot quite spectacularly corrupt).

By the end of 1585, Elizabeth, besides subsidising Henri de Navarre in France, had sent 6,000 men to the Low Countries and had also authorised the adventure which brought Francis Drake at length to Roanoke. He had cleared for the Main with thirty ships and a force of over 2,000 sailors and soldiers – all equipped by joint stock, the Queen contributing one-third of the total. Drake damaged Spanish prestige, cheekily finishing off his fitting out in a port on Spanish soil, capturing and sacking San Domingo and Cartagena, but he missed the treasure fleet, the enterprise made no profit, and this discouraged any attempt to repeat it.

On his way homewards he crippled the small Spanish colony in Florida, probably by prior arrangement with Ralegh. Then he breezed up to Roanoke itself, laden with slaves captured from the Spaniards and flush with all kinds of useful looted supplies. He offered Lane food, arms and clothing, a ship, boats and sailors to man them. But before these could be handed over a fierce thunderstorm struck his fleet in its insecure anchorage, then raged for four days. As it cleared, the ship Drake was offering ran away; no doubt its crew had lacked relish for their proposed service. Drake offered another, less suitable vessel, but the colonists now had wholly lost their nerve, and eagerly scrambled away in Drake's fleet.

A few days later, the first supply ship despatched by Ralegh arrived, found no one, and sailed home. Then Grenville turned up with a second and larger instalment, men as well as supplies. He left fifteen men on Roanoke, to keep a foothold, but the Indians soon struck, two colonists were killed, the rest took off in a small boat and were never heard of again. Meanwhile, Grenville rubbed home what many investors would take to be the main lesson; the prizes he brought back defrayed much of the cost, and would seem to prove that robbery on the high seas offered rich gains while colonies in a wilderness got nowhere. Nevertheless, Ralegh tried again, on an improved basis designed to produce a more stable, self-supporting community than Lane's party could ever have been.

Shareholders in the new joint-stock company would be drawn largely from those who were prepared to go in person. Each would get 500 acres of land on the strength of his undertaking to go, and further land in proportion to his investment. All would enjoy rights of self-government, while leaving representatives behind in England to use part of their investment in keeping them supplied through the difficult early stages. For governor of 'the City of Ralegh in Virginia', John White the artist was chosen. He was given twelve 'Assistants' in this office, obscure people of middling class in England, who nevertheless acquired coats of arms in honour of their appointment; a foretaste of what America might offer the common man.

Only three of Lane's men were willing to venture again, but scores of new colonists came forward. They must have been people with some property, as farmers, tradesmen or such-like, which they could sell in order to buy their equipment. In the event, 113 settlers arrived in America in May 1587, of whom 17 were women and 9 were children.[84]

They found the fort rased, but the houses still intact, and the Indians still shunning the island. On 18 August, a month after their coming, John White's daughter Eleanor, who was married to an Assistant, Ananias Dare, gave birth to a daughter, the first known English offspring on North American soil, who was duly christened 'Virginia'. But the colonists were already feeling a shortage of livestock, salt and various other items, so they prevailed upon White himself to sail, most reluctantly, back to England to expedite fresh supplies. Meanwhile they would move to the mainland; the objective agreed was possibly Chesapeake Bay.

White was home by early November, and Ralegh pressed ahead with plans for relief. But when Grenville was almost ready to sail in the following March, the Privy Council ordered him not to go. A Spanish invasion was threatening. England needed his ships. White was allowed to set off, but with two little pinnaces only. He seems to have been a weakish though decent man, and he could not prevent the crews embarking on piracy, even against allied ships. A French privateer paid White's ship back, and it staggered into Bideford badly mauled. The other pinnace returned some weeks later, having been nowhere near Virginia.

And now events ruled out any chance of relief for the moment. This was 1588, year of the great Armada. Philip II had gradually realised that he must come to declare war on England. The execution of Mary Queen of Scots early in 1587 left him, as he saw it, the true Catholic claimant to England's throne, her son, James VI of Scotland, being a heretic. The new Pope, Sixtus V, was willing to subsidise Spain to attack Elizabeth. Drake's raid on Cadiz in the spring of 1587, destroying 24 ships and many stores, held up the invasion fleet, but only for one year. In late July 1588, it was at last sighted off Cornwall, 130 ships, with 22,000 seamen and soldiers aboard, bent on linking up with the Spanish forces in the Low Countries and thereafter escorting troops who would cross the Channel in barges.

Against Parma's crack troops from Europe, if landed, Elizabeth would have mustered only an inexperienced militia. On paper the overall Spanish marine, now joined with the Portuguese, outweighed that of England by six or eight times.[85] But the Channel was a great barrier. So was the quality of the ships which England now had. A high officer of the Spanish fleet had confided to a papal envoy, ironically, that while Spain must win, since God was on her side, it would only be because God must provide one of His miracles: the English ships were so much faster and handier.[86] Since the 1560s, Sir John Hawkins had been pressing the need for speedy manoeuvrable ships of the latest design. For ten years, he had been in charge of the Navy's dockyards and building programme. England now had, besides many armed merchant ships, 25 war galleons built and armed in the newest fashion.

Despite their advantages, the English made little impression on the Armada in nine days' running fight as it sailed up the Channel and anchored at Calais. There fireships broke it up. Mauled by the English, the papists fled in disorder before a south-west wind and reached home round the coasts of Gaelic Scotland and Ireland, where several ships were wrecked. Yet two-thirds or more of the whole fleet got back. Though Spanish sea-power was hurt, the wound healed quickly. If anything, Spain was stronger at sea in the 1590s than before the Armada. More silver flowed in from the New World than ever, in fleets still imposing and well guarded. But the blow to Spanish prestige was great; England's allies in France and the Netherlands were heartened. In England itself relief was exhaled in much boasting in verse and prose, with Hakluyt's large compilation of English voyages, his *Principal Navigations*, arriving from the press in 1589 to inject further bubbles into the national mood. The crepuscular sequel, Elizabeth's last years, the decline of English sea-power under her successors, would only make patriots cling more fondly to the myth of the Great Armada destroyed by an epic band of seadogs, Drake and Frobisher to the fore. The myth confirmed emotionally what Ralegh had settled on intellectually: that England had a destiny and it was fathered by God's will upon the Sea. God blew, so men piously said, and the Armada was scattered.

Counter-Armada was attempted next year, the so-called 'Portugal Adventure', a shameful disaster. Drake commanded, and bungled, a sorry attack on Lisbon and a desultory swipe at the Azores. After 1588, in fifteen years, England would gain no big victory over Spain. The war was frustrating for both sides, nerve-racking and ruinous for the English Crown. There was never a straightforward confrontation on land, though Englishmen fought in the Netherlands and in France, where Spanish troops opposing Henri de Navarre occupied Britanny, fearsomely close to English shores. Spanish naval might, through the 1590s, would pose constant threat of invasion, and God would be kept hard at work blowing to scatter Armadas, lest the finest soldiers in Europe should land in England and confront the militia of Dogberries, Bottoms, Mouldies, Shadows, Warts, Feebles and Bullcalfs which was the far from plausible defence of the homeland of His favoured people.

Meanwhile, Ralegh tried to salvage White's colony, egged on by Hakluyt and supported by a rich London merchant, Sanderson, who had invested heavily in the venture. Ralegh had learnt much already from his mistakes, and in 1589, in his third attempt, he rallied a score of London merchants whose backing, given in return for comprehensive control of the trade of the area claimed under Ralegh's patent, might have been strong enough to nurse 'Virginia' into real life. But privateering now seemed to obsess all seamen. When poor White finally sailed again early in 1590 in quest of his grandchild and those with her, it was in a spree mounted by the great John Watts, most noted of all sponsors of privateering. Watts's captain would take White only, no planters and no supplies, and then he ranged the West Indies hunting prizes for four months of precious sailing time before he made for Virginia late in the season.

White had agreed with his fellows three years before that if they departed from Roanoke in distress or under duress, they would leave a cross as a signal. He 'found the houses taken downe, and the place very strongly enclosed with a high palisado of great trees, ... and one of the chiefe trees or postes at the right side of the entrance had the barke taken off, and 5 foote from the ground in fayre Capitall letters was graven CROATOAN without any crosse or signe of distresse.' Croatoan was an island in the Bank to the south where there had been friendly Indians. Why had the colonists written its name there? Why had they left White's three chests of belongings, which he found in the ditch, clearly rifled by Indians, 'my things spoyled and broken, and my bookes torne from the covers, the frames of some of my pictures and Mappes rotten and spoyled with rayne, and my armour almost eaten through with rust ... ': that armour which would have symbolised his status as Governor of the City of Ralegh?[87]

All questions stay unanswered. White could make no search, as his Captain would not linger. Their idea was then to return to the Caribbean and then come back to 'Virginia' in the spring, but the ship was blown off course and ran all the way home. White, after so many frustrations, gave up. Certain authorities think that the colonists merged into local Indian tribes. D. B. Quinn now holds that some of them did reach Chesapeake Bay and were eventually wiped out by a chief named Powhatan, of whom more later. Firm proof of any notion is not to be had.[88]

After 1600, Ralegh tried again to locate them. But meanwhile he became John Watts's partner in privateering. In 1591, they netted a profit, on one voyage to the Caribbean, of more than 200 per cent, despite a quarrel with the Queen over their prize money.[89]

XII

John White went to Ireland, where several of Lane's men, including Thomas Hariot, also settled in Munster, pioneers nearer home. Grenville was a great 'undertaker' in this colony, and Ralegh was the most outstanding organiser of all. The largest seignory was supposed to be 12,000 acres, but thanks to the Queen's favour Ralegh got no fewer than 42,000 acres of arable land near Cork and Waterford, at an especially low rent. Munster was not properly mapped, and there was confusion as natives returned to claim lands which colonists had earmarked. However, by 1589 there were over 600 male English settlers, many with families.[90] They brought English tools and stock and built farmsteads in the English style, but the original concept of a little England was sabotaged from the outset by undertakers who, to save trouble, broke the rules and gave Irish natives their land back as tenants. Edmund Spenser, who became lord of 3,000 acres in County Cork, wrote disapprovingly of the tendency, always marked in Irish history, for the English to fall into Hibernian habits. ' ... Having been brought up at home under a strait rule of duty and obedience, being always restrained by sharp penalties from lewd behaviour, so soon as they come thither, where they see laws more slackly tended, and the hard restraint which they were used unto, now slacked, they grow more loose and careless of their duty; and as it is the nature of all men to love liberty, so they become flat libertines and fall to all licentiousness . . . '91

The settlers, Ralegh above all, seized on the woods of Ireland as a source of quick profit, and the government was worried by the speed with which they were denuded for timber. While able tenants within reach of towns or navigable rivers probably did pretty well as commercial farmers, 'many preferred to live on rents from Irish tenants and to engage in land-jobbing and commercial speculation.'92 The colony was from the first harried by Irish outlaws and men deprived of their land, and was swept away in the torrent of rebellion which flowed over Ireland from 1594 onwards.

This trouble stemmed from Ulster, fastness of Gaeldom, where the dominating figure was Hugh O Neill, Earl of Tyrone. The son of that Baron of Dungannon done to death by Shane O Neill's men, he had spent eight years in England as a youth and on his return to Ireland had collaborated with the Dublin government – even with such a menacing enterprise as Essex's attempt to colonise Ulster itself. By the late 1580s, Ulster seemed tamed. Lord Deputy Perrot had established three garrisons there and had confirmed a settlement between Tyrone and his wily and drunken relative Turlough Luineach, the O Neill, by which the former acknowledged Turlough's captaincy and became his *tanaiste* (successor-designate). When Perrot, accused by Spenser and others of being too soft on the Gaels, left in 1588, Turlough Luineach stood on the quay watching his ship till it disappeared, and then burst into tears. As ships of the shattered Armada passed by the Irish coast, where many were wrecked, English fears were pacified; not a rebel stirred, though some chiefs did help survivors to escape. Two henchmen of Tyrone's, on the other hand, butchered hundreds of shipwrecked Spaniards, performing on behalf of the government the vicious job which the English elsewhere did for themselves.93

Perhaps that enigmatic figure was merely biding his time, or perhaps it was chiefly personal pique which began to edge him towards revolt. He fell out with Bagenal, the Queen's Marshal in Ulster. He eloped with Bagenal's sister Mabel in 1591, made her his third wife, and then, to complete the insult, disenchanted his bride by openly flaunting his mistresses before her. She went back in tears to her brother at Newry. But most likely it was a helpless instinct for self-preservation in the face of inexorable pressures which pushed Tyrone against his will into the cul-de-sac of revolt. For behind Bagenal, that angry intruder who could use the Crown's power to thwart Tyrone locally, stood a Dublin government which was gradually pressing ahead with the eradication of Gaelic Ireland, its customs and its political institutions on which the power of Tyrone himself depended. He had aimed to become the O Neill, and in 1593 the ageing

Turlough Luineach relinquished that ancient title to him, a claim to traditional kingship in its own right. But meanwhile there had been ominous doings in Monaghan, on Ulster's southern edge. When Sir Ross McMahon had died in 1589 without a legitimate son, the Dublin authorities had backed his brother Hugh who was legal successor by English law, against his *tanaiste*, Brian. The English had given the land to Hugh, lent him troops and then, when Hugh had proceeded to act in the style of a Gaelic chief and had used the government's soldiers to raid and burn, the Deputy had tried and executed him and had divided McMahon's country between various local Gaels, whose tenants became freeholders. The area was converted to English law and the Gaelic chiefship officially died.

Meanwhile, Tyrone's son-in-law Hugh Roe ('Red Hugh') O Donnell had been kidnapped by Perrot and imprisoned in Dublin Castle. After five years, in 1592, he made a remarkable escape. The O Donnells now had a handsome, heroic, fresh chief. Tyrone himself liked the young man. The old rivalry of O Neill and O Donnell was shelved, and Red Hugh allied with another hothead, young Hugh Maguire, chief in Fermanagh and also Tyrone's son-in-law. For the first time the main Ulster chiefs would face outward together. Red Hugh began to form a confederation which involved leading Catholic churchmen and was in touch with Philip of Spain.

Yet when Maguire threw off the traces in 1593 and raided in Sligo and Roscommon, Tyrone accepted the government's order to quell him and co-operated with his arch enemy Bagenal to this end. He was not, in his own opinion, sufficiently thanked. Early next year he submitted a long list of grievances to the government, and Elizabeth tried to conciliate him. Now, as Red Hugh joined Maguire in revolt, it was Tyrone whom the English, rightly, saw as the great danger. Early in 1595, when they reckoned Tyrone himself had 6,000 soldiers, the government shipped over to Ireland 1,600 veterans from the wars in France, and 1,000 fresh levies from England.[94] A great drain of English treasure and lives was beginning.

Elsewhere, England had had little success against Spain. Disillusion was setting in. Veteran warhawks were dying – Leicester in 1588, Walsingham in 1590 and then, in the next year, Sir Richard Grenville, following the *Revenge*'s famous last fight, an episode in the not very effectual attempt, over several years, to cut off the Spanish treasure fleets by a blockade in the Azores. A huge Spanish force approached. The outnumbered English fled, all save Grenville, who could have escaped but instead fought a bloody action all night against a whole fleet, alone, until, when he was mortally wounded, his men arranged a surrender. Drake, in disfavour after the Lisbon disaster, was given the chance to make, with Sir John Hawkins, another raid on the Caribbean in 1595. The old targets were aimed at, but the old flair for assault had gone. The Spaniards were forewarned; the attack was botched. Hawkins died at sea off Puerto Rico, Drake of dysentery at Porto Bello.

There were two further big naval expeditions. A successful commando raid on Cadiz by an English Armada in 1596 was followed in the next year by the total failure of the 'Island Voyage' to the Azores. But in each of those years, Protestant winds broke up Spanish Armadas aimed at Ireland, and thereafter, though there were still English troops in the Low Countries, Ireland became the main theatre of the war.

XIII

The rebellion there confirmed Ralegh's loss of interest in his Irish lands, which he made over to a friend in 1598 and finally sold altogether in 1602 to a sharp young adventurer, Richard Boyle, who founded the greatest of Irish colonial fortunes. By 1595, Ralegh had a new love, Guiana.

He had long known something about the land between the Amazon and the Orinoco which neither Spain nor Portugal had bothered to occupy, and which was already attracting English merchants and privateers. What spurred him to act was his loss of favour at court. Already frustrated by the rise in Elizabeth's favour of a dazzling new favourite, the young Earl of Essex, Ralegh had made the mistake in 1592 of marrying one of the Queen's maids of honour and of lying to keep it secret. When she found out, the Queen imprisoned both for a while. Brooding in his mansion in Dorset, Ralegh came to see a Guiana enterprise as the stroke which might restore him to glory.

He had heard of the Spanish quest for the Empire of the Gilded One, 'El Dorado', so named from its king who was supposed on feast days to coat himself from head to foot in gold dust. It was a second Inca realm, civilised, rich beyond dreams, yet utterly vulnerable to invasion, and it was supposed to lie in the Guiana Highlands. A Spaniard, Don Antonio de Berrio, had taken up the search some years before and had now, as official 'Governor of El Dorado', established a base on Trinidad. To cut him out and to find the golden realm would give the English a counterweight to Spain's American bullion, and the beginnings of their own tropical empire — this, Ralegh would argue, was a far sounder strategy than Hawkins's idea of blockading against the treasure fleets. Besides, it would bring the new Cortés as much wealth and fame and power as even Ralegh could wish for. In 1594, he sent out a ship to spy on the Spaniards in Trinidad. It lost eight men in a brush with Berrio's force but Ralegh went ahead, without royal support. In February 1595, he set off with four ships and three hundred men. His idea was to examine the strength of the Spaniards, ally with local Indians, reach El Dorado and verify its opulence, come to terms with its emperor, and then persuade his delighted Queen to send him back with an official expedition.

He swiftly destroyed the Spanish town on Trinidad in a surprise attack, captured Berrio, found him a fine old man, 'very valiant and liberal' and treated him well. The local Indians seemed pleased at the rout of the Spaniards. Ralegh, supposing that he had their consent, formally annexed the island, with its remarkable pitch lake which, he averred, could load 'all the ships of the world'. Then he set off to explore up the Orinoco.

One of his aims was to prove to the Queen and his enemies that he was no weakling, and he plumed himself later with his sufferings during the fifteen days which it took him to pass, with a hundred men, through the stifling Orinoco delta, lying on hard boards under the burning sun, living mostly on fish and afflicted with the stench which rose from the wet clothes of his people. ' ... I will undertake there was never any prison in England, that coulde be founde more unsavory and lothsome, especially to my selfe, who had for many yeares before beene dieted and cared for in a sort farre differing.' There were compensations. ' ... We sawe birds of all colours, some carnation, some crimson, orenge tawny, purple, greene, watched, and of all other sorts both simple and mixt, as it was unto us a great good passing of the time to beholde them ... ' Then came a view of a great highland escarpment ahead, and the huge rolling plains of the Orinoco valley beside their route, park-like, with short green grass, and deer who 'came downe feeding by the waters side, as if they had beene used to a keepers call'.

On the way, he was careful to treat the Indians well; his men, he would swear later, never touched one native woman, though these were very handsome and 'came among us without deceit, starke naked'. But the Englishmen stole on occasions and when he could do so Ralegh made restitution and punished offenders in full view of the villagers. There was self-interest in this. Ralegh could claim later that he had everywhere shown the Indians his Queen's portrait, so she was now very famous in that part of the world, where they venerated her as 'Ezrabeta Cassipuna Aquerewana, which is as much as Elizabeth, the great princesse or greatest commaunder.' Thousands of loyal subjects would make a most handsome present. He knew how Drake had made good use of 'cimaroons', and how Cortés had worked wonders with Indian allies. Yet he seems to have hated truly the 'cruelty' which he attributed to the Spaniards, and to have viewed the Indians with genuine respect, not the naïve self-deceiving idealisation which some other writers expressed and which would erect the European myth of the 'Noble Savage'. He wrote of a chieftain's wife, 'with blacke eies, fat of body, of an excellent countenance ... knowing hir owne comelines, and taking great pride therein', as if she might indeed be a fellow-subject with him under Gloriana: 'I have seene a Lady in England so like hir, as but for the difference of colour I would have sworne might have beene the same.'[95] Ralegh's eyes, like John White's, were clearer, franker and friendlier when they met people of other races than would be those of most of their successors.

Ralegh heard stories which made him believe that El Dorado was truly ahead. He pressed up the tributary river Caroni looking for a passage through the escarpment, but found the way blocked soon by huge waterfalls. He would come back and try again, he decided. He left two English residents with a chief whom he much liked, Topiawari, and took the latter's son on with him to England. Here, his reception was chilly. The Queen was not won over. He badgered high-placed friends for support, harping, perhaps sincerely, on the danger that the good relations which he had established with Indian 'kings' would be undone by the robberies of English privateers, if he himself were not sent back there soon.[96] Then, with the Queen still deaf, he wrote and published his tale, *The Discoverie of the Large Rich, and Bewtiful Empyre of Guiana*, extolling the fine climate, the bounty of nature, the mineral wealth, of 'a Countrey that hath yet her Maydenhead, never sackt, turned, nor wrought, the face of the earth hath not beene torne, nor the vertue and salte of the soyle spent by manurance, the graves have not beene opened for gold, the mines not broken with sledges, nor their Images puld down out of their temples.' A small expeditionary force would be enough to persuade the Emperor of El Dorado to pay tribute to England. Ralegh envisaged what would be called later a 'protectorate' over the natives. The Emperor's people would be instructed in the use of European weapons and in the 'liberall arts of civility'.[97]

Early in 1596 Ralegh sent Laurence Keymis back to Guiana. Keymis found a new Spanish fort at the mouth of the Caroni, and just missed the start of a disastrous Spanish attempt to sow the Orinoco basin with European settlers. When Keymis reached home, Ralegh was out of disgrace. He distinguished himself as Vice-Admiral of the Cadiz fleet, and though he sent out a further ship to explore, he was soon absorbed in a multitude of new duties. However, his book sold hugely. He helped turn English minds towards tropical countries. Others would soon pursue the direction he pointed in.

And meanwhile, to Ralegh's gold-haunted coastline, the privateers continued their visits.

XIV

The term 'privateer' was not in fact used till the seventeenth century, when it came to denote a ship sailing to take plunder from the enemy in compensation for goods lost by its owner through that enemy's depredations. The privateer was distinguished from the pirate by the fact that he acted by licence under some recognised authority. Philip II's seizure of English merchant ships in 1585 gave many people a real basis for privateering, but in practice the pretext of reprisal became little more than a legal fiction, and many dispensed with licences anyway. The system of licensing was very loose and corrupt even by Elizabethan standards – not surprisingly so when Ralegh and other Vice-Admirals for the southern and western counties were themselves great promoters of privateering.

So genuine ships of reprisal mingled, in the guerrilla host which took to the sea from the summer of 1585, with private men-of-war equipped by gentlemen and merchants, and with pirates, who would not be treated as such so long as they stuck to Spanish shipping. There were about a hundred privateering voyages a year down to the end of the war in 1603. Seamen notoriously preferred these ships, though they were overcrowded (for the sake of strong boarding parties) and, hence, sadly disease-ridden, to those of the Queen's Navy where discipline was stricter and the rewards were lower. Men gambled their lives for loot, and the proceeds were on occasion enormous. In 1592 privateers captured a huge Portuguese East India carrack off the Azores, laden with jewels, silks and spices. A cargo worth perhaps £500,000 was ransacked by the mariners – and even so about £140,000 was left for the promoters, of which the Queen, a shareholder, took about half. Such bonanzas were of course rare, but most of the many expeditions to the West Indies seem at least to have covered their expenses.[98]

This was, then, a popular sea war, waged in a roughly democratic fashion, with crews consulted on all important matters. The cumulative results were remarkable. There were some great individual blows. In 1595, James Lancaster and his men occupied Recife, the main port of Brazil, for a whole month. In 1598 a fleet of twenty vessels sent out by a consortium led by the Earl of Cumberland captured Puerto Rico, though with half the men dead from disease or ill, they soon had to leave. In the course of the war, Spain and Portugal must have lost over a thousand ships, and as they ran short of vessels they became dependent on foreign carriers – the efficient Dutch were the main beneficiaries. Spain neglected the defence of the West Indies as a whole so as to safeguard the main treasure route which was the privateers' chief target. Parts of the mainland coast, and the islands of Hispaniola, Jamaica and Puerto Rico, were left at the plunderers' mercy.[99]

Some of the privateering promoters were gentlemen-amateurs inspired by notions of derring-do and chivalry, like Thomas Cavendish, a young Suffolk squire who sold or mortgaged much of his lands to help pay for the voyage (1586–8) which made him the second English commander to circumnavigate the globe. George Clifford, 3rd Earl of Cumberland, claimed in 1600 that he had spent £100,000 on sea voyages, and he had indeed sent out several fleets comparable in strength to squadrons of the Royal Navy. A contemporary said they were 'bound for no other harbour but the port of honour, though touching at the port of profit in passage thereunto'. But this semi-quixotic coeval of Don Quixote so overstrained his resources that he was drawn into co-operation with London merchants for whom the port of profit was the sole target.[100]

Ralegh's sometime colleague John Watts was probably the most active of these. One of the chief losers by Philip II's confiscations in 1585, he died Sir John Watts, having been Lord Mayor of London, and also governor of the East India Company. Perhaps there could have been no British Empire without men like Ralegh and Cumberland who set sail for the port of honour. It is absolutely certain that without Watts and his unromantic like, America could not have been colonised, nor could the English have gained a foothold as traders in India. As the war dragged on, the great London merchants took a larger and larger share of the risks and proceeds of privateering, and this helped confirm the dominance of their city in English trade. The merchants financing privateering were not shady little fellows scrabbling in small windfalls – they included members of the City's élite whose fortunes, stemming in very great part from sea plunder, would be available, early in the new century, to finance colonies and long voyages on a scale hitherto impossible.[101]

Privateering gave life to an otherwise depressed economy. While cloth exports languished, the import trades steadily advanced, largely thanks to plunder, which may have accounted for 10 or 15 per cent of England's total imports during the war. Capital was concentrated, in London, in the hands of men skilled in the problems of long-distance enterprises. The building of ships – and of large ships – was stimulated. Few English sailors before the war had much experience of transatlantic sailing; such men were abundant by its end. Captain Christopher Newport was the epitome of a new kind of professional specialising in far voyages. He lost his right arm trying to capture two Mexican treasure ships in 1589, but went back to the Caribbean year after year. He came to know its coasts and waters better even than Drake, but unlike Sir Francis he did not project great schemes on his own account. He sailed where his employers sent him, though he seems to have taken his own pious pleasure in removing church bells and destroying papist images every time he captured a Spanish settlement. He became a prosperous and respected man, who after the war took colonists to Virginia (where the town of Newport would be named after him) and finally died in Java on his third voyage for the East India Company.[102]

The exotic luxuries brought in by privateering stimulated new tastes in England, and also the industries which served them. Ben Jonson satirised the extravagant cravings which had begun to seize Londoners in his creation of Sir Epicure Mammon:

> My shirts
> I'll have of taffata-sarsnet, soft, and light
> As cob-webs ...
> My gloves of fishes, and birds-skins, perfum'd
> With gummes of *paradise*, and easterne aire ...[103]

Perfume became the fashion. Sugar began its long march from the tables of the few to those of the many. Before the war, sugar imports, mainly from Morocco, had run at £20,000 or £30,000 a year. In three years, 1589–91, privateers alone brought in sugar worth £100,000, and a Spanish spy could report, 'sugar is cheaper in London than it is in Lisbon or the Indies themselves.' The Portuguese in Brazil were rapidly increasing their output of sugar in the last quarter of the century, and now that their Spanish King had dragged them into war their ships became an especially popular target.[104]

And the English captured altogether three of the vast Portuguese carracks which came home laden from Golden Goa with Eastern delights. For a while London merchants found it cheaper to bring in such goods as plunder than take the risks of direct trade in the East. Two expeditions which they did send around the Cape of Good Hope in the 1590s were wholly unprofitable, and were in any case aimed at piracy rather than trade. But the Dutch showed that it could be done. Already the seamen of Holland and Zeeland, with their revolutionary new *fluitschips* to carry bulk cargoes, were penetrating deeply as traders and carriers in the West Indies, Guinea, Brazil, where the English still went mainly for loot. In 1598 the Dutch sent no fewer than 22 ships to the East; 4 sent earlier came home lavishly laden next year. The bowels of men like Watts yearned.

In September 1599 over a hundred London merchants promised a total of £30,000 'to set forthe a vyage this present year to the Est Indies and other the ilandes and cuntries therabouts ...' They elected their own committee of fifteen and sought a charter, which they received at the end of 1600. So the East India Company began, a new initiative opening a new century. In its councils, the privateering magnates provided effective leadership. They were used to organising far expeditions. They had the capital and the large and powerfully armed ships which the new company needed. And of course the depredations which they had sponsored had helped considerably to weaken any Portuguese counter-challenge against English intrusion.[105]

The redoubtable James Lancaster set off with four ships for the East in February 1601. They would all come home safely and profitably three summers later, after trading in Sumatra and Java. The East India Company, infant giant, foreshadowed the end of the epoch of petty stabs towards far continents by individuals and small partnerships. The Newports, managerial skippers, were replacing the Hawkinses and Drakes. London merchant interests, and those who could best work with them, had taken over the lead from the West County gentry. Now, on the bigger ships which sailed East, discipline would be exacting, the crews would no longer have a voice. A new style of merchant capitalism stepped portentously out of the violence and muddle of war.

XV

The harvests from 1592 to 1596 were bad in England. Famine or near famine resulted. Prices rose sharply. Plague raged. Returning soldiers – sick, wounded, discharged, deserting – complicated all social problems. The government, nearly helpless, turned for a scapegoat to the black servants and paupers brought into Britain as surplus from slaving voyages and as loot from the Spaniards. In 1596 Elizabeth licensed a German merchant to ship them to Iberia, and ordered her subjects to turn them over to him: 'thoose kind of people may well be spared in this realme, being so populous.' The order, however, was typically ineffectual.[106]

Meanwhile, the war was ruinous for the Crown. Costs were rising, as longbows gave way to muskets. Elizabeth had to call six parliaments during the war, and while subsidies were readily granted, M.P.s grew cocky and truculent. In 1601, the royal prerogative itself was questioned, and the monopolies held by men like Ralegh were bitterly attacked. Even £2 million voted in taxes could not pay for the war. More royal lands had to be sold. Vigorous and unpopular actions raised crown income from its normal level of £200,000 per annum to £300,000 – but the minister Robert Cecil alleged in 1599 that Ireland alone had cost £4,300,000 since the Armada year.[107]

England could not yet afford foreign mercenaries and the strain on a population smaller than that of the Low Countries, less than half that of Spain, was severe. Of 20,000 men raised for France, barely half returned. Rather more went to the Low Countries, almost as many were levied for three great naval expeditions, but Ireland was the greatest drain, drawing perhaps 25,000 men. Trained militiamen were kept in England for home defence; it was raw pressed men who were sent abroad.[108]

In 1559, Shane O Neill's time, little more than 1,000 regular troops had been at the Viceroy's disposal in Ireland. At the height of Desmond's rebellion, nearly 9,000 had been employed. To put down Tyrone would call, at peak, for double that number. The quotas demanded from Lord Lieutenants of English counties were largely filled with men of whom the authorities wished to be rid. A critic complained, 'We disburden the prison of thieves, we rob the taverns and alehouses of toss-pots and ruffians; we scour both town and country for rogues and vagabonds.' One method of raising troops was to surround a fair and to seize all able-bodied men who were not following occupations thought respectable.[109] The masterless men of England were sent to put down the unmastered men of Ireland. To desert was for many the first and final ambition. At least half the troops probably died in service, but this would have been true in France or the Low Countries. What made Irish service uniquely unpopular was the absence of rich towns to loot in the dysentery-ridden island, and the presence of an enemy who did not follow the rules of war which Englishmen thought fair.

Soldiers' pay was usually in arrears. Half a year sometimes elapsed between pay days. So troops leeched ferociously on the natives, seizing food, drink and money wherever they could. Even so they went short. 'Most part of the army', one captain reported from Munster, 'seem beggarly ghosts, fitter for their graves than to fight a prince's battle.'[110] Men sold their equipment, even their clothes, while corrupt captains encouraged their English troops to desert and filled their ranks with Irish who would accept still worse terms, then drew full pay for them.

Irish rebels before this had been quite easy to beat. English cannon, though cumbersome on the march in a land without roads, served well to reduce Irish strongpoints. English cavalry were at a disadvantage in bogs and woodlands, but they had been able to break up any opposing body of Irish foot. Now success was far harder. A gloomy official told Robert Cecil in 1596 that Tyrone's unprecedented forces 'could now affront the royal army in the open plain, instead of as formerly only in defiles and forests.' Earlier O Neills had relied on an erratic supply of 'Redshanks', seasonal mercenaries from the Hebrides. But Tyrone had officers with him who had served the English. He had a steady flow of deserters and the expertise of a scattering of Spaniards. He got some munitions, as well as gold, from Spain, and much from the Lowland burghs of Scotland, but another important source were the Crown's supposedly loyal Irish subjects. Gentlemen sold to Tyrone munitions which they had drawn from royal stores under the pretext that they were fighting the Gaels. ' ... By the pretended subject the Kingdom is put to sale', the Chief Justice of Munster complained in 1599, alleging that merchants in the port towns were buying arms, armour and ammunition in England and selling them to the rebels at a profit of '6d for a penny'. The townsmen, another observer wrote, wished 'nothing more than a continual war.' Kerns became musketeers. Tyrone's rebels could put together a force approaching English standards in arms and in discipline. Yet the Irish retained such advantages as their mode of life gave them. Roaming cattle readily fed swift-moving horsemen. Forests and bogs and mountain passes gave ample scope for guerrilla tactics.[111]

Tyrone's own leadership may have counted for much, but his aims will always remain obscure. Like Fitzmaurice before him, though perhaps less sincerely, he made the cause of Catholicism one with that of preserving Irish chiefship. He must have thought of uniting the country under his own rule, but in the last resort he depended on Spanish troops for victory, and if they had come in sufficient numbers, Ireland would have exchanged the rule of England for the hegemony of Spain. The scanty known facts give one licence to make contradictory judgments of the man. Some make him seem like a tragic victim, half English by culture yet captured by Gaeldom. Negotiating before his move into outright rebellion, he burst into tears as he spoke of the Queen's favours to him and acted out a strange scene which made it appear as if his Irish clansmen and allies were dragging him away from his deep loyalty to her. At the height of his rebel power, an English visitor saw him with his two sons, who wore English clothes and spoke English. Tyrone assured him that he was not ambitious, 'but sought only safety for himself, and freedom of conscience, without which, he said, he would not live, though the Queen would give him all Ireland.'[112] Yet both scenes may have reflected a genius for buying time, via truces and negotiations, which would enable him to build up his forces for the next battle. Ambitious clan chief or Catholic statesman, cynical self-server or Gaelic patriot, Tyrone's massive vague figure exposes all the internal contradictions of a dying Celtic order which could only submit to its own dissolution, or seek to arrest change by taking sword in hand, so hastening its own destruction. But for all this, Tyrone was the skilful and undisputed leader of a uniquely wide confederacy when he came off the fence at last in 1595.

In October that year, he and Red Hugh O Donnell appealed to Spain for two or three thousand soldiers to help them 'restore the faith of the Church' and to secure Philip II 'a kingdom'.[113] The weather frustrated Spanish expeditions. Without foreign help, Tyrone's aims stopped short at defence. He mixed diplomacy shrewdly with aggression, sporadic confrontations with specious negotiations. After several months of formal truce, he and his allies burst out in Ulster and Leinster during the summer of 1598, and his old foe Sir Henry Bagenal marched north rashly to relieve a strategically vital fort on the Blackwater which Tyrone was attacking. The English force, over 4,000, was a large one for Irish warfare, but on August 14, in sight of the fort, at a place called 'the Yellow Ford', it was utterly shattered. Bagenal himself was killed, only 1,500 men got back to Armagh, and this was a worse disaster than English troops had ever suffered in Ireland, or would ever suffer again.[114]

Tyrone could have struck at Dublin and captured it. Fatally, he did not, but with his allies he now dominated most of Ireland. He himself was master of almost all Ulster. O Donnell, with Burke allies, controlled Connacht. The O Mores were up in Leinster and Owney MacRory O More and Captain Tyrrell (an Irish renegade from the royal army) broke into Munster with a large force to raise support for James Fitzthomas Fitzgerald, nephew of the last Earl of Desmond and now, as claimant to his position, nicknamed the 'Sugane' (straw-rope) Earl. Those Munster colonists who could flee did so. Those who could not were slaughtered or mutilated, 'divers sent into Youghal amongst the English, some with their throats cut, but not killed, some with their tongues cut out of their heads, others with their noses cut off ... '[115]

Elizabeth withdrew hundreds of troops from the Low Countries, called out new levies in England, and, as a likely-looking response to a desperate situation, sent to Ireland, as Lord Lieutenant, her prime favourite, the handsome, dashing and greatly ambitious Earl of Essex. Gentlemen adventurers flocked to his popular standard. He was to have 16,000 foot and 1,300 horse, with 2,000 reinforcements to follow every three months. No commander in Ireland had ever led such a force.[116] Essex arrived in the spring of 1599, carrying with him exceptional hopes, which he dashed with exceptional suddenness.

He dawdled through Leinster and Munster, wasting men's lives in skirmishes, but bringing not one rebel to submission. Elizabeth insisted that Essex must move to Ulster and put an axe 'to the root of that tree which hath been the treasonable stock from which so many poisoned plants and grafts have been derived.'[117] He duly marched north with 4,000 men, but he did not fight Tyrone. In September the two men talked for half an hour without witnesses at a ford. It is quite likely that Tyrone played on Essex's ambitions to rule in England and inveigled, or half-inveigled, his support for the Gaelic cause.

5 Captain John Smith with part of a map of New England

6 John White's drawing of an Algonquian mother and child

7 The arrival of the English in 'Virginia' — De Bry's engraving, after John White

8 'Their dances which they use at their high feasts' — another White drawing of 'Virginian' Indians

9 'The Town of Pomeiock', in 'Virginia', drawn by White

Certainly six weeks' truce was arranged on terms which favoured Tyrone. Then Essex received a note from the Queen ordering that no truce should be made. He at once, breaking all commands, dashed to London, to throw himself at her feet. She imprisoned him. The sequel is well-known. Essex, deprived of most of his offices, plotted treason and became a magnet for all malcontents. Early in 1601, he attempted to raise London in rebellion, failed, and was executed; Ireland had ruined him, as it had killed his father.

His successor there was a man of most different mettle. Charles Blount, Lord Mountjoy, arrived as Lord Deputy early in 1600. Though 36, he had never commanded large bodies of troops in the field before. His personal habits hardly seemed apt for Irish conditions; he was a valetudinarian, finicky about his food, who wore three waistcoats in cold weather. (Fynes Moryson, who left a famous prose portrait of him, thought his abundant use of tobacco helped to avert the ill effects of Irish provender, bogs and climate; certainly, it must have helped ward off the insects.) A model Protestant gentleman, he prayed always morning and night and scowled fiercely when men swore at his table, but he was averse to religious persecution and saw that it merely encouraged the views which it sought to extirpate. He argued intelligently with priests and Jesuits 'as upon divers occasions with other Papists his friends.'[118]

Yet for all his cultured and quiet tastes, he proved most efficient, and ruthless. He spent longer in the saddle than any previous viceroy, soldiering five days a week in the depths of winter. There would be no more truces, or even parleys. The aim was complete conquest; the means, force applied without qualms. Whenever Mountjoy passed through a defile he had it cleared of trees so that progress would be easier next time. He planted garrisons shrewdly so as to pin rebels down in their own localities and thus prevent them from co-operating. His winter campaigning aimed to push the Gaels into starvation. It 'brake their hearts', Fynes Moryson wrote, 'for the air being sharp and they naked, and they being driven from their lodgings, into the woods bare of leaves, they had no shelter for themselves. Besides that, their cattle (giving them no milk in the winter) were also wasted by driving to and fro, and that they being thus troubled in the seed-time, could not sow their ground. And as in harvest time, both the Deputy's forces, and the garrisons, cut down their corn, before it was ripe, so now in winter time, they carried away or burnt all the stores of victuals in secret places, whither the rebels had conveyed them.'[119]

Mountjoy had able lieutenants. Sir George Carew, who came over with him, had almost pacified Munster within a year. Ulster itself, hitherto almost impregnable, now began to fall to attack from three sides. Sir Henry Docwra garrisoned Lough Foyle and created a base in Tyrone's rear, and both he and Sir Arthur Chichester, governor of Carrickfergus, played skilfully on rivalries among the Gaels. In the summer of 1601, Mountjoy was able to enter the township of Tyrone itself. He left strong forces in Ulster, then headed south

E

again. A Spanish landing was imminent at last. Mountjoy had ensured that it came too late.

There were too few Spaniards anyway. Another Protestant gale had reft nine ships from their fleet. Aguila, commanding the Spanish force, had under 4,000 men. They landed at Kinsale in late September, occupied the town, and stayed there. By the end of October, Mountjoy had opposed them with nearly 7,000 foot and over 600 horse. The necessary withdrawal of troops from other parts made it easy now for Tyrone and Red Hugh to bring their men south. They moved only slowly. Red Hugh, true to his Gaelic tradition, wasted three weeks ravaging Tipperary. But by early December, some 700 further Spaniards had arrived at another Munster port, Castlehaven, and had got much support from the local Irish, while Tyrone and Red Hugh were virtually besieging the English besiegers of Kinsale.

Despite 5,000 reinforcements from England, Mountjoy was now down to little over 6,500 fit footsoldiers, no more than the encircling Gaels. Sickness and large-scale desertion had withered the English army. Tyrone's view now, as before, was sagely Fabian; no need to attack, let the Sassenachs rot away. But the ardour of Red Hugh and the pressure of the besieged Spaniards overcame his caution. A plan for simultaneous attack on the English was worked out, and was fusionlessly betrayed by Brian MacHugh Oge MacMahon, whose son had been a page of Sir George Carew's in England. He ran out of whiskey, sent to ask Carew for a bottle, and, on receiving it, paid for it with a warning. In any case, wrangles over precedence meant that the Gaelic attack on December 24 began late. Aguila, missing them at the expected time, stayed put in Kinsale. Mountjoy left 4,000 men to confront the Spaniards and sent only 1,100 against the Gaels. But one daring English cavalry charge was enough. The Gaels ran headlong, leaving hundreds of dead, while the Spaniards who had joined them from Castlehaven stood rock firm and fought till three-quarters of them were killed. The English lost just one man.[120]

As his followers streamed homewards, Red Hugh took ship to Spain to seek further aid; he died there, perhaps by poison, leaving sorrowing tales of the most glamorous of young rebels. The Spaniards soon surrendered and were duly shipped home by the English; there was no massacre this time. Despite the sickness which now carried off thousands of Mountjoy's men, the war was almost over. When the Deputy came north again in the summer of 1602, Tyrone took to the fern. Mountjoy systematically ravaged his lands, destroyed all the standing corn, and smashed the 'stone of the kings' used for centuries in the inaugurations of the O Neills at Tullaghoge.

The symbolism was apt. Gaelic Ireland was beaten. The English must now decide how to rule the land they had conquered. There had of course been suggestions. Edmund Spenser, some years before, had advocated the settling of Ulster rebels in Leinster, rebels from Leinster in Ulster, all to be tenants under English colonists. Cattle herding should be restricted to those unfit for field labour – 'look into all countries that live in such sort by keeping of cattle, and you shall find that they are both very barbarous and uncivil, and also greatly given to war.' Gaels should be compelled to follow useful trades. Schools should be set up in every parish to convert children to Protestantism. The surnames beginning with O and Mac should be 'utterly forbidden and extinguished'. In short, all that was distinctively Gaelic should be destroyed. Another writer, about 1599, went even further. Almost all natives should be removed from Ireland to England. The few remaining would be a small servile minority under alien English and Flemish colonists.[121] It was far from the last time that a 'final solution' would be suggested for that troublesome island.

XVI

Ireland had left Elizabeth with very scant resources for England's northern border. Good relations with Scotland were assured after 1586 and this encouraged the Queen to cut costs, while the still more impecunious Scottish King stopped paying salaries to his frontier wardens altogether. The level of violence and rapine perhaps rose. In 1589–90 men from Liddesdale alone, Armstrongs, Elliotts and the like, were averaging a raid a week; in that winter they stole more than eight hundred and fifty beasts, captured some sixty prisoners, wounded ten men, killed one, burned five houses, and took £200 worth of household goods (children's coats and cooking utensils not excepted).[122]

The Scottish wardens, local magnates, were commonly ringleaders in feuds, but on the English side the Carey family were specialist forerunners of the colonial service. Henry Carey, Lord Hunsdon, served his cousin the Queen on the Border for nearly thirty years. When his son John, deputy governor of Berwick, had a horse stolen by one Jock Dalgleish, he sent fifty riders to gain revenge, and they killed the man. Elizabeth was shocked; this was, she said, 'verie barbarous and seldom used emonge the Turckes.' Carey pleaded with Burghley, ' … it was not so barbarouslie nor butcherlie don as you thinck it to be, it should seeme your honor hath bene wrongfullie enformed, in sayinge he was cutt in manye peeces, after his deathe – for if he had bene cutt in many peces, he could not a lived till the next morninge, which themselves reported he did – which shewes he was not cutt in verie many peeces.'[123]

Another of Hunsdon's sons, Robert, gives in his *Memoirs* a most vivacious account of his life among the Border tribes. In 1601, when he was warden of the English Middle March, he resolved to have it out with the Armstrongs for good and all. They withdrew to Tarras Moss beyond Liddesdale, a forest stronghold surrounded by bogs, marshy ground and wilderness. They sent Carey word 'that I was like the first puff of a haggasse, hottest at the first', and that he would never get them. But the haggis stayed hot. Carey sent 150 troops to encircle the Tarras by night and lay ambushes, then he attacked openly at dawn with 300 horse and 1,000 infantry. As the outlaws fled the ambushes were sprung and five Armstrong leaders were captured, whose value as hostages Carey exploited so thoroughly that he had no more trouble with the surname afterwards.[124]

Visiting the Queen early in 1603, Robert Carey saw she was dying and took serious thought of his own future. He wrote to James VI telling him how things were and promising that when death came, he would be the first to bring news. 'On Wednesday the twenty-third of March she grew speechless. That afternoone, by signes, she called for her Councill, and by putting her hand to her head, when the King of Scottes was named to succeed her, they all knew hee was the man she desired should reign after her.' By ten the next morning, Carey was in the saddle madly riding north. He reached Edinburgh on Saturday evening, having covered 400 miles in 60 hours, though he 'gott a great fall by the way' and was kicked in the head by his horse. James was roused from his bed. Carey knelt and saluted him 'by his title of England, Scotland, France and Ireland.'[125]

A few days later Tyrone came in and submitted, to Queen Elizabeth. Mountjoy had heard of her death and had no right to accept the surrender, but did so. Tyrone was promised, and got, a pardon, his earldom restored, and most of his old lands back. When he did hear that the Queen had gone, he wept.

Perhaps he wept because he thought that new political complications in England might have favoured his now-dead rebellion. But in fact the Crown changed hands smoothly. James borrowed 10,000 marks from the City of Edinburgh and his family lashed out on new clothes. Then he sped south with his followers for the fat lands of England somewhat himself like the last of the great reivers. His Proclamation of the Union of the Crowns of Scotland and England announced, ' ... The Isle within itself hath almost none but imaginary bounds of separation, without but one common limit or rather guard of the Ocean sea, making the whole a little world within itself, the nations an uniformity of constitutions both of body and mind, especially in martial processes, a community of language (the principle means of civil society), an unity of religion (the deepest bond of hearty union and the surest knot of lasting peace.)'[126] This was, of course, over-optimistic. The Highland Gaels of Scotland still did not share in the 'community of language' and were outside 'civil society'. Religious divisions would yet be involved in new wars between Scotland and England. But the Union of the Crowns would survive, and with it the Border problem melted like snow on the Cheviots in spring.

The Marches became the 'middle shires'. Trading replaced raiding. Galloway cattle travelled south safely to England. The Border hills produced more wool for market. The 'auncient waste ground', as one contemporary put it, was now found 'to be very good and fruitefull', so that the local gentry began to quarrel over land boundaries in the law courts.[127] Poor cottagers were thrust out and sheep came in. The days of Fingerless Will Nixon, Archie Fire the Braes Elliott and other reivers of their like were over. The Union was followed at once by wholesale hangings. The gentry entrusted with mopping up saw the chance of helping themselves to confiscated land, and found ample chance in a region where men had developed settled habits of breaking inoperable laws. Ancient charges were dragged up and no one was given the benefit of the doubt. Of all riding families the English Grahams of Esk suffered worst. They had some good land on which the privateering Earl of Cumberland's eye had fallen. These acres were confiscated. Scores of Grahams were sent to serve in the Low Country garrisons, but most quickly stole back, and a clutch of the surname holed up in south-west Scotland and resumed the trade of reivers. By 1606 the Commissioners appointed to pacify the Border were gaoling even innocent Grahams, as 'their restraint will not a little bridle their friends who are out.' Now it was first decided that the internal colonisation of Britain would provide colonists for overseas. The Grahams were to go, not to Canada or Australia like certain distant successors, but to Ireland, where a gentleman in Roscommon wanted settlers. The gentry of Cumberland and Westmorland subscribed £300 to the cost of transportation. Some fifty families were shipped off in 1606 and 1607. Scottish Elliotts were forced out in the same way. Great men whose feuds had troubled the peace kept their land; small malefactors were hanged and drowned and transported until the Borders were, in the word of the time, 'purgit'.[128]

Peace on the Borders; and peace with Spain. The Treaty of London in 1604 ended the long war. Regarding the New World it seemed to do no more than re-establish the exact status quo of the days before Hawkins had butted in there. But the balance of power shifted so that all was transformed. Spain remained a great power but her northern enemies, Dutch and English, had won, and were still winning, the battle for commerce. The Mediterranean was already an 'Anglo-Dutch lake'.[129] Now peace meant that England's Western sailors could establish the first of the classic 'triangular trades', catching cod off Newfoundland and North America, taking it direct to Portugal, Spain and the western Mediterranean, then bringing home oil and fruit and wine from sunnier climes than their own. The great problem broached in the 1550s by crisis in the cloth trade was on the way to solution. England was escaping from undue reliance on markets in northern and central Europe into trades like those with Russia and Turkey which had a 'quasi-colonial' character and into others, just dawning, with India, with Brazil, with the West Indies, which would imply colonial expansion, and bring great profits resulting from the gap between buying and selling prices of exotica, common where they were made or grown but dear and prized at home.[130]

' ... Golde is more plentifull there then copper is with us', says a sea-captain in *Eastward Ho*, a comic play of 1605. ' ... Why man, all their dripping Pans, and their Chamber pottes are pure Gold ... and for Rubies and Diamonds, they goe forth on holydayes and gather 'hem by the Sea-shore, to hang on their childrens Coates, and stick in their Cappes ... Wilde Boare is as common there, as our tamest Bacon is here: Venison, as Mutton. And then you shal live freely there, without Sergeants, or Courtiers, or Lawyers, or Intelligencers, onely a few industrious Scots perhaps ... You may come to preferment enough, and never be a Pandar; to riches and fortune enough, and have never the more villanie ... ' He is telling folk of a (satirist's) Virginia where Ralegh's colonists have interbred with the Indians.[131] Such jokes only work if, like that prod at the King's tribe, the Scots, they take up some widespread topical buzz. Ralegh's vision had not been ignored.

Ralegh himself was now in the Tower, and would be for ten more years. James had disliked and feared him from the start. Ralegh had pressed for continued war against Spain. The King wanted peace. A ridiculous charge of treason was trumped up. To contemporaries Ralegh's imprisonment came to symbolise all their regrets for the old Queen's reign, now superseded by the graceless cavortings and craven diplomacy of an ill-favoured northern foreigner. A poet declared in 1616,

> Time never can produce men to o'ertake
> The fames of Grenville, Davies, Gilbert, Drake ... [132]

Pygmies had followed giants. The papists were getting off lightly. Ralegh's patent rights in America had passed into the hands of King James himself.

But in fact he used them towards the foundation of colonies which, unlike Ralegh's, endured. The epic first phase of expansion was ending as joint effort replaced individual flair and as commerce took over from plunder. But whereas Elizabeth had never been keen on colonies, James eagerly fathered them in Ulster and in Virginia. He came to the throne with ideas on the subject and with some, hard, experience. While Elizabeth's men had been fighting in Ireland, some of his had been trying to colonise the Hebrides. The lure there was fish, not gold, but James was right to think that nets cast for such things would eventually haul in bullion.

Thomas Smythe's Expansion

What reason is there why the income from business should not be larger than that from landowning? Whence do the merchant's profits come, except from his own diligence and industry?

JOHN CALVIN[1]

I

James VI and I grew up in a chaos of faction and internecine violence and then, despite his physical timidity, secured a grip on Scotland in the 1580s which he held for forty years. He raised up lesser landowners, especially men who gave him loyal service, so as to balance the great feudal magnates. He brought to submission the group of Catholic lords led by the Gordon Earl of Huntly. He persuaded the Kirk to bow to his authority, despite its strong Presbyterian faction. But he could not boost the royal revenue to the point where he could pay his own way. Used from infancy to deficit and bungling, he developed irresponsible habits which he took with him to England and which proved fatal to his son and heir. He scrounged when in pressing need. He devalued the Scottish coinage to his own short-term advantage. He made extravagant gifts to his favourites.

In the Highlands and islands James maintained the policy of using certain great clans whose own lands fringed the Lowlands to keep raids into the English-speaking areas down to a minimum. Thus, he connived in the attempted destruction by his Campbell allies of Clan Gregor. The MacGregor had been a chief of note, extolled by bards – 'gold gleameth on their hilts, the weapons of the Lion of Loch Awe.'[2] But his estate, in truth, had been small, and his clansmen, scattered tenants of other chiefs, had become rightly notorious for their plunderings in the Lowlands. In 1610, a campaign of extermination was mounted. Twenty-eight nobles and lairds who had MacGregors as neighbours received a commission of fire and sword to 'ruit oute and extirpat all that race'.[3] A fat price was put on the head of every MacGregor, and their name was outlawed until the late eighteenth century.

Meanwhile, the Campbells completed the destruction of the Macdonalds of Islay, symbolised by the erection (1609) of the royal burgh of Campbeltown in the Kintyre peninsula. The Campbell empire now stretched from there through the Central Highlands to Calder (Cawdor) in the north-east. Further north, in

Ross, the Mackenzies had risen by similar methods, serving the Crown in Edinburgh, and appearing to do so in the Highlands, while by judicious marriages and by business cunning they engrossed a large belt of territory. As one Gordon put it, 'Thus doe the tryb of Clankeinzie become great in these pairts, still incroaching upon ther nighbours who are unacquented with the lawes of this kingdome.'⁴ But meanwhile the Gordons themselves, led by earls of Huntly and Sutherland, built up a similar empire in the north-east.

For lesser Gaels, James had no sympathy at all. His justification, in 1608, of his policy towards them slithered swiftly from routine pieties via racial contempt to calculations of economic self-interest. 'First in the cair we haif of planting of the Gospell amang these rude, barbarous and uncivill people, the want whairof these yeiris past no doubt has bene to the grite hazard of mony poore soullis being ignorant of thair awne salvatioun. Nixt we desire to remove all such scandalous reproaches aganis that state, in suffering a pairt of it to be possessed with suche wilde savageis voide of Godis feare and our obedience, and heirwith [now he comes to it] the losse we have in nocht ressaving the dew rentis addebtit to us furth of those Yllis, being of the patrimonie of that our crowne.' An Act of 1597 ordered landlords and clan chiefs to produce title deeds to the lands which they held and to find security for regular payments of the royal rents and for the peaceful behaviour of themselves and their men, on pain of forfeiture. Since many chiefs would be unable to meet the conditions, its clear intention was to provide the Crown with large tracts of land. The preamble complained that by their 'barbarous inhumanity' the occupants had made unprofitable, both to themselves and others, lands 'most commodious in themselves as well by the fertility of the ground as by the rich fishings by sea ... '⁵ The view that there was great wealth to be tapped in the glens and lochs informed another Act of the same year which ordained the erection of royal burghs in Kintyre, Lochaber and Lewis. Nothing came of the Lochaber project. The struggle to realise the Lewis one makes a significant story.

Sixteenth-century geographers had lavished praise on the economic resources of the Hebrides. Mixed in with fanciful details – a certain spring on Mull, or, some said, Barra, gushed forth in profusion 'verie small' eggs, shining like pearls, which turned into edible shellfish – were hyperbolic accounts of the aptness of the isles for 'corn' and perfectly factual assertions about the prospects for fishing.⁶ The fish trade was already important to Scotland's Lowland burghs. The profits to be made from fish bulked large in the arrangement which James made in 1598 with a group of twelve men headed by his cousin, the Duke of Lennox, and mostly composed of Fife barons, hence known as the 'Fife Adventurers'. These men were granted the remote isle of Lewis and Harris, with parts of Skye. Harris and also Dunvegan on Skye were held, though in James's view illegally, by a very shrewd customer, Rory Mor Macleod, chief of the branch of his clan called Siol Tormod. But the Macleods on Lewis, the Sior Torquil, were embroiled in a characteristic Gaelic succession dispute. So thither the Fife-men sailed at the end of the year, with five or six hundred soldiers and some craftsmen.

The King's plans involved 'ruiting out the barbarous inhabitantis'. These latter, however, had their own view of affairs. 'Barbarous, bludie, and wiket Hielandmen', led by one Neil Macleod, opposed the settlers from the first. So did Mackenzie of Kintail, though he was overtly obedient. He wanted Lewis himself. When the colonists, despite hostile arrows and dysentery, had begun to erect their town at Stornoway, Mackenzie shrewdly released the young man, Tormod, whom most of the clan regarded as rightful chief and whom he had been holding captive. Inspired as Gaels always were by the presence of their true leader, the Macleods attacked and forced the Adventurers to surrender with heavy losses. In 1602, after just three years they sailed abjectly away.[7]

James was incensed by this indignity. A fresh expedition was sent in 1605, led by Sir James Spens and Sir George Hay. Tormod Macleod seems to have picked up too much 'civility' for his own good. He accepted the offer of these men that they would send him to London to get a pardon from James. He duly went to the court, but was sent back to Edinburgh and imprisoned for ten years without trial. However, Neil Macleod, after waging guerrilla war against the new colony, attacked decisively in April 1607, destroyed £10,000 worth of property and forced a second evacuation. When a third attempt was made in 1609, Mackenzie of Kintail was entrusted with the duty of assisting it. He tricked James neatly, sending supplies of food but tipping off Neil so that the ship which carried them would be captured. Hay and Spens hurried back to Fife for reinforcements and provisions, and Neil assailed the small garrison which they had left, killed some, and packed the rest off home.[8]

Mackenzie, in a contemporary's words, now 'catched his long-wished and expected prey'.[9] Hay and Spens sold their rights in Lewis to him. When he died in 1611, the inveterate Neil still held out, but he met his end on a gallows two years later and Mackenzie's son had undisputed possession of Lewis, to which he soon added the new title of Earl of Seaforth. The Earl brought Dutch merchants to Stornoway, where they traded in tallow, hides, plaiding and the like. But great fleets meanwhile came yearly from Holland to reap silver harvests in Scottish waters, and Lowland enterprise could not compete with them. A series of undertakings intended to operate the Lewis fisheries in Scottish interests failed in the face of opposition from local Gaels.[10]

However, the attempt at colonisation had given neighbouring Gaelic chiefs a bad shock, and this assisted James's policy. In 1608 Lord Ochiltree trapped, on the King's behalf, a number of chiefs whom he had invited to dinner on his ship off Mull, and they were imprisoned, in Lowland castles. They all made abject submission. In the summer of 1609 they and others signed, on the island of Iona, the so-called 'Statutes of Icolmkill' presented to them by the government. Macleod of Dunvegan, Macdonald of Dunyveg, Macdonald of Sleat, MacLean of Duart, MacLaine of Lochbuie, MacLean of Coll, MacKinnon of Strath and

MacQuarrie of Ulva agreed, implausibly, that they would support kirks and Protestant ministers, establish inns, limit the number of followers they maintained, stop entertaining bards, and send their sons to school in the Lowlands until they could speak, read and write English. They were to be answerable for the doings of their followers and must report in person every year to the Privy Council.[11]

The statute which forbade drinking of wine by common people merely encouraged the islanders in the perfectly legal distillation of whisky.[12] While the now submissive Rory Mor Macleod was given a charter for his lands, and acquired a knighthood, he continued to keep court at Dunvegan in high traditional style, and was duly praised for it by Gaelic poets:

> We were twenty times drunk every day,
> To which we had no more objection than he had.[13]

But the Isles did become relatively peaceful.

James could not prevail upon his new English subjects to accept his suggestion of a union of Parliaments, a union of Churches, and free trade between England and Scotland, and the Scots, rather than flocking south as English prejudice insisted that they had done, continued to maintain and extend their own links with the Continent. Scores of thousands emigrated there in the seventeenth century, as mercenary soldiers, pedlars and farmers, depositing Scottish names all over northern Europe (amongst them those of the German philosopher Kant and the Russian poet Lermontov, ex Learmonth). The poverty of their homeland spurred them. James himself was glad enough to be out of the draughty, hand-to-mouth life which he had led in Edinburgh, and did not revisit Scotland till 1617. But his very absence, which lifted him from the reach of factions, probably helped tame the country. Through a governing élite of professional officials, James had the Parliament, the General Assembly of the Church, the Court of Session and the Convention of Burghs under effective control. Townsmen, lawyers and smaller landowners supported the royal authority, and the influence of the Kirk, cutting across old divisions, also favoured a new tranquillity. The Scots were now, by their standards, docile: the English Parliament certainly was not.

II

It didn't like James much. The new King was homely, clumsy, fearful and uncouth. He was genuinely learned and highly intelligent, but he speechified too often and too long for the patience of his subjects. He was often drunk and could not disguise his homosexual proclivities. His quirks and idiosyncrasies might have been found endearing, had most not been, very typically, Scots ones. English prejudice against a Scots dynasty soon surfaced; an M.P. was sent to the Tower for saying that the union of England with Scotland which James wanted was as natural as the union of a prisoner with his judge. It could not be suppressed; in 1640 a Kentish preacher declared that if a Scotsman ever went to Heaven, the devil would go too.[14]

James was extravagant. His ordinary expenditure doubled that of Elizabeth. Such vanity weighed far more in the eyes of tax-hating landed gentlemen than James's assertion of the divine right of kings, in which Elizabeth had believed, and which his Puritan opponents in Parliament also accepted. But what counted for most of all in the eventual intensification of the struggle between Crown and Parliament was probably the arrival, around 1620, of a long phase of economic depression, bringing frustration for well-to-do men and poverty for the many which may have been worse than any conditions ever endured by the mass of the English people.

The peace with Spain in 1604 gladdened the hearts of many merchants, and rising prosperity, at first, followed. James shared in it; customs revenue more than doubled in the first eighteen years of his reign and in 1621 provided three times as much income as crown lands. There was no conflict between the Crown's interests and those of merchants in general. The cloth trade rose to a new peak by 1614, when perhaps 144,000 pieces left London as compared to 104,000 at the turn of the century.[15] Then came a crisis in European trade which lasted for generations and which has been held responsible for a wave of revolutions over the Continent in the 1630s and 1640s. The population rise of the sixteenth century was checked, and there may even have been a general decline. The great price rise jolted to a halt by the 1640s. Trade suffered a check before 1620, when the conflict now known as the Thirty Years War began to rack the centre of the Continent. When the tumult and the shouting died down in the second half of the century, Europe was transformed. The Mediterranean had ceased to be the hub of world trade. Italy had slumped from urbanised prosperity towards rustic decadence. German development had been set back for two centuries. The Spanish Crown, its New World silver flow dwindled, was a shadow of its former self, chased out of Portugal in 1640. The French monarchy had emerged from a period of anarchy as the strongest in Europe, Louis XIV a model for absolutists everywhere. The Dutch and the English were now setting the commercial pace, and the latter, in 1649, had chopped off the head of James's royal son.

The general picture then, was one of English advance through difficult times, and by revolutionary methods. European capitalism burst through the feudal shell in which it had been nurtured. ' ... The decisive shift from capitalist enterprise adapted to a generally feudal framework to capitalist enterprise transforming the world in its own pattern, took place. The Revolution in England was thus the most dramatic incident in the crisis, and its turning point.'[16]

Tonnage of English-owned shipping (the figures cannot be certain) seems to have risen from 67,000 in 1582 to 115,000 in 1629 and somewhere between 150,000 and 200,000 by 1660. Let us say that it may have trebled in eighty years.

Transatlantic and East India trade played some part in this growth, but carrying coal from Newcastle should not be forgotten. The coastal coal trade, above all to London, waxed importantly, engaging 1,400 large ships by 1700 where it had used only 400 smallish ones at the start of the century.[17] And trade with Europe still far outweighed fancy traffic in far continents. Here was the heart of a crisis. The Thirty Years War provoked the sudden collapse of traditional markets for English cloth. A difficult readjustment had to be made.

The so-called 'New Draperies' now became crucial. These lighter cloths, such as the 'bays' and 'says' of East Anglia and the serges and 'perpetuanas' which Devon made out of wool from Ireland, growingly dominated the heavy old broadcloth which was the forerunner of our blankets and baize. They did well in the Mediterranean, where the collapse of the native textile industries in Spain and Italy was obvious by the 1620s, leaving open rich markets not only in Southern Europe itself but in the Spanish colonies and in the Levant. Trade in the Mediterranean grew until it reached saturation point in the mid-eighteenth century. By 1700 only half of English cloth exports were going to the traditional markets in Northern and Central Europe.[18]

The Dutch were both coadjutors and rivals. Eighty years of war from the 1560s to 1648 established the independence of the seven United Provinces of the Netherlands. In the fifteenth and sixteenth centuries, the ports of Holland and Zeeland had won a main share of the carrying trade between the Baltic and Western Europe. The war with Spain had not impeded their rise. By the 1590s the Dutch had evolved a basis for world power, the *fluit*, a cargo ship which because it employed fewer hands, and carried greater bulk – of Baltic grain, of timber or of sugar – could undercut all competition. In the first half of the seventeenth century, the Dutch dominated the Baltic trade so thoroughly that their ships passing through the Danish Sound outnumbered those of the English by roughly thirteen to one. During their struggle with Spain, they continued to supply their papist enemies with grain and naval stores which the latter could simply not do without, and their cynical dedication to profits became a byword among their English competitors, on whom the lesson was not wasted. The great philosopher Hobbes claimed that many Englishmen, especially in trading towns, were inclined to think that Dutch prosperity actually stemmed from their revolt against their lawful sovereign, Philip of Spain.[19] Here was a still more subversive lesson. By 1648, the Netherlands were a republic effectively dominated by an oligarchy of some 10,000 rich men.

Amsterdam now had a status as an international commercial emporium never matched before or, arguably, since. Yet its ruling townsmen staggered foreigners by their very lack of ostentation, their 'parcimonious and thrifty Living'.[20] The great seaman de Ruyter would dress like the plainest sea-captain, the great statesman Johan de Witt like the commonest burgher, and neither was ever seen attended by more than one manservant, indoors or out. These men were not yet 'bourgeois' in the full nineteenth-century sense, but self-confident, self-ruling townsmen they certainly were, and to a surprising extent even the people of the rural Netherlands – those narrow lands largely hard won by reclamation from the North Sea – shared in the values of town-dwellers. So far had they travelled from ideas of self-sufficiency, that frugal Dutch farmers were said to sell their high quality cheese and butter for export and buy for themselves 'the cheapest out of Ireland or the North of England.'[21]

This was the most densely populated part of Europe. Agriculture had responded by concentrating on crops grown for cash and on cattle breeding – those cows so respectfully painted by seventeenth-century Dutch masters were fit inhabitants of a townsman's best room; they were at as far an extreme from the black beasts of the Scottish Highlands as the Dutch burgher was from a Gaelic tribesman. For centuries the Dutch had been pioneers in agricultural technique. The crop rotations which they had developed raised yields of corn remarkably. Now in the seventeenth century their efforts at land reclamation reached a peak; and they introduced high-yielding artificial grasses which enabled them to feed more animals and, at the same time, to grow more crops with the help of the manure which their livestock gave them. This was the revolution which made the later Industrial Revolution possible; more people could by their methods be fed on the same, or even a smaller, acreage.

The wealth won from the land helped support a Dutch empire overseas. While they harried the Spaniards in the New World – in 1628, for the Dutch West India Company, Piet Heyn achieved Drake's dream and captured the Mexican silver fleet – they overran the preserves of Portugal. They dominated the carrying trade between Europe and Brazil and then, in 1630, invaded that country. For some years they controlled the sugar of north-eastern Brazil at source, until revolt drove them out in 1654. In the East sporadic warfare between 1605, when the Dutch seized the principal Indonesian spice islands, and 1663, when they captured the Portuguese settlements on the Malabar coast of India, deprived the papists of all but a few outposts, though they kept their capital, 'Golden Goa'. The Dutch Albuquerque was Jan Pieterz Coen, a servant of the Dutch East India Company (VOC). The VOC directors wanted peaceful trade. Coen told them in 1614, 'we cannot carry on trade without war nor war without trade.'[22] As good as his word, he took Jakarta in Java five years later. Renamed Batavia, this became the Dutch capital in the Far East and was the thin end of a long wedge. And amongst his other exploits he 'extirpated', to use James I's word, the people of the unhappy Banda Islands. 'The Dutch have a proverb', it was said, 'Jesus Christ is good, but trade is better.'[23] Spain and Portugal had poured priests into the tropics. The Dutch made no real missionary effort, and Indonesia under their dominance became steadily more Muhammadan, as its rulers reacted against Christian aggression.

Forward-looking English landowners, most famously in Norfolk, followed the Dutch example and planted turnips to feed to their cattle. The Dutch lead was pursued in crop rotation, vegetable growing, the use of windmills. But the

Dutch were hard to catch. 'They had cornered the most profitable economic activities. They dominated world markets, standing at all points between the English and their suppliers and customers.'[24] Norfolk barley was brewed in the Netherlands. Dutch herring boats plundered British waters from the Shetlands to the Thames. In view of the shores, they took fish which they sold to the English and Scots themselves and the humble kipper, it could be claimed, was the pebble in the sling with which the Dutch David felled the Spanish Goliath.[25]

The Dutch loudly preached the freedom of the seas. They must be able to go where they wanted, papal bulls notwithstanding. When they had got there, they strove to exclude all competitors, with almost complete success in Indonesia, and totally in Japan, where they were the only Europeans allowed to trade between 1639 and 1854. Against them, the merchants and intellectuals of England and other countries began to refine the ideas which we call 'mercantilist'.

James I was something of a mercantilist himself. Having failed to forestall the Dutch in Lewis, he promoted another aggressive project in 1614. Dutch dyers were finishing English broadcloths and taking perhaps half the total profits from their ultimate sale. In return for a promise of £300,000 a year to himself, James withdrew the Merchant Adventurers' privileges in favour of a new company, directed by Sir William Cokayne, which was licensed to export finished cloths only. Disaster followed. The Dutch banned the import of English dyed cloths. The new company could not match their technical skills, nor do without their marketing channels. English cloth exports slumped by a third and ruin spread through the West Country. In 1617 James restored the Merchant Adventurers to their former privileges. However, the 'Cokayne Project' had not been fatuous, merely premature. By the 1660s the English finishing industry had so far caught up that two-thirds of the broadcloths going to Holland were dressed and dyed.[26] The English were the Dutchmen's aptest pupils.

English mercantilist thinking came to its first maturity in the 1620s as the government took the novel step of calling in merchant experts to advise it about the deep and complex depression which had struck English trade and industry. How was it, men were asking, that Spain, with so much 'treasure' at its disposal, could not hold on to it and was growing poor, while its Dutch enemies had built up Europe's largest commercial fleet, 'those multitudes of Ships,' Thomas Mun wrote, 'which unto them are as our Ploughs to us, the which except they stir, the people starve ... ' (thus Mun, an East India merchant, rises unconsciously into blank verse as he contemplates the achievements of 'such a small Countrey, not fully so big as two of our best Shires ... ')[27] His credo, *England's Treasure by Foreign Trade*, quite likely written in the 1620s, though not printed till 1664, would eventually become a kind of Old Testament for English economic thinkers.

The term 'mercantilism' was in fact unknown before Adam Smith in 1776 launched his attack on the system which he called 'mercantile', associating it with two ideas which he thought especially erroneous. One was the emphasis placed on the accumulation of gold and silver, which seemed to confuse money with wealth. A second idea, found in Mun and in his successors, was that the nation must maintain a favourable balance of trade; this promoted what Smith thought vicious state interference to discourage imports and boost exports, sacrificing, Smith would say, the interests of consumers to those of producers. But now that Smith himself is no longer uncritically cited, we can see mercantilism as an adequate, if unlovely, response to the challenges of seventeenth-century Europe, and its central doctrine of the balance of trade as the key to a nationalistic economic policy which, in the case of England, worked in practice to build up 'greatness'.

Mun was one of the state-appointed Commissioners who put forward in 1622 a prophetic set of proposals. English raw materials should be reserved to the native cloth industry by the prohibition of exports of wool, fullers' earth and so on, especially to Holland. England should reduce her need for imports by developing manufactures of her own — linen, for instance, should be made with home-grown flax. Native fishing companies should be formed and the Dutch ousted. Goods imported from abroad should come only in English ships or in ships belonging to the country which had produced them, so eliminating the Dutch middleman. Each of these beggar-my-neighbour ideas, though they could not be implemented at once, was 'a root from which elaborate later policies were to stem.'[28]

While in France 'mercantilist' policies would be forced by rulers on merchants, and while in the Netherlands they arose, in effect, spontaneously, in England they became a conscious programme shared, as the century wore on, by monarchs, state servants, theorists, and, of course, merchants. There would be differences of particular opinion — East India merchants like Mun, for instance, who were committed to exporting bullion, would be much criticised on 'mercantilist' grounds. But a 'mercantilist' way of viewing the world would dominate for a century and a half those who pressed forward expansion beyond Europe. Each European power concerned would develop a system of trade 'composed of all the devices, legislative, administrative and regulatory, by which societies still predominantly agrarian sought to transform themselves into trading and industrial societies, to equip themselves not only to be rich but to be strong, and to remain so.'[29]

In an age of growing national consciousness and deepening national rivalries, when the zeal generated by religious conflicts began to transfer itself to the conflicts between 'states' which were beginning to be called by that name, mercantilism emphasised, not wrongly, the link between trade and power. The power of a strong state intervening forcefully in economic affairs could promote trade which in turn would breed power. Exports, and re-exports, were seen as crucial to 'treasure by foreign trade', the acquisition of a surplus of bullion. Exports to colonies were more securely maintained than exports to alien markets. Colonies meanwhile could make England (say) self-sufficient in necessities and in certain luxuries (sugar, tobacco) which would soon come to seem necessities. A surplus for re-export could be available. And Mun and others favoured internal colonialism within the British Isles themselves. Waste grounds should be used to grow commodities which would otherwise be imported.[30]

All this may now seem no more than a sometimes quaint system of rationalisations to justify what was happening anyway. Mind, as usual, limped after reality. Yet the crystallisation of these ideas involved a revolutionary shift in the consciousness of men which in turn came to affect the reality they were making. The cult of the national state, which now seems to us natural, is a human invention. So is the notion, not always well based, but eagerly propounded by mercantilist thinkers, that 'national' power and wealth benefit the poorest sections of the community. A novel faith was emerging, both cynical and naïve, which asserted the glory and dignity of trade. Mun talks of the 'nobleness' of the merchant's 'vocation', confusing 'degree' as his forefathers had seen it. ' ... Wee ought to esteem and cherish', he says, 'those trades which we have in remote or far Countreys.' Why? What is, after all, so estimable about wresting spices from Asian cultivators? 'As for example,' Mun goes on; 'suppose Pepper to be worth here two Shillings the pound constantly, if then it be bought from the *Dutch* at *Amsterdam*, the merchant may give there twenty pence the pound, and gain well by the bargain; but if he fetch this Pepper from the *East-indies*, he must not give above three pence the pound at the most, which is a mighty advantage, not only in that part which serveth for our own use, but also for that great quantity which (from hence) we transport yearly unto divers other Nations to be sold at a higher price: whereby', he concludes, with what may now seem refreshing frankness, 'it is plain, that we make a far greater stock by gain upon these *Indian* commodities, than those Nations doe where they grow, and to whom they properly appertain, being the natural wealth of their Countries.'[31]

The good of England, or rather the power of England, sanctifies such amoral book-keeping. And the interests of England and those of men making several hundred per cent profit are hailed as identical. The merchant, as Mun eulogises him – the master of the mysteries of trade, 'The Steward of the Kingdom's Stock' – is a crusader chivalrously bearing the grave risks of trade in the interest of Great England. Devoted and penny-counting, he is, in Mun's view, entitled to scorn the mass of his fellow countrymen who still share in 'the general leprosie of our Piping, Potting, Feasting, Fashions, and mis-spending of our time in Idleness and Pleasure (contrary to the Law of God, and the use of other Nations.)'[32] Nationalism, profit and piety mesh together. Warren Hastings, Samuel Smiles, and Gradgrind, are all foreshadowed in a single sentence. Puritan dedication to work is good not only because God likes it, but because the Dutch have shown its commercial advantages. Hobbes sneered that the great art of merchants was no more than that of 'making poor People sell their Labour to them, at their own Prices; so that poor People, for the most part, might get a better Living by working in Bridewell ... '[33] But for Mun and his co-thinkers the now 'noble' merchant had the same kind of prescriptive right to profit from others' work as the feudal nobleman had enjoyed in respect of his serfs.

This ideological merging of trade with nobility was very English. It reflected, for instance, and no doubt encouraged, the coalition of merchants with landed gentry and peers which was in Mun's day pressing forward maritime expansion. The surge of prosperity up to about 1615 was accompanied by a rush of investment in overseas trade and colonies. East Indian and American trade remained for the moment puny compared to the volume of commerce with Europe – in Tawney's words, they did 'more for the imagination of England than for its stomach or its industries' – but they lent prestige to all who ventured in them.[34]

The main engine of advance was the joint-stock company, based on London but commonly raking in money from elsewhere. Initiatives started in Plymouth and other provincial centres generally had to turn for help before long to the capital which now dominated the English economy as never before. The country gentleman bumping up to London in his coach – such vehicles came within reach of the middling pocket by the 1590s – so as to vent his hatred of his neighbours in the law courts or his suspicions of the King from his seat in Parliament, was often attracted there to invest in some fine-looking scheme for colonies or discoveries. His surplus from rising rents, his profits from agriculture or from the sale of land, were made available for expansion through joint-stock companies which (unlike the regulated companies) gave him the chance of participation without expertise or responsibility. He was rarely attracted by purely commercial aims. Nor was he likely to think of emigration himself. Mercantilist arguments might have some intellectual sway over him. Patriotism moved him. And glory beckoned; gentry were far more willing than merchants to invest in the relatively small companies which promoted wild schemes, as they seemed, for settlements in Guiana or bitter New England, or for the expansion of trade with Africa. It would be an honour to share in some exotic project brought to reality. Though Sir Edwin Sandys, a substantial landowner, was egregious in the degree of his commitment – he devoted the last twenty years of his life largely to colonial interests, and achieved positions of responsibility in three major trading companies – there is a sense in which this enthusiast, suddenly seized by visions in his mid-forties, typified the whole remarkable breed of gentlemen-investors which had no counterpart on the Continent.

The middling gentleman's contribution in gross financial terms was, however, outweighed by that of peers and great courtiers, whose interest in colonies can be related to their passion for gambling at cards, and who siphoned some of the profits of office into overseas expansion. Men about court were as much involved under James I and Charles I as under Elizabeth, and their interest was shared by the malcontent 'Puritan' faction of the nobility. Professor Rabb has been able to classify 5,184 investors in overseas and similar enterprises between 1575 and 1630, out of an overall total of 6,336. Over 1,000 of these were knights and gentlemen. Also involved were 179 peers. Almost 40 per cent of the members of both the 1604 House of Commons and its 1614 successor were investors, and Commons men actually composed about a fifth of the Virginia Company, of which nearly three-quarters of the directorships were held by gentry rather than merchants.[35]

But almost all East India Company directorships down to 1630 were held by merchants, and 85 per cent of the capital in that organisation seems to have come from trade. 'The commercial classes naturally dominated the entire overseas effort ... ' Most money went into fields where merchants and their quest for immediate profits were dominant — into privateering and into the East India Company.[36] Merchants were naturally glad to have men at court and in Parliament who shared their interests. They might well have abandoned North American settlement had it not been for the plans and enthusiasm of gentlemen. But in the annals of expansion from this period even Sandys or the privateering Earl of Warwick is outweighed by the great merchant Sir Thomas Smythe, son of a notoriously successful customs farmer, who had been not implausibly accused of corruption on a huge scale in Elizabeth's day.[37] And the very big merchants in general were those who put most in.

Merchant oligarchs, above all in London, were driving craftsmen down from proud independence into a proletarian subjection. It was claimed in 1622 that two-thirds of England's trade was handled by only fifty men. Noblemen might dabble in far commerce, but 'handicraftsmen' and other small Londoners were excluded, as much by their lack of means as by the tough restrictions on membership made by the great monopolistic corporations.[38] Such hardening, widening class divisions deprived England of much of its 'merriness'. Without the concentration of financial resources in the hands of men like Smythe who were prepared to switch them from old to new fields of enterprise, from one quarter of Earth, indeed, to another, overseas Empire could not have existed. But while mercantilism, the cult of trade, rationalised rapacity in the Indies, it also favoured expropriations at home — in the Borders and Lewis, as we have seen; in Ireland, naturally; and in England's own Fen country.

III

A writer of 1586 described the distinctive way of life of the 'rude uncivill' people who dwelt in the peat fens of Cambridgeshire. Their region was 'over-flowed' by rivers in winter, and 'sometimes most part of the yeere', but when the streams retired to their own channels they left excellent feeding for cattle. The people mowed as much of the rich hay as would serve them, then, in November, burnt the rest to fertilise the soil, so that it was a sight to wonder

at, 'this Fennish and moyst Tract on a light flaming fire all over every way.'
The inhabitants had adapted superbly. 'Stalking on high upon stilts' — one man
so provided could drive hundreds of cattle to pasture — they devoted themselves
to grazing, fishing and fowling. There were similar areas in Lincolnshire to the
north where men went forth to milk their cows in little boats.[39]

In 1600, Parliament passed a 'General Draining Act'. The Fens were the
largest area involved. There were few large estates there, so capital from outside
was essential, and could only be attracted by the promise that those who provided it would get a portion of the acreage to be reclaimed. Areas now enjoyed
in common by the Fenmen must pass into the hands of outsiders. The natives
were not prepared to co-operate in the extinction of their way of life, since
lands which seemed drowned and worthless to the mercantilist mind were a
source of coarse plenty to their inhabitants. Throughout the year the Fens gave
employment to multitudes of cottagers, who gathered reeds, fodder, turves and
many other useful things. Fish and edible fowl were God's bounty. 'The fens',
said an objector in 1622, 'were made fens and must ever continue such.'[40]

Amongst the numerous undertakers who set to work was that great privateering magnate, Alderman Watts. Another was Cokayne of the famous textile
project. Their syndicate did exploit reclaimed land for several years, but was
then turned out by the 'uncivill' Fenmen after the waters broke their banks and
'drowned all again'. The King declared in 1621 that the 'Honour of this kingdome' would not allow the Fens to continue 'wast and unprofitable' and said
he would undertake the work himself in return for 120,000 acres. But nothing
came of this.[41] Dutch expertise would be needed before the trick could be done.
And meanwhile his Majesty's Irish colonies were presenting him with problems
enough.

IV

Ireland when James I came to the throne was a ravaged land where wolves
dominated great waste tracts, merchants refused to accept the debased currency
except at far below its face value and Algerian Muhammadan pirates preyed in
the long inlets of Munster. Mountjoy had made a desert and called it peace. Yet
the simple Irish economy had natural resilience. Herrings and salmon knew
nothing of soldiers and oppression. The herds and flocks which grew by natural
increase would sustain export trades in wool and sheepskins, cattle, hides, tallow
and beef. Great woods still covered perhaps an eighth of the land, waiting to be
ripped down by English settlers, to fuel the making of iron or to provide pipe
staves for exports to the Continent, where they would be used to make wine
casks. The axe opened up new lands for settled cultivation. Seeing connection
between the trees and the old chiefly families and castes of learned men, a Gaelic
poet would lament,

What shall we do henceforth without timber,
the last of the woods is fallen ... [42]

While the trees fell, the Gaelic order fell too. But, as economists measure life, the first four decades of the seventeenth century were for Ireland a phase of growing prosperity.

Conquest completed, the Pale's legal system was swiftly extended over the whole country. Gavelkind and tanistry were declared void of legality. The common law of England, it was ordained, must prevail without competition from native Brehon Law. The Gaelic upper classes were learning English and adopting the conquerors' style of clothing, though in Ulster at least the old *braccae* or trews persisted among the common people down to the 1640s, despite the denunciations of papist clergy.[43]

The Counter-Reformation had now come to Ireland in force, and its austerity was in sharp conflict with Irish custom. A Spanish captain had remarked of the Donegal wench who had helped to rescue him from the wreck of an Armada ship that she was 'Christian in like manner as Mahomet'. Confronted by cheerful polygamy, by funeral wakes which turned into orgies marked by what seemed obscene songs and gestures, and by general ignorance of the main tenets of Catholicism, Jesuit missionaries now tried to civilise the Irish and, as one bishop put it in 1617, to 'eliminate barbarous customs, abolish bestial rites, and convert the detestable intercourse of savages into polite manners and a care for maintaining the commonwealth.' However, Irish Franciscans working at Louvain in Europe created a Gaelic press which printed not only religious works but also books which preserved as well as could now be done the Gaels' traditions of their own history.[44]

Irishness and Catholicism were to become identified, and the so-called 'Old English', products of several centuries of alien settlement, but still Catholic, would be driven into 'Irishness' by religious discrimination. The Gaels themselves now distinguished these *Sean-Ghaill* from the *Nua-Ghaill*, 'New English', the fiercely Protestant, curtly supremacist men who had recently come as colonists or officials and whose main vested interest was in preventing the Catholics from taking any share in political power. A shilling fine for each non-attendance at Anglican church was laid down by law and the favourite 'New English' solution to the chronic financial problems of Ireland's government was a simple one; let all the fines be collected. The greatest New England magnate was Richard Boyle, first Earl of Cork, who had picked up Ralegh's Irish domain and who came to enjoy, by 1629, an income of £20,000 a year from rents alone.[45]

Sean-Ghaill ('Old English') seems to refer to race but in fact defined a political attitude. Some Gaels, leading O Briens, for instance, shared it with some Hibernicised descendants of Norman settlers, with the 'lords of the Pale' whose forbears had come from England long since, and with members of recent settler families (including Spenser's, of all men's) which had slumped into papistry.

All these were propertied Catholics still loyal to the Crown and fearful of the 'Gaelic Irish' who might rise and dispossess them. They were a minority under pressure from two sides, but some two thousand Old English families owned much of the best land in the country, and their sort controlled most of the trade of the Irish ports. Though all were excluded from high office, they had a natural majority in the Irish Parliament which the government had to counteract by creating new boroughs to return Protestants. The Old English had enough influence to ensure that religious conformity was not strictly enforced. An uncomfortable half-tolerance prevailed. Meanwhile Old English unease was accentuated by government schemes for 'plantations', which made all titles to land in Ireland seem insecure.

In Leinster, grants made by Elizabeth, even by James himself, were over-turned or rendered shaky in several areas. The poorer Gaels of course bore the brunt. When details of a proposed plantation in Kavanagh country were announced in 1611, the natives who held the land were shocked and angry, and some turned brigand. In 1618, three-quarters of it was in fact set aside for native proprietors, but while the chief landowners got estates good in law, the lesser ones were robbed of everything. David Rothe, a Catholic bishop, expounded in Latin the plight of these 'unlearned men without human help or protection', and emphasised that they were dangerous. 'They have been deprived of weapons, but are in a temper to fight with nails and heels and to tear their oppressors with their teeth.'[46]

Even some Dublin officials were uneasy about this Wexford operation, yet further schemes proceeded in Leitrim and Longford. Sir John MacCoghlan of Delvin had served Elizabeth in her wars; O Dunne of Iregan had a grant from James; both were amongst those deprived of lands. In Longford, where the O Farrells were dispossessed, it was said that some of the victims, before they died of grief, asked to be taken out of their beds 'to have abroad the last sight of the hills and fields they lost ... ' Bitter grievances were created without real gain. Very few British families were settled outside Ulster.[47]

The leading Ulster rebels had all been pardoned, though Sir Arthur Chichester, who succeeded Mountjoy as viceroy in 1605, deported several thousand 'swordsmen' for military service on the Continent. Tyrone kept almost all of his vast estates and Rory O Donnell, successor to Red Hugh, was confirmed as lord of most of Donegal and ennobled as Earl of Tyrconnell. But while they attempted to reassert the arbitrary power of Gaelic chiefdom, English feudal land tenure marched in, with English officials ready to enforce it.

Tyrone wearied of life in a conquered Ireland. O Cahan, chief over fertile lands, had defected from his allegiance to him in 1602 on promise of a grant of them from the Crown. Tyrone still tried to treat him in the old chiefly style as a mere tenant of will of his own. Officials favoured O Cahan, who was shortly to be knighted. Tyrone received a summons to London that James I might settle the dispute. Meanwhile Tyrconnell was implicated in intrigues with

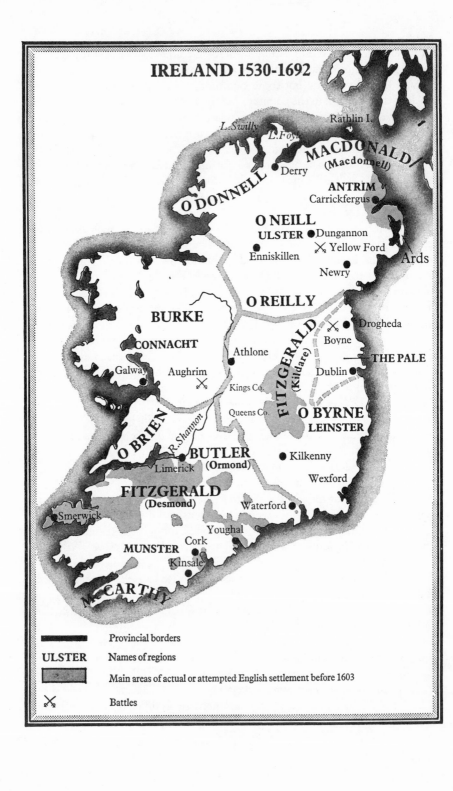

IRELAND 1530-1692

Rathlin I.

L. Swilly

L. Foyle

MACDONALD/
(Macdonnell)

O DONNELL

Derry

ANTRIM
Carrickfergus

O NEILL
ULSTER   Dungannon
             ✗ Yellow Ford

Enniskillen   Newry

Ards

O REILLY

BURKE   Drogheda
                                    ✗
CONNACHT   Athlone   Boyne

Galway   Aughrim   THE PALE

                    ✗   Dublin

              Kings Co.

              Queens Co.   O BYRNE
                              LEINSTER

O BRIEN   R. Shannon   BUTLER
                        (Ormond)

           Limerick   Kilkenny

FITZGERALD   Wexford
(Desmond)

Smerwick   Waterford

                    Youghal

MUNSTER   Cork

           Kinsale

McCARTHY

FITZGERALD
(Kildare)

━━━━━   Provincial borders

ULSTER   Names of regions

▨▨▨▨   Main areas of actual or attempted English settlement before 1603

✗   Battles

Catholic powers abroad, and the government heard of it. The two Earls decided on flight. On 3 September 1607 they sailed from Lough Swilly with almost a hundred followers. They made their way to Rome, where Tyrone died, aged and blind, in 1616. 'Woe to the heart that meditated, woe to the mind that conceived, woe to the council that decided on, the project of their setting out on this voyage ... ', was the lament of the annalist over the 'Flight of the Earls' which seemed to complete the defeat of the Gaelic social order.[48]

In the spring of 1608 Sir Cahir O Doherty of Inishowen, annoyed by an insult from the governor of Derry, broke into revolt and burnt the town. The rising was quickly suppressed, with copious hangings, and one man who tasted the full bitterness of English treachery was O Cahan, no longer useful to the government now that his enemy Tyrone had fled. Arrested and charged with presumption of treason, he ended his days in the Tower of London. O Cahan's lands joined those of the Earls in a pile of forfeitures.

Further cynical shifts increased the scope for plantation. Thus Sir John Davies, the Attorney General (a Welshman, and yet another important poet to play a part in Ireland), had, as lately as 1606, adjudged clansmen, not chiefs, to be owners of Cavan and Fermanagh. Now he said that they had never been more than tenants at will. So the Crown could claim to have at its free disposal six whole counties—Tyrone, Donegal, Coleraine (later Derry), Armagh, Cavan and Fermanagh. Three or four leading Gaels were given large grants and about 280 lesser Irish proprietors received between one-eighth and one-ninth of the rest. All the remainder went to English and Scottish settlers.[49]

Chichester, one of the more decent of viceroys, regretted the injustice done to the Gaels. He had 'conceived that one half of each county would have been left assigned to natives; but now they have but one barony in a county and in some counties less.'[50] James I's scheme was short-sighted. The Gaels, mostly left landless had nothing to lose if they rebelled again. Yet the plan for a strict segregation in miniature Bantustans must break down because planters needed tenants and labourers to make the lands which they had acquired pay.

Early in 1609, Scottish and English 'undertakers' were invited for tracts of 1,000, 1,500 and 2,000 acres, rent free for two years then costing a penny farthing an acre. The needs of defence would be costly, though. Undertakers must build stone or brick houses with 'bawns' (defensible courtyards), and keep, train and arm a sufficient force. Only English and Scottish tenants were allowable. Another class provided for were 'servitors', men, mostly soldiers, who had worked for the Crown in Ireland. They were permitted to have Gaelic tenants, but would have to pay higher rent for any land leased to natives. Gaels granted land of their own would also have to build 'castles' and bawns, and would pay twice as much rent as the British undertakers.[51]

It was important for strategic reasons that the towns of Derry and Coleraine should be strong. Early in 1610 the City of London acquired from James the area which became County Londonderry. O Cahan's fertile lands, the dense woods of Glenconkeyne, the rich fisheries of the rivers Foyle and Bann, enjoyment of customs, military support from the King – all these were to be the City's in return for building up their two towns. The territory would be run by a so-called 'London Company', later known as the 'Irish Society', which was in effect a standing committee of the City's common council.

The City was thus the largest of the 'undertakers' who in the event secured over two-fifths of the land granted in the six escheated counties. The established Church received over one-fifth. Servitors and native Gaels shared most of the rest. As in Munster years before, individuals acquired far larger estates than anyone was supposed to hold. Lord Audley (Sir John Davies's father-in-law) received 3,000 acres for himself and his wife and 4,000 for two sons. The results of such greed were predictable. It was reported in 1619 that on all the Audley lands there were no bawns or strong houses, no British freeholders had been established, discontented British tenants were leaving, and a score of Gaelic gentry rented the remainder of the land.[52] Such delinquency was common. Wild wolves and wilder robbers discouraged settlers. The Englishmen who 'undertook' were mostly unsuitable, gentlemen with too little capital who were often ready to sell their claims and retreat. The Scots, momentously, did rather better, in spite, or because, of a penchant which much distressed James, for marrying Gaelic girls, as some of them might just have done at home.

James's keen interest in Ulster prompted repeated surveys. That of 1619 confirmed a picture of partial successes and overall failure. Nearly 2,000 British families were settled. But Gaelic graziers, craving continued hold on the land, offered better rents than could be got from English tenants, so much of Ulster was still roamed by natives with their deplorable cattle. 'Londonderry', now so called, was in sad condition. The City of London had been bound to erect 200 houses, but there were only 102 families in the place, and too few men to defend its (very strong) wall. The surveyor, Nicholas Pynnar, doubted if the plantation could last. 'My reason is, that many of the *English* Tenants do not yet plough upon the Lands, neither use Husbandrie, because I conceive they are fearful to Stock themselves with Cattle or Servants for these Labours. Neither do the *Irish* use Tillage, for that they are also uncertain of their Stay upon the Lands; so that, by this means, the *Irish* ploughing nothing, do use greasing [grazing]; the *English* very little; and were it not for the *Scottish* tenants, which do plough in many places of the country, those Parts may starve ... '[53]

Matters got no better. After numerous ultimata had failed to oust the Gaels, James conceded at last in 1625 that they could be admitted as tenants on a quarter of the undertakers' lands. The vision of a strongly planted Ulster devoted to tillage had not been realised. Meanwhile, the City men had poured in money to little effect; John Rowley, their chief agent during the first three years managed, it seems, to squander and embezzle more than half the £30,000 they raised in that time. James, having tempted the City with hopes of profit, then set about reminding it of its obligations and discouraging profitable enterprise. The Londoners seem in the end to have lost about £40,000 over the venture. Their most significant energy was seen in the slow rise of Londonderry to a population of some 500 able-bodied British men in 1630, when it was by far the largest town in Ulster.[54]

Scottish undertakers also had done something to ensure that the Ulster plantation, with all its falterings, would make a permanent mark on Ireland. Ulster was much easier to reach from south-west Scotland than from any part of England. The first Lowland Scottish incursions preceded the main plantation, pursuing the tracks of those Highland Gaels, Macdonalds, who had in Elizabeth's reign captured the Route and the Glynns and held them against all others. Sir Randal Macdonnell (the Irish form of the name) was confirmed in his possessions by James in 1603. Meanwhile two Lowlanders, Hugh Montgomery and James Hamilton, had managed by sharp practice to get their hands on most of the area held by Con O Neill. By the summer of 1606, a flow of Lowland settlers into County Down had begun. Montgomery gave estates to lairds from his own district and brought over smiths, masons and carpenters to build houses on the devastated land. His wife, the prime organiser of the estates, supervised the building of watermills and, with prophetic instinct, encouraged the making of linen cloth. There was soon a thriving community. Macdonnell also brought Lowlanders into his Antrim lands, and these two eastern counties of Ulster were said in 1618 to be better planted with English and Scottish settlers than some of the six which had been escheated. Private initiative succeeded where James, overall, had failed, in creating dense plantations with deepening roots.[55]

Meanwhile, within the Ulster plantation proper, over 60 Scots, mostly lairds, were granted land. General poverty in their homeland made lesser Scots ready to try their luck as tenants or servants in a barbarous country. They were soon exporting corn and beef back to Scotland. By the end of James I's reign there were no fewer than 8,000 Scots males capable of bearing arms settled in Ulster, mainly coming from the south-west and from the Borders – whence many reivers fled James's justice. Scots quickly captured most of the export trade of Londonderry, and came to outnumber the English inhabitants there.[56]

Irish Protestantism, where it existed, was already strongly puritanical. The influx of Scots reinforced this. Scots became bishops in Ulster and numbers of them got livings in the Established Church. But some of these were Presbyterian enemies of the episcopal order itself, and by the 1630s they would bring a vexatious third factor into Irish religion and politics. For the moment, however, James I could be satisfied that his Scottish countrymen were finding an outlet in Ulster to match that which his English subjects were making in the New World. The two movements were closely linked in men's minds at the time. There is still a place in Ulster called 'Virginia'.

V

While Ralegh studied and experimented in the Tower, his lost colony had practical effects for the activities of others. The Spaniards who negotiated the peace treaty with England in 1604 believed that it still existed and that it would be hard if not impossible to get the heretics to abandon land which they had actually possessed for so long; this helped to explain why there was no provision about the Indies in the treaty. The way was left open for colonisation without war.[57]

But privateering was now outlawed. While merchants in the West Country ports were encouraged by the rapid growth of the triangular trade in Newfoundland fish with Southern Europe to take an interest in the cold shoreline of New England, great men in the City of London who had grown up with the ideas of Hakluyt saw 'Virginia', lying in similar latitudes to Spain and the Levant, as a possible alternative source of fruits and wines, as well as of timber, and of the tobacco and dyes which were currently acquired from the papist Indies.

Numerous voyages prospected the North American coast. Soon after James's succession, two Indians gave on the Thames an exhibition of their prowess at canoeing. In 1605 a skipper, George Weymouth, who had studied the coast of Maine, came back with five more Indians, who were taken under the wing of Sir Ferdinando Gorges, governor of Plymouth. He sent a couple of them to Sir John Popham, the aged, vast and pompous Lord Chief Justice. Popham had been an undertaker in Munster and was now involved in draining the Fens. Furthermore, he had taken a special interest in the problem of vagabondage. He saw a North American colony as an outlet for the 'infinite numbers of cashiered captains and soldiers, of poor artisans that would and cannot work, and idle vagrants that may and will not work, whose increase threatens the State ... '[58] James's chief minister, Robert Cecil, Earl of Salisbury, was also interested, so that the State itself was, for the first time, officially involved in transatlantic colonisation.

Certain London merchants, headed by Sir Thomas Smythe, were clearly attracted. But Gorges and merchants of Bristol, Plymouth and Exeter were jealous of the City men. So in April 1606, James chartered two Virginia Companies. Each would be entitled to choose a spot for a colony within the vast area between 34° N. (the Cape Fear River) and 45° N. (Passamaquoddy Bay, where the boundary between Maine and New Brunswick now runs). The Londoners might settle up to the 41st parallel and the Plymouth Company as far south as the 38th, but even in the area of overlap, neither might plant within 100 miles of the other.

A Royal Council in England was to have overall government of both colonies – this was the step which ushered in a new era of expansion, making it clear to Spain that she could move against the settlements only at the risk of another ruinous war. Each colony was to have a local council of thirteen men, appointed by the Company, who were to elect their own president. Settlers were to be guaranteed all the liberties of native-born Englishmen, including, for instance, trial by jury. The new lands opened up would be legally part of the King's demesne and would be held in 'free and common socage' as if on a royal manor in England.

But settlement was still not necessarily the main aim. The first expeditions would be exploratory. Both companies were organised on a semi-joint-stock basis in which each voyage was expected to pay for itself. The investors wanted the largest and swiftest return for their money that could be found. Some hoped for gold and silver, or for easy access to the Pacific Ocean – the Virginia adventurers were advised to select for settlement the river running furthest into the interior, and if this river had two branches, to choose that which bent most towards the north-west, 'for that way you shall soonest find the other sea.'[59]

The Londoners actually moved first, but the fate of the Plymouth enterprise may now be mentioned. In May 1607 the Western Company sent out 120 men under George Popham (the old man's nephew) and Ralegh Gilbert (son of Sir Humphrey and nephew of Walter), who founded a settlement at Sagadahoc in Maine. They lacked enough food for the winter and quarrelled bitterly among themselves. (This last was true in the opening phases of most early colonies, and it is perhaps surprising that historians have been so censorious of the spites and rages of sick and starving men.) Popham died and Ralegh Gilbert sailed home to claim his inheritance when he heard of the death of his elder brother. The experiment was abandoned in the next year, but West Country interests in fur and fish could be served just as well by transient visits to the coasts, and the Plymouth Company went on sending out ships.

The Londoners had more capital and more luck. They wisely chose Christopher Newport to command their first expedition. He had a little fleet of three ships, the largest, the *Susan Constant*, only 100 tons, which sailed from London on December 19, 1606. No one there can have realised its significance – since Gilbert's day there had been so many forlorn-looking parties bound for the New World. A hundred and forty-four men set forth. Only 105 disembarked after five unpleasant months on the still-standard route via the Canaries and the West Indies; only 38 were alive at the end of 1607. The party included labourers and craftsmen but was top heavy with 'gentlemen'; over half of those whose names are known were recorded as such. It was drawn mainly from Suffolk and London. The phase of West Country dominance in transatlantic schemes was now ending.[60]

Chesapeake Bay was carefully investigated and a site for a fort picked at 'Jamestown', on the most impressive river they encountered. It was low-lying, marshy and malarial, but there was deep water close inshore for an anchorage and, important for purposes of defence, it was all but an island. Chesapeake Bay itself was to prove a most apt amphitheatre for exploration, trade and further colonisation. It was over 200 miles in extent from north to south and at its widest about 40 miles across. Great navigable rivers flowed into it north, west and south – the 'James', the 'York', the Rappahannock, the Potomac and the Susquehanna.

But Newport's exploring party found in the rapids on the James, at what is now Richmond, a formidable barrier to further progress, while in the week of its absence local Indians struck and only a startling burst of fire from the ship's guns saved the settlement from extinction. Before Newport sailed home with a cargo of timber, disappointment was settling in.

These early colonists themselves tell us what very little we know of the world they found. The Algonquian Indians, who had possessed the area for perhaps three hundred years, had not interfered greatly with the fecund woodland which they inhabited. Oaks and walnuts were the most common trees. The many squirrels were grey, not red like the English ones. Beavers and bears abounded. Wild turkeys ran in the woods and the rivers teemed with sturgeon. The summers were as hot as in Spain, though the winters at times might be bitter.

The red men shaved the right sides of their heads (with shells), leaving the hair on the left to grow long. While the 'better sort' had mantles of deerskin, lesser tribesmen wore grass or leaves. The women, some heavily tattoed, always wore skins about their waists and were 'very shamefast to be seene bare'. Both men and women had 'three great holes' in each ear. Some warriors wore in them small live snakes, or dead animals. A bird's wing, a stuffed hawk, a piece of copper, or even the dried hand of an enemy might provide a head-dress. Heads and shoulders were painted red, a protection against summer heat and winter cold. 'Many other formes of painting they use,' wrote Captain John Smith, 'but he is the most gallant that is the most monstrous to behold.'[61] Even when many such tribal peoples had been encountered in every part of the world, even when serious books had explained native customs with sympathy, there would still be a violent shock for the average Englishman when he confronted his first 'savages', fearsome in visage, uncouth in smell. Much brutality would begin from the simple facts of repulsion and terror.

And at this stage, informed sympathy was almost impossible. The English spoke of Indian 'towns' – they were in fact groups of twenty or thirty wooden buildings made 'like an oven with a litell hole to cum in at', in each of which six to twenty people would sleep. There were no metal tools, land was painfully cleared by scorching growing trees at their roots, beating up weeds with a crooked stick. Holes in the earth were made, also with a stick, and beans, corn and pumpkins were planted and tended by women and children. The men fished with weirs and with boats made from burnt-out trees; they hunted; and they fought wars, not usually for land or possessions, but to take women and children captive. Their code of war was elaborate, though their swords were wooden, their very sharp arrows were tipped with stone and their axes, till trade with the white man brought them the iron tomahawk, were headed only with stone, or with horn. They took scalps. Malefactors were 'broyled' to death. A hated enemy would be quartered and flayed alive, then burnt. Horrified whites rarely asked themselves whether tortures and hangings in Europe were any more humane; though, with one of those flashes of understanding which render briefly more cheerful the bleak perspective of early American race relations, one colonist who lived for a time with the red men did notice that their dancing at feasts was like a Derbyshire hornpipe and that when women and boys played football, 'they make ther Gooles as ours only they never fight nor pull one another doune'.[62]

Their code of hospitality made Europeans who came in peace welcome, at least formally. Each guest was offered 'a woman fresh painted red with *Pocones* and oyle, to be his bedfellow.'[63] They worshipped, it seemed, whatever they feared – fire, water, lightning, thunder or Newport's cannon. But their religion evaded European categories, and so did their political system. These Indians had a remarkable leader, Powhatan, born in the 1540s, who had inherited control of some half-dozen villages but had in time established suzerainty over an 'empire' of eight or nine thousand people. Perhaps the impact of the whites had helped him build up this power, red men drawing together against a common menace. Spaniards had first visited the Chesapeake as early as 1560. Powhatan himself may have been involved in the eradication of a Jesuit mission later sent to the area, and of the survivors of Ralegh's lost colony.[64] Certainly, he had long known about whites and their strange capacities and the challenge which these posed to his own people's well ordered and comfortable culture. His motives now, confronted with Jamestown, must have been almost as complex as those of his contemporary Tyrone. Could he ally with them, perhaps, against his enemies beyond the falls of the James? If he was not friendly with them would they themselves ally with these foes? It seems unlikely that he wished to annihilate them, and more probable that he hoped, somehow, to make them of use to his own power.

In any case, Powhatan could not fully control all the villages under him, while, exploring to the north, Smith encountered the gigantic Susquehannock Indians, with huge clubs to match their stature and words which came from them 'as a voyce in a vault'. Conveniently the red men were disunited as well as few. Various languages were spoken within a few score miles of Jamestown. Smith noted down words and phrases of that used by Powhatan's people. One sentence he recorded as 'Kekaten Pokahontas patiaquagh niugh tanks manotyens neer mowchik rawrenock audowgh': 'Bid Pokahontas bring hither two little Baskets and I will give her white Beads to make her a Chaine.'[65]

There is an irreducible ground of fact beneath the haunting story of Smith and Pocahontas, of the friendship of a little Indian princess for a short, stocky, deep-bearded Englishman, much embroidered though this has been. Even if it were exposed as essentially an invention, it would still be significant that the man so central in the early days of the Virginia colony was capable of devising an archetypal tale of affection across the races, embodying a wistful notion of the universality of unselfish feeling. In fact, romantic as Smith's account of his own life must seem, recent research suggests that it may be substantially true. He was born in 1580, son of a fairly prosperous Lincolnshire yeoman, and apprenticed at fifteen to a merchant. He escaped to become a soldier of fortune and fought against the Turks on Europe's eastern frontier. Pillagers found him groaning but still alive among the corpses on a battlefield, and sold him as a slave to the Crimean Tartars. As Smith recounted it, he beat out his master's brains with a threshing bat and rode off across the Steppe, reaching a Muscovite garrison which freed him of his irons. He travelled back across Europe and through Spain to North Africa, whence he sailed for a while on a pirate cruise under a French captain. Yet plunder never seems to have been his aim. He was not mercenary. Establishing colonies interested him, not the pursuit of gold mines. He handled the Indians whom he met forcefully, but he was never wantonly cruel and seems to have desired, like Ralegh before him, a kind of peaceful if unequal co-existence with savages whom he saw as having their good points. He was a man with qualities rare in his own or any other period – disinterested in his zest and zeal, a quick-witted observer, a good writer. He was also, clearly enough, a boy who never wholly grew up, and our imaginations sometimes insist on the truth of his stories, against our judgment, because they embody so many staples of adventure fiction. He aims at knight-errantry, quests for glory. Time and again, he effects hair'sbreadth escapes from death. Mysterious foreign ladies of high birth, of whom Pocahontas is not the first, give him succour. If Smith had not been real, somebody would have been certain to invent him.

Though he arrived in Virginia under arrest, on suspicion of plotting to usurp control, Smith became one of the colony's first Councillors when his name was produced with the others from a box which had remained sealed during the voyage. The President elected by the Councillors was Edward Maria Wingfield, a veteran of Irish wars, conscious of his own status as a gentleman, resentful of such a jumped-up commoner as Smith. The latter in turn sneered at gentleman-colonists who lost heart 'because they found not English Cities, nor such faire houses, nor at their owne wishes any of their accustomed dainties ... ' The first months were desperate. Sickness and famine took a fearsome toll. Another colonist wrote, 'There were never *Englishmen* left in a forreigne Countrey in such miserie as wee were ... ' There was constant fear of the natives. 'Wee watched every three nights, lying on the bare cold ground, what weather so ever came; warded all the next day: which brought our men to bee most feeble wretches. Our food was but a small Can of Barlie sod(den) in water, to five men a day. Our drinke, cold water taken out of the River; which was, at a floud, verie salt; at a low tide, full of slime and filth: which was the destruction of many of our men.' The colonists squabbled over such things as a spoonful of beer, a plateful of pease and pork, a roasted squirrel. When Wingfield was deposed by the Councillors, they accused him of atheism, because he had no bible with him, and also of conspiring with the Spaniards, but his defence of himself centred largely on food. 'Of chickins,' he insisted, 'I never did eat but one, and that in my sicknes. Master *Ratcliff* had before that time tasted of 4 or 5.' Be that as it may, Ratcliff succeeded him.[66]

Smith emerged as the cardinal leader, however, a resolute explorer and clever trader of trinkets for food with the Indians. In December he was captured on one of his trips and taken to see Powhatan, the first Englishman to set eyes on that potentate. He found him flanked by more than two hundred 'grim Courtiers', a tall, well-proportioned man with a 'sower looke', old, but very hardy-looking, with a young girl on each side of him. He feasted Smith in Indian style. Then two great stones were brought before him. Smith was seized, and his head put on the stones; he thought they would beat his brains out. But '*Pocahontas* the kings dearest daughter when no intreaty could prevaile, got his head in her armes, and laid her owne upon his to save him from death: whereat the Emperor was contented he should live ... ' Smith almost certainly misinterpreted this incident; it was very likely a rite of mock execution and salvation to signify Smith's adoption into Powhatan's tribe, with Pocahontas, aged about 12 or 13, acting the pre-arranged role of foster parent. However, some bond of friendship undoubtedly developed between the two. Since she often came down to Jamestown later with embassies sent by her father, and since food came with these embassies, Smith was able to describe her as 'next under God ... the instrument to preserve this Colonie from death, famine and utter confusion', and on a later occasion she slipped alone through the night to warn him that her father planned to surprise and kill him.[67]

Smith got back to the fort in January 1608 on the same day as Newport arrived with the first 'supply' from England. He was under pressure to come back with real gold this time – the 'ore' shipped home the year before had proved worthless. To Smith's disgust, there was soon 'no talke, no hope, no worke, but dig gold, wash gold, refine gold ... ' and Newport's sailors consumed all the food which they had brought for the colonists during their stay of fourteen weeks.[68]

The Councillors bickered; starvation impended; Smith explored up the Bay until, in September, as the only man left eligible, he was almost automatically chosen President. Newport, that most reliable of seamen, was back again later that month. His instructions were various. The merchants in London had still not made up their minds for what, if anything, Virginia was good, and, while they were still interested in minerals, Newport was to look for Ralegh's lost colony, explore the river towards the presumed Passage, and with the help of eight Polish and German experts, try to determine the prospects for industries making glass, pitch, tar and soap ashes. Also, Powhatan was to be persuaded to accept a copper crown, whereupon, in the eyes of legalistically-minded men in

London, he might be understood to have become King James's vassal. Against Smith's better judgment, a farce was transacted. Powhatan was presented with a basin and ewer, with an English bed and other 'civilised' furniture. Somehow they got him into the scarlet robe provided, but then weary persuasions failed to make him kneel. ' ... At last by leaning hard on his shoulders, he a little stooped, and three having the crowne in their hands put it on his head ... ' A salute of guns was then sent off in his honour, at which Powhatan started up in a 'horrible feare', till he was reassured that no murder was intended.[69]

Newport left behind him seventy new colonists, including the first two women to reach Jamestown, and also continuing grave problems. Powhatan had not been alchemically converted into a loyal subject of the Crown. Smith had to use strong-arm methods to persuade the reluctant Indians to trade corn. Death and departures had now left him the only Councillor and he was free to exercise his personality against his bugbears, colonists who wouldn't work, 'Gluttonous Loyterers'. He ordained that except for the sick 'he that will not worke shall not eate ... '[70] Thirty or forty acres were dug and planted with food crops, under the instruction of two captive natives. Then in April 1609 it was found that the casked corn on which the settlers relied for food until their own produce grew had gone rotten or had been eaten by rats. Smith copied the practice followed by Indians in the lean months. While the two captive Indians, now firm friends, brought in something by hunting, Smith reduced the food problem at the fort itself by sending parties off to live off the land and sea as best they could, by fishing, gathering shellfish or eating berries and acorns. He somehow brought the colony through its crisis with only a handful of deaths. This was enough to secure its survival. There were ambitious new plans for Virginia.

VI

In 1609 a new charter for the Virginia Company increased the bounds of the colony, to stretch 400 miles along the coast to north and south, and from sea to sea. The authority of a 'Treasurer' in England was to be matched in Virginia itself by that of a Lord Governor appointed for life and authorised to name all members of the local Council. While the merchant Smythe became Treasurer, the governorship went to a prominent statesman, Lord De La Warr. A craze for Virginia had begun. Books had been opened to enter subscriptions from the public and within three weeks an alarmed Spanish Ambassador was writing to Philip III that 'there is no poor, little man nor woman, who is not willing to subscribe something for this enterprise.' When the Charter received the royal seal in May, 56 City companies and over 650 individuals had subscribed, and hundreds of men, women and children had volunteered to go in person. Clergymen, physicians, soldiers and gentlemen, and above all craftsmen had been subjected to an advertising campaign which emphasised religious and patriotic sentiment as well as economic opportunity.[71]

The 'Adventure' of one's own person was regarded as equivalent to the standard £12. 10s. share taken out by those who stayed in England, and would entitle the settler to a dividend after seven years. Colonists, who were thus putting their labour into a common terminable joint stock with the capital of investors at home, would depend for their diet on a common store which their joint labours would replenish. Out of this also craftsmen would be paid, while land was cleared, fortifications erected, and so on. In 1616, the land already opened up would be divided. Individual shares were promised a return of 100 acres at least, and the common herd of cattle would be partitioned among the settlers.

The fleet of nine ships which sailed with 800 crewmen and colonists in June 1609 has been called 'the true beginning of one of the great folk movements of history.'[72] Reconnaissance was over. The hopeful settlers took with them the makings of a new society on English lines. Besides their axes and hatchets, spades and hoes, bellows and grindstones and other tools, they had locks and hinges for doors, kettles and frying pans, clothing and sheets, soap and candles. The ageing Sir George Somers was admiral, Newport went yet again as Vice-Admiral. De La Warr, coming later, sent an old soldier, Sir Thomas Gates, as his deputy.

The fleet was assaulted by a tempest. The *Sea Adventure*, which carried all the leaders, was separated from its fellows, and its passengers and crew pumped 'for three dayes and foure nights' together, without sleep or food. But the ship ran safely aground on rocks close to shore, and 150 people were taken off it. Luck had brought them to those uninhabited, heavily wooded islands discovered by one Juan Bermudez in the early sixteenth century but little visited since. For the moment, the 'Bermudas' became 'Somers' Islands'. During ten months they supported the castaways beautifully. Certain birds, called 'cahows' after their 'strange hollow and harsh howling', which had made earlier visitors think that the isles were haunted by devils, now proved as fat as partridges and very easy to catch. There were plenty of wild hogs and turtles, good to eat. Only five of the company died, a remarkable rate for the period, before it sailed on in pinnaces which had been built from the local cedar. They reached Jamestown towards the end of May 1610.[73]

Here, they confronted catastrophe once more. The rest of the fleet had arrived in the summer of 1609 to find eighty survivors at Jamestown. In the absence of written orders—lost with the *Sea Adventure*—Smith refused to yield up the Presidency. A period of chaos followed in which 'no man would acknowledge a superior'. Smith in disgust arranged his own passage home and George Percy, the brother of an Earl, took over as President. Appalling hardships resumed. Four hundred new colonists had arrived too late to help grow the provisions which they would need to survive. The Indians were not prepared to feed whites through yet another winter, and Powhatan massacred all but one of a party of thirty men sent to bargain for food. The animals brought to breed stock

F

were eaten, then rats and mice. According to Percy, corpses were dug from their graves and devoured. 'And amongst the rest, this was most lamentable, that one of our colony murdered his wife, ripped the child out of her womb and threw it into the river, and after chopped the mother in pieces and salted her for his food ... ' When the sleek, hog-fed castaways arrived from Bermuda, only just over sixty out of some five hundred people had survived and Jamestown, Gates noted, 'appeared rather as the ruins of some antient fortification, than that any people living might now inhabit it. The pallisadoes he found tourne downe, the portes open, the gates from the hinges, the church ruined and unfrequented ... '[74] Gates decided to abandon the colony, and he and the survivors were actually headed homewards down the Chesapeake when they met De La Warr, sailing in with 150 new settlers.

His Lordship restored some order, but he himself fell victim to disease, and by the time he left ten months later, epidemics, hunger and Indians had carried off 150 more whites. Mortality rates which shock us now were not enough in themselves to deter Jacobean Englishmen who were used to the visitations of plague and hunger in their own country. A fresh appeal for investment in 1610 raised £18,000 and two new consignments of settlers arrived in the following summer. In spite of all setbacks, the idea of a colony of settlement had now aroused the enthusiasm of enough people to make Virginia's future safe. Indeed, it seemed that Divine Providence had clearly displayed itself, watching over the fates of God's Englishmen. The Indians had been strangely kind in the first winter. Somers's landfall in the Bermudas had, surely, been miraculous. De La Warr's arrival just as Jamestown was being abandoned showed God's continued favour. The Virginia Company had been able to divulge, in their circular letter of March 1610, that the will of God and the interests of their nation marched neatly in step with their own material gain. 'The eyes of all Europe are looking upon our endeavours to spread the Gospell among the Heathen people of Virginia, to plant an English nation there, and to settle a trade in those parts, which may be peculiar to our nation, to the end we may thereby be secured from being eaten out of all profits of trade by our more industrious neighbours' [those busy Dutch!].[75] However, no missionary work had in fact been attempted, and commercial prospects were still uncertain.

The lesson of early colonisation was that a staple product must be found and reft from the soil or the forests so as to give a heavy continuous trade to the merchants at home who could supply the settlers with the clothing and tools which they needed. Virginia, goldless, silverless, lacked bait. Lieutenant Governor Gates and his deputy, Dale, both old soldiers, meanwhile held the colony together only by a draconian discipline. The death penalty was prescribed for petty insubordinations, and compulsory attendance at church thirteen times a week was part of a strict regime designed to keep the little settlement fed. A drum rolled at 6 a.m. to call all those not assigned to other duties out to labour in the common fields behind palisades designed to keep off the Indians. In the autumn of 1611, Dale moved with 300 settlers to form a second township at 'Henrico', so named after Henry, the King's eldest son. Trade up the Potomac River brought, in exchange for trinkets, hatchets and so on, not only meat and corn but also deerskins and furs which were shipped home to reward the merchants in London. Timber, however, was still the main freight. The search for exotic staples continued and Dale began the first of countless experiments in wine-making, using the native grape.

Dismayed by the sick De La Warr's return, many subscribers had flatly refused to pay up. But James's royal favour kept the enterprise going. For instance, he authorised the Company to raise money by lotteries, which became an important standby. Partly to attract new investors, the Company was reorganised so as to give them more say in its affairs. Powers were transferred from the Council to a 'Court and Assembly' of all the Adventurers which selected officers for both Company and Colony. This weekly assembly of a commercial enterprise was, not at all inappropriately, one seed from which would eventually stem the Constitution of the U.S.A.

Meanwhile, the Company was able to exploit Somers's rediscovery of the Bermudas which, introduced to the English public through that captivating story of shipwreck (Shakespeare employed it in his *Tempest*), had for the moment a stronger appeal to investors than Jamestown. The 'Somers Island Company' formed as a subsidiary was not legally separated from its parent till 1615, and even thereafter its affairs were so interwoven with those of the Virginia Company that the two courts sat virtually as one body. Smythe was governor of the Somers Island Company – as also of the East India Company, whose guns and anchors he lent to Bermuda – and profits from Asian trade were probably most important in helping the frail western colonies stay alive.

By 1615, Bermuda was thriving more than Virginia. It had over 600 colonists, and the Chesapeake Bay settlements would not outstrip those numbers for several years. Even more than plain John Smith's important role in Jamestown, it was a portent of New World democracy that the first governor of Bermuda, duly appointed, should be a ship's carpenter. After a phase of squabbles and cheerful anarchy – the Adventurers in London heard with dismay of 'the revells, and the perpetuall Christmas kept' on the island – Bermuda settled down to prosper.[76] Its main product was the new wonder-staple, tobacco.

All over the world, the taste for tobacco was growing. Indians in the Americas had, in divers regions, invented the pipe, the cigar and the cigarette. Portuguese sailors had picked up the craving and spread it along their trade routes, so that by now coastal Africans, for instance, were already greedy users. A Frenchman named Nicot had hailed the plant's medicinal properties in the 1560s and it would take centuries for science to recognise that tobacco was at best useless and at worst lethal. Meanwhile some three score maladies would be held, by one expert or other, to be at the mercy of this botanic avenger. It was extolled as emetic, as cure for coughs. But it was the weed's flavour, of course, which attracted most customers.

Ralegh's explorers had met in 'Virginia' natives smoking an acrid plant, *Nicotiana Rustica*. But it was the delicious herb, *Nicotiana Tabacum*, cultivated by Spaniards in the West Indies, which established the habit in England. Ralegh smoked. Others copied the great man. By the onset of the seventeenth century, some blamed tobacco for the London fog. In the pamphlet war which ensued, James I himself smote hard with a *Counterblaste to Tobacco* (1604) which contemporaries put down to his dislike for Ralegh. By 1615, however, it was reported, 'There is not so base a groom, that comes into an alehouse to call for his pot, but he must have his pipe of tobacco, for it is a commodity that is now as vendible in every tavern, inn, and alehouse, as either wine, ale or beer ... '[77]

About 1611, John Rolfe, a Jamestown colonist, somehow acquired seeds of *N. Tabacum* from the West Indies. In 1612 he exported a first crop to England. It was to be several years before the implications of his initiative manifested themselves, but meanwhile he did Virginia more service. He married, in 1614, the princess Pocahontas, who had been captured, held as a hostage, and meanwhile instructed in Christianity. The long letter in which he describes to the acting governor his 'mighty warre' with his own conscience over this decision shows how in Stuart Englishmen practical sense might co-exist with self-torturing piety. Rolfe was a Puritan. His bible seemed to warn him that God's displeasure had fallen on 'the Sonnes of Levie and Israel for marrienge of straunge wyves'. Yet, though the Indians were a 'cursed' generation, was it not clearly his duty to save the girl's soul? The believing husband would sanctify the unbelieving wife. For the sake of her soul, not for lust, then, he would marry her. And also for the good of the colony.[78] This singular trophy of proselytising success was excellent propaganda back home, and the Virginia Company showed its pleasure by granting Pocahontas an annual stipend; while Powhatan himself accepted the match, and several years of peace with the Indians followed. When in 1616 that hard man Dale came home, he brought the couple and their infant son Thomas, so as to give Virginia the revived public interest which it badly needed.

Rolfe, now secretary of the colony, wrote a brief account of it which was sent to eminent men. He praised its wide spaces, its climate, that fertile soil where the settlers grew all manner of vegetables (and also, showing already the characteristically English devotion to gardening, cultivated flowers 'for pleasure'). Tobacco had swiftly become Virginia's 'Principall commodytie' but the colony which Rolfe described was still military in its main character. There were three classes of people — 'officers', 'labourers' fed and clothed from the company store, and a smaller and more independent class of 'farmers' who had to provide a quota of maize to fill that store and also to give a month's service to the Company when they could best spare the time. There were now six little settlements of which Henrico, '90 odd myles' from the mouth of the James, was furthest inland. Altogether they numbered 351 souls – 205 officers and labourers, only 81 'farmers', and 65 women and children. Rolfe's call to the English to swell these numbers sounds the terrible peal of puritan pride. Though married to one, he valued the Indians lightly. 'There are no *greate nor strong Castles*, nor men lyke the *Sonnes of Anack* to hinder our quyete possession of that *Land*. Godes hand hath bene mighty in the preservation thereof hetherto. What need wee then to feare, but to *goe up at once* as a *peculier people* marked and chosen by the *finger* of God to *possess* it? for undoubtedly he is with us.'[79]

Meanwhile Pocahontas was making in London the stir expected of her. She was well received at court, and took part in a spectacular masque devised by Ben Jonson for Twelfth Night. But from John Smith's account of a visit to her, it seems clear that she was unhappy and confused, and when Smith later met one of her train of Indian followers, this man, who had been at court, flatly denied that he had seen England's king. After Smith convinced him that he had, his complaint was, 'You gave *Powhatan* a white Dog, which *Powhatan* fed as him-selfe; but your King gave me nothing, and I am better than your white dog.' Pocahontas, who had told Smith bitterly, 'your Countriemen will lie much', died, of what it isn't quite clear, at Gravesend, awaiting passage home. Her son by Rolfe survived to help populate Virginia.[80]

The colony now shifted to a new basis. When the seven-year term of the Company's joint stock expired, there was just land, and less of that than had been promised, to portion out among the investors who were offered merely 50 acres per share, with more to come later as settlement expanded – but this only if they paid another £12. 10s. to meet the cost of sending out a new governor and a commission of survey. The London Adventurers would soon be torn between three factions – that of Smythe, that of the Earl of Warwick, and that of Sir Edwin Sandys, a quarrelsome visionary who was able in 1619 to take over the Treasurership with momentary backing from Warwick's supporters. But Smythe and Sandys were at one over the so-called 'Great Charter' of 1618. The land policy which this promised was complex. Adventurers still in England and 'ancient' (pre-1616) planters got initial grants of 100 acres per share with more to follow when those were 'sufficiently peopled'. Men who had gone out as Company servants would get the same when their seven years of service expired. But post-1616 settlers would be under different rules. Those who went at the Company's expense would serve seven years as tenants keeping a half share of what they produced but without promise of land at the end. Men migrating at their own cost could claim land under what historians call the 'headright principle'. This would be a fundamental basis of English settlement in several North American colonies. A settler would get a quota of land (50 acres in the first place) for each person whom he brought to Virginia at his own cost. Since one's own head counted, anyone who could afford to cross the Atlantic could claim fifty acres, and the principle further encouraged planters to bring in the labour – at first, white indentured servants – which the colony needed.

Portentously, a 'generall Assemblie' was created, corresponding to that of the shareholders in London.[81] All male inhabitants could, at this stage, vote to elect its members, and it would meet annually to make laws, to advise the governor (who retained a veto) and to serve as a court of justice. One object was propagandist, to reassure prospective settlers who would have heard bad tales of bullying arbitrary governors on that far malarial shore that they would retain in the New World the fundamental rights which Englishmen liked to think that they possessed.

The first Assembly met in Jamestown in July 1619 in the choir of the church, and consisted of six councillors appointed by the governor and twenty-two 'burgesses' representing eleven districts. In six days it produced a code of laws. Everyone must grow food crops. Everyone must go to church on Sunday. In the same year, a new governor went to Bermuda with instructions to call an Assembly there, 'because every man will more willingly obey laws to which he hath yeilded his consent.'[82] This duly met in 1620. Precedents had been set which would be followed in every English colony in the New World.

James I, who disliked Sandys, refused to permit his re-election as Treasurer in 1620, but he remained the guiding spirit as an attempt was made to drive Virginia forward into prosperity. Tobacco was not thought sufficient. The search for staples to supersede it involved rash expenditure on attempts to set up an iron industry and the emission of a stream of expert craftsmen who were supposed to help build up trades in naval stores, guns, dyes, timber, salt, glass and shipbuilding. Besides wine, silk and indigo were essayed. And there was a little torrent of emigration.

In three years 3,570 people were sent out. Scores of pauper children were swept off the London streets and shipped out to serve as apprentices. A batch of convicts was sent. To meet the shortage of women, parties of girls were consigned; a colonist could take one to wife in return for 120 lb. of tobacco. In the summer of 1620, the Company began the traffic in indentured servants which would last for a century and a half. A colonist paid a lump sum to acquire an immigrant's labour for an agreed number of years.[83] The servant who signed indentures wrote away his own freedom. The English had entered a new commerce in human flesh.

Fresh mouths came out so fast that Virginia could not feed them. Jamestown was still swampy. The death rate remained stupendous. A census in 1624 showed only 1,095 people in the colony—yet over 7,500 had come out since 1607, about 4,000 since 1618 alone. And only 347 deaths could be put down to the Indian massacre which shocked the settlers in March 1622.[84]

As the colony grew and encroached on lands where the Indians hunted and gathered berries, fresh friction was inevitable. It is a (convenient) myth that North American Indians were people genetically too frail to fight back against white intrusion; in fact, their tenacity, if tragic, was remarkable. Powhatan's brother Opechancanough had succeeded him as 'emperor' in 1618. As Indian complaints went unheeded, he united the tribes for a major assault such as Powhatan had never tried, or perhaps had never been able to muster. The colonists had become careless and overconfident. On Good Friday, the red men who came to trade meat and furs as usual suddenly turned on the whites, slaying them in their homes or where they worked in the fields. Perhaps a fourth of the colony were wiped out. But those who survived had an ideal excuse for the seizure of more land. One exulted, 'Our hands which before were tied with gentlenesse and faire usage, are now set at liberty by the treacherous violence of the Savages ... So that we, who hitherto have had possession of no more ground then their waste ... may now by right of Warre, and law of Nations, invade the country ... Now their cleared grounds in all their villages (which are situate in the fruitfullest places of the land) shall be inhabited by us, whereas heretofore the grubbing of woods was the greatest labour.' The Company's council in London urged 'perpetual war' against the Indians, without mercy, sparing only 'the younger people of both sexes, whose bodies may by labour and service become profitable.' But of course the men on the spot had begun their campaign of attempted genocide without the need for any such promptings. They boasted in letters home of the treachery which they employed – 'Stratagems were ever allowed against all enemies, but with these neither fayre Warr nor good quarter is ever to be held ... '[85] Proportionately the Indians lost more than an eye for an eye. After a two-year fury of burning villages, killings, destruction of crops, only shreds of Powhatan's former 'empire' were left to regroup themselves. By then, the colony's rudimentary economy was restored. Tobacco was the mainstay, and would remain so. It was a crop which ate acres and asked for more. Bermuda, with little more than twenty square miles of land, could not satisfy that plant's appetite, nor those of the London smokers. Now Virginia's destiny lay with N. Tabacum rather than in the hands of the God of the Israelites.

James I had not scrupled to profit from the crop which he detested. It could, and can, be grown in England itself. In 1619 James's Lord High Treasurer made a deal with the Virginia and Bermuda Companies whereby all planting in England was forbidden, in return for their agreement to pay a far higher customs duty than their charters laid down. Both companies were now controlled by the Sandys faction. In 1622, they secured from the King a monopoly of tobacco importation in return for a revenue from the sales, but the details of the agreement did not please Sandys' enemies. The Warwick and Smythe factions combined against him. The rows in the Companies' courts became a public scandal. Meanwhile, Sandys' ambitious schemes for industries in Virginia bore no results and colonists were protesting against mismanagement from London. Sandys' opponents demanded, and got, a Privy Council inquiry.

The Company, now bankrupt, stood no chance of surviving it. In May 1624 its charter was declared vacated. The Crown itself took over. Virginia became Britain's first royal colony. A weed, rampant, might well have served for its coat of arms.

VII

A suitable emblem further north would have been a codfish, couchant. Off the shores of the territories which became 'New England' and 'Nova Scotia', and off the ragged coastline of Newfoundland, there were 'banks', submerged plateaux where the rich growth of marine life lured immense numbers of fish into shallow waters. Plankton attracted the cod and the cod drew in mariners from Europe. The Spanish and Portuguese had fallen behind leaving the English and French to compete. The French, who had plenty of cheap solar salt in their own country, practised 'wet fishing', salting the cod as soon as they caught it and rushing it back to the metropolitan market. The English were short of salt at home. Theirs was a 'dry fishery'. Cod were exposed on American shores to sun and wind which rendered them into a product much to the taste of those Mediterranean Catholics whose religion insisted on fish on Fridays. Durable lodges and platforms and stages had to be erected on land, and favoured spots were re-occupied annually by West Country fishermen. The French were soon copying English techniques and selecting their own summer nests on the shores.

Newfoundland's many bays made it a fine base despite the ice which locked it in during winter and the fogs which haunted it all year round. Inland, it was rugged and uninviting. White men rarely if ever strayed more than a few miles from the coast, and no European, it seems, crossed the island from east to west till the nineteenth century. The interior was left to the aborigines, Beothuk Indians, who visited the bays in summer, to catch the flightless great auks which, like themselves, would become extinct long before our own day.

By 1610, about two hundred ships crossed from England each year. An early Act of the reign of James I recognised the importance of Newfoundland fisheries as a 'nursery' for the Royal Navy, for which they were said to supply most of the crews in wartime. Fishermen came when the harbours were ice free in May and were usually gone by mid-September. Besides fish, they lived on hard biscuits and salt beef from England. Scurvy was commonplace, drunkenness general, and fires were frequent. However, there was rough equality. The West Countrymen worked on shares, with merchants, ship masters and crews bearing losses or taking profits proportionately. But their hold on the industry was now challenged by the great men of London and their allies in other major ports. 'In the west-country', Gillian Cell points out, 'a small fishing ship could be hired for as little as £16 a month; a London sack might cost as much as £220 a month. The first might be freighted by a small merchant who needed to see a modest return on his investment within six months; the second by a speculator who could afford to wait a year or two for his very substantial profits.'[86]

In 1610, a settlement was planted in Newfoundland by a powerful London–

Bristol consortium which had obtained a royal charter for colonisation. Alderman John Guy of Bristol led two score men. Their beer froze in the winter. The West Country fishers, of course, were at odds with them. Nevertheless, there were takers when the Newfoundland Company, left short of money by their struggle and unable to get the revisions to their charter which would have given them control of the fishery, set about raising new capital by selling large grants of land. A Welsh knight, Sir William Vaughan of Lllangyndeyrn, depressed by the barrenness of his native soil and moved by envy of Devonshire enterprise, decided that Newfoundland had been 'reserved by God for us Britons' (the Welsh), got land from the Company and sent out in 1617 a party of Welsh men and women who throve so badly that their first governor packed all but six of them off home. Nevertheless, 'Cambriol', as the patriot Vaughan named it, may have maintained a ghostly existence into the 1620s.[87] It was joined by some other spectral settlements, making half a dozen in all. The most significant, founded by George Calvert, first Lord Baltimore, who bought land from Vaughan in 1620, has, as will be mentioned later, a special place in the story of Stuart empire-making. But none amounted to more than a handful of folk grouped round a bleak harbour, and all soon faded away, leaving only specks of permanent settlement.

Meanwhile, an English sailor named Henry Hudson had written his name bold on the map of North America. Setting out for the Muscovy Company to sail to China over the North Pole, in accordance with a theory of his own that the sea would grow warmer in very high latitudes, he was of course blocked by ice. He tried again for the same backers in 1608, this time aiming at a North East Passage, but could not get beyond Novaya Zemlya. Then the Dutch East India Company bought his services. His mixed Dutch and English crew did not like their north-eastern course and forced their captain to sail west instead. Hence he entered what is now New York harbour and explored north up the great river which he found there. On his return, he proposed a further north-western voyage to the Dutch EIC, but the English authorities would not now let him voyage 'to the detriment of his own country'.[88] A consortium, including the ubiquitous Sir Thomas Smythe, rose up to back new exploration in England's interest. Hudson set off in the *Discovery* in the spring of 1610 and entered the vast Bay which now bears his name. This seemed to be the Passage at last. Hudson wintered there and next year proposed to sail further. His crew quarrelled with him and left him behind in a little boat. No more was heard of Hudson, but the mutineers were not punished after they came home with such exciting news. A fresh expedition under Captain Button found that the Bay, alas, had a western shore, but even so explorations continued yearly.

The less visionary Dutch now claimed, on the basis of Hudson's voyage for them, the whole coastline from Cape Cod to Delaware Bay. A Dutch West India Company, set up in 1621, sent out a colony three years later to 'New Netherland' on the 'Hudson' River. In 1626 Manhattan Island was bought from

Indians for sixty guilders' worth of trade goods and 'New Amsterdam' was established there. But commerce, not settlement, was the Dutch proclivity. Farming was neglected while quick profits were sought from furs.

The New World fur trade had achieved much importance even before the end of the sixteenth century. The main emphasis was on beaver. Craftsmen developing techniques of making hats out of felt were able, with that animal's unwilling help, to create a vogue which lasted in Europe for generations and shaped the history of North America. When the outer layers of guard hair on the beaver's pelt were discarded the soft downy fur underneath was full of tiny barbs which helped the felt to mat securely and gave a lustrous finish. It made, like tobacco, a light cargo commanding high prices, which could well support the heavy overhead costs involved in long sea voyages. And as with tobacco the market was elastic, as more and more men could be found to purchase what had been an exclusive commodity. The forests of North America sheltered perhaps ten million beaver. This charming, ingenious creature was easy to find. He travelled over land very slowly and migrated as little as might be. He built his elaborate dams and lodges on lakes and streams in the deciduous forests where his diet was found. Europe was running out of beaver, and North American fur was in any case better. The Indians had been catching a few and wearing their skins. French traders active on what are now Canadian coasts in the late sixteenth century had been able to trade for them metal tools and weapons which made the beast's capture quite easy. The beaver's house had resisted spears and stone arrows, but now the metal hatchet could pierce it, the dam could be cut, the water run off, the beaver's underground burrows exposed in the banks.

Planters had no use for Indians, since native men disliked agricultural work. But where the fur trade flourished, the accumulating effect of native dependence on European trade goods was compensated for by the white man's dependence in turn on Indian hunters and on the preservation of the beaver's (and natives') woodland habitat. The vaunted French superior skill in race relations really stems in great part from this simple fact of life. The French were already, by the end of the sixteenth century, closely allied with Algonquian Indians in the fur trade, and so also with the Hurons who supplied their partners with corn. This in turn implied that the French were at war with the famous Iroquois of the 'Five Nations'. It also meant that the colonies which they established would be strictly ancillary to the fur trade and that their growth would be limited and slow.

Monopoly was another natural outcome. The Indians realised that if they waited till several competing ships showed up, they could get more goods for each beaver. Meanwhile, Henri IV of France wanted a great American colony. The monopoly of the fur trade was therefore granted to a company in return for a commitment to take out settlers. In 1604 Samuel Champlain, an ex-soldier who had become Henri's geographer-royal, went out under the Sieur de Monts, a Huguenot nobleman. Over a hundred colonists travelled with them, and Port Royal, on the Bay of Fundy, in the region which the French called 'Acadie', was founded as a factory in 1605. It proved impossible to enforce a monopoly from there. Champlain saw the possibilities of the place where the great St Lawrence River narrowed so that a cannon could block the passage. In 1608 he and de Monts began to settle the site of Quebec, one of the best natural military strong-points in the world, on the only great river system which led from the heart of North America to the Atlantic seaboard. To south and west of Quebec lay the Great Lakes in an area teeming with beaver; beyond them the plains of what is now the Midwest and the vast Mississippi river.

The French at Quebec were at once embroiled with the Iroquois, who were soon able to get guns from the Dutch on the Hudson. The French traders, pre-pared to explore immensely and to reside with the Indians who procured the furs, were far more forward than any European rivals, and unlike the Dutch and English they took conversion seriously. Champlain envisaged a Canada populated by a mixed race of Christians. The Jesuits began missionary work in 1611, the Recollect fathers followed soon afterwards. Heavy settlement, driving the tribes west, would militate against the aim of conversion. Still more impor-tant, 'French commerce, in Canada being only the fur trade, was incompatible with colonisation, because every colonist was a charge on the profits of the trade and also a potential free trader.'[89] The royal aim of settlement was neglected. There was no ploughing at Quebec until 1628.

Despite the French presence in 'Acadie', a Scottish courtier and poet, Sir William Alexander, was granted by James I in 1621 a vast area of what is now maritime Canada, which he endowed with the name 'Nova Scotia'. His first efforts, from 1622, produced nothing but a little unoriginal exploration of the coastline, but he persevered and in 1624 published *Encouragement to Colonies*, scattering the map of his New Scotland with familiar place names, including a River Tweed (the St Croix River) to divide it from New England. James I, in his chronic financial difficulties, had long since turned to the sale of peerages – English, Scottish and Irish – and had invented the new hereditary title of baronet; by this time it usually cost only a couple of pounds sterling. Now he gave Alexander permission to confer it on any gentleman who would furnish six settlers and 1,000 Scottish marks towards the proposed New World colony. So that these men could get formal possession of 'earth and stone' from their new estates, part of the Castle Rock in Edinburgh was designated Nova Scotian territory. This device created numerous new baronets, but did not in fact provide settlers; a serious start on Alexander's scheme could not be made without merchant backing.[90]

One of the aims was to establish a buffer 'New Scotland' between 'New France' and 'New England'. The latter invented name was already beginning to mean something. The namer had been Captain John Smith, and he had also provided much of the impetus for its first colonisation.

VIII

In 1614, some merchants sent Smith out whaling. He explored the coastline from Maine down to and round Cape Cod and pronounced what became Massachusetts a 'Paradise'. On his return he laid plans for colonisation before Sir Ferdinando Gorges of the Plymouth Company which had been chartered in 1606 and which could still claim the area. Gorges and his associates designated Smith 'Admiral of New England', and sent him off in 1615 with the nucleus of a settlement. He fell foul of French pirates off the Azores. But Smith retained all his zest and became till his death in 1631 primarily a professional writer propagandising for the New World. His *Description of New England* (1616) had much influence, notably on the so-called 'Pilgrim Fathers'.

This body of ordinary, remarkable men have a special status not because they were the first successful English colonists in North America — they were not even the first comers in New England — but because it has seemed proper that they should have been. They have appeared a much more suitable seed for a great democratic nation obsessed with its own destiny than the idle, quarrelsome squirelings of Jamestown. And religion was, without question, their main driving force. They belonged to the school of thought labelled 'Brownist' and persecuted in England during the 1590s as dangerously subversive. Brownists held that each congregation should organise itself under a mutual covenant to 'forsake & dame all ungodliness and wicked felloship', and should select its own pastor and officers. Brownist congregations remained independent of each other and found no warrant in the Bible for any hierarchical church structure. There had already been one wholly abortive attempt by the Government, before the end of the sixteenth century, to settle some of these gently troublesome souls on the Magdalen Islands in the gaping mouth of the St Lawrence River, where the French were already whaling, sealing, fishing and trading in furs.[91]

Meanwhile a Brownist congregation had been established at Scrooby, a village in northern Nottinghamshire, under the lead of the manor's bailiff, one William Brewster. The Reverend John Robinson was their beloved minister. Imprisonments and fines followed. They emigrated to tolerant Holland and settled down in Leyden. As William Bradford, an orphan boy whom Brewster had virtually adopted as his son, would put it in his famous account of their lives, they were 'not aquainted with trade nor traffique' but had 'only been used to a plaine countrie life, and the inocente trade of husbandrey.' But bustling mercantile Holland opened their eyes and — it proved to be crucial — their leaders learnt how to deal with businessmen. In Leyden they had their own permanent place of worship by 1611. They worked in various crafts and in time many became citizens. But their lives were mostly impoverished and hard. While some grew old, children fell into Dutch ways, a grief to their very English parents, who 'saw their posteritie would be in danger to degenerate and be corrupted'.[92] And the truce between Dutchmen and Spaniards clearly would not last—indeed, fresh war did break out in 1621. The decision which some took to go to the New World was, as Perry Miller puts it, 'a shrewd forecast, a plan to get out while the getting was good ... '[93]

They made terms with a very worldly Londoner named Thomas Weston who combined an ironmonger's business with smuggling cloth to the Netherlands, and who led a group of merchants, 'John Pierce and Associates', which had acquired a patent for land in Virginia. Yet that Anglican colony would hardly suit these separatists. Weston came up with a fresh plan, that they should get a grant from the 'Council for New England' which Gorges was now organising as a successor to the moribund Plymouth Company. But Gorges's Council did not get its patent till 1621. Those Pilgrims who had sold their property could not wait. They began their journey with only the old 'Pierce' patent entitling them to settle in Virginia. In this case, there was no charter linking the New World colony with London, though the Pilgrims' deal with Weston bound them in what can be defined as an unincorporated joint-stock organisation, with capital and profits to be divided between merchants and planters. What the merchants imagined was that the colonists would labour on their behalf in America. What the Pilgrims wanted, and quite soon would get, was a situation where every man would work his own land to feed himself and his family. Disagreement boiled up when the Leyden party arrived in England to join the other colonists whom Weston had recruited. Despite it, the *Mayflower* sailed on its famous voyage on September 6, 1620.

The chunky, sluggish ship of only 180 tons left with inadequate provisions, crowded with 102 passengers and 30 or more seamen. There was sickness, and there were storms, but in a voyage of over nine weeks, only three crewmen and one passenger died. Bradford was pleased to note the death of one sailor, 'a proud and very profane yonge man' who mocked the passengers in their sickness and told them that he hoped to help 'cast halfe of them over board before they came to their jurneys end, and to make mery with what they had ... ' For all his lusty physique, he was smitten himself, the first to be dropped into the sea. 'Thus his curses light on his owne head; and it was an astonishmente to all his fellows, for they noted it to be the just hand of God upon him.'[94]

But less than half the passengers were in fact self-styled 'saints' from Leyden — sixteen men, nine women and sixteen children. Only five were Scrooby people: William Brewster, his wife, their boys named Wrestling and Love (daughters Patience and Fear would come later) and the redoubtable Bradford himself. The most prominent of the majority of non-Brownist 'strangers' was Myles Standish, a middle-aged soldier, short in stature, fiery and red-haired — 'Captaine Shrimpe' one enemy would dub him, and he would command the colony's little army. Most of the 'strangers' came from London and the southeast and were conforming Anglicans.[95] The first problem of the Leyden contingent would be to impose their authority on those who were not of them.

Their aim to settle on the Hudson River (still within bounds of the Virginia patent which they carried with them) was thwarted by shoals and breakers as they tried to round Cape Cod. So they made landfall there on November 11. The problem of self-government had to be faced at once. Within the Virginia Company's allotted area they would have come under the Jamestown governor. As it was, they had no legal status whatever. Some of the 'strangers', according to Bradford, began to mutter that 'when they came a shore they would use their owne libertie; for none had power to command them ... ' But the Pilgrims had a model to hand, in the covenants by which separatist congregations were founded. Still on shipboard, forty-one adult men among the colonists signed the famous 'Mayflower Compact':

> We whose names are under-writen, the loyall subjects of our dread soveraigne Lord, King James ... doe by these presents solemnly and mutualy in the presence of God, and one of another, covenant and combine our selves togeather into a civill body politick, for our better ordering and preservation and furtherance of the ends aforesaid; and by vertue hearof to enacte, constitute, and frame such just and equall lawes, ordinances, acts, constitutions and offices, from time to time, as shall be thought most meete and convenient for the generall good of the Colonie, unto which we promise all due submission and obedience.[96]

There were eighteen indentured servants and five hired men aboard, and the prime object of this covenant was to show them their place, to make it clear that they would have to keep it, and to maintain hierarchy as Jacobean English people valued it. But to further this purpose, it would seem, several servants were invited to sign, and did so, and the Compact deserves more credence as a first document of American democracy than a cautious and cynical generation of historians have recently been prepared to give it. The main question is not, what was it meant to do? but, what was it? The medium in the end would be the message. The transposition of the idea of a compact (or in a phrase famous later, 'social contract') from the separatist Church to civil government was a response to the bleak and unwanted exigencies of American pioneering. Since it sprang from the actuality faced by a little group of diverse Englishmen all alone in a wild place, something much like it would happen again, several times in the next few decades, as settlements were founded outwith the scope of traditional authority. Only twelve of the *Mayflower* signatories could even claim the title of 'Mister', most being mere 'Goodmen', and none of these 'Misters' had much pretension to rank.[97]

The compacted settlers now chose Mr John Carver to be their first governor; but their own landfall must have struck all present as far more momentous than this precocious political act. They fell on their knees and praised God who had brought them again at last to the 'firme and stable earth, their proper elemente.' Yet the first sight of the new land, as Bradford would movingly describe it, was in itself painful. ' ... What could they see but a hidious and desolate wildernes, full of wild beasts and willd men? ... If they looked behind them, there was the mighty ocean which they had passed, and was now as a maine barr and goulfe to seperate them from all the civill parts of the world.' They had despised civil worldliness, now they faced the consequences, not even sure, having left Weston so angry, that they would get any succour from home. 'What could now sustaine them but the spirite of God and his grace? May not and ought not the children of these fathers rightly say: *Our faithers were English-men which came over this great ocean, and were ready to perish in this wilderness; but they cried unto the Lord, and he heard their voyce* ... '[98] Few men have been less 'imperialist' in temper than these, but Bradford struck up in passing a theme which would be useful to later builders of empire, who could persuade themselves and others that shivering grateful piety stood at the fount of all.

After a month of exploration, they settled upon a harbour which Smith had named 'Plymouth'. It was large, well sheltered, ringed with stately woods. They pushed up cottages of wattle and daub and thatched them, laying out a village on a field where Indians had previously grown corn, with a single street running up from the harbour. Here the privations of sea-voyaging took their toll as frost, rains and winds assailed them. Six died in December, eight in January, seventeen in February, and by the end of March of more than a hundred people scarcely fifty still lived. More than half the heads of households died, but the quality of these good people is suggested by the fact that just three out of twenty children perished.[99] At the worst moment there were only half a dozen strong enough to work and care for the others. Indians had been glimpsed, and were feared. Then a brave strode into 'new Plymouth' and, amazingly, spoke English, which he had learned, he said, from fishermen up the Maine coast. What he told them made clear why so few red men had been sighted; the local tribe had been wiped out a few years before by a plague.

Not long after this, Massasoit, the great 'sachem' of the Wampanoag Indians of the region, appeared in the colony and with Governor Carver concluded a treaty which, often renewed and never seriously jeopardised, would endure till the chief himself died more than forty years later. Pilgrims and Wampanoags pledged themselves to support each other in war. Through Massasoit, the settlers met Squanto, an Indian who had seen even more of the world than themselves. Carried to England by Captain Weymouth in 1605, he had returned in 1614 with John Smith, but had then been seized and then sold into slavery by a subordinate while Smith himself was off exploring. Sent to Spain, he had escaped, arrived in London and spent several years there, returning only in 1619 with another explorer, Captain Dermer, to find all his people dead or dispersed by the plague. He preferred the company of the English to that of Massasoit's people and seemed to Bradford 'a speciall instrument sent of God' to help the Pilgrims.[100] He taught them how to plant maize and where to fish.

In April 1621 Governor Carver came from the fields very sick one hot day, lay down, and soon died. William Bradford was chosen to succeed him. He remained governor, with few intermissions, till his death in 1657. The orphan from Scrooby, 'fustian maker' in Leyden, became the sagacious father of his people, respected by them and by outsiders alike. The Pilgrims soon found that what became Boston Harbour would have been a better place to settle than the sparse area which they had selected. But they cared for sufficiency rather than wealth. Harvest was celebrated with Massasoit and scores of his braves in October 1621. On this first Thanksgiving Day, there were venison, duck, goose, clams and eels, white bread and corn bread, green vegetables, wild plums and dried berries, all washed down with wine made from wild grapes. Then they went on short winter rations again. In November a small ship came with thirty-five new settlers, some of them 'saints' from Leyden, and with a chideful letter from Weston. The merchants were impatient for profits. 'A quarter of the time you spente in discoursing, arguing, and consulting, would have done much more ... ' But there was also the news that their settlement had been legalised, under a grant from the Council for New England. The colonists loaded the ship with timber and beaver and otter pelts worth, according to Bradford, nearly half what the merchants had advanced. It fell to a French pirate on the way home.[101]

Friction with the Narragansett Indians to the west—a dangerous people whose ambition had made Massasoit welcome the Pilgrims as allies—led Bradford to set Plymouth Colony on a militant basis. A strong pale was built round the village, and action stations allotted. When Standish treacherously massacred some unfriendly Indians, the revered pastor Robinson, still in Leyden, stiffly denounced this white barbarity. Meanwhile, the Pilgrims permitted no church but their own. An Anglican minister arrived. He was admitted to their congregation and even to their pulpit, but was found to be baptising children privately with Anglican rites, under the obnoxious sign of the Cross, and like certain other malcontents, he was expelled. This scandal confirmed the disillusionment of most of the colony's merchant backers. They pulled out, and in 1627 the colonists made a new deal with a few of the Londoners who still saw promise in furs. These men agreed to pay off the original London adventurers. A partnership joining Bradford with seven associates in New Plymouth and four in England took on responsibility for the colonists' debts, which they proposed to meet by monopolising the fur trade. Meanwhile, the Pilgrims divided the colony which they had, in effect, bought on mortgage. Each family got 20 acres for each of its members, plus an extra share for every £10 which it had invested in the joint stock. Each share carried with it one-sixth of a cow and one-third of a goat.

When some planters earlier had demanded immediate division of the land, Deacon Cushman had lectured them on the 'Dangers of Self Love'. Who, he had asked, had 'brought this particularization into the world. Did not Satan, who was not content to keep that equall state with his fellows, but would set his throne above the stars?' This egalitarian-seeming colony of subversives had attracted such rumours in England that Bradford had had to write home in 1623 to reassure shareholders that women and children did not, in fact, have the vote. All male freemen (most adult males) could vote in the annual meetings of the General Court, and on other occasions when Bradford summoned them, but essentially he ruled as a benign autocrat, with the help of five, later seven, assistants.[102]

Plymouth, reinforced several times in the 1620s, grew to 300 people by 1630, 579 by 1637. A second street crossed the original one at right angles. Four cannon stood at the intersection, commanding all approaches. The houses were made of planks now, standing with gardens behind them, neat to the eye. The hill overlooking the village carried a wooden fort, with six cannon on the roof, where a sentry paced day and night. It served as arsenal, gaol, court of justice, town hall and church. Twice on Sunday and early on Thursday evening ('Lecture Day') the Saints and their families assembled at the beat of a drum, each man with a musket, at the foot of Fort Hill, then marched up three abreast for worship. 'Behind', a Dutch visitor reported, 'comes the Governour, in a long robe. Beside him, on the right hand, comes the preacher, with his cloak on, and on the left hand, the Captain, with his sidearms and cloak on, and with a small cane in his hand.'[103] It is a vignette of a society orderly, militant, ceremonial, yet small and intimate. Worse ways of life have been seen, though many less frugal.

Bradford and his trading associates learnt from the Dutch in New Amsterdam how avid the Indians were for *wampumpeag*, white and purple beads. With 'wampum' for currency, the Pilgrims were able for several years practically to monopolise the commerce in beaver skins from large regions. They disposed of a troublesome competitor close to home, one Thomas Morton, who had taken over a settlement at what is now Quincy, Mass. A gentleman-lawyer, with Clifford's Inn education, he gleefully shocked the Pilgrims with views of right behaviour quite the reverse of their own. He rechristened his settlement 'Merry Mount', and celebrated this with an apt festival. A gross maypole was erected. A barrel of beer was brewed and everyone round invited, including the Indians. Morton's servants danced round the pole with red-skinned laughing girls singing a lay composed by their master:

> Drinke and be merry, merry, merry boyes;
> Let all your delight be in Hymen's joys ...
> Make green garlons, bring bottles out,
> And fill sweet nectar freely about ...
> Lasses in beaver coats, come away,
> Ye shall be welcome to us night and day.

'As if', Bradford sourly remarked, 'they had anew revived and celebrated the feasts of the Roman Goddes Flora, or the beasly practieses of the madd Bacchinalians.' (Like Morton, he knew his classics.) Morton was ready to enlist any

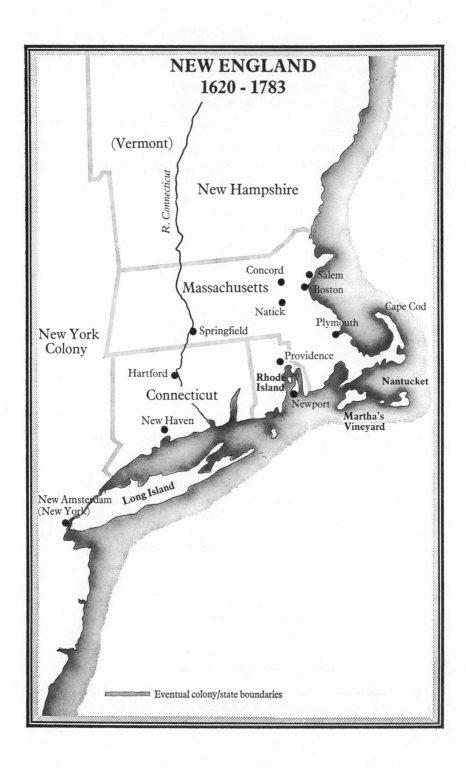

NEW ENGLAND
1620 - 1783

(Vermont)

New Hampshire

R. Connecticut

New York
Colony

Massachusetts

Concord

Salem
Boston

Cape Cod

Natick

Plymouth

Springfield

Providence

Hartford

**Rhode
Island**

Nantucket

Connecticut

Newport

New Haven

**Martha's
Vineyard**

New Amsterdam
(New York)

Long Island

Eventual colony/state boundaries

malcontent from another plantation, 'how vile soever', and to trade guns to the Indians so they could shoot beaver for him. The peppery Standish moved in to deal with this shrewd commercial rival, captured him in a bloodless and farcical little affray, and pleaded before Bradford and his council for the rogue's execution. Instead, the Pilgrims shipped him off to England; he was soon back and causing trouble again.[104]

Morton was only one of the opportunists from England who tried his hand in the Massachusetts area. 'New England', defined as the vast area between the 40th and 48th parallels, was now theoretically under the sole ownership of Gorges and his Council. Gorges's schemes had little purchase on reality. At first there were no merchants at all in his Council of forty, though some had to be admitted later as the need for their wealth became obvious. Though an elderly man, Gorges imagined himself as feudal overlord in America with a colonial *noblesse* beneath him. But in fact the Council could not even enforce its fishing monopoly. On paper Gorges himself and Captain John Mason acquired a grant to Maine in 1622; on paper they divided it in 1629. In 1623 Gorges did send his son Robert with a large expedition to make a principality for him. They settled at Wessagusset in Boston Bay but soon tired of the struggle and dispersed. Yet if Gorges's antique visions were as impractical as Gilbert's had been before him, there were reasons now attracting hard-headed men to the idea of permanent settlements in New England. Colonies might cut costs and increase profits in the fishing and fur trades. Weston and his fellows had seen that colonists might feed themselves and meanwhile, all year round, catch cod, gather beaver, hew lumber, and ship cargoes back to England. Though the Pilgrims disappointed their sponsors, the pattern, with variations, was attempted elsewhere. And in every case the outcome was similar — baulked of quick profits, the merchants involved lost interest. By the late 1620s there were abandoned colonies, stray settlers left to fend for themselves in small groups, at several points on the New England coast.

What was needed to make 'New England' a thriving reality was just a fraction of the sustained effort and capital which had been put, over many years now, into the East India trade. In its whole career, the Virginia Company had raised only some £200,000. The Pilgrims' backing and debts were in scant hundreds and thousands. Yet by 1632 the East India Company would have found £2,887,000. The City of London's commercial élite was not ready to make the long term, fixed capital expenditures which were needed to sustain North American plantations. But sending big ships out for spices, despite the great risks, retained its appeal.[105]

IX

The Dutch, sending fleet after fleet East from the mid-1590s onwards, at first had a good reception from native rulers almost everywhere in South-East Asia, who looked to them for support against the Portuguese. The Dutch East India Company (VOC) was founded in 1602 and before the end of the decade had won the upper hand in the Moluccas, that scatter of islands which gave the world its cloves, mace and nutmegs. They brought a new ruthlessness with them. The Portuguese had spread the cultivation of cloves; the Dutch, in pursuit of high monopoly prices, cut trees down.

The Portuguese had never been able to stem the stream of eastern goods which reached the Mediterranean overland through the Levant. But the English Levant traders took alarm at the Dutch threat to their supplies of spices, and their money helped make the EIC a powerful consortium. A longstanding role was foreshadowed as James I soon began to turn to the Company for loans. Royal co-operation was essential. Besides providing the monopoly of English Eastern trade which was essential when risks were so great and costs were so high, the king provided continual exemption from laws which restricted the export of bullion and was called on for support when international complications arose. He showed his esteem for the EIC by knighting the commanders of each of its first two voyages. But the Company was left to organise itself. The 219 original shareholders formed its first General Court and elected a 'Court of Committees' of 24 members. Sir Thomas Smythe (who else?) was chosen first governor and held the post for most of the EIC's first twenty years of existence, aptly, for this was very much a merchant body, and at the outset the 'committees' rejected a suggestion that command of the first expedition should go to a gentleman, picking instead James Lancaster who had captained an epic, if wholly abortive voyage into the East in the early 1590s. With hardly any gentleman members till 1609, the EIC, by contrast with the more idealistic Virginia Company, was single minded in its pursuit of profit. ' ... Even the tracts written in its behalf dealt more with economics than glory.'[106]

The endeavour launched by this cold-brained body of commoners would, in the very long run, exalt Britain's vainglory prodigiously, but its members wasted no time in discussion of national prestige as they probed cautiously into the dark, not yet on a full joint-stock basis. They still formed an association of individuals, with no capital as a corporate body. Each voyage would reward only those members who personally backed it. Yet the first voyage called for no less than £70,000, sending out, as the wherewithal of trade, over £20,000 in money but less than £7,000 in trade goods – a controversial proportion which would be roughly maintained.[107]

Of five vessels leaving London in February 1601, four were home fully loaded by September 1603. The destination had been Indonesia. Few thought much about India yet. Good relations had been established with the rulers at Achin, in Sumatra, and at Bantam, in Java, where a first 'factory' had been established. The first ship home alone brought 210,000 lb. of pepper, besides other spices. The market was glutted, and some of the adventurers could not dispose of their pepper for six or seven years. But the twelve 'Separate Voyages' down to 1612 brought an average profit of 155 per cent. A fresh charter in 1609 extended the EIC monopoly indefinitely. By 1613, the disadvantages of 'separate' voyaging had become obvious – different ventures were in effect in competition with each other – and a new subscription was raised on the under- standing that the capital would be used over several voyages. This 'First Joint Stock' worked its way over ten years, eventually yielding a profit of 87 per cent.[108]

In 1624, when the EIC had exported £750,000 in bullion but only £350,000 in English commodities, its apparently unpatriotic character was producing rowdy scenes in Parliament. Thomas Mun and others had to defend the export of bullion. Spices, they said, would always be in demand and would be imported, so 'treasure' would be lost by them anyway. The crucial matter was the overall balance of English trade, not the export of bullion in one direction, which was compensated for as the EIC re-exported most of its imports, so that these earned precious metals abroad. The argument would go on for many lifetimes. Meanwhile, the EIC was mastering a complicated trade in three interrelated sections. The main part of it seemed to be the commerce between the Indies and England direct. But in fact this was made economically viable only by two less glamorous sorts of venturing – firstly, by the re-export, just mentioned, of East Indian goods to Europe, where they could be used to acquire the naval stores and silver which the EIC needed; and secondly by the so-called 'country trade' in Asian waters.

Silver was the current monetary standard in Asia and its real price was much higher than in Europe; that is, a given amount of it would buy more goods. The incentive to export it would thus have existed even if English goods had been in greater demand. But while the famous English woollens might serve a potentate for the covering of his elephant, they were too heavy, and too expensive, to find a wide market. Meanwhile, supplies of silver from the New World were dwindling, and the Dutch and English between them were soon sending far more bullion East than Italians and Portuguese had ever done. Involvement in the Eastern port-to-port trade became essential as a way of reducing bullion exports. The EIC, from its Third Voyage (1607 onwards), branched out in search of Asian commodities which could be used in trade within Asia itself.[109] The importance of India was soon clear; the Dutch showed the way there, founding four factories between 1605 and 1612 on the west coast of the subcontinent. Indian textiles were coveted in the islands of the Indonesian archipelago. The EIC was lured to India not by any sense of national destiny but by the exigencies of the spice trade.

Known English journeying in India went back as far as the 1580s when a London merchant, John Newbery, reached Goa as a prisoner of the Portuguese, was released on the intercession of an English Jesuit, traded there for a while, then absconded and viewed the domains of the 'Great Mogul'. He died some- where on the way home, but his companion, Ralph Fitch, came back – after more than eight years, having travelled down the Ganges and reached Malaya.

The Mughal Emperor, it was well known, would be a harder man to impress than any Indonesian king. The dynasty had been launched in 1517 when the remarkable Babur, descendant of the great Mongol conqueror Timur, had turned from his realms in what is now Afghanistan to intervene in North India, then ruled by a confederation of Afghan chieftains. By his death in 1530 he had achieved a loosely-knit empire stretching to the borders of Bengal. His grandson Akbar, charismatic, tolerant, witty, humane, in a reign of nearly fifty years (1556–1605), built vastly on Babur's foundations. His victories extended Mughal rule from Kashmir in the far north into much of the Deccan, where the great Hindu empire of Vijayanagar was hit hard; and from Sind across to Bengal, richest area of the north, with its rice, with its silk, with its most essential saltpetre. Control of Bengal's resources was one basis of Mughal power, along with profits siphoned from the rich trade between India and the Middle East.

There were thirty-three grades in the Mughal imperial service. Most holders in Akbar's day had been born outside what we now know as 'India', but nationalist feeling against an 'alien' conqueror could hardly be a factor when Akbar himself married a Hindu (Rajput) princess and gave natives, both Hindu and Muslim, high office and honours in return for loyal service. Mughals, Afghans and 'Indians' alike were all under strong influence from Persia, reflected in literature, architecture and painting as well as in the use of the Persian language for administrative purposes. Like the Ottoman Turks far to their West, the Mughals opened a career to any young adventurer of talent, who could become a *mansabdar* (holder of command) in their service. After Akbar's day, the *mansabdar* came to be paid by an assignment of land revenue rather than by cash, but had no hereditary claim to the land which supported his ostentation along with the troops which he was bound to supply.

Akbar divided his empire into twelve provinces; later there were eighteen. These in turn were subdivided into *sarkars* (say 'districts') and *parganas* ('subdistricts'). 'The government appeared to the people in the countryside mainly as a revenue collecting agency.'[110] While it took in general one-third of all produce, or its value, each local community in the intricate Indian racial and religious jigsaw was left to administer its own law. The contrast between rich and poor was already acute – the highest *mansabdar*, commander of 5,000, with a salary roughly worth £24,000 a year in Stuart sterling, could live in a style to fill James's courtiers with envy. But it must be stressed that the divergence between 'developed' West and 'underdeveloped' East still lay far in the future, and that the average peasant probably ate more than his European counterpart while being no more subject to war's disasters, and no more steadily oppressed.[111] Under Akbar's able successor Jahangir (1605–1627), Mughal India was overall as cultured, well-governed, and comfortable as any part of the world.

The first English vessel to reach an Indian port anchored near Surat, on the north-western coast, in August 1608. Aboard was one William Hawkins with a polite letter from King James addressed to the now-dead Akbar. He went to the Mughal court at Agra to try to secure trading concessions at Surat, which lay in a major textile-producing region. He spoke Turkish, and made a good impression. Jahangir created him *mansabdar* of 400 and married him to an Armenian girl, but kept changing his royal mind about whether he would yield the requested privileges for English trade. Meanwhile Portuguese Jesuits did their best to ensure, by the influence which they had at court, that the English would not be admitted. After more than two years, in November 1611, Hawkins finally quit. Soon after, Sir Henry Middleton arrived off Surat with ships of the EIC's Sixth Voyage. Attacked by the Portuguese, then refused permission to trade by the Mughal's official, he stormed off to the Red Sea and seized every Indian ship he could find there, forcing them to trade on his own terms and exacting high ransoms. Piracy paid where diplomacy had failed.

The news of Middleton's depredations arrived at Surat soon after Captain Thomas Best had appeared there with the EIC's Tenth Voyage. It provoked thought as well as anger. The Red Sea trade was important to Gujerat, and it now seemed the English could prey as they wished on almost defenceless Indian ships. Best was promised permission to trade, and while confirmation from the Emperor was still awaited, he pushed the lesson home by beating off with his two merchantmen four large but weakly armed Portuguese warships which had been sent from Goa to capture them. Early in 1613, the imperial *farman* arrived and the first English factory in Western India was duly established under Thomas Aldworth. The factors began with delicious illusions, writing home, 'our hope is you shall not neede to send any more mony heather, for heere and in the neighbour citties wil bee yeerly sould above a thowsand broade-cloathes and five hundred peeces of Devon keirsies, for ready monies.'[112] The demand for woollens soon proved almost non-existent, but the seizure by some Portuguese frigates of a Surat ship belonging to the Emperor's mother greatly helped the English position in India. Jahangir ordered the arrest of all Portuguese in his realm and sent an army to attack his new enemies at Daman. Early in 1615, the Viceroy of Goa sent north a strong fleet to oust the English from Surat. Captain Nicholas Downton, with only four ships, beat them off and the Mughal governor, duly impressed, gave him a sword 'with hilt of massie gold' in exchange for his English sidearms.[113]

But the English footing was still insecure. The EIC had persuaded James I to despatch to India an ambassador-plenipotentiary of far greater standing than the mere merchants who had so far tried to deal with Jahangir. Sir Thomas Roe, a great courtier, arrived at Surat in September 1615, in a ship skippered by Christopher Newport (of privateering and Virginian prowess), to attempt to negotiate a formal treaty of commerce between the 'Great Mogul' and his own royal master. For two years and nine months he followed the emperor from place to place, but found that Eastern potentates were not interested in haggling over the details of trade with a man from a faraway nation which had so little to offer. Roe wrote to James, 'I have sought to meyntayne upright Your Majesties greatenes and dignitie, and withall to effect the ends of the merchant; but these two sometyme cross one another, seeing ther is no way to treate with so monstrous overweening that acknowledgeth no equall.'[114] When he left India early in 1619 all that he had secured was a *farman* providing favourable conditions for English trade at Surat in return for English protection of Mughal commerce and Indian pilgrims bound for Mecca. The EIC had found a role as naval auxiliary to the Mughal power which would last through the seventeenth century. Besides whatever vessels from England might be to hand, the Surat factory built up a local flotilla of small sea-going warships. In the early 1620s, EIC vessels helped the Shah of Persia against the Portuguese and played a major part in the capture of Ormuz from them in 1622. So in Persia, too, the EIC gained a fairly secure footing, with local headquarters at Gombroon, on the Gulf.

But elsewhere in Asia there were disappointments. Permission to trade in Japan was gained, but after ten years, in 1623, the EIC closed down its factory at Hirado as unremunerative. Short-lived posts in Siam were abandoned in the same year. A factory which did last was founded in 1611 at Masulipatam on the Coromandel Coast of eastern India, outwith the Mughal realm, but Surat and Bantam became the main centres of trade, with 'Presidencies' established in each place by which the principal factors held authoritarian sway. John Jourdain, the first English 'President' in Bantam, proved to be the most notable victim of a miniature undeclared war with the Dutch in Indonesia.

As in Europe, so in the East, the English viewed the Dutch with a mixture of fellow feeling, admiration and jealousy. Brawling soon started in Bantam itself. Then, in 1609, Captain Keeling was ordered out of the Banda Islands when a Dutch fleet arrived to establish a fort there. Yet in general the Dutch behaved generously towards their weaker, but Protestant rivals, and when the EIC petitioned the English government to intervene with the States General in 1611, complaining of 'uncyvell and inhumaine wrongs',[115] the Netherlanders were able to show that the English themselves had much to answer for. At conferences in 1613 and 1615 where the English turned against the Dutch their own favourite argument that the seas should be free and open to all, nothing was achieved for the EIC. And in the Moluccas the Dutch began to show unmistakeable ruthlessness, spurred by the fact that competition would make the risks of the spice trade unprofitable, forcing up prices and bringing the danger of glut in the West. While the Dutch tried to enforce total monopoly, the English were able to trade with natives resentful of Dutch rapacity.

The Banda Islands, specks lost on most maps, with a total land area of only 17 square miles, where, however, the nutmeg was indigenous, now become a centre of rivalry. Here in 1615 the natives of Wai sided with the English and drove off the Dutch. Next year a Dutch fleet of ten confronted four EIC ships there and dictated terms, by which the English must remain neutral while the

Dutch fought the natives, and must abandon the island if the Dutch won. Richard Hunt, in command of the English factory, breached these terms and persuaded the people of Wai and its neighbour Run to haul up English colours; and even after the Dutch had captured Wai decisively, the English held Run ('Pularoon') till 1620 and finally dropped their claim to it only in 1667.

Jan Pieterszoon Coen arrived in Java as Governor General of the Dutch East Indies in mid-1618 with expansionist plans and instructions to expel all foreign Europeans from places where the Dutch traded. John Jourdain, from Devon, was another determined man. He founded a factory at Macassar in Celebes, half way between Java and the Moluccas, which ensured a copious leakage in the Dutch spice monopoly till it was lost half a century later. The English seizure of a Dutch ship at Bantam provoked Coen to burn the EIC factory at Batavia. Undeclared war followed. The rivals' fleets fought an inconclusive engagement in December 1618, with Sir Thomas Dale, formerly governor in Virginia, in command on the English side. When Dale went back to India to refit, Coen swept in with a powerful fleet. Jourdain was treacherously killed under a flag of truce, but the English were ready to resume battle, early in 1620, when word came that an agreement had been reached in Europe. By an Anglo-Dutch treaty of 1619, the rival East India Companies were to share the trade of Indonesia and to bear the costs of defence jointly. The EIC were to have half the available pepper and a third of the spice trade of the Moluccas, Amboyna and the Bandas. Coen of course disliked this deal and busily made it unworkable. The Dutch seized all the Bandas, and Coen executed his own plan for rooting out the islanders and replacing them with settlers from outside. Boats were destroyed. Enslaved captives were sent to Java. The people of Run tried to escape in mass but were rounded up and the grown men among them all killed. Coen used similar methods on the larger island of Ceram. Meanwhile, co-operation with the Dutch was coming to seem to the EIC factors in Indonesia only a 'kind of slavery', and they had already decided to quit the Dutch settlements when word came of the 'Amboyna Massacre'.[116]

On Amboyna (Ambon), close to Ceram, the English traded under protection of a Dutch fort. The EIC factory here was larger than most of the English settlements now dotted across the Far East, though it was petty enough — eighteen white men scattered between several posts: twelve 'factors', two clerks, a barber-surgeon, a tailor, a couple of servants, together with the six boy-slaves these held. The Dutch, they reckoned, had two hundred white soldiers and three or four hundred native troops; the steward of their factory, it is worth noting, was an Aberdeen Scot named George Forbis, and they employed some thirty Japanese among their mercenaries. At the very time when orders were on their way from Java that the EIC men should evacuate, a Japanese soldier suspected of conspiracy incriminated the English under torture. The Dutch built up a story that the English had decided to seize the fort on the arrival of an English ship or during the Dutch governor's absence, and had employed

their drunken barber, one Abel Price, to corrupt the Japanese. Price too confessed, under torture, and in mid-February 1623 the governor, Van Speult,
swept in all eighteen Englishmen. Twelve were tortured by water, two also
with fire. Confessions were made, retracted, then reaffirmed under fresh torture:
a cloth would be bound tightly about the victim's neck and face, then water
was poured softly on to his head until the cloth was saturated up to the mouth
and nostrils. Slow suffocation was combined with horrible swelling of body and
cheeks. Though Van Speult got word while the English awaited trial that they
were now to be withdrawn on Company orders anyway, he went ahead and
executed ten EIC men as well as nine Japanese and a Portuguese captain of
slaves. Horrors were almost as common in the world then as now. The Dutch
had lawful jurisdiction, which the English had always recognised, and the use
of torture was not only permitted but even directed by the law of the settlement.
But even if the English had actually been conspiring, which though rash can
hardly be thought impossible, the judicial procedures used were hasty and
farcical, and Towerson, the English chief, was a pious, honest enough fellow,
thoroughly apt for the status of martyr. When the news reached England fifteen
months later, in May 1624, James I was outraged and 'sundry of the greatest
shed tears' at the royal council table.[117] The EIC bayed for reprisals, but Dutch
help was now needed against Spain. War with Holland was out of the question.
However, for fifty years and longer, the 'Massacre' would retain its place in
English consciousness as a prime aggravator of anti-Dutch feeling.

Meanwhile, in the East, the English tried for a time to make their headquarters on an island in the Sunda Straits, but need drove them back to Java,
first to Batavia, then to Bantam, where a ruler at odds with the Dutch gave
them protection. Willy-nilly, though, India was confirmed as the EIC's main
resort. And this was a blessing, though for the moment heavily disguised (the
Second Joint Stock of 1617–32 was a near disaster for the Company, with
investors losing heavily). The Dutch commitment to a spice monopoly involved
the VOC in large military costs which kept profits low, and in the not very long
run the demand for Indian wares in Europe would prove far more elastic and
important than the market for cloves and spices.

Except in certain unhappy Moluccan islands and, growingly, in Java, the
total European impact in the East was still puny. Wherever fair competition
existed, Arab, Persian, Indian or Chinese traders could still hold, and even
improve, their position against Europeans. The 27 vessels sent back from Surat
to London in the first 15 years of the factory (1615–29) amounted to a tiny
proportion of India's total seaborne trade, and EIC factors there, slow to grasp
monetary systems, weights and measures, and to learn the local languages,
stayed reliant on native brokers as well as remaining subject to the whims of the
Emperor and of his officials in their port, though they could always, at a pinch,
use the threat of blockade as a makeweight.[118]

But in England itself the Eastern trade was gathering some importance. The

EIC disposed of its cargoes at 'Candle auctions' in London. A public notice was hung at the Royal Exchange. An inch of lighted candle was set up in the dark in the EIC's mart, and goods were knocked down to the man who bid highest before the wick guttered out. Pepper was in this early phase by far the most valuable import. Dividends were paid in pepper down to 1627. Indigo, that rich dye, was also significant, but it was the rapid increase, from the 1620s, of Western demand for Indian calicoes which pointed the way forward. Cotton textiles from the subcontinent ranged from arse-clouts for black slaves to super-fine products coveted by great ladies, and they would find markets, re-exported, in Africa and in the Middle East. In England itself, besides lovely garments, they made napkins and table linen, bed-furnishings and wall-hangings, being easy to wash, brightening life, and raising the standards of comfort and elegance of growing numbers who found that they could afford them.

The EIC had become one of the largest employers of labour in the London area. Till 1639, its policy was to own the ships it sent East, and in the second decade of the seventeenth century each of its dockyards, at Deptford and Blackwall, turned out over 30 ships of some size. Ranging from 300 tons upwards as a rule, these were some of the largest vessels owned in England. (Ships sent out to the West Indies, by contrast, ranged from only 100 to 200 tons.) The Venetian Ambassador reported in 1618 that the EIC fleets were 'so well constructed and armed as to cause amazement.' Keeping them active spawned new industries — the EIC had its own iron foundries, and cordage manufactures, and also slaughterhouses to kill its own beef for its sailors. A growing proportion of ships came back — while over half the tonnage sent out was lost in the first twenty years, almost all got home thereafter, reflecting partly the abatement of friction with the dangerous Dutch. Yet there were complaints from opponents that the EIC, besides depleting England's woods for its vessels, was murdering rather than 'nursing' English sailors. And indeed, despite a progressive policy which sent ships East with lemon water aboard as a specific against scurvy, the assumption was that disease would kill many hands, so extra men were always shipped on the outward voyage.[119]

The round trip to Surat generally took eighteen months, that to Bantam about two years. Hence the interest of Smythe and other East India merchants in the spate of expeditions, down to 1616, which searched for a North West Passage. Attempts were resumed in 1631, when Captain Luke Foxe, a shrewd Yorkshireman, sailed for some London merchants, and Captain Thomas James for a rival Bristol consortium. Foxe established that there was no westward channel in Hudson's Bay, then, late in the season, ran into his more gentlemanly but less experienced competitor on the Bay's southern shore. ' ... I found that hee was no Seaman,' Foxe wrote. He asked James why he kept out his flag. 'To this was replide, that hee was going to the Emperour of *Japon*, with letters from his Majestie, and that, if it were a ship of his Majesties of 40 Peeces of Ordnance, hee could not strike his flag. "Keep it up then," quoth I, "but you are out of the way to *Japon*, for this is not it." '[120] With this exchange, the search was dropped for a century. East Indiamen continued to make their painful way round the long and still enigmatic coastline of Africa.

X

The trade with Africa itself begun in Tudor times by the Hawkins family came to little before 1618 when, inspired by the success of the EIC, thirty-seven 'Adventurers of London' launched a Guinea Company which would last in various forms for over forty years. It established a factory on the Gambia River which later developed into a fort and also, probably in 1631, the first important English settlement on the 'Gold Coast', at Kormantin. Between these two points, it developed a useful trade in the dye called redwood with peoples in Sierra Leone and on the Sherbro River. So far, slaves were not the bait and an English captain, Richard Jobson, who explored far up the Gambia in the early 1620s, responded starchily when a Mandingo trader named 'Buckor Sano' offered to sell him some black girls. ' ... I made answer, We were a people, who did not deale in any such commodities, neither did wee buy or sell one another, or any that had our owne shapes ... '[121]

Such self-esteeming virtue would not long survive the successful placing of English colonies in tropical America. Following Ralegh, several attempts were soon made in the stickily hot coastlands between the Orinoco and Amazon deltas. In 1604, Charles Leigh took a party to the River Wiapoco (Oiapoque), which later became the eastern border of French Guiana. They managed to grow some flax and tobacco, but Leigh died of a fever and the venture was abandoned in 1606. Three years later a Catholic, Robert Harcourt, was back with sixty men at the same place. Son of an Oxfordshire knight, he had obtained a royal commission, and he formally annexed a vast tract for King James, but his colony soon melted away and even the proprietary grant of the whole of 'Guiana', received from the King in 1613, failed to attract investors to his company. Meanwhile, Sir Thomas Roe, later ambassador to the Great Mogul, pushed inconclusively three hundred miles up the Amazon in 1610–11. He was a friend of Ralegh, who backed him with £600, and his aim was El Dorado. He left, at the mouth of the river, the first of several English settlements which flickered and died there.

Ralegh himself was allowed one last attempt. He used his time well in prison, conducting chemical experiments and writing, amongst other things, a *History of the World*, which, published in 1614, became the century's most printed book after the King James Bible. Its iconoclasm prompted an effort by James I to suppress it, and this simply increased its popularity. But the ageing man wanted freedom, and to return to Guiana, where he was convinced that he had found a huge gold-mine. He harped for years on the subject, playing on the cupidity of the King and his court, and after the 1614 Parliament had failed to grant him supplies, James, desperate now for money, decided to give Ralegh his way. He was released early in 1616. He sold all his own possessions and most of his wife's, and secured generous backing from friends and admirers, so that a vast force of 14 vessels and 1,000 men was possible. The Spanish Ambassador, Gondomar, saw this as a threat to his nation in the New World. He had great influence over James, who hoped for a rich Spanish match for his son Charles, and prevailed on him to announce that Ralegh would forfeit his life if he fought the Spaniards or meddled with their property. James told the Spaniards all about the expedition and where it was headed; yet Ralegh could still gamble that if he did secure gold, the King would forgive him everything.

However, the old man had lost the knack of command. Well-received by Indians on the coast, where he was still remembered, Ralegh was too ill to set out in person to find his mine. Lawrence Keymis, commanding 400 men, disobeyed orders and captured the Spanish town of São Thomé in an affray in which Ralegh's own son was killed. After a month his men forced him to return. Chided by a heartbroken Ralegh, Keymis committed suicide. The expedition fell apart in desertion and mutiny and Ralegh reached England again to find Gondomar's influence unabated. He was duly beheaded in October 1618. He made a fine end, with pious talk and brave jokes, and when his head was held up a voice broke through the shocked silence, 'We have not such another head to be cut off.'[122] To contemporaries it seemed that a cowardly king had sacrificed the last veteran of the Armada battle to appease an arrogant Catholic Spain. Ironically, James did not get the Spanish dowry which he coveted, and his son Charles, succeeding him in 1625, went to war with Spain, a satisfactory outcome for the patriotic country gentry who hankered like their fathers for the destruction of papist power in the New World. But the Stuarts themselves could not be identified with this English patriotism, and the memory of Ralegh, victim of Scottish faithlessness, was kept alive when such leaders of the Puritan party as Hampden, Cromwell and Milton made his *History* their favourite reading. As prisoner, still more as corpse, above all as symbol, he was popular as he had never been in the peacock heyday of his glory. And in the 1650s Oliver Cromwell would revive the Elizabethan project for mastery in the Caribbean with which Ralegh, like Drake, had been associated.

Puritans

The Lord hath done such things amongst us as have not been known in the world these thousand years.

OLIVER CROMWELL, 1654[1]

I

English colonising in South America was ended, for the time being, in 1631, when the Portuguese wiped out a short-lived settlement on the island of Tocujos in the Amazon delta, the second such plantation attempted by one of Ralegh's former officers, Roger North. But the many small and frequently beautiful islands of the Caribbean, still covered with sumptuous virgin forest unoccupied by the Spaniards, had started to beckon. If there were any black faces there yet, they were only strays shipwrecked or escaped from the Spanish lands. For the moment, it was red men whom the white pioneers saw and feared, those brave and ferocious Caribs whose customs, by a slight change of consonant, gave the word 'cannibal' to the English language.

The Caribs had destroyed an English settlement on St Lucia as early as 1605, and had thwarted an attempt by English merchants to colonise Grenada with two hundred white men four years later. Both these islands were in the 'Windward' group, but there were Caribs also on the speck in the 'Leewards' which Columbus had named St Christopher and which, under that name, 'St Christophe' to the French and finally as 'St Kitts', was to become the most fought-over eggshell of land on earth. In 1622 Captain Thomas Warner, a Suffolk man of good family, rising towards fifty, quit North's first colony in disgust at 'the disorders that did grow in the *Amazons* for want of Government' among the English there and with some companions sought a place of their own where they could be 'quiet'. They found St Kitts, shaped like a tadpole, 28 miles from end to end, 68 square, dominated by mountains which rose to a peak of 3,800 feet at 'Mount Misery'. Warner made friends with the Caribs, planted a crop of tobacco, and six months later sailed away with enough of it to get London merchant backing for his proposed settlement. He returned in January 1624 with a small party (not more than nineteen men). They built homes of logs thatched with palmetto leaves and planted tobacco in clearings painfully hewn from the dense forest. Their first crop was destroyed by a hurricane, but a second had grown when Warner's Suffolk neighbour, John Jeaffreson, arrived in March 1625 with provisions and reinforcements.[2]

The Caribs grew understandably restive as the English erected a fort, which the settlers tried to pass off as a fowl-house. Pre-emptively — 'Like a wise man and a good Souldier he tooke the advantage of theire being druncke' — Warner massacred the adjacent Indian village;[3] but there was still danger as St Kitts was easily reached by Carib canoes from other islands. When a damaged French privateer appeared, the English welcomed white allies. For the first few years, English and French settlers helped each other against the common enemy, and in 1627 a formal agreement divided the island. The French took both ends, the English retained the middle. Warner already confirmed as 'King's Lieutenant', ruled the English section until he died in 1649, a shrewd and ruthless squire who had the advantage that he could pack dissidents off to colonise fresh Leeward islands. Nevis (50 square miles) was settled by Englishmen from St Kitts in 1628, Antigua (108 square miles) in 1632. In the latter year Montserrat (32½ square miles) was occupied; before long it filled up with Irish papists. Though two rebellions would force Warner to concede an elected assembly to the St Kitts planters in the 1640s, he contrived to weather a period which had seen the second English West Indian colony, on Barbados, several times reduced to anarchy.

Barbados was (from one point of view) a fortunate isle, never changing hands in international wars after its initial settlement by Englishmen in 1625. It was the most easterly of the Lesser Antilles, to the windward even of the Windward Islands, so that the Caribs had never settled it and could not now attack it, and even Spaniards and Frenchmen would find it hard to reach from their Caribbean bases. In 1627 a London merchant, Sir William Courteen, sent out about eighty colonists. The settlement soon throve and by 1629 there were said to be 1,800 whites (and 50 blacks) on the island.[4] Such rapid success contrasted with the slow progress of Virginia. As with Bermuda, an island gave ease of defence. The tropical soil was lavishly fecund. For nearly two hundred years English colonies in the Caribbean would matter far more to people at home, would seem worth more, and indeed, would be worth more, than those on mainland North America. Where we see a flurry of dots on the map, the mercantilist mind conceived wealth and power. As a major source of commercial opulence, the West Indies would help mightily in the political transformation of England, of which the revolt against Charles I was an early conspicuous symptom.

II

The King grew poorer while the propertied classes represented in Parliament were getting richer. The Crown was sustained by land in an age when rents fell behind rising prices, and though James I avoided war, he had, over his reign, to dispose of much land. Power drained from the centre. From 1614 James did not summon Parliament for seven years. His favourite, George Villiers, Duke of Buckingham, was vastly corrupt, extravagant and incompetent. When

James turned to Parliament again in 1621, it recovered its power, not used since the fifteenth century, to remove those of the King's ministers whom it disliked. Then it insisted on debating foreign policy; the King dissolved it and imprisoned a number of truculent members, including a man named John Pym.

A new fight with Spain was launched in pique after the humiliating failure of Prince Charles's quest for a Spanish bride. Parliament, summoned again in 1624, voted supplies for the war, but insisted that they must be administered by a committee chosen by the House of Commons. With the accession of Charles next year, strains were intensified by the new King's theological views; he was 'Arminian', following the views of a Dutch sage who undermined the cherished Calvinist doctrine of predestination and believed that salvation depended partly on what men did. The Parliament of 1626 tried to impeach Buckingham; when Charles angrily dissolved it, this meant that he got no subsidies. The war went badly, and Buckingham's rash diplomacy soon embroiled England in the dangers of fighting France and Spain at once. Charles had to sell more crown lands; when he tried to exact a forced loan from his subjects, numerous Puritan M.P.s refused to pay it and several were imprisoned.

The Parliament of 1628 produced the resounding Petition of Right against arbitrary imprisonment, arbitrary taxation, billeting of troops and martial law. The aim was to bring the monarch under the rule of law. Faithless Charles accepted it, and got his subsidies, but the assassination in the same year of Buckingham, who had enthralled son like father, made political friction if anything worse — Charles now fell in love instead with his own wife, a papist Frenchwoman. And he took into his service Thomas Wentworth, once a leader of Parliament, soon to become the King's most abhorred secular henchman. Charles's meddlings with the Church inspired frantic fears and revulsions. High office was becoming impossible even for moderate Puritans. In 1629, Charles lost patience with the House of Commons and adjourned it, provoking a famous demonstration where the Speaker was held firmly in his chair while resolutions were passed against the King's views on religion and taxation. Having dissolved Parliament and tried and imprisoned its leaders, Charles now essayed to rule without it. Thousands of his subjects fled, in effect, to the New World, in a movement involving all classes of pious Puritan people.

Those who opposed Charles believed that they stood for the liberties of Englishmen. It is easy for any schoolboy to sneer that 'liberty' for the property-owners who sat in early Stuart parliaments meant, precisely, the rights of property-owners. Yet the potential electorate may have embraced, by the critical year of 1640, a third or more of the adult male population.[5] Parliament itself, not yet fearful of all lower orders, acted to extend it and even some quite poor men could vote, since inflation had in effect degraded the property qualification which restricted the franchise in the counties to those with a forty shilling freehold. Political consciousness was wide and growing, albeit within a social order where most people still accepted that hierarchy was natural and

10 A wood carving of a wounded seaman of the early Stuart period

11 Scottish mercenary troops in Germany, c. 1630

12 Tellicherry (India) in 1731

13 Ternate, East Indian isle of cloves — an early-eighteenth-century engraving

good. While taxation seems a selfish enough grievance, that does not mean that the Puritans were hypocritical when they focused attention on Church affairs. Even excluding the papist Queen, there really were Catholics now in high places. Though Charles's religious mentor, Laud, who became Archbishop of Canterbury in 1633, refused a Cardinal's hat when it was offered to him, Charles really did, in 1636, accept a resident papal agent in his court. As Laud systematically denied preferment to Puritan clergy, and as his attempt to stamp out predestinarian ideas led to a ban on the reprinting of that anti-papist classic, Foxe's *Book of Martyrs*, men could be excused if they fancied a forewarning sniff of new fires of martyrdom. Puritans emphasised preaching. Laud, in contrast, exalted the sacraments, and revived what seemed superstitions: bowings, genuflections, altars.

Charles was favoured in his attempt to rule without parliamentary votes of money by the dwindling out of the long inflation, and also by the expansion of trade. His attempts to increase his income showed ominous success, though royal extravagance meant that even when Charles's income had soared to the unheard-of height of £900,000 a year in the second half of the 1630s, he still was not solvent. Old laws were disinterred and the breaking of them exploited (thus, Charles enforced fines against enclosers, but not because he opposed enclosures). What could have been Charles's master stroke was the decision in 1635 to call for the tax of Ship Money, levied in ports to support the Royal Navy, from inland towns as well. His success in raising it over the next three years showed how he might escape altogether from parliamentary control, even perhaps finance his own wars. In 1637 a rich Puritan, John Hampden, was taken to court for refusing to pay Ship Money. Seven judges out of twelve decided for the King against Hampden. Hampden paid up. What now could check the drive towards absolute rule?

III

In 1637, a local gentleman named Oliver Cromwell took the part of poor protesting commoners in the Ely Fens, deprived of much of their grazing land and of the chance to fish and to fowl by the operations of a syndicate led by Francis, 4th Earl of Bedford. A famous Dutch expert, Vermuyden, had been called in to supervise the draining of that expanse of the southern Fens which later became known as the Bedford Level. He straightened river channels so as to increase their gradient. Different syndicates were at work farther north. A Fen poet wrote angrily:

> Away with boats and rudder, farewell both boots and skatches,
> No need of one nor th'other, men now make better matches;
> Stilt-makers all and tanners, shall complain of this disaster,
> For they will make each muddy lake for Essex calves a pasture.

G

The feather'd fowls have wings, to fly to other nations;
But we have no such things, to help our transportations;
We must give place (oh grievous case) to horned beasts and cattle
Except that we can all agree to drive them out by battle.[6]

And in fact, in more than one place, fenmen, after the adventurers had started to exploit the drained land for corn and cattle, rose up, broke sluices, and seized possession again.

Charles I himself took over the undertaking of the Bedford Level in 1638, on the pretext that the syndicate was not doing its job properly. He kept on the hated foreigner, Vermuyden, and the disorders increased. A general movement of opposition was seen now over the whole area, in Lincolnshire as well as at Ely, whence, in June 1638, the local Justice reported threats to break open the gaol and added, 'Our warrants that we send in his Majesty's name are resisted by some, neglected by others, and some that are charged to aid the constables make light of it and refuse it ... ' It was resistance, in effect, to colonialism. Charles proposed to create 'several new plantations' and to build 'an eminent town in the midst of the Level, at a little village called Manea, and to have called it Charlemont' – as 'Londonderry' had been renamed, as 'Jamestown' had been created, and vastnesses to the west christened new at the whim of kings and settlers.[7]

'Maryland', for instance, had just been born in North America, named after Charles's French wife, Henrietta Maria. It realised the vision, much flirted with since Humphrey Gilbert's day, of a refuge in America for Catholics fined for their faith in England. George Calvert had become the King's principal Secretary of State in 1619, but had resigned when anti-Catholic measures were proposed and had announced himself a Roman convert. He had long had interests in Ireland and America, and his religious faith now marched with his attraction to colonies. In 1620 he had purchased land in Newfoundland, where he had established a small colony. Then in 1623 he had acquired a royal patent, enlarging the grant and erecting it into the 'Province of Avalon', so named after the traditional birthplace of Christianity in England. This was the prototype of many other patents for 'proprietary colonies'.

Basically, the 'proprietary' patent gave its lucky recipient powers within the area concerned as great as those exercised by the Bishop of Durham in his border palatinate in the fourteenth century. The idea of handing a difficult frontier over to a single viceroy had been obsolete in England since Thomas Cromwell's day, but no other precedent existed to give legal shape to so large a grant as James made to Calvert. Charles I, after reaching the throne, usually favoured proprietary patents over the other idea of making a grant to a company. In one important instance, in 1627, he gave the 'Caribee Islands' to a spendthrift favourite, the Earl of Carlisle, over the head of Sir William Courteen who had just opened up Barbados. A nice wrangle followed, as Courteen's patron, the Earl of Pembroke, exploited royal insouciance over geography and spelling to acquire an independent grant of 'Trinidado, Tabago, Barbudos & ffonseca', the last named being wholly imaginary. Carlisle responded by getting from Charles a fresh grant clearly referring to 'Barbadas alias Barbades alias Barbudos alias Barbadus'.[8] In 1629 Sir Robert Heath was granted 'Carolana' (*sic*) to the south of Virginia and Sir Ferdinando Gorges got Maine. The idea was that the new colonies should be established under individual owners with vast feudal power. All land was to be held directly or indirectly from the proprietor who was himself tenant-in-chief under the king. He could set up courts and appoint officers for the enforcement of laws which he endorsed himself. He might grant pardon to offenders and make war, if he wished, against native Indians. All this in theory; in practice, the difficulty of control from a distance and the need to attract liberty-loving English settlers, meant that the proprietary domains would evolve elective assemblies and other institutions matching those found in colonies under chartered companies.

Yet unlike the inane Carlisle, Calvert actually wished to live abroad himself. Having twice visited his 'Avalon' settlement, he concluded that he should remove where 'the winters be shorter and less vigorous'.[9] In 1628 he left for Virginia with his family, but his refusal to take the anti-papal Oath of Supremacy made residence there impossible, and he returned to England to seek permission to found a separate colony. In 1632, just after his death, his son Cecilius, second Lord Baltimore (this was an Irish title acquired in 1625), got a charter for 'Maryland', viewed it seems as a buffer colony between Virginia and the 'New Amsterdam' Dutch.

Father Andrew White, an English Jesuit, helped to publicise the colony with a letter in which he proclaimed Baltimore's main aim to be 'not to think so much of planting fruits and trees in a land so fruitful, as of sowing the seeds of religion and piety. Surely,' the good man went on, exposing that deep patriotism which would induce papists to settle outwith yet within the realm of the English King, 'Surely a design worthy of Christians, worthy of *angels*, worthy of *Englishmen*. The English nation, renowned for so many ancient victories, never undertook anything more noble or glorious than this.'[10]

Yet sailing was held up as the Virginian settlers, outraged by a venture which blocked one frontier against them, appealed to the Privy Council and tried to seduce the seamen whom Baltimore hired, and as the Council itself insisted that all passengers took the (Anglican) Oath of Allegiance. Many evaded this somehow. But while the leading men in the expedition were Catholics, the followers whom they took with them seem to have been mostly Protestant, and Baltimore issued orders to Leonard Calvert, his brother, who went as governor, that on shipboard and in the settlement papists should practise their own rites discreetly and give no offence to the others, whose complaints, sent home, might jeopardise the whole venture. From the start religious toleration, even religious harmony, were seen as essential to the colony. So might the New World begin to correct the Old.

Arriving in the Chesapeake in February 1634, the colonists pitched, as a place to settle, on 'St Mary's', a site on the broad Potomac which even that patriot Father White conceded was 'the sweetest and greatest river I have seene, so that the Thames is but a little finger to it.'[11] The local Indians were friendly, and no famine confronted the two to three hundred settlers led by sixteen gentlemen with their families. These gentlemen were at once granted land and a unique attempt was made to transplant English feudalism lock, stock and barrel to the New World, though it was moribund in England itself. It failed. The Baltimore proprietors would in the end create more than sixty 'manors', but freeholders with plots up to 1,000 acres were much more numerous than the manor lords; and those few lords who bothered to exercise their jurisdictive prerogatives, in manorial courts and so on, soon gave it up as a waste of time. In practice, local government followed the Virginian pattern, and the 'head-right' system here also became the basis of development. The interior began to fill up with tobacco farmers who made wealth the measure of status and struggled against the proprietors' controls. Despite Leonard Calvert's theoretically almost absolute powers, an assembly met in 1635 and quite frequently thereafter. Frontiersmen insisted on 'English liberty'.

The same factors, of course, applied in Virginia, now a 'royal' colony, where the settlers themselves soon came to enjoy the new laxness of administration by a governor and council appointed in England, as opposed to the former close control of the Virginia Company. An impecunious monarch could hardly do much with people many weeks distant across the ocean, while the colony's problems huddled so smokily around tobacco that it would have been absurd for the governor not to consult the people who grew it. In its early days, when it was fashionable, Virginia had attracted men like Wingfield and Percy from noble families. But by the 1620s, almost all its 'natural' élite had gone home, and the political void had to be filled by planters of humble origins who had come out, for the most part, with no more than one or two servants, even by some who had been servants themselves. 'Tough, unsentimental, quick-tempered, crudely ambitious men,' as Bernard Bailyn describes them, 'concerned with profits and increased landholdings, not the grace of life',[12] they sought the maximum freedom to pursue their own interests. These easily defined themselves. They wanted aggressive expansion at the expense of Indians and, as these came along, of other colonies also. They wanted unrestricted access to land and legal endorsement as they acquired it. All this implied their own control over the colony, and that was why they quarrelled with Governor Harvey, just as a partly similar class, the grasping 'New English' of Ireland, fell out, at the same time, with Charles I's viceroy, Wentworth.

Sir John Harvey arrived in 1630, a proud, stubborn and ill-tempered man who wanted to be more than mere chairman of the Council. A scenario now sketched itself out which would serve, with adaptations, in many colonial situations down to the mid-nineteenth century. Harvey, like later agents of London, did not want war; he wished for stable relations with the Indians, and so he held out against expansion. He also brought to men who were now perfectly happy to concentrate on tobacco the still-official policy that the economy should be diversified. Colourful scenes resulted. Harvey outdid even his royal master in 1635 when, without consulting his Council, he imprisoned his leading antagonists and made plans to finish them off with the help of martial law. The Council deposed him, but Charles I sent him back, so he charged his opponents with treason and shipped several of them to England in their turn to be tried by the much-feared Court of Star Chamber; then he began to seize his enemies' property. But he was replaced at last in 1639, and his antics had not checked the steady development of the colony.

A census in 1625 had shown 1,478 inhabitants, of whom 269 were women, and 23 were Negroes. Plantations had by then spread along both sides of the James River. Two factors helped to keep them close to the waterside — Indian pressure, and the advantage of nearness to deep water when shipping came. But tobacco exhausted the soil swiftly, and the crop's boundless appetite for land led to steps to spread settlement across to the York River which formed the other side of the Jamestown peninsula. This is turn called for a strongly-held line of settlement between the two rivers, and by 1634 a six-mile palisade connected them (a Pale, in fact — one thinks again of Ireland) excluding the Indians and any question of their rights to the land. Roughly 300,000 acres had thus been digested. The flow of immigrants increased. By 1635, Virginia had nearly 5,000 people: by 1640, 8,000: by 1660, 33,000. Eight counties were drawn in 1634, three new ones in 1648-51, and by 1660 Virginia had expanded into the Pamunkey Valley and along the Chesapeake coastline from the Potomac to Hampton Roads, while settlements were approaching, in various places, the 'fall line' which interrupted river navigation and still seemed to impose a natural limit to expansion.[13]

The 'headright' principle, which brought a man new land in return for his having paid the cost of importing a fresh labourer, gave a consistent momentum to immigration, though Virginia in the 1630s attracted proportionately far fewer people than Ulster, than the West Indies, or, indeed, New England. What emerged, here as in Maryland, was a unique society of modest or small landowners, living quite simply, growing tobacco to pay for imported goods and some corn chiefly for their own consumption. Urban life did not develop importantly, Jamestown never became a centre of residence for planters. The Assembly had 'detailed and almost complete' control of the colony's finances, since the costs of government were met by public levies for which its votes were essential. Universal (white) male suffrage was not abandoned till 1655, after which all men who held houses qualified. While Justices of the Peace, as in England, became responsible for local government, the post of sheriff began to

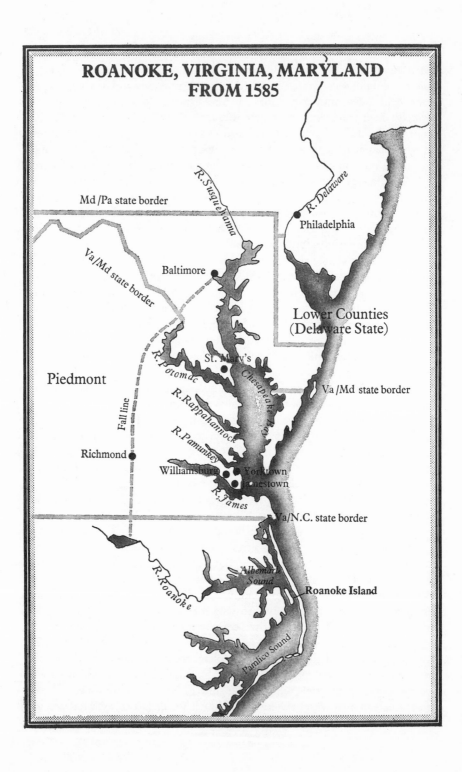

ROANOKE, VIRGINIA, MARYLAND FROM 1585

Md/Pa state border

R. Susquehanna

R. Delaware

Philadelphia

Va/Md state border

Baltimore

Lower Counties
(Delaware State)

R. Potomac

St. Mary's

Chesapeake Bay

Va/Md state border

Piedmont

R. Rappahannock

R. Pamunkey

Fall line

Richmond

Williamsburg   Yorktown
   Jamestown

R. James

Va/N.C. state border

R. Roanoke

Albemarle
Sound

Roanoke Island

Pamlico Sound

develop a greater importance than at home. There was no bishop, and hence there were no ecclesiastical courts, so marriages, wills and probates were dealt with in ordinary secular courts from the first. Virginians were reluctant to grant tenure to their clergy, and in practice ministers came to be 'hired' annually. Naturally, they were paid in tobacco. All trade in the colony rested on the exchange of tobacco for other goods. Other products – furs, skins, timber, provisions, livestock – were occasionally exported, but the seductive weed was overweening.

There was of course a self-confirming, inexorable tendency; the use of tobacco as currency virtually forced men to plant it in order to buy goods and to pay taxes. But tobacco had spontaneous appeal. It was a crop through which a poor man could prosper. Captain John Smith argued that a man's labour on tobacco was worth as much as £60 a year, where expended on grain it would produce only £10.[14]

The man depending on tobacco alone was in dire case when, as periodically happened, markets were glutted and prices plummeted. In 1630, for instance, Virginia tobacco sold at less than 1d. a lb. But planters would not be deterred. The English government helped them, imposing an adverse duty on Spanish imports – 2s. a lb. in 1631, as compared to 9d. on Virginian – and the colonists through their assembly tried to regulate the crop – for instance, a code of 1633 laid down that no one might grow more than 1,500 plants and that only the finer grades might be raised. Yet prices remained low as production expanded, and the practice grew up of destroying inferior tobacco. In 1640 the Assembly accepted a proposal from the English merchants concerned and made the draconian ruling that not only all the bad but also half the good tobacco in that year's crop should be destroyed, while a production limit of 170 lb. per head was set for the next two years.[15]

Meanwhile, tobacco had become a cause of bitter dissension in rural England, where Charles I in Virginia's interests had repeated his father's ban on its planting and had set off a phase of dogged resistance among the growers in Gloucestershire and Wiltshire, during which cultivation steadily expanded to other counties. In the West Indies, too, small men had rushed to feed the new taste.

IV

The Earl of Carlisle, having secured his proprietorship of 'Barbados', in practice performed as a front man for his merchant backers. To one merchant syndicate he granted a subcontract for 10,000 acres on the island, with very favourable terms; he used other merchants to found a plantation for himself and others again to exploit his rights on St Kitts. Though the 'Carlisle Patent' endured in name for more than thirty years, it was always unpopular with the colonists.

But then on their lush green frontier they would certainly have resented any form of government at all.

They sent the first 'Carlisle' governor back to England in chains. The second, Henry Hawley, was less frangible; he was a prototype of one characteristic Caribbean breed of seventeenth-century colonial viceroy – tough, unprincipled, bullying, quick on the draw. The planters had set up one John Powell as their governor. When Hawley arrived, this man rashly accepted an invitation to board the newcomer's vessel. He and his fellow guests were stripped and chained to the mainmast, where they stayed for nearly a month till the ship was captured by a Spanish force off St Kitts. Hawley himself somehow made his escape and contrived also to outmanoeuvre, and then have shot, yet another 'Carlisle' governor sent out to replace him. The wild hogs of Barbados had all been eaten. In 1630–1 the island went through a 'Starving Time'. But Hawley survived, forcing people to work on his own land, imposing arbitrary fines, and even ordaining that 'noe strong beere should be sold but to the Governor and Councell, and such as he pleased'. When Carlisle, in the late 1630s, at last got a royal commission for Hawley's recall, the latter nimbly erected a 'parliament' on Barbados which, duly packed with his supporters, elected him governor (and yet this opportunistically improvised organ was to prove the most enduring of all colonial assemblies). The King sent commissioners to force Hawley out in 1640. He went quietly, managed to hang on to his lands on the island, and died there at last, in 1677, at the ripe age of 80.[16]

No frontier ever moved faster. By mid-century, Barbados and St Kitts would be among the most densely settled places on earth. This was far friendlier country than the North American mainland. (Although Barbados had no river and few springs and, as on Antigua which was completely without running water, cisterns had to be used to capture the rain.) A castaway could flourish in the West Indies – Defoe would not err in having his hero Crusoe build for himself here a replica of the English middle-class lifestyle. The species of palm tree had their various easy uses. Leaves made buckets and covered houses. Sap gave palm wine, and one remarkable sort rising to over 100 feet had a bushlet on top which looked and tasted like cabbage and could be eaten like it. Wild pigeons were easy to catch. Turtles provided delicious meat, and one gourmet of this period exulted over 'little lobsters, but wanting the great claws afore, which are the sweetest and fullest of fish, that I have seen; *Chichester* Lobsters are not to be compared to them.'[17] Nets and rope could be made from the bark of certain trees, and early Barbados colonists could export profitably the dyewood which they hewed down as they cleared land for planting. Except for the plaguing mosquitoes and midges, there were few things about which did not come in handy.

Ecological revolution came with the white men. Captain John Smith had described how virgin Nevis looked in 1607 – 'It is all woddy ... in most places the wod groweth close to the water side, at a high water marke, and in some places so thicke of a soft spungy wood like a wilde figge tree, you cannot get through it, but by making your way with hatchets, or fauchions.' Yet sixty years later it could be said that 'at the Barbadoes all the trees are destroyed ... '[18] Besides shortage of fuel, soil erosion and loss of moisture would result from the massacre of trees. The land, however, would remain rich and pleasant. The climate, while somewhat enervating, was gentle – 'not very hott, but that which I like well off',[19] a man reported back to New England in 1646. The temperature in the Caribbean rarely exceeds 80°F, though it did provide a rationalisation for the excessive drinking which at once became a feature of island societies. A visitor of 1631 claimed that after a short time in Barbados, he got used to swallowing 30 drams of spirits with each meal.[20] Plantains and sweet potatoes, wild 'plums', oranges, and pineapples all yielded interesting alcoholic beverages, before rum became the poor man's drink. Fruits and food-crops imported from all over the tropics grew fast and well in the black 'mould' soil of Barbados and the still more valuable dark grey loam of St Kitts, which was 'so light and porous as to be penetrable by the slightest application of the hoe ... '[21]

Half an ounce of tobacco seed would produce 15,000 to 25,000 plants ready for harvesting after four or six months. Tobacco was the obvious staple to grow. But it murdered the soil; after a few years, more land was essential, so tobacco was intrinsically far more suitable for a mainland colony like Virginia than for a breast-pocket island. It also demanded skill in the tending which Barbadians did not acquire. Their first attempts at the crop were 'so earthy and worthless, as it could give them little or no return from *England*, or elsewhere.'[22] St Kitts did better, exporting nearly half a million lb. in 1638. But by now the London market was glutted, and West Indian exports tailed off rapidly. The need for diversification had long struck some planters, amongst whom let James Drax be sung. Astute and fortunate, he did well from his first crop of tobacco, invested the proceeds in forty-odd servants and brought them back to Barbados, then led a switch to cotton among some planters. By 1640 cotton equalled tobacco in value among the island's exports and had virtually succeeded it as the chief commodity used instead of coins in exchange. Drax, shouldering forward, began to buy small parcels of land from little freeholders and to convert them into cotton plantations.[23] As holdings consolidated, landless and unlucky whites formed a human residue which flowed into buccaneering or into the colonisation, sponsored or freebooting, of further islands. Barbadians spilled eagerly into the Earl of Warwick's attempt to colonise Trinidad, aborted, as was the first colony on St Lucia (1638–41), by vigorous Carib Indians.

Frenchmen settled the two largest among the Lesser Antilles, Guadeloupe and Martinique, in 1635. But there was as yet no rivalry with England. The nationals of north-western Europe were colleagues in the invasion of the Spanish monopoly, and the ingenious Dutchmen, of course, were their leaders, trading, financing, dominating everywhere. The humble herring explains their presence, like so much else. They needed salt to cure fish. They had begun to exploit the great deposits at Araya in Venezuela. A Spanish fort there in 1622 drove them off to the Lesser Antilles, where salt could be had at St Martin and St Kitts, and at Curaçao, which last became their chief base. They soon took over several small Leeward Islands and a Dutch presence emerged in Guiana. It is probably true that without Dutch traders the English could never have launched their colonies. Dutchmen provided roots, seeds, capital, expertise, slaves, and provisions, and ships to carry the produce away; they were the main dealers in English West Indies tobacco and were commercially strong enough to buy it even after prices had slumped in 1638. Meanwhile, the Dutch were gaining a hold of Brazil, the Portuguese colony which had become Europe's main source of sugar. From this, well-known consequences would follow.

V

As events in the Caribbean showed, Spanish power was declining. Even the population of Castile was falling. The coinage was debased time and again to help finance the endless war against the Dutch. Heavy taxation bore down on merchants and manufacturers. Industry after industry wilted and Spain's overseas trade passed largely into the hands of Protestant foreigners. A soldierly ethic and religious zeal had once combined to motor Spanish expansion. Now, they helped foster contraction. The mass of petty *hidalgos* refused to work with their hands or in trade. (One day, the cult of the 'English gentleman' would do similar damage.) Fertile young people swarmed into the impotence of holy orders. From being ruthless conquerors, Spaniards were becoming gallant losers.

War with Spain was, and would long remain, a most agreeable idea to many Englishmen. When it came in 1625–30, Puritan peers and London merchants were swift into action, and the orgy of privateering eclipsed that of Elizabeth's day in volume, if not in fame. Perhaps £2,400,000 were invested in this field before the war ended in 1630 with an agreed stalemate; a return, in effect, to the terms of 1604.[24]

France was on the way to becoming a far tougher enemy. A remarkable minister, Cardinal Richelieu, was laying foundations for a state which before long would lead Europe. In 1627 he moved, in a mercantilist spirit, to reorganise Canada, aiming at large-scale settlement in the St Lawrence Valley. The Company of New France was set up to run the colony, under Richelieu's own patronage. But England and France were at war when a French fleet sailed with hundreds of colonists, and some privateering brothers named Kirke struck a blow of long-term significance. In 1628 they captured the French expedition in the Gulf of St Lawrence and went on to seize both Quebec and Port Royal. Sir William Alexander, who had never been able to do anything with his grant of Nova Scotia, promptly asserted his right to the area which the Kirkes' boldness had opened up. An Anglo-Scottish consortium was founded when he did a deal with some London merchants, and in 1629 settlers were landed at Port Royal and in 'New Galloway' (Cape Breton Island). Charles I encouraged Alexander to export whole clans of Gaelic Highlanders there – 'deburdening that our kingdome of that race of people which in former times hade bred soe many troubles ther ... ' But nothing seems to have come of this novel alternative to genocide.[25]

The French got Quebec back by treaty in 1629, and Port Royal was surrendered in 1632 when Charles swopped it for 400,000 crowns still owed to him from his French wife's dowry. But the Kirkes had done fatal damage to Richelieu's project of settlement. With the Company almost ruined and the French Crown unable to give further help, the Society of Jesus became Quebec's most effective supporter, attracting funds which helped its members build up the colony. They were not much interested in farmers and saw their task as lying with the Indians – more specifically with the Hurons who were the middlemen in the growing commerce in pelts, and whose conversion would bind them to France. The fur trade and true religion marched together as the Jesuits (founders of Montreal in 1643) aimed to maintain New France as what one of them called 'a holy and sacred temple built by God'.[26] They were quite as sincere as the body of English Puritans who, in the 1630s, created 'New England' farther south.

'Puritanism', of course, is hard to define. It can be applied to those men (and women) within and outside the Church of England who held fast by the Calvinist insistence on man's sinfulness and his impotence to draw to himself God's grace; a joyless creed, it might now seem, and associated with censure of jolly habits. Yet puritanism produced marvellous writers, Milton the greatest of them; it did not preclude a taste for music, which Cromwell loved; and it certainly did not always rule out drinking and dancing. It defined itself by contrast with what it hated. Puritans were sober men, or tried to be, in an age of drunkenness and of gluttony when a certain peer, in 1621, spent £3,000 on one day's meals. They extolled holy, serious living while Cavaliers made a sport of ravishing and deemed rash swordplay essential to their honour.[27] They hungered for long intellectual sermons at a time when Laud and his followers were shifting the emphasis back to rituals which Puritans thought idolatrous, and their detestation of Laud pushed them towards rejection of episcopacy as an institution. Intolerant of any views but their own – since their opinions seemed right in the most vital matters, they reckoned all others wickedly wrong – their claim for religious liberty for themselves led some of them widdershins towards toleration.

That puritanism energised men – and women – in momentously heroic endeavour is still an obvious fact, never veiled for long by debate over the scope of the term itself or the feuds of enschooled historians. Though the 'classic' Puritan view deplored individualistic greed and was more prone to look back towards medieval communalism than forward to a commercialised world, and though Calvinist Scotland in the seventeenth century won booby prizes for economic ineptitude, the famous theory, associated with Weber and Tawney, that Calvinism and capitalism, Puritan values and business success, march significantly together has much palpable truth in it, so far as England and North America are concerned – however much one must emphasise the qualification that involvement in commerce pushed saints from orthodoxy towards heresy. Values had practical use where doctrines didn't. Frugality, sobriety, hard work, keeping one's word, were qualities both of good Puritans and of good businessmen. If many Puritans believed in witches and looked to portents, the movement's inherent contempt for idolatry and mystique helped agile minds within and outwith it towards scientific understanding of nature and a new realism about purely human affairs. Most importantly – and this goes for rustic-minded Pilgrims and Scottish lairds as well as for colonisers in Ireland and London merchants – puritanism gave the devoted, with stiff-necked self-righteousness, hypermanic courage. In the midst of politics, commerce, warfare, colonisation, Puritans struggled to discern the will of the Lord, His purpose in history, and their own relation to it. Once they thought they knew these, they were ready to act as befitted the chosen instruments of divine power – as daring adventurers across the oceans, as soldiers resolved and valiant in battle, as ardent and reckless propagandists for heterodox opinions. Milton's mighty ambition stubbornly building *Paradise Lost*, the tenacity of the Fathers of New Plymouth, the unconquered arm of Oliver Cromwell, drew power from the same psychological source – the electric interaction between humble obedience before God's omnipotent and manifest will and proper pride in one's being a member of the Lord's invincible party at a decisive time in human affairs.

Besides many ordinary people – gentry and merchants, artisans and seamen – Puritan values attracted some of the great. Francis, Earl of Bedford (the Fen drainer) led one of the major Puritan connections. Robert Rich, Earl of Warwick, who 'for forty years had a hand in every important overseas enterprise, Puritan or not, legitimate or not',[28] fronted another important family grouping. Deprived by Charles I of Parliament, their main outlet of opposition, Puritan leaders fostered a surge of emigration calculated at once to provide a refuge for good men outwith Laud's grasp and to advance overseas the true interests of England, which were, of course, in their eyes those of Calvinist Protestantism. They carried forward the empire-building ideas of Hakluyt and Ralegh.

Early in the 1620s, when New England was under the nominal control of Sir Ferdinando Gorges and his Council, Puritan interest arose in the south-western town of Dorchester which was much involved in the transatlantic fisheries. The town's Puritan clergyman, John White, saw a chance to combine greater hauls from the New World seas with the diffusion of the Gospel among the Indians. With a patent to hand from the Council, a syndicate was formed of people from West Country towns and countryside: gentry, ministers, merchants. A first party of fourteen men was left at Cape Ann in 1623, and additional settlers followed, but the site chosen was too far from good fishing and the survivors migrated to Naumkeag, renamed 'Salem', where they struggled through two bitter winters while White and others organised a new company to take over the enterprise. Londoners and East Anglian Puritans were brought in, and only six of the original West Country adventurers were found among the nearly ninety members of the 'New England Company' which received a grant from Gorges's Council in March 1628, embracing a slice of what became Massachusetts.

A fiercely intolerant Puritan, John Endecott, led reinforcements out to Salem. One of his first actions was to descend on the Pilgrims' old bugbear, Thomas Morton's settlement at Merry Mount, to drive out its profane inhabitants, to hew down the notorious maypole, and to rename the place, biblically and bitterly, 'Mount Dagon'. The Salem colony's position was jeopardised by a number of previous grants made in the area by the Council, so its backers went over the Council's head to get a charter of incorporation direct from the King. The Company represented a formidable array of mercantile and landowning interests, and prominent Puritans such as the Earl of Warwick still carried impressive weight. In March 1629, the King chopped a large section out of the Council's territory and approved the charter of the Massachusetts Bay Company.

The model was the Virginia Charter of 1612; a governing body of twenty was to be chosen by all the Company's members. The shrewdness and wealth of these men, as well as the lessons hard-learnt by previous colonies, helped to make the five ships sent out in 1629 the best equipped expedition yet to sail for New England. Meanwhile, the crisis at home, as Charles dissolved Parliament and the Arminians tightened their grip on the Church, moved many Puritans to think deeply and fearfully. One such was John Winthrop, a gentleman-lawyer from Suffolk, aged over 40, who was in debt and had to provide for a large family. He had already sent one son to plant in Barbados. Now poor health, financial worries and the condition of England oppressed his mind. 'My deare wife,' he wrote in May 1629, 'I am verly perswaded God will bringe some heavye Affliction upon this lande, and that speedylye ... If the Lord seeth it wilbe good for us, he will provide a shelter and a hidinge place for us and ours as Zoar for Lott, Sarepthah for his prophet, etc. ... ' He threw up his job in the Court of Wards and Liveries and retreated to his Suffolk estate. His troubled vision fastened on Massachusetts. 'Whoe knows but that God hath provided this place to be a refuge for many whome he meanes to save out of the generall callamity, and seeinge the Church hath noe place lefte to flie into but the wilder-nesse, what better worke can there be, than to goe and provide tabernacles and foode for her against she comes thether.'[29]

Some members of the Massachusetts Bay Company feared for the future of their colony. The Charter of course did not restrict membership to Puritans. The ungodly might be able to buy control. A daring scheme was evolved. The

whole Company, with its precious Charter, its legal warrant, should be transferred to the New World, out of Charles I's reach. In August 1629, at Cambridge,
Winthrop and eleven other gentlemen solemnly agreed to transport themselves
with their families to America, so long as they could get by legal transfer the
whole governance of Massachusetts. This was soon secured at a special meeting
of the Company, when only a fifth of the members were actually present.
Winthrop was elected governor. Through the winter, a great fleet was prepared. The first seven ships sailed next March, and before the end of 1630
seventeen vessels had taken out a thousand passengers, pioneers of the 'Great
Puritan Migration'. Their leaders were the most formidable body of Englishmen
ever to arrive in the New World together — men of some wealth, well-educated,
politically conscious, and with firm and on the whole canny ideas about how to
run a colony. A flood of newcomers pressed steadily behind them, not less than
20,000 by 1643.[30]

Winthrop stands in his well-known portrait like an incarnation of all the
severe vitality of puritanism — dark-haired, with a wide pale forehead, long nose
and pointed beard, the eyes seeming to mix hauteur with other-worldly medita-
tion, to stare across a world of sinners towards Zion. On shipboard, he lectured
his fellow passengers. Massachusetts must be a model for men everywhere.
' ... We must Consider that wee shall be as a Citty upon a Hill, the eyes of all
people are upon us; soe that if wee shall deale falsely with our god in this work
wee have undertaken and so cause him to withdrawe his present help from us,
wee shall be made a story and a by-word through the world.'[31] He was planning
to transmute the institutions of a chartered trading company into a model
Puritan commonwealth, and where the Charter contradicted his aim, well, as
events would prove, he would bend it. Many men would fall out with Winthrop
and his ways, but his bleak integrity would remain above question. He was no
would-be feudal overlord, no impatient profiteer. He had a godly mission and
a strong will to accomplish it. The famous journal which he kept till his death
in 1649 testifies to his self-control, his superstition, his heroic view of men and
events in a world where everything was a sign of God's pleasure or displeasure
towards His people. Unlike the Knoxian Scots, the embattled French Huguenots, or their own divided co-thinkers in England, Puritans in Massachusetts did
not have to struggle against any metaphorical forest of existing institutions,
only with the real forest which God had allotted to them. Doctrine could
inform practice. It was an epic experiment, deeply antipathetic, of course, to
the twentieth-century mind, yet lavish with latencies which would help shape
that mind and change the whole of human consciousness.

Could the human material, even then, have matched Winthrop's exalted
vision? If 80,000 English people left the country between 1620 and 1642, nearly
60,000 of these avoided the safer outlets, Holland, say, or Ireland, and crossed
the Atlantic.[32] Sir William Petty reckoned that over 40 years down to 1660,
from his own home town of Romsey in Hampshire, with a population which

he put at 2,700, 'about 400 went to *New-England*, the *Caribe-Islands*, and *New-found-Land*.' Romsey was the main centre of puritanism in the county, yet even from here one cannot imagine that all who departed were self-conscious saints.[33]

Why did people go? The voyage would be disgusting—perhaps 200 people crowded on board a ship of normally around 200 to 250 tons. Storms were common, seasickness certain amongst landlubbers who had never voyaged before. There would be five weeks at least, and perhaps several months, on a nautical diet of bad food and stinking beer. After such torture the New World itself would probably be a sad disillusionment. What was there in New England, after all, but small villages sketched on a rocky coastline, wild sea before and dark forest behind? William Wood, at Massachusetts in 1634, heard new arrivals complaining 'they could see nothing but a few Canvis Boothes and old houses, supposing at the first to have found walled towns, fortifications and corne fields, as if townes could have built themselves.' The soil was ungenerous, the fauna horrific. One dejected woman exclaimed: 'The air of the country is sharp, the rocks many, the trees innumerable, the grass little, the winter cold, the summer hot, the gnats in summer biting, the wolves at midnight howling, &c.'[34]

The pull of America then, at first, was not too strong. We must look to the push of conditions in England itself. 'This lande', John Winthrop wrote in 1629, 'growes wearye of her Inhabitantes, so as man which is the most pretious of all the Creatures, is here more vile and base, then the earthe they treade upon: so as children, neighbours, and freindes (especially if they be poore) are rated the greatest burdens, which if things were right, would be the cheifest earthly blessings.'[35]

'Canvis boothes' on Massachusetts Bay were hardly more rebarbative than the crude cotes commonly put up, windowless, with no floor but the earth, by evicted labourers on England's own wastelands. A great many people in Coventry lived in vaults and caves. The dogs did bark and the beggars came to town, as at Exeter in December 1625, when a reputed 4,000 destitutes roamed in, and many citizens abandoned the place. Food was short, and so was firewood. It took 2,500 trees to make one ship, and while this and other indus-tries ravaged the groves, enclosures in some areas cut peasants off from supplies of free firewood. Winters were colder than now. A Massachusetts planter wrote pointfully in 1630, 'all Europe is not able to afford to make so many great Fires as New England. A poore Servante here that is to possesse but 50 Acres of Land, may afford to give more wood for Timber and Fire as good as the world yeelds, then many Noble Men in England can afford to doe.'[36]

American rattlesnakes could not outvie the plague, which stalked England seeking whom it might devour. In the town of Cambridge, through the seventeenth century, plague struck every five years or so, and in overcrowded London, a bad year like 1625 would carry off one-fifth of the population. Every outbreak produced a bewildered residue of parentless children, masterless journeymen, tradesmen deprived of their customers, to whom migration beckoned. Meanwhile, the woollen industry was depressed. In 1630, the accounts of merely one Surrey parish reported 1,100 idle people who depended on the clothiers for their livelihood, and 3,000 more in surrounding villages.[37]

Yet these facts operate best to explain migration in general, the lure of the West Indies, expansion on the Chesapeake. New England was a special case. Very few servants went there under indentures. If the very highest ranks were absent, so were the very lowest, and this was the only area in which the English family was rooted from the outset; the Massachusetts courts dealt hard with men who came over without their wives and failed to send for them soon. Only here did all ages muster, children and grandparents too. And only here was there no general shortage of clergymen. Thanks to Laudian pressure on the Puritan minority of preachers, and thanks also the overproduction of graduates, in an age when higher education was strikingly open, ninety-two scholarly ministers flocked to New England, often drawing admiring parishioners with them. William Stoughton, son of a Dorset emigrant, preaching at Boston in 1668, was entitled to cry, 'God sifted a whole nation that he might bring choice Grain over into this Wilderness.'[38]

A kindly satirical ballad of the period displays Cousin Hanna leaving England and Ruben persuading his sister Susanna to go. Tom the Tyler, 'the smith as black as a Cole', Raph the cobbler, 'honest Symon' the weaver, and so on and so forth are going — villages are on the move — and the refrain is 'Then for the truth's sake come along. Come alonge! Leave the place of supersticion.' The Bible showed that the Jews had left a land which wanted them not. John Dane of Bishop's Stortford in Essex decided in 1636 to uproot for New England. His parents, though they were Puritans, opposed him. He told his father, 'if whare I opened the bybell thare i met with anie thing eyther to incuredg or discouredg that sould settell me. I oping of it ... the first I cast my eys on was: Cum out from among them, touch no unclene thing, and I will be your god and you shall be my pepell.' So he went, and his parents soon followed with the whole family, no doubt persuaded, as so many others were, by letters from him, good news from a sure source.[39]

For others, good news was a business proposition. Besides the tracts and sermons, the handbills and promotional ballads which spread it, there were merchants who profited from the shipping of migrants and who sent agents into the countryside to incite custom. As time went on, the like of Tom Tyler and Raph Cobler heard of the high price which skilled labour could claim in New England, just as pious merchants noted the profits on furs. Even Winthrop's thoughts of God did not exclude care for his debts. Puritans understood that God's favour to his elect would be revealed in earthly blessings. New England aimed at practical success. A tension was there from the start between Puritan idealism and the brusque business drive of some Puritans. But such drive built up the new colony fast. Massachusetts had 6,000 settlers by 1636, perhaps 15,000 by 1642.

The largest quota from any one area came from within a radius of 50 miles from John Winthrop's home, Groton, in Suffolk. But there was no overwhelming regional bias; about one-fifth overall seem to have parted from Essex and East Anglia, but almost as many again from the West Country, nearly one-fifth also from London.[40] The names of new settlements harped on nostalgia. 'Boston' succeeded Salem as the chief centre. 'Weymouth' and 'Dorchester' followed, and so on. By 1642 there were twenty-one villages. Population still mostly clung to the coast. Intellectual life was vigorous from the first. Schools were quickly erected. Harvard College was founded in 1636, and from 1639 the colony had a printing press proffering sermons, psalm books and almanacs. A *fait accompli* had been made; from England, it looked like revolt and subversion.

Gorges did not learn till 1632 what the Massachusetts Charter provided; then he made a fuss. He found allies who had fallen out with the Puritans in America, amongst them Thomas Morton of Merry Mount who wrote a satire ridiculing 'King Winthrop' and his 'Fantastical ordinances'. Demon Laud headed investigations; in 1634 the Privy Council virtually abdicated its powers over all colonies to his 'Commission for Regulating Plantations'. Winthrop, convinced that this was out to destroy his Commonwealth, was horrified when the impulsive Endecott cut the red cross of St George out of a royal ensign flying at Salem, saying that the Pope had given the King this cross. This might be interpreted as rebellion. Endecott was debarred awhile from public office. But two years later, as the cold war proceeded, Massachusetts removed the cross from all military ensigns and for half a century flew its unique flag, a red ensign with a plain white canton. The colony actively prepared for armed struggle. Its clergy in 1635 declared that it would be lawful to defend its 'lawful possessions' against any royal governor sent out from England. 'The first overt rebellion against Charles I might have taken place in Boston harbour instead in Edinburgh.'[41]

About this time it was discovered at last that the colony's charter was not in England. In 1637 the Court of King's Bench found the Company guilty in its absence, and Charles soon announced that he was taking over the management of New England and that Gorges was to be his governor. But Gorges was seventy. Charles had no funds to provide him with soldiers. Across the Atlantic a new and distinctive society went on, most impudently, creating itself.

VI

The New England spirit was seen at its sweetest in Plymouth colony, which, after the founding of Massachusetts, became a sleepy satellite of its neighbour, squeezed out of the fur trade by the early 1640s. Unable, despite repeated efforts, to get a charter, Plymouth worked out its own form of self-government. The governor and his 'assistants' were elected by all the freemen at a yearly meeting. Laws were enacted by a general court or assembly, in which, until 1638, every freeman could sit. When the spread of settlement compelled introduction of the representative principle, there was no property qualification for voting, and the great majority of men were electors.[42]

Smoking was forbidden. People were fined for lying, for letting their servants drink and play shovel-board on the Lord's Day, even for 'needles walkinge on ye Sabbath'. When Goodwife Mendame of Duxbury was found guilty of seducing an Indian brave, she was sentenced to be 'whipt at a cart's tayle through the towne's streets, and to wear a badge with the capital letters AD cut in cloth upon her left sleeve ... ' But the death penalty for adultery was never exacted. No witches were ever burnt here. By comparison with England's, justice in Plymouth was mild.[43] This good-tempered society of simple, mostly ill-educated people found it hard to attract qualified ministers. Clerical influence was small. Here was one major contrast with Boston.

Another was that Massachusetts was direly embattled. It was threatened by the government at home, by Indians, and, so its rulers felt, by the enemy within represented by non-Puritans and heretical Puritans. Strong authority was needful to preserve the commonwealth and to maintain its purity. In the early days, Winthrop and his 'assistants' (the magistrates) ruled in disregard of the Charter, levying taxes for which it did not provide and leaving the freemen no role save to re-elect them. In 1634, resentment among the freemen forced Winthrop out of the governorship for three years, though he regained it and held it, with two short interruptions, till his death in 1649. The 'General Court' of shareholders was domesticated as an assembly. The whole body of freemen was to be present only at the elections in May; to the other three quarterly Courts towns should send deputies to represent them, and these would help to make laws and dispose of lands. Both a majority of magistrates and a majority of deputies had to vote favourably before a motion could go through, and this meant that the former could thwart the will of the latter, who outnumbered them. Friction resulted, and in 1644, after a wrangle over the ownership of a sow, in which most of the magistrates backed the rich merchant Robert Keayne and nearly all the deputies favoured the poorer plaintiff Mrs Sherman, the General Court was divided into two houses, which were to sit apart and communicate formally; a measure would pass when both reached agreement.

Ministers were not permitted to serve also as magistrates, but in practice civil and religious affairs were inseparable. Clergy were consulted by magistrates on difficult matters. Magistrates intervened in the life of the Church and in moral questions; they enquired into the fitness of the clergy, examined quarrels within the congregations, sought out heresy, and sentenced people for it. To grumble against the churches was in effect sedition. Heretics threatened Church and commonwealth equally, and if Massachusetts was the best-schooled place in the world, this was partly because of the wish to implant conformity in the minds of the young.

But common sense modified would-be theocracy. Winthrop's diary records how in 1633 one Captain Stone, who had arrived in Boston via the West Indies and Virginia, 'carried himself very dissolutely in drawing company to drink, etc., and being found upon the bed in the night with one Barcroft's wife, he was brought before the governor, etc., and though it appeared he was in drink, and no act to be proved, yet it was thought fit he should abide his trial ... ' This was interfering, but not arbitrary rule. The 'great jury' at the Court could not convict Stone of adultery, though it fined him £100 for his other misdemeanours and ordered him on pain of death to come to Massachusetts no more.[44] The fine was not actually levied, and was presumably meant to deter Stone from coming back. Here also, justice was gentler than in the home country. The colony, short of men to work and to defend it, found it prudential to be lenient. It was common to remit in part or in whole the sentences of those who acknowledged their guilt and said that they would reform. There were few hangings, and prisoners served only short terms.

But justice, predictably, favoured the well-to-do. Gentlemen were rarely whipped, drunken masters were rarely punished, and it was not until 1648 that the pressure of the deputies was able to secure a written code of laws so that men could plead its letter in their own defence. No one in Massachusetts was a 'democrat', and John Winthrop voiced the conventional wisdom of his age when he said that democracy was 'the meanest and worste of all formes of Government.'[45] Only church members could be freemen, though non-freemen were by the late 1640s allowed a share in local government. Women and indentured servants did not count. But the townships were run by 'selectmen' with an occasional 'town meeting' exercising veto power. There was a degree of self-government here approached in Stuart England only within those villages, say a fifth of the total, where there were no gentry in residence and the yeomen and husbandmen ran all themselves.[46] These English villages perhaps gave the model, but to such a practical basis, New England added the ideological impulse of its own brand of revisionist Calvinism, tending towards later 'democratic' ideas.

The 'covenant theology' favoured by New England leaders related in economic life to the business deal, and in politics to the idea of social compact. God makes a fair bargain with man. If man will believe in Christ the mediator, he has fulfilled the contract and God must redeem and glorify him. 'You may sue him of his own bond written and sealed', one divine had declared, 'and he cannot deny it.'[47] Each man makes his own individual covenant with God, renouncing his liberty to do anything but what he has promised. The tendency of this view is to push aside the feudal view of society, where each man's place is determined historically and he cannot avoid being defined by his status at birth. Extended into Puritan notions of government, the 'covenant' temper of mind had portentous implications, at home as well as in Massachusetts. Men enter freely into covenant with each other, as each has done with God. Thereafter, they must show absolute obedience to godly magistrates as they should to God. But neither God nor magistrate can be arbitrary. Both rule by reasonable agreement with consenting individuals. Furthermore, the magistrate is not God. Any other 'saint' chosen by God is clearly as good a man as any magistrate. Thomas Hooker, a representative New England divine, argued: ' ... Take the meanest Saint that ever breathed on the earth, and the greatest scholar for outward part, and learning, and reach and policie, the meanest ignorant soule, that is almost a naturall foole, that soule knowes and understands more of grace and mercy in Christ, than all the wisest and learnedst in the world, than all the greatest schollers.' And any saint must obey his own conscience, which one Puritan thinker defined as 'a man's judgement of himself, according to the judgement of God of him.'[48] Authority thus becomes internalised. No king can command the saint to do what his conscience eschews – no preacher – no magistrate ... So Winthrop's commonwealth was early racked by internal tension between authoritarian and proto-democratic emphases.

The aim of the godly in Massachusetts was to establish a purified Church which would come to the rescue of the mother Church in England. Yet from the outset their congregations looked oddly like those of the Pilgrim 'separatists'. When the first church at Salem was made, in 1629, the minister and the 'teacher' (whose role in instructing the congregation in doctrine was in practice hard to distinguish from the pastor's) were elected by written ballot, after they had described their callings and had 'acknowledged ther was a towfould calling, the one an inward calling, when the Lord moved the harte of a man to take that calling upon him, and fitted him with guiftes for the same; the second was an outward calling, which was from the people, when a company of beleevers are joyned togither in covenante, to walke togither in all ways of God, and every member (being men) are to have a free voyce in the choyce of their officers, etc.'[49] As new settlements grew up, this pattern was repeated (with female 'saints' still excepted). Though, after 1637, synods were held at various times, each Massachusetts church was independent of all others.

However, a common view spread. John Cotton, teacher at the Boston church from 1633, a brilliant luminous divine, argued that a church must include only those who had 'saving faith', and this was the basis of the so-called 'New England Way'. A candidate for church membership was grilled by an elder and had to show not only that he knew the correct doctrines but that his religious experience was such as to suggest that he was saved. Then the whole congregation would join in the inquiry. In 1636, the General Court restricted freemanship in Massachusetts to those who had passed such examination. The 'sanctified', those whose actions seemed to confirm that they were in enjoyment of grace, 'dramatised their solidarity in Sabbath observance, sober dress, oathkeeping, sexual propriety, and so on ... '[50] In England these had been marks of non-conformity. Here, the 'saints' were conformists and their manners stamped the whole society. Delinquents were first admonished, then censured by the vote of the whole church. If they persisted, they were excommunicated and the pastor in the name of Christ delivered them over to Satan. But again, there was nothing arbitrary about this. Debate, painful and thorough, surrounded each case. The whole society was alive with argument. There were sermons morning and afternoon on Sundays, lectures on weekdays. An earnest spirit could move from lecture to lecture, church to church, comparing what different divines were saying. Notes taken in sermons were discussed at home afterwards. Debate was as characteristic of these people as discipline.

VII

Doctrinal disputes led to some breaking away. But splits were inherent also in the economic basis of settlement. Most colonists aimed to create a self-sufficient agriculture like that of rural England – and, incidentally, to perpetuate already obsolescent 'open-field' methods – rather than to prosper through planting staple crops, as in Virginia and Barbados. Yet the soil was sparse, and good land round the Bay soon filled. Meanwhile, only trade with England could bring the clothes, tools and so forth required by an English type of society; and only furs offered a ready item of exchange for such manufactures. The Bay area, with its short rivers, was not good beaver country. Local furs were soon exhausted and from 1633 there was a rush for the wilderness which lay between Massachusetts and the Dutch settlements on the Hudson. As first Plymouth, then Boston fur traders moved in there, word came to the Bay of rich meadows along the Connecticut River. John Winthrop's son, also John (the first notable Jr in North American history), with backing from Puritan lords and gentry in England, including the famous names of Pym and Hampden, proposed to set up a plantation at its mouth and acquired a dubious patent to the area. He arrived in Boston in mid-1635 and declared that Connecticut lay outside Massachusetts' jurisdiction.

It was swiftly agreed that an independent government should be established. The Reverend Thomas Hooker led thirty-five men and their families overland through rugged country in the summer of 1636. The white man's westward drive in North America had begun as the settlers prodded their cattle before them, fed on the milk which they provided, and slept in the open, 'having no pillows to use to take their nightly rest but upon such as their father Jacob found in the way to Padan-Aram.'[51]

Connecticut grew slowly, to only about 3,000 people by 1654. Its communities, in heavily wooded country, were much exercised by wolves, bears and wildcats. Without much sea-going trade, they developed a way of life based on grain-growing and the rearing of cattle, the latter providing meat, and milk, leather, and strength for ploughing and hauling. A man's status was measured by his herd. There were, in effect, neither rich nor poor. Without a charter, the settlers, like the Pilgrims before them, made their own social contracts, evolving in 1639 their famous 'Fundamental Orders', from which all reference to the authority of the King was omitted, perhaps deliberately. Despite the modern-sounding ring of Hooker's pronouncement that 'the foundation of authority is laid in the free consent of the people',[52] only church members could be freemen, and the system of government was much the same as in Massachusetts.

Another new colony to the westward was founded at New Haven by the Reverend John Davenport in 1637. Several wealthy London merchants provided the backing and the site chosen (in Long Island Sound at the mouth of the Quinnipiac River) seemed to promise, with its spacious harbour, a busy trade and fat profits from beaver skins. But the river was narrow and short, beavers were few. As the colony's once-hopeful merchants scattered and the remaining settlers farmed the poor land, New Haven became the most theocratic of New England colonies, under the virtual dictatorship of Theophilus Eaton. Dancing and singing were forbidden, small misdemeanours met severe punishment, and there was at least one execution for adultery.[53]

Rhode Island, by contrast, developed as a true 'haven' for various kinds of heretic. Its pioneer was the most attractive of all Puritans, Roger Williams, a young divine from a London merchant background, who was a centre of storms from his first arrival in Massachusetts in 1631. His sincerity was respected by all his adversaries, while his charm made them sorry to censure him, but his very own way of reading the Bible equipped him with a range of horrific ideas. An orthodox Calvinist, but an extreme purist, he denied that the New England settlers could consider themselves a chosen people – ' ... In respect of the Lord's special propriety to one country more than another, what difference between Asia and Africa, between Europe and America ... ?' Massachusetts, he said, had no scriptural right to persecute dissidents. Its churches contained hypocrites; elect mingled in them with non-elect, the 'herds of the world' with the 'flock of Christ'. Church and State, he held, should be completely separate. No commonwealth could by 'spiritual rape' force all consciences into conformity, and only Jesus had the right to judge men in spiritual matters; they should be left alone, their opinions tolerated, till He made His harvest and sinners were properly punished. But Williams's Christ was not stern. He had been 'a beggar's brat laid in a manger and gallows-bird.' God's son represented all the earth's dispossessed. He also exemplified love for all men and unconcern for worldly possessions. The Christian's task was to imitate him.[54]

Worse still, perhaps, from the orthodox point of view, Williams's ideas regarding the Indians raised in a most embarrassing form the niggling matter that Puritans who had proclaimed the aim of converting the red man, were doing little or nothing about it: and meantime encroaching on Indian lands. While their doctrine instilled a contempt for all people outside their own covenant with God, Williams assumed that all men were sons of Adam and Indians were no worse than white men. He liked many of them. He traded among them from his first arrival. He journeyed, he said, hundreds of miles through their lands without danger, sharing their diet of parched or boiled maize, their dried chestnuts, their strawberry bread and currant bread, their dried smoked fish, the clams which they boiled to make broth. He sold them the Dutch and English cloth mantles which they preferred to their own furs, and noted their shrewdness in bargaining – they would travel for miles to find a trader who would pay sixpence more. His *Key into the Language of America*, published in London in 1643, was in effect the first objective anthropological study of Indian culture, as well as the first textbook by an Englishman on any Indian tongue. He respected even the Indian way of government. Their chiefs, he said, would do nothing 'unto which the people are averse, and by gentle perswasion cannot be brought'; and *they* persecuted no man for his religion.[55] Williams made little attempt to convert them to his; his Calvinist logic taught him that there was no point in getting them to submit to set forms of worship.

He moved from his first post as teacher at Salem to Plymouth, where he shocked Governor Bradford by telling him that the colony's patent from James I was worthless, since the country had belonged to the Indians and James had had no right to give it away. Returning to Massachusetts, he made the same point to Governor Winthrop – only purchase from red men could make the Puritan presence valid. These and other opinions were too much to stomach; he was banished. In January 1636, with one companion, he headed south, through the hardships of bitter winter. Four others came to join him in founding, at a site bought from the Indians in Narragansett Bay, a new place called 'Providence', where land was shared on principles of equality, people governed themselves through a social compact, and liberty of conscience was an agreed principle.

Ironically, Williams's move suited Massachusetts real-politics pretty well. John Winthrop, who liked him, continued to correspond with him and saw his usefulness as a mediator with the Indians. Trouble had long been brewing with the Pequot tribe which had moved into the area between the Connecticut River and Narragansett Bay. Pequot attacks on fur traders and then, in 1637, on the Connecticut settlements (thirty people were massacred at Wethersfield) prompted a war of extermination, in which whites joined with Indian allies. Williams, settled amongst them, helped to keep the Narragansett Indians loyal, literally sweetening their chief with gifts of sugar. At the climax of the brisk campaign, several hundred Pequots were surrounded in their fort at Mystic, which was set on fire; those who ran away were hewn down and run through. The Puritans attributed this pleasant outcome to the general fast ordered in Massachusetts for the previous day, and their Lord wore his Old Testament face. 'It was a fearfull sight to see them thus frying in the fyer, and the streams of blood quenching the same, and horrible was the stincke and sente ther of; but the victory seemed a sweete sacrifice, and they gave the prays therof to God ...'[56]

Meanwhile tensions within Massachusetts produced the 'Antinomian Controversy' of 1635-8. Its background is found in the uneasy position within the godly commonwealth of two groups: women, at large, and the merchant class.

In the Puritan farm, workshop or business, the wife worked alongside her husband as partner. And in Winthrop's Boston, women actually outnumbered men among the 'elect' who were church members, though three male colonists, it would appear, arrived in New England for every two women. Shortage of women on the frontier, which contrasted with a surplus of them in England, made for easier marriage and higher status. Puritans eschewed the idea that marriage was a sacrament as a 'Popish error', and the civil, contractual basis of union was one of the legal differences between New and Old England which helped give women a measure of security and, in effect, of independence which they could not enjoy at home. Yet the family was conceived as a sphere where the father's role was to teach and chasten servants, women and children alike. Winthrop's journal shows more than one instance suggesting that puritanism could drive wives to desperation, such as that of the woman who fell out with her husband, was expelled from the Salem congregation, was whipped at the magistrates' order, and later, 'possessed with Satan', broke the neck of her 3-year-old daughter that she might save her from future misery. Yet puritanism, encouraging ideas of spiritual equality even as it denied women an equal share in church organisation, was 'subtly and unconsciously an underminer of that very patriarchalism it publicly championed.'[57]

The businessmen likewise suffered, though less painfully, from the ambivalence of Puritan social doctrine. Puritanism was ready to aver that, for one of the elect, any calling was as good as another, there was nothing corrupting in trade; and Edward Winslow, one of the Pilgrim Fathers, had described America as a place where 'religion and profit jump together'. But the founders of Massachusetts retained a traditional belief in the 'just price' and were ready to regulate both prices and wages. This proved impossible. While scarcity of skilled workmen pushed wages up to the point where a carpenter or a mason could find himself as prosperous as his social superiors, people were willing to pay almost anything for imported, manufactured necessities. No merchant already in the front rank emigrated from England. Mere tradesmen from London became merchants and dominated Boston and neighbouring towns, yet they did not control the government of the colony as a whole and provided only two out of the twenty-two magistrates elected over the first ten years. In 1639, Robert Keayne was fined £200 in the General Court for 'taking above sixpence in the shilling profit; in some above eight pence; and in some small things, above two for one.' He was also severely admonished by the Church. Since he was a devout man, this pained him deeply.[58]

Anne Hutchinson was the wife of one prominent early merchant, the sister-in-law of another, the parent of a third, as well as the mother of fourteen other children. Her family had followed from England the preacher John Cotton, whom Anne idolised. From his insistence that, for one whom God had chosen, union with Christ was complete before and without any work or act of faith on his or her part, Anne developed her own 'antinomian' doctrine that the saint who felt the presence of God in his or her own heart was freed from the shackles of moral law, since whatever he or she did must be God's will – 'I live but not I but Jesus Christ lives in me.'[59] In her forties, with powerful mind and attractive personality, Anne gathered women around her for regular meetings. Some men were coming too. The Holy Ghost within her, as she understood it, gave her the right to preach to both sexes alike. All authority was threatened, that of magistrate, minister, along with that of the male head of the family. One of the orthodox sourly defined her allure. ' ... The weaker Sex prevailed so farre, that they set up a Priest of their own Profession and Sex, who was much thronged after ... Come along with me, says one of them, i'le bring you to a Woman that Preaches better Gospell than any of your black-coates that have been at the Ninneversity ... and for my part, saith hee, I had rather hear such a one that speakes from the meere motion of the spirit, without any study at all, then any of your learned Scollers ... '[60]

But her doctrines also appealed to rich merchants, to men curbed by a coalition of magistrates with country farmers from handling business as they thought best. Why shouldn't the saved merchant do as he liked? Most of the Boston church came round to her way of thinking. So did Sir Harry Vane the Younger, a man of distinguished family who was elected president of the colony in 1636. But clergy and magistrates struck back, with the country people behind them. Next year, Vane was voted from office and Winthrop, re-elected governor, led a thorough campaign against Mrs Hutchinson and her followers. After a trial for sedition before the General Court, Anne was sentenced to be banished as a 'woman not fit for our society'.

One of her followers was William Coddington, a merchant and probably the richest man in Boston. He and eighteen others incorporated themselves as a 'Bodie Politick' under Christ and moved southwards. With Roger Williams's help, Coddington bought the island of Aquidneck, similar in shape to Rhodes, from which the colony would eventually get its name. Here Anne and her family settled in 1638 in the town of 'Portsmouth'. Deposed as chief magistrate in favour of Anne's husband, Coddington moved on with his faction to found 'Newport' on the same island. The two embryonic towns merged next year in a miniature state which, like Providence, proclaimed religious toleration. 'Rhode Island' for Anne Hutchinson proved as quarrelsome as Massachusetts, and she ranged on after her husband's death to settle a remote spot in the Dutch territories. Her six youngest children were with her. In 1643 she was murdered, with five of them, in an Indian rising. The sole survivor, a daughter, lived several years with her captors. Restored at a truce, she was loath to leave them; she had forgotten her own language.

Another great troublemaker had entered Williams's sphere, Samuel Gorton, radical spokesman for the lower orders, who founded a settlement at 'Warwick' which fizzed with so many dangerous ideas that the Massachusetts authorities moved in to stamp it out in 1643 and took him and twenty-five fellow colonists to Boston. The sympathy of the poor there made it impossible for them to punish him, and he was back before long. So there were now four independent towns in the area where Williams had been the white pioneer. That seeker of lost Zion had been joined by some Baptists and had communed with them for a while, then had broken away (while maintaining friendly relations) to make a church of two with his own wife. Sick Indians, Indians wanting shelter, Indians asking advice constantly came to his house. The wilderness was not only a fact which he lived with at Providence, it was his image of the world, through which men of all races moved seeking the truth. England was spiritually as waste as the Narragansett country. Papists, Jews and Muhammadans all had consciences which could not be forced by persecution. What an abomination, Williams thought, and would write, were wars between absolutist religious creeds; how pointless, alien to Christ's own spirit.

Williams was a trader. As his neighbour Coddington would have agreed, toleration was essential in trade. How could Englishmen do business in Italy or in Constantinople if they could not co-exist peacefully with papists and brown infidels? How could they trade in India save by the forbearance of Muslim rulers? Eventually, the advance of commerce would help to secure general acceptance for the Rhode Island view.

VIII

Charles I's reign was a dim time for the East India Company. Profits were disappointing. The trade with Persia launched in 1628 soon languished. Famine stifled commerce in Gujerat in the early 1630s, making times hard for the Surat factory. Whereas 50 ships had been sent East between 1620 and 1630, only 37 went in the following decade.[61]

The Dutch overweened more than ever. They gained an ascendancy in Siam which would last for decades and intervened in Ceylon, whence they ousted the Portuguese by 1663. Malacca fell to them after a long blockade in 1641, and in the same year they became the sole Westerners allowed to trade with Japan. From 1642 to 1661, they controlled Formosa. Their sea-explorer Tasman followed up earlier Dutch sightings of the coast of Australia (first noticed in 1616) and in 1642–3 reached Tasmania and New Zealand. These had as yet no economic significance, but the Dutch colony founded in 1652 at the Cape of Good Hope was directly useful in provisioning ships on the way East. It is hard to realise now how enormous seemed the scope of Dutch enterprise. Faced by such might, the Portuguese willy-nilly grew friends with the English. A Convention signed at Goa in 1635 was followed by a treaty seven years later; lasting peace between the two nations began in the East.

By 1620 the EIC organisation there had achieved a definitive form. The factories at Surat and Bantam each had a 'president' with near absolute authority. Persian affairs came under the Surat Presidency; the Coromandel Coast of south-eastern India was part of the Bantam President's province. The 'factors' sent East had to execute a bond or security which specified their terms of duty and guaranteed their good behaviour by a financial penalty; this meant that the senior factors, who stood to lose most, had to be men·of some means and the junior ones had to find rich and willing patrons. Nevertheless, the EIC was chronically, rightly suspicious of its people, and was constantly involved in litigation with them. They were well paid; they were encouraged to invest in the Company, and some came to have quite large holdings, but it was quite impossible to prevent them from going in for private trade on their own account and so in effect competing with their employers. Almost every factor was accused of it. In 1628, the EIC persuaded the Crown to issue a proclamation threatening offenders with severe punishment, but this also conceded that Company servants might trade freely in some commodities, and gave them a limited quota in all others.

The EIC, true to its age, spliced business with piety. Its coat of arms bore the sanctimonious pun *Deus Indicat*, 'God Points the Way'. In 1611, it sent East for the 'better comfort and recreation' of its employees the works of the famous Puritan thinker William Perkins, as well as Foxe's *Book of Martyrs* and Hakluyt's *Voyages*. Its instructions to its servants mixed concern for economy (thus, there should be no unnecessary shooting-off of salutes when captains went ashore) with more directly puritanical maxims. Gaming and dicing were forbidden. Excessive drinking was denounced. Company servants were placed under a collegiate regime which in theory, if not in fact, made it possible to enforce temperate behaviour, and one foreign observer was impressed in 1638 with the discipline and piety of the Surat factory, where divine service was held twice daily.[62]

But the English vied even with the notorious Dutch in the depth and frequency of their compotations. A seventeenth-century tombstone in Coromandel makes the point:

> The Dutch and the English were here
> And they drank Toddy for want of beer.

The word 'punch' entered the English language from the Marathi *panch*, meaning five, which signified the five ingredients of an insidious brew mixing sugar, lime-juice, spice and water with arrack, the local spirit. In five years, 1630–1634, 48 out of 190 EIC factors died, and one modern authority would suggest that drink accounted for most of them.[63]

Without drink, how bearable would life have been? Three Bantam factors complained to the Company bitterly in 1618: 'At home is content; abroad nothing so much as grief, cares, and displeasure. At home is safety; abroad no security. At home is liberty; abroad the best is bondage.'[64] To relieve their 'displeasure', since white women were absent, EIC servants turned, like the Dutch and Portuguese, to native women. A British proverb in India one day would be, 'Necessity is the mother of invention and the father of the Eurasian.'

Controlling whole territories, Portuguese and Dutch had comported themselves with racialist arrogance, holding many slaves and living, in Goa and Bantam, with great ostentation. This the English could not do. Nor were they tempted to missionary endeavour. Portuguese priests, helped on occasion by force, gained many thousands of converts in India and Ceylon (now Sri Lanka) and had for a time surprising success in Japan. Even the Dutch sent out preachers, though these were inferior both in number and calibre and the austerities of Calvinism were harder to peddle than papistry with its pomp, its lavish imagery and its incense. The English, with no territory to speak of, acquired a habit of concentrating on trade and leaving the natives to their own religion.

Their scope was enlarged greatly in 1640, when Fort St George was established at the village which later became Madras, on the Coromandel Coast. The English centre on that coast, from 1611, had been at Masulipatam, with sub-factories growing up elsewhere later. But cotton chintzes were cheaper to southward, and the English eagerly accepted the invitation from a local ruler which gave them a new headquarters. By 1652 Madras was so important that the 'Eastern Presidency' was transferred there from Bantam. The English had meanwhile moved into Bengal, a rich land of raw silk, of sugar, of saltpetre. There was a factory at Hugli from 1651, and soon sub-factories in the Ganges valley.

Long afterwards, this slow and gradual expansion would seem to have been begotten by manifest destiny out of inevitability. Yet the EIC's very existence was still fragile. The system of terminable stocks had encouraged a search for quick profits at the expense of long-term interests. By 1637, the Company was in debt for £100,000. Its appeal had faltered. By contrast with £1,600,000 subscribed for the second joint stock of 1617, in the 20 years after 1636 four successive joint stocks aggregated only about £600,000 between them.[65] And the Company had in effect lost its monopoly, thanks to Charles I's own drive for money.

In 1628, Charles had used a troublemaker within the EIC called Smerthwicke as his agent in a scheme to get himself admitted as adventurer for a fifth of the EIC's whole stock and profits, without any payment by him, in return for taking the Company under his protection. The shareholders would have none of this. But in the mid-1630s Charles backed the interloping 'Courteen Association', in which he was credited with £10,000 worth of free stock. The chief actors in this enterprise were a famous courtier, Endymion Porter, and two London merchants, Sir William Courteen and Sir Paul Pinder, who had lent the King vast sums of money. Courteen will be remembered as the founder of Barbados. The Association did not thrive. All the ships of its first expedition (1636) were taken or destroyed by the Dutch. But a few short-lived factories were established in India, and meanwhile the EIC was weakened not only at home but in the East, where the piracies of Courteen's ships in the Red Sea led to the imprisonment, by way of retaliation, of its own servants in Surat.[66]

Just as Charles I's shortage of cash prevented him from having any effective foreign policy — with no parliament to back him, he could not afford war — so, as the Courteen Association showed, it distracted him from establishing any coherent 'mercantilist' policy. There were haverings over the important Newfoundland fisheries. The West Country interests involved were able to claim to the Privy Council in 1634 that this remarkable 'nursery of seamen' employed about 10,680 mariners annually. In that year they obtained a charter from the King regulating the industry and confirming their fishing rights in Newfoundland. The old custom that the master of the first fishing ship to arrive became 'admiral' and ruler of the harbour was now confirmed in writing. The right to enforce regulations was vested in the mayors of nine West Country ports — Southampton, Weymouth and Melcombe Regis, Lyme, Plymouth, Dartmouth, East Looe, Fowey and Barnstaple. This seemed to be victory for their merchants over the handfuls of planters who lived on Newfoundland all the year round, and over the London interests which supported them. But in 1637 Sir David Kirke, once the privateer captor of Quebec, came up with a scheme, backed by London merchants, which would give him and three great noblemen proprietary rights over practically the whole fishing area of north-eastern America. They could not get all they wanted. The proprietors' privileges were greatly restricted and the freedom of all Charles's subjects to fish at Newfoundland was clearly affirmed. Even so, the West Countrymen, after Kirke had gone out as governor in 1638, complained not only that planters were bagging the best fishing places and destroying their property, but that Kirke was licensing taverns in despite of his charter and making their fishermen unfit for work.[67]

Kirke was a staunch Royalist. But Charles was prepared to permit noted Puritans to essay an imaginative plan in the Caribbean. Though it failed, the 'Providence Island' scheme was second in significance only to Massachusetts among new overseas ventures of Charles's reign. Its first mover was Robert Rich, second Earl of Warwick, that jolly Puritan whose fortune matched his name. Besides being active in the Virginia, Somers Island and East India Companies, the Guinea Company and the Plymouth Company for New England, Warwick had helped finance North's Guiana expedition in 1619; in the same year one of his ships had landed the first cargo of black slaves ever sold in Virginia; he had helped to get the Pilgrim Fathers their patent; and in the late 1620s, authorised to privateer against Spain, had joined with London merchants to launch a whole fleet of predators. He now conceived that Santa Catalina, a speck off the coast of what is now Nicaragua, would be a good place for a Puritan colony. The name 'Providence' was invented for it. It looked a fine base for privateers. In 1630 a company was chartered.

The list of its investors might serve also for a roll-call of leaders of Puritan opposition in Parliament. Its treasurer was none other than John Pym, who made its affairs his main interest through the 1630s. Through family and business connections, the Company's leaders were linked with John Hampden, with the Winthrops, and with Oliver Cromwell, who at one time thought of going to Providence Island himself. As in West Indian pioneering generally, there was an East Midland and East Anglian bias in this group, as marked as the West Country flavour in Elizabethan New World adventure.

The Providence Island Company was the link between the anti-papist zeal of the 1580s and the aggressive Protestant imperialism of the 1650s. Its base was six miles long and four miles wide, large enough for purposes not unlike those of an aircraft carrier. Ninety Englishmen landed in May 1631. Their governor, Philip Bell, had instructions to confiscate and destroy all cards and dice, and he forbade mixed dancing, which became possible next year when women and children arrived. His mace had a silver plate at one end on which was portrayed the Company's seal: ' ... viz. three islands and the words written about it *Legem ejus expectabunt*, taken out of Isaiah, 42., 4, "The islands shall wait for his law", which prophecy we hope', added the Company, 'may in some sort be fulfilled by planting the Gospel in those islands.'[68] Tobacco, cotton, madder and indigo were planted as well. The Dutch were indispensable here as elsewhere, buying the first year's crop and imposing themselves as traders despite complaints from the directors in England. Piracy was on the agenda from the first, and the vision of a godly commonwealth rapidly broke down in practice. When the last group of distinctively Puritan immigrants arrived in July 1633, the minister who led them was so shocked by the gulf between project and reality that he shortly went home to voice the complaints of the more sincere settlers. The next batch sent out were indentured servants recruited by paid agents.

By 1635, 'New Westminster' had church and governor's house built of brick, and the island bore 500 white men, 40 white women, a few children; and 90 black slaves. One Samuel Rishworth had protested against the introduction of these last and had assisted a number to escape. The Company sneered at his 'groundless opinion that Christians may not lawfully keep such persons in a state of servitude during their strangeness from Christianity.' Religion, he should learn, consisted 'not so much in an outward conformity of actions as in truth of the inward parts.' (Respectable Puritan men could, when their profits were touched, sound as 'antinomian' as Mrs Hutchinson.) As privateers brought hijacked ships to the island, these provided cheap Africans a-plenty. By 1637 there were almost as many blacks as whites on Providence, and planters were showing reluctance to accept white servants. The process by which black slavery lowered the cost of labour and so destroyed the dignity of work swept on more rapidly here th in it had done or would do anywhere else in the English New World. The Company complained that the increased use of slaves 'brought down the bodies and labours of men to such cheapness that we shall not be able to supply servants as we have done formerly', and attempted to stem the black influx. Too late. The sale of slaves to other plantations became an important trade for Providence. A large body of runaway Africans took to the woods. A slave revolt at the end of 1638 was suppressed only with great difficulty.[69]

The Company also busied itself with the island of Tortuga, off the north-west of Hispaniola. A body of settlers from St Kitts and Nevis had found their way there after a Spanish attack on those islands, and their leader, a rascal named Anthony Hilton, was able to secure from the Company an official governorship and a splendid mask for the new trade of 'buccaneering'. The island was renamed 'Association', but the Spaniards moved in and crushed its pirates in 1635. Meanwhile, the Company sought trade with the Moskito Indians of the Central American coastline. There was more than Christian principle involved when Pym ordered the captain of the vessel sent there, 'You are to endear your-selves with the Indians and their commanders and we conjure you to be friendly and cause no jealousy.'[70] The natives of this part had been viewed since the days of Drake as likely valuable allies against the Spaniards. And in fact, besides a small settlement at Cape Gracias á Dios, trading in flax or 'silk grass', the Company somehow established genuine good relations with the Moskitos, who were allied with the English, more and more unequally, down to our own century.

A Spanish attack on Providence, beaten off in 1635, came most opportunely. The Company asked for, and Charles gave, permission to make reprisals. Its promoters, who had been losing heavily on the colony, now reorganised it for blatant depredation. Settlers were encouraged to privateer and to pay for their own defence out of the profits. When the Spaniards failed again in 1640, the deputy governor executed papist prisoners who had been promised their lives; then, when both the island's ministers of religion protested, shipped them home in chains, consigning them to the hands of Archbishop Laud as 'disaffected' from Anglican conformity.[71] It was an odd outcome from all the colony's pious aims. Tough though Providence Island was — with six hundred men able to bear arms and a great many cannon — the Spaniards compelled its surrender in 1641. They were merciful. The women and children were sent home to England, the men taken as prisoners to Spain. Vast hauls from privateering were now exposed to the eyes of its victims. The loss of Providence rankled among its promoters and their allies in England, though these Puritans were by now embroiled in climactic struggle against the King at home. They would deal with Charles first, and then with the papists later. Events in Scotland and Ireland had swept the ball to their feet.

IX

Ireland saw Charles I's regime at its most vigorous, Scotland the King at his weakest and silliest. Here were the flashpoints of revolutionary civil war.

As the half-closed back door, still, to England, Ireland demanded a strong army. By 1622, the force which existed was pitiful and its pay was two and a half years in arrears. From that year, to help the Crown's quest for money, the work of the Irish Court of Wards was expanded. It bore hard on the Catholic 'Old English' landowners. Minors from Catholic families were brought up as Protestants, the greatest example being James Butler, later first Duke of Ormond, a dominating figure in seventeenth-century Irish history. Catholic heirs were forced to take the oath of supremacy or to leave themselves at the Court's mercy. Most of the land of Catholic wards was leased to Protestants. The 'Old English' were now faced with piecemeal destruction.

Yet this was the very class to whom Charles I had to turn for financial support as war, from 1625, reopened the danger of Spanish invasion of Ireland. Hence the bargain summed up in the 'Graces' of May 1628. In return for three annual subsidies of £40,000 each, the King offered fifty-one concessions, which he promised would be confirmed by a parliament. Grace 24 met the fears of landowners that their property could be snatched from them – except in King's and Queen's Counties the Crown would renounce all titles to land of more than sixty years' standing. Grace 25 covered the only area, Connacht and Clare, where this guarantee was not enough. Here, in 1585, all freeholders had surrendered their lands to have them regranted with new and secure titles. The resulting grants had never been enrolled in the Court of Chancery. Charles now offered that the enrolments would be made.

These and other Graces showed that the Old English had some bargaining power, but what followed exposed their essential frailty. They were so frightened of the native Gaels that they felt a desperate need for the King's army. The parliament promised to them was not summoned, yet the subsidies still came in. The faithless Charles realised he need not call one. While most of the Graces (probably) were implemented, Articles 24 and 25 were not, and as relations with Spain eased, the Dublin authorities launched severe anti-Catholic policies. For three years, 1629–32, Ireland was ruled, in the absence of a viceroy, by two 'New English' Protestants, Adam Loftus and Richard Boyle, Earl of Cork, as Lords Justices. Then Charles appointed as Deputy, Thomas, Viscount Wentworth, who was already a species of viceroy in England, where he was President of the Council of the North.

Wentworth was forty years old when he came to Ireland, a strong administrator at the peak of his powers, a man of angry, self-interested determination to enhance the power of the king whom he served, and whose full confidence he enjoyed. Writing to Laud, Charles's other prime henchman, in 1633, Wentworth called for a common policy of 'Thorough' – driving 'through'

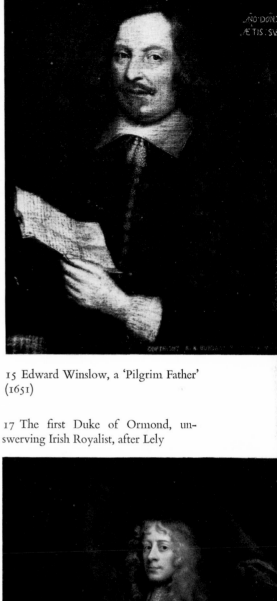

14 John Winthrop the elder

15 Edward Winslow, a 'Pilgrim Father' (1651)

16 Archibald Campbell, eighth Earl of Argyll – the Covenanting hero

17 The first Duke of Ormond, un-swerving Irish Royalist, after Lely

18 William Petty as a young man, by I. Fuller

('thorough') all interests which lay in the way of the religious and administrative unity of the realm. Ireland, it seems, was being consciously used as a testing ground for policies to be tried later in England. Laud, Wentworth and Charles alike aimed to override the common law which secured English landowners in their property, of which a version operated in Ireland, and to root out the 'puritanism' which expressed the resistance of landowners and others to hierarchy in State as well as in Church.

The spirit of Wentworth is expressed in an image we have of him soon after his arrival in Ireland in 1633. Aiming to bring the King's wretched Irish army back to discipline, Wentworth, although no soldier, set an example by drilling his own troop of sixty in person. A letter writer described him at this work 'on a large green near Dublin, clad in black armour with a black horse and a black plume of feathers ... '[72] Saturnine, militant, burnished and autocratic, the black man's goal was a French-style absolutism. Pursuing it, he was ready to bully and lie with as strong a conviction as his untrustworthy master.

The subsidies granted in 1628 were about to run out. The Irish government was running at an annual deficit of about £20,000 and had a gross debt of £76,000. Cork and Loftus in 1632 had proposed to meet this situation by reimposing the fines levied on papists for not attending the right church on Sunday. Typical Caroline deviousness ensued. Charles, at Wentworth's instigation, sent a letter to the Lords Justices authorising this step, though only as an alternative to subsidies, but smearing responsibility for it on them and ordering that his letter be made public. The aim was to persuade the Irish Commons to vote money. Cork, never outdone in shiftiness, concealed the letter, began to levy fines and tried to fix the blame on Wentworth. Wentworth, however, made sure that Cork was held responsible, then graciously withdrew the threat of fines, which sufficed to persuade the grateful Old English to renew the subsidy for another year. This was the classic policy of divide-and-rule, which Wentworth later described as being to 'bow and govern the Native by the Planter and the Planter by the Native'.[73]

He despised the self-interested New English clique who formed the Irish Privy Council – 'a company of men the most intent upon their own ends that ever I met with.' His struggle with them matched, in exaggerated form, his royal master's contest with English Puritan landowners, and every victory which he scored over them seemed ominous to their counterparts in England. To his unscrupulous victims, his methods appeared shockingly unscrupulous. Cork had acquired his vast fortune largely by cheating Crown and Church. Wentworth had him prosecuted and fined to the tune of £15,000. Cork had long leases and fee farms of various episcopal lands and other church lands, and enjoyed the tithes of numerous livings; these gains were protected by the accepted principles and practices of Irish law. But Wentworth fiddled the law and smashed Cork's carefully built-up position to fragments.[74] He dealt equally brusquely with other great men; Loftus spent sixteen months under arrest.

H

But Wentworth, it was rightly said, while 'violently zealous in his master's ends' was 'not negligent of his own.' He chased and very swiftly got wealth by the methods of his age—selling offices which were in his gift and taking every chance which his high position afforded for helping himself, and his friends, to what was going. He profited vastly from the Irish customs. His income from Irish sources was £13,000 a year. The vast house which he built for himself near Naas cost £22,000. Besides 14,000 acres granted him by the King he bought, for a total of £35,000, some 20,000 acres of Irish land.[75] Sheer jealousy must gather men against him.

The parliament which he summoned in 1634 unanimously voted subsidies, to cover six years, of £120,000—neither 'Planter' nor 'Native' daring to seem remiss and give cause for him to favour the other side. But Wentworth did not intend to fulfil the King's promise. With the subsidies safely granted, he gave out that only ten of the Graces would pass into law and the most important of these confirmed the titles of Protestant undertakers in Ulster and Leinster. The rest would continue only at His Majesty's discretion, and on the vital Articles 24 and 25 he made no promise of action at all. An Old English pamphleteer depicts him 'In a scoffing and jeering manner telling the committee appointed to attend him in blunt terms that they had more already than their six little subsidies were worth ... '[76]

Wentworth proceeded to violate Article 25. 'Plantation' was pushed forward into Connacht. Under the Burke Earl of Clanrickarde and the O Brien Earl of Thomond, the province had been generally 'loyal' in Tyrone's war, but now that the threat of the Ulster Gaels seemed vanished, the value of allies in Connacht was much diminished. The Crown had a specious claim to the province. Wentworth now proposed to confiscate lands even in Clanrickarde's county of Galway, which Boyle himself had never thought of touching. Three other counties were affected. Under the 'stern looks' of Wentworth in person, juries in Sligo, Roscommon and Mayo 'found' for the King. But in August 1635 the Galway jury stood fast and refused to find the King's title except for part of the lands, even though Wentworth himself was there, staying impertinently in Clanrickarde's house, and, it was angrily noted, 'casting himself in his riding boots upon very rich beds'.[77] The Sheriff of Galway died in the prison where Wentworth flung him. His jurymen were tried in the Court of Castle Chamber (Ireland's equivalent of the notorious Star Chamber) and each was fined £4,000, plus imprisonment. When at last they gave in and agreed to the King's title, their fines were reduced and they were released. Instead of the quarter or third originally intended, Wentworth vindictively now proposed to plant half County Galway with new settlers. Observing the fear of the Old English, he wrote gloatingly, 'they within the Pale beginn now to find his Majestie hath the same title to a great part of Meath which he hath to Conaght and that many other places amongst them alsoe are upon other faire and just claims subject to plantation.'[78]

In fact, Wentworth could not recruit settlers, and Clanrickarde sustained a successful fight at the royal court, where his family had influence. The plantation made no progress; all Wentworth's brutal deployment of arbitrary power had done was to drive the Old English towards desperation. Otherwise, certainly, his rule seemed effective. His government's debts had been cleared, the army revitalised, administration reformed. Algerine pirates in 1631 had sacked Baltimore in the south-west and carried off over a hundred people to slavery;[79] but Wentworth could claim that he had cleared the seas. Trade throve, enriching the Crown from rising customs, and Wentworth pursued the clever 'mercantilist' line of trying to stimulate a linen cloth industry which would complement English success in woollens. Yet everything he did alienated someone. Merchants were worried by tightening royal control. The Ulster planters also were agitated.

One cause of grievance in Ulster was not Wentworth's fault. In 1635 the English Court of Star Chamber found that the London men concerned in Derry had failed to comply with the conditions of the City's agreement with the Crown. In 1637 they yielded up their rights and agreed to pay a £12,000 fine in return for a pardon. The King's agents, sent into Ulster, raised rents and dispossessed certain important proprietors. Meanwhile the Ulster Scots were shocked by the Laudian programme which Wentworth had brought over for the Irish Church.

Except around garrisons and plantation settlements the established Church of Ireland had little life or influence. Its only real centre of relative strength was Ulster, and this was because the inflowing Scots had found no trouble in joining a Church which, by articles adopted in 1615, was strongly Calvinist in emphasis. Meanwhile, toleration had been sufficient over the years to permit the Roman Church to strengthen itself. Priests were trained by hundreds in Europe. Most dioceses now had resident Catholic bishops.

Into this froward ambience, Wentworth imported his chaplain, one John Bramhall, an ardent Laudian, who grimly wrote back to Laud after a fortnight that one parish church in Dublin was the viceroy's stable, another a tennis court where the vicar acted as keeper. The lower established clergy, he reported, were 'below all degrees of contempt, in respect of their poverty and ignorance ... ' Bishop of Derry from 1634, Bramhall became the effectual primate of Ireland. The nominal primate, Archbishop Ussher, was helpless, as Laudian bishops fresh from England were rushed into vacant sees, as the 39 articles and the English canons were introduced, and as fines and imprisonments enforced conformity. The Earl of Cork had raised an immense monument in black marble to his late wife, at the spot in St Patrick's Cathedral, Dublin, where the High Altar had formerly stood. In the interests of Laudian ritualism, he was compelled to take it down stone by stone and to re-erect it elsewhere.[80]

But it was in Edinburgh that revolt against Laud took fire. Revolution in Scotland preceded, and made possible, revolution in England. As an English historian writes, 'King Charles's government did not fall by any mistakes in its dealings with the English opposition, but through over-confidence in its handling of the poor and despised kingdom of Scotland.'[81]

James VI and I had boasted once that he governed Scotland with his pen in London, though others had failed to do so with the sword. But he had lived in Scotland as child and man, and this largely explains the contrast between his success and his son's ruin. Charles, though he kept a Scottish accent till his head fell, understood his compatriots even less well than he understood the English, his tactlessness and high-handedness were naked in his dealings with them, and he compounded all errors by his failure to explain either to Scots or to southrons what aims informed his policies north of the Border. Incomprehension bred suspicion which fuelled hatred.

In England, by 1637, Charles had few real friends left. He had alienated most of the peerage and gentry and could not rely even on all his bishops. But his enemies seethed in impotence. There was no rival claimant to the Crown whom they could support, there was no military force to speak of except that controlled by the King, and Puritan peers like Bedford and Warwick grudgingly played ball with Charles rather than risk their great possessions. Defiant squeaks from New England frightened no cats.

But in Scotland a magnate like the Earl of Argyll would have a family tradition of thinking himself, in most respects, as good a man as the king. Divide-and-rule might have worked here if Charles had ingratiated himself with the lesser landowners and the plebeian ministers of the Church whose interests were not those of the great peers. Instead, he achieved a miracle rarely matched before or after; almost the whole Scottish people united; against him.

He ruled Scotland, by the pen, through a feeble Privy Council in Edinburgh. There were few Scots now at his court (the debt-ridden Alexander, laird of Nova Scotia, being one main and fairly distinguished exception). Such Scots as sought him out there found their accents and penury mocked by the ceremonious elegance of that extravagant ambience on which the painter Van Dyck conferred so much vapid nobility. They went back to join those who grumbled that the King was dominated by Englishmen, nursing their grievance that they were absented from the rich pickings (for instance, whole empires in the New World) which fell, plop, plop, from the King's plate, while their country was denied any share in England's expanding overseas trade. When Charles visited Scotland in 1633, he loathed his own down-at-heel, uncouth people and those who met him disliked him for showing it.

He had started his reign with a blundering show of power. Approaching half of the landed income of Scotland came from former church property. By his 'Revocation' of 1625, Charles reasserted the Crown's right to all these and to the teinds (tithes) which they yielded. He intended only to take back a little, paying compensation to those who lost it, and in fact he could not afford to proceed thus in more than a few cases. But he insisted on full surrender although he had no intention of taking advantage of it. Great landowners were outraged, and not without cause, since Charles's aim was not only to fatten the Church and the Crown, but also to reduce landed power by taking over tithes and tenants. He jolted even the lesser lairds who might, with diplomacy, have been brought round to his side. As in Ireland, the feeling arose that no rights to land were secure, and watching Wentworth at work, it was not absurd to suppose that the same sweeping methods might be tried in Scotland. Above all, the 'lords of erection' were troubled, those numerous peers of recent creation who held former church lands granted by Charles's father.

Presbyterian ministers were now a smallish minority, many of them abroad in Ulster. Most Scots accepted the compromise evolved under James VI and I, whereby the Kirk (after 1610) had bishops, but these acted as moderators of synods. James had offended many with his 'Five Articles of Perth' of 1618, which had prescribed kneeling at holy communion and celebration of Christmas and Easter as holidays, but thereafter had had the sense not to press too hard against Puritan prejudice. The Scottish Church was in better shape than the English, its ministers were better paid and probably better educated; Scots liked it the way it was.

Charles didn't. Dogmatically Laudian, he tried to enhance the pomp of the Scottish bishops, and he pushed them forward as agents of his own power, making them take an increasingly large political role. Realising that he could not force the English liturgy as it stood upon Scotland, he ordered the Scottish bishops to suggest alterations. The result was a new Anglicised prayer-book imposed with amazing casual recklessness; neither Parliament nor Church Assembly was consulted. Here was a prime case of arbitrary rule. Substantial, non-Puritan Scots feared for their property, even for their lives, and meanwhile increased taxation was spreading anger. When the new prayer-book was introduced into St Giles' Cathedral, Edinburgh, in July 1637, the lower orders assuaged their own feelings by hurling stools and bibles at the Bishop. Petitions for the withdrawal of the new liturgy flooded in from other places. The Bishop of Brechin read the book to his congregation with a loaded pistol in each hand.

Malcontent nobles were willing to lead popular anti-Laudian agitation, amongst them the charming and gifted James Graham, Earl of Montrose. A revolutionary junta, 'the Tables', emerged, representing nobility, lairds, ministers, townspeople. By February 1638 a document had evolved, the 'National Covenant', which yoked both patriotism and holy fervour. Its lengthy text appealed to the anti-popery of the masses. It invoked the rule of law, as established through Parliament. Its aim was conservative, to defend the Church as preferred by the nation and the property rights of the Scottish subject. It pledged those who signed it to oppose innovations and all, including the King, who sought to make them. Changes would be the 'subversion and ruine of the true Reformed Religion and of our Libertie, Law and Estates.'[82] The signatories, however, might also conceive themselves as bound, with all true Scots, in a special treaty with God. The Scots could be seen as a chosen people. Whereas to those pondering New English history the word 'covenant' would eventually come to seem rather gentle and lovely, almost the same thing as 'democracy', the results which flowed from a parallel theological view in Scotland gave the word 'covenanter' bloody and tragic significance, mixing it with intolerance and massacre.

In the Greyfriars church in Edinburgh, on February 18, leading nobles and lairds signed. Next day ministers and townsmen came forward. Copies were sent to every burgh and parish and, willingly or unwillingly, a great proportion of the whole people subscribed, or lifted up hands in church to signify assent. Ministers accepting the new liturgy were deposed. The Tables began to buy arms abroad and to drill troops.

Charles reacted as ineptly as possible. He withdrew the offending prayer-book, yet planned nevertheless to suppress the insolent Scots. He sent a Scots favourite, the Duke of Hamilton, north to lie, temporise, and pretend to negotiate. Meanwhile he had to grant the General Assembly of the Church which the Covenanters demanded — and then packed. This met in November, defied Hamilton, annulled the new liturgy and other 'popish' innovations, and deposed the bishops. The Scottish Privy Council's feckless rule had collapsed. All but one of its members walked out of the revolutionary Assembly. The one who stayed was squinting Archibald Campbell, 8th Earl of Argyll and perhaps the most notable man in all his line, who combined Presbyterian zeal with the familiar Campbell trait of dynastic ambition.

Where could Charles find an army? In the summer of 1639 he at last scraped one together, drawn largely from the English militia and financed by loans and gifts from rich papists and various office-holders and toadies. While Montrose, for the Covenanters, marched north to capture the resolutely episcopalian city of Aberdeen, the main Covenanting army sang its way south to oppose Charles. It was too strong for him. He did not fight. At Berwick, he promised the new rulers of Scotland a free Parliament and a free Assembly. Victorious in a crisis, men are tempted towards extremism, and zealots have their chance. Predictably, the new Assembly was still more defiant, declaring episcopacy to be contrary to the Law of God, and the new Parliament confirmed its acts. It made subscription to the Covenant compulsory and there was nothing which Charles could do to close its proceedings. Meanwhile, he had turned to his trusted strongman, Wentworth.

Numerous Ulster settlers had subscribed to the Covenant. Wentworth had acted quickly, expanding his army and stationing a large force at Carrickfergus to prevent any alliance with Scottish rebels. In May 1639 he imposed a 'Black Oath', repudiating the Covenant, on all Scots in Ulster. Many took it, unwillingly. Many fled to the woods and hills, or to Scotland. Many were gaoled in Dublin:

one family of four, with their servant, were fined a total of £13,000 and con-demned to life imprisonment.[83] Wentworth thought of expelling every unpropertied Scot from Ulster. But then he was summoned back to London. He became Earl of Strafford and Charles's chief minister. With Charles he drew up a fatal plan for an army of 9,000 men, to be created in Ireland and used against Scotland. Despite the obvious dangers, Catholics were given command of companies. Many junior officers, most of the rank and file, were self-confessed papists. From this desperate scheme, the wreckage of Charles's power in all three countries would follow.

In Massachusetts, now that the Scots were up, Governor Winthrop's position was easier. Since Charles was preoccupied, Winthrop could disobey orders from England that he must return his colony's charter, hinting in his reply that the settlers, if deprived of their patent, would set up an independent state else-where. In fact, Massachusetts was now virtually independent, politically, though not economically. Charles had tried, absurdly, to drive a common programme 'thorough' vested interests in three very different countries. In both the major islands of the British archipelago, the motley array of enemies whom he had raised up now moved to revenge themselves. Scottish Protestant zealots and Irish priests, offended English gentry, cantankerous London traders in fur and tobacco, got their various blows in. The monarchy staggered.

X

Even now, when Strafford (as Wentworth now was) returned briefly to Ireland in March 1640, he was able to get new subsidies from the Irish Parliament. But Charles was less fortunate. His need for money compelled him to summon an English parliament, which met in April and May and was so truculent that he dissolved it without getting any money. Again, he managed to scrape an army together to face the Scots. It was routed. The Covenanting army occupied Newcastle and Charles had to agree to pay them £850 a day while they stayed there and waited for him to come up with terms that would satisfy them. Short of conceding all their demands, Charles could do nothing but call another parliament. There followed perhaps the first general election to centre on national politics. The large electorate was impassioned. Of sixty-six candidates nominated by Court agencies, all but fourteen were defeated. The 'best educated' House of Commons in English history 'before or since', met in November for what became the famous 'Long Parliament', its members in effect under Scots protection and, like the King, subject to Scots blackmail.[84]

Presbyterians had seized their chance and had made their ideas dominant in Scotland. The Scots leaders seem to have agreed with Pym's men, the Provi-dence Island Party, that they would delay concluding a treaty with the King until Parliament got what it wanted from him. In return they demanded not only their £850 per diem but a pay-off of £300,000 and the abolition of bishops in England. Under Pym's management, Parliament pushed through legislation removing hated grievances — Ship Money, the Star Chamber — attacking Laud and his bishops, and trimming the royal prerogative. The question was whether Charles could be trusted to implement these laws, which he now formally approved. Parliament must press on till, by getting right-minded men in high positions, it could control a king to whom almost all its members were still loyal and whom it believed to be led astray by evil counsellors. Strafford was impeached for high treason, and in May 1641 his career ended on the executioner's block.

His enemies in Ireland had gleefully fed Pym's party with evidence useful towards his impeachment. Once his back was turned, the Irish Parliament jumped out of its characteristic subservience. Many supporters of Strafford's regime who sat in it were preoccupied with raising his famous army. Old English Catholics and New English dissidents combined in an alliance which could not last long but which was sufficient to give them a majority for a year. Strafford's deputy was forced to drop the scheme to plant Connacht. The subsidies recently granted were whittled down by nearly three-quarters. Then, with the common enemy dead, this movement, which had begun to agitate for a new independence for the Irish Parliament and a positive law-making function, promptly petered out. The Old English had got what they wanted. Charles, in desperate need of Irish support, had confirmed the Graces. But no one thought to appease the Gaelic Irish.

Wentworth's splendid financial policy was in ruins. By June 1641, crown debts in Ireland stood at £140,000. The English Parliament insisted that the vast new Irish army must be abandoned, as Charles himself could not possibly afford it. Though a thousand men were shipped off to serve under the Spanish Crown, thousands more lingered in Ireland and Charles secretly schemed to keep them intact, and even expand them, as a weapon against the English Parliament. But meanwhile a conspiracy sprouted among the Gaels, promoted by Roger Moore from Kildare and involving Lord Maguire and various prominent Ulstermen. With so many papists armed by the King, tinder awaited the match. Army officers were drawn in. A two-pronged plan was devised. Dublin Castle, with its store of arms, was to be seized and at the same time Sir Phelim O Neill was to raise rebellion in Ulster. Sir Phelim, a vain and silly man, nevertheless had great influence. He aspired to the pre-eminence once achieved by his namesake Tyrone.

The strike at the Castle was aborted by treachery, but Sir Phelim rose as planned and captured Charlemont and Dungannon, the two key points of central Ulster, on the night of October 22, 1641. The aim of the Gaelic leaders was not revenge with the sword for their injuries. Charles's intrigues made them think that he wanted a rising and would reward those who rose. They hoped rebellion would achieve a bloodless coup which would put them in a strong position to bargain over their grievances. Their chief object was religious liberty, though they must have nursed some confused hopes of regaining land once theirs. They intended to attack English positions but to leave alone the Ulster Scots. But their followers had no time for political sophistication. As they assailed a plantation which was already weakened, physically and morally, by Wentworth's policies, revenge tempted them irresistibly. Atrocity stories flowed into Dublin with refugees from Ulster. An eye-witness reported their coming in – 'Many persons of good rank and quality, covered over with old rags, and some without any other covering than a little to hide their nakedness, some reverend ministers and others that had escaped with their lives sorely wounded. Wives came bitterly lamenting the murders of their husbands; mothers of their children, barbarously destroyed before their faces; poor infants ready to perish and pour out their souls in their mothers' bosoms; some over-wearied with long travel, and so surbated, as they came creeping on their knees; others frozen up with cold, ready to give up the ghost in the streets; others overwhelmed with grief, distracted with their losses, lost also their senses.'[85]

It was said that a priest in Longford, when the rebellion spread there, had given the signal for massacre by 'ripping up the parson with his own hands'. Such stories were believed. They confirmed racist prejudice – Gaels were beast-like as well as Catholic. Hence, when the chance arose, Protestant reprisals were beast-like in turn. Yet in Cavan, O Reilly's country, the desire of Gaelic leaders to spare needless bloodshed was apparent. The Scottish vicar of Lurgan, Andrew Creichton, received a message that no Scot would be harmed, and was able to help the refugees moving south. He made friends with a leading O Reilly's mother on the grounds of common kinship with the Earl of Argyll, and this kindred, he said, 'stood me in great stead afterwards, for although it was far off and old, yet it bound the hands of the ruder sort from shedding my blood.' And when Bishop Bedell, Englishman and Protestant, died of typhus, the O Reillys overruled the Catholic Bishop of Lismore. Bedell had been well-liked in his district – he had been the first to translate the Old Testament into Gaelic – and many weeping Gaels were present when he was buried by Protestant rites.[86]

This is a dismal recurrence in Irish history: tokens of co-existence and friendship from quiet times overlaid and forgotten in the recital of massacres. Very few people in England or Scotland would have believed in the O Reillys' humaneness, or would have been prepared to reciprocate it. The atrocity stories reached England most opportunely for Pym and his party. Parliament had lost its Scottish protection. The King had gone to Edinburgh in August and had made his peace with the Scots leaders, conceding all their demands and confirming rebels in office, Argyll amongst them. Before his return, the Irish 'news' struck. No one in England had expected rebellion. Ireland had seemed peaceful and prosperous. Charles's most determined opponents in Parliament were, probably, shocked in all sincerity as they heard tales of Protestants roasted and eaten alive, Protestant prisoners fed on garbage and offal. But they did not follow courses designed to get swift relief to their co-religionists. They used the commotion for their own ends.

The myth of the papist massacres would be elaborated over the next decade. Many contemporaries would believe that within a couple of years of the insurrection, some 200,000 Protestants had been murdered, otherwise done to death, or expelled from their homes in Ireland – and a Jesuit, stupid man, would gleefully claim in 1645 that by this time 150,000 heretics had been killed. More temperate commentators would talk of the massacre of some 37,000, 40,000 or 50,000 Protestants at the start of the rebellion alone.[87] These figures, coined in the mewling infancy of statistics, were, of course, nonsense.

But the notion of a plan to slaughter all Protestants suited the Pyms and Cromwells very well, especially as Charles I was implicated by a forged royal commission which Sir Phelim O Neill flaunted. Thousands of miserable colonists had crossed to England for refuge. Most M.P.s had friends if not kindred in Ireland. Could any true Christian be safe from the diabolical schemes of the King's papist controllers? How could Charles be trusted to handle the army which must be sent to repress this rebellion? Pym, in the Commons, now proposed, with success, that Parliament must make it a condition for giving financial support to this end that the King should appoint only such great officers as Parliament was willing to trust. Then, more narrowly, the Commons carried their 'Grand Remonstrance' which identified the Irish rebellion as part of a Catholic plot threatening all three kingdoms, and accused Charles of setting up arbitrary government and relying on the support of a popish and malignant party. Charles attempted to arrest five M.P.s for high treason, Pym among them. They fled into the City of London, now dominated by their supporters.

Thanks partly to the troubles recently facing the cloth trade with northern Europe, the merchants who traded to the Middle East and to the East Indies had ousted the Merchant Adventurers as the leaders of London. They faced in turn the challenge of a third group of traders, preoccupied with the new transatlantic colonies and resentful of the oligarchy, meshed by inter-marriage, which was based on the monopoly privileges of the Levant and East India Companies. Few East India merchants had shared Sir Thomas Smythe's breadth of interest. It had been left to hundreds of pettier men to keep trade with Virginia, Massachusetts, Barbados, speeding. The leaders who had swiftly emerged among them, dominating the trades in tobacco and provisions, were closely linked with Warwick and Pym. They were frustrated by the high customs duties, which Charles I could not afford to lower. They chafed over England's failure to challenge Spain more directly, they interloped as they could in the preserves of the hated monopoly companies.

Hence, while the aldermen-oligarchs of the City establishment were mostly supporters of King Charles – despite the Company's problems with the 'Courteen Association', only two EIC directors are known to have favoured Parliament – the 'colonial-interloping group', as Robert Brenner has called them, were 'overwhelmingly' on Parliament's side. These men and their allies, in a kind of coup, broke the power of the City establishment and controlled England's commercial and financial centre. 'A French King', Lawrence Stone lobserves, 'could and did survive the loss of Paris, but it was far more difficult for an English King to survive the loss of London.'[88]

The King found the metropolis too hot for him and retired to Windsor. The army for Ireland which Parliament now set out to organise became a pretext for preparations for conflict with the King.

The Ulster rebels had soon moved south to seize Dundalk, though with few arms and little military experience they had been unable to root out several dogged centres of Protestant resistance in their rear. Risings of Gaels in parts of Leinster followed. The Old English leaders in the Pale had protested their loyalty, but the government was slow and reluctant to mobilise their support and handed out very few arms to them. The whole of the standing army in Ireland remained in Dublin, except for one garrison at Drogheda. There would, of course, be no timely reinforcements from England. Landowners all over Ireland were thus left unprotected. The Old English gentry knew that the authorities distrusted them. They could only save their estates by some kind of bargain with the advancing rebels. Two incidents late in November completed Old English alienation. One government force, on the way to relieve Drogheda, was routed at Julianstown, while another, commanded by Sir Charles Coote (a surname that India would one day know) relieved Wicklow swiftly, then fell to summary execution of the townspeople. Julianstown seemed to show that the government was too weak to defend loyal subjects, and Coote's actions that it would not be too careful in its choice of papists to slaughter. Within a few days the Old English of the Pale were up in rebellion, still protesting their loyalty to King Charles. Wentworth's policies and Charles's intrigues had helped drive into one camp the descendants of Tudor settlers and those of Gaels whom they had expropriated, but the Catholics thus combined still saw themselves as the King's allies against the English Parliament and its Puritan managers.

In August 1642, the King raised his standard at Nottingham. Civil war in England began. It was partly a war between life-styles. Parliamentarians, called 'Roundheads' although their leaders wore long hair, distrusted the fashionable, extravagant ways of the Royalist 'Cavaliers' and tended to favour sober, hardworking habits. It was more importantly, of course, a war over religious ideas. Puritans generally fought for Parliament, Laudian Arminians and papists on the King's side.

But it was also a revolutionary war, the product of great and cumulative changes sweeping England away from feudalism into a new phase where the operations of the market would dominate social relationships. The numbers of men in the landed class of gentry had multiplied three times (to about 15,000) in the century since Henry VIII had put monastery lands up for sale, while the population as a whole had scarcely doubled.[89] The gentry, and their relations and counterparts in the professions and in large-scale trade, had grown in wealth as well as in numbers, and many were no longer prepared to fawn on peers or to give unquestioning respect to an impoverished and discredited Scottish dynasty. Parliament's defiance expressed the desire of some upper-middle-class men for a reordering of the polity which would give them greater legal and economic scope – freedom of speech, freedom from arbitrary arrest, free consent to taxation, emancipation from monopolies granted at the royal whim. The 'Country' stood against the 'Court'. Puritanism defied the antique mystiques of king and bishop. Pym and his allies led a brief but world-changing coalition in which otherwise discrete ideals cohered – the bellicose nationalism which harked back to Drake and Ralegh combined with bitter resentment of Laudian 'Idolatry'; a passion for the spirit, as gentry conceived it, of English law and constitution matched with the craving of landowners to have things their own way in their own areas.

The rural poor and the urban wage-earners on the whole seem to have stayed neutral in sympathy, so that both King and Parliament had to resort to conscription. But while the rich merchant oligarchs, as in London, were likely to favour Charles, artisans and shopkeepers, like small freeholders and yeomen, were drawn to the other side. Prominent Parliamentarians tended to be older than their opponents – the well-born young were perhaps less repelled by the centralising ideas now widely favoured in Europe, as well as less attracted by the puritanism which had clarified itself as long ago as Elizabeth's day – but New England had drawn away much youthful vigour from the Parliamentarian side, and returning Puritan exiles, some from Holland, others, like Hugh Peter and Roger Williams, from America, provided much of the most original thinking. Meanwhile, Parliament gathered behind it, not to the taste of most of its members, a mass of religious and political sectaries, brandishing every heresy known to man, drawn in great part from the lower-middling orders.

Parliament took the lid off. Censorship was relaxed. In the two decades after 1640, many thousands of sermons, speeches, pamphlets and newspapers swarmed from the presses. Speech in the taverns was even less bridled than formerly. The favourite heresies of the common people, long cherished in secret in town and countryside, now erupted into public debate. Anti-clericalism and hatred of religious images were respectable enough these days; but men and women were also heard denying the doctrine of the Trinity, espousing the 'mortalist' doctrine that the soul died with the body, and wedding far-out theological notions with unmistakeable 'levelling' class feeling. The Bible could be cited in support of almost any idea, including, of course, polygamy. The book of Revelations was favourite study among artisans as well as university-trained intellectuals; both sorts of reader could equate Charles and the Pope with Antichrist, and might expect the imminent reign of God's saints on earth, the millennium. Amongst Baptists and Quakers, Ranters and Levellers, Diggers,

Fifth Monarchists, Muggletonians and a myriad other groups, much super-stitious absurdity might be found.

But also ideas which even the twentieth century would find challenging or disturbing. Some women preached in public. Free love had its antinomian advocates. Fair and equal access to land was demanded. Roger Williams and Anne Hutchinson were moderate, old-fashioned persons compared to many of the new prophets, and the 'classic' puritanism of men like John Winthrop was swiftly outflanked and outmoded. Presbyterianism, though still a revolutionary force in Scotland, became a conservative one in England. Denying man's inherent sinfulness and emphasising man's freedom of choice, 'popular' versions of Arminianism emerged, utterly different in bearing from Laud's, appealing to confident men of the urban middle classes like the poet Milton, or like Anne Hutchinson's erstwhile supporter Coddington.

New freedom of speculation in religion, a new optimism regarding man's destiny, abetted acceptance of the revolutionary insights and discoveries of scientists. If Laud's or Calvin's authority should not prevail, why should Aristotle's or Galen's? Earlier in the century, Francis Bacon had argued that modern men could advance beyond ancient knowledge. By careful study of the world around him, by co-operative research, scientists could change man's earthly condition for the better. Like William Harvey's discovery of the circu-lation of the blood (1628), Bacon's thought gained wider hearing after 1640; by the 1660s the new scientific outlook would have official state backing, and its relationship to industrial and commercial advance would be obvious to most reflective men. One implication was that nothing earthly was sacred because it was mysterious. The challenge to the traditional view of an earth-centred uni-verse marched with a rejection of absolute royal authority and with uninhibited exploitation of near-virgin America.

Meanwhile, as conflict spread over three kingdoms and into the colonies, many men, rich and poor, picked their sides not out of deep conviction but as opportunism or old quarrels dictated. Longstanding contests between gentry families were sanctified. Winds of decentralisation blew through the three realms (to be checked in the 1650s by centralisation such as the islanders had never dreamt of). In Ireland anarchic confusion resulted. In Scotland, class con-flict boiled up along with a great revival of feuding. Wales, mainly Royalist, regained strategic importance. The petty campaigns, the side-shows, with which narrative cannot cope succinctly (rebellion on the Leewards in 1642, a popular rising on the Isle of Man nine years later) were as much of the period's essence as the great battles which must be mentioned. And out of the mêlée it was possible that a fully separate Calvinist kingdom of Scotland, an independent Catholic Ireland, might have emerged, to what length of life no one can say.

In England, there was stalemate at first, despite the organisational genius which Pym brought to his side. He and his friends could see only one way to break the deadlock. The Scots must be won as allies. They would be difficult yoke-fellows. The Scottish noblemen who had supported and, in effect, launched the Covenant were finding the Kirk which they had helped to refresh most uncomfortable. Puritan presbyterian ideals now had hypnotic sway. Zealous plebeian ministers presumed to dictate behaviour to the mighty. But Archibald Campbell, Earl of Argyll, was prepared to co-operate with their godly aims while exploiting the situation to further his own house's inveterate ambitions. Other noblemen, full of justified suspicion, began to shift back towards King Charles, and one of these was the able Montrose. Argyll used the Covenant as a pretext for taking fire and sword to his clan's foes. The Ogilvies, kinsmen of Montrose, suffered, and in the summer of 1641 he himself was briefly imprisoned because he had been corresponding with the King.

Extremists were jumping into the saddle. They wanted to exalt the ministers over the laity, noble and commoner alike; to create a theocracy. They had a grandiose vision of national destiny. Their remote ancestors in the Celtic Church had been good Presbyterians, it was believed, long before Rome and its bishops had touched Scotland. In 1581, in 1590 and 1596, the Scots, as it seemed to these enthusiasts, had covenanted as a whole people with each other and with God to defend the best of all reformed Churches. Now the National Covenant had confirmed the status of the Presbyterian minority as prophets of divine inevitability, who had foretold a new intervention of God in Scottish history. Archibald Johnston of Warriston, a lawyer who had helped write the Covenant, was not alone in seeing a 'verrie near paralel betuixt Izrael and this churche, the only two suorne nations to the Lord' – nor in talking as if Church and nation were one and the same thing.[90]

The sworn nation was swift to send troops to Ireland, at the request of the English Parliament. Most of the Old English had followed the lead of the Lords of the Pale. Except for pockets in Ulster and Munster, Drogheda, and Dublin itself, almost the whole island was soon beyond Protestant control. A proclamation from Charles I denouncing the rebels arrived in February. Properly used, this might have swayed the Old English back. But the Protestant Lords Justices did not want submissions. They deliberately discouraged them by throwing the first who surrendered into prison. Swayed by the characteristic New English avarice, they wanted Catholics to stay out in rebellion so that their lands would be forfeited. The English Parliament thought on the same lines. Their idea, evolved by February 1642, was to make Ireland pay for its own suppression. Though at this time little was really known of the rebellion save that it had been violent, it was agreed that the papists had risen all over the island, so there would be forfeited land in every province, and plenty of it to go round. Two and a half million acres, Parliament thought, nearly one-fifth of all the profitable land in Ireland, could be promised as security to English 'Adventurers' who were now invited to put up money to support the war. Pym and Cromwell invested £600 each. Altogether 1,533 'Adventurers' came forward to assist in this revival of Elizabeth's method of fighting the papists on a joint-stock basis. They would get their reward only if the rebels were defeated, and almost unconditionally defeated; thus, only a drastic and punitive settlement could suit them. But for the moment, the whole Adventure was the tool of an English party. The first £100,000 raised, and the forces gathered for Ireland, were cynically diverted for use against Charles at home. Meanwhile, the Old English were bound in the last resort to support Charles, since only a royal victory could secure their lands.[91]

So the struggle was going to be long and bitter. Major General Robert Monro, who arrived in Ulster with 2,500 Scots in April, could not do enough to break the stalemate. A veteran of the Thirty Years War, like many mercenaries who had returned to Scotland at this promising juncture, he was ruthless even by the standards of his profession. He soon captured Newry. As a shocked subordinate said, the rebel garrison surrendered 'upon a very ill made accord, or a very ill keepd one; for the nixt day most of them, with many merchands and tradesman of the toune ... were carried to the bridge and butcherd to death, some by shooting, some by hanging, and some by drowning, without any legall processe; and I was verilie informed afterwards, that severall innocent people sufferd.'[92] The rebels were not cowed by such barbarism; they retaliated in kind by murdering prisoners. And though they were too poorly armed and led to stand against regular troops, there were not enough of the latter to hold down whatever territory might temporarily be won from the rebels.

In this situation, the Catholic hierarchy moved towards the creation of an Irish state. At a meeting of bishops with leading nobles and gentry in July 1642, a provisional government was set up. The aims of the war were defined as defence of the Catholic religion, and of the King's prerogative. An oath to association was agreed on, to be administered to all and sundry by the clergy, binding the swearers to restore Catholicism as it had been established before the Reformation. Ironically, there was evident influence from the Scottish Covenant – and in this case also, a conservative rebellion by landed men was pushed towards zealous extremism by the influence of the clergy.

The provisional government itself soon had the services of two famous mercenary soldiers. Owen Roe O Neill, nephew of the great Tyrone, came back to his native land with a reputation, earned fighting for Spain, which he did little to justify. Colonel Thomas Preston, of distinguished Old English family, returned about the same time and was given command in Leinster to match Owen Roe's in Ulster. The two men mistrusted each other, and this was bad for discipline, which was weak anyway: an Irish Jesuit lamented, 'one of our birth attributes is never to submit ourselves willingly to any of our own nation ... '[93]

The Supreme Council had summoned a General Assembly, elected like a parliament, to meet at Kilkenny in October. Its business was conducted in English, which shows how far Gaelic leaders had already been weaned from their native culture. The 'Confederation of Kilkenny' was to be a union of all Catholic Irish, with no distinction of race. However, the new Supreme Council, or ministry, was dominated by the Old English element, which craved an agreement with the King at all costs, and the Assembly voted an 'Old English' solution to the land question – ownership should be stabilised as it had been in October 1641. There was an inherent contradiction from the outset between Old English moderation and the aims of Gaels who had long since lost their land and who were willing to fight indefinitely in the interests of the true religion. The coins which the Confederation ordered to be struck had Charles I on one side, but St Patrick on the other.

The Protestant side was also disunited. James Butler, 12th Earl of Ormond, commanded the government forces. Handsome, punctilious in dress and display, Ormond was not a great soldier or a brilliant politician, but he was able to get on with Catholics, and in the fifty years of political life ahead of him, he would never swerve from support for the Stuart dynasty. He was able to prevail over elements on the Council which favoured Parliament, and he acted as Charles's agent in negotiations with the Confederation which continued over months of indecisive fighting, until in September 1643 a truce was signed. The Confederates agreed that each side would keep what it had, and they would pay Charles £30,000. The Dublin government was then free to send 2,500 troops to England, where they were swiftly routed.

Meanwhile, Parliament had bought the Scots, or some of them, at a heavy price. The cost of hiring 21,000 troops was a less grievous burden than the Solemn League and Covenant of 1643 upon which the masters of Scotland insisted. As the Scottish Covenanters saw it, this agreement meant that they and Parliament would work in harness to establish Presbyterianism not only in their own countries, but also in Ireland, and would punish all who opposed this aim, which they further implied should be extended into a European crusade. Covenanting pride supposed that the forms of the Scottish Kirk could be extended to two kingdoms each larger and more populous than Scotland. Many English intellectuals and radicals believed that the chosen nation was their own: John Milton wrote of England's 'precedence of teaching nations how to live' and subscribed to the concept of 'God's Englishmen'.[94] But Parliament set up the so-called Westminster Assembly to discuss the reform of the English Church. Though the eight Scottish envoys present were disappointed by what seemed the lukewarmness of the English, who wouldn't let their Church assembly legislate in its own right as theirs did, and still thought that the idolatrous Christmas holiday should be observed, the Scottish Kirk accepted the Calvinist 'Westminster Confession of Faith', so that, ironically, its chosen creed would forever bear the name of an English place and originate from a conclave where Scots had had no vote.

The English Presbyterians adopted the Scottish model of organisation with the important difference that they favoured lay supremacy rather than clerical.

Even so, their implicit intolerance put them at loggerheads with 'Independents'
like Cromwell who looked to New England rather than Scotland and favoured
a Congregationalist basis. But all who wanted to beat the King were, if
grudgingly, glad when the Covenanters crossed the Border in January 1644 and
besieged Newcastle.

XI

Charles had given Montrose the titles of Lieutenant Governor of Scotland and
Captain General. While the Covenanting army was occupied in England,
Montrose joined in the Highlands an army sent over from Ireland by the
Royalist Earl of Antrim, and partly armed and supplied by the Catholic Confederates. Its commander was Alasdair Macdonald, a giant (seven feet high, so
they said), styled 'Colkitto' by English writers, including Milton, who couldn't
spell Gaelic. 'Colkitto' had had no trouble, once in the Highlands, in raising his
own tribe, the Macdonalds, against their hereditary foes, Argyll and the Campbells. The clans now divided, for or against Montrose or the Covenant, on their
own bases, not in response to principles. Macleans and some Macleods sided
with Macdonalds and hence with Montrose, while Frasers, Grants and Munroes
to the north fought against him, and the Mackenzies dithered. Montrose,
immensely handsome and charming, a competent poet, pursued the cause of the
King along with his own ambitions, the perfect Cavalier, and a future godsend
to lady novelists.

Few writers of fiction could have invented a better story than the one which
he acted out in the Highlands in 1644–5. Europe hailed him as a great commander, but his effectiveness derived from his understanding that with a force
mostly of Highlanders the normal rules of soldiery could, and indeed must, be
flouted. To their rapid mobility in their own habitat, Highland Gaels had in the
sixteenth century added a new technique, the ferocious mass charge on foot
with drawn claymores. (Afghans who used similar methods would one day find
the Macdonalds' descendants armed with traditions of courage which stemmed
from Montrose's time.) Montrose was able to hold together a medley of men,
united by nothing but hatred of the Campbells, on amazing marches which
time and again turned hopeless retreat into a base for savage surprise attack.

But the capture of Aberdeen which he soon effected showed the limitations
of his kind of campaign. The city and the area round it were stubbornly Royalist
and episcopalian in their sympathies. Here was the best available reservoir of
broad-based support for the King. But for three days Colkitto and his tribesmen
plundered, murdered and raped, hating the Lowlander more than they loved
the royal cause.

Argyll came up in pursuit. Montrose led him a wearisome chase round the
Eastern Highlands, beat him at Fyvie when he at last caught up, then vanished
into the mountains. In dead of a bitter Caledonian winter, he brought his men

unexpectedly down upon the Campbell stronghold at Inverary. Argyll himself escaped in a boat, just in time, but his lands were ravaged. Soon three armies converged to trap Montrose in the Great Glen. In snow and wind he escaped by a march into the pathless mountains, from which he fell on the Campbells massed at Inverlochy. Argyll had to flee again as his clansmen were slaughtered. Even this feat was exceeded next summer when Montrose, having captured Dundee, got his men out of town just as pursuers came up, doubled back on his tracks to evade another army which cut off his retreat to the Highlands, and then reached the hills by skirting Dundee again. Then, reinforced, Montrose struck south, crossed the Forth and crushed a Covenanting army at Kilsyth. This was August 1645. He was master of all Scotland. The Covenanting leaders escaped the country. Edinburgh, Glasgow, the landowners, submitted.

But this time his Highlanders weren't allowed to plunder. They had joined him to beat Argyll. Now Argyll was beaten. They dribbled homewards. A Gaelic force, it was thus proved, could not hold Scotland.

The kind of army which could do so was being created south of the Border. As Montrose's guerrilla campaign had got under way, Parliament's Covenanted allies had marched to battle at Long Marston Moor in Yorkshire, singing, so tradition would have it,

> When to the kirk we come,
> Wee'l purge it ilka room
> Frae Popish relics and a' sic innovation,
> That a' the warld may see
> There's nane in the right but we,
> O' the sons of the auld Scotish nation.[95]

In the biggest battle ever fought on English soil, on July 2, 1644, Scottish reinforcements arrived at just the right moment to help Oliver Cromwell, commanding the horsemen of eastern England, recover and break the Royalist cavalry for the only time in the war. Charles's defeat at Marston Moor gave Parliament control of the North. It confirmed the stature of Cromwell as soldier, and preceded the creation of his New Model Army, the first force to wear the red uniform which the British would carry to battlefields in every continent.

Cromwell thus looms as large in the history of the army as he does in the history of the empire which that army would extend and defend, and in the development of all three British kingdoms. His name by modern reckoning would have been Williams. He was descended from a sister of the famous Thomas Cromwell who had married a Welshman. Their son had deserted his name for hers; but when heralds came to devise a crest for Oliver, they would include the arms of the last Prince of Powys. However, to look at and hear Oliver was *echt* English, a ruddy-faced man with long brown hair and a big nose, careless of clothes and appearance, devoted to horses and hawking, a pithy phrasemonger on many occasions but blurting and tortuous when it came to oratory; a bluff 'Anglo-Saxon' hero for Thomas Carlyle. 'I had rather be overrun', he once declared, 'with a Cavalierish interest than a Scotch interest; I had rather be overrun with a Scotch interest, than an Irish interest ... all the world knows their barbarism.' Yet his loathing of religious intolerance (bar papists, of course) was as deep and sincere as Milton's or Roger Williams's. Like them he was his own man in religion, a searcher. He prayed, he would say, for 'union and right understanding between the godly people (Scots, English, Jews, Gentiles, Presbyterians, Independents, Anabaptists and All)', and once said that he would rather permit Muhammadanism in England than risk the persecution of one of God's children.[96]

By birth and background he was an English Puritan gentleman, born in 1599 in the East Anglian heartland of puritanism, and educated after the fashi onof his religion and class at Cambridge University and at the Inns of Court. Plenty of relatives were in the House of Commons when he entered it in 1628. He shared their enthusiasm for New England; he came near to emigrating in the 1630s, pined often to live in a godly New World commonwealth, and corresponded when at the height of his fame with the pastor of Boston, Massachusetts, John Cotton. His temperament suited Calvinism well. He was a manic depressive, his life marked by bouts of wild glee and phases of deep indecision. He would rise to the top as a practical politician showing more sense than the fretful idealists, yet he took the Calvinist doctrine of providence literally and made it the basis for his actions. Every event came about because God willed it to happen. Slow to decide what God's will might be, he was swift, decisive and ruthless in action once he presumed that he had discovered it.

Yet he had a genuine breadth of sympathy, shown in the 1630s when he took up the case of the poor fenmen of Ely despite the vested interest which his own class had in drainage. He was not really greedy for lands or money. He cared for the welfare and interests of his common soldiers. He made men of low birth officers, so long as they were godly. 'I had rather have a plain russet-coated captain that knows what he fights for, and loves what he knows, than that which you call a gentleman and is nothing else.'[97] The New Model Army which Parliament created so as to have a national force independent of the regional preoccupations of the gentry would be the most revolutionary item in British history. Cromwell did not create it alone, but he showed that he could lead it best.

At Naseby in June 1645, the New Model Army defeated one of the King's forces. At Langport on July 2, the other royal army was shredded. Charles's only hope now was Montrose, whom he ordered to march south to meet the Covenanting contingent led by the brilliant David Leslie. At Philiphaugh in the Borders, Montrose was caught off guard. His infantry, after surrender, were massacred in cold blood on the orders of the godly ministers who dominated Leslie's army. The humiliation of God's chosen race by a band of Gaelic savages was savagely avenged. Montrose escaped, and was raising new troops in the north early in 1646 when Charles, preferring Scots rebels to English, surrendered himself to the Covenanting army encamped at Newark.

The Covenanters could do nothing with this king who would not be a Presbyterian and in January 1647 they sold him to the English Parliament for £200,000, half the money now due to them, and went home. The victorious English revolutionaries were now split between the factions to which the rough and misleading labels 'Presbyterian' and 'Independent' attached themselves. 'Right' and 'left wing' will do, roughly, as well. The 'left wing' army, 'independent' in bias, hijacked the King in June 1647 from the Presbyterian-dominated Parliament. In August the army occupied London. The troops had elected 'agitators', shop stewards as it were, to voice their demands for pay and for religious toleration. The influence of the 'Levellers' was growing among them. These men formed, in effect, the first secular party in English history. Their leaders – John Lilburne, Richard Overton, William Walwyn – stood for the lower-middling people, attracting, besides the rank and file of the army, yeomen, small businessmen, and craftsmen. They wanted the franchise extended to all except servants and beggars. They wanted a republic, no king. They wanted the House of Lords abolished, along with excise and tithes. They wanted free schools and hospitals, general reform of the law, the election of magistrates. They prefigured not only the far later socialist movement, but also (and more exactly, in some respects) some views of the Victorian middle class. They worried Cromwell deeply, and those to the right of him still more so. What could one make of these people who saw the common masses of Irish as fellows in just rebellion rather than innate monsters?

Class feeling was hardening in Scotland also. To most of the nobility, it seemed that the only way to safeguard their traditional dominance of society was to save the King. But the General Assembly of the Kirk was under the control of men for whom the terms of the Solemn League and Covenant were as indestructible as the stone of their hills. The King's refusal to accept them damned him. In December 1647 three Scottish lords, amongst them the learned and pliable Earl of Lauderdale, made an agreement with Charles, who refused to swear to the Covenant but agreed to establish Presbyterianism in England for a trial period of three years, and to give Scots the same commercial privileges as his English subjects. While the Scottish Parliament supported this 'Engagement', Argyll and the standing Commission of the Kirk opposed it, and did their best to prevent the recruitment of an army. The blink of Scottish unity was over.

The 'Engagers' took a force of 20,000 men into England where Cromwell cut them to pieces near Preston in August 1648. The 'Second Civil War' was brief. Royalist risings in support of the Scots in various parts of England and in South Wales were swiftly suppressed – the New Model Army was by now probably Europe's most efficient fighting force. But Cromwell was furious at this new and unnecessary effusion of blood. Charles's faithlessness was responsible. Now he had failed, God's witness against the King seemed confirmed. The rout at Preston triggered coups in both England and Scotland.

For reasons which have never been adequately explained, the heartland of support for Presbyterianism and the Covenant was in south-west Scotland. Clydesdale, Ayrshire and Galloway bore their crop of opinionated small men – petty lairds, owner-occupying peasants. Recruiting for the King had sparked a rebellion here in June. The insurgents had been dispersed, but now they rallied again and marched on Edinburgh. When they went to the capital to buy corn in the summer, the Westland men drove their horses with the cry 'Whiggam! Whiggam!'[98] Hence their seizure of Edinburgh was the 'Whiggamore Raid', and the word 'whig' entered the English language. The lay government fled and the militants of the Kirk were left in power. Cromwell came up and lent them troops, and they were able to impose their minority opinions on the country. A rump of the Scottish Parliament passed, early in 1649, an 'Act of Classes' excluding from all public office and military command not only supporters of Montrose and 'Engagers' but even those who had not actively opposed them, as well as all guilty of immorality. The Church itself was purged, and there was what one contemporary called 'daylie hanging, skurging, nailling of luggis ... and boring of tounges' for moral as well as political offences.[99]

So 'whigs' now ruled Scotland. The word 'tory' came, in this period, from Ireland, as we shall see later. That island, in the mid-1640s, was in extreme confusion. Monro's Scots were still in Ulster to fight for the Solemn League and Covenant and in Munster a noted Protestant Gael, Lord Inchiquin, known as 'Murrough of the Burnings', had swung his force on to Parliament's side. Neither of these subscribed to the truce which the third Protestant leader, the Royalist Ormond, maintained with the Catholic Confederacy, as he continued to negotiate with it on the King's behalf. Within the Catholic camp, there was growing division. While the aristocratic Old English tended to favour the truce, many of the Gaels opposed it and provided recruits for a clerical faction headed by Pietro Scarampi, the Pope's envoy. Desperate for Confederate support, Charles secretly gave the Earl of Glamorgan, an English papist, a rash commission to treat with the Confederation behind the back of Ormond who, as a Protestant, would not concede the religious terms they demanded. In the autumn of 1645, Glamorgan made a deal whereby Catholics in Ireland would get possession of all churches and church property not actually in Protestant hands in return for supplying Charles with 10,000 troops. When word of this agreement leaked out, Charles had to repudiate it, but the suggestion – not unfair, at this time – that he was in conspiracy with Irish papists, did him enormous harm in England. The deal which Ormond finally made with the Confederation in March 1646 said nothing about church property or a new status for Catholicism.

This compromise outraged the man who had recently arrived in Ireland as papal nuncio, Giovanni Battista Rinuccini. Elderly, unworldly, unbending, he had the treaty condemned at a synod which threatened all who accepted it with excommunication. Catholic noblemen were unimpressed, but the common Gael was easily stirred by the priests; as in Scotland, the clerisy threatened aristocratic leadership. The veteran Owen Roe O Neill had just gained the one major victory for the Catholics in the war. At Benburb his pikemen had routed Monro's over-confident Covenanters. ('The Lord of Hosts', wrote Monro characteristically, 'had controversy with us to rub shame in our faces ... ')[100] Now, instead of pressing his victory home, O Neill piously hurried to help Rinuccini, who with his support entered Kilkenny in September, deposed and imprisoned the Supreme Council, and made himself the Confederation's new president.

The Confederate forces now prepared to attack Dublin. In despair, Ormond appealed to Parliament for aid. But before any deal was made, he was saved by a quarrel between the Irish commanders, O Neill and Preston. O Neill withdrew. Preston intrigued with Ormond. The failure to take Dublin discredited Rinuccini, but the Assembly which he called early in 1647 was still obdurate against the peace treaty, and Ormond saw no chance to hold the capital. He handed the city over to the English Parliament and, in July, with the takeover complete, he left the country.

The new Parliamentary commander, Michael Jones, soon routed Preston when the latter advanced again towards Dublin, and Inchiquin was so successful in Munster that, in May 1648, the Confederate Council had to make a truce with him. Rinuccini once again proclaimed excommunication against all who adhered to it. The Council retorted by formally sacking his follower, Owen Roe O Neill, and the Confederation fell into internecine strife. The baffled Rinuccini retreated to Rome, lamenting that the Irish were 'Catholic only in name'.[101] He had done his unwitting best to wreck their cause, and the Pope made his displeasure plain on the nuncio's return.

Confusion was now compounded as the Second Civil War blew up in England. The Scots in Ulster fell out with the local Parliamentary commander and he had to seize their garrisons. Inchiquin declared for the King and begged Ormond to return, as the latter did, in September, to head a new Royalist alliance. After coming to terms with him, the Confederation was formally dissolved in January 1649.

This was a famous month, regarding which John Milton rejoiced that 'God has inspired the English to be the first of mankind who have not hesitated to judge and condemn their king.'[102] It was true. Other European monarchs had been killed by their subjects. But a group of Englishmen were the first to try and condemn in a court of law a man whom they recognised as king. In December 1648 the army 'purged' Parliament, which had been negotiating with Charles. Colonel Pride, a former brewer's drayman, new man of a new era, arrested 45 members and turned back 96 others. The 'Rump' which remained passed an ordinance for the King's trial. The proceedings which followed were justified in terms which would later resound through the entire Atlantic arena. Ultimate authority lay with the people. The King held office only as their trustee. And on January 30, to Europe's astonishment, the King was beheaded.

The Scots, even hard Covenanters, were shocked, and proclaimed the dead man's son Charles II. They would have to be dealt with, but England and Ireland came first. Cromwell suppressed the Levellers in his army, then crossed to Dublin in August with 3,000 Ironsides.

Jones, his predecessor as Parliamentary commander, had just shattered the Royalist army near the capital. Ormond sent the best of what was left to garrison Drogheda, so Cromwell's first stroke was to besiege that town. It fell after eight days, on September 11, 1649. What followed made one of the reddest stains on the Irish historical memory. Cromwell himself wrote, ' ... Our men getting up to them were ordered by me to put all to the sword; and, indeed, being in the heat of action, I forbade them to spare any that there were in arms in the town.' Cromwell was within his rights. The garrison had refused to surrender. But another English witness reported that 'The slaughter was continued all that day and the next', and some townspeople and several priests were among the slain, though there is no evidence to support the legend that the whole civilian population was massacred. The killing of virtually all the garrison was, however, a savagery without precedent in the English civil wars. Altogether between two and four thousand people were slain. Cromwell was normally a humane and merciful man. It seems clear that at Drogheda he was possessed by one of his manic rages. Beyond that, he shared the view of Ireland which most Englishmen held. Irish papistry was maliciously evil. Ireland had been (under Wentworth! but after all, the man had at least been English) a most pacific and prosperous country. Then the wicked papists had risen. 'You, unprovoked, put the English to the most unheard-of and most barbarous massacre (without respect of sex or age) that ever the sun beheld', Cromwell would later write in a 'Declaration' addressed to the Catholics. 'And at a time when Ireland was in perfect peace, and when, through the example of the English industry, through commerce and traffic, that which was in the natives' hands was better to them than if all Ireland had been in their possession and not an Englishman in it.'[103] This sounds like the voice of the white man in India during the Mutiny, or in Southern Africa now.

The atrocity shocked Owen Roe O Neill into alliance with Ormond; but the old warrior died only three weeks later. The North was soon almost wholly in English hands. Cromwell marched south and besieged Wexford from October 1 to October 11. When his troops entered the city they ran amok. He made no attempt to check them. Between 1,500 and 2,000 people were butchered. Again civilians suffered. The once-thriving seaport was almost emptied of people and Cromwell was pleased by the thought that it was now open to English settlement — 'it were to be wished', he ruminated, 'that an honest people would come and plant here ... '[104]

Though outnumbered three or four to one by Ormond's forces, Cromwell's Ironsides overran most of the country before he himself left in May 1650. His nine months in Ireland were enough to secure what later became known as the Protestant Ascendancy. There had been, in the 1640s, a chance that an Ireland of legal Catholicism might have emerged, with, or even without, a Stuart King at its head. Divisions among the Irish had thrown that away. Cromwell's ruthlessness and skill completed the work.

Before the end of 1650 the beaten Ormond had sailed for France. By mid-1652 the major remaining Royalist forces had been defeated or had surrendered. The rebellion was officially said to be over in September 1653. Some Irish troops with their officers had been allowed, on surrender, to go to serve on the Continent. But many soldiers turned brigand. The word 'tory' was now being applied to such men who linked their robberies with political resentment, and 'toryism' would be for decades a major problem in Ireland.

'Tory' Charles II would later say that Calvinism was no religion for a gentleman. But in June 1650 he had perforce to subscribe to the Scottish Covenant. An invasion on his behalf by Montrose, from the Orkneys into northern Scotland, had been quickly defeated and Montrose himself had been hanged in Edinburgh like a common criminal. Now the Covenanting regime had a king whom they had sworn to their cause. Cromwell, whose attitude to Protestant Scots was quite different from his view of papist Irish, pleaded with them to be more tolerant – 'I beseech you in the bowels of Christ think it possible that you may be mistaken ... There may be a Covenant made with death and hell.' Failing, he invaded, and on September 3, 1650, seemed to have met his match at last. He was trapped at Dunbar by a Scottish army led by David Leslie, once his able colleague. But there was a committee of godly ministers advising Leslie. Their knowledge of military affairs came from close study of the Old Testament. They advised that the Scots should desert their impregnable upland position and fall on the English, whom they outnumbered two to one. They came down, shouting, 'The Covenant!' The English cried 'The Lord of Hosts!' and slaughtered them. The Scots, one contemporary said, were 'driven like turkeys'. Three thousand were killed, ten thousand captured – more than half the Scottish army. It was the greatest victory of Cromwell's career.[105]

The rout at Dunbar made Argyll and other relative realists inside the Covenanting party ready to co-operate again with the 'Engagers' whom they had spewed out of their mouths. By the following summer the 'Act of Classes' had been in effect rescinded and the King had been crowned; by Argyll himself, who else? But Cromwell had occupied Edinburgh. He let the new Scottish army, 'Engagers' within it again, pass him by to invade England, where, at Worcester, exactly a year after Dunbar, he defeated it utterly. English forces thereafter conquered Scotland more thoroughly than the nation's own kings had ever been able to do. The country stood on the brink of famine and had no effective leadership. In October 1651 the London regime announced that

England and Scotland were henceforward one country.

In the same year was published the greatest work of English political philosophy, Thomas Hobbes's *Leviathan*. Inspired both by the new scientific learning which had been making headway through all England's troubled years, and by loathing of civil war and its insecurity, Hobbes brought a startling realism to the discussion of political power and of human society. Here was a man with no time for ghosts or fairies or for the notions that the 'soul' might have any existence apart from the body and that heaven and hell could exist anywhere save on earth. This confident materialist described man as an automaton who could act only out of hope of advantage to himself. Religion was only valuable as a means of securing submission to secular authority: reason, not revelation, was the way to the truth: God was merely the first mover who started the universe going. All sovereignty was based, not on divine right, but on covenants made by men, who, so Hobbes argued, must give complete obedience to the sovereign king or assembly which they had set up. Though the orthodox, of course, could not stomach such stuff, Hobbes, prophet of reason, represented the wave of the future. Men were growing sick of wars for religion. The new science showed those who understood its findings that nature might be made to serve man and vastly increase the prosperity of individuals and of society. Let the world then be exploited. Let Ireland be put to good use. Let overseas empire flourish. Let enterprising men cease to argue about free will and instead apply such wills as they might have to their own enrichment under whatever form of government would make that possible. The State had nothing to do with God or morality. Born out of fear, it existed as power. Let power be used on behalf of trade.

The first Cromwell, Thomas, had read Machiavelli. The second had not read Hobbes, yet his status might have seemed to exemplify what Hobbes meant. He had success. He had the army behind him. Men agreed that he must rule them. Even the Scots were mostly too tired and cowed to stir.

Under the Rump Parliament England was governed by a Council of State of forty-one men, with a quorum of nine. The royal arms came down. There was new coinage, a new Great Seal. Monarchy and House of Lords were abolished. Political sovereignty was stripped of mystique. All men could see that men unmade kings, even if men could make them again. Experimentation continued. At the army's urging, in 1653, Cromwell turned out the Rump. Now came the 'Barebones Parliament' with 144 members selected by the army. An extremist minority of millenarian 'Fifth Monarchists' pushed hard for radical reform, and the majority, propertied men, voted its dissolution to safeguard their class. So Cromwell became Lord Protector, much, in effect, like a constitutional monarch, and as such often at odds with his parliament. Though unprecedentedly high taxation gave it double the income Charles had ever commanded, Cromwell's state was still not solvent. The army and navy were costing too much. With its new armed power, England was now far more of a force in European affairs than it had been under the Stuarts. As always, such power faced two ways and weighed also on people at home.

XII

At least, after the queasy 1630s and the disrupted 1640s, there was now plenty of employment in England. There was less impetus to emigration. The great folk movement across the Atlantic was over, and would not resume in spate (except from Ulster and the Scottish Highlands) before the mid-nineteenth-century. But the rulers of Republican England were enthusiasts for empire, and they took measures to ensure that planters got able bodies to labour for them.

The idea of 'transporting' felons was old. The governor of Virginia in 1611 had been willing to welcome convicts as a 'readie way to furnish us with men and not allways the worst kind of men.' In an age of cruel punishments (for instance, in 1641 a woman was sentenced to be pressed to death for the theft of a table cloth and sheet), transportation commended itself as a lenient course. In 1615 James I had authorised judges to reprieve convicts 'whoe for strength of bodie or other abilities shall be thought fitt to be ymploied in forraine discoveries or other services beyond the Seas.'[106] But only a few score had been thus trans-ported to the New World before Cromwell's day. Then in 1655 a relatively straightforward procedure was introduced. Felons could be pardoned on con-dition that they left the country for a certain term of years. Scores were now succeeded by hundreds.

Another source of supply was prisoners, mostly Scots, taken in battle. Wild statements about thousands of Scots being sent into slavery by Cromwell have featured in print. The truth was not so dramatic. Perhaps several hundred were despatched into servitude – not slavery, quite – after the battle of Preston in 1648. Of the 1,250 Scots prisoners intended for America after Dunbar and the 1,610 so allotted after Worcester, only a small proportion reached the colonies (where, lean, hungry, hard-working, they commonly thrived).[107] Some English rebels and conspirators were despatched as well, like the considerable number who were 'Barbadoed' after Colonel Penruddock's Royalist rising of 1655.

The Scots were not shocked at the time by the loss of a few hundred young men; far more had gone to serve and die overseas in the Thirty Years' War. National pride was affronted by defeat, and under the Cromwellian constitution of 1653 Scotland was allowed only thirty M.P.s (the same number as Ireland) to sit with four hundred Englishmen at Westminster. Yet Union with England was 'not in itself unpleasing to the Scots'. After all, the Solemn League and Covenant had envisaged it. Scots had long craved to trade freely with the English colonies, and with England herself, and were now permitted to do so; but the stunted and war-torn Scottish economy was in no shape to profit much. Trade with Barbados was begun, then abandoned; the voyage out there was too long to be financed by men of small capital.[108]

Zealots within the Church of Scotland abhorred the toleration of other Protestant views which the Cromwellian Union entailed. Deviant sects crept in and established themselves — for instance, a small body of Scottish Quakers emerged. But apart from an abortive Royalist rising in the Highlands in 1653–4, the years of Union were years of calm. Under the largest army Scotland had ever seen, even the Gaels were uncannily peaceful. Cromwellian rule was, for the most part, both fair and efficient. Feudalism was temporarily abolished, and with it the arbitrary power of local magnates and barons. In the years of civil war, lairds, burgesses and lawyers had figured with a new prominence, while religious doctrines had come to seem more important than kinship and clannish loyalties. Feuding was obsolete. The last fortified house to be built in Scotland dates from 1661.[109] A hundred or more years later than his counterparts south of the Border, the Scottish landowner was ready and able to put comfort before security. Cromwellian rule furthered the work of transformation begun in the 1640s, when the power of aristocratic magnates had for the first time yielded, before that of ministers and the lairds supporting them. And in another respect also, the English regime carried forward the work of the Covenant. An Act of 1656 took Scottish sabbatarianism to its highest pitch. It forbade anyone to frequent taverns, dance, hear profane music, wash, brew ale or bake bread, 'profanely walk' or travel or do any worldly business on a Sunday. Most Presbyterians, then, could co-operate with a regime so much more austere than that of Charles I.[110]

The Irish were less amenable, despite and because of the horrors which they had endured. Sir William Petty, the pioneer statistician (of whom more later), estimated that when the war ended in 1653, 616,000 people had perished, leaving 850,000 survivors. These figures are certainly wrong, but they show how a very intelligent and well-informed man conceived the losses. He reckoned that 167,000 people had died from sword, famine, 'and other Hardships' and 450,000 from the outbreak of plague which swept Ireland in 1650. And certainly, land worth 30s. an acre in 1641 fetched only 2s. 6d. in 1653, thanks to underpopulation and to continued insecurity.[111]

The four Parliamentary Commissioners who ruled Ireland under the Rump reported most gloomily back to London. The numbers of tories were 'daily increasing'. Cattle stocks were so run down that four-fifths of the best land in Ireland lay waste and uninhabited. Even County Clare, less touched by the war than most areas, was 'totally ruined and deserted', with only 40 of its 1,300 ploughlands actually peopled.[112] The task of reconstruction lay in English hands. The Irish Parliament was done away with and the M.P.s who sat for Ireland in Westminster were largely English army officers.

In theory, many Englishmen were enthusiasts for Ireland, though not for the Irish. Advanced social reformers and scientific thinkers hoped, like Wentworth before them, to use Ireland as a kind of laboratory in which ideas could be tested for later application to England. Such institutions as Ireland had had in

Church, law and education had been decayed or swept away by war, and whereas England bristled with powerful vested interests, in Ireland the natives could mostly be ignored. One of the Parliamentary Commissioners thought that God had led the Cromwellians 'into a strange land and to act in as strange a work, a work that neither we nor our forefathers knew or heard of: the framing or forming of a commonwealth out of a corrupt rude mass ... ' A government chaplain saw Ireland as 'clay upon the wheele, ready to receive what forme authority shall please to give it', and the Chief Justice of Munster likened the country to a 'white paper'.[113] 'New English' Protestant landowners had their own hopes of improving their fortunes by scientific agriculture and by the exploitation of the mineral wealth which the island was falsely supposed to contain, and several of the most prominent were drawn to the ideas of the advanced circle of Baconian thinkers which centred on the Puritan sage Samuel Hartlib. Puritans in general believed that the historical drama of their time was the prelude of a new age in which man's dominion over nature would be restored, and many looked forward to the 'Great Instauration'. Hartlib's circle directed Baconian thinking to practical ends – universal education, experimental medicine, general economic reform, the world supremacy of England. Hartlib himself hoped to establish in Ireland a clearing house for scientific and experimental ideas, and though this was not achieved, several of his associates were busy and prominent on the island in the 1650s, involved in educational schemes and above all in the surveying of lands preparatory to a resettlement.[114] In Elizabeth's day the finest of English poets had been drawn to the country. Now forward scientists trended thither. But the island was not a white paper. There were people there. And the English arriving among them as rulers fell willy-nilly into traditional policies.

There simply was not enough money for visionary schemes. Ireland was a horrid financial burden. In 1649–56 over £1,500,000 had to be transmitted from England to help govern it, while under £2 million were raised in the island itself.[115] This subsidy was progressively snipped, and the Irish came under swingeing taxation, so heavy that it was a deterrent to new immigration from England. Cromwell kept members of his own family in charge. A son-in-law, Ireton, was dominant after he left, then in 1652 another son-in-law, Fleetwood, took over, and finally in 1655 his son Henry came out to hold charge. But the Protector and his Council and Parliament were too busy with English and foreign affairs to give Ireland close attention; they never even got round to passing an Act of Union formally joining the two islands in one state. Meanwhile, not one native Protestant was appointed to the Irish government. This was foreign rule, sluggish, inept and unfeeling. Till 1655 the emphasis was on making the Catholic Irish pay for their 'crimes'. Under Henry Cromwell, it changed. He conciliated the native Protestant elements and adopted policies suited to their interests; hence some accused him of being 'too gentle to ye Scotch and revolting English of Ireland.'[116] Presbyterianism in Ulster flourished under his rule.

As in Scotland, strange new sects came in with the Ironsides. Fleetwood looked very favourably on the Baptists, as did many garrison commanders. Cork had a Quaker governor, Robert Phaire, and this sect established a permanent presence, attracting artisans, craftsmen, smallholders and shopkeepers in the Munster and Ulster plantations. Protestant Ireland had its belated taste of the radical debates which had helped transform the way people thought in England. But those who argued kept their backs turned to the papists. In theory, the Cromwellians wanted to build a new Protestant Ireland. In practice, they couldn't find enough preachers of an approved kind willing to serve there, and efforts were made to get ministers from the American colonies. Despite Cromwell's hatred of popish priests and the price that was put on their heads, their numbers actually grew during his reign. The few efforts made to convert the natives from their Catholicism were pitiful even compared with those of the Church of Ireland in the days before the war, when the good Bishop Bedell had worked at translating God's word into Gaelic and the learned Archbishop Ussher had preferred ministers who could speak that tongue. Official hostility to the language continued. Only one book in Gaelic was published in Dublin in the 1650s. There was the aim of a national school system which would teach the Gaels 'civility and pious behaviour', but only thirty-five schoolteachers were employed by the State in 1659 and these, like the approved preachers, were concentrated in the garrisons.[117] There were a good many nominal converts to the reformed religion, since Catholics were, for instance, threatened in 1656 with the loss of two-thirds of their property unless they abjured papal supremacy. But the hold of Rome was essentially stronger than ever.

The old attack on the Irish way of life was resumed. Lord Deputy Fleetwood denounced the 'odious practice' which the Gaels had of 'promiscuous lodging and lying together in one room, contrary to the manners of all civilised nations ... ' The seizure of 'vagrants' was enjoined in a stream of orders recalling Elizabethan resentment of nomadism. Now the idea was to transplant these nuisances to the 'Caribbee Islands'. In a typical case, in June 1654, Colonel Stubbers was 'authorised to transport out of Connaught for the West Indies, three score Irish women that are vagrants, idlers and wanderers ... '[118] Some Irish soldiers, as they surrendered, were sent to Barbados, to make their contribution to the delightful accent of speech on that island.

It may be that life for some poor people was better under Cromwellian rule. The simple Irish economy was resilient. By 1655 the effects of war had worn off sufficiently for the government to permit export of the traditional produce — tallow and hides, butter and meat and livestock — though Ireland did not enjoy the same freedom of trade as Scotland. Customs revenue soon returned to its high level of the 1630s. Agricultural prices stayed up while rents were extremely low, depopulation meant that landlords were eagerly seeking tenants, and the arbitrary authority of old proprietors had commonly vanished. Perhaps the lesser Irish found new opportunities. Nobody knows. There is no record of their opinions.[119]

What is indelibly written into history is the Cromwellian scheme for the mass transportation of all Catholic natives to the west of the island. The spirit was Philip II's or Stalin's. The execution fell somewhat below modern standards.

The decision taken in 1642 that the repression of Ireland should be paid for out of forfeited estates had always implied a general resettlement of Irish lands. In fact the 'Adventurers' of that year — mostly merchants, with Londoners predominant — had put up only £300,000, and the repression had cost perhaps ten times that amount. Their entitlement came to less than a million acres and it was now assumed that ten million — half the land of Ireland — would be escheated. How could the rest be used? The solution lay to hand in the vast army of 33,000 to 35,000 English soldiers now occupying the country. Land values had spiralled downwards and Irish acres, no longer attractive to English investors, could still be the means of paying soldiers cheaply.[120]

An amazing Act of 1652 was the basis of the resettlement. It condemned perhaps 100,000 Irish rebels to death (which only a few hundred actually suffered) and to total forfeiture of their lands. In addition three or four more classes of Irish defined as relatively 'innocent' were to lose a third or two-thirds of their holdings and to be given lands equal to the remainder wherever Parliament chose they should go. While about 180,000 acres were confiscated from Royalist Protestants, the chief effect of the Act was to dispossess almost every Catholic landowner. The citizens of Dublin were the only large body of papists never to have contended with Parliament, yet even they lost their houses, forcibly leased to republican soldiers. Elsewhere no more than twenty-six Catholic landowners seem to have proved 'constant good affection'. Lunatics, invalids and minors suffered confiscation because they hadn't given positive help to Parliament. Descendants of Tudor planters suffered with Gaels. Bagenals, Raleghs, even a Cromwell, were included in this almost clean sweep, and Oliver himself had to intervene on behalf of Edmund Spenser's grandson, whose family had slumped into papistry.[121]

A further Act in September 1653 provided that all Catholic Irish, including those technically 'innocent', were to be barred from the whole country east of the Shannon. Even in the territories of Connacht and Clare which were reserved for them, the Irish were not to live within four miles of the sea or the Shannon, nor on any island. They were to be cut off from all direct contact with Europe and the wider world. All natives entitled to lands under the 1652 Act were to remove west of the Shannon by May 1654, and any who lingered thereafter would be put to death.

Families, livestock, dependants were to be uprooted to Connacht with the landowners. But the scheme was impractical as well as brutal. The English planters who were to take over would need Irish labour. Even if it had been possible to find hordes of English people prepared to work in Ireland, their labour would have been much more expensive, and they would not have been prepared to pay such high rents as the natives. Irish labour was cheap labour. The 'final solution' ran counter to the best interests of the Protestant landowning classes.

The original deadline was perforce extended. After much debate, it was agreed that only landowners and those who had borne arms were to be transplanted. It seems that while most Catholic landowners were unable to prove enough 'innocence' to entitle them to any Connacht acres at all, and so lost everything, some 2,000 were assigned, between them, about a quarter of the whole area of Connacht and Clare. But the mass of natives stayed east of the Shannon. A census of 1659 shows that even in Ulster there were only four English and Scots to every ten Irish. In Leinster the ratio was under one to six, in Munster less than one to ten. The intention had been to settle over 1,000 English Adventurers and perhaps 35,000 soldiers, in Ireland, but it seems that only 500 Adventurers and 7,500 soldiers actually established themselves, having their estates confirmed in 1670. This was a large influx compared with earlier plantations – but whereas those had been concentrated in compact areas, the newcomers now were scattered over three provinces.[122] The Scots in effect had transformed Ulster; the Cromwellian English could not exert such influence. The vision of a 'civil' Protestant Ireland was still, and always would be, chimerical.

The rank and file soldiers who had been thought of as a resident garrison, not only settled in smaller numbers than had been hoped but showed a distressing, inevitable propensity to go bush; it was reported in 1659 that many had 'married Irish Papists, contrary to sundry Declarations made in that behalf'.[123] But of course there were important outcomes. Officers commonly bought up allotments given to rank and file and even those granted to papists in Connacht; many of these men founded great landed families. Altogether about a third of the land of Ireland, some 6½ million acres, was divided up among new Protestant owners. Meanwhile, the leading towns were subjected to Protestant takeover. Numerous Catholic merchants now decamped to the Continent. The purge went furthest in Waterford, whence all papists were expelled by an order of March 1651, and in the once-thriving port of Galway. Here and elsewhere it proved impossible to get the right kind of settlers to move in. A contemporary complained, regarding Galway, that the newcomers replacing Catholics were merely 'a few mechanick barbers and taylers ... mean persons unfit to carry on the trade of soe great a porte.'[124] Suitable English failing, attempts were made to attract New Englanders, Huguenots, Dutchmen, all without much success. Dublin, already a mainly Protestant town, profited from the problems of the outports to confirm its dominance of Irish trade.

Though a Catholic merchant community would grow afresh, Protestant grip of the rule of the towns was another enduring legacy of the Cromwellian period. The papist 'Old English' had now been driven down into one mass with the

Gaels. Catholics had owned three-fifths of Irish land in 1641; in 1660 they had under one-tenth.[125] Here was the basis of the 'Protestant Ascendancy' which would prevail in Ireland until the nineteenth century.

Cromwellian treatment of Wales was in extreme contrast, though no area had given more support to King Charles. Puritanism had had very few adherents in Wales before the civil war. The Welsh gentry were generally Royalist, and the commoners so responsive to Charles's call that one Cavalier called the country 'the nursery of the King's infantry'.[126]

The conversion of Wales to a better religion was now made a high priority. In 1650 an Act for the Propagation of the Gospel in Wales was passed, and that famous Fifth Monarchist general, the millenarian Thomas Harrison, headed a commission of seventy set up to implement it. For three years Wales, under this body, had a degree of autonomy not known since 1536, or after 1653, but self-government did not come into it. Several of the Commissioners were English, and the Anglicised border counties were heavily represented, and the proportion of Welsh gentry was very small. The aim was Anglicisation. The conversion of Welsh Celts evoked far more purposeful effort than that of Irish Gaels. There were three editions of the New Testament, and one of the whole Bible, in Welsh between 1647 and 1654.[127] But the day when Calvinism would dominate most Welsh hearts and minds was still very far distant. Nearly three hundred unsatisfactory clergymen were ejected by the Commissioners, but with so few Welsh Puritans it was impossible to replace them and itinerant preachers, often English in speech, were all that could be provided. The sixty or more schools now set up by the State, free and open to both sexes, were entirely English in character and had little effect. Though Quakerism, Baptism and Presbyterianism made some inroads in the more Anglicised parts of the country, the net result of the Commissioners' work was to prolong Welsh 'backwardness' by leaving many parishes without regular church services. While many of the Welsh gentry were ruined by their outlays on behalf of the King, and by fines after the war, so slumped to become mere farmers, the more fortunate families which kept their heads above water and formed for generations thereafter the country's small ruling élite remained mostly reactionary in their outlook.

Under the Protectorate centralisation of government came to an extent never felt in Britain before. In 1655 Cromwell put England and Wales under the direct rule of eleven Major Generals, plenipotentiaries who confronted the local gentry with powers of interference comparable to those of French *intendants* or of Turkish satraps. Justices of the Peace, now overborne in their own patches of rule, loathed these incomers, who were often men of humble origin (thus, Berry, who ruled Wales, had been a mere clerk in an ironworks, and the pedigree-conscious native gentry were deeply insulted). The civil war phase had given the various countries and regions of Britain much greater independence. But now old Councils in the north and in Wales were abolished. The Major

Generals carried a common policy into every district, organising militia, enforcing punitive taxes on Royalists, executing the poor laws, purging the J.P.s and even 'promoting virtue': they were, for instance, told to suppress horse-racing.

The economic counterpart of republican centralism was the way of thought which would later be called 'mercantilism'. National aims must prevail over local feelings. England must be heavily armed, and must use its arms to further projects thought to be in the nation's interest. Cromwell, who had once spoken up for the fenmen, was the chief advocate after the civil war of an Act designed to complete the drainage work on the Bedford Level. The wording of this legislation is textbook mercantilism. The Fens are to be made 'fit to bear coleseed and rapeseed in great abundance, which is of singular use to make soap and oils within this nation, to the advancement of the trade of clothing and spinning of wool, and much of it will be improved into good pasture for feeding and breeding of cattle, and of tillage to be sown with corn and grain, and for hemp and flax in great quantity, for making all sorts of linen cloth and cordage for shipping within this nation; which will increase manufactures, commerce, and trading at home and abroad, will relieve the poor by setting them on work, and will many other ways redound to the great advantage and strengthening of the nation.'[128]

Despite more riots by the common fenmen, the work was finished by 1652, after Scots prisoners captured at Dunbar had been drafted in to alleviate shortage of labour. So one great wet area was conquered, though the civil war had enabled the commoners to triumph in the northern Fenlands and traditional Fen ways of life would prevail over a large area into the eighteenth century; the process of bringing unamenable local cultures within Britain to heel and of making their provinces serve the interests of capitalism would not be completed till Queen Victoria's day.

Central power was still too small to police rural England, as the case of the West Country tobacco-growers showed. During the civil war years, they had got on with illegal planting untroubled. Cromwell moved against them again. But soldiers sent down in 1654 to the great tobacco centre of Winchcombe in Gloucestershire found themselves faced by a local force of three hundred horse and foot. Four years later at Cheltenham a body of cavalry ran into 'an armed multitude guarding the tobacco field', and had to retreat. So it went on. The list of counties where the authorities were ordered to put down tobacco lengthened from year to year as cultivation spread from Wales to Essex, from Devon to Yorkshire. In 1674 there were estimated to be 6,000 plantations in four western counties alone (Gloucestershire, Devon, Somerset and Oxfordshire), and when the home industry died out in the 1690s this was probably due to the improved quality and lower price of the Virginian product rather than to any government action.[129]

But while it is important to realise that the mercantilist 'Old Colonial

I

System', which was established by law from this time on, was not and could not be watertight – the State, as we have seen, could not yet consistently enforce laws against any body of subjects determined to evade them – the first Navigation Acts passed by the Rump in 1650 and 1651 did mark a crucial shift in policy, away from the old idea that trade was best controlled through the grant of particular privileges to particular companies, towards a new concept of general regulations which formed, as it were, an arch through which individual traders might wend as they thought best. 'With the Navigation Act,' writes Charles Wilson, 'we have arrived at a fully fashioned conception of economic policy in an essentially national form.' It belonged to the same region of mind as Hobbes's *Leviathan*. The old aim that royal power should check the private greed of enclosers, usurers and profiteers was giving way to the notion that national interests existed beyond morality. Success and power, however come by, would be self-justifying. 'Mercantilist logic was the logic of violence in an age of violence.'[130]

The first Navigation Act, in 1650, forbade all foreign ships to trade in any English colony. The second, in 1651, prohibited the import of any goods from Asia, Africa or America except in ships from England, Ireland or the colonies in which a majority of the crew also came from these areas. No European commodities were to be imported except in English, Irish or colonial ships or in ships of the country in which the goods had been produced. One aim of the two Acts was to prevent the Dutch from trading into the empire as middlemen. The context which gave rise to them was one of rebellion in the New World colonies, which had dealt happily with the Hollanders in the centrifugal 1640s.

The influence of the 'colonial-interloping' men trading out of London with the New World was now at its highest point. 'Indeed, in its formal republicanism and its relative religious toleration, as well as in its militant commercial imperialism, the Commonwealth was the near-embodiment of their interests and ideals.'[131] When the City of London feasted Parliament, Council of State and the Army officers after Cromwell had suppressed the Levellers in 1649, its Lord Mayor was Thomas Andrews, a leading American trader and interloper in the East Indies. Such men helped directly to frame the new mercantilist-expansionist policies, and gratefully acted to organise and supply naval expeditions sent out to oust their Dutch competitors. In 1651–2 a Republican naval force toured the more southerly plantations – Barbados, Bermuda, Virginia, Maryland – knocking Royalist truculence over. Another such force soon after cowed Congregationalist Massachusetts.

XIII

Parliament, late in 1643, had entrusted the government of the colonies (in so far as they could be governed from London) to a commission headed by the Earl of Warwick, who held the title of governor-in-chief of all plantations.

This Puritan peer was of course sympathetic to New England, but he used his influence on behalf of principles of toleration which were not generally accepted there. Roger Williams arrived in London in 1643, seeking a charter for the Rhode Island colonists. He plunged into the controversies of that exciting time and published *The Bloody Tenent of Persecution*, a great affirmation of liberty of conscience, then returned in September 1644 bearing a parliamentary patent. The assorted heretics, his neighbours, came to meet him with a flotilla of fourteen canoes, the highest pomp which their settlements could afford him. Rhode Island – or 'Providence Plantations' as it was still called – evolved its own constitution, with all freemen entitled to sit in the assembly which joined its four constituent townships, and with toleration of all religious views. In this small, disputatious polity Baptists were prominent. Quakers soon came in and made it their base for forays into the rest of New England, though Williams loathed their opinions and raged that they 'preached not Christ Jesus but themselves'.[132]

The Rhode Island heretics had been excluded from the New England Confederation set up in 1643, with the aim of common defence against the Indians at a time when civil war made assistance from Old England impossible. As the fur trade dwindled, so did the usefulness of the Indians to the New England economies. Their land was increasingly desired. Miantanimo, chief of the Narrangansetts, tried to convince neighbouring tribes that they must all unite against the whites, and one of the Confederation's first triumphs was to deliver this awkward customer into the hands of his foe Uncas, who duly slaughtered him.

In the 1640s, the sudden ebb of immigration affected all the New England colonies greatly. It was disastrous for Plymouth, which had been selling its cattle to new settlers. As the price of a cow slumped from £20 to £5, colonists began to move on, searching for better luck elsewhere, and Plymouth was practically a ghost town in 1646 when, most ironically, it was relieved by the arrival of a pirate (one Captain Cromwell or Crumwell), driven in by a storm with three shiploads of Spanish loot. His eighty crewmen 'did so distemper themselves with drinke as they became like madd-men', Governor Bradford observed sourly; but he also noted that in their stay of some weeks, 'they spente and scattered a greate deale of money among the people.'[133]

New England had relied on the cash brought in by new migrants to pay for its imports of English goods. With a chronic shortage of specie, barter had to suffice and people hoarded commodities as a form of capital; one Plymouth lady who died in 1654 left no fewer than eighteen tablecloths and sixty-six napkins.[134] Massachusetts responded to the crisis with ambitious attempts to establish a self-sufficient economy. The fur trade was no answer: there were already too few beaver left in eastern New England to make a staple. If imports of clothes and utensils from England could not be paid for, native manufactures must be encouraged. In 1641 the Massachusetts General Court began a drive to develop local resources. But what followed illustrated why Americans would not be able to flourish in manufacturing till the nineteenth century. John Winthrop Jr went to England and got backing there for a company which set up ironworks at Braintree and Saugus. There was from the outset a ruinous tension between the desire of English investors for profit – they wanted to be allowed to export the iron out of New England – and the colonists' wish to keep for their own use all the pots, pans, anvils, scale weights and so on which Saugus was soon producing. All they could offer for them were corn and chickens. Investors had to send necessary equipment from England, and local labour was expensive, thus costs were so high that losses rather than profits increased as production expanded. In 1652 the concern was bankrupt, and by the mid-1660s the works were abandoned.

The younger Winthrop had other schemes, for salt-making and graphite-mining, which also failed. The attempt to foster a local cloth industry was hardly more successful. John Pearson built New England's first fulling mill at Rowley, Massachusetts, in 1643. Local wool production was encouraged. But the industry could not compete with imported English cloth. The one field in which real advance was made was shipbuilding. A 300-ton ship – large for the day – was made at Salem as early as 1641.[135] This industry throve because it met local needs in the overseas commerce which in fact proved to be Massachusetts' salvation. Self-sufficiency was impossible, but the Boston merchants worked out for themselves a middleman role within the evolving Atlantic system of trade. Once the furs were gone, New England would have little to offer which Old England did not produce herself. So exchanges had to be made in places outside England, and profits turned into credits in England.

The civil wars at home disrupted normal traffic, as sailors, fishermen, and their ships were swept into service. With fewer West Country vessels visiting New England fisheries, the settler merchant class moved in. Massachusetts fishermen were so disreputable and unruly that in 1647 it was prudently enacted that 'noe wimin' should live in one of their bases, the Isle of Shoals. But Boston merchants were happy to back these ungodly persons. Old Sir Ferdinando Gorges had tried, after 1639, to build up his colony of Maine but the few settlers in this remote area were another ungovernable lot. Gorges died in 1647. Five years later Massachusetts took control of the region; though it could not enforce Puritan morals on the coast's scattered fishing communities. (' ... When Wine in their guts is at full Tide, they quarrel, fight and do one another mischeif, which is the conclusion of their drunken compotations.')[136] However, the Boston merchants could and did trade with them.

They began to infiltrate the commerce in dried cod which English merchants carried on with Southern Europe and with the 'Wine Islands' – Madeira, the Azores, the Canaries. They formed partnerships for this trade with merchants in London, or set up consortia of their own. Since English merchants kept their grip on the initial outward voyage of boats laden with trade goods for New England colonists, the Bostoners could never control the whole triangle of trade. But by 1660 they were masters in their own fisheries, and a fleet of locally owned and run ships were plying to Iberia and the Wine Islands. Having used fish to get their foot in the door, they learnt of demand there for foodstuffs and for timber (wine makers always needed wood for their casks) and they began to export these too. In 1644 one ship went further. After calling at the Canaries it proceeded to the Cape Verde Islands for slaves, took these on to Barbados and exchanged them there for tobacco. This was the small beginning of a trade with the Caribbean which within a few years was vital both to New England and to the Islands.[137]

Such energetic merchant activity tugged at the seams of the godly commonwealth. The magistrates did not like it. In 1648, seeing that corn was being exported to the Wine Islands and Caribbean, they presumed that this must be causing shortage at home and banned the practice. Governor Winthrop could not understand why prices had not risen higher and people had not felt the dearth more. The truth was there had been no shortage. The rulers of Massachusetts were still trapped in a medieval view of economics. The merchants did not have political power to match their economic predominance – even in the House of Deputies, men from the rural inland towns were in a majority. But a losing battle was fought against the effects of trade which menaced the Puritan ideal. Overseas trade, for instance, implied constant contact with the ungodly – papists in Spain, drunken planters in Barbados – and brought undesirables into Massachusetts itself. The fear of contamination produced laws like that which in 1651 required every stranger over sixteen to present himself on arrival to two magistrates for scrutiny. An old-timer cried in the 1650s, 'Let not any Merchants, Inkeepers, Taverners and men of Trade in hope of gaine, fling open the gates so wide, as that by letting in all sorts you mar the worke of Christ intended ... '[138]

While trade made the ideal commonwealth impossible, it also made Massachusetts separatism unviable. In the late 1640s, Massachusetts made the spectacular claim that it was beyond the reach of English law – 'our allegiance binds us not to the laws of England any longer than while we live in England ... '[139] The context of this was the General Court's quarrel with seven 'Remonstrants' in the colony who had demanded toleration for Presbyterianism and had taken their case to London. In the outcome, Warwick's Commission upheld the Massachusetts position, but the remark, like the episode, spotlighted how far the Bay Colony was now out of step with English Puritans. In the 1630s, Massachusetts men had been conscious of themselves as heroes of the movement. Now they realised that their old friends in England regarded them as performers in a small side-show. New England puritanism had grown more rigid while puritanism at home had relaxed and diversified. Many of the best left the colony – more than a third of the men who graduated from Harvard between 1642 and 1656 went to England, and former New Englanders took ecclesiastical posts at home, officered in the English army or even (like Edward Winslow of

New Plymouth) found high government office. The ardent proponents of national interest had small opinion of New England. Cromwell himself now looked on the area 'only with an eye of pitie, as poore, cold and useles.'[140] He wanted to get its colonists to resettle in Ireland or in the Caribbean. Tropical islands suited the aim of national greatness far better than a truculent base for cod-fishing, so independent-minded that in the 1650s a Massachusetts mint was producing its own coins with a pine tree emblem on them; and when, in 1654, Cromwell's Council asked the New England colonies to proclaim the Lord Protector, only Rhode Island complied (since it needed support from home against its larger neighbours).

But the English government sent out in 1653 vast orders for New England tar, turpentine and timber. The reason was war with the Dutch, who had enough influence in the Baltic to shut off their enemy from the 'naval stores' which that area, crucially, provided, and who rubbed the lesson in by shooting high and destroying masts and rigging. England won that first Dutch War of 1652–4. This was really the most significant happening of the Interregnum. The Stuart kings had taken an interest in sea-power. The navy had improved somewhat after 1618, following years of decay and corruption. But James I and Charles I had never had enough money to build a force strong enough to cope with the Barbary pirates who preyed on England's Levant trade and marauded even in English waters. The navy was under Parliament's control during the first Civil War of 1642–5, and this was crucial, both in preventing foreign interference and in securing London from blockade. Warwick, commanding the fleet, was popular with his men and perhaps did as much as Cromwell himself to secure victory. The new Republic of 1649 acted swiftly to build up English naval potential.

A new body of Naval Commissioners under Sir Harry Vane took over administration and organisation. Three colonels of the New Model Army were made 'Generals at Sea', and one of these, Robert Blake, born in 1598 as the son of a Somerset merchant, enjoyed for eight years an almost unequalled record of naval success. Between 1649 and 1651, the strength of the fleet was virtually doubled, with forty-one new ships added. Never before had a large standing navy been 'kept continuously in being and efficiently administered'.[141] In 1650 a Convoy Act was passed for the better defence of trade. Later that year, Blake's squadron appeared in the Mediterranean. For the first time the English state's power was strongly felt there. French ambition was checked. Diplomatic recognition from Spain and Portugal for the new English Republic was promptly secured. And the regular defence of the Levant trade against pirates was begun.

Now the English could take on even the Dutch. The context of war was longstanding commercial rivalry. The pretext was a quarrel over protocol at sea between Blake and Admiral Tromp. Amboyna was avenged. The English captured 1,500 or so prizes, more than double their own total merchant tonnage.[142] These ships were now used by Englishmen. In 1653, Blake's blockade of the coast of Holland thwarted Dutch trade and fishing and threatened Amsterdam with ruin. By the Treaty of Westminster the Dutch agreed to pay compensation for the Amboyna massacre, to acquiesce in the Navigation Acts, and to make an annual payment for the right to fish in English waters.

Though New Haven and Connecticut had been ready to help fight this war, Massachusetts refused. Cromwell sent west an expedition designed to attack the Dutch in New Amsterdam, but also to overawe the Massachusetts magistrates. The war ended before much could be done, though the French were flushed out of Nova Scotia, which became English again for thirteen years. And the rulers of Massachusetts had seen English force on a new scale, and could recognise that their old style of defiance of English governments was no longer practical.

The same sermon had been preached to the north and the south. Sir David Kirke, the Royalist governor of Newfoundland had been arrested in 1651. The Republic appointed Commissioners to rule the island and instituted a convoy service for the fishing fleet. Meanwhile, Barbados, Virginia and Maryland had been brought to heel by the English navy.

XIV

Whereas in New England religious dissidence was confined to Puritans who were natural supports of Parliament, the southern colonies were split as England itself was. Even Bermuda, which under the Earl of Warwick's influence had had Puritan preachers and Puritan governors, saw a 'Country Party' rise up in 1649 and declare for Charles II. The leading Roundheads were banished, but three years later Puritan dominance was restored.

In Maryland rivalries between Protestants and Catholics had been latent from the beginning. Till 1642 they shared the same chapel in St Mary's, the chief town, but in that year the Catholics locked the Protestants out, till the Assembly ordered their re-admittance. Squabbles persisted, with shady adventurers using the time's controversies to equip them with pretexts. In 1644 the master of a tobacco ship took on the role of Protestant champion and enemy of arbitrary rule, driving Governor Calvert into temporary exile. But the oily Lord Baltimore, at home in England, was able to defend himself against the charge that he was a foe to Parliament and held on to his charter, though with difficulty. He provided asylum in 1648 for several hundred Puritans who left Virginia for religious reasons and next year proposed for his colony an Act permitting general toleration. (It was a way of meeting the charge that Maryland was a snake's nest of papists, and at the same time of attracting fresh settlers.) The Maryland Assembly amended his Act, refusing to tolerate non-Trinitarians, but it laid down fines for people using 'in a reproachful manner' such names as 'heritick, Scismatick, Idolator, puritan, Independent, Prespiterian popish prest, Jesuite, Jesuited papist, Lutheran, Calvenist, Anabaptist, Brownist, Antinomian,

Barrowist, Roundhead, Sepatist, or any other ... ' The aim of abating religious strife failed.[143]

Matters in Virginia went far less waspishly. In 1642 the most durable of colonial governors, Sir William Berkeley, arrived to take charge there. He was still quite young, well connected, much travelled, well educated, a courtier and believer in the Divine Right of Kings. The colony was much of his way of thinking, but even here quite a large body of 'schismatics' emerged. There was, however, no great repression of Puritans, and a fresh Indian rising emphasised the common problems of settlers of all views. Powhatan's successor, old Opechancanough, engineered it in the spring of 1644, in response to a generation of creeping encroachment upon the lands of his people. About five hundred settlers were killed. Two and a half years of slaughter and burning by whites followed before the Indians came to terms and 'ceded' the whole peninsula between the Falls and Hampton Roads. In return they were promised, faithlessly, undisputed possession of all land north of the York River. Trading was from now on to be confined to certain forts and neither party was to enter the other's lands. Thirty years of unstable peace followed.

In 1651, two Commissioners for the Commonwealth turned up with a strong force. Berkeley, anxious to keep his Royalist record straight, displayed the intention of resisting, but negotiations soon began. Generous terms were granted in March 1652. The control of the colony by the Assembly was confirmed, and Berkeley stayed on, though a Puritan governor succeeded him. For Maryland matters did not go so well. In this colony of a few thousand souls, the actions of the Commissioners and the intrigues of Baltimore precipitated a miniature civil war.

But the revolutionary period, for all these alarums and excursions, was one of steady expansion for the tobacco colonies. Virginia had ten counties in 1643, nineteen by the mid-1660s when population had risen to 40,000.[144] Maryland waxed alongside it. The nucleus of the 'Southern Aristocracy' arrived in the 1640s and 1650s. Governor Berkeley himself was a good representative of the smoother-tongued men who came in to succeed the rough-diamond 'plantocracy' which had fought Governor Harvey in the 1630s. His family had interests in Virginia dating from investments back in the days of the Company, and his switch from the life of Charles's court to colonial administration exemplifies the motives which brought out others, the first bearers of names which were to become famous, Bland and Carter, Byrd, Mason and so on. Like him they were 'younger sons of substantial families well connected in London business and governmental circles and long associated with Virginia.' They took over family claims to large tracts which had already been brought under cultivation. They had no need to pioneer. Though middling in class, they were close enough in their origins to the top to nurse aspirations to aristocratic standards. On them the unique Virginian ruling class was founded.[145]

They were farmers, and gentlemen, yet also merchants. They had for a while the pleasures of free trade. With English commerce disrupted, the Dutch and New Englanders moved into tobacco. Of 31 ships trading in Virginia at the end of 1648, 12 were from Holland, 7 from New England, only 10 from London and 2 from Bristol.[146] Dutch commercial expertise enabled Dutch captains to offer prices for which planters had ceased to hope, and they rejoiced, like their counterparts in Barbados.

Both Governor Bell on Barbados and old Warner on St Kitts were too canny to declare for either side during the civil war, when the Caribbee Isles, or rather their richer men, flourished. But in 1647 their owner, the Earl of Carlisle, leased them to Lord Willoughby of Parham, who shortly broke with Parliament and fled to Holland. In 1650 he sailed to the West Indies with a commission from Charles II to govern Barbados. He arrived to find the island riven by faction. The established planters in general seem to have had Puritan leanings, but from the mid-1640s a stream of Royalist exiles chose Barbados rather than prison, men with the means to prosper and make their presence felt. The Cavaliers prevailed over the Roundheads, whose biggest man was that clever James Drax whom we have met before, and after Willoughby's arrival scores of pro-Parliament men were expelled or left. Antigua also declared for King Charles. Then, in the autumn of 1651, came the Republic's naval squadron under Sir George Ayscue. It was big enough, eight hundred men in seven ships. The Barbadian leaders, deciding to fight, showed that Massachusetts had no monopoly of libertarian rhetoric. 'Shall we be bound to the government and lordship of a Parliament in which we have no representatives? ... In truth this would be a slavery far exceeding all that the English nation hath yet suffered.' Willoughby's style was more archaic. Told of Cromwell's victory at Worcester, he still refused to surrender: 'I never served the Kinge in Expectation soe much of his Prosperous Condition as in consideration of my Dutye.'[147] After several score Barbadians had been killed or captured, Colonel Thomas Modyford, one of the Cavalier newcomers, showed the opportunist flair which would give him a lucrative career in the Caribbean and went over to Ayscue with his whole militia regiment. The terms were generous here, as in Virginia soon after. They seemed to guarantee to the island free trade with all friendly nations. This was not Ayscue's intention – he seized most of the seventeen foreign ships he had discovered in Barbados harbours. But the Navigation Acts were for the moment a dead letter here. The new governor put in by Ayscue actually encouraged illegal trade and when Admiral Penn arrived in 1655 to further Oliver Cromwell's 'Western Design', he in turn found fifteen foreign vessels in port.

The 'Western Design' followed English naval muscle-flexing in the Mediterranean. In 1654 Blake had smashed a squadron of Barbary pirates and had exhorted by gunboat diplomacy a satisfactory settlement from the rulers of the pirate ports of Tripoli and Algiers. Portugal in the same year conceded such rights by treaty to England that she virtually became an English protectorate. Englishmen were to have freedom to trade in Portuguese Africa and India, and also, with some restrictions, in the rich land of Brazil. Portuguese would hire English ships, but not those of any other nation. Cromwell asked for similar concessions from Spain. Spain refused. Cromwell launched war. His Design pointed backwards and forwards. The aims — conquest, plunder, trade and colonisation in the West Indies — took up those of Ralegh and of the Providence Island Company, many of whose ex-members were prominent in the Lord Protector's entourage. The object was permanent settlement on Spanish-owned land and an invasion of Spain's commercial monopoly. But in its bad organisation, the expedition sent to achieve this prefigured a long series of clumsy English forays into the Caribbean. Cromwell grossly under-estimated Spain's strength in the New World. Of the 2,500 men sent, many had no military experience. Command was divided, between Admiral Penn and General Venables, and this as always was a source of weakness.

War was not declared before the expedition was sent in November 1654. (No less a hand than John Milton's was later employed to write a justification of this subterfuge, in Latin, which invoked a long catalogue of examples of 'cruel and barbarous' behaviour by Spaniards.) The force arrived on Barbados and came to a standstill there, 'eatinge up the island', as one of its members put it: food ships failed to arrive from home, so local supplies were commandeered. Money was seized from the island's excise revenue and of nearly 4,000 whites recruited to fight, some were indentured servants who had not completed their time, and whose owners were very displeased.[148] A feature of island planting mentality which would hamper the English in war for generations thereafter now manifested itself; the Barbadians clearly feared that any new colony set up by the expedition would rival their own in production of staples, and this made them indisposed to co-operate.

The commanders had wide discretion as to which Spanish land they might aim at. They plumped for Hispaniola. With a further 1,200 recruits from the Leewards, they made quite a force. But they landed in the wrong place, too far from the island's capital, Santo Domingo. In two attempts, its walls were never reached. The local colonial levies were quite good enough to frustrate them. Navy and soldiers fell out so badly that army officers would not allow the embarkation of sailors who had been ashore until every soldier was on board; they feared that the fleet might abandon them. After three useless weeks the expedition headed for Jamaica, a fairly large island which might, conquered, be enough to defend Penn and Venables against the Protector's terrible wrath. It was easy to capture. There were about 1,500 Spanish subjects on the island, most of whom lived by keeping or hunting cattle. On 17 May 1655, after only a week, most gave in. But one native of the island, Cristobal Ysassi, held out with a small band in the hills until 1660, helped and fed by black cow-catchers who had been slaves of the Spaniards. Complete victory came only when the leader of these black 'maroons' deserted to the English, but other blacks held out and formed the nucleus of a guerrilla community which would trouble settlers for eighty more years.

Penn and Venables scurried home, each anxious to make his excuses first to Cromwell; both were clapped in the Tower for a few weeks. Epidemic flamed through the force they had left behind. Of the original 7,000 English soldiers, half died within six months and barely 1,500 survived the first two years. Their conduct matched their wretched condition. Discipline collapsed. They killed in a few weeks some 20,000 cattle, generally leaving the carcasses to decay. There was soon a shortage of food. Hundreds of men were despatched or captured by the resourceful maroons, who came into the garrison at 'Spanish Town', caught soldiers in their beds, and burned down their houses. Eventually, after two commanders had died, the able Colonel D'Oyley was left in charge and he wore down and finally drove out Spanish resistance. Colonisation meanwhile proceeded slowly. To join the soldiers, who were intended to settle there, 1,600 to 1,800 colonists came from the Leewards in 1657, of whom, after shocking mortality, not 80, it was said, remained alive there three years later. Others arrived from Barbados, Bermuda and New England. But good planters were now hard to find. Jamaica's agricultural progress would be extremely sluggish. Its immediate future was more as a base for naval aggression and robbery. The English Navy ravaged a number of the smaller Spanish towns on the mainland. Then in 1659 one Captain Myngs swept through four such places and came back to Jamaica with loot worth £300,000. A new age of plunder was dawning for Englishmen.[149]

XV

With a strong navy, and overweening army, things which had once been hard were now easy. In 1656 Captain Stayner captured two ships of a Spanish plate fleet and destroyed four others, picking up booty worth rising £700,000. Blake made naval history by spending the whole winter off Spain blockading Cadiz, and then, in April 1657, with brilliant aggression, destroyed another plate fleet in the Canaries. He died at sea soon after, but his exploits had shown that England could now challenge Holland, humiliate Spain.

Such success had cost money. High taxation and military rule made English gentlemen hope for a change. When the Lord Protector himself died in September 1658, his position passed to his unforceful son, Richard Cromwell, and the monarchical Republic could not long survive. Parliament and army tussled again for control, till General Monck, commander in Scotland, marched south as the strong man bringing hope and order. A Scottish Assembly had voted him £50,000. He could pay his troops; General Lambert, sent to oppose him, couldn't. Arriving in London, Monck got on good terms with the merchants, and wisely did not seek supreme power. In May 1660 Charles II returned as King with the agreement of a new Parliament.

Monck's Scottish provenance had significance. Britain had been tightly centralised. Now the periphery triumphed over the centre. The local gentry got their way. The J.P. returned to his own. What was restored at the 'Restoration' could be seen as the constitution of 1641. In England the king was to rule with the Lords and Commons in Parliament. Scotland reverted to being a separate polity under the Crown. Conservative elements, landed men, wealthy merchants, had survived the challenges to their position made by Royalists, 'whigs', and Levellers, then by Fifth Monarchists, Quakers and Major Generals.

And yet so much had changed, over more than twenty years of crisis and revolution, debate and experiment. An institution restored is never the same as one which has merely developed. 'After the Restoration,' Lawrence Stone observes, 'the clergy and the Tory gentry spoke incessantly of their devotion to the principles of Divine Right and Non-Resistance to a lawful king, but the very stridency of their professions betrays an inner insecurity.'[150] Disruption had swept through both islands. Ireland was now secured for Protestant greed. In Scotland lairds and lawyers were poised to draw power from the great feudal magnates. In England, still moving fastest, feudal moulds were at last broken for good. Land worth millions of pounds had changed owners, lost by the Crown, lost by the Church, or lost by more than seven hundred Royalist proprietors. Much of this remained in the hands of its purchasers, and all lands formerly held from the king by feudal tenure had been converted to freehold. At the same time, the effort, canalised by the Levellers, aimed at securing the tenure of copyholders, had been vanquished along with the parallel movement to protect common rights to common land. The yeoman and peasant, defeated, were on their way out. The big men who could extrude them from their holdings were now independent of all check save that of legislation which, through Parliament, they could themselves influence.

Puritanism had done revolutionary work, yet was itself shattered and, in its classic form, outmoded, by the revolution which it had made. From the loins of Calvinism heresies and worse had been born. The sons of John Winthrop epitomise much of what happened. The younger John was brilliant, restless, and pliable, greatly concerned with the things of this world. Stephen fought for Parliament, then became a loyal adherent of Cromwell and of his policy of toleration. Samuel settled in the West Indies, and, most delinquent of all, turned Quaker. Old John, as we have seen, had views on economic affairs which were in essence still medieval. Profiteering was sin. Usury was evil. Such views now died with such men. After 1660 in England, 'public discussion no longer entered into the moral or ethical question of whether interest was permissible or not, but dealt with the practical economic problems of how *high* the rate of interest ought to be and whether its height should be limited by a legal maximum.'[151]

'The idealists, on both sides, were sacrificed.'[152] Many loyal Royalist gentlemen never recouped their losses. The visionary Puritans Vane and Harrison were quickly disembowelled. The free-thinking sectarians, Baptists as well as Quakers, were after 1600 harried along with the die-hard Covenanters. The men who emerged triumphant from the upheaval and joined the ruling class, setting the pace at court, dominating the administration, were those who had known how to trim and when to change sides. We have met their like in the colonies—John Winthrop Jr in Connecticut, Modyford in Barbados, 'mutable and slippery' men. Now such persons would dominate Charles II's colonial policy. Viscount Saye and Sele, 'Old Sublety', had once been a member of the Providence Island Company, but he survived to sit on Charles II's Committee of Trade and Foreign Plantations, alongside Anthony Ashley Cooper (Lord Shaftesbury) who had begun his political life in the Barebones Parliament, that assembly of zealots, yet himself did not believe in more than the cool deism of the advancing 'Age of Reason'. Then there was George Downing, more than any other one man the architect of the 'Old Colonial System' — one of the first strokes of legislation after the Restoration was a revised Navigation Act. Downing's parents had emigrated to Massachusetts. His mother was John Winthrop's sister. He himself had been Harvard's second graduate. He had served in Cromwell's army in Scotland and had 'represented' Edinburgh in the Cromwellian parliament of 1654. A jealous admirer of the Dutch, he had been sent as a diplomat to the Hague. In 1660 he made his peace with Charles, blaming his former alignment on his New England training. He sold his old associates to the King's executioners and in return received a baronetcy. In New England thereafter they said that a man who betrayed his trust was an 'arrant George Downing'.

Such people often took patriotism as lightly as religion. Yet they continued the policies for developing colonial trade to the aggrandisement of England which the commonwealth had inaugurated. 'Although new men came into power in 1660, there was no departure from the principles already in force.'[153] The strong navy created by regicides would be a force in the world from now on. Cynicism endorsed what idealism had done.

For a further case study, let us take Sir William Petty. Born in 1623, son of a Hampshire weaver, he went to sea at twelve as a cabin boy, picked up some education from Jesuits in France, studied medicine in Holland and when still in his twenties became in succession Professor of Anatomy at Oxford and Professor of Music at Gresham College in London. In 1652 he went out to Ireland as physician-in-chief to the army. He wormed his way into the post of surveyor of confiscated lands. He executed the task wonderfully in the famous 'Down Survey' which took little more than a year, a triumph for science and also a gold-mine for Petty: he made a profit of £10,000 in cash. Through purchase and graft he now turned himself into a major Irish landowner. By the Restoration he held perhaps 100,000 acres, having meanwhile occupied high political office in Dublin. His success caused a bitter political storm and in 1659 he had to defend himself before the House of Commons.

He had once been the great Thomas Hobbes's research assistant. He shared Hobbes's political philosophy. In the forefront of science in his day, he valued all knowledge by its practical usefulness, hence finding René Descartes lacking. He wrote once, 'I ... never knew any man who had once tasted the sweetness of experimentall knowledge that ever afterward lusted after the vaporous garlick and onions of phantasticall seeming philosophy.' His main pioneering was in social science. Marx and Engels would one day regard him as the founder of political economy. Mercantilist in his view of foreign trade, he innovated in seeing labour as the source of wealth, going on to argue that the labourer should be given 'just wherewithall to live' – if he were paid double he would do only half as much work. The principle of the division of labour was one which Petty developed in practice in ways which prefigured industrial revolution. His Down Survey was masterly in its management. He procured about 1,000 soldiers to do his legwork for him and proved that humble minds performing simple operations could, if efficiently organised, undertake large-scale scientific research out of the reach of the cleverest individual. These soldiers used simple but adequate instruments mass-produced by Petty's craftsmen.[154]

This remarkable man had one characteristic which barred his way to the high office he craved. He 'did not much notice other human beings.'[155] The trait would of course become commoner, and more widely acceptable, as mercantilism and capitalism marched on. It coloured his interesting plan, perfected in 1687, for the treatment of Ireland. This was beautifully simple. A million Irish should be transplanted to England, leaving just enough people to manage as many cattle as the country could feed. He reckoned some 300,000 herdsmen and dairywomen would suffice. No other trades would be needed, and no imports save salt and tobacco. The total destruction of the Irish culture must follow. Anyone staying in Ireland must take an English name. Everyone should wear the same clothes, those 'most commodious' for their employment. The Highlands of Scotland, he added, somewhat prophetically, should get the same treatment.[156] These sagacious suggestions were buttressed by Petty's statistics. He was not, as some have said, the inventor of statistics, but he gave them a new name, 'political arithmetic'. We have noted some of his calculations before now. Scholars can't trust them, but can't find any better. One example of his methods deserves full quotation. He is deliberating upon the loss of people in the Irish rebellion of 1641–53. They had cost rather less, he was able, he fancied, to show, than the 'impairing of the worth of lands', which he estimated at £11 million. 'The value of people, Men, Women and Children in *England*, some have computed to be £70 *per* Head, one with another. But if you value the people who have been destroyed in *Ireland*, as Slaves and Negroes are usually rated, *viz.* at about £15 one with another: Men being sold for £25 and Children £5 each; the value of the people lost will be about £10,355,000.'[157]

Here Petty shows his kinship of spirit with that able Roundhead, James Drax, who had pioneered cotton production in Barbados. About 1642 Drax saw a new scope for self-interest and led the movement on that island to sugar, helped by his Dutch acquaintances. In their way, such men as Drax were as revolutionary as any regicide. The sugar plantation, as we shall see, was already in essence almost the nineteenth-century factory. Here division of labour was taken to peaks achieved nowhere else in the seventeenth century, save perhaps by the ingenious Petty. Slave labour was ideal for the plantation's monotonous, killing routines. As Petty wangled his wealth among the white non-men of Ireland, black non-men were starting to give a firm base to England's coming mercantile greatness. The old expansion of plunder and spices was giving way to the new imperialism based on systematic exploitation of slaves to produce sugar, and, later, tobacco and rice.

BOOK TWO:
1660–1763

King Sugar

As the goodness of God and the progressive nature of man are unquestionable, and as God has permitted every nation to undergo the state of slavery, so we may be sure that slavery has not been an evil unmixed with good. Slavery appears to have been the step by which nations have emerged from poverty and barbarism, and moved onwards towards wealth and civilisation.

EDWARD GIBBON WAKEFIELD, 1835[1]

I

Imperialism has transformed the world. But the world would not have been transformed merely by the growth of the trade which brought Eastern spices to Europe, nor even by the exploitation of silver-mines in America. The crucial fact in modern history – it is indeed the fact which creates 'world history' – is the industrial revolution launched in north-western Europe, initially in Great Britain, by the 1780s. For this to happen, discoveries alone, colonisation alone, technical change alone, were not enough. The social structure of societies still agrarian and feudal had to be revolutionised. Workers had to be detached from the land and made available for labour in industry – agricultural enclosures had this result. Because dispossessed people no longer grew their own food, brewed their own beer, made their own clothes, they provided the swelling market for the products of industry which was a precondition of technical revolution. As industrialism emerged, a new attitude to profit would also emerge. If by mass-production one could make a small profit per sale on a very large number of identical items, this gave one more in the long run than a very large profit on each of a small number of luxury goods, and the man of capital was released from dependence on the richest consumers, the old ruling class, and could begin to reshape the world after his own bent.

Into the seventeenth century an older attitude to money still ruled. The object of merchants and manufacturers was not to expand the market but to corner it. The trade in cloves and pepper for which four European nations fought in the East Indies was one where very high profits could be made on a small bulk of goods. When they won the battle, the concern of the Dutch was not to increase the output of spices in the Moluccas but, on the contrary, to restrict and monopolise it. However, a different kind of colonial trade had grown up side by side with the fort-and-factory style, the middleman role, which the Dutch had inherited from the Portuguese. The tobacco plantation, still more the sugar plantation, were harbingers of revolution. Both products, momentously, were habit-forming. The market for them was virtually limitless. This encouraged increased production, which drove down the price and so spread demand further. The sugar plantation was in essence already the factory of the industrial revolution, exploiting labour with cruel efficiency. Concentration on one product made agrarian self-sufficiency out of the question. The plantation had to depend on a flow of tools, clothing and even food and drink from industries in Europe which thus gained a large new market for such items, sold and exported in bulk. The slave trade on which plantations were founded involved increasing recourse to African coasts where cheap metalware found many buyers, and so did textiles, some made in Europe, others acquired by growing trade in India.

This new system created, and came to depend on, what we would now call a 'rising standard of living' in Europe, as demand for tropical produce grew to the point where luxuries like tobacco and tea became virtual necessities. The Englishman's taste for tea with milk and sugar in it is more than an endearing national quirk; it is a legacy of the process by which, from the seventeenth century, the everyday lives of ordinary people became more and more involved with international trades which Britain more and more dominated. The milk would come from efficient dairy farming for the increasing urban market, as traditional rural ways were dissolved into agrarian capitalism. The tea came, of course, from the East, the sugar from the West Indies. We can only speculate vaguely about the extra energy which cane sugar must have injected into the bodies and minds of Europeans. It must have been quite an important factor in Europe's rise to world dominance, along with the stimulant effect of tea and coffee, replacing alcoholic drinks which fuddled consciousness.

Large-scale production of sugar had been pioneered in Brazil in the last quarter of the sixteenth century. The carrying trade, like so many others, had fallen into Dutch hands, and between 1621 and 1654 the Dutch tried, for a time with success, to seize the Pernambuco region which produced the crop. But the Amsterdam refineries were finding a growing market in Europe, and the Dutch were in general piling up surplus capital, shipping, and manufactured goods which needed an outlet. Hence Dutch merchants encouraged English and French settlers on the Caribbean islands to start cultivating the canes. And sugar answered the planter's problems. Its price was rising, while that of tobacco slumped. ' ... Unlike tobacco, it could be grown only in the tropics. It could be grown by unskilled labour, for long periods on the same ground, without exhausting the soil.'[2]

On Barbados, the most developed of the islands, concerted efforts to grow sugar began about 1642, and the lead was taken by the same planters as had pioneered cotton a decade before – above all by the sagacious James Drax, whose success encouraged others to copy him. By 1644 he had done so well that he could bear the cost of importing thirty-four new black slaves. The crop boomed as planters found they could make four times as much from it as from tobacco, and sugar penetrated the Leewards also, though its development there would be far less dramatic. The Dutch were most happy to supply the rollers, coppers and so on needed for processing; they could provide slaves also, and they were willing to give credit before the first crop. Several planters went to Amsterdam to seek financial aid directly. London merchants also began to pour in capital, though they could not match the easy terms of the Dutch. By the late 1640s the 'sugar revolution' was under way. The surgery done on King Charles's neck was not more significant in its long-term effects.

From the first there had been some large plantations on Barbados. But before sugar came the landed proprietors on the island were typically small men farming five to thirty acres. Now people already rich took an interest in sugar; some of the Royalists who moved into the island in the late 1640s were men of considerable wealth. By its very nature, sugar production demanded large estates. The mill – 'ingenio', as it was called – was a quite costly assemblage of equipment, and it needed to draw cane from a wide area if it was to be kept occupied. Successful sugar men soon saw that leasing lands on the one hand, or on the other, persuading small men, whom they could not directly control, to grow cane to feed their mills, could not be the best answer. Large units using slave labour would be more efficient and profitable. Slaves were expensive, and were needed in mass. 'For sugar cultivation one slave was required for every two acres, as compared with one slave to from five to ten acres of cotton, and one slave to thirty or forty acres of corn.'[3]

Richard Ligon, a Cavalier who came to Barbados in 1647 and helped the astute Colonel Modyford manage his land, reckoned that a man needed at least £14,000 to get settled in a 'sugar work'. By mid-seventeenth century standards, a sugar plantation was big business. The one which Ligon worked on contained '500 Acres of Land, with a faire dwelling house, an Ingenio plac'd in a room of 400 foot square; a boyling house, filling room, Cisterns, and Still-house; with a Carding house, of 100 foot long and 40 foot broad; with stables, Smiths forge, and rooms to lay provisions, of Corn, and Bonavist; Houses for *Negroes* and *Indian* slaves, with 96 *Negroes* and 3 *Indian* women, with their Children; 28 Christians, 45 Cattle for work, 8 Milch Cows, a dozen Horses and Mares, 16 Assinigoes.' [These last were donkeys.] Modyford paid £7,000 for a half share in an estate which eight years before had been worth only £400 altogether.[4]

Thanks to the war between Dutch and Portuguese in Brazil, prices of sugar were most temptingly high, and they remained so during the 1650s. James Drax, knighted by Cromwell in 1658, lived 'like a Prince', according to Ligon, who described an amazing feast where the meats of Europe and the fruits of the tropics met in an epic profusion sickening merely to read about. Drax's Royalist rival Walrond matched his style. As men such as these consolidated holdings of several hundred acres each, yellow fever, probably brought in slave ships, raged through Barbados from 1647 to 1650 and carried off perhaps a third of the total population. Many petty men died. Rich men took over their land. The character of the colony was transformed within a single generation, from one where most white planters had farmed modestly with the help mainly of indentured white servants, to one where fewer white men controlled a growing mass of black slaves. In 1645 there were said to be 11,200 proprietors, holding an average of less than ten acres each and outnumbering their Negroes two to one. In 1680 there were still just over 3,000 property holders, but the 175 big planters each of whom owned more than 60 slaves had over half the total acreage and formed the richest ruling class in the English New World. The rough equality of the frontier had given way before a small 'plantocracy' of wealthy men, utterly dominant even though one white male in four or five had the vote.[5]

By 1661, the trade of Barbados employed 400 ships a year and the island's annual exports to England were worth £350,000. From now on England's imports of sugar would always exceed its combined imports of all other colonial produce. Though prices for sugar inevitably fell, there was not the least danger that the limits of the market would be reached and Barbados, followed by other islands, drove towards monoculture. A correspondent told Governor Winthrop in 1647, 'men are so intent upon planting sugar that they had rather buy foode at very deare rates than produce it by labour, soe infinite is the profitt of sugar workes after once accomplished.' Planters neglected the fine and abundant local fish; it would mean diverting labour from sugar to get it. Cane cultivation took priority even over the building of decent habitations for the plantation owners themselves. According to Ligon, ' ... Though the Planters talk of building houses and wish them up, yet when they weigh the want of those hands in their sugar work, that must be employed in their building, they fall back, and put on their considering caps.' This austere dedication to profits at the expense of comfort would not endure, but reliance on seaborne produce would become permanent. In the early 1670s Barbados had to import three-quarters of the food it required.[6]

By the end of the seventeenth century King Sugar would have unchallenged reign over the island colonies. His rule meant terrible labour, fierce discipline, foul stenches. Canes were planted on ground painfully hoed – ploughs could have been employed, but that would have meant leaving servile labour unused for much of the year. The five dry months from January to May were a period of frantic harvesting. After a growing period of fourteen to eighteen months, the canes were taller than the men who slashed them down. Their sugar would spoil unless they were swiftly processed, preferably within a few hours. Unloaded from the backs of donkeys, the canes were fed between vertical hardwood rollers geared together with cogs and attached to a vertical axis which was rotated by long sweeps commonly yoked to horses or oxen. (Camels were tried, but few planters knew how to feed them. Where streams existed water power could be used. Barbadians soon saw the advantage of windmills.) The juice crushed out by the rollers was borne away down a pipe to a cistern. In the boiling house, it was expertly ladled from copper to copper until, in the fourth or fifth, it was ready for crystallisation. Then it was ladled into a cooling tank. While still lukewarm it was put into large earthenware pots with holes in the bottom then passed to the curing house, a large building where the molasses slowly drained from the crystals of sugar and was collected as a valuable by-product. The pots drained for at least a month then, in the 'knocking room', the golden cones of crystals were released.

Making sugar imposed such hard conditions on all involved that Thomas Tryon, writing about 1700, found it in him to pity even the master – his lot was 'to live in a perpetual Noise and Hurry and the only way to render a Person Angry, and Tyrannical too; since the Climate is so hot, and the labour so constant, that the Servants night and day stand in great Boyling Houses, where there are Six or Seven large Coppers or Furnaces kept perpetually Boyling; and from which with heavy Ladles and Scummers they Skim off the excrementatious parts of the Canes, till it comes to its perfection and cleanness, while others as Stoakers, Broil, as it were alive, in managing the Fires; and one part is constantly at the Mill, to supply it with Canes, night and day ... '[7] The sugar mill prefigured the later cotton factory. It required a large, disciplined, strictly controlled labour force, concentrated around fairly expensive fixed capital. Men were tortured by machines and conditions which men had created.

Various qualities of product emerged. To simplify a rather bewildering topic, we may distinguish between 'muscovado' – basic raw sugar – on the one hand and, on the other, two sorts of refined sugar. 'Clayed' white sugar could be produced on the plantation by covering with wet clay the pots where the muscovado stood draining; as water seeped down, it would remove much impurity. Fully refined white sugar could be made by melting muscovado, boiling it again, and then claying it. In the interests of sugar refiners in England itself, refining in the colonies was eventually checked by an Act of Parliament in 1685 which taxed imports of white sugar very heavily in relation to brown. Hence the staples of the English West Indies came to be muscovado and its by-products, molasses and rum.

Sugar culture also produced two different kinds of human being: masters, and slaves.

II

Its governor reported in 1681 that Barbados was 'one great Citty adorned with gardens.'[8] Like a city, it depended on heavy imports of food. Like the cities of that day, it killed people fast and so required continuous imports of people.

Though there were no natives on Barbados, Indians could be imported from other islands and from the mainland. While the men could be used as footmen and fishermen, the women were set to making cassava flour and bread and to making sailcloth, tents and hammocks out of the local cotton. But the docile Arawaks were not very numerous and the Caribs seemed to offer no medium way between armed co-existence and total extermination.

The story of 'Indian' Warner, old Sir Thomas's son by his Carib mistress, casts much sinister light on relations between white and red men. He lived among the English on St Kitts till his father died. Thereafter his English step-mother treated him like a slave. He escaped and joined his own mother's people on Dominica. The English, hoping to gain control of that island, made him official deputy governor there for the Crown, in 1664. But ten years later he perished along with some eighty other Caribs at the hands of an expedition from the Leewards led by his own half-brother Philip Warner, following Indian raids on Antigua. It was said that Philip enticed his half-brother and some others aboard his boat, made them drunk with rum, then butchered them. He was tried on Barbados. Charles II ordered the governor there that 'speedy and exemplary justice' should be done for the massacre and that heads should be sent to the Caribs as palpable proof to appease them. But a Barbados jury acquitted Warner, and though Charles ordered his exclusion from public office, his fellow planters on Antigua strongly supported him and elected him Speaker of their House of Assembly.[9] The story can illustrate one persistent factor in English imperial expansion. To the home government, thinking in large strategic terms, good relations with native peoples would always seem desirable; they saved money by cutting defence costs. To the settler on the frontier, the native was always a savage who should be murdered before he murdered the whites.

For labour, anyway, red men would not suffice; this the English deduced like the Spaniards before them. Founded as white plantations on lines like those of Virginia, the English (and French) islands progressed, if that is the word, towards a society based on slavery to an extent never seen before, through an inter-mediate stage where the recruitment and domination of white indentured servants established commercial and managerial precedents for the later and greater handling of black men.

At home in England, temporary indentured labour was not necessarily demeaning – it was perfectly normal for the sons and daughters of artisans and yeomen, even of parsons, in effect not unlike apprenticeship. The system did enable some people to emigrate who had sound reasons for wanting to go – a valid hope of self-betterment, for instance. But Edmund S. Morgan has shown that the lives of servants under get-rich-quick tobacco planters during the Virginia tobacco boom of the 1620s were notably more onerous and degrading than at home in England. 'A servant in Virginia, as long as his term had not expired, was a machine to make tobacco for someone else.' Most servants went to the West Indies and North America because of the blandishments or pressure of entrepreneurs who had a pecuniary interest in the valuable business of ship-ping, and of deceiving, them. The voyage out would most likely be appalling. One ship in the 'servant trade' lost 130 out of 150 on board.[10]

The 'indenture' was a form of legal contract by which the servant bound himself to do what his master told him well and faithfully for a given length of time. In return the master undertook to transport the servant to a colony, and to give him shelter and clothing and food, perhaps also a reward in clothes, equipment, or land at the end of his term. The time specified varied upward from four years. Servants were almost always indentured in the first instance to a merchant, an emigration agent, a ship's captain or even a common seaman rather than to a planter, and when they arrived were sold off to the highest bidder. While their terms lasted they were chattels; they could be won and lost at cards, their legal status was far lower than that of freemen, though they were not quite slaves. From the 1670s the English government constantly found cause to instruct its colonial governors to take measures to stop masters treating them cruelly. The planter, having paid a large sum, had every incentive to work his possession hard for the limited time which he had it.

The trade flourished from early Jamestown days on towards the end of the eighteenth century. From first to last most of the victims were young. The Virginia census of 1624–5 showed the average age of servants as only twenty-three. In a shipment of thirteen servants from Liverpool in 1705, five were still in their teens. The proportion of women rose markedly as time went on, and all but one of this batch were women, the sole male being a Scots lad of fifteen. Ten came from Lancashire, two from Wales. The oldest, a Liverpool woman, was thirty, and she was to serve only four years while ten of the others were down for five, two for seven.[11] Most women, if they survived disease on shipboard and after landing, stood some chance of pleasure in life, employed as domestic servants rather than in the fields and quite likely to marry the master or his son. But, especially where the West Indies were the goal, the records of this large exodus of young people generally reek of misery, pathos and waste.

It cost a merchant from £4 to £10 to ship a servant to the colonies, where he or she would sell for from £6 to £30. Besides this tempting direct profit, there was the point that live human bodies could replace worthless ballast in ships sent out to load tobacco or sugar.[12] There could thus be a double gain, on people as well as on produce. Hence the eager activities of the so-called 'spirits', emigration agents.

Some were commissioned officially by the promoters of colonies, others were hired by merchants or ships' captains, others still were free-enterprisers on their own accord – the 'crimps' who brought candidates for servitude before magistrates for legal registration, then turned them over to a merchant or skipper. Around the turn of the seventeenth and eighteenth centuries, Ned Ward described the look of the business in London. 'We peep'd in at a Gateway, where we saw Three or Four Blades well Drest, with Hawks Countenances, attended with half a Dozen Ragamuffinly Fellows, showing Poverty in their Rags, and Despair in their Faces, mixt with a parcel of Young Wild Striplings like Run-Away Prentices ... That House, says my Friend, which they are entring is an Office where Servants for the Plantations bind themselves ... '[13]

The 'spirits' were generally loathed. One reason was that they were the recourse of runaway prentices, runaway wives, runaway husbands, escaped prisoners, desperate thieves and so forth – of anyone anxious to evade justice or responsibility. But it was the practice of kidnapping which earned them most odium. It had begun early; in 1618 a civil servant had been executed for counterfeiting the Great Seal of England and using a forged commission 'to take up rich yeomen's daughters ... to serve his Majestie for breeders in Virginia.' Blackmail seems to have been this man's main object, but kidnapping did become a regular business. Shipowners and captains anxious to make up a load would pay a pound or two and ask no questions. Wandering children would be lured with sweets, drunks picked out of the gutter. The victims were made amenable, with strong drink or with wild tales of the little work done by servants in the New World and of 'the pliant loving natures of the Women there'. By the 1640s there were depots in the sleazier quarters of London where kidnappers stabled their prey, perhaps for a month or more, before they were shipped. For decades, the authorities struggled fitfully against the practice. Ships were searched in the ports. In one lying in the Thames in 1657, ready to sail for Virginia with 19 indentured servants, not less than 12 were found to have been illegally detained. A drover from Yorkshire had been made drunk at Smithfield market, then enticed on ship at night under the notion that he was returning to his lodgings. A young woman in search of work had been told that if she went aboard she would find it in Virginia, which was described to her as a town a few miles below Gravesend. Elizabeth Smalridge had been inveigled onto the ship by a soldier, who had then sold her into bondage.

An informer in 1671 was able to name sixteen well-established 'spirits' in London. John Steward, for instance, made a comfortable living, paying twenty-five shillings to anyone who brought him a victim and selling at once to a merchant for forty shillings. Public concern mounted. In the 1680s, Chief Justice Pemberton launched a fierce campaign against kidnappers. The result was that merchants ceased altogether to ship servants; there had been no wholly legitimate trade in them. After a petition from some merchants trading with Jamaica, a royal order of 1682 laid down that all servants for export should be taken before magistrates and a record kept of their binding. By the eighteenth century, crude kidnapping seems to have abated, though there were still cases of it (most notoriously in 1728, when the son and heir of the Earl of Anglesey was seized) and, as we shall see, a subtler form flourished in parts of the Scottish Highlands. It was always hard to draw the line exactly between persuasion and coercion, and perhaps very few went wholly against their own will.[14]

Certainly, the 'Caribbees' early acquired a bad reputation which made servants harder to attract there. So the Irish, who were very poor, perhaps more gullible, and certainly less protected against kidnappers, came to provide the main source of labour. Montserrat was virtually an Irish colony from the late

1630s, and a little later the population of St Kitts also seems to have been preponderantly Hibernian. The Dutch, opportunist as ever, competed briskly with English merchants in the trade in servants from south-west Ireland, and it was in vain that the Barbados Assembly tried to prohibit it in 1644. One authority estimates that Irish made up more than half the population of the English West Indies by mid-century. Their governor remarked drily in the 1660s that the Irish of Montserrat had sworn to be true to Charles II, 'and I believe them till an enemy appear.' Besides their tendency to defect in times of war, Irish servants more than once (on Bermuda in 1661, on Barbados in 1692) were found to be plotting insurrection with black slaves. The servant trade from Ireland at last grew too gross for the Cromwellian Council there to stomach and in 1657 it revoked all the Orders which had been granted to various persons for carrying 'idle and vagabond' Irish to the plantations, remarking that kidnappers had been sweeping in not only Irish innocents but English residents as well.[15]

By this time it seemed clear that white servants were likely to be, if not Irish, otherwise disreputable. 'This Illand', noted one observer on Barbados in 1655, 'is the Dunghill wharone England doth cast forth its rubidg: Rodgs and hors and such like peopel are those which are generally broght heare. A rodge in England will hardly make a cheater heare: a Baud brought over puts one a demuor comportment, a whore if handsume makes a wife for some rich planter.' Hundreds of women, in fact, were not long after this seized in the London brothels and houses of ill repute and shipped to Barbados to make themselves useful as breeders. But the flow of white men was not adequate for a booming island — 2,331 indentured servants in the seven years from 1654 to 1660.[16]

The legal code governing treatment and rights of servants which the Barbados Assembly passed in 1661, and which was shortly imitated on other islands, was not savage by the standards of the day, but hardly offered inducement to emigration. The servant could not leave the plantation without a pass. He could not marry without his master's consent, and the father of a bastard child would have to serve the mother's master three years beyond the end of his indenture, while the mother would serve an extra two years. The worry shown here was not about morality; a pregnant woman or nursing mother could not work so hard. And word got home that work on a tropical plantation was almost uniquely unpleasant.

Richard Ligon alleged that white workers were worse treated than black: 'The slaves and their posterity, being subject to their Masters for ever, are kept and preserv'd with greater care than the servants, who are theirs but for five years, according to the law of the Island.' His own account of Barbados hardly bears this out — thus he notes that when cattle died by accident or disease the servants were given the meat, the blacks only the skin, head and entrails. Yet the treatment of whites which he describes was severe enough. A bell summoned them to work at six in the morning, they laboured until eleven, then were given a 'dinner' of 'Lob-lolly' (maize porridge), 'Bonavist' (beans) or potatoes, washed down with 'mobbie', made of fermented potatoes. (The blacks, however, got nothing better than water.) At one o'clock they returned to the fields, they worked till six, then they returned to have more of the same fare for their supper. They slept in crude cabins, in hammocks or on bare boards. 'And if it chance to rain, and wet them through, they have no shift, but must lye so all night. If they put off their cloaths, the cold of the night will strike into them: if they complain, they are beaten by the Overseer; if they resist, their time is doubled. I have seen an Overseer beat a Servant with a cane about the head, till the blood has followed, for a fault that is not worth the speaking of; and yet he must have patience, or worse will follow. Truly, I have seen such cruelty there done to Servants, as I did not think one Christian could have done to another.'[17] While poor food and hard work were the common lot in England, vicious continual discipline was not.

The evidence is that most of those who survived servitude were wrecked by it. A visiting physician in the 1680s remarked on the 'yellowish sickly look' of the poorer whites.[18] When new colonies were formed partly out of the human leavings of old ones, such 'seasoned' West Indians proved far less fit in mind or body than fresh recruits from Britain. Whereas in mainland North America there was always a chance, slim but enticing, that a servant who lived would come to own land of his own, in the West Indies the acres swiftly ran out. The normal allotment to freed servants in Barbados was three to five acres until 1647 when the Lord Proprietor was compelled to rule that since the island was fully owned, land would have to be accepted on one of the Leewards instead. Then supplies dwindled in the Leewards in turn, and the only compensation for years of toil offered as 'freedom dues' anywhere by the 1680s was a few hundred lb. of sugar or (on Jamaica) forty shillings in cash.

Yet the islands needed white men, not simply as labourers, but as militiamen ready to serve against the French or to put down a black uprising. Hence as the years went on their assemblies passed codes unmatched on the mainland, prescribing amounts of food and clothing which servants must be given that were, by current standards, lavish indeed. Ideally, they shouldn't be Irish or even English. 'Scotchmen and Welchmen we esteeme the best servants', a St Kitts planter, Christopher Jeaffreson, wrote in the 1680s. But he indicated, in this letter to London, that the Leewards would accept anything. ' ... If Newgate and Bridewell should spew out their spawne into these islandes, it would meete with no lesse incouragement; for no goale-bird can be so incorrigible, but there is hope of his conformity here ... ' And Jeaffreson shortly, returning to England, became the Leewards' agent in an attempt to secure a consignment of 300 'malefactors' for which the governor had long been begging. This was a hard task. Gaolers preferred to sell to merchants trading with Jamaica, who took women as well as men, weaklings as well as the strong, in job lots. Besides the gaolers, the Recorder of London and Mr Blathwayt, the Secretary at War, wanted bribes before they would co-operate. Eventually Jeaffreson (who was expecting for himself a third of the profit from their sale in the islands) was able to send no more than 66 felons, in two shipments in 1684–5. Of his second batch, he wrote, ' ... They certainly are a parcel of as notorious villaines as any that have been transported this long tyme ... As they went down to the water-side, notwithstanding a guard of about thirty men, they committed several thefts, snatching away hats, perrewigs, &c, from several persons, whose curiosity led them into the crowd.' They had cost him £1. 11s. a head, and after all his trouble he found that planters were not keen to buy them.[19]

There was now only a limited future for white labour in the West Indies. White servants were prone to insubordination. Barbados saw an attempt at concerted rebellion in 1634, and in 1649 many of the servants on the island agreed to rise and cut their masters' throats. Like the former plot, this was betrayed, and 18 ringleaders were executed. After earning their freedom, servants would form a sediment of 'loose, idle, vagrant persons', a blot on the prestige of white men, a burden on the parish, broken in health and morals, sodden in rum, unemployable. Blacks, owned from cradle to grave, would be more efficient, and also less hard to discipline. That shrewd man of the future, George Downing, visiting Barbados in 1645 as the sugar revolution began, saw at once how things would go. He wrote to his relative, John Winthrop Jr, governor of Connecticut, 'A man that will settle ther must looke to procure servants, which if you could gett out of England, for 6, or 8, or 9 yeares time, onely paying their passages, or at the most but som smale above, it would do very well, for so therby you shall be able to doe something upon a plantation, and in short tim be able, with good husbandry, to procure Negroes (the life of this place) out of the encrease of your owne plantation.'[20] In short, indentured labour was good enough to begin with, cheaper in the first instance, but once a planter was launched he would clearly buy blacks. A Barbadian planter wrote simply, not quite half a century later, 'of all the Things we have occasion for, *Negroes* are the most necessary, and the most valuable.'[21]

III

So black slavery became the central feature of Caribbean society. Even in early days there were too few white workers or docile red men, and those who could afford it bought slaves from the Dutch. The association of heavy manual labour with black slavery helped to discourage white emigrants of good calibre. Slavery meant that even the cheapest white freeman was not worth hiring unless he had very special aptitudes. The absolute number of white emigrants coming out as servants fell off just as the introduction of sugar made servile labour essential and its rapid expansion created a great and growing demand for hands. Contrary to the myth which grew up, Africans were not better fitted, in mental or even in physical nature, for the torment of labour in the canefield. But they were available; culture-shock made them docile. As hard and degrading tasks were more and more commonly done by black men under the overseers' lash, the idea gained force that Africans were servile drudges by nature, and that the work which they did was morally and physically impossible for white men.

And by that time slavery as a legal concept had been more or less clarified. For the English, this was quite difficult. Some English people had still been 'bond' in the sixteenth century, but they had been few in number and their status had been a legal technicality rather than the dominant fact in their lives. In any case, it was soon obsolete. Indentured servitude had existed before English colonies were founded, but, as we have seen, this was not quite the same thing as slavery. The planters had to work the distinction out for themselves. By 1705 we find an easily recognisable definition in the *History of Virginia* by a colonist author, Robert Beverley. 'Their servants they distinguish by the Names of Slaves for Life, and Servants for a time ... Slaves are the Negroes, and their Posterity, following the condition of the Mother.'[22] In other words, all slaves are servants, but not all servants are slaves. It is lifetime duration of servitude which distinguishes slavery. Furthermore, all Negroes are assumed to be slaves.

Like other Europeans, the English saw the origins of slavery as lying in the capture of prisoners of war. To spare a prisoner's life was to acquire power over it, virtually absolute power. Slaves were commonly treated like beasts. They were commonly infidels or heathens. Therefore African prisoners were in every way apt as slaves. Their defeat in war was presumed. They were thought to be beastlike – by an unlucky coincidence Africans and chimpanzees were seen together by Europeans in West Africa and the assumption that there was some affinity between black men and apes became commonplace. This encouraged a lack of concern over their religious condition – while in the early days of English colonisation there were many ardent professions of hope for the conversion of red men, there was very little interest in the conversion of African pagans until the late eighteenth century. African infidelity seemed ingrained, inherent. 'Blackness', the African's salient quality, was in English culture deeply associated with evil. It was hard to explain why the Indians of Brazil were 'red' yet Africans on the same latitude were black; clearly, greater closeness to the sun did not determine pigmentation. The curse of Noah upon Ham and Canaan in Genesis (9:19-27) seemed to provide an answer. Since Ham has seen his father Noah naked, the old man curses Ham's son Canaan – 'a servant of servants shall he be unto his brethren.' Nothing is said about blackness, but the biblical text clearly implies slavery. The curses of blackness and of slavery could be conceived as working together upon all Africans, seen as descendants of Ham. Thus many concepts and prejudices clustered conveniently, so as to make it seem natural to most Englishmen that Africans should be slaves, and slaves should be African; that slavery was part of God's justice.

The Bermuda Assembly in 1623 produced the first statute in the English-speaking world which clearly tended towards the creation of a special legal code for slaves; blacks must not 'walke abroad at any undue houre in the night tyme', carry weapons, or engage in trade without their masters' knowledge. In 1636 the governor and Council in Barbados resolved that blacks and Indians brought to the island for sale should serve for life 'unless a Contract was before made to the contrary'. There had been blacks in Virginia since 1619, though their numbers reached only 300 within the next thirty years. By mid-century, both here and in Maryland, some blacks were serving for life and some black children were inheriting servile status, although other Africans worked under indentures, and some were free and were property-owners. In 1640 a Dutch servant, a Scots servant and an African ran away together in Virginia – one of several seventeenth-century episodes, here and in the West Indies, which show that white and black labourers could feel some community of interest. But while the two whites, on recapture, were sentenced to four years' extra servile labour, the African was to remain a slave for the rest of his life. In the same year blacks were specifically exempted from a Virginian law which required all other men to be armed.[23]

The New England Puritans showed characteristic scruples over the issue. In 1641, the Massachusetts General Court laid down that there should be no 'Bond-slavery Villenage or Captivity' except in the case of 'lawful Captives taken in just Wars'. Thus the enslavement of conquered Pequot Indians was acceptable, and so somehow was their exchange, in 1638, for African slaves from Providence Island; but when, in 1646, James Smith and Thomas Keyser brought two blacks direct from Africa for sale, they were arrested, and the General Court decided to free their victims and send them home. Smith was tried for murder, man-stealing and Sabbath-breaking because the slaves had been captured by unjust force on a Sunday. But close commercial and personal ties with the West Indies made acceptance of slavery in New England inevitable. A celebrated but quite ineffectual Rhode Island statute of 1652 prohibited slavery. Here, too, practicalities would outweigh passion for rectitude and the 'common course' (as this statute called it) would be followed.[24]

As it was, indeed, in England. Blacks were a common sight in London after the Restoration. To have one as a domestic was fashionable. They spread widely over the country – twelve black slaves lived with their families in Nottinghamshire in 1680. In the previous decade, the recognition that men might be judged commodities had decisively entered English law. The wording of the charter given to the Royal African Company in 1672 showed the new readiness of Englishmen to drop the phrase 'Negro-Servants' and talk of black slaves as chattels. Five years later the Solicitor General gave his opinion that 'negroes ought to be esteemed goods and commodities within the Acts of Trade and Navigation' and in the same year a court gave common law backing – Negroes, 'being usually bought and sold among Merchants', were, accordingly, 'Merchandise'.[25]

IV

In the seventeenth century, somewhere over 1,300,000 slaves seem to have been imported into the New World from Africa, as sugar cultivation spread from Brazil to the Caribbean. Between 1701 and 1810 another 6 million would make the 'Middle Passage', then approaching 2 million more before the trade ended in 1870. Altogether, the best estimates suggest that between 8 million and 10½ million black slaves entered the Americas – excluding those others, certainly millions, who perished at some point in transit. The great majority of immigrants into the New World up to the end of the eighteenth century were in fact black. The economy of the continent, from Maryland southwards, was at its base a mainly African creation. Though Brazil, over the whole period of the trade, was the greatest single digester of slaves, the English colonies in North America and the Caribbean absorbed about 2 million, more than the whole of Spanish America and more than the French Caribbean.[26]

The Portuguese had begun the trade and for approaching two centuries, despite the efforts of such as John Hawkins, had virtually monopolised it. Wars and raids in the region now known as Angola destroyed, by the 1660s, their hapless client Kingdom of the Kongo. On the east coast, the powerful Shona kingdom of the Mwenemutapa in the Zambesi valley had been wormed by estates (*prazos*) established as private slave-worked concessions by Portuguese adventurers. Slaves crossed the Atlantic from this region too. But the coast of Guinea was pre-eminent. Here other Europeans picked up the jargon of slaving as the Portuguese had established it. Negotiations became 'palaver'. The headman or official who sold slaves was a 'caboceer' (*caboceiro*). To kidnap someone for slavery was to 'panyar' him, to bribe a native ruler was to give him a 'dash'.

The Dutch founded their first base in Guinea in 1611 or 1612. Twenty-five years later they seized the main Portuguese fort on the Gold Coast, Elmina. The Dutch West India Company, started in 1621, was imitated by other North Europeans. The English 'Gynney and Bynney' (African) Company had a permanent fort on the Gold Coast from 1631. The Danish West India Company (1625) and the Swedish African Company (1647) were both mainly umbrellas for Dutch capitalists who resented the Dutch West India Company's monopoly. The Baltic German Duchy of Courland developed interests on the Guinea Coast. A French West Indian Company pitched in during the 1660s, a Brandenburg Prussia company in the 1680s. The squabble between all these rivals was indecisive and fitful. European rulers esteemed the African trade highly, but it was not quite valuable enough to justify the expense of constructing and keeping up all the forts which were needed to uphold an effective monopoly. In any case, there were African powers far too strong to be trifled with. Hence, 'A policy of live-and-let-live, born of weakness and exhaustion not of principle, came to prevail and even to cut across the lines of international enmity in Europe.'[27]

19 Sir Josiah Child of the East India Company

20 Sir Henry Morgan, the buccaneer

21 William Blathwayt, Whitehall's colonial expert

22 Graham of Claverhouse, first Viscount Dundee, and first hero of the Jacobite cause

23 Malay slaves at Bencoolen (Sumatra) by Alexander (1794)

24 Sugar-making in the mid-seventeenth century. Slaves feed cane into the roller mill which is powered by cattle. The juice runs to a cistern (E) and is ladled into coppers (K) for boiling.

In the first phase of sugar production in the Caribbean the Dutch were the main suppliers of slaves, as of most other things needful. The English Guinea Company was weak. After the Restoration, the Stuart Crown took swift steps towards improving matters. Charles II chartered in 1660 the 'Royal Adventurers into Africa', a monopolising company, with his brother James, Duke of York, as governor. Though the Duke of Courland had helped Charles in his exile, Admiral Robert Holmes shooed his tiny settlement out of the Gambia, and James Island in that river was occupied and fortified. Other posts were established on the Gold Coast. The 'Second Dutch War' was sparked off by further aggression by Holmes, who swept down the Gold Coast capturing Dutch forts after the Dutch had obstructed English trade. Admiral De Ruyter, following quickly behind him, knocked the English in turn out of all their settlements save the just-captured Cape Coast Castle. This showed that the game of beggar-my-neighbour was not worth playing in this region, where any strong naval force of whatever nation would be able to throw ill-defended posts down like nine pins. The Dutch thereafter mixed cold war and peaceful co-existence with the English, who made Cape Coast their main base. But the war had ruined the Royal Adventurers, who found themselves unable to exploit their own monopoly. Hence the emergence in 1672, as already noted, of the Royal African Company, favourite child of the Royal house of Stuart. Charles's charter granted it all the lands and trade of the West African coast between Cape Blanco and the Cape of Good Hope for a thousand years, and with these the more practical, most exceptional privilege (which the East India Company did not get until 1683) of erecting its own courts of justice on the coast to try interlopers. The advertised target of £100,000 for subscriptions to the new company was, not surprisingly, swiftly passed.

The RAC, with such wholehearted royal support, had great prestige and unlike the Royal Adventurers, top-heavy with peers and courtiers, it was dominated by merchant capital. But big City men were cautious, with good reason. In its first twenty years, its fattest, the RAC paid an average annual dividend of only about 7 per cent — a small return for speculation in distant trade — and it had to borrow money in order to fork out even this much.[28] And monopoly depending on the royal prerogative was, in these heady new days of booming commerce, a controversial notion, hated in many quarters. Manufacturers complained that the RAC artificially stunted their exports. They wanted free trade with Africa; so did merchants outside the RAC, above all the men of Bristol. And West Indian planters insisted, it seems rightly, that the Company simply could not meet their demand. The development of Jamaica was retarded. In its most successful phase, the 1680s, the RAC supplied over 5,000 slaves a year to the English West Indies; yet towards the end of that decade it was estimated that Jamaica alone needed 10,000 a year, the Leewards 6,000 and Barbados 4,000.[29]

Expectation of life was generally lower then everywhere in the world, but

K

there seems no doubt that sugar production killed men exceptionally fast. 'Much has been written on the planter's need to conserve the slaves who represented a heavy capital investment for him,' Ralph Davis has noted, 'but the facts say that he worked them to an early death.'[30] No other crop was so lethal as sugar, and this was especially true in the 'frontier days' when a class of *nouveau riche* planters rose up suddenly, mostly exempt from those paternalist feelings on which some of their inheritors would pride themselves, and, even outside the ferocious demands of harvest time, ready to work their slaves at a brutal rate clearing virgin land for more canes.

The average slave survived no more than ten years of plantation life. A man owning a hundred slaves would have to buy eight or ten every year to keep numbers up. Home-grown slaves were not economical. It was cheaper to import fresh men than to have women wasting their time rearing families. Traders normally brought two men from Africa for every one woman. Female slaves in the West Indies had remarkably low fertility; only in colonies on the North American mainland, where conditions, as we shall see, were generally different, did blacks achieve a natural net population increase. In the Caribbean the net natural decrease was commonly 20 in the 1,000 per annum, rising as high as 40 per 1,000. The low cost of African labour, Philip Curtin concludes, led the South Atlantic system of trade 'into a pattern of consuming manpower as other industries might consume raw materials.' In 1695 a slave could be bought in Jamaica for £20. He had roughly the same money value as 600 lb. of muscovado sugar sold in London, or as the cost in Europe of sixteen 'trade guns'. But at this time eight trade guns would buy a slave on the African coast, while a good labourer purchased in Jamaica could be expected to add more than 600 lb. to the plantation's production in his first year of work.[31]

Unable to get all the slaves for which they were avid, West Indian planters turned to Madagascar for more. That area lay outside the RAC's monopoly, within that of the EIC, who made no effort to stop the trade. And interlopers moved in on the Guinea Coast itself. In 1679–82, while only about 70 Company ships arrived in the West Indies, at least 32 interlopers, probably many more, turned up carrying slaves. The RAC could seize only four of these. Neither owners nor captains nor crew could be prosecuted simply as interlopers, while leading planters and officials in the West Indies favoured the illicit traders, and no jury was likely to give a verdict in the Company's favour. A report from a RAC agent on Jamaica, in 1681, exposes not only the Company's impotence but also the greatly varying rates of mortality for slaves on shipboard, as between voyage and voyage. The Royal Navy intercepted a 'great Interloper' with 'two hundred and twenty Negroes the remaines of six hundred and odd taken in at Guiny ... ' But while the frigate was tied up coping with this intruder, another illegal trader landed elsewhere 'about 250 brave Angola Negroes which were dispersed and secured before we could have any timely notice to prevent it.

They are like to make a great Voyage of it having lost but three or four Negroes in their whole Passage from Angola.'[32]

The RAC's forts in Guinea cost about £20,000 a year in upkeep, and this expense helped to make it uncompetitive. Interlopers could offer more for slaves on the coast and still undersell the Company in the West Indies. From 1686, the RAC licensed private ships to voyage to Africa, and this was a tacit admission that its monopoly was unenforceable in spite of all the help given it by the Crown. Its troubled history exemplifies an era of renewed struggle, within Britain, between forces aiming at autocratic centralisation and other elements anxious to weaken the State.

V

In Elizabeth's day and in those of the early Stuart kings, monopolies had been a consistent grievance. The monarch had sold to favourites the right, in effect, to tax item after item; bricks and buttons, butter and beer, paper and pepper, herring and hats – in 1621 there were said to be, all told, 700 monopolies. Three years later Parliament had invaded the royal prerogative and declared them illegal, but Charles I had continued to grant them. They interfered with the natural channels of trade and they hurt manufactures by raising the cost of industrial needs like coal and alum. The Civil War swept them away, along with the old monarchy, and with paternalist ideals in government. There would be no more laws against enclosures. The Poor Law, after 1660, was more harshly applied. The 1563 Statute of Apprentices, which had excluded three-quarters of the rural population from employment in the clothing industry, was no longer enforced. Labour could move more freely to where it was wanted. Meanwhile the role of the 'regulated company' in overseas trade was increasingly suspect. The early seventeenth century had seen a great expansion in the trade with Iberia which was unregulated and in colonial trades open to more or less everyone. The need for overall State control, on mercantilist lines, was still generally admitted, but the trend from 1650 on was towards 'free trade' carried on by individual merchants. Regulation had aimed to secure the highest possible prices in trades seen as intrinsically limited; markets, it had been thought, did not grow. Now it was clear that markets could grow.

By 1660 overseas trade had become an obsession, even a fetish, with England's rulers. The Commonwealth had initiated a comprehensive plan for developing trade with the colonies. Now Charles II's government carried it forward. His first parliament of 1660 passed a revised Navigation Act. This was in essence a combination of the Acts of 1650 and 1651, to which a list was added specifying those goods which were to be sent from the colonies only to England and not to other countries. All the main colonial products were listed except the fish of Newfoundland which found such a lively market in Southern Europe. The

Staple Act in the same year made illegal the taking of goods direct to the colonies from any foreign country, even in English ships; Dutch linens, for instance, or French brandy, must now first be landed in England and then reshipped. So, according to law, the colonies must now market nearly all their produce in or through England and must buy goods only from England. But within England their sugar, tobacco and dyestuffs were given an effectual monopoly by the imposition of duties several times higher on any of these things imported from foreign sources. The colonists were regarded as Englishmen and the Acts were supposed to be to their advantage. The Acts protected the trade and industry of their compatriots based at home, and fostered English sea-power for everyone's benefit.

The tonnage of English shipping seems indeed to have soared in the next quarter century, by 75 or even 100 per cent. From about 115,000 in 1629, it had risen to some 150,000 or 200,000 tons by 1660. By 1688 it stood around 340,000. In the last forty years of the century, exports increased by more than half, imports by just under a third, and a deficit of £300,000 on foreign trade was transformed into a surplus of £600,000. This has been called 'the Commercial Revolution'. By 1700 shipping was one of the largest employers of labour in the country, involving perhaps 10 to 20 per cent of the total working population outside agriculture.[33]

In the early seventeenth century, the Netherlands had been 'the chief source of English imports, the principal market, finishing depot and retail centre' for English exports and a main supplier to England of shipping services. By 1700, Holland was still the main market for exports, but England was drawing more imports from her own plantation colonies. Nearly two-thirds of England's re-exports now came from outside Europe. Woollen cloth down to 1640 had been the only major English export, yet by 1700 it counted for only half, and two-fifths of the export trade was composed either of re-exports of non-European goods or of exports to India and America. Imports from Asia and the New World had made no more than 7 per cent of the total in 1621. By 1700, they were accounting for 34 per cent. Even by 1640, tobacco had been the greatest single item in London's import trade; then imports quadrupled by the 1660s. In that decade English West Indian sugar, undercutting that of Brazil, captured the North European market. By the end of the century half of English imports of sugar were being re-exported to the Continent, along with most of the tobacco coming from the colonies, and with Indian calicoes brought home by the EIC which found avid customers in Europe.[34] African trade was, of course, important as well. The slaves shipped by the RAC and others were a portent of great days ahead for the town of Liverpool.

Liverpool's rise from the obscure life of a small fishing village began within the seventeenth century, but at this time the revival of Bristol was still far more striking. The growth of the western ports in general is a main feature of the period, reversing the trend which had made London utterly dominant. The new

American direction of English overseas trade brought prosperity back to declining towns. Customs revenue at London increased well over five times between 1614 and 1676. Over the same period, that of Hull and Newcastle nearly tripled. But Exeter's quadrupled, Plymouth's multiplied eight times. The revenue of Bristol multiplied twenty times. By the late 1660s, this town seemed to Pepys 'in every respect another London.' At the end of the century, roughly half of the vessels entering its port came from the New World.[35]

Bristol had a share in the classic triangular trade which took Newfoundland cod to Southern Europe and brought back oil, fruit and wine. By the 1630s, its trade with Ireland had been gaining a new vitality. Bristol men purchased there not only skins and coarse cloths but also foodstuffs – beef and bacon, fish, pork and barrelled butter – which found good markets in Europe, among the Newfoundland fishermen who needed them during their long voyages and their summer labours, and also, of course, among West Indian planters now growing sugar at the expense of food crops. Sugar was the main basis of Bristol's growth. John Knight showed the way in 1654 when he set up the town's second sugar refinery, linked with an estate on Nevis which he bought at the same time. Other refineries followed. Tobacco, as we shall see, mattered greatly as well, and Bristol men added a further colonial interest by interloping eagerly in the new slave trade. Bristol's carrying and re-export trade were matched now by lively processing and manufacturing industries. In the first half of the eighteenth century, the town's population doubled, to 100,000.[36]

This left it, however, still far behind London, which even now handled between two-thirds and three-quarters of all overseas trade. In the early seventeenth century London's quarter of a million people had spilled out beyond the old City walls to east, west and south. A hundred years later, when population stood around 675,000, the central areas alone held as many people as more than one quite impressive foreign state. Its dominance within England's life was unchallengeable, its role in the origins of industrialism one of incalculable but huge importance. ' ... Out of 140 companies whose capitalisation could be estimated for the year 1695, only five – the East India Company, the Royal African Company, the New River Company, the White Paper Makers, and the Bank of England – had capital conspicuously in excess of that probably invested in the largest colliery on the Tyne.' There was no industry in Europe like Newcastle coal. Demand from London drove the owners to dig increasingly deep pits involving expensive drainage systems and still more expensive pumping machinery. Investment was needed in timber, in horses, in wagonways, and in wharves. Large capital became the rule, so did large labour-forces. By the end of the seventeenth century, in England and Scotland combined, there were perhaps 15,000 to 18,000 pitmen, and nearly half of these were working for collieries which employed a hundred or more hands.[37] The great burnings of coal brought by sea from Tyneside drove wealthy people in London to settle in the west of the city, whence the prevailing winds drive, and symbolised the city's significance as a centre of mass consumption unequalled anywhere in the world.

Here was a vast market to tempt rural landlords into improvements in transport and in agricultural efficiency, and to draw brewers and other industrialists into technical innovation. Meanwhile, the concentration of wealth in the hands of London merchants supported risky trading far overseas and made possible by the end of the century the development in England of financial institutions as good as, or better than, those of the Dutch. English financiers after 1660 invented the banknote. From London, its use spread slowly outward till by the mid-eighteenth century such paper money equalled about a third of the amount of circulating silver and other coin.[38]

Without a vigorous home market, concentrated precociously in London, England's expansion overseas could hardly have taken place at all. The English poor were still very poor indeed. But demand for what had been luxuries was spreading as the export trades fostered rising incomes which stimulated fresh investment in industry, providing in turn increased employment and opportunity. Growing trade with the Mediterranean brought back, in exchange for cloth, luscious things — raisins and figs, silks and oranges. Turkey, for instance, could offer almost nothing but trifling exotica. Growing frivolity and materialism in England after 1600 must have in part reflected the fact that such goods were now abundant and cheaper. Tobacco, by 1680, cost only $3\frac{1}{2}d$. a lb. The price of sugar fell by half in the forty years after it was first planted in Barbados. Because labour in India cost so little, calicoes could be carried 10,000 miles and remain inexpensive compared to European textiles. English brewers, in Charles II's day, were so worried by the appeal of imported Near Eastern coffee that they put out knocking copy claiming that this new drink caused impotence and warning wives that it would make men 'as unfruitful as those Desarts whence that Unhappy Berry is said to be brought ... ' They missed for a moment the real enemy, which was tea. In response to the menace of that delicious beverage, London brewers developed, in the first half of the eighteenth century, porter, a black beer which kept better and cost less than pale ale and was the first of their wares suitable for mass-production.[39]

An important law of 1701 would forbid the EIC to bring calicoes into Britain where they would harm the native textile industry. Over the previous century an industry had grown up in Lancashire using cotton, mixed with flax, to make 'fustians'. The Middle East had once been the main source of cotton, but the West Indies were taking over. The Lancashire industry was from its early days in the seventeenth century dominated by merchant capitalists. Weavers in Europe and in London had long defied the 'Dutch looms' which quadrupled ribbon output per man but in Lancashire, hitherto rural, without well-organised crafts, the capitalists had their way and the new machines came into use soon after the Restoration. By the 1680s they were a common sight in the small town of Manchester, where the industry's organisers could act without restraint, since there was no corporation. Looms were grouped in batches of half a dozen to a dozen in what were already small-scale factories, though no power was yet used save human sinews.[40]

The English, not hitherto notably inventive, were now initiating technical advances. In Charles II's reign they were recognised as masters in the delicate art of making watches and clocks, a prototype of all precise engineering. They had learnt this craft from French immigrants, but by the early eighteenth century the French authorities were inviting English clockmakers over to set their own craftsmen an example. The foundation in 1662 of the famous Royal Society in London symbolises the new zest in England for what we now call science and technology. The impact of this on agriculture was obvious. One John Houghton wrote in 1682, 'Since His Majesty's most happy Restoration the whole land hath been fermented and stirred up by the profitable hints it hath received from the Royal Society, by which means parks have been disparked, commons enclosed, woods turned to arable, and pasture lands improved by clover, sainfoin, turnips, coleseed, purslane, and many other good husbandries, so that the food of cattle is increased as fast, if not faster, than the consumption ... '[41] Yet at the same time as animal fattening took over large areas of the Midlands and East Anglia and as fruit-growing increased near London and in the west, English production of corn was pushed up by larger yields per acre. In France there was no general improvement in corn yields until the mid-eighteenth century. Agricultural practice there was still mostly controlled by peasants; in England this class was being swept away.

Charles II's land settlement gave to those who had. The stronger Royalists got their lands back. The stronger among those who had bought confiscated lands in the interregnum were able to hold on to them. The consolidated class of haves set about making strong defences against any fresh invasions of the gentry's status. The fact that England, one of the first countries to break from feudalism, now seems among the most feudalistic and backward-looking lands in the world, with its monarchy and its House of Lords and its quaint old universities, reflects the strength of reaction after 1660, which froze the country's institutions at a transitional point. The dominant landowners were commercially minded. From the 1660s, corn laws protected them against foreign competition in their main cash crop. They exploited the timber and gravel and coal they found upon their estates, they allied themselves by marriage as well as in interest with merchants and with the growing professional classes. Beneath them, their leases created a middle class of tenant farmers. The poor stared at them across a social ravine. The notorious Game Laws date from this period. By a law of 1671 only a freeholder worth more than £100 a year was allowed to kill birds or beasts even on his own land. Game was reserved for the wealthy. The poor were disarmed. Gentlemen hunted across country without any respect for the lesser man's boundaries. The parson rode to hunt along with the squire, no longer a zealous independent theologian but a parasitical spokesman for the ruling class.

That class blamed education for what had occurred between 1640 and 1660. Literacy had spread too widely. Too many clever clergy and lawyers had been allowed to spring up from the lower orders. Entry to Oxford and Cambridge and to the Inns of Court was now generally reserved for the children of the well-off. Proportionately, higher education in England did not reach again the student numbers achieved in the 1630s until well into the twentieth century. The grammar schools were left to stagnate, village schools withered.[42]

Puritan Scotland and New England would put English education to shame. That the English remained a thinking, inventive people was largely due to the new breed of 'Dissenters' created by Charles II's religious settlement. Inclined to papistry, Charles was himself not a deeply religious man and probably meant it when, before his return, he promised his subjects 'liberty to tender consciences'. Nor was it wholly denied them. For the first time in English history, heresy became legal. Sephardic Jews opened the first synagogue in London in 1662 and were soon playing an important part in finance and commerce. But Protestantism of any except the kind now defined as Church of England came to relegate its professors to at best mediocre social status. The squires in Parliament, from 1662, pushed through a string of Acts excluding nonconformists from any share in central or local government, barring them from the universities, and penalising more directly those who continued to worship outside Anglican forms. Persecution raged in the 1660s, when thousands of Quakers, for instance, were gaoled, and again in the early 1680s. Presbyterians, Baptists, Congregationalists clung to their faith by sheer strength of character. In the countryside where men were scattered this might not be enough, and the pattern was for dissenting towns to form brick islands in seas of green Anglican land dominated by squire and parson.

The self-interest of merchants, whose ever-more-intricate trade demanded political stability, and the fear of landlords that social conflict would fire revolution again, both created drives towards settled government. Yet England was still riven by political conflict. It was not yet settled how England should be ruled. The King had been summoned home by a parliament which he had not himself summoned. A conflict existed between the privileges of Parliament, now confirmed, and the royal prerogative, now reasserted. The latter could beat down the Irish and Scottish Parliaments into impotence, but it could not control the English Commons, or stop the English gentry ruling their own localities. The King could not reign, or, at least, could not pursue any active foreign policy, without money. Unable to get his way with the Commons, he turned to Louis XIV of France for cash. From 1670 till 1678, when he fell out with Louis, Charles was taking secret bribes from France. In the next phase, 1678–81, his quarrel with the Commons brought England close to revolution again. For the last four years of his reign, he did without Parliament, and became a client of France once more.

Perhaps the devotion of writers and thinkers and statesmen during his reign to promoting England's greatness through overseas trade arose in part from the fact that home politics were miserably unsettled; the quest for profit abroad could seal differences and harmonise interests, enriching not only the King's luckier subjects, but, through the customs returns, the monarch himself. The group of efficient civil servants which emerged in this period was orientated towards external aggression. Among its most striking figures were William Blathwayt, secretary to the Committee for Plantations, and Samuel Pepys, ablest man on the naval board. Both were friends of Sir William Petty. Both prized prosperity over ideas, both saw knowledge of facts and a mastery of them as the true basis for good decisions, both were attracted by the new science of statistics. Thanks to such men, despite all political turbulence, England by 1714 'probably enjoyed the most efficient government machine in Europe.'[43] But it was a machine built for war, tested by war and improved by war. Trade meant war. The question was, who to fight?

The Iberian powers, excellent trading partners for England, seemed well beaten, though buccaneering war with Spain continued 'beyond the line' till 1670. Good relations with Lisbon were confirmed by Charles II's marriage in 1661 to a Portuguese princess, whose dowry included the island of Bombay, which Charles II made over a few years later to the EIC, and also Tangier, in Morocco, which was potentially almost as valuable, but which proved too costly to keep up. It needed a garrison of 3,000 men. The attacks of the Moors were too hard to repel. In 1683 the English withdrew.

The Dutch seemed to many prominent Englishmen both the best exemplars to follow and the most obvious target. Nothing is more characteristically 'English', we may now feel, than a church by Sir Christopher Wren. Yet the architecture of Charles II's day, Wren's included, reflects the spell cast by Holland over English culture. Englishmen loved what they fought. The second Dutch war, launched, as we have seen, by deliberate English aggression in West Africa, has been called 'the clearest case' in English history of a 'purely commercial war'.[44] The great aim was to seize Dutch shipping, though New Amsterdam was acquired as well. The war (1664–7) coincided with two immense disasters for England. A great epidemic of plague in 1665 was followed by the burning of over 400 acres of densely populated housing in London in 1666. English finance was stretched to the limit; Pepys was distracted from work 'because of the horrible Crowd and lamentable moan of the poor seamen that lie starving in the streets for lack of money', having been left unpaid.[45] Dutch blockade stifled London's trade and Dutch ships broke into the Thames and the Medway. After so much disaster, the English modified the Navigation Act in Holland's favour, returned Surinam to the Dutch, and kept New Amsterdam. From this point, the natural drift of Anglo-Dutch relations seemed to be towards lasting peace. The Dutch were still strong, but the English could more or less match them, and the two countries had obvious things in common. The Dutch feared French power on land, and many English merchants and manufacturers were coming now to realise that France, the largest country in Europe, must be England's most dangerous competitor. As he swam against the tide into dependence on France, Charles II could carry with him the City merchants involved in the great trading companies which depended on royal charter and favour, but not the City as a whole, whose turbulent anti-establishment politics would be a problem for English kings for a hundred years more.

Louis XIV's example had a hypnotic allure. He took personal charge of his kingdom from 1661, and used its immense resources to back a successful drive to add new lands to it. The pageantry of his court, the lavishness of his public buildings, the great palace which, from 1671, he erected at Versailles, had splendour to dazzle lesser monarchs and goad them to emulation. But Louis was also a hardworking king, and not indifferent to trade. His great minister, Jean-Baptiste Colbert, was obsessed with the need to humble the insolent Dutch. He made the French navy into a dangerous force. French industry was encouraged in many ways – by subsidies, by outright nationalisation and by protective tariffs; this was classic mercantilism. French manufactures won at this time a reputation for fashion and high quality which they have never lost, though it was based on luxury goods and the economic future lay more with humbler products like sugar and iron. Colbert's East India Company (1664) failed commercially despite huge royal investment, and his West India Company went bankrupt and vanished in the 1670s.

Charles would have liked, of course, to be absolute like Louis. His own character was an impediment. He was a genial man, but lazy and profligate, witty but short on dignity, giving the lead to a court which flaunted its idle lewdness and lived as if it must be aware that the restored Stuarts could not last for very long. Besides, Charles had no strong standing army, and could not afford one. The navy was no help to him at home; the very basis of England's rising prosperity, since it was sea-power, acted against absolutist ambitions, by diverting money from soldiers to ships.

Even the navy was hardly impressive when Charles's alliance with Louis launched England into the third Dutch War (1672-4). Charles spent £6 million and gained nothing. It was over a hundred years before England fought Holland again. Catholic France was surely the proper enemy. In 1678, Titus Oates, a disgusting liar, electrified Britain by his pretended discovery of a 'Popish Plot' to kill Charles II, massacre Protestants, and install Charles's brother James, who was avowedly papist, upon the throne. Charles lost control of the Commons and of the country. A reign of terror followed against those imagined to be in the 'Plot'. The Commons struggled to outlaw James's succession to the throne. The words 'whig' and 'tory' were snatched from the Celtic fringe and hurled as terms of abuse. 'Tories' supported the royal prerogative which was Charles's greatest weapon, 'whigs' aimed to exclude James from the heritage of his childless brother. In 1681, Charles dismissed his last parliament and, helped by

Louis, proceeded to rule on his own and to lay the basis for absolutism. Magnates as well as old revolutionaries were implicated in the 'Rye House Plot' to seize the King in 1682, and its discovery prompted fresh persecution of Dissenters. The Bench of Judges was purged, and Charles set about winkling the whigs from their bases in the town corporations, calling in ancient charters and granting new ones. When Charles died in 1685, England was drawing closer to the French model.

It was the time of Purcell, England's greatest composer. In Charles's reign Wren devised St Paul's Cathedral as a central symbol of empire. An Englishman, Newton, was at work on ideas in mathematics and physics which revolutionised all human thought, and John Locke, in opposition to Charles, shaped the theory that governments must rule with the consent of their subjects. This was not a barren age in England. Yet the tone of its life disgusted good men. To adapt the Earl of Rochester's earnest *Satire Against Mankind*, a most unhappy courtier's testament, men preyed on men and betrayed each other, committing adultery with their own wives. John Bunyan, a Baptist field-preacher imprisoned for his beliefs, produced in 1678 a fable eschewing the world's ways which became a seminal work in English popular culture. In *Pilgrim's Progress*, Christian and his companion Faithful are put on trial in the town of Vanity Fair. Faithful is tortured and finally burnt after one Pickthank has testified that he had 'railed on our noble Prince Beelzebub' and had spoken contemptibly of that Prince's good friends, 'the Lord Old Man, the Lord Carnal Delight, the Lord Luxurious, the Lord Desire of Vain-Glory, my old Lord Lechery, Sir Having-Greedy, with all the rest of our nobility ... '[46]

The ideals and ideas of the revolutionary 1640s were driven down with the radical sectaries into the middle and lower orders of society. Lord Hategood and Sir Having-Greedy might battle each other in paranoiac factions, yet the reign of their kind seemed secure. Dissenters, however, cherished notions which, transmuted by passage through years, would one day challenge the rulers again, as democracy, liberty, equality, fraternity. Meanwhile, blocked from using their talents in politics or in the professions, their cleverest men turned their energies to trade and industry. Contemporaries soon saw and announced the connection between Dissent and business success. In the early years of the next century one Baptist, named Newcomen, would further the mining industries by his invention of a steam engine, and a Quaker ironmaster, Abraham Darby, would revolutionise his concern by the introduction of smelting by coke. What other Quakers would do in America, we shall soon see. Meanwhile, similar repression of Christian radicalism in Scotland had helped towards creating a nation which would one day become signally wedded, not to a Covenant with Yahweh, but to advance through technology and trade.

VI

On the face of it, Charles II's Restoration brought a return to the system by which his father and grandfather had governed Scotland. The Earl of Argyll was executed, along with a few other figures identified with rebellion. Charles ruled through a Privy Council in Edinburgh, a parliament firmly under control, a tame convention of Royal Burghs, and a Church to which bishops were now restored, though as before they had to work with presbyters. But much had in fact changed. The fractious nobility had been chastened and tamed. ' ... It would have seemed ludicrous by 1688 should a landlord in Lowland Scotland have proposed to call out his dependents either to pursue a feud or to challenge the crown. Opposition to the government, as well as government itself, was increasingly finding expression through constitutional machinery ... '[47] The magnates, having seen how their own power stood or fell with the King's, were content to make trouble only through 'loyal' opposition in Parliament. Charles II's reign saw a great systematisation of Scots law, and quarrelsome men now found in litigation satisfaction for which they could no longer risk armed feuding.

The lawyers, mostly of lairdly origins, were a powerful new element in society, and a far more modern-minded one, for the most part, than the burgesses of the old-fashioned Scottish towns. But trade now spilled out of the burghs as landowners became commercially conscious, promoting new towns of their own and in many cases turning traders themselves. Agriculture flourished as the amount of land under cultivation was extended. The administration in Edinburgh tried very hard, though with scant success, to promote manufacturing industries and to strengthen native trade and fisheries.

As the western ports rose in England, so rose Glasgow. In 1612, Glasgow was only the fifth burgh in Scotland in wealth. By 1705 she was easily second, a bustling town with handsome new buildings, catching up with Edinburgh. The stimulus provided by commerce with the Scottish colony in Ulster was for the moment perhaps the main factor in Glasgow's elevation. The relative pacification of the Highlands helped to open up trade with that region. And Glasgow merchants were early ready to seize chances of semi-licit trade with England's New World plantations. The town had the foresight to construct down the Clyde, in 1667, Port Glasgow, a harbour able to take the large vessels which were needed to brave Atlantic storms. By the 1680s, Glasgow was getting six or seven American cargoes, of sugar and tobacco, per year.[48] The English would soon be seriously worried about Scots interloping in the New World.

Yet the immediate hinterland of Glasgow, in south-west Scotland, was a centre of political trouble throughout Charles II's reign. The vast majority of ministers in this region refused to accept the restoration of bishops, though elsewhere even in the Lowlands most conformed, and acquiescence was all but universal north of the Tay. The rebels of the 'Whiggamore' country were, of course, ejected from their livings, and because they continued to find a loyal following, the ideals of pure presbytery and of the Covenants still held menace to the Scottish authorities. Some noblemen remained Presbyterians, but none were now ready to revolt for the cause. So the lower classes of the south-west went ahead against the bent of their feudal superiors; this was a novelty in Scotland's history. ' ... After the Covenant lost its appeal to the magnates, it survived as the rallying point of the humbler folk, and it was the "very mean persons" who were most obstinate.'[49]

The reaction of petty landowners, who were abundant in the south-west, to the reimposition of feudal ties broken during the Cromwellian occupation may have been one basis for the emerging movement. The first crisis, however, was triggered by the Dutch War of 1664-7, which was widely unwelcome to Scots, as it deprived the country of its main Continental trading partner. The government had laid down that nonconformists must pay fines if they absented themselves from the approved churches. Now they sent troops in to collect these fines as a way of paying for Scotland's share of the forces required for the war. The soldiers quartered on the south-west abused their position. Extortion provoked revolt. A body of about 3,000 'whigs' headed for Edinburgh in November 1666. They were easily dispersed at Rullion Green in the Pentlands, but the authorities stupidly over-reacted, hanged over 30 captured rebels, and gave this new Covenanting movement its first consignment of martyrs.

The Duke of Lauderdale now came to the fore in a political struggle among Charles's ministers in Scotland and for a dozen years, as Secretary for Scottish Affairs, he was virtually ruler of the country. A former Covenanter turned Royalist, he was patriotic and learned but also immensely, inventively corrupt, and his flagrant exploitation of his office discredited his regime. However, like his royal master, he preferred toleration to bullying. The 'indulgences' of 1669 and 1672 which permitted Presbyterian ministers, if they accepted certain terms, to preach legally, split the opposition between the intransigents and those who followed 'indulged' clergy. The die-hards continued to worship in open-air 'conventicles', swords at the ready, and before long repression was renewed. In 1677, landowners were told they must sign bonds for the loyal behaviour of all persons living on their lands. For many in the south-west this demand was impossible to meet; nonconformity was too general. To discipline the area, Lauderdale sent in the famous 'Highland Host' of 1678. Six thousand Gaelic-speaking clansmen, as well as three thousand Lowland militiamen, were told to take up free quarters on all who refused to sign a promise of conformity. Peers suffered along with commoners. The host plundered at will. No one was killed in a month or so of pillaging, but the 'whigs'' anger at their immense losses was inflamed further by the fact that Highland savages had been the cause of them. One Covenanter wrote that as the clansmen passed Stirling on their way home, 'every man drew his sword to show the world they had returned as conquerors from their enemy's land, but they might as well have shown the pots, pans, girdles, shoes and other bodily and household furniture with which they were loaded.'[50]

A new rising could hardly be long delayed. In May 1679 the spark was provided by the murder of the unpopular Archbishop Sharpe on a moor in Fife by a band of self-righteous men who firmly believed him to be the devil's agent. They fled to the south-west where others massed to support them, and soon captured Glasgow. Charles II sent his illegitimate son, the Duke of Monmouth, with a large force, to help suppress them. The rebels fell into furious factional dispute and were easily routed at Bothwell Bridge near Glasgow. Monmouth, a friend of English Dissent, presided over a short period of relative leniency, when most of the 1,400 or so prisoners were set free on promise of not rising again. But as white hope of the English opposition, Monmouth became suspect to Charles at the same time as the furore over the 'Popish Plot' made it necessary for James, Duke of York, to leave England. Monmouth was exiled to the Continent; James went to Edinburgh where the Privy Council organised a reign of terror which continued and even intensified after his return to England in 1682. Peaceful Presbyterians as well as extremist rebels were harried and hunted and merely to have shown friendship towards a man who had fought at Bothwell Bridge could cost a Lanarkshire or Ayrshire farmer his life. John Graham of Claverhouse was the commander chiefly identified in later popular lore with the policy of driving people back to the official Church and quelling resistance by brutal summary methods. He went down in Lowland legend as 'Bluidy Clavers', persecutor of sainted martyrs.[51]

Two points need drawing out here. The first is that trouble in Scotland, by tying down troops, weakened Charles II's position in England and on the Continent. The second is that a potent myth was born out of persecution. Charles II himself remarked once that 'there was no natione or kingdome in the world, where the tenants had so great a dependance upon the gentlemen, as in Scotland.'[52] Events in the 1680s helped to create a counter-tradition, of self-reliance as against subservience. Deserted by nobles and gentry but cherished by common folk, the hunted minority who followed the few remaining field-preachers injected doctrines which cut against feudal and clannish dependence. They became known as 'Cameronians' after their leader Richard Cameron who died in a skirmish in 1680. Cameron was a merchant's son and one of his hearers recalled him saying 'after these defections and judgements are over, ye may see the nettles grow out of the bed-chambers of noblemen and gentlemen and their homes, memorials, and posterity to perish from the earth.'[53] His successor, Donald Cargill, had the gall to excommunicate Charles II and all his ministers. A moderate Presbyterian minister complained of such men as these that they extolled 'the ignorance, simplicity, indiscretion, and infirmities of the poor vulgar, a thing not to be gloried in, nor boasted of ... '[54] In other words, they thought the ideas of the poor might be worth more than those of the rich. One day Lowland Scots named Watt and Burns and Cook would prove them right.

SCOTLAND TO 1745

FRASER Gaelic clans

Scott Border families

⚔ Battles

Lewis

● Stornoway

Loch Broom

MACLEOD

MACKENZIE

MACDONALD

FRASER

⚔ Culloden

● Inverness

Dunvegan ●

Skye

GORDON

● Aberdeen

Killiecrankie ⚔

Highland line

Glencoe

MACLEAN

CAMPBELL

Dundee ●

Perth ●

⚔ Sherrifmuir

Stirling ●

Inveraray ●

Islay

MACDONALD

Prestonpans

⚔ ⚔ Dunbar

● Glasgow

Edinburgh ●

⚔ Bothwell Brig

Home

⚔ Philiphaugh

Scott

Kintyre

Border

Elliott

Liddesdale

Armstrong

Debateable

Galloway

Graham

land

● Carlisle

Behind the tobacco magnates of eighteenth-century Glasgow, behind an artisan class which would make two successive industrial revolutions, stood ancestors who had fled from Bothwell Bridge.

The same may be said, however, of many Protestant Ulstermen. Self-righteousness and boastful intolerance would be another inheritance from the Cameronians. The Ulster Scots grew greatly in numbers in Charles II's reign. Preachers outlawed at home sought refuge in Ireland, where Alexander Peden, one of the best-loved Covenanting ministers, prophesied 'hunger, hunger in Derry, many a black and pale face shall be in thee.' Or so it was said, after such things had come to pass.[55]

VII

Protestant planters in Ireland had given Charles II valuable backing in the preliminaries to his Restoration, and he had to accommodate their interests. He announced late in 1660 that the Cromwellian newcomers were to keep what they had acquired, although Irish deprived of their lands on the grounds of religion or Royalism were to get back what they had lost. While, furthermore, soldiers who had served Charles abroad would also have claims to reward in Irish acres. Ormond, now created a duke and re-appointed Lord Lieutenant, commented wrily that they would need to discover a new Ireland, as the present one wasn't large enough. So it proved. Under the Act of Settlement passed in May 1662 by the Irish House of Commons, now exclusively Protestant, dominated by recent settlers, 'innocent' Protestants and papists were to be given their lands back. The Court of Claims now set up found 'innocent' a vast majority of those who came before it, and fears of dispossession made some Protestants plot an abortive coup. When the Court ended its work in August 1663, over 700 'innocents' had been certified, but thousands of claimants were still waiting to be heard. If most of these also proved 'innocent', the Act would be unworkable. A squalid deal followed. The more prominent Catholics threw over the rest. Even so, large surrenders of land were required from Protestants and there were fierce words and half-drawn swords in the Irish Commons before Ormond soothed tempers and the angry newcomers realised that the proposed arrangements at least gave them security. A series of inquiries and crown grants thereafter did help to restore more of what Catholics had lost. Total Catholic share of the land had been reduced to under 10 per cent by 1660. By 1685, it had risen again to 20 per cent.[56]

But most Catholics had been cheated. Old English and Gaels now shared a feeling that the settlement had been a great betrayal. Petty, who was most certainly not one of the losers, observed in the 1670s that the old distinction between Gael and Catholic settler was 'asleep now, because they have a Common Enemy.'[57] Protestants held almost all Ulster and four-fifths of Leinster and Munster, but Catholics still owned half the lands beyond the Shannon and there were influential papist peers and landlords scattered elsewhere in sufficient numbers to worry newcomers who feared, quite rightly, that any good chance would be taken of throwing the settlement into the melting pot again.

As in England, the Church of Ireland became 'part of the defensive structure of a ruling class', turned outwards against Dissenters now as well as against Catholics. Petty reckoned that little more than a third of the 300,000 Protestants whom he calculated to be in Ireland belonged now to the Church by law established. (And he estimated that there were 800,000 papists.)[58] Though Charles from 1672 gave a *regium donum* (royal subsidy) to the Presbyterian ministers whose flocks dominated Ulster, their relations with the authorities were and remained uneasy.

For most of Charles II's reign, Catholics were not persecuted, and at times the Roman hierarchy 'was able to function more freely than it had done for over a century'. But Titus Oates's 'Popish Plot' led to pressure on the easy-going Ormond. Though he evaded the extremes of persecution urged on him, action was taken to expel bishops and regular clergy. Those who remained were hunted. Oliver Plunket, Roman Archbishop of Armagh, a saintly man who had co-operated with the government against the 'tories', was seized and, since no Irish jury would have convicted him, was sent for trial to London charged with treason. He was executed there in 1681 despite the wishes of the King and the disgust of Ormond at perjured witnesses who 'went out of Ireland with bad English and worse clothes and returned well-bred gentlemen, well caronated, periwigged and clothed.'[59]

Even in good times, Catholics forced to pay tithes to Protestant clergy had little left for their own priests. Catholic education was tolerated only locally and spasmodically, though a Jesuit school which flourished awhile in Drogheda was good enough to attract many sons of Protestant gentry. The transition was not yet complete to an Ireland where an alien aristocracy would rule over natives with whom it had nothing in common. Gaelic poets lamented that in the great houses now the harpstrings were untouched and the pipes unplayed, that dancing and mirth were no more and that penny-pinching oafs had usurped the places of old chiefs, yet some were prepared to write in praise of Protestant newcomers, so it must be presumed that some of the latter were ready to pay them.

Against Irish custom, of course, some Catholic clergy were as militant as any Anglocentricist would have wished. Missionary clergy continued to struggle against irregular marriages, drinking at wakes and succouring of tories, though the native priests were commonly prone to indulge in whiskey in public and were mostly ill-educated men. A visitor to the south-west in 1703 would report that the poor there rarely spoke English 'unless forced', but the alien language continued its progress and most people were coming to understand it. When an Irish translation of the Bible was at last published under Protestant auspices in the 1680s, this was too late either to further the Reformation or to halt the ebb of the tide of Gaelic. But the poor retained their pre-Christian superstitions.

'On St John's Eve it was customary to make small bonfires in the principal gaps and tracks frequented by cattle to prevent the fairies passing there; on May Day, the pails of milk were adorned with garlands of flowers; and rings of mountain ash were often attached to cows udders to safeguard them against the spells of fairies.' The custom of fosterage long survived the social order it had come from, providing a bond between gentry and tenants. Reverence for superiors lingered from chiefly days. A writer of 1674 observed that 'a tenant fears as much to speak against a Lord of the manor, or their next powerful neighbour, as wise men would dread to speak treason against a prince ... '[60]

For the moment, only the endemic tories were in active revolt. They were popular heroes. The prime Robin Hood was Redmond O Hanlon, famed on the Continent and among the poor, an educated man who had lost his land under the Restoration Settlement. He haunted the mountains north of Dundalk, in Ulster, till he was betrayed and executed in the early 1680s. Richard Power in Munster was described as 'an absolute ubiquitous ... He is sometimes in the county of Waterford and sometimes in Kilkenny, and immediately after we hear of his pranks in the county of Limerick and in Kerry and Cork.' He too died on the gallows, bravely, after despatching three bottles of wine.[61]

Toryism reflected not only the dying Gaelic tradition of reiving, but also the growing traffic which flowed along Ireland's roads and could be preyed upon with profit. Dublin, like London, was spreading its commerce to hitherto isolated parts of the country. With around 60,000 people by 1685, Dublin was the second city of the empire, sustained by its dominance in the trade with England and by the demand of country landowners for skilled craftsmanship and imported goods. Besides its vast number of taverns and alehouses, it boasted numerous coffee houses and bookshops, a learned Philosophical Society (1682) and a new theatre (1662). Ormond had acquired in France a taste for architectural grandeur and encouraged Dublin's transformation towards the impressive capital which it became in the eighteenth century. Cork, no less than half its size, throve on trade with the New World. And Ulster, hitherto poor and backward, was beginning to rise. A spate of new settlers from Scotland, and England, helped to build up the linen industry from the 1680s, and Belfast, by 1700, was the fourth port in Ireland, eclipsing Limerick and Galway.[62]

Perhaps many Irish were better off than before. The potato, established from the 1650s, certainly strengthened, at this stage, the national diet. Petty raged against the chimneyless hovels in which the poor lived, full of soot and smoke, vermin and damp, and against the fact that the Irish poor still remained self-sufficient, rarely buying anything made outside their own village. But he noted one breach in the rule that they ignored foreign commodities. 'Tobacco taken in short Pipes seldom burnt, seems the pleasure of their Lives, together with Sneezing: Insomuch, that 2/7 of their Expence in Food, is Tobacco.'[63]

War and confiscations had shaken land loose from communal control, and landlords in Ireland now found it relatively easy to direct their production towards foreign markets. Deforestation doomed the iron industry, since the island had little coal. But as land was won from the forests, it fed sheep and cattle and Ireland sent butter to the Continent, supplied wool for the English textile industry, and sold salt beef to sea captains and to West Indian slave-owners.

By the early 1660s there was a thriving trade in live cattle and sheep exported to England. The squires at Westminster would not stand for this competition, and the 'Great Cattle Act' of 1667 forbade it, as well as the import of Irish beef, butter, and pork. This left Ireland dependent on trade outside British markets, and so exceptionally vulnerable to wars. But Frenchmen and Spaniards eagerly purchased the cheap and excellent Irish salt beef and it gained 'a maritime and colonial monopoly it held almost to the end of the eighteenth century'. Perversely, some of the most backward parts of the British Isles became largely dependent on markets far overseas. In 1666 nearly three-quarters of all Irish exports had gone to England, but by 1683 the proportion was less than a third, though French tariffs then reduced Irish trade with France, and the rise of linen, which found a market only in England, swung the pendulum back. Ormond encouraged the industry, which was complementary to English woollens rather than competing with them.[64]

Petty pointed out how inconvenient it was that 'a Ship trading from *Ireland* into the Islands of *America*, should be forced to unlade the Commodities shipt for *Ireland* in *England*, and afterwards bring them home.' For ten years from 1671 the direct import of various products, including sugar and tobacco, from the colonies into Ireland, was banned, and the prohibition was resumed in 1685. But the Navigation Acts bore hard only on a few importers. Direct and indirect trade with the New World flourished. Consumption of tobacco in Ireland almost doubled between 1665 and 1686.[65]

Indeed, by the mid-1680s, Irish prosperity was beginning to worry some people in England, not just because they were crudely jealous, but because of its political side-effects. Charles II in 1665 had been granted by the Dublin Parliament customs and excise in perpetuity. He did not thereafter need to summon this body, and his increasing income from Ireland helped him defy his London Parliament. The situation looked ominously like that of the late 1630s. An Englishman wrote in 1684, 'though it sound harsh to the merchants in England to hear that Ireland thrives and that the revenue makes near £300,000 per annum, yet it is much more so to those that are discontented at his majesty's prosperity, since his royal authority is there more absolute and his power on that side does by consequence make him more powerful on this.'[66]

VIII

So the interests of Protestant landowners and merchants in Ireland were no more easily reconciled with those of their counterparts in England than were the ambitions of kings with the liberties of some of their subjects. Nor, as time would momentously prove, could the King's New World subjects always pull happily at the same wagon with his metropolitan ones. But for the moment expanding overseas trade was of some benefit to all alike, and consolidation and expansion overseas were carried forward by a wide coalition of interests.

A powerful group of courtiers, politicians and peers gave a strong lead. Amongst them were the King's brother James, Duke of York, whose work for the navy redeems him from the historian's general charge of ineptitude; his cousin, Prince Rupert, once the dashing leader of the Royalist cavalry and the Royalist fleet; George Monck, now rewarded for his part in the Restoration with the title of Duke of Albemarle; and Anthony Ashley Cooper, soon created Earl of Shaftesbury. Closely associated with this group were the leaders of the new bureaucratic class, including Blathwayt, Pepys and another famous diarist, John Evelyn. The City merchants were more than just in attendance; in Sir Josiah Child they threw up the most remarkable man of his age, so far as England's overseas interests went. Born in 1630, probably a London merchant's son, he made his way in the 1650s by furnishing stores for the navy. Already a rich man, he bought £12,000 worth of East India Company stock in the early 1670s, made himself probably the Company's largest shareholder, and came to rule it absolutely as its governor in the 1680s. When he died in 1699, his estate was well over £200,000. His brother-in-law became Duke of Chandos, one granddaughter a Duchess of Bedford, and a grandson Duke of Beaufort. Far-sighted and domineering, he once remarked that all trade was 'a kind of warfare'.[67]

No man grew so great in the colonies themselves, but here too expansion was strongly pursued by men who had either been born to or had acquired links with persons of influence in London — Willoughby, Modyford, Berkeley are names we have met already. Beneath them the lesser appetites of settlers and traders carried frontiers forward, dragging behind them, in effect, the economic thought of the age.

'Mercantilist' views now reigned. 'Acquisitive trade' had become an ideal.[68] The temper of thinking was amoral, its values materialistic without shame. Some of the old arguments for colonies now disappeared or became unimportant. The search for precious metals in the New World, and for a North West Passage to China were now dropped in favour of the more tangible benefits which stemmed from buying tobacco and selling ironware. Only a few almost eccentric people cared any longer about converting savages and barbarians to Christianity. Strategic considerations now weighed infinitely more, reinforced by a series of wars with Spain, Holland and France. At very least colonies could be justified as a safeguard against the balance of power shifting counter to England. They provided footholds for attack on the enemy. They helped England's rising naval power by providing bases and by encouraging trades which were 'nurseries of seamen'. And if they were worth having for such reasons, further acquisitions would be useful where they protected the frontiers or lifelines of existing colonies.

Advanced economists placed a new emphasis on the value of labour. The brilliant Petty suggested, in 1662, that compulsory labour – 'slavery' – should be substituted for the death penalty in cases of theft. Child emphasised in his famous *New Discourse of Trade* that besides being a 'Duty to God and Nature', to find employment for the poor would greatly enrich the country, just as 'Lessening the Number of our Holly-Days would encrease the days of our Working, and Working more would make us Richer ... ' Mun's themes were varied and elaborated; the gospel of work was further developed. Since labour at home was now seen as so valuable – and the more there was of it, the lower wages would be – the desire for greater population in England might seem to conflict with any call for emigration. Some writers actually argued that colonies were an evil, on such grounds. The reply from men such as Child was that, if potentially evil, they were necessary. Child reasoned that the plantations absorbed people who wouldn't have stayed anyway, such as religious dissidents who would otherwise have gone to Europe, or people who would have been hanged or have starved – 'loose vagrant People'. He argued that population went as employment went. If jobs were lacking, there would be fewer people at home. The plantations, buying English goods and employing 'near two thirds of all our *English shipping*', had actually increased population in England. Every Englishman in Barbados or Jamaica created employment for four men at home.[69]

Child was a strong and consistent advocate of religious toleration, which reminds us that 'mercantilism' took different forms in different countries. In England, the force of the Dutch example was accepted. A tolerant country would attract skilled people – Jews, Huguenots – from abroad. Petty thought highly of the economic value of schism: ' ... Trade is most vigorously carried on, in every State and Government, by the Heterodox part of the same ... '[70] Robinson Crusoe's island, where three religions co-existed, would be an apt myth for the England of Defoe's day, where the idealism of Milton and Roger Williams no longer cut ice, but the practical value of toleration was commonly accepted. By contrast, in France, Colbert's mercantilism was accompanied by religious persecution more thorough than any seen in England, and the great exodus of skilled Huguenots in the 1680s would be a vast gain for Britain, Ireland and North America.

England stood halfway between Holland, where there were no Navigation Acts and mercantilism was more spontaneous and informal, and France, where mercantilist policies were ruthlessly enforced. English authorities press-ganged men for the navy; the French condemned criminals wholesale to labour for decades in the state galleys. England, from 1700, would prohibit the import of printed calicoes; in France even their manufacture at home was forbidden in the interests of the traditional textile industries, and some 16,000 people are said to have lost their lives through the enforcement of this ban between 1686 and 1759.[71] The English State never developed a bureaucracy capable of such cruel enforcement, and a very few people, if any, wanted it to. Colbert's mercantilism, and that of his successors, was imposed on the French nation from the top, whereas in England, merchants were commonly to the fore, demanding freedom from certain controls at the same time as they urged the State to fight in the interests of mercantilist goals. Child inelegantly but strongly urged that 'Giving such Honour and Perferment [sic] to Merchants in the Affair of the Nation, as their Experience & Education hath fitted them for, will doubtless encrease their number.'[72] He was right, in effect, and England would outstrip France commercially.

Cromwell had acted as if he thought Child's way. In 1656 he had created an advisory council of army officers and London merchants to take general cognisance of Jamaica and the West Indies. The merchants involved formed what came to be known as the 'Committee for the Affairs of America', forerunner of the later Board of Trade. In 1657, Cromwell granted the East India Company a new exclusive charter which set its affairs on a far firmer basis. By 1647 the Company had been so short of funds that it had admitted new members for as little as £5 a head. The rival Courteen Association had faded after an abortive attempt to colonise Madagascar (1645–6) but a new consortium had emerged, headed by Lord Fairfax, the famous commander. The Council of State had forced the companies to amalgamate their stock, but in the First Dutch War many ships were lost and English prestige in the East reached its lowest point. However, the treaty with Holland in 1654 brought financial compensation for the company as well as damages at last for the representatives of the Englishmen who had suffered at Amboyna. Cromwell's new charter ended the old system of terminable joint stocks. From now on stock was to be permanent and non-returnable, and this meant that the long-term interests of the Company could be advanced free of the clamour for quick profits.

The fresh charter granted by Charles II in 1661 did not break continuity, though it widened the EIC's powers, giving the Company the right to make war against any non-Christian prince within the limits assigned to it. In return for such generosity Charles II asked for, and got, a loan. The EIC was beginning its long career as an indispensable prop of government finance. Charles seems to have received over £300,000 in gifts and loans from the Company. The shareholders would not mind. Royal support was ensured. Meanwhile, subscribers to the new joint stock were richly rewarded. A £100 share was worth £245 in 1677, £360 or even £500 in 1683. In January 1682 shareholders received a dividend of 50 per cent and a bonus of 100 per cent. Dividends had been averaging nearly 25 per cent per annum. All this reflected the spectacular gains of Eastern trade. In 1675 Company exports worth £430,000 brought back produce worth more than £860,000.[73]

Charles II had returned to confront a huge deficit and exiled courtiers anxious to make up their losses had flocked home at his heels. Despite Parliament's grant of £1,200,000 annually, the King's difficulties persisted and he still had to sell manors for ready cash like his royal predecessors. He and his courtiers found overseas expansion a partial answer to their problems. Virginian trade alone came to bring Charles £100,000 a year, and this was equal to his secret subsidy from Louis XIV.[74] Loyal followers could be rewarded with grants and offices overseas. The empire was beginning to be what one Victorian radical would denounce, a system of outdoor relief for the upper classes.

Merchants did not recover under Charles the dominating role in expansion which they had had under Cromwell. They were used. Their brains were picked. But except in the EIC, the City was not allowed to lead. Government policies suited, however, many if not all merchants, and the class fell into a 'position of comfortable subordination'.[75] Merchants were well represented on the large Councils of Trade (62 members) and Foreign Plantations (48 members) which were set up in 1660, but these were advisory not executive bodies, and the former in any case died of neglect by 1667. Meanwhile, at home and abroad, Charles II's reign saw the nascence of a small sub-class of administrators specialising in colonial government. William Blathwayt, Secretary to the Lords of Trade in 1679, auditor general of the royal revenue in America in 1680, has been called 'the first among Whitehall's bureaucrats to find a way to power by becoming a specialist on colonial questions.'[76] But it would be a grievous mistake to suppose that Blathwayt conformed to the ideal of incorruptibility which was crystallised in the nineteenth century. He used office to enrich himself. Crown servants overseas likewise saw office as a source of personal profit. The governors of the colonies now became sole responsible agents for carrying out the Acts of Trade there. They had in their gift, furthermore, public offices making the holders responsible for collecting taxes, for allocating grants of land and for regulating customs. They and their chosen few, creaming the system, became a focus of jealousy for those excluded, and this largely explained the character of 'politics' in all the colonies down to the late eighteenth century and, in some cases, beyond.

There were already fears that the colonies must eventually crave and assert independence. And Ireland and New England presented problems to mercantilist thinking which were, in effect, insoluble. Neither could produce much that could not be grown or made at home; each was thus a potential competitor. Both, in particular, acted as suppliers of produce to the West Indian islands so that Child amongst others argued that English landowners were suffering. Another point which weighed with Child was that neither used black slavery. The mass demand for clothing, tools and produce from slave plantations seemed to Child the major benefit of empire. On top of this, the New Englanders smuggled colonial wares into foreign markets and took foreign goods back to the colonies, undercutting English merchants in both spheres. For such reasons

Child argued that New England was 'the most prejudicial Plantation to this Kingdom.'[77]

It was mostly New England activities which explained the new Act of 1673 aimed at tighter control of colonial trade. A loophole in earlier Acts permitted colonists to transfer tobacco or sugar to some other plantation, thence to export it wherever they wished. This was now blocked. A customs duty – 'plantation duty' – was imposed on shipments of 'enumerated' commodities from one colony to another, and new requirements were introduced for the bonding of shipmasters. The Act also provided for the appointment of customs officers in the plantations who would act under the jurisdiction of the Commissioners of the Customs in London. So governors were deprived of one area of patronage and a beginning was made towards what became the colonial civil service.

This was part of a general trend, from the late 1660s, towards greater central control of the colonies. A new body, the 'Lords of Trade' (Lords Committee of Trade) was set up early in 1675, comprising nine Privy Councillors. Though this, like earlier bodies, was advisory, it contained powerful ministers able to translate advice into action. Its aim from the outset was to make the colonies wholly obedient to the Crown. The colonies at this time were seen alternatively as 'possessions of the nation' or as 'dominions of the king'. Charles II favoured the latter view, of course. Overseas his absolutist proclivities could find expression. In the 1670s and 1680s, A. P. Thornton argues, 'the monarchy was testing its strength in a field far removed from the scrutiny of a factious, turbulent Parliament.'[78] Under the Lords of Trade, an inquiry was started into the conduct of governors. The navy was ordered to seize all foreign ships found in the colonies and to send additional ships to colonial waters. An attack on colonial charters was launched. The Bermuda Company lost its charter in 1684, and in the same year Massachusetts at last was deprived of its quasi-independence.

The new policy swaggered fiercely. The conquest of New Amsterdam in 1664 had been effected by methods essentially like those of Queen Elizabeth. Charles II had provided the ships, but the soldiers, somewhere over 300 of them, had been recruited for the service of an individual, James, Duke of York. By 1676, by contrast, rebellion in Virginia was swiftly met with a royal force of 11 ships and over 1,100 soldiers.[79] At about the same time, Edward Randolph was making himself deeply unpopular as royal superintendent of customs in Boston, and in 1677 an attempt was made to apply 'Poynings' Law', that veteran device for shackling the Irish Parliament, to the assembly of the island of Jamaica.

But royal power wasn't sufficient. Parliament wouldn't give positive help to the King in such huffing and puffing. The Jamaican planters successfully called the bluff of the Lords of Trade. Virginia, garrisoned for five years by royal soldiers, eventually sent them away when the Assembly simply refused to pay for them. The new royal customs collectors could not, of course, stamp out smuggling, and they ran into clobbering opposition from local ruling cliques.

The King himself calmly created a new vested interest which was potentially at odds with his own authority when, in the 1680s, he gave a vast proprietorial grant to the Quaker William Penn. Royal policy was neither consistent nor effectual.

Another contrast with French mercantilism would emerge in this sphere. Colonies were expected to raise the costs of their own administration. In return, they would demand, and it proved that they must be given, substantial self-government. Rhode Island could thus be as tolerant as it wished; neither here nor elsewhere were English religious policies imposed. In the last phase of Company rule in Bermuda, the assembly had been summoned only once in fourteen years, and governor and council had taken taxes without the inhabitants' consent. But the first royal commission to a governor of the island after the Company's ousting in 1684 specifically authorised the calling of an assembly as in other colonies.

The effectual unifying bond of the empire was the growing English navy. In 1665–6 well over half of all government spending was on the navy. This was exceptional, a year of war, but in the fifty years after the Restoration an average of about a quarter of State expenditure was directed to naval needs, with more beyond this spent on naval ordnance.[80] In 1649–60, over two hundred new ships had been added. This formidable new force was institutionalised after the Restoration 'so successfully that its administrative structure, the build of its ships, the methods by which it was officered, manned and supplied, continued without fundamental change until half way through the nineteenth century.'[81] Increasing drill marched with a hardening class structure. In the days of Blake and Cromwell, 'tarpaulins' (lower class sailors) had risen to become captains and admirals. But along with the formal creation, in 1677, of a professional corps of officers – no one could become a lieutenant unless he passed an examination in seamanship and navigation – there came an almost complete blockage of this kind of upward mobility. The days of the Drakes and Blakes were over. The better-off classes made the navy a source of secure careers for their sons.

But common seamen, as before, served in the navy or merchant service as times demanded or as their luck ordained. Only a small proportion spent all their lives in royal service. Since Elizabeth's time, 'impressment' had been used to gather in hands in time of war. The procedure now became standardised. The Privy Council would issue an order to the Admiralty for a general impress. The naval authorities then sent down warrants to local authorities. These in turn appointed 'presters' to recruit men either on sea or on land. Sailors were taken off colliers in the North Sea and returning merchant ships in the Channel. Kidnapping was commonplace. Once in the service, seamen found discipline savage. By Act of Parliament captains would give the death sentence not only for murder but for striking an officer, even for sleeping habitually on watch. Men preferred the merchant service, where pay was not always better, but where it was less likely to be delayed. Edward Barlow, who joined the navy in 1659, wrote, 'we seldom in a month got our bellyful of victuals, and that of such salt that beggars would think scorn to eat ... There are no men under the sun that fare harder and get their living more hard and that are so abused on all sides as we poor seamen.'[82]

The fact that the Newfoundland fisheries were seen as prime 'nursery of seamen' largely dictated the attitudes of the home government towards the sketchy colony on the island. Settlers could live, it seemed, only by fishing. But their little boats gave them no experience of deepwater sailing, and in any case they were too far away to be easily pressed as need arose, whereas the ships which voyaged from English West Country ports came back regularly every year. The colonists were a lamentable nuisance. In the mid-1670s there were, in any case, merely 523 of them, scattered in 30 or 40 settlements, mostly just hamlets, which were linked only by steep pathways through thick woods. Around this permanent nucleus of families, there was a shifting population, generally well over 1,000, left behind by the West Country vessels so as to save freight and food on the return voyage. All told there were only 167 houses and the inhabitants outnumbered their own livestock. This scene was in sharp contrast with the French settlement on the island at Placentia. The French Crown subsidised the colony, as it did the fish merchants of the French ports. Placentia was strongly governed and had three churches and a garrison. The French had overhauled the English in the fisheries – in 1670 it was estimated that they had 400 ships and 18,000 seamen at Newfoundland, as against 300 and 15,000 from England.[83]

The Newfoundland settlers lost even the ghost of a stable government when the Calvert family, unable to assert its proprietorial rule effectively, backed out in the 1660s. They didn't mind this at all, but the London, and later Bristol, merchants who supported them against the West Country interests which retained a monopoly in the fisheries set up a cry at home for strong civil government. The home authorities came down on the side of the West Countrymen, whose charter was confirmed, and strengthened. Besides the 'nursery' theory, there was a fear that Newfoundland, if given stability, might become another New England. New regulations in the 1670s denied the colonists right to settle within six miles of the coast. The effective 'governor' was the commodore of the naval convoy which came each year to help the fishing ships get home safely. The commodore of 1675, Sir John Berry, told the inhabitants for the second time that they must either leave the island or settle inland. But this was wholly impracticable, and Berry sensibly became a spokesman for the settlers. Many couldn't afford the passage to other colonies and must become public charges wherever sent. Settlers might be driven to seek French protection. And besides feeding and helping the fishermen out of England, they were actually catching more and more fish themselves. The home government let them stay there.

Meanwhile, the New England merchants had moved in, along with some

Scots and Irishmen. This incursion alarmed the government more than French competition. The New Englanders traded tobacco, sugar, provisions, tackle and so on for cod, then exchanged the fish on the spot for wines and other items brought direct from Southern Europe, or carried it off themselves to their markets in Iberia and the Caribbean. A provision of the 1663 Navigation Act was that salt could be freely imported to Newfoundland for the sake of the fishery. This made smuggling easy, since Southern Europe was the prime source of salt. By 1680 the commodore was reporting 100 vessels engaged in illegal trade. Newfoundland had become in effect an entrepôt for smugglers and interlopers. Here Scottish merchants could acquire tobacco, and from here Virginian planters could draw supplies of French liquor; one master of a brigantine seized in 1688 with brandy aboard innocently explained that 'he took it up floating in the Sea and might have taken up a great deal more.'[84]

New Englanders even tried to enter the fur trade of Hudson's Bay, the vast icy area which Charles II made over to the most long-lived of all chartered companies. English interest was attracted by two French trader-explorers. In the 1650s the Sieur des Groseilliers, a slow, quarrelsome, daring man, and the talkative, boastful Pierre Esprit Radisson found that superb furs could be had far to the north of the French settlement at Quebec, and proposed a direct trade by sea into Hudson's Bay. The French authorities were not attracted; characteristically, they insisted on funnelling all trade through the St Lawrence, where it could be taxed; and the governor of Quebec alienated the two explorers by despoiling them of most of their profits. They turned to the English. In London, they were given an audience and pensions by the King, and a consortium was formed to take advantage of their knowledge and experience.

The fur trade, valuable in its own right, had a certain strategic significance. Russia, once an exporter of furs, now showed a strong demand for beaver. The Dutch were supplying Muscovy with the French surplus. If England broke into this trade, it would reduce dependence on Dutch intermediaries for vital supplies of 'naval stores' from the Baltic. The project for Hudson's Bay appealed greatly to the group round the King who took a general interest in expansion. Rupert, James Duke of York, Albemarle, Shaftesbury were drawn in. City financiers co-operated. Nevertheless, the capital raised in ten years – £10,500 – was less than was needed to buy one sugar plantation. Two ships were sent in 1668. Only the *Nonsuch* reached Hudson's Bay, with Groseilliers aboard, but that proved enough. 'Mr Gooseberry', as the English called him, hauled in beaver skins at rockbottom prices through a winter so bitter that the Bostonian master of the ship observed that all the world seemed frozen to death. 'Fort Charles', a pallisaded house, was erected at the southern extremity of James Bay. 'Gooseberry' brought back furs which sold in London for £1,379. 6s. 10d.[85]

In 1670 Charles granted the 'Governor and Company of Adventurers of England trading into Hudson's Bay' a charter which, despite many attacks, survived for two hundred years. Its affairs were to be managed by a governor –

Prince Rupert for the first dozen years, then James, Duke of York — with a deputy and a committee of seven. These men were to control the 'sole Trade' of an area, 'Rupert's Land', which proved to comprise nearly 1,500,000 square miles. The aims were diffuse at first. Groseilliers and Radisson had talked of an easy route, part overland, to the Pacific. Colonisation was on the agenda. But the fur trade swiftly proved to be the only practical way of exploiting the grant, and the company, uniquely, kept a charter for a colony which was used in effect purely for trade.

Profits were slow to come. Within a decade, City men took over control from the original courtier-promoters, but there was no dividend till 1684, when 50 per cent was given. Another 50 per cent four years later and 25 per cent in 1689 meant some reward at last for patience.[86] The Company survived because of its growing mastery of a very difficult trade, which was always useful but never opulent. Hudson's Strait provided the only route in and out of the Bay, and currents, tide and ice restricted navigation to a few weeks in mid-summer. By August, ice was drifting in the Bay again. There were forested coasts in James Bay and in the west, but the eastern shoreline was treeless and rocky and gave little shelter. Of the three or four ships a year which came from England, one or more would commonly be lost. The stubbornness of such conditions deterred illegal traders. The first two English ships to attempt inter-loping, in the 1680s, were wrecked, though New England freebooters briefly established a post on the Hayes River. Serious danger came from France.

The French were very worried by English rivalry. The rivers draining into the Bay were natural arteries for the fur trade. The English had cheaper trade goods and the advantage of low ocean freights. A letter of 1686 from Quebec noted 'All the commerce of the Bay ... is of no value except as it could be carried on by sea since it saves the infinite expense of carrying provisions and merchandise by land. But our merchants are in no position to compete with the English in this way since they have good seagoing boats well armed and well equipped. It is much to be feared that our company could not be successful in saving the best furs of Canada since certainly the greater part of "castor gras" comes from the North and besides the fur there is very much finer.'[87] ('Castor gras' was what the hatters of London and Paris coveted. The high-crowned beaver hat was now in fashion all over Europe. A beaver robe worn by an Indian for a long time, until the guard hairs fell off and a soft down was exposed, became 'castor gras'; a fresh fur was mere 'castor sec', which the hatters mixed in only in the proportion of one to three.) The French responded to competition by direct aggression — thus, Fort Charles was seized in 1671 — and by a more subtle and dangerous method; their 'wood-runners', *coureurs de bois*, wooed Indian tribes back by taking trade goods direct to them rather than leaving them to find their own way to the English.

Some of the goods which the latter were offering can be seen from a list of supplies sent out in 1684: ' ... 300 guns for Bottom of the Bay, 100 guns for

Pt. Nelson etc., to be made by 3 different gunsmiths ... 1000 hatchets from 10d to 14d each, 1800 long knives at 2/9 per doz., 900 long small knives, 1000 Rochbury large knives, 500 Rochbury small knives, 1000 Jacknives.' By this time there were several posts on the Bay, though their combined population in 1687 would be only 89 men in the Company's employ. The first governor at Charles Fort had been Charles Bayly, a Quaker released from imprisonment in the Tower of London on the surety of its governor, who was one of the initial investors. The committee in London was insistent that Indians must be mildly treated, and long-term interests thus prevailed over two-fisted swift exploitation. Bayly was liked and trusted by Indians, and built up a good trade with them. His successor (1679), John Nixon, was perhaps a Scot, and certainly advocated the use of Scots in the Bay rather than the 'London childring' whom the committee were recruiting. Hudson's Bay was a frontier of (modest) opportunity for men who could tolerate its conditions. James Knight entered Hudson's Bay Company service as shipwright while still a boy. In the Bay from the early 1670s, he became boatswain, landsman, trader, deputy governor, finally member of the Committee and Governor of all the Company's posts.[88]

Such men developed specialised skills which made them indispensable, and gave the Company its strength. It had no other commanding advantage, certainly no monopoly, since, besides the French, it had to compete, even on the English market, with the fur traders of the province now known as 'New York'.

IX

The conquest of New York was involved, as we shall shortly see, with fresh attempts to discipline New England. That difficult province, or rather the Boston merchants who dominated its economic life, had found a place in the evolving Atlantic economy which made links with Restoration England vital, no matter now corrupt Charles II's court might be. While merchant families in Boston retained 'umbilical' links with London, New Englanders transplanted to the West Indies and became factors for Boston merchants there. The great Hutchinson network will illustrate how matters worked. Richard Hutchinson, brother-in-law of the 'antinomian' martyr Anne, exported manufactured goods from London to brothers and nephews of his in Boston who sold them in the Bay area and, through middlemen, to more distant settlers. They maintained a large trade with the Caribbean, exchanging provisions and cattle for cotton and sugar which they sold for credit in London. Their West India trade was largely handled for them by Richard's nephew Peleg Sandford of Portsmouth, Rhode Island, who exported their horses and produce to Barbados, where they were sold by two brothers of his own.[89] The fact that in a trustless age ties of kinship and a common language made it easier to establish and to maintain commercial relations kept New England tethered to Old England despite its merchants' utter disrespect for the Navigation Acts; the colonies depended on the goodwill of a small group of Londoners for their supplies of manufactured goods.

Though the men of Connecticut and Rhode Island sent a small but steady flow of produce to Virginia and Maryland and sometimes to the Caribbean, they were right out of touch with the English sources of manufactured goods. Three towns only, all in Massachusetts Bay, were in continuous commercial contact with the metropolis, and of these Charlestown and Salem were far less important than Boston. That port within 30 years had grown to 3,000 people. Into it, foodstuffs, timber and livestock drained from the whole of New England. It had plenty of good shops and able craftsmen. The houses were mostly on the sea-banks, 'wharfed out with great industry and cost' and handsomely built in brick and stone. The streets were 'many and large, paved with pebble stone' and the south side of the city was 'adorned with Gardens and Orchards'. The Town House was an imposing two-storey building which contained law courts, an armoury and a library, and provided space beneath them in which merchants could discuss business.[90]

The Boston merchants exploited their virtual monopoly greedily. One witness reported that if they did not make 100 per cent profit on their dealings with the settlers in Maine they would 'cry out' that they were 'losers'. The fishermen there, who bought cloth from them at three times the price it commanded in England, and who relied on them wholly for cables and cordage, anchors, lines, hooks, nets and canvas, fell into a kind of slavery. They would get ruinously drunk on a merchant's wine and, once in his debt, would be at his mercy. The farmers of Rhode Island were also resentful; the colony's General Court complained in 1658 that the Bostoners could 'make the prices, both of our commodities, and their own also, because wee have not English coyne, but only that which passeth amonge these barbarians [i.e. the Indians], and such comodities as are raised by the labour of our hands, as corne, cattell, tobbacco, and the like, to make payment in, which they will have at their own rate, or else not deal with us.'[91] This same shortage of currency meant that Bostoners anxious to expand could only do so by getting increasing control over valuable natural resources. They looked for timber inland and established sawmills. They raised horses and sheep themselves instead of relying on small farmers. They built ships for themselves to save freight charges, and to earn carriage fees. Avid for real estate, they acquired properties piecemeal; they purchased land from natives, they foreclosed on debtors, and they obtained grants from colonial governments. And they speculated in land, acquiring blocks of wilderness in New Hampshire, Maine or western Massachusetts for the sake of timber or possible furs, or in the hope that it would increase in value as settlement expanded.

New England life was losing its quasi-egalitarian character. In 1658 Massachusetts introduced a property qualification for voters. In Plymouth ten years later the qualification was set at £20 rateable estate. Connecticut, by the Restoration, had introduced a higher one, £30, for full citizenship. From 1657 till his death in 1676, this colony had as its governor the ingenious John Winthrop Jr. After Charles II's return, the status of the lesser New England colonies was problematical. Connecticut had only scant legal basis, New Haven no basis at all. The latter settlement was too poor to send an agent to London to negotiate with the new government, and so had perforce to rely on the offices of Winthrop, who went, and performed a dexterous double cross. He obtained a charter for Connecticut which sanctioned its exceptional degree of self-governing autonomy. It also defined boundaries which digested New Haven. The Rhode Island agent was resourceful enough to defeat Winthrop's bid to take over his colony also, and obtained a fresh charter for Roger Williams's settlement. But boundary disputes would rankle on for decades.

Hence the need to sort out New England squabbles on the spot provided an effective cover, in 1664, for an expedition aimed at the unsuspecting New Amsterdam Dutch. Three Commissioners for New England went with the conquering force, with the aim of bringing the area for the first time effectively under royal government. They were civilly received in the lesser colonies, but when they presented their credentials in Boston the Massachusetts General Court stonily declared their commission invalid, since the authority which it conveyed conflicted with that of the Massachusetts charter which the King had renewed three years before. Faced with such opposition, they could do little, though the beginnings of a Royalist party in Massachusetts were seen as local dissidents rallied to their side.

The capture of New Netherland was a far easier matter than the taming of Massachusetts. The town itself housed 1,500 people in 1664, but the whole colony had a white population only one-fifth of New England's. It was a polyglot arena. Besides Dutch, French and Portuguese, and Jews, there were the remnants, digested in 1655, of an abortive Swedish colony on the Delaware which had in fact been mostly composed of Finns. From the 1630s, English people had been settling Long Island, and Peter Stuyvesant, the famous governor who arrived in 1647, had had much trouble with their characteristic demand for an elective assembly. New Amsterdam was so placed as to create a very serious leak in the English colonial system. The Dutch had settled land long claimed by England. Charles II presented his brother with the whole region from the Connecticut to the Delaware (and also with a vast tract of Maine) before sending the expedition under Richard Nicolls. Only a handful of people were killed in the swift conquest.

For the first time Englishmen were faced with the problem of ruling alien colonists. Nicolls, now governor, followed generous policies. All who would swear allegiance to Charles were promised denizenship, religious freedom was given to Dutch Reformed and Lutheran settlers. Only a few colonists left, and even the ousted Governor Stuyvesant, after a trip to Holland to clear the record, came back in 1667 and lived in 'New York' until his death. No elective assembly was set up. There was a gradual transition, under military government, from Dutch to English law. The Dutch Reformed Church remained the most influential denomination in the colony for a long time after the conquest, and the upper Hudson River settlements stayed Dutch in language, custom and law for many years. In 'New Netherland', land had been granted free of quit-rents. Fresh colonists from England and New England would hardly be happy to live side by side with the old settlers whose grants were now confirmed if they themselves were asked to pay quitrents. Hence the quitrent in 'New York' was no more than a formality. James, Duke of York, could extract scant pickings from his vast colony, and his interest in it must have been primarily political rather than economic. Indeed, even before Nicolls reached New Amsterdam, James had granted away for a nominal consideration the whole area which became New Jersey.

The beneficiaries of this largesse were Sir George Carteret and John, Lord Berkeley (the latter a brother of the governor of Virginia). Carteret had seized and held the Channel Island of Jersey during the civil war, and had given Charles II shelter there: hence the territory's chosen name. The two proprietors sent out a governor in 1665. By 1668 the new colony had a general assembly. Two years later, a demand for quitrent sent settlers into open rebellion. New Jersey life was largely shaped from the outset by truculent men from New England, who introduced the town meeting style of local government, but there was also an important influx of settlers from Barbados, some of whom were destined to be very influential.

Barbadians had taken the initiative in the projecting of another proprietary colony far to the south in 'Carolina'. There was no idea in this case of any significant shipment of colonists from the mother country. Overspill from existing settlements was expected to provide planters. The main aim of the lucky proprietors was the collection of quitrents from them.

Charles I's grant of 'Carolana' to a courtier in the 1620s had been abortive, but by the 1650s the coastline between the Chesapeake and Florida had attracted Virginians, percolating southwards. In the early 1660s, New Englanders set up an outpost near the mouth of the Cape Fear River. But the prime mover in proposals for a new proprietorship was Sir John Colleton, a Royalist planter from Barbados who came home at the Restoration. In 1663, Charles granted the area to a powerful eight-man consortium, which included the Earls of Claren-don, Albemarle and Craven, and Sir Anthony Ashley Cooper, not yet Earl of Shaftesbury, besides Carteret, Colleton and the two Berkeley brothers. Though the pre-emption of Spanish occupation was no doubt a valid national aim, the chief motive of the proprietors was pecuniary, and it was greed, hoping to attract settlers, which dictated the promise of religious freedom into the charter. Elected assemblies were also promised. The longstanding desire to make England self-sufficient in Mediterranean products underlay the provision that settlers would be exempt from customs duties on all wines, silks, raisins, currants,

25 The great Rembrandt paints 'Two Blacks' as human beings

26 But the Red Indians attacking Deerfield, Mass. (1704) are, in Alexander Anderson's woodcut, faceless homunculi

28 Richard Talbot, Earl of Tyrconnell, James II's viceroy in Ireland

27 A posthumous portrait of the younger Christopher Codrington, by Sir James Thornhill — strangely arrayed in semi-Roman costume

29 Anthony Ashley Cooper, first Earl of Shaftesbury, and Carolina proprietor, after J. Greenhill

capers, wax, oil, olives and almonds imported into England for a term of seven years; but as in Virginia, this proved chimerical.

The avarice of the proprietors was their undoing. They demanded ½d. an acre rent, and that 20,000 acres should be reserved for them in every settlement undertaken. In return, they were not prepared to spend much. In 1664 a governor was named for 'Albemarle County', as the existing settlement near Virginia was now styled. But movement thither was quickly deterred by a sliding scale for headrights which meant that colonists entering in 1667 would get less than the standard 50 acres per head given in Virginia, while they would have to pay a higher quitrent. Meanwhile, that same sandlocked coast on which Ralegh's colony had been lost cut Albemarle off from any easy supply of labour or goods. So development in northern Carolina was very halting. The Barbadian adventurers who provided the main drive in this phase were more attracted by areas further south, where they set up a colony on the Cape Fear River. By 1666, 'Charles Town' was said to have 800 people, but settlers in this area also were soon restive. Because much of the land was swampy and sandy, settlements were dangerously scattered along some sixty miles of the river. The local Indians were aggressive, and the proprietors asked the same rent for waste as for fertile land. By the autumn of 1667 the colony was abandoned.

The future Earl of Shaftesbury now gave a lead, with the help of his assistant, later famous, John Locke. In 1669, the proprietors agreed that each would contribute £500 to a fund to found a settlement in the 'Port Royal' area south of Cape Fear. An expedition was sent out that year, but it included not much more than 100 colonists; the aim was still to draw seasoned planters from older colonies. Headrights were more generous than before, and the rent of a penny an acre was not due till 1689. The proprietors planned to reserve a fifth of the land to provide seignories for themselves, while another fifth would give baronies to a hereditary aristocracy. Locke helped Shaftesbury draw up 'Fundamental Constitutions' which were as outlandish as they were ineffectual. The noblemen were to be called 'landgraves' and, using the Spanish word for Indian chieftains, 'caciques'. Though freeholders with more than 50 acres would elect an assembly, only men with more than 500 could serve as deputies in it. The aim was to attract rich men to the colony by the promise of great acreages, honour and power. Black slave labour was expected and invited, and the ruling class which would eventually emerge in South Carolina would in fact be an opulent plantocracy on the West Indies model, not a European-style nobility. Meanwhile, such 'landgraves' and 'caciques' as arrived normally hastened to shed their ridiculous titles.

The colonists who reached the coast in 1670 built a new 'Charles Town' at a site which they called Albemarle Point. A Spanish expedition from Florida tried and failed to flush them out. Fresh settlers came from the West Indies. Since access to waterways was so crucial to planters, the colonists ignored the proprietors' orderly plan of settlement in squares of 12,000 acres each, 40 such

L

to constitute a county; they followed instead the natural highways, the Ashley and Cooper Rivers, and yet a third 'Charles Town', later to be the remarkable, sinful city of Charleston, grew up where the two rivers converged. (The name was transferred to it in 1680.) Meanwhile South Carolina colonists struggled to find an economic future. The hoped-for Mediterranean staples did not flourish. The Chesapeake settlements, in times of glut, provided too much competition for a new tobacco colony, and neither cotton nor indigo worked at first, though both would eventually be very important. Cattle, exported to the West Indies, became the commercial standby; in 1682 some planters were said to have seven or eight hundred a head.

X

In the mid-1670s 'King Philip's war' in New England and 'Bacon's Rebellion' in Virginia marked, after two generations of relative peace, a crisis in the relations between red men and white in North America. It is time to inquire what had been happening to the Indians in and near the English settlements.

In theory, most English settlers believed that they had a clear right to the land they took in America. The rationalisations were various. God, John White the Puritan had argued in 1630, intended that 'man should possesse all parts of the earth', so that occupation of waste was not only lawful but pious. The elder John Winthrop urged that the red men had no title or property, 'for they inclose no ground, neither have they cattell to maintayne it, but remove their dwellings as they have occasion.'[92] Even Roger Williams was in the end prepared to seek, and accept, charters from the English government as a basis for his colony. Yet in practice, despite the Crown's all-inclusive claim to North America, colonial governments recognised the 'Indian title' to lands which red men actually occupied and most colonists were as scrupulous as Williams himself to 'quiet the Indian title' by purchase. Outright expropriation would provoke war, and this was hazardous in the early days when red men outnumbered whites greatly.

To begin with, then, the English did not displace Indians, they moved in among them. In southern New England the Indian population, of about 20,000, was little if at all lower in 1675 than it had been at the beginning of the century. But by now there were about two Europeans for every one Indian.[93]

So colonists lived everywhere close to Indian neighbours – and intermarriage was not uncommon. From Maine southwards to the upper part of Carolina the Indians of the coastal plain all belonged to the linguistic family of Algonquians and Siouans. Despite Winthrop's convenient notion that they were nomads, almost all tribes lived in villages and practised agriculture, though hunting, fishing and gathering shellfish and other wild foods were important to them. Seasonal migration was part of the way of life; in summer Indians might live near the planted fields while in winter they would find a more protected site and in spring they would camp to fish near the falls of a river. But each tribe occupied territory with clearly understood boundaries. The fields and garden plots belonged to particular families and groups, and the rest was common hunting ground. However, land was not 'owned' as the English thought of ownership. 'It was merely occupied and utilised under a temporary arrangement that might be altered whenever conditions warranted a change. In a transfer of land from one group or family to another, only the right to make use of the land was granted, and the agreement was valid only so long as it satisfied the particular Indians affected.'[94] Here was immense scope for interracial misunderstanding, and a basis for the myth of Indian dishonesty. Nor could the English, or most of them, make sense of Indian political systems, which tended to be far more 'democratic' than their own. In various parts of the coast Algonquian peoples had formed loose confederacies for mutual protection against the dangerous Iroquois of the interior. But the Powhatans of Virginia and the Delawares of what became the 'middle colonies' were exceptional in the strength of their leadership and organisation, and everywhere Indian life was less hierarchical and more loosely organised than Europeans supposed when they spoke of native 'kings' and 'emperors'.

As, from the 1650s, the English settled south of Virginia, they came into contact with a variety of language families. The south-eastern Indians, whose ultimate fate provides the saddest chapter in American frontier history, depended still more on agriculture than the Algonquians, and their political organisation was generally stronger. There were numerous strong confederacies, some under absolute rulers. The largest tribe, the Cherokees, gathered some 20,000 people in 60 towns, while to the south of them the Creek confederacy numbered some 50 towns. These peoples, with the Choctaws, Chickasaws and Seminoles, would become the 'Five Civilised Tribes' of the early nineteenth century, demonstrating that Indians could adapt in the face of the challenge of European culture. But in the early days, there was almost no contact between the world-views of Indians and of whites. Each to the other seemed unpredictable; each thought the other profoundly treacherous. To most whites, Indians seemed obviously and intrinsically 'savage'. Even their hospitality might be interpreted simply as a sign that the white man's God was well disposed towards His white men – 'God caused the Indians to help us with fish at very cheap rates.' Friendliness was assumed from the start to be a mask for treachery. Nor was the idealistic Christian counter-view necessarily less racialist. It projected the red men as naturally good children, more moral than spoilt Europeans. The kindly Jesuit Father White who went out with the first colonists to Maryland reported, plausibly, that Indians had far sharper sight than Europeans but claimed less shrewdly that, 'For chastity I never see any action in man or woman tendinge to soe much as levity...'[95]

To superimpose such an ideal on reality did no more good than the commoner habit of equating Red Indians with the 'Wild Irish', who were seen as primitive, lazy, cruel and deadly. White observers, no doubt enviously, saw Indian males hunting while their wives worked in the fields and accused them in their minds of being idle sportsmen, whereas in fact the Indians had an equal division of labour in which women produced grain and men meat. Just as the Irish, as wandering herdsmen, were self-evidently barbaric, so the Indians as huntsmen were wicked wasters of the land which they traversed. John Locke was the most distinguished exponent of the idea that hunters might justly be forced to alter their economy by an agricultural people. And in a most revealing way, the conversion of the Indians to Christianity was seen as somehow inseparable from their conversion to European dress and agriculture. Only the fur traders, who had a vested interest in the Indian way of life, could find their deviance (partly at least) tolerable. The most famous missionaries to figure in the sparse annals of English efforts towards conversion — Father White and the Reverend John Eliot — both identified change of dress with change of heart. White referred to 'Christian apparrell'.

Enthusiasm among serious Christians in England for missionary work would always, down to our own day, be markedly greater than among colonists. When in 1618 the Virginia Company set aside 10,000 acres to support a 'University and College' for training Indian children in 'true Religion moral virtue and Civility', large sums were raised from charity. But nothing came of the idea. Nor did the English Jesuits get very far in Maryland. White lived with an Indian 'Emperor', cured him of disease, and accepted his grateful conversion. 'The Emperor', as the Jesuits proudly reported, 'has exchanged the skins, with which he was heretofore clothed, for a garment made in our fashion.' He also changed his name, from Kittamaquund to 'Charles'. White later converted the principal men of another village and by 1642, after eight years, the mission was reporting quite considerable successes. But in the religious and political confusion of the mid-seventeenth century, this effort petered out.[96]

In the Caribbean, the English did virtually nothing. The Reverend John Eliot in New England was, along with certain neighbours, the only English missionary in the New World to get the steady and relatively heavy support from England which was essential to success (and which Canadian priests had from France). In the charter of the Massachusetts Bay Company, the conversion of the natives was proclaimed to be the 'principall ende of this Plantacion' and the colony's seal displayed a native with a label issuing from his mouth, 'COME OVER AND HELP US'. No effort was made to validate these manifestoes until the mid-1640s, and even then political expediency seems to have far outweighed warm commitment, except among the missionaries themselves. New England puritanism was as ill-adapted to missionary work as any religion could be. Ministers could be ordained, so its doctrines held, only by a congregation of believers; therefore a corps of specialist evangelist ministers was impossible. Because of the Puritan insistence on rigorous preparation for church membership, long years of labour would be required to bring the natives up to standard.

Quick conversions would be as undesirable as forced baptism. Beyond all this, Puritans shared a scorn of the Indians. Perry Miller points out that 'the Theology of the covenant inevitably bred a contempt for lesser breeds outside the covenant … ' Calvinism held that even those who had never seen a bible and had had no chance to hear the gospel preached were damned, just as surely as any saint was saved. And Puritans deeply distrusted the natural world and natural, 'carnal' feelings. The Indians, for instance, seemed to spoil their children with kindness and many Puritans came to lament the 'indianising' of the colony in this respect, assuming that the native family was acting as a bad example.[97]

The first Indian convert seems to have been made by Thomas Mayhew Jr, son of the owner of the island of Martha's Vineyard, in 1643, three years before Eliot began his mission. By 1652 the Mayhews had nearly three hundred professed converts and had opened a school. But Eliot, rather than either Mayhew, became the hero of the hagiographers, not only because he was the most successful missionary in English North American history, but also because he was just the man whom Massachusetts colony found ready to hand at a tricky political moment when it was potentially at odds with both the Presbyterian and Independent factions in the English Parliament. The charter was vulnerable, hence the colony's rulers were sensitive to the charge that its 'principall ende' had been neglected.

Eliot, minister at Roxbury, aptly so named in its rocky neighbourhood, emerges from the accounts of those who knew him as a 'cheerfull', friendly, selfless but rather sententious man. ' … His whole breath', according to Cotton Mather, 'seemed in a sort made up of ejaculatory prayers … By them he bespoke blessings upon almost every person or Affair that he was concerned with; and he carried every thing to God with some pertinent *Hosannah's* or *Hallelujah's* over it.' He acquired the heterodox idea that the Indians were descended from those lost tribes of Israel who would be gathered in before the overthrow of Antichrist; their conversion was ordained in the scriptures, and to press it forward would hasten the time when the Son of God would rule the world in person.[98]

In 1646, when he was forty-two, he began to preach to the Indians at their nearest village in their own language. He won friendship by handing apples and cake to the children, tobacco to the men. News of his work was before long published in England and the Rump Parliament, in 1649, chartered the 'Society for the Promoting and Propagating the Gospel of Jesus Christ in New England' ('New England Company'). Its members were chiefly wealthy Puritan merchants. Every parish minister in England and Wales was obliged to make a house to house canvas for funds. Remarkable sums flowed in; by 1660 nearly £16,000 had been contributed.[99] But the Company's operations were muddled with commerce in a way which gave grounds for suspicion. It shipped two kinds of goods to New England. Some were for distribution among the Indians themselves; others, notably large supplies of arms and ammunition, were for sale, the proceeds going to fund the work of Eliot, Mayhew and others.

Eliot's programme was an expensive one. He wanted to get the Indians to live in settled townships, to farm in a European way with English tools, to use European clothes and to learn in European-type schools. At Natick, eighteen miles south-west of Boston, he built up a village, from 1650, where he organised his 'Praying Indians' into a little scriptural commonwealth, with a constitution based on the eighteenth chapter of Exodus, under which they elected rulers of tens and of fifties. Eliot himself preached at the meeting house there fortnightly while remaining minister at Roxbury. So rigorous were the tests applied that Indians were not allowed to form their own church until 1660. Meanwhile, however, Eliot found so few whites to join him in the work of conversion that he had to use Indian assistants. An 'Indian College' was built as part of Harvard to house Indians who would train as ministers. But students were hard to find. Only one actually graduated, Caleb Chesschanmuk, in 1665; he died of tuberculosis next year. The Indian college was pulled down in 1698. However, a handpress in the building produced Eliot's most remarkable legacy, his MAMUSSE WUNNEETUPANATAMWE UP-BIBLUM GOD, a translation of the Bible into Algonquian which he completed in 1658. This was the first Bible printed in any language on the American continent, and was followed by a stream of other devotional works and primers for Indians.

After the Restoration, the New England Company was renamed and rechartered. From 1662 to 1689 its governor was the learned and influential Anglo-Irish scientist, the Hon. Robert Boyle. Eliot would refer to Daniel Gookin, lay superintendent of the Praying Indians from 1661, as his 'only cordial assistant'. However, by 1674 there were seven 'old' Praying Indian townships in Massachusetts, while nine more 'new' ones had recently been founded in the Nipmuc country to the west, fifty to seventy miles from Boston and far beyond the then frontier. Altogether Gookin could claim some 1,100 Praying Indians in Massachusetts, besides several hundred more in Plymouth Colony and the Christian Indians of Martha's Vineyard and Nantucket. Each soul had cost something like £10 to win; the Catholic missionaries in Canada had won far more souls far more cheaply.[100]

The price which the Indians paid for conversion is indicated by the humiliating terms of a loyalty oath imposed on red Christians along Cape Cod at around this time. 'Forasmuch as the English and wee, the poor Indians, are of one blood, as Acts 17th, 26, for wee doe confesse wee poor Indians in our lives were as captives under Sathan and our sachems, doeing their wills whose breath perisheth, as Psalmes 146.3.4; Exodus 15,1,2 &c; but now wee know by the word of God that it is better to trust in the great God and his strength, Psa. 118,8,9; and besides, wee were like unto woulves and lyons, to destroy one another ... therefore wee desire to enter into covenant with the English respecting our fidelities, as Isai; 11.6.'[101]

Indians settled under white magistrates and dependent on supplies of English goods had lost all basis for pride and independence. To convert Indians, in English eyes, must be to 'civilise' them. To 'civilise' them was in effect to destroy them. The point is neatly implied in a little doggerel written in Eliot's honour:

> Eliot, thy name is through the wild woods spread,
> In Indians mouths frequent's thy fame, for why?
> In sundry shapes the Devills made them dread;
> And now the Lord makes them their Wigwams fly.

If the Wigwam was conceived as a work of the devil, the whole of Indian culture needed eradication, and any Indian who sincerely converted must live with a view of himself as a Christian being only on probation and by sufferance. The Indians at Natick in the mid-1680s said that they preferred their (white) preacher to use English rather than their own language, because English people then came to hear him and this made the occasion more respectable.[102]

Old Massasoit, friend of the Pilgrim Fathers, refused steadfastly to turn Christian, and in 1653 when he agreed to give up a large tract of land to the English sought (in vain) for an assurance that there would be no missionary work among his people. To be Indian was to be 'savage'. To retain self-respect was to be Indian.

To be English was to want to sell woollen cloth. It had long been urged as a motive for colonies that Indians could be brought to want woollens though they produced none themselves. ' ... This want of cloth,' remarked a tract of 1609, 'must alwaies bee supplied from England, whereby when the Colony is thorowly increased, and the Indians brought to our Civilitie (as they will be short time) it will cause a mighty vent of English clothes.'[103] And as Indians lost their hunting grounds and the fur trade decimated the animal population, to wear 'Christian apparrell' would in fact become almost essential. Meanwhile, to be Indian was to be ready to trade furs. The Indian had to. If he refused, his Indian enemies would get the guns and destroy him. Guns anyway made hunting easier, which in turn made it easier to supply white men with furs in exchange for more guns.

Guns and alcohol were the great staples of the traffic, though textiles, beads and metalware also figured. To be English was to fear arming the natives. But if the English did not arm them, the French or Dutch would. In 1659 Virginia repealed its policy of prohibiting sales of arms, which, since other colonies did not follow it, had put Virginia at a disadvantage in trade without actually increasing its security. Supplies near the coast were running out, and tribes there could only retain economic independence as middlemen in the trade with the interior or by seizing in warfare a new hunting ground. But those who did remain in the fur trade became captives rather than partners, 'much as a drug addict becomes bound to his supplier.' They specialised as hunters, forsaking other aptitudes, swiftly destroying their own means of subsistence. Unused to alcohol, Indians had no social conditioning to control its use and easily became utter drunkards. 'If they are heated with Liquors they are restless till they have enough to sleep; that is their cry, "Some more, and I will go to sleep ... " ' Drunk Indians were potentially very dangerous. But as with guns, the first whites to stop supplying alcohol must lose custom. When the governor of New France in 1686 chided the governor of New York on this question, the latter sharply retorted, ' ... Certainly our Rum doth as little hurt as your Brandy and in the opinion of Christians is much more wholesome ... '[104]

But the fur trade alone would not have destroyed the Algonquians. Advancing white settlement was a more dangerous enemy, leaving pathetic scraps of once confident tribes in its wake. By the late 1640s Virginia, after its second Indian rising, was clearly moving towards the invention of the 'reservation', which would remain over three centuries the white man's only answer to the 'Indian problem', save genocide. The colony passed laws to protect the Indians and to define mutual responsibilities. From 1656 it was laid down that Indians must not be treated as slaves; from 1662 the great man of each Indian township was made answerable for the misdeeds of his people, who had the right to gather seafood, berries and fruits outside the bounds allotted to them by law only if they acquired a licence from two justices.[105]

Mistrust and fear of Indians would persist, one basis for inappeasable racial prejudice. In Virginia, the date of the 1622 massacre was annually commemorated to remind people of the need for vigilance, and emigrants at midcentury were advised that a complete suit of light armour was necessary. Every settlement in New England came to have its garrison house, or houses, with walls that could stop arrows and unusually heavy doors, where people could resort in times of danger. From the very earliest days, Englishmen – Jamestown settlers, Pilgrims and Puritans alike – did not scruple to make ruthless preemptive strikes. The almost ceremonial character of warfare between Indian tribes much amused English observers. ' ... They might fight seven years and not kill seven men,' one wrote. 'They came not near one another, but shot remote, and not point blank, as we often do with our bullets ... This fight is more for pastime, than to conquer and subdue enemies.' The Indians in turn objected to the English way of fighting – 'it is too furious and slays too many men.'[106]

From the 1640s onwards there were nearly two generations of general peace on the frontier. In New England, terrible conflict at last exploded just when the region's furs were virtually exhausted. The Indians now had no economic role to play in the colonies' development. They could not by barter get access to white goods; their standard of living had fallen and with it their status in the eyes of whites. 'King Philip' preferred a desperate, doomed attempt to drive the whites into the sea, over the prospect of slow extinction.

The long peace between Plymouth Colony and the Wampanoag Indians had endured without fatal strain till the death of the ancient sachem Massasoit in

1661. Before he died, he had asked the General Court of Plymouth to give English names to his two eldest sons. They thought of the two kings of Macedonia. Wamsutta became Alexander and his younger brother Metacom was named Philip. Alexander had to struggle to exert his authority over tribesmen who were increasingly restive about white encroachment. His truculent postures made the authorities over-react. They seized him and took him to Plymouth. On his return to his own people, he died – some Indians said of bitterness, others blamed white man's poison. Philip, succeeding him, nursed a deadly grievance. For thirteen years he kept the settlers on edge with rumours of war, till conflagration broke out in 1675.

The spark was the murder of a 'Praying Indian' named Sassamon, who had attended Harvard but had later served Philip as an adviser. A few days before his death, he had told the governor of Plymouth that Philip was forming a general conspiracy. Three Indians were hanged for his murder. Philip's people did not see how the white men had a right to try Indians for crimes against other Indians. On June 20, a group of young Wampanoags rampaged into the township of Swansea, shooting cattle and ransacking houses, but it was an English youth who spilt the first blood three days later, provoking Wampanoag retaliation.

Plymouth called other colonies to help. Philip and his people lived in the Mount Hope Peninsula, where swift action could have bottled them up. But the colonists let him escape and he found his way to the country of the Nipmucks in western Massachusetts. Heartened by Philip's example, they joined in. The townships of the Connecticut Valley were ravaged.

This was now, on both sides, a war aimed at extermination, as in September when Indians trapped a provision train and killed 68 colonists with it. Philip's lead was followed by some – but not all – of the New England tribes. The colonists, rightly, doubted that the Narragansetts would stay neutral. The tribe had gathered on a fortified island. On a Sunday, of all days, white troops moved in to massacre them, men, women and children. The 'Great Swamp Fight', in bitter December weather, also killed perhaps a fifth of the English involved, by exposure as well as by native arrows. The whites retained the support of several tribes, and Cononchet, the Narragansett chieftain, was shot by a Pequot after he had been captured by native auxiliaries. Englishmen watched as his corpse was quartered and burned by representatives of his Mohegan, Niantic and Pequot enemies; then they themselves sent his head to the Connecticut government.

The Indians responded in kind. Town after town was burnt. Of the 90 white settlements in New England, 52 were attacked and more than a dozen almost completely destroyed. Providence was burnt in March and Roger Williams, now over seventy, limping, was one of twenty-seven men who 'stay'd & not went away' and painfully rebuilt the town. His forty years of conciliation had failed. So had John Eliot's idealism. He and Gookin were reviled for having provided the 'new' Praying Indians with arms. The 'old' Praying Indians were loyal almost to a man, and some proved useful as scouts and auxiliaries. But most were rounded up and interned on a 'bleak bare Island' in Boston Harbour, where they spent three winters living mainly on shellfish and under constant threat from the town rabble.

The hastily mobilised forces of the rusty New England Confederation could not easily control an enemy who was desperate and moved fast. But Indian mobility had been achieved at the cost of abandoning fields and foodstores. Like the Gaels of Scotland, Indian tribes aimed in warfare at plunder and at immediate gain. They rested between raids. They could not sustain a long campaign. By the spring, braves hiding out far from their homelands were leaving the war parties to look for places where they could fish or grow corn. Philip was driven from his winter camp near Albany by hostile Mohawks, and, as through the summer his allies were wasted by slaughter and by defection, he fatalistically trekked back to his homeland at Mount Hope. Here in August he was tracked and shot by an Indian traitor (who was given Philip's hand as a reward and for several months exhibited it in a pail of rum 'to such gentlemen as would bestow gratuities on him').[107]

Philip's skull stared for decades from the spike where it was stuck in Plymouth. His people were sold into slavery, mostly in the West Indies. Groups of Indians who had not joined him, and had put themselves under the protection of the colonial authorities, were packed off to be sold as slaves in Tangier. 'This useage of them is worse than death', was the horrified comment of John Eliot, who now had to begin all over again, with only four 'Praying' townships surviving.[108]

Roger Williams, like other pioneers, had long been lamenting the way things had been going. 'Sir,' he had written to the younger John Winthrop in 1664, 'when we that have been the eldest die, and are rotting, (tomorrow or next day) a generation will act, I fear, far unlike the first Winthrops and their Models of Love: I fear that the common Trinity of the world, (Profit, Preferment, Pleasure) will here be the *Tria omnia*, as in all the world beside: ... that God Land will be (as now it is) as great a God with us English as God Gold was with the Spaniards.'[109] The Wampanoag lands were now open to white settlement. Their sales helped to finance a new meeting house in Plymouth.

The colonies estimated their total war expenses at over £100,000. Thousands of whites were killed—between 5 and 8 per cent, it is said, of the men in Plymouth Colony.[110] Many others were maimed or crippled. But the God Land rewarded his devotees. Men had been encouraged to enlist in the militia with the promise of land afterwards. They had fought for land. Those who survived got land. An economic boom followed in the decade after the war.

The North American mind was permanently affected. As settlement moved westwards, elements from the scenario of 'King Philip's War' would be re-enacted over and over again. It was all very well for ministers to explain that war was God's judgment on New England for its backsliding (Eliot ascribed divine wrath to the new fashion of wearing wigs). The lesson which people insisted on learning was that the only good Indian was a dead one. Inter-marriage was now taboo. By the first years of the eighteenth century, hatred was so ingrained that we find one pastor recommending to the authorities that Indians should be hunted with dogs – 'they act like wolves & are to be dealt withall as wolves' – while another, the famous Cotton Mather, compared the red men to rattlesnakes and denounced them as 'the veriest *Ruines of Mankind*, which are to be found any where upon the Face of the Earth.'[111]

In Virginia, godly principle had always offered less obstruction to racialism. News of 'King Philip's War', reaching the southern colonies, swiftly convinced people that there was a general conspiracy of Indians all along the frontier. Nat Bacon's Rebellion followed.

XI

After Virginia had suppressed Opechancanough's rising, in 1646, the assembly had voted to build four forts inland which became posts from which fur traders sent expeditions deep into the interior. In 1671 two men exploring on behalf of Abraham Wood made the first recorded passage by whites over the Appala-chians into the Ohio basin. Two years later, another pair of Wood's people, moving south-west, reached the land of the Cherokees. The fur trade, as always, called for good relations with Indians. It was in the hands of a few rich men – Wood, William Byrd I and others – who depended on the favour of Governor Berkeley, ultimate regulator of the trade. The treaty of 1646 which had pro-mised Indians land and hunting grounds north of the York River had soon been violated, as tobacco farmers pressed impatiently on.

Tobacco insisted on fresh land, and then on more fresh land. By the 1670s, exaggeration could claim that although the population of Virginia did not exceed that of the single London parish of Stepney, they owned plantations spreading over an area equal to the whole of England. Tobacco quickly exhausted the soil it grew on. After the third crop, planters replaced it with maize or wheat. Then they let the land grow up again in underwood. Few men bothered to pen their cattle so as to fertilise weary soil, and the value of the vast beds of marl found in the colony was not recognised until the mid-eighteenth century. Cultivation became habitually reckless and wasteful simply because so much land was available. The natural tendency to expand into virgin territory was restrained only by the equally natural need for access to the sea over which the crop must be transported – and the many rivers branching off the Chesa-peake offered a superb service.

In both Virginia and Maryland the characteristic economic unit remained a small plantation. As the very bulk of Virginia's production drove tobacco prices down, some farmers began to think that a larger scale of plantation could compensate for a low rate of profit. Larger units of production would favour the introduction of slaves drilled by overseers. By 1681, however, Virginia had only 3,000 blacks. The main source of labour was still the annual supply of about 1,500 indentured servants from England.[112]

With a river providing direct access to traders and smugglers, the planter felt no want of urban life. Individualism, even isolationism, grew with his patriarchal independence. Good fences made good neighbours. Preferring to give their livestock free range, planters fenced in their crops instead, and since there were few stones to be had they developed the characteristic fences made of three-sided rails, wood split with the grain, set in a zigzag pattern with stakes driven at each interlacing or 'corner'. It saved nails (to the detriment of suppliers in the English Midlands) and the fence could easily be torn down and reassembled. Livestock had their important place in a modest way of life which centred on tobacco, cattle and work. Pork was the staple meat, and pigs rooted for themselves in the woods until hog-killing time in the autumn. Since there were relatively few mills, characteristically 'Southern' dishes developed, like succotash, roasting ears and hominy, which employed the whole grain. Horse raising developed only slowly, and the growth of sheepflocks was restricted by the ravages of wolves, a serious and persistent problem; in 1668 York County paid 2,200 lb. of tobacco for 11 wolves' heads brought in, and an Act of Assembly next year required the tributary Indian communities to deliver 145 heads annually.[113]

The slowness with which ploughs came into use was an index to the character of the whole way of life. There was little call for them. As forest was cleared, stumps were left in the ground which would have held up a plough. By the time these had rotted, the ground had been exhausted and abandoned. Tobacco was mistress; tobacco didn't linger. Legislation demanded that each farmer must cultivate a certain acreage of maize and wheat, and Virginia did not fall like Barbados into reliance on imported food. But no substitute for tobacco as a cash crop proved acceptable.

Tobacco was the effective currency. Virtually all accounts were carried on the books till the tobacco crop had been cured. Then they all fell due at once, and payment was largely a matter of book-keeping transactions. ' ... A hogshead of tobacco, or even a portion of it, might be accepted by the sheriff in payment of taxes, then assigned by him to another planter in return for services rendered the county or the province, and by him in turn paid over to a local merchant without out the tobacco having been so much as once moved from the tobacco house of its original producer until, properly marked or sealed, it was collected for direct shipment to England.'[114] A fresh immigrant had to plant tobacco to pay his way. A poor farmer had to sell tobacco to live. The English government, because it was a vital source of customs revenue, opposed schemes to stop or stint its planting aimed at forcing up the price. And if the Virginians slowed down the Dutch and others who bought their leaf might start growing their own supplies. In any case, Maryland and Carolina would seize their chance.

Tobacco was first planted in sheltered beds in the woods about mid-January, then transplanted to the fields, usually early in May. It required watchful care. So that the plant's vitality was not dissipated, settlers adopted the Indian practice of removing its seed head ('topping'). Then they 'suckered' it, taking away the shoots which grew to compensate for the lost top. Careful weeding of the earth around was essential, and the plant remained very vulnerable to diseases and to the weather. Cut as soon as it was ripe, it was stored in large barns, up to 60 feet long. Fire was not yet used to hasten the curing, which was left to the air itself and took five or six weeks. When the leaves had been taken down, stripped from their stalks, and assorted according to grade and quality, the tobacco was packed into casks which ran up to 1,000 lb. in weight. A planter not committed to merchants by previous advances of goods to him could sell as he wished, to some local trader, or to a correspondent in England or in another colony. But most tobacco was delivered to receivers acting on behalf of merchants to whom the planter was already indebted. Some planters, the best placed, themselves acted as merchants, distributing imported goods and taking crops in payment. In any case, the casks went to the water, pushed by sweating and cursing servants or slaves or seamen down rudimentary colonial roads to the landings. Special ships were built to carry as much tobacco as possible, with huge holds and tiny cabins. The largest might take 600 casks, or 300,000 lb. Grumbling planters were at the shipowners' mercy. If too few vessels arrived, the crop might be spoilt waiting collection. Masters were unwilling to take any hogsheads except those consigned to the merchants in England who owned their vessels. When shipping was scarce, as in wartime, freight charges soared and the planter might be compelled to pay whatever a master demanded. In the end the selfishness of English merchants would be their partial undoing: Glasgow men, willing to give better prices, were infiltrating before the close of the century.

Smuggling, largely through Scottish ships, was endemic. Virginia itself taxed tobacco, imposing an export duty of 2s. per hogshead from 1658 to supplement the colony's poll tax. The duties in England were very heavy. Fourteen ships in two fleets brought so much tobacco into Bristol in 1662 that there was insufficient cash in the city to pay the Customs. It was alleged in 1671, that one of the first ships to take tobacco to Liverpool brought in 300 hogsheads and paid duty only on 60.[115] With the planter selling tobacco for as little as 2d. a lb., temptation, for him as well as for merchants, was irresistible.

Tobacco, by hook and by crook, supported the emergence of a society subtly divergent from that of England. Berkeley, chosen as governor again by the Assembly in 1659, ruled as a planter among planters. Titular aristocrats were absent, but the wealthy man, as in the West Indies, would acquire the dignified name of 'Colonel' from his command in the militia. The governor's personal clique, by the 1660s, formed the 'Council'. In the colony's bicameral legislature this corresponded to the House of Lords, as the House of Burgesses matched the House of Commons. By contrast with New England, Virginia at this time showed little or no common purpose or idealistic public spirit. ' ... Men thrown back on their own resources had proceeded to build a society that gave as free play to individualism as any America was to know.'[116] This produced a political tradition which emphasised individual liberty, and an economic one characterised by prodigal, heedless waste. Neither showed the least charity for the Indians or for their way of life.

Though the Susquehannock Indians had long been allies of Maryland, guarding the colony's northern approaches, their lands were encroached on as tobacco expanded. In 1674 the Maryland English abandoned the Susquehannock and made peace with the Seneca, who were traditional enemies of both. The Susquehannock fell back to the north bank of the Potomac river. Their presence stirred up the Indians in that area; overcrowding led to shortage of food, and thence to raids on the colonists. In 1675 a planter in Northumberland County, Virginia, was murdered by a party of Doeg Indians. 'People in their Way to Church, saw this Hen lying th'wart his Threshold, and an Indian without the Door, both Chopt on their Heads, Arms and other Parts, as if done with Indian Hatchetts. Th'Indian was dead, but Hen when ask'd who did that? Answered "Doegs Doegs", and soon died ... ' The county militia rode furiously into Maryland after the Doegs. A Doeg chief and ten of his people were pistolled to death, but another white party, blinded with rage and fear, fell upon some Susquehannocks and had slaughtered fourteen before an Indian ran up to the colonel and 'with both hands Shook him (friendly) by one Arm Saying *Susquehanougs Netoughs i.e.* Susquehanaugh friends, and fled. Whereupon he ran amongst his Men, Crying out, "For the Lords sake Shoot no more, these are our Friends the Susquehanoughs." '[117]

Friends no longer. The Susquehannocks rose and fought, and the combined militias of two colonies could not contain them. They fell on Virginia's frontier plantations. Governor Berkeley ordered a punitive expedition but then, for reasons not clear, retracted the decision and persuaded the assembly to settle for a defence. His refusal to yield to popular pressure as the Indians burnt and slew as far south as the James set a spark to discontent over a complex of other grievances.

Tobacco prices were low, and on top of that the 1676 crop was nearly ruined by bad weather. Like all New World colonies, Virginia was full of debtors who resented their creditors. Berkeley's personal clique, over his long years in office, had grabbed much of the best land as well as the most lucrative offices. Leading fur traders were closely identified with him and, though he does seem honestly to have favoured justice and mildness in race relations, he was not immune to the charge that he was holding back reprisals against the Indians in his friends' interests. Meanwhile, forts on the Chesapeake, built with the colonists' taxes after a Dutch raid in the 1660s, had been allowed to fall into disrepair, despite expensive work on them. The Dutch had returned in 1673 and had captured several vessels. There was a suspicion that other taxes and levies were going to fill the pockets of Berkeley's cronies. While the important class of country magistrates grumbled over the favouritism shown to Council members, the ordinary planters boiled with resentment against the local privileges of these same magistrates. Berkeley's softness towards the Indians and his proposal for more expensive forts now came as the last straw. In his own words, Berkeley governed 'a People wher six parts of seaven at least' were 'Poor Endebted Discontented and Armed.'[118]

The cry went up for slaughter. 'Nor would the people understand any distinction of Friendly Indians and Indian Enemyes ... ' What use was the fur trade to them? It was, they said, 'monopolised by the Governour and Grandees.' The 'common cry and vogue of the Vulgar was, away with these Forts ... wee will have warr with all Indians which come not in with their armes, and give Hostages for their Fidelity and to ayd against all others; wee will spare none.' Nathaniel Bacon, emerging as leader of the malcontents, exclaimed, 'these traders at the head of the rivers buy and sell our blood.'[119]

Yet Bacon himself belonged not with the 'meaner sort', but to the class of well-to-do men who felt cheated of their due by Berkeley's clique. He had been less than two years in the colony. His father was a wealthy Suffolk squire who had packed him off to Virginia with the colossal nest egg of £1,800 after his shocking behaviour had caused scandal in England. As a cousin of Lady Berkeley's, he had promptly acquired a seat on the Council, but the governor had proved unamenable to his joint bid, with William Byrd, for a monopoly of trade with the Indians. Still in his twenties, Bacon was clearly unstable, if not actually mad, a man of 'an ominous, pensive, melancholly Aspect ... despising the wisest of his neighbours for their Ignorance, and very ambitious and arrogant.'[120]

In the spring of 1676, Bacon accepted command of a vigilante group which aimed to force the governor's hand. It moved against the Pamunkey Indians, whom Berkeley rightly regarded as faithful allies. The governor denounced this as rebellion. Bacon led his force into the forest. As support rallied to his adversary, the governor tried to propitiate the populace. The franchise had been restricted in 1670 to freeholders only; now Berkeley issued writs for a new assembly for which all freemen would have the vote. Bacon, after indiscriminate slaughter of friendly Indians in the forest (he declared they were 'all alike'), came out and gained election to this new assembly. Before long he was captured, submitted to Berkeley, was given back his seat on the Council and, probably, was promised command in the war against the Indians.

Then, while assemblymen tried to appease their poorer constituents' grievances by a string of populist Acts, Nat Bacon flounced out of Jamestown. Back home in the upper parts of the colony, people learnt that he had not yet got his commission as leader against the red men. A party of armed men followed him back to town. The scenes which followed anticipated both Grand Opera and the Hollywood Western. The rebel confronts the governor. Old Berkeley bares his bosom, urging his men to shoot him if he ever gives a commission to such a rebel as Bacon, then offers to measure swords with his young adversary and to settle their quarrel by single combat. 'God damne my Blood,' swears Bacon, 'I came for a commission, and a commission I will have before I goe.'[121]

Berkeley had to give way to armed force. Next day Bacon, commission in hand, was off to shoot more innocent Indians. However, just as he was ready to move, word came that Berkeley had again proclaimed him a rebel. He turned back to settle the matter. But Berkeley had failed to get support. According to one, as it were, savoury account, when the governor summoned up the militia of Gloucester and Middlesex counties, there 'arose a Murmuring before his face "Bacon Bacon Bacon" and all Walked out of the field, Muttering as they went "Bacon Bacon Bacon" ... ' The governor fled to the eastern shore of the Chesapeake. Bacon, now master of most of Virginia, bound people to follow him by an oath, and unleashed them to loot his opponents' estates. 'And for the next three months Virginians of all ranks vied with one another in plundering.' Berkeley, returning, likewise offered plunder as bait for support. Bacon left off his rather indecisive operations against the hapless Pamunkeys, and marched in to capture Jamestown, which he burnt, church, statehouse and all. After this last wild gesture he died of 'a Bloody Flux'. His lieutenant soon submitted to Berkeley and the rebellion ended many weeks before troops arrived from England, in January 1677.[122]

Confronted by over 1,000 soldiers, with Colonel Jeffreys, new governor-designate, at their head, Berkeley still displayed his inveterate tetchiness, and sailed off to die in England after insulting his replacement. The rebellion, his personal disaster, had been a cataclysm for the Virginian Indians. Some tribes were completely extinguished. Though the dependent tribes within the colony were given a treaty in May 1677 by which their chiefs held thrones and lands of the king of England, Indians who survived in the tidelands and piedmont found it increasingly hard to maintain their traditional way of life. Malnutrition and demoralisation were deadlier than muskets. A clergyman wrote in 1687, ' ... The Indian inhabitants of Virginia are now very inconsiderable as to their numbers and seem insensibly to decay though they live under the English protection and have no violence offered them. They are undoubtedly no great breeders.'[123]

As for the planters, Bacon's episode was no more than a somewhat extreme symptom of the frontier condition of life. Berkeley's loyalist followers vastly enriched themselves by legalised pillage of the estates of real or purported rebels, but otherwise there was no greater lasting significance than can be found in the squabble in 1677 among the scattered, anarchic settlers of North Carolina which some historians have dignified with the name of 'Culpeper's Rebellion'. Everywhere, even in parts of New England, colonists in the New World were

undisciplined and always hard to rule. This was, after all, the heyday of a sort
of men who took to extremes the democratical tendencies of the frontier – the
'buccaneers' of the Caribbean.

XII

'Privateering', 'buccaneering' and 'piracy' are three shades in a continuous
spectrum. 'Privateering' was legal. 'Buccaneering' became so for a while in the
Caribbean. The 'buccaneers' were a cosmopolitan, rootless body of men. It is
characteristic that the classic account of their doings should have been written
by one Exquemelin, who sailed with them, of whose nationality no one is certain. Was he French, Flemish, Dutch, a Breton? The buccaneers took to an
extreme prevalent features of West Indian life. Like those English who settled
on French islands, those Dutch who traded with all comers, in their pursuit of
fortune they did not mind whom they served or pillaged. Like sugar planters
who died rich and honoured, they sacrificed all moral considerations to quick
profits. Their shifting communities absorbed shipwrecked sailors, runaway servants, deserting soldiers, escaped criminals. Though the bulk seem to have been
'English' or 'French', two of Exquemelin's minor heroes are the always-
unlucky 'Bartolomeo el Portugues' and 'Rock the Brazilian', who was in fact a
Dutchman born in Groningen.

The word 'buccaneer' derives from a Brazilian Indian name for the wooden
gridiron on which strips of meat were broiled. On Hispaniola, towards the
mid-seventeenth century, a body of men gathered who lived by hunting the
great herds of pigs and cattle descended from those escaped from Spanish settlements. They sold the hides and smoked meat to planters or passing ships. As the
herds declined, more and more men took to piracy. Then, as the century wore
on, English and French governments sought their service. The 1660s were their
heyday.

Though famous leaders arose – Henry Morgan, most celebrated Welshman
of his time; a Dutchman, Scot or Englishman named Mansfield; an especially
cruel Frenchman nicknamed 'L'Ollonais' – the buccaneers remained essentially
anarchists recognising only their own code. They had their say in the destination
of a raid and in the share which the leader was to get. They agreed in advance
on rewards for those wounded; the loss of an arm to strike with would, for
instance, be repaid with six hundred pieces of eight or six slaves; a mere eye
earned only a hundred, or one slave. The remaining spoil would be shared
equally. As Exquemelin said, they 'only cared to fight for booty',[124] but in its
pursuit they were as brave, perhaps, as any soldiers ever have been. Even when
they marched overland, women and children went with them, and as their
polyglot tribe approached, a Spanish town would be warned of its danger by
the flocks of carrion birds which flew over the column, rightly anticipating a
feast of dead beasts and men. If we believe Exquemelin's account, the capture

of a town would be followed by cruelties rarely matched before our own century, as women were raped and every person who could be found was tortured to disclose where the Spaniards had hidden their treasure. If a buccaneer fell dead in the water, his comrades would fish out the corpse and hack off the fingers for the sake of the rings; then throw him back for the sharks to eat.

Many of them found a patron in Colonel Thomas Modyford, representative Englishman of this phase of frontier history, who went to Jamaica as governor in 1664, from Barbados, where his pragmatism had prospered in the sugar boom. He was, in effect, a Hobbesian, game for any device which worked. He welcomed the immigration of Jews. He would have been happy to see Dutchmen planting on his sparsely settled island, where he himself and his family came to hold many thousands of Jamaican acres. He ruled for seven years as an independent autocrat, disregarding instructions from home and summoning only one assembly. Meanwhile, the island throve as a base for buccaneers, who sacked scores of ill-defended Spanish towns and villages around the main, some of them over and over again.

The Spaniards still wanted Jamaica back. For the moment there was no strong English naval or military presence in the Caribbean. In 1657, Governor d'Oyley had invited the buccaneers to transfer their base from Hispaniola to Jamaica. The freebooters, some 1,500 strong, were Jamaica's only defence. When the second Dutch War broke out in the mid-1660s, there was really no alternative to using them. A force was sent out to capture the Dutch islands of St Eustatius and Saba, and was then called to help St Kitts, where the French had attacked their English neighbours. The difficult character of these auxiliaries was demonstrated as the buccaneers, enraged by the death of their leader in fierce fighting and angry about the lack of co-operation shown by the timorous local militia, sacked the house of the English governor as they retreated. Finding little enthusiasm among them for attacking the Dutch, Modyford concluded that he must give them letters of marque against the Spaniards. He was able to get the tacit permission of the English government. For five years or so Harry Morgan hammered the Spaniards as he pleased.

Morgan, born about 1635, came from a substantial South Wales family. One uncle had returned from mercenary service in Europe to soldier as a Cromwellian general; another, Edward, had been Charles I's commander in South Wales and after the Restoration was made lieutenant-governor of Jamaica, where young Harry had settled as a member of the English invading force and was becoming a major planter as well as the buccaneers' favourite leader. By the mid-1660s Harry had rampaged across thousands of miles on a privateering commission issued by Modyford's predecessor, Lord Windsor, the first royal governor (1662). Under Modyford, Morgan became the right arm of English rule in Jamaica. He was given a free hand, and his followers paid themselves in plunder. Modyford put up excuses and took his cut, while the King received his fifteenth and James, Duke of York, Lord High Admiral, his tenth of all the rich booty taken.

In 1668, Morgan raided Cuba, then struck at Porto Bello on the Isthmus, with a force of 460 buccaneers. This was a strongly defended town; Morgan encouraged his little band by telling them 'if they were so few in number, each man's portion would be so much the greater,' then his ruthlessness proved irresistible. According to Exquemelin, he blew up a fort with its garrison inside it, used captured monks and nuns as a screen as he seized the town, then, confronted by a force from Panama, refused to leave without a ransom and threatened to put all his prisoners to death. Only eighteen buccaneers lost their lives. The booty worked out at £60 per man. The pickings would never be quite so rich again. An assault on Maracaibo next year gave only half as much profit per head.[125]

Morgan's commission was against Spanish shipping; it did not license him to land and to sack Spanish towns. The outraged Spanish authorities proclaimed war in retaliation against all English south of the Tropic of Cancer. Modyford now had to commission Morgan as admiral and commander-in-chief to fight the Spaniards on land and sea. Ironically, in the same year, 1670, negotiations in Europe produced the Treaty of Madrid by which Spain at last conceded to the English a right to exist in the New World. ' ... It is agreed that the Most Serene King of Great Britain, his heirs and successors, shall have, hold, and possess for ever ... all the lands, regions, islands, colonies, and dominions situated in the West Indies or in any part of America that the said King of Great Britain and his subjects at present hold and possess.'[126] There had long been hopes of a peaceful trade with the Spanish possessions. Now the way seemed open. Modyford was ordered to suppress privateers. But Morgan had already sailed, for his most remarkable exploit, the sack of Panama, with a force of thirty-seven ships and several smaller vessels.

He took 1,200 men on a gruelling march across the Isthmus. A scorched earth policy forced them to eat leather bags and stray dogs. Yet with desperate strength they routed in pitched battle a Spanish army which was picturesquely but ineffectually reinforced with two herds of wild bulls, and captured the city in a couple of hours. 'Whenever a beautiful prisoner was brought in,' Morgan 'at once sought to dishonour her.' After three weeks of rape, carousing and plunder, the buccaneers left with 175 mules laden with silver plate and coin and with several hundred prisoners. But the Spaniards, forewarned, had shipped off most of their treasure. Profits were smaller than hoped, only £50 a head, and Morgan's career of grand larceny ended in bitter arguments over shares with his men.[127]

The buccaneers had two uses for money: drink, and women. Their hauls poured straight into the hands of the traders of the town of Port Royal, which duly flourished like the green bay tree. Exquemelin reported of his companions on Jamaica, 'They are busy dicing, whoring and drinking so long as they have anything to spend. Some of them will get through a good two or three thousand pieces of eight in a day – and next day not have a shirt to their back. I have seen a man in Jamaica give 300 pieces of eight to a whore, just to see her naked.' Tavern keepers would commonly give ample credit on the unspoken security that the toper himself could be sold into servitude if his debts were not met.[128] Yet the buccaneers served cold-sober political strategies. Besides helping Spain's rivals force doors in the Caribbean still wider, they put into circulation lots of that scarce commodity, ready money. And Morgan was greatly admired in England. The diarist John Evelyn recorded in 1671 that at a meeting of the Council for Foreign Plantations in London, 'The letters of Sir Thomas Modiford were read, giving relation of the exploit at Panama, which was very brave ... Such an action had not been done since the famous Drake.'[129]

However, the English government was now on friendly terms with Spain, and gestures had to be made. Modyford was recalled in 1671 and spent two years in the Tower. Morgan was soon after shipped home, though he was not imprisoned. After the new governor, Sir Thomas Lynch, had offered the buc-caneers a pardon and land, Morgan, who must have had charm, was sent back by the King with a knighthood and the office of lieutenant-governor. Modyford also returned, as chief justice. Left as acting governor in 1678, Morgan, though no longer for roving himself, gave help to an old associate, Captain Coxon, who accomplished remarkable feats of plunder on Spain's Pacific coast. But in 1680 a further treaty with Spain was signed at Windsor, and thereafter even Morgan seems to have worked to repress privateering in the interests of trade with the Spanish colonies. The end of his career as public servant, if that was ever the right name for him, came in 1682 when he and his clique were pushed out of office by Lynch, returning for a second term. In his early fifties, he died six years later, sallow, pot-bellied, 'much given to drinking ... '[130]

From the mid-1660s the French had been turning the quarter of Hispaniola occupied by 'their' pirates and planters into a regular colony, St Domingue. Since Spain refused to recognise their rights of possession, the French authorities went on employing buccaneers long after the English had stopped. Morgan, unable to issue letters of marque himself, used to recommend buccaneers whom he liked to the French, in return for a commission. But by the end of the century, all 'official' buccaneering was over. Piracy remained, preying impar-tially on ships of all nations without any gloss of legality whatsoever. By the mid-1680s, Lynch had a fleet of small ships on Jamaica to counter the pirates, but the problem would persist for decades.

The buccaneers had furthered, rather than held back, Jamaica's development. The real check was shortage of slaves. The Royal African Company could not meet Jamaican demands. On an island with many wild acres, and an established colony of fugitive maroons, to hold slaves once they were bought was more of a problem than elsewhere in the English Caribbean. Between 1673 and 1694 there were six sizeable slave revolts on the island. But Port Royal, thanks in great part to the buccaneers, was an impressive town in 1692, with perhaps 10,000 people, the largest English settlement in the New World. It had hundreds of four-storeyed brick buildings and rents were said to be as high as in central London. In this great entrepot for trade with Spaniards and with Indians, craftsmen were said to earn three times as much as they could get in England, there were large warehouses and shops, and there was even, of all things, a grandiose church, though sots, whores and gamblers swirled around it. Then, on an almost cloudless June day, retribution struck. In a couple of minutes of earthquake, most of the town was 'swallowed into the Sea'. Corpses floated for days in the harbour. Scavengers stripped the dead and their houses. Masterless slaves ran free. Port Royal never really recovered, and Kingston usurped its position. A Sodom had been chastised, though seeing what went on elsewhere in the Caribbean, the Lord was oddly selective in his vengeance.[131]

With Spanish power curtailed and the Dutch increasingly on the defensive, rivalry between France and England was beginning in Charles II's reign to become important. (The Danes, with their foothold in the Virgin Islands, and the Brandenburg Prussians, who followed them there in the 1680s, were never numerous enough to cause much diversion.) But no power had at this time resources in ships and soldiers to dominate the whole area. One shrewd Stuart governor of the Leewards observed, 'Whoever is master of the sea, and has good soldiers, from October to June, can carry or destroy the strongest islands.'[132] The outbreak of war in Europe was followed by a game of general post in which various ill-defended islands changed hands. Then at a peace treaty in Europe whatever had been gained was handed back or swapped. It would be pointless to give full details of so many intricate little conflicts. They did, however, have quite serious local effects. The destruction of the enemy's sugar works, and still more the theft of his slaves, were consistent aims, and St Kitts, divided between French and English and so always fought over, was stunted in its development by wars.

A typical swap at the Treaty of Breda in 1667 gave the English title to New York in return for handing over Surinam, which had been colonised by Lord Willoughby of Parham from 1652 and had attracted thousands of English settlers. But the practical internationalism of this frontier meant that the Dutch did not scruple to call in English craftsmen to help them develop their acquisition. It also made Jews conspicuous all over the Caribbean. Their numbers and success were provoking protests and discriminatory legislation in Barbados by the 1650s — in 1680 there was about one Jewish household in Bridgetown for seven English. Their role in Jamaica also became important; by 1693 the council there was complaining, 'the Jews eat us and our children out of all trade.' The Sephardic network of contacts made Jews expert and invaluable in trades legal and illegal.[133]

Thus, Jews led in trade with the Spanish colonies, which was an essential source of bullion, so much sought in that mercantilist age, and greatly needed

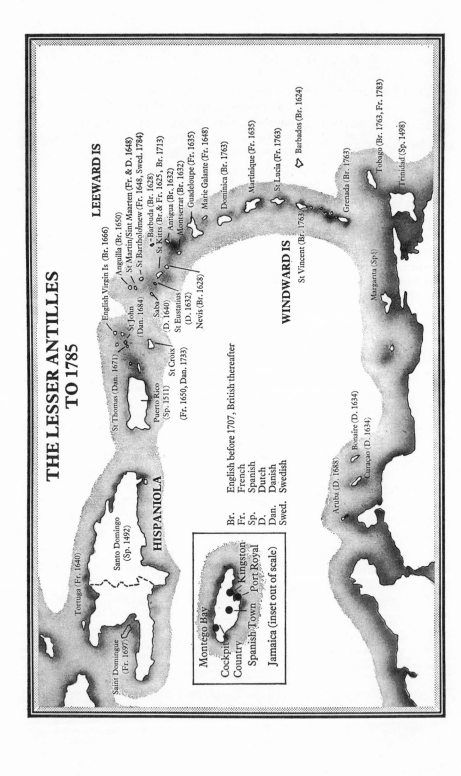

THE LESSER ANTILLES
TO 1785

Toruga (Fr. 1640)

HISPANIOLA

Santo Domingo (Sp. 1492)

Saint Domingue (Fr. 1697)

St Thomas (Dan. 1671)

Puerto Rico (Sp. 1511)

St John (Dan. 1684)

St Croix (Fr. 1650, Dan. 1733)

English Virgin Is (Br. 1666)

Anguilla (Br. 1650)

St Martin/Sint Maarten (Fr. & D. 1648)

St Bartholomew (Fr. 1648, Swed. 1784)

Barbuda (Br. 1628)

St Kitts (Br. & Fr. 1625, Br. 1713)

Antigua (Br. 1632)

Montserrat (Br. 1632)

Guadeloupe (Fr. 1635)

Marie Galante (Fr. 1648)

Saba (D. 1640)

St Eustatius (D. 1632)

Nevis (Br. 1628)

Dominica (Br. 1763)

Martinique (Fr. 1635)

St Lucia (Fr. 1763)

LEEWARD IS

Barbados (Br. 1624)

Grenada (Br. 1763)

St Vincent (Br. 1763)

WINDWARD IS

Tobago (Br. 1763, Fr. 1783)

Trinidad (Sp. 1498)

Margarita (Sp.)

Aruba (D. 1688)

Bonaire (D. 1634)

Curaçao (D. 1634)

Br.   English before 1707, British thereafter
Fr.   French
Sp.   Spanish
D.   Dutch
Dan.   Danish
Swed. Swedish

Montego Bay
Cockpit Country
Spanish Town — Kingston
Port Royal
Jamaica (inset out of scale)

to provide coinage in the New World. In 1685, English governors were authorised to give it all possible encouragement, so long as the Spaniards themselves inserted nothing which might compete with English manufactures. The Navigation Acts achieved their objects rather as a leaking tank may still hold enough petrol to run a car. Trade between English and Dutch colonists went on even when the two countries were formally at war. The Dutch were still ahead of the English in sugar refining and could process the product more cheaply, so they could offer a good sum to the planter and still get sugar at lower prices than those they paid for re-exports from England. St Eustatius ('Statia') in the Leewards was well placed for illicit trade. Dutch ships on their way to Holland called at all the English islands on the pretext of watering, and privily conveyed goods to English planters. Then they went to St Eustatius, whither the Englishmen shipped them their sugar. A Royal Navy officer detailed to enforce the Navigation Acts pointed out in 1687, 'Most of the islands have so many bays and inlets that it is impossible for the Customs-house Officers to check the shipping off of the sugar, and the Dutch ships generally send their long boats to St Christopher's once or twice a week on pretense of getting water, though one boat load of water would last them a month ... '[134]

The logwood trade which attracted buccaneers and others to the Central America mainland was another lucrative business which could not be contained within the Acts. Despite its confusing name, 'logwood' was cut in sticks a yard long and two or three inches in diameter from a certain gnarled tree. In Europe, these were ground to powder and used by dyers to give cloth a good base or foundation for other colours, which it made brighter. The wood was readily found on the stretch of shoreline running from the Gulf of Campeche around the Yucatan peninsula and down to the coast inhabited by Moskito Indians in what is now Nicaragua. 'British Honduras' was the eventual legacy of centuries of English involvement there. The discharge of Morgan's privateers stepped up a trade which had gone on casually for decades. By the mid-1670s scores of ships went annually from Jamaica, and hundreds of non-Spaniards, mostly 'English', settled permanently on the coast and perpetuated some of the buccaneer tradition. Merchants paid them £5 a ton in rum or sugar, and they drank up to eight times that sum while a ship was in, then retreated to cut more wood. The Spaniards of course claimed the whole coast, the English retorted that the 1670 Treaty of Madrid gave them a right there, and the logwood cutters became a source of friction for generations. The English authorities established a form of loose protectorate over the Moskitos. In 1687, the governor of Jamaica, in token of it, gave a commission to their chief under the English king, and a traveller a few years later found that 'King Jeremy', as the native principal called himself, cherished a laced hat as his crown, while his people esteemed themselves Englishmen.[135]

New Englanders, of course, would not resist a valuable trade which could hardly be policed from Jamaica. By 1678 they were said to be taking 1,000 tons off annually, and they sold the logwood in Holland and France at below the English re-export price. Their vital role in maintaining the English islands should already be clear. In the 1680s nearly half the ships supplying the English West Indies came from New England, and over half the ships entering and leaving Boston were in the Caribbean trade. They brought in 'refuse fish' for slaves, grain for masters, horses to drive mills and heavy timber to build them, prefabricated frames of houses, and above all oaken shooks to be coopered into hogsheads for sugar and molasses.[136] They made life extremely difficult for the theorists of mercantilism.

To such thinkers, the West Indian sugar colonies otherwise seemed ideal both in notion and practice. Sugar was the perfect commodity. 'The Kingdom's Pleasure, Glory and Grandure ... are all more advanced by that,' wrote Dalby Thomas, 'than by any other Commodity we deal in or produce, Wool not excepted ... '[137] As the emphasis of mercantilist theory shifted from bullion towards manufacturing industry, the islands, which bought all their manufactured needs, seemed more and more exemplary. A Barbadian pamphleteer of 1689 offered a litany of wares which the islands purchased. ' ... An infinite Quantity of Iron Wares ready wrought ... all sorts of Tin-Ware, Earthen-ware, and Wooden-ware', hoes and hinges, soap and rope, cloth, hats, shoes – 'How many Spinners, Knitters, and Weavers are kept at work here in England, to make all the Stockings we wear?' – saddles and bridles, locks and muskets, flour and beer, cheese and butter and candles. And also, every year, 'thousands of Barrels of *Irish* Beef.'[138]

There was a rub. Weren't the Irish, and the New Englanders, draining profits away which should have gone to Englishmen? The paradox was that the sugar colonies, pampered prodigies of mercantilist theory, provided infinite scope for evasion of the Navigation Acts, both in letter and in spirit. The planters themselves, whining and truculent by turns in their addresses to the home government, wanted to trade with the Dutch and sell sugar direct to Europe. The monopoly of the Royal African Company roused them to heartfelt wrath. They were very hard to govern at all. Vessels carrying vital letters might be lost at sea, and with bad weather or enemy action, ships might take months to get from London to Barbados. Instructions might be out of date and inapplicable before they arrived. And governors sent out with strict instructions to enforce royal authority would find it difficult to resist the arguments, and still more the favours, of wealthy planters.

Apart from an assured market for their sugar in England, what the evolving 'Old Colonial' system offered the planters was military and naval protection. But England, in the seventeenth century, had few or no ships to spare for colonial defence. Only one fleet sent out – Sir John Harman's to the Leewards in 1667 – actually accomplished much, and Harman and the governor had to pawn their shirts to pay its seamen. For permanent help, an island would get at best a couple of Royal Navy frigates, and when, in 1679, the Government considered an estimate prepared by Pepys which reckoned that three frigates in the Leewards would cost at least £43,400 a year to maintain, the response was not only *not* to send them, but to recall, so as to save money, the two frigates actually stationed at Jamaica. The Dutch and French were consistently more powerful at sea. Regular troops were hardly in better supply. Planters retained the Englishman's suspicion of standing armies and, still more to the point, were furious at the thought of having to pay for one. A hundred or so soldiers stationed on the Leewards in the mid-1670s were said to be 'naked and starving' under the eyes of their French enemies. Jamaican planters, anxious not to pay for it, forced the disbandment of a regiment sent to their island in 1678, insisting that it was a threat to their liberties.[139]

The cry of 'no taxation without representation' originated in the West Indies. As early as 1652, influential planters on Barbados were demanding M.P.s at Westminster and some were going further to claim what would later be called 'dominion status'. In 1660, the island council, formerly nominated in England, was made elective in response to colonists' pressure.[140] What was largely at issue in all this was not a precocious passion for democracy, but the fear of a return to effective proprietary rule under the old Carlisle Patent. Hardfaced men who had done well out of the sugar revolution were afraid of detailed investigation into their rights of tenure, and they were not unhappy when Charles II, in 1661, announced that he was taking proprietorship himself. When the first royal governor arrived in 1663, they swiftly made a deal with him whereby the proprietary dues and rents were cancelled, they were confirmed in their estates, and they gave in return a 4½ per cent duty on all exports, on the understanding that the moneys accruing to the King would be used to pay the cost of royal government. But this duty, which also applied to the Leewards, was to become a recurrent grievance during the 175 years of its charging.

In theory, the islanders might now have been at the Crown's mercy. In practice, Charles II characteristically diverted the 4½ per cent duty into other purposes than administering colonies, so the governor still had to rely on the Assembly for revenue. This thwarted a serious attempt by Charles to assert his authority in the 1670s, when the number of offices to which appointments were made by the Crown in London were greatly increased and West Indian governors lost their right to appoint their own councils, which would now be named by the King. In 1678, the Lords of Trade began their abortive attempt to impose Poynings' Law on Jamaica. The plan was to recast the entire government of the colony, raise revenue without an assembly, and make Jamaica as tame and profitable as Ireland. One Samuel Long, an old Cromwellian soldier, friend of Sir Harry Morgan, led the planters' opposition and was brought to London a prisoner in 1680. Patrick Henry would have been proud of his rhetoric. He argued vehemently that the Jamaican settlers, 'as Englishmen, ought not to be bound by any laws to which they had not given their consent.' The Lords of Trade backed down. Long was acquitted. In Barbados as well as in Jamaica, the attempt to impose closer control was abandoned, in face of the obstinate facts of distance and of rebellious self-interest.[141]

Samuel's descendant, Edward Long, would write in the 1770s that a 'faithful description' of the royal governors of his island 'would be little better than a portrait of artifice, duplicity, haughtiness, violence, rapine, avarice, meanness, rancour, and dishonesty, ranged in succession … ' He reflected the traditions of planters of his own class, of whom an exasperated governor of Jamaica reported in 1700, that they believed 'what the House of Commons could do in England, they could do here' – while they sat in assembly they thought that 'all power and authority was only in their hands.' A counterpart in the Leewards, about the same time, wrote of the St Kitts planters that they were 'a parcell of Banditts, and would willingly be without government, religion, or any appearance of order.'[142]

One rather exceptional governor, Sir William Stapleton, who ruled the Leewards for thirteen years down to 1685, did show a vision transcending his own interests; that is, he was a proficient bully in the wider English interest, though he was, in fact, a Catholic Irishman. His ferocious temper did not impair his popularity in the islands, where rage was no uncommon thing. He bullied the Caribs, mounting two expeditions against their bases. He practised gunboat diplomacy against the Danish governor of St Thomas when a pirate found refuge there – 'If you do not deliver him or make some atonement for the injuries you have inflicted on the English, I warn you, have a care. I shall come from the Leeward Islands with an armed force [and] blow you up … '[143] Rather amazingly, he even contrived to persuade the four principal Leewards to send representatives to a common general assembly.

But he could not eradicate the planters' resistance to the idea that all four islands should logically share the same laws. Planters were furthermore rootedly reluctant to share in the cost of military operations which were good for the English power in general, rather than merely in their own local interest. Barbados men were perfectly happy to see their compatriots on the Leewards battered by the French or raided by Caribs, regarding them not as fellows but as competitors. And when the Nevis Assembly was asked to participate in an assault on the Caribs, who had recently ravaged Antigua and Montserrat, they objected on the grounds that their own island had not been troubled by Indians 'these twenty years'.[144] On another, later occasion, the Nevis planters surrendered their stronghold to the French rather than see their canes burnt. When it came to the point, not even personal pride, let alone royal authority or patriotic feeling, could often distract a sugar planter from his prime purpose, making money.

As the Royal African Company found, such men were adept at avoiding payment. Extracting debts from defaulters was often impossible. Coins were in short supply, for a start, and payment in sugar offered scope for fine little tricks as valuations fluctuated. Even where coins were in use, the chronic debtors who manned the island assemblies had a standing temptation to overvalue them, and deliberate clipping, as well as much wear created abundance of 'light' money. The courts were slow, and if their machinery worked at all it favoured debtors. Besides, planters made the laws. On Nevis and St Kitts, they even found a way of making the creditor pay the debtor; someone distraining on an estate had to accept goods at the valuation set on them by his debtor's neighbours, and if their reckoning exceeded the debt, he had to refund the supposed surplus. Planters administered the law. On some islands, there were no prisons.

Yet the 'groans' of the plantations, as one writer called them, were constantly relayed to England. When sugar duties were raised in 1685, the planters and their allies set up a shriek till the addition was repealed eight years later. The basis of their despair was merely that after the great sugar boom ended with the 1650s, men who had been getting rich very fast had to be content with getting rich slowly. For muscovado worth perhaps 35s. per hundred lb. in London in 1657, the price fell to 25s. in 1674, 15s. 9d. in 1686. The planter was meanwhile paying his 4½ per cent duty, and slaves were costing more, so his profits shrank quite painfully. Furthermore, Barbados was beginning to confront problems of soil erosion and soil exhaustion which would become more widespread in the next century. Dung was used to revive the soil. ' ... We rake and scrape Dung out of every Corner,' exclaimed our groaning pamphleteer of 1689, Edward Lyttelton. 'Some save the Urine of their People (both Whites and Blacks) to increase and enrich their Dung. We make high and strong Walls or Wears to stop the Mould that washes from our Grounds: which we carry back in Carts or upon *Negroes* heads.' The planters, he insisted, with more force than truth, were ruined. He appealed to England, ' ... Hath our dear Mother no *Bowels* for her Children, that are now at the last Gasp, and ly struggling with the pangs of Death?'[145]

This was colonial rhetoric as it would be heard many times thereafter. (Ian Smith and his kind are our latest exemplars.) Men used loud words partly through fear of not being heard far away, while they inflated or even invented 'facts' secure in the knowledge that these could not easily be checked. But the clamour over the 'Impositions' of 1685 showed how absolute a master sugar now was in Barbados. Because investment in plant and in slaves had been so heavy, it was no longer possible to switch swiftly to another crop when prices fell. Barbados had led the drive towards monoculture; St Kitts lagged behind, and Jamaica remained for a long time a frontier island with various possibilities.

There were still thousands of small English freeholders in the West Indies, farming up to a dozen acres with the help of their children, indentured servants and one or two slaves. While great planters dominated in sugar, small men could eke out a living from the minor staples. The Irish on Montserrat still grew much tobacco. Jamaica found a ready market in England for ginger and pimento, dyewoods, preserved fruits; and for cotton. Even after sugar had become the leading product on Jamaica, cotton increased its acreage there, and everywhere in the West Indies cotton now stood second to sugar. Much was used in the islands themselves, for clothing, sails and hammocks; also, by 1690, the Lancashire fustian industry seems to have been drawing about seven-tenths of its ginned raw cotton from the West Indies, where Barbados was still the leading producer.[146] Indigo was a crop, yielding a valuable blue dye, which needed quite a lot of equipment and labour, and it was grown on middle-sized plantations; there were three or four score of these in Jamaica in the 1680s. Finally, chocolate was now becoming known and appreciated in England. When the English conquered Jamaica in 1655, they found 'cocoa walks' there, orchards, as it were, of ten or twelve acres. This was the most aesthetically pleasing of staples. The island exported quite large quantities.

But despite the opportunities given to small men by the minor staples and by the demand for provisions, white numbers in the older colonies fell in the third quarter of the seventeenth century. Barbados stabilised at around 20,000 whites, a drop of perhaps a fifth in twenty-odd years. The Leewards by the 1670s had two or three thousand apiece.[147] Disease was not the only determining factor, though yellow fever came in with black slaves, and the islands developed a distinctive local malaise, the 'dry belly ache' or 'dry gripes' which produced fearful pains in the stomach and loss of use of the limbs, resulting (but this was not realised till the mid eighteenth century) from poisoning caused by the distillation of rum in leaden pipes. Re-emigration and war seem the main explanations for white population decline. Colonists were caught up into armies, lost heavily in French raids, or sold out to wealthier men and sought better luck elsewhere. A writer of 1667 claimed that at least 12,000 whites had emigrated from Barbados, 'wormed out of theire small settlements by theire more suttle and greedy neighbours ... Between 1643 and 1647 to New England, 1,200; to Trinidado and Tobago, 600; between 1646 and 1658 to Virginia and Surinam, 2,400; between 1650 and 1652 to Gudaloupe, Martinique, Marie-galante, Grenada, Tobago, and Curazoa, 1,600; with Colonel Venables to Hispaniola and since to Jamaica, 3,300.'[148] The figures are most unlikely to be accurate, but the general impression is credible enough. While New England provided food and ships for new colonies, Barbados gave men.

Poor men ventured in the abortive colony on St Lucia (1664-7) or set off to seek out plunder in Jamaica. Rich men looking for land for younger sons interested themselves in Carolina and in Antigua, the latter still only one-third settled around 1690. And new black labour far outweighed the trickle of fresh indentured servants. By the end of Charles II's reign, Barbados had reached the ratio of whites to blacks — roughly one to three — which would be maintained there throughout the eighteenth century. On the Leewards, taken as a group, the ratio was still about one to one, but in Jamaica some 15,000 whites were already outnumbered by slaves. The implications deeply worried administrators, who saw the need to maintain a white militia which could overawe and defeat black rebels.

Black slaves were quite rapidly replacing whites even as carpenters, and masons; in 1682 the white coopers of Nevis persuaded the assembly there to pass a law prohibiting slaves from being taught their trade.[149] The rich planters who sat in the assemblies were divided in their own minds. As capitalists, they had no use for white servants, who cost more to keep and were said not to work so hard. But fears of slave revolt made them pliable. In 1672, with war in the offing, the Jamaica assembly passed a law requiring each planter to keep one white servant for every ten Negroes. Other island assemblies also imposed quotas and efforts were made by the authorities to force and even, in effect, bribe planters to accept servants. Never to much avail. The ratio of blacks to whites overall went on rising.

The stratification of classes on the islands was fixing itself in the repulsive shape it would keep as long as the 'Old Colonial System' endured. The majority were black slaves. 'Above' them, but hardly better off, was a morass of poor whites who, if they retained any energy, went in for fishing, smuggling or piracy. Otherwise they lounged, and drank crude rum till they died and the land crabs nibbled their corpses in the gutters. There was a largish, middling class of white shopkeepers, artisans and petty planters. At the peak of the pyramid were the rich sugar men, whose life, at this time (its features were softened later), presented as little graciousness or real dignity as that of any successful class in history.

By 1680, on Barbados, as we have seen, 175 individuals (one in sixteen of the landholders) owned more than half of the white servants, slaves and acreage. On Jamaica the top men were probably fewer, their holdings bigger. One of the greatest of all West Indian fortunes was founded there by Peter Beckford, whose father was said to have been a tailor. He began as a petty trader in 1662. When he died an old man in 1710 he was said to have twenty estates, 1,200 slaves and £1,500,000 in bank stock.[150] Rich planters came from many sources. Some were ex-Roundhead soldiers, some Royalists. Some came from landed, others from merchant families. Their chief common characteristics were the constitutions which permitted them to survive the white West Indian life-style, and the mentality of the entrepreneur. They found no high culture on the islands, and had no wish to create any. Their most attractive quality might appear to be their religious tolerance, except that it seems on examination to have amounted to no more than acceptance of different styles of laxity. Priestless Catholics planted alongside lapsing Dissenters and nominal Anglicans. Clergymen were few, ill-rewarded, and mostly of poor human quality. One governor of Barbados increased his unpopularity by ousting a parson, not really in orders at all, whose offices had been accepted for a quarter of a century; he had married many islanders, and the legitimacy of their offspring was now suspect, which was a dangerous matter in law.[151]

Law was, in effect, the planter's religion. Since there were no surveyors to run the boundaries and conveyancing was rudimentary, titles to land were always extremely uncertain. ' ... Every one is a lawyer in these partes', one St Kitts planter wrote in the 1670s, asking for law books from home. Most colonial assemblymen had no legal training. Many laws were passed which were badly drafted, or even absurd. Besides their own laws, the islands were bound by English Acts of Parliament and by the common law of England. 'As far as I have observed,' one governor noted, 'the laws of England and the customs or pretended customs of the islands take place by turns, according to the fancy of the judge.' The courts were scenes of brawling disorder, with pleaders and judges often drunk – 'more like a Horse-Fair or a Billingsgate,' Governor Modiford once remarked. But governors, like chief justices, were frequently under suspicion themselves of using their public authority for private ends.[152]

The greatest English historian to have written about the West Indies of that day observes that life there 'seems to have been one long quarrel, in which business, law and politics were all mingled.'[153] There were few books but law books. Jamaica, even in 1690, seems to have had no schools at all. Richard Ligon, around the mid-century, had found some Barbados planters talking of bringing expert musicians·out from England, 'yet, I found others, whose souls were so fixt upon, and so riveted to the earth, and the profits that arise out of it, as their souls were lifted no higher; and those men think, and have been heard to say, that three whip-sawes, going all at once in a Frame or Pit, is the best and sweetest musick that can enter their ears; and to hear a Cow of their own low, or an Assinigo bray, no sound can please them better.'[154] Such attitudes became more common rather than less.

If anything raised the planter's soul somewhat above the earth, it was military or civil ceremony. Great planters paraded as colonels of the militias, and uniforms were in use from the 1680s. Salutes of guns and gluttonous public dinners greeted new governors. Protocol was always a problem; men stood on what they imagined was their dignity. Meanwhile, the slaves ate dried fish and played their own music, which few except Ligon among the masters had ears to find interesting.

The cruelty of the laws bearing on slaves has to be set in perspective. In Barbados, by legislation of 1688, a black man who stole as much as a shilling might be executed for the crime, but this was no more than standard English law of the period, when some three hundred crimes were designated felonies, punishable by death. While in England royal pardon would save half or more of the offenders from the gallows, in the West Indies planters were unlikely to execute a creature belonging to one of their fellows without what seemed to them some overwhelming reason. The death rate among slaves must likewise be set against that among the plantocracy. The Price family which became the wealthiest on Jamaica was prolific in children above the average, yet expectation of life in its first three generations in the West Indies seems to have been no more than 24 years; 35 years or so was the general run in England.[155]

These facts allowed, the treatment of blacks must still be seen as exceptionally cruel. Slaves, if not executed, were punished sadistically. Lash wounds were rubbed with melted wax. Half a black's foot might be chopped off; he might be castrated. Most planters seem to have accepted that the best way to make use of the slave who cost them so much was to drive him hard for as long as he could stand. Huts were exiguous and almost unfurnished. Diet — corn, plantains, beans and yams — was minimal at the best of times; the convenient myth was establishing itself that black men were somehow content and even happy with far less food than whites. And when profits shrank, the slaves were given still less and were worked harder yet, in dangerous conditions. The groaning planter pamphleteer whose voice we have heard already waxed obtusely eloquent on the wastage of lives. A third of all freshly imported slaves, he suggested, would die before they did any work at all (demoralised, we would now add, in a strange place, and subject to novel diseases and hardships.) 'When they are season'd, and used to the Country, they stand much better. But to how many mischances are they still subject? If a Stiller slip into a Rum-Cistern, it is sudden death: for it stifles in a moment. If a Mill-feeder be catch't by the finger, his whole body is drawn in, and he is squeez'd to pieces. If a Boyler get any part into the scalding sugar, it sticks like Glew, or Birdlime, and 'tis hard to save either Limb or Life. They will quarrell, and kill one another, upon small occasions: by many Accidents they are disabled, and become a burden: they will run away, and perhaps be never seen more: or they will hang themselves, no creature knows why.'[156]

Such unaccountable beasts: in some ways it would have been convenient if they had been able to explain themselves better. But to teach them English, or, still more, to convert them to Christianity, was fraught with a fearful risk; property would be transmuted into humanity. A slave named 'Sambo' asked Ligon to help him become a Christian. But when Ligon enquired of his master, the latter replied that under the laws of England, a Christian could not be made a slave. Why not though, asked Ligon, make a slave a Christian? 'His answer was, That it was true, there was a great difference in that: But, being once a Christian, he could no more account him a Slave, and so [they would] lose the hold they had of them as Slaves, by making them Christians; and by that means should open such a gap, as all the Planters in the Island would curse him. So I was struck mute, and poor *Sambo* kept out of the Church; as ingenious, as honest, and as good a natur'd poor soul, as ever wore black, or eat green.'[157]

A black man made Christian could not be made to work on Sundays. And he would have to be taught in English; the 'Gentlemen Planters' in London, approached on the subject of conversion by the Lords of Trade in 1680, insisted that 'the disproportion of blacks and whites, being great, the whites have no greater security than the diversity of the negroes' languages ... '[158] Hence the Jamaican law of 1675 which laid down that each master must instruct his slaves in the Christian religion was and remained a dead letter.

The whites paid the price of their greed in constant fear. The first slave revolt on an English island had occurred on St Kitts as early as 1639, when scores of black men and women had escaped into the woods. As land was cleared, this recourse became impossible on the smaller islands. On Jamaica, flight to the wastelands remained an outlet for rebels. Elsewhere, blacks would have to conspire to seize the whole island. Such conspiracies were rare, and were always betrayed by timorous slaves. Blacks had good cause for fear. The whites had guns and would show no mercy. A conspiracy on Barbados in 1675 was savagely punished, property or no property. Six slaves were burnt alive and eleven beheaded. The dead bodies of these latter were dragged through the streets, and there were twenty-five more executions later. Eight years after, a black was burnt alive merely for using threatening language.[159] The whites were as vigilant as brandy-soaked men could be, and as the years went on they were more and more cast in the mould made by their own oppression. There were fewer and fewer men like Ligon who could, at least fitfully, perceive blacks as individual people.

Sensitive men were repelled from the islands by their lack of faith and learning. A planter who wished to attend plays or to worship in a seemly church would retire to England after making his fortune. Those who remained were adapted to the specialised pleasures of a slave society; drunkenness, gluttony, gambling, sleeping with terrified black girls, feuding with neighbours, and, for some temperaments, the licence given to sadists who could lash and mistreat men and women absolutely under their power. Only a few stood against the prevailing mores, amongst them Morgan Goldwyn – an Anglican clergyman who, after living on Barbados, published in the 1680s tracts attacking the planters for their fear of baptising their slaves – and also quite a number of Quakers.

Like Anne Hutchinson's 'antinomianism', Quakerism, which extolled the inner light found within each individual, had strong appeal for some men whose economic activities took them beyond the boundaries of what had been acceptable to any church. Numerous prominent planters on Barbados were early converts and there were six Quaker meetings on the island in 1680. Some Quakers were rich; most Quakers owned slaves. Persecution set in almost at once. Some 237 Friends suffered between 1658 and 1695 at the hands of Barbadian authorities who fined and in many cases imprisoned them for refusing to bear arms, to swear oaths, to pay clergymen's dues. The story was similar on Antigua, and in Jamaica, where George Fox, the sect's founder, set up seven meetings. His followers most perversely stood for humane standards. Quaker midwives gave their services free to poor people and even to slaves; as if the islands wanted black babies when strong black men could be bought. In Bridgetown, Barbados, Quakers established a school where poor children were taught gratis. Though George Fox when he preached to slaves on Barbados in 1671 was careful to tell them to remain faithful to their masters, he rounded on the planters there and asked them, 'is not the Gospel to be preached to all creatures? and *are they not Men*? And are they not part of your families?' To no avail; five years later a law was passed against the Quaker practice of having slaves at their meetings. Any slave found at one would be forfeit and half his price would go to the informer. It seems the Quakers had been drawing hundreds of blacks, but they stood to lose their property if they persisted in their principles and their witness in the islands faded from prominence.[160] They now had a large scope for activity elsewhere in the New World.

<h1 style="text-align:center">XIII</h1>

Except for the traffic in indentured servants, mostly to the tobacco colonies, emigration from England to America was slack after the Restoration. New England now showed little or no interest in attracting further settlers. In 1680 the governor of Massachusetts was reporting that few new colonists had arrived over the past several years, and about the same time Connecticut authorities declared that no more than one or two immigrants a year were coming from Britain.[161] Carolina, as we have seen, drew primarily from already established colonies. But in the 1670s a large new wave of migration began. It was aimed chiefly at the middle area of the seaboard between New York and Maryland, and its most obvious element was Quakerism.

The Society of Friends had grown under George Fox's leadership from the 1650s. In its early days it shocked Royalists and orthodox Puritans alike. Its adherents took the logic of Protestant individualism to an extreme, giving women a leading role, with virtual equality, and not hesitating to preach radical doctrines to servants. The refusal of Quakers to take off their hats before magistrates, and their insistence on using the levelling 'thou' or 'thee' when addressing others of whatever station made them alarming deviants in a status-conscious age.

Their organisation was ideally adjusted to the demands of expansion across the Atlantic. There was no specialist priesthood, but Fox built up a system of monthly and quarterly meetings of representatives from local groups, and from 1668 there were great Yearly Meetings in London. A sort of standing Executive Committee there, the 'Meeting for Sufferings', corresponded with Friends across the Atlantic and acted as a pressure group in official circles.

The roots of Quakerism were chiefly among the lower orders, amid yeoman farmers, husbandmen, artisans, shopkeepers and hired servants, and it had strongholds in the poorest sections of England, the remote west and hilly north. There was also a concentration in the south-east, where London alone was said to have 10,000 Quakers in 1678, but in the great city also, the sect drew from the poorest classes. There were between six and seven hundred families of Quakers in Ireland in the 1680s, largely concentrated in and around Dublin, but also dominating the trade of the great New World-facing port of Cork.[162]

M

The Quakers in fact swiftly began to spawn immensely successful business communities. They were hardworking, frugal, horrified by idleness, cautious and strictly honest in their dealings; and like other dissenters they were wholly barred from lucrative careers except in trade. As Fox himself observed, 'Friends had double the trade, beyond any of their neighbours. And if there was any trading, they had it.' By the end of the seventeenth century it could be said, quite correctly, that the Gracechurch Street Quaker Meeting in London was composed of the City's richest trading men, including such pioneers of banking as the Barclays, Gurneys and Lloyds. Hence the curious paradox that the Quakers, appealing to poor men and savagely persecuted, soon developed political influence.[163]

Their eruption in New England in the late 1650s was dramatic. One young woman Friend entered the church at Newbury, Massachusetts, stark naked, and walked down the aisle, explaining afterwards at her trial that her aim had been to show those present the nakedness of their rulers. In 1658 the New England Confederation ruled that all heretics must be banished on pain of death. Four Friends were in fact hanged in Massachusetts, but popular opposition to such savagery ensured that when a fifth was condemned the authorities dared not execute him. Governor Prence in Plymouth Colony went no further than fines, whippings and imprisonments, and Governor Winthrop would not permit any slaughter in Connecticut. Judicial murder ceased on orders from England in 1661, but by then the trauma of plebeian Quakerism had helped to push the New England colonies into tightening up their franchises so as to exclude the poor.

Rhode Island became a Quaker base. 'They begin to loath this place', it was wrily noted there, 'for that they are not opposed by the civill authority.' They converted William Coddington, founder of Newport; by 1690 nearly half that town's population were Friends, and the whole colony was under their dominant influence. Meanwhile, in 1671, Fox, with the suitably apostolic number of twelve companions, arrived in Barbados, and, starting from there, ranged the whole of English America. These missioners were followed by a constant stream of 'public Friends' — Quakers who felt the call to travel across the Atlantic, and who kept scattered groups in touch as they pressed indefatigably through pathless wilderness. In 1700, when there were perhaps 50,000 Quakers in Britain, there were at least 40,000 in the New World.[164]

This remarkable expansion would help to determine, as much as New England Congregationalism or Southern tobacco culture, the character of English society in North America. Its most concentrated drive produced in West New Jersey and Pennsylvania two distinctively Quaker colonies. In 1674 John, Lord Berkeley sold his interest in New Jersey to a Quaker named Edward Byllinge. Since the already-settled eastern section belonged to Carteret, Berkeley's former colleague, what was acquired was an extensive wilderness. Byllinge went bankrupt and quarrelled with a Quaker associate in the enterprise. It was policy among Friends that disputes should be settled privately rather than in the courts, so trustees were appointed for West New Jersey and Byllinge's half-interest was divided into 100 shares, of £350 each, which were mostly purchased by well-to-do Quakers. The trustees drafted 'Concessions' which embodied the most advanced concepts of personal liberty, since they reflected the drastic experience which Quakers were having of the perverted operations of English law. ' ... We put the power in the people.' An assembly elected annually was to have full control of its own sessions and procedures and was to choose ten commissioners to rule. Individuals were given exceptional protection against the law, and freedom of conscience was guaranteed as an absolute and unqualified right belonging to all men.[165] Byllinge violated the Concessions in the early 1680s, proclaiming himself governor and sending out a deputy, but this man proved tactful enough to gain acceptance from the colonists.

East New Jersey in 1683 came under the control of twenty-four new proprietors, including five Scots, one of whom was a very prominent Quaker, Robert Barclay of Urie. A surge of some five hundred Scottish settlers crossed to join the thousands of Englishmen already there; these newcomers were mostly not Quakers, but persecuted Presbyterians. By 1692 a Scot, Andrew Hamilton, would be governor of both the New Jerseys, now combined again.

William Penn was a proprietor both in East and West Jersey, but from 1681 his main interest was in the province which Charles II granted to him personally. Born in 1644, he was the son of the Admiral Penn sent to the West Indies by Cromwell. Having acquired an Irish estate from the Protector, the Admiral prudently switched to support Charles II in 1660. Not only did he serve the Stuarts, he also lent the royal brothers money, of which £16,000 was still unreturned in 1681, eleven years after his death. Dying, he had asked James and the King to show goodwill to his son; hence the most famous sectarian of his time could move and get a hearing in the highest circles at Court.

Young Penn had turned Quaker in his early twenties, though not before he had made a Grand Tour of the Continent and had come back, according to Pepys's wife, 'a most modish person ... fine gentleman', with an affected manner and Frenchified clothes.[166] Such a rare bird was bound to become one of the sect's main leaders. He was gaoled several times, though James, Duke of York, intervened in 1669 to get him released from the Tower. The death of the Admiral next year left him a wealthy man, and as such he naturally moved at the front of the Quaker drive to found colonies. Yet his motivations cannot in whole be distinguished from those of the Carolina proprietors. Whereas most Quakers showed their own hair, Penn wore a wig. He was attracted to the life of a free-spending country gentleman surrounded by servants. He achieved it in England, and took it with him to America, where the city he founded, Philadelphia, would become a major centre of attempts by others, also, to replicate that life-style. His own writings blend, in the Quaker way, mysticism with practicality.

His argument that people should act according to the rules of nature which are 'few, plain, and most reasonable'[167] take us towards the centre of eighteenth-century secular Enlightenment, with which judicious Quakerism, as the hot sect cooled, would harmonise remarkably well. In his arguments for toleration Penn was closer to Sir Josiah Child than to Roger Williams. Toleration was right. It also promoted prosperity. Persecution was bad for trade.

So Penn is a cryptic figure, a man of self-contradiction and compromise, in whom the heroic and radical consciousness of the sects of the Civil War and Cromwellian period can be seen making a blurred transition into the genteel nonconformity of the eighteenth century. Bishop Gilbert Burnet was often unjust in his verdicts on contemporaries, especially on those close to James Stuart, but there is probably truth in his suggestion that Penn was 'a talking vain man' with 'such an opinion of his own faculty of persuading, that he thought none could stand before it, tho' he was singular in that opinion.'[168]

However, there is no need to question Penn's sincere wish to provide a refuge for his own sect where Quaker ideals could be put into practice. A Quaker paper of 1680 enumerates the sufferings of Friends since the Restoration: 243 had died in prison, 276 were currently in gaol and some had been there for years. Nearly 200 had been banished. What with imprisonments and seizures of property, 10,778 Friends had suffered directly.[169] This was the context in which Penn asked that the King's debt to his dead father should be met by the grant of a province in America.

Charles II complied but then, it would seem, enjoyed himself teasing the well-bred Dissenting bore. Penn wanted the land to be 'New Wales' or, in view of its forests, 'Sylvania'. Charles insisted upon 'Pennsylvania', out of respect for the late Admiral, and so worked a commoner's name into the title of lands half as large again as Scotland. It was, as Penn felt himself, a strange designation for the site of a 'holy experiment' on behalf of an egalitarian creed.

What was Charles II up to? Was he governed by respect for the Admiral his creditor and by his personal tolerance of Dissent? Did he hope to decant his most difficult subjects into the New World and so ease the way to absolutism in Britain itself? Was there some strategy based on the fact that a royal grant, once made, could always be taken back, and that meanwhile Quaker wealth would extend the King's empire? Whatever his own interest was, the Lords of Trade resisted this new charter. Their policy was that no more such grants should be made, and it was perhaps due to their protests that the last of the great proprietary charters contained several novel limitations. The Navigation Acts must be strictly observed, laws were to be forwarded to England for royal confirmation or veto, the rights of the Anglican Church were to be respected. But Penn had all the authority which attached to the ownership of the soil. He went on to invest in his new lands more heavily than any other Restoration proprietor.

This was, as he saw it, to be a 'colony of heaven', where a whole society would live in accord with the Quaker apprehension of Inner Light within all men, under a government whose fundamental law would be the Sermon on the Mount. Quakerism, unlike earlier puritanism, took an optimistic view of human nature. By contrast with Winthrop's Massachusetts, toleration and pacifism were to be cardinal principles.

The project was an instant success. By July 1683 as many as 3,000 people may have entered the beach-head of the new colony on the Delaware river. At the end of the century, Pennsylvania was not far short of 20,000. Persecution alone could not explain this. Quaker meetings were schooled to accept suffering and were not readily inclined to grant the necessary credentials to members proposing to go to America merely to evade trouble. Poverty may have been a stronger push; men from the bleak northern dales were drawn in such numbers to the rich uplands of Chester County, Pennsylvania, that as late as the mid-eighteenth century a broad Yorkshire dialect prevailed there.[170] An important group of Welsh Quakers, probably fairly prosperous, were pulled by the vision of a New Wales where, as they said at the time, they could try to decide disputes among themselves 'in a Gospel order', and not 'entangle' themselves with 'laws in an unknown tongue' – the obnoxious language, of course, being English.[171] In general the appeal of Pennsylvania seems to have been less the negative one of a refuge than the positive one of a sphere where Quaker ideals and energy could find full scope.

The offer of land was imaginatively made. While Penn prudently reserved a tenth part of all for himself and his heirs, a well-to-do man could buy 5,000 acres for £100, a poorer one could rent 200 acres for a penny each, and those poorer still were offered a stake of tools, stock and seeds upon an agreement to develop an assigned acreage through seven years, at the end of which they might buy the land; while large blocks could be purchased by groups wishing to settle as whole communities. Penn was famous in Europe as well as at home and his very clever propaganda campaign was conducted in Dutch, German and French as well as in English.

All migrants need not be Quakers. Toleration was assured to any believer in the one God, though only Christians could vote or hold office. The legal system was as liberal as West New Jersey's. But the constitution was aristocratic; the elected assembly was to have no power except that of yielding or refusing consent to laws proposed by the governor and council, and while the latter was elective, Penn seems to have expected that social convention would ensure the choice of wealthy men. He believed, with other Quakers, that all men were inwardly equal, but, like Barclay, accepted current social ideas about the natural existence of inferior and superior men; just as, in nature, cedars were higher than brambles.[172]

He wished sincerely, however, that dealings with Indians should be peaceful and just. Like toleration, good race relations were economically shrewd; they could save his colony the costs of defence which were borne elsewhere. He wrote unctuously and no doubt incomprehensibly to the Indians of his province in 1681, evoking the 'great God' who had written his law in the hearts of all men and had been 'pleased to make' Penn 'concerned in your part of the world', and proffering friendly co-existence.[173] Penn and his agents purchased each tract in turn from native holders in such a cordial way as to convince the red men that justice was being done. The Delaware Indians were in fact docile until the 1730s; the Quakers were lucky to have them as neighbours rather than the belligerent Iroquois, who might have made pacifism less feasible.

Penn landed in his new kingdom in 1682, fully intending to reside there permanently. He supervised the building of a gracious mansion for himself and the laying out of 'Philadelphia', so named from two Greek words meaning 'brother' and 'love', on a spacious rectangular plan; with straight streets running parallel, two wide avenues bisecting each other. Quakers from urban backgrounds in London and Bristol gravitated to this fast-growing settlement, while rural Friends sought the farmlands beyond. The early Quaker townsmen were generally manual workers, and Penn himself noted with gratification that Philadelphia started its life with 'most sorts of useful Tradesmen'. Merchants flocked in, chiefly Quakers not from England but from other colonies where they had grown wealthy. The richest man, Samuel Carpenter, came from Barbados; Isaac Norris, noted in politics, from Jamaica; the very wealthy Edward Shippen from Boston; and the new town's first mayor from New York.[174]

From his friend James, Duke of York, Penn in 1682 acquired a title to the area which became the state of Delaware, but which for many years to come was known as the 'Lower Counties'. This tract west of Delaware Bay already had a few hundred settlers, and besides some English, there were relics of earlier settlements made by Swedes, Finns and Dutch. 'German-town', founded near Philadelphia in 1683, was actually first settled by Dutchmen, though Quaker settlers from the Rhineland were shortly attracted by Penn's propaganda and acquired, in Francis Daniel Pastorius, a remarkable intellectual to lead them. But the great influx of Germans would come only in the next century; up to 1700, it is reckoned, settlers in Pennsylvania were roughly two-thirds English, one-tenth Welsh and one-tenth Irish – only one in twenty or so came from Germany and the Netherlands.[175]

The Colony of Heaven and the City of Brotherly Love soon fell into factions. The Welsh, led by John Ap John, were given a tract of 50,000 acres variously known as 'New Wales', 'Cambria' and 'the Welsh Tract', with the understanding that they would be left to speak their own language, practise their own customs and hold their own courts, but before long Penn's governor ran a county line through the middle, which had the political convenience of splitting the solid Welsh bloc of voters. A controversy with Lord Baltimore over his border with Maryland forced Penn to sail home in 1684, and he did not return for fifteen years. His hopes of wealth from the quitrents due to him were disappointed as they proved very sticky to collect. The 'Pennsylvania Company' which he set up to help establish and supply the colony and which had some 200 stock holders in England soon ran into trouble with its own inefficient and dishonest officials in Philadelphia and with opposition in the Colony, though it staggered on unprofitably till 1723. The Land Office was badly managed. The Lower Counties were restless. As soon as Penn left, his fellow Quakers, who were securely in a majority of the population and in control of both Assembly and Council, fell out among themselves, and in the 1690s there was even a doctrinal schism amongst them. One thing only seemed to unite everyone — hot resentment of proprietorial government.

One deputy governor put in by Penn would before long be recalled in humiliation after friction with the colonists, remarking of the Philadelphia Quakers as he departed that 'each prays for his neighbor on First Days and then preys upon him the other six.'[176] But political quarrels, as this remark rather suggests, did not affect success in trade. The Quaker merchants of Philadelphia came to control the growing commerce of West New Jersey and of the Lower Counties, as well as that of their own province.

The town of New York suffered from the success of Penn's colony, losing, along with several of its leading merchants, its trade in tobacco and peltry with the Delaware River. Philadelphia soon outstripped the older port, which depended chiefly on Boston for its supply of English goods and had no established contacts with London of its own. Governor Dongan of New York (a Catholic Irishman) now found Penn's agents looking for a share in the fur trade and creeping up behind his province to try to buy the upper Susquehanna valley from the Iroquois — with whom Dongan accordingly allied his own colony. The revenue of New York, since settlement was still sparse, had to depend on the fur trade, and Dongan aimed to capture control from the Canadian French. But he lacked the resources to do so. His colony was a cartographical nonsense. Long Island, which belonged historically and geographically with New England, was its main centre of population; the governor had the expense of defending and trying to govern his royal master's territories in Maine, and Albany up-river was jealous of New York City. There was great resentment among the scant, but polyglot, colonists over the powers concentrated in the hands of the governor and his council. New York was still the only English colony which had no representative assembly. Dongan, when he arrived in 1683, had borne instructions to set one up. Eighteen representatives, mostly Dutch, now drafted an ambitious 'Charter of Libertyes' for the colony, which James confirmed next year. But he had not sent it back when his brother died, and New York automatically, as he ascended the throne, became a royal colony. To give its leading men what they asked for would set a precedent for Virginia and Massachusetts. The Charter was aborted, as James developed his own extensive plans, in the New World as well as at home.

Parcels of Rogues

Fareweel to a' our Scottish fame,
Fareweel our ancient glory!
Fareweel ev'n to the Scottish name,
Sae famed in martial story!
Now Sark rins o'er the Solway sands,
An' Tweed rins to the ocean,
To mark where England's province stands —
Such a parcel of rogues in a nation!

What force or guile could not subdue
Thro' many warlike ages
Is wrought now by a coward few
For Hireling traitor's wages.
The English steel we could disdain,
Secure in valour's station;
But English gold has been our bane —
Such a parcel of rogues in a nation.

ROBERT BURNS

I

The succession in 1685 of this Catholic monarch was bound to arouse fear and rage. James, while his brother had been taming England, had been working to secure his own position in Scotland, where a parliament in 1681 passed, at his suggestion, two Acts. The first declared that no difference in religion could disqualify a rightful successor to the throne. The second was the notorious Test Act which imposed an oath on all persons engaging in politics, who must now swear that they would never try to make any alteration in the government of Church or State. The Earl of Argyll, son of Montrose's great rival, was one of those who refused to take it. He escaped to Holland. On James's succession, Argyll returned with three hundred supporters and attempted to raise rebellion, but he was swiftly caught and, like his father before him, executed. Meanwhile, the Duke of Monmouth, with even fewer followers, sailed from Holland to Devon, and rallied an army of some 7,000 among the Dissenting freeholders and unemployed clothworkers of the south-west. But his inexperienced soldiers were routed by James's regular troops. Lord Chief Justice Jeffreys dealt out punishments brutally in his 'Bloody Assizes' on the western circuit. Besides perhaps 300 sentences of death, some 800 people were condemned to be transported to the West Indies, and various courtiers were granted the right to sell them. The Queen, amongst others, made a considerable profit.[1]

The militia had proved ineffectual in operations against Monmouth's rising. This suited James well; he could argue that a strong standing army was essential. But he insisted on his right to have papist officers in it. The parliament summoned early in his reign had at first been complaisant; the elections had proved the value of his brother's purge of the boroughs, and the whigs were now broken and dispirited. But James asked too much. The Commons would not stand for Catholics in civil or military office. James prorogued Parliament in November 1685 and thereafter went his own way. The purge of officeholders which he now mounted was in effect an attack on the power of the aristocracy and the major gentry. Most Lord Lieutenants of counties were deposed. Nearly half the J.P.s were ousted, tories as well as whigs were alarmed as papists, even a Jesuit, found high places in government and as the commander of the Royal Navy was turned out in favour of a Catholic. A huge army, some 16,000 troops, was quartered on Hounslow Heath each summer, as if intended to overawe London, and in Ireland a great Catholic force was being created by James's subordinates. With Anglican opinion thoroughly alienated, James turned to court the nonconformists, amongst whom William Penn was his close associate. The tests which since the 1660s had barred Dissenters from office were suspended, and as the remodelling of corporations was pressed forward, jumped-up sectarians joined obscure Catholics in the government of proud old towns.

This was in effect an attempt at revolution from above. It offended almost every powerful vested interest. The clergy were the first to show open defiance. When a second Declaration of Indulgence towards nonconformists was proclaimed in May 1688, they generally refused to read it aloud in church as ordered. Seven bishops were arrested. A jury acquitted them. Now came the last straw. James had hitherto lacked a male heir. He was elderly. Men could console themselves that things must change soon. In June his wife produced a son.

The threatened ruling class was in no mood for heroics. The situation recalled that of 1640 in so far as a papist army in Ireland hung as a threat over England; but, unlike his father, James had a strong force at home and the Commons had voted him revenue for life. Besides, the 1640s had shown that great men who raised rebellion ran the risk of inflaming lesser men; levelling ideas would be at work again. But a deus ex machina was available. William, Prince of Orange, ruler of the Netherlands, was James's nephew and also his son-in-law. He was moving towards war with Louis XIV of France, to whom James was a client, though not a very reliable one — there was a strong streak of bluff English patriotism in his make-up. William had moved carefully, making it clear to prominent men in England that if they wanted him to come, he must have a written invitation. This was duly provided, with seven names on the document from great aristocratic families.

James saw what was impending and hastily reversed all his policies. But he was too late. On 5 November 1688 William disembarked at Torbay in Devon with the largest army ever to land in England, some 15,000 men. The cowardly English ruling class gave him little military support, but James's army retreated before him, riddled with disaffection, and virtually everyone looked on agreeably as William moved steadily up to London. James ran away. By Christmas, he was in France, and 'Jacobitism' had been born.

England had no king, if James was held to have abdicated. A 'convention' met early in 1689, Parliament under another name, and drew up a Declaration of Rights which outlawed James's practices and with them absolutism. William and his queen, Mary, James's daughter, were jointly offered the Crown. A set of transactions marked by extreme caution on all hands, and with gross personal betrayal by many of those closest to James, would be awarded the name of the 'Glorious Revolution'. John Locke had returned from exile and he could rationalise what had happened in terms which would be accepted by men all over the English-speaking lands. His *Essay of Civil Government* argues that government is based on contract. Men agree to form an ordered society. When the king whom they have entrusted with government flouts his trust, revolution is the ultimate safeguard of law. The aim of government is to preserve property.

England became a constitutional monarchy, though the constitution was not codified. Government policy was from now on restrained by specific appropriations of money made by Parliament. Most of the country's political men endorsed the war against France into which William promptly pulled England. Such a war had never been waged from the island before, with the enemy engaged not only at sea but on frontiers in the colonies and, in association with allies, on the continent of Europe itself. The hundred-year squabble between Crown and Parliament was over. Spending on the navy had hovered in the 1680s at between £330,000 and £470,000 a year. In 1696–7 it stood at £2,821,931 – and yet the proportion of public money being used in this field was not much greater.[2] State spending vastly increased as Parliament voted money without inhibition. To keep William's war going, Parliament had to meet every year to grant funds. This habit was never broken. The king's prerogative of summoning Parliament lapsed. And since William had to accept, in 1694, an Act by which an election must be held at least once in three years, the next two decades saw a preposterous effusion of political faction, as whigs and tories, regrouped, contended for power.

Religion remained a bitter topic. But toleration was now made law. Nonconformists, as the ruling class wished so fervently, were barred again from public affairs, but they were made free to have their own places of worship under certain conditions. Catholics in England reverted to their position under

Charles II – or perhaps they were slightly less disadvantaged. In Ireland, of course, the tale was a very different one.

II

James sent over his brother-in-law, the Earl of Clarendon, to replace the aged Ormond as viceroy, but the real ruler of Ireland during his reign was his friend Richard Talbot, a prominent Irish Catholic landowner, to whom he gave the title of Earl of Tyrconnell and the command of the army. A purge and reconstruction of this force began in the summer of 1686. By the autumn there were 5,000 Catholics out of 7,500 private soldiers, and within a couple of years most of the officers were also Catholics.[3]

Some of his fellow papists disliked Tyrconnell, who was arrogant, quicktempered and blustering. To Protestants, of course, he was a bogeyman. When, in January 1687, he formally succeeded Clarendon as Lord Lieutenant, the appointment produced a famous song, 'Lillibullero'. Set to a lively tune (probably not by Purcell), it caught on so well that the author of the words, Thomas Wharton, could claim later that he had sung a king out of three kingdoms:

> Ho, brother Teig, dost hear the decree
> Lilliburlero bullen a la
> Dat we shall have a new debittie:
> Ho, by my soul, it is a Talbot,
> And he will cut all de English throat.

The lumpen-Hibernian spokesman, it will be observed, was given a pidgin much like that attributed to black men; 'Teig' and 'Sambo' seemed very alike to fearful English-speaking masters, and would do so down to our own century. As Catholics reappeared in the Irish Privy Council, in town corporations, as local magistrates, even as judges, a trickle of perturbed Protestants began to emigrate from Ireland, while a Gaelic poet exulted over Tyrconnell's new army:

> Behold there the Gael in arms every one of them,
> They have powder and guns, hold the castles and fortresses;
> The Presbyterians, lo, have been overthrown,
> And the fanatics have left an infernal smell after them.[4]

One of James's most serious mistakes was to call over Irish troops in 1688 to support him. While their drafting weakened Tyrconnell's force in Ulster, the civilian populations of London and Portsmouth hated the papist barbarians and there were scuffles in the streets. Deep resentment within the English army helps to explain its later reluctance to fight for the King. After James's overthrow, Irish Protestants, fearing a repetition of the 1641 rising, began to quit hurriedly in spite of Tyrconnell's efforts to calm them. In the north, those who stayed formed armed associations which effectively controlled large areas, and Derry went into open rebellion. Presbyterians were heartened by the news from Scotland.

The Revolution of 1688 was a purely English initiative, and it was not until James called the Scottish army south that the south-western Covenanters rose against the hated episcopalian clergy and a mob in Edinburgh drove the Jesuits out of the Palace of Holyrood and sacked the royal chapel. A Convention of Estates met in March 1689 and heard a moderate letter from William and a threatening one from James. The majority settled for William. Amongst the minority, Graham of Claverhouse, newly ennobled as Viscount Dundee, took the lead. Though he was Protestant, he stood no chance at all of making his peace with a Williamite regime; his reputation as persecutor (like Jeffreys's) was too well-established. He withdrew from the Convention, which declared him a rebel and went on to offer terms to William and Mary. Tolerant William shied for a moment at a clause in the oath proposed to him which obliged him to root out heretics, but was assured that this was mere form. In July 1689 prelacy was formally abolished in Scotland and Presbyterian government was restored. The ministers ejected since the Restoration were reinstated and dominated the General Assembly of the Church, which they purged of more than half its clergy. But the heady conditions of the 1640s could not be revived. The Kirk was now subject to parliamentary statute, and civil penalties could not now be enforced for ecclesiastical excommunication. The Covenants, overtly reaffirmed, were tacitly conceded to be a dead letter. Though the newly ousted ministers formed the basis of an underground episcopalian Church, the days of religious warfare were over. The more ardent Cameronian Covenanters split, and while some stuck to their creed in a series of little sects, others joined the new Cameronian Regiment which was set up to fight for William.

Dundee had rallied an army in the Highlands. The Campbells, of course, were for William—James had executed their chief, the Earl of Argyll, and other clans had accepted the failure of his rising as delicious opportunity to pay off old scores. Now various chiefs feared the coming revival of Campbell power. Though James, while king, had been as unsympathetic to the Highland Gaels as any of his predecessors, Macdonalds, Camerons, Stewarts, Macleans and others were now ready to fight for him. Dundee showed he could lead them well. At the pass of Killiecrankie late in July a classic Highland charge destroyed the Williamite army sent against them, though at the moment of victory Dundee himself was killed. Jacobitism had won its first battle in Scotland, and found its first hero. But Dundee's successor, Colonel Cannon, could not match his flair. In August, the Jacobites were repulsed at Dunkeld, a gate to the Lowlands, by the Cameronian Regiment, whose Colonel had fought for the Covenant in the Bothwell Bridge rising. The Presbyterians showed impressive courage. Scotland was saved for their creed, and for William. Next year, the Jacobites were beaten again, and their challenge collapsed.

In Ireland, the Williamites found success far more difficult. Tyrconnell manoeuvred skilfully for control, playing for time by suggesting that he might go over to William while actually raising 40,000 more troops for James. In March 1689 his army defeated an Ulster Protestant force in the 'break of Dromore' and soon only Derry and Enniskillen held out. Tyrconnell's success helped to persuade Louis XIV that he should support James in an attempt to regain his throne through Ireland, and just before Dromore a French fleet of 22 ships brought their king to the Irish, along with supporters from all three of his kingdoms, besides French officers, arms and ammunition. He made a triumphal progress from Kinsale to Dublin, welcomed, as one contemporary witness put it, 'as if he had been an angel from heaven'. As he entered the capital on March 24, pipers were playing 'The King Enjoys His Own Again'.[5]

But James was not interested in the prospect of reigning over Ireland in Ireland. He wanted to cross to Scotland as soon as possible and thence strike into England. Meanwhile, he showed his mortification when his beloved English navy was bested by the French fleet which landed further troops for his cause at Bantry Bay. Irish Catholics were soon disillusioned with him. The foreigners who had come with him did not disguise their contempt for the Gaelic rabble who would fight on his side. An English Catholic, for instance, declared that these troops would 'follow none but their own leaders, many of them men as rude, as ignorant, and as far from understanding any of the rules of discipline as themselves', and a French leader wrote to Louis XIV, 'The Irish recognise … that the Englishmen close to the king, even the Catholics, are their greatest enemies.'[6]

So James could not hope that the Irish Parliament which he summoned for May 7 would produce legislation acceptable to opinion in England. But he had to call it. He was short of arms, of supplies, of money. Thanks to Tyrconnell's purges, this 'Patriot Parliament' contained only six Protestants in the Commons and five in the Lords – but the Church of Ireland bishops were summoned in preference to the Catholic ones. James thwarted its attempt to repeal Poynings' Law, but was compelled to agree to an Act declaring that the English Parliament had no right to pass laws for Ireland, and to give his sad consent to a Bill, odious to his English supporters, which swept away the land settlement of the 1660s and authorised dispossessed papists to take steps to get their property back. Those who had rebelled against James, or had even had correspondence with rebels – that is, virtually every Protestant who could write – were to forfeit their estates. All James could do was to postpone the setting up of a Court of Claims, alleging, plausibly, that army officers were deserting their posts and hurrying to inspect their ancestral property.

James's first stroke on arrival had been to proclaim freedom of religion for all, and an Act of the Parliament now made this law. He hoped to pursue a conciliatory policy, leaving Church of Ireland vacancies unfilled and using the

money to subsidise Catholic priests, while providing that Catholics and Protestants should each support their own clergy. Later he tried, without much
success, to stop Catholics seizing Protestant churches. His moderation pleased
neither side.

The Patriot Parliament set aside the restrictions imposed by the English
Navigation Laws, and James had to block Bills which attempted to give special
favour to France. Trade had in fact collapsed, and this bore hard on the royal
revenue. The Parliament was generous with its grant, but the amounts raised
fell far short of what had been granted and with expenditure on the army
running at ruinous heights, James turned to minting brass and copper money,
about £1 million in a year. Guns were melted down to provide coinage. Yet
this devalued so rapidly that by the spring of 1690 it was common to give
50 shillings of brass money for a guinea.[7] Protestant toasts later would include
brass money, along with popery and with wooden shoes, among the horrors
from which William III had delivered the British isles.

And the men of Derry would become the prime heroes of Protestant
mythology. When James advanced towards the town in April 1689, it was
packed with refugees. About 30,000 people were crammed within its narrow
walls, 500 yards long by 300 wide. There was some ill feeling between Presbyterians and episcopalians, and the governor, Robert Lundy, a Scots Protestant,
gave only hesitating allegiance to William and did not believe that the place
could be defended. But Derry, reinforced from London, had proclaimed
William and Mary, and its denizens were braced to resistance by fears of a
repetition of 1641. Lundy was ousted and replaced by two new governors,
Major Baker and a die-hard Church of Ireland minister named George Walker.
A siege of fifteen weeks began. Before the end dogs and cats, rats, hides and
tallow would be eaten, 'a handful of sea-wrack or chickweed fetched a penny
or twopence.' The defenders had only new regiments of inexperienced soldiers.
The enemy killed just eighty, but famine and sickness reduced the force from
7,500 to about 4,300, of whom more than a quarter were unserviceable. The
supply of cannonballs eventually failed, and pieces of brick were covered with
lead. But the defenders were never short of powder, and though they were
easily bombarded from the high ground round the city and the Jacobite mortars
damaged many houses, the besiegers had only one gun heavy enough to make
any impression on the famous walls.

The Jacobites were fewer and sickness and desertion quickly eroded their ill-
equipped force. Their best hope was to starve Derry into submission. But
James showed reckless clemency, ordering that non-combatants should be
permitted to leave; then repented when he heard that several thousand had
departed. Food and four regiments were on the way from England and the
Jacobites built a boom across the river Foyle to block their passage. On June 30
their commander threatened that if the city hadn't surrendered by the next day,
he would drive all the Protestants in the surrounding area under the walls and

leave them there to starve. The defenders retorted by erecting a gallows on which they threatened to hang their prisoners. The herded Protestants were allowed to go home. The relief ships, thwarted by the boom, sailed round to Lough Swilly, and the knowledge that they were close by stiffened resistance. On July 28 two ships broke the boom, laden with peas, flour, beef and biscuits. The Jacobites now could do nothing but raise the siege, which is said to have cost 15,000 lives altogether, mostly from disease and starvation. The stubbornness of Derry had baulked James's plan to cross to Scotland.[8]

Meanwhile, the Protestants of Enniskillen had harried the Jacobite communications, had carried off thousands of cattle and sheep, and, in their mounted raids, had seemed to threaten Dublin itself. Soon after the siege of Derry ended, they routed a much larger Jacobite force at Newtownbutler. Jacobite morale was low when, on August 13, 10,000 troops in William's service arrived in Ulster under the command of Marshal Schomberg, a famous French veteran. More soon followed. While all Catholics between 16 and 60 were ordered to arm themselves, James's own French generals advised him to retreat. But on this occasion, he was courageous. Late in August he marched north. Schomberg had been joined by three fearsome regiments from Enniskillen, brave, insubordinate volunteers mounted on scraggy little horses and looking, as one witness reported, 'like a horde of Tartars ... half-naked with sabre and pistols hanging from their belts.'[9] But Irish disease, that inveterate foe, had weakened the Williamite force so severely that Schomberg for the moment refused battle. His retreat encouraged an unsafe optimism in the Jacobite camp, and with it a continued failure to train and equip James's army.

French and Irish officers quarrelled continually. James, unimpressed with his native soldiers, shipped 5,000 off to France, where they formed the nucleus of the famous Irish Brigade, and received 6,000 troops sent by Louis XIV in exchange. Many of these were Walloons and Germans, some of them actually Protestant. This was becoming a most cosmopolitan struggle. William, to add to his Dutchmen and Germans and Huguenots, had hired 7,000 Danes, and Jacobite propaganda, recalling the Norsemen, deplored this calling in of 'the old invaders of our country'.[10] Ireland, as never before or since, was a theatre of European war, waged by William and his allies against Louis. To mark its importance, William came in person in June 1690. Ireland had seen no king since Richard II. Now it was honoured with two at the same time, but just as James thought of Dublin as a stepping stone towards London, so William counted Ulster an outpost of Holland. Neither had real sympathy with the preoccupations of any of Ireland's inhabitants.

James fell back before William to the River Boyne. On June 30 an engagement took place which, overrated, became the most famous event in Irish history. James had about 25,000 men. William's 36,000 were far better equipped, especially in artillery. The Williamite right wing, crossing the river upstream, turned most of James's force to face it, expecting the main thrust there, but

William launched his Dutch Blue Guards straight across the river at 10 a.m. The struggle was fierce for a while, Tyrconnell's cavalry charged time after time. Schomberg was killed. William kept saying, 'my poor guards, my poor guards.' He lost about 500 men, James twice as many. The Jacobites were forced into disorderly retreat. And James lost face. While his rival had shown reckless courage and had been slightly wounded, James had fled from the battlefield in haste, and took ship for France next morning. On July 5, William rode with great pomp to St Patrick's Cathedral in Dublin and the Protestants there, as one of them wrote, 'ran about shouting and embracing one another and blessing God for his wonderful deliverance as if they had been alive from the dead ... '[11]

A saying of James's most dashing commander, Patrick Sarsfield, went around Europe. 'As low as we are now,' he told some English officers, 'change but kings with us, and we will fight it over again with you.'[12] James's supporters were left resentful and disillusioned. He himself blamed the Irish for running away, and his instructions to his infant son, written two years later, advised him to root out the Gaelic language and to tell the Os and Macs of Ireland firmly that their forfeited lands would never be restored; nor should natives be trusted with high office.

The Jacobite army retreated to Limerick. Tyrconnell was now for surrendering. But Sarsfield, idol of the army, 'a man of an amazing stature, utterly devoid of sense, very good natured and very brave',[13] still insisted on dying hard. William wanted to offer generous terms, but the revengeful Irish Protestants would not let him. The Jacobite leaders had to fight on if they wished to retain their estates. A desperate three-week defence of Limerick, in which unarmed men threw stones and women fought in the breach with broken bottles, forced William into retreat.

But James's French troops went home, and his Irish warriors were confined behind the line of the Shannon. Sarsfield, now named Earl of Lucan, resented Tyrconnell's authority and neither got on with the new French commander, St Ruth, who arrived to lead the army in May. The Jacobites, probably due to treachery, lost the key town of Athlone and the Irish troops there were butchered. Recriminations and a spate of desertions followed. But St Ruth still had about 20,000 men, equal to the numbers commanded by a Dutchman named Ginkel for William, when the two sides met in decisive battle at Aughrim in County Galway on July 12. Williamite writers praised Irish courage – one declared that the battle was the 'last effort' in which 'the gasping honour of all the Catholic nobility and gentry of the kingdom struggled to do its utmost.' But there seems to have been fresh treachery on the Jacobite left wing, and after St Ruth's head was blown off by a cannonball, massacre followed. Over 7,000 Irish were dead before night stopped the slaughter. Corpses were strewn for almost four miles around. 'It isn't the loss of Aughrim' became the Irish way of saying that a misfortune was bearable. This one was not. Four hundred officers died and many of the Jacobite aristocracy were captured. It was the worst defeat in Irish military history.[14]

The French, wishing to lock up a Williamite army as long as possible, sent reinforcements after Aughrim, and there were still over 20,000 Jacobite troops in the field, concentrated around Limerick, when Ginkel marched to besiege that town late in August. But within a month even Sarsfield was ready for surrender. His own chief interest in the negotiations which began on September 23 was to get permission for the Irish army to go to France, and Ginkel readily conceded not only this, but also transport to take them there. The hard bargaining took place over the Irish who would remain. In the event, the terms given left most estates held by Jacobites liable to forfeit, but promised the Irish such privileges in the practice of their religion as they had enjoyed under Charles II or were consistent with the laws of Ireland; which was vague enough. People in the Limerick garrison and in the four counties of Clare, Kerry, Cork and Mayo which were under Jacobite protection, together with officers and soldiers still in arms, would be pardoned and allowed to keep their property and carry on their professions if they submitted to William and took a simple oath of allegiance.

The military articles were faithfully executed. By Christmas an estimated 12,000 Irish troops had been taken in English ships to France, where they gave James II his own army till the European war ended, but thereafter were absorbed into the French forces. Sarsfield himself died in battle for the French a couple of years later, and the 'wild geese' whom he led earned a reputation for ill-rewarded bravery on the battlefields of Europe. Many Jacobite Irish, it is worth remembering, opted to serve William, who consigned a select 1,400 of them to fight for his ally the Emperor.[15]

The civil articles, however, were never fully honoured, despite William's own wish that they should be. They did help to regain or preserve the property rights of several hundred Jacobite landowners. But Protestant opposition was so bitter that confirmation by the Irish Parliament came only in 1697, and the Bill then presented bore little resemblance to the original treaty. The articles giving Catholics back their position under Charles II were wholly overridden by the notorious penal legislation against them which began in William's reign. By an Act of 1697, which William had to approve, Catholic bishops and regular clergy were banished.

The land settlement, though the scale of transfers was small compared to those of 1652 and 1665, rounded off a century of confiscations. William struggled with his English Parliament over the forfeited estates. He was at first able to make vast grants to his personal favourites. To the son of his friend Bentinck went 135,000 acres; another Dutchman, Keppel, received over 100,000, and, most notorious of all, the King's clever, squinting mistress, Elizabeth Villiers, Countess of Orkney, was given the 'private estate', formerly James II's personal property, of nearly 100,000 acres. The English Commons fought back and regained control of the forfeited lands by an Act of 1700. Matters were finally settled only in 1703. By that time, the Catholic share of profitable acreage was reduced from 22 per cent in 1688 to only 14 per cent, and as penal legislation drove many landowners into Protestantism, it fell further still, to a mere 5 per cent or so by 1776.[16]

The results of the Battle of the Boyne and the events surrounding it are still felt in Ireland. As in Scotland, traditions of military valour stem from this period. The Enniskillen Fusiliers would match the Cameronian Regiment in reputation. Meanwhile William's birthday, November 4, became a holy day in Ulster. Year after year the renegade Lundy would be burnt in effigy and the brave defenders of Derry would be extolled. While Ulster Protestants nurtured a potent mythology, Catholic resistance in Ireland was almost broken, though 'rapparees', ex-soldiers from the 1689–91 war, succeeded the 'tories' for a time as patriotic brigands. It would be a century before Catholic Irishmen once more sought to recapture their own country by arms.

Meanwhile, what was left of the old Gaelic order would die rather more peacefully than that of the Scottish clans. Some chiefs now lived in hovels, but west of Galway, about the end of the seventeenth century, an English traveller named Dunton visited the O Flaherty, chief of a famous fighting clan, who still kept something like traditional state in his 'long cabbin', a booley or summer dwelling, with 'walls of hurdles plaister'd with cow dung and clay'. He was surrounded by a 'greate company of his relations ... a parcell of tall lusty fellows with long hair.' Nine brace of ferocious wolfhounds mingled quietly with the company. A whole sheep was devoured at supper, and afterwards all present, 'even the lady herself', enjoyed Dunton's tobacco; she said they needed something like that in such a moist country. 'I enquired about the customs of ploweing by their horses tayl, and burning the corn in the straw. They told me the former was wholy disused as a thing too injurious, their cattle often loosing their tayls thereby, but they still burn their corn to save themselves the trouble of thrashing ... ' O Flaherty apologised for their 'barbarous' way o f life; he had been to Dublin and had seen how things should be done, but old habits, he confided, died hard.

Since there was no chimney, everyone suffered from sore eyes. The house was a single long room without partitions. The whole company lay down to sleep here, on green rushes (full of 'white snayles'), but Dunton was given sheets and soft white blankets. 'I wonder'd mightily to heare people walkeing to the fire place in the middle of the house to piss there in the ashes, but I was soon after forced to doe soe too for want of a chambrepot ... ' Next morning, O Flaherty, after a breakfast of meat and rough whiskey, invited him to 'walk a small mile to view theire deer'. Dunton was surprised that there should be a deer park in so wild a place. But indeed, there was not. After a trek over mountains and through bogs, 'modestly speakeing as farr as half way from Whitehall to Barnet', they came to an untouched vale amid 'lovely green mountaines' and there on the hillsides were 'hundreds of stately red dear'. They returned to the cabin for a vast dinner, with a whole carcase of beef, mutton as well, and tall heaps of oatcakes, a delicious cold milk drink, whiskey and ale 'such as it was'. Then they rode back to hunt the deer with 'above thirty footemen' following them. There was venison besides beef and mutton and fish for supper.[17]

The new Ireland retained only hospitality from this dying, archaic way of life. The thriving city of Cork greatly impressed an English merchant in 1703. 'They drive a very great trade to the West Indies with their provisions, chiefly by Bristol men who flock hither to load about September and October for Jamaica, Barbadoes, Antegoa, and the other islands of the West Indies, with beef, pork, butter, candles, etc.' They also kept up a contraband commerce with France. ' ... The people are generally given to hospitality, civil and courteous to strangers; follow pretty much the French air in conversation, bringing up their children to dance, play on the fiddle, and fence, if they can give them nothing else.'[18] Their prosperity was, of course, quite largely based on that of the slave economy in the West Indies.

III

The monopolies of the East India Company and of the Royal African Company were under attack from the 'interlopers' and their allies. Both were closely identified with the royal family and hence were imperilled by the 'Glorious Revolution'. Of the EIC and its survival, more later. The RAC was beaten by its opponents within the quarter century after 1689.

James II was the governor and largest shareholder in the RAC until his flight. It now lost confidence in the legality of its own charter, stopped seizing interlopers, and had to settle with traders whose goods it had impounded before the Revolution. So the African trade was opened up. The Company's forts, however, were seen as essential safeguards of English interests in Africa. A ten per cent duty was imposed by Parliament on exports to Africa by non-Company ships – henceforward known as 'Ten Per-Centers'. In return these would have the same privileges at the forts as RAC vessels. The money raised by the duty would help to pay for the upkeep of the forts.

The Company made great efforts to compete. It sent out Sir Dalby Thomas, a formidable aggressive man, who was also a well-known expert on trade, as its Agent General at Cape Coast Castle from 1703. But war with France weakened its position; about a quarter of its ships in the war years were taken by the French, and losses in this way ran up to about £300,000 by 1713. The French drove the RAC out of its posts on the Gambia for five years in the 1690s. And despite the appearance of Dutch William on the English throne, the cold war with the Netherlanders on the Gold Coast warmed noticeably, involving expensive intrigues among the African coastal powers. The Dutch encouraged the RAC's English rivals; Sir Dalby complained picturesquely in 1705 that the Dutch general on the coast was the '10 per cent mens Diana, and they pay all adoration, with great presents, to him.' Intensified competition led to reckless bidding which forced up the price of slaves. But the 'separate traders' or 'Ten Per-Centers' still throve. An official enquiry showed that between 1698 and 1708 they had imported about 75,000 slaves into the New World colonies as compared with the RAC's 18,000.[19] In 1712 the Act of 1698 expired and was not renewed. The men of Bristol had triumphed and in their wake followed the ships of Liverpool. The RAC now had no monopoly – and no ten per cent. Yet it retained its forts.

These explained its defeat. A chartered company had been set to do work which later was seen as the State's. Its forts were the RAC's main justification, but commercially they were a liability. Because it was committed to keeping up a continuous trade between Africa and the New World, the RAC could not pick and choose its time like the interlopers, and so its losses through war were more serious. Like its Dutch and French rivals on the coast, it was 'asked to perform the most difficult of all commercial feats, the reconciliation of the capitalist ethic with public duty ... '[20]

It is necessary to understand that, apart from the Portuguese in Angola and Mozambique, no European power, at this stage, was able to control more than a scrap of Africa. John Barbot's view of Accra, on the Gold Coast, about 1680 represented the general position even where forts existed. Though the Dutch, English and Portuguese were all installed there, Barbot remarked, 'The three *European* forts have but little authority over the *Blacks*, and serve only to secure the trade, the *Blacks* here being of a temper not to suffer any thing to be imposed on them by *Europeans*; which, if they should but attempt, it would certainly prove their own ruin.'[21]

The myth that West African societies were at this time hopelessly backward, infantile in comparison with those of Europe, must now be totally dismissed. The vast region embraced, indeed, a number of societies which was perhaps even larger than Europe's, and just as men in the Highlands of Scotland or in Lapland were very different from people in London or Bordeaux, so there were simple cultures as well as highly sophisticated ones in Guinea. Overall, there was a range of industries – cloth-making, mining, metalwork, building and so forth – comparable to that found in other pre-industrial societies. Since before the foundation of Rome, trade across the Sahara had linked the region with other continents. In its risks and its character, it was like the overseas trades of Europe. As in the long-distance trade with the East Indies, only luxuries, dear in relation to their weight, could economically be carried on the long journey, up to three months, across the blazing desert. Slaves, along with gold and leather goods and high quality African cloth, were among the suitable merchandise. Perhaps one-fifth of slaves died as they crossed the Sahara, in a trade which endured until well into the twentieth century.[22] In exchange, rulers south of the desert acquired the salt, weapons, and horses required to sustain their own dominance, along with luxuries which they consumed as tokens of their rank.

Africans, as well as Arabs, Berbers and Jews, were prominent in trans-Saharan commerce, which from the eleventh to the seventeenth centuries had been the main source of gold for the international economy.

South of the shoreline, as it might be called, between desert and savanna, Mande, Hausa and Yoruba traders had ranged widely, linking forest and plain. There were many markets in Guinea, and merchants were highly regarded men. There were cities, in the forest region as well as in the savanna, which matched those of Europe. A Dutchman who penetrated Benin in 1602 was impressed with the size of the great central street, the good order of the houses, the vast extent of the Oba's palace, and thought it comparable with Amsterdam. At this time Benin was probably larger than any English town except London. For some African rulers, trade in slaves was vital even before the European impact was fully felt. In the city-states of Hausaland, according to R. A. Adeleye, 'Slaves seem to have supplied the life blood of commerce. They were central to the economic life of the states. As domestic slaves they supplied manpower for generating profit. They were employed for agriculture as well as in war. They were in themselves an international currency as well as a means of earning currency.'[23]

The key to the role of slaves in West African economies was underpopulation, the very factor which would make servitude seem essential in Virginia. Because land was plentiful, hired labour would be too expensive. Despite the vision which many Europeans had of Africa as a place where natural fecundity meant that a man could live by merely gathering wild fruit and grains, soils in Guinea were commonly hard to work. Many West African cultures were based on arduous and sophisticated agriculture. Draught animals, ploughs and wheeled vehicles were not generally used, though Africans did know about them; they were unsuitable in local conditions. Their absence, however, created a great need for diggers wherever agriculture moved beyond peasant subsistence, and for carriers where trade developed. Chattel slavery was a consequence. Many slaves worked in large gangs in gruelling and perilous roles – as roadmakers, front-line soldiers and, most taxing of all, as cutters of rock salt in the Saharan mines. However, the institution was commonly far milder than in the West Indies. The slave's colour was the same as the owner's. In some contexts slaves rose to important positions in the State or engaged in skilled work, and there was a general trend towards their assimilation into society as they gained certain rights in return for their loyalty. In the Bambara state which had evolved on the Niger by the eighteenth century, slaves – who included hereditary slaves as well as captives, debtors and criminals – were not precluded from owning slaves themselves. Among the Mande up the Gambia, an English factor would note in the 1730s, 'Some People have a good many House-Slaves, which is their greatest Glory, and they live so well and easy, that it is sometimes a very hard Matter to know the Slaves from their Masters or Mistresses ... '[24]

Few white men got so far inland. The Senegal and Gambia rivers were exceptional in the chance they provided for contact with Africans of the interior. The great artery of the Niger was hidden from white understanding until the nineteenth century, and there were otherwise no rivers which could take a trader far into the continent. The power and pugnacity of the African states which existed behind most parts of the coast meant that far forays on land were almost impossible. Disease also sapped European initiative. Between a quarter and three-quarters of any group of Europeans arriving fresh on the coast would die within a year; thereafter, the death rate would be about ten per cent. Guinea was, unbelievably, four times as dangerous to whites as the West Indies or India. Its swamps harboured a species of malaria far more virulent than that still found in those days in the English fens and the Irish bogs. European medicine was at this stage no more efficacious than that practised by Africans (nearing his predictable death from liver disease, the buccaneer Henry Morgan actually dismissed his white doctor in favour of a black one). It failed to distinguish malaria from yellow fever, another persistent killer. Most Africans acquired immunity to these diseases in childhood; a white would become unscatheable only if he survived his first attacks. Meanwhile, the role of insects in carrying disease was not understood, the value of quinine against malaria was only fitfully appreciated from the 1670s on, and the favourite white doctor's technique of bleeding sufferers would commonly help to hasten their deaths. The only safe place to be in Guinea, if you were English, was on a ship well offshore.[25]

However, the RAC maintained its sometimes spectral footing on the coast. Besides its James Fort at the mouth of the Gambia, the RAC on occasion established factors quite far up the river, but scattered individuals were easily over-awed by native rulers, and trade from sloops or yachts commonly seemed a safer proposition; five such vessels were in use in the mid-1680s. 'Senegambia', as this region is commonly called, had once provided a great proportion of the slaves shipped to the New World, but its importance in that respect had, relatively, much declined. Ivory, beeswax and hides were valuable items of trade, along with a substance named 'gum Senegal' which came from acacia trees and was prized in textile manufacture. The RAC, in the reign of James II, tried to give up buying slaves altogether in this region, but in 1691 its agent reported from James Fort that when he refused several hundred slaves offered to him, African merchants did not bother to come down river with other goods. Slaves had to be bought, he said to 'keep up the credit of the trade'.[26] The James Island fort led an especially vexed existence. Deserted after French attack in 1695, it was resettled in 1699, abandoned again ten years later, resumed in 1713. (Then in 1719 it was vacated once more, for a couple of years, after a raid by a Welsh pirate named Howel Davis.)

Further south, the RAC had posts in Sierra Leone – at Bence Island and at York Island on the Sherbro River. Around here the main attraction was red-wood, a coveted dye. From the Sherbro to the Gold Coast stretched the 'Wind-ward Coast' where no Europeans settled and trade was conducted solely from ships; yet in the 1680s more goods were consigned from England by the RAC to this region than to any other section of Guinea, and the Company's agents in the Gold Coast were very jealous of the 'Windward' trade.

However, the Gold Coast remained far and away the chief centre of European competition. By 1700 there were about thirty-five white posts there, several meriting the name of 'castles'. The Swedes had dropped out early. The Danes by the 1680s were reduced to a precarious trade with interlopers, and in 1685 they sold one of their bases to the RAC; but about this time the Brandenburg Prussians set up shop at 'Gros Friedrichsburg', purchased in turn by the Dutch some thirty years later. The RAC, besides Cape Coast Castle, had several smaller factories. Slaves from this region had a remarkable reputation in the West Indies, where they were known as 'Coromantees'. They often led revolts there, and some planters eschewed them, but experts valued them highly. ' ... Very bold, brave and sensible,' noted one slaving captain. Christopher Codrington, governor of the Leewards, wrote of them in 1701 with the affection which men normally reserve for good horses or motor cars. 'All born heroes,' he called them, adding, 'My Father, who had studied the genius and temper of all kinds of negroes forty-five years with a very nice observation, would say, noe Man deserv'd a Corramante that would not treat Him like a Friend rather than a Slave.'[27]

So the RAC aimed to get as many slaves as possible from the Gold Coast. But its vessels cammonly had to fall back on other sections to make weight. They would press on towards the despised human wares of the 'Slave Coast' and Angola. East of the River Volta, slaves were virtually the only item brought to trade. The RAC were established at Whydah (Ouidah) from 1683. It became a free port where factors from several nations competed. Captain Thomas Phillips, who sailed for the RAC in 1694 and wrote the most vivid picture we have of conditions on the Guinea coast at that time, bought 1,300 slaves in nine weeks there in 1694. Though the 'King' of the place walked barefoot through the mud and water of his palace yard 'with as little concern as any of his poor subjects', Phillips was told that he could raise 40,000 of the latter within a day, and when he gave audience he was surrounded by 'nobility upon their knees'. Phillips, however, was not overimpressed. 'When we were entered, the king peep'd upon us from behind a curtain, and beckon'd us to him; whereupon we approach'd close to his throne, which was of clay, raised about two foot from the ground, and about six foot square, surrounded with old dirty curtains, always drawn betwixt him and his cappasheirs [headmen], whom he will not allow the sight of his handsome phiz. He had two or three little black children with him, and was smoking tobacco in a long wooden pipe, the bole of which, I dare say, would hold an ounce, and rested upon his throne, with a bottle of brandy and a little dirty silver cup by his side; his head was tied about with a roll of coarse calicoe, and he had a loose gown of red damask to cover him.'[28]

But this disagreeable man was amply strong enough to dictate terms to Europeans. He and his kind, the quite petty rulers of towns on the Gold and Slave Coasts and in the Niger Delta, were certainly not helpless victims of white rapacity. They were as shrewd in their dealings as the city fathers of London or Bristol.

In other places, individual African merchants became virtually 'kings' in their own right, like John Claessen, de facto ruler of Fetu in the late 1650s, or John Konny, who from 1711 controlled the possessions of the Brandenburgers whom he served; when they sold out to the Dutch in 1717, he refused to hand over and successfully resisted for several years. Dutch and English competed for the good will of John Kabes of Komenda, a merchant prince whose profits came not only from the slaves and ivory which he bought from inland traders and resold to Europeans, but also from the flotilla of canoes which he hired out to the whites to enable them to move their goods from fort to fort, from the salt-making industry in which he engaged, and from his maize farms, worked by slave labour, which supplied both factories and ships with their daily bread.

In many respects, such African middlemen had the whip hand. Europeans did not at first like advancing credit to men who could supply them with slaves, but they had perforce to do so, and found them no more and no less honest than themselves. Slaving was no crude exchange of human beings for rum; Africans were selective, demanding customers. When the English tried to sell them bad trade guns, they insisted on better. Nor were they easily fobbed off with rum adulterated by sea-water. They were, after all, up to tricks of their own, filling the middle of cast ingots with lead, mixing brass filings with gold dust and treating the skins of sick slaves with palm oil and lime juice so as to give them the gloss of health. Their demands for goods were extremely various; an experienced trader reckoned that 150 different commodities were required for trade on the Gold Coast alone, and from there the RAC received a plea in 1707 (mentioning several different species of textile), 'It is true that we are well supplied with perpetts and sheets, which are the two staple commodities, but we humbly conceive that it would be for your interest always to supply us with some of every sort of more current commodities such as gune [sic], gunpowder, tallow, knives, sayes, blankets, carpets, pewter basons, lead bars, iron bars, India and Guinea stuffs, niconees, brawles and tapseels ... '[29]

Even on the Gold Coast, where it was relatively thickest, European population at the end of the seventeenth century was minuscule. The Dutch were most numerous, with something over 350 in this area. The Danes and Brandenburgers had perhaps 170 men between them. The English in this part numbered somewhere over 200. (Though at peak, in the 1680s, the RAC had had over 300 men between James Fort and Whydah.) Captain Phillips was contemptuous of the 'small white square house' at Succandy, which was supposed to be a fort, though its eight or ten little guns were 'good for nothing but to waste powder, being all honeycomb'd within, and the carriages rotten and out of order', while the Agent was raving mad in his bed on account of a quarrel with a Dutch merchant over a mulatto girl. But Cape Coast Castle was quite impressive, with brick walls 14 feet thick, plenty of great guns, rum vaults, workshops, repositories for up to 1,000 slaves. The white garrison here was always over 50 and sometimes over 100, apart from 'castle slaves' and African artisans. The Agent General, based here, commanded RAC employees elsewhere on the Gold Coast, and normally at Whydah as well – some fourteen or fifteen settlements.[30]

The aim of such forts was threefold – to facilitate trade by installing experienced staff with a permanent stock of goods, to impress the natives, and to act as a defence against pirates and enemies. None of these advantages was conclusively achieved. Goods rotted in the climate. Even Cape Coast Castle could not have stood up to a determined drive to push whites into the sea. Ironically, the forts' main effect may have been to create and preserve a balance of power, as between Dutch and English, which enabled interlopers to flourish by playing one company against the other. The forts had some power over the African settlements which grew round them. But Sir Dalby Thomas, Agent General early in the eighteenth century, was a would-be Cortés or Clive in the wrong place at the wrong time. He told his employers in 1706 that if he had a hundred and fifty good soldiers he could destroy the Kingdom of Fetu which ruled around Cape Coast and 'foarse an inland trade'. But even when he succeeded in installing a supposedly pro-English Queen of Fetu, against the Dutch candidate, he shortly had to report that the lady in question was 'very villainous in turning the trade from us underhand.' There was no question of 'forcing' trade with the interior when middlemen at the coast could successfully block the whites from any direct contact with their sources of slaves and could always find means to starve out a cantankerous garrison. Here and elsewhere, the Europeans paid tribute to native rulers in return for possession of their forts. Even the sizeable mulatto population which had arisen from natural incontinence could not be relied on to be subservient. Sir Dalby had to drive away a remarkable mulatto named Edward Barter whom the RAC had educated in London and sent back as an agent; he had made himself an independent trader, controlling all the commerce of Cape Coast, and flaunted his own miniature fort and personal army.[31]

Cohabitation with black or mulatto 'wives' – very cheap to keep, Phillips noted, and docile because they could be turned away at pleasure – was almost the only solace available in the notorious climate, which, in their different seasons, provided scorching heat, torrential rain, thick fogs and piercing cold Harmattan winds. Men drank from fear of death, and so hastened their deaths. Phillips entertained a Dutch factor aboard his ship, 'and after dinner we found him to be a boon companion, taking his glass off smartly, and singing and dancing by himself several jiggs, capt. *Shurley* and I being indisposed, and in no dancing humour; I was glad to see he could be so cheerful that had liv'd so many years in such a dismal country ... ' He noted that the place where dead whites were buried by the factory of Whydah was 'call'd, very improperly, the hog-yard'.[32]

Survivors were hardly likely to be remarkable for their refined feelings. Nor were men of high culture easily drawn to the coast. The RAC, unlike the EIC, banned 'private trading' by its agents after 1680, but there was very little local coastwise trade anyway, and scant chance of an agent growing rich. The ban encouraged factors in their general proclivity to bad faith and fraud, and meanwhile added to the disincentives which made personnel hard to find. Left short of English employees, the RAC had to turn to foreigners. In the 1690s, about three-quarters of the men at Cape Coast seem to have been non-English, and Phillips found that of the three chief merchants in charge there (this triumvirate was an unsuccessful device by which the RAC aimed at saving an Agent General's salary) one was a Roman Catholic Irishman and another was a Scot – 'a very sober quiet honest man, and understood accounts to perfection.' The chaplain was Irish (presumably Protestant), the surgeon was another Scot.[33]

The nature of the main business, slaving, was itself a deterrent, of course, even then. Captain Phillips returned from his slaving voyage in 1694 so ill that he gave up the sea and retired to his native Wales, where he wrote that blacks 'excepting their want of christianity and true religion, (their misfortune more than fault) are as much the works of God's hands, and no doubt as dear to him as ourselves ... I can't think there is any intrinsick value in one colour more than another, nor that white is better than black, only we think it so because we are so ... ' Such humility and freedom from prejudice were, of course, exceptional even in his day, yet others, like him, would have found the trade physically disgusting.

He haggled at Whydah every day for nine weeks at the 'trunk' where the African middlemen collected their slaves, and he often fainted with the stench, 'it being an old house where all the slaves are kept together, and evacuate nature where they lie, so that no jakes can stink worse ... ' To meet growing European insistence on speedy delivery, African traders took to storing slaves in such warehouses, 'barracoons', and in some cases whites themselves established floating barracoons in hulks off shore. The slave had to survive conditions in these places after a journey from his point of capture which seems often to have been very long indeed. Once purchased, each slave was carefully scrutinised, with the aim of discarding the elderly and the diseased, especially those who suffered from V.D. 'Our surgeon,' Phillips wrote, 'is forc'd to examine the privities of both men and women, with the nicest scrutiny, which is a great slavery, but what can't be omitted.' The Captain's problems did not end there. 'The negroes are so wilful and loth to leave their own country, that they have often leap'd out of the canoes, boat and ship, into the sea, and kept under water till they were drowned ... they having a more dreadful apprehension of Barbadoes than we can have of hell ... ' Sharks swarmed round the slave ships and, according to Phillips's information, followed them to the West Indies in expectation of dead blacks thrown overboard.[34]

On the voyage, white men had to supervise blacks who vastly outnumbered them. Big ships were used. They had to be heavily manned – thirty or forty seamen at least, and sixty or seventy in the largest vessels which could carry four or five hundred slaves. Proportionately, it seems, more white seamen than slaves would lose their lives, commonly to the killer mosquito. 'Beware and take care, Of the Bight of Benin,' sang the sailors, 'For one that comes out, There are forty go in.' This was a 'grave of seamen, rather than a nursery.' Crews were hard to find; men were commonly pressed aboard against their wills, and many deserted once the West Indies were reached. On shipboard, slave revolts were frequent, and savage measures were taken by frightened whites. 'I have been inform'd', wrote Phillips, 'that some commanders have cut off the legs and arms of the most wilful, to terrify the rest ... I was advised by some of my officers to do the same but I could not be perswaded to entertain the least thoughts of it ... ' From the early eighteenth century, however, comes the horrific case of Captain Harding of Bristol, who made slave mutineers eat the heart and liver of one of their number, and hoisted a woman rebel up by her thumbs so that she could be whipped and slashed with knives in full view of the rest, until she died. In the early days, 'covetous' captains overcrowded their ships, and the death rate on the Middle Passage in the 1680s may have averaged nearly 25 per cent. (It fell markedly during the eighteenth century.)[35]

Phillips was overloaded. The 'white flux' killed 320 out of the 700 slaves aboard his *Hannibal*.[36] This mortifying loss no doubt enhanced his disillusionment with the trade. But the purely physical horrors of the Middle Passage should not be exaggerated. White indentured servants, even free immigrants, suffered appalling conditions on shipboard in the Atlantic, and often their mortality rates were as high. Seamen were brutally treated as a matter of course, and sadistic captains were certainly not confined to this one trade. Transmitting slaves became an expert craft as time wore on. The captain's job was to get his cargo to port; he would be rewarded accordingly. A sensible slaving skipper made sure that his valuable freight received plenty of food and exercise and kept his ship as clean as he could. Even Captain Harding merely whipped the ringleaders of the rebellion, since their price would be high in the West Indies. The worst horrors of the trade were psychological. Africans suffered extreme shocks, while the Europeans who stayed in the trade were inured to the treatment of other people as items of merchandise. One slaver noted laconically that, when slaves had tried to starve themselves to death, he had been 'necessitated sometimes to cause the teeth of these wretches to be broken ... and thus have forced some sustenance into their throats.' The same man observed (and other evidence bears him out) that the Africans thought that the white men were cannibals and that they were being carried like livestock to the slaughter.[37]

Phillips remarked of his fellow slaving captains that 'they would deceive their fathers in their trade if they could.' Yet their profession carried little or no stigma, at this time. There seemed to be no way of doing without the trade.

The RAC, noting that its monopoly of African products imported direct to England was far more profitable than its trade in slaves, would have preferred, from the mid-1690s, to give the latter up altogether. Sierra Leone dyewood could be bought for goods worth about £3 a ton and sold in London for £40 or more; the direct voyage there and back was shorter than the 'triangular' passage via the West Indies, and there was no need to give credit to cheating planters. Why could not plantations be established in Africa itself? The answer was that cheap African labour was more valuable in the New World; the temptation to export any worker was too high. The RAC's attempt to plant indigo in Sierra Leone from 1687 was abandoned within fifteen years. West Indian interests were in any case jealous. Sir Dalby Thomas experimented with seeds in the Gold Coast, but the RAC, under pressure from the West India lobby, asked its factors not to cultivate any more cotton or sugar cane.[38]

Some Africans wanted to sell slaves; New World planters were clamouring for them; between the two, the relative unimportance of trade in African produce was confirmed. Triangular, not direct trade was to be the prevailing pattern. At first the RAC terminated the contracts of its hired ships in the West Indies, but full triangular voyages became common after 1689. Such a voyage generally took between nine and eighteen months. The slaving part was not a source of secure profit. Slavers required larger crews than other ships, expensive provisioning, heavy armaments, and after the outlays on these there remained a risk of disastrous loss among the perishable human cargo. Furthermore, the trade was intensely competitive. But such competition shows that contemporaries saw it as a way to grow rich.

While the English share in the slave trade would grow, English dominance in sugar production would be lost to the French in the second quarter of the eighteenth century. But for the moment it was assured. Production in the English islands doubled or trebled between 1660 and 1700, and at the latter date, they seem to have been providing nearly half the sugar consumed in Europe, while the Caribbean trade accounted for 7 per cent of all English merchant tonnage and 11 per cent of the value of the country's overseas commerce. The islands exported to England commodities worth over £700,000 per year (1698–1700); by comparison, goods from Virginia and Maryland were worth only £230,000.[39]

The stimulus which the triangular trade gave to English manufactures can be inferred from the pattern of RAC exports. Besides re-exporting East India textiles to Guinea, the Company depended in early days on goods acquired in Europe – iron and copper from Sweden or Germany and trade guns from Holland rather than the inferior English ones which the Africans would not take. But this dependence was outgrown very rapidly. English rum replaced French brandy. Knives and the like, once bought in Amsterdam, were made in the English Midlands, where between 1690 and 1701 Samuel Banner of Birmingham supplied the RAC with over 400,000 knives and 7,000 swords.

Demand for long runs of identical, cheap items harbingered industrial revolution. By the beginning of the eighteenth century, guns of the Dutch type were mass-produced and the cheap fabrics once obtained from Dutch suppliers gave way to Devonshire serges.[40]

The importance of Africa to England was symbolised by the making of a new coin, the 'guinea', from the fine gold which the RAC imported; half a million were issued between 1673 and 1713.[41] Large numbers of people in and around London and Bristol profited directly from the slave trade; this was a time when great men and little liked to invest in a one-eighth, or one-sixteenth, or smaller share in a ship. Liverpool men were now moving in, led by the Norris family, lords of the manor of Speke Hall yet also most active merchants, who dominated life in and around the port. Thomas Norris was Sheriff of Lancashire and M.P. for Liverpool. Sir William Norris was ambassador to the Great Mogul. Richard Norris was Lord Mayor of Liverpool in 1700. Instructions to the Captain of a slaving ship, the *Blessing*, which the family sent out in October of that year reveal 'the combination of Christian piety, ruthlessness and commercial *savoir faire*' with which the Norrises did business. He was ordered to go via Kinsale in Ireland and pick up provisions and other necessaries for his voyage there. He was to sail on to Africa. 'I hope you will slave your ship easy and what shall remain over as above slaving your ship lay out in teeth [ivory] which are there reasonable ... ' Then he was to proceed to the West Indies and load up with 'sugar, cottons, ginger if to be had ... We leave the whole management of the concern to you and hope the Lord will direct you for the best ... Endeavour to keep all your men sober for intemperance in the hot country may destroy your men and so ruin your voyage ... We commit you to the care and protection of the Almighty ... '[42]

Cotton, 'if to be had', would have served the growing Lancashire textile industry. The African trade was essential to its rise. A third of Manchester's textile exports went there up to 1770, while half went to the West Indies and the American colonies.[43] The industry might have been strangled in infancy by the competition of Indian textiles. But there was a vast demand for these latter in Guinea. Hence both the Lancashire clothiers and the EIC could thrive.

IV

The East India Company had acquired its first territory in 1659. The tiny island of Pulo Run in the Bandas had been returned by the Dutch under the treaty of five years earlier. It was never in fact reclaimed. The expedition sent out to occupy it was diverted instead to the uninhabited island of St Helena in the South Atlantic. The excellent climate had made this a place of refreshment for Company ships since the earliest days. The aim now was to countervail Dutch occupation of the Cape of Good Hope and to secure a base from which homeward bound ships could be convoyed. The EIC put in a resident governor, though at first it was hard to find settlers. The spot was excruciatingly lonely. By 1670 there were no more than forty-eight whites and eighteen blacks on the island.[44]

The value of this diminutive possession should not be underestimated, even though its future would be eclipsed by that of Bombay, a second island which the EIC acquired from Charles II in 1668. It lay well south of the factory of Surat, which within twenty years it had supplanted as the centre of EIC operations in Western India. It offered a superb harbour. It also gave independence; on this small patch the EIC was supreme and the Mughal emperor or his governor could not seize its possessions as he pleased. Merchants of all races were attracted to such a promising site, and within a few years the population, so it was said, rose from 10,000 to 60,000, which would have made it, after London, the second city of the empire. Yet its early days under EIC rule were fraught with problems. The spot was extremely unhealthy for Europeans. The English there soon acquired a proverb, 'Two Monsoons are the Age of a Man.' Of twenty-four passengers who arrived in one ship at the start of the rainy season, twenty had been buried before it ended.[45] Bombay stood among tidal marshes. As in Africa, the English failed to identify their real enemies; they blamed the 'unhealthfulness of the air' on the local practice of manuring coconut trees with small fish, named 'Buckshoe', which putrefied and were held to cause a kind of fog.

The pirates of the Malabar Coast were a menace to shipping. The mainland, which itself produced little of commercial value, was held by pugnacious Marathas who were at war with the Mughal. Beyond this, the Dutch remained a danger. Gerald Aungier, President at Surat from 1669 to 1677, lined the shore at Bombay with Martello towers, completed a main fortress with heavy ordnance and sixty light fieldpieces, and drummed up a militia among the residents, which he stiffened with over 400 regular soldiers, mostly European or Eurasian, telling his masters in London that trade here could only be carried on sword in hand. Then, in 1672, he moved to Bombay himself. The show of force which the place made deterred a Dutch fleet from pressing its attack the next year. But Aungier could not prevent the Mughal and Maratha forces from bringing their naval war into the harbour.

A Fellow of the new Royal Society, John Fryer, who travelled to India in the early 1670s, looked wryly upon Bombay. Aungier, when he dined, had 'Trumpets usher in his Courses, and Soft Musick at the Table'; he went out in a coach drawn by large milk-white oxen, or was carried in a palanquin. Yet, Fryer observed, 'for all this Gallantry, I reckon they walk but in Charnel houses ... ' The EIC had sent out Englishwomen, but their children were 'sickly', more so than those of mixed race. Fryer noted that the natives and seasoned Portuguese lived to 'a good Old Age' and plausibly attributed this to their temperance. The English, here and at Surat, as he portrayed them, were almost at the mercy of the native trading class, the *Vani*, whom they called 'Banyans', and who, Fryer said, hung on them 'like Horse-leeches' sucking both '*Sanguinem*

& Succum (I mean Mony) ... ' At Surat, when the ships were in, the factory was 'in a continual hurly burly, the *Banyans* presenting themselves from the hour of Ten till Noon; and then Afternoon at Four till Night ... below stairs, the Packers and Warehouse-keepers, together with Merchants bringing and receiving Musters, make a meer *Billinsgate*; for if you make not a Noise, they hardly think you intent on what you are doing.' The EIC maintained a master to teach its young servants to read and write the native language, and there was some financial incentive to learn. Yet few tried, and fewer succeeded. In ignorance of the speech of the country, the English remained under the thumbs of native brokers.[46]

The position at Madras was similar, the EIC's Chief Merchants at Fort St George were Indians. Of these, Kasi Viranna ('Verona') came in the late 1670s to be head of a joint stock known as 'Cassa Verona and Company'. He purchased all imported English merchandise, and all orders of native goods for export were given to him for execution through his agents. This remarkable man could neither read nor write. He passed as a Muslim among Muslims, but as a Hindu among Hindus, and the EIC relied on his good standing with officials and courtiers. When he died in 1680, thirty guns were fired in tribute at the fort.[47]

At Madras the EIC controlled a strip of land some six miles long by one broad, acquired, as we have seen, in 1639. For this it paid a quite stiff annual rent to a local ruler, but it was able to administer its own justice. Inside the walls of the 'White Town' Europeans enjoyed trial by jury before the Agent and Council. In the 'Black Town' which had sprung up alongside, the junior of the three Councillors acted as magistrate, flogging, fining and gaoling at discretion, but the role of keeping order and presenting offenders was carried out by an Indian known as the Pedda Naik. Here, as in Bombay, the English chief spared no expense to impress orientals with his dignity; the Agent, in 1674, was described as having a personal guard of three or four hundred 'Blacks' and as never going abroad 'without Fifes, Drums, Trumpets and a Flag with two Balls in a Red Field; accompanied with his Council and Factors on Horseback with their Ladies in *Palenkeens*.' He hanged natives when he pleased, and Englishmen for 'piracy' — an offence which could be broadened to include crossing a strip of water (the fort had a river behind it) with property which might be presumed stolen. Yet such pomp and powers were accorded to a man whose salary stood at no more than £300 a year.[48] Middle-class Englishmen were already picking up strange habits in India.

The Agent was chief over all the scattered English factories on the East Coast. Madras itself had perhaps 40,000 people around 1670. Many Portuguese had taken up residence there. It was a most cosmopolitan town, and extremely remote from England. In the mid-1660s, Sir Edward Winter, superseded by a new Agent sent from home, seized and imprisoned this intruder, charged him with treason, and stayed in control for nearly three years, till a fleet with a royal mandate persuaded him to hand over peacefully; he was let off scot free. Insubordination continued. In 1678 the redoubtable Sir Streynsham Master became Agent. Though he had first seen India at the age of sixteen, he was the son of a country gentleman, and rather more polished than most EIC servants. In his three years of rule, he erected, at Madras, the first Anglican church in India (it would remain unique for many years) and attempted to bring some order in among the EIC servants in Bengal.

The Bengal factories were reputed the laxest in India. The main EIC settlement, dating from the mid-century, was at Hugli, long the chief mart of Western Bengal and a renowned centre of weaving. By Master's day there were two other main factories at Cassimbazar and Balasore, three outlying ones, and one small agency. The chief of all was an unscrupulous person named Matthias Vincent. The EIC accused him of 'Diabolical arts with Braminees', of exercising charms and of using poisons, but what worried them most was his bold trading in his own interest, his ready palm for a bribe, and the countenance which he gave to interlopers. The thirty-odd men under him were a drunken and quarrelsome bunch, who showed little respect for the collegiate regime under which EIC servants in India were still supposed to live; Master attempted to fine them for drunkenness, for staying out after 9 p.m. and for failing to turn up to prayers, and threatened 'condigne punishment' for 'Adultery, Fornication, uncleanness ... ' The general tendency, in this humid place, was for Englishmen to take to Indian ways of living, wearing native dress and marrying Indian wives.[49]

The trade pursued here grew and grew in importance. Bengal, besides its abundance of wheat and rice, sugar and hemp, flax and opium, teemed with weavers producing desirable textiles — silk 'taffaties', the striped or checked cotton cloth known as 'gingham' and a variety of other cotton wares plain and patterned. The EIC's servants slid into a role much like that of merchant clothiers in English country districts. They organised, and exploited, native weavers. Vincent reported in 1676 that 'taffatyes' were procured by 'sending round the Towne and other adjacent places' to the individual weavers, whose numbers had so much increased in recent years that a piece of cloth costing 15 rupees a dozen years before was now 'made and sent home at between 6 and 7 ... ' To these weavers the EIC men advanced money, thus getting them under their control; it was now becoming easier, Vincent wrote, to persuade them to comply with the written contracts which specified quality, colour and so forth best suited to meet demand in England.[50] Beyond all this, the Company, in the 1670s, actually sent out skilled English silkworkers to Bengal — throwsters, dyers, and weavers — to orientate, as it were, the production of goods for the European market.

Bengal also provided saltpetre, a commodity vital to English interests, both in India and in Europe, during an age of almost continuous warfare. By 1680 the EIC's annual investment in Bengal had reached £150,000.[51] And the area

30 In this racist depiction (published in 1803), a cowering Cudjoe makes peace with the British

31 Africans carrying slaves to ships off the Gold Coast, by Johannes Kip

32 Prince of Wales Fort, Hudson's Bay, as seen in the 1770s

33 An eighteenth-century view of Sandy Point, St Kitts, looking across to the smuggler's paradise, St Eustatius

was a magnet for interlopers. Technically, any Englishman sailing the eastern seas without EIC permission was an 'interloper', including the pirates who preyed on all comers from bases in Madagascar and elsewhere. But serious traders were also involved; they could drive a lucrative commerce, selling their ships in the East and remitting the proceeds covertly through the Dutch East India Company, or taking the risk of bringing their rewards home in the form of diamonds and pearls. And EIC servants and agents were commonly friendly; interlopers could provide them with freight for their own private commerce.

EIC servants were barred from trade in the most valuable Indian commodities. But this did not stop them from amassing large fortunes, if they lived and were lucky. They could buy goods which they then sold at a profit to the EIC, and could throw onto the Company bad debts advanced in their private trade. The worst goods might be sent home in the EIC shipments, the best reserved for their own use in the 'country trade'. This commerce along the Asian coasts was engaged in by the EIC on its own account – Sir Josiah Child reported in 1681 that 25 EIC vessels were trading from port to port in the East. In any one of these, as Master had noted, there might be no more than half a dozen English sailors, the rest of the crew being made up of thirty or forty 'INDIANS called LASCARS'; the latter word would remain in use down to our own day.[52] The profits from 'country trade' remained essential to the Company because they reduced the quantity of bullion which it had to export.

Apart from precious metals, the chief EIC exports into the East remained lead, iron and cloth. Woollen exports to India quadrupled in value between 1664 and 1685,[53] but even now English cloth could not command markets to match those found in Britain and Europe by the products which the EIC fleets brought back.

Tea was first imported in the mid-seventeenth century. Trade with China provided it. EIC servants in Surat had used it since the 1630s at least, though strictly as an auxiliary to harder liquors. It was first purchased or drunk in England in the 'coffee houses' which opened in London from the early 1650s. After Catharine of Braganza brought the tea-drinking habit with her from Portugal, it acquired high fashion. The EIC drew in regular shipments from about 1670. Thus in 1685, the directors wrote to Madras, 'In regard *Thea* is grown to be a commodity here and wee have occasion to make presents therein to our great friends at Court, we would have you to send us yearly 5 or 6 canisters of the very best and freshest Thea. That which will colour the water in which it is infused most of a greenish complexion is generally best accepted.' At this time, tea was thought a fine medicine and had 'the Repute of prevailing against the Headach, Gravel, and Griping in the Guts ... '[54] It was heavily taxed in England, and this restricted its popularity, but by the late 1690s, imports were running at between 70,000 and 100,000 lb. a year. Then, from the early years of the eighteenth century, the spread of tea-drinking made the leaf (still generally Chinese in origin) prime among all the smuggler's choice wares.

N

Pepper, indigo, and cotton yarn also found buyers but textiles, in Charles II's day, were the EIC's chief, and most controversial, import, rising from an average of 160,000 pieces a year in the 1660s to 750,000 by the 1680s, with a peak total of no less than 1,700,000 in 1684. As well as taffetas and ginghams, there flooded in chintzes and quilts and 'Bastards', 'Cassaes ... Mulmulls ... Silk Romalls ... Nillaes ... Fine Humhums'. 'In some things,' a parson who visited Surat wrote, 'the Artists of *India* out-do all the Ingenuity of *Europe, viz.* in the painting of Chites [chintz] or Callicoes, which in *Europe* cannot be parallell'd, either in the brightness and life of the Colours, or in their continuance upon the Cloath.' Besides, Indian labour was cheap. English woollen interests inveighed against 'Heathens, who work for a penny a day and destroy Christians', as one of their spokesmen in the House of Commons put it in 1677. The class-conscious complaint was heard that even kitchenmaids could afford to wear Indian scarves.[55]

The English silk industry seemed imperilled. The EIC in the early 1680s was, from one side of its mouth, ordering raw silk from Bengal with the unctuous explanation that it would 'set the poor on work' at manufactures at home, and with the other, clamouring for wrought silk – 'there is nothing so difficult but may be effected where the material & Silk, and midwife labour are so cheap, as with you.' The merchants in London who traded with Turkey were as aghast as the English silk manufacturers. With the woollen interests, both joined the powerful coalition which was assembling against the EIC, along with whigs suspicious of the Company's close relations with the Stuart Court, economists who deplored its bullion exports, and interlopers and others who wanted a free, or freer, trade with the East. A pamphlet of 1676, which advocated a 'regulated' trade, denounced the EIC for its '*Monopoly* of *Monopolies*, that restrains almost all *English men* from their lawful Visiting, and Trafficking into so many parts of *Asia, Affrica*, and *America* as includes *half* the *world*.' It violated the rights of 'Free-born Englishmen' that the Company should have arbitrary power to punish Englishmen and seize their goods in '*half* the *world*'.[56]

There were thus two bizarrely conjoined trends of attack. One suggested that all trade in textiles with the East was injurious. The other, taken by those who wanted to enter that very trade, denounced the EIC, its monopoly and all its works, with the aim of securing a new and less exclusive organisation. The EIC could count on the firm friendship, sweetened with annual cash gifts, of Charles II – who once asked the Company to fetch from India for him 'one Male, and two Female Blacks, but they must be Dwarfs, and of the least size that you can procure'[57] – and then of James II. It also had, in Sir Josiah Child, a pamphleteer as fertile, sage, and inventive as any who might be found to enter the field against it.

Child was a director of the Company from 1673, its governor in 1681–3 and again in 1686–8, its deputy governor during the rest of the 1680s, and then as a grey eminence, dominant figure in its councils until he died in 1699. His power was based on his vast individual shareholding and he justified his virtual dictator-ship on the grounds that 'a small interest will never awaken a man so often in the night.' He was, justly, accused of defending his policies with the help of lavish bribes, and also of manipulating the market in EIC shares by putting about rumours of losses at sea. He would send one set of brokers out shaking their heads and implying bad news, with shares of his own to sell, then, as people rushed to unload, another set of his brokers would begin to buy. By selling say £10,000 worth at a small loss, he would be able to buy up ten times as much at a far lower price. Then, a few weeks later, he could reverse the procedure and as everyone fell to buying, sell at a great profit.[58]

This was, it should now be clear, one of the deeper minds of that era. He was too much for his rival, the whiggish Thomas Papillon, deputy governor under him, when the latter in 1681 manoeuvred to wind the Company up and to open a new subscription book to all and sundry. Child met the general arguments against East Indian trade by conceding, as he had to, that his Company imported more than it exported, and carried out of the land much gold and silver. But he had the point on his side that EIC re-exports to Europe, running at £500,000 or so per year, brought home considerable profit. Anyway, no English goods would be sold in the East at all if the EIC did not export them. The 'twenty five to thirty Sail of the most War-like Ships in *England*' which it constantly employed were, like its imports of saltpetre, a great addition to national strength. Its exotic imports gave employment, in their handling, to as many people in England as they deprived of work, while textiles from the East were cheaper than those which would otherwise be bought from actual or potential enemy countries in Europe. ' ... The Taffities have so great an Advantage of Florence Sarsnets and French Avignions, that they have caus'd a general disuse of them throughout the Kingdom.' Child could sum up impressively the posture of EIC affairs in 1681. The year before, the Company had sent out four three-deck ships, each carrying over a hundred seamen, to the Bay of Bengal and the Coromandel Coast, three of like size to Surat and the West Coast of India, two more big ones to Bantam and two smaller ones to China and the South Seas. The total stock contained in all these had been £479,946. 15s. 6d.; this year, it would be raised to £600,000.[59]

These figures, of course, would not appease those whose prime grudge was against monopoly. But Child's case for monopoly proved, in effect, unanswer-able. In casuistic defence of the EIC's restrictiveness against those who argued that there were not more than eighty real merchants in it, he argued both ways at once, that there were in fact 556 stockholders, and anyway, why shouldn't some people have vast holdings? – such gripes must come 'out of the mouth of an Old Leveller'. But he had the strong points to put that England must have a powerful company in the field to match those of Holland and France; that joint stock was the only safe way to carry on the trade; that the EIC's factories and forts had cost it over £300,000; that it had to deal in the East with over 100 kings and rajahs and that if it were abolished at least forty ambassadors, each carrying large presents, would be required to support the English position. He professed himself a foe to monopoly in general, but this, he insisted, was a special case.[60] He was quite right.

The aggressive policies followed by the EIC in the East during the 1680s have normally been attributed to Sir Josiah in person. Yet it is hard to see how the Company, whoever led it, could have resisted the pressures insisting on muscularity. The areas where it traded had once more become violent and competitive. In India itself, the Mughal Emperor Aurangzeb, who ruled for forty-eight years, fought campaign after campaign in the south from 1681. In 1686-7 he crushed two independent powers, Bijapur and Golconda, which had survived in the Deccan, but then he spent the rest of his life struggling with the Marathas. He smashed their unified kingdom, and before his death in 1707 ruled, between Kabul and Madras, a larger political unit than the subcontinent has seen since; but bands of tough, ruthless Maratha horsemen continued to raid over vast areas. Meanwhile, the French were increasing their ambition in the East. Colbert's East India Company (1664) tried in the early 1670s to establish new posts in Ceylon and India, and by 1673 was settled in Pondicherry, south of Madras. It was poorly supported by businessmen at home. Fryer said of its factory at Surat in 1675 that it was 'better stor'd with *Monsieurs* than with Cash; they live well, borrow Money, and make a Shew.'[61] But French activities in South-east Asia looked very dangerous.

The Dutch were expanding their power in Indonesia. Over the Moluccas, they exerted a sordid tyranny, destroying cloves, nutmegs and mace, which they now monopolised, in the interest of keeping up prices. The English had long been established at Macassar, in Celebes, but in 1667 the Dutch prevailed on the local ruler there to expel all other Europeans except themselves. In Java, they took the first, portentous, involuntary steps towards conquest. To maintain their position at Batavia, they had to involve themselves in local politics. Called in to help the ruler of Mataram, they acquired great commercial privileges and much territory. The realm became virtually subject to them. In the early 1680s a similar intervention in the Sultanate of Bantam established Dutch control there also. The English were forced to leave their Bantam factory.

However, the EIC found a new base on Sumatra. The Dutch had just broken the control over the pepper trade there which had been exercised by the city-state of Atjeh. In 1685 the local rulers at Bengkulu – a place which the English would call 'Bencoolen' – anxious that the Dutch should have competition, signed a treaty giving the EIC a large tract of ground and a great measure of control over local supplies of pepper in return for a guaranteed price. The site was, to say the least, unhealthy. After a little over three months, in constant rain, the English chief was reporting: 'The Sick Lye Neglected, some cry for remedies but none to bee had: those that could eate have none to Cooke them victualls, soe that I may say the one dies for hunger & the other for want of

Remidies, soe that wee now have not liveing to bury the dead, & if one is sick the other will not watch, for hee Sayes that better one then two dies, Soe that people dies & noe notice taken thereof.' Yet the settlement survived, and others in West Sumatra followed. The English soon found enough heart to begin bullying the natives, enforcing compulsory planting of pepper and putting local rulers in the stocks when they failed to produce enough at the low price which was offered. An English visitor in 1690 thought the chief at Bencoolen 'brutish and barbarous'; this man later was recalled to Madras, which controlled the Sumatra factories, after many complaints against his treatment of the Indonesians.[62]

Meanwhile, in 1687, the EIC, under French provocation, went to war with Siam. King Narai (1657–1688) had welcomed English traders, and also French Catholic missionaries. The EIC bungled and wasted their chance. Their factory was short-lived, expiring after ten years in 1684. In that year, Louis XIV sent an ambassador with a large suite of priests and Jesuits. One aim was to convert Narai to Catholicism. Another, which was fulfilled, was to extract trading concessions. The cession of a garrison on the east coast of the Malay peninsula was, however, a disappointment for the French, who coveted Mergui on the west coast, a fine depot for shipbuilding and repairs and well placed for trade with the Coromandel Coast. It was currently a nest of English pirates and inter-lopers who flew the Siamese flag. Their chief surrendered to a pre-emptive EIC expedition, but Siamese forces then massacred the English, who had given themselves up to orgies on the shore. James II, despite his pro-French postures in Europe, was convinced by the EIC that Mergui must not fall into French hands. Elihu Yale, the Agent at Madras, was instructed to send a ship to seize the place, but the frigate which he despatched found that the French had already taken control. Louis XIV had sent six warships with orders to seize Mergui and also Bangkok. Narai had capitulated without a fight. However, in 1688, the Siamese rose against the foreigners, and the French had to evacuate. From then on, the rulers of Siam would, sensibly, be most chary of granting privileges to Europeans.

Baffled at Mergui, the Madras authorities found the dockyard they wanted at Syriam in Burma. The rulers of that country were uninterested in overseas trade and a short-lived EIC factory there had petered out in 1657. The EIC directors at home were against any new establishment at Syriam, but its servants in Madras obtained consent from the Burmese authorities and operated an unofficial factory and dockyard there for half a century from the 1690s. In this case, and at Bencoolen, the logic of events in the East dictated expansionist EIC policies on the spot against the wishes of the directors in London. Madras had no suitable harbour. Needs must.

Yet, with all this said, the London EIC's policies which were associated with Child, were aggressive, and came from the same stable as those followed in America and the West Indies by Child's royal friends and masters. In both cases the exercise of power proved rash and premature.

Child wrote to Madras late in 1687 that the EIC's aim was 'to establish such a politie of civill and military power, and create and secure such a large revenue to maintaine both ... as may bee the foundation of a large, well-grounded, sure English dominion in India for all time to come.'[63] This must not be misinterpreted as a precocious manifesto of conquest. Dominion 'in' India meant no more than the rule of certain safe places, Bombay, Madras, as centres of trade. The real thrust of the new policy was towards 'a large revenue' to support 'civil and military power'. The Company's rule over its servants and others must be asserted. The factories must be fortified and garrisoned till they were strong enough to repel Dutch, French, Marathas, Mughals, all-comers. The cost must be met through increased rents and customs dues and through municipal taxation. The new policy provoked resistance. In Bombay, the garrison revolted and its commandant, Keigwin, for a time ruled the settlement. In Madras, the inhabitants, now asked to pay the full cost of repairs and fortifications, went on strike against the house tax and were only brought to submission by the threat of expulsion. St Helena had seemed promising to Child. He thought of planting sugar, tobacco and indigo there. But the few hundred islanders were habitually mutinous, and the fourth rebellion there, in 1684, was the worst so far. Four ringleaders were hanged and other severe punishments were inflicted, but Child upbraided the governor for being too lenient and another high EIC official was ordered in to try the rebels. Jeffreys's Bloody Assizes were fresh in men's minds. St Helena saw a miniature counterpart, in 1685, with fourteen mutineers tried and condemned and five duly executed. The EIC's opponents at home raised a cry of tyranny.

Sir John Child, Sir Josiah's namesake but not his close relative, was a heavy-handed president in western India. When he was appointed, in 1686, to the new title of Captain General and Admiral and Commander-in-Chief of all the EIC's forces throughout its possessions, including Madras and Bengal, his powers matched those of Tyrconnell in Ireland, and, as we shall shortly see, of Andros in New England. Sir Josiah's new policy for Madras was shrewdly Machiavellian. He recognised that the people there would more willingly pay 'five shillings towards the public good, being taxed by themselves, than sixpence imposed by our despotical power – notwithstanding they shall submit to [it] when we see cause.' The EIC used its own authority, in 1687, to grant Madras a charter, erecting a corporation of a mayor, twelve Aldermen and sixty or more burgesses. The first aldermen appointed were an even stranger crew than the mixtures of papists and Quakers which James II was foisting on English towns. Only three were EIC servants. There were two Portuguese merchants, one French, three Jews, and three Hindus. This might look like a remarkable recognition of the right of coloured peoples to share in their own government, but Elihu Yale, in fact, overruled them as he pleased, and by 1690 the number of English aldermen had risen to eight.[64]

Charles II in 1683 had given the EIC permission to set up Admiralty Courts in the East and to confiscate the ships and goods of interlopers. The lengthy trial of one avowed interloper, Thomas Sandys, was used by the Company's opponents to raise in the English courts the whole question of the royal prerogative to create a monopoly in the India trade. Lord Chief Justice Jeffreys (who else?) gave judgment in 1685 for the King and for the EIC. Next year, with a new charter, James II confirmed the EIC in possession of all the jurisdiction, civil and military, which it could possibly want. Royal admirals and officers of justice were commanded to help the expression of its powers on land and at sea. Child boasted that the King had turned his Company from 'mere trading merchants' into 'the condition of a Sovereign State in India'.[65]

But it still couldn't repress Thomas Pitt, the most flamboyant of all interlopers. He was born in 1653, the son of a Dorset rector of gentle origins. He first went East in the EIC service as a seaman, but settled at Balasore in Bengal in 1674 and drove a lucrative trade there for seven years despite repeated commands from the EIC directors that he should be arrested and deported. Pitt sensibly married the niece of Vincent, the EIC chief at Hugli. In 1681 he boldly came home with his wife and their infant son, whose own son would one day be Earl of Chatham. The EIC procured a writ to prevent him leaving England, but he evaded it and sailed off again in the same year with chests full of money, to operate on a still larger scale. The EIC had already sent off William Hedges as Agent in Bengal, with orders to arrest Vincent. But Pitt caught him up on the way, entered Balasore eleven days before Hedges's arrival, and spread the report that there was a new Company and that he, Thomas Pitt, was its Agent.

Vincent took himself off into the Dutch factory with all his papers, under the protection of a guard of soldiers in his own pay. The EIC raged in vain against Pitt, this 'fellow of a haughty, huffying, daring temper', who paraded into Hugli with four or five files of well armed troops in red coats and 'great attendance of Native Soldiers with Trumpeters'. Hedges could make no headway against him, nor against Captain Alley, another interloper, who flaunted equal pomp in the Agent's face and who was privily visited by 'every considerable person' in the EIC factory.[66]

It was no use appealing to the Mughal's Bengal viceroy; Pitt could out-bribe the EIC. He and Vincent went home rich men in 1683. When they were arrested at the EIC's suit, each was able to give £40,000 security. Wealth, however gotten, must have its way. Vincent was knighted by James II, and Pitt, after four years' litigation, paid only a trifling fine. He became an M.P. in 1690 and bought control of two Commons seats, one of them the later notorious 'rotten borough' of Old Sarum. He was in fact the first of the great 'nabobs', using the wealth of the East to make himself powerful at home.

Meanwhile grand troubles, long maturing, came to the EIC in Bengal. Mughal officials demanded constant presents and bribes. (They were perhaps quite as avaricious as Blathwayt, the secretary of the Lords of Trade, or as Governor Dutton, who was currently making himself wealthy in Barbados.)

Shaista Khan, Aurangzeb's veteran viceroy, troubled the EIC with what they, and imperialist English historians after them, would choose to call 'exactions'. There was persistent friction over way dues and customs. The English tried to pull a very fast trick, manipulating a full stop in their translation of an edict (1680) by Aurangzeb which added a poll tax of $1\frac{1}{2}$ per cent to customs of 2 per cent, so as to make these charges seem to apply only in western India, not in Bengal.[67]

Hedges had come to agree with the leading EIC men in the province that 'the trade of this place could never be carryed on, and managed to the Company's advantage', till they 'fell out', quarrelled, with the Bengal government, and forced it 'to grant us better termes'. He had thought of seizing an island at the river mouth and trading from there. The Court of Directors in England, sublimely ignorant of the commerce and geography of Bengal, thought that Chittagong, which they believed to be on the Ganges, but which was in fact well to the east, would be a better bet. In any case, the aim must be a fortified settlement to which the English could withdraw when they were threatened and whence they could exercise a blockade to put pressure on the viceroy.[68]

Early in 1686, the directors decided to fight. The actions which followed were sometimes farcical, yet were of most serious importance. As a great historian has observed, one may recognise a major event by the fact that it has a sequel, and few have had sequels more impressive than those which stemmed from the foundation of Calcutta.

An expedition was equipped, six companies of infantry with ten warships. On the west coast of India, it was to cut off native shipping and declare war on the Mughal Emperor. On the east coast, it was to pick up, if possible, 400 more soldiers at Madras, bring away the EIC servants from Bengal, capture and fortify Chittagong (meanwhile seizing all Mughal ships at sea), then advance up the Ganges and extort a treaty from the viceroy of Bengal. In addition, it was to punish (by seizing his ships) the King of Siam for certain wrongs done to the Company, and was to drive the Portuguese out of certain dependencies of Bombay where, by treaty, they had no right to be. 'Of this vast programme, conceived in ludicrous ignorance of the geographical distances and with astounding disregard of the opposing forces, not a single item was carried out.' In the autumn of that year, just two ships with a few lightly armed tenders entered the Hugli with some 300 soldiers, intended to make war on an empire where the viceroy of Bengal alone could lead 40,000 men into action.[69]

The EIC chief in Bengal was now a resourceful man named Job Charnock. His birth had been obscure; his life was invested with romance. The English told after his death the story, perhaps even true, of how he had rescued a Hindu widow from the flames to which the custom of *sati* consigned her, had lived with her happily for many years, had set up a magnificent tomb for her, and sacrificed a cock there every year to her memory. Local Indians would fable show 'Chanak', facing great Mughal forces with only a few men and a single ship, caught the sun's rays with a burning glass and burnt the river face of the city of Hugli as far as Chandernagore. He had arrived in India in the mid-1650s, had been chief at the Patna factory for many years, and was an old hand thoroughly seasoned, to the point of adopting native customs and losing most traces of his own religion. Hedges, whose coming temporarily blocked his way to the overall headship in Bengal, was deeply suspicious of him, believing that he embezzled saltpetre, practised extortions upon the weavers and was in league with interlopers. All this seems likely, nor do the scandals related to Hedges about his dealings with native women seem implausible. Charnock certainly kept as his servant a white man, named Harding, whom the Company had dismissed for 'Blasphemy and Athisticall Tenetts' and who was, it appears, most adept at fornication. Charnock certainly bragged that 'never no chief was yett able to contend with him.' But he was also noted for his truculence towards the Mughal authorities, and he was uniquely esteemed by the directors at home, who lavished praise in their letters on 'our old and good servant Mr Charnock' and his 'integrity'. They must have thought that on balance he was worth money to them.[70]

The Mughal governor of Hugli moved against the English factory there in October 1686. Charnock commanded a strange assortment of soldiers – Hindu Rajput warriors who retained their own dress and customs, under their own officers, together with some native Christians who were known as 'Portuguese', and with a handful of English troops united with these in one company, which wore red uniforms trimmed with blue. Altogether, there were less than 400. They were now locked in by a Mughal force of 3,000 foot and 300 horse, virtually under siege, and forbidden to resort to the market. Three who did so, near the end of the month, were beaten up and imprisoned. An attempt to rescue them led to a skirmish. The English captured the Mughal battery and spiked its guns, but the Mughals burnt the factory and many small English craft. A truce followed. Charnock led his forces down river to a place called Sutanuti, some seventy miles from the sea, with a good anchorage for ocean-going ships which had long made it a centre of trade. The settlement stood on swampy banks with brackish malarial lagoons inland which stretched for over 100 square miles and made assault from the east impossible. It was an obvious place to go. It became the site of one of the greatest cities in the world. But not immediately. The viceroy would not come to terms and Charnock retreated to Hijili, on the coast, an island swamp full of wild beasts where a local landowner had previously agreed that the English might set up a fort and factories. From here, Charnock's men sacked the important town of Balasore.

Aurangzeb heard about this several weeks later. He was in the south, busy capturing Hyderabad. We may infer how little the news hurt him from the fact that he had to call for a map in order to find out where Hugli and Balasore were. Meanwhile, as the heat intensified through March and April, the English at Hijili began to run out of provisions and die. Mughal troops beset the island closely, and fired on it from a powerful battery. In mid-May, thousands of Shaista Khan's soldiers came up. The town of Hijili was seized, and only desperate fighting saved the English fort. Charnock now had scarcely 100 fit men, but he held out for four days, and then, by luck, 70 new English soldiers arrived, fresh (if that is the word) from Europe. These sallied with great effect next day. So Charnock cunningly sent men out in ones and twos, assembled them at the landing place, and then marched up what looked like another fresh body. The Mughals conceded an honourable truce, and the English left after three months' siege with drums beating and colours flying. By September, Charnock was installed at Sutanuti once more.

For a year he worked at building his factory there, while letters from the directors chided him for not proceeding to fulfil their grand design. Then Captain Heath arrived with a fresh naval force and ordered that Charnock's surviving troops must sail with him to Chittagong. Around the time that James II was deposed at home, but all unwitting of that event, Heath and Charnock abandoned Sutanuti again and set off down river. Early next year, the English arrived at Chittagong. Bathos supervened. The place was far too strong to attack, and Heath shortly sailed off for Madras. The Mughal Emperor was neither much amused nor much displeased. The English were no more to him than moles in his garden; and like moles, they had their uses. Aurangzeb first punished them; having conquered Golconda, he turned his local officers loose. The remaining Englishmen in Bengal were driven out. The factories at Masulipatam and Vizagapatam on the east coast were seized, as was Surat on the west. Bombay was attacked. But the English were still a danger to Indian sea-borne commerce and to the routes which took Indian pilgrims to Mecca. When Sir John Child, from Bombay, sued for peace at the end of 1689, Aurangzeb was not long in granting it. His conditions were that Child should be expelled (in fact he had just died), that the English made humble submission, that they paid a fine of 150,000 rupees, that they restored all the goods they had plundered, and that they promised to behave better in future.

So Charnock returned to Bengal after a new viceroy had released the English factors there and had guaranteed the English freedom from customs, as long as they kept up their old payment to him of 3,000 rupees a year. In August 1690 he was back at Sutanuti, where, by contrast with Hugli, the English could always bring up sea-going ships and use the guns of these to defend themselves. The former buildings had been burnt and Charnock's contingent had to live in boats while the rain fell on them steadily day and night. Next summer, those who survived fever were still dwelling only in 'Tents, hutts, and boats' and clamouring for their comfortable houses in Hugli.[71]

But within a decade, there was a busy new town with '1200 English inhabitants, of whom 460 were buried between the months of August and January in one year'. Indian and Armenian merchants congregated in 'Calcutta', as the place came to be called, and doomed Englishmen kept coming to try to profit from its commerce. Its effectual founder, Charnock, died early in 1693. His last years had been no more edifying than his earlier ones. His temper, never good, had grown worse. His successor as chief in Bengal accused him of having enforced no discipline and of having no regard for Christianity, so that 'severall of English men's black wives turned Papist that were not soe before.'[72] This man, Sir John Goldsborough, ejected the papist priests and pulled down their mass house. (Then he promptly died himself.) It is one of the charms, for us, of such a hard-boiled, courageous old rogue as Charnock, that pious Victorian hagiographers of the English in India would find it so hard to make his career yield suitable reading matter for young persons.

Besides creating Calcutta, the war against the Mughals confirmed the EIC in a new, and wiser, outlook. Land war against the emperor was now conceived to be impossible, though it was realised afresh that sea-power could in the end secure terms. The EIC 'made up its mind, once and for all', that it must trade from fortified places. But the war had cost the Company £400,000, over and above huge losses by shareholders, and by the King, through the interruption of trade. Shares fell in value (though a £100 share was still worth £190 in 1692).[72] The EIC was weakened at a critical moment in its struggle with its enemies in London.

The Glorious Revolution was in itself a dangerous blow. The new parliament was clearly hostile. The chorus of complaint from English textile interests mounted; the House of Commons was besieged at one point by thousands of wives of textile workers. A mob of 3,000 weavers assembled to attack Child's mansion, and the EIC itself nearly lost its treasure when East India House was assailed. The woollen interests would seem to win their point in 1701, when a famous Act was passed which forbade the use or wear in England of Indian and Chinese silks and of Indian prints, printed calicoes, striped or checked cottons, though this would be a Pyrrhic victory, since the Lancashire cotton industry would thrive on the production of local imitations. A powerful association of merchants outside the EIC was formed by 1691, in effect as a rival organisation. In October that year the House of Commons resolved that a joint-stock company with exclusive privileges was the best means of trading with the East, but the question remained, which company? Child put his trust in bribes, and spent £80,000 on corrupting the King's ministers and his court. He was able thus to secure a new charter in 1693 – but one which doubled the Company's capital and restricted individual members to no more than £10,000 in stock. Any merchant could now join on payment of £5, and the Company must export £100,000 worth of woollens annually.[74]

Thomas Pitt had suffered losses as a patron of privateers in the French war, and so returned to the East to shake the money-tree once more, this time with the tacit knowledge and consent of William III. He was soon flourishing at Hugli again. The EIC had no stomach for a fresh fight. Word of Child's bribes had reached the public, and its then governor had been committed to the Tower.

The House of Commons had in effect endorsed interloping. The Company now came to terms with Pitt's co-partners in England and sent orders to Bengal that he should be given all assistance in getting home. According to the Bengal Council, Pitt 'to the last made a great bounceing' and 'carried himself very haughtily'. He would be back before long, a poacher turned gamekeeper, as the EIC's governor in Madras. Child was strongly opposed to the choice of that 'roughling, immoral man', but had to accept strange allies in the struggle against the rival 'Dowgate Association'.[75] And it was striking how most warring interests in England seemed to have no hesitation in shelving their differences in face of the challenge of the proposed Scottish East India Company, a prime stimulus to the great debate over trade which marked the year 1696.

V

A dozen general elections between 1689 and 1715, rubbed home the new importance of Parliament as the main road to power, to office, and to the profits of office.

In the 1680s it might still cost only a few pounds to contest the election for a small borough; by the 1720s to fight there would demand hundreds. Direct bribery was not widespread, but the candidate would be expected to give his supporters food and drink, and to promise fine things to the electors — a town hall, a school, a water supply, plate for the corporation. Votes were traded, also, for patronage. Sir Henry Johnson, a rich East India merchant whose daughter married an earl, became M.P. for Aldeburgh after the Glorious Revolution. To consolidate his position there, he plied the local gentry with exotic presents from India. He also entertained applications for the East India Company clerkships which were known to be at his disposal. ' ... Aldeburgh,' observes J. H. Plumb, 'seems to have been teeming with ambitious young men with a passion for the East; they were all relations of voters.'[76]

Since votes were now so valuable, borough after borough acted to cut down its own number of electors. As party conflict bruised on, the swollen electorate was trimmed. It was now the tories who were commonly elected in the seats with the widest franchises, and who tried to defend the broad spread of votes among the people, whigs who acted time and again in Parliament to restrict the franchise. The tories spoke for the 'Country' against the 'Court', for small squires, yeomen, the cheated and the unlucky against the great and fortunate. Yet when in office they used their opponents' methods, lavishing lucrative posts on their supporters and so undermining their own position; the whigs floated on the wave of the future. The new whig party was in a minority in the country, but had a majority among the peers. A clique of propertied men 'either aristocrats or linked with the aristocracy, whose tap-root was in land but whose side-roots reached out to commerce, industry, and finance' now moved towards dominance.[77] Titled whig families were leagued with financial interests in the City of London. They sought, in the end successfully, for control of the vast new scope for patronage which the expansion of government opened up.

By the first years of the eighteenth century the Navy, with over 200 ships and about 50,000 seamen, was a grand reservoir of lucrative employment. In 1711 England had at least 70,000 soldiers in the field. Both these organisations, quite monstrous by prevailing standards, had to be clerked, had to be kept posted, had to be victualled. To support them, governments had to raise unheard-of sums in taxation. A Land Tax (1694) was one device which lasted; its inequitable collection bore hard on minor tory squires. There were taxes on salt and servants, on trawlers and hackney cabs, on plate, paper and glass, and so on; all these required gatherers. Customs collection grew with trade; by 1718, there would be 561 full-time customs officers in the Port of London, besides over 1,000 part-timers. Plymouth and Liverpool would have over fifty full-time officers each; even the tiny port of Fowey in Cornwall would have twelve. There was a growing number of customs officials in the colonies, which also required postal clerks, army officers, judges, and formed quite an important field of patronage. 'The number of men employed by the government grew faster between 1689 and 1715 than in any previous period of English history, and perhaps at a rate not to be equalled again until the nineteenth century.'[78] Only the royal court actually shed posts; and though it remained an important fountain of status and cash, it was far outstripped in size by the personnel employed in the Treasury, which now came to dominate domestic affairs, securing control over all the sub-departments of state concerned with revenue and taxation. The new administrative system was not a 'machine'. It was corrupt from top to bottom. While the numbers of people employed to collect taxes rose, the yield of each tax steadily fell. Commissions in the army were bought and sold while promotion of men without riches or influence became increasingly rare, and the soldiers went short of food, clothing and arms as their officers reimbursed themselves. Old-fashioned whigs, like tories, shuddered at the cancer of venality which spread with the State's growth and which was exposed in scandal after scandal. Yet the system worked. England did not lose her wars.

'King William's War' did not, on the face of it, go very well. The English army was locked in a war of entrenchments and sieges in Flanders. Louis XIV's fleet was trounced at La Hogue in 1691, but this was small gain, as the French diverted their seamen into privateering, and England tasted the same punishment which its mariners had once meted out to Spain. Thousands of ships were lost, and an elaborate system of convoys was required to protect English trade. ' ... Their Privateers swarm and cover the Sea like Locusts,' one English writer declaimed, 'they hang on our Trade like Horse-Leeches ... '[79]

But even the check to commerce was a gain for English industry. Strengthened by Huguenot expertise and capital which had migrated from France in the 1680s, it began to produce local substitutes for goods imported formerly from the Continent; paper and silk, cutlery and glass. There was an astonishing surge of speculation in new projects. 'There were copper and mining companies', Sir John Clapham tells us, '... saltpetre, leather, diving machine, pumping machine and fire hose (Sucking Worm Engine) companies; brown and white and blue (wall) paper; plate and bottle glass; various kinds of munitions; water supply ... ' The number of joint-stock companies in England and Scotland rose from 22 in 1688 to nearly 150 by the end of 1695.[80] Besides prompting the rapid development of marine insurance, in which England would lead the world for so long, the war led to the creation in 1694 of the Bank of England. The government was in dire need of money. There were plenty of Englishmen so avid to invest that they were putting their money into hare-brained projects. Now approaching 1,300 shareholders came together in one grand finance company. In return for raising £1,200,000 to be lent to the government at 8 per cent, the company was incorporated as the first English joint-stock bank and empowered to issue notes, to discount bills and so forth. Its loan paid for William's one great victory, the capture from the French of the strong fortress of Namur after three months' siege in 1694. After peace came three years later, the Bank was rewarded with increased privileges. A stronghold of whiggery from the first, it brought a new flexibility and security to the nation's monetary system. The war, which cost about £40 million, left a debt of over £14 million, and a vital role not only for the Bank, but also, as we shall see, for the East India Company.[81]

That England could shoulder such enormous financial burdens was a sign of the country's real wealth. Yet in 1695, with the war going badly again, the French privateers at their work, and men's minds still not adjusted to England's new power, there were cries that trade was ruined. The great minds of the day, Newton and Wren among them, were called to advise the government on the economic crisis.

Though few men-of-war could at the moment be spared to enforce the existing Navigation Acts, a new one was passed in 1696. Its aim was to tighten up the entire system. Colonial governors were made liable to a fine of £1,000 and dismissal for allowing breaches of the Acts. Vice-Admiralty Courts were shortly set up in the New World to try infringements.

The Lords of Trade who had kept watch over the colonies from the mid-1670s had faltered in the commotions since 1685; the industrious Blathwayt, secretary to their board, had become its one effective moving part. Clearly, a new organ of state was required. The question was who should control it. Parliament wanted a Council of Trade controlled by itself. The Crown fought back to protect its prerogative. The new Board of Trade which emerged, though its name survives to this day, and though it was a precursor of the far later Colonial Office, was merely an 'awkward compromise'.[82] It included two peers and five experts, amongst whom the relatively idealistic John Locke balanced the thoroughly self-interested Blathwayt. Its role was advisory, not executive. Real power rested with the Treasury. The Board's permanent staff consisted only of a secretary and four, later seven, clerks, although its brief covered the whole world. It assumed, and maintained the right to nominate Council members in the colonies, and had some influence in the appointment of governors. At first its members showed energy — in 1697 they met more than four days per week — but in the early years of the new century, this fell away, and the Board became increasingly insignificant. New men who came on it were chiefly concerned with the £1,000 a year it paid them.

Meanwhile, the committee of the House of Commons which conducted a full-scale inquiry into trade in 1696 turned, in effect, into a court before which the EIC was tried. Its opponents raked up grievances old and new. The virtues of the 'joint stock' and of the 'regulated' sorts of company were proclaimed by their respective adherents. Yet what emerged was not decision upon the form of English trade with the East, but the impeachment of Lord Belhaven, William Paterson and others for 'high crimes and misdemeanours'. Their offence had been to organise the 'Company of Scotland for Trade with Africa and the Indies'.

VI

Scotland was not for the moment a military danger, though it would seem for generations that it might become one. After Dundee's Jacobite followers had gone home or had been beaten, garrisons had been put into the Highlands. At Inverlochy, where the Great Glen of Loch Ness, cutting the Highlands in two, debouched to the south-west, Fort William was erected, for rather different purposes than the strong building of the same name which would shortly arise at Calcutta. The aim was not to repel civilised might but to restrict the disorders which might be caused by those clans of Gaelic barbarians who had still not sworn allegiance to the Dutch King and whose mistrust of the now-triumphant Campbells still made them dangerous to the state which the Campbells supported.

In this context came about the most notorious of Highland massacres — most famous not because it was the worst but because it was ordered from London rather than from Edinburgh. William's chief agent in Scottish affairs was a clever lawyer, the Master of Stair. A scheme was set afoot to resolve the conflicts arising from the Campbell Earl of Argyll's claim to lands which were actually held by the Camerons, Macleans and others, through the purchase of the disputed glens by the Crown. But it was not carried out. Harsher, less sensible courses were followed. The dissident chiefs refused to take an oath of allegiance to William without the consent of the exiled James II. William offered pardon for all offences if they came in to swear by January 1, 1692. James's letter authorising his followers to do so was not received in the Highlands till just before Christmas. Even so, some chiefs came in by the stated time, and a minor Macdonald chieflet, MacIain of Glencoe, was able to give good excuse when he had his oath taken only six days late. But Stair, long before this, had decided to make an example of some Highlanders. The Macdonalds, as the 'only popish clan', seemed to him suitable victims – 'it will be popular to take a severe course with them.' Whether the Glencoe men were in fact Catholics is doubtful. But their sept was small, and relatively easy to get at. They were notorious raiders and rustlers, 'the worst', Stair alleged, 'in all the Highlands'. They were also famous for their Gaelic poets, but this would not deter a Lowland Scot like Stair. He decided that no one must escape. The passes out of their glen must be sealed. All must die. 'It's a great work of charity to be exact in rooting out the damnable sept ... '[83]

A regiment of Campbells was now in existence. Soldiers from it, under Campbell of Glenlyon, were ordered into the bleak glen to do the job. For nearly a fortnight they enjoyed Macdonald hospitality. Then, one snowy morning in February, the trustful MacIain was shot down from behind as he called for a dram for his guests. But the massacre was botched. The passes were not sealed. Though thirty-eight Macdonalds were killed, ten times as many escaped to skulk on the bare hills. Colonel Hill, an old Cromwellian soldier who commanded at Fort William, an Englishman, was ordered to kill the remainder but pleaded for them instead, and after six months the sept occupied Glencoe once more.

On the face of it, the massacre worked. The remaining chiefs were quick to submit. But the atrocity, which shocked Scotland, was a gift to Jacobite propagandists and helped ensure that the Stuarts would find troops in Britain again. Stair's political enemies used it to oust him from office. He had by-passed the Scottish Privy Council with orders direct to the reluctant Hill, and feeling against rule from London was inflamed.

Most important Scots were trying to move away from the nation's violent past. The last wolf in the country seems to have perished about this time, though the last witch would not be executed until 1727 (fifteen years after England's last witchcraft case). Scots of the upper and middle classes were attempting to emulate the comforts of civilisation as Dutch and English displayed them. The modern dining-room was taking the place of the baronial hall. Even on Skye, Macleod of Dunvegan now ate in private, to the dismay of his bards. The wealthier classes cherished Dutch linen and, though there were few roads fit to drive them on, imported English coaches to show that they could afford them. As in Ireland, even the poor now chewed, smoked and sneezed tobacco.

The English were noticing that some tobacco now slipped in through Glasgow. But well-to-do Scots themselves were perturbed by the country's lack of success in overseas trade. The native shipbuilding industry was minimal, and merchants relied on vessels bought in Holland or Norway. In any case, they owned only a fifteenth or a twentieth of the number of ships employed by Englishmen. 'Had the whole of the northern kingdom been suddenly engulfed in a tidal wave,' T. C. Smout remarks, 'the catastrophe would hardly have troubled the economy of her neighbours.'[84] Yet imports were, or seemed, essential. Scottish coopers bought staves from Ireland and ready-made iron hoops from Flanders. The Dundee linen weavers used Polish flax. French claret was virtually a national drink – a 'most pernicious trade', as one writer moralised, 'because founded chiefly on the price of the wool and skins which we exported into France, so that it may be said we exported the substance of our country and subsistance of the poor for a sorry liquor which nature never intended for us ... '[85]

England was, and growingly so, the most important area for Scottish foreign trade – the only place where Scots cattle would wend on the hoof for sale, and the only place where Scots could find an outlet for their poor-quality linen. But the English put up, then increased, tariffs against Scottish linen. They protected the Tyneside coal-mines against competition from the Forth. Scottish governments did their best to retort in kind. A Scottish Navigation Act in 1661 had matched the English one. In 1670s, amid hopes and fanfares, a Royal Fishery Company was established with a monopoly, but it collapsed within eleven years. The government tried to stimulate the manufacture of better woollen cloth, but the products could not compete with the English for price and quality even on the home market. Of new industries founded, only sugar refining had much success.

An independent Scottish foreign policy would have ruled out war with France, an important trading partner. But the Union of the Crowns, and William III's war against Louis XIV, exposed Scots merchants to privateers against whom they had no fleet to protect them, while the relatively small body of Scottish seamen was depleted to fill the English navy. The 1690s were years of dire crisis. Bad harvests in 1695, 1696 and 1698 produced such horrors that it was said that in some rural areas a third or even a half of the population died or left the country. On top of this, all the main export commodities, except cattle to England, were now affected by tariff barriers and prohibitions abroad. The French forbade the import of Scottish woollens and fish. Tariffs since 1670 had blocked the export of Scottish corn to England; now they were raised against it in Norway, too, a vital source of ships and timber. Competition from Belgian mines, a reduction of export duties by the English, and prohibitive rates imposed in the Spanish Netherlands themselves, stemmed the traditional trade in coal to the Low Countries. The English in 1698 increased the duties on Scots linen, while the new Navigation Act passed two years before had been largely aimed at Scottish interlopers, and raised questions about the legality of Scots holding office in English colonies.

Besides Scottish involvement in New Jersey, there had been a Scottish outpost, 'Stuarts Town', founded in 1684 to protect the southern flank of South Carolina, but wiped out by the Spaniards only two years later. There had been quite large involuntary emigration to the New World. Daniel Defoe (not the most reliable of sources) claimed that 1,700 Covenanters had been transported to servitude in America, and one of the most prominent episodes in Covenanting martyrology was the wreck off Orkney in 1679 of a ship with 200 intransigents so destined. Sober, hard-working, hard-headed Scots servants, more grateful than English ones because their homeland was poor, had, as we have noticed, a high reputation in the Caribbean, and the demand from colonial governors for such men to swell the militias was such that many were kidnapped and sold for cash. But the promise of the New World was growingly obvious. A settler in East New Jersey reported home in 1685 that he had met a man 'who was sent away by Cromwell to New England, a slave from Dunbar. Living now in Woodbridge like a Scots Laird, wishes his countrymen and his Native Soyle very well, tho' he never intends to see it.' Andrew Hamilton, governor of New Jersey from 1692, a Scot, was accused of being a 'great favourer of the Scotch traders his countrymen', and was temporarily robbed of his office on the grounds that he was not a 'natural born subject of England' as the terms of the Navigation Act of 1696 demanded.[86]

Yet all Scots born since the Union had been regarded as such 'natural' subjects. Growing English paranoia met growing Scots jealousy on collision course in the 1690s. Scotland, small, poor, culturally divided, with few decent highways, offered little home market. Only foreign trade could make Scots rich, 'the one really flexible element in an otherwise inflexible economy'.[87] Everywhere outside the Highlands, landlords were becoming commercially minded, aiming to sell their agricultural surplus when there was one, to make textiles, to profit from coal and lead. The country thus with remarkable solidarity pitched itself into a rash bid for effective economic independence. What would abort it before long was the fact that trade across the Border in linen and cattle was the most useful of Scotland's real assets.

Scotland already had a share in one important colony, in Ulster. There was a brisk trade exchanging Scots coal and manufactures for the produce of the settlers there. But Ulster farmers could offer nothing not grown or made already on Scottish estates, and the landowners who dominated the Scottish government did everything possible to stop imports of victuals from Ireland. A tropical colony giving Scotland its own source of sugar and of tobacco would be far more acceptable. And some Edinburgh merchants were taking an interest in the possibilities of trade with Africa. In 1693, then, the Scottish Parliament passed an Act giving permission for the formation of joint-stock companies to trade with countries not at war with the Crown. This opened the way to a further Act of 1695 establishing the 'Company of Scotland for Trade with Africa and the Indies'.

At this stage, some London interlopers saw a Scottish company as a means of attacking the RAC and EIC monopolies, and the primacy given to Africa in the name suggests that the weaker RAC was the main target. That Guinea was forgotten and the 'Indies' became paramount had much to do with the personality and ideas of a prominent London-based Scot, William Paterson. He had recently taken a leading part in the formation of the Bank of England, but he had nursed for years the dream of an entrepôt on the Isthmus of Darien, that narrow neck of land where Central and South America join. Paterson – pious Christian and pushful businessman, patriot Scot and ardent internationalist – was a man whose apparent self-contradictions would often recur among his Caledonian compatriots. He had left his homeland young and had knocked about as a trader in the Caribbean before settling in London. When he was consulted by those creating the new company, the intention was to find half its capital in England, and an equal number of London-based and Scottish-based directors were appointed. Paterson assumed leadership at the London end. From the outset his thinking was idealistic and grandiose. He wanted European participation – nationality and sect were immaterial, though Paterson hoped that Almighty God would 'make some use of Scotland also to visit those dark places of the Earth, whose habitations are full of Cruelty.'[88]

To Paterson it was 'this great and noble Undertaking.' To others it seemed no more than a squalid fiddle by certain people aiming to break the EIC monopoly who, when they failed in that aim, went on to deceive the Scottish people with impossible promises. In the words of a shrewd Scot, Clerk of Penicuik, 'they were either so short-sighted or so obstinatly set on their privat advantages that they did not discover how improbable the success of such a scheme was.' Anyone could have seen, Clerk argued (but this was years later) that the English would never 'suffer Scotland to grou rich in a seperat state because it was more than probable that this increase of wealth would sometime or other be made use of to the prejudice of England ... ' And only an 'army of men', he pointed out, could have stopped the smuggling of tropical goods across the Border if they had come into Scotland free of duties, or at low rates.[89]

The aim was to raise £300,000 in each country. Subscription books opened in London first, in November 1695, and were closed after little more than a fortnight with that much money promised. But the House of Lords intervened and summoned the London directors for questioning. The Commons as we have seen, resolved to impeach twenty-three people, but since an essential witness, the Company's secretary, had prudently removed himself to Edinburgh, the trial could not go forward. But the London investors took fright and withdrew their money. The few directors who remained loyal retreated to Scotland. And in that country, there was a surge of feeling recalling the Covenant of 1637. The cause of a trading company now united a people as the reformed religion had once done. As one judge wrote, ''Twas the notice the parliament of England first took of it made the whole nation throng in to have some share ... ', and when William dismissed the Scottish ministers who had, he said, 'ill served' him, this news fanned the enthusiasm.[90]

The Company's Scottish directors, a few months before, had thought £300,000 was more than their nation could raise. Now they threw caution away and appealed for £400,000 (sterling), in effect about half the total capital

which was available at that time in Scotland. They got it. Covenanter and
Cavalier, whig and Jacobite subscribed together. Scotland was united over trade
with the tropics as it had never been before. The Earl of Argyll put up £1,500,
the Viscount of Stair £1,000, the landed classes together nearly half the capital.
The merchants of Glasgow and Edinburgh found another quarter, those of the
lesser burghs joined in, and the rising class of lawyers added their piles. In less
than six months, by early August 1696, the subscription books were filled and
a first call on the subscribers had already produced £100,000.[91] Yet this was a
year of famine, the second in succession.

The directors still toyed with ideas of the African slave trade. But the persuasive tongue and epic imagination of William Paterson convinced them that
they, the Scots, must now try to realise his vision of an entrepôt on the Isthmus
which could gather, he argued, the trade of the whole world. Darien was the
'door of the seas and the key of the universe'; it would enable its proprietors to
'give laws to both oceans', Atlantic and Pacific, and 'to become arbitrators of
the commercial world, without being liable to the fatigues, expenses and
dangers, or contracting the guilt and blood of Alexander and Caesar.'[92] Paterson
was a forerunner in spirit of those Victorian free-traders who eschewed conquest
and saw commerce as the solvent of all divisions between mankind. Only a
country so recently haunted by old-fashioned violence as Scotland could at that
time have produced a leader like Paterson stressing the pacific nature of trade.
Sir Josiah Child knew better: 'All trade is a kind of warfare.'[93]

Paterson showed his fellow directors an account of Darien written by a young
pirate, who proclaimed the soil fertile, the Indians friendly, the whole country
a leafy El Dorado, rich in colours and scent. Why had the Spaniards not troubled
to occupy this paradise? The directors convinced themselves that this must be
because they had no valid claim to it. In any case, hadn't Morgan and other
buccaneers quite recently shown how weak Spain was in this area? There was,
furthermore, nothing that the English could do to prevent a settlement on the
Isthmus; though John Locke, on the Board of Trade, was hot for action against
the Scots, the legal position was so tricky that direct opposition was impossible.[94]

However, when Paterson went abroad to seek capital, the Dutch East and
West India Companies blocked his way in Holland, and the English consul in
Hamburg baulked him there by threatening the city's rulers with King William's
displeasure. The first wise impulse of the directors in Edinburgh was to wind
up. Their second was to appeal to the King. William equivocated. No German
money came in. The Darien venture went ahead.

Twelve hundred men, a quarter of them 'gentlemen', were gathered. Soldiers
recently discharged at the end of William's war with France made up much of
the party, and one of the more resourceful members, as it turned out, was
Thomas Drummond, who as a grenadier captain had played a grim and notable
part in the massacre at Glencoe. In November 1698 the fort and township of
'New Edinburgh' was founded in Darien, now renamed 'Caledonia'. The

commonplace horrors of first settlement in the New World, and the East, at that time, were repeated. The Scots suffered as the Jamestown settlers had suffered and as Englishmen had done, more recently, at Bencoolen. Disease raged; food was short; the Council squabbled. But the first messages home were optimistic. The Indians were friendly. Ships from New England and Jamaica were willing to trade. What destroyed the colonists' spirit was the news that the governor of Jamaica, in common, as it turned out, with all the English colonial authorities, had ordered that the Scots must not be dealt with or helped in any way whatsoever. William, anxious for friendship with Spain against France, had disowned the Scots in face of Spanish protests. In June 1699 the survivors abandoned their cluster of huts and rude fort on the Isthmus. More than 300 had died already. Many more perished on a dreadful journey via Jamaica to New York; the English authorities in both places were unable to help and were obliged to obstruct. In the end, only 300 sailed from New York home.

In Scotland, public demonstrations of joy had marked the news that the settlement had been made, followed by rage when word came of the English proclamations against 'Caledonia'. An expedition to reinforce it, with 1,300 people, including 100 women and 4 ministers of the kirk, was sent out in the summer of 1699. This new party, after a few demoralising weeks, had to meet a determined Spanish attack by land and by sea. Resistance would have been crazy. Surrender on generous terms, in April 1700, was followed by a second, and final abandonment of 'New Edinburgh'.

Meanwhile, shame and despair in Scotland had turned outwards as indignation against the King and the English. The Scottish Parliament was hastily adjourned, in May 1700, when it tried to insist that the Darien settlement was within the terms of the Act of 1696, though William now said it was not. News of the capture of a small Spanish fort by the second party of colonists arrived next month and provoked a glad riot in Edinburgh, gleefully fanned by the Jacobites, in which the windows of unpopular peers were smashed. But word of the final surrender arrived a week later. Four great ships had carried the second party of colonists. None returned, and only a handful of the people whom they had carried. The Company's largest vessel, the *Rising Sun*, had gone down, with symbolic aptness, in a storm off North America. Now Scotland's sun seemed set.[95]

There was little the Company could do. Africa was remembered. Four ships were sent. One came back, and its cargo of gold dust and ivory brought the Company its only trading profits, some £48,000 (Scots).

It was its own folly, not English hostility, which had led to the Company's wasting complete over £150,000 (sterling), perhaps a sixth or a quarter of Scotland's total liquid capital. It had attempted an enterprise which even the English or French could have pulled off only in favourable circumstances, yet it had come nowhere near to assembling the financial resources required. The annals of illicit trade in this period suggest that the English, and even the Spaniards, in the Caribbean might have traded with Caledonia had it been worth their while, but the colonists had only inferior trade goods and lacked the money, or letters of credit, which would have brought them provisions all proclamations notwithstanding.[96] But in Scotland, where hardly a family of substance had not lost money or kin through Darien, rage against the English seethed.

VII

In Scotland there would always be many detractors, indeed haters, of William III, whose reign was marked by famine, by Glencoe, and by the disaster at Darien. For the New England colonists, by contrast, the Glorious Revolution of 1688 would become a sacred moment, the writings of Locke a species of holy writ. To understand why this was so, we must return to the scene in Boston in the 1670s, and observe the course of a long contest between the Stuarts and certain habitually truculent subjects.

The so-called 'plantation duty' introduced by the English Parliament in 1673 was largely inspired by complaints received against the New England carriers. It exacted a new tax at the point of clearance on enumerated goods, about equal to the duty on the same goods when they entered England. It was meant to cut profits on cargoes shipped illegally to Europe. It could be interpreted to mean that unless New Englanders took goods immediately from the port where they laded them to England, they would have to pay on them twice over, once in the New World, again in England itself. English merchants, sending ships out which then went directly home, paid duty only once, and had part of the tariff refunded if and when they re-exported goods to Europe. The Massachusetts government backed the Bostonians' protests against this discrimination.

Meanwhile the heirs of Gorges and Mason, whose stake dated back to the earliest days of New England, were pressing their claims to Maine and New Hampshire respectively. The Lords of Trade decided to demand that Massachusetts sent agents to London to respond to these claims, and Edward Randolph, a young man related by marriage to the Masons, was given the job of special courier. He was hard up, ambitious and grasping, too tactless to find a secure position at home and anxious, like many another emigrant, to better himself in the New World. His long struggle with the Boston merchants began when he first arrived in their city during King Philip's war.

He wanted the Crown to intervene in Massachusetts so that he could receive office under it, and he reported home accordingly. The colony's leaders, he said, were 'inconsiderable Mechanicks', merely front men for Dissenting zealots who were 'generally inclined to Sedition'. Freely admitting traders of all nations – Randolph saw ships arrive direct from France with brandy – the Massachusetts government 'would make the world believe they are a free state and doe act in all matters accordingly.' The Crown, he reckoned, was losing over £100,000 a year in customs.[97]

At first Randolph did not have things all his own way. In 1677, the Lords Chief Justices in London upheld Gorges's right to Maine but decided against the Mason claim and found the Massachusetts Charter valid despite Randolph's propaganda against it. But then the colony overplayed its hand. It made what was almost a unilateral declaration of independence. The General Court declared that the Navigation Acts were in force 'by the authority of this Court'. It was argued that since Massachusetts was not represented in Parliament, laws passed there could not bind its trade; however, its assembly would humour the English by passing the Acts itself.[98] The Lords of Trade were soon clear that only revocation of the Charter and the appointment of a royal governor would suffice. Meanwhile, Randolph was appointed collector of customs for New England, and came back in December 1679 as the first salaried civil servant ever stationed by the Crown in Boston.

He found some support. There were many wealthy merchants who looked socially and culturally to England for models, who recognised their dependence on the English trading system and who resented – this was an old grievance – the fact that rich men were outvoted in the General Court by the representatives of petty traders and country cultivators. Those who hoped for religious toleration also sided with Randolph, as did opportunists of all sorts. So a 'moderate' faction emerged. In New Hampshire, an area of vast forests and few white denizens, Randolph was able, in 1680, to bring to birth the second royal colony in North America. But in Massachusetts he met frustration. His salary was only £100 a year. His aim was to augment it with the 50 per cent of confiscated goods which would be due to him as informer against smugglers. His rapacity ran up against the stolid defiance of Massachusetts juries, who decided for the defendants in all the ten cases he brought between March and December 1680. Next year, he returned to England to seek an increase in his powers. He came back in 1683 with a writ of *quo warranto* to be served against the Massachusetts authorities.

In October 1684 the Massachusetts Charter was declared vacated in the court of Chancery. The years during which this threat had overhung the colony had seen the strains in its life emphasised. A synod of clergy and lay elders which met in Boston in 1679 to discuss God's controversy with New England reported a vast mass of iniquities. Heretics were numerous. Swearing had increased. Pride and extravagance in attire were flaunted. Lawyers were thriving, a sign of contention between folk who should be united in mutual love. The disposition to slumber during sermons was growing. Mixed dancing was rampant and women were baring their shoulders and even their breasts. Men were becoming liars, especially when they were at the business of selling. While the wealthy speculated in land, workmen demanded unreasonable wages. In fact, all these abominations were symptoms of a prosperity based, though chiefly for town dwellers, on trade.

But rural die-hards still dominated the General Court. To such men the willingness of the 'moderates' to negotiate over the Charter and to accept even its disappearance was base dereliction and blasphemy. The Charter was the safeguard of the Congregational Church system, and men whose lives centred on the land feared that if it was voided, their holdings would revert to the Crown; at best they would have to pay quitrents, at worst they would be pushed off. What was at stake was the character of Massachusetts village life, in which religious intolerance consorted with the co-operative farming of land still held in strips in open fields, and with the herding of animals communally. The 'moderates' ran into furious vituperation. Joseph Dudley, son of a founder of the colony, went to England on a mission of negotiation in 1682 and on his return was dismissed from his seat as a magistrate and described as an enemy of the country by vote of the Boston town meeting. But God was extremely quarrelsome. In May 1686, this same Dudley became president of a temporary Council of quislings, dominated by rich merchants, which was appointed to run the colony while the government in England made up its mind what to do with the North American plantations.

Richard Dunn has commented on the 'overbearing executive style of the 1680s'.[99] In each colony Charles II's agents aimed to prise out of power which-ever local interests were in control and to substitute a new combination of persons prepared to work under the governor who served the King. In the West Indies, Dutton in Barbados, the Duke of Albemarle in Jamaica, Sir Nathaniel Johnson in the Leewards, all called on the grumbling small farmers to help them push the bigger landowners from their entrenched positions in council, assembly and judiciary; this was a counterpart of the attack on the corporations in England which, under James II, produced an Anabaptist Lord Mayor of London. In Virginia, Lord Howard of Effingham denied the Assembly the right to act as highest court of appeals or elect its own clerk. The most striking exemplar of the drive against local particularism in favour of royal absolutism would be Edmund Andros in the novel 'Dominion of New England'.

Andros had first arrived in America in 1674 as governor of New York, and had soon outraged New Englanders by reviving James, Duke of York's claim to the western part of Connecticut. Only a show of force on their part had stopped him from making this good with his troops. Now, in December 1686, he appeared in Boston, marched portentously through a local guard of honour into the Town House dressed in laced scarlet coat, and began a revolution from above which matched in miniature his royal master's work in England. James broke with the English Parliament; Andros did away with representative bodies in New England. 'While James II whipped up religious hysteria in England by appointing Catholics to high offices, Sir Edmund was fostering the Anglican service in Boston, which in Puritan eyes was little better than the Whore of

Rome. Andros was buttressed by a troop of redcoats in Boston, equivalent to James's standing army on Hounslow Heath.'[100]

Other motives beside the drive towards absolutism helped prompt the creation, under Andros, of the 'Dominion of New England'. James was aware, as he showed in regard to Siam, of the need to protect English gains overseas against his French allies, who had in Quebec a united command which the English colonies facing them lacked. Divided defence against Red Indians was only one of a range of further problems arising in whole or in part from the fractionalisation of England's northern colonies. New York was in a poor state. The first royal governor in New Hampshire had come close to provoking rebellion. Massachusetts still had long-distance jurisdiction over part of Maine. The scope now given to Andros might resolve many nagging issues at once.

Andros was empowered to govern Plymouth Colony and to annex Rhode Island. Both were smoothly taken over. Connecticut was soon added to the list; here, Andros's old enemies showed more resistance until he simply seized control there. New York and New Jersey were brought in during 1688. But Andros was moving too fast, like James at home. He alienated the well-to-do 'moderates'. He spoilt the fun of the men on Dudley's provisional Council (who had been granting each other title to large tracts of unoccupied land and assigning themselves and their cronies all the plum offices) when he named a new Council on which they were outvoted. He alarmed landholders in general when he ordained that all new grants of undeveloped land should be subject to a quit-rent of 2s. 6d. per 100 acres, and that all existing titles were to be reviewed for confirmation subject to such payment as he, Andros, might decide. And all pious Puritans feared for the safety of their own church system.

New England learnt only slowly and piecemeal of the 'Glorious Revolution'. Official confirmation of the accession of William and Mary did not arrive until 26 May 1689, three months after they had accepted the Crown. But already, on April 18, the townspeople of Boston, getting wind of events in Britain, had dealt with Andros and his Dominion. Dissident 'moderates' like Wait-Still Winthrop, grandson of the founder, joined with unreconciled supporters of the old Charter such as the famous minister, Cotton Mather. Under the guidance of these men, over a thousand Bostonians rose in arms, forced a bloodless capitulation, and had the satisfaction of imprisoning Andros, Randolph and Dudley. A provisional 'Council for the Safety of the People' took over while the other New England colonies went ahead and re-established their former governments.

In Virginia, the revolution was transacted peacefully. In Maryland, rebellion forced the surrender of Lord Baltimore's governor and his Catholic-dominated council; the insurgents formed a 'Protestant Association' and petitioned the new King to take over the province. In New York, more drastic conflict happened. At the end of May, a large part of the militia, led by a malcontent merchant of German birth named Jacob Leisler, and supported by 'mob' action, seized

Fort James at the lower end of Manhattan island. Andros's lieutenant there, Francis Nicholson, unwisely decided to leave them to it, and sailed home to England to report in person. A representative convention gave authority to a Council of Safety and named Leisler Commander-in-Chief. The former ruling clique opposed him fiercely. The new governor, Henry Sloughter, nominated in England in September 1689, took a year and a half to reach his post, and Leisler, who had assumed the title of 'Lieutenant Governor', had to meet the shock, early in 1690, of the sack of Schenectady by a French and Indian force.

He appealed for help from other colonies as far away as Barbados, and was able to arrange a concerted attack on the French with the New England colonies. Massachusetts, in April 1690, had sponsored a successful venture against Port Royal in Acadia, where a weak French garrison had promptly surrendered and much plunder had been taken. Sir William Phips, leader of the expedition, was an archetype of the local boy made good. A native of Maine, illiterate till his teens, he had risen as seaman and trader and had become famous after he had found, on behalf of an English syndicate, a sunken Spanish treasure ship off Haiti. (The Syndicate had given a dividend of 10,000 per cent. Phips had cleared £16,000 himself, and James II, receiving £40,000, had knighted him.)[101] Now the sack of Port Royal made him a popular hero in Boston, plunder in hand begot a taste for more, and the northern colonies were emboldened to mount an ambitious joint plan for the conquest of Canada. An overland strike from Albany against Montreal was to coincide with an amphibious assault on Quebec led by Phips, who took 32 ships and 1,300 soldiers with him. But his attack failed, and the other invasion aborted below Lake Champlain.

Early in 1691, a company of royal troops arrived to take over New York on behalf of Sloughter. Leisler refused to hand over except to a lawfully commissioned governor in person. The King's soldiers were fired on, two were killed, and after Sloughter's arrival Leisler was hanged for treason. But New York at last got a representative assembly to match those now restored elsewhere.

The delays which had undone the luckless Leisler reflected the fact that the new regime in England had at first no time to spare for the plantations. When it moved, the results were somewhat paradoxical. William had no prejudice against men with a reputation for upholding the royal prerogative, and Andros, sent home for trial, soon returned to the New World as governor of Virginia, while Dudley became president of the Council in New York and Randolph was commissioned as surveyor general of customs for the whole of North America. The Catholic Lord Baltimore was deprived of political control of Maryland, which came under royal rule for a quarter of a century until another Lord Baltimore prudently converted to Anglicanism in 1715. William Penn stood in greater danger, as one of James II's most conspicuous favourites. In 1689, there was a warrant out for his arrest under suspicion of high treason, and he was indeed involved in Jacobite intrigues towards an invasion from France[102] before he finally submitted to William III in 1694, and won control of his colony back.

Massachusetts was given charge of the whole of Maine and digested little Plymouth Colony. A new charter in 1691 ensured that existing titles in land held and that colonists need not, as Andros had threatened, pay quitrents to the Crown, but William III insisted there must still be a royal governor, who would exercise a veto in the election of council members by the General Court, and would have power to adjourn, prorogue and dissolve the House of Representatives and to veto its legislation, all of which must now be sent to England for approval. This emaciation of Massachusetts liberty did not worry the thriving merchants, who through alliance with the governor could now make the Council their political voice.

Phips, still a local idol, was made governor and arrived in May 1692 to find the notorious Salem witch-hunt in progress. This episode is remembered today, like the almost-contemporary affair at Glencoe, because it jarred with a new and more rationalistic temper which made it the last of its kind in the English-speaking world. It coincided with deeply-felt outrage among traditionalists over the new charter and reflected deep social unease in the colony. The mania began when two sick children in Salem claimed that a black servant, Tituba, was bewitching them, others cried out against her, and she 'confessed'. Children, servants and women, all underprivileged in Puritan society, fed the growing hysteria which began with informers, mainly girls, naming lowly neighbours as witches who were afflicting them and swept on till the accusations struck at Lady Phips and other prominent people. Some fifty persons who 'confessed' were spared. Those subjects who denied guilt suffered. A court, opening on 2 June, had by 22 September condemned 27 people to death, of whom 20 had been executed. There were 100 people in gaol awaiting trial and double that number had been accused but not yet imprisoned. At this point Phips at last called a halt.

Larzer Ziff has seen the craze as originally a spasm amongst the weakest elements of Massachusetts society 'whose lives were no longer of public consequence as the politics of empire took hold ... The old charter had gone under, the dignity of rural labour had gone under, the unopposed superiority of the Congregational Church had gone under, and the legal protection of the agricultural producer through fair-price and fixed-wage laws in opposition to his being an involuntary victim of international market conditions had gone under ... But the Lord had other ways of manifesting His special interest in His folk.' The fact that the accusers were frail and lowly showed that even the least of the people which God had chosen mattered.[103] Massachusetts retained an unearned notoriety (in persecution of 'witches' it had never matched Scotland, or England) and Cotton Mather justly earned the obloquy of posterity by writing to whitewash the trials for English readers.

Yet a recent writer has claimed that the arrival of William III on the throne meant that ' ... a New England more closely bound to the mother country than ever before had now emerged.' The colony from its beginnings had been alienated from the Crown, but with the Stuarts ousted, all seemed different. Massachusetts divines poured sycophantic praise on their Calvinist new Dutch monarch; Mather hailed him as 'the Phoenix of this Age' and William became a symbol of Protestant virtue, the champion of truth against papist France. However, Massachusetts leaders still showed a very good conceit of their colony's special status in the eyes of God. They often spoke as if New England — with about one person for every fifty living in England and Wales — was on more or less equal terms with the old country, and though Mather conceded 'It is no little Blessing that we are part of the English Nation ... that brave Nation', he also boasted that his fellow colonists had 'proportionately more of God among them than any part of mankind beside'.[104]

Such pronouncements cannot have helped abate the continuing disposition of Englishmen in authority to regard New Englanders as a stiffnecked, machinating people, and so perhaps to underrate their current zeal for the broader English interest in the New World. While Boston merchants, true to form, throve on the wartime conditions which deflected so much English shipping from the New World trades, frontier settlers fought deadly war against French and Indians.

English outnumbered French in North America by about twenty to one. The Acadian colony (Nova Scotia) was neglected by the French authorities. The area was still dominated by Abenaki, Micmac and Malecite Indians and though its fisheries were important, Port Royal was the only considerable settlement. But 'New France' was a formidable and persistent danger. It was in the St Lawrence valley that French effort was concentrated.

When the Canada colony was taken under direct royal control in 1663, New France had only about 2,500 settlers. By 1676 there were 8,500. An influx of colonists sponsored by the French state included consignments of young pauper girls (*filles de roi*) who were expected to breed, promptly. There were rewards for early marriage and penalties for bachelordom. Families were rather larger than in metropolitan France and the number of children surviving to marry was twice as great; so the Canadian population doubled in each generation.[105] Other policies were far less successful. Colbertian mercantilism aimed to create on the St Lawrence a replica of rural France, chiefly devoted to sending flour, provisions and timber to the French colonies in the West Indies. The fur trade stood in the way. Its rewards exceeded those which any other industry could offer. Its lure took Frenchmen through the unexplored continent and established claims to enormous territories almost in Louis XIV's despite.

The Comte de Frontenac was governor in Quebec from 1672 to 1682, and from 1690 until his death in 1698. A brave old man with a violent temper, he was also extremely greedy and fostered the fur trade, from which he himself profited greatly, in spite of the orders which he received from home. Under his governorship, the Sieur de la Salle explored the Mississippi valley down to the river's mouth and claimed the whole for the Crown, committing France to struggle, eventually, for a continent. The society which Frontenac ruled was, like him, insubordinate and obsessed with furs. Even the Jesuits who dominated its religious life were tied to the fur trade by their interest in the conversion of the Indian sellers and middlemen. In theory government was royal and auto-cratic. The Council and the officials were all chosen by the King. But in practice the colonists were as free as they wished to be. 'Since the only taxes levied in the colony were an import duty on wines, spirits, and tobacco, an occasional tax for local improvements more easily agreed to than collected, and until 1717 an export duty on beaver pelts and moose hides, there was no need for an elective assembly on the British model.'[106]

The land was divided among feudal *seigneurs*. These granted holdings in turn to vassals who paid very modest dues and whose position was far superior to that of the heavily-taxed peasantry of metropolitan France. Every concession had to have access to the St Lawrence, which created, as grants were subdivided through sale and inheritance, the characteristic pattern of narrow fields running at right angles back from the river. Canadian feudalism ruled out land specula-tion. The *seigneurs* stood to make little. Those who were not content to labour with their vassals on the land, or who could not find jobs under the colonial government, were drawn into the fur trade, and helped to swell the numbers of the *coureurs de bois* who met the competition of the Hudson's Bay English and the Albany Dutch by undertaking long voyages to trade with remote tribes, cutting out the middlemen and spending as much as two or three years at a time away from the colony. English trade goods were generally cheaper, and English woollen cloth was superior in quality. But other French goods were better made and better adapted to Indian needs than those of their English competitors. The red men sensibly liked brandy better than rotgut rum. The French *coureurs* would deliver the goods to the Indian in his own village, could speak his language well, and probably understood native economic values more thoroughly than their competitors sitting in Hudson's Bay posts. (In the first eighty-four years of the Hudson's Bay Company's existence only one employee is known to have struck far into the interior: Henry Kelsey, who ventured hundreds of miles during 1690-2, to the Saskatchewan River and the prairies beyond.)

The *coureur*, whether a hired *engagé*, an entrepreneur in his own right or a freebooter interbreeding with red women and trading shamelessly with the Albany men, was a counterpart, in the forests, of his contemporary, the buccaneer. ' ... The Batchelors,' wrote one English observer, 'act just as our *East-India-Men*, and Pirates are wont to do; for they Lavish, Eat, Drink and Play all away as long as the Goods hold out; and when these are gone, they e'en sell their Embroidery, their Lace, and their Cloaths. This done, they are forc'd to go upon a new Voyage for Subsistence.'[107] But they were heroes in New France, a markedly individualistic society. Peasants resisted attempts by the Crown to gather them into villages for defence. Their lone farms were easy targets for Iroquois enemies. 'Every Canadian male became an irregular soldier, an expert guerilla fighter in a war that had a very high casualty rate.'[108] The military instincts which the St Lawrence French had developed made them, with their Indian allies, a match for the English when, in the 1680s, the government in Quebec moved them into aggression.

Three times in the 1680s and 1690s the legendary D'Iberville, who almost always fought against odds and was never beaten, led parties of Canadians which swept the Hudson's Bay Company out of its forts; leaving on each occasion only one. In 1696, he also ravaged the English settlements in Newfoundland. Meanwhile Frontenac waged *la petite guerre*, sending raiding parties against English frontier townships and hostile Iroquois villages, successfully aiming to impress Indian trading partners with the powers of New France. Frontenac seems to have used the war as a pretext for expanding the fur trade at the expense of the Paris government – beaver exports boomed as garrisoned trading posts were established. New France overdid it. By 1695 supplies of furs were running at four times the demand of the French market, and next year clear orders were sent from Paris that the up-country trade must be stopped.

Meanwhile the English were learning, like the Canadians, methods of forest fighting from the red men. Each side provoked Indian allies to massacre. Raids were cruel as well as destructive. When Schenectady was sacked in February 1690 almost every dwelling was burnt, a great deal of booty was taken and, besides many deaths, twenty-seven captives were led away. This became commonplace, and the sufferings of English men, women and children, taken on long marches through the snows and then forced to work for the Indians as slaves, confirmed the stereotype of the red man's inhuman ferocity. Scalp hunting was seen by the North-east American Indians as the way a young brave gave proof of his entry into manhood. The English were shocked by it. Yet they encouraged it, offering bounties in King Philip's war and thereafter for the heads of their own enemies, and they allied with the Iroquois, a people detested by their red neighbours for their cruelty. The Iroquois, though they were not steady man-eaters like the Caribs, did on occasions devour the hearts of their enemies, believing that their courage would thus be ingested. They also tortured captives, for instance sticking short pieces of wood all over a man's body, then setting them alight; or they might tear all his flesh off while he was still alive. On the other hand, they neither burnt witches nor employed the cat o' nine tails.

The so-called 'Five Nations of Iroquois' – Mohawks, Oneidas, Onondagas, Cayugas and Senecas – lived across upper New York colony. There were other Iroquoian-speaking peoples. Amongst these, the Hurons and Susquehannocks were cardinal enemies of the Five Nations, but the Tuscaroras migrated north to join them in the second decade of the eighteenth century after losing a war with Carolina, and became the sixth member of the league, which controlled the Mohawk valley, the easiest route between the eastern seaboard and the fur-filled heart of the continent.

The Iroquois lived in an area where competition between several European peoples for furs had made guns easy to get. As the beaver was wiped out on their own lands, they had to invade those of other tribes to north and west. Involved with Dutch traders, they fell out with the French and with the Huron middlemen used by the French. In 1649, an Iroquois war party broke into Huron country, and shattered their rivals' position. By 1675 the Five Nations made themselves the only significant power along the whole frontier of English settlement, pushing the Mohicans out of the strategic junction between Hudson and Mohawk Rivers and finally in a long struggle defeating the Susquehannocks (and thus indirectly sparking Bacon's rebellion). In decades of fighting, they replenished their power with large numbers of defeated Indians whom they absorbed into their own tribe, while other groups sought their protection voluntarily.

The solidarity of the Five Nations was attributed by legend to the efforts of a Mohawk chief or shaman named Hiawatha in the late sixteenth century. The constitution of their league may have influenced that of the U.S.A.[109] At the annual summer conventions, the fifty Council members voted by tribes, each tribe having one vote. The five nations only rarely agreed to unite against a common enemy, but blood-feuds and serious internal strife were avoided. The fifty federal Sachems or Peace Chiefs were appointed by women and could only be deposed by women; this was because the basic Iroquois social unit was the mother with her children. Women headed the groups of related families (ohwachiras) from which the clans in turn were built, and the senior woman ruled in each of the longhouses, covered with slabs of elm bark, sixty feet or more in length, where ten or a dozen families dwelt together. So the League linked five republics in which women had a crucial position at every level of decision-making.

Allied with the English in the 1690s, the Iroquois suffered heavy losses from casualties and from defection to the French, whose priests converted numerous tribesmen to Catholicism. The main body stood by the English, who asked for fewer beaver skins for their guns. But it was the far more numerous English whose greed for land threatened them in the long run. Hence the Iroquois in the early eighteenth century tried to play the two white peoples off against each other, hoping that this would leave room for themselves. They renewed their friendship with the English but also promised the French to remain neutral in future wars. They would go down in ruin in the end, but not before they had provided an impressive example of Indian military and political prowess.

Existence alongside Indians in terrains which red men had mastered was helping to change the English character in North America. The novelty of New England, the virginity of Virginia, showed in the place names, of which many were Indian. The first rivers on which Englishmen settled had been given, and would retain, English titles – James, Charles, Cooper. But their tributaries, and rivers beyond, kept those which the red men had accorded them. The names of almost-extinct tribes would stay on the map to jostle those borrowed from towns in England and those expressing religious vision. 'Providence Plantations in Narragansett Bay' – any colonist setting such words on paper was unconsciously fertilising habits of thought which would modify his sense of himself as intrinsically English. Yet no distinctive American accent of speech seems to have emerged in the seventeenth century. The idiom in New England quite likely derived from that of East Anglia. There is no evidence of a Southern drawl. However, the digestion of Dutchmen and Swedes into the empire from the 1660s, and the readiness with which English governments admitted foreign immigration, had brought some cross-breeding in manners and language. Boston and Newport were still sturdily English in character, but New York remained cosmopolitan after the conquest, Charles Town in Carolina sheltered Huguenots and Scots, and Pennsylvania had its Germans and Welshmen.

By 1700 'English' colonists possessed the coastline from Maine to South Carolina, though there were still large gaps in effective settlement, notably the several hundred miles between the North Carolina and Charles Town colonies. Most people still clung to the shorelines and navigable rivers which gave a direct link with Europe. Boston, at or near 7,000, was the largest town. Virginia and Maryland had perhaps 90,000 colonists, New England about the same number, the 'Middle Colonies' something above 50,000 and the Carolinas perhaps 16,000; altogether, about a quarter million – far fewer than the population of London. However, numbers – as in New France – had doubled, perhaps trebled, since 1660. The New World, in temperate regions, was healthier and more evenly prosperous than the old. There were no ill years for food. The abundance of land, the lack of economic constraints, meant that colonists married younger than English people, they married for love, not money, they married more happily. Families seem to have been on average twice as large as in England. More children survived infancy.[110]

This was in spite of some difficulties and hazards. Rattlesnakes, common then even in the northern colonies, especially horrified the pioneers. Most of the seaboard where the English settled was originally covered with hardwood forest, though in many areas there was relatively little underbrush since the Indians, besides clearing some fields, habitually burnt over large areas to make hunting easier. The soil around Boston was said to become 'barren beyond belief' after five or six years' cultivation, but Pennsylvania pioneers were more fortunate. Rich land abounded there, and an account of 1685 could point out that 'The Trees grow but thin in most places and very little under-Wood.'[111]

Original settlers might favour the new unitary farm or might come from areas in Britain where open-field cultivation in strips was still taken for granted. New England was more old fashioned than Virginia; farming in strips was still

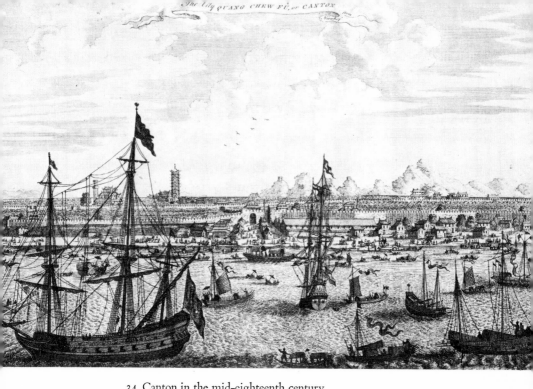

34 Canton in the mid-eighteenth century

35 An early impression of Savannah, Georgia

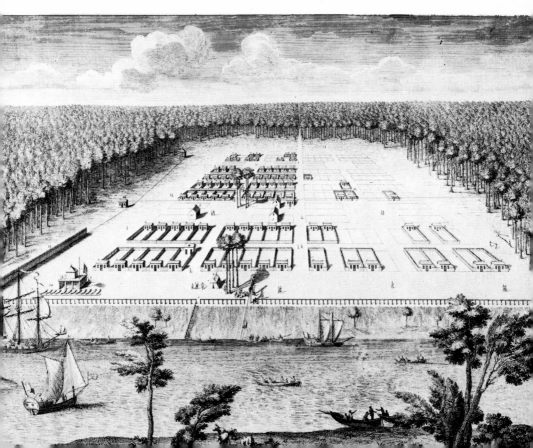

36 'Blackbeard the Pirate'—Edward Teach

37 Jonathan Swift, by C. Jervas

38 James Oglethorpe, after W. Verelst

39 Jonathan Edwards, of New England's 'Great Awakening', by Joseph Badger

general, and settlement expanded as whole groups of people applied for land on which to set up new townships. But the differences between north and south were no more striking than those between coastline and frontier. Every frontiersman carried, except at his peril, a flintlock musket, rather inaccurate beyond fifty yards, but deadly enough at close quarters. While modest comfort on well settled land was quite easily attained, the newcomer clearing virgin forest was sometimes so poor and ill-equipped that he must use a sledge instead of a cart, or make wheels from sawn slices of logs. A large bush dragged across the field might serve as a harrow. However, abundance of timber was an immense advantage, and venison and wild turkey from the forests, supplementing beef and pork from domestic animals able to graze widely, meant that new colonists ate far more meat than people back home. There was plentiful maple sugar and, to southward, native exotica such as peaches. Abundance of land made tillers extremely careless. Even the thrifty New Englanders seem to have discarded the more difficult English agricultural practices, without, however, adopting the best Indian ones.

Established farmers, except in New England, soon acquired more land than they could work with their own hands. The labour of free whites was from the outset extremely expensive. The unskilled worker could command two or three shillings a day compared to a shilling in England, while artisans and craftsmen could ask as much as 8s. 6d. Free workmen could soon afford to buy land themselves and would ride away to independence. As with such industrial concerns as ironworks, the richer colonists had to rely on indentured, servile labour. Furthermore, under the 'headright' system, those who imported large numbers of servants could secure enormous tracts of land. In 1676, 122 labourers entitled William Byrd, the Virginian fur trader, to no less than 7,351 acres; larger scoops were known, and the demand for servants was so hot that numerous Turks were imported into the Chesapeake.[112]

New England, with no headright system, and few large holdings, scorned the servant trade. After the great influx of the 1630s, its population grew by natural increase, supplemented by seamen glad to resign or desert from shipboard life. But land grants in New York were very large, and the inhabitants clamoured for all the servants merchants could bring them, and more. That they were left short reflected the greater attraction of Pennsylvania, where the Quakers, furthermore, frowned on the use of black slaves. Maryland and Virginia had a steady supply from the tobacco ships. The only North American colony which had to offer special inducements to bring in white servants was South Carolina which, with an actual majority of black slaves by 1708, was in the same predicament as Jamaica and Barbados.

Even so, no North American colony was glad to accept felons, of whom some 4,500 were destined to transportation from England in the last four decades of the seventeenth century, though far fewer would have been shipped or would have arrived. Virginia's legislators halted imports in 1671, expressing

o

the fear that it would harm the colony's reputation if it was 'believed to be a place only fitt to receive such base and lewd persons'.[113] By 1696 the Board of Trade found that only Barbados would still accept them, and even there women and children were not wanted. The problem was temporarily mitigated by renewed war early in the eighteenth century, which gave felons alternative employment in the forces.

The only advantage of buying convicts was that they served seven or fourteen years. By the end of the seventeenth century, a five-year term for indentured servants over a certain age was laid down by law in Virginia and Maryland, and a similar law was made in South Carolina by 1717. Other conditions, as legally imposed, varied greatly from colony to colony. Though the bait of free land was dangled to draw servants to Virginia, by those in England who stood to profit from them, the 'custom of the country' in that colony was to give none. Maryland ceased to offer free land at the end of indentures from 1683; New York never promised any; the Carolinas continued to give it until well into the eighteenth century. But since wages were so high, a freed servant might soon be able to buy land, if, that is, he had survived physically.

It can be argued that the greater rarity of active unrest shows that even people under indentures felt better off in America than in England. But Maryland court records show that a significant number of servants committed suicide. Clearing virgin forests under duress was punishing. The master, having paid up to thirty pounds for his labourer, stood to profit exceedingly over four or five years if he worked him hard enough. Runaways in Virginia had to serve double or more the time of their absence; Maryland exacted ten days for one, Pennsylvania five, and South Carolina seven for one day, a year for a week. Most runaway servants, being white, made good their escape, but newspaper advertisements commonly described them as having collars round their necks.[114]

On the face of it, servants once freed should have been able to prosper. In Pennsylvania and the colonies southward, the authorities, to encourage expansion, granted land on easy terms. Some servants in fact did well. Up to 1666, it would seem that a third or more of landholders in Virginia had come in under indentures. But then, three-quarters of all colonists had entered in that condition. Not less than 5,000 servants arrived in Maryland in the 1670s. Only 1,249 – a quarter – proved their right to the 50 acres which custom still allotted as freedom dues, and most of these sold out at once to other people. Only one servant in twenty-five emerged as a landowner. A. E. Smith has calculated that over the whole colonial period in North America, out of ten servants eight either died during their time, returned to England afterwards, or became 'poor-whites'. Only one would become a landholder, and the last would go to work for wages. A tiny minority of indentured servants became important men or founded famous families, but America, for most, was no land of opportunity; it was the scene of destructive and demoralising toil.[115] Yet there was never much hint of concerted rebellion amongst servants in any mainland colony. Running away was easy in early days. Later the influx of black slaves helped to pacify truculence, giving the hardest-ground white servant a consciousness of status.

In 1671 there were still only a couple of thousand slaves in Virginia. Tobacco did not insist on slaves like sugar. Why did slavery and North American society become inseparable? The overspill from the Caribbean of slaves re-exported or entering with white masters would have ensured some black faces in the southern, as in the northern colonies; but what, beyond this, led to steady imports? Greed for acres is one major explanation. 'The God Land' ruled in Virginia still more strongly than in New England; the headright system ensured that land could be claimed in respect of slaves imported; the supply of servants from England was never enormous; shipmasters could supply black people on the spot in return for tobacco and other produce. By 1700 slaves in Virginia were the chief basis of the acquisition of title to land, and the colony had perhaps 6,000 blacks.[116]

With peace opening sea lanes and raising hopes of new markets in Europe, with higher prices for tobacco, and with the Separate Traders now licensed to compete with the Royal Africa Company, a spate of purchases had begun. In 1700 the governor of Virginia reported that a slaver direct from Guinea had sold about 230 blacks, in the York River area, at the highest prices yet fetched. 'There were as many buyers as negros, and I think that, if 2000 were imported, there would be substantial buyers for them.'[117] Within the next decade, Virginia's slave population doubled.

South Carolina had been under West Indian influence from its beginnings. In the last decade of the seventeenth century, rice became the colony's chief staple, and this crop was slave-cultivated from the outset. South Carolina borrowed from the already mature slave code of Barbados, and legislation there was the harshest on the mainland; blacks had no rights at all.

Virginia codified its slave laws in 1705. By now quite small landowners were committed to the institution. In 1716, when two-thirds of taxpayers in Virginia's Lancaster County were slaveholders, three-quarters of these had four blacks or fewer. (Only four planters had more than twenty, though one of these, Robert Carter, may have owned 126.) The flogged-out indentured servant and the poor white failure could see that at least they were not niggers. To be Christian was to be white. To be black was to be a slave, unless proof could be shown. From 1691, Virginian law, which had previously borne hard on the practice, outlawed interracial sexual liaison completely as 'abominable mixture'. At this period, a white woman giving birth to a coloured child had to pay £15. If she could not pay she was to be sold into servitude herself for five years.[118]

There were, and had long been, free people of colour in Virginia. In 1654, 100 acres had been granted to a Negro carpenter on the basis of headrights conferred in respect of two whites. In 1697, John Nicholls left by will 500 acres to two mulattoes, presumably his own children. But when another Virginian planter in his will had not only emancipated a slave, bequeathing him a house and as much ground as he could cultivate, but had also appointed him guardian of a girl ward of his, and overseer of her property, a court had not allowed him to fulfil such offices. Free blacks could own Indian or black slaves, but no longer white servants. In 1723 black freemen, along with mulattoes and Indians, would be specifically excluded from voting. Meanwhile, emancipation was frowned on. A Virginian law of 1699 required the exportation of every African freeman within six months of his emancipation, on penalty to the planter of a levy upon his own property.[119]

By this time, Massachusetts law also was overtly prejudiced, distinguishing mulattoes as well as Negroes in a separate category. A traveller of 1687, commenting on the scarcity of white labour there, alleged that every household in Boston, 'however small may be its Means', had one or two blacks. But the governor reported in 1708 that of 550 blacks in Massachusetts altogether, 400 were in that town. The first printed protest against the slave trade in New England seems to have come in 1700 when Samuel Sewell produced a pamphlet, *The Selling of Joseph*, which argued on archaic Puritan lines that an unlawful war could not make lawful captives and that, for all New Englanders could tell, the wars in Africa which were supposed to provide the source of slaves were in fact unjust ones. Nevertheless, we find him thereafter advertising for sale 'Negro boys' to 'be disposed of' by himself. A patently racialist Massachusetts Act of 1705 'for the Better Preventing of a Spurious and Mixt Issue' imposed a duty of £4 a head on all blacks imported.[120] This was of course a discouragement, not a ban, but the Board of Trade was very angry when it found out that the colony was interfering in this way with one of England's prime lines of commerce. There was later some smuggling of slaves into Massachusetts to evade this duty.

One of the most perfected expressions of prejudice to be found at this time comes from the wife of a Boston merchant, Sarah Kemble Knight, who travelled through Connecticut in 1704. She wrote sharply that the people there were 'too Indulgent (especially the farmers) to their slaves: sufering too great familiarity from them, permitting them to sit at Table and eat with them, (as they say to save time,) and into the dish goes the black hoof as freely as the white hand.' She went on to relate with disgust an anecdote regarding a farmer instructed by arbitrators to pay 40s. damages to his black slave for failing to fulfil a promise punctually; the 'poor master' had actually done so.[121] Of course, if this story was true, or merely thought possible, it showed that in rural New England Africans, because rarer, might be more readily accepted as individual human beings.

Mrs Knight's worldly snobbery was symptomatic. Boston now had scores of public houses. New England and Pennsylvania were chaste places compared with Barbados or Jamaica, but the whores of Boston were famous throughout the colonies and the Philadelphia Quakers sometimes tippled quite heavily. Dress among Puritans and Quakers was decorous, but black was not general, let alone uniform. Puritans approved of athletic sports (including cricket, an early passenger to America) and had no objection to secular songs if they were not bawdy. And in any case strict Puritans no longer dominated New England society; the great John Winthrop's grandsons were more devoted to real estate than to godliness and were 'always exceedingly anxious to hear about the latest London fashions in waistcoats and wigs'.[122]

The Puritan was turning into the Yankee, byword the world over for commercial sharpness. There is a fascinating and often-discussed transition from the Calvinism of New England's founding fathers, through the non-Calvinist, more humanistic vision of Philadelphia and Newport Quakers who remained Puritans in dress and manners, towards the almost wholly secularised ethics of that Philadelphian, Benjamin Franklin, in the eighteenth century. Puritans and Quakers alike believed that idleness was the mother of vice, and put profits back into business which men of other creeds might have wasted in conspicuous consumption. Sobriety, thrift and frugality – 'credit-making virtues' – dominated in Boston and Philadelphia.

But the seemingly inexhaustible acres of virgin land on which successful traders would cast lustful eyes gave American capitalism an especially marked tendency, which it has never lost, to the reckless, improvident exploitation of natural resources. The beaver were steadily massacred. In the north, the great fur-trading centre was Albany, up the Hudson, completely surrounded by a palisade, with lodges outside its gates for Indians bringing in furs, where town officials jealously strove to guard a monopoly of commerce with the Iroquois first established in days of Dutch rule. In the south, lead in the trade in furs and skins was passing from Virginia to Charles Town, Carolina, which was nearer to the hunting grounds of the Catawba and Cherokee. As the valuable beasts were wiped out, so Indians would become redundant and their lands would attract planters and farmers who had spoiled their old holdings by careless methods.

Resilient optimism was to be a more pleasant outcome of the scope for westward expansion. Toleration, if not always tolerance, was another liberating force at work. Proprietors anxious to find settlers wrote religious liberty into their promises and their constitutions; it was rare for any one denomination to have a clear majority in any single polity, and so, as Richard Hofstadter puts it, America 'stumbled into virtue'.[123] In 1660 only Maryland and Rhode Island had been officially tolerant, and other colonies had been under theoretically tight State-Church rule. Yet by 1700 even Massachusetts, thanks to pressures from England, had made ample concessions, religious compulsion was aberration, not norm, and the colonies were moving well beyond the cramping toleration accorded to dissenters in England itself. Trade swayed their leaders in the seaports. Toleration suited trade.

Though New England Congregationalism differed markedly from Virginian Anglicanism, each was remote in practice from the Church of England. Neither colony had bishops. While in New England marriage was from the outset a civil contract, in Virginia, where the civil authority issued licences, it tended to become so. Where Anglicanism was not established, it appealed chiefly to a self-conscious élite, hopefully sycophantic before the English governor, anxious to emphasise the gap which new-made wealth had set between themselves and the ordinary colonist.

There were people in North America who saw themselves as gentlemen and were seen to be so. Deference was still given readily to a Winthrop or Carter. But though the wealthiest men in Virginia were quite impressive plantocrats, though New York's cosmopolitan oligarchy kept firm control, and though some of the rich Quakers who emigrated to Philadelphia in its early days at once began to live in 'brave brick houses' with balconies overlooking the Delaware River, such people were not lords or baronets; in terms of English society then, they were what we would call middle class. 'No house in New England hath above 20 Rooms,' it was reported in the 1670s. 'Not 20 in Boston, which have above 10 rooms each ... The worst cottages in New England are lofted. No beggars. Not 3 put to death for theft.'[124]

This was at the other pole from the West Indies, where contrasts in wealth were sharp, as in the homeland. The difference has been established by Richard Dunn, comparing probated estates in Jamaica and Maryland in the late seventeenth century, as these are shown in inventories. Three-quarters of property owners in the tobacco colony were worth less than £100; only a third of those in the sugar colony. In Jamaica 5·5 per cent were worth over £2,000, in Maryland there were none at all in that highest category, and only 3·7 per cent were worth over £500. Proportionately, there were ten times as many wealthy men in Jamaica, and the wealthiest there were very much richer. The contrast with New England was stronger still. There were thirteen servants or slaves per household in Jamaica and the richest men could put some blacks in livery and give them ceremonial tasks. Even Sir William Phips, when governor of Massachusetts, kept only three blacks and four white servants at his Boston mansion — and all of these slept in bedchambers in the house, whereas a rich West Indian planter had his extensive retinue stabled, as it were, in huts outside, or strung up in hammocks in the hall.[125]

But whereas few planters in the Caribbean owned more than a handful of books, Massachusetts could boast many sizeable libraries, partly because New England clergymen were commonly well-to-do, whereas West Indian parsons were almost poor-whites. William Fitzhugh, holder of a large estate in Virginia, kept his property on the market in the hope that he might end his days in England, explaining in 1687 that 'society that is good and ingenious is very scarce and seldom to be come at except in Books'.[126] But even this would-be absentee revealed intellectual as well as social aspirations, and, largely because very few mainland colonials were rich enough to support a position in English society as prestigious as that which they could enjoy, big fish in small pools, in America, absentee landownership never became common, as it was in the West Indies and in Ireland. Cultural standards reflected this fact. By the 1670s Harvard was managed by its own graduates rather than by men trained in England. The College of William and Mary in Virginia was founded before the end of the century, and Yale just into the eighteenth, taking its name later from Elihu Yale, born near Boston in 1648, who served for five years as governor of Madras and assisted the college in Connecticut with a gift of books and pictures worth £560.

Boston had its own printing press before the Civil War, Philadelphia almost from its inception. Literacy, unusually widespread in England itself, was even more so in the northern colonies. But New England produced at this time little literary prose except sermons and little poetry of the least distinction. There was not much call for light literature; Virginian planters seem to have been almost as fond of reading sermons as Massachusetts magistrates. The great Anglo-Welsh religious poet George Herbert was far more popular in North America than any writer of love lyrics. Almost every learned man in New England seems to have composed didactic verse, generally for private use; but ideas mattered more than gracefulness — as, notoriously, in the 'Bay Psalm Book', a metrical version first published in Boston in 1640 which aimed at literal accuracy at the expense of all else ('O give yee thanks unto the Lord, because that good is hee:/because his loving kindenes lasts to perpetuitee').[127] The most striking colonial poet, Edward Taylor (c. 1645–1729), wrote 'metaphysical' verse for his private purposes long after the style had lost all favour in England, and found no audience till our own century.

Good books, after all, could be imported from England, along with kettles and cloth. Verbally fluent young men in North America would aspire in politics rather than literature. As in ancient Athens or Renaissance Italy, the abundance of servile labour helped to support a remarkably widespread partici-pation in the running of affairs, both in Church and State.

Though all colonies now had a franchise based on property, 'property, like Godliness, could be widely distributed'.[128] Massachusetts with, after 1691, its new 40s. freehold qualification, still had almost universal male suffrage, and this at a time when the franchise in England itself was being cut back. However, no one talked about democracy, at least, not with approval. Power was usually centred in the Governor's Council of about a dozen men. Except in Massachu-setts, Connecticut and Rhode Island, Councillors were appointed by royal or proprietary authority, and even in New England the general rule applied that the wealthier families were represented. The governor had to struggle against local men with a good conceit of themselves, and with useful connections in London, while colonists themselves accepted the idea received in all European societies that, as the Virginian House of Burgesses put it in 1706, some must be 'highe and eminent in power and dignitie; others meane and in subieccion.'[129]

These same Virginian burgesses, however, were ready to side with the governor, on occasion, against overweening Council members. The divide between Council and lower house was roughly that between upper-middling and middling people. Bicameral legislature had become standard in the 1690s, when Rhode Island, Connecticut and South Carolina had been brought into line. The desire to produce a replica of the English Parliament with its Lords and Commons was probably as weighty as any other motive. Everywhere, by 1696, representatives in the lower house had, as in England, the right to take initiative in legislation. The colonists had borrowed the English title of 'Speaker' for the chief officer of the lower house, and asserted after the English manner the privileges of assembly members, whether these were called 'burgesses', 'deputies' or 'representatives'. Such men sat for 'townships' in New England and for 'counties' elsewhere; an occasional 'borough' or 'manor' surviving from the grandiose neo-feudalist visions of proprietors would also have representation.

However, proprietorial Pennsylvania came to provide an exceptional instance of assembly-power. Penn returned in 1699, planning to live out his days in the New World; two years later he reluctantly conceded a 'Charter of Privileges' by which the Council was excluded from legislation, though the governor would still have a veto. The assembly here thus obtained unique control over legislation, taxation, and its own organisation and membership, while the 'Lower Counties' (Delaware), acquiring their own assembly in 1704, though they still came under Pennsylvania's governor, lived in a rather delectable constitutional twilight, with no crown charter, no defined status, and no need to send laws to England for approval.

But even Pennsylvania was not 'democratic'. In practice, its politics were dominated till 1756 by an oligarchy of wealthy Quakers, of whom Penn himself, an authentic English gentleman, wrote sarcastically, 'There is an excess of vanity that is apt to creep in upon the people in power in America, who, having got out of the crowd in which they were lost here, upon every little eminency there, think nothing taller than themselves but the trees, and as if there were no after superior judgement to which they should be accountable; so that I have sometimes thought that if there was a law to oblige the people in power, in their respective colonies, to take turns in coming over for England, that they might lose themselves again amongst the crowds of so much more considerable people at the custom-house, exchange, and Westminster Hall, they would exceedingly amend in their conduct at their return, and be much more discreet and tractable, and fit for government.'[130] He was bitter not only against the anti-proprietorial opposition led by a Welshman named David Lloyd, but also over the fact that his quitrents did not come in.

While Quakerism became the religion of plump merchants who still dressed plainly, but in the finest cloth, a revived and rather militant Anglicanism tried to regain lost ground in America. From 1685 James Blair, a Scottish Anglican clergyman, settled in Virginia as Commissary for the Bishop of London. This was the first appointment in the colonies to an office with general supervisory authority over Church and clergy. Blair married into Virginia's élite and was strong enough, with the Bishop's help, to get Governor Andros removed from office in 1698; then he engaged, with other Council members, in a furious struggle with the new governor, Francis Nicholson. The Church in Virginia had been virtually Congregational in form. Local landowners, as vestrymen, had hired and fired clergymen. The house of burgesses backed Nicholson against Blair, but the latter's connections in London finally unseated this governor also. Blair's counterpart in Maryland was Commissary Thomas Bray, founder of the Society for the Propagation of the Gospel which began Anglican missionary work, chiefly among whites, from 1701, supported by donations from English clergy and laity. After a long struggle with local Quakers (and their lobby in London), Anglicanism was established by law in Maryland from 1702. Two years later the South Carolina Assembly excluded Dissenters from membership and provided for an Anglican establishment, but the noncon-formists, with more houses of worship in the colony than the Church of England, made such a powerful fuss that revised legislation in 1706 removed Church membership as a test for office. Anglicanism, as established here, drew on pro-vincial revenues, rather than tithes, for support, and gathered to itself the élite families of the colony.

New York in 1691 fell back into the hands of the grandees who had been Leisler's enemies. They received eager collaboration from certain notorious governors, who favoured them with huge land grants; so much the worse, historians have concluded, for the development of New York, which remained under-settled; so much the better, however, for the Iroquois. The big men helped push through a proposal for an Anglican establishment in 1693, but it was restricted to four counties near New York City itself.

In Massachusetts, Joseph Dudley, the villain of the 1680s, schemed to get hold of the governorship and succeeded in 1701. He bullied the lower house and challenged its privileges. They hit back, as they well could do, controlling the purse strings, and refused him more than a meagre salary. For the next three-quarters of a century this pattern would recur—a detested royal governor warring with niggardly assemblymen, scorning the latter socially as well as politically, and allying with Boston merchants against the country people.

New England clerical families intermarried, and only a few exceptional men could penetrate their caste. Against the Congregational tradition, they began in the 1690s to organise themselves as a professional group, and to strive for control of the churches. In Connecticut, in 1708, a quasi-Presbyterian system was adopted by law, under which neighbouring churches formed 'consociations' and parcels of ministers were to examine and license candidates for their own pro-fession. Village Hampdens thwarted a movement towards this in Massachusetts, but rustics could not prevent the formation of Boston's fourth church in 1698–9 by some of the richest merchants, who adopted a refined and ritualistic degeneration of Calvinist practice. A local satirist called out:

Saints Cotton and Hooker, Oh look down and look here ...
Our churches turn genteel
Our parsons grow trim and trig with Wealth, Wine and Wig
And their heads are covered with meal.[131]

The merchants who went to this polite place had the farmers under their thumbs. In debt with them for imported goods, the latter could only pay with produce, and their labour was thus exploited with classic directness. Yet it must be emphasised, over and over again, that this colony and Virginia were, and would remain, far more homogenous and socially open than any European society. The novelty of the political culture which was emerging across the Atlantic was not understood in the colonies, where men still thought of themselves as English, and it could hardly have been grasped by men on the Board of Trade in London who had never themselves crossed the Atlantic.

The system of rule was self-contradictory. In the colonies the royal prerogative was still not trammelled, as it had been in England after 1689. The Reverend John Wise, who led a short-lived tax strike against Andros in Massachusetts in 1687, invoked the rights of Englishmen 'according to Magna Charta' at his trial. Dudley slapped him down firmly: he 'must not think the laws of England follow us to the ends of Earth ... you have no more privilidges left you, than not to be sold for Slaves.'[132] This remained, in theory, true. If king or parliament at home chose to overbear the colonists, they had hardly a legal leg to stand upon.

Yet the Board of Trade was not powerful at home. While monarch, or Commons, or Lords, or a Secretary of State, could take an initiative in colonial affairs, depending upon the matter involved it would engage the admiralty, the war office, the treasury, the customs commissioners, the law officers, the high courts, or the Bishop of London. Delays and inefficiencies were inevitable; by virtue of this the colonists were not over-governed and could successfully play one authority off against another.

The chief parcel of people who had an interest in strong and uniform rule were the small group of professionals in the colonial civil service. That experienced governor Francis Nicholson backed the Board of Trade as, after peace came in 1697, it commenced a drive to resume for the Crown all the proprietory charters. For Blathwayt, who found in the colonies quite lucrative posts for six of his relations, and for Randolph, who was piqued by the fact that courts in chartered colonies commonly adjudicated against him and robbed him of his reward money, jobs for the boys and cash in hand would be the pay-off if royal government were extended. Penn went home in 1701 to fight. His parcel, the well-to-do Quaker lobby in London, was too strong for the Board. Though New Jersey's 72 proprietors finally surrendered their political rights to the King in 1702, the Board could not get its grander aims passed by a not-very-interested Parliament, at three attempts in six years. Penn's triumph was somewhat Pyrrhic. He fell disastrously into debt and spent eleven months in prison in

1708. He attempted to sell his province to the Crown, and agreement (£12,000) had actually been reached in 1712 when a partial stroke prevented him from completing negotiations. He lingered in rural England, fuddled and quiescent, until his death six years later left Pennsylvania to his heirs. The return of Maryland to proprietary rule in 1715 was balanced by the King's purchase of Carolina a few years later, so the shape of the North American empire was substantially that which it would retain till the last quarter of the century.

Vice-Admiralty Courts were erected between 1697 and 1701 in eleven jurisdictions in the New World. The aim was to cope with pirates and smugglers. The Board dealt quite successfully with piracy. This was a major problem, as peace demobilised seamen trained in maritime combat. The Indian Ocean was the main centre. Most of the pirates there were said to be English. Pirate ships were fitted out in the North American colonies, manned there, and supplied by colonial vessels at their bases in Madagascar. The New World colonies themselves suffered; John James, in 1699, plundered the coast at will from North Carolina to New York. But pirates were otherwise welcome for the coin they brought in. Governors often accepted bribes; so did jurymen. The Board of Trade obtained royal permission to have the rogues shipped for trial in England, and the notorious Captain Kidd, captured in New York, was brought to London in 1700 with 31 of his fellows; he and 11 others were duly hanged, as were 26 out of nearly 100 pirates whom Governor Nicholson sent from Virginia.[133]

All this was of great importance to the East India Company; or rather Companies; there were now two. The Mughals blamed them for all piracies. The problem abated for a while when a Royal Naval squadron was sent into Eastern waters. But a Scottish merchant in the Orient, one of confusingly many Hamiltons to appear in colonial history, claimed that a fellow-countryman of his, a certain Millar, 'did the Publick more Service in destroying them, than all the chargeable Squadrons that have been sent in Quest of them; for, with a Cargo of strong Ale and Brandy, which he carried to sell them, *in Anno* 1704 he killed above 500 of them by carousing, tho' they took his Ship and Cargo as a Present from him, and his Men entred, most of them, into the Society of the Pirates.' It was an ill wind which blew no one good; Hamilton also observed that one effect of the pirate presence in Madagascar was to stop the EIC seeking slaves in that island.[134]

VIII

In 1698, the monopoly of the East India trade was, in effect, put up for auction. The EIC, weakened by losses to the French, offered to loan the government £700,000, at 4 per cent interest, in return for confirmation of its charter. The rival 'Dowgate Association' offered £2 million at 8 per cent, and won. Parliament ordained that a 'General Society' of the subscribers to their loan would have the monopoly until at least 1714. Its members could either trade separately or unite in a fresh joint stock. Most chose the latter, and in September 1698 a new East India Company was incorporated by royal charter.

However, the old EIC bought its way into dominance in the new company, subscribing, through its treasurer, no less than £315,000 to the loan, and carried on perfectly legally. The New Company, having lent its original capital to the government, found it hard to raise more from its members. The squabbles which arose in the East did neither any good. The rulers of India, while taking little interest, tended to favour the Old hands. Thomas Pitt in Madras sneered at his namesake and relative John Pitt, now installed as King's Consul and New Company president up the coast at Masulipatam, for his 'Sugar Candy how-doe-you-doe letters' trying to seduce Old Company personnel, and had distinctly the better of the confrontation.[135]

William Norris, M.P. for Liverpool, was created a baronet and sent out as Royal Ambassador to Aurangzeb. He went with a large retinue in gorgeous liveries, thinking that he could march across war-torn India and approach the Emperor in fine style. In fact, he was stuck for several months in Masulipatam, where John Pitt could not produce the escort and supplies he promised. Realising his error, Norris sailed round to Surat, where he wasted 1,800 gold mohurs on bribes designed to secure him the honour of a public entry into the town. He finally obtained an audience with Aurangzeb in April 1701, nineteen months after his first landing in India. Six months later, having got nowhere, he quit without taking personal leave of the monarch. He died on the voyage home. His embassy cost vast sums and achieved only negative results; after his impolite departure from the Mughal court there were imperial proclamations that the goods and persons of Englishmen should be seized. The New Company suffered heavily in Bengal, but the Old Company held out in Calcutta, and in Madras Pitt survived three months' siege by Daud Khan, the Nawab of the Carnatic.

As the King himself wished, the Old and New Companies amalgamated in 1702. After a transition period of half-and-half, the Old Company surrendered its charter in 1709 and made its possessions, Bombay and St Helena, over to a 'United Company of Merchants of England Trading to the East Indies'. Sir Nicholas Waite, New Company president in Bombay, learning that his Old Company rival Gayer had been preferred by the joint board at home, bribed the Mughal governor heavily to keep Gayer in prison and ruled on for six years – meanwhile, although he had a wife at home, contracting an incestuous marriage with his niece.[136] But by the second decade of the eighteenth century, most of the dust had settled. The 'Separate Adventurers' permitted under the 1698 arrangements were bought out and monopoly in the Eastern trade was fully restored. In return for concessions by Parliament, the United Company was required, in 1708, to lend the exchequer a further sum of £1,200,000, making £3,200,000 in all, on which it would get only 5 per cent interest. The right of Parliament to control the conditions under which monopoly operated was thus established, and the EIC ranked alongside the Bank of England as one of the indispensable pillars of national finance.

As the situation stabilised for the English in the East, an essential feature was that, like the French and the Dutch, the EIC at Surat was compelled to sign a security bond for the payment of any losses from piracy by Mughal subjects. The three nations divided these losses, and policed the waterways between them, the Dutch taking the coast from Surat to the Red Sea, the French the Persian Gulf and the English the Bengal and Coromandel coasts. After Norris's rudeness and its repercussions no more ambassadors were sent. The Emperor left the English to govern themselves.

The politics of the presidencies were infinitely sordid long before the days of Warren Hastings. The governor would always be under the suspicion of the directors at home and liable to supersession when the next ship arrived. He chaired a small council whose members he could not override, and who commonly amused themselves writing spiteful letters to London behind his back. Underlings owed promotion to the directors, not to him. His main duties were tediously commercial; goods must be inspected and checked, the annual cargoes home must be prepared. The pomp which the governors always adopted masked their practical lack of power. The tone of their remarks upon council members suggests an ambience where the finer flowers of human nature bloomed rarely if at all. 'I shall not rake into his dirty ashes', Elihu Yale once commented on a young man whom he was accused of poisoning. 'All the custome he ever paid the Company never defrayed the charge of bringing the water he drank' was Thomas Pitt's characteristically odious valediction for another defunct councillor.[137]

Of Governor Weltden of Calcutta (1710–11) the Scots trader Hamilton remarked: 'His Term of governing was very short, and he took as short a Way to be enriched by it, by harassing the People to fill his Coffers ... Yet he was very shy in taking Bribes, referring those honest Folks, who traffick'd that Way, to the Discretion of his Wife and Daughter, to make the best Bargain they could about the Sum to be paid, and to pay the Money into their Hands.'[138] Embezzlement by EIC servants was quite frequent, and subtler chicanery was commonplace. Company money was used to finance private trade, and many EIC servants seem to have contrived to sell their own goods to their employers at prices set by themselves, using the cover of native names. Every Englishman was out to make as much as possible as fast as possible. More than one chaplain was dismissed for engaging in private commerce. Gambling was the favourite amusement, in which even 'gentlewomen' indulged. Still more than the Caribbean, this was a track where men raced against premature death.

Feasting remained as gross, and as suicidal, as compotation. We read of twelve or fifteen courses as a rule served for both dinner and supper. Thomas Pitt's correspondence 'teems with references to his strong drinks.' He and his son went out to Madras with no fewer than fifty-two chests of wine. Madeira became a common English tipple in the East, but 'Shiraz wine' from Persia was also used, and so, to disastrous effect, was the local spirit, *arrack*. Immoderate habits abetted disease in its scything. It can be assumed that virtually every Englishman wanted to quit as soon as he had acquired enough to sustain him in comfort back home. But of forty-six men appointed to serve the EIC in Bengal between 1707 and 1711, twenty-nine perished in India, and this rate, around two-thirds, remained standard thereafter.[139]

On the face of it, it seems hard to understand why people went East. The United Company settled on a series of graded ranks for their covenanted servants. After five years as a 'Writer' one became a 'Factor', then, three years further on, a 'Junior Merchant' and finally, after three more, a 'Senior Merchant'. Promotion was strictly by seniority. Pay was piffling. Writers got £5 a year, Senior Merchants £40, and even various extra allowances brought the rewards given by the EIC no higher than £34 and £225 respectively. Only the governors received enough to subsist on.[140]

Nevertheless, Writerships were coveted in Britain. Certain highly respectable commercial families which often intermarried between themselves and seeded an Anglo-Indian 'caste' habitually sent their sons East. They expected that the profits of private trade there would bring them, if they survived, quite ample fortunes. And a trickle of independent merchants were attracted by the same lure. The EIC licensed them to trade within the area of its monopoly, though these so-called 'Free Merchants' were in fact sharply restricted – for instance, they were not allowed to operate inland, away from the main English settlements.

The EIC let its servants ship very little to England on their own account, but since the 1660s it had given them almost complete freedom to trade in Asian waters. For various reasons, it was not economical for the Company to engage in the 'country trade' between Asian ports on its own behalf. It encouraged its underpaid hirelings to do so. The French and Dutch companies did not allow their servants such liberty till well into the eighteenth century, and there is no doubt that the EIC's attitude greatly furthered the spread of English trade in Asia by unleashing its employees' initiative. They competed, of course, with native merchants and shipowners in meeting local requirements. Some operations were humble and routine. Thus, we read of a ship sent, in 1714, from Calcutta to Junk Ceylon in Malaya for tin and dried fish. It was to sell the fish at Malacca for sugar and rattans, and these in turn were to be disposed of on the Malabar Coast of India, whence pepper could be procured for sale in Madras. But there were also valuable long-distance trades westward to Persia and Arabia.[141]

Surat, under native control, was still regarded as India's greatest port, but Calcutta was rising very fast, ousting Hugli as Bengal's main outlet. The growing success of English shipowners over their Asian competitors in the carrying trades at this time owed nothing to technical superiority. They too employed mostly Asian crews on ships built in Asia, which were no better armed than native-owned vessels, and which asked for much higher freight charges. The chief factor seems to have been the diplomatic prowess of the EIC, under whose vast umbrella all Englishmen in the East sailed and traded. It had won striking privileges at such key ports as Achin in Sumatra, where the concessions granted to the EIC in 1602, on its very first voyage, were still in force; as Gombroon in the Persian Gulf, where it paid no customs as compared to 9 per cent generally demanded from Asian merchants. Indians despatching merchandise on risky long voyages preferred English-owned ships, not just because of these direct benefits, but because the EIC's reputation would deter customs collectors and other officials from high-handed exactions and might even hold the ubiquitous pirates back from attack.

But it must be stressed that EIC personnel, and their competitors from other European countries, still played only a small role relative to the vastness and variety of Asian commerce. In their small communities, there was as yet little disposition to harp on racial superiority. Attitudes to miscegenation were genial. Of 119 Englishmen on the Coromandel coast in 1699, fourteen had wives who were 'castees' (as pure Portuguese were called), four were married to 'mustees' (who mixed Portuguese and Indian parents), two had French wives and one had espoused a Georgian. The number with English wives was only twenty-six. Availability was limited. There were at this time fourteen widows to choose from, but only ten single English young women. It was arduous and risky to sail to India. 'A modest Woman,' one clergyman-traveller, Ovington, observed, 'may very well expect, without any great Stock of Honour or Wealth, a Husband of Repute and Riches there, after she has run all this Danger and Trouble for him.' It was perilous and unpleasant to live there. One young lady wrote to Govern or Pitt, 'Could I have got home to England, I wod not have staid here for the best husband in India.'[142]

The yellow malarial Englishwoman could barely compete in allure with the native dancing girls, so accomplished, as Ovington conceded, 'that a grave *European* will scarce adventure himself in the sight of their insinuating Temptations, and charming deportment'.[143] The EIC servants and other English traders tended to go the way of Calcutta's unhallowed founder, Job Charnock. They liked these *Nautch* girls, and otherwise borrowed whatever Hindu and Muslim customs they fancied. At home they ate in the English way at table, but among natives would lie on carpets in the Indian fashion. They buried their many dead in elaborate tombs designed, it would seem, to outmatch those of Muhammadans. They wore native clothes indoors, chewed pan and betel, and smoked hookahs. They ate kebabs and pulaos and mango pickles as well as dishes cooked in the English or Portuguese style. Like the barbarians who had conquered Rome, or the Manchus who had in the seventeenth century mastered China, they would be well acquainted with local habits when the time to assert themselves came.

But that was not yet. When their hour struck, their descendants would be less affable than the Huns. Meanwhile, unlike Norris, experienced India hands comported themselves discreetly. Even the 'roughling' Thomas Pitt wrote obsequiously to Daud Khan, the Emperor's viceroy, in 1701: 'I have with great impatience waited for your arrival at Arcot which being informed of two days ago I celebrated with great joy, preparing my people to wait on you with such acknowledgements of respect as I was capable of providing.' Sheer laxity, as in the Caribbean, must have bred tolerance among them; but the overwhelming numerical mass of adherents of non-Christian religions would have compelled them anyway to be modest about their own. There was no missionary effort. 'In *Calcutta*,' remarked the Scot, Hamilton, wrily, 'all Religions are freely tolerated, but the *Presbyterian*, and that they brow-beat.'[144] Latent racialism peeped out in tell-tale signs. The half-caste sons of EIC servants would be employed as of right by the Company; however, not in the highest posts. Most Europeans learnt the Portuguese pidgin which was the *lingua franca* of white and off-white India; few even now bothered to learn native tongues.

Much of the character of the EIC at this time can be understood from observing the way things went in its non-Indian colonies at St Helena and Bencoolen. The first was an island paradisal in climate. The islanders, white and black, were notably healthy. The girls ravished the eyes of landsick sailors. Just as well; they were pining to get away by marriage to a seaman or passenger. ' ... The minds of the Inhabitants,' wrote Ovington, 'are generally as Uncultivated as the neglected Soil.' Remoteness compounded the effects of poverty and drunkenness. The garrison mutinied, shooting the governor, in 1693; this was promptly followed by an attempted slave rising. Roberts, governor from 1708 to 1711, brought the island to some kind of order, but Governor Boucher who followed him let everything slide. He spent six hours a day in the saddle, believing himself to be in poor health, riding on donkeys from his large stud, which he insisted must be called his 'horses'. So that bad weather need not prevent this pastime, he built at the Company's expense a covered shed 400 feet long. When he resigned in 1714, his last act was to strip Government House of everything portable, not excluding the locks on the doors.[145]

Bencoolen in Western Sumatra remained even unhealthier than the EIC's Indian settlements, but it had the compensation that the natives could be bullied. Joseph Collet, governing six or seven garrisons scattered over about 300 miles of coastline, noted with gratification in 1712, 'Severall Kings profess themselves to be our Subjects. I always receive them with the forms and air of a Superiour.' York Fort, impressive seen from the sea, was not truly formidable, and in 1714 Collet abandoned it and set up headquarters at Fort Marlborough, built a couple of miles to the south. Even this stronger place was captured by natives in 1719 and returned only when the English agreed to exact less pepper. The garrison was a problem. English soldiers died quickly. Slaves from Madagascar proved unsatisfactory. Here as in India the half-caste Portuguese 'Topazes' were the mainstay, supplemented in this case by Bugis from Celebes. The surrounding country was wild. Relations with the natives were bad. Food was scarce. Labour costs were high. The whites had nothing to do but squabble. Collet reported on the shortage of white women: 'There are but 5 White things in Petticoats upon the Coast, one I am sending away with her husband, tho' she petitions to stay behind in the Quality of Nurse alias Bawd. Another is sent away by her husband with my consent because she is so free of Tongue, Tale and Hands that the poor man can't live in quiet with her. A third is non-compos and actually confin'd to a Dark room and straw. A 4th is really a good Wife and a modest Woman but the malitious say, that her person never provok'd any one yet to ask her the question. The 5th is a young Widow suppos'd to have a little money, of the rt. St Helena breed, as well shap'd as a Madagascar Cow, — and so much for Women.' Not quite. With such scarcity of white females of any shape, interbreeding with natives was commonplace, and here, in contrast with India, Eurasian half-castes came to fill even senior posts in the Company's service.[146]

Bombay, after the war with the Mughal, stood only above Bencoolen among the EIC's settlements; there seem to have been no more than seventy-six Europeans there in 1699. Madras had about twice as many. Though it was scorchingly hot from April to September, this was a healthier place than Bombay or Calcutta. But it had its drawbacks. The beach was continually pummelled by high surf. English boats were no use for landing or shipping goods, so the local flat-bottomed 'Mussoolas', held together with twine, were hired instead. Fort St George with its red laterite walls, the colour of rusty iron, its four bastions, mortar and fifty-six guns, was built on sand. A salt river flowed round behind it; there was no drinkable water within a mile. But the White Town within its walls had half a dozen 'strait handsome streets' of brick houses with flat roofs where the denizens might take what air was to be had. The 'better sort of People' went about in palanquins carried by six or eight native coolies. The EIC servants were supposed to keep apart from the scores of thousands of natives in the 'Black Town'. Collegiate discipline still survived; EIC men could not live outside the fort without special leave and had to attend morning and evening prayers. Clerks and Writers who were unruly were sometimes sent home by the next ship.

But the barracks was, in 1711, described as the 'scene of many a drunken frolick'. About that time, it numbered some 250 Europeans, some 200 'black Mungrel Portuguese' and 200 natives. The white soldier could live well on his pay; meat, fish, poultry and clothing were cheaper than at home. ' ... Not a common soldier in the place but has a boy to wait on him.' Soldiers might marry papist women so long as the children were brought up as Protestants, hence there was a school in Madras intended to imbue them with the correct principles. But the Portuguese were allowed their own Catholic church in the White Town, and an Armenian Christian church rose among the Black

Town's pagodas, few brick houses, many hovels. Elihu Yale had encouraged Armenian merchants to settle, egged on by that prophet of tolerance, Sir Josiah Child.[147]

Yale's father was Welsh and he himself retired, aged just over 50, to Plas Grono in north-east Wales. It was probably for this reason that a new stronghold built by the EIC near Cuddalore, well to the south of Madras, in 1690, was given the name 'Fort St David'. Madras itself was expanded. Three adjoining villages were rented from 1693, five more during Pitt's reign (1698–1709). But the Mughals resumed these latter in 1711, and did not return them for six years. As in Calcutta, the English had no absolute possession.

Calcutta was fortified with the Mughal's leave in 1698. The EIC became *zemindar*, tax collector, in three villages, which altogether covered only a fraction of the area later occupied by the city. For an annual rent of 1,200 rupees to the Mughal, the Company was free to tax and govern almost as it pleased. Next year, the Bengal EIC was given its own presidency, based on Fort William in Calcutta. Governor Beard was able to resist an attempt to seize the Company's goods in 1702, and showed skill in the art which was still most essential to any English leader here; calculating the size of bribe which would be just sufficient to placate an official.

In 1706, Calcutta's population was reckoned at 17,000. The underpaid native collectors employed to take taxes were from the outset prone to fraud and extortion. The EIC also relied on native policemen. The regular garrison at Fort William was only 150 men of all races. But the brick fort was solid above a town of thatched hovels built among stinking pools of water, with large wastes of unreclaimed land all around it. Collegiate discipline here was never strong. EIC servants were commonly given permission to live apart, and the 'General Table' where all were supposed to eat together was ended in 1713. Hamilton was impressed with the splendid and pleasant way of life enjoyed by white people here. Men worked in the morning, rested in the afternoon, and took recreation over the fields or on the river in the evening. There was ample fishing and fowling, and one could make a pleasure trip upstream to sample the life of French and Dutch factories. Good books were as scarce as in the West Indies, and social life as riven by quarrels and faction, though the church of St Ann was completed by 1709, its naming a tribute to that most Anglican of English queens.[148]

IX

Early in 1702, William III's horse stumbled on a molehill and threw him. He died shortly afterwards, and Jacobites then and much later cheerfully toasted the mole who had slain him. His sister-in-law and successor, Anne, had no heir, and was well on in years. But Parliament had already ruled against a Jacobite inheritance. The Act of Settlement, 1701, fixed the succession in the ruling house of the German Electorate of Hanover, who were descended from James I's daughter Elizabeth.

It was an era of explosive succession problems. In 1700, Charles II of Spain had died, leaving his crown to Philip of Anjou, Louis XIV's grandson. The prospect that France and Spain, with their overseas empires, might share the same king, aroused understandable fears in England. A French company now acquired the *asiento* from the Spanish Crown, the monopoly of selling slaves to Spanish America. In 1701, Louis XIV prohibited English imports into France, and requested Philip V of Spain to do the same. When James II died in the same year, Louis recognised his young son as James III. With Dutch and Austrian allies, England now fought 'Queen Anne's war', which lasted eleven years, in Europe and in the New World.

Almost everywhere else in Europe, warfare nowadays enhanced the grip of military despotism. Monarchs personally controlled large armies. In England, by contrast, the navy was run by an independent board, the Commons had control of the army, and the Secretary to the Forces sat in their House. The troops 'came home only in small units, and in order to disband'. There was no general conscription. Foreign mercenaries were hired for use in Europe. Over such English forces as existed, parsimony reigned. While officers defrauded their soldiers, and also the government, Whitehall cheated both officers and rank and file. In Cromwell's day, the common soldier had had status. Now he was despised and rejected of men. Condemned criminals were drafted, as were debtors and unemployed. All were subject to horrifically brutal punishment; scores or hundreds of lashes with leather thongs might be given; the tongue might be bored with a hot iron for swearing. (But the army still swore, and it looted and raped without mercy.) Casualties on troop transports at sea were commonly higher than on slave ships. 'Of 5000 men shipped from the West Indies to Newfoundland in 1702-3, only just over 1000 survived the voyage.' Even on the shorter voyage to Spain, losses of over a third were suffered.[149]

Yet, under Marlborough, the English army was the best force in Europe. His ruffians were victorious over the French at Blenheim in 1704, at Ramillies two years later, at Oudenarde in 1708. Meanwhile, the Methuen Treaty with Portugal (1703) gave English manufacturers a virtual monopoly of trade with that ally and her empire, and the capture of Gibraltar in 1704 assured the English and Dutch command of the Mediterranean.

The main show was in Europe. Marlborough and Anne's chief minister, Godolphin, would spare few vessels to protect colonial trade, and colonists in Virginia were required to pay themselves for the small-arms which their governor requested. The tories now stood for the 'blue water' policy of Drake, Hawkins and Cromwell, deploring war on the Continent and advocating expeditions to hit the enemy far overseas. But the fitful application of this strategy brought in this age no notable victories.

The quarter century of wars which began with the Glorious Revolution had opened badly for the English in the Caribbean. The Irish on Montserrat stood by King James; the Irish on St Kitts rose on his behalf, killing, burning and destroying 'all that belongs to the Protestant interest'. The French temporarily seized the whole island. 1693 saw an expedition from England designed to drive the French out of both the Antilles and Canada. By the end of its failed attack on Martinique, fleet and soldiers had lost half their men and most of their officers from wounds and sickness. Sailing on to Boston they found the governor there unwilling to help and the survivors went home having accomplished nothing.

But Queen Anne's war was even more badly bungled in the West Indies. In 1706, the colony on the Bahamas, established since the mid-seventeenth century, was temporarily wiped out, and St Kitts and Nevis were devastated. Montserrat's turn came in 1712. There was little effective retaliation. An expedition from England in 1702 was still more ambitious than that of 1693. The object was to destroy the French colonies in Martinique and Guadeloupe, to attack the Spaniards on Cuba and, if possible, on the mainland, and then sail north to hit the French in Canada and Newfoundland. The wrong kind of ships were sent, without enough artillery. The troops were lamentably equipped, and, as usual, the naval commander was at odds with the general.

This general was a planter, the third Christopher Codrington. His grandfather, the first Christopher, had been an early planter on Barbados. The second Christopher had moved on to the Leewards, where he and his brother acquired the entire small island of Barbuda. He fought the French ably during King William's war, but he died in 1698 under the shadow of disgrace for his involvement in illegal trade with the enemy. His son succeeded him as governor of the Leewards, and also as the wealthiest English landowner in the West Indies, with holdings on Barbados, Nevis and Antigua.

The second Christopher had been a rumbustious and self-serving planter politician of a familiar type. The third was a rarer case. If he had not existed, V. S. Naipaul would surely have invented him to personify certain melancholy potentialities of the Creole psyche. The Caribbean was first his springboard, then a trap. To the autocratic temper which his father had left him, he added the arrogance which came from acceptance in England as one of the most gifted young men of his day—a success no doubt much eased and furthered by his immense wealth. Educated at Oxford, he became a Fellow of All Souls, and used his boundless resources to buy rare books from all over Europe. He wrote verse, and was a friend of Locke, of Addison, and of Matt Prior, the poet, who, later, as a member of the Board of Trade, gave him useful political support. Meanwhile, Codrington gained a high reputation as a soldier in the Low Countries.

He did not return to the Leewards till 1701. In the interim they had been ruled by a greedy and violent planter named Norton, who on one occasion had bullied the governor of Anguilla into signing indentures. 'After which he was forced to work in the fields as a slave, almost naked and half starved. Once or twice a week Col. Norton caused him to be whipt in the pillory and the pickle of beef brine to be put on his sores.' Codrington, whose letters were marked by an acid and graceful wit, added characteristically that Norton would 'condescend to plunder even for a pound of soap, as well as sho buckles.'[150]

Men like Norton were not exceptional. Attempting to enforce the Navigation Acts, Codrington found that he could not trust a single official under him and discovered 'so generall a Conspiracy in People of all ranks and qualitys here to elude the Acts of Trade, that I have the Mortification of Knowing a hundred things are done every day, (which I cannot possibly prevent), prejudicial to the trade and interest of England.' He claimed that to be an honest governor was costing him £1,500 a year out of his own pocket, and told the Board of Trade, 'If you knew who were the leading men in the several Assemblys, you would be convinced that Governors ought to have better salarys and not [be] permitted to take any presents from the people. Whilst they doe, there will be illegal indulgences in point of trade, Justice will be bought and sold, Chancery pro-tracted and the poor opprest.' With donnish hauteur he referred to the officials who administered justice as 'Little animales who call themselves Lawyers'.[151]

His attempts at reform, which seem to have been sincere, ran up against intractable opposition. He went too far when Mead, the customs commissioner on Antigua, was clearly obstructing justice in his own favour. As governor, Codrington intervened directly in the business of the court. Caught later in the act of smuggling, Mead went to London to vilify Codrington, who wrote savagely, that if a governor must stand by and see oppression without daring to interpose for fear of a complaint, then he himself was not the right man, 'And they must ev'n send from home a Tom Turd or a Tom Fool ... or any other wretch fit to be bribed or aw'd by such an overgrown raskall as Mr Mead.' Though a House of Commons enquiry acquitted him of all imputations, Codrington was permanently embittered by the calumny of his opponents.[152]

Meanwhile his health had broken down during the unsuccessful attack on Guadeloupe which was made by the expedition of 1702-3. The home govern-ment decided to replace him. Colonel Daniel Parke was given the governorship as a reward for bringing the news of Blenheim to Queen Anne. Parke resented his predecessor and showed it. Tired of feuding, Codrington retreated to Bar-bados in 1707 and applied himself to the study of Church history and meta-physics. When he died three years later, only 42, Parke wrote savagely at the news, 'They say he broke his heart, not being able to gett the better of me.'[153]

His will epitomised Codrington's aberrancy. To All Souls he gave his collec-tion of books and £10,000 to build and stock a library. Two plantations on Barbados, and the greater part of Barbuda, went to endow a college to be established under the care of the recently founded Society for the Propagation of the Christian Religion in Foreign Parts. Though he specified that 300 slaves 'at least' should be kept at work on these lands, his aim was the absurd and dangerous one, in the eyes of his fellow-planters, that blacks should be converted to Christianity. The man had been sick of the world and all its works. His college was to be monastic, its clergy under vows of poverty, obedience and chastity.[154] The Society, while accepting the gift, and the slaves, scotched the notion of monasticism, and planters on Barbados, led by their governor, resisted the creation of the college, which did not materialise till 1745, when it became the only significant secondary school for boys in the English West Indies.

Parke's end was still more startling, though less edifying. On his day of triumph at Blenheim, Marlborough had promised Parke, one of his aides-de-camp, the governorship of Virginia, where the latter had been born. Parke was disappointed with the Leewards, which seemed to offer only slim pickings. He whined in official letters home that he was 'roasted in the sun, without the prospect of getting anything.' He also denounced the behaviour of the rich planters. 'A poor man is in a miserable condition for he cannot arrest any freeholder they haveing greater previleges than a Duke in England; every rich man among his neighbours is more absolute than a Bashaw, he may beat, nay murder him, and not fear any punishment.'[155]

Planters made more than one attempt to assassinate Parke. The regiment of soldiers which he had was divided against him after his complaints had compelled officers who were absentees in England to come out to fulfil their duties. He used those soldiers who sided with him to commit outrages on his planter enemies. He made the wife of a prominent islander his mistress, then tried the man for his life after he had killed someone 'by accident'; the jury, of course, acquitted Parke's rival. In 1710 he dissolved the Antigua Assembly. Armed planters rallied to its support. Parke gathered the soldiers he could trust, mounted a field gun in Government House and refused to surrender. The place was stormed. Four of the rioters died, with eleven of Parke's supporters. The governor himself was butchered. Accounts varied as to the details. The most colourful had the maimed governor hauled naked along the road and left to die under that sun which he so detested. A more moderate version was that the rioters tore his clothes off, dragged him about his house by his testicles, beat him on the head and broke his back with the butt ends of their guns. Then one of them 'spitt in his face in the agony of death.'[156]

Governor Douglas, his successor, took no action until he had pocketed bribes from everyone anxious to be exempted from nomination as ringleaders. Only three men were arrested and tried, and they were not executed. After a notable course of corruption, Douglas himself was recalled to England and given a five-year gaol sentence.

The violence of life on Antigua was far from unique. In the year after the rising against Parke, the always tumultuous politics of the few and impoverished planters of North Carolina erupted into a little rebellion. This was followed by two years of war with the Tuscarora Indians, in which South Carolina was also involved. The Charles Town colony had before this been embroiled with European enemies. In 1699 D'Iberville, on Louis XIV's orders, had occupied the Louisiana delta, so South Carolina now feared French as well as Spanish attack. The Florida Spaniards drove overland in 1702 and were beaten off. Four years later a combined French and Spanish force struck without success from the sea.

But both Carolinas profited from the bounties on the production of 'naval stores' offered by Parliament in 1705, when Sweden was unfriendly and Baltic supplies were at risk. In the previous year the importance of rice, Charles Town's staple, was recognised when that grain was 'enumerated' under the Navigation Acts. It was eaten by people in Europe who could not afford wheat, and there was plenty of market for it. Charles Town prospered, the hub of a slave society similar to those of the West Indies.

But not identical. Various factors combined to make absenteeism more and more common among the richer West Indian planters. Life on the islands was lavish, but ungracious. The struggles against overweening royal governors in the 1680s had sapped the confidence of the plantocrats. French wars made the islands more dangerous and less appealing. Above all, with sugar prices falling and French competition increasing, the advantages of being closer to Westminster were clear. Henry Drax, whose forbear had pioneered in the introduction of sugar, led a movement in the 1680s of big Barbadian planters back to permanent residence in the motherland. The sugar lobby had always outpointed others in imperial politics. In the late 1660s, tobacco had paid in England customs duty which was 150 per cent of the price realised by the Chesapeake planter; the corresponding figure for sugar was only 10 per cent. ' ... By 1700 the home tobacco tax was six times the market value of leaf in Virginia.'[157] The power of sugar interests at home was now reinforced by opulent absentees. The government, as we have seen, was prepared to send large expeditions to die in the Caribbean. It was far slower to give military help to North American colonists. A significant contrast of attitudes was the result. English West Indians slumped ungratefully into dependence on aid from home, while North Americans were beginning to develop their own military traditions.

Luckily for them, New France during Queen Anne's war was starved of military assistance. But Albany had a most profitable clandestine trade with Montreal, so New York Colony was not very interested in fighting the French. Massachusetts was left for years to shoulder the burden almost alone. Paradoxically, Boston boomed, with the stimulus given by war-funds disbursed by Whitehall. In 1714, Massachusetts had 1,100 ships, of which 678, nearly two-thirds, had been added during the war years. The colony's shipbuilding industry, while meeting local demand, was also supplying vessels to the West Indies, to Newfoundland, and to England itself.[158]

On the frontier line of defence which stretched some 200 miles from western

Massachusetts into Maine, local inhabitants were reinforced by drafted militia-men and by volunteers, who were drawn by the prospect of plunder, by the liberal bounties paid for Indian scalps, and by the chance to sell young red captives into slavery. Undiscriminating sweeps were made into Indian country. Villages were burnt, crops destroyed in the fields, red men were cut off from their fisheries.

War had important effects in the mainland colonies. It reduced social tensions, directing aggression outwards and giving an occupation to poor whites. As in England itself, it enhanced the power of lower houses in the assemblies; governors could get funds only by making concessions, while war fostered a certain financial precocity which indirectly increased control by representatives over the revenues. The colonies were always short of coins. They were not allowed to mint their own or to prohibit the re-export of those that reached them. The balance of trade drew coins towards England. Hence the attraction, for governors and others, of the pirate laden with pieces of eight. But now the pirates were being effectively curbed. Massachusetts showed the way when it supported Phips's expedition, in 1690, with an issue of paper money. It resumed the practice in Queen Anne's war. Before peace returned, seven other colonies had followed suit. The basic device, which worked on the whole pretty well, was a bill of credit through which future revenues were anticipated.

From 1709, the home government was committed to a renewed attempt to destroy the French position in Canada. This implied the emergence of mainland North America as a major theatre of Anglo-French conflict, which it remained for three-quarters of a century. Since the prime mover of the scheme was a Scot, it also marked the beginning of 'British' Empire. In 1707, Scotland and England became one country.

X

Cromwell's Union of the two countries in 1654 had been imposed by an army of occupation. But a pro-Union lobby developed in the northern kingdom. The restored Stuart monarchs no longer had the capacity to prevent their English parliaments passing laws, like the Navigation Acts, which were preju-dicial to Scotland. The Scottish Convention which ratified the Glorious Revolution approved – unanimously, according to one source – overtures to England for Union. At this juncture even Fletcher of Saltoun, of whom more shortly, favoured 'uniting with England in Parliaments and Trade', though not in Church or law. Meanwhile Scottish aristocrats more and more commonly tried to narrow the gap between their standard of living and that of English magnates by marrying English brides with lush dowries.[159]

The Darien episode produced awkwardly matched swings of opinion. On the one hand, it made William III an enthusiast for Union; in February 1700 he urged the English House of Lords 'very earnestly' to seek this solution. On the other, it helped make the Scottish Parliament evil-tempered and difficult to manage. Even a fairly lavish outlay in bribes could not stop it passing an address to the King, early in 1701, which denounced English 'intermeddling in the affairs of this kingdom'. Anti-English feeling was inflamed by the blatancy with which Scottish ministries were now manipulated by the London government. It was written of James Ogilvy, first Earl of Seafield, who was Scotland's Chancellor in 1702, that he was a 'blank Sheet of Paper, which the Court might fill up with what they pleas'd.'[160] The English Commons were huffy enough themselves. They refused to accede to William's wish for Union. As a dying man, in 1702, he renewed his plea, and Queen Anne echoed it in her first speech to Parliament. For her, both English houses passed a motion empowering the government to appoint commissioners to negotiate with the Scots. But after a few weeks negotiations broke down. The Darien Company was an impassable obstacle.

The single-chambered Scottish Parliament was 'rigidly feudal in its composition'.[161] The great nobles sat with 'barons' representing the shires who were in general much under their influence, and with burgh members sent up by narrow, self-elective town councils which spoke only for the merchants and master craftsmen. But organisational changes since the Revolution had given it the right to initiate legislation, and greater scope for troublemaking. In the parliament of 1703, there were three loosely defined parties. The 'Court Party' consisted of the 'ins' who held the great public offices and of others who followed these men from self-interest either gratified or hopeful. They were professed 'revolutioners', claiming commitment to the 1689 settlement. The 'Country Party' rallied the 'outs' and expressed the patriotic anger lit by Glencoe, then turned to a blaze by Darien; they wanted adjustments which would give Scotland the benefits of free trade with England and her colonies but without any loss of Parliament or separate identity. The third faction, the 'Cavaliers', were Jacobites and episcopalians. Trouble between England and Scotland suited the cause of the exiled Stuarts well, though many with Jacobite sympathies had a soft spot for Anglican, Stuart, Queen Anne. The Cavaliers stood with the Country Party and both groups looked for leadership to the Duke of Hamilton, one of the most striking, but also one of the most slippery, of a line long renowned for its shiftiness. He had a distant claim to the Scottish Crown, and was a hero of the Edinburgh 'mob', but he had heavy debts and large estates in England as well as an aversion to any development which might bar his own way towards the throne, now that Queen Anne's lack of direct heirs left both kingdoms up for grabs. Under such direction, the opposition could no more be decisive, at crucial moments, than it could ever be united on possible solutions.[162]

Among so many parcels of self-seeking men, Andrew Fletcher of Saltoun was able to give the last years of Scottish independence a few unexpected touches of rhetorical dignity. He had no family whose interests he must promote. Therefore, he could ignore the temptations of office and denounce those who felt compelled to scramble for them. 'He was Bless'd,' one Jacobite, Lockhart of Carnwath, wrote, 'with a Soul, that Hated and Despised whatever was Mean and Unbecoming a Gentleman, and was so Stedfast to what he thought Right, that no Hazard nor Advantage, no not the Universal Empire, nor the Gold of *America*, could tempt him to yield or desert it.'[163] An East Lothian laird, born in 1653, Fletcher had gone into exile after opposing James, Duke of York, in Parliament, had joined in Monmouth's rebellion and had then, like so many Scots of his day, roamed Europe, roving in Spain and fighting the Turks in Hungary. He had returned with William III in 1688, but within a few months had joined the opposition to the new king, though he remained staunchly anti-Jacobite.

'A great Admirer of both Ancient and Modern Republicks', he hated the royal prerogative; if the nation must have a monarchy, it should be strictly constitutional. His fundamental ideal seems to have been a republic dominated by landowners. (He had his counterparts among the 'Country' whigs now in opposition in England. Like him, they detested standing armies and looked back to Ancient Rome.) Confronted by the famine of the late 1690s, he had noted the vast increase of beggars – there were 200,000 in Scotland he reckoned – and had argued that these idle people should be compelled to work as slaves. He was not a narrow nationalist. He admired the English and their love of freedom and sketched a vision of Europe divided into ten portions, each to contain ten or twelve sovereign cities under one monarch. Small governments could not bully their neighbours, so the scourge of war would be lifted. In small societies the 'corruption of manners' was less likely. ' ... Whatever contrives to make people very rich and great, lays the foundation of their misery and destruction ... ' Elevating the classical ideal of honourable simplicity, Fletcher anticipated some characteristic views of the late eighteenth century.[164]

Behind his time and ahead of his times, the pedantic Fletcher was no politician. Compromise was beyond him. His hot temper involved him in ludicrous quarrels in Parliament. He had no gift of extempory debate. But the speeches of this 'low thin man, of brown complexion, full of fire, with a stern, sour look ... '[165] made much impression on the house, where his arguments – in part – were useful to other persons who wished to cause trouble.

The succession question gave them a chance to create serious problems. The English government was, of course, very anxious that the Scottish Parliament, like the English, should choose the House of Hanover. The Duke of Queensberry who, as the Queen's Commissioner, 'managed' (that is, bribed) the Scottish Parliament, tried and failed in 1703 to do a deal with the Jacobite members. Thereafter, Parliament could not be controlled. It refused to discuss the voting of money until it had dealt with the succession question, and then evolved an Act of Security which laid down that the Queen's successor should be nominated in Scotland by the Estates, should be a Protestant, and should not be the successor to the throne of England 'unless that in this Session of Parliament there be such conditions of Government settled and enacted as may secure the honour and independency of the crown of this kingdom, the freedom, frequency, and the power of Parliament, and the religion, liberty and trade of the nation from the English, or any forraigne influence.'[166]

Unable to carry the Hanoverian succession, Queensberry fell for the moment from office. Factions shuffled themselves. A 'New Party' replaced the old 'Court Party', drawing 'in' some of the former 'outs'. But when the new Commissioner, the Marquis of Tweeddale ('a rarity in that age, an honest politician')[167] confronted Parliament in 1704, it still refused to vote money until the Act of Security was accepted. A French invasion of Scotland seemed at this juncture quite likely. The English ministry gave in to Scots blackmail. The Act was made with a touch of Tweeddale's sceptre.

Daniel Defoe's contemporary verdict is worth noting. The Act, he believed, was well aimed so as to bring the English over to the idea of letting the Scots share in their trade, 'for either England must comply with Scotland ... or else she might have the satisfaction to see clearly, Scotland by this act was placed in an intire separate State from her.' The Act 'effectually settled and declared the independency of Scotland, and put her into a posture fit to be treated with, either by England, or by any other nation.'[168]

France, for instance. Unless the two British kingdoms were united, England would have an open back door again. The Act of Security called on landowners and towns to arm their people. Rumours came south that the Scots were buying arms in Holland. Anne's chief minister, Godolphin, was worried enough by the threat to remind the Scots that they had rarely beaten the English in the past. Military considerations also preoccupied the Earl of Roxburghe, a clever young twister adhering to the 'New Party' who wrote around Christmas 1704 to another 'New' man in the code which these scheming people thought it needful to use. 'I am thoroughly convinc'd that if we do not go into Z, or Y, very soon, 20 will certainly be, upon the first qf bdf; for supposing E durst go into such GG as were yielded last, 22 will never suffer 21's enjoying 30, 34, 27, and what is necessary for maintaining of those.' This meant that he thought that England would turn round and conquer the Scots rather than let them establish effective independence.[169]

The English Parliament now used blackmail in turn. The 'Alien Act' of February 1705 was a well-measured ultimatum. It would make all Scots except those already settled in England, Ireland or the plantations into 'aliens'. It would prohibit the import into England of Scottish cattle, sheep, coals and linen. The Scots would thus be conclusively shut out of colonial trade and deprived of their vital market in England. But the Act would not come into operation until Christmas. Meanwhile the Scots were offered a last chance to negotiate for 'entire and compleat union', or at least to accept Hanoverian succession.[170]

The first, predictable, result of this Act was to intensify Scottish anger. This was demonstrated in a grisly incident. One of the Darien Company's ships had recently disappeared. It had in fact been seized by a Madagascar pirate and destroyed off the Indian coast. But drunken talk by some of the crew of an English Indiaman which was unwisely docked at Leith convinced the Company's secretary that the captain of this ship, the *Worcester*, had been responsible for the loss of the Scottish vessel, and had killed its commander. This was totally false, but Captain Green and two subordinates were convicted and hanged on Leith Sands in April 1705, against Queen Anne's clear wishes; the Scottish Privy Council felt obliged to permit the lynching rather than risk the fury of the Edinburgh 'mob'.

So the 'New Party' fell from Anne's favour. Politicians manoeuvred for office again. The 'Old Party' came back, with a 25-year-old soldier, the Duke of Argyll, as Queen's Commissioner. Despite his youth, Argyll was tough and insistent, showing the self-confidence to be expected in a hereditary ruler of great lands. After several weeks of struggles, Parliament agreed, first that there should be negotiations with England, secondly that the Commissioners undertaking it should be nominated by Anne rather than by itself. A volte face by Hamilton settled the matter. Even so, he was not included in the list of thirty-one Commissioners. Almost all were safe 'Old Court Party' figures. A solitary Jacobite, Lockhart of Carnwath, was included, because he was nephew to the English Lord Wharton and thought to be amenable to influence.

When the two sets of Commissioners met in April 1706, the English suggested 'Incorporating Union', with one parliament serving both countries; the Scots wanted 'Federal' Union by which their nation would retain its own Parliament and institutions but mutually hostile laws would be repealed and Scots would enjoy free trade with England and her colonies. After a fortnight, matters were squared. The Scots got free trade – a principal aim – at the tolerable expense of losing their parliament. Scotland would keep its own laws and lawcourts in matters concerning 'private right'. A so-called 'Equivalent' was devised to heal the raw wound of the Darien venture and to compensate Scots for taking on the burden of helping to pay for England's fast-growing National Debt. A sum of just under £400,000 would be used to pay the public debt of Scotland, to reimburse the Darien Company's shareholders, and to make good losses incurred through the conversion of Scottish coinage to the English standard. A second, smaller 'Equivalent' was also offered; when, as was expected, Scottish revenue expanded as a result of the Union, the increase would be creamed off to be used for the stimulation of Scottish industries. 'On the whole,' William Ferguson concludes, 'the fiscal and financial provisions of the treaty were fair, in some respects generous, and were calculated, in both senses of the word, to recommend the treaty to the Scottish parliament.'[171]

Representation in Parliament was settled by some clever arithmetic. Scotland was thought to have two million people to England's six million, giving a ratio of 1:3. But her people were far poorer, and Scotland's contribution to the Land Tax would be only about 1:40. This ratio would give Scotland only 13 M.P.s, while the first one would suggest 170. A medium was fixed at 45. Only 16 Scottish Lords, chosen by their own peers, would sit in the Upper House. The crosses of St George and St Andrew were to be joined in a new flag to represent the whole kingdom; so the Union Jack was created.[172]

By 23 July 1706 the Commissioners were able to announce to the Queen the end of their labours. Lockhart and, on the English side, the Archbishop of York, had refused to sign the proposed treaty, but each was outnumbered thirty to one. That the Treaty would be accepted by the English Parliament was a foregone conclusion. The outcome in Scotland was unpredictable.

A swarm of pamphleteers got to work to help the Scottish Parliament make up its mind. Defoe came to Edinburgh as a propagandist for the Union, and as a spy for Godolphin. William Paterson, the visionary of Darien, laboured on the same side. They had the arguments of commercial hard-headedness. Their most voluble opponent, an industrious hack named Hodges, could only appeal to sentiment – Scotland was the oldest kingdom in Europe, never conquered by arms, he inaccurately asserted – or argue by dubious analogy: Portugal was richer now she had moved from union with Spain.

In taverns and market places the noes had it. Defoe observed that hatred of the proposed treaty was such that if the articles had been published before the Commissioners had reached home, few of them would have ventured into Scotland 'without a guard to protect them'. But he also remarked on the disunity of the opposition, who could agree only on the negative. While in England High Tories had opposed Union because it would mean digesting an established Presbyterian Church, in Scotland the zealots of that Kirk feared the loss of all that had been won in 1689. The Treaty said nothing about religion. Now, as Defoe remarked, 'It was the most monstrous sight in the world, to see the Jacobite and the Presbyterian, the persecuting prelatic Non-juror and the Cameronian, the Papist and the reformed Protestant, parle together, join interest, and concert measures together – To see the Jacobites at Glasgow huzzaing the mob, and encouraging them to have a care of the Church! the high-flying Episcopal dissenter crying out, the overture was not a sufficient security for the Church!'[173]

The men who had to breast the wave of anti-Union feeling were Queensberry, now re-appointed Commissioner, and the Secretary of State, the Earl of Mar. They did very well. The attitude of the New Party, now nicknamed the 'Squadrone Volante', was crucial; twenty-five or so in number, they held the balance in Parliament. The court lured them with baits of office and money. They decided to support Union. 'After all,' wrote one of them, 'considering the temper of this people, how unfit to govern ourselves ... I must be convinced that the Union is our onlie game.'[174] Parliament met on October 3rd. On the 15th, Queensberry got a majority of sixty-six for the vital motion to go ahead to consider the articles of the treaty.

But a week later the Edinburgh 'mob', drums beating, ran riot, maltreating every known Unionist it saw. As voting proceeded clause by clause, there were constant threats against Queensberry's life. Over a third of the shires, and a quarter of the royal burghs, sent in addresses against the Union; not one came in for it.[175] In Glasgow, where the magistrates had decided not to petition for continued independence (what innocents they would have been to do so, considering the legal trade in America which the Union would open up to them) rioters pillaged the provost's house and compelled the city fathers to sign an anti-Union address. The Covenanting west fizzed once more. Hundreds of farmers gathered at Dumfries and burnt the articles of Union at the market cross. There were plans for a new 'Whiggamore Raid', at which a cross-bred alliance of Cameronians and Jacobites would evict the parliament and declare for King James III. But the Duke of Hamilton declined the leadership offered to him, pointing out that the English had massed troops on the Border. Hamilton was still the hero of the Edinburgh 'mob'. (This term, then as now, had pejorative implications. No substitute is available, but it must be understood that in the eighteenth century, quite well-to-do people commonly took part in mob action, that they, like the poor, had no other way of making their opinions felt, and that 'mobs', though destructive, were selectively so, and could be remarkably self-disciplined.) If the Duke had wanted to use physical force to thwart Union, he might have done so. But he was not a revolutionary, nor cut out to be a hero. When Fletcher and the Duke of Atholl, effective leaders of the patriot opposition, summoned hundreds of country gentry to protest in Edinburgh, Hamilton's hedging baulked the proposed deputation to Queensberry, and the disappointed lairds went rhubarbing home. Later, Hamilton himself proposed an opposition walk-out from Parliament. But on the day he refused to come to the House, pleading a severe toothache. Frog-marched there all the same, he still did not make the gesture expected of him. His vacillation demoralised his followers and made the Union certain.

With various minor amendments, the whole Treaty was passed. The English Parliament swallowed all changes, together with a further Act embodied with the Treaty and guaranteeing the continuance of a Presbyterian Church 'without any alteration ... in all succeeding generations' and laying down that all office bearers in the Scottish universities would have to be Presbyterians. 'Now, there's ane end of ane auld sang,' Seafield said, as he signed the English Act of Ratification and formally wound up Scotland's independence.[176] In April 1707, the Scottish Parliament dissolved for the last time. On May 1st the Union was inaugurated with a service in Wren's new St Paul's Cathedral.

There is no way of knowing now whether most Scots were adamant against Union. Parliament represented the views of privileged classes, and its members gave Queensberry comfortable majorities. In the case of Article IV, which embodied freedom of trade, the voting was 156 in favour, only 19 against. There was less enthusiasm, of course, for the abolition of Parliament itself, but even here the majority was two to one.[177] Why did the same Parliament which had seemed so anti-English in 1703–4 now vote consistently for Incorporating Union?

One traditional answer, given enduring currency by Robert Burns, was that Union was 'bought and sold for English gold'. Some politicians certainly asked a price and were given it. The Duke of Argyll received a generalship for himself and a peerage, the earldom of Islay, for his brother. 'In an effort to win votes all sorts of inducements were held out. Payment of arrears of salaries to office holders was made conditional on their supporting the treaty. Partly for this end, a sum of £20,000 sterling sent up from the English treasury was secretly disbursed by the Scottish treasurer, the Earl of Glasgow.'[178] But payment for votes was now part of the British system of government. The fact that it was used in this case does not prove that men voted as they did merely because they were bribed. One could argue as plausibly that politicians had passed the Act of Security so as to put up their own selling price.

There were powerful negative reasons impelling leading Scots towards Union. The alternative was to strike for independence under a non-Hanoverian king, presumably Stuart. A Stuart king would have tried to reclaim the English throne. If he had succeeded, Scotland would have returned to square one; a Union of the Crowns and management from London. If he had failed, the English would have enforced Incorporating Union on their own terms. As Fletcher himself put it: 'This country must be made a field of blood in order to advance a Papist to the throne of Great Britain. If we fail we shall be slaves by right of conquest; if we prevail, have the happiness to continue in our former slavish dependence.'[179]

And the economic spurs working Scotland towards Union were decisively important. Roxburghe pointed to them in a letter of 1705 in which he predicted that the Edinburgh Parliament would swallow Union, 'The motives will be, trade with most, Hanover with some, ease and security with others, together with a generall aversion at civill discords, intollerable poverty, and the constant oppression of a bad Ministry, from generation to generation ... ' The present position had no advantages. Trade did indeed weigh heavily with most Scottish politicians. The English Alien Act of 1705 showed what a heavy penalty independence would carry. Scotland's main exports were linen and black cattle, which could be sold only in England, and wool, which went largely to France, but was in great part smuggled out of England first. If the Border were policed, the wool trade would be stunted. Worse still, landowners all over Scotland would suffer – 'unless our cattle and linen can be otherwayes disposed on, we are utterly ruined should those laws take effect,' Roxburghe had exclaimed in another letter. Trade with England, running at about £114,000 (sterling) per year in 1698–1700, had fallen to £54,000 per year in 1704–6.[180]

In the last Scottish Parliament, barons from the shires were only four to three in favour when the whole Treaty was passed. The burgesses from the towns were three to two in favour. But the peers, great landowners, voted more than two to one for Union. Landowners had shown their interest in colonial trade when they had subscribed half the capital of the Darien Company. Those who sold corn or coal, salt or cattle from their lands, and who had linen industries on their estates, had a vital need of the English market. On the face of it, the peers lost through Union. The automatic right to sit in Parliament was denied them. But without the Union, they would be cut off from the amenities of the upper-class life-style which money acquired directly or indirectly from trade could provide.[181]

The Scots were poor, and getting poorer. The English upper and middle classes waxed fatter every day. The disparity in wealth between the two countries, marked in 1603, was still greater now. This partly explains how the English could be generous. What were a few hundred thousands disbursed to whining Scotsmen compared to the millions of the National Debt? Besides improving the chance of a safe Hanoverian, Protestant succession, the Union gave England certain striking rewards. Economic historians of the future would applaud the 'creation of a British common market embracing almost 7 million people, much the largest free trade area in contemporary Europe ... '[182] Contemporaries were perhaps more impressed by the prospect sketched by Daniel Defoe. 'Scotland is an inexhaustible treasure of men, as may be demonstrated by the vast numbers they have in our army and navy, and in the armies of the Swede, the Pole, the Muscovite, the Emperor, Holland and France. What might not England now do, had she in her pay all the Scots actually in the service of these princes, where they are daily cutting one another's throats, and, at the expense of their country's impoverishment, gain the empty reputation of being the best soldiers in the world. This is a treasure beyond the Indies ... '[183]

This implication of Union was at once grasped in the 'Indies' themselves. Governor Daniel Parke, that old soldier, wrote from the Leewards in January 1707 asking for 10,000 Scots whom he could throw at the throats of the French and Spaniards, 'with otemeal enough to keep them for 3 or 4 months'. The warm sun, he thought, might thaw out their Calvinism, and 'if I gett them all knock'd on the head, I am off the opinion the English Nation will be no great loosers by it.' With Union shortly impending, his joke was sternly rebuked; Queen Anne, he was informed, thought the Scots good subjects and good Christians.[184]

And so Whitehall was prepared to hearken to Samuel Vetch, a Scot with a record which would have distressed it before the Union. He was the son of a famous Covenanting minister exiled in Holland under Charles II. He had joined the Darien expedition and had the luck not only to survive but, landed in New York, to marry the daughter of a Scots trader, Robert Livingston, who was also the son of a Covenanting exile, and whose wealth and consequence were already enormous. However, Vetch had felt it needful to better himself further by some illicit trade with the French, for which the General Court of Massachusetts convicted him in 1706. Partly to clear himself, he set off for England.

Here was another Scottish visionary, less idealistic than Fletcher or Paterson.

The paper, 'Canada Survey'd', which Vetch laid before the Board of Trade in 1708 made frequent and no doubt exultant use of the terms 'Great Britain', 'British trade' and 'British Empire'. It gave a persuasive picture of the fragility of the French position in North America, where a handful of men were spread from the Gulf of St Lawrence to the Gulf of Mexico. 'Britain' should strike now while the enemy was still weak. The price would be trifling, less than half, Vetch reckoned, of one year's loss of 'British trade' incurred through the mischievous French presence. The two battalions of regular troops required would cost the Crown no more than 'they now doe in Scotland, where they are idle'. The capture of Canada would 'not only afford a booty to the captors farr exceeding all the expence of the undertaking, but infinitely advance the commerce of the Brittish over all America, and particularly make them sole masters of the furr, fish and navall stores trade over all the Continent ... ' Canada would become 'a noble Colony, exactly calculate for the constitutions and genius of the most Northern of the North Brittains.'[185] Time would prove Vetch correct in this last view. The Scottish 'genius' would indeed thrive in that region. In the short run, however, his ideas proved less apt.

Queensberry and Hamilton used weight on behalf of their compatriot's scheme, and it gained remarkably swift acceptance. By February 1709, Anne had approved it and Vetch was commissioned as colonel and charged to raise forces in the colonies. New England greeted him with great enthusiasm. There were soon some 1,500 men in arms along the Hudson River-Lake Champlain corridor and the veteran Francis Nicholson was on hand to command a march upon Montreal. However, the promised expeditionary force from England was cancelled. Nicholson went to London to try to revive the government's commitment, but returned, in July 1710, with only 400 marines and two men-of-war. With colonial assistance these proved enough to effect with ease, and with permanence this time, the conquest of Acadia, now 'Nova Scotia' once more, which was agreeable no doubt for the new 'North Britons' of Vetch's homeland.

Useful though the long war had been to English traders (there was a general upswing of commerce from about 1705) the squires and populace at home wanted peace. A tory ministry rose in 1710 on a wave of war-weariness, reflected in mutinies, riots and resentment of taxation. Marlborough was dismissed. The 'blue water' strategy was in favour. With the French fleet now virtually inactive, ships could easily be spared. Nicholson's walkover at Port Royal made Vetch's final solution to the problem of Canada seem plausible. In May 1711, 64 ships, including 11 men-of-war, sailed to Boston with over 5,000 troops, mostly veterans of Marlborough's campaigns, as well as 6,000 seamen.

The force outnumbered the population of Boston. New England farmers and traders had a heyday supplying it with provisions. A thousand more fighters were found in New England, and Nicholson was to command a separate force of more than 2,000 white colonists and over 800 Indians (mostly Iroquois) who

P

were to strike overland while the great Armada attacked up the St Lawrence. But Admiral Sir Hovenden Walker, the tory appointed to command, had not been well chosen. He placed unwise trust in French pilots, and had no reliable charts. In bad weather late in August nine transports were dashed to pieces on the north bank of the St Lawrence. Nearly 800 lives were lost, Walker gave up and sailed home, and Nicholson stopped his march in disgust.

English and French came finally to terms with the Treaty of Utrecht in March 1713. The whigs claimed that this was a treacherous tory sell-out. Yet Britain, as we may now call the nation, had won great advantages. Philip V of Spain was to renounce any claim to the throne of France; the two realms must never be united. Britain was to possess the whole of Hudson's Bay and the whole island of Newfoundland, as well as Nova Scotia and, at long last, St Kitts complete. From Spain, Britain received Gibraltar and Minorca and — most coveted prize of all — the *asiento*, conceded for thirty years; a monopoly right to ship 4,800 black slaves a year to Spanish America. Besides these direct gains, there was the indirect bonus that Britain's Dutch allies had overtaxed themselves. They had sacrificed naval strength in favour of military effort on land. Holland was no longer a great naval power. The Dutch struggle gained them little at the treaty. It lost them dominance in transoceanic trade, in which the British now rode supreme.

Scots swarmed eagerly into the wide-open world. Too greedily, in the case of Governor Douglas, Parke's successor in the Leewards; but his successor was also a Scot, yet another Hamilton. Not surprisingly, lands in the former French part of St Kitts found their way into Scottish hands. In the Leewards, from now on, 'The contribution of the Scots was far out of proportion to their numbers.' Their superior education helped. Scots professional men turned planters in time and founded dynasties. Thus, Walter Tullideph, son of a Kirk minister, went out to Antigua about 1726 as a doctor. Several friends and relatives were already established in their professions there. He sold Scottish linen and other goods to the planters, carrying merchandise on his doctor's rounds. After ten years he married a widow who owned 63 slaves. After forty he had over 500 acres and 271 slaves. He brought in other Scots as doctors, plantation managers, attorneys and lessees. He died an absentee, on the laird's estate he had purchased in his homeland. One of his daughters married a baronet.

Similar stories could be told about other islands. Barbados retained a markedly English character, but within fifty years of the Union Scots owned around a quarter of all the taxable land on Jamaica, and throve there in general better than the English.[186] William Paterson, in a sense, stood vindicated, though his 'key to the universe' had been found not at Darien but in points east. And north. We shall soon see them in action in Virginia. Scots were clannish still. Family feeling overflowed into fellow feeling. Paranoid, sober, industrious and thrusting, Scots clustered together far overseas and helped each other forward, summoning recruit after recruit from the bleak homeland to lusher pastures. While Scots seized new opportunities, the English gained from the long-delayed release of Scottish intellect and commercial energy.

Ireland was not so lucky. The Navigation Act of 1696 placed it clearly 'beyond the pale of commercial privilege'.[187] Trade had recovered swiftly from the Jacobite war of the Boyne and Aughrim. Ulster, where merchants had done well from provisioning William's armies, moved forwards especially fast; famine in Scotland brought immigrants flooding into the region, bringing their capital with them. The island had long found markets abroad for cheap woollen friezes, which did not compete directly with higher class English goods. Now, with the stimulus of an influx of Huguenot craftsmen and Huguenot money from France, Ireland began to export 'New Draperies'. This competition incensed clothing interests in south-west England, and after three years' effort, in 1699, they secured an Act from the English Parliament which forbade the export of woollen goods from Ireland to foreign countries; duty on their import into England was already prohibitive. Irish production of woollens continued to rise slowly — the home market was, after all, sizeable — but a shock had been vindictively administered.

Why did not the Irish use blackmail like the Scots? The answer was simple. The Protestant propertied men who now monopolised the Dublin Parliament represented only an insecure minority, which must depend in the last resort on English arms. At the same time as the Scots were cockily taking on the English with the Darien scheme, the Dublin Parliament tried, in 1698, to appease the fears of English clothing interests, laying new export charges on Irish woollens themselves.

An Irish counterpart of Fletcher, William Molyneux, did publish in 1698 a pamphlet which argued, as West Indian planters had done long before, that the English Parliament had no right to make laws for people not represented within it. ' ... To tax me without Consent, is little better, if at all, than downright Robbing me.' The pamphlet, often reprinted, would fuel the partial patriotism of later spokesmen for Protestant Ireland against Westminster. But Molyneux was slapped down easily enough. The English House of Commons condemned his 'bold and pernicious assertions' and went ahead to pass its Act against Irish woollens.[188] They were quite safe to do so. Irish Protestants saw themselves as essentially English. Their claim was that they should enjoy the same liberties as the Englishmen in England. Their attitude to the mass of Irish, the Catholics, was made clear enough by the laws passed in Dublin.

British governments were normally more tolerant than the parcel of colonists ruling across the water. But for the sake of getting money Bills through the Irish Parliament, Westminster was ready to let Dublin have its punitive way. The Irish Catholics, after all, were natural rebels. A great part of their aristocracy was now fighting in Europe in the armies of Britain's enemies. ' ... Virtually all the Irish clergy and the sons of the more prosperous laity were educated at one or other of the Irish colleges scattered throughout Europe.'[189] Until 'James III, died in 1766, his advice on Irish ecclesiastical matters was taken by the papacy. The association of Catholicism with Jacobitism and treason provided a rationale for the so-called 'Penal Code' constructed against its adherents in Ireland. The code waned only after James III's death.

A Dublin Act of 1704 'to prevent the further growth of popery' laid down that no Catholic might buy any interest in land, except in a lease of no more than thirty-one years. He could not bequeath land in a will, so his property would be split among all his sons at his death; but if the eldest conformed to the Church of Ireland he would obtain all of it, and, by a further refinement of legislative viciousness, if he did so during his father's lifetime, the latter would become merely his life tenant. Catholics were barred from all public employment. They might not send their children for education abroad and had to take an oath abjuring the Jacobite Pretender before voting in parliamentary elections. (In 1728, they were deprived of the franchise altogether.) Let the great historian Lecky take us further: 'They could not be sheriffs or solicitors or even game-keepers or constables. They were forbidden to possess any arms; two justices, or a mayor, or a sheriff, might at any time issue a search warrant to break into their houses and ransack them for arms, and if a fowling piece or a flask of powder was discovered they were liable either to fine or imprisonment or to whipping and the pillory. They were, of course, excluded on the same grounds from the army and navy. They could not even possess a horse of the value of more than £5, and any Protestant on tendering that sum could appropriate the hunter or the carriage horse of his Catholic neighbour. In his own country the Catholic was only recognised by the law, "for repression and punishment". The Lord Chancellor Bowes and the Chief Justice Robinson both distinctly laid down from the Bench "that the law does not suppose any such person to exist as a Roman Catholic." '[190]

The aim of the code was not to destroy Roman Catholicism. It would have been most inconvenient for its framers if it had done so. A Church of Ireland archbishop observed ruefully, 'There are too many amongst us who had rather keep the Papists as they are, in an almost slavish subjection, than have them made Protestants, and thereby entitled to the same liberties and privileges with the rest of their fellow subjects.' The vast majority remained Catholic; hence, that majority were subordinate and open to easy exploitation. Like the apartheid system to which it was so close in spirit, the Penal Code brutally ignored the humanity of those upon whom it bore down. The Parliament, Lords Lieutenant, Lords Justices, all those who wielded power in Ireland, referred to the papist mass as 'the common enemy'.[191] Religion, not race, was the dividing factor by which Protestant landowners sought exclusive privilege, but the drive of the Code was virtually to create two different races, identified with two different classes, the haves and the have-nots.

Many landed families deserted Catholicism so as to enjoy the rights of Anglicans. A few preserved faith and fortune together by the good luck of

having no more than one son, or through the collusion of Protestant neighbours. Others, like English Dissenters, found an outlet in trade. The Irish
Catholics were, at least, white. The letter of the law was more savage than its
execution. However, it achieved its ostensible object. Many Catholics who
might have led rebellion went abroad. Those who stayed, and retained property,
shunned political activity for fear of attracting attention to themselves. Such
Protestant gentry as called themselves 'tories' disliked the native papists far
more than they loathed English whigs. In 1715, no one in Ireland moved on
behalf of James III.

Empire of the Oligarchs

It is astonishing the wealth that can be extracted from territories of the poor, during the phase of capital accumulation, provided that the predatory elite are limited in number, and provided that the state and the law smooth the way of exploitation. One thinks of the maharajahs of petty Indian states in the nineteenth century, or of the great servants of the East India Company fifty years before. The fortunes of the great speculators, politicians, generals and courtiers of the early eighteenth century in England have the same baseless, insubstantial air: they exist, but, in a country where wages, salaries, rent and tithes are counted in tens of pounds, it is not clear what these fortunes of thousands per annum rest upon. In many cases — Cadogan, Cobham, Chandos, Walpole — the fortune rested in origin upon access to public money, lands, perquisites of office, sinecures, percentages on public transactions.

E. P. THOMPSON[1]

I

Defoe had prophesied that the Scots would more and more bless God for the Union which had removed them from 'the petty tyranny of their own constitution' to be 'made one with the freest nation in the world'.[2] In the short run, it did not seem like that at all. Just after the Union, the French launched 25 ships and 12 battalions of infantry, carrying the Stuart Pretender James III with them, and designed to land in Scotland and enlist local Jacobite help. The British navy, and contrary winds, thwarted this attempt of 1708. The Scots closed their ranks in face of English enquiries, but habeas corpus was suspended and numerous noblemen and gentlemen, from the Dukes of Hamilton and Gordon down, were arrested in a sweep which bundled notorious Roman Catholics together with such Protestant anti-Jacobites as Fletcher of Saltoun. The government could not find enough evidence to convict a single prisoner, and the feeling south of the Border that Scots had been let off lightly produced a Treason Act in 1709 which extended harsher English laws to Scotland. After the tories gained a Commons majority, the vengeful feelings of Anglicans against Scots Presbyterians were released. The Toleration Act of 1712 permitted Anglican worship in Scotland. The Patronage Act restored to lay patrons the right to appoint ministers to livings which they owned, reversing the settlement of 1690, and for seventy years, the General Assembly of the Kirk would regularly protest about this. Then, in 1713, despite an article in the Treaty of Union which ruled out the extension of the English malt duty to Scotland during the present war, there was an attempt to do just that. Scots in Parliament moved the repeal of the Union, and the motion was lost merely by four proxy votes.

All this helped to give Jacobitism a persisting natural base in Scotland considerably broader than it could now find in England, though in the second-hand palace which Louis XIV had given the Stuarts at St Germain, young 'James III', whose father had died in 1701, had much correspondence from leading English statesmen. James's 'reign', for those who acknowledged him, would be the longest in British history, ending only with his death in 1766. But piety would be his undoing. He promised English tories that, if he ruled, he would secure the Church of England, but he would not give up his own Catholicism.

The Treaty of Utrecht which ended the long war in 1713 was popular. A general election in that year increased the tory majority. But whereas the whigs were quite tightly organised, and were solid in defence of the Revolution Settlement of 1689 and in support of a Protestant succession which would secure a limited monarchy, their tory rivals were divided. Some were Jacobites, some were Hanoverians, some sat on the fence. Some supported the centrist Harley, Earl of Oxford, some followed the brilliant, eloquent, hard-drinking, lecherous Henry St John, Viscount Bolingbroke. As Queen Anne's health failed, defection of tories to the whig side began. When she died in 1714 the whigs were able to seize control and to ensure a peaceful succession for George I, Elector of Hanover. They expected, and got, their reward.

Having won the General Election of March 1715, they purged tories great and small from public office and its sweets, and they threatened the tory leaders with impeachment for treason. Bolingbroke's panic flight to France could be represented as an admission of guilt. Yet the triumph of Hanover, whiggery and hard cash was not going to prove easy. The mood of those people whom eighteenth-century writers called the 'mob' or the 'populace' was ugly. Peace with France had brought unemployment in crafts geared to war and had flooded the streets with discharged soldiers. Jacobite mobs were out in London that spring, and though the south-east and east remained quiet, violent pro-Stuart demonstrations burst out through the summer in other parts of England.

The popular, brave but stupid Duke of Ormond, Marlborough's tory successor as commander, began to prepare a rising in the west then, hearing that troops were coming to seize him, he too fled to France, leaving a leaderless and confused movement behind him. While the whigs had the backing of the City of London, English Jacobitism drew what strength it had from archaic or defeated classes — impoverished gentry in the north, depressed peasantry in the south-west, clergymen in the old universities of Oxford and Cambridge.

According to James III's plan, a rising in the south-west, centred on Bath, would be supported by sideshows in the north and in Scotland. But in the autumn the whig government acted decisively to smash the south-western organisation, and so the Scottish insurrection went forward alone. Its leader was 'Bobbing John', the Earl of Mar, who had helped to get the Treaty of Union through and had held office in the tory administration. Having tried, but failed, to ingratiate himself with George I, he had returned to his base in north-eastern Scotland. Here, after a fine day's sport in the deer-hunt which was traditionally held at Braemar by the peers of his line, he told the Jacobite nobles and chiefs whom he had invited to shoot with him that his eyes were opened. The Union had been a mistake. He would do his best to make the Scots a 'Free People' again.[3] In spite of the Pretender's own wishes, the cause of the Stuarts and that of Scottish independence were now, and would remain, confused together.

A few days later, on September 6, the standard of James III and VIII was raised at Braemar. Mar soon led a formidable force of clansmen and men from the episcopalian north-east. Meanwhile, Thomas Forster, M.P. for Northumberland, with the young Earl of Derwentwater, mustered in northern England what one malicious contemporary called 'an army of fox-hunters armed with light dress swords'.[4] Scottish Lowland Jacobites crossed the Border to join them.

Between the two Jacobite armies, 'Red John of the Battles', the Duke of Argyll, had wisely concentrated at Stirling the government's few regular troops in Scotland. Historians commonly write that unsuccessful commanders are 'irresolute' (whereas those with the luck to be winners are praised for their 'caution'). But Mar's 'irresolution' probably deserves its notoriety. With ten or twelve thousand men, far outnumbering Argyll's forces, he fussed and fiddled at Perth while the English-Lowland combined army wandered into Scotland, failed to take Dumfries, then marched vaguely off towards Liverpool. Forster thought Lancashire would revolt. But textile industries were already reducing the backwardness of the county. Cotton and lost causes would not, in Britain, mix well together. England would see no more 'Northern Risings'. The rebels were stuck in Preston with armies advancing against them from south and east. After losing only about seventeen men, they tamely surrendered on November 13. Seventy-five English and 143 Scottish noblemen and gentlemen were captured, along with over 1,000 Scottish troops and a few hundred English common soldiers.

On the same day, one of the oddest of all battles was fought north of Stirling. Mar had at last decided to march past his adversary and Argyll, outnumbered three to one, moved to oppose him at Sherrifmuir. Neither side showed much zest for killing. Argyll's forces drove Mar's left wing in rout, but Mar's chased the government left almost as far as Stirling, and the Jacobites should have turned to annihilate the whigs. Mar dithered as usual. The chance was lost. Since the Jacobites did not enter the Lowlands, Argyll could justifiably claim the victory.

As usual, the Highlanders in Mar's army now drifted home. However, James III, with a few companions, arrived in the north-eastern bleakness at Peterhead on December 22. Before long, he had set up a chilly court at Perth. He was disappointed in his supporters, and they with him. He was pale-faced, gloomy and sanctimonious. One rebel wrote, 'Our men began to despise him; some asked if he could speak.'[5] As Argyll advanced, the retreat from Perth was ordered and on February 4 James took ship for France again. The Jacobites scattered for safety and English and Dutch troops looted the north.

The whigs had had a fright and reacted vengefully. Nineteen Scottish and two English peerages were forfeited and seven lords were condemned to death, though only two were in fact executed; young Derwentwater and the Scottish Viscount Kenmure. There was the usual mass transportation of hundreds of lesser rebels to the New World. But the harshness of the English authorities was not matched in Scotland. As Duncan Forbes of Culloden wrote, there were 'not 200 Gentlemen in the whole Kingdom' who were not 'very nearly related to some one or other of the Rebels.' The rank and file were pardoned as briskly as possible. Judges connived at ensuring that forfeitures were not effective. Mackenzie, Earl of Seaforth, went into exile and his great estates were put under a government commission, but its agents were terrorised, rents continued to find their way to the Earl, and when in the 1720s the land was put up for sale, pressure from the clan kept bids so low that it went to Mackenzies who passed it back to the Earl's family. Finally, Seaforth was pardoned himself and came home. The story illustrates the persistence in Scotland of feudal and family loyalties now outmoded in England.[6]

Under English pressure, James was expelled from France. In 1718 he took up residence in Rome, where he stayed for the rest of his life, a papist at the heart of papistry. Spain was at war with Britain and a plan was devised whereby Ormond would go with a Spanish force to raise the west of England, while a smaller expedition would rally the Scottish clans. The winds were, as usual, Protestant. Ormond's armada was broken up by a gale. The luckless Earl Marischal, reaching the isle of Lewis with only 300 Spanish soldiers, found little support among the Hebrideans. When it came to a fight, in Glenshiel on the mainland, in June 1719, his Highlanders soon ran away and the Spaniards, who stood firm, had to surrender.

Bolingbroke fell out with James and was permitted in 1723 to return to England. No politician of his stature and gifts would be found on the Stuart side again, though a drunken blusterer named Shippen maintained a charade of 'Constitutional Jacobitism' in the House of Commons, with perhaps fifty followers there. The Septennial Act which the whigs had passed in 1716 had ushered in something like a one-party state. Extending the maximum life of a parliament from three to seven years, it reduced the frequency with which the tories might appeal to the electorate and raised the value of parliamentary seats since men were prepared to pay more for benefits which they could enjoy longer. The whigs had wealth on their side. Their rich men bought up the boroughs, while the larger county electorates commonly favoured the tories who came to form a permanent minority in the Commons. Governments for nearly fifty years would change only as a result of faction among the whigs as they quarrelled over the spoils. To ensure their own dominance they were prepared to desert old whig principles; thus they shamelessly made use of the royal prerogative and of the Crown's resources of patronage. Fearful of the Pretender, they favoured, and kept up, a long peace with France, and swallowed the Treaty of Utrecht which they had once denounced as a tory iniquity.

As we have seen, Britain had won great advantages through this Treaty, amongst them, the monopoly right to ship 4,800 black slaves a year to Spanish America. This *asiento* was in fact worth less than men supposed. But it helped to inspire the manic excesses of speculation known as the 'South Sea Bubble'. The tories in 1711 had set up the South Sea Company as a counterpoise to the great whig moneyed corporations, the Bank and the East India Company. Its nominal orientation was towards the Pacific. In practice, it acquired the *asiento* and all its promise. The whigs now tried to use it to cope with the National Debt, which had risen five-fold between 1695 and 1713. The interest on the Debt was paid from taxation. The whigs wanted to reduce the hated Land Tax and so make it easier for them to reconcile tory squires to their supremacy. A scheme was floated by which the South Sea Company was to take over the whole National Debt, except for the stocks held by the Bank and the EIC. Holders of government stock were to be persuaded to exchange it for South Sea stock, at a lower rate of interest, but with the prospect of fabulous profits from the Company's trade. The rush of stockholders after this bait pushed up the price of South Sea stock till it reached £1,050 for a £100 in midsummer 1720. The boom enabled the Company's directors to engage in sharp practices; ministers, and the King's mistresses, were implicated. Meanwhile, the great sums realised by those who bought South Sea stock on the up and sold it as it climbed further, encouraged a wild burst of speculation. All kinds of bogus and chimerical companies were floated to take advantage of people now eager to invest but unable to afford the South Sea prices.

When the bubble burst and South Sea stock plunged, former holders of government annuities were left holding paper worth far less and confronting with rage the vast fortunes which lucky investors had milked from the boom. At this point Robert Walpole, whose hands were – or seemed – clean, emerged from the lower ranks of the government as the man who could save the situation. He was close to the directors of the Bank of England, and was able to pull off a solution which minimised the loss of South Sea investors and set the Company itself on the road to becoming a stalwart financial corporation, dealing mainly in gilt-edged securities, and only marginally concerned with trade. He preserved certain great persons from punishment by the judicious sacrifice of some lesser ones to the rage of the Commons. With the gratitude of King and Court on his side, he arrived in the spring of 1721 as Chancellor of the Exchequer and First Lord of the Treasury, to dominate politics for a generation, as one of the last of the great royal favourites and as the first 'prime minister' in anything like the modern sense.

Walpole was 'the epitome of the successful whig, who took full advantage of all the economic opportunities of the post-Revolution era.'[7] His origins were not exalted, but typical of those of the gentry who sat in the House of Commons, except that he came from the county of Norfolk which had taken the lead in applying the new agricultural techniques introduced from Holland in the seventeenth century. His father had been an 'improving' landowner who had enclosed land, enriched the soil by marling, and begun the new rotations which obviated the need to leave part of the land fallow each year. The agriculture which used turnips and clover and looked to the expanding market belonged to an ambience very different from that of the tory squire. Its proponents were natural whigs.

Walpole's appetite for power was matched by his greed for wealth. His tastes were notoriously extravagant, and he built himself a palace on his ancestral estate at Houghton. Politics made him rich. While he sat on Queen Anne's Admiralty Council he did not refrain from indulging in smuggling. Under George I, he gained the coveted post of Paymaster General to the forces, a rich one even in peacetime, since its occupant, receiving moneys in bulk, could invest them and pocket the interest before he paid them out to the troops. By the standards of his day, Walpole was never blatantly corrupt; he operated in the gloaming between due reward and outright theft. No one could deny his real ability. He was hard-working and hard-headed. Coarse-featured, stocky and forceful, seemingly frank and open, he was in fact devoid of principle, but his sun of cordiality never set, and his powers of persuasion kept the Commons under his control. He operated with cheerful mendacity and with moderate, common-sense brutality over the most graceless phase of British political history, which spawned minor counterparts in most parts of the empire; subtle Islay in Scotland, perdurable Speaker Boyle in Ireland, opulent Charles Price in Jamaica.

The system of rule over which he presided was both strong and (in a sense) cheap. The J.P.s, unpaid, still ran their localities; central government was still largely oiled with fees and perquisites rather than salaries. 'It was a *laissez-faire* state, whose chief internal function was to hinder hindrances to the sway of the "natural rulers", just as in the economy there was internal free trade and external protection.'[8] These rulers now defined themselves as whig. Every man who wanted office had to call himself a whig. The whigs of the 1720s were a 'curious junta of political speculators and speculative politicians, stock jobbers, officers grown fat on Marlborough's wars, time-serving dependants in the law and the Church, and great landed magnates.'[9] Each politician sought to reward his family, friends and supporters by finding them places — real jobs, or sinecures — where they could sip or gulp at the public revenues.

Walpole allied himself with Thomas Pelham Holles, first Duke of Newcastle, the greatest owner of borough seats in the country (controlling perhaps a dozen or sixteen), with Newcastle's brother Henry Pelham; and with a rising lawyer, Philip Yorke, who later became Lord Hardwicke. These men helped themselves and their cronies manipulate elections with large sums of money from the government's secret service fund. Even so, and even despite the large 'Court and Treasury Party' of office-holders who sat in the Commons, the government could not reliably control more than about 150 votes in the 558-member House.[10] There were many backbenchers, not professed tories, who prided themselves on their 'independence' and it was Walpole's capacity to persuade these gentry to vote for his policies which sustained him in power for twenty years. The 'prime minister' and his clique of some four close associates, forming a kind of inner Cabinet, were able in general to get the King to accept their advice, but the monarch retained real power. Walpole's standing at court depended on his control of Parliament; the latter in turn required continual royal favour, providing him with the bait which would draw ambitious men to his side. He came, through his use of the Crown's resources, to command a wider scope of patronage than any minister before him. Even minor officials in the revenue service would owe their positions to him, while high office in the law or the Church seemed conditional on the acceptance of his policies.

Had there been less to hand out, the stability which Walpole gave Britain might have been impossible. Perhaps the existence of an empire, with the field of patronage, military and civil, which its administration created, may have been vital to the achievement of the one-party state which determined so much of the character of modern Britain. (Even now, lawyers wear eighteenth-century wigs.) The political dominance of the landed classes was perfected in the reigns of the first two Georges, and certain results are still with us. 'What Sir Robert Walpole and the Whigs did was to make certain that political and social authority should devolve by inheritance,' J. H. Plumb wrote in the 1960s, adding, 'the methods have been purified, and tortuous by-ways evolved for talent, but birth still remains a broad highway to power.'[11]

The mighty English landed class encouraged artistic forms which directly enhanced or mirrored its own grandeur. Magnificent country houses testify to the skill of the architects employed, and to the self-esteem of the owners. A fine school of native portrait painters was beginning to flourish. Young lords sent abroad to be polished, on the 'Grand Tour' of Europe, pillaged that continent's art-works, bringing back oil paintings, statues, Roman remains.

The English milord was becoming a byword for wealth. The biggest British landowners, with £40,000 or £50,000 a year, were richer than many small independent rulers in Europe. In the English social pyramid, a top group of some four hundred great families surmounted perhaps twice that number of gentry families who were distinctly wealthy, three or four thousand families below them of middling landowners and perhaps 15,000 or more petty gentlemen with only a few hundred pounds a year. Land was more and more an aristocratic-cum-gentle monopoly; the class of small owner-occupying free-holders was in decline. Very few merchants or bankers could as yet match the wealth of the territorial magnates, and these latter dominated political life. Power begat money which begat more power. 'In 1726 a quarter of the peerage held government or court office and most other places were in the hands of their relatives or dependants.'[12] High office provided more pelf than could be extracted from any other source, even from law, even from military command, even from most branches of trade.

Landed politicians were also investors. The quarter century of French wars before the Treaty of Utrecht had given Britain the strongest financial institutions in the world. Land was no longer the sole safe investment for men with surplus income. Parliament guaranteed the National Debt. Taxation wrung from the gentry in part, but increasingly from the poor, was used to pay interest to investors thus able idly to fatten themselves. The 'financial revolution' which had begun in the 1690s largely explains why 'stability' settled upon English politics, and why the Jacobite cause was doomed. The moneyed classes, able to lend to the government profitably, had more than any others a vested interest in the avoidance of civil upheaval. Underwriters, bankers, insurance men and the members of the great companies acted to prop up governments which in turn were highly sensitive to their interests.

Money was taking on new and preternatural life. Money battered down that yeoman class which had formed the backbone of Cromwell's army. Money had less and less time for the crafts of the old-fashioned urban artisan. Money sneered at Jacobite squires and lairds. Money was up-to-date in its ideas, accepting the thinking of Hobbes and Newton and Locke, who in various ways helped Money to explain why it was that God (who still existed, and would punish those who defaulted on payments) had no objection at all to Money. Money was, Money opined, in accordance with the natural order of things which God had created and left, as was now understood, to its own development. The laws of Money were like those of gravitation; God had little more to do with them; He was like the king of a *laissez faire* nation; He might intervene if He wanted, but it would be bad form. The earth revolved round the sun; Britain and her colonies revolved around Money. Money didn't mind Moneyed Dissenters and papists, and saw no cause to fight religious wars. 'The splendour of this Monarchy is supported by commerce,' a merchant named Hanway would write in 1749, adding, 'and commerce by naval strength.'[13] Money in his younger days might have doubted if this were the whole truth, might have mentioned the glory of God and the strength of true faith. But Money now fought, without hypocrisy, for the sake of trade, for Money.

Money's alternative name, when it sat on the bench of justices, was Property. Property had no trouble explaining what crime was; crime was an attack on Property. The prophet Locke had proclaimed that government had 'no other end but the preservation of Property'. As David Ogg has written, if Property is seen as the foundation of civilisation then England was the most civilised state in Europe, 'because property was protected there by a penal code more brutal than any to be found elsewhere.' By the end of the eighteenth century, there would be more than two hundred felonies, punishable by death, on the statute book. 'Men were executed for stealing five shillings; a girl was hanged for stealing a handkerchief.'[14]

The sacredness of Property was now proclaimed in terms formerly reserved for human life. 'Banks were credited with souls, and the circulation of gold likened to that of blood.'[15] As Property, alias Money, confirmed his sway, all economic and legal relations between men of different classes became more impersonal. The justice of Tudor and early Stuart days had not been lenient, but its values had been human. Now, as E. P. Thompson observes, 'In place of the whipping post and the stocks, manorial and corporate controls, and the physical harrying of vagabonds, economists advocated the discipline of low wages and starvation, and lawyers the sanction of death ... What was now to be punished was not an offence between men (a breach of fealty or deference, a "waste" of agrarian use-values, an offence to one's own corporate community and its ethos, a violation of trust and function) but an offence against property. Since property was a thing, it became possible to define offences as crimes against things, rather than as injuries to men.'[16] While the black slave was defined as a thing, was 'property', the English labourer was now 'free' of feudal ties. But what he grew or made with his hands was more and more conceived as something alien to himself. It was the property of the landlord or of his employer; he had no claim to what he produced, and could be hanged if he asserted a claim.

Britain had no regular police force — landowners themselves loathed the idea. In the absence of such, the ruling classes resorted to terror. During the 1720s, a little war developed in the forests of Berkshire and Hampshire between the authorities and armed men who blacked their faces to poach deer. It reflected the pressure on the traditional way of life of forest dwellers — craftsmen, yeomen, petty gentry — exerted by the actions of great Hanoverian bigwigs who cherished deer parks as a symbol of status and who were coolly encroaching on royal lands and common lands as they created country seats for themselves. For instance, Thomas Pitt, his huffing and roughling career not yet over, bought an estate in the Windsor area in 1719, cut down ten acres of trees without licence, and enclosed without anyone's permission a park three miles round which included twenty-three acres of covert and wood belonging to the Crown. Such big thieves were not, of course, brought to book. They felt themselves much inconvenienced by little thieves. In Hampshire, 'King John' with his band of perhaps 100 men — the 'Black Chief and his mock negroes', one journalist called them — exerted folk justice, Robin Hood style, intervening on the side of the poor in disputes over debts, over timber rights, over grazing rights, over fishing rights, until he declared his own reign at an end as the government reaction became intimidating. Other 'Blacks', less prudent, died on the gallows, or in gaol, or were transported. A couple of keepers were killed. Walpole retorted, in May 1723, with the 'Black Act' which created at one stroke some fifty new capital offences – not only such 'Black' offences as poaching, the maiming of cattle and the cutting down of young trees, but almost every conceivable kind of action against Property. It was periodically renewed, with death penalties added for yet more offences, until it was made perpetual in 1758.[17]

When Jonathan Wild, thief-taker and also gang boss, was exposed and executed in 1725, writers seized at once on the analogy with Walpole. This was, with good reason, the great age of British satire, with Swift and Pope, Gay and Hogarth striking at the perversions of life around them. The finest talents of the time were deeply alienated from Walpole's 'Court' regime and tended towards the 'Country' opposition represented in Parliament by a queasy alliance of whig 'outs' with the remnant of the tory party. Under the leadership of the returned Bolingbroke, a recension was produced of the 'Country' ideology latent or present everywhere in the English-speaking world. (Fletcher of Saltoun had been spokesman in Scotland for one variant.) The voice of the English opposition, expressing the anger and fears of the lesser gentry, the lower clergy, the threatened craftsmen and the petty merchants, was also eagerly heard across the Atlantic. It did not attack the Hanoverian settlement, and it paraded a patriotism which extolled the glories of commerce and empire, anticipating, as we shall see, the much later 'jingoism'. It endorsed the Revolution Settlement and attacked, not Walpole's policies, but his political methods.

English liberty, as these men explained, depended on a balanced constitution. Crown, Lords and Commons each had a proper role. Now Walpole was using, so the theory went, the patronage of the Crown to undermine the independence of Parliament. Corruption was spreading over the face of the green and pleasant land. The true English virtues were industry, simplicity, honesty and patriotism; Walpole sapped them all with his encouragement of idle luxury and excessive wealth. Paper money figured moral decline, as did the succession of scandals (in 1725 the Lord Chancellor was convicted for embezzling over £100,000) through which Walpole alias Jonathan Wild successfully protected his corrupt and corrupting supporters and instruments. The call was for legislation against corrupt practices, for shorter parliaments, for the exclusion of placemen and pensioners from the Commons, and, as of yore, for a reduction in the size of the standing army in peacetime. North American colonists would remember the doctrines expounded in Bolingbroke's mouthpiece, *The Craftsman*.

Walpole did his best to muzzle his critics. A tax on newspapers (1725) put up their price. Editors were harried and gaoled and from 1737 the stage was censored and effectively gagged. And yet those French thinkers who were advancing the movement of ideas which we call the 'Enlightenment', against a regime and Church far more repressive, looked with admiration towards an England which seemed to them already 'enlightened'. Voltaire, twice imprisoned in the Bastilel for his writings, stayed three years in England in Walpole's day and applauded the religious tolerance which he found there, the absence of press censorship and the mysterious lack of a legally closed and privileged class of noblemen. 'This is a country where all the arts are honoured and rewarded, where there are differences in rank, but only those based on merit. This is a country where one thinks freely and nobly without being held back by any servile fear.'[18] Montesquieu's great *Spirit of the Laws* (1748) would applaud the English constitution and the liberties enjoyed by Englishmen, and would approve of the separation of powers, as the author saw it, between Legislature, Executive and Judiciary. This also was noted in North America.

And the English themselves believed firmly in their own liberty. The law was on paper savage but the judges and gentry who administered it were sticklers for legal forms. A well-founded prosecution could fail on a minor error in the indictment, and foreign visitors were deeply impressed by the solicitude shown by English judges for the rights of the accused man. Gentlemen were occasionally sentenced to death or transported; in 1760 a peer of the realm would be executed at Tyburn. The common people retained a fervent belief in the impartial justice of the law, and this faith propped up the Hanoverian state. And with almost all prosecutions initiated, not by the State, but by private individuals, a luscious power of mercy was enjoyed by the gentry, who, in the case of a poacher, say, could decide whether or not to prosecute and, if so, upon what charges. Displays of kindness and lenience, winning popularity for the countryside's rulers, helped to legitimise their position in the eyes of their inferiors.[19] The lower orders were heartily glad not to be French or Spanish, not to be under despots.

Nor was this the worst age in which to be poor in England. Population was still growing more slowly than trade, crops, and wealth. Corn was cheap. While the cottagers who had eked out a living from livestock kept on common land were hit by the remorseless advance of enclosure, and the small freeholder was hurt by low prices for grain which suited others well, the countryman was commonly better off than before or later. Diet was healthier. Real wages were higher. The prosperity of English tenant farmers, and even of English labourers, was envied by visitors from Europe. In the favoured home counties, female servants were now getting tea, no less, both in mornings and in afternoons. Rural women of the poorer classes could earn useful money carding and spinning in their own homes for the mighty English textile industry. Trade could now be seen to benefit even the lowly.

Compared to the great boom after the Restoration, and the stupendous one which commenced in the mid-eighteenth century, English trade grew languidly at this time. Tonnage of English-owned shipping increased only slowly, from 323,000 in 1702 to 421,000 in 1751. But it grew; and the annual average of exports and re-exports combined rose about 50 per cent between the first decade of the eighteenth century and the fourth, from £6.1 million to £9 million. The special relationship with Portugal forged in the first years of the century gave

Britain access not only to that country's home market, but to her colony of Brazil, where gold had been found in the 1690s. Both became virtually part of the English colonial system. European Portugal took Newfoundland fish and English cloth in exchange for oil, oranges and wine; it was now that 'port' wine became a standard British tipple. The gold rush to the Minas Gerais region of the Brazilian back country, which made Lisbon one of the wealthiest cities in Europe again, was of still greater advantage to the British. While export of gold from Portugal was theoretically prohibited, British warships in fact loaded it regularly, as did the packet boat from Falmouth which maintained a weekly service to Lisbon from 1706 onwards. In the first half of the eighteenth century, something between £1 million and £2 million a year entered England. Meanwhile, it was notorious that the British merchants who handled wine exports made far larger profits than the growers. ' ... The high living of the prosperous English merchants at Lisbon and Oporto was what struck most foreign visitors to those places ... '[20]

Between 1721 and 1742, the value of British exports probably rose by a third, imports by just over a fifth.[21] Yet it was the relative stagnation of the British economies in the age of Walpole which impressed many contemporaries. The avid expectations of the Bubble days had come nowhere near realisation. Britain's industries lacked the stimulus provided by war conditions, and its traders could not see the Royal Navy seizing new markets and opportunities for them. Hence, by the late 1730s, a chorus baying for war.

Walpole did not want war. The Hanoverian dynasty was still insecure. In 1733 Walpole's failure to carry his Excise Bill brought students into the streets of Oxford crying 'King James for ever'. Peace was essential to Walpole's clever attempts to balance all interests in harmony and reconcile all possible groups to the Georges. For most of his rule, Walpole kept the Land Tax as low as 2s. in the £ — in 1731–2 it was only 1s. But the threat of war in 1728–9 sent it up to 3s., and the actual arrival of war in 1727 and 1740 brought it back to 4s.[22]

France, with a child, Louis XV, on the throne, had for the moment an equal interest in keeping things cool, and between 1717 and 1740 understanding between the two countries, steadily wearing threadbare because they were natural rivals, maintained a precarious balance of power. Britain's imperial interests, though they were not advanced, were not undermined. By sending fleets to the Baltic nine times between 1715 and 1727, Britain safeguarded the naval supplies from that region, which was made unstable by the rise of a new power, Peter the Great's Russia. When Spain in 1727 declared war and besieged Gibraltar, British diplomacy averted all-out conflict. In an age of petty and futile diplomacy, when alliances in Europe shifted rapidly at the whim of monarchs, moved by vainglory or dynastic ambition, Walpole's foreign policy had the merit of consistency. The classes represented in Parliament made sure that authentic national and imperial interests were never overlooked. Money dictated its wishes to diplomats and ministers.

And in these quiet days, Walpole brought the 'mercantilist' system to its apogee. With Scotland digested and Ireland and Massachusetts under secure control, old frowns unwrinkled. The most prominent 'mercantilist' writer of the time, William Wood, secretary to the commissioner of customs, expressed in his *Survey of Trade* (1718) the now widespread view that New England and Pennsylvania were not, as Child had thought them, a menace to England, but a useful market for manufactured goods and an indispensable source of supplies for the more southerly colonies. The tropics and sub-tropics called out for linen clothing, as did increasingly fastidious taste in Britain itself. Rising demand had perforce been met, since England produced little, by fine linens acquired in France and Flanders, coarser cloths from Germany and Holland. Now the linen industries of Ireland and Scotland were deliberately encouraged. These provinces of the empire, during the first half of the eighteenth century, made Britain self-sufficient in this important commodity.

By 1730 or so, England had outstripped France industrially.[23] Walpole tried to assist in this development. His policy was consistently protectionist. In 1722 he abolished export duties on nearly all manufactured articles, so securing lower prices for British goods on foreign markets, while reducing or abolishing import duties on foreign raw materials required by British manufacturers and offering financial bounties for the export of various British products. The import of some foreign manufactures was banned altogether, and high duties were set on others.

British manufacturers were also protected against British workers; Money had no sentimental notions in favour of giving them a fair share of increased prosperity. Walpole's day saw legislation to keep wages low, to make it harder for unemployed men to obtain poor relief, and to outlaw nascent trade unions ('combinations'). By a law of 1726, any contract demanded by a combination of workers was made illegal.

There was no labouring 'interest' recognised at Westminster where well-organised lobbies now jockeyed for position, using pressure in and outside Parliament. Walpole was always attentive to the wishes of the great City companies; the Bank, the East India Company, the South Sea Company and the Russia Company. Adjustments to the navigation code reflected the strengths of lesser competing lobbies. The Irish lobby showed its power in 1731 when the Navigation Acts were revised to permit direct imports of non-enumerated goods from the colonies to Ireland. The West India lobby had plenty of muscle. The North American colonies, with their diverse and divergent interests, were weaker. This was reflected in a series of measures which emphasised their auxiliary status in the empire. White pines from New England forests were prized by the Navy; in 1722 it was enacted that no such tree should be felled or destroyed without a government licence. In 1732 the English hatters won a significant bout – colonists were forbidden to export hats or felts, a particular instance showing the general intention that colonists should import British goods, not create their own manufacturing industries. And the Molasses Act of 1733 was a triumph for the West Indian planters over the New Englanders.

However, North Americans showed few signs of pique over Acts which in practice had little effect on them. This was the period of 'salutory neglect'. The colonies were the responsibility of the Secretary of State for the Southern Department. From 1724, this office was filled by the Duke of Newcastle, who took a lively interest in matters to do with patronage but was hardly concerned with much else. With the Board of Trade now dozing ineffectually, there was no group of men in London actively pressing for tighter control of the colonies. The empire looked rather like the later 'commonwealth of nations' with various quasi-independent polities prospering (for most did, most of the time) in their own different ways, each with its distinctive political patterns, all benefiting from the secure markets which the system provided for their produce.

In England itself, however, and also in Scotland, taxation, seen as oppressive, provoked quite dangerous opposition at times. Looking for ways of relieving the 'landed interest' of as much of the burden as possible, Walpole shamelessly made up his mind to squeeze the poor, taxing virtual necessities – malt, beer and salt. In 1724 he replaced the import duties on tea, coffee, cocoa and chocolate with excise paid inland, aiming in part to check smuggling. He did not succeed in this, but revenue increased and in 1733 he tried to extend the idea to tobacco and wines. He had to back down in face of violent popular outrage and fierce opposition in Parliament.

Ordinary people hated Walpole's excise and thought it no crime to evade it. The eighteenth century really was the heyday of smuggling which romantic history makes it seem, and the smugglers, everywhere in Britain, were much admired and zealously supported by the common people. Most smugglers were themselves manual workers. One could earn five or ten times as much in a night as a labourer won in a day, and this might mean that a man from a poor family could arrive at a certain modest wealth.[24]

There was much smuggling out, of wool to the Continent. The staples of smuggling in were brandy and tea. Duties on French brandy were prohibitive. Till 1723 there was a customs duty of 14 per cent by value on all tea imported by the EIC, plus a further tax of about 5s. per lb. Walpole replaced these with an excise duty of 4s. per lb. which lowered the price only a little. But the habit was spreading fast and wide. While a rich man might pay 36s. a lb. for the finest 'Hyson' and a middle-class lady perhaps 12s. for her 'Bohea', the poor were beginning to buy small quantities which they drank very weak, or to fall for nasty adulterated products – unless they could get good cheap leaf from the smugglers.[25]

The scale of smuggling was so enormous that all statistics purporting to show imports and exports in the eighteenth century must be used with cautious reservations – Adam Smith would dismiss figures such as these as 'those public registers of which the records are sometimes published with so much parade, and from which our merchants and manufacturers would often vainly pretend to announce the prosperity or declension of the great empires.' Between 1723 and 1732, 250 Customs Officers were beaten up or otherwise abused; six were murdered. Of boats engaged in smuggling, 229 were confiscated, and about 2,000 people were prosecuted. Nearly 200,000 gallons of brandy were seized. Yet these impressive totals represent only the government's direct confrontations with smugglers, and its very limited successes. Witnesses before Parliament in 1745 estimated that over 3 million lb. of tea were coming in illegally every year – more than three times the amount 'fairly' imported.[26]

The salaries of rank and file customs and excise men were low and irregularly paid. They were easily bribed or intimidated. The jagged coastlines of Scotland made smuggling easy. The Isle of Man was still 'part of the crown but not of the realm of England'; duties were lower there, and the rise of Liverpool and Whitehaven as ports on the nearby mainland had a very great deal to do with the ease with which small boats slipped across to make landfall at dusk. Kent and Sussex, close to France, were estimated to have more than 20,000 professional smugglers. From Lydd, in Romney Marsh, an official reported in 1734 that 'The smugglers pass and repass to and from the seaside, forty and fifty in a gang in the day time loaded with teas, brandy and dry goods; that above two hundred mounted smugglers were seen one night upon the sea beach there waiting for the loading of six boats and above one hundred were seen to go off loaded with goods; that they march in a body from the beach about four miles into the country and then separate into small parties ... ' Reaching London in the small hours, smugglers could dispose of their goods to the waiting tea dealers and be out of town again before morning. Some had special coats into which they could 'quilt a quarter of a hundred weight of tea'. Soldiers sent into the area to cope with its resolute, armed gangs commonly shirked combat and sought collaboration instead. A magistrate might not dare send a smuggler to gaol for fear of having his house burnt down or his own life taken. Even after pitched battles between the gangs and the law, no convictions followed. A customs officer wrote to the treasury from Folkestone in 1744 comparing the situation there to that of a 'frontier town in a state of war'.[27]

Next year, the excise on tea was cut to 1s. a lb., though a 25 per cent tax was put on sales at EIC auctions. Thereafter, however, duties rose again and the war between government and smugglers went on with little abatement for decades. In its own way, it represented the growing importance of foreign trade to the whole United Kingdom. The colonies and the East Indies, in particular, counted for more and more. Exports from England and Wales to mainland North America rose from around £250,000 per annum in 1701–5 to £1.8 million by 1766–70. Exports to the British West Indies started higher (£305,000) but rose less fast, to £1.4 million. In the first period, these New World markets took nearly 10 per cent of metropolitan exports – in the latter, nearly 25 per cent. The colonial share of imports entering England rose from 15 per cent in

1700 to 40 per cent in 1760. Direct trade with Africa remained relatively small, but exports to the East Indies rose from £100,000 per annum to over £1 million in the first seventy years of the eighteenth century.[28]

Textile materials (linens, calicoes, silk, flax, hemp, cotton wool) made up about 30 per cent of English imports in 1750 as in 1700. But over the same period 'groceries' (tea, coffee, rice, sugar, pepper and other non-European products) rose from about one-sixth to over a quarter; by 1772 they would contribute over a third. Imports of coffee and sugar waxed enormously, imports of tobacco considerably, but tea, taking merely the figures for legal imports, was the most spectacular acrobat: 70,000 lb. a year in 1700–4, 3,550,000 lb. in 1750–4. British exports, meanwhile, were growing far more varied. Woollens in 1700 still made up approaching three-fifths of all exports; by 1750 they were contributing less than half.[29] The captive markets in the colonies were an immense, perhaps a decisive, stimulus to home industry. There was no demand in Europe, which had its own manufacturers, for most of the goods which Britain could offer; cloth, grain and coal were the main exceptions. But fast-growing populations on the North American mainland cried out for nails and pans, ploughshares and buckles, anchors and soap, knives. The British metal industries profited in particular. Meanwhile, West Indian planters required large stocks of identical garments for their slaves, and the East India Company placed orders in bulk, nagging and prodding industry towards mass-production even in years when the armed forces which fought the empire's battles were not in search of great supplies.

Three world-transforming events were in the making; one within Britain itself, in industry, one on the North American mainland, the third in Bengal. All three would burst out during the astonishing upward sweep in British trade fuelled, after 1739, by world-wide war. Meanwhile, under Walpole, the empire, most misleadingly, gave an appearance of solid, even of stolid, stability. Only one new colony was added, Georgia in the 1730s. The slave trade grew and grew in old channels, without flooding, and the Lancashire cotton industry rose quietly in response, as Liverpool, from the 1730s, moved up to dominate the commerce in Africans.

Europeans, from the fifteenth century, had invented a transoceanic pattern of commerce which linked four continents; their own, America, Africa and Asia. With English and other traders nesting at Canton, in China, from 1700, the pattern was nearing completeness. The 'South Sea', the Pacific, was still no more than a highway linking the Philippines with Mexico; its peoples and islands awaited discovery, as well as exploitation; men still theorised about a great Southern Continent there, a new, as it were, 'New World', while Jonathan Swift could fantasise *Gulliver's Travels* in that last of unknown quarters of the globe. Europe, monopolising trade by sea between continents, would clearly send men one day to open it up. But there was no hurry. There were almost enough markets, and the accounts of strange places collected in Churchill's

Voyages (a sequel to Hakluyt, in four, six, and finally eight volumes, which had four editions between 1704 and 1752) were for the moment sufficient to gorge the curiosity of most people, and to provide 'Enlightened' thinkers with means of speculation about human history, human society; also—this was a new concept beginning to crystallise—about human progress from barbarism to Walpole and, it was to be hoped and inferred, onwards.

Africa was the source of cheap labour. America was the continent where it was needed. The northern red man still brought in furs as a prelude to his own liquidation. Amerindians, and blacks, in Latin America, laboured to mine the bullion which European traders needed for commerce in the East. India had no gold of its own, but used a gold and silver currency. The world's bullion drained towards the realm of the Mughal emperor, where it commanded more real goods in exchange than it could do elsewhere—hence the cheapness of Bengal textiles for foreigners. China's money was copper, but 'Silver valued by weight was a sort of superior currency', the basic instrument of large-scale exchanges. Chinese production of silver was too low for the Manchu empire's needs, as it had been for that of the Mings before it. Hence tea merchants sent silver to Canton. Even a poor Chinaman would carry around with him scissors and a precision scale, as one European reported in the 1730s, so that he could cut and weigh silver, originally put into circulation in loaves, to make the exact sum required for exchange.[30] The ingenious heathen could snip off half a farthing with preternatural exactitude, but his economy, settled in such ways, was now beginning to look old-fashioned compared to that of the realm of George II and Walpole. The world was still the world's world; within a few lifetimes it would become Europe's world.

II

Cathay had been the original goal of European seafaring. But the scholar-officials of the Chinese empire scorned trade and regarded commerce with foreigners not as a normal and obvious activity but as a deviant one, to be permitted as a privilege only under close restriction. The Portuguese were established at Macao from 1557 and the East India Company's first attempt at trade with China came only in 1635, after friendly relations with Portugal had been established. A ship was then sent to Macao, but even after Charles II's marriage to Catharine of Braganza the use of her fellow-countrymen as intermediaries had proved difficult and disappointing. In the years which followed the conquest of Ming China by the Manchus in 1644, the isolation of the country became, for a time, still more complete.

But in 1670 the EIC chief at Bantam made a deal with the Ming regime which still held out on Formosa and which momentarily held Amoy, an island harbour off the Fukien coast. An EIC base was established here, and even after the town's conquest by the Manchus ten years later, English trade was still tolerated. In

1684, thinking of China's need for Japanese copper, the great Manchu emperor K'ang-Hsi decreed the South China ports open to foreign commerce. Local officials remained obstructive, but eight English ships did business on the coast between 1690 and 1696, twenty in the next seven-year period, by which time the French were also sending vessels direct to China. And in 1699 a 'New Company' ship, the *Macclesfield*, arrived in Canton and began a trade there. This port soon replaced Amoy as the main focus of English activity. The so-called 'Ostend Company', based on the Austrian Netherlands but largely a screen for British and Dutch interlopers, arrived there in the second decade of the eighteenth century, and after diplomatic pressure, in 1727, persuaded the Austrian Emperor to suspend the Ostenders' charter, the Dutch East India Company moved in and provided the British with their hardest competition.[31]

While the rewards for Europeans were great, so were the difficulties of this trade. What would the Chinese take, apart from silver? The British used their position in Bengal to advantage, sending thence to Canton raw cotton, cotton yarn and then, in spite of prohibitions by emperors from 1729 onwards, opium to fuddle the Manchu's subjects. With the vaulting demand for tea, the China trade in the course of the eighteenth century outstripped the trade with India itself, the proportion of EIC tonnage devoted to it rising from less than one-eighth to more than half.[32] Yet the conditions imposed in Canton were humiliating. The city stood forty miles up the Pearl river, at the apex of a vast estuary. Europeans dropped anchor at Wampoa, twelve miles below the city, and their movements were more and more restricted to this anchorage and to the water-front street in Canton itself where their factories stood side by side. Europeans could deal only with a selected group of merchants, which came to be called the 'Co-Hong', and the 'Hoppo', the local imperial functionary, pressed hard on both groups of traders. It was forbidden that foreigners should learn Chinese, so bargaining through interpreters here was the outcome of necessity rather than laziness. 'Pidgin English' developed through informal communication, of which there was precious little. No white women might be introduced into Canton, and even the men were not allowed to reside there except during the season when the ships were in. The EIC after a time ordered one senior employee to stay in the area all the year round as Chief of Council, and eventually, from 1770, a permanent establishment, as in India — council members, supercargoes and Writers — would work at Canton during the permitted period, then retire to Macao for the interim.

The round trip at best took nearly two years. EIC ships carrying textiles, lead and silver coin left England in December or January and arrived, with good luck, on the South China coast in the following August or September. Having collected their tea and coped with the Chinese officials, they would sail around the New Year. One or two might get to London in time for their tea to be offered at the EIC's December, or even its September, sales, but most took longer, and some much longer. The value of the cargoes, which grew steadily richer, supported this huge consumption of time and effort. In 1722, for instance, two EIC vessels between them took off tea worth £40,000, as well as £28,000 of silk.[33]

The law of 1700 which had forbidden the use in England of Asiatic silks, printed calicoes and dyed calicoes had actually increased the demand for raw silk, cotton yarn and plain cotton pieces. Eventually, protests from woollen and silk manufacturers secured legislation in 1720 forbidding the use even of calicoes dyed and printed in Britain, with certain exceptions. (A relaxation in 1736 permitted printing on cotton stuffs with a linen warp, but it was another forty years before British calico printers were once again allowed to dye and print cloth wholly made of cotton.) Tea supplanted cotton piece goods as the EIC's most valuable import. The amount of leaf brought home multiplied five times in forty years after 1718. Raw silk from Bengal, where the EIC fostered its cultivation, was another great source of profit.

EIC trade more than doubled in value in the forty years up to the half century, when, by official returns, exports and imports stood at just over £1 million each per annum, and the real figures were rather higher. After a great upsurge in the early days of the United Company, when it paid dividends of 10 per cent annually, progress slowed down and dividends fell to 8 per cent in the 1720s, 7 per cent in the 1730s. A new Act of 1730 prolonged the EIC's monopoly, but this was after a fresh attack on it, which had prompted the alarmed Company to reduce the rate of interest on what the government owed it to 4 per cent. In 1744, the price of a further forty-year extension was the loan of a further £1 million at 3 per cent. This was worth affording. In the last years of Anne's reign the Company had been sending an average of eleven ships East every year; by the mid-1740s, the average was twenty, and their tonnage was much larger. However, the EIC did not fit out monstrous Indiamen like its European competitors. One reason belonged to the Age of Reason, when religion had lost its compulsive hold. A clause in its 1698 charter obliged the Company to provide a chaplain for every ship over 500 tons. Prudently, so as to save the expense of a salary, it never chartered a vessel of more than 499 tons, until the clause was repealed in 1773. Its ships at Wampoa were dwarfed by 1,200-ton Danes and 1,500-ton Frenchmen.[34]

The East, like the West Indies, had its influx of Scots after the Union. Cordially, but with patient discretion, Walpole as early as the 1720s found ways of using East India patronage to gratify his Scottish supporters, while enterprising mariners and professional men inserted themselves by their own efforts. An Ayrshire seaman named Macrae governed Madras with success in the late 1720s, and a list of surgeons in the fort during that decade shows Munro, Ramsay, Lindsay and Douglas following each other in quick succession. The Scots moved into a concern which was now running more or less smoothly; a couple of generations passed with few dramatic events. Each presidency went on its own way except in 1714 when all three combined to send an embassy to the emperor Faruksiyar, which after three years won an impressive new *farman* (imperial grant), after a Scottish surgeon had luckily cured that potentate of V.D. The emperor confirmed that the EIC in Bengal had the right to trade free of customs in return for an annual payment of 3,000 rupees. This was, P. J. Marshall declares, 'the most spectacular confirmation of privileges ever to be obtained by a European nation.' But the EIC faced fresh competition in India from Europeans. The Ostenders' settlement on the Hugli was abandoned in 1744 and the Swedish East India Company, founded in 1731, traded almost exclusively with China. A Danish Company had been settled on the south-east Indian coast for more than a hundred years. An up-turn in the fortunes of the French Company was of most moment. Between 1720 and 1740, its trade increased ten times, to become nearly half as great as that of the EIC.[35] This new rivalry coincided, a fateful conjuncture, with a general crisis in the Mughal empire.

The pomp of Aurangzeb's successors remained imposing. But decline was obvious by the 1720s when the Mughal empire was virtually divided in two; Asaf Jah, a frustrated chief minister, returned from Delhi to the Deccan provinces and became in effect independent there. In 1738, the Marathas burst into the suburbs of Delhi and dictated a peace which divided the northern and southern portions of the empire by the cession to themselves of the province of Malwa. Next year, the Persian King, Nadir Shah, invaded India and plundered Delhi. Wholesale distintegration would soon set in. The Marathas were the chief solvent. By the mid-century they had spread right across central India, occupying Orissa and attacking Bengal, making the entire empire their field for plunder and for the exaction of *chauth*, tribute taken with a strong hand. Yet they themselves would be more and more divided into five distinct sections, with the authority of the Peshwa who ruled in Poona rivalled by those of the Gaekwar at Baroda, the Bhonsla at Nagpur, the Holkar at Indore and Sindhia at Gwalior.

Apart from the Maratha incursions, other, internal reasons can be suggested for the collapse of Mughal power. Hindus are said to have been alienated by Aurangzeb's Muslim orthodoxy. The able young adventurers from central Asia who had provided the empire with fresh leadership were now diverting themselves to Persia. The loss of the will to rule, a factor impossible to measure, can also be proposed. All empires come to an end, except China's, and the Mughal power, based on the spread of alien Muslim adventurers, had never founded itself on native loyalty. But it seems clear that trade with Europeans was not, before the 1740s, a cause of the re-division of India. About its effects in West Africa, historians are less certain.

III

Now that it had lost its monopoly and had none the less to maintain its forts, the Royal African Company could not effectively compete with the slavers of Bristol and Liverpool. Its forts decayed and from 1730 it was given a State subsidy of £10,000 a year to help with their upkeep. After 1746, the subsidy was withheld and four years later Parliament replaced the RAC with a 'regulated' company which took over the general management of the African trade and the forts. Any man could join it on payment of a small fee.

The RAC's establishment of settlements on the Gambia, in Sierra Leone, and on the Gold Coast, goes far to explain why these areas later became islands of British rule in a sea of French territory. In its first four decades, to 1713, it had delivered 100,000 slaves to the plantations, coined more than half a million 'guineas' and built or rebuilt eight forts in Africa. Only the Dutch West Indies Company, among its foreign counterparts, came near to equalling its success.[36] The booming 'open' trade built on monopoly's thankless achievements.

While London merchants had been ensnared in two monopoly companies – the RAC which acquired slaves, then the South Sea Company which sold them to the Spaniards in the New World – Bristol merchants, followed by those of Liverpool, had moved in to seize most of the African trade. In the second quarter of the eighteenth century, Liverpool began to overhaul Bristol. Closeness to the Isle of Man, as we have seen, made evasion of duty on produce brought home easy. Lancashire textiles were better suited to tropical markets than the woollens of Bristol's hinterlands. The lean and hungry acumen of the outsider helped to enable the Liverpool men to undercut their rivals by £4 to £5 a head and still show a profit. Smuggling into the Spanish New World brought them coin which increased their capacity to give credit to British planters. Before long they were settling factors on Jamaica and showing themselves superior to their competitors in what we now call marketing. Besides this, Liverpool traders had commonly started as seamen themselves and were readier to show a prudent meanness towards their captains, crews and agents than Bristol merchants of the second and third generation who liked to think of themselves as gentlemen. While Bristol and London skippers could eat ashore on occasion and drink Madeira, their Liverpool counterparts gnawed salt beef on shipboard and washed it down with rum punch – though after virtual monopoly was secured, the port came to regard slaving captains as a special breed, indulged and even honoured, whereas skippers in other trades were still treated as parsimoniously as before.[37]

Liverpool, with 35,000 people by the 1750s, was something like a frontier town still, graceless and raw. Slaving captains and the merchants who sent them were commonly pillars of the local churches. Practically everyone had some direct stake in the town's characteristic trade. The ships employed were typically 250 to 300 tons, heavily armed, built for speed, and carrying a larger crew than normal. The son of one respected Liverpool slaving captain would recall how his father had a body of loyal seamen who went on voyage after voyage with him. 'The men used to make much of me. They made me little sea-toys, and always brought my mother and myself presents from Africa, such as parrots, monkeys, shells, and articles of the native workmanship.'[38]

No one in Liverpool was likely to challenge a trade of such value, when hard-headed thinkers on economic questions concurred on its prime importance. An anonymous pamphlet of 1749 set forth a long settled British view. 'The most approved Judges of the Commercial Interests of these Kingdoms have ever been of the opinion that our West India and African Trades are the most nationally beneficial of any we carry on. It is also allowed on all Hands, that the trade to Africa is the Branch which renders our American Colonies and Plantations so advantageous to Great Britain: that Traffic only affording our Planters a constant supply of Negro Servants for the Culture of their Lands ... The Negroe-Trade, therefore, and the natural consequences resulting from it, may be justly esteemed an inexhaustible Fund of Wealth and Naval Power to this Nation.' This was not an absurd standpoint. Between 1709 and 1787, while British shipping engaged in foreign trade quadrupled, vessels clearing for Africa multiplied twelve times. And up to 1770, one-third of Manchester's textile exports went to Africa, one half to the New World.[39]

Appropriate attitudes to race hardened. In the sixteenth century there had been little attempt to distinguish between the sorts of mankind on anatomical, physiological or cultural grounds. ' ... As long as all men were considered brethren in the family of God, *as long as no efforts were made to classify some men among the beasts*, as long as no political or economic interest called for a theoretical imputation of debasement with respect to any group of dependent people, neither skin colour nor the natural anxiety caused by conflict with enemies such as the Muslim or the Tartars led to anything like what we now know as racial "tension".' The Book of Genesis still explained everything. All men were descendants of Noah, even if he had cursed Ham. But we have seen how colonising and trading practice modified Christian principle in Ireland, in Africa, in America. Meanwhile, the 'scientific revolution' of the seventeenth century had fostered a tendency among advanced intellectuals – Sir William Petty, for instance – to play with polygenetic theories which presumed that different species of men had different origins. By the 1720s the idea that savages (that is, Red Indians and Africans) were a link in a chain between apes and men and so were inferior biologically, had gained a great deal of ground. The medieval hierarchy of being, in which King, Lion and Sun had stood clearly above lesser men, lesser beasts, lesser planets, was in the process of conversion 'from a spatial arrangement of forms into an historical, developmental or evolutionary series.' Thus a British doctor wrote of Africans at this time that, 'As for their Customs, they exactly resemble their Fellow Creatures and Natives, the Monkeys.' Another traveller, in 1735, wrote of 'A Colour, Language and

Manners, as wide from ours, as we may imagine we should find in the planetary Subjects above, could we get there', going on to suggest that 'the black and white Races have, *ab origine*, sprung from different-coloured first Parents.'[40]

The paradoxes are piquant. 'Racialist' rationalisations emerged in close conjunction with the new scientific thinking which, within two and a half centuries, would indeed take men into space and their hardware on to 'planetary Subjects', while the destruction of medieval concepts of hierarchy was indispensable to the rise, by the late eighteenth century, of modern democratic ideas. All three tendencies relate to an intellectual movement from Christian orthodoxy which made Deism intellectually fashionable, and, in effect, ushered God out of a universe which He was still supposed to have created, but which He had left to the operation of comprehensible and consistent natural laws. (Of these 'Gravity' was well established by Newton; 'Evolution' was, so to speak, still evolving.)

Loss of faith in miracles and in the possibility of supernatural events meant, in effect, that, from the early eighteenth century, few learned men really 'believed' in God in the old way. Will to believe replaced instinctive belief. The excesses of evangelical Christianity, as these were breaking out, in Walpole's day, in Britain and the American colonies would seem largely to have stemmed from the desperate wish of the intellectuals who promoted them to go on believing, to go on worshipping, in the teeth of the cool sceptical acceptance of outward forms in religion simply because they were socially desirable, which was now dominant in the English-speaking countries. Man, the rhapsodists of revival insisted, could not live by Newton and sugar alone. They appealed to the lower orders, who had never heard of Newton, and still got precious little sugar. The price of salvation was cut. Everyone might be saved. Doubt, creeping always upon the most pious now, like a thief in the night, could be kept at bay by the manic indulgence of emotion. The urge to cultivate rapture and awe and joyful release also helped create, from the mid-century, the Protean 'Romantic' movement with its tempting array of alternative new religions. ('Nature' or 'Homer' or 'Motherland' might do instead of Jehovah.) Like evangelicalism, this current in literature and the arts bore men away from easy acceptance of slavery.

Yet Deism too might encourage kind words for the savage, emphasising his reason or good manners rather than his wildness, because it was one way to undermine Christian superstition. Voltaire extolled the cool Chinese religion. Of course, men must conceive the polished and pale (if haughty) mandarin to be a very different fellow from the naked African. But did not the red prince, the black priest, worship the One God in his own way? Had not the revered poets of Rome extolled the virtues of shepherds? Was not the simple life, amid unspoilt nature, in most agreeable contrast to that of the corrupt cities, some of which were beginning to grow monstrous in size as well as in immorality, or to the luxury of a cynical court? Mrs Aphra Behn's play *Oroonoko*, first published in 1688, held the stage throughout the eighteenth century. It portrayed an African prince of most elevated feelings who died a slave, tortured to death, in Surinam. Esteemed essayists and poets – Addison, Steele, Pope, common reading among the middle and upper classes – had begun in the early eighteenth century to develop a potent rhetoric of (condescending) sympathy for the blackamoor. Defoe, characteristically, wrote both against the slave trade, in verse, and in its favour, in prose.

The source of a cliché may be no more than a little spring bubbling out among rocks and bushes, but before long it will feed broad rivers in flood. The literary novelties of one generation create stock judgments in the next, or the next after that.

In 1733 distinguished intellectual circles in London encountered a literate African, Job ben Solomon, son of a Muhammadan priest among the Fula people of Senegambia, who captivated them with his stories of slaying lions with poisoned arrows, and his explanations of how he coped with two wives. The circumstances of his arrival in Britain were equally dramatic. He had been kidnapped into slavery – ironically, on a journey made to sell two boys as slaves. From Maryland, he had written to his father, and the letter had come into the hands of General Oglethorpe, founder of Georgia and at this time, despite his hatred of slavery, deputy governor of the Royal African Company. The philanthropic General had secured his release. After being introduced to the Hanoverian royal family, Job sailed back to the Gambia a free man. In 1747 a veritable African prince appeared in England. His father, King of Anomabu on the Gold Coast, had sent one son to France, with gratifying results, and so tried to despatch another to England. An English sea-captain, however, sold the young man into slavery. When English ships bombarded the King into agreeing to exclude French traders, it was settled that in return the English would find his son. So he was tracked down in the West Indies, redeemed, and much admired in London; he was taken to see a performance of *Oroonoko* and was said to have been deeply moved. As an African of 'noble' birth he himself matched the literary stereotype of 'Guinea's captive kings'.[41]

By the second quarter of the eighteenth century, Quakers, especially in America, were starting to protest. 1735 saw the publication of a first-hand account of the trade, by John Atkins, which included a long and unqualified attack on it, drily demolishing the apology put forward that slaves lived better in the New World than they could have done at home: ' ... who is to judge of their Wants, themselves, or we?' Active opposition to the slave trade did not begin, except among Quakers, until the 1780s. But there is no reason to doubt the sincerity of the sentiments expressed by Horace Walpole, youngest son of Sir Robert, in 1750 when, as an M.P., he was involved in the debates which ended the RAC. 'We have been sitting this fortnight on the African Company;'

he wrote, '*we*, the British Senate, that temple of liberty, and bulwark of Protestant Christianity, have this fortnight been pondering methods to make more effectual that horrid traffic of selling negroes. It has appeared to us that six-and-forty thousand of these wretches are sold every year to our plantations alone! — it chills one's blood. I would not have to say that I voted for it for the continent of America!'[42] Horace Walpole was a leader of taste. His queasiness on this subject would eventually become as fashionable as the neo-Gothic style of architecture which he pioneered at his house at Twickenham, 'Strawberry Hill'.

Francis Moore, who had been an RAC factor in up-country Gambia, published an account of that region in 1738. He portrayed the Fula people as hospitable and generous to neighbouring peoples when famine struck. They were strict Muhammadans who would not touch alcohol; they were rarely angry, yet very brave; they were skilful herdsmen, great huntsmen and good agriculturalists. But Moore also said that rulers near his post used the slave trade to provide themselves with pocket money and to dispose of unwanted subjects. 'Not only Murder, Theft and Adultery, are punished by selling the Criminal for a Slave, but every trifling Crime is punish'd in the same manner. There was a Man brought to me in *Tomany*, to be sold for having stolen a Tobacco-Pipe.' He further described the comportment of the King of 'Barsally', a drunkard who would shoot at passing canoes for sport and, to satisfy his 'insatiable Thirst' for brandy, would set fire to villages of his own people and seize them for sale into slavery as they ran out. There is no reason to disbelieve Moore. Children were hanged in England for petty crimes, and chiefs in the Scottish Highlands were selling their own followers into indentured servitude in the New World. But as Moore showed, most slaves were not bought direct from source. African merchants were bringing down to the Gambian posts 'in some Years Slaves to the Amount of 2000, most of which, they say, are Prisoners taken in War. They buy them from the different Princes who take them.' Many, he said, came from 'a vast Way inland. Their Way of bringing them is tying them by the Neck with Leather-Thongs, at about a Yard distance from each other, 30 or 40 in a String, having generally a Bundle of Corn, or an Elephants Tooth upon each of their heads.'[43]

It seems that one way or another, virtually every people in West Africa lost men through the trade. There had been no reservoir of slaves surplus to local needs before the Europeans arrived. The demands of the white traders encouraged rulers to set about increasing greatly the numbers of slaves and other saleable subjects beneath them. By the end of the eighteenth century the servile class in Guinea was much larger and more closely defined than two hundred years before, though A. G. Hopkins concludes that most of the slaves shipped were in fact not slaves already; they were ordinary cultivators and their families, generally gathered in by raids, warfare and tribute.[44]

Europeans on the coast listened anxiously for news of wars inland; though they would dislocate trade for a time, prolonged peace might halt the flow of supplies altogether. Thus in 1706 the English on the Gold Coast were 'in daily expectation of the Arcanians coming to fight the Cabesterra people.' They hoped that if the Akani won there would be 'a glorious trade' in slaves. It would be hard to say where normal, as it were 'natural', warfare ended and deliberate raiding for slaves began. Certainly, much commercial raiding went on. Since both raiding and trading required much labour and capital, they were generally financed and directed by a few big men — 'kings, rich men, and prime merchants', as one observer noted. Among a people which engaged in slaving, a species of mercantilism might evolve — 'The firm acquired political functions; conversely, the state acted like a huge corporation.'[45] Oligarchs in such African ports as Whydah and Old Calabar collaborated with other oligarchs in London, Liverpool and Nantes in the shipping of thousand upon thousand of African men, women and children. It is difficult to judge which continent, Europe or Africa, was immediately more sharply affected by the actions of these men: how does one weigh the rise of the Lancashire cotton kings and the Glasgow tobacco barons against the evolution of slaving states in Guinea?

To some historians it has seemed obvious that the demand for slaves transformed the interior of West Africa and pulled wealth and power towards the coast where new states were formed. It has also been held that the exchange of slaves for firearms meant that the latter became decisive in African political history. The first proposition is doubtful, the second more so. The cavalry of the Yoruba empire of Oyo was able in 1726, without firearms, to defeat the King of Dahomey's musketeer footsoldiers. African potentates certainly valued muskets, and local soldiers and blacksmiths became adept in their use and repair. But the Maxim gun lay far in the future; trade muskets took a long time to reload and were not always triumphant, as the famous Asante power also found.[46]

The Asante ('Ashanti') burst unexpectedly into the view of Europeans in 1701, when they humbled the state of Denkyira, on the Gold Coast, with which the whites were in touch. The Asante state, based on Kumasi, had been created in the late seventeenth century by a remarkable leader named Osei Tutu. It bound together various Akan clans and family groups around the symbol of the Golden Stool of its rulers, the Asantehene. Exploiting the major gold-workings of the interior and expanding their power in all directions, the Asante were greatly respected by Dutch and English alike, and their successful wars brought many captives to the coast for shipment.

Further east the Yoruba empire of Oyo had been established on the savanna since before the fourteenth century. Oyo had no guns until the nineteenth, and its rulers did not encourage dealings with Europeans. Yet it was able more than once to conquer the slaving kingdom of Dahomey which had been created about 1625 and which became a byword in Europe for militarism and despotism. Agaja, who ruled Dahomey from 1708, started a remarkable military training scheme for young boys and established a body of spies to bring word

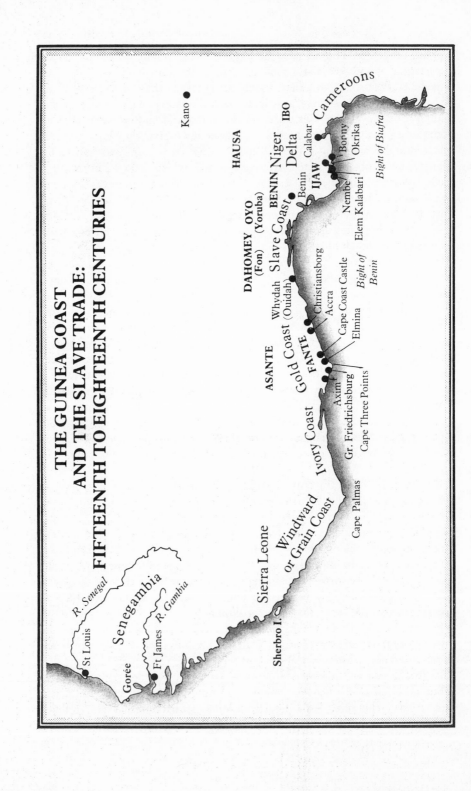

THE GUINEA COAST
AND THE SLAVE TRADE:
FIFTEENTH TO EIGHTEENTH CENTURIES

R. Senegal

Senegambia

R. Gambia

St Louis

Gorée

Ft James

Sierra Leone

Sherbro I.

Windward
or Grain Coast

Ivory Coast

Cape Palmas

ASANTE

Gold Coast

FANTE

Cape Three Points

Gr. Friedrichsburg

Axum

Elmina

Cape Coast Castle

Accra

Christiansborg

DAHOMEY OYO
(Fon) (Yoruba)

Whydah
(Ouidah)

Slave Coast

BENIN

Benin

HAUSA

Kano

OYO

Bight of
Benin

Niger
Delta

IBO

Cameroons

Calabar

Bonny

Okrika

Nembe

Elem Kalabari

IJAW

Bight of Biafra

40 (*above*) 'Success to the Africa Trade', a 'Delft' punch-bowl made in Liverpool

41 (*right*) Olaudah Equiano, Ibo slave turned anti-slave trade propagandist

42 (*below*) Sea-captains carousing in Surinam in the mid-eighteenth century, by John Greenwood

ROMANS: 43 A classical Clive, by
Peter Scheemakers (1764)

44 Robert Adam's design for
Admiral Boscawen's tomb

45 'The Death of General Wolfe', by Benjamin West

of doings in neighbouring kingdoms. In the 1720s he conquered two coastal kingdoms, Allada and Whydah. In 1730, he accepted the suzerainty of Oyo, under which Dahomey continued for almost a century, but he also drove a strong bargain with the Europeans.

All trade in slaves was concentrated at Whydah. On the African side, the Dahomeyan state assumed a monopoly. An oligarchy of chiefs profited from it; some were allowed to participate directly in raiding and trading, others received a percentage of the taxes deriving from foreign commerce. The slave trade increasingly became the basis of Dahomey's economy. The creation of the King's famous army of Amazons, several thousand fighting women, seems to reflect a shortage of men. Civil dissensions meant that Europeans turned to other ports, and Dahomey became too poor to pay its tributes to Oyo regularly. Tegbesu, who succeeded Agaja in 1740, expelled Europeans who defied him, but took the advice of other whites on national policy and encouraged slaving to replenish his kingdom's wasted treasury. By the 1760s trade was in decline again — it seems that Dahomey's involvement had exhausted the human resources both of itself and of its neighbours.[47]

The trade shifted eastwards. Planters, perhaps because they were used to slaves from other regions, tended to sneer at 'Angola' slaves (who in fact came from regions both north and south of the Congo river) — in the 1720s they were said to be a 'Proverb for worthlessness'.[48] Opinion about the Ibos who came from the Niger Delta and Cross River trade varied extremely; they were popular in some parts of the New World for their gentleness but distrusted elsewhere for their despondency and proneness to suicide.

The Bight of Biafra, relatively unimportant as a source of supply until the 1730s, became the main slave-shipping region before the mid-century. There were no factories here. Traders stayed as briefly as possible in the steamy, unhomelike delta-world of rivers and mangroves. Reliance on Africans ashore was essential. The Ijo city-states of the Niger Delta — Bonny, Elem Kalabari, Okrika and Nembe — and the rather similar Efik state of Old Calabar on the Cross River developed, quite clearly, in response to European demand for slaves. Fisherfolk turned into middlemen-traders. The old Delta institution of the *wari* (household) was adapted to serve new ends. Traders were able to build up large households, including many beyond their immediate families, and weld all into a united labour force with its own war canoes. House rulers were members of the king's council. Succession in the houses was determined by the vote of all adult members and since slaves were integrated (at the price of accepting Ijo culture) they too might be elected to house headship. Large canoes with cannon cruised up the creeks looking for slaves, but most came in through peaceful trade. Iboland was the main source of supply. An Ibo clan, the Aro, formed towards the mid-eighteenth century, used their possession of an oracle, the 'Long Juju' of Arochuku, which was venerated by all of their people, so as to make themselves monopolists in the trade. Litigants came from

Q

far away to hear the Juju's judgment, and were made to pay a fee or a fine in slaves, whom the oracle allegedly ate. But, in fact, these passed to the coast down a grapevine of Aro traders (along with other slaves whom the clan had bought). The Aro used mercenary soldiers, against trading rivals and against people who defied their oracle, taking over the war captives for sale as well.[49]

There was mutual adaptation of whites and blacks on the coast. Some African slave traders became Christians; conversely, some Europeans joined African associations. Elsewhere, most people in Guinea remained untouched by European influence and values. Bornu and the Hausa kingdoms, the middlemen states in the trans-Sahara trade, grew steadily more Islamic. In the western Sudan also, Islam expanded fast, especially after 1750. Literacy entered the Asante empire not through contact with Christians but from Islam, and by the end of the eighteenth century the Asantehene would be making use of Muslim scribes.[50]

Meanwhile, the Society for the Propagation of Christian Knowledge gave up Africa as a bad job after an unfortunate experience with two youths from Mozambique whom it 'converted'; one hanged himself in an English port, the other refused to have anything to do with their missionary after his return home. An Irish factor, Nicholas Owen, at York Island on the Sherbro in the mid-eighteenth century, wrote morosely in his diary: 'It seems to mee that the blacks on this coast retains their ancient custums without alteration in any thing, except thier cloathing, which alters a good dail by the help of Europain cloath, swords, and househould furneture, likewise has made some adition to thier granduer with our goods in general. As to our religion it has made no impression in the least otherwise then a matter of redicule or laughter in so many years as they have had us among them ... '[51]

Some Africans grew rich from the slave trade and added to their 'granduer'. The politics of some states were certainly affected. But there was no general transformation of the African economy or of African views of life. Even in the New World, Africans retained much from their own cultures, mixed with elements borrowed from their masters', or imposed by them. In South and Central America, and on a small scale in Jamaica, runaway slaves had established polities of their own. In the West Indies, most of the population was now black, and African gods and legends found a home. Survivals were weakest in mainland North America, where slave population was based more on natural increase than on fresh imports; yet it has been argued that the blues singers of the twentieth century have maintained something of the tradition of the *griots* of the West African savanna; South Carolina planters showed a preference for slaves from Senegambia. A Jamaican white was less impressed. He conceded that blacks from this region were 'of better understanding than the rest, and fitter for learning trades, and for menial domestic services', but remarked, 'they are unfit for hard work; their bodies are not robust ... '[52]

IV

There was one white to six blacks on Jamaica in 1698. By 1778 the ratio was about one to eleven. Antigua had one white to four slaves in 1707, one to fifteen in 1774. Yet over the whole period of the slave trade, Barbados acquired some 350,000 slaves, and its unfree black population in 1809 was only about 70,000; in the mid-eighteenth century this island still required an importation of 3,000 a year, or about 5 per cent, to compensate for excess of deaths over births. In the first three-quarters of the eighteenth century, Jamaica imported close on half a million slaves, but its slave population rose by only a little over 15,000.[53]

So Caribbean slaves had a very high mortality rate, and they did not replace themselves. The relationship between these two facts was both more direct and more complicated than might be supposed. The planter did not 'break even' on a slave born on his land until his third decade of life. ' ... Child-rearing was profitable only if the expected life of slaves at birth was greater than the break-even age.' On the North American mainland, children were valuable. In the West Indies, people commonly died younger. Planters preferred to buy grown slaves from Africa rather than rear them. They consciously discouraged fertility. Pregnant women were neglected, the workload of nursing mothers was not reduced, and the imbalance between the sexes, with male slaves outnumbering female by about four to three, was deliberately maintained.[54]

In the 1740s, men on Jamaica would cost £50 or £100, women only £20 or so apiece. The great planter with several plantations commonly moved slaves at will from one to the other without any concern for settled family life. The slave women seem to have known techniques of contraception, and frequently, it was said, took 'specifics to cause abortions'. Such babies as survived birth more often than not would die in early childhood. Maltreatment of mothers and children was a far more decisive factor in keeping demand for imports high than that which the planters chose to emphasise themselves, the great death-rate among people fresh from Africa. It was true that perhaps a third perished within three years of arrival, some of disease, but others, it seems, chiefly of sheer bewilderment and demoralisation. (Hence, an overseer on Nevis in the 1720s advised that slaves should be bought young: ' ... Them full grown fellers think it hard to work never being brought up to it they take it to heart and dye or is never good for anything.') But given the chance, those who survived would have multiplied. 'I will not deny,' wrote Edward Long, the planter-historian, 'that those Negroes breed the best, whose labour is least, or easiest.' Black domestics, he said, were more fertile than those who tended cattle, 'and the latter, than those who are employed on sugar plantations.'[55]

As this remark emphasises, conditions for Caribbean slaves varied quite markedly. The head boiler, head distiller and head cooper, vital craftsmen, would form a black élite, along with the black drivers of field gangs, better fed, better clothed and (not always to their advantage) better supplied with rum than field labourers. The diet of slaves on Jamaica, where land had not run out, was probably better in general than on other islands. Slaves could grow provisions for themselves, saving their masters money, and were given a day and a half to themselves each week for that purpose. ' ... What renders their slavery tolerable to them,' a white inhabitant wrote in 1757, 'is that little shadow of property and freedom which they seem to enjoy, in having their own little parcels of ground to occupy and improve; and a great part of its produce they bring to market, there to dispose of it; which, besides supplying the white inhabitants with a great plenty of wholesome provisions, enables the negroes to purchase little comforts and conveniences for themselves and their little ones.' The repeated word 'little' is salient. Heavy work required a more generous diet than the unripe roasted plantain which became the 'staff of life' even on this favoured island.[56]

Compared to semi-starvation, deliberately sadistic treatment was a minor influence on the death-rate. Atrocious things were done, by some planters. An Act was passed in Antigua in 1724 to 'prevent the inhumane murdering, maiming and castrating of slaves by cruel and barbarous persons (as has been too much practiced) ... ' The viciousness of Jamaican whites became especially notorious. The wife of a planter there, though despising the blacks and feeling that they required 'a whip for every Trifle', added, 'yet I don't think that Sufficient excuse for the Barbaritys exercized upon 'em here.' The custom was that if a slave was executed for a crime, his owner would receive compensation, and an investigation in 1739 disclosed that in some parts of the island planters were commonly having sick or lame slaves falsely accused in the hope that they would be put to death.

Planters dealt out 'justice' to planters. Though in theory a Jamaican master who wilfully killed a slave might be gaoled (for three months), in practice he would always get off with the claim that his victim had been caught in the act of stealing or running away. Two magistrates (planters) and three freeholders (planters) could form a court to hear the most grave cases, and there was no appeal against their judgment. 'A slave might be condemned one hour and executed the next. In cases of murder or rebellion the favourite vengeance of the planters was to hang the criminal in chains until he starved to death, or to stake him to the ground and burn him with a fire which was begun at the feet and slowly consumed the whole body.'[57]

Yet the death penalty was dealt out far less often in the Caribbean than in England. The slave was part of his master's capital. To whip him was usually preferable to killing him. Punishment was left to the discretion of the magistrates; thus under a Jamaican law of 1749 it was up to them whether death should punish a slave who harboured a runaway, and the island's whole code was open to the objection that, falling over itself to leave room for mitigation, it left slaves unclear as to what might await them if they offended and were caught.[58] In Britain, as we have seen, more and more offences against property were liable to severe punishment. But a black slave was property.

A Jamaican law of 1696 had laid down, with typical tentativeness, that slave owners should try 'as much as possible' to instruct their slaves in Christianity and to have them baptised. The planters were unimpressed, and the slaves were left for the most part to make what they could of their own cultural resources, as generations of fresh incomers had brought these from many parts of Africa.

Even the hostile Edward Long could not but concede slaves some musical talents. He noted the songs of derision improvised against white overseers, the African musical instruments which they had recreated, the 'just time and regular movements' of their dances.

Melodies of songs changed over time, but construction, rhythm and form remained basically African:

> If me want for go in a Congo,
> Me cant go there!
> Since them tief me from my tatta [father],
> Me cant go there!

The cultural shifts adopted by African first-comers commonly influenced later arrivals. Thus, though the English lost Surinam in the 1660s, the creole there, while much influenced by Dutch, remained English in main vocabulary. Dialect words picked up by sailors from Cornwall or Yorkshire or Scotland would be preserved in creole tongues into the twentieth century, when they would be obsolescent in Britain itself. But African words also survived in great numbers. Even now, more words in Jamaican creole are drawn from the Twi language than from any other African tongue, reflecting the preference of Jamaican planters for slaves from the Gold Coast.[59]

'Creoles' – slaves born in the Caribbean – looked down on natives of Africa, but the most feared and respected black on any plantation would be the obeah-man, who was usually an African. Religious beliefs were generally similar over the whole area from which slaves were drawn, and 'Obeah' emerged as a form of sorcery which all blacks alike considered effective. The obeahman did harm to people at the request of clients who paid him for his 'bad medicine'. He caught and impaled shadows, used fetishes and charms, and on occasion simply resorted to poison. If slaves rebelled, it was he who administered oaths of secrecy.

Ancestor worship, as used in Guinea, persisted to some extent in the New World. So did belief in spirits; the cottonwood tree, for instance, was venerated on Jamaica down to the present century. The funeral rites of the slaves combined elements from diverse African cultures. Long was shrewd enough to observe the parallels with a Gaelic Wake – the slave funeral was 'a kind of festival', with songs sung in praise of the deceased. Other occasions were found for communal recreation, at nights, at weekends, and during the seasonal holidays granted by the masters. These last – Christmas, Easter, 'Crop-over' –

anticipated the later West Indian carnival. On a few days each year, the slaves could release their pent-up aggression and sense of injustice, in ritual forms which left the planters unscathed. They would dress as finely as possible, speak to their masters with impolite familiarity, and assume gala-day names borrowed from those of the leading whites on the island. While creole slaves mimicked white recreations, tribal groups would identify themselves and appoint their own kings and queens. The rites of 'John Connu' emerged on Jamaica from memories of the customs of West African secret societies and the bands of entertainers which they hired. 'In the towns,' Long wrote, 'during the Christmas holidays, they have several tall robust fellows dressed up in grotesque habits, and a pair of ox horns on their head, sprouting from the top of a horrid sort of visor, or mask, which about the mouth is rendered very terrific with large boar-tusks. The masquerader, carrying a wooden sword in his hand, is followed with a numerous croud of drunken women, who refresh him frequently with a cup of aniseed-water, whilst he dances at every door, bellowing out *John Connu*! with great vehemence ... '[60]

In one arena, at least on Jamaica, the slaves were dominant all the year round. The Sunday markets were cheerful social occasions. From early dawn long lines of slaves with baskets on their heads moved towards them. They sold the pigs, goats and hens which they had reared and the crops which they had grown — bananas and fruits and yams and so on. They also purveyed stolen sugar, and their markets, paradoxically, were the main local source of this staple substance, for urban whites as well as for free non-whites. With the proceeds of trading, the slave would probably earn just enough to enable him to purchase necessities — salt and fish and beef, on occasion cloth. Very few could save anything, but markets permitted 'Quashee' to escape for a day from the shadow of 'buckra', his white owner.[61]

'Quashee' was the West Indian's counterpart of the white North American's black 'Sambo' and of the Englishman's Irish Gael 'Teague', later 'Paddy'. He was the stereotype figure evolved so as to relieve the planter from the necessity of questioning who his alien labourer really was, and then, out of defeatism or with cunning, accepted as a model by the victim himself. Quashee, like Paddy, was always evasive, and could not help lying. He was capricious and unpredictable; generally lazy and childlike, happy-go-lucky and cheerful, but also viciously revengeful, and tyrannical when he was placed in authority. He mistrusted all innovations in technique; he had no judgment, and always did everything wrong; he either was, or let himself seem, very stupid; yet he was also a sharp judge of character. This convenient monster was not merely a product of white imagination. Slavery hardly encouraged its victims to show any eagerness to work or any sense of responsibility in their master's business. To be able to turn a good lie might save a man's life, and the alien language of the whites, as the slave used it, offered ample scope for irony, reservation, double-meaning and whimsy. Long noted that the 'better sort' of slaves were 'very fond of improving their language' and caught at any 'hard word' which the whites used in their hearing, to 'alter and misapply it in a strange manner'. Quashee, like Paddy, could see that the master subconsciously wanted him to conform to the stereotype. He could get a wry pleasure from deceiving the tyrant and could play Quashee to serve his own ends – for instance, by bungling so as to wreck the arrangements of an obnoxious overseer till the man was exasperated into resignation.[62]

'Anancy the spider man' became Jamaica's folk hero, derived from the *Ananse* of whom the Akan peoples of the Gold Coast told stories. He was voracious, selfish and lazy and callous, but he was a brilliant trickster. To survive at all, the slave needed to show some of the cunning and resourcefulness of the Maroons at large up in the mountains.

There had been Maroons, slaves escaped from the Spaniards, before the English conquest of Jamaica. A second sizeable group was formed in 1690 after an uprising of slaves, which included, perhaps, the Gold Coast 'Coromantee' named Cudjoe who became the most famous Maroon leader. Other fugitives – mainly, it has been said, Coromantees – joined this body later. The outlaws became a serious problem. They kept in touch with blacks in the plantations who gave them food in lean times and warned them of the movements of militia and soldiers. They stole cattle and carried off slaves from the lands of isolated settlers. In 1720 the Jamaican authorities brought in some fifty Moskito Indians to act against the Maroons, but most of these were either killed or forced into the guerrilla groups. Cudjoe, flanked by his two 'brothers', Accompong and Johnny, commanded a dangerous force, though his group and the 'Windward Maroons' in the east of the island cannot have numbered much more than 1,000 altogether. Since the Maroons relied on what arms and ammunition they could capture, or purchase by posing as fowlers or traders, they had perforce to become expert marksmen. Trackers as fine as the Amerindians themselves, they also became skilled in the use of camouflage and at setting ambushes in dusky forest trails.

By 1730 the whites were acutely worried. Governor Hunter sent three major militia expeditions against the Maroons in that year; all were farcically unsuccessful. The first came to a halt when its commander was illegally arrested for some petty debts and then 'barbarously murdered' in custody. The second was ambushed by the Maroons and driven back with the loss of fifteen men. The third, under an incompetent leader appointed by the Assembly over Hunter's objections, got lost in swamps, where over a quarter drowned or died of fever. Hunter had been clamouring for regular troops, and the home government heeded his request at last and despatched two regiments from Gibraltar. Malaria and yellow fever ran through this force, and left the survivors wholly demoralised – at one funeral, a colonel, a major, two captains and a lieutenant were buried. Within nine months of their arrival, the Duke of Newcastle ordered their return though Hunter was able to persuade over 200 to stay by the promise of special bounties. The crisis grew. Nanny Town, headquarters of the Windward Maroons led by Quao, was three times captured by the militia, three times retaken. A large expedition of 600 men, half of them regular sailors or soldiers, was ambushed by the Maroons and routed. A letter from a planter in May 1734 depicted 'the insecurity of our country occasioned by our slaves in Rebellion against us whose insolence is grown so great that we cannot say we are sure of another day and Robbings and Murders so common in our capital Roads that it is with the utmost hazard we travel them.' Newcastle soon ordered the despatch of 600 more regulars.

In 1735, Quao's Maroons were at last checked. Nanny Town was captured by the whites, for the fifth time, and on this occasion some progress was made towards building a defensible barracks there. Quao's men were themselves ambushed and suffered their heaviest losses yet, thirty men. They trekked west to join Cudjoe. That formidable old man was jealous of his own power and did not wish to unite the two groups. The Windward men went back to their old country, but it was two years before serious raiding was resumed.[63] In 1738 a new governor, Edward Trelawny, arrived with a sensible new policy settled in Whitehall. The Maroons could not be defeated, so a treaty must be made.

Cudjoe himself was ready to negotiate. The Maroons had been hard pressed. Two hundred Moskito Indians had been hired and deployed with their dogs, advanced posts had been built near Maroon strongholds, well stocked, well garrisoned, and joined by footpaths. The Maroons' provision grounds had been destroyed one by one, and Cudjoe had retreated west into the Cockpit Country, a tract of some 500 square miles sliced by deep depressions between precipitous towers of rock. He had established himself at Petty River Bottom, which had one of the area's few springs of water, and could be approached only through a long pass which would reduce soldiers to single file. His brother, Accompong, had founded another township to the south of him.

A grand military push was prepared, but first the soldiers sought to bring Cudjoe to terms. One Dr Russell was with the advanced party who first clapped eyes on the legendary Coromantee. 'Cudjoe was rather a short man, uncommonly stout, with very strong African features, and a peculiar wildness in his manners. He had a very large lump of flesh upon his back, which was partly covered by the tattered remains of an old blue coat, of which the skirts and sleeves below the elbows were wanting. Round his head was tied a scanty piece of white cloth, so very dirty, that its original use might have been doubted. He had on a pair of loose drawers that did not reach his knees, and a small round hat with the rims pared so close to the crown, that it might have been taken for a calibash, being worn exactly to the rotundity of his head.' He was shirtless, and his clothes and skin were coated with the red earth of the Cockpits. His men were 'as ragged and dirty as himself', but like him they had guns and cutlasses.[64]

A treaty was made—this was March 1739—under a large cotton tree in

Cudjoe's town. The leader and his people were confirmed in their liberty and were to hold 2,500 acres of land. They would have redress if injured by whites. Two Europeans nominated by the governor were to reside with the Maroons, and in miniature, this was to be what was later called 'indirect rule', though Cudjoe was to be chief for life, with power to punish his own people, but not to use the death penalty. The Maroons undertook not only to send back at once any slaves who ran away to join them, but also to help actively in operations against rebels. Not long after, Quao, leader of the Windward Maroons, a more shadowy figure than Cudjoe but perhaps even more remarkable, made a similar treaty with the whites.

The Maroon leaders, now 'captains' regularly commissioned, were given silver chains and medals with their names on them and paid regular visits to the governor's mansion. Their followers settled down in their villages and came to terms with the money economy. They hired themselves to planters for wages, grew provisions which they sold to neighbouring settlements, vended their jerked pork and made large profits from trading in tobacco. They became studious in their respect for the whites. Maroon chiefs assumed the names of gentlemen on the island and wore old military coats which such persons gave to them. If white guests arrived, they did not presume to eat at the same table, but sat at a respectful distance and spoke only when spoken to. They remained a distinct people, with no religion which the whites could recognise, practising polygamy and using a dialect which mixed African languages with Spanish and English.[65] But they were now of immense use to the planters. Had they been exterminated, fresh groups of runaways would have sprung up in the woods and would have proved just as dangerous in time. Now they policed the interior themselves, and co-operated with what seemed like zeal in the suppression of slave revolts.

Jamaica, nevertheless, had relatively more of these than any other slave society in the New World except perhaps Brazil. Its insecurity reflected the temptations offered by its mountainous interior, and the high proportion of Africans, men who had known freedom, among its slaves; about half the population were newcomers in the middle of the eighteenth century, more than a quarter even at its end. Furthermore, the proportion of whites in Jamaica was uniquely low and absentee ownership was unusually common. Perhaps the planters' quixotic preference for fierce Coromantees was also important – certainly, Gold Coast slaves were commonly to the fore in risings. It was Coromantees who planned the great rebellion of well over 1,000 slaves which lasted for months in 1760, till its leader Tacky was killed by a Maroon, and which brought death to 60 whites and three or four hundred rebels; afterwards, 600 slaves were executed or transported, and Long estimated the colony's loss at no less than £100,000.[66]

Though Barbados was now quite calm, the Leewards had two severe shocks in the 1730s. On the Danish island of St John rebel slaves took control for six months. Fearing that the example might be infectious, volunteers from the British islands went, unsuccessfully, to quell the blacks; a strong French force from Martinique eventually did the trick. Three years later, in 1736, a lurid and interesting conspiracy was uncovered on Antigua, where some 3,000 whites and 150 regular soldiers confronted 24,000 blacks. Certain privileged slaves seem to have realised how weak their masters' position was. Court, said to be 'of a considerable family in his own country', was a Coromantee, well treated by his master. 'Tomboy' was a master carpenter who was allowed to take black apprentices and to make all the profit he could from his craft. Another principal, 'Hercules', was 'an Excellent Tradesman and all most the Support of the poor family that own'd him.' Like Tomboy, he was a creole, island-born, and so were other leading insurrectionaries, Jack and Scipio, Ned and Fortune, Toney, Secundi and Jacko. 'The chief measures taken to corrupt our slaves were entertainments of dancing and feasting under colour of innocent pretences; those corrupted were bound by oaths. A new government was to be established when the whites were extirpated: Court was flattered by all with being king, but the creoles had privately resolved to settle a commonwealth and make slaves of the coromantees.' Court, however, used African rituals to bind his force together, 'the coromantees knowing but the creoles not understanding the engagement entered into.' An oath was taken by 'drinking a health in liquor with grave dirt and sometimes cock's blood infused, and sometimes the person swearing laid his hand on a live cock. The general tenour of the oath was to kill the whites.'

Tomboy was to get the job of carpentering seats for a great ball to be held in the capital, St John's, on 11 October 1736, the anniversary of George II's coronation. All the leading whites would be present. He would lay gunpowder in the house and this could be fired as the dancing went forward. Several hundred slaves were to enter the town and put the whites to the sword. The forts, and the ships in the harbour were to be seized. But the ball was postponed until 30 October. In the interim, several slaves gave the plot away. The resulting frenzy of judicial enquiry brought many interesting things to light. A freed black, Benjamin Johnson, was said to have bragged, 'he had thought of going for England to marry but now he hoped to get a white wife here, that Damn them (meaning the Christians) he did not get his freedom from them, Damn them, his mistress gave him his freedom.' At least fifty blacks proved to have taken the oath *after* the execution of ringleaders had started. By 18 February 1737, the toll of executions was huge. Five men were broken on the wheel, six were 'gibbeted alive', seventy-seven were 'burnt'. The shock of discovery was for the whites compounded by the fact that skilled and trusted slaves had been to the fore. Many could read and write well and had been baptised. No fewer than twenty-three drivers, twelve carpenters, and seven coopers were amongst those convicted, along with musicians, masons, coachmen, waiting men, a sugar boiler, a drummer.[67]

We can now see that the gravest danger to the whites in all slave societies came not from fresh Africans running into the woods, but from such talented and frustrated men, who could imagine themselves as commanders and magistrates. The West Indian planters took a great risk in training blacks as craftsmen and so driving away poor-whites who might otherwise have been artisans, and militiamen. Yet the Antigua outbreak was exceptional. The black élite was generally quiescent. It would seem that its members commonly found their own condition comfortable enough to reconcile them to white dominance. Eruptions of violence were more inevitable than they were typical. The races lived together, in the colonial towns, without murdering each other so often as to make life intolerable for either. Besides the slave élite, a free non-white middle class began to emerge, trammelled though it was by jealous restrictions.

Freedmen were commoner on the French than the British islands; towards the end of the eighteenth century, the ratio of free 'persons of colour' to slaves would be 1:64 on Jamaica, 1:25 on Martinique. But a slave woman who slept with a British planter and produced a child stood a fair chance of freedom. Planter fathers were often ready to acknowledge their mulatto children and even to bring them up under the same roof with their legitimate white ones. Rich coloured inheritors were a disturbing thought. Jamaican law, from 1762, laid down that no white person could leave more than £2,000 to a negro or mulatto (though private Bills could still be brought to get round it). The well-off mulatto, even if educated in England, would not be treated as an equal by whites. In most of the British islands, his evidence would not be received in a criminal case against a white, and he could not serve in public office.[68]

But on Jamaica, uniquely among British New World colonies, the passage of generations could turn a mulatto white. This was because of a shortage of British women. On Barbados white women outnumbered men now, in the Leewards the sexes were roughly equal, but on Jamaica there were two British males for each white female, and open concubinage with black girls resulted. Under a law of 1733, all who were 'above three degrees removed in lineal Descent from the Negro ancestor' could exercise the rights of whites. The catalogue of colours ran like this: the daughter of a white man and a black woman would be a 'mulatta': if she cohabited in turn with a white man, their offspring would be 'tercerons', and the child of a daughter marrying a third white man would be a 'quateron'. The fourth stage was critical. A fourth white man must bed the quateron to produce a 'quinteron'. Any true quinteron passed as white.[69] With matters arranged like this, black and mulatto freemen would naturally seek brides of the palest shade available, and the atrocious colour snobbery of the Caribbean was under formation.

Faithful domestics rewarded by manumission, blacks who saved enough to purchase their liberty, and others who fought well against rebels or informed against slave conspiracies, joined mulattoes in a small class of coloured freemen. There were 'upward of three thousand seven hundred' on Jamaica by the 1770s. The most famous of such people was Francis Williams, son of two free Jamaican

Negroes. A philanthropic English peer sent him to Cambridge University in an experiment to find if a Negro might be educated to the same level as a white. He then tried to have him appointed to the Council of the island, but the governor objected and Williams set up a school in Spanish Town. He defined himself as a '*white* man acting under a *black* skin'. But the whites never accepted him at his own valuation despite his habit of addressing a Latin poem to every new governor of the island.[70]

Jamaica alone still imported sizeable numbers of white indentured servants, but even here, the frontier of opportunity was now effectively sealed, as great planters secured exorbitant grants of virgin land; it was reported in 1739 that freed servants could find no employers and generally remained in 'a low abject State, thro' the whole Remainder of their Lives.'[71]

One Jamaican Act of 1703 ineffectually laid down that each planter must employ one white for every ten blacks; another in 1720 raised the ratio to 1:30. But the total yearly fine of 270s. was much less than the cost of maintaining a servant. Planters paid up, and within a few years the Act was essentially a revenue measure, raising thousands annually. Attempts were made to revive the small farming class. In 1735 the British government put pressure on the Jamaicans to release uncultivated land from the grasp of the great proprietors, and an Act shortly vested 30,000 acres in the Crown for the use of new settlers. Nearly 100 families from the Leewards came to take these up. A further act of 1749 offered £145 to any planter who would bring in and settle a white family on 20 acres of land, and over five years nearly 350 people came in under this scheme.[72] But the influx of new slaves was far outstripping that of fresh whites. There was, of course, a steady call from the estates for white clerks, slave drivers, and craftsmen. White employees, however, were hardly more charmed by plantation life than the slaves. They were free to go and most quickly went.

There were still Caribbean frontiers to attract whites impatient with life on the sugar islands. The logwood cutters of the Central American coast continued to supply a valuable trade. In 1716, the Spaniards flushed the British out of the Bay of Campeche, but the settlement at Belize, though attacked by Spain and destroyed time and time again, still remained a base for the cutters. The Moskito Coast further south was a safer place. A fertile and healthful territory stretched about 300 miles along the coasts of Honduras and Nicaragua, abundant in game and famous for its turtles, with mountains behind it which helped to keep out the Spaniards. Little was exported — mahogany, tortoise-shell, sarsaparilla, a few mules — and the colonists on Jamaica (which exercised vague control over the area) had no wish to see plantations set up there which might rival their own. Paradisal anarchy prevailed. The 8,000 or so Moskito Indians, and the tribe of Samboes of mixed Indian and African blood who rather outnumbered them, were not over-deferential to the 'kings' who were recognised in Jamaica. Amongst them lived some 150 whites, some 170 half-castes and

800 slaves; about half of these incomers were concentrated in and around the main settlement on the Black River, where the whites lived comfortably in neat framed houses with thatched roofs. There was no real authority among them until 1749, when a 'Superintendent of the Shore' was appointed, under the governor of Jamaica.[73]

A more violent temperament might have picked the Bahamas. This group of 29 islands, 661 cays and 2,387 rocks totalled in land area just a little more than Jamaica, but the limestone islands had no rivers or streams and the soil, though fertile, was extremely thin. Dangerous reefs fringed all. A Puritan named William Sayle had sought, in 1648, to establish an ideal community on an island named 'Eleuthera' after the Greek word for freedom. The first colonists had eked out a quarrelsome existence on the proceeds of braziletto wood, ambergris and gleanings from wrecks. The group had then been granted to the proprietors of Carolina, but the governors they had sent in had never been able to cope with the truculent rogues who lived there. Governor Trott in the 1690s laid out Nassau on New Providence and built a fort there. Then he was dismissed for providing sanctuary for Captain Avery, perhaps the most prodigious of all pirates, who had captured the Mughal Emperor's daughter in the Indian Ocean and gave Trott a cut of his immense booty. Sacked by a Franco-Spanish expedition in 1703, Nassau was left almost deserted. The islands had long attracted pirates; now pirates took them over completely. Even before the peace of 1713 released, as usual, a spate of unemployed privateers into outlawry, there were at least 1,000 active pirates on the Bahamas, outnumbering the two hundred or so settler families. Amongst the desperadoes who used this base, Benjamin Hornigold and Charles Vane have now faded from general recollection, though they were just as dangerous in their heyday – the classic phase of piracy – as Edward Teach, 'Blackbeard', who is still well remembered.[74]

There was so much competition that Blackbeard took no great pickings. But in the summer of 1718 he blockaded Charles Town, South Carolina, and terrorised the colony and its shipping for a week, seizing passengers from merchant vessels and holding them to ransom. Further pirates followed him there, and the colony was in fear for months. Governor Spotswood of Virginia sent out two sloops at his own expense. They found Blackbeard's ship, with its crew of twenty-five, lurking in Ocracoke Inlet (Cape Fear). Blackbeard took a bowl of liquor, 'drank damnation to anyone that should give or ask quarter' and then proceeded to wreak havoc with his guns. He boarded one of the opposing vessels and fought its commander hand to hand till he himself fell, pierced by twenty sword wounds and five pistol shots. Nine pirates died with him, but so did eleven of the governor's force.[75]

Meanwhile a seaman of subtly different stamp, Captain Woodes Rogers, had arrived at Nassau. He was famous for a privateering voyage around the world in 1708–11, during which he had rescued Alexander Selkirk, the prototype Robinson Crusoe, from an island in the South Pacific. He had later fallen on hard times, and had come up with a project, backed by merchants, for developing the Bahamas as a base against the Spaniards. Thomas Pitt was a member of the company which he founded. The Carolina proprietors surrendered the civil and military government of the islands to the Crown and leased the quitrents and royalties to Rogers and his associates. Duly appointed governor by George I, Rogers arrived in New Providence in July 1718. Vane, skull and crossbones hoisted, at once sailed off and never came back. Other pirates acknowledged Rogers's reputation by firing muskets into the air and shouting huzzas for the King. Most of them after a time skulked away, and Hornigold helped Rogers round up those who were not wise enough to do so. Before the end of the year, Rogers had sent three pirates to England for trial and executed nine more himself at Nassau. The notorious 'Calico Jack' Rackham surrendered next year.[76] Though piracy in the New World persisted intermittently into the nineteenth century, its heartiest days were over.

Rogers was not impressed with the non-pirates under his rule. ' ... For work,' he wrote, 'they mortally hate it, for when they have cleared a patch that will supply them with potatoes and yams and very little else, fish being so plentiful ... They thus live, poorly and indolently, with a seeming content, and pray for wrecks or pirates; and few of them have an opinion of a regular orderly life under any sort of government, and would rather spend all they have at a Punch house than pay me one-tenth to save their families and all that's dear to them.' When the Crown bought out the proprietors and the company in 1733, there were still little over a thousand people on the three inhabited islands, but they included a fair number of slaves, and it was in a way of a mark of the arrival of Property and civilisation that there should have been a black conspiracy, next year, to rise and destroy the whites. Though as late as 1788 the islands' assembly would include, besides four planters and five merchants, six 'licensed Wreckers', the Bahamas gradually evolved into a minor but fairly respectable Crown Colony, prospering in wartime partly in the old manner, as a privateering base, and as a mart for illicit trade with the enemy.[77]

Further south, Anguilla in the Leewards, and a couple of the Virgin Islands, had become a refuge for small white planters, debtors and criminals. Pardoned pirates joined them there. The governor of the Leewards reported in 1728 that he had a lieutenant governor on each of the British Virgins, 'but if his cudgell happen to be a whit less strong than a sturdy subject's, Good night, Governour.' However, cotton became a profitable export; in 1743 Tortola, Virgin Gorda and Anguilla between them had 3,000 slaves, made about 1,000 hogsheads of sugar, and produced a million lb. of cotton.[78]

Cotton was a crop for small men. The grip of sugar on the main British islands grew more and more absolute. In 1770, sugar, rum and molasses would make up 93 per cent of exports from Barbados, 89 per cent of those from Jamaica. Sugar was more than ever a crop for the rich. A bigger plantation meant lower unit costs, greater ease in procuring credit and more chance of riding over the dangers of hurricanes, floods, glutted markets, and slave rebellions. In 1670 only 47 individuals had held more than 1,000 acres on Jamaica. By 1754, 467 people, about three in ten of the patentees, owned between 10,000 and 22,000 acres each, some three-quarters of all patented lands. In St Andrew's parish near Kingston at this time, there were 154 estates, ranging from a truck garden of three acres to Philip Pinnock's plantation, the biggest on the island. Of these estates 128 produced no sugar and the owners cultivated provisions, grew the minor staples — coffee, ginger, or cotton — or raised livestock on a moderate scale. The 26 sugar plantations ranged from 257 acres up to Pinnock's monster of 2,872, and in slaves employed from 30 to 280; only 3 of them gave any land to the minor staples, and 8 had no area at all set aside for provisions or pasture. The tendency was for slave work-forces to grow still larger. In the early 1740s the median estate on Jamaica had 99 slaves; thirty years later it had 204.[79]

The Caribbean white's obsession with owning the labour-force which he employed created grave problems, as slave prices rose, and as he continued to neglect the welfare of his workers. There is evidence that the waste rate among slaves declined over the eighteenth century, but it remained very high. The growing exhaustion of the soil in Barbados and the Leewards was met by asking for harder labour from still more slaves and by applying more and more manure. The industry grew less efficient. Antigua, though half its worthwhile land was uncultivated as late as 1734, followed the same downhill (or dunghill) course as Barbados, but more rapidly. By 1756, when it was said to be completely cultivated, it was still crying out for slaves because, as the governor said, of 'the Necessity the Planters are under to manure their Lands, which are getting impoverished by long Culture.'[80]

French Martinique, though larger, was likewise showing signs of exhaustion after mid-century. Not so Jamaica. To keep prices up, three-quarters of the good land on that island was still deliberately left unused in 1752. The island could have produced more sugar, or could have become self-sufficient in food, but neither aim suited its magnates, who were content to exploit the captive British market. They had enormous advantages. 'Ratoon' canes grew spontaneously from roots where cane had been cut. On virgin soil, these would continue, without the expense of fresh planting, to produce for five or ten years as much sugar as plant canes, and that of better quality. On old soil, the yield from ratoons was so much smaller that it was better to plant anew each year, but in Jamaica, a planter exhausting one tract could move on to another. Here, in the first three-quarters of the century, sugar production went up ninefold while the slave labour force increased only fourfold. Population rose from 7,000 whites and 45,000 blacks in 1703 to 18,420 whites and 205,261 blacks in 1778. The other British islands were left far behind. Jamaica was clearly Britain's most valuable New World colony.[81]

But the attitude of the Jamaican plantocracy was, in effect, handing the lead to France. While the French had acreage on their side – St Domingue was more than twice the size of Jamaica, Martinique was bigger than all the British Lee-wards put together – this need not have been decisive so early. In 1720 Jamaican sugar exports roughly equalled St Domingue's, but by 1740, the latter was producing well over double Jamaica's output and more than all the British colonies combined. British merchants were eager to smuggle French sugar, which was cheaper; thus, amongst other devices, ships would leave port in a British island ostensibly to load at some seaboard plantation, would be met at sea by French sloops, and would return to secure the necessary clearance papers by declaring their freight as English. Everywhere in the Caribbean, the 'old colonial system' leaked like a sieve. Meanwhile, British re-exports of raw sugar to Europe dropped by two-thirds in the ten years after 1717, and by the mid-century French sugar was selling there at half the price charged for the substance in England.

Two things made this position tolerable. Firstly, the market for sugar in Britain itself was relatively huge. British planters were supported by the high prices paid by more and more consumers at home, where consumption per head was eight times as high as in France. Secondly, since the French trading system was even more porous than the British, people in Britain and in her North American colonies could cream off profits from the booming French islands. These depended on Irish beef and New England provisions. Nor could French merchants supply all the slaves they needed. In 1722, a French force expelled yet another British attempt to settle St Lucia in the Windwards; neutral there-after, it became the centre of what can aptly be called a 'black market', where French planters sought out British slave traders. Though, by the 1740s, the French were creating two-fifths of American sugar production, and the British only a quarter (not much more than Brazil), this did not undermine British supremacy in New World commerce and at sea.[82]

And even on Barbados, it was still worthwhile to grow sugar. Paradoxically, sugar created huge fortunes at a time when even great magnates were chroni-cally in debt. The planter's position needs some explanation. The resident mer-chant class in the West Indies, except at Kingston and Bridgetown, had withered away, so the planter typically sent his produce home to be sold by a merchant there who disposed of his sugar and bought stores for the plantation on his order, taking commission on both operations. To make a large payment, the planter would draw a bill of exchange on his factor, and use this to satisfy a New England fish salesman or a Liverpool slaver. Payment for new slaves was a constant drain, which cancelled out more than half the favourable balance of trade which the Caribbean colonies had with Britain. Planters loaded their estates with large legacies for younger sons and lavish marriage portions for younger daughters, but settlements made when sugar prices were high became ruinous when they slumped. From the 1730s mortages were more and more common, and as the local merchant class fell away, local loans became less frequent, sterling loans usual. The planters were therefore deeply dependent on British merchants. It suited these to have colonists in their debt; they could be sure of commissions on future consignments of sugar, and the sugars which reached them acted as good securities. The merchants became in effect the planters' bankers, loaning them money which in the last resort came from the planters themselves, and charging high rates of interest for doing so.[83]

This meant that division of opinion between merchants and planters was almost ruled out. Their combined 'West India interest' was made still harder to defeat by the fact that the most unlikely people depended for at least part of their income on sugar. Comparatively few great merchants were not trading with the West Indies in one way or another. Numerous gentry families, predecessors of Jane Austen's Bertrams, had interests in the Caribbean. The major absentee planting families – Long, Codrington, Lascelles, above all Beckford – were amongst the wealthiest in England. Their interests coalesced in the Planters' Club founded in the third decade of the eighteenth century. Their opulence, and its employment in politics, helped force up the price of parliamentary seats. William Beckford, twice Lord Mayor of London, was noted for the lavishness of his civic entertainments. His son, also William, would be remembered as the pioneer of 'Gothic' fiction and as the builder of an amazing and extravagant 'Gothic' mansion at Fonthill. Mario Praz has remarked that when this Beckford was an old man, he used to ride through Bath dressed in the style in fashion during his young days, and 'people would point him out as the relic of a fabulously remote age, the time of feudal aristocracy.'[84] Yet his was new wealth; its basis was capitalism and slavery; what he exemplified was the extent to which sugar money helped to fashion such very English institutions as the eccentric milord and the taste for medieval architecture.

The sugar lobby worked against what a later age would consider the 'national interest', making its product needlessly dear to consumers. In 1721, the Board of Trade directed that Tobago might be settled only if planters on Barbados agreed and only if no sugar were planted there; and similar instructions were made regarding St Lucia and St Vincent. Yet despite such restrictive behaviour, the trade figures seemed to justify sugar's claim more or less to *be* the 'national interest'. From 1660, imports of sugar always exceeded combined imports of all other colonial produce. Rum imports soared during the eighteenth century. Over the sixty years after the Treaty of Utrecht, the tiny islands of Montserrat and Nevis, combined, were a better market for British exports than the giant colony of Pennsylvania. Imports from Montserrat alone were three times higher than those from Pennsylvania, and imports from Nevis were almost double those from New York. As a consumer of British goods, Jamaica equalled New England, and it exported to Britain six times as much as all the northern and middle colonies on the mainland put together.[85] And these figures take no account of the magnitude of the slave trade.

The sugar interest had worrying times in the 1720s and 1730s, as re-export markets were lost to France and the domestic market was glutted. The average price of brown sugar at the London Customs House was 25s. a cwt. in 1728, only 17s. in 1733. In the depression, which went on through the 1730s, many planters were ruined and many debunked, notably to South Carolina, where the law protected debtors especially well. Rising consumption in Britain came to the rescue. Sugar went nicely with tea. British demand alone was enough to force prices back to 35s. a cwt. in the mid-1750s. But meanwhile, the House of Commons enquired anxiously into the sugar trade and, in 1733, produced the Molasses Act, hitting directly at the puny North American colonists. The New Englanders under this legislation would have to pay 6d. a gallon on molasses and 5s. a cwt. on sugar imported from foreign colonies; the aim was to check their trade with the French. The importation of French colonial produce into Ireland, where French sugar, brought in New England ships, had captured the market, was now forbidden. Not satisfied with this, the sugar planters clamoured for freedom for their own trade. The Sugar Act of 1739 was a remarkable concession to them. Its ostensible object was to open up European markets again; planters might ship sugar direct to Southern Europe. Its real aim was to raise the price of sugar in Britain, where the mere possibility that more might be sent abroad would have an effect.[86] And in 1753, the West India lobby beat out of the Commons a Bill, backed by the British sugar refiners, which was intended to force the cultivation of new lands in Jamaica.

The West India lobby also crushed the attempt of the Jamaica Assembly to subject absentees to extra taxation. This was the one rift in the sugar interest, widened as more and more successful planters left the islands to build Palladian houses and keep graceful horses in some gentler English landscape. 'Whenever any Person has made his Fortune,' a writer of 1740 commented, 'he seldom fails to transport his Family and Effects to England.'[87] This was bad for the white community on the island, bad for the soil, and commonly bad for the absentee himself or for his heirs. Renting to tenants had many dangers. The usual policy was to leave a manager in charge, with perhaps a planter appointed attorney to watch over him. The manager was likely to compensate himself for the stench and danger amid which he worked by keeping a retinue of slaves off the fields to wait upon himself and by charging what he ate and drank to the plantation accounts. If, as was often the case, he was paid with a percentage of the crop, he would have an overbearing impulse to achieve the largest production possible in the short run, sabotaging his employer's long-term interests as he drove slaves to death, over-ratooned the soil and raced the estate through mounting debts towards foreclosure.

However, absenteeism did provide opportunities for industrious persons to build up fortunes from nothing on the islands as agents, attorneys or overseers. For the Scots, at any rate, Jamaica was still a frontier. Edward Long reported in the 1770s that there were reckoned to be a hundred people of the name of Campbell residing on the island, all claiming relationships with the Duke of

Argyll. He thought 'very near one third' of the island's whites were Scots by birth or descent. Many Scots had arrived as indentured servants, 'actually kidnapped by some *man-traders*' or sold by their Highland chiefs. The Scots, Long wrote, thinking of Lowlanders, were especially zealous in service, 'sober, frugal and civil; the good education, which the poorest of them receive, having great influence on their morals and behaviour.' It was a strange place for the ideals of John Knox to bear fruit, but so they did. Scots who were skilled craftsmen, coming out under indentures, often acquired 'very handsome' fortunes.[88] Scots also provided some of the ablest surveyors, a rare and necessary skill in an island where ownership of land was so obsessively interesting.

Free coloured people, and creole slaves, who sought to assimilate white culture, are said to have digested Scottish influence as they did so — Scottish fiddle-playing, Scottish dances. But Scottish forms were often hard to distinguish from Irish, and the Hibernian presence in the West Indies had older and wider strata than the Caledonian. In Jamaica during the eighteenth century the preponderance among servants of Irish Catholics posed a serious political problem, since it was feared that they would not stand as militiamen against their French and Spanish co-religionists. Montserrat remained an essentially Irish colony — in 1768 slaves there would sensibly plan a rising on St Patrick's Day, when all the whites would be deep in drink.[89] Here there were some rich Catholic planters, but most of the Irish who entered the Caribbean élites were of course Protestants. On Jamaica, men named Kelly and Concanen figured notably in the factional squabbles which historians dignify with the name 'politics'.

Jamaica, as Britain's most important New World colony, took over from Barbados the lead in exposing issues within the Old Colonial System such as would have a momentous outcome further north. The constitutional struggle begun under Samuel Long's leadership in the 1670s wrangled on deep into the eighteenth century, over the freedom of the Assembly to pass its own laws and over the question of whether the governor should have a permanent revenue and thus become independent of the planters. Two Revenue Acts, the first in the 1680s, the second in the new century, represented a compromise; government income had been voted for twenty-one years in each case.

A traveller had remarked in 1711 that 'the Late Governor lived the meanest of any Gentleman in the Island.' Even though commissions and fees in respect of the granting of licences, passes and so forth could bring in over £6,000 a year, the governor would find it hard to make his standing felt among so many rich men. Many posts in what we would now call the civil service were, furthermore, outside his control. Important positions were held by patent direct from the Crown, mainly by absentees who creamed off most of the salaries and farmed out the actual work to the lowest respectable bidder, usually a Jamaican colonist. The governor could not easily oust one of these hired deputies. The dearth of trained lawyers meant that judicial posts, even the most powerful, had to be bestowed on local planters or merchants, whose jealous squabbles over them added factional bitterness to the governor's tribulations. But the House of Assembly was his greatest trial. Every freeman with at least £10 a year in income could vote in the elections for its forty-one members, who had themselves to be worth more than £300 a year. So far as the whites went, this was government far more representative than Britain's, and the governor could not hope to buy or suborn a majority of the colonists.[90]

When the 21-year Revenue Act expired in 1725, the constitutional battle was renewed. So seriously was Jamaica taken that the home government took the amazing step of appointing a new governor on the basis of merit rather than patronage. This was Robert Hunter, a great success formerly as governor of New York and New Jersey; a cool, urbane Scot with literary interests, highly efficient, and greatly in sympathy with the North American way of life. He swiftly evolved a satisfactory new compromise. In 1728 the Assembly agreed that the imperial government should have its permanent revenue, at last, in return for its confirmation of all the laws and privileges of the colony. But the £8,000 a year granted was inadequate and over the next twenty years the colony was constantly at war, first with Maroons, then with European enemies. A standing army was required, and the money for this was voted annually, so any measure to which the House of Assembly thought the governor might object, under his secret instructions from home, was tacked on to the Bill which provided the cash. Time and again, the planters and the governor grimly played chicken against each other. Whose nerve would break first? If the governor rejected the Act he would run the risk of mutiny among the troops, slave rebellion, French or Spanish conquest. But then, so would the planters.[91]

Edward Trelawny, governor from 1738 to 1752, began his career unembarrassed by any former experience or known talent. He was a member of the Cornish mafia which played a large role in the politics of Walpole's England because of the quite disproportionate number of borough seats, guaranteed rotten, which were at the disposal of local gentry. (And the 'common sort of people' in Cornwall, as an opposition leader exclaimed peevishly, thought they had as much right to sell their votes as they had to sell their corn and their cattle.) Hence the career of Trelawny, fourth son of a bishop and M.P. for the family borough of East Looe, had been cordially advanced by Sir Charles Wager, another Cornishman who was Walpole's First Lord of the Admiralty, and Trelawny was able, though with much difficulty, to triumph over the faction opposing him on the island because of his clan's weight at Westminster, even though Rose Fuller, his chief opponent, came from a family allied with the Duke of Newcastle himself. One county in Jamaica is still called Cornwall.[92]

But Trelawny, a supple, intelligent operator, succeeded at the cost of compromising himself pretty completely with the planter class. To please them, he let through Assembly Acts prohibited by his instructions from the British government, knowing, of course, that they would be annulled when they reached London. He evaded a direct clash, relying heavily on the talents of Charles Price, greatest planter of his day, whose younger brother had had the prudence to settle in Cornwall for his health, so that the absentee branch of this family also carried, as it were, the southpaw punch which was so useful at Westminster. Charles Price was Speaker of the Assembly almost continuously for eighteen years from the mid-1740s. It was not public spirit alone which sustained his concern with the sordid, faction-ridden affairs of the island. Control of the government was a key to cheap land. By an Order in Council of 1735, no grant should exceed 1,000 acres, yet in some thirty years Price patented no less than 8,707 acres. He bought up adjacent land when it came on the market cheaply and at his death, besides about 1,800 slaves, he owned 26,000 acres, quite likely the largest individual holding in the island's history. However, his interest in the huge tracts of crown land which his standing secured him was not always to plant them, but, often, to speculate in them; he disposed of much in due course in smaller parcels. In 1760 he sold the Jamaican government 240 acres for £3,880; his brother had bought them twelve years before for only £98.[93]

Edward Long, the Jamaican historian, wrote admiringly of his cultivated friend Price, of his 'delicacy of humour', of his 'inflexible' love of 'truth'. The English language at this period had a convenient penchant towards abstraction. But Sir Charles, as he became, did indeed live graciously. He built himself a mansion 'of wood, but well finished' with a lake in front frequented by wild ducks. The elegant garden had walks shaded with coconut trees, cabbage palms and sandbox trees. The octagonal garden-house was 'richly ornamented on the inside with lustres, and mirrors empanneled.' (Why, one wonders; what curious doings went on there?) From the great triumphal arch at the end of one walk there was a fine view across a vale to the sea, and Price owned a local beauty spot, the White River Cascade, a fall of 300 feet or more. Long, who noted that 'theology seemed his favourite science; and the Great Author of nature, the chief object of his study', praised Sir Charles for recognising the fall's natural beauty and for refraining from making any 'improvement'. Price formed a club of gentlemen which met every year for some weeks at the Cascade 'during which, they took the diversion of shooting the ring-tail pidgeons, which in this part of the country are very numerous ... ' The black people of Jamaica found their own way of remembering this pioneer of Romantic taste and worshipper of that deistical whig God who had arranged the world so wisely; a certain species of large rodent, which he is supposed to have imported to wipe out the native breed, is still known as the 'Charles Price rat'.[94]

Though few, if any, could have matched Price's opulence, every substantial planter had his 'great house' on the edge of his estate, usually in a commanding position equally conducive to fine views and to defence. Built of wood, on stone supports, it stood one storey high. Cool and spacious piazzas ranged along its sides. 'Friends, acquaintances, and even strangers, walked in and out at random; so evidently did pigs and poultry.' Hospitality was no hardship when households commonly employed twenty or thirty servants. On Antigua, in the early 1770s, a Scotswoman, Janet Schaw, would share with a fellow countryman who owned five plantations 'a family dinner, which in England might figure away in a newspaper, had it been given by a Lord Mayor, or the first Duke in the Kingdom.' Turtle – 'young, tender, fresh from the water, where they feed as delicately, and are as great Epicures, as those who feed on them' – were served with splendid fish, 'generally dressed with rich sauces', with guinea fowl, turkey, pigeons, mutton, 'the finest Vegetables in the world, as also pickles of everything the Island produces.' Then came a second course of as many dishes – pastry, puddings, jellies, preserves – followed by a 'dessert' of thirty-two different fruits. Liquor, of course was never wanting.[95]

The planter might have to work very hard during the harvest, but otherwise riding round his estate to look at his gangs at work was more routine or amusement than serious labour. He hunted, he fished, he spent all day in a tavern, he raced horses, he gambled on them, played billiards, cards and backgammon, and gambled on those too. He cheerfully eschewed public spirit; if roads or bridges had to be built for the good of all, he would undertake them resentfully and would be satisfied with the most minimal makeshift. On Jamaica, Long observed, 'Drunken quarrels happened continually between intimate friends; which generally ended in duelling. And there were very few who did not shorten their lives by intemperance, or violence.'[96]

Spanish Town, Jamaica's capital, offered amenities but it was eclipsed by Kingston, where thirty-five wide and regular streets had many houses aspiring to elegance and where, by the 1770s, 11,000 or more people lived. St John's, Antigua, smaller than either, was a lively place, thanks to an unusually high proportion of resident landowners. West Indian society was no longer wholly philistine. Long, and a younger Jamaican, Bryan Edwards, emerged in the late eighteenth century as remarkable writers, able students of culture and society, of history and natural science. Barbados acquired a printing press in the 1730s and with it a newspaper, in which gentleman planters could publish their lamely derivative verses. What now most clearly distinguished Bridgetown or Kingston from Boston or Philadelphia was the almost complete lack of educational facilities. Provision existed in Jamaica for schooling fewer than fifty boys. 'The Office of a Teacher,' it was reported, 'is look'd upon as contemptible.' Because there were no schools, children were sent away; because they were sent away, there were no schools. Unlike their North American counterparts, West Indian planters could commonly afford to ship their offspring to England and keep them there. They went, as Long lamented, 'like a bale of dry goods, consigned to some factor'; and commonly, he observed, they emerged 'vicious, idle and prodigal ... rolling on the wheels of money into every species of town debauchery ... ' Many never returned to the islands, and even for those who did, Britain remained 'home'.[97]

Yet crowds of black servants influenced growing children in other ways than by making them spoilt. ' ... A Boy till the Age of Seven or Eight', it was said of Jamaica in 1740, 'diverts himself with the Negroes, acquires their broken Way of talking, their Manner of Behaviour, and all the Vices these unthinking Creatures can teach ... ' Long directed the same complaint, rather later, against girls, who picked up from slaves not only their 'drawling, dissonant gibberish' but also 'no small tincture of their aukward carriage and vulgar manners.' He drew a depressing picture of life on a 'sequestered country plantation' with its stunted Tatiana, 'a very fine young woman aukwardly dangling her arms with the air of a Negroe-servant, lolling almost the whole day upon beds or settees, her head muffled up with two or three handkerchiefs, her dress loose, and without stays. At noon we find her employed in gobbling pepperpot, seated on the floor, with her sable hand-maids around her. In the afternoon she takes her *siesto* as usual; while two of these damsels refresh her face with the gentle breathings of the fan; and a third provokes the drowsy powers of Morpheus by delicious scratchings on the sole of either foot. When she rouses from slumber, her speech is whining, languid, and childish. When arrived at maturer years, the consciousness of her ignorance makes her abscond from the sight or conversation of every rational creature. Her ideas are narrowed to the ordinary subjects that pass before her, the business of the plantation, the tittle-tattle of the parish; the tricks, superstitions, diversions, and profligate discourses, of black servants, equally illiterate and unpolished.'[98]

Even creole girls brought up with more pretensions commonly struck observers as languid and spiritless. Among the innumerable casualties of empire, we should not forget these idle women, often married very young, for whom the highest fulfilment would be to coquet with H.M. sailors, while their drunken husbands played with mulatto mistresses. Janet Schaw was impressed with the ladies of Antigua. Society was less opulent here; even the richest women carried the keys and supervised their households closely. But she noted the pallor of their cheeks — from childhood they were 'entirely excluded from proper air and exercise'. If they went out, they were covered with masks and bonnets and when Miss Schaw took a two-mile walk up hill with her friend Fanny, she realised that 'This was truly a British frolick, and what no creole would ever dream of.'[99]

But she liked the Leewards men very much — 'the most agreeable creatures I ever met with, frank, open, generous, and I dare say brave ... Their address is at once soft and manly ... their whole intention is to make you happy.' White Caribbean society was more easy-going than Britain's and, perverse though this may seem, more democratical in temper. Only sailors, and maybe some Irish servants, mingled with any black men as equals. Otherwise, all whites stood together, and class divisions between them were felt to be narrowed. Bryan Edwards would remark on the 'independent spirit' they showed and the 'display of conscious equality throughout all ranks and conditions. The poorest

White person seems to consider himself nearly on a level with the richest, and, emboldened by this idea, approaches his employer with extended hand ... '[100] In the character of its social relationships, as in the ideas of its political leaders and in the quality of its best intellectuals, British West Indian society was closer to that of British North America than people now generally suppose.

V

But whereas West Indian planters wanted no new frontiers, in the mainland colonies many people – speculators and governors as well as farmers, would-be farmers and fur traders – were coming to covet the vast, almost virgin acreage rolling up to the mountains and then on beyond them. The idea was gaining ground that the whole continent, as far as the still uncharted coasts of the Pacific, could rightfully be occupied by Englishmen. Colonists had their imaginations drawn to the interior by the growing French threat on their undefined borders. A swelling chorus of alarm prompted the Board of Trade to produce a report in 1721 which would eventually serve as a basis for British policy. 'Nova Scotia' should be fortified and the Acadian French expelled. Defensive forts were needed in the passes through the Appalachians, and also military posts on the Great Lakes, with more than defence in mind; they would secure the future advance of British settlement.

There was basis for fear. The French, aware that pre-eminence over all North America might grossly increase British power in Europe, were now committed to struggle for the continent. The Treaty of 1713 was a setback, but far from crippling. Though they were denied any sovereignty in the island, the French retained valuable fishing rights on the northern and eastern coasts of Newfoundland. 'Nova Scotia' was absurdly misnamed. There were few if any Scots there, and virtually the only British settlements were Annapolis Royal, a village capital where a small garrison held a neglected fort, and Canso, a fishing station with some dozen permanent residents. About 5,000 French-speaking Acadians either refused to take an oath of allegiance to the British Crown or did so with qualifications, including exemption from military service against the French or their allies. They were fishermen, or they quietly farmed rich dyked lands by the Bay of Fundy, and they were in themselves no great source of trouble. But most of the area was still dominated by Micmac and Abenaki Indians who remained loyal allies of the French.

The French held Cape Breton Island (Île Royale), commanding the entry to the Gulf of St Lawrence. A few score settlers crossed from Newfoundland and made this bleak spot a dominating competitor in the fishing industry. The waters were ice free, and ships could seek cod as early as February and go on as late as Christmas. Here, at Louisbourg, from 1720, at vast expense, the French Crown erected what was, or seemed to be, the strongest fortress on the continent. A fleet based here could guard Canada, protect the French fisheries, and pose a threat to New England shipping. Meanwhile, since farming did not much develop on the island, Louisbourg depended on the British colonies for provisions, and became an important centre of shady trade, where Massachusetts flour was exchanged for St Domingue sugar.

Travelling past Louisbourg, up the St Lawrence, and on, the French reached their vast, vague empire stretching to the Gulf of Mexico. Around 1740, there were only some 50,000 French subjects in North America. But they were far more unified than the British confronting them. In theory, the governor general and intendant in Quebec commanded all. Though in practice Louisbourg and Louisiana had separate governments in direct communication with Paris, there was far less chance of dispute than existed between a dozen or so British regimes. And French motivations were simpler. Furs, and, increasingly, war, were the key to all. The French Crown poured in money and soldiers, yet there was no conflict between its aims and the gratifications of the white native Canadians. Royal money buoyed up the local economy. Whereas in the British colonies few locals owed advance or title to the home government, the French King gave colonials commissions in the officer corps of the regular colonial force, in preference to incomers from France. An aspiring Canadian family, having acquired wealth in the fur trade, could find commissions for its sons and finally gain the legal status of nobility. As the military character of New France was thus confirmed, the humbler Canadians got on with their farming without much direct contact with France – only twenty ships a year reached Quebec from the metropolitan country, compared with up to 600 sent to the French West Indies – but enjoying a comfortable self-sufficiency which permitted, on some occasions, exports of grain.[101]

Quebec, with 8,000 people in the mid-eighteenth century, was not eclipsed by the British New World ports. Its churches and public buildings were striking; a Swede, Pehr Kalm, the only man who left his impressions of both, thought upper-class Canadians better read, and very much more polite than their counterparts in the mainland British colonies. Montreal, however, was merely a frontier town, dominated by soldiers and fur traders. While Canada had over 40,000 people by 1740, to the south, via the Great Lakes to the Mississippi basin, there were very few French indeed. At vast expense the Crown maintained half a dozen military posts. Settlement round them was scant; Detroit, where a few hundred colonists farmed, was exceptional. A little group of agricultural villages in the 'Illinois Country' along the Mississippi had 1,536 French settlers, 890 blacks and 147 Indian slaves in 1752. So much for the vast province of 'Louisiana', except that in the far smaller area which still bears that name, a few thousand whites, whose slaves outnumbered them, sweated, squabbled and perished without much profit amid swarms of mosquitoes, propped up by the French Crown lest the British move in. New Orleans, founded in 1718, became the seat of government four years later.[102]

During Queen Anne's war, the French beaver-hat trade had lost its export markets and the nation's warehouses had filled with surplus furs turning rotten. The greater cheapness of British trade goods, furthermore, was asserting itself strongly among the red men. That the French fur trade recovered was largely, perhaps chiefly, due to the support and persistence of the French State. The Crown wanted Indian allies. The Indians wanted European goods; furs were what they could give in exchange. The French Crown subsidised high prices to draw the Indians from Port Oswego, set up by New York in the 1720s, to its own fortified posts, Frontenac, Niagara and Detroit. The Montreal French acquired cheap British goods in commerce with their rivals in Albany, a practice prohibited by a New York Act of 1720, but then authorised by the British Crown nine years later. The French retained greater skill in interracial relations. They did not get on with all Indians; far from it. There were several bitter wars, including one with the Fox people which lasted for nearly three decades. But they were more generous than the British and more companionable. An envious competitor echoed an old plaint around the mid-century: 'The French talk Several Languages to perfection; they have the advantage of us in every shape ... '[103]

In the early 1730s, the explorations of the Sieur de La Vérendrye greatly strengthened the French in competition with the Hudson's Bay Company. Followed by the erection of several forts, they won the trade of Lake Winnipeg's drainage basin and the Saskatchewan river valley. *Voyageurs* setting off each spring to take trade goods and military supplies to New France's far-western outposts started to father a future nation of half-castes, the Métis, on the plains. The best furs were diverted to Montreal away from the HBC's York factory.

It is amazing now to think how many beaver there were. Indian methods of hunting were as rapacious as anything a Yankee might have devised; while baited traps were employed in summer, in winter the beaver's lodge would be destroyed and nets used to capture the fleeing beasts, and in spring, most destructively of all, hunters broke dams and drained ponds, catching the animals as they escaped. Around 1730, before La Vérendrye's exploits, York Fort alone was sending 50,000 beaver furs per year to Britain. English fur exports rose from £44,000 in 1700 to over £263,000 by 1750. Beaver hats accounted for more than 85 per cent of this latter figure. The main markets were in the New World itself – the British West Indies and the Spanish and Portuguese colonies. Nothing mattered much to the Hudson's Bay Company except beaver. Some small furs – those of martens, in particular – could be very profitable, but never became more than a sideline. In the early 1720s, the furs of white foxes were not even thought worth sending home. So the massacre of beaver continued. The Hudson's Bay Company prospered, despite the French. Mercantilists gloated that hats, passing through Spain to the Spanish New World, were contributing, like the slave trade, to 'dispersing the wealth of the Indies' into British hands. And this was achieved by a company which in the mid-century had only about 120 officers and servants and brought home only three or four ships a year.[104]

Overheads were high, and French competition pushed them up. The cost of carrying on the trade and maintaining half a dozen factories ran at four or five times that of trade goods sent out. The outgoing cargo of manufactures and supplies was heavy, though the furs brought back were light. Hence the Company was mean with its employees, expecting them to live as much as possible off the bare lands around them, to cut their own timber, to brew their own beer and even to manufacture and mend trading goods. Prospects, for those who could stand the climate, were not bad; the chief officers in the Bay were still generally promoted servants, 'typical products of the artisan class'.[105] In the eighteenth century, Orcadians — they must not simply be called Scots, as the islands had their own special history and still retained much of their Norse heritage — were recruited in preference to Londoners, who drank too much and were hard to discipline. The Orkneys were a port of call on the way to the Bay. Stromness retains an eighteenth-century character which bears pleasant witness to the modest prosperity which the Hudson's Bay ships brought with them. They took off peasants and fishermen who were used to inclement weather and short rations, like the local breeds of cows and sheep which were also introduced to the Bay. Compared with the affable French Canadians, the Orkney men were tightfaced and unenterprising, but they gave the forts a most solid backbone.

In the summer months (mid-May to late August), British dress could be worn, but winter garb was voluminous — a beaver coat reaching to the calf, a double lined waistcoat and a flannel shirt beneath that, buckskin breeches, cloth stockings over worsted stockings which reached up to the crutch, three socks on each foot under deerskin shoes, a beaver cape over the shoulders, tying under the chin, and a piece of duffel covering the whole face, with apertures only for nose and eyes. Beneath this, 'a Beard as Long as Captain Teache's, and a face as black as any Chimley Sweepers.' If a sudden gale caught a man unsuitably dressed, he would freeze 'as hard as a Rock'. The rocks themselves would be split by frost. Then there were sudden thaws in spring when the waters released would burst banks and tear down trees because the river mouths were still blocked.[106]

In the end, the Bay put paid to that tough veteran James Knight, an important and well-to-do member of the HBC's committee when he agreed to return in 1714 and govern the posts now relinquished by the French. He survived a flood which struck York Fort in the next spring, a deluge six fathoms deep in which ice tore to pieces a French brigantine and knocked down one side of the trade house, where there were two feet of water in the upper room. He led his men out to shelter on trees and platforms. Rebuilding was difficult; when Knight had pitched his roof three times it still leaked, and the old man had a miserable winter in 1715–16 with weak knees, colds, gout, fever and ague. 'I must have gone,' he wrote, 'if Nature had not been very Strong.' Yet he went ahead in 1717 to establish a post at the mouth of the Churchill River, a place of ill omen to the north where a shipload of Danes under Jens Munck had wintered and died a hundred years before. 'I never see such a miserable place in my life,' he reported. He and his twenty-five helpers, pestered by mosquitoes, raised the fort on a diet of mouldy oatmeal and cheese, with the occasional partridge or goose, having to drag timber, he wrote sarcastically, 'as farr as it is from the Hudson's Bay Company's house to Ludgate.'[107] The new post would rely almost completely on Britain for provisions, and the Eskimos were close at hand and dangerous.

But the French did not compete at these northern limits of the beaver's range, and Knight and the Company had another motive which weighed even more with them: copper. Now in his seventies, the governor saw visions of a far-northern El Dorado. He heard talk of yellow metals, and came to believe that he could reach the copper and gold mines the Indians spoke of by sea and that the North West Passage could be found at the same time. The Company gave him two ships. He vanished completely.

James Isham, a promoted clerk, was in charge at Churchill from 1741–5, and wrote a vivid account of life on the Bay. HBC orders from London denounced the practice of keeping Indian mistresses – wives, or squaws, in effect – but Isham like many others went on regardless, and eventually left all his property to his half-breed son Charles, who found employ with the Company and became very useful. (Another half-breed, or perhaps full-blooded Indian, was actually put in charge at Churchill in 1759–60.) Isham, understandably, declared that 'those Indians that has had copulation with the English, has Brought forth into the world as fine Children as one wou'd Desire to behold'; such children, he added, were 'pretty Numerious' in the forts. Yet though he found Indian women 'very Bewitchen', he reckoned their race in general to be a 'lud' (lewd) and vicious lot, cheats, thieves and liars, and very greedy; 'the more you give, the more they Crave ... '[108]

Company policy was to restrict most servants from having more than a minimal contact with red men. The aim, commercially shrewd, was to thwart the 'private trade' which was so commonplace in the East Indies. Indians were not to enter the factory itself. Trade was carried on suspiciously, through a window or hole in the wall. Isham reported a typical speech of an Indian chief to a factor: ' "You told me Last year to bring many Indians, you See I have not Lyd, here is a great many young men come with me, use them Kindly! use them Kindly I say! give them good goods, give them good Goods I say! – we Livd hard Last winter and in want. the powder being short measure and bad, I say! – tell your Servants to fill the Measure and not to put their finger's within the Brim, take pity of us, take pity of us, I say! – we come a Long way to See you, the french sends for us but we will not here, we Love the English, give us good black tobacco, moist & hard twisted. Let us see itt before op'n'd, – take pity of us, take pity of us I say! – the Guns are bad, Let us trade Light guns small in the hand, and well shap'd, with Locks that will not freeze in the winter ... – Let the young men have Roll tobacco cheap, Ketles thick high for the shape, and size ... – Give us Good measure, in cloth ... Do you mind me!, the young men Loves you by coming to see you, take pity, take pity I say! – and give them good, they Love to Dress and be fine, do you understand me!" – here [added Isham] he Leaves of and they all say ho!'[109]

The special relationship of Britain with Portugal was, as this speech illustrates, the Company's prime advantage. The Indians loved strong, black Brazil tobacco, and the French found it hard to get them to accept any other kind. But the chief's plea for good measure was commonly ignored, and the Company exported from London a trade 'brandy' which was probably gin, coloured to look like the genuine French item.[110] The Indians truly did depend on trade goods – relying on white men's weapons, they might die in the winter for want of powder and shot, and the failure of a ship from Britain to get through could mean disaster for tribes around the posts. Conversely, the white men depended on Indian hunters to reinforce their monotonous diet of flour and cheese, pease and small beer.

Some of the British were acquiring a taste for the Indian food 'pimmegan' (pemmican – pounded dried meat mixed up with fat and cranberries). Isham reckoned beaver tail 'the finest Eating in the Country, Cutting firm, itts all fat Except a bone in the midle and Very Lucious food.' But the great standbys were partridges and, still more, the white geese which the British called 'weyweys'. So-called 'Home Guard' Indians, in return for oatmeal and other supplies, slaughtered birds in vast numbers. With a ration of half a goose per man six days a week, 700 birds would feed for only ten weeks the twenty-four men at Moose Factory (which post, incidentally, was once destroyed by fire when all its inmates were 'stupified' by drink).[111] So far as fending for themselves went, the British showed little enthusiasm for gardening in this unfecund clime.

Nevertheless, the region was alluring enough to Arthur Dobbs, a prominent Irish Protestant landowner, who around 1730 became interested in the quest for a North West Passage, which the Company had neglected, and began a twenty-year assault on its monopoly. He made sufficient impression for the government, in 1741, to send Captain Middleton out to explore. Middleton announced there was no Passage. Dobbs insisted the man had been bribed. A pamphlet war developed, Parliament was moved to put up a £20,000 reward for discovery of the Passage, and Dobbs founded a company which sent out two more ships. They confirmed Middleton's judgment. But Dobbs was at last able, in 1748, to obtain a House of Commons inquiry into the monopoly. Though the Royal African Company went down at this time, the Hudson's Bay Company stood up. M.P.s were swayed above all by the need to maintain a united front against France.

And the HBC was now stirring from what one former employee dubbed its 'Sleep by the Frozen Sea'. French success had provoked the establishment, in 1743, of its first inland post, 'Huntly House', wiped out by indignant Home Guard Indians eleven years later because the Company's employees, while taking red women to bed, would not admit red men to share their victuals.[112]

From 1754 onwards the Company ordered a stream of inland voyages. In that year, Isham, now at York Fort, sent an outlawed English smuggler, Anthony Henday, with his resourceful native 'bed-fellow' and a band of Crees, to persuade the Indians of the Plains to trade with the Company. He travelled over a thousand miles altogether, probably saw the Rocky Mountains, got on well with the Blackfoot Indians, and established for the first time the hitherto unsuspected extent of French influence in the interior.

And the French, as we have seen, remained serious competitors in the fisheries, even with Newfoundland in British possession. There was now what historians euphemistically call a 'commercial community' at St John's, Newfoundland. (A contemporary described it as a 'nest of little pedlars'.) The New Englanders who drove a roaring contraband trade with Europe through this village found that factors resident there made operations easier. Under an Act of 1699, the admiral of the incoming fishing fleet was in charge of the island; he was kept so busy on the banks that he had no time to regulate the harbours. In 1723, some fifty leading men, inspired (it is alleged) by the writings of John Locke, attempted to found a civil government by social contract, to operate while the naval convoys and their commander were absent. Anarchy proved too well established for this experiment to succeed.[113] The British government had been baulking over the expense of providing all-year-round authority, but in 1729 a royal governor was at last appointed. A Vice-Admiralty Court was set up in the mid-1730s and actually checked illegal trade somewhat. But government remained careless and sketchy.

In 1726 it was reported that 65 out of 420 families on the island kept public houses. ' ... A race almost worse than savages,' one visiting French priest had called them. 'Crime of the most loathsome nature is quite public among them ... ' The fishing masters recruited seamen in Ireland and by the mid-century perhaps a quarter of the island's 3,000 or so inhabitants were Irish Catholics. Most people were in the strong grip of merchants. The New Englanders could demand high prices in winter, make profits of up to 400 per cent, entice people into contracting large debts and then sell them as indentured servants, sometimes shipping as many as sixty in a single sloop. The truck system was general in the shore fisheries, with men paid in cod or in bills, both of which were only convertible in the merchant's store. Since conditions were so much better in the mainland colonies, there was a willing exodus besides the involuntary one, the two together estimated at 1,200 to 1,400 men a year, of whom many were sailors left behind by English ships at the end of the season.[114]

Though salmon fishing and sealing had begun to develop, cod remained the colony's reason for being. An estimated 450,000 quintals (hundredweight) of codfish a year were cured and exported around 1740, six or seven times as many as were caught off New England. The Newfoundland trade was supposed to be worth £225,000 or £300,000 annually about this time, and nearly £500,000 in 1753, when it employed over 15,000 men and some 1,675 ships and boats. The

Channel Island of Jersey, a paradise of smuggling, actually had a larger stake in the trade than either Bristol or London.[115] This was a commerce unlike any other except that in South Carolina rice; both commodities went direct to Southern Europe, there being little market for either in Britain itself. But rice grew on land, if not dry land. Newfoundland was almost like an oil rig out at sea, one with a few permanent inhabitants. Its ties with the mother country were uniquely close, and its character was completely different from that of any North American mainland colony.

VI

Newfoundland, it will be clear by now, was merely one of the many places where the 'old colonial' system leaked rather copiously. Perhaps it only worked so well because it leaked and desired commodities found their vents somehow. The British government itself had no quarrel with those subjects who sucked gold in from Lisbon or surreptitiously introduced British manufactures into Spanish America. Smuggling cleared for itself channels into which legal trade would one day flow in spate. It is not merely liberal delusions which make us suppose that the current in Britain already, in the early eighteenth century, ran towards freer, then still freer trade. The New Englanders were to the fore in a general movement. The expansive energies of the British economies, in the New World as in the home islands, were outgrowing the very system set up, successfully, to promote their expansion.

Colonial customs were not at this time expected to produce a significant revenue. The aim, rather, was to regulate trade. The customs ran at a loss; at mid-century, the returns of some one or two thousand pounds per annum would be nowhere near meeting the costs of enforcement, £7,000 or £8,000. In Walpole's day, the increase of population and trade in British North America were not met by a proportionate rise in the numbers of officials appointed to enforce the regulations. These were scattered along the seaboard, in forty-seven different ports, where approaching ninety surveyors, riding surveyors, comptrollers, collectors, searchers, prevention officers, land waiters, tide waiters performed their various tasks, or failed to do so. The force came under 'surveyors-general' – three from 1709, covering the West Indies as well as the mainland; later, there would be three for the mainland alone. Breaches of the Acts of trade were tried in Vice-Admiralty Courts, of which there were eventually a dozen. Since these courts had no juries, local prejudice in favour of smugglers was less likely to sway their decisions; but common law courts in the colonies claimed authority over ships seized by the Royal Navy in adjoining waters, and they were prone to discharge convicted traders and generally to obstruct the work of the Vice-Admiralty Courts. Meanwhile, it was impossible to prevent customs officials (and even naval officers) from engaging in trade on their own account. It was common for one official to hold several posts. Salaries were inadequate, and the use of ill-paid deputies by absentee office-holders further weakened enforcement. Abuses were especially blatant at Newport, Rhode Island. A traveller noted in the 1740s, 'Collectors and naval officers here are a kind of cyphers. They dare not exercise their office for fear of the fury and unruliness of the people, but their places are profitable upon account of the presents they receive for every cargo of run goods.'[116]

The situation was not, after all, very different from that in various ports in Britain. Colonial administration was still conceived at home as no more than part of the normal government of the king's realm. 'Except in the case of the papers of the Board of Trade and the Secretary of State, no special files of documents were set apart containing the record of business done with America and the West Indies. In the various offices of the Admiralty, Treasury and War Office, in the Custom House, Post Office, and High Court of Admiralty, the details of colonial administration were entered in the regular books or filed in the regular bundles that contained the record of official business done in England or elsewhere as part of the ordinary routine of the day.'[117]

Decisions were taken by the Privy Council sitting as a Committee, usually acting under the advice of some other board or department. The Treasury was now clearly the most powerful department under the Crown, but it had no 'colonial policy'; its interests were financial, and its normal view was that colonial governments should be financially self-sufficient. There was precious little money raised in the New World. Virginian planters since the 1680s had paid an export duty of 2s. a hogshead on their tobacco. Barbados and the Leewards still produced their 4½ per cent duty on exports. Jamaica from the late 1720s paid its £8,000 a year towards its own government. The Crown drew petty sums from various sources – quitrents and treasure trove, fines and mines, waifs and strays and so forth. Whatever revenue the Treasury spotted, it would take away from the New World and apply to non-American purposes. Virginia was the only colony where quitrents produced a sizeable surplus; this was mostly siphoned off to Britain, while the 4½ per cent duty from the West Indies was used to pay the salaries of officials on the islands concerned and in other colonies, but never applied, as once promised, to defence. The colonies received as little naval and military protection as could decently be provided. Once troops got to the New World, they were 'neglected and almost forgotten',[118] and despite the call from devout Anglican circles for colonial bishoprics, these were never set up; they would have cost too much. Walpole's brother Horatio, Auditor General of the colonies from 1721, was even more devoted to the profits of office than his predecessor Blathwayt.

However, the colonists, lightly governed and taxed, rarely felt in a mood to complain. The Molasses Act, under Walpole, was not pressed in practice. Virginians, paying their small export duty and seeing that Whitehall vetoed their own Acts on occasion, and sought to prevent them from developing manufactures, might, like coddled West Indian planters, declare themselves to

THE HARDY RACE:
46
(*right*) Lord Dunmore,
last Royal governor of
Virginia, by Reynolds,
in Highland tartan

47 (*far right*) Corporal
Samuel Macpherson,
leader of a mutiny of
Highland soldiers, 1743

48 (*below*) Fishermen
and their wives near
Inverness in the 1720s

49 Henry Grattan, patriot orator, by Francis Wheatley

50 Cork in the mid-eighteenth century

be oppressed and 'enslaved', but their popular governor, Spotswood, was flowery rather than fatuous when he told the burgesses in 1720: 'I look upon Virginia as a rib taken from Britain's side and believe that while they both proceed as living under the marriage compact, this Eve must thrive so long as her Adam flourishes, and I'm persuaded that whatever serpent shall tempt her to go astray and meddle with forbidden matters will but multiply her sorrow and quicken her husband to rule more strictly over her.' At about this time, an Anglican clergyman in the colony reckoned that Virginian planters got tea, coffee and clothing 'as cheap or cheaper than in England'. He pointed out that they were allowed to import wines direct from Madeira, 'and other Commodities are brought from the West Indies, and the Continent, which cannot be brought to England without spoiling.'[119] The marriage, despite occasional tiffs, stayed warm.

Virginia and Maryland tobacco, like Carolina rice, was clear gain to Britain in mercantilist eyes. Another positive virtue of North America was that it promised greater self-sufficiency in naval stores. The New England forests abounded in tall trees suitable for the production of masts and timber for ships. In Massachusetts, from 1691, and eventually in the whole region from Maine to New Jersey, all trees above 24 inches in diameter standing on land not privately owned were reserved to the British Crown. Lumbermen ignored this ruling, and were backed by forceful colonial leaders. In 1721 a law was passed forbidding the felling of any pine whatsoever on land not included within the bounds of a township. Evasion continued, and in 1729 Parliament authorised royal surveyors to mark trees reserved to the Crown with a 'Broad Arrow', made with three blows of a hatchet. However, many officials took bribes and connived in evasion of the law by favoured colonists, much to the indignation of those not favoured.

Colonial white pine trees were excellent, but the Navy Board in Britain rated American pitch and tar much lower than the products obtained from Sweden. The Swedes made their tar patiently from green trees. In America, after a standing pine had had channels or hollows chopped in it from which turpentine was collected, the tree was commonly allowed to drain and dry for several years till it fell down. Only then was the wood burnt slowly in a kiln so that the hot tar ran out. (Pitch was created by boiling or burning the tar itself.) The long war between Sweden and Peter the Great's Russia deprived Britain of most of its 'naval stores' from the Baltic. An Act of 1705 offered bounties for the production in the colonies. The response was enthusiastic; to the surprise of theorists, it came not from New England but from the Carolinas, where access to pitch-pine from rivers was still easy and where cheap slave labour was abundant for the lengthy and skilful processes involved. By 1715, America was producing almost half Britain's supplies of tar and pitch; over the next eight years the proportion was four-fifths — more than sixty thousand barrels a year.[120] Then the Board of Trade, convinced that the Swedish product

R

was better, persuaded Parliament to reduce the bounties on naval stores produced by American methods. South Carolina now switched its main attention decisively to rice, and North Carolina, with no such alternative staple, became the main producer of tar and pitch.

Other colonial industries were tolerated, in practice, but the Southern colonies were obsessed with agricultural staples and where slaves were less common, labour was too expensive to make colonial manufactures, for the most part, temptingly competitive with Britain's. Besides, nature was naïvely prolific. Buckskin and leather abounded, and served for clothing. Wood met a vast range of needs; colonists could live in wooden houses, use wooden tools, draw off maple syrup, and boil salt from seabrine with wooden fuel. The better-off in the port towns burnt coal sent from Britain as paying ballast in ships, and 'good fire-wood being so plentiful that it encumbers the land', there was no incentive to mine local coal deposits.[121]

Wood also made ships. New England oak was abundant and excellent. With other necessities easily to hand, the colonial shipbuilding industry was more than competitive; it cost about twice as much to create a merchant ship in Britain as it did in Massachusetts. Boston in 1720 had fourteen yards turning out about 200 ships a year. Philadelphia and Newport were already catching up, and other New England ports would quite soon outstrip Boston. Further important industries spun off from the nature of American trade. By the 1730s, New England and New York had several sugar refineries. But rum was the pride and shame of Yankee enterprise. Massachusetts merchants near mid-century declared it to be 'the great support of all their trade and fishery; without which they can no longer subsist'. The rum made in Boston and Newport drove Red Indians mad, enserfed rough fishermen from Cape Cod to Newfoundland, traded for slaves on the coast of Guinea, and found its greatest outside market of all in the southern mainland colonies. William Byrd II, travelling in North Carolina, reported an impromptu roadside meal of half a dozen very fat rashers of bacon fried up in a pint of rum. The liquor here, he noted, mostly came from New England, 'so bad and unwholesome that it is not improperly called "kill-devil".'[122]

A report that 10,000 beaver hats were being made annually in the northern colonies pressed Parliament into the 'Hat Act' of 1732. It was ineffectual, like Acts restricting the production of woollens and, in 1750, colonial iron. Charcoal was still the basis of ironmaking. With wood in Britain itself running short the colonies could exploit a natural advantage. Governor Spotswood of Virginia set the pace for the colonists there. By the early 1720s, his crude, heavy metalware was on sale in Williamsburg, his pig iron was being exported to Britain. The Virginia Assembly encouraged iron mining and the making of pig, and one of Spotswood's successors, Governor Gooch (1727–49), also had a direct interest in the business. The Pennsylvanian Quakers were not behind, and by 1740 Philadelphia had a steel furnace.[123]

As, in the period after Utrecht, an increasing American population produced more, and in greater variety, from its farms and crafts and industries, it was starting to outgrow the capacity of the British and British colonial markets to absorb its exports. The restrictions of the Navigation Code might soon begin to seem to outweigh its advantages. As it was, the mounting wealth of the well-to-do in American seaboard towns owed a great, if incalculable amount to illegal operations. One governor wryly noted, early in the century, that while poor pirates were hanged, 'rich ones appear'd publicly, and were not molested in the least.' Their cash and cargoes were very welcome. Smugglers, as in Britain, perhaps still more so, were admired rather than deplored. A merchant thought nothing of landing tobacco after dark, reshipping it as 'salt fish', a licit export, to Madeira, a licit venue, then loading up in Vigo or in the Canaries with illicit Spanish wine, touching at Madeira on the way home to pick up a few casks of the local tipple for the customs in Boston to sample.[124] His attitude did not differ in essentials from that of a London tea merchant purchasing leaf from a Sussex smuggler in the dead of night, but whereas Parliament would slowly bend to accommodate thrusts of British commerce which strained and made absurd the laws of the land, Yankee go-getters could expect little or no sympathy.

Especially as they showed greater and greater independence of ties with London. Rich colonial merchants, instead of insuring ships through London, began from the 1720s to insure American vessels themselves. Only wealthy Virginia planters still depended on London or Bristol credit; farmers elsewhere were chiefly in the grip of local merchant classes. Since the British government refused to supply even a modest copper coinage to the colonies (minting a special set of coins for America would have been an expensive task and a strain on Britain's bullion supply) and since American trade balances with Britain were adverse, the countryside lost coin to the seaboard towns, and these in turn saw it drain away to England.

Certain major consequences stemmed from this, as well as some ludicrous events. (In 1740–1, Philadelphia, short of small change, imported large quantities of English halfpence. These passed as pennies. Bakers refused to accept them, and went on strike. Two nights of mob activity ensued before the Corporation proclaimed a rate of fifteen English halfpence to the shilling.) The use of printed money had spread through most colonies during the wars of 1689–1713. Colonial credit banks were still maintained by several governments, who would print blocks of notes, make loans in them to farmers on the security of their lands, and draw interest which gave them useful income – Rhode Island, for thirty years, needed to levy no taxes. Though the Pennsylvania currency never depreciated materially, over-issue of paper money elsewhere led to very swift debasement. The resulting rise in price levels benefited debtors, mostly farmers, as against creditors, mostly merchants. The former, dominating colonial legislatures by weight of numbers, pressed for more loans, more notes, more inflation.

Friction resulted, notably in the furious struggle in Massachusetts from 1739 over the proposal for a 'land bank'. Creditors everywhere looked to London for help, and the British Parliament at last, in 1751, banned all future note issues in New England except those tied to tax collections.[125]

Meanwhile, since there was no market yet in Britain for transatlantic food-stuffs – they were too bulky to bear the costs of transport – colonial capitalists had perforce to continue devising schemes, licit and illicit, for triangular or polygonal trades which sent their skippers roaming the Atlantic in search of bills. A Quaker merchant wrote in 1741: 'We make our Remittances a great many different ways sometimes to the West Indies in Bread, Flour, Pork, Indian Corn, and hogshead Staves, sometimes to Carrolina and Newfoundland in Bread and Flour sometimes to Portugall in Wheat, Flour and Pipe Staves sometimes to Ireland in Flax Seed Flour, Oak and Walnut Planks and Barrel Staves and to England in Skinns, Tobacco, Beeswax, staves of all Kinds, Oak and Walnut planks, Boat Boards, Pigg Iron, Tarr, Pitch, Turpentine, Ships, and Bills of Exchange.' In other words, having taken provisions and timber to the Caribbean, Lisbon or the 'Wine Islands', vessels might go on to Britain either in ballast or laden with sugar, molasses, rum or Madeira. The ship itself might then be sold; otherwise it would come home laden with British (or bootleg European) manufactures. A typical homeward cargo might consist of twelve crates of earthenware and twenty casks of nails, six dozen scythes, twenty reams of paper, three gross of ink powder and bolts of various textiles, including Persian and Chinese taffeta.[126]

Rising consumer demand in mainland America for such commodities made the Caribbean more and more vital to the prosperity of colonists further north. So far, in mercantilist terms, so good. The interdependence of the British New World colonies was satisfactorily represented by the large numbers of yellow-visaged Jamaicans, Antiguans and Barbadians to be seen mingling with the ruddy-faced locals in North American seaboard towns. The trouble was that the British West Indies did not increase their demand for provisions and wood at the same pace as mainland production rose; and in any case French or Dutch sugar and molasses were cheap enough to smother any freakish strength of national loyalty among the Bostonians or the Quakers of Newport and Phila-delphia. Mainland interests were therefore increasingly tied to those of the foreign islands with which mainlanders more and more traded.

Meanwhile, over the vast and growing area of mainland white settlement, there was more trade than one port could dominate. Boston was losing its pre-eminence. Its population, 16,258 in 1742, had by then started to decline some-what. Its growth was being checked by the rise of other ports. Its immediate New England hinterland, which included Connecticut and New Hampshire, remained comfortable rather than opulent, but smaller coastal towns even here were flourishing and competing. John Barnard, minister at Marblehead, looked back in 1766 over more than fifty years spent in what had been a simple fishing community. Now the place abounded in craftsmen. It had thirty or forty ships engaged in foreign trade; there had been none when he arrived. 'The people contented themselves to be the slaves that digged in the mines,' he remarked, metaphorically, 'and left the merchants of Boston, Salem, and Europe to carry away the gains; by which means the town was always in dismally poor circumstances, involved in debt to the merchants more than they were worth; nor could I find twenty families in it that, upon the best examination, could stand upon their own legs, and they were generally as rude, swearing, drunken and fighting a crew, as they were poor. Whereas, not only are the public ways vastly mended, but the manners of the people greatly cultivated; and we have many gentlemanlike and polite families, and the very fishermen scorn the rudeness of the former generation.'[127]

Newport was Boston's most formidable New England rival, with over 6,000 people by the 1740s, by when its merchants had started their own direct trade with the Old World, and had intervened on the Guinea coast. New York (11,000) was the liveliest place in British North America. A Scots doctor, Alexander Hamilton, who left a vivid account of his travels through the colonies, observed that one had to be a 'good toaper' to get on well with the inhabitants. 'To talk bawdy, and to have a knack att punning passes among some there for good sterling wit.' Apart from its excessive drinking, he liked the place. A great deal of Dutch language was still used there, and most houses were built 'after the Dutch modell with their gavell ends fronting the street ... the greatest number of brick, and a great many covered with pan tile and glazed tile ... ' New York was also breaking away from Boston's hegemony. But its growth was outstripped by that of Philadelphia, which was now, with some 13,000 inhabitants, clearly becoming the North American capital.

It did not impress Hamilton unduly. Most of the houses seemed to him 'mean and low', and the streets 'very dirty, and obstructed with rubbish and lumber.' He had never been in a town of this size where there was so little taste for 'publick gay diversions ... Their chief employ, indeed, is traffick and mercantile business which turns their thoughts from these levitys.'[128] The rich farming lands around and behind were now the granary of the southern colonies; the port even shipped flour to Boston. It dominated, besides Pennsylvania, the trade of Maryland, Delaware and West New Jersey, with its own home-built merchant fleet. Its men took the lead in the colonial production of pig and bar iron which was leaving Britain's own behind.

About 800 families of Quakers made up little more than a quarter of the town's population by the mid-century: but they dominated the place. The whole Quaker community had shifted upward socially over the years. Artisans and labourers had fathered merchants and master craftsmen. The jealousy of the Yankee Congregationalists was heartily reciprocated, fed not only by rivalry in trade but by memories of Puritan persecution. The élite of Quaker traders felt less in common with their non-Quaker fellow citizens than with those other prosperous Quakers in Britain and the colonies with whom they corresponded ceaselessly regarding 'prices current and the prosperity of Truth'. And a growing distance was emerging between simple country Friends in Pennsylvania and these Philadelphia grandees whose ways were suspiciously worldly. Though Isaac Norris, for instance, decided after all not to have his coat of arms on his coach, his wife insisted on liveries for the servants who drove with it, so he ordered them 'Strong and Cheap, Either of a Dark Gray or Sad Coullour ... or any Grave Coullour thou likes.' Norris wrote furtively to London for battledores and shuttlecocks for his children, 'to keep 'em out of the dirt'.[129] The beauty of Quaker gardens matched in fame the copiousness of Quaker degustations, and the 'slyness' of Quakers in business dealings.

Hamilton dined at a Philadelphia tavern where a 'knott of Quakers', characteristically, 'talked only about selling of flower and the low price it bore.' But in this place, a 'great hall well stoked with flys', he also found a 'very mixed company' – Scots and English, Dutch, Germans and Irish, 'Roman Catholicks', Anglicans, Presbyterians, 'Newlightmen, Methodists, Seventh day men, Moravians, Anabaptists, and one Jew.'[130] This represented the range of peoples and sects now settled in the hinterland. There would have been Africans there as well, although Hamilton did not mention them. Pennsylvania's population included several thousand blacks.

The intellectual life of Philadelphia was enormously enhanced by so many diverse influences, as it took over from Boston the cultural leadership of the colonies. The town pioneered in the 1720s a native style of Georgian architecture. Its grandees built themselves impressive country houses. The larger American ports were now ahead of their British counterparts in amenity. Boston and Philadelphia had underground sewers at a time when Bristol still suffered from unpaved gutters running down the centre of its streets. But while the North American towns were absolutely bigger than they had been, the proportion of population now living in them had declined: 5.4 per cent in 1742 compared to 9 per cent fifty years before.[131] This was still mainly a territory of planters and farmers, and as the frontier was extended, so its overall rural character grew more, rather than less, pronounced.

It was, however, a rural ambience modified from its beginnings by commercial capitalism. This was true even in the Chesapeake colonies, which still lacked really substantial towns. Williamsburg, capital of Virginia, was a village with some two hundred houses, a few good shops, a College, a Capitol. The Virginian population was thinly dispersed. Socially and culturally the area stood somewhat apart. Few New England ships called there and the tobacco planters seldom travelled to other colonies. But the whole region was concerned with commerce. Tobacco production mounted fast – 20 million lb. in 1700, 80 million in the mid-1730s, 220 million in 1775. With the crop exhausting the soil so rapidly, the tidewater lands of the first comers were worked out. Planters aimed at large holdings, with plenty of land in reserve, to be cleared when slack times came. (Hence a writer of the 1720s could say that the 'whole country' was a 'perfect forest' except where scratched by white or Indian occupation.) As early as 1709 good land in Virginia was selling at 20s. an acre, very high by North American standards.

However, by contrast with sugar, tobacco remained a crop for the small man as well as the great planter. Even in the longest-settled counties of Virginia, two-thirds of white landholders had farms of 200 acres or less. Settlement now surged past the fall line which limited navigation, into the 'Piedmont', where most of the pioneers were small producers using the labour of themselves, their families, with one or two indentured servants or convict labourers. With tide-water land failing in productivity, the old advantage of nearness to the sea was outweighed by those of virgin soil. The patterns of Chesapeake life began to modify. Real towns – Baltimore, Richmond and so on – emerged on the fall line towards the mid-century. And the character of trade changed. By navigable water the pattern had been for large planters to deal direct with agents in London; small men commonly sold their crops to the great, who received in return goods from Britain which they traded among their neighbours. Now, in the Piedmont, the enterprising tobacco merchants of Glasgow led the way in opening stores which sold British goods to planters on the security of their tobacco and reduced them to a more obvious dependence.[132]

But Carters and Byrds in Virginia, Dulanys and Carrolls in Maryland, could still set the tone of society and dominate politics, owning thousands of acres and hundreds of slaves. An English traveller of 1742 wrote of Yorktown, 'You perceive a great air of opulence amongst the inhabitants, who have sometimes built themselves houses, equal in magnificence to many of our superb ones at St James's ... The roads in the neighbourhood are infinitely superior to most in England ... The planters live, in a manner, equal to men of the best fortune ... '[133] The qualification – 'in a manner' – as we shall see, mattered greatly. But whereas the petty farmers enjoyed, in their neat timber houses, a coarse plenty in cows and pigs, corn and vegetables, growing just enough tobacco to meet their needs for goods from outside for the next year, the rich men, in their fine brick mansions, formed one of the most remarkable ruling classes in history, and aimed at an almost visionary ideal of self-sufficiency which was far more than sufficiency.

Their most eloquent spokesman, William Byrd II (1674–1744), who inherited 26,000 and more acres, and owned 180,000 at his death, presented the ideal, in a letter to the cultivated Earl of Orrery just as if it were actuality. 'Besides the advantage of pure air, we abound in all kinds of provisions without expense (I mean we who have plantations). I have a large family of my own, and my doors are open to everybody, yet I have no bills to pay, and half-a-crown will rest undisturbed in my pocket for many moons together. Like one of the patriarchs I have my flocks and my herds, my bond-men and bond-women, and every soart of trade amongst my own servants, so that I live in a kind of independence on everyone but providence.' It was true that the plantation would be like a small village, with, in an extreme case, its own mill, its wheat silo and ironworks, its forge, turner's shop, wheelwright's shop, carpenter's shop, shoemaker's shop, with tanners and sawyers and weavers, with slave children busy making nails and veteran slave women spinning yarn, with distillers making peach brandy, with excellent home-grown cider, with beer as good as any from England made in the planter's brewery. But Virginia also imported 'vast quantities' of Bristol beer, and this was less esteemed than such foreign potions as wine and arrack, brandy and rum.[134]

What Byrd wrote next hinted at the other side of the radiant moon he had hoisted. 'However this soart of life is without expense, yet it is attended with a great deal of trouble. I must take care to keep all my people to their duty, to set all the springs in motion and to make everyone draw his equal share to carry the machine forward. But then 'tis an amusement in this silent country and a continual exercise of our patience and economy.' In his rustic 'silence' Byrd sought to console himself for the much-missed gossip and chatter of England, where he had been educated from the age of 7 until he was 22, where he had been elected to the Royal Society, and whither he had returned as agent for his colony for spells totalling some twenty years. Only as an old man did he settle in Virginia, complaining that his daughters yearned for the London theatre. And the role of plantation owner was, as he said, 'a great deal of trouble'.[135]

Other large planters, like Byrd, conceived themselves as 'patriarchs'. It was the slave's 'duty' to serve his master well. The master preferred to call his blacks 'servants' and the whippings he gave them 'correction'. He took an obsessive interest in the characters and activities of his 'family' of slaves, doctoring them devotedly when need arose, and, conversely, exercising stern parental authority. This was a more intimate attention than an English landed gentleman commonly accorded to his domestics and labourers. But, it was also sound business, or appeared so.

The planter, however 'opulent' he might seem, was, like his West Indian counterpart, always in debt. As Thomas Jefferson would note wryly, debts had become hereditary from father to son and many Chesapeake estates were 'a species of property annexed to certain mercantile houses in London'. The delightful sensation of coin resting undisturbed in the pocket was the result of living on credit; the planter, since he did not disburse directly, was tempted to draw goods from Britain beyond his means. His chosen role of serene, luxurious, generous patriarch was in sharp conflict with the reality of his position. He was, in fact, a trader himself, snared in a most complex business. Robert Carter ('King Carter'), who died with 300,000 acres, wrote once to his London factor, 'I cannot allow myself to come behind any of these gentlemen in the planter's trade.' No Virginian 'gentleman' scorned 'trade'. Even Byrd had been sent by his father to study business methods in Holland and had served a brief apprenticeship to London merchants. The real sources of the great planter's power were his roles as middleman slave dealer reselling to petty planters and traders, as retailer of European goods, as contractor hiring out slave artisans, and as manufacturer bringing on to the market the products of his home industries. And, of course, as an entrepreneur making tobacco, and looking, as King Carter's son put it, 'into every hole and corner' of his plantation, counting seedlings, stores and crops to make sure that slaves and overseers did not cheat him, working, in fact, a long, hard day. Tobacco profits were too low to make absenteeism practicable. The enviable way of life was won by effort no less than that of a Scots factor and, in terms of hours spent, not remote from that of his slaves.[136]

The contrast with such Jamaicans as Charles Price is obvious. What was it, however, that made the Virginian 'gentleman' different from the English iron-master or clothier? Clearly the paradox that he belonged to a 'bourgeois' class orientated to the land. He was not an 'aristocrat' — one writer familiar with both England and America described George Washington as the son of 'creditable Virginia Tobacco Planter (which I suppose may, in point of rank, be equal to the better sort of Yeomanry in England).' The only significant titles in his world were those — 'colonel', 'major' and 'captain' — which derived from status in the Militia. Council members and some persons given appointments by the Crown were acknowledged as 'esquires', but in the 1720s there was only one baronet's family known in the colony. The basis of the Virginian planter élite was sharply different from that of the English gentry. In the years since the Restoration, the latter had developed legal devices designed to ensure that estates passed on intact from eldest son to eldest son; by now half or more of England, probably, was held under 'strict settlement', to the disadvantage of younger offspring. This in part reflected the growing shortage of land. In Virginia, there was no deficiency. Younger sons, even younger daughters, could be granted landed inheritance, receiving tracts outside the home county while the eldest son took the 'home' plantation. But where was 'home'? This class was not rooted. With soil so quickly exhausted, its members would not be tied to a single place. And entail was ruled out by the fact that the slaves without whom land would be worthless had to be moved to fresh land and could only be kept in one place at the cost of economic suicide. Hence, four male Carters in the third generation were equally important. In 1750 seven Lees of the same generation were sitting together in the Assembly. The great families, expanding amoeba-like, intermarried incessantly with each other and produced a ruling class, compacted into a cousinry, in which every man was the equal, and no more, of every other. This provided an arena for easy give and take of ideas in debate, and for common action in the defence of the ideals of the group, which included the belief, rarely found in the West Indies, that every substantial man should play a responsible part in public affairs and do his duty in the commonwealth. Such was the background of Washington and Jefferson.[137]

Yet the class rarely produced intellectuals. 'They are more inclinable,' a clergyman wrote, 'to read men by business and conversation, than to dive into books.' In a muted, more dignified mode, the Virginia gentleman's pleasures were the same as those of the Irish squireen or Jamaican buckra. Hospitality was free and easy, extended visits were 'almost the only kind of group life the region afforded.' Men hunted, raced the excellent local breed of horses, gambled away their acres, danced until they dropped. Byrd's intellectual curiosity was as freakish as Thomas Jefferson's. The great passion, shared by both Byrd and Jefferson's father, was for speculation in land. Governor Spotswood showed everyone the way. In 1722, getting wind of the fact that he would shortly be dismissed, he and his cronies hastened to patent nearly 179,000 acres in the new frontier county of 'Spotsylvania', in a period of less than twelve weeks. Spotswood himself carved out 85,000 acres and, when relieved of the cares of office, settled in the Piedmont and led a movement of Tidewater gentry away from the worn-out maritime lands.[138]

South and North Carolina were separated by the proprietors in 1712, and continued to develop in markedly different directions. North Carolina was perhaps the most rural of all colonies, where the largest 'town' had only 150 buildings, and only about one colonist in fifty lived in an urban settlement. Albemarle County in the north was a small-fry extension of the Chesapeake tobacco region. The Cape Fear area in the south-east went in for rice, and later indigo, like South Carolina. In the west, the rich forests of the 'Pine Barren' belt were the basis of the naval stores industry. All these areas used slaves, but mostly in small parcels. Wealth here was distributed with relative even-ness among many petty but well-fed farmers. The colony preserved for a long time its reputation as a haven for criminals, debtors and runaway blacks. Children remained unbaptised, government feeble. William Byrd II sneered with stilted Latinate hauteur at Edenton with its forty or fifty houses. 'A citizen here is counted extravagant if he has ambition enough to aspire to a brick chimney.' He painted a would-be satirical, in fact attractive picture of a 'Lubberland' where provisions were easily raised in a kind climate. 'When the weather is mild, they stand leaning with both their arms upon the cornfield fence and gravely consider whether they had best go and take a small heat at the hoe but generally find reasons to put it off till another time.'[139]

South Carolina, in extreme contrast, became the closest equivalent on the mainland to Jamaica. (Contemporaries still on occasions referred to this colony as being in the 'West Indies'.) This was not inevitable. Though rice cultivation had begun in the 1690s and slave population had overtaken white in the first decade of the eighteenth century, Carolina had remained a frontier society, heavily committed to the trade in deerskins. A bitter war with the Yamasee Indians (1715–17) fed growing resentment of the Colony's proprietors in England. The war cost £116,000 in two years, yet the proprietors by their own admission sent less than £1,000. Then they claimed the conquered lands for themselves. In December 1719, the 'Commons House' in Charles Town moved into near revolution, declaring themselves a 'Convention, delegated by the

People, to prevent the utter Ruin of this Government', electing their own governor, and petitioning for South Carolina to be made a royal colony.[140]

The home government took effective control and sent out the vastly experienced Francis Nicholson as governor. The colony's teething pains were not yet over. In 1727 a serious economic depression following the reduction of bounties on naval stores provoked virtual rebellion by the small farmers. In 1729, the Crown at last purchased the colony from the proprietors. Parliament was persuaded to permit direct shipment of rice to Spain and Portugal, the colony's natural markets. A boom followed. Between 1732 and 1738, the market value of rice rose by 75 per cent and exportation from the colony nearly doubled, to 67,000 barrels per year.[141] With deerskins, livestock and timber to export, as well as rice and, later, indigo, South Carolina became the richest of all the mainland colonies, and the one most favoured by legislators in London.

The cypress swamps of its 'Low Country' by the coast were excellently suited to rice. Much capital was needed for irrigation works and, like sugar, this became a crop for grand slave-owners. The richest planters each had a dozen or more rice plantations. African labour was more obviously desirable than it had been in the early days of sugar. Much rice was grown in West Africa. Some slaves would be more familiar with its planting, hoeing, processing, cooking than, in the first instance, their masters were. 'In summer, when Carolina blacks moved through the rice fields in a row, hoeing in unison to work songs, the pattern of cultivation was not one imposed by European owners, but rather one retained from West African forbears.'[142] The environment was a paradise for mosquitoes. Africans commonly had inherited immunity to malaria, as well as acquired resistance to yellow fever, which periodically decimated the white population of the Low Country.

Rice prices fell low in the mid-1740s, but indigo, a recent re-introduction, became extremely profitable after Parliament, in 1748, offered bounties for its cultivation. The crop complemented rice; it grew best on higher and better-drained soils. Overall, in forty years from the mid-1730s, the value of South Carolina produce multiplied five times, to over £500,000 a year.[143]

Although it possessed other possible harbour sites, the colony depended on Charles Town to take off its produce, and became a kind of city-state. With approaching 7,000 inhabitants, Charles Town rose from the ashes of a fire in 1740, which destroyed many crude old wooden buildings, with an elegant architectural manner of its own, mixing West Indian notions with the classical style now prevailing in Europe. Nowhere else in the New World was urban life more gracious, for the rich. Planters commonly contented themselves with modest wooden houses on their plantations and flaunted their new wealth in their elaborate town residences, drinking fine wines in airy high-ceilinged rooms. There were dances twice a week in the Assembly rooms, public concerts from 1732, a theatre from 1735, and, by the mid-1760s, three newspapers. The ethos of the élite was bourgeois as well as quasi-aristocratic. ' ... It was almost as if the Carolinian was so ardently genteel because he was so adept at business and a little ashamed of it ... '[144] But he worked far less hard than his Virginian counterpart. Overseers were given more scope. The planter escaped to Charles Town or to his favourite resort, Newport, Rhode Island, towards the end of April, returning only in November or December when the rice country climate was at its best, and there was good hunting to be had there.

The Carolina élite, some 2,000 people, was 'full of money' but empty of public spirit. Few people bothered to vote, though suffrage was, among whites, virtually universal. 'Many parishes had to hold elections two or three times before they could find men who were willing to serve, and some assembly seats were never filled.' Twice in the late 1740s it proved impossible even to muster a quorum in the Commons House, and assemblies were dissolved without effectually having met at all. The great planters left the politics of the assembly to the merchants and lawyers of Charles Town, where the only courts of justice in the entire province were found. Local government was non-existent. Half or more of the parishes had no ministers.[145]

Granted that two-thirds of the population were slaves by 1720, and that blacks came to outnumber whites by as much as eighteen to one in certain parishes, South Carolina might seem to have been no more than a flashier, faster Jamaica. But there were important points of difference. There was frontier acreage. Farmers inland supplied grain and pork to the rice and indigo planters. The colony was more than self-sufficient in food. Though schools were far less numerous than in more northern provinces, and in all its hundred-year life as a colony, less than twenty natives of South Carolina bothered to acquire university degrees, private tutors were abundant. Absenteeism was rare. And in the 1740s, the colonial legislature actually checked the importation of slaves.[146]

Only temporarily. South Carolina retained a predominantly black population. In Virginia, blacks made up 40 per cent or over, in Maryland over 30 per cent, in North Carolina only about a quarter. From Pennsylvania northwards, blacks were concentrated in the port towns. Early in the eighteenth century, they made up approaching a quarter of the people of New York City; in 1720 one Bostonian in six was black. However, in the mid-century, taking New England as a whole, blacks were 3 per cent only of the people. In New Jersey and Pennsylvania the figure was about 8 per cent. Rhode Island and New York, the latter with one black face among seven or eight, were the two northern colonies most concerned with slavery at home – though all, of course, drew benefits from slavery in the West Indies.[147]

Ironically, it was in Rhode Island, which had once, long ago, outlawed slavery, that the closest Northern equivalent to Southern plantation life existed. In the Narragansett country, ranchers ran sheep, cattle, and the famous local breed of horses, on parcels of between three hundred and three thousand acres, each employing from half a dozen to forty slaves. The largest dairy milked 100 cows and made 13,000 lb. of cheese annually, besides much butter. Such prowess suggests that large-scale slavery might have been profitable north of the Chesapeake. As it was, slave labourers, seamen and craftsmen played a role out of proportion to their numbers in Northern economies where white workmen could not be checked from moving on to acquire land.[148]

In Queen Anne's day a French Huguenot named Elias Neau, who had himself served seven years as a galley slave, started a school for blacks in New York City, which soon had scores of pupils. Many New England churches had blacks as full members. Interracial marriages occasionally occurred in the Northern colonies, though both Massachusetts and Pennsylvania had laws against miscegenation. In New York free blacks, and in New England even slaves, could testify against whites in court. A few free Northern blacks and mulattoes voted in elections. But even here, many slaves ran away. Slaves were forbidden in New England to wander beyond town limits without a pass, to remain on Boston common after sunset, to build bonfires or drink in taverns. What might be defined as the first known American lynching occurred at Roxbury, Massachusetts, in 1741, and the first serious slave revolt on the mainland occurred in New York City in 1712.[149]

New York slaves were commonly craftsmen – a dangerous class, as we have seen. Some two dozen slaves erupted, coupling arson with butchery. Several committed suicide rather than submit; seventeen were executed. The town remained edgy. In 1741 a purported plot was unearthed, thirteen blacks were burnt, eighteen were hanged and seventy were shipped out of the colony. Alexander Hamilton, not long after, noted that 'Ever since the negroe conspiracy, certain people have been appointed to sell water in the streets, which they carry on a sledge in great casks and bring it from the best springs about the city, for it was when the negroes went for tea water that they held their caballs and consultations ... '[150]

The fear of servile insurrection cannot be dissociated from the precocious beginnings of anti-slavery argument in North America. The first published protest against the institution had been made by a small group of Pennsylvania Quakers as early as 1688. The first true 'abolitionists', men who devoted a great part of their lives to agitation, were Philadelphia Friends. William Sandiford (1693–1733) was ostracised by other Friends and boycotted in his shop. Benjamin Lay, an eccentric hunchback who died in 1759, refused to use slave-grown produce, lived in a cave outside the town in preference to a man-made building, denounced slave-holding Friends at Meetings dressed in sackcloth, and stood barefoot outside in the snow to draw attention to the plight of slaves who had to spend the whole winter thus. His Meeting disowned him in 1738. But by the time of his death, a genuine anti-slavery movement, powered by idealism and fear, was emerging in America, led by Anthony Benezet, a Quaker schoolteacher and a powerful scholar.[151]

Yet meanwhile Rhode Island Quakers had played a part in the growing colonial participation in the slave trade. In the mid-eighteenth century, Newport had roughly half its merchant fleet, perhaps 170 ships, engaged in slaving. The American vessels—mostly about 40 or 50 tons—were far smaller than their British rivals and were amongst the most cramped and least seaworthy involved in the commerce. Their share was never great (6,300 out of 97,000 blacks carried from Africa in 1768). However, Southern merchants and planters commonly bought an interest in African voyages undertaken by English slavers.[152]

In the first sixty years of the century, British North America seems to have imported altogether some 170,000 slaves. Between 1740 and 1760 by when there were 41,000 blacks in the colonies northward from Maryland, and 284,000 in the others, 100,000 came. Nearly 60 per cent of all blacks lived in the two Chesapeake colonies; Virginia alone had 140,000.[153]

How did conditions compare with the West Indies? Smaller farmers, in North and South, worked, with their sons and white servants, beside their slaves; this meant both constant social intercourse and constant surveillance. Even large planters of tobacco and rice, worried about problems of supervision in their absence, divided their land into portions with never more than thirty slaves to a 'quarter', creating a different environment from their Caribbean counterparts. But not an idyllic one. At the peak of the harvest season, a fifteen-hour day was demanded in Virginia. Rice was even more exacting than tobacco. Banks, ditches and sluices had to be kept in constant repair so that the fields could be flooded three times a year. Indigo was perhaps most laborious of all, with two crops every summer and a difficult process required to extract the dye. Field slaves, whatever the crop, were commonly housed in barrack-like structures. Their diet was dominated by maize. They wore coarse uniform clothes made of linen. However paternalistic the master, the overseer was likely to be impatient and cruel and here too there was much passive resistance—idling, sabotage, pilfering, feigned illness.[154]

Mainland slave codes, in some particulars, were more repressive than Caribbean ones. Only Antigua, in the West Indies, made castration a lawful punishment, yet it was prescribed for certain offences in the Carolinas and in Virginia and also in Pennsylvania and New Jersey. All the Southern mainland colonies legislated against miscegenation, even, by 1717, South Carolina. Free blacks and mulattoes were worse off than in Jamaica. The sole hope of social acceptance for someone of mixed descent was actually to pass as white.[155]

In the West Indies, a black culture was developing which was shared by a black majority and which had considerable impact on white habits. The North American slave or freeman was commonly less hard used physically, but psychologically his position was perhaps even more humiliating. Typically he worked in a smaller unit, and had more contact with whites, who were increasingly proud of their own American ways and saw him as a regrettable aberration. He himself was more distanced from African culture, because of a feature which made slavery on the Northern mainland unique in the New World: the rapid increase, by breeding, of numbers of native slaves. By 1720 the annual rate of natural increase in British North America was surpassing the annual rate of importation, and by the 1780s, only one slave in five would be African born. In 1800 there would be a million blacks in America. If the birth- and death-rates had matched those of the West Indies, there would have been only 186,000.[156] Besides relative freedom from lethal diseases, the main reason seems to have been attitudes among planters, at least north of Charles Town, which were not, always, more truly humane, but which made interbreeding among slaves easier. The contrast between Virginia and South Carolina bears this out.

The Virginians, as we have seen, were not men who found wealth easy to come by. Even in 1699, at the peak of a mania for purchasing slaves, the Assembly prudently put a duty of 20s. a head on each import, specifically towards the rebuilding of their Capitol in Williamsburg, which had been burnt down. In 1705 they continued the Act, for the sake of the public revenue which it pro- vided. They were beginning to guess that their speculative euphoria had been not entirely wise. When, in 1710, the House of Burgesses passed an Act creating a duty of £5 per slave, its members, according to Governor Spotswood, 'urged what is really true, that the Country is already ruined by the great number of negros imported of late years; that it will be impossible for them in many years to discharge the debts already contracted for the purchase of those negros if fresh supplys be still poured in upon them while their tobacco continues so little valuable ... ' The Act was in force till 1718, and it effectively stopped importation. In 1723 the Assembly tried to impose a duty again, this time only 40s. But British slave traders now protested so strongly that the colony's legis- lation was vetoed by the King in Council. The attempt was repeated five years later, and the veto was applied again (with an adviser to the Board of Trade urging that since slaves were purchased in Guinea 'in Exchange of Our own Manifactures', it was as if the Virginians were trying to lay an import duty on British goods). An acceptable formula was found in 1732; the duty was to be paid by the buyer, *ad valorem*, and this measure became virtually permanent.[157]

It was not effusive love of black people which made Virginians uneasy about the trade. On the contrary, they showed growing prejudice. In the same year as they ran foul of British merchant interests, 1723, they passed Acts making manumission more difficult, and barring free blacks and mulattoes from voting. The Board of Trade was very annoyed when it noticed this latter enactment a dozen years later; Governor Gooch hastened to explain that the aim was to 'fix a perpetual Brand' on these people, since it was well known they would always side with the slaves. They must be made to feel that there was a distinction between their children and those of Englishmen. Virginians were very worried at this time by the risk of slave uprisings; two hundred slaves had attempted insurrection in 1730, and trepidation flavoured a now famous letter which Willaim Byrd II sent to the Earl of Egmont six years later. Byrd feared a revolt which would 'tinge our Rivers as wide as they are with Blood.' He wished

Parliament would stop 'this unchristian Traffick of makeing Merchandize of Our Fellow Creatures.' If it went on, there would be so many blacks in Virginia that he feared it would become known as 'New Guinea'. He deplored slavery itself, on grounds partly racialist, partly humane. He regretted that the 'base Tempers' of the blacks being what they were, they had to be disciplined and chastised; it was 'terrible to a good naturd Man, who must submit to be either a Fool or a Fury.'[158]

Such men as Byrd were inwardly divided on the issue of slavery. It did not suit their exalted image of America as an Utopian land of self-sufficient gentleman farmers. Indians, by contrast, were romanticised in their minds as true native Americans; Byrd fulsomely advocated inter-breeding with them, and laws against miscegenation did not apply to them. Feeling this way, the plantocrats' attitude towards 'creole' slaves was in effect quite generous. They believed that American natives *should* be baptised, and this view was unique among British New World planters. Such blacks were suitable for training in white skills, and this, in Virginian eyes, more or less implied conversion. Planters had slaves taught to be expert forgemen, blacksmiths, sawyers, bricklayers and so on. Many were able to read and write, and could hold their own in every respect except skin colour with white artisans in the same crafts. But their growing numbers posed dangers. Skilled men were hard to discipline, and were likely to be sold by one exasperated master after another. Many ran away, a common aim being to pass for free in one of the towns. That so many escaped recapture for so long shows that Virginian slave society was uniquely permissive and open. Those whites prepared to accept and employ runaways violated the slave code, like many blacks, with impunity. Numerous domestics and skilled slaves were smooth-tongued and spoke excellent English.[159]

South Carolina was very different, with its rush of wealth, its careless rulers, its spate of fresh imports – 32,233 slaves between 1724 and 1739. In these years, attitudes prevailed which exactly matched those of Jamaican planters. Planters came to value fresh imports above the survival of people whom they already owned. The lot of slaves therefore grew worse. With a persisting imbalance of male slaves over women (eighteen to ten on the larger plantations by 1730) natural increase almost disappeared. Most blacks bore large and visible scars from their whippings. 'Mr Hill, a dancing master in Charleston, whipped a female slave so long that she fell down at his feet, in appearance dead; but when, by the help of a physician, she was so far recovered as to show some signs of life, he repeated the whipping with equal rigour, and concluded the punishment by dropping scalding wax upon her flesh: her only crime was overfilling a tea-cup!'[160] The militia, from 1721, was transformed from an army into an internal police force; by 1740 all its members were supposed by law to take part in regular patrols. To check runaways, scout boats ranged the coasts, and garrisons were set up on the edge of settlement inland, while the Creek Indians in 1721 and the Cherokees in 1730 signed agreements to bring back slaves alive or dead.

The aim was to make this mainland colony as difficult to escape from as any island.

The effort defeated itself. Increasing white control was met with increasing black resistance. In the late 1730s the Spaniards in Florida shrewdly published a decree granting liberty to black fugitives reaching them from the English colonies. Runaways responded in spate. In September 1739, a score of slaves, many of them newly-arrived Angolans, rose near the Stono river in South Carolina, seized arms, burnt houses and killed more than twenty whites. Rebel numbers grew, and it was almost a week before the largest party was beaten in pitched battle thirty miles to the south, clearly heading towards Florida. The whites remained fearful for months and then, the next summer, some sixty-seven slaves were brought to trial for a fresh conspiracy. The shock was such that the government laid down penalties for harsh masters, and, while blacks were put under more restrictions than ever, a prohibitive duty was temporarily set on fresh imports, which were cut by nearly nine-tenths during the 1740s, the money raised being used to encourage white immigration. The proportion of new arrivals among slaves was never so high again.[161]

But the black to white ratio did not alter markedly. Someone travelling south from Virginia in 1774 would notice that Carolina gentlewomen talked 'like Negroes'. (Whereas in Virginia some slaves talked like gentlemen.) This seems to have been the origin of the 'Southern drawl', reflecting, like the white Jamaican accent, irresistible influences on the white minority. Christianity rarely touched Low Country slaves. A South Carolina lady asked her Anglican minister, 'Is it Possible that any of my slaves could go to Heaven, & must I see them there?' This was the only part of North America where, as in the Caribbean, Africans were thrown together, from different tribal backgrounds, in areas where they greatly outnumbered whites who took little or no interest in their personalities. A creole language, 'Gullah', evolved as their common tongue, retaining strong African elements. There were quite large numbers of Red Indian slaves in the colony – 1,400 were counted in 1708. Domiciled alongside them and more at home than their white masters in a sub-tropical environment, Africans played a mediating role vital to South Carolina's development. Besides their skill in rice-planting, they were often adept at fishing with nets. Expert African canoemen became the backbone of the transport system; and blacks, used to crocodiles, coped far better with alligators than Europeans. They became pathfinders, guides and interpreters. Indian and African skills fused in such crafts as the weaving of baskets from palmetto leaves. Blacks created the bases of the colony's material life, and were essential to its expansion.[162]

But this was true, if less obviously so, in most other North American colonies. In 1700 there had been, at most, one black to ten whites in British North America. By 1770, the proportion would be one to five, the highest in the history of the northern mainland, despite a remarkably high white birth-rate in the colonies, and a renewal of heavy white immigration.[163]

VII

Thomas Malthus would call it 'a rapidity of increase probably without parallel in history.' Between 1700 and 1760, while the population in England and Wales grew by about 23 per cent, that of the American mainland colonies multiplied six times. 'In 1700,' Richard Hofstadter has observed, 'the colonies were small outposts of Western civilisation, an advance guard on the fringe of the raw continent numbering about 250,000 souls. By 1750 there were 1,170,000 ... ' And those would increase fivefold again in the next half century. In 1700, colonists in North America outnumbered blacks and whites in the British West Indies by at most two to one. Three-quarters of a century later, the ratio would be over six to one, and there would be more whites in sparsely settled New Hampshire than in Jamaica, the largest Caribbean colony. Taking whites alone, the disproportion between the two groups of colonies would be about forty to one.[164] The mainland white population passed that of Scotland and would, by 1800, stand at half that of the whole island of Great Britain.

Men of the time did not make or use many statistics, but they were aware of changing balances within the empire, of a vast area already settled and of the far vaster area which might yet be settled; Virginia, within its present state boundaries, is nearly seven times as large as Yorkshire, the biggest English county. They could also appreciate the astounding fertility of the North American family. Better diet than in Europe implied lower infant mortality and less disease among children. The ease with which land was acquired encouraged parents to have more offspring, since their labour, before they were ten, would be useful. Patrick Henry, born in Virginia in 1736, was one of nineteen siblings. One Rhode Island woman who lived to be 100 could count 205 descendants surviving before she herself died. The average number of births per fertile marriage may have been as high as seven.[165]

Rising population pushed the frontiers forward. In Pennsylvania land increased in price from £5 per hundred acres to £10 in 1719 and £15 in 1732. It was cheaper further south. In the 1720s movement began into the Cumberland Valley, an avenue leading from Pennsylvania to the back-country of Virginia.[166] By 1716 rangers from that colony had found a passage over the Alleghenies. Governor Spotswood himself led an expedition to follow up their discoveries, taking several leading gentlemen with him. Reaching the Shenandoah River in the Valley of Virginia, they drank the King's health in champagne, the Princess's in burgundy, then those of the rest of the royal family in claret, firing off a volley after each toast. On their return after much fishing and hunting, Spotswood presented each gentleman with a golden horseshoe. Lesser men soon followed these 'Knights of the Golden Horseshoe' westwards. By 1724 there were immigrants, Germans, in the Valley of Virginia. Within a quarter of a century, the whole Valley was settled, with movement west from Virginia itself having met there a spate, about double its volume, of pioneers flooding south from Pennsylvania.

The God Land ruled unabashed now even in New England. The practice of limiting land grants for new townships to congregations had broken down in Connecticut at the end of the seventeenth century. The New England township system had limited inequalities among settlers. But now communalism was fading as families consolidated their holdings of scattered strips into unified farms and as more and more families lived away from the nucleated villages. In 1727 the Massachusetts General Court initiated a policy by which new townships were authorised not singly but in groups. The aim was to secure the frontier, while meeting the demands for land promised to war veterans. However, veterans or their heirs commonly sold their rights to speculators, and the passion for gambling in land began to inflame even ordinary farmers. New England villagers now showed the same restless urge to move on which characterised other colonists.

Virgin land was worthless without occupants. Speculators often pulled settlement forward – offering inducements, providing the capital needed to buy out the Indians, constructing defensive works, and so on. Competition between them for buyers helped to keep the price of land low, as did competition between colonies. All provincial governments, like that of Massachusetts, came up with schemes of group settlement on the frontier. Besides inter-colonial jealousy, and the aim of defence against French and Indians, trade with the red men remained valuable. South Carolina alone sent Britain perhaps a million and a quarter buckskins in twenty years from 1739 – they were in great demand for riding breeches – and they were so much used as a form of currency in the back-country that their value became a standard measure in Pennsylvania; hence one surviving usage of the word 'buck', for dollar.[167]

But pressure for fresh land grew spontaneously. Expansion away from the weary tidewater lands into Virginia's Piedmont accelerated in the 1730s, and a Scottish planter-parson, the Reverend Robert Rose, helped it forward mightily by inventing a way of transporting tobacco down river; two canoes fastened together, but still easy to manoeuvre, could take eight or nine heavy hogsheads. New Englanders were moving eastward into Maine in quest of lumber, and reserves of cultivable land in Massachusetts, Connecticut and Rhode Island were almost exhausted by the mid-century. So pioneering in New York accelerated as the shortage of acres in New England made the terms of the great landowners there more acceptable. Thus the Iroquois now felt the pinch. New York's Secretary for Indian Affairs wrote around the mid-century, 'The injustice the Indians have suffered with regard to their Lands has contributed to drive Numbers to the French in Canada ... ' Iniquity towards red men was now casually committed almost everywhere. Speculators often had no conscience. As one chief complained in 1745, 'when a Small parcell of Land is bought of us a Large Quantity is taken instead of it.'[168]

Even in Pennsylvania, where a tradition of just dealing had been established, time eroded red-white relations. In the 1720s the Delaware Indians from eastern Pennsylvania began to trek westward in face of white pressure. The Pennsylvania authorities now preferred to deal direct with the Iroquois and use them to keep the local Indians in line. As Delawares moved west, so did the fur traders who battened on them. Pennsylvania's trade reached as far as the shore of Lake Erie.

Men from the eastern seaboard colonies seem to have cheated the Indians far more flagrantly than the Hudson's Bay factors or the Montreal French. Further north, those who controlled the trade looked to the future; here, the rapacious individual's quest for 'a fast buck' had freer rein. Like many other observers, Governor Spotswood attributed Indian unrest chiefly to the bad character of the traders who 'made no scruple of first making them drunk and then cheating them of their skins, and even of beating them in the bargain.'[169] But his own attempt to regulate the trade was crushed by the influence of merchants in Britain and by the Virginian House of Burgesses.

Missionaries, what few there were, often explained poor results by pointing out that the behaviour of whites seeking furs was the worst possible advertisement for Christianity. But they also admitted to encountering apathy and resistance among the Indians themselves. Governor Spotswood opened a school for Indian children on the frontier, and at one point it had nearly fourscore pupils, but distant chiefs prepared to leave children there 'would not relinquish their barbarity'. They explained that 'they thought it hard, that we should desire them to change their manners and customs, since they did not desire us to turn Indians', though they were ready to let their children sample the white men's ways. In any case the school soon perished 'through the opposition of trade and interest', while alumni of the hall set up for Indians around 1723 at the College of William and Mary commonly chose to 'elope' back to their skins and their own 'savage' customs.[170]

The Society for the Propagation of the Gospel in Foreign Parts, founded in England at the start of the century, began with optimistic views characteristic of the Age of Reason. Its missionaries were told, when instructing Indians and blacks, to commence with 'the Principles of Natural Religion, appealing to their Reason and Conscience; and thence proceed to shew them the Necessity of Revelation, and the Certainty of that contained in the Holy Scriptures, by the plainest and most obvious Arguments.' But in practice, its personnel were mostly devoted to the needs of under-clergied white colonists. In 1710 four Iroquois chiefs were presented to Queen Anne in London and seemed to ask for a mission among their people. A special fort was built, but the missionary installed there resigned in exasperation in 1719 – 'Heathens they are, and heathens they will still be.'[171] The most brilliant of eighteenth-century missionaries, David Brainerd, was a young Connecticut minister supported in the 1730s by the Scottish Society for the Propagation of the Christian Gospel, whose travails in the Pennsylvania wilderness were cut short after only four years by his death before he was 30.

A New England Company mission to the Indians of Maine aborted after three years in 1720 — here as elsewhere the red men were 'in such a ferment about their Lands, lest the English should entirely engross them', that they were unwilling to hear the white God's word. But John Sergeant in 1734 started a successful venture among the Housatonic Indians on Massachusetts' western frontier. The Assembly granted land and a township called Stockbridge was created. White families moved in as well. Numerous Indians qualified to vote in elections. In 1763 the whites captured control of local government. The Indians protested. A committee of the General Court declared the election legal, but recommended political separation between the races, what would later be called, elsewhere, apartheid.[172]

A few Indians adapted successfully to white culture. Alexander Hamilton, *en route* from Connecticut to Rhode Island in the 1740s, came upon the house of George Ninigret, sachem of the remaining Narragansetts. Though his people were 'servants and vassals' to the whites, he himself seemed a prosperous rancher. 'His queen goes in a high modish dress in her silks, hoops, stays, and dresses like an English woman. He educates his children to the belles lettres and is himself a very complaisant mannerly man. We pay'd him a visit, and he treated us with a glass of good wine.' But at Kingsbridge near New York, Hamilton watched about ten stark naked Indians fishing for oysters, and their miserable estate was more typical of the dwindling numbers of red men in areas of well-established white settlement.[173] There was, as we have seen, much use of Indian slaves in South Carolina. Inland tribes in that region came to own black slaves, and provided red ones to the British for shipment out of Charles Town to the West Indies. But this did not imply easy relations.

The so-called 'Yamasee' war of 1715–17 arose out of South Carolina's failure to regulate its Indian trade. Practically every Indian nation which did business with the colony was involved. The Yamasees themselves were chased into Florida, but ten years of diplomatic struggle between British and Spaniards followed for the control of the Creek nation. Meanwhile, the French in Louisiana seemed menacing. By 1730 the Board of Trade had made up its mind that colonisation must be effected south of the Carolina settlements.

Enter James Oglethorpe, soldier and philanthropist, shrill and unbearably garrulous, nevertheless commanding respect as a man of courage, integrity and idealism: in short, because he was not a Walpolian whig. His father had led the Stuart cavalry which had chased the Covenanters away from Bothwell Bridge in 1679, and after the Revolution had been for several years an active Jacobite intriguer, making his peace with William III only in 1696, the year in which James Oglethorpe was born. An elder brother was given a Jacobite barony by the Pretender, their three sisters settled in James's court, and their mother, a friend of Jonathan Swift, continually intrigued on behalf of the Stuarts. Till his dying day (1785) James Oglethorpe supported the doctrine of the Divine Right of Kings, but he sat in the House of Commons from 1722 as a loyal Hanoverian tory.

In this period, the defence of humane values largely depended on such tories. Oglethorpe spoke up for the oppressed British seaman and published in 1728 a pamphlet attacking the press-gang. A close friend had been sent to gaol for debt and had died of smallpox there. Oglethorpe pressed for a parliamentary enquiry into the state of the prisons, succeeded, and chaired the committee set up. Fearsome extortions and cruelties were exposed, but the several gaolers put on trial were all acquitted; the whig state looked after its own. Oglethorpe now devised a plan for a colony which would give harbour to debtors who would otherwise suffer in prison. Parliament approved the project in 1732. A new kind of charter was granted. Oglethorpe and nineteen associates were made 'Trustees for establishing the colony of Georgia', on territory between the Savannah and Altamaha Rivers, but the composition of the governing Council would be controlled by the Crown, and the colony would revert to the King after twenty-one years. Besides money given to them by charitable individuals, the Trustees were provided with £10,000 by Parliament, the first such grant ever made. Oglethorpe's publicity beckoned to the 'unfortunate', who could now be 'carried gratis into a land of liberty and plenty', and the Trustees indignantly rejected an application from a rich contractor who wanted to settle with his servants, but they hearkened to the plight of Protestants recently expelled by the Archbishop of Salzburg from his lands in Germany. By the end of their term, the Trustees would have sent 2,127 people to Georgia 'on the Charity'.[174]

Oglethorpe himself sailed with the first batch of 130 lucky unfortunates (and '10 tons of Alderman Parson's best beer'). In February 1733 they began to erect 'Savannah' on the river of that name, ten miles from the sea. Since the Yamasee war, the region had been deserted. The coastal plain stretching south had good fertile soil, but it was mixed in with large tracts of 'Pine Barren' land, and was replete with malarial mosquitoes. The colonists found scalding droughts and drenching rains, with frosts in winter which led to 'Chamber-Pots frozen under the Bed'. Yet under Oglethorpe's guidance, the settlement started well. He had a sincere respect for Indian rights. He got on very well with the Creeks, helped greatly by a remarkable Indian woman, a princess of their nation, named Mary Musgrove, whose white husband kept a store in Savannah.[175]

The philanthropic vision of the Trustees prompted a quixotic and ineffectual ban on rum in the colony. Their prohibition of slavery, however, was not simply due to the growing revulsion felt in certain circles in Britain, and by Oglethorpe himself. Experience had shown that plantation colonies were hard put to defend themselves. This must be a white man's buffer settlement, unworried by dangers of servile rebellion, always ready to take up arms. Silk, the proposed staple, did not require slave labour. Plantations, besides, would spread people too widely. A single colonist might hold in Georgia only fifty acres, and these were granted in 'tail male', so that women could not inherit, lots could not be split by inheritance into uselessly small sizes, sale would be impossible, and great holdings would not come about. As a scheme for settling a white yeomanry of resident soldiers in a hot climate, this, so far, was perfectly sensible. However, from the outset, men entering at their own expense, with a certain number of servants, could get 500, later 2,000 acres.[176]

At first the settlers were buoyed up by their trust in Oglethorpe and their gratitude for the new chance he offered. 'The general Title they give him,' an observer reported, 'is FATHER: If any of them is sick, he immediately visits them and takes a great deal of Care of them: If any Difference arises, he's the Person that decides it ... He keeps a Strict Discipline.'[177] Even after Savannah had forty houses, Oglethorpe continued to live in a tent. He accepted hard rations, was last in bed and first out.

He was soon at odds with South Carolina over the Indian trade. He told the Chickasaws that he was himself a red man, 'an Indian, in my heart that is I love them', and his popularity with them struck against the influence of Charles Town traders.[178] On a visit home in 1734, he took several Indian chiefs with him, repeating the coup Dale had once made with Pocahontas; a dazzled government gave him £25,800 to set up a chain of twenty forts against the French and Spaniards. He recruited Highland Scots and settled them on the Altamaha, where their village gained the nostalgic name of Darien; to please these people, characteristically, Oglethorpe used on occasion to wear plaid and tartan. He set up garrison after garrison, village after village. In 1737 he wheedled £20,000 more out of Parliament, and permission to raise a regiment with himself as Colonel. In military terms, the colony was a success But the settlers were now turning sour.

Oglethorpe was preoccupied with his role as soldier. While the Highlanders zealously kept to their clearing and planting of land, most of the rest grew lax. The village capital, Savannah, was ridden with quarrels, bootlegging and pilfering. Elsewhere men gave up in disgust and towns were abandoned. New settlers would not come. The colonists who remained grumbled about rum, tail male and, above all, the prohibition of slaves. Even the parson, a young Oxford scholar named John Wesley, embroiled himself in a feud with a great rogue named Causton, the colony's storekeeper, which split Savannah into two parties.

William Stephens, a former M.P. who emigrated to the colony when the quarrel was at its height, 'found it manifest the first Rise of it was upon young *Williamson's* marrying Mr *Causton's* Niece, whom the Parson had a Liking to for himself ... ' The spurned Wesley refused to administer the Sacrament to the new bride. And he preached against the magistrates, of whom Causton was one, calling out from the pulpit that the colonists should remember they were Englishmen and 'insist upon their Rights, when they found themselves oppressed ... ' A later sermon, in effect still more subversive, went far above the heads of the congregation; Wesley argued, against the cold and reasonable religion now orthodox, that the several kinds of passion, except for hatred, were consistent with Christianity. Soon, however, this ineffectual firebrand gave out that he was returning to England. Williamson, his successful rival, put up a public advertisement of an action against him for £1,000 damages and threatened to prosecute anyone who helped Wesley leave. The magistrates ordered the constables to apprehend him if he tried to go. But the parson slipped away with three others, all of whom left large debts behind them, and one of whom was deserting his wife and child.

However, the next summer there was a new clergyman in the colony, George Whitefield. This very young man had no trouble at all in 'captivating the People with his moving Discourses'. His manner was open, jovial and easy. The church was soon far too small to hold those who wanted to hear him, and the colony's labour was soon being diverted from its lethargic agricultural pursuits to build the orphanage which he proposed near Savannah.[179]

The Scots and the Germans kept Georgia going. But even the Salzburgers, at New Ebenezer, worried Oglethorpe by their eagerness to grab the rich lands held by the Uchee Indians. In 1746 they had their way, and by the 1750s Oglethorpe's treaties with Indian nations were being ignored by the colonists in general. The other ideals of the Trustees had also gone by the board. After 1740 the land laws were relaxed, the tail male principle was abolished, larger holdings were permitted, the habit of rum-drinking was legitimated. Then, from 1750, slaveholding was legalised. When the colony reverted to the Crown in 1753 it still had only 2,381 whites and 1,061 blacks. But rapid growth followed. Rice, indigo, lumber found markets. Within ten years the population had trebled. Then it trebled again, to about 33,000 by 1773, by which time 'Scotch-Irish' settlers had completed the long trail from Philadelphia through the back-country and were invading lands in western Georgia which the Creeks and Cherokees had to cede.[180]

The 'Scotch-Irish' were a people with vivid traditions of emigration. By 1672, an estimate had suggested 100,000 Scots in Ireland; most were Lowlanders, most were concentrated in Ulster. In the fifteen years after James II's defeat at the Boyne, when Lowland Scotland was huimliated by famine and shocked by the Darien disaster, and when land in Ulster left tenantless was going cheap, tens of thousands more went over. In 1715, Ulster had perhaps 600,000 people, a third of them Presbyterians and most of these of Scottish origin. The appellation 'Scotch-Irish' had been used by an American colonist as early as 1695, when there were already a few Ulstermen in the New World. It stuck, despite the chagrin expressed by the inhabitants of Londonderry, New Hampshire, in 1720, at hearing themselves called *Irish* — 'when we so frequently ventured our all for the British Crown and Liberties against the Irish Papist.' It was the badge of one of the most remarkable folk movements in history. Some writers have claimed that between about 1717 and 1775 as many as a quarter of a million Scotch-Irish entered North America, and though this figure must be too high, we can say with some certainty that during their last and greatest surge, in 1771-4, approaching 40,000 people emigrated from Ulster in four years.[181] They brought to North America not only a passion for whisky, but also stock which would eventually father a disproportionate number of U.S. Presidents, and the militant traditions of Londonderry and Enniskillen from the Jacobite war of 1689. Their part in the opening up of the continent was enormous. They formed the largest single ethnic group emigrating to North America during the colonial period.

The home government did not encourage emigration from the British Isles. Mercantilist thinking now emphasised the value of labourers and a large population. The aim was maritime power, and maritime colonies; no obvious good could come to Britain from settlements deep in the American interior, far beyond the reach of sea-going vessels. To dump convicted felons in the New World made sense; to ship in black slaves to grow tobacco and rice made more; to lose artisans in the textile industries and Protestants from the minority in Ireland was not in the least desirable. Until the 1770s, there was no legal check on emigration from Britain or Ireland. But foreign settlers were actively encouraged. While the Spanish authorities, till 1717, restricted settlement in the New World to Castilians only, while Brazil discouraged non-Catholic colonisation and while the French colonies were barred, not very effectively, to Huguenots, British policy accepted all sorts of emigrants.

In the case of Georgia, for strategic reasons, English migration was positively assisted. But with dissenters tolerated and civil strife abating, voluntary colonists from England were relatively rare after 1689. The coming of peace in 1713 brought back the old problem of surplus convicts. An Act four years later established official policy for the rest of the century. Transportation for seven years was introduced for the first time as a punishment for English people convicted of certain lesser offences, while men and women pardoned for greater crimes would be transported for fourteen or twenty-four years. The penalty for premature return would be death. Convicts themselves seem to have had a horror of transportation. They were handed over to official contractors who were paid £5 a head for taking them but expected to make a good profit from selling them in the New World at £8 to £25, they were kept chained below decks throughout the voyage, and deaths in transit seem to have averaged 15 per cent or more, a rate bad by the standards of the slave trade. Approaching three-quarters of those convicted at the Old Bailey were transported, besides many others from provincial courts, and altogether some 30,000 felons seem to have been despatched in the eighteenth century. Two-thirds, probably, went to Virginia and Maryland. The assemblies in both colonies tried to block the flow in the 1720s, but the home authorities would not let them. Benjamin Franklin suggested that the colonists should export rattlesnakes to Britain in return. But most planters, especially on the frontier, were glad enough to have convict labour.[182]

Meanwhile the trade in indentured servants remained 'the backbone of the whole migratory movement'. White servitude did not end in North America until the nineteenth century. Its continuing importance is obscured by the greater numbers of black slaves. In Maryland there were 3,003 servants and 4,657 slaves in 1707; by 1755 the respective figures were 6,871 (excluding 1,981 convicts) and 46,356 blacks and mulattoes. Around this later date the President of the Council in Pennsylvania averred that 'every kind of Business here, as well among the Tradesmen and Mechanicks as the Planters & Farmers, is chiefly carried on and supported by the Labour of indented Servants.' There was little slavery in Pennsylvania and New Jersey, and most of the eighteenth-century trade in servants went there. Conditions for servants were now, perhaps, rather easier. There was less collective unrest among them.[183] The great majority now were non-English. There was a trickle of Welshmen and Scots, but most of the incoming servants in the mid-eighteenth century were 'Irish' of one sort or another. Maryland, from 1699, tried to restrict the entry of people from Ireland by a heavy tax on their import. Pennsylvania, following suit in 1729, also put a tax on Germans.

By now the influx of Germans was alarming colonial English chauvinists. Benjamin Franklin would denounce these 'Palatine Boors' in 1753, asking, 'Why should Pennsylvania, founded by the English, become a Colony of *Aliens*, who will shortly be so numerous as to Germanize us instead of our Anglifying them ... '[184]

The first large wave, which lent Germans in general the misleading name of 'Palatines', began from the Rhineland in 1708–9. This region had suffered twenty years of war. Various Protestant sects endured persecution. An exceptionally bad winter was the trigger. Some 13,000 Rhinelanders, by invitation, arrived in England. Many went on to the colonies. The German lands, including Switzerland and Austria, now seemed to others, as they had done to Penn, an abundant reservoir of likely settlers. Agents ('newlanders') were sent through the area. Colonial governors and prominent landowners sometimes intervened directly – thus William Byrd II wrote a pamphlet, published in 1737, to attract Swiss settlers to his *Neu-gefundenes Eden*, a holding on the Roanoke River. 'In Rotterdam and Amsterdam the lucrative business of gathering and trans-shipping emigrants was soon concentrated in the hands of a dozen prominent English and Dutch firms.' A new form of servitude was devised. As people turned up in the ports without enough money to pay their passages, merchants took what they had, put them on board with their families and possessions, and contracted to deliver them. After arrival, the emigrant would have a short period in which to 'redeem' himself by finding the balance of money owing. If he could not, he was sold into servitude for a time depending on the size of his debt. The system was adopted in Britain, especially in Ireland, but it never wholly replaced the old one there, whereas almost all Germans went out as 'redemptioners'.[185]

The Scotch-Irish often fared badly. A height between decks of 4 feet 6 inches was thought worth boasting about in advertisements; the *Sea Flower*, leaving Belfast with 106 passengers in 1741, lost 46 of them at sea from starvation, and when help arrived six of the corpses had been eaten. But of all white immigrants to North America, the Germans probably suffered the worst horrors. Their vessels were so commonly swept with typhus that it became known as 'Palatine fever'. Because most of them could not understand English they were easily victimised by merchants and captains – overcharged, and sold for longer periods of servitude than a just reckoning would have required.[186] Yet the 'redemptioner' was commonly a more substantial immigrant than the ordinary indentured servant. He had some goods, a wife and family, and very often a valuable skill. Germans kept coming over because they thought they could thrive better in the New World than the Old. They were frequently right, and in any case they enjoyed religious freedom.

Most Germans were members of a Lutheran or Reformed Church – 'church people'. From 1736 there was a small but highly significant influx of 'Moravians', adherents of a pietistic and pacifistic sect which had broken away from Lutheranism. In North America, as in the West Indies, they had important influence as missionaries. They were the most civilised of frontiersmen, skilful craftsmen and engineers who insisted on education for both sexes and cultivated choral and instrumental music. Their missionary zeal distinguished them from a range of other immigrant German sectaries – Mennonites from 1710, 'Dunkers' (who baptised by dipping) from 1719, Silesian 'Schwenkfelders' from 1733, and so on. Such people, clinging on to their European peasant culture, commonly kept to themselves, and became the best farmers in the colonies.

Between 1727 and 1742 at least ninety-five shiploads of Germans arrived in Philadelphia; in 1738 alone, about 9,000 German immigrants entered Pennsylvania through the port, which now had German signboards over many of its shops and even a German newspaper. By 1775 at least 100,000 Germans had arrived in North America and the 'Pennsylvania Dutch' (*Deutsch*), may have made up a third of that colony's population. As they settled there, or moved south along the frontier, they brought agricultural and other techniques superior to any the British had used. Though the Conestoga wagons which they made were the ancestors of the prairie schooners, and it was they who developed the frontiersman's long rifle, other pioneers seldom imitated their sensible iron stoves.[187] Their inventiveness, and their care in agriculture, put the Scotch-Irish greatly to shame.

The Scotch-Irish were not forced across the Atlantic by persecution. Many Presbyterian fears had been set at rest by the successful Hanoverian Succession of 1714. Under George I their religion enjoyed complete toleration and Irish Presbyterians who wanted political office seem to have got their share of it in spite of the Test Act.[188] Meanwhile Ulster was clearly becoming the most advanced province in Ireland. The growing linen industry gave small farmers extra income from weaving in their homes. What seems to have been at the root of the emigration is the combination of a moderate push with a strong and growing pull. Life in Ulster, by Irish (or Scottish) standards, was not impossible. Life in America, however, sounded better.

Nevertheless, economic conditions certainly moved the westward waves of 1718–20 and 1724–30, and underlay the later steady flow. Ulster depended so heavily on linen that any adverse fluctuation in its price meant hardship for whole communities. But when linen prices were high, landlords raised rents. In parts of Ulster, these quintupled in the second and third quarters of the eighteenth century; but the average price of Irish linen cloth advanced by only one-fifth over the longer period from 1710 to 1770. The strong competition of Catholics for land forced rents up to the highest possible level, so even a small shortfall in the harvest would result in destitution. Meanwhile, year after year, fleets came from Philadelphia and New York bringing flax seed to the Irish ports. This was bulky. The linen goods taken back were less so. There was plenty of space for emigrants on the ships bound for America.[189]

During normal times, it was mostly farmers who went, but when food was very dear wage-labourers predominated. There was a good proportion of skilled craftsmen. The price of a passage fell over the years as trade with America increased – from £5 or £6 at the start of the century to £3 5s. in 1773. But before the 1770s most emigrants did not pay their own way; they went as indentured servants. The Charles Town *Gazette* in 1734 advertised, 'Just imported and to be sold ... Irish servants, men and women, of good trades, from the north of Ireland. Irish linen, household furniture, butter, cheese, chinaware and all sorts of dry goods ... '[190]

One hears of a rascally ship's captain in the 1730s making specious promises to farmers and labourers and assuring a weaver 'that he would get a guinea sterling for weaving a ten hundred piece of cloth, which according to the labour of a good workman in linen of that sort, would produce above £100 sterling a year',[191] but in Ulster, by contrast with Germany, the emigration business was usually a sideline for merchants and shipowners meeting spontaneous demand, and relying on newspaper advertisements. From the mid-century, American land speculators would be markedly active, vying to draw settlers with some means as tenants to their holdings, but they had much less impact than letters from Ulster emigrants to their friends, and the steady draw of relatives who had gone. At times, the close-knit Presbyterian minority would be seized by an epidemic of wanderlust.

As a series of natural and man-made calamities struck Ulster from 1715 to 1720 – drought, dear food, epidemics, rising rents – a first, smallish spate of something over 2,000 emigrants headed west to try their luck in Boston. A few Scotch-Irish had recently been welcomed as frontier settlers in New England.

But they had aroused sharp ethnic and religious prejudice. The Bostonians began to grumble, 'these confounded Irish will eat us all up.' When one ship arrived with forty-nine intending immigrants in 1719, they were warned to leave immediately. Over the next couple of decades, Boston successfully shooed off Hibernian aliens. The Irish authorities, also, were starting to worry about this effusion of Protestants. 'No Papists stir ... ', Archbishop King lamented in 1718. 'The papists being already five or six to one, and being a breeding people, you may imagine in what condition we are like to be in.'[192]

But of roughly 15,000 emigrants to North America leaving Ireland in the 1720s, northern Protestants made up the great majority. A fever set in about 1724. The long thirty-one-year leases given after the end of the Williamite war were now expiring, as twenty-one-year leases had done in the previous decade. On one estate near Lisburn, thirty-four farms which had rented for a total of £90 in 1719 were let for £223 in 1728, and this coincided with near-famine. This time the wave toppled on to the ports on the Delaware. As with the Germans, Philadelphia became the main port of entry for the Scotch-Irish, who continued to come in at an average rate of one or two thousand per annum until, by 1769, some fifty or seventy thousand more had settled.[193] Then, another fever set in.

James Logan, Provincial Secretary of Pennsylvania, who was an Ulsterman himself, shared the general local alarm and disgust over the incoming Scotch Irish hordes. By 1729, he was reporting a 'common fear' that they would 'make themselves Proprietors of the Province. It is strange that they thus crowd in where they are not wanted.' Remembering Londonderry, he tried to make use of them as frontier warriors to defend the Quaker colony, but he found that 'the settlement of five families from Ireland gives me more trouble than fifty of any other people.' For a time, he refused to grant them land. This merely encouraged them to squat wherever they saw vacant ground. When the authorities burnt down their cabins, the Scotch-Irish simply squatted again. From 1743, the proprietors tried, with some success, to decant them into the Cumberland Valley in western Pennsylvania. This became almost their exclusive preserve, a reservoir of Scotch-Irish which 'after having been filled to over-flowing, sent forth a constant stream of emigrants ... '[194]

Scotch-Irish families were ready to move, settle awhile, move on again. During the 1730s, encouraged by land speculators and by the Virginian authorities, they began to stream into the Chesapeake back-country. Part of it became known as the 'Irish tract'. The Valley of Virginia was mostly a vast prairie, easy to settle. Governor Gooch gave the Presbyterians full toleration. Meanwhile, the Carolinas were looking for settlers. By the 1740s, the Scotch-Irish were fanning into North Carolina; by the 1760s their southward sweep met fresh westward waves of immigration from Ulster through Charles Town, incited by South Carolina's offer of bounties to white incomers.

A novel society was coming into being in the area which has been called

Greater Pennsylvania' – the hilly southern back-country stretching about 600 miles from the northern boundary of Maryland to the Savannah River. In 1730 the only white men seen there had been occasional traders or hunters. By 1775 it contained about 250,000 people of European, American and African birth.[195] The dominance of the sea over patterns of settlement was broken. The 'Great Philadelphia Wagon Road' followed old Indian tracks from Pennsylvania down to Georgia, linking lands claimed by six colonies. By the 1760s it was the most travelled way in America, with towns springing up along its route, and with large covered wagons pressing down it, sometimes a hundred at a time. Welshmen and Englishmen used it, and Scots traders, as well as the large caravanserais of Germans and Ulstermen. But once settled, peoples did not mix or interbreed much. Each community kept up its own way of life, reinforced by fresh settlers from home.

Many parts of the back-country swiftly became more thickly populated than the Tidewater and Low Country plantation lands. Small and medium-sized farms predominated. Stunted cattle – a gallon of milk a day was thought a decent average for a cow – grazed freely on natural meadows. The better soil was two feet deep, and rich. The pioneer would sow newly cleared land with Indian corn for several years until the yield notably declined. Then he might turn to black-eyed peas or beans, or try wheat. The Germans, all witnesses concurred, were the best farmers. They used stone for building when they could and were better than others at making neat and weathertight log cabins. Meanwhile, the Scotch-Irish pioneered in the making of whisky from rye or barley. Such cash crops as hemp, flax, tobacco and indigo were variously cultivated where the soil was suitable, and after about 1750 the back-country moved beyond subsistence farming and began to send food surpluses to the ports. Iron mines and furnaces arose at some places in the interior. The lead deposits found in the Valley of Virginia in the 1750s were of the most immediate value. Lead bullets defended the frontier.[196]

Though the Scotch-Irish from the outset showed no respect for the Indians or their rights, most of the land they moved through was not permanently settled, and serious conflagration was avoided until the 1750s. When it came it was terrible. The score seems to have varied between three and fifty dead whites for every dead Indian. But the red men were outnumbered, and the Ulstermen proved matchlessly savage fighters. Inspired by the discovery that killing of red men freed new lands for whites, they 'wrought desolation at every opportunity'.[197] Irish traditions of genocide found new expression in a New World.

Women, perhaps outnumbered three to one in the early days, had to be tough under frontier conditions. Though the Germans tended to treat marital bonds with European solicitude, the Scotch-Irish became notorious for cohabitation and wife-swapping. An Anglican clergyman, Charles Woodmason, would leave a vivid if prejudiced picture of life in the South Carolina back-country in the 1760s. His parish was 150 miles broad by 300 long. He rode miles day after day, eating rough food – sometimes no more than corn bread and water – in dirty smoky cabins or alone in the woods. Lost 'amidst Bogs, Rocks, Defiles, Swamps, Thickets and Morasses', he would sleep on the bank of a swollen creek in his wet clothes. In winter he forded icy rivers, in summer crossed 'scorching sands'. Flies and mosquitoes abounded. The people seemed hardly less pestilential, though curiosity would always muster him a congregation. At a place named Granny Quarter Creek he confronted 'the lowest Pack of Wretches my Eyes ever saw ... As wild as the very Deer – No making of them sit still during Service ... How would the Polite People of London stare, to see the Females (many very pretty) come to Service in their Shifts and a short petticoat only, barefooted and Bare legged – Without Caps or Handkerchiefs .. ' (This was, incidentally, the depth of winter.) Wild Presbyterians mustered to harass him, set up drunken whoops and halloos outside the doors of the makeshift buildings he preached in. However, he had a still greater aversion for Baptists. He wryly observed that one thing which united jarring denominations was a common passion for strong liquor. ' ... Married many Rogues and Whores on Beaver Creek,' he noted once in his journal; elsewhere he remarked that the girls he hitched were almost invariably pregnant. Mating took place early. Girls married at fourteen. He would often see ten or fifteen children in a single cabin, 'Children and Grand Children of one Size – and the mother looking as Young as the Daughter.'[198]

But after a few years, such ill-fed savage-looking persons would be making a modest profit from cash crops and aiming to build comfortable frame houses and imitate the comforts they had seen among classes above them in Europe or on the east coast. They were followed into the back-country by planters with their slaves, merchants and craftsmen, lawyers and ministers, and, of course, land speculators. When it came to elections, pioneers were quite happy to vote for such gentry, near-gentry and pseudo-gentry. In Lunenburg County, Virginia, as it emerged from its pioneer phase in the 1760s, the richest ten per cent of men held forty per cent of the acreage. Though social relations were more fluid on the frontier, communities there were no more, if no less, egalitarian in temper than those in settled areas to the east.[199] Perhaps one man in twelve on the frontier was a slave.

Everywhere in the mainland colonies, both appointive and elective public offices were securely in the hands of wealthier men. As in all other English-speaking cultures, 'mobs' on occasion asserted the views of the poor. There were near-insurrections, as when farmers, in 1741, marched on Boston in anger over the Land Bank issue. But there was never a widespread call for basic changes in the prevailing patterns of upper-class leadership. Rival factions among the élite appealed to the electorate, seeking to gain control of the very palpable fruits of office.

In Virginia, these were widely enough dispersed to keep the colony free of faction from about 1720. Massachusetts was fairly quiet after 1741 under the fifteen-year rule of Governor Shirley, who used patronage cunningly to exalt a powerful oligarchy and to end half a century of factionalism. New York politics from the 1720s showed a kaleidoscope of shifting factional alignments based on 'family rivalries, conflicting economic interests, ethnic and national differences, religious tensions, sectional antagonisms, personal ambition and political alliance with the royal governors.'[200] Pennsylvanian divisions were stabilised in the same period, as squabbling factions among the Quakers united to form, by 1736, a single well-disciplined party, staunchly supported by the Germans of the rural hinterland. Its main plank was opposition to Penn's heirs, the proprietors. Scotch-Irish frontiersmen worried about Indian attack adhered to the rival 'Proprietory Party'.

But diverse though the scenarios of colonial politics might be, there was a common factor which would one day assume prime importance. In England some politicians were 'in', others were 'out'. 'Ins' in Jamaica had close links with 'ins' at home. But vis-à-vis London, every substantial man in North America was an 'out'. Colonists had, of course, contacts and allies in Britain and might with their help intrigue strongly against royal governors, but they lacked a wealthy, solid absentee lobby. Personal inconvenience resulted. For instance, because the fount of power was so distant, even the richest North American would find it hard to transfer an office held by one kinsman to another when death or resignation made this necessary. Everywhere except in Rhode Island and Connecticut, the governor was appointed in England, and wielded prerogatives and powers greater than those now allowed to King George in Britain. Whether his own faction was 'in' or 'out' of the governor's favour, the colonial bigwig was always aware of the need to defend his provincial assembly's status. He was, in a sense, always in opposition, and would very likely adopt his own brand of 'Country' ideology.

The rhetoric of Bolingbroke and his allies, extolling the balanced constitution and the ideal of the disinterested patriot, suited especially well the would-be-Roman would-be-virtue of the Virginian native élite, and also found receptive imitators in other colonies. The continual struggle of the lower houses in the assemblies to check the prerogative and to diminish executive authority ensured a 'roughly uniform pattern of constitutional development in all of the colonies'.[201] The authorities in London refused to recognise the parliamentary status which the assemblies insisted they had, but they would not pump in the money required to free governors from dependence on local complaisance. Most assemblies came to control the appointment of the agents who officially represented their colonies in London, and they regulated colonial courts of common aw. So they were, in effect, little parliaments; yet their electoral basis was strikingly, and increasingly, different from that of Walpole's loot-fed assemblage of clients at Westminster.

Governor Spotswood of Virginia wrote in 1715, ' ... I cannot forbear regretting that I must always have to do with the representatives of the vulgar people ... for so long as half an acre of land, (which is of small value in this country,) qualifys a man to be an elector, the meaner sort of people will ever carry the elections...' A political leader in New Jersey told the peripatetic doctor Hamilton that the House of Assembly there was 'chiefly composed of mechanicks and ignorant wretches, obstinate to the last degree ... ' William Byrd II observed of the North Carolina farmers, 'They are rarely guilty of flattering or making any court to their governors but treat them with all the excesses of freedom and familiarity.'[202]

In Virginia, probably well over half, perhaps 85 per cent, of all adult white males had the vote at any one time. The Massachusetts qualification for electors – a 40s. freehold or £40 worth of property – could pretty easily be met by any farmer or artisan. In other colonies also, the vast majority of white men could expect to acquire enough during their lifetimes to meet the requirements for suffrage. Inequalities as between colonists may have been increasing in the towns – two-sevenths of adult males in Boston had no taxable property in 1771, compared to only a seventh in 1687. But the contrast with Britain was obvious. Snobbish colonists found it hard to accept. With an Anglican clergyman, Alexander Hamilton visited a small log cabin up the Hudson River occupied by man, wife, and seven children. These were poor people by colonial standards, yet their 'very neat and clean' dwelling contained 'a looking glass with a painted frame, half a dozen pewter spoons and as many plates, old and wore out but bright and clean, and' – pregnant detail – 'a set of stone tea dishes, and a tea pot'. The parson thought these things 'superfluous and too splendid' for such a cottage; they ought to be sold to buy wool for making yarn.[203]

Hamilton had earlier fallen in with a Pennsylvanian dressed like a ploughman or carman, in a 'greasy jacket and breeches and a dirty worsted cap'. Yet this man was anxious to pass for a gentleman, and told his hearers repeatedly, in between oaths and animadversions on the iniquity of Robert Walpole, 'that tho he seemed to be but a plain, homely fellow, yet he would have us know that he was able to afford better than many that went finer: he had good linen in his bags, a pair of silver buckles, silver clasps, and gold sleeve buttons, two Holland shirts, and some neat night caps; and that his little woman att home drank tea twice a day ... ' A Rhode Island sea-captain, about this time, remarked that 'A man who has money here, no matter how he came by it, he is everything, and wanting that he's a mere nothing, let his conduct be ever so irreproachable.'[204]

The status which money conferred could be earned by hard work. The effective ethos of American society was 'bourgeois', middle class, meritocratic. 'The people of this province,' the *Pennsylvania Journal* declared in 1756, 'are generally of the middling sort, and at present pretty much upon a level. They are chiefly industrious farmers, artificers or men in trade; they enjoy and are fond of freedom, and the *meanest among them* thinks he has right to civility from the greatest.' Wealthy and poor men alike looked towards the middle. While the labourer could see his way open to middle-class prosperity, the rich man,

S

as Richard Hofstadter observes, 'had to exercise his power in the knowledge that his way of doing so must not irritate a numerous, relatively aggressive and largely enfranchised middle class public.' There were, he goes on to point out, only 'shadowy substitutes' for the basic institutions of Old World society: a governor, but no court; rich men, but no peers; churches, but no bishops. Institutions which reflected middle-class values of enterprise, self-help and practical public spirit, were salient as they could not be in Britain.[205]

'Dissenting', not Anglican, churches dominated in most areas. The towns spawned flourishing newspapers: Boston, which led the way, had its first in 1704, six by 1734. The public concert, that quintessential product of middle-class culture, had arrived in Boston by 1729. As other colonies followed the lead of New England and Virginia, half a dozen new colleges, all of which later became universities, sprang up along the seaboard between 1746 and the mid-1760s.[206] America shared in the eighteenth-century 'Enlightenment'. Philadelphia became the local centre, and Benjamin Franklin, citizen of that place, one of the movement's leading prophets and ornaments.

Franklin epitomised the land of opportunity which America had become. Born in 1706, the tenth son of a Boston tallow-chandler and soap boiler, he had less than two years' formal schooling. Apprenticed at 12 to his elder brother, a master printer, he became nominal editor of the Boston *Courant* when still only 16 after his brother was gaoled for publishing a satiric news item, but struck off on his own soon after and migrated to Philadelphia. By 1730 he was sole proprietor of a press and newspaper. Shopkeeper, paper dealer and book importer as well, he throve together with his chosen city. His writings gave voice to the ethos of middle-class America, above all his *Poor Richard's Almanack* (1733–57), which sold 10,000 copies a year. 'Work hard and count your pennies.' 'He that hath a trade hath an estate, and he that hath a calling hath an office of profit and honor.' 'Love your neighbour, but don't pull down your hedge.' Franklin expressed a secularised puritanism. As a young man, he made it his business to shun places of idle diversion and seem an 'industrious, thriving young man'.[207] To *seem* such was good for one's credit. The gist of this brilliant, witty, nauseous moralist was: fornicate and cheat by all means, but don't be caught at it. However, his public spirit was perfectly genuine. In 1727 he and some friends — silversmiths, glaziers, printers, shoe-makers, ironmasters — formed a club, the 'Junto', dedicated to civic improvement: which came.

Five years later, thanks to the Junto, Philadelphia acquired the first subscription library in America. Before long the place had several more. Labourers read books. Almost everyone read books. The city had eight printing shops in 1740, twenty-three by the mid-1770s, churning out almanacks, sermons, pamphlets, textbooks and pirated English bestsellers. Over the same period, newspapers increased from two to seven, full of new ideas, of controversy on all subjects, of schemes for civic and philanthropic good works. The town acquired a police force, seventeen fire companies, a hospital, as well as dozens of clubs of all kinds and no fewer than three masonic lodges. Evening schools also flourished, offering practical instruction for working men and apprentices in such skills as book-keeping and surveying. Genteel perusal of ancient authors, as practised at English universities, had no obvious use to such people. 'Can there be anything more Rediculous', a newspaper piece asked in 1735, 'than that a Father should waste his own Money and his Sons Time, in setting him to learn the Roman Language, when at the same Time he designs him for a Trade?'[208] The more practical, democratical Scottish view of higher education made better sense to middle-class America. When a college was set up at Philadelphia in the 1750s, its curriculum tended towards utility, and its provost came from Aberdeen University. In 1765, the city founded the first medical school in America, with a professor who had studied in Edinburgh.

Franklin's own interest in electricity was aroused by another Edinburgh-trained scientist. The pioneering experiments which he published in London in 1751 gave Franklin a European reputation as a 'natural philosopher'. He was, in the Philadelphia of his own day, far from alone in intellectual eminence. Benezet's writings on slavery greatly influenced British and European thinking; David Rittenhouse was a renowned astronomer; John Bartram, a versatile naturalist, was much admired by Linnaeus himself and helped Franklin to found, in 1744, the American Philosophical Society, a counterpart to the Royal Society of London.

Yet meanwhile the country estates around Philadelphia, with their groves, parks, formal gardens and kitchen gardens, but without droves of black slaves in attendance, provided the closest replica anywhere in the colonies of the life-style of the English gentry. The aping of English fashion was taken to almost ludicrous lengths. When a fox-hunting club was formed in 1766, Philadelphians brought in English red foxes – to no avail, since they swiftly interbred with the local variety. Bostonians who could afford it were equally servile to metro-politan 'standards'; one merchant sent his watch to be cleaned in England. Virginian planters modelled their habits and ideas on those of the area round London, which they considered their 'home', despising Bristol, Scotland, and other provincial parts of Britain. They, and their blacks, spoke extremely 'pure' English, with no trace of a regional accent – as, it seems, did refined Philadelphia circles.[209]

But the Scotch-Irish and German presence was waxing yearly, and slave numbers were running into hundreds of thousands. The colonies were ceasing to be more or less wholly English in speech and in origin, and Franklin disliked this vociferously. At the mid-century he, like his fellow colonials, had no idea of a wholly novel 'American' identity. They had no bards to sing about such a fancy. Colonials were preoccupied with the business of getting on. Such cultural excellence as they displayed was, like Franklin's, dedicated to practical matters and to observation of Nature's material phenomena. They produced no distinctive creative writing. Before the 1760s, they found no spokesman to spell out grievances against Britain who was remotely comparable in passion and power to the great Irishman, Jonathan Swift. And Swift's bitter writings found few colonial readers. The facts of life in thriving America contradicted his innate pessimism. Colonists there had no causes for complaint which were as urgent as those of Ireland.

VIII

Ireland was an extremely unhappy country in the second and third decades of the eighteenth century. Others besides Ulstermen were hurt as the long leases of the 1690s fell in, as harvest failures were frequent, and as the short upsurge of agricultural prices aggravated all problems. William III had given vast estates to his favourites. George I and George II both gave pensions to their mistresses drawn from the Irish revenues. The London regime gave an Irish peerage, an Irish estate, an Irish pension, as usual rewards for political and military service. (There were nearly fifty holders of Irish titles who had in fact no land in the country.)

Since most new, and many old, owners lived all or most of the year in England, capital drained from the poorer island. An estimate of 1729 showed, beside £300,000 a year paid out of Irish taxation to English holders of Irish office or pensions, a further £300,000 going to some fifty-four peers and eighty-three other wealthy absentee owners. Such payments were not taxed. The absentees contributed nothing towards the expenses of the Dublin government, and their suction gave Ireland a difficult balance of payments problem. Since rents rose fast — Lord Rockingham's income from his many acres increased from a little over £5,000 to nearly £18,000 in sixty years from 1724 — the well-fed absentee felt under no pressure to 'improve' his Irish lands or to concern himself with his tenants' condition. In G. E. Mingay's words, such men saw Ireland as 'a subordinate province or colony' and assumed that they 'drew their revenue by right of conquest over an alien people'.[210]

The effects on agricultural standards were deplorable. An Act of 1695 had eliminated the customary rights of tenants of confiscated lands. Most English tenants held their lands 'at will', but in practice they were given security by various conventions. In Ireland such conventions rarely arose. The sitting tenant could not expect preference when a farm was re-let; a Catholic would very often be turned out in favour of a Protestant. Hence there was no point in trying to farm well, or to improve the property. Meanwhile, the absentee, to save himself bother, commonly let large tracts of land on long leases to 'middlemen', sometimes themselves absentees, who in turn had recourse to under-agents and stewards. These in turn employed bailiffs, petty despots, to wring profit from helpless papist tenants living on very small parcels of land for which they paid the highest conceivable rents.

The local agents of distant landlords swelled a notorious class of quarrelsome squireens. Like any parasite class in an undeveloped country, they revelled in exceptional freedoms. Servants' wages cost next to nothing. Provisions were very cheap. There were fine local horses to hunt with and race. Swift's friend Lord Orrery, though Anglo-Irish himself, found even the famous hospitality horrible. 'Drunkenness is the touchstone by which they try every man, and he that cannot or will not drink, has a Mark set upon him.' The Protestant roisterer, he reported, would toast 'the glorious and immortal memory of King William in a bumper without any other joy in the Revolution than that it has given him a pretence to drink so many more daily quarts of wine. The person who refuses a goblet to this prevailing toast is deemed a Jacobite, a Papist and a knave.'[211]

Great parts of the island looked, and were, ruined. There were many actual ruins — 'broken abbeys, roofless churches, battered castles, burnt houses, deserted villages ... ' The cabins of the poor were famous for their decrepitude. They were commonly made of sods and mud, thatched with bracken or furze or fern, chimneyless, full of choking smoke. Livestock still shared such quarters with man, wife and children. 'A cabin with no place to sit down,' the Gaelic poet Brian Merriman would write:

> But dripping soot from above and oozings from below,
> No end of weeds growing riotously,
> And the scrapings of hens across it,
> Its roof tree sagging, its couples bending
> And brown rain falling heavily.[212]

The roads teemed with beggars, many of them blind. In the seventeenth century, the lives of the Irish poor had not been obviously harder than those of many in England. Now the growing contrast invited sensitive men to compare the condition of the poor Gaels with that of blacks in the West Indies. ' ... The poor people in Ireland,' Lord Chesterfield wrote of the 1740s, 'are used worse than negroes by their lords and masters, and their deputies of deputies of deputies.' An anonymous writer of 1757 described the peasant as a 'slave' whose labour propped up 'the idleness, perhaps, of twenty superiors', and alleged that 'more than two thirds parts' of the immediate landholders had barely enough food 'to support the day's fatigue'.[213]

As in Jamaica, the 'Big House' dominated the landscape. In some parts of the remote and mountainous west, where Gaelic Catholics of old lineage had hung on to some land, bonds between gentry and commons might be traditional, strong and affectionate. The landlord would talk English to visitors, but he could use Gaelic with his own people. The secret economy of the smugglers who naturally favoured the rugged Irish coasts brought wine and brandy from France, and friars and soldiers slipped in from the Continent with news of relatives serving in armies abroad. The exploits of the Irish Brigade were toasted. The work of the Gaelic poet still had its natural setting.

People from settler families, even Protestants, were not always aloof from

Gaelic culture. Slaves influenced planter habits in the New World; likewise Ireland had always seduced its conquerors. 'English' children learnt Gaelic from their nurses. Gentry needed it to direct their workmen. Arthur Young in the 1770s would find English spoken without admixture of Gaelic only in Dublin and in some parts of Wexford.

Yet he would also emphasise the cruelty of social relations. 'The landlord of an Irish estate, inhabited by Roman catholics is a sort of despot who yields obediance in whatever concerns the poor, to no law but that of his will.' Such a member of the Protestant Ascendancy could 'scarcely invent an order' which a servant, labourer or cottier would dare to refuse to carry out. He could use his cane or his whip on anyone answering back with as little fear of punishment as Sir Charles Price. ' ... A poor man would have his bones broke if he offered to lift his hand in his own defence. Knocking down is spoken of in the country in a manner that makes an English man stare. Landlords of consequence have assured me that many of their cottars would think themselves honoured by having their wives and daughters sent for to the bed of the master ... It must strike the most careless traveller to see whole strings of cars whipped into a ditch by a gentleman's footman to make way for his carriage; if they are over-turned or broken in pieces, no matter, it is taken in patience, were they to complain they would perhaps be horsewhipped.'[214]

And the cottier's life at subsistence level was also endured patiently, with the help of the tuber which God had given His island. Archbishop King of Dublin reported in 1717 that 'One half of the people of Ireland eat neither bread nor flesh for one half of the year, nor wear shoes or stockings ... '[215] But by this time, the words 'Irish' and 'potato' already fitted together as naturally as 'Virginia' and 'tobacco', while the crop was still almost unknown in Scotland and hardly used in England except in the north. The potato adapted well to poor bog lands. It was easy to cook on the customary cauldron over the traditional peat fire; it could be stored through the hungry winter; it was not hard to cultivate with simple peasant tools. On one Irish acre (equalling 1.6 English) a man could grow enough for a family of six to subsist on.

But the poor also ate grain. Ireland was normally more than self-sufficient in oats, its main food cereal. The very poor relied on oatmeal from the spring onwards after the store of potatoes had run out. At this stage in Irish history, famine only came when harvests failed in other countries and grain could not be imported. But strike it did, long after England and even Scotland had ceased to know it. A disastrous harvest in 1728 brought famine to many parts of the island. In 1740–1, deaths may have reached 200,000 or even 400,000. 'Want and misery are in every face, the rich unable to relieve the poor, the roads spread with dead and dying bodies, mankind the colour of the dock and nettles they feed on ... '[216]

Such was the Ireland to which, as his native land, Jonathan Swift came reluctantly back in 1713, Dean of St Patrick's Cathedral, Dublin, to be confined there for life by the utter defeat of his English tory patrons. His never-equalled gifts as pamphleteer found scope as economic and other issues, from 1719 to 1725, brought a new phase of constitutional conflict between the Irish and British Parliaments.

The subservience of the Dublin Commons was usually not too difficult to secure. As at Westminster, patrons controlled representation. There was no Act ensuring regular elections, so one sufficed for George I's reign, and one parliament only sat through the 33-year reign of George II. The Irish Commons had no control over the Dublin executive, made and unmade no ministries, had no settled party divisions or coherent 'Country' opposition. Yet the British Parliament managed, for a few years, to unite this caucus of toadies and squires against it in a precocious outburst of 'patriotism'. A disputant in an Irish lawsuit appealed, with success, to the Irish House of Lords. His opponent appealed to the House of Lords at Westminster, which decided in his favour. The Irish Lords refused to execute the decision and insisted on their right to final jurisdiction in their own island. The British Parliament, in 1719, retorted with an Act declaring that it could bind the Irish with whatever laws and judgments it pleased. Though this was no more than an emphatic re-statement, the 'Declaratory Act' was enough to incense every Protestant in Ireland. Political differences were submerged in a common 'cry of Independency'. Archbishop King, erstwhile an eager whig, had even before this concluded that 'As to Oppressing Ireland, a Whigge and Tory Parlement and Ministry are much at one', and found himself in the same camp as Swift, who launched himself into Irish politics with an anonymous pamphlet proposing a boycott of English imports and arguing that Westminster's mercantilist policies were responsible for Irish poverty. When the government prosecuted the printer, a jury, despite severe pressure, refused to convict him.[217]

The ground was prepared for the struggle over 'Wood's halfpence'. Ireland was offered a favour denied to the American colonies, but in such a manner that England received no credit. The island was chronically short of coin of small values. In 1722 the King's mistress, the Duchess of Kendal, was granted a patent to issue copper coin to the total of over £100,000. She sold it to a Midlands ironmaster named William Wood. No one in Ireland had been consulted. The vast sum Wood was to coin, the vast profit he was to make and the necessity for so many halfpence – why not, Archbishop King asked, sixpence, halfcrowns and so on? – were all violently questionable. As the coins arrived, many refused to accept them. The Dublin Parliament drew up angry protests. As furore followed, Walpole's miscalculations, and Wood's own insolence, gave Swift his chance to make the debate unforgettable. The newly-appointed primate of the Church of Ireland, Boulter, marvelled that 'people of every religion, country and party here, are alike set against Wood's halfpence ... '[218] Even the Irish Privy Council would not comply with Walpole's government.

Swift, inventing a low-born opponent for the plebeian Wood, launched the first of his 'Drapier's Letters', purportedly by a Dublin tradesman, in March 1724. He averred that the Irish were paying £90,000 of good gold and silver for coins so small and of such base metal, that they were really worth no more than £9,000. He pictured Conolly, the immensely rich Speaker of the Irish Commons, sending 'Two Hundred and Forty Horses' to bring up his half-year's rental in halfpence. He called 'stand to it One and All, refuse this Filthy Trash.' Swift moved on, in his fourth 'Letter', to seditious animadversions on the constitutional ties between Ireland and Britain, and though the new viceroy, Carteret, was a friend of his, the authorities could not forbear to offer a £300 reward to anyone who would reveal the author's identity. The secret was in fact perfectly open, but in words of Scripture much quoted at this time, 'the people rescued Jonathan and he died not.' A jury refused to find a true bill against his printer. Before long, the government had to capitulate. In September 1725 the Irish Parliament was told that Wood's patent had been ended. But the ironmaster ('Brazier', Swift had called him) privately had the last laugh; Wood was compensated with a pension of £24,000 issued to a fictitious Thomas Uvedale Esq., and drawn from the public funds of Ireland.[219]

Though his birthday was hailed in Dublin with bells and bonfires, Swift despised even Protestant Ireland:

> Remove me from this land of slaves
> Where all are fools, and all are knaves
> Where every knave & fool is bought
> Yet kindly sells himself for nought.

But he spoke out for Protestant Irish grievances in a stream of further tracts. Why did the Navigation Acts prevent Ireland from exporting her produce and wares wherever she pleased? Why were men born in Ireland overlooked for office in Church and State in favour of Englishmen? Why were the Irish revenues decanted to bribe English politicians? 'One third Part of the Rents of *Ireland* is spent in England; which, with the Profit of Employments, Pensions, Appeals, Journeys of Pleasure or Health, Education at the *Inns* of Court, and both Universities, Remittances at Pleasure, the Pay of all Superior Officers in the Army, and other Incidents, will amount to a full half of the Income of the whole Kingdom, all clear Profit to *England*.'[220]

Swift was a favourite and spokesman of the poor weavers in Dublin amongst whose dwellings his own deanery was set. His compassion took the application of his writings beyond the narrow self-interest of the Ascendancy class. His 'Modest Proposal for Preventing the Children of poor People in *Ireland*, from being a Burden to their Parents, or Country, and for making them Beneficial to the Publick' forks with appalling ferocity at the rooting assumptions of Whiggery, Money, Property and Commerce. The Irish economy was so weak that 120,000 children born annually must become beggars or thieves. But why not breed babies for the table? — 'a young healthy Child, well nursed, is, at a

Year old a most delicious nourishing and wholesome Food, whether *Stewed, Roasted, Baked,* or *Boiled*; and I make no doubt, that it will equally serve in a *Fricasie,* or a Ragoust.' Children would be a food 'very *proper for Landlords,* who, as they have already devoured most of the Parents, seem to have the best Title to the Children', while England, Swift suggested, would gladly eat up the whole Irish nation – without salt. Swift deftly parodied Petty's 'political arithmetic' and took the logic of the slave trade only a bare step further. His later 'proposal', that the whole of Ireland should be turned into a single sheepwalk, to be managed by 67,200 graziers, hardly exaggerated views formerly held by Petty and other Englishmen, and anticipated rather exactly the future advance of capitalism in the Scottish Highlands.[221]

But the prophet was not fully understood in his own country, and Swift's moral victory over Wood's halfpence soon counted for little enough. A resentful Walpole made sure that less patronage went to natives of Ireland. The administration and Church became increasingly alien. Archbishop Boulter was the main whig catspaw; as soon as he heard that a judge or bishop was ill, he would write in haste to warn Westminster not to appoint a 'native' replacement and to suggest a candidate of his own. The Lord Lieutenant was now as a rule nonresident. This lucrative office was bestowed on discarded whig politicians or on noblemen down on their luck – as one contemporary put it, 'the indigence of Ireland was considered as the appropriated fund to compensate the losses of the gaming table.'[222] Many important Irish Protestant families found themselves shut out of office. Swift's rhetoric lodged in their minds. One day Anglo-Irish landowners would mouth again the language of resentment and 'patriotism'. For the time being, however, quiet returned. The Dublin Commons was 'managed' for the London government by a group of local politicians who received coveted posts and dealt out spoonfuls from the jampot of patronage. Henry Boyle, Speaker of the Commons for twenty-three years from 1733, was the most powerful of these 'undertakers'. The Irish Assembly had its conceit, flattered by the erection on College Green of an opulent new Parliament House, started in 1728.

Other imposing buildings came to grace the capital, giving Dublin its stilldelightful eighteenth-century character. They reflected an improvement in the general economy which made the grievances of the rich easy to bear and so deprived the poor of spokesmen. With its university, three good theatres, and fine musical life (Handel's *Messiah* had its première here) Dublin was lively enough for its resident upper and middle classes. It had 200,000 people by the end of the century. The city dominated Irish trade, collecting over half the revenue from imports and exports. Britain, of course, was Ireland's main trading partner, and Dublin was the chief port in dealings with Britain.

By the 1730s, Irish exports were surging upwards, and linen led the rise. 'The Irish linen industry was perhaps the most remarkable instance in Europe of an export-based advance in the eighteenth century.' The chief centres, in Ulster, still relied on Dublin for their working capital, and that city handled most of their products. In 1698, Ireland had exported less than half a million yards of linen; by the 1790s the figure would be over forty million yards annually.[223] Even in Ulster, Catholics had their share of the weaving, and the spread of the industry did a little to relieve the poverty of smallholders in other parts of the island.

Cork, somewhat over a third the size of Dublin, looked, by contrast, outward across the ocean. Irish beef gave the town importance to the entire Atlantic economy. Between 1727 and 1741, French mercantilism relaxed so far as to permit vessels bound for the New World to call at Irish ports to load beef. Exports boomed as the French expanded their sugar plantations in St Domingue. And in 1739 the call of the English woollen industry compelled the repeal of import duties on yarn from Ireland, so that for a while spinning supplemented the incomes of landless labourers in the south-west.

So the Irish economy was on the upswing from the 1730s. Dublin government action often aimed directly at stimulating it. The landed men in Parliament had a direct interest in the extension of cottage industries on their estates, and the Linen Board established in 1711 worked usefully to develop weaving. An Act of 1730 appointed four 'Commissioners of Navigation', and a canal from Newry to Lough Neagh was soon put under construction in the vain belief that supplies from deposits in County Tyrone could break the English monopoly in coal. The Grand Canal between Dublin and the Shannon followed (1756–1804). The 1730s and 1740s were periods of rapid roadbuilding, and the excellence of the Irish highways would be much admired later in the century. Internal trade increased, inland towns grew, though slowly.

Inevitably, a Catholic middle class grew as fast as industry and trade. Able papists, barred from the professions and from government, and hard-pressed to operate as landowners, gravitated, like Jews and English Dissenters, into commerce, and as early as 1718 Archbishop King was complaining that they had 'engrossed almost all the trade of the kingdom'. The wealth which was gradually amassed among them made the Penal Code seem more and more archaic and ridiculous, even to intelligent Protestants. There was toleration of papistry, up to a point. Under an Act of 1703, more than 1,000 secular pirests had been registered and given legally recognised status, but bishops, along with regular clergy, were banished, so that in theory no new ordinations were possible. In 1719 the Irish Privy Council tried to enact that illicit priests should be castrated, but English ministers insisted that branding on the cheek with a red hot iron must be sufficient.[224] In practice, however, unregistered clergy managed to operate, and new recruits were smuggled in from abroad.

The established Church of Ireland was infiltrated, like other denominations, by coolness, tolerance, scepticism and politeness. One of its bishops was Berkeley, the famous philosopher, who asked in a work of 1749, 'Why should disputes about faith interrupt the duties of civil life? or the different roads to Heaven prevent our taking the same steps on earth?' The Penal Code relaxed as Protestant fervour waned. But there were still no papist churches. People worshipped in barns, in houses, and in the open air. One Sunday an Anglican observed 'several hundred people' attending Mass on a mountainside in Donegal. Andrew Campbell, illegal Catholic Bishop of Kilmore from 1753, could only travel among his flock in the guise of a bagpiper and hold confirmations for children secretly at fairs.[225] So the Penal Code, indirectly, and paradoxically, reinforced Catholicism in Ireland, creating a special, perhaps unique, closeness between the priests and the folk who protected them.

In 1732 there were, in spite of the laws, 51 friaries, 9 nunneries and at least 549 popish schools, according to an official report. These last were in no way weakened by the foundation, from 1733, of Protestant 'Charter Schools' by voluntary subscription, supported also by public funds, and aimed at rescuing children of the 'poor natives' from 'ignorance, superstition and idolatry' by instruction in the 'English tongue and manners, and the Protestant religion'. They spread widely, but their obvious propagandist intent alienated the people from them, their management was as bungling and corrupt as that of many eighteenth-century institutions, and they dwindled on with the most ignominious of reputations. That Irish labourers could strike judicious observers as better educated than their English counterparts must be attributed to the 'hedge schools', meeting in huts or in barns or in ditches, where children of poor parents could acquire literacy, and even Latin.[226]

L. M. Cullen has recently argued a strong case which makes the mid-eighteenth century seem, as Irish history goes, a prosperous interlude. 'Under the penal laws the rent of land let to a Catholic was to be not less than two-thirds of the annual value of the property leased. In fact, this was unenforceable. Otherwise the substantial investment by Catholics in livestock in grazing and dairying districts could not have taken place.' The restriction of leases to Catholics to thirty-one years mainly affected the well-to-do. While the old dispossessed proprietors saw any lease at all as a symbol of confiscation, to lesser countrymen it represented a measure of comfort and security. The worst excesses of the middleman class were not general outside the bitterly poor south-west.[227]

The famine in 1740–1 was not soon repeated. Irish population rose from something like 2½ million in 1700 to 4 million in 1780. It is true that the upward movement was world-wide; but in the late nineteenth century, Ireland would show how one country might lose people steadily while the rest of Europe trended quite otherwise. Though the Irish cultivator under George II was generally far worse off than his English counterpart, conditions were not absolutely so bad as they later became. Absenteeism actually diminished; 'Between the 1720s and 1770s the rent roll of Irish landlords perhaps trebled. Rents to absentees doubled.' And some absentees were among those landlords who showed zeal for 'improvement'. Ireland, moreover, was uncannily peaceful. Protestant hotheads who might have caused trouble left Ulster, as we have seen, in spate. The 'rapparees', successors to the 'tories', found plenty of scope in the mountains and bogs of the west, but after the 'Houghers' who terrorised Connacht in 1711–13, destroying cattle and sheep in protest against the extension of pasture, there was no violent movement of agrarian defiance for half a century. All countrymen, Protestants as well as papists, large farmers as well as smallholders, grumbled against the tithes paid to the Church of Ireland clergymen. Otherwise, the people seemed lost for a grievance. Exports rose from £992,832 in 1730 to £1,862,834 in 1750. Over the whole century, they multiplied six times in value.[228]

A modern visitor to Dublin sees in its fine buildings signs of an eighteenth-century heyday. Yet what, he asks himself, did this culture produce? The Georgian paintings by local hands in the art gallery are at best engagingly derivative. Apart from Swift, the most famous native writers – Goldsmith, Burke, Sheridan – flourished not in Dublin but in London, and as a distinguished and sympathetic student of eighteenth-century Anglo-Irish culture has recently acknowledged, 'Their writings show no common stamp of a distinctively national character.'[229] How was it that mounting prosperity in Ireland brought so little glory to that country itself? Why was Dublin more provincial, in certain respects, than Philadelphia, Cork a less vital town intellectually than Newport, Rhode Island? Proximity to England is not the only answer. We must look to the divisions among the island's people. Catholic Ireland, in close touch with Europe, received not the brave new ideas of the Enlightenment but, from its clergy, the counter-arguments to them. Its horizons were narrowed by its cherished priests. Its Gaelic poetry took on during this century an increasingly more democratic character, escaping from parasitism upon a dying aristocracy. But though some Protestant gentlemen went to the funeral of the famous blind Connacht poet Carolan in 1738, and others began to take a genteel proto-Romantic interest in Irish scenery and in native antiquities, the culture of the Ascendancy stood remote from that of the Catholic masses. *Pace* Yeats, it drew no strength from the soil. Serious thinking would undermine its cause, by showing its life-style to be unjust. Its favourite art-forms were architecture and oratory. Like the style of its grander country houses, rhetoric dressed with classical dignity its ignoble rootless provincialism. Trinity College, Dublin, with its fine new buildings, lagged intellectually far behind the University of Edinburgh for all the barebones scruffiness which the latter's premises shared with the rest of that surprising northern city.

IX

Adam Ferguson (1723–1816), one of Edinburgh's intellectual luminaries, would illustrate the differences in tone between Scottish and Irish culture by his deprecation of Europe's obsession with the 'grammar of dead languages' and with 'beauties of thought and elocution' now remote from the active and vivid life of the Greeks and Romans whence they had sprung.[230] Never, anywhere, have remarkable collective experiences found better match in fresh and radical theory than in the Scotland of Ferguson's long lifetime. A Highlander, he stood on a cultural watershed, regretting the loss of the heroic virtues found among 'primitive' peoples like his own as commercialism surged forward, yet extolling the struggle and energy which now drove man on.

In Lowland Scotland likewise, the casualties of historical advance had seemed to many immense and insufferable. The aristocracy largely favoured the Episcopalian Church which had gone down in defeat in 1689–90 and which was now deeply involved with Jacobite intrigues. Jacobitism, both hardline and sentimental, had become a focus of patriotic feeling; the cause of the Stuarts was rather perversely equated with Scotland's nationhood lost at the Union. 'Cameronians', ultra-Presbyterians, also regretted that event – Patrick Walker, for instance, who wrote in the 1720s of 'the Scots blood gone out of our veins, honesty out of our hearts, and zeal off our spirits; and the English abominations drunk in as sweet wine with pleasure...' But Walker's chapbook lives of his heroes, the Covenanting martyrs and prophets, joined the folk songs and old poems now collected and published by Allan Ramsay amongst the elements making for cultural continuity. Just before the Union, Fletcher of Saltoun had written that 'if a man were permitted to make all the ballads, he need not care who should make the laws of a nation.'[231] Old ballads were still sung; new songs were written, and so traditional stories of feudal violence persisted alongside those of a persecuted Kirk to give Lowland Scottish culture a flavour still unique, as different strains in the country's historical heritage worked with amazing speed towards modernisation.

An intellectual dawning had begun among 'landed' and 'professional' classes in the late seventeenth century. In practice, in Scotland as in Virginia, the two classes were hard to distinguish. Lawyers were drawn overwhelmingly from the landowning class. Because Roman Law was at the basis of Scots Law, and this was to be studied on the Continent, not in England, many young men went for training to France and Holland, where they were exposed to the best Continental thinking. They were also, of course, in touch with the best English thought. From the study of the law branched interests in moral philosophy and in political science; in 1719 the Faculty of Advocates sponsored the appointment of a lawyer as first Professor of Civil History in the University of Edinburgh. That institution and its Glasgow counterpart hummed with advanced European ideas, and by the 1720s their students were outraging staunch old-time Presbyterians by their freedom of thought.

Fresh thinking among men of high status met and meshed with growing demand from the townsmen and even the country people for education. Though the ambition to see a gifted son in the pulpit was still strong, more practical preoccupations had welled up along with that avid interest in commerce and expansion which had produced the Darien débâcle. As in Franklin's

Philadelphia, such subjects as navigation, book-keeping, geography, modern languages, medicine, seemed roads to prosperity. The striving of Scottish surgeons in the employ of the Royal African Company and the East India Company anticipated the rise from the 1720s of the Edinburgh Medical School to international pre-eminence. In England the 'modern' curriculum, as distinct from the classics, was left to the Dissenters in their famous Academies, and to private initiative generally; the ancient Universities eschewed it. In Scotland, free enterprise raced with official action by universities and town councils. With medicine, science was welcomed into the highest planes of education, and the Knoxian tradition opened these altitudes to others besides gentlemen. The idea gained ground that even classical scholars should have training in practical subjects. Teachers at all levels competed for pupils; the earnings of professors as well as dominies depended on the classes they could attract. Since Kirk sessions and town councils fixed on the lowest possible fees in the schools they provided, so as to give the able poor the greatest possible chance, and since inflation ate these away as the century progressed, masters were spurred to keep up their incomes by teaching, cheaply, the practical subjects demanded by traders, farmers and even landowners for their sons.

In 1752 a minister of the Kirk could be heard announcing, ' ... In proportion as the scale of science rises or falls, that of the kingdom rises or falls with it.' The old religious zeal for education modulated so that learning itself became a kind of religion. By the mid-century, almost everyone in the Lowlands seems to have been able to read and write. Very few other cultures could then match this achievement, though Calvinist New England was one competitor. Parents were glad to pay for their children's instruction and private 'adventure' schools supplemented those offered by the parishes. The Lowland peasant, it has been observed, 'was not merely able to read, but apparently loved reading'.[232]

His zeal for self-improvement marched with the drive of Lowland landowners to catch up with England. To crave assimilation was an expression of patriotism. Economically, Scotland seemed plainly inferior. An English sojourner of the 1720s could sneer, 'A pedling Shop-keeper, that sells a Pennyworth of Thread, is a *Merchant* ... an enclosed Field of Two Acres is a *Park*; and the Wife of a Laird of fifteen pounds a Year is a Lady ... '[233] Such taunts must be rendered impossible. The most gifted Scots of the day shared the common inferiority complex. Robert Adam, the architect, who migrated to England, told his sister that he thought it a pity that 'such a genius 'as himself 'should be thrown away upon Scotland where scarce will ever happen an opportunity of putting one noble thought in execution.' The great philosopher David Hume remarked in a letter to Adam Smith, the founder of economics, 'Scotland is too narrow a place for me.' We can now see that it must have had breadth to hold both of them; yet Hume shared in the general, abject contempt of the middle and upper classes for their own Scottish accent, and he strove to eliminate Scottish turns of phrase from his writings. Such men ardently wished that the English would accept them as fellow 'Britons'. James Thomson, the major Scottish poet, another migrant to England, wrote 'Rule, Britannia!' But the many displays of English prejudice, ranging from cheap jokes to violence, often spun Scots away rebuffed. Hume, feeling slighted, sneered at 'Barbarians who inhabit the Banks of the Thames.'[234] Scots, unable to consummate the Union as they wished, tried harder than ever to surpass the southrons.

The way in which Scotland was now governed gave them room to do so. N. T. Phillipson characterises its position as being, like that of the American colonies, one of 'semi independence'. Draft legislation about Scottish affairs was generally vetted by Scottish lawyers in Scotland. Though Walpole brought Scottish patronage firmly under the British Treasury, the few Englishmen given posts north of the Border were greatly outnumbered by Scots preferred to positions in England. There was a kind of implicit bargain (sweetened, as we have seen, by colonial and East India patronage) whereby Scottish M.P.s and peers propped up Walpole and his cronies with their votes, but the Scottish 'managers' controlled their own patch. Two factions of Scottish whigs contended over the spoils, the old 'Squadrone' versus the grouping, largely Campbell, which was led by the Duke of Argyll ('Red John of the Battles') and his brother Archibald, Lord Islay. The 'Shawfield Riots' in Glasgow against Walpole's Malt Tax made Scotland, in 1725, seem close to rebellion. In their wake, the 'Squadrone' Secretary of State for Scotland was deposed, and his post was not filled again. Walpole relied on the Campbell brothers. Islay would earn the nickname 'King of Scotland', though he exercised his strength discreetly. ' ... Slow, steady, [and] revengeful', Horace Walpole would call him. 'He loved power too well to hazard it by ostentation, and money so little, that he neither spared it to gain friends or to serve them.' He worried over minute matters of patronage and managed elections by skilful horsetrading; the Duke of Newcastle, who could appreciate such skills, saw Islay as 'the absolute Governor of one of His Majesty's Kingdoms'.[235] He was too astute to create an exclusionist 'in' faction. A gifted outsider need not appeal to him in vain. In his dark and devious mode, he can even be styled a Scots patriot. His brother, an impulsive and generous man, certainly stood forth in that role to effect. Argyll displayed his independence in 1733 by voting against Walpole over the excise, and had to be won back by offers of fresh preferment. As Campbell chief, he had the reflexes of an independent potentate, and over the famous 'Porteous Riots' he made himself spokesman for Scotland's honour.

The riot arose from Scotland's extreme addiction to smuggling. In 1736, after the execution of a smuggler, an Edinburgh 'mob' threatened Porteous, the captain of the City Guard, who ordered his men to fire. Several people were killed. Porteous was tried and condemned, but during six weeks' respite given to him, the well-disciplined 'mob' took over the city, forced the prison, and lynched him. Despite Argyll's protests in the House of Lords, Scotland's capital city was fined and its provost deposed.

Yet, as a rule, Lowland Scotland, after the Union, was the section of the empire which gave Westminster and Whitehall least trouble. The myth that the Scots are a naturally radical people is not borne out by the eighteenth-century record. One exception proves the rule. In 1724 there was a brief revolt of hundreds of so-called 'Levellers' in the old Covenanting strongholds of the south-west, a reaction against evictions and enclosures by landlords enlarging their stock farms to profit from the thriving trade in cattle with England. After dykes had been overthrown and cattle killed and maimed, six troops of dragoons were sent in. But this outbreak was never matched elsewhere. Lowland Scots in general seem to have accepted, even with gratitude, the ending of traditional ways of life. The anti-paternalist strain which had emerged with the Cameronians expressed itself fanglessly in schisms within the Kirk, creating a sizeable body of 'dissenters'. But a quasi-feudal respect for lairds still prevailed, and helped them transform the country's agriculture.

Scottish lairds were distinguished sharply from English gentry by their relative poverty, made worse by the Darien disaster. Grand Tours were out of the question; even London or Bath outpaced their means. They stayed in their bleak homeland and made Edinburgh their social centre. The place was little more than a grotesque procession of huge tenement buildings down the spine of its Castle Hill, and in an age of filthy cities it was notorious for its slovenliness. But the taste for new ideas was becoming as strong as the passion for claret. Lowland landowners, conscious now of a novel unity, which was cemented by jealousy of the English, turned their minds to making Scotland prosperous.

The economy had not flourished as had been promised. Around 1730, a devoted Hanoverian and Unionist, Clerk of Penicuik, still had to argue defensively – things were much the same as before 1707, they hadn't got any worse. Some direct benefit was seen from 1727 when the 'Equivalent' bargained for in the treaty was at last extracted from 'British' funds; it came to provide a steady income for the new Board of Trustees for Fisheries and Manufactures, which strove to promote the linen industry, already important but lagging behind Ireland's. Scottish scientists were encouraged to help with the industry's problems, growers of flax were subsidised, foreign craftsmen were brought in to teach the natives, 'factory' methods were pioneered. But there was no great headway in this field until the 1740s.[236] Before that, some landowners had begun to make revolution.

England had no 'agricultural revolution'. The term is misapplied to a country where novel techniques came in gradually from the seventeenth century onwards. But it suits eighteenth-century Scotland. The rallying cry of the revolutionaries was 'improvement'. Their new methods were called 'English husbandry'. Notable early 'improvers' tended to be more idealistic than businesslike. They were patriots with a vision which more and more of their countrymen came to share and which embraced, as well as new crops and tools, manufacturing, schooling and the reform of manners. What they launched was, in effect, a movement for self-colonisation.

As in England, the old communal methods of cultivation must go. Capitalist farmers must emerge with consolidated holdings. So fewer tenants could hold land, yet remodelled farms would produce more food. To meet the twin problems of surplus produce and surplus people, the improving laird conceived the planned village. Scotland, outside the Lothians, lacked villages of the English type. Country people were scattered in hamlets. A movement began to create villages. It is reckoned that in the century after 1745 no fewer than 150 were made. Eventually most parts of Scotland would be affected. The Duke of Perth pioneered in the Highlands, laying out Callender and Crieff in the early 1730s. John Cockburn in the Lothians created, from 1738, a more accessible model at Ormiston. Within a couple of years, a contemporary was writing of the place with excitement, 'His toun is riseing exceedingly ... ' Besides blacksmiths and shoemakers, candlemakers and bakers and maltsters, Cockburn had forty linen looms with weavers to work them, ten spinners providing yarn for each weaver. So much work was offered that there was 'not a boy or a girel of 7 years old' but was busy — 'ye will not see ane in the toun except in ane hour of play.'[237] This was the impression of industrious thriving which later improvers would strive to create. As at Ormiston, new geometrical nicety would rebuke the haphazard character of the old hamlet. The laird would provide attractive stone houses of two or three storeys, with front doors opening directly on to the pavement so as to check the habit of piling midden heaps before dwellings. He would seek to let houses or feus, not only to his own people displaced by enclosure, but also to respectable skilled men from outside. Industries would be projected from the outset — textiles above all, brewing, distilling. The village was to become a centre of education, to have a refining effect on the vicinity, introducing new habits of consumption, selling tea to rustic wives.

Cockburn was harbinger of changes which would rush to a head later in the century, preached and pushed forward by clergymen, hailed, if sometimes uneasily, by intellectuals. The titles of the master works of the 'Scottish Enlightenment' suggest the struggle of brilliant men to come to terms with the time's divisions as they experienced them in person: Francis Hutcheson's *System of Moral Philosophy* (published posthumously in 1755); Hume's *Treatise of Human Nature* (1739–40) and *History of Great Britain* (1754–63); Ferguson's *Essay on the History of Civil Society* (1767) and Adam Smith's *Wealth of Nations* (1776). 'These thinkers', Duncan Forbes writes, 'were primarily humanists and moralists, but as such they were deeply concerned with the nature of that commercial civilisation which had begun to change the face of Scotland so dramatically, for better and for worse.' Ferguson would regret that in the capitalist world 'man is sometimes found a detached and a solitary being: he has found an object which sets him in competition with his fellow creatures, and he deals with them as he does with his cattle and his soil, for the sake of the profits they bring.' Like that of other Scottish philosophers, his thinking emphasises warm counter-values – sympathy, heroism, love of mankind. It was from these scholars that the movement against slavery in the English-speaking countries would receive most of its intellectual energy – almost all the leading Scottish thinkers deplored it. Yet they sought to balance the claims of humanism with those of economic advance. Hume, before his friend Smith, argued for free trade against the mercantilists. The achievements of eighteenth-century Scots which lie at the base of modern understanding in the fields of economics, political science and sociology as well as in history, in psychology and in philosophy proper are, limited (as Sidney Pollard has argued) by their devotion to those boureoisg ideals which produced Adam Smith's implicit assumption that 'every man was by nature a Scotsman on the make'.[238]

An equivalent to the Lowland Scottish self-colonisation of the eighteenth century may be found in the Japanese self-westernisation in the late nineteenth, which was still swifter and equally successful – but the Scots helped to pioneer the industrial revolution which the Japanese adapted wholesale. Meanwhile, Scottish thriving in most parts of the empire suggests a different comparison, with the Jews. The English had plenty of anti-Scottish jibes to match their anti-Semitic ones. In Jamaica, 'Scotch Attorney' or 'Scotchman hugging a Creole' became the local name for a species of vine which twined round the trunks of trees and destroyed them. A writer of 1740 reported that the slaves there correctly held that 'England must be a large Place, and Scotland a small one; for Scots Bacceroes (which they call all white Men) all know one another, but *English Bacceroes no know one another.*' As peasants and ministers collaborated with lairds at home, Scots merchants and professional men carried overseas a precious readiness to help each other out. St Andrew's Clubs sprouted in major American towns. Alexander Hamilton, travelling through the mainland colonies, easily found his fellow countrymen everywhere; thus, the landlady of a tavern in Albany, 'happening to be a Scotswoman, was very civil and obliging to me for country's sake. She made me a present of a dryed tongue.'[239]

Until the 1760s there was little emigration to the New World by Scots people wishing to become farmers, though Scots judges shipped beggars, gypsies and the like to the colonies under indentures, and at least 639 Jacobite rebels, most of them Scots, were transported in 1716. Some pockets of Highland settlement were established; besides the Gaels at 'Darien' in Georgia, a none-too-scrupulous gentleman named Lachlan Campbell brought over some 500 Highlanders to New York colony in the late 1730s.[240] Lowlanders, by contrast, generally went to the colonies as transients, planning to stay for as long as it took them to grow wealthy. There were clusters of Scots merchants in the cities, and, more famously, the Glasgow tobacco men who invaded the colonies on the Chesapeake.

In 1769, Scotland would actually take more imports from Virginia and Maryland than did England. By then it would be rare to find a storekeeper, agent or factor in Virginia who was not a Scot. Their incursion was gradual until the

1740s, rapid thereafter. Illegal traders from Scottish ports had been roaming the Chesapeake for a quarter of a century before the Union. Those who followed after 1707 found London merchants in control of the business of the Tidewater and pushed, with advancing settlement, into the back-country, where they established chains of stores depending on collecting and distributing points in the towns – Richmond, Fredericksburg, Petersburg and so on – which grew up along the fall-line. Meanwhile, they ousted the English from much of the tide-water trade. Their lean and hungry enterprise made them hated and affluent and Glasgow a great and wealthy town. Scottish imports of tobacco, $2\frac{1}{2}$ million lb. a year in 1715, rose to 10 million in 1743 – then, by 1753, to 24 million, and by 1771 to 47 million.[241]

Scots had more than their fair share of colonial patronage. Most of the early missionaries of the Anglican Society for the Propagation of the Gospel seem to have been Scots – by a pleasant irony, the first bishop in English-speaking North America would eventually, in 1784, be consecrated by episcopalian clergy at Aberdeen. The three-quarters of a century after the Union saw some thirty governors and lieutenant governors of Scottish birth appointed in North American colonies, while Jamaica had as many Scots governors as English.[242]

But perhaps the main sphere of distinctive Scottish impact was intellectual and was epitomised by that Dr William Small, Professor of Mathematics and Philosophy in the College of William and Mary, who taught there, around 1760, a young Virginian named Thomas Jefferson. 'It was my great good fortune,' Jefferson wrote later, 'and what probably fixed the destinies of my life ... '[243] Scottish teachers and professional men put North America in touch with the Enlightenment of their own homeland. And Scotland was still the main centre of that Presbyterian creed which was becoming one of the most widespread religions of the mainland colonies.

Romans and Hardy Races

> To overawe, or intimidate, or, when we cannot persuade with
> reason, to resist with fortitude, are the occupations which give its
> most animating exercise, and its greatest triumphs, to a vigorous
> mind; and he who has never struggled with his fellow creatures, is
> a stranger to half the sentiments of mankind ... Sentiments of
> affection and friendship mix with animosity; the active and strenuous
> become the guardians of their society; and violence itself is, in their
> case, an exertion of generosity as well as of courage. We applaud,
> as proceeding from a national or party spirit, what we could not
> endure as the effect of a private dislike; and amidst the competition
> of rival states, think we have found, for the patriot and the warrior,
> in the practice of violence and stratagem, the most illustrious career
> of human virtue.
>
> ADAM FERGUSON[1]

I

The 1730s and 1740s saw the ebullition, in North America and in Britain, of a
movement which conditioned all future events in the Atlantic world. It was led
by young men, some very young indeed. It gave the English-speaking countries
most of their common hymns, learnt by generation after generation of children.
It created modern Wales, bringing religious reformation at last to an inchoate
and backward-looking country. Explosive and partly subversive in itself, it pre-
empted revolution in Great Britain while it prepared bases for revolt in America.
One direct result, over some fifty years, was the creation, in Methodism, of an
important nonconformist denomination. But its first character was ecumenical.
The movement swept across most of the divisions between Protestants, drawing
in Anglicans and Dissenters with others who had known no serious creed.
Calvinist and Arminian believers embraced for a while in the vivid dawnlight
of evangelicalism.

Evangelical Christians laid drastic emphasis on the 'conversion' of the individual and on his personal faith in Christ. They had no taste for the intricate
theological wrangles which had obsessed the seventeenth century. What they
demanded was the experience of passion, despair and joy, gushing tears, a vital
religion, to counter and oust the empty rituals of whiggish Anglicanism and the
tepid restraint of old-fashioned dissent, by the revival of religious awe and the

cultivation of 'enthusiasm'. 'God inside oneself'; we have met this interesting heresy before, in Anne Hutchinson's 'antinomianism' and in the Inner Light revealed by George Fox to the Quakers.

Prototype evangelicals can be detected in the early eighteenth century wherever zeal still ran high among clergy and laity; for instance, amongst the founders of the Society for the Propagation of the Gospel. The characteristic impetus of the movement was in fact missionary, the urge to reach out to the godless — English or Celtic, red, even black — left to their 'ignorance' and 'depravity' by Property and its hard-drinking, pluralist parsons. Before the end of the century, evangelicalism would be giving English-speaking Protestantism its first enduring successes among tropical pagans. But the flashpoint, the real beginning of the movement, came in the mid-1730s as news reached Britain from Massachusetts which inspired serious Anglican clergy and deeply impressed such Dissenting leaders as the hymn-writers Watts and Doddridge.

The state of religion in North America was complex. In 1740, taking all colonies together, 246 Anglican churches were greatly outnumbered by 'dissenting' places of worship — Congregationalist (423), Presbyterian (160), Quaker (approaching 100), and those of the fast rising sect of Baptists (96) whose anti-intellectualism went well with conditions on the frontier where learned preachers were rare, and whose stress on adult conversion (and immersion) suited places where children grew up with little or no religion. There were in addition something over 200 Dutch and German Protestant churches, apart from the European pietist sects. Catholic places of worship were few, something over a score, mostly in Maryland and Pennsylvania, and the groups of Jews in the seaport towns were as yet less prominent than in Jamaica.[2] So America was overwhelmingly Protestant, and the greatest bulk of its religious people were found in Calvinist denominations. New England Congregationalism had, in Connecticut at least, come close to Presbyterianism in form and the two bodies tended to affiliate in self-defence in colonies further south where Anglicanism was established by law.

Even in New England, it seems, not more than one person in seven was now a church member, in the Middle Colonies this was one in fifteen, and further south participation was lower still. Virginia was plagued with drunken, incompetent parsons. In its first eighty years, the Society for the Propagation of the Gospel sent out 309 clergymen, but these made overall little impact. Here was a natural arena for 'revival'. In the 1720s, a smouldering started in the middle colonies. A Scotch-Irish Presbyterian divine, William Tennent, began to train ministers and to demand from them the experience of 'conversion'. His son Gilbert, from 1729, established himself as a great revivalist preacher, a fiery man who scorned polish and gentility. He would soon split the Presbyterian Church with his attacks on 'unconverted' ministers whose dull sermons, he said, proved them worthless.[3]

The Congregational Church in New England, though still established by law, had lost vitality. 'Arminianism' (that is, open-mindedness) had been infecting its intellectuals. The churches had ceased to make rigorous demands of their members, admitting now all whose character was not scandalous and who were ready to go through appropriate motions. As in England itself, doctrine had superseded heart-felt belief. Once the force of complete conviction which had produced the doctrines had faltered and failed, revival could only take shape from deliberate excitement of emotion to the point of ecstatic delusion. There was a basis for outburst in New England in the unsettlement of country people by the decline of the old communal spirit and by the alienating, divisive operations of speculation and commerce.

About 1734, strange things happened in several individual congregations, notably that of Jonathan Edwards at Northampton, Massachusetts. Edwards, the most formidable theologian of his day, was too much an intellectual to be a typical revivalist, but had special stature as a subtle apologist for enthusiasm. A spontaneous mania in his congregation, after a young woman 'of easy ways' had undergone a surprising 'conversion', fed a craze which swept up and down New England's western frontier. After the great surge of emotion, a bitter aftermath set in, marked by suicides among people desponding over the states of their souls. For a few years, revival abated in New England. Initiative shifted to Englishmen and Welshmen.

Two mighty Welsh preachers, both in their early twenties, were launched in 1735 with the separate conversions of Howel Harris and Daniel Rowland. These men combined forces a couple of years later. Meanwhile, Oxford had formed, and Georgia was transforming, the cardinal English evangelists: John Wesley, his younger brother Charles, and George Whitefield.

The Wesleys' High Church, tory father, a zealous parson in that wild country, the Lincolnshire Fens, was greatly drawn to missionary work, and would at one time have been glad to go to the East Indies for the Society for the Propagation of the Gospel. Hence he was naturally an early and eager supporter of the scheme for Georgia colony. John, born in 1703, became a fellow of an Oxford college, and was drawn into the 'Holy Club' founded in 1729 by his brother Charles within that university. So was George Whitefield, son of a tavern-keeper, who supported his studies at Oxford by working as a serving-man. The club, which never had more than twenty-five members, emphasised personal discipline, charity and frugality. John Wesley drew up 'methodical' rules of behaviour, a 'scheme of self-examination' ('Have I prayed with fervour? ... Have I daily used ejaculations? ... Have I been zealous to do and active in doing good? ... ').[4] So the Club's denigrators described it as 'Methodist'. Membership did not imply 'conversion'. Whitefield experienced the joy of 'conversion' in 1735. For the Wesleys, release proved harder. The brothers sailed with Oglethorpe, founder of Georgia, when he returned to his colony late in 1735, eager to minister to debtors and Red Indians. Both were disillusioned. John was unable to start an Indian mission and his prim devotion to

Anglican ritual was not much appreciated in Savannah. Charles became Ogle-thorpe's private secretary, quarrelled strongly with him and left after five months.

Yet Georgia gave the brothers experience and ideas which determined the subsequent character of 'Methodism'. Huge American parishes meant that clergy had to ride almost incessantly from one settlement to another. The idea of the Methodist 'circuit' stems from this. And the colony had attracted a band of Moravians, who influenced the Wesleys profoundly. Moravians stressed the value of hymn-singing; during his stay, John wrote or translated several, and Charles went on to become the most effective hymn-poet in English. John seized on Moravian methods, 'select bands', the 'love feast', and practised them in Savannah, along with such innovations as lay assistants, extempore prayer, extempore preaching. 'It is not too much to claim that in Georgia the main features of Methodist ecclesiastical policy were first outlined.'[5]

'Conversion' came in the aftermath of shame. 'I went to America,' John Wesley cried, 'to convert the Indians; but O! who shall convert me?' A Mora-vian, Peter Böhler, was on hand in London to console both young men. 'Preach faith till you have it,' he said; 'and then because you have it, you will preach faith.' The preacher, once he had tasted the power which came from moving others, could constantly renew his own 'faith' by new experience of the excite-ment of preaching, which in turn renewed and 'converted' his hearers. The problem was to get started. On 21 May 1738 Charles underwent a dramatic 'conversion'. Three days later, John, hearing something by Luther read aloud, 'felt', as he put it, grace for the first time. ' ... I felt my heart strangely warmed. I felt I did trust in Christ, Christ alone for salvation; and an assurance was given me that He had taken away *my* sins, even *mine*, and saved *me* from the law of sin and death.' All sense of strain and effort left him. He found from now on that he was 'always conqueror'.[6] A slight, morose and neurotic young man became the cheerful, unresting leader on horseback who rode and preached his way to the centre of English history.

Whitefield, an even more prodigious traveller, came back to Britain for a short time and began to evangelise round about Bristol, addressing thousands in the open air. In March 1739, John Wesley went down to hear his old friend. Early next month, he began his own career as mass orator there, preaching to some 3,000 in a brickyard. Whitefield was a self-styled 'Calvinist', but admitted that he had not read Calvin, and in practice believed like Wesley that all who came might be saved. Their missions were equally offensive to most of the establishment. 'It is monstrous,' a Duchess complained, 'to be told that you have a heart so sinful as the common wretches that crawl upon the earth.' In the 1740s, the 'Methodists' were smeared with the bogey-word 'Jacobitism'. Magistrates, in some places, permitted riots against them. But where clergymen were slack, where, as in certain industrial areas, population growth had out-moded old parish boundaries, where the unwashed and unwanted were not catered for by the Church of England, Methodism gathered its converts together. Wesley created a mass movement, the first organisation of its kind. Between his conversion and his death in 1791 he preached no fewer than 52,400 times. He would leave behind him a body of 136,000 'people called Methodists' with some seven times as many 'adherents'.[7] The converts were grouped in 'classes' each with its 'leader', while lay 'stewards' managed the movement's temporal affairs. Besides Wesley, other itinerant preachers rode their own 'circuits'.

Though by 1784 he was ordaining clergymen under his own authority and his movement had acquired clearly separate legal status, Wesley thought of himself as an Anglican till his last day. Anglican evangelicalism grew up in free and easy commerce with Methodism. Various ardent Anglican clergymen — amongst them, for instance, Samuel Walker and George Thomson who jointly 'evangelised' Cornwall — were in close, even daily, touch with other revivalists — ordained and un-ordained, beneficed and itinerant, Calvinist and Arminian, dissenters and loyal members of the Church. The tours with which George Whitefield shocked North America into its 'Great Awakening' reached members of every denomination.

His voice was magnificently apt for his purpose. The great actor David Garrick remarked that Whitefield could make an audience weep or tremble merely by pronouncing the word 'Mesopotamia'. He said much about hell fire, he could be heard over vast distances, and almost at will, it seemed, he could send people into fits. They turned pale, they wrung their hands, they flung themselves on their faces, they cried to God for mercy. As the orphanage he had set his sights on rose in the bush near Savannah, he went about raising funds outside Georgia. In 1739–41 he ranged the entire North American seaboard, meeting and encouraging Tennent and Jonathan Edwards, setting other itinerant preachers in motion, spreading hysteria wherever he went, then leaving others to cope with its consequences. Whitefield even dampened the merriment of Charles Town, until, as he noted with pleasure, 'the jewellers and dancing masters' began 'to cry out' that their craft was in danger. Though he soon transferred his energies back to Britain, he returned to America several times to keep 'rebirth' booming, and eventually died there in 1770.[8]

When he first visited Wales, early in 1739, Whitefield was only 24 and the local revivalists who met him, Harris and Rowlands, were 25 and 26 respectively. By the time these men were old, the character of the Welsh people would be well set on the way to transformation. In the 1730s the country, still generally Welsh-speaking, was dominated by not very wealthy, mostly tory, gentry and was infested with Jacobitism. The Society for the Propagation of Christian Knowledge had turned its attention to this near-heathen land, and in the first four decades of the eighteenth century founded almost 100 schools, where instruction was usually in English. One of its teachers was the Reverend Griffith Jones (1683–1761), a shepherd's son who had become a clergyman only with difficulty, and who ran into trouble with the hierarchy for preaching in parishes other than his own, and even in unconsecrated places, as he tried to take Christianity to a people with few parsons. In 1731 Jones launched his own educational campaign, sending out itinerant teachers who would stay for three months in any one place, long enough to teach local children to read. By the time of his death, over 150,000 people had passed through these 'Circulating Schools', besides unregistered adults who came at night; and the movement went on and even grew thereafter.[9] The passion for learning rooted itself.

It was under Jones's ministry that Daniel Rowland experienced 'conversion'. Whitefield himself witnessed Rowland's effect in 1743: 'At seven of the morning have I seen perhaps ten thousand from different parts, in the midst of sermon, crying *Gogunniant – bendyitti* – ready to leap for joy.' While Rowlands was an ordained minister, Howel Harris, a Breconshire schoolteacher, never regularised his position. This little man, who has been called 'the greatest Welshman of his age', exemplified the obsessional 'method' of the revivalists; as his diary shows, he would ask God 'about buying a pair of gloves' and even inquire 'His will if I should take tea'. No scholar, he felt that the substance of his preaching 'was all given unto me in an extraordinary manner, without the least premeditation.' He could extemporise 'without any subject' before huge crowds for hours on end. ''Tis the presence of the Spirit only that is my all to preach.' The Lord would come upon him even in London bustle, 'overpowering me with love like a mighty torrent', and once in such a mood he 'sang and triumphed all the way through the streets to the Tower. Preached to all the whores I met, being in God out of self.'[10]

Harris joined with other Welsh evangelists in an association in 1742, but eight years later, after about 400 'Methodist' societies had been founded in South and Central Wales, a split came between his followers and Rowland's. Harris went on to form a 'Family', a kind of commune, at Trevecca, where more than 100 people joined him, giving up all private possessions. He repudiated the name 'Methodist', but his organisational gifts helped to ensure that Calvinistic Methodism would become almost the national Church of Wales. Other forms of dissent flourished in the climate of fervour which revival created and canalised – Baptist and Independent churches were soon spreading even faster than Methodist ones. The gentry continued to favour Anglicanism, and their alienation from the nonconformist masses grew clear and unbridgeable. Between 1716 and 1870, no Welsh-speaking Anglican bishop held any Welsh see, but evangelicalism boosted the Welsh language wherever that was still dominant, in particular by encouraging hymn-writing. The distinctiveness of Wales became more, not less, marked as a result of the revival.[11]

The distinction of Lowland Scotland, by contrast, was that enthusiasm made little mark on its industrious and quiescent people. The Covenant of the mid-seventeenth century had in effect done revival's work pre-emptively. The Kirk was in very different case from the Church of England. Its organisation remained comprehensive. Its central role in Scottish life was accepted. For geographical reasons – clergy and elders from far away found it hard to attend – its annual Assembly, now Scotland's only national forum for debate, fell under the control of 'moderates' from Edinburgh and the Lothians, cool men, new 'whigs' as opposed to old 'Whiggamores'. The restoration of lay patronage after the Union rankled with many ministers and laymen, and a struggle over this issue, 1732–40, led to the secession of Ebenezer Erskine and three other ministers who founded their own denomination. The 'Seceders' invited Whitefield to Scotland, but finding that he would not swallow Presbyterianism, they denounced his 'wild enthusiasm'. Preaching in Established churches, he made his impact. There was one spectacular outburst, in 1742, in the Clydeside parish of Cambuslang, where the minister had been impressed by news of the New England revival. After several months of daily sermons, tears and conversions, Whitefield himself came in June and characteristically preached three times in one afternoon, finishing after 1 o'clock next morning. In August 30,000 people gathered for an open-air rally. Whitefield reported that he had never seen such a 'commotion', not even in America. However, excitement died away, and for half a century evangelical influences penetrated Scottish life by degrees, without much further dramatic incident.[12]

Ireland was still less touched. Since the character of Catholicism was so different, it would be misleading to say that its priests conducted a non-stop religious revival. But religion was close to the people as nowhere else. Belief had never been lost or suspended or challenged by the queries of Reason and Enlightenment. 'Enthusiasm' could find few crannies to enter. Its provinces lay where existing churches were failing the people.

A reasonable religion was of no use to the men and women, largely uneducated, whose unregeneracy drew evangelical missionaries to the margins of Britain and the empire. Evangelical theology, if it deserves that name, was optimistic and easy to understand. It could be preached like thunder and sung with fervour:

> Simple folk and undiscerning,
>   Nothing we Know but Thee,
> Love is all our learning:
>   We with loving hearts adore Thee,
> This is our deep Scholarship,
>   This is all our glory.

This hymn, which Charles Wesley wrote for colliers, represents both the egalitarian and the anti-intellectual tendencies of the movement. It made outcasts feel true men. It devalued the scholarship which the well-to-do had paid to acquire. Whitefield told his flock in Georgia 'that he was firmly persuaded in himself, very few great and rich Men, and as few of our learned Doctors, for an Age and more past, could ever see Heaven … ' 'I bear the rich and love the poor ... ,' Wesley said. He wrote a tract addressed to smugglers, he founded schools and devised many cheap textbooks, and when, in his respectable old age, at Whitehaven, all the local clergy and most of the gentry turned out to hear him, his comment in his journal was that 'they all behaved with as much decency as if they had been colliers.'[13] In 1774, he published an attack on slavery.

Though Whitefield himself became a slave-owner, his 'Great Awakening' touched many black people. As he left Philadelphia in 1740, he found that 'near fifty negroes came to give me thanks for what God had done to their souls.' In a pamphlet of that year he declared that blacks were no less, but no more, 'conceived and born in Sin', than white men. Other evangelists also preached to mixed crowds. The Baptists in particular had an influx of black members. As a major Presbyterian revivalist, Samuel Davies, noticed in Virginia, blacks delighted in singing revivalist hymns; they took 'a kind of ecstatic delight in Psalmody'. Some Indians, also, were drawn into the fold.[14] No one could be turned away or excluded; and anyone slighted and aggrieved by his treatment could set up as a preacher on his own account. Blacks began to preach. Women were known to preach.

Like the spate of immigration which in itself was one cause of its effervescence (more immigrants in the back-country meant more churchless people awaiting conversion), the Great Awakening flowed across the borders between colonies and stirred many people into a consciousness of common concern. Yet it was also divisive. Many who disliked 'enthusiasm' drifted towards Anglicanism, which therefore increased its hold among the wealthier. Even New England colonies, like the others, emerged riddled with sects — 'New Lights' versus 'Old Lights', Baptists rampant. America was already precociously tolerant; now with more sects, more dissenters, the pressure to do away with remaining discriminations increased. Popular initiative in social and political life was heightened. The American social structure had been loose by European standards before this. Now, although slavery grew no milder, and though no one yet liked the idea of 'democracy', it became yet more fluid and novel.

In Wales also the long-term effect would be to inflate the uppishness of the low and to bring snobs into contempt. Scotland remained comfortably under the control of its lairds and ministers. But why did Methodism not shake the English class structure more strongly? Why has it seemed to so many scholars that it helped to preserve it? The answers must be complex.

Wesley himself despised gentlefolk, and he was as savage as Marx about the idiocy of farmers and agricultural labourers. Hence he mostly ignored the south-eastern counties, heartland of agriculture and squirearchy. This area was dismissed in Methodist circles as a 'wilderness'. Penetration here, although it came, came slowly. The chief centres of Wesley's own activity were London, with its sprawl of suburban poor, Bristol, and Newcastle. Hence his regular journeys took him from south-west to north-east and back, from the tin-miners of Cornwall, through the seamen and colliers of Bristol, among the industrial workers of Staffordshire, Lancashire and Yorkshire, and up to the classic Northumberland coalfield. These regions, where Methodism grew fastest, would within Wesley's own lifetime begin to receive the impact of novel industrial growth. Before and while the impact was felt, Methodism brought people a new sense of their own worth, and training in leadership and organisation, but also integration into a movement anxious to emphasise its non-subversive character. In the 1740s, Wesley's own toryism had been in opposition to insolent well-heeled whiggery. When he died, 'toryism' itself, mutated, had become the blazon of order and Property.

The revival in early days generated real frenzy. It is hard for us to imagine how exciting it must have been to encounter young Whitefield, or Wesley's piercing eye. The great revivalists sought to induce, in themselves as in others, not merely one experience of self-transcendence, but renewed, and again renewed exultation. An early Anglican evangelical prayed 'that God would give us new bread not stale, but what was baked in the oven on that day.' Men must weep and cry out in terror and penitence and joy again and again. Tears flowed not only at great open-air gatherings, but indoors, over the sacraments – one was saved, one was saved – the tears proved it. Whitefield worked for his tears, one might say, like a black. This thought in fact occurred to an African seaman, Olaudah Equiano, who arrived in Philadelphia in the mid-1760s to find a church crowded with people, its yard full, folk mounted on ladders peering in at the windows. He was told Whitefield was preaching. He had 'often heard' of him. He pressed into the gathering and beheld the 'pious man' holding forth at full pitch, 'and sweating as much as I ever did while in slavery on Montserrat beach.'[15]

Such displays were not genteel. They were 'primitive'. They were atavistic. They were meant to be so. Wesley extolled the 'primitive Christianity' of the earliest centuries of the Church. Excited readers were discovering Homer. Winckelmann was about to deify ancient Greek sculpture. Macpherson would soon unveil the spurious beauties of his *Ossian* poems purporting to come from ancient Gaelic tradition. Mountainous scenery, hitherto sensibly shunned as barren and dangerous, was beginning to draw cultivated men with its inexplicable appeal. The cult of the 'sublime' was emerging; it was good to be frightened.

Many factors beside the decline in Christian faith and the call for revival, or for substitutes, must explain the shift in the consciousness of educated Europeans and colonists, about the middle of the eighteenth century. The artificiality of life amid the teacups in towns which grew bigger and bigger, or in country houses with more and more amenities; the thought, nobly expressed by Adam Ferguson, that commercialism was at the work of destroying the springs of passion, of generous, fine behaviour; the growing knowledge of regions outside Europe where men might look uncouth, but still seemed heroic; all these must have prodded thinkers to seek out the unspoilt, to masturbate their passions, to cherish tears. So must, in England, the sordid nature of politics dominated by 'interest' and by the quest for safety, by Walpole. In the age of Wesley, many men craved war. They yearned for heroes, Plutarchian, Roman, noble. So they invented the radiance of William Pitt.

II

More powerful, palpable interests demanded war. When it came it would be brazenly, nakedly fought for the sake of trade. British commerce seemed not to be growing fast enough. In thirty years after 1710 French trade between colonies and metropolis rose from 25 million livres to 140 million livres a year. France appeared to derive an 'unfair' advantage from the connection of her ruling Bourbon dynasty with the Bourbon monarchy of Spain; most of the goods exported through Cadiz to Spanish America had been manufactured in France. Beside merchants, British commerce employed clerks and dockers, and, less directly, weavers and iron-workers, so the cry of 'our trade in danger!' could be sure of wide support. Ironmasters could look forward to supplying the cannon. Contractors would be required to meet huge orders for military and naval supplies. This was a time when, in Lewis Namier's words, 'Fortunes were made and the greatness of families founded in army magazines and bread wagons.'[16] While the big City men of the Bank and the East India Company were closely allied with Walpole and accepted his pacific policy, lesser merchants clamoured for war and forged links with the opposition of 'outs' who sincerely or cynically called themselves 'Patriots'.

The opposition craved war because it seemed that so long as Britain was prosperous and at peace, no crisis could arise drastic enough to unseat Walpole. A stream of pamphlets through the 1730s called for war with Spain. There seemed to be ample pretext. The hostility of the Florida Spaniards to the new Georgia colony was now added to the longstanding uncertainty of the valuable British logwood trade. The Treaty of Utrecht had not pacified British greed. The British wanted from Spain a freedom of trade which they would not accord foreigners in their own colonies.

Under the Treaty, the South Sea Company had been given the right to send one ship a year of 500 tons (later 650) to Porto Bello, laden with British merchandise. Its goods would be exempt from duties, but the King of Spain would have a quarter share in each vessel and would take 5 per cent of the profits on the rest. This provision had been negotiated for Britain by a naturalised Dane named Manuel Manasses Gilligan, who had been in his day a great smuggler. The first ship sailed only in 1717, and a mere eight voyages were undertaken altogether. But whenever a South Sea Company vessel was in port, it served as a depot for contraband trade. Carrying neither provisions nor water, it was necessarily accompanied by sloops from Jamaica. These secretly carried merchandise. Unloaded during the day, the big ship was reloaded at night. But the Company, operating its own racket, faced competition from British freelances who picked their own time and place for selling all year round and could offer lower prices to the Spanish colonists. The Spaniards acted against smugglers. The freelances made their own reprisals. These would be punished in turn by confiscation of Company property – so the Company would often dissuade the Navy and the British government from taking action to protect shipping in the West Indies. The freelances execrated the Company. The Company complained about low profits. The King of Spain suspected the Company of hiding its real gains so as to cheat him of his share. Everyone, therefore, was prone to short temper.

The Spanish authorities claimed the right to stop and search ships anywhere in American waters, and coastguard vessels (*guarda-costas*) were fitted out and manned by shady persons who got their pay from the sale of the prizes they brought in. A ship might be seized and condemned merely because it was carrying logwood or seemed headed towards an unlawful destination. Probably some of the British traders who suffered were actually innocent. Seizures were not very numerous, thirty-eight over seven years. But the *guarda-costas* were commonly violent.[17] In 1738, the opposition rejoiced, and the public shrieked, over the tale of Captain Jenkins's ear.

William Beckford M.P., West India merchant and wealthy absentee planter, proudly produced before the House of Commons one Robert Jenkins, who claimed that seven years before a coastguard, ransacking his ship, had cut off his ear with a cutlass. He happened to have it with him, pickled. He was wearing a wig, which he was not asked to remove. Beckford himself later cast doubt on the story. But this ear was what the warmongers needed. Other atrocities were announced, or invented. There was a collection at Lloyd's Coffee House in the City 'for the support of the wives and children of those poor unfortunate sailors who are now made slaves and prisoners by the Spaniards.'[18] But Walpole coolly negotiated a new Convention with Spain, signed early in 1739. Spain agreed to pay £95,000 as the estimated excess of Spanish over British depredations.

Enter the hero. William Pitt, aged 30, made his reputation as the greatest orator of his time by denouncing the Convention of Pardo in the House of Commons: ' ... Is this any longer a nation, or what is an English parliament, if with more ships in your harbours than in all the navies of Europe, with above two millions of people in your American colonies, you will bear to hear of the expediency of receiving from Spain an insecure, unsatisfactory, dishonourable convention?' The agreement was 'nothing but a stipulation for national ignominy ... The complaints of your despairing merchants, the voice of England has condemned it.'[19] This performance marked the first emergence of blatant imperial boasting as a factor in British public affairs. The empire had been seen as a useful business proposition. Pitt, though a spokesman for merchants, would give it the glamour of heroic myth.

In 1702, Thomas Pitt, governor of Madras, had bought a huge diamond from an Indian merchant for £24,000. He hoped to dispose of it for ten times as much. It was still unsold when he was dismissed from the East India Company's service in 1710 and came home, and its fate obsessed him until, seven years later, the Regent of France took it for a mere £125,000 or so. The nabob's rough temper bore hard on his own children – 'What hellish planet is it that influences you all?' – as well as upon their estranged mother.[20] His son Robert reacted by turning tory. William, Robert's second son, was a favourite with his brutal grandfather. He did not in later life display much liking for East India men; his vision of empire centred in the New World, and William Beckford became a close ally. Nevertheless he could not escape his heredity. Gout struck him down in his late thirties. In the eighteenth century gout was a hold-all name for diseases, and while Pitt undoubtedly had gout proper, his contemporaries attributed other illnesses, and his long phases of deep depression, to 'gout in the stomach', 'gout in the bowels' and 'gout in the head'. He shared in the strain of neurotic disorder, even madness, which appeared elsewhere among old Thomas Pitt's descendants. It helped to account for the spell cast by his oratory.

In private life he was charming, a dazzling talker. His tastes reflected the current shift in sensibility. He pressed a young nephew to read the epic poets of antiquity, Homer and Virgil: ' ... They contain the finest lessons for your age to imbibe; lessons of honor, courage, disinterestedness, love of truth, command of temper, gentleness of behaviour, humanity and in one word virtue in its true significance.' One of his friends was 'Capability' Brown, the celebrated land-scape gardener. Pitt's own talents in this field were recognised by his friends. Nothing pleased him better than to be building bosky bowers and Temples of Pan, to design a walk or judiciously place a rotunda. He loved country rides and strolls by the seashore. But his public manner was stiff and formal, a mask. The stilted language of his speeches was won by hard labour. Upright and graceful in posture, he transfixed the Commons with an eye 'that would cut a diamond'.[21]

His elder brother controlled several boroughs. Anxious to have the votes of their M.P.s, Walpole gave young William an army commission, which he still held when he came to sit in the Commons in 1735. But he had connections, through his family, with the great men of the opposition, and his patron was Viscount Cobham, who was sacked by Walpole for stepping out of line over the excise controversy. As one of 'Cobham's Cubs', Pitt made needling speeches. Walpole accordingly stripped him of his commission. Pitt's hostility was con-firmed. He became a rising young star of the opposition which centred itself on the separate court of George II's heir Frederick, whom the King loathed. His part in the 1739 debates made him a politician to reckon with.

'Had he lived four centuries earlier,' one biographer writes, 'miracles would have taken place at his tomb.'[22] Oratory was in his day a source of real power. M.P.s had been saturated during their education in the orators of antiquity. They adored a dramatic style allied to language controlled in the interests of aesthetics rather than reason. They did not mind Pitt's artificial manner, and

forgave his dishonesty and opportunism as they drank in his 'ornamental eloquence'. It may be compared to what Whitefield did for the vulgar. It helped
vinous, self-interested M.P.s to believe that they sat in an imperial 'senate' as
dignified as they thought that of Rome to have been. 'Wonderful as was his
eloquence,' one observer wrote, 'it was attended with this most important effect,
that it impressed every hearer with a conviction that there was something in
him even finer than his words.' Horace Walpole described his power thus: 'His
language was amazingly fine and flowing; his voice admirable; his action most
expressive; his figure genteel and commanding. Bitter satire was his fort: when
he attempted ridicule, which was very seldom, he succeeded happily; when he
attempted to reason, poorly.' He spoke 'to the passions' rather than 'to the
question'.[23] Since most M.P.s were uncommitted and their votes could be
swayed, such performances could help a man to office, if that was the only way
to keep him quiet; and word of them reaching outsiders all over Britain, could
focus public opinion, of which governments had to take account.

However, Pitt, as contemporaries sensed, was not after power as an end in
itself, but as a means. He would become great by making Britain greater. Trade
was one imperative; when the City after his death raised a vast monument to
him in the Guildhall, the inscription acclaimed him as the first statesman by
whom 'commerce was united with and made to flourish by war'. And he had
a strategical vision which could foresee and work towards large strokes in the
interests of clear British pre-eminence. As Richard Pares has observed, he was
the only leading politician who 'considered colonial acquisitions as something
more than so many debating-points for or against the Ministry ... the one living
figure among a generation of shadows.'[24] He symbolised for parts of the public
at large their own growing appetite for world power, their wish to emulate and
surpass the feats of ancient Rome. He was on excellent terms with a group of
poets, attached to the opposition, who were now striking up imperial themes.

One must be careful not to equate too closely the 'patriotism' of Jenkins's
Ear days with the 'jingoism' of the 1880s. There was as yet no assimilation of
war with sport; indeed a satirist in 1740 wrote contemptuously of the peace-
mongers:

> Safe let them sleep, unhurt by scattering balls,
> Unless when football or when cricket calls;
> Frenchmen may mediate or Spaniards plunder,
> While Britons generously withhold their thunder.

However, crude prejudice against other peoples was easily fanned. In 1753 there
would be a nasty outburst of anti-Semitism when the government carried a
Bill providing for the naturalisation of foreign-born Jews after three years'
residence. (British-born Jews were citizens already.) Six months of agitation,
with 'mobs' bawling 'No Jews, no wooden shoes', in allusion to the allegedly
ill-shod papists of the Continent, forced the ministry to repeal their own Bill.

51 An early-eighteenth-century view of Dublin from the North

52 Dublin's magnificent Custom House, as it appeared in 1792

53 Siraj-ud-daula by an Indian artist 54 Sir Eyre Coote, East India Company general (attributed to H. Morland)

55 Fort William, Calcutta, in the early 1750s

The more positive aspects of English patriotism were seen in the vast increase among ordinary people of interest in their own country's past. A translation of Rapin's *History of England* made in the late 1720s had had enormous success. Shakespeare's history plays were greeted with fresh delight — Garrick made his name in 1741 with a performance as Richard III. Propagandists for war against Spain invoked Oliver Cromwell. Samuel Johnson, still a struggling young writer, turned out short lives of Drake and of Admiral Blake.[25]

Proto-imperialism, like jingoism later, was probably dependent on the existence of literary hacks. With popular publishing and journalism flourishing in a new and regular way, a class of mercenary writers arose, the denizens of London's Grub Street and like squalid suburban purlieus, whom Pope denounced as upstarts and bores in his *Dunciad*. Such men were commonly failed professional people — lawyers and so forth — and, as Pat Rogers has argued, 'must have thought of themselves as outsiders. Insecurity bred, as it usually does, defensive techniques of abuse and exclusion.'[26] Under constant danger of pillory, gaol or fine for obscene and seditious libel, this class was likely to revel in bombast and war-whoops against safely-distant foreigners.

But respectable writers of large talent had long been turning to imperial themes. The early and mid-eighteenth century produced little good love poetry. While the Muse expressed her disgust at the base days of Walpole in satire, her inveterate bent to ennoble and to praise sought outlet in celebration of commerce. The wool trade and even the sugar plantation were sung through extensive poems. But commerce as an end in itself could not satisfy. Trade was perceived in great vistas of future tranquillity, opulence, universal brotherhood, as the agent of civilisation. This modulated in turn into celebration of empire, as in Thomson's anti-Walpole poem, 'Liberty' (1735–6):

> Gay colonies extend; the calm retreat
> Of undeserved distress, the better home
> Of those whom bigots chase from foreign lands.

The same poet, in 1749, produced an early intimation of nationalism proper, a new religion, suggesting that the whole community of the 'ever-sacred country'

> ... consists
> Not of coeval citizens alone:
> It knows no bounds; it has a retrospect
> To ages past; it looks on those to come.

'Britannia's empire' was still seen as involving dominion over the seas rather than over fresh territories, but the term and others like it was growing 'in emphasis and in breadth of reference', and as it did so its usage became more arrogant.[27] The 1740s saw a climax of patriotic self-praise. Arne produced his definitive setting of 'Rule, Britannia!' in 1740, and 'God Save the King' was first printed four years later.

T

War had finally come in October 1739. Huge crowds cheered the proclamation in London. Enthusiasm ran just as high in Bristol and Glasgow, Liverpool and Edinburgh. The opposition clamoured for seizure of colonies – Carteret, one of its leading figures, told a Swedish diplomat, 'We shall take from Spain some countries in America, and we shall keep them in spite of the whole world.' It was hoped that Spanish colonists, or their Indian victims, would rise and throw off the yoke of Madrid, that they would rush to make themselves British subjects and share in the unique benefits of the English constitution. One of the noisiest voices baying for war in the Commons had been that of Admiral Edward Vernon. Now he had his chance. By 20 November he was off to Porto Bello with six ships. It was not hard to bring the neglected fort to capitulate. Vernon seized all the vessels in the harbour, blew the fort up, and threw the town's trade open. Both Houses of Parliament voted their thanks. London gave Vernon the freedom of the City. Countless crude medals were manufactured, all showing Vernon's head with the legend, 'He took Porto Bello with six ships.' That head became a favourite decoration for inn signs, and districts in many different parts of England and Scotland were dubbed 'Porto Bello', while far off in Virginia Peter Jefferson, whose son Thomas was not yet born, applied that name to a small tract which he had purchased.[28]

Vernon found fame fickle. Absurdly overrated, he soon fell under excessive denigration. Though it was able to choke Spain's trade with the New World, and open new fields to illicit trade in the Caribbean, the British navy was in a muddle. The army faced the usual problem that troops sent to the West Indies died like flies – one regiment stationed quietly in the Leewards was given 960 men between 1739 and 1745, yet had at the end no more than 492 effective soldiers. A combined operation was planned against Cartagena. Hacks wrote premature ballads extolling its capture. But the town did not fall. Yellow fever scourged the forces. Vernon quarrelled with the army commander. Another attack launched at Cuba failed, and then an attempt to seize (shades of the Scots) the isthmus of Darien, also proved abortive. By the end of these failures, nine-tenths of the force had been laid low by disease.[29]

Meanwhile, undeclared war with France had begun. Then a jangling of dynasties in Europe produced the 'War of the Austrian Succession'. France attacked Austria. Britain supported her. A second front was opened. Foreign troops were hired to fight on land. But Walpole was hardly the man to run a war which he had entered so reluctantly. He had recently stripped the Duke of Argyll of his posts. In the election of 1741, Argyll sided with the 'Squadrone', and Walpole lost seats in Scotland, while Cornish borough-mongers swung away from him. He soon found that he could no longer control the Commons securely, and went at last in January 1742. The new ministry drew some of the 'outs', including Carteret and Argyll, into coalition with a Walpolian core centring on the two Pelhams, Newcastle and his brother Henry. By the end of 1744, Argyll was dead, Carteret had been twisted out, and Henry Pelham had achieved primacy. The war had been going badly, both in Europe and in the New World. Pitt, still 'out', insisted that Britain should not waste money on allies in Europe, but should attack France and Spain on the high seas. When the Commons were asked to sanction the taking of 16,000 of George II's own Hanoverian troops into British pay, Pitt declaimed that 'this great, this power-ful, this formidable kingdom, is considered only as a province to a despicable Electorate.'[30] The last phrase, to define Hanover, was a neat one, but George II would be very slow to forgive him.

Meanwhile, those American colonists whose virtues Pitt proclaimed so loudly were given a chance to show their own relish for empire. In 1740 troops from Georgia and South Carolina besieged St Augustine in Florida, which would not fall. Two years later the Spaniards riposted with an attack of their own, but Oglethorpe, with luck on his side, ambushed a large part of their force at 'Bloody Marsh' and catastrophe was averted. In Pennsylvania, the paci-fist, Quaker-dominated Assembly voted to send 'grain' to the battlefronts and the governor slily took it that gunpowder was a form of 'grain'. But it refused to take defensive measures, even though French and Spanish privateers threatened the Delaware, and that ardent British patriot, Benjamin Franklin, inspired the creation of a voluntary 'Association' of men ready to fight.

When formal war with France began in 1744, a *petite guerre*, raiding and counter-raiding, broke out again in the northern borderlands, but there was only one striking event. The trade and fisheries of Nova Scotia and Newfound-land were now of importance to Massachusetts. Governor Shirley devised, and the General Court accepted, a scheme for the capture of the French fort at Louisbourg which threatened all British interests in the region. The British government sent four ships from the West Indies to help, but this was essentially a New England operation. William Pepperell, a merchant, sailed as leader of 4,000 colonists. The famous fort proved far less formidable than legend had made it. After six weeks' siege, in June 1745, it surrendered. The good news reached England as that country faced its most obvious peril since the Armada. Prince Charles Edward Stuart, son of the Jacobite Pretender, landed in the Hebrides.

III

'The Young Pretender', at 25, was not in fact much younger than his father had been during his sojourn in Scotland in 1715, but his ardent high spirits were in extreme contrast with James III's moroseness. Charles was martial, fond of out-door sports, not much interested in religion, and able to win men's hearts with his charming familiarity of manner. His father was an Englishman brought up in France, his mother was a Polish princess, but 'Charlie's' own name always evokes Scotland.

O Theàrlich mhic Sheumais, mhic Sheumais, mhic Theàrlich,
Leat shiubhlainn gu h-eutron 'n am éighlich bhith màrsal ...

'O Charles son of James, son of James, son of Charles, With you I'd go gladly
when the call comes for marching', a Gaelic poet, Alexander Macdonald, now
wrote, and he, or one of his fellow-clansmen, describing how this 'tall youth
of a most agreeable aspect in a plain black coat with a plain shirt not very
clean ... ' landed on the Scottish mainland, would add, 'at his first appearance
I found my heart swell to my very throat.'[31]

English Jacobitism was virtually dead. Wesley was now taking a different
creed to the very regions where it had been strongest. Sir Watkin Williams
Wynn M.P., greatest landowner in North Wales, had helped revive a Jacobite
club. This 'Cycle of the White Rose' and its South Wales counterpart, the 'Sea
Serjeants', bringing together local magnates, had great political influence. The
Earl of Barrymore, with lands in Cheshire, a general of the British army, was a
Stuart sympathiser. The French King had been told in 1743 that the whole of
Wales was ready to rise if Barrymore gave the signal. But Barrymore had been
arrested. Sir Watkin was down to his last £200 in ready money. Few Welsh
Jacobites made any move.[32] Of the 'Seven Men of Moidart' who landed with
Charles Edward, four were Irish. Yet Ireland, as in 1715, was quiet, under the
rule of its cleverest eighteenth-century viceroy, Lord Chesterfield, who gave
official permission for the opening of Catholic churches and encouraged the
landed classes to wear clothes made of Irish materials at official receptions. Gaelic
Scotland was the last support of the Stuarts.

As an Englishman, Edward Burt, had observed in the 1720s, Highlanders
loved a leader. Though there had been no pitched battle between clan armies
since the 1680s, the chief was still looked to as a commander in war. Cattle
stealing was still endemic, and while chiefs now stood aloof from rustling themselves, many protected raiders and saw the habit as a useful means of keeping
men fit for military service. The whole clan was still conceived as an armed
force; its officers were the 'tacksmen', close relatives of the chief who lived on
the difference between the rents they collected from his followers and those they
paid over to him. A good chief represented his people before the civil authorities,
taking their cases through the higher courts, winning them compensation for
raids and for other injuries suffered from hostile clans. He succoured the old and
looked after surviving dependants of those who had served him. He chartered
grain for his clan when the harvest failed.

In return for his dutifulness, he exercised simple pomp. On a formal visit to
an equal, he took with him a 'tail' — his Henchman (a foster brother), his poet,
his spokesman, the gillie who carried his sword, another whose job was to
carry his own person over fords, another to lead his horse in difficult paths, his
baggage man, his piper, the piper's own gillie, besides other hangers-on, and
gentlemen-kinsmen to keep him company. He would brag to supercilious

Lowlanders of the number of men who served at his table. Burt deplored the advantage which the chiefs took of their followers' 'Slave-like' devotion. 'The ordinary Highlanders esteem it the most sublime Degree of Virtue to love their Chief, and pay him a blind Obedience, altho' it be in Opposition to the Government, the Laws of the Kingdom, or even to the Law of God.'[33]

So a tribal way of life was maintained in a corner of whig Britain, bending the prongs of 'civilisation' thrust into it. According to Burt, a Cameron magistrate in Inverness would never let a Cameron suffer for a crime if the clan wanted him to be saved. Lowlanders rarely entered the region; Burt said that if one had to do so he made his will 'as though he were entring upon a long and dangerous Sea Voyage.' Few polite persons yet had a good word to say for the mountains, whence eagles still commonly swooped to seize lambs or even calves. Sheep could be seen grazing on top of squalid turfed houses. Women at work on the harvest, girls fulling cloth with their feet, men launching a boat, were incited to effort by the strains of the bagpipe. Wooden ploughs and spades broke such ground as was cultivated, but the way of life was still pastoral. The clansman kept goats and sheep mainly to feed his household, black cattle to pay the rent. Many beasts signified a substantial man, so the glens were chronically overstocked with weak animals. Cattle were still driven up to summer shielings. In spring, as stores of food failed, people still bled their beasts and boiled the blood into cakes. Everyone wore the plaid. Though Burt saw a 'Laird and his Lady, without Shoes or Stockings, a good Way from Home, in cold Weather', the chiefs and tacksmen commonly wore leather brogues, besides tartan trews, short tartan coats, and slightly longer tartan waistcoats. The commoner frequently had nothing but his plaid, and used it also as bedding at night, so that it reeked to Burt's nose most offensively. 'A small Part of the Plaid ... is set in Folds and girt round the Waste to make of it a short Petticoat that reaches half Way down the Thigh, and the rest is brought over the Shoulders, and then fastened before ... ' This belted plaid or 'kilt' was generally worn 'so very short, that in a windy Day, going up a Hill, or stooping, the Indecency of it is plainly discovered.'[34]

Inverness, the one sizeable place, was a frontier town. The people there, Burt remarked, would not call themselves Highlanders 'not so much on account of their low Situation, as because they speak *English*.' Yet 'within less than a Mile of the Town', few people spoke 'any English at all'. Trade, as carried on at the town's four or five fairs every year, did not impress Burt. A small roll of linen cloth or a piece of coarse plaiding was relatively big business, and most Highlanders brought in no more than two or three small cheeses, a bit of butter, a few goatskins—to buy with the proceeds 'a Horn, or wooden Spoon or two, a Knife, a wooden Platter, and such like Necessaries for their Huts ... '[35] Candles were made from the cores of living pine trees, rope from wood-roots. Archaic self-sufficiency still seemed dominant.

Yet Highland society was fast changing. The Gaelic script had gone out of use. The bardic caste had been eclipsed as new forms of verse were used by gentlemen, even by working people. Education was eroding the traditional clan solidarities. From Civil War days, the Presbyterian synod of Argyll had striven to supply Gaelic-speaking ministers, and had given the Western Highlanders books of devotion in their own language (though the New Testament was not translated till 1767, nor the whole Bible till the nineteenth century). It had established numerous schools, and from 1709 onwards the Scottish Society for the Propagation of Christian Knowledge, set up in imitation of the London body, had complemented the work going forward in Wales, founding 176 schools in fifty years.[36] All these taught English, and forbade the use of Gaelic. Meanwhile, the Highlanders had bred a native professional class of clergy and dominies, and kinsmen of chiefs were practising law in Edinburgh.

Thus many chiefs were uneasy in their position. It was irksome for a man of education, with aspirations to live like an English gentleman, to find that the reverence of his followers, while deep, was also conditional. He had to pretend a warm familiarity with clansmen all of whom claimed to be blood relations. ' ... They insist upon the Privilege of taking him by the Hand, whenever they meet him,' Burt noted, and he reported the discontent aroused when one chief was ashamed to accept such marks of brotherhood in front of an Englishman of high station. Nor could a chief lightly marry a Lowland girl. When one matched himself with an Edinburgh goldsmith's daughter, 'no Way deriv'd from the Tribe', his people felt that he had disgraced them all. If he must marry beneath him, weren't there smiths enough with daughters within the clan?[37]

Burt also encountered a chief who maintained the traditional ruling that his followers must not go in for trade or put their children out to learn crafts, either of which would weaken his hold. But the sordid market at Inverness did not tell the whole story of the Gaelic economy. Glasgow now had a serious trade with the Western Highlands. Even before the end of the seventeenth century, clansmen had followed the herring south down the coastline in summer, docking at last at Greenock on the Clyde, where they acquired in exchange wares from Glasgow. There had long been a regular traffic in cattle from the islands. Macleod of Dunvegan, on Skye, was sending, by the early eighteenth century, large droves to market and this trade provided his tacksmen's main income. The beasts crossed the narrow sea to Kyle of Lochalsh at low water; a boat with four oars would pull five swimming cows joined jaw to tail with withes, on their way to the Perthshire town of Crieff where the great stream of livestock stemming from the isles converged with another moving down from Caithness in the far north. The yearly fair at Crieff had started in 1672; fifty years later it was said that 30,000 beasts sold there in a single autumn, bringing in 30,000 guineas. Some of the Gaelic drovers then took cattle on to Norfolk, where they would fatten for the London market.[38]

The chief's taste for fine wine and excellent linen depended for satisfaction on the cattle trade. Traditional rustling was a brake on it. Military attitudes faltered before commercial ones. Some chiefs came to prefer cash to men. Burt met one who was selling 'troublesome Fellows' from his clan as indentured servants for the New World, out of Inverness: ' ... I have been well assured, they have been threatened with hanging, or at least perpetual Imprisonment, to intimidate and force them to sign a Contract for their Banishment.' Norman Macleod, 22nd chief of his name at Dunvegan, would run up vast debts with his gambling, his tastes for books and mangoes, his mansion near Edinburgh. As early as the 1720s, he was dabbling in 'improvement', introducing clover to Skye, growing exotica such as cauliflowers and cherries in his garden, trying to work a lead mine, and adventuring money in a fishery company. In 1739, it emerged that one of his tacksmen had abducted more than a hundred men, women and children from Skye and Harris, some of them plucked from their beds at night, so that they could be sold as servants in America; when the ship was refitted in Ulster, they escaped and told the tale. Macleod of Dunvegan and his neighbour Macdonald of Sleat were implicated in this sordid operation.[39]

Chiefs who sold their clansmen to keep their cellars full violated the old ethos more crudely, but no more decisively, than the great house of Argyll. By the early eighteenth century, this had at least 500 square miles of rent-paying land. The Duke was, on top of this, overlord, or feudal superior, of most of the chiefs and landowners in Argyll itself and in parts of Inverness-shire, whose estates covered about 3,000 square miles. He was the law in the Western Highlands. As hereditary sheriff of Argyll, he administered justice. As hereditary lord-lieutenant, he had legal control of armed forces. From his clan and vassals, he could muster an army of well over 5,000. His territories were an enclave of relative civility and of 'improvement'. The second Duke, Red John, con-structed new towns, new villages, new piers and new canals, and established new industries. Though his clansmen still revered him as 'son of Great Colin', he lived in London during most of the year, and needed all he could get from his lands to support a life-style as lavish as that of other whig magnates. Tradition snapped. First in Kintyre about 1710, then in his other estates in 1737, Red John offered tacks — leases — of farms in open auction to the highest bidder· Campbell or non-Campbell, Gael or Lowlander, he would now take as tenant whoever offered most money.[40]

The dominance of Argyll gave the London government what hold it had in the Highlands, yet it was also a source of weakness and danger. Bitter resent-ments confronted Campbell success. On lands taken over from the MacLeans in the late seventeenth century, Campbell colonists had faced incessant native hostility — outright resistance, cattle-maiming, arson. Macdonalds, Camerons, Stewarts nursed their grudges. Argyll was a whig, so these clans were Jacobites, regardless of what Stuart kings themselves had done or attempted to do to the Gaels. Nor could the government buy their leaders over. The pot of patronage was not full enough to feed faceless little men so far from London. Whiggery north of the Highland line dealt out little. Simon Fraser of Lovat had captured

Inverness from the rebels of 1715, and had been rewarded with chieftainship of his clan over the ousted Jacobite incumbent. In 1733 he received the Sheriffdom of Inverness-shire. Then there was no more in the cupboard, and he began to intrigue for a Jacobite dukedom.

However, during a Jacobite scare of the early 1720s, Fraser had given useful advice to the government, describing a clearly dangerous situation. As soon as possible after the 1715 rebellion, the government had disbanded Highland Companies raised officially by clan chiefs and had neglected the region. Various clans still levied blackmail in adjacent Lowland areas. Outside Argyll's territories, there were hardly any justices of the peace. The government did now stir itself. General Wade was sent to investigate the position and then allowed to implement his own report. He began to build military roads, though 250 miles of these by 1740 still barely touched the problem of Highland communications. Six new Highland Companies were created. But by the 1730s, the State's presence in the Highlands was weakening again. Argyll's innovations on his estates made danger greater, as Campbells who lost tacks wavered in their loyalty. By 1740, cattle raiders were attacking Inveraray itself, presumably with the connivance of local Campbells.

The French of course took an interest. The Jacobite intriguer Murray of Broughton arranged for massive support in the Highlands if Charles Edward would cross with 10,000 French troops and adequate arms and money. But when Charles, in February 1744, joined two regiments of cavalry and twenty battalions of foot assembled at Gravelines under Marshall Saxe, the aim was to land in Essex. It was only after yet another Protestant gale had shattered the expedition in harbour, and the French government had lost interest, that the Young Pretender struck out for the Highlands. He had only two frigates and 700 troops. The ship carrying his soldiers was disabled by a British man-of-war and returned to France. Hence Charles's arrival with so few companions, and hence the news which greeted him that Macleod of Dunvegan and his neighbour Macdonald of Sleat would not give the support which they had promised.

But others were less cautious. Anti-Campbell clans rallied. Sir John Cope, the government's commander in Scotland, went north, dithered, and then let the rebels pass him. At Perth, Charles was joined by the brilliant Lord George Murray, who became joint commander of an army now 2,400 men strong. The dragoons left to guard the Lowlands retreated before them. Charles took Edinburgh without bloodshed. According to someone present, two-thirds of the men there were whigs, but two-thirds of the women were for Prince Charlie; in any case there was no overt opposition when James III was proclaimed from the Market Cross. His son promised that the established Churches of Scotland (and of England) would be maintained, and denounced the Act of Union for making Scotland 'no more than an English province'.[41]

Cope, who had reached Inverness, came back by sea and took up a strong position near the coastal village of Prestonpans to the east of Edinburgh. His

2,200 men nearly matched Charles's force in numbers and far surpassed it in equipment; some of the Jacobite troops had only scythes mounted on poles. But Charles's Highlanders surprised Cope's force, on the morning of September 21, with a charge on their classic model; men stripped off their plaids, fired their muskets, and raced in headlong, sword in one hand, round shield in the other. It was all over in about ten minutes. While the Jacobites lost some thirty-odd men, Cope fled with only four or five hundred.

> When Johnnie Cope to Dunbar came,
> They speer'd at him, 'Where's a' your men?'
> 'The deil confound me gin I ken,
> For I left them a' this morning.'[42]

Charles was master of Scotland by default. The coalition government of 1742 had revived the office of Secretary of State for Scotland and had given it to a veteran of the Squadrone faction, the Marquis of Tweeddale. He was fussy, infirm, and ignorant of Highland geography; furthermore, his appointment vexed the Campbell faction. Lord Islay, who had inherited the Dukedom of Argyll from Red John in 1743, had acted shrewdly on his own patch, amending his brother's policies over tenancy, but he was not going to help Tweeddale, and the latter in turn had shrunk from precautionary reorganisation in the Highlands for fear of giving power to political enemies. So Charles had been able to march south without serious opposition.

For five weeks, wearing always a Highland plaid waistcoat, he held court at Holyrood Palace. His army grew. But very few Lowlanders joined, and no Presbyterians. His force, it is reckoned, numbered three Catholics to every seven episcopalians. It came mainly from the central and west Highlands and from the episcopalian Lowlands of the north-east, where Jacobite lairds had called in bands of clansmen to bully reluctant tenants into arms. Less than half the Scottish Gaels supported Charles, and the ex-Covenanting south-west was emphatically against him.[43] But if this was not the 'Scotch rebellion' which distant English imagined, neither was it a Scottish civil war. The propertied classes largely sat on the fence. They might not have minded a Jacobite victory, though they were not going to risk rebellion. If Charles had wanted no more, he could perhaps have made his father king of an independent Scotland. But that was not his conception at all.

In November, against the judgment of most of his advisers, he marched 5,000 men into England, where three Hanoverian armies awaited him. He reached Lancashire without resistance, but he was drawing no English recruits of note. When Manchester was captured, the pro-Stuart townspeople, who welcomed him, provided only a few score soldiers. But a brilliant feint by Murray outwitted the Duke of Cumberland, George II's second son, who was commanding an army twice as large as the Jacobites'. By early December, Charles's troops were at Derby, only 127 miles from London.

There was a run on the Bank of England. The capital was in some fear. Charles was for pressing on. But Murray saw that any further advance would be opposed by overwhelming force as the three Hanoverian armies united. Though Charles raged at his Council, it overbore him. Retreat began on December 6. The districts which the Jacobites passed through were now hostile rather than apathetic. General Oglethorpe failed to cut off the Scots as ordered, and people remembered his Jacobite family background; he was court-martialled, and though he was acquitted, the founder of Georgia never saw active service again. Charles got safely across the Border, leaving most of his guns behind.

In November Argyll had at last persuaded the King to recognise his own hereditary Lieutenantship. The Campbells were raised in arms. Eighteen new Highland Companies had been formed, and wavering chiefs had been won over by the offer of commissions. Edinburgh had been reoccupied by the Hano-verians. Another great Highland charge brought Charles victory at Falkirk in January, but then his clansmen, as always, began to flock home with their booty.

Murray favoured a Highland guerrilla campaign. But when Cumberland marched to meet the Pretender in April with troops thoroughly trained in new tactics to quell the terrible Gaelic charge, Charles chose confrontation in pitched battle. He still had approaching 5,000 men, but very little artillery. Cumberland, with 9,000, including many pro-Hanoverian Gaels, reached him on April 16 at Culloden, near Inverness, on Drummossie Moor. He had plenty of guns. For an hour, Charles's Highlanders stood and fell under Cumberland's cannonade. When the time came to charge, Macdonalds refused to move because Lord George Murray's own Atholl men had been given the place of honour on the right which Clan Donald claimed had been granted them in perpetuity by Robert the Bruce. A ragged charge, bloody fighting, were followed by a general rout. No quarter was given, on Cumberland's orders. Dragoons hacked down rebels and bystanders alike on the road to Inverness. With a price of £30,000 on his head, Charles began those wanderings through the Highlands and Isles which fused him with that region in myth forever. Highland traditions of hospitality served him well as Hanoverian troops combed land and sea for him. He got away on September 19, with 130 other fugitives. That was the end of Charles Edward as a leader. France had lost interest in him. The Jacobite cause petered out in a few shadowy plots. When James III died in 1766, even the Pope would not recognise his heir, who lingered in Italy as a pitiful drunkard prac-tising in seclusion upon the bagpipes, till his misery ended in 1788.

Seventy-seven Jacobite rebels were formally executed, 610 were transported to the New World.[44] Meanwhile, 'Butcher' Cumberland's reign of terror in the Highlands affected far more people. The search for fugitives was a pretext for burnings and seizures of cattle. Most of the chiefs of the disaffected clans now went into exile, and the government acted to ensure that the Highlands would never again be a base for rebellion. The Highland dress was banned, kilt and tartan. A new Disarming Act was fiercely enforced. An Act of 1746 abolished the military nature of Scottish feudal tenures, and next year the heritable juris-dictions of Scotland were ended. (Few clan chiefs had in fact wielded justice under such legal forms, but their disappearance in Highlands and Lowlands alike helped to tidy up Scottish administration.) A commission of Lowland gentry was put in to run estates forfeited by rebels. Both the Jacobite generals of the '45 were 'improving' Highland landlords, and one of them, the Duke of Perth, had controlled the Crieff cattle tryst. The old order had been decaying within. Now it was systematically smashed from without. Clan feeling remained strong among the poor, but chiefship in the old style was no longer possible and gave way, at best, to paternalist landlordship.

Perversely, the poorly-supported tribal rising in 1745 provided new symbols of lost Scottish nationality:

> Mony a gallant sodger fought,
> Mony a gallant chief did fa';
> Death itself were dearly bought
> A' for Scotland's king and law.

> Will he no come back again?
> Will he no come back again?
> Better lo'ed he'll never be,
> And will he no come back again?[45]

Pathos, yearning and fatalistic defiance, these feelings expressed by the many fine Jacobite songs made them a harmless surrogate for nationalism. They evoked heroism untainted with interest, and feudal values which seemed far more noble than the ethics of Money and Property. Lord George Murray had written to his brother, 'My Life, my Fortune, my expectations, the Happyness of my wife & children are all at stake (& the chances are against me), & yet a principle of (what seems to me) Honour, & my Duty to King & Country, out-weighs evry thing.' Old Macdonald of Keppoch had cried out as his followers hung back at Culloden, 'My God, have the clansmen of my name deserted me', and rushed forward, pistol and sword in hand, to be shot down.[46] Such men seemed to redeem the most squalid era of British public life, providing examples more estimable than those of 'Butcher' Cumberland and of Islay-Argyll.

This was the want of uplift and heroes which made Pitt indispensable to the British. He would one day boast that he had been the first English Minister to arm 'the hardy and intrepid race' of the northern mountains and direct the 'valour' and 'fidelity' of Highlanders against the enemies of his own country. Earlier ministers had in fact used Gaels to fight British battles overseas. But people believed Pitt and that was most significant. With the last tribal region of Britain now tamed, Pitt would seem to focus an inchoate sense of united, self-confident British identity in which almost every section of Scottish society soon came to participate with some zeal. 'I have no local attachments; it is indifferent to me, whether a man was rocked in his cradle on this side or that side of the Tweed.'[47]

Henry Pelham needed the dangerous Pitt as a colleague; after the Jacobite rising he threatened to resign unless Pitt received office. George II still refused. Pelham resigned. No one else could form a government. So Pitt was given an Irish sinecure position, and then, just after Culloden, he succeeded to the notoriously lucrative post of Paymaster to the Forces. Not for the last time, Pitt seemed to have sold out. His reputation faltered. However, he turned disadvantage to triumph. Ostentatiously, he refused the perquisites of office. Instead of using the balances passing through his hands for his own profit, he lodged them with the Bank of England for public use. No other eighteenth-century statesman made such a gesture.[48]

Pitt had developed important contacts with merchants. Urged on by William Vaughan, a New Hampshire fish merchant, he now argued unavailingly that the capture of Louisbourg should be followed by an attack on Quebec. His more regular Sancho Panza would later be William Beckford, opulent, vulgar, rather absurd, but well able to enhance Pitt's awareness of the nature and importance of West India trade and so to help him develop his vision of world empire resting on sea-power.

IV

One ocean remained unmastered, the Pacific. The British had attempted little there. William Dampier, a former buccaneer, sent out to explore the east side of Australia in 1699, had not reached it or done much else of importance. The South Sea Company had accomplished nothing. But war with Spain prompted a bold incursion. In the autumn of 1740, Commodore George Anson set off with half a dozen ships and a general commission to do what he could where he could against the Spaniards in the Pacific. If possible, he should possess and fortify some port or island as a permanent British base. The tale of this expedition is macabre. As troops, Anson was provided with 500 pensioners from the army's hospital at Chelsea. But 'all those who had limbs and strength to walk out of Portsmouth deserted', so that the 259 who came on board were mostly decrepit invalids over sixty.[49] Numbers were made up with raw marines. Struggling round Cape Horn, the squadron suffered terribly from scurvy, that vile disease which brought spots and ulcers all over the body, swollen legs, putrid gums, extreme lassitude. The survivors took some prizes along the Chilean and Peruvian coasts, and captured a galleon from Mexico as it approached the Philippines. Anson returned in June 1744, after nearly four years, with loot valued at £1,250,000. But 1,051 men had perished, over half the total, amongst them all the pensioners who had set out.

A Scottish doctor, James Lind, was moved to make researches which, in his

Treatise of the Scurvy (1753), at last proved the power of lemon juice to prevent the disease, guessed at by some since Elizabeth's day. The Admiralty did not order a regular issue of lemon juice till 1795, after which the scourge swiftly disappeared. But another lesson of the circumnavigation would be acted upon much sooner. It had been impossible to keep Anson's intentions secret, because he had had to stop for refreshments on the Brazilian coast. Hence people began to talk of the value of seizing the Falkland Islands as a stepping-stone to the Pacific. Thirdly, Anson himself was a hero despite his party's misfortunes, and was enabled to make his mark as a reformer within the navy. From 1751 to 1762, with just one short break, he would be in charge at the Admiralty. Improvements in tactics and personnel would stand to his credit. He would resist the prevalent custom of patronage and insist on promoting officers solely on merit.

There was plenty of room for reform. French and Spanish naval vessels were faster and better proportioned. An admiral complained during the war of 1739–48, 'The unthinking populace are too free to censure without enquiry into the reasons of things, and imagine it strange that an English ship of war of 70 guns cannot take a French ship of the same force, whereas it is pretty apparent that our 70 gun ships are little superior to their ships of 52 guns.' The navy's growth increased problems of manning. It had 302 ships, 43,537 men in 1744. By 1762 there would be 432 ships and 81,929 men.[50]

'No man,' Dr Samuel Johnson remarked, 'will be sailor who has contrivance enough to get himself into a jail, for being in a ship is being in a jail, with the chance of being drowned.' The scale of wages in the navy was not altered between 1653 and 1797. The Able Seaman was supposed to receive 24s. a month, less deductions, the Ordinary Seaman only 19s. This was half or a third of what could be earned on merchant ships, less even than was given to common soldiers. Food was monotonous and often disgusting; it was said that seamen turned the cheese into buttons for their jackets and trousers. The ships were disease-ridden, with typhus killing even more people than scurvy. Discipline may have been less savage than in the army, but in the war of 1739–48, there were twenty occasions when a sailor was 'flogged round the fleet', that is, whipped alongside every ship, with the rigging manned so that everyone could see the lash fall in the boat where the culprit was tied to a scaffold. After more than a hundred strokes, the man was usually maimed for life. In less serious cases a captain could give up to five dozen lashings with the cat o' nine tails, and could order the same man the same dose next day, and the day after, if he wished. The vicious punishment of 'running the gauntlet', where the entire ship's company were given knotted cords to strike at a man's bare back as he ran between their lines, was not abolished until 1806. Not surprisingly, the navy suffered such heavy desertions in the 1740s that clemency had to be offered to lure men back. Because of the risk of desertion, shore leave could rarely be granted in home ports, and boatloads of whores were needed to slake the lust of sailors who were in truth near-prisoners. No pressed man could be trusted to stay in the service, and half of the navy were pressed.[51]

The army filled its ranks by enticement rather than force. Bounties were offered. Likely recruits were made drunk. The navy also offered bounties, but to insufficient effect. At the outbreak of war, the government issued warrants to local authorities, admirals and captain who then organised 'press-gangs' of hired thugs. Men without experience at sea were in theory exempt, but in practice were commonly pressed, so that Cornish miners, for instance, would prudently take themselves off to hide on Lundy Island. Masters and officers of merchant ships were generally invulnerable. Otherwise, no seaman was safe, and the men in charge of pressing could therefore extort plenty of bribes. The gaols were raked for men. Liverpool crimps brought over poor Irish and sold them to the gangs. But most impressment was done on the water. While outward-bound ships were normally exempt, vessels returning home would be accosted. Violent affrays were common. Thus, in 1740, returning East India ships, met by press-men in the Downs, fired on their boats and wounded several. Most of the merchant seamen aboard escaped.

Those who were captured were consigned to 'pressing tenders' in the ports where, until they could be distributed to ships, their lot, kept under strict guard behind barred portholes, was not markedly better than that of black slaves. Popular feeling execrated the press-gangs, and always sided with their victims. Philanthropists like Oglethorpe denounced the system — and so even did Admiral Vernon. When he protested in the Commons and asked for some more humane method, he was told that the Lords of the Admiralty hated impressment too, but could see no other way; they could not 'expose the nation to danger from reasons of private tenderness'. Like slavery, pressing remained legal. A register of seamen had once been attempted as an alternative, but it had failed, and attempts to revive the idea were always sunk by the shipping interest. The philanthropist Jonas Hanway, in 1756, would found a 'Marine Society' to channel vagrant and destitute men and boys into the navy, and this would provide some thousands of recruits. But the need would still run to scores of thousands, and 'free born Englishmen' would continue to walk in peril from press-gangs. The freeborn white in the New World colonies was luckier. Acts of 1708 and 1746 gave him virtual immunity. One admiral was arrested for pressing in Antigua and another was exasperated into making the threat that he would bombard Boston unless he got the men he wanted.[52]

But the colonies were a major source of strength at sea. North America provided masts and naval stores. The mainland's abundant produce made it easy to victual British squadrons in the West Indies. The French, by contrast, were cut off in wartime from normal sources of supply in Ireland. French campaigning in the West Indies was sharply limited. In some years there was no French naval presence at all. The British had permanent squadrons; the one based in Jamaica since Queen Anne's reign had ten or fourteen men-of-war in the 1740s, and there was a 'station' in the Leewards established in 1743. There were dockyards in Jamaica and Antigua, and the squadrons were regularly relieved by convoys from home. Their blockade of the French islands, though never wholly efficient, increased the shortage of victuals there. If a superior French force momentarily appeared, the British could retire into port until it went home, and then resume their normal business of attacking enemy commerce and defending British merchant ships.

The French system of recruitment was superficially more sophisticated than the British, but conscription was so unfair in practice that men forsook the sea in disgust and the maritime population of France actually declined in the eighteenth century. The French could not maintain their commerce and man their navy at the same time. The British could manage both, largely because from Queen Anne's day the Navigation Acts were amended to permit three-quarters of a merchantman's crew during wartime to be foreign-born. Aliens were swept into the navy also, leading to frequent diplomatic protests.

The French spent far less on their navy, which in the 1740s was at best little more than half the size of their main rival's. Its permanent officers, the 'Navy of the Red' were an exclusive aristocratic élite, despising the bourgeois 'Officers of the Blue' drawn in wartime from the merchant marine; quarrels between the two classes frequently interfered with tactics. The British navy was somewhat more meritocratic, as befitted a country with a more fluid social system. Chances of promotion from the lower deck were now small. But commissions could not be bought. While cadets could enter the service from the Royal Naval Academy at Portsmouth, founded in 1732 and catering for the sons of nobility and gentry, most officers began their careers between the ages of thirteen and sixteen as captains' servants. Promotion to midshipman depended on the captain's approval. No one could be commissioned lieutenant until he had served six years as midshipman or mate and had passed an examination. Competition was strong. Further promotion might go by merit as well as by influence. The British navy was probably the best-officered in Europe.[53]

Nevertheless, its commanders were cramped and on occasions paralysed by the code of practice embodied in 'Permanent Fighting Instructions' and by the sacrosanct doctrine that the line of battle must always be maintained. Warfare at sea as a rule was neither daring nor, by the standards of earlier and later days, savage. Commanders aimed to avoid action whenever they could honourably do so. They conducted war with a constant eye for pecuniary gain. Once a man had achieved the rank of captain, he received only half pay except when he was actually used. Hence a general avidity for prizes, shared by the ordinary seamen, whose zeal was kept up by the chance of a share in a sacked port or a captured treasure ship. Anson was only one seaman who made a huge fortune from prize money. A renowned admiral of this period, Boscawen, wrote to his wife, 'If these French gentry do not escape me this time, they will pay for the house and furniture too, besides something to save hereafter for all our dear children.'[54]

Providing convoys for merchantmen was a major duty for the navy. The system was far from perfect. Merchantmen would break and run as they neared home so as to avoid the press-gangs or be first to market, and might then fall easy prey to French privateers. But the French could not really check British trade so long as the British navy remained intact, while the weaker French mercantile marine was simply swept from the seas once the chief French naval squadrons were smashed. More than 3,000 British ships were taken in the war of 1739–48, nearly as many as those lost by France and Spain together, but they were a much smaller proportion of the island nation's whole tonnage.[55]

A British force deployed in the Channel could hope to choke enemy commerce. Blockade of Europe severed the French from their colonies. The French convoy system broke down. Neutral vessels became vital to the French sugar islands; in 1745, only one ship from France itself called at Guadeloupe, 168 came from the Dutch island of St Eustatius.[56] Next year a great French fleet – nearly half the whole navy – broke out and crossed to operate in harness with the army in Canada, but plague, famine and shipwreck devoured it, and thereafter it was difficult to get supplies to the St Lawrence, and impossible to recapture Louisbourg. British power at sea had already doomed the Young Pretender to failure, and had clearly established superiority over France and Spain combined, when Anson, in May 1747, caught a French fleet off Cape Finisterre and chased it till six men-of-war and several Indiamen were forced to surrender. The French forces now engaged against the British in India were denied timely succour.

V

Under the emperor Muhammad Shah (ruling 1719–48) Mughal India had lost coherence. The flow of revenue to Delhi dwindled as provincial governors (*nawabs*) asserted de facto independence and founded dynasties of their own. Military adventurers, above all the ranging Marathas, found in the growing anarchy a chance to establish new, ill-defined and predatory realms. The situation in the Carnatic epitomised the whole.

Nizam-ul-Mulk, the viceroy of the Deccan, based at Hyderabad, while technically still a subject of the Mughal, had reared himself up as an expansionist potentate in his own right. He made a deal with the Marathas, by which they would have a free hand in North India provided they did not attack his territories. This enabled him to assert his authority over the Carnatic, where the Nawab in turn was converting his official post based at Arcot into hereditary rule, and was interested in absorbing two principalities to the south, the Hindu realm of Trichinopoly, which was conquered in the late 1730s, and Tanjore, which had a Maratha raja. A major Maratha force took sides in this latter struggle, killed the Nawab in 1740, destroyed his army, and forced his son and heir to make terms. Vicious succession crises characterised Mughal India at every level. The new Nawab was murdered by his brother-in-law in 1742, but the latter failed to establish himself and local feeling favoured the 'legitimate' line now represented by a young boy. The aged Nizam, intervening, found a chaotic situation where every subordinate governor and commander had assumed the title of Nawab. He installed his own man, Anwar-ud-din Khan, but adherence to the old dynasty persisted, and even after the murder of the 'legitimate' boy, a relative, Chanda Sahib, launched a fresh succession struggle.

Three European powers held cities in the Carnatic, in each of which a few hundred white men ruled unknown thousands of Indians. These were, in the whole Indian pattern, no more than petty states established, like others, by alien opportunists. South of the British headquarters at Madras, the French held Pondicherry, and further south still, the Dutch possessed Negapatam. The Dutch had problems enough in Java. Involvement in native politics and in succession disputes there would give them by 1772 complete control of the island. But overall, their strength was clearly waning in the East as it was in Europe, where the famous textile industries were in decline, where even Dutch agriculture was now technically stagnant, and where foreign competition had weakened traditional dominance in the fisheries. The Netherlands were even beginning to suffer from a shortage of sailors. The Dutch East India Company had lost confidence in its own capacity to compete with the British in Asia.[57]

That left the French to duel with the EIC. The struggle was not for territories, let alone empire. Both sides, when war was declared in Europe in 1744, sought nothing in India save commercial advantage and security. During Queen Anne's war there had been an unofficial truce in India, and the English at Cuddalore had successfully asked the governor of Pondicherry to mediate in their dispute with a local raja. Though the French company was supported by the State (which guaranteed its dividends from 1723) its personnel in India aimed straightforwardly, like the British, at private wealth. This was true, during his early career, even of the formidable Dupleix.

But Dupleix, who had been in India since 1722 and had married a woman partly of native descent, was transformed from a man preoccupied by his own private trade into an ambitious military schemer by what seemed to him British treachery. As governor of Pondicherry, he hoped, when undeclared war developed in Europe, to arrange a mutual pact of neutrality with the British as in Queen Anne's war. He thought that he had achieved agreement. Then, at the end of 1744, a small British squadron arrived in Indian waters where the French for the moment had no warships. The EIC men had rightly pointed out that they could not control the Royal Navy, but Dupleix was furious when news came that Commodore Barnett's squadron had captured the French China fleet, and several ships in the French 'country' trade.

The French held Île de France (now Mauritius) and under its governor, La Bourdonnais, Port Louis there had become a well-equipped naval base. La

Bourdonnais's improvised fleet of armed commercial ships arrived on the Coromandel coast in June 1746. Barnett was dead and Peyton, his stodgy successor, commanded a weary and weakened force. French sea-power momentarily ruled the coast. Madras swiftly surrendered, after only six casualties. If the treaty which La Bourdonnais now concluded with the Madras Council were followed, he would receive a handsome cash reward, but Dupleix would get nothing. The two Frenchmen quarrelled. Another hurricane forced La Bourdonnais to return to base, leaving Dupleix with 1,200 extra soldiers, brought from Île de France, and his chance to denounce the treaty and plunder the town. The British were expelled. Dupleix attempted to transfer the entire trade of Madras to Pondicherry but native merchants were not eager to move and the French had to content themselves with extorting bribes from those who remained.

The immediate military sequel had epochal implications. Dupleix had kept the Nawab out of the contest by suggesting that he was taking Madras only in order to hand it over to him. Anwar-ud-din Khan now demanded the city. Dupleix retorted that since the British had owned the place by absolute sovereignty, he himself had a perfect right to keep it. The Nawab sent troops. Twice, with ease, the French repulsed them.

How was it that Paradis, a Swiss engineer officer, with 230 'European' soldiers, 700 Indian troops, and no artillery, was able to attack and rout the Nawab's force of over 10,000 men, which had the support of guns? 'National spirit' was hardly the reason. Robert Orme, who knew India at this time, wrote that 'The European troops in the service of the colonies established in Indostan, never consist intirely of natives of that country to which the colony belongs: on the contrary, one half at least is composed of men of all the nations in Europe. The christians, who call themselves Portuguese, always form part of a garrison: they are little superior in courage to the lower casts [sic] of Indians, and greatly inferior to the higher casts, as well as to the northern Moors of Indostan; but because they learn the manual exercise and the duties of a parade with sufficient readiness, and are clad like Europeans, they are incorporated into the companies of European troops. From wearing a hat, these pretended Portuguese obtained amongst the natives of India the name of Topasses; by which name the Europeans likewise distinguish them. The Indian natives, and Moors, who are trained in the European manner, are called Sepoys: in taking our arms and military exercise, they do not quit their own dress or any other of their customs. The Sepoys are formed into companies and battalions, and commanded by officers of their own nation and religion. These troops of the natives, who bring with them their own arms, and continue in their own manner of using them, retain the names they bear in their several countries. On the coast of Coromandel the Europeans distinguish all the different kinds of undisciplined militia by the general name of Peons ...'[58]

The key to European success from the 1740s lay in the training which, as Orme stressed, all these troops save the 'Peons' were given. Whether Pathans or South Indian Hindus, 'Topasses' or Germans, Swedes or Irishmen, the men in the cosmopolitan armies gathered by Dupleix and by his British enemies, though prone to desert from either to the other, depended on their current employer for pay, and were prepared to be drilled. Even the most mediocre white commander in India now had assets denied to the forces deployed by the Childs in Bengal in the 1680s. Then, a third of the East India Company army had carried pikes and their artillery could fire no more than fifteen rounds to the hour. Now, all 'Europeans', and Sepoys, had musket and bayonet, while field-pieces could discharge ten or twelve shots a minute.[59] The native-led armies which met them also had muskets, but they were not trained to use them in the disciplined way which now brought momentous results. Native rulers had guns, but set greatest store by unwieldy pieces of vast size. Their traditions of warfare were antiquated and uneconomical.

The Mughals and their viceroys had adopted the classic form of the Indian army, more than two thousand years old, a core of elephants surrounded by a crowd of brave but undisciplined cavalry. Infantry was despised and its best use not understood. A charge of the mail-clad horsemen who made up the bulk of the army was the favourite tactic in battle; these warriors, often superb as individual fighters, were unwilling to risk their mounts against guns, and their tremendous surges forward were quite easily smashed by smaller European squadrons riding with discipline stirrup to stirrup. Indian armies were commonly huge — in 1750, the Nizam's camp exceeded twenty miles in circumference and was thought to contain a million people.[60] But they were correspondingly clumsy in movement. Few of the troops, proportionately, would be directly recruited and paid by the leader. The mighty-seeming hosts would be composed for the most part of loose groups led by vassals and allies, each of whom was quite likely awaiting the chance to sell his defection for a good price. There was hardly a battle in which great lords did not stand aloof or change sides. But while loyalty to a common cause was rare, and national feeling in effect unknown, the death or flight of a leader, conspicuous on his elephant, was enough to precipitate rout. Both sides would use, and expect, treachery. Unless a leader commanded overwhelmingly superior forces, he would seek to win by ruse or intrigue. Men who played war as a deadly game in this way were suddenly, in the 1740s, shown to be highly vulnerable when faced with Europeans, whose attitudes to fighting were more direct and whose disciplined infantry was a factor hitherto unknown in Indian battle.

The most remarkable of these Europeans, Robert Clive, had arrived in Madras as a 'Writer' in the EIC service in June 1744, just before war broke out. Two years later, disguised as a native interpreter, with his face blacked, he escaped from the city after the French had captured it. Like others, he made his way to Fort St David, the second-ranking British settlement, only a dozen miles from Pondicherry. In just over eighteen months, this place experienced five French attacks. Dupleix was thwarted by the arrival of Admiral Thomas Griffin, who blockaded Pondicherry itself. Anson's action off Finisterre preserved the British command of Coromandel waters. Three vessels from France which were able to reach Île de France in October 1747 managed to distract Griffin a while, but the fifth French attack on Fort St David was beaten off by the garrison there, amongst whom Clive was now commissioned as Ensign, at the age of 21. 'Be sure,' the Court of Directors wrote from London when it heard of his change of vocation, 'to encourage Ensign Clive in his martial pursuits, according to his merit ... '[61]

St David was relieved of all danger by the arrival in July 1748 of the strongest British squadron yet seen in Indian waters, thirteen ships of the line and a score of smaller craft, under Rear-Admiral Boscawen. The French were now besieged in turn. The British massed 4,000 'Europeans' (half of them genuine articles fresh from Scotland, Ireland, and the English gaols) and about 2,000 native foot. Dupleix had less than 5,000 men to oppose them. Disease more than equalised matters. While the French during six weeks of siege lost only about 250 men of all races, over a quarter of the 'Europeans' on the British side died or were incapacitated, chiefly by sickness. Ensign Clive displayed some 'merit'. A French sally sent the British troops flying from their trenches. Only one platoon remained, and this was about to run away when 'their officer, ensign Clive, reproached them sternly for their pusillanimity, and represented the honour they would gain by defending the trench ... All the company's troops had an affection for this young man, from observing the alacrity and presence of mind which always accompanied him in danger ... ' and the thirty or so soldiers, 'animated by his exhortation', fired with such deadly aim upon the confident enemy that the French in turn fled back to town.[62] If there was an element of classical embellishment in Robert Orme's account of the incident, it served to encourage the faith, which Clive himself shared, that the British were now finding heroes to emulate the ancient Romans. However, the monsoon approached. The British retired. News came of peace made in Europe.

Within that continent, French arms had triumphed everywhere. 'We are beaten and shall be broke,' Henry Pelham lamented. But the British navy had redressed the balance. Anson's successor in the Channel, Rear-Admiral Hawke, had caught another outward-bound French convoy off Finisterre in October 1747. All but two of the warships guarding it had been forced to strike by nightfall. The impact of the rout of the navy on France's colonial commerce can be measured; worth 24 million livres in 1743, its value sank to 7 million in 1748.[63] The Nantes slave trade had been almost destroyed. So England was able to gain surprisingly good terms at the Treaty of Aix la Chapelle. Frederick the Great of Prussia kept Silesia. Otherwise, all conquests were handed back. The original cause of war between Britain and Spain was not settled at all. Jenkins's Ear had produced effects as absent as itself. A treaty of 1750 put formal end to the South Sea Company's trading career. The *guarda-costas* resumed their work. The logwood controversy went on.

When Britain handed back Louisbourg in return for Madras, there was fury in New England. The conquest of Cape Breton Island had already nurtured ill feeling, as the British commander had kept colonial troops there over the winter on garrison duty and had replaced American officers with British. This was a colonial conquest, after all. What right had London to give it away? Governor Shirley of Massachusetts had his own reason for wishing the place to be kept; it would, he argued, serve to restrain the colonists, 'if ever there should come a time when they should grow restive and dispos'd to shake off their dependency upon their Mother Country.' (There was indeed renewed sign of the ancient truculence of Massachusetts; the General Court about this time tried to stimulate local manufactures, and produced an Act, disallowed, of course, to restrict such 'unnecessary' imports as tea, snuff and china.) Even in England, the concession of Louisbourg was disliked. Tobias Smollett would complain that the British government had given up 'the important isle of Cape Breton, in exchange for a petty factory in the East Indies, belonging to a private company, whose existence had been deemed prejudicial to the commonwealth.'[64] But in North America, as in India, British and French alike saw the inconclusive treaty as only a truce.

VI

Besides the Treaty of Aix la Chapelle, 1748 saw the death of the Mughal emperor Muhammad Shah, the usual wave of upper-class murders in Delhi and a falling apart of things at the centre in India. Marathas and Afghans, moving in, vied for power in Hindustan. Though this had no immediate bearing on the position in the Deccan and the Carnatic, it established a context in which, sooner or later, European trading companies in India must have been drawn into politics and warfare. To Londoners and Parisians, Yankees and Canadians, India and the affairs of its 'petty factories' formed a remote arena of exotic and mysterious sideshows. White men in Pondicherry and Fort St David, hearing about events in Europe and the New World only months after they had occurred, continued to act as local circumstance and personal greed and ambition seemed to dictate. By mere and yet most portentous coincidence, the first climax of Anglo-French imperial rivalry in America deposited small forces of national rather than company troops in India at just the juncture when, as it happened, their deployment could begin to revolutionise the subcontinent and world affairs.

In the words of Robert Orme, ' ... The war had brought to Pondicherry and Fort St David a number of troops greatly superior to any which either of the two nations had hitherto assembled in India; and as if it was impossible that a military force, which feels itself capable of enterprizes, should refrain from attempting them, the two settlements, no longer authorised to fight against each other, took the resolution of employing their arms in the contests of the princes of the country: the English with great indiscretion, the French with the utmost ambition.'[65]

Dupleix, somewhat cocksure after his capture of Madras and successful defence of Pondicherry, resentful of the part played by the Nawab of the Carnatic, Anwar-ud-din Khan, and short of money to support the large force which he now had on his hands, decided on a gamble. He accepted the proposal from Chanda Sahib, representative of the old ruling family, that the French should help him oust Anwar-ud-din in return for reimbursement after the event. There was no guarantee, of course, that the French would ever be paid, yet the enterprise went forward, drawing in an important ally, Muzafar Jang, a claimant to the viceroyalty of the whole Deccan. Meanwhile, the British, amongst whom Boscawen's voice was probably decisive, executed a smaller project of their own. Boscawen, both admiral and general at Fort St David (EIC headquarters were not transferred back to Madras for several years) had the taste for loot, and the sharp eye for it, of successful men of his class. He liked the proposition made by Shahaji, a former raja of Tanjore, who was seeking to regain his throne and promised the fort of Devikottai, some land around it, and payment of expenses, if the EIC would give him mercenaries. The first attempt, by land and sea, was a disastrous failure. To regain prestige, the EIC sent a fresh expedition under Major Stringer Lawrence.

Lawrence, already fifty when he had arrived in India, had fought in Europe and at Culloden, and his experience, tough constitution and adequate pugnacity probably made him a bargain at the price ($£250$ a year) which the EIC were paying him.[66] He had created an adequate little army. In June 1749 he took Devikottai. The British, finding that Shahaji had no popular support, made terms with the actual ruler of Tanjore, and duly acquired the fort and a lakh of rupees. But Dupleix was after bigger stakes, and his schemes now forced the EIC into a strange, sluggish war at second hand where each European side backed rival native princes and pretenders.

British and French forces remained small. Dupleix began with some 1,200 'Europeans' in his garrison, the British with only some 800. Over the four years 1750–3, 2,500 reinforcements despatched by the French company reached India, while his EIC rivals received over 1,800, of whom 500 were Swiss.[67] Dupleix, acting far beyond his instructions, was then drawn deeper and deeper in by the need to justify his policies with the unanswerable argument of grand actual success, and by the consideration that only victory could pay his troops. The fact that his officers, like himself, looked always to immediate personal profit, made the problem of remunerating the rank and file still more difficult. Intervention in native affairs brought jewels, rupees, the gold coins called 'pagodas', in delectable plenty to French adventurers. The windfalls of war also allured the British, but their overweening motive was self-defence. It looked as if Dupleix might manage to drive them out of South India. While directors of the two companies in Europe wanted only the profits of peaceful commerce, Dupleix's schemes involved their employees in a life and death struggle.

In August 1749, the French and their allies defeated and slew the Nawab. Chanda Sahib was thus installed, and Dupleix's rewards were large grants of land for the French. The EIC had to secure itself, and supported Muhammad Ali, the dead Nawab's son. Dupleix sent troops to attack him, but the constant problem of finance asserted itself, and at the suggestion of their allies his men turned off to try to exact tribute from Tanjore. The British encouraged the raja there to resist, which he did for several months, till the intervention of Nasir Jang, viceroy of the Deccan, further widened the scope of the contest. The French quit the siege of Tanjore. Months of manoeuvre followed, in which the British openly sided with Nasir Jang against his French-backed nephew, Muzafar Jang. Then in December 1750 Nasir Jang was defeated and killed by a French army. The French now seemed all-powerful, with Muzafar Jang recognising Dupleix as governor of all India south of the river Krishna and with their most notable soldier, Bussy, installed at Hyderabad as the viceroy's chief support. The British now had to build up their own coalition against Dupleix and his allies and puppets. Saunders, the president at Fort St David, sent, in May 1751, eight or nine hundred troops to support Muhammad Ali at Trichinopoly. Dupleix in turn despatched an army to capture that place, officially in the interests of Chanda Sahib. As a long siege proceeded, Robert Clive marched into fame.

He came from a long-established but now hard-pressed family of country gentry in Shropshire. He was one of eight children, and was packed off to Madras at the age of seventeen. He seems to have shown till then no great promise, and his impecunious father was willing to risk him on the off-chance that he might get rich out there, and so repair the family fortunes. The declassed youth was reserved and aloof during his early days in the East as a 'Writer', oppressed, it seems, by his consciousness of the need to economise and thrive for the sake of his family, and hoping for a transfer to the richer pastures of Bengal. War came as a relief, but as fighting ceased after the capture of Devikottai, Lieutenant Clive was glad enough of the lucrative position of commissary to the EIC troops, which soon brought him a fortune of £40,000.

In 1750 he suffered what seems to have been his first attack of an illness combining nervous depression with physical symptoms, probably gallstones, possibly chronic malaria, to counter all of which he employed opium. It recurred throughout the rest of his life. His manic-depressive temperament baffles brief description; though he had some taste for books, and would write powerful letters, deeds rather than words expressed his full character, and his deeper motivations elude his biographers. He was certainly very ambitious, and no more unconcerned with his personal interests than any other European in India at that time. Yet an almost morbid streak of fatalism seems to have powered the rashness with which he dashed into danger, a spirit wholly remote from the patience of the counting-house. He was neither a handsome man nor a likeable one. His most attractive side was shown to his family. He was a devoted son and brother, and an affectionate and faithful husband. His strengths and his limitations alike reflected the old-fashioned area on the marches of Wales where he had grown up. Stringer Lawrence, who liked and encouraged the young soldier, and who in return awakened his devotion, was also a 'Marcher' by birth. Neither man would have risen high in conventional English society. Both found scope in India. The elements of Clive's personality may have been quite simple. He loved pomp, luxury and pre-eminence, and projected himself robustly into an antique mould of heroism. His manners suited war and command and Sepoys. In the drawing-room he appeared uncouth. The reflexes of class-conscious England would eventually repudiate such straightforward animal power, once his fellow countrymen realised that he was not of the species of Roman whom they loved to imagine and to extol, but uncomfortably like the real pre-Christian item. By 1752, he owned a gold coat, and a gold turban.

This was after Arcot, which gave him reputation to match his own exorbitant taste for finery. Muhammad Ali, encircled in the great rock fortress at Trichinopoly, wanted his British allies to make a diversion towards Arcot, Chanda Sahib's capital, some three-score miles south of Madras. Clive was selected to lead the expedition. He was given 210 'European' troops and 600 Sepoys. Of the eight officers with him, only two had seen action and four had come straight from merchant life. Ten miles from the city, the expedition marched into a violent thunderstorm. Clive led them on regardless through rain and lightning. This was too much for the garrison at Arcot, which saw such egregious progress as an omen. The fort was abandoned. On September 1, 1751, Clive took possession of the citadel.

In his first burst of enthusiasm, Clive sent to Madras for a Union Jack. But President Saunders there would have none of that; the place must be held in the name of the Mughal emperor, who was in theory Muhammad Ali's overlord. Chanda Sahib could not let Clive stay there endangering his own revenue collection. On September 24, his troops took over the town itself. Fifty days of close siege of the fort by them made Clive a hero. His defence was sometimes rash but always brave. The fort was dilapidated. The moat was easily forded. His troops were in danger of starvation and under constant fire from a force of 10,000. Four men were shot dead when at Clive's side; such luck in a leader impressed Muslims and Hindus. According to one of his white sergeants, his fellow countrymen 'solaced' themselves 'with the pleasing reflection of having maintained the character of Britons in a clime so remote from our own.' Climax came on November 14. The besiegers were worried by news that a Maratha chief had agreed to come to Clive's aid. They decided to storm the fort, and attempted to batter down the gates with elephants which had pikes fastened to iron bands around their heads. Clive's men fired at these unlucky creatures, which turned and trampled on the troops behind them. Though Clive had only

240 men of all races fit for duty, fighting went on all day and the enemy was repelled at every point. Besides the Marathas, there was an EIC relief force advancing, and the besiegers now suddenly withdrew.[68]

Connoisseurs of slaughter, captious historians, and liberals anxious to demote Clive's achievements have argued that he was never a good general. Their doubts are wholly irrelevant. How Clive would have performed in the set-piece battles of Europe cannot be known or guessed. Under Indian conditions, where reputation might by itself bring victory, he had shown himself fortunate, and an effective leader of men. 'Sabit Jang', men called him: 'Steady in War'. After Arcot, the tide turned against the French. Clive soon won his first victory in the open field, at Arni, expelled the French garrison from Conjevarum and then, early in 1752, at Caveripauk, routed a force, larger than his own, which Dupleix had sent against Madras. He was about to lead an army to Trichinopoly when Stringer Lawrence, who had been to London to argue about his salary, re-appeared and took over command, but it was the magical coloration of Clive's rapid series of successes, marked by many cat's-whisker escapes from death, which was now inducing native commanders to switch their assistance to the British side British success was soon completed by the surrender of several hundred French troops at Trichinopoly and the death of Chanda Sahib, be-headed by a Tanjorean general after he had given himself up In September Clive's capture of two important French forts made Muhammad Ali the effec-tive ruler of the whole Carnatic. Then the young Clive *Bahadur*, Clive the Brave, as the Nawab had officially styled him, suffered one of his phases of illness and asked for home leave. He arrived in England again a famous man, in October 1753, rich enough to redeem the mortgages on his family's home, to pay his father's debts, to give his sisters allowances, to buy a Cornish borough seat in Parliament and to set up a genteel establishment in the West End of London. The public acclaimed him. The EIC directors gave him a gold-hilted sword set with diamonds.

But Dupleix was not yet beaten. Bussy still dominated the viceroy's court at Hyderabad. Dupleix's diplomacy lured key native allies from the EIC and in December 1752 he resumed the offensive. Trichinopoly came under siege again, and the French were still trying to take the place in August 1754 when one Godeheu arrived at Pondicherry, sent to replace Dupleix by authorities at home who had long disapproved of his unofficial war. By the end of the year, Dupleix was on his way home and the two companies had agreed a provisional treaty by which both would cease to meddle in the quarrels of native princes. It is hard to believe, however, that this could have stabilised matters, even if fresh war had not broken out between England and France on the other side of the world.

Horace Walpole noted in 1754 that people in England were beginning to think 'that an East Indian War and a West Indian war may beget such a thing as an European war.'[69] They had just heard of the defeat of a very young

Virginian colonel named Washington in the Ohio country, south of the Great Lakes.

The growth of Britain's seaboard colonies had now shifted the whole balance of empire so as to give ministers in London, on the one hand, somewhat dizzying visions of vast markets opening up as the land beyond the mountains was settled, and, on the other, acute consciousness of French jealousy and French pressure. Louisbourg, handed back, had been made stronger than before. To match it, the British government took a strikingly novel step. Halifax, Nova Scotia, was to be built up as both military base and naval station. In a year over 3,000 settlers were sent out at public expense. Even Georgia provided only partial precedent for this act of strategic colonisation. There was now a dispute over how much of 'Acadia' France had actually ceded in 1713; Paris claimed that only the Nova Scotia peninsula had been intended, and the French proceeded to fortify the northern end of the Isthmus of Chignecto. French priests incited the Micmac Indians to attack isolated British settlers. French-speaking Acadians refused to take the oath of unqualified allegiance to George II which was demanded of them.

Meanwhile, the governor of New France, De la Galissonière, was attempting to make good the French claim to the entire Mississippi basin by linking Canada and Louisiana with a line of forts which would shut the British off from the west. In 1749 he despatched 200 people to the Ohio valley, where they claimed the territory for France and expelled British traders found in Indian settlements. Such behaviour might thwart the taste for land speculation which now engrossed big and middling men alike in the British colonies. Two great consortia in Virginia were now competing for western lands. A coterie of prominent families – Lee, Mason, Fairfax, Washington – had organised the 'Ohio Company' in 1747. This was granted 200,000 acres, providing that within seven years it built a fort near the Ohio River's 'forks' and settled a hundred families. The Loyal Company, which included Thomas Jefferson's father, was granted, without obligation to colonise, 800,000 acres in 1749–52.[70]

The successful British naval blockade in France had gravely damaged French trade with the Indians, interrupting the flow of trade goods to the St Lawrence. Traders from Pennsylvania had penetrated the Ohio Valley and had drawn the red men there into the British trading sphere. The French had to act. In 1752 they sent a party of Ottawa Indians led by a Wisconsin half breed to chastise the Miamis for their defection. Then an expeditionary force of 2,200 went in the next year to cut and fortify a route from Lake Erie to the upper Ohio and to build forts on that strategic line.

Hence the first fame of George Washington, six years younger than Clive, also a man of action rather than eloquence, but better adapted to neo-classical taste: the noblest Roman, time would reveal, of them all. Slow in thought, marmoreal in his silences, six foot two, with huge feet and hands, immensely dignified in his bearing, his 'Character of Convention' as one contemporary would style it, would eventually make him not the least striking monarch to reign in the English-speaking world. He had no talent for oratory to match his taste for pomp and circumstance, but he was a splendidly graceful horseman, incapable of fear, or at least of revealing it. In habits he typified his own planting class. He was devoted to fox-hunting, horses, dancing and cards, rarely seen with a book but obsessively interested in farming technique; an excellent businessman of that special Virginian breed, regretful that he had to own slaves but prepared to work them as hard as might be. He attended church because everyone did so and worried very little about spiritual or moral issues. Manners, however, exercised his attention; in his fourteenth year he had drawn up a hundred or more 'Rules of Civility', which he employed to subdue his raw-boned provincial gaucheness: 'SHAKE not the head, Feet or Legs, rowl not the Eyes, lift not one eyebrow higher than the other, wry not the mouth and bedew no mans face with your Spittle, by approaching too near him when you speak.'[71] But his predisposition to become a statue was not wholly evident in the early 1750s, when his career as warrior began with his colonelcy, in the Virginian militia, acting directly in the interests of his class. Born on a 1,000-acre plantation along the Potomac, protégé of Thomas, Lord Fairfax who owned almost a quarter of Virginia and had employed him to survey the frontier lands, inheritor of the large estates of his brother, who had helped found the Ohio Company, Washington volunteered to beard the French. The Ohio Company wanted to set up its own fort on the Forks. Members like Washington wanted those foreigners out.

French forts at Presquisle and Le Boeuf now commanded a line pointing south to the Forks. Governor Dinwiddie of Virginia, another member of the Ohio Company, sent the 21-year-old colonel on a 500-mile journey to warn the French off Company territory. Washington was no diplomat, and never learnt French. The hated rivals were gentlemanly, but frank. 'They told me,' Washington recorded, 'That it was their Absolute Design to take Possession of the Ohio, and by G—— they would do it ... '[72] He trekked home across the mountains in freezing weather with nothing to show but a polite brush-off.

The British government gave Dinwiddie permission to repel force by force. With a small sum obtained from the grudging Virginia Assembly, he sent an ill-equipped force of 400 to protect a party which was now building the Company's fort on the Forks. The commander died on the way and Washington, second in command, took charge. He proved himself a resourceful leader of raw troops in frontier conditions. Word came as he proceeded that the uncompleted fort at the Forks was already in French hands and had been named Duquesne in honour of the current governor of New France. But he went on and ambushed a party of French soldiers in May 1754, killing the leader and nine other men. This small affray by the Monongahela River can be called the start of the new Anglo-French war. As the French advanced, Washington fell

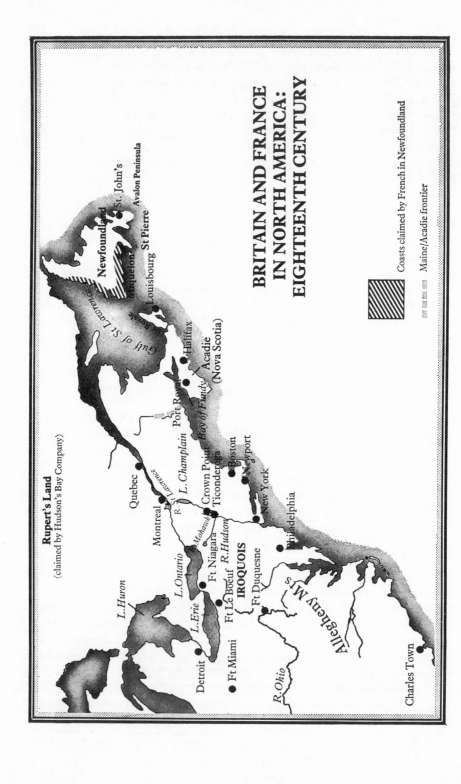

**BRITAIN AND FRANCE
IN NORTH AMERICA:
EIGHTEENTH CENTURY**

Coasts claimed by French in Newfoundland

Maine/Acadie frontier

Rupert's Land
(claimed by Hudson's Bay Company)

L. Huron

Detroit

L. Erie

Ft Miami

R. Ohio

L. Ontario

Ft Niagara

Ft Le Bœuf

Ft Duquesne

IROQUOIS

Allegheny Mts

Charles Town

Montreal

Quebec

R. St Lawrence

Mohawk

R. Hudson

L. Champlain

Crown Point

Ticonderoga

New York

Philadelphia

Boston

Newport

Port Royal

Bay of Fundy

Halifax

**Acadie
(Nova Scotia)**

Gulf of St Lawrence

Port Royal

Louisbourg

Miquelon

St Pierre

Newfoundland

St. John's

Avalon Peninsula

back to an improvised fort where, in July, he was besieged and forced to surrender after nine hours and a hundred casualties.

Other colonies were not ready to back Dinwiddie in the informal war which he had started. South Carolina, with its large slave population, could not spare troops. New Jersey had no frontier. Pennsylvania had an assembly still dominated by pacifist Quakers, and much jealousy of the activities of Virginian speculators. New York interests feared the effect of war on relations with the Indians. The Iroquois were now restive and were complaining of lack of British protection. The Board of Trade in London had pressed for a conference of colonists with Iroquois to forge a new understanding, and while Washington was engaged with the French, this met at Albany. It was unsuccessful. Only seven colonies were represented. The treaty made with the Indians was harsh and led to trouble later. Pennsylvania and Connecticut officials tricked Indians into deeding them a vast tract including the lands of tribes whose representatives had not signed the document. Meanwhile, they busily cheated each other. The Indians, unimpressed by British behaviour, would generally side with the French in the coming conflict.

An attempt was made at Albany to find a basis for union between the colonies. The common danger from French and Indians made this seem desirable; so, in some minds, did grandiose new ideas of 'empire' in the New World. 'Empire' was now outgrowing its old limited, Thomas-Cromwellian sense and was gathering to itself the amplitude suggested by the now-cherished comparison between imperial Britain and the Roman *imperium* of Augustus.

Benjamin Franklin was the leading imperialist in the colonies. He had pointed to the swift increase of population in British North America, he had voiced the demand for *Lebensraum*, and he had been calling for a voluntary union of the colonies as a basis for federal empire. He wanted the abolition of British Acts 'restraining the trade or cramping the manufactures of the colonies', and a federation in the New World which would be mightier yet, becoming one day the dominant force in the empire. Anticipating favourite ideas of the early twentieth century, Franklin's was the first vision of 'the Empire' as a worldwide political system held together by the mutual affection and harmony of its constituent parts.[73]

At Albany, he was one of a steering committee of seven which, after four days, unveiled a plan combining his draft with that of a high-minded, ambitious man from Massachusetts named Thomas Hutchinson. There should be a federal union of the colonies from South Carolina to Maine, with an annual 'Grand Council of Delegates' elected by the colonial assemblies and a 'President General' appointed by the Crown. This central government would control Indian affairs, declare war and make peace, raise and equip soldiers, and levy taxes.

The plan, however, was not accepted by even one of the colonial assemblies, and while the British government was sympathetic, it thought that the present crisis was not the time to attempt a novelty like this. Parliament never considered the scheme. Political attention in Britain was absorbed by the lengthy manoeuvres within the whig ruling élite which had followed the death, in March 1754, of Henry Pelham. His brother, Newcastle, more or less took charge.

The government now decided to undertake a limited campaign in North America, to which both British and colonists would contribute. The aim was to drive the French back to the position established in 1714 without launching a general war. Some petty forts were to be captured in four distinct offensives; that was all. But the decision had great significance. ' ... Great Britain for the first time was assuming responsibility for the defence of the colonial frontier.'[74] In retrospect, the commitment would seem fateful.

A force of 6,000 colonials failed to flush the French out of Crown Point on Lake Champlain. In Nova Scotia Fort Beauséjour was captured. Meanwhile, in April 1755, General Braddock had arrived in Virginia from Ireland with two regiments, which were to be augmented in the colonies, and then to strike at Fort Duquesne on the Forks. The colonists were not very helpful. Braddock found himself direly short of transport till the patriotic Franklin provided him with what he described as 'almost the only instance of ability and honesty I have known in these provinces'. In a fortnight, Franklin collected 150 wagons and 259 horses from Pennsylvania farmers by offering generous, rates and pledging £1,000 of his own resources. Franklin, however, by his own later account, was much less impressed with Braddock than the general was with him. Franklin reckoned Braddock a brave man who 'might probably have made a Figure as a good Officer in some European War. But he had too much self-confidence, too high an Opinion of the Validity of Regular Troops, and too mean a One of both Americans and Indians.' Franklin warned him of the danger of ambush on the march by pro-French Indians, but Braddock scoffed at the notion that these 'savages' could make any impression 'upon the king's regular and disciplin'd Troops ... '[75]

With Washington as his aide-de-camp, Braddock left Fort Cumberland on the Potomac in June on a 122-mile march to Fort Duquesne through mountains and primeval forests such as his British regulars had never seen before. Besides his two regular regiments, he had recruited several hundred colonial troops. Sensibly, his plan was to build as he proceeded a road through the wilderness fit to bear heavy artillery. This meant slow progress. About half way, he decided to press ahead with the better two-thirds of his force. Within nine miles of Fort Duquesne, a couple of hundred French Canadians and some 600 Indians trapped him, firing rapidly from cover behind trees and ridges. Out of 1,460 men on the British side, 863 were killed or wounded by this unseen foe. Their bare bones and battered skulls still littered the field twenty years later. Braddock himself died of his wounds.[76]

Repercussions were manifold. Letters captured in Braddock's baggage warned the French of the fourth prong of attack, a colonial force under Governor

Shirley of Massachusetts which was advancing to capture Fort Niagara. That too aborted. Secondly, colonists had their eyes opened to British vulnerability. 'This whole Transaction,' Franklin would write, 'gave us Americans the first Suspicion that our exalted Ideas of the Prowess of British Regulars had not been well founded.' The *Boston Gazette* charged the British troops with cowardice and compared them unfavourably with New Englanders. There was much friction between Britons and colonials in the Nova Scotia campaign – it had been some time before British regulars had conceded that ranks in the colonial forces should be counted equal to theirs. Washington himself, now left with 1,500 colonial troops in charge of protecting a frontier 400 miles long, was involved, not for the first time, in a dispute over seniority when a petty Captain at Fort Cumberland claimed to take precedence by virtue of his royal commission, and the Virginian had to go 500 miles to headquarters at Boston in order to get a ruling in his own favour.[77]

Thirdly, the danger from Indians, now attacking along the whole frontier, was such that the Quaker pacifists of the Philadelphia Assembly could not defeat a clamour for retaliation. By the spring of 1756 the colony was committed to war for the first time. Within a few weeks six leading Quakers resigned from the Assembly; others followed, and the so-called 'Quaker Party' now came under Benjamin Franklin's leadership.

Fourthly, the British Cabinet put behind it ideas of limited war. New France, like Carthage, must be destroyed. The way to all-out war with Old France was cleared by the so-called 'diplomatic revolution' in the early months of 1756 when the alliances of the 1740s were reversed; Britain came to terms with Prussia, and the enraged French King reached an understanding with Austria. Formal declaration of war came in May, after the French had attacked British-held Minorca. The 'Seven Years War' followed.

VII

Fifteen thousand French troops had landed in Minorca. Port Mahon, the capital, was blockaded. The British government, concerned about the Channel, could spare insufficient reinforcements for the Mediterranean. Rear-Admiral John Byng, arriving with only ten vessels off the island, had rather the worse of an engagement. Instead of remaining at hand to interrupt French reinforcements and supplies, he retreated to Gibraltar. At the end of June the small British garrison on Minorca surrendered.

Pitt, a sick man wandering from watering place to watering place in the early 1750s, had recently taken on a new lease of life, making a belated marriage and razoring Newcastle and his Cabinet with oratory as high pitched as ever, enhanced now by the bandagings and strange clothing which he employed to advertise his supposed decrepitude, and to dramatise himself as a prophet battered by fate but still mustering voice on behalf of his country. Towards the end of 1755 he had reminded the House of the 'long-injured, long-neglected, long-forgotten people of America', in an oration which finally cost him his post as Paymaster General. Cassandra-like, he had predicted the fall of Minorca, and the violence of his recent speeches contributed greatly to the mood of panic and rage which now gripped, it appears, British 'public opinion'. 'Never did the English nation suffer a greater blot,' a Sussex shopkeeper wrote in his diary. In the latinate words of Tobias Smollett, 'The populace took fire like a train of the most hasty combustibles ... ' Mobs erupted all over the country, burning the admiral in effigy, chanting 'Hang Byng or take care of your King.' The Lord Mayor of London presented an address to George II demanding punishment of 'the authors of our late losses'.[78] Why so much anger? Partly it was irrational, like the ferment over the 'Jew Bill' a few years before. Minorca had been important, but not essential; Gibraltar would still serve as a base for blockading the French Toulon fleet. But Port Mahon had been a useful centre for British traders, and naval weakness in the Mediterranean shocked and frightened merchants dealing with Italy and the Levant. Trade again demanded vigorous war. Trade now hoisted Pitt to power.

Newcastle and his colleagues, blamed for the disaster, offered the over-cautious Byng as a scapegoat, employed agents to blacken his name in the alehouses and hired mobs to whip up fury. Shamefully, Byng was court-martialled and executed for what had been, at most, an error of judgment. But meanwhile bad news from America was confirming the dread Pitt's prophetic status.

In a remarkably drastic measure, in 1755, ten thousand French-speaking Acadians, refusing a last chance to take the oath required of them, had been rounded up and shipped off from Nova Scotia to various parts of the New and Old Worlds. But attempted British blockade failed to prevent large reinforcements reaching Canada, and in 1756 a new commander, the Marquis de Montcalm, arrived in the St Lawrence.

He seemed successful at once. Yet if the gods had not reserved for him a touching and heroic death quite soon after, Montcalm might be remembered, like Braddock further south, as a man who had fatally impaired relations between colonists and metropolitan country. An 'enlightened' aristocrat, lively, impassioned, generous and rash, he disliked the cynical profiteering and the rude colonial habits which he found in Quebec, as well as the barbarousness of France's Indian allies and the tactics of *petite guerre* which the Canadians had learned from them. The governor, Vaudreuil, a native Canadian, was for his own part resentful of Montcalm, of French neglect and of French condescension. Canadians were as free-spirited as Yankees, and the French army in the New World was weakened, like the British, by quarrels between regular soldiers and Colonial militiamen. Montcalm's aide-de-camp, Bougainville, wrote of the Canadian attitude, 'It seems that we are of a different nation, even an enemy one.'[79] Nevertheless, using Vaudreuil's strategy rather than Montcalm's, the

56 The Palmer family, by Zoffany — an Englishman in India with his native wife and children

57 An Indian artist depicts a European smoking a hookah

58 Noble savages—an idealised version, from the 1790s, of the Caribs of St Vincent

French were able to thwart an attempt by Lord Loudoun, the new British commander, to drive them back in the critical Hudson-Montreal corridor.

Such news swelled the clamour for Pitt now heard in England. Men with interests in New World trade sang along with tories who liked Pitt's 'blue water' policy of naval rather than military aggression. The King had to give way, and in November a new government emerged with Pitt as Secretary of State and the Duke of Devonshire at the Treasury, to whom Pitt roundly said, 'I know that I can save this country and that no one else can.'[80] On one main point he swiftly compromised with the King. For years he had been denouncing the subsidising of foreign allies and the hiring of foreign troops, but he was now prepared to apply British funds to the support of a huge army on the Rhine, and to lavish financial assistance on Frederick the Great of Prussia. His idea was that while Frederick tied down the French in Europe Britain would further assist him by diversionary raids on the French coast. Spain should be kept neutral while the traditional blockade of the French navy supported major attacks on French colonies and commerce. While Pitt swiftly adopted the idea put to him by a Quaker merchant named Cumming that an expedition should be sent to chase the French from their West African posts, he prepared for a major effort in America. An 'expedition of weight' was to go which, by the summer, would give Loudoun 17,000 troops to attack first Louisbourg, then Quebec.

As a safeguard against invasion, Pitt now got the reactivated militia which he had been demanding for some time. Men were to be selected by ballot and were to train once a week through every summer. Each man was to serve for three years. The militia was to be paid for out of the rates and officered by volunteer landowners. Such a gesture pleased the lesser squires, but since men who could afford it could buy their way out of service, this was not a 'national' citizen army and until a fresh invasion scare came in 1759 response was only grudging. A bolder step was the arming of Highlanders who had been 'out' in the 1745 rebellion. Newcastle was seriously alarmed when one of Pitt's first actions was to raise two regiments of Gaels. At the time, Pitt insinuated cynically that it was best to kill such creatures off in Canada; but the prowess of the Highland troops made him proud of what he had done. 'I sought for merit wherever it was to be found ... ' he would brag one day, 'I found it in the mountains of the North. I called it forth ... '[81]

Despite the vigour which he showed in his first weeks in office, Pitt did not satisfy George II, who found the long speeches which his minister made to him in private both affected and incomprehensible. At the first chance, in April, he thrust Pitt out again. Pitt retorted with an elaborate publicity stunt, in which a dozen cities and towns testified their esteem for him by conferring their free-dom upon him, and in some cases making him presents – 'the rain of gold boxes'.[82] Twelve weeks of especially intricate factional intrigue followed his dismissal. The crisis was resolved when Newcastle agreed to combine with his

U

enemy Pitt. Newcastle's job was to find cash and provide secure majorities in the Commons. Pitt was to run the war. He had, in the phrase of the time, 'stormed' the King's closet.

He was the first politician to achieve such power by systematically playing upon imperial pride and commercial greed. His position seems to present-day thinking most paradoxical. He represented the older, popular strain of whiggery against the oligarchs led by Newcastle. He stood for the Commons against the Lords. He spoke up for quasi-democratical Americans, and in some measure did understand their point of view. Noises raised outside the imperfectly representative Parliament had helped to hoist him where he was. Yet 'at no time during his 31 years in the House of Commons did he, the idol of the Empire, represent as many as 100 electors.' He sat in succession for four 'rotten' boroughs, where the electorates ranged from seven to seventy-five.[83]

However, he held aloof from the borough-mongering which gave Newcastle his influence. He found it hard to work with other politicians and his more or less permanent 'party' of firm supporters was always small. 'Merit' in the form of rhetorical virtuosity had raised him to indispensability; the merit of hard and skilful work now helped him to seem to justify his supporters' faith. Few politicians of that era laboured, as he did, into the night. 'He worked like a clerk and spoke like a monarch.'[84] Pitt was Secretary of State at the Southern Department (which dealt with France, Southern Europe, the Far East and all the colonies). He made his 'Northern' counterpart no more than a cypher, and domineered over the titular First Minister, Newcastle. He gave orders direct to naval and military commanders, often without taking time to get the formal approval of a full Cabinet.

His strategical talents are questionable. In any case, his capacity to affect events was limited. The steamship and the telephone did not exist. Even if Pitt had taken more interest in India, his actions could have had only fortuitous bearing on events there. Letters from India took six months or a year to reach London. While orders for America might get to ports there in six weeks, they might then have to make a long journey up country. But Pitt had a simple objective – crush France – and this gave a certain unity and drive to what were in effect almost four different wars in four continents.

France's population was more than double that of Great Britain. The cost of fighting such an enemy put a severe strain on Britain's resources. Supplies voted at home and in the colonies rose from £7 million in 1756 to nearly £19 million in 1761. Houses and windows were taxed. Heavy duties on malt hit everyone. The money was squeezed from a British population 'of between five and a half and six million, many of them desperately poor and living barely at subsistence level.' In 1748 Britain had had 49 regiments of infantry; by 1761, there would be 115, and the strengths of battalions would have been greatly increased. All this did not imply 'total war' as a later century would know it, but Pitt was attempting to concentrate the efforts of the whole people on one end as no leader had done before him. A navy of 70,000 men, an army of 140,000, were prodigious by earlier standards.[85]

Britain had striking advantages. Votes of the Irish Parliament paid for over twenty regiments. And the large colonial population of British North America made the task of the French in the New World daunting. The problem was to mobilise it effectively. Pitt's policies made this easier. Colonial assemblies were promised some repayment for the cost of raising armed forces. In the end about two-fifths of the whole military outlay of the colonies was returned to them.[86] Furthermore, the home government would supply free arms and artillery, tents and provisions, if a colony found adequate numbers, clothed and paid them. In 1758 Pitt laid the bogey of precedence; henceforth, he ordained, a colonial captain would rank above a regular lieutenant. But grave problems persisted. The Albany Plan had aborted. Each colony went its own way.

Most colonists did not like the war, which was so patently being fought in the interests of men like Franklin — expansionists, speculators, ambitious politicians — and of fur traders and Yankee merchants. While assemblies in Connecticut and New York were ready to give generous support, and Massachusetts, required to raise 2,300 troops, actually found 7,000 and even offered to send men to help defend Britain against invasion, Virginia and Maryland showed less eagerness. The three colonies — Rhode Island, Maryland and Delaware — which had no foreign frontiers were not interested. New Hampshire and North Carolina pleaded poverty. In any case, local feelings made sound strategic deployment of colonial troops impossible. Virginia always refused to provide a garrison for Fort Cumberland because it lay in land claimed by Maryland — which latter colony, however, refused to admit any obligation, so that regulars had to be used. New England militia regiments elected their own officers. Assemblies sometimes laid down that their troops must serve only under such-and-such a commander and be used only for such-and-such operations. The troops themselves seemed of poor quality. 'They fall down dead in their own dirt,' a British officer named James Wolfe reported, 'and desert by battalions, officers and all.'[87] Most colonies had no effective law for enforcing military discipline. Men would serve only for liberal bounties and pay.

On top of all this, British regulars saw assemblies, as in previous wars, seizing the chance to increase their own powers. Thus Pennsylvania's tried yet again to tax the proprietors' estates by including the measure in a Bill granting money. The governor vetoed it, and a struggle ensued. The colony sent Franklin to London to present its case, achieving success in 1760. Such behaviour might well be resented in tax-racked Britain. A British writer sneered at the lucky American, 'deliberating for a year or two, whether he will pay six-pence in the pound, to save himself and family from perdition?'[88] Pitt's obligingness towards his 'neglected' Americans meant trouble for his successors in office, who would be subject to odious comparisons with his magnanimous Roman self.

Meanwhile, naval power, not weight of numbers on land, was still the key to success in America. Manning was harder than ever. Over the whole war, 133,708 sailors would be lost through disease or desertion, as compared with 1,512 killed in action. But British command of the seas was soon such that the French government gave up even trying to keep its colonies fully defended. By 1763, France would have lost 109 warships to Britain's 50. If British losses of trading vessels exceeded those of her foes, in 1760, by three to one, this was because French trade was almost annihilated while British ships, more numerous than ever, presented themselves in thousands for capture. The value of French colonial trade slumped by nine-tenths in five years.[89]

Though France's defeat in the New World would imply vast extensions of British territory, it was trading dominance which Pitt desired. Conquest was not seen as an end in itself. Fisheries, factories, naval bases, were the objectives. The capture of a French colony would give Britain an extra counter in peace negotiations. If Martinique could be exchanged for Minorca, this might save handing over Cape Breton Island again and thus would give Britain control of New World cod. Like the Dutch before them the British aimed to be masters of every sea. They were already reckoned to own a third of all the tonnage of shipping in European hands. It seemed as if Pitt wished to engross all. When the beleaguered French threw their Caribbean islands open to ships of all nations — otherwise French planters could not have disposed of their sugar — the self-righteous British denounced this as cheating. Neutrals should not be allowed to engage in trades closed to them in peacetime. Neutral ships were searched. British privateers attacked neutral vessels. Dutch and Swedes, Danes, Russians and Spaniards were bitter.

Pitt's colleague the Duke of Bedford objected farsightedly, 'The endeavouring to drive France out of any naval power is fighting against nature, and can tend to do no good to this country; but, on the contrary, must excite all the naval powers of Europe against us, as adopting a system, viz: that of a monopoly of all naval power, which would be at least as dangerous to the liberties of Europe as that of Louis XIV was, which drew all Europe upon his back.' But City interests doted on Pitt's war. Wealthy businessmen gathered more wealth by financing the loans on which Pitt depended. Ironmasters throve on the making of cannon. Traders gloated over the capture of fresh markets and the expansion of access to raw materials. In 1759, when a new tax on sugar was proposed in the Commons, Pitt's ally Beckford opposed it with a tedious speech about sugar, sugar, again sugar, which drew 'horse laughs' from the House. When Beckford sat down, Pitt rose. 'Sugar, Mr Speaker,' he began. Another laugh. 'Sugar, Mr Speaker,' Pitt thundered. Hush supervened. Then Pitt whispered in his sweetest tone, 'Sugar, Mr Speaker: who will laugh at sugar now?'[90] On behalf of men like Beckford the press-gangs went out, the contracts flowed, soldiers were lashed into discipline, slave ships flocked to the Bight of Biafra, sad ballads grieved for those gone to the 'wars of Germany'.

For all this, 1757 went badly for British interests. Frederick the Great lost a third of his army at Kolin in Bohemia. Most of Hanover was overrun by the French. Loudoun, reinforced too late and hearing that there were twenty-two French battleships in harbour at Louisbourg, called off the attack on that fort, then learnt, on his way back to New York, that Montcalm had taken Fort William Henry at the south end of Lake George. Blockade of the French ports was not yet effectual. A well-equipped raid on Rochefort failed because of quarrels between the commanders. The new Militia Act provoked dangerous riots in many counties; the poor rightly feared that militiamen might be sent to fight overseas, as had in fact happened in Huntingdonshire. Amid all this word had arrived, in June, that a year before the Nawab of Bengal had crushed the British factory at Calcutta.

VIII

Even after Dupleix's recall, the viceroy at Hyderabad was still in effect a French puppet. Bussy's role as his adviser was a direct threat to the British in both Madras and Bengal. In 1754, for the first time, Royal troops, 900 of them, were sent to India, with a small squadron commanded by Admiral Watson. An attack on Hyderabad through Bombay, with Maratha allies, was projected.

Within a decade or so, Europeans had lost all awe of native power in India. The French, from Dupleix downwards, had formed a contemptuous view of the double-dealing and decadence of the aspirants whom they manipulated. Their example was not lost on the British, nor was the lesson of Clive's successes.

Clive came back for the new round. He went to Bombay with a fresh consignment of troops. He now had a royal commission as Lieutenant-Colonel as well as the East India Company rank of governor of Fort St David, second man on the Coromandel Coast. EIC servants in Bombay, a relatively modest and prudish establishment, were not attuned to the new, grandiose, *realpolitik*. The Council there shied away from the attack on Bussy now proposed, and it was not made. To appease the frustrated Marathas, Watson and Clive, in collaboration with them, attacked and seized, with much loot, the west coast pirate stronghold of Gheria some 180 miles south of Bombay. Then Clive proceeded to the Coromandel Coast, and had just taken up office at Fort St David when word came of shameful events at Calcutta.

Bengal was, in Robert Orme's word, 'the paradise of India', abounding in rice, cattle and fish, and in skilled weavers. Earlier in the eighteenth century, up to three-fifths of British imports from Asia had originated here. The British enjoyed, under the 1717 *farman*, exceptional privileges in a region relatively much more stable, and hence more propitious for commerce, than the war-torn Carnatic or than Surat and Bombay under the Maratha shadow. The Bengal *zemindars* (revenue collectors) were in some cases rulers of huge areas, though others were quite small fry. They governed on the whole equitably, under Nawabs who had in the past rarely much annoyed the British. Cotton and silk textiles of unmatched quality were widely produced, as well as such precious crops as sugar-cane, indigo, tobacco, betel nut and opium. Salt and saltpetre also abounded. Bengal was one of those tropical areas where Europeans supposed climate and soil to combine to create such fecundity that the inhabitants hardly need labour to live. Orme and others attributed to this the 'general effeminacy' of the small, slender Bengalis, patient and skilful traders though some of these people were.[91] Prejudice apart, it was true that they had shown no disposition to resist their Mughal overlords.

Though still nominally subject to Delhi, the Nawab ruling the three provinces of Bengal, Bihar and Orissa had for some time been effectively independent. In 1740 the title had been usurped by an able soldier of fortune from Turkestan, Alivardi Khan. Almost at once, he faced heavy Maratha incursions. In the words of a Bengali poet, 'After looting in the open, the bargis [horsemen] entered the villages. They set fire to the houses, large and small, temples and dwelling places. They constantly shouted "Give us rupees, give us rupees, give us rupees." ' Those who would not pay were drowned.[92] After years of fighting, Alivardi Khan was forced, in 1751, to concede them Orissa and to pay them tribute. His constant need for money to fight wars created resentment and instability. Merchants and landholders were squeezed, while Muslim commanders chafed as Alivardi raised Hindus into positions of power. A dominant force in Bengal was the family of Jagat Seth, 'Banker of the World', the title bestowed in 1715 on a Jain named Manik Chand after he had lent the Emperor ten million rupees. His adopted son had controlled the mint at Alivardi's capital, Murshidabad, and the EIC had been among the Seths' clients.

Bengal, for all the antiquity of its civilisation, had become a kind of frontier. Marathas and Afghans hovered over an arena where Persians and Armenians, Punjabis, French, Dutch and British schemed for wealth and intrigued with well-to-do Bengalis. The soil was generous. Its tillers were quiescent. The prizes were lavish, and EIC men, who had gambled their lives in a deadly climate, were not disposed to resist their temptation.

There were only some 750 white men in the whole province. But Calcutta's population now stood at maybe 120,000.[93] Outside its rather handsome centre built in European style, where whites and rich Asians resided, sprawled a sordid collection of villages, shanty towns and *bazars* where robbery and murder were commonplace and European officials and their agents flogged and extorted unmercifully. However, the god Property was respected here as it was everywhere that people spoke English, and its veneration lured more and more of the Nawab's richer subjects, who found British 'justice' to their taste and settled in Calcutta with their dependants. The whites relied in their trading on Asian middlemen, Asian agents and even on Asian capital. While ambitious Indians were commonly attracted to serve EIC men as personal factotums – *banians* – almost every European was deep in debt to wealthy natives.

White merchants still smoked the hookah and copied other Indian habits.

They kept many servants and were carried about in palanquins. But they longed to reach home again and, if possible, to live in Britain in an equally grand way. The Nawab now seemed to be blocking their ways to wealth. The Emperor's *farman* of 1717 had left much to the Nawab's discretion. Permission to acquire some two score villages round Calcutta had been made conditional on the Nawab's sanction; when this was not given, the EIC had bought land through its native employees but had continued to offer revenue only for the three villages granted in 1698. The Nawab, understandably, asked for more. A greater vexation, since it bore on private trade rather than on the Company's interests, was friction over customs duties. EIC men claimed that the *farman* implied that their private trade should be free of them. The ruler's officials did not agree, and strove furthermore to block altogether British participation in the valuable internal trades in salt, betel nut and tobacco from which the Nawab drew much revenue.

British enterprise in Bengal was faltering. Around 1750, Bengal's share in the EIC's total Indian trade had been as high as two-fifths; in 1753–6 it slumped to little over a quarter. Prices of goods in Bengal had once been lower than else-where in Asia. But recently this had ceased to be true. In some sixteen years, the price of rice in Calcutta had tripled or quadrupled while that of textiles had risen by nearly a third.[94] Coinciding with disruptive wars and political problems in Western India, in Persia and in Arabia, this inflation had helped produce a slump in the 'country trade' with points west on which EIC men had depended for their private fortunes. Bankruptcies of Company servants had become quite common. Whites in Calcutta therefore were more avid than ever to profit from the rich internal trades of Bengal itself. At the same time, they were compelled to find excuses for their poor performance which would satisfy the EIC directors. The Calcutta Council blamed the 'exactions' of the Nawab as well as the competition of French and Dutch.

In 1754, higher demands for commission from native brokers prompted them to replace these independent intermediaries with agents employed full-time by the Company. Discontented ex-brokers joined the voices at Alivardi's court which condemned Europeans for whatever went wrong with the Bengal economy. But Alivardi did not want to tangle with the whites. Calcutta was now Bengal's main port. He told one of his generals, Mir Jafar, that the Euro-peans were like a hive of bees; their honey was good, but if one disturbed them, they would sting one to death.[95] News of what was happening in the Deccan and the Carnatic proved that these persons had a sting. The French in Bengal were suaver and more obedient than the British, who constructed fortifications without the Nawab's permission, and insisted on their sovereignty on their own patches, collecting taxes, charging their own customs duties, operating their own courts of law, and, it might be added, bullying any Bengalis in their grasp.

Yet they were fragile. There were about eighty covenanted EIC servants at

Calcutta and the four subsidiary factories, Kasimbazar, Dacca, Balasore and Jugdea, under a governor, Roger Drake, of sordid reputation. The least mediocre were probably William Watts, in charge at Kasimbazar, and John Zephaniah Holwell, born in 1711 the son of a timber merchant, trained as a surgeon, who held the lucrative post of *zemindar* (revenue collector) at Calcutta. Holwell had been in Bengal for nearly a quarter of a century, and his capacity to survive had brought him exceptional opportunities to adjust his temperament to local notions of graft, extortion, corruption and intrigue.

In 1756 Alivardi Khan died at a great age. His chosen successor was Siraj-ud-daula, his grandson, still in his early twenties. Siraj was volatile, lustful, and tactless, and alienated veteran Muslim commanders by his dependence on Hindu ministers. He seems to have been unsure of his own judgment; as well he might have been, in these difficult days, with Bussy's intrigues reaching out from the Deccan, and Afghans and Marathas threatening Bengal's borders. Those who attribute what followed to his character fail to explain what courses he could have pursued to save his skin. Within his own family, his succession was opposed by his aunt, Ghasita Begum, and by a cousin who was governor at Purnea.

He was marching against the latter in May 1756 when he heard that the man had recognised him as Nawab. At the same time he received an insolent answer from the EIC to an order, issued to all Europeans, that any new fortifications must be demolished. The French and Dutch replied with due courtesy. Having just overawed his native enemies, Siraj did not need to accept British bluster, and he would have lost face if he had done so. He returned to Murshidabad and ordered the seizure of the EIC factory at Kasimbazar. He stated several perfectly just reasons for moving against the British. Besides their illicit fortifications, they had abused their privileges by granting *dustucks*, certificates which exempted goods from toll, to persons who were in no way entitled to them, so whittling at the Nawab's revenues. And they had given shelter to fugitives from justice; thus, recently, one Krishna Das, the son of an official suspected of embezzlement, had arrived in Calcutta with treasure worth over 5 million rupees, and Drake had refused to hand him over.

Though Siraj himself did not allege this, it seems possible these were funds set aside to finance a coup in which the British would have been implicated. While the EIC directors in London were certainly not planning to conquer Bengal, that idea had been advanced not long before by Caroline George Scott, chief engineer at Calcutta, who had argued that if the EIC did not act, the French would.[96] The case of pre-empting the French, by plotting if not by arms, was always likely to strike men on the spot. But quite what was cooking, no one will ever know. In the miasma of intrigue shrouding Bengal, only one fact will ever be wholly clear: that almost everyone of importance, Christian, Muslim or Hindu, was plotting, suspecting plots and ready, at a pinch, to betray or cheat fellow-plotters. That said, much tedious and debatable detail may be avoided. Others besides Siraj must have been changing their minds from day to day. Events fell confusingly because men were confused.

Siraj, mindful of happenings further south, feared the Europeans. But he did not wish to expel them. Their honey fed courtiers, bankers, merchants, the Nawab himself. He proposed merely to teach the British a lesson. Their trade was prevented from moving up and down river. Watts, encircled at Kasimbazar by a vast army, had less than fifty troops, and swiftly submitted. He was politely treated in captivity. Drake, however, refused to be reasonable. Diplomacy failing, Siraj moved against Calcutta.

Either Drake was convinced that Siraj was bluffing, or he must have believed that the Nawab's army was so riddled with treachery that harm would come only to Siraj himself. Calcutta was in no state to be held. It was true that Drake had strengthened its defences, but only against attack by water. The city now had hundreds of thousands of people and the approaches to the feeble fort were masked by buildings. The garrison of only 180 fit soldiers, under an incompetent leader, had no cartridges ready, no shells fitted, no fuses prepared. There was little powder and most of that was damp. The militia, untrained, numbered about 250, largely half-caste 'Portuguese' and Armenians. Siraj's huge force appeared on June 16. Three days later, Drake, the commandant and several Council members prudently took themselves off to the relative safety of ships on the river. In a panic flight of whites and Eurasians, numerous Portuguese women were drowned with their children. Holwell was left in charge of the fort, but he and all the rest would have been evacuated had not ships summoned on their behalf run aground. With the houses around the fort in flames, scores of soldiers deserted. On June 20, after puny resistance, the fort fell. Through folly, or over-confident scheming, Drake had almost undone the psychological impact of the success of Dupleix and Clive. The French, who generously gave clothes and food to thousands of refugees in Chandernagore, were scandalised by the behaviour of Drake and his colleagues, men 'unworthy to bear the name of Europeans'. All whites in Bengal felt dishonoured. Contemptuous natives now called them 'sister-fuckers'.[97]

It was thanks to John Zephaniah Holwell that a signal instance of cowardice or worse was eventually alchemised into the classic fable of white heroism and heathen devilishness. Holwell's good would be interred with his bones; almost no one remembers that he was one of the first whites in India, who, however obtusely, made serious efforts to understand Hinduism. But the tale, as he wrote it, of the 'Black Hole of Calcutta', became and perhaps remains the most famous single episode in the whole history of the British Empire. Holwell was something of a pioneer in the evolving genre of 'sentimental' pseudo-documentary which would shortly be raised to eminence by Laurence Sterne. His literary skills were sufficient to create a story later too useful to be discarded. Whatever atrocities the British might justly be charged with, not merely in India, but anywhere in the tropical world, the 'Black Hole' would serve to show that dusky fiends had surpassed them. The bodies of suffering Christian martyrs at its base seemed to transform the edifice of British power in India from counting-house or barracks into cathedral.

When Siraj-ud-daula entered Calcutta on June 20, he admired the buildings, remarked that the British must be fools to oblige him to drive them out of so handsome a place, and ordered that the captive Holwell be released from his irons and that the prisoners should be decently treated. Many simply walked out and escaped. Some drunken soldiers remained and began to be a nuisance. Siraj asked if a dungeon was available. Of course there was one; every British garrison needed a place to confine disorderly men, and until 1868 such a lock-up would always be known, officially, as a 'Black Hole'. Prisons in England were at this time foully insalubrious. Calcutta's 'Hole' must have been a nasty place at the best of times; eighteen feet long by fourteen or fifteen wide with two barred airholes opening into a low veranda. Siraj probably did not realise how small it was when he ordered that all the prisoners, Holwell included, should be confined in this noisome den. Several wounded officers and a sick chaplain were among them, but even Holwell exempted Siraj himself from any charge of deliberate cruelty.[98] The Nawab left the fort in the early evening, and did not return till the following morning.

The stifling tropical night overpowered men drunken, wounded and sick. The gaolers did not go beyond their orders to relieve their suffering. When the cell was opened, a number of men had perished horribly, leaving 23, or 21, survivors. What is not known is how many had gone in. The maximum number of Europeans left in Calcutta, it can be shown, was no more than 64, but Armenians and Eurasians may also have been present. Recent scholars accept figures of between 18 and 43 deaths, though precision will never be possible, and the real total may have been lower. Early reports in the London press a year later reflected rumours which pushed the number of people confined up as high as 250. But accounts which present themselves as first-hand evidence hover about 146 prisoners, which seems to have been the figure decided between Holwell and a couple of others soon after the event. Released from the Hole on Siraj's return to the fort, Holwell had little time to recover from what had happened before he was taken up river to Murshidabad. On this man in low physical condition, the deaths of friends must have weighed somewhat, along with humiliating fetters, recollections of the shameful loss of Calcutta, and cal-culations of how his own future prospects, within or without the EIC, might be affected by the débâcle. Perhaps calculation, even in this phase, predominated; Clive, no softie himself, would remark, 'Mr Holwell has talents, but I fear wants a heart.'[99]

There is no moral difference to be drawn, of course, between the death of 18 prisoners of war through a sort of negligence and the holocaust from the same cause, of 123. But by raising the figure beyond what is conceivable, Holwell achieved several literary ends, which were also political ends in his own struggle for reputation. All sight of Siraj's easy conquest is lost in the horror of the narrative. Holwell himself emerges as a prodigious hero. He urges calm upon his shocked companions as they realise what hell they have been forced into. When the guards respond at last to the call for 'water, water' everyone else in the Hole falls into 'agitation and raving' at the mere sight of it. Holwell foresees that its effects will be 'fatal', yet nevertheless he passes it on to the rest in hats, keeping up this strenuous action for nearly two hours, while his comrades trample each other to death in their lust for it and the guards, 'brutal wretches', laugh at the scene. But when he finally lays his weary form down on a bench and cries out for water himself, the others, crazed though they may be, still have 'the respect and tenderness' for him 'to cry out, "GIVE HIM WATER, GIVE HIM WATER!"' and not one will touch it until he has drunk. However, finding this relief insufficient, he sucks away at the perspiration collected in his shirt. Since almost all the others have stripped (at his own prudent suggestion) his colleague Lushington sucks at the same source, afterwards assuring Holwell that he believes 'he owed his life to the many comfortable draughts he had from my sleeves.' Crushed, as the night proceeds, under three other sufferers, Holwell, sucking away, retains enough presence of mind to keep consulting his watch to note the time for the sake of posterity. But towards two o'clock he can bear it no more and faints. Next morning the survivors cannot persuade the guards to open the door, so one of them prudently thinks of searching for Holwell in the hope that he may have influence enough to gain their release. They find him under a heap of dead, but alive.[100]

This summary deprives the reader of many not unhilarious fatuities (with what Olympic skills in gymnastics, for instance, does Holwell, hemmed in as he describes, contrive to sample and reject the refreshing qualities of his own urine?) The absurdities of his tale are such as almost to reinforce its authority. What man in his senses would hope to be believed, unless such improbable episodes were in fact true? But it would seem that the writer invented each detail in turn so as to forestall obvious questions. Why don't they take off their clothes? Holwell says they did. But how does he himself survive? By keeping his clothes on and gushing with perspiration. Why don't the Indians bring water? They do, but only to mock at the prisoners' agonies. And so on. To point his fable, Holwell thoughtfully adds to those present a woman; the 'country-born' — that is, native or Eurasian — wife of a sailor named Carey pathetically insists on sharing her husband's imprisonment. An account in an English newspaper of the fate of the crew of a British privateer seized by the French, who were confined in the hold of their captors' ship, where twenty-seven out of eighty-three suffocated, clearly spurred Holwell's imagination, supplying one of his more poignant details. But his finest stroke was without doubt to acknowledge that other survivors would not confirm his story, observing that their accounts were 'so excessively absurd and contradictory, as to convince me, very few of them retained their senses ... ' Only Holwell remained sane. Only Holwell should be believed.[101]

Believed he was. Tobias Smollett at once paraphrased the tale without question in his own standard *History of England*. Robert Orme in his authoritative *History of ... The British ... in Indostan* (1778) likewise repeated Holwell, with the embellishment that the woman (mentioned by no other survivor) was 'English' and that she was taken afterwards into the harem of one of Siraj's generals, Mir Jafar. But for its full effect, the legend had to await a writer of genius, Thomas Macaulay, who in his essay of 1840 on Clive related it as a tale surpassed by 'Nothing in history or fiction, not even the story which Ugolino told in the sea of everlasting ice, after he had wiped his bloody lips on the scalp of his murderer ... But these things – which, after the lapse of more than eighty years, cannot be told or read without horror – awakened neither remorse nor pity in the bosom of the savage Nabob.'[102] As time wore on, Mrs Carey would become not only English, but blonde into the bargain.

Drake and his fellows had fled down river to Fulta. Holwell eventually joined them there, and signed the Council's letter to the directors in London which gave a summary account of the fall of Calcutta. This letter does not mention the 'Black Hole'. At the time, in Bengal and Madras, the alleged event made no stir. The British did not denounce Siraj for this war crime. No compensation was ever demanded for the victims, real or purported. Much Company property had been lost in Calcutta and the other factories – valued at over three and a half million rupees. But nearly two million rupees' worth would be recovered intact in due course; Siraj looked after what fell into his hands.[103]

He renamed Calcutta 'Alinagar', ordered the erection of a mosque inside the fort, and demanded large tribute from the French and the Dutch, who agreed to pay 800,000 rupees between them. The Nawab wrote to Madras in conciliatory fashion, blaming the 'wicked and unruly' Drake for what had happened.[104]

The Madras authorities still hoped to move against Bussy in the Deccan and were expecting a fresh declaration of war in Europe. However, British prestige in Bengal had to be reasserted. Even before the end of July, a small force from Madras under Major Kilpatrick arrived at Fulta, a most unhealthy spot, where refugees and soldiers wasted away. Kilpatrick felt he could not recapture Calcutta, and awaited further help from the south. When it came, Clive was in command. Clive's ambition was far from slaked with the governorship of Fort St David, and he was fired by the prospect ahead. He wrote to his father, 'This expedition if attended with success may enable me to do great things. It is by far the grandest of my undertakings.'[105] The object of the expedition was indeed large – not only to regain Calcutta but also to recover all the EIC's privileges in Bengal and to force reparation for all losses, while trying to oust the French from Chandernagore. He set off with eight ships and more than 1,700 troops, most of them natives, in mid-October, but stormy weather caused delay and before he arrived at the mouth of the Hugli early in December, 673 soldiers had been lost on the way, when two vessels had turned back. Even with Kil-patrick's men, and natives recruited locally, this would not be a large force. Neither Clive nor anyone with him had really the least idea of what Siraj's military capacities might be.

But they moved purposefully up river. Their first objective was the fort of Budge Budge. After one of Siraj's armies had been beaten off in a fierce skirmish, the place was captured by the drunken bravado of a lone Gaelic sailor, one Strahan, who scaled the walls and cried 'The place is mine', upon which others rushed forward and the fort fell with only one British casualty. Though Strahan was severely rebuked by Admiral Watson for his anarchic behaviour (muttering as he left, 'If I am flogged for this here action, I will never take another fort by myself as long as I live, by G——d') the swagger of the British sailors, like the great guns on the great ships they manned, struck fear into the Nawab's forces. Calcutta was reoccupied without fighting on 2 January 1757 and a week later the town of Hugli was captured and plundered. Clive recruited two or three hundred fresh Sepoys, meanwhile quarrelling with his British associates. His right to command was disputed by Captain Coote, a prickly Anglo-Irishman who was trying to live down the disgrace of having been court-martialled and cashiered (though then pardoned) for alleged cowardice against the Jacobites at Falkirk in 1746. Coote would eventually earn fame enough in India. The petti-ness of the Calcutta Council disgusted Clive more. They seemed to think of nothing save punitive compensation for their personal losses. ' ... They are bad subjects and rotten at heart,' he wrote to Governor Pigot of Madras. ' ... The riches of Peru and Mexico should not induce me to dwell among them.' The flash of exotic ambition is seen for a moment. Clive was thinking of Cortés and Pizarro.[106]

His conduct in 1757 seems to display, besides his usual alternations of zest and depression, a tug between golden dreams and responsible business-like apprehen-sion. The latter made him wish to attempt a treaty with Siraj without further fighting. But Clive's embassies were unavailing. Early in February, the Nawab came to Calcutta with 40,000 troops. Clive had less than 2,000 and was virtually confined to camp, in danger of starvation if he did not submit. Then a surge of rashness saved him. He mounted a night attack, probably aiming to capture or kill Siraj. Technically, it misfired. The British missed their aim in fog and found themselves in the morning forced to make a day-long circuitous march back to base. About a tenth of the troops were killed or wounded, very heavy losses for so small a force. But the bungled action worked. Its psychological effect was immense. In skirmishes, Siraj had lost over 1,000 men, and Clive had given him a serious fright. He retreated about six miles and swiftly came to terms. A treaty of February 9 gave the British almost all they had hoped for—their privileges confirmed, compensation for the Company, presents for Clive, Kilpatrick and others. Clive thought his business in Bengal was done. Now it was time to go back to Madras. He confided to his father that he wished to become governor-general of all the British in India and had already written to prominent statesmen at home towards this end.[107]

But Siraj was inclining towards the French, and the British position was full of risks still. Admiral Watson had heard in January that Britain and France were officially at war. He wanted to attack the French in Bengal and refused to sign a treaty of neutrality which they offered. This boisterous seaman threatened Siraj horridly: ' ... I will kindle such a flame in your country, as all the water in the Ganges shall not be able to extinguish.'[108] But Watts, the EIC emissary at the court, was a subtler diplomat. At last Siraj, jolted by rumours of Afghan invasion and anxious to have British help against it, gave what Watson took to be tacit permission for an attack on Chandernagore.

In March, Watson's guns overwhelmed the French fort. When the news reached London, East India stock would go up by 12 per cent. The French company, now deprived of its largest source of profit, was at once weakened all over the subcontinent. And Siraj had lost any chance of substantial French support. He now wrote to Bussy for help, but by his concession to Watson he had weakened himself fatally.

Matters moved quite swiftly towards a dénouement. The Nawab's court was now wormed with French and British bribes. One leading Frenchman summed it up later: 'We were much engaged in opposing corruption by corruption in order to gain the friendship of scoundrels ... ' An EIC man at Murshidabad, Luke Scrafton, could not resist a Roman analogy, writing to Calcutta that Siraj's court might be 'compared to that of Ptolemy's that reigned in Egypt when Pompey fled there after the battle of Pharsalia, that is that the head and members are all as corrupt and treacherous as possible ... ' Clive, he suggested, 'should be the Caesar to act as Caesar then did, take the Kingdom under his protection, depose the old and give them a new King to make his subjects happy.' Scrafton showed this was more than a pleasant fancy when he added, 'How glorious it would be for the Company to have a Nabob [nawab] devoted to them.'[109]

Clive himself was now coming to agree that Siraj could not be depended upon to fulfil the treaty. He stayed in Bengal despite urgent calls from Madras for his return. He wanted to chase out the French completely. Siraj would not deliver them up to him. By April, the EIC men in Bengal had made it their definite policy to depose Siraj.

They hardly required to start from scratch. There was a galaxy of actual and potential conspirators, many of them long involved in dealings and intrigues with the British. In one of his tantrums Siraj, most unwisely, had struck Jagat Seth across the face. The central force in the plotting came from the Seth bankers. Their hatred of the Nawab and their resources powered intrigues which drew men of all races. Two other key figures were Rai Durlabh, Siraj's Bengali treasurer, and a senior general, Mir Jafar, brother-in-law of the late Alivardi Khan, who had set him an example of usurpation. The British now fell in with the Seths' suggestion that Mir Jafar should be installed as Nawab. They demanded a very high price for their soldiers. All the chief EIC men, like the Indian plotters, were to receive lavish rewards. Watson was not averse to taking his share. On June 12, Watts, his conspiratorial work complete, fled from the Murshidabad court. Next day Clive began to march on the Nawab's capital.

It was confidently said then, and has often been said since, that Siraj was almost universally loathed. Certainly, very few of the chief people under him were reliably loyal. What the weavers and farmers of Bengal thought about events is anyone's guess. Their reactions were not considered a factor. Everything rested on a few men. The British were gambling. Calcutta was left almost undefended. If their fellow-plotters had turned upon them, they might have been swept from Bengal. The EIC had a treaty with Mir Jafar. Watts had had him swear to it on the Koran and the head of his son. But Clive could not be sure that the man would keep faith. Mir Jafar was terrified when Siraj, warned by the French of the plot against him, dismissed him from his post of commander-in-chief, though the Nawab himself was too fearful and irresolute to have the conspirators put to death. The plot might have broken down in timidity and confusion. But the British had bold leaders. Coote and Kilpatrick were martially avid for loot. Watson's determination had knocked the French to touch-line. Now Clive's fitful daring would be critical.

As the British had prepared to push north, even Watson had advised Clive that he could not be too cautious. Clive had 613 European infantry, about 100 Eurasian Topasses, 171 artillerymen and 2,100 Sepoys. He had no cavalry and could deploy only eight fieldpieces and two howitzers. Nor could he or anyone guess what might happen. The monsoon was coming. A crisis must be forced quickly. The pretext for aggression was simple: Siraj had not fulfilled his treaty and he was intriguing with the French. But the nature of the climax ahead was hazy. The British officers, Clive included, did not know whether they would fight a battle, make new terms with Siraj, or merely rendezvous with Mir Jafar.

On June 19, Clive reached Katwa, a fortified town on the west bank of the Hugli, about eighty miles north of Calcutta and forty from Murshidabad. Now it was hard to decide what to do. Word from Mir Jafar was eagerly awaited. Clive sent to tell him that unless he proved his good faith by coming to Plassey, a place fifteen miles to the north-east, the British would not cross the river. The reply came at last at 3 p.m. on the 22nd. Mir Jafar's note urged Clive to proceed. The British began at once to cross the Hugli, which contemporaries would match with Caesar's Rubicon, and marched on towards Plassey, where Clive hoped, but was not certain, to meet Mir Jafar.

He met more than he expected. His men, having marched through heavy rain, had in some cases bivouacked only at 3 a.m. Daybreak on June 23 revealed an unnerving panorama. On the wide, lush plain, the Nawab had assembled, by Clive's own reckoning, 15,000 horse, 35,000 foot and forty pieces of artillery. ' … What with the number of elephants,' Luke Scrafton recorded, 'all covered

with scarlet cloth and embroidery; their horse with their drawn swords glistering in the sun; their heavy cannon drawn by vast trains of oxen; and their standards flying, they made a most pompous and formidable appearance ... '
There was more behind this appearance than some cynical modern accounts suggest. Siraj had proved in the past that he could win battles. Fifteen thousand of his troops were his own personal force, whose loyalty was not suspect. The cavalry were dangerous men, mostly Pathans from the north-west of the subcontinent. The foot were equipped with matchlock muskets. Clive's fieldpieces were small six-pounders; the Nawab's cannon were mostly twenty-four- or thirty-two-pounders, and native artillerymen were directed by a force of French experts. Finally Siraj's position was strong; his camp lay behind entrenchments which sealed off a loop in the river. Clive could only deploy his small army in a thin line, Europeans to the middle, from the river to the west as far as the edge of a grove to the east. As the vast body of men and beasts advanced, Clive, like most of his officers, was at first daunted. When someone asked him what he thought would happen, Clive replied, 'We must make the best fight we can during the day, and at night sling our muskets over our shoulders and march back to Calcutta.'

At 7 a.m. he sent a desperate note to Mir Jafar — 'Whatever could be done by me I have done, I can do no more. If you will come to Daudpur I will march from Placis to meet you, but if you won't comply even with this, pardon me, I shall make it up with the Nawab!' But the Nawab's forces took the initiative out of his hands. The heavy guns began to crack at about eight. Thirty men fell in half an hour. Clive could only withdraw his men behind an embankment where they were relatively safe. For hours the cannonade continued, with the lighter British guns retorting. One howitzer shell did signal work, mortally wounding Mir Madan, the main general still faithful to Siraj.

About noon, a heavy monsoon shower stopped the guns. With desultory artillery fire resumed, Clive went to change his wet clothes at Plassey House, a hunting lodge of the Nawab's which he had made his headquarters. In his absence, the battle was transformed. Siraj had ordered his men to withdraw to their entrenchments. Seeing the enemy gunners beginning to leave their advanced position by a water tank, Major Kilpatrick at once moved up with two guns. Clive reappeared very angry and threatened to arrest Kilpatrick for taking an undue risk. But the initiative had passed to the British. Clive realised that to retire now would encourage the enemy. He ordered Kilpatrick off, took charge himself, and called up reinforcements.

At this point the Nawab's cavalry and foot made their first move towards active intervention. Accurate British fire warded them off, but some of the enemy found a strong position near a second water tank. Clive sent Coote to deal with them. The attack succeeded. Then the British troops charged. Bravado once more brought reward. The enemy fled.

Siraj, long harried by fears and suspicions, had entered the battle in trepidation.

Astrologers, possibly bribed by the plotters, had reported bad omens. Mir Madan had been brought back to die in the Nawab's own tent. Siraj pleaded with Mir Jafar to attack. Mir Jafar played canny. His force, a huge body to the east of the British position, did advance during the afternoon, but fell back promptly in face of British fire. As the British attacked, Siraj's nerve broke. He rushed away from the field. By 5 p.m. Clive was victorious. Only then did he receive a note from Mir Jafar, advising him sagely to do what he had already done. Clive, exploiting Kilpatrick's advance, had won an astonishing victory.

Perhaps 500 of the Nawab's troops had been killed, amongst whom the death of Mir Madan may have been virtually decisive. The British had lost twenty-two men, and had another fifty or so wounded; these casualties, Clive himself noted, were 'chiefly blacks'. But despite quite small carnage, Plassey was a serious battle, and not merely the 'transaction' or 'skirmish' which some have styled it, even though the chief forces prevailing were psychological ones.[110]

So much for the 'Roman' heroics. Now came 'Egyptian' sordor, or rather an unattractive conjunction of European greed with Asian mores. Siraj found himself friendless. Within ten days of the battle, he was brutally murdered and hacked to pieces by Mir Jafar's son. His mother and aunt were cold-bloodedly drowned. Mir Jafar reigned in his place at Murshidabad, where Clive followed him with 500 soldiers. The secret treaty with Mir Jafar confirmed the EIC in its privileges, ceded to it twenty-four *parganas* south of Calcutta, provided compensation for past losses and promised support against all British enemies. Clive assured Mir Jafar that the British did not intend to interfere in any way with his government. British aims, as distinct from British imaginations, still stopped short at peaceful trading.

So far as the EIC was concerned, a commercial problem had been solved. But with things in Bengal as they were, only British armed force could guarantee that the new agreements would be kept; so it seemed, anyway, to the Calcutta Council which now wrote home to London asking for a 'sufficient number of recruits to make a respectable garrison in Bengal, which should consist of a body of two thousand Europeans at least ... This, we are of opinion, will be the only method of preventing in future the encroachments of the country government, to make our friendship and alliance courted, to carry on our trade on the securest footing, and to oppose the resettlement of the French in these provinces.'[111]

Many British involved in Mir Jafar's takeover did not survive long to enjoy the profits. Watson died in the sultry heat of August, after a day when birds dropped dead from the sky. Kilpatrick followed him in October, when of 250 men who had come with him from Madras fourteen months before, only five survived, and these were thin and sick. But for numerous others the gamble paid off richly. 'The first fruit of our success,' Scrafton wrote, 'was the receipt of nearly a million sterling, which the Soubah [Mir Jafar] paid us on the 3d July, which was laden on board two hundred boats ... ' The triumphant progress of this treasure past French and Dutch to factories to Calcutta, 'with music playing, drums beating, and colours flying', was an apt symbol of the exorbitant appetite now growing by what it fed on. In the end, Clive personally received £234,000. Members of the Calcutta Council got handsome cuts. The army and navy shared fifty lakhs of rupees (over £500,000). Altogether, at least £1,238,575 was handed out to Europeans. And Rai Durlabh took, as agreed, a commission of 5 per cent on all he had negotiated during the plotting for the British.[112]

This man had misled them. As treasurer he should have known that the Nawab's coffers could not afford all that was promised. Though Clive would later profess himself 'astonished at my own moderation' when he could have ransacked Bengal's gathered riches, he like the others pressed for the full claim.[113] No one saw anything wrong in taking huge presents, which Eastern potentates commonly made. EIC regulations did not forbid them. The King's army and navy depended on booty and such-like for the incentive to fight at all. Clive was never furtive about his spoils.

But the sheer scale of the gifts accomplished psychological revolutions. At home, men accustomed to the slow plunder by Walpole and his whigs of Britain itself, were nevertheless outraged as well as envious. Perversely, the hauls of Clive and his colleagues helped to stimulate a growing movement in favour of cleaning up British public life. In Bengal, as commonly happens, men who had made much wanted to make more, while those British who had not grown rich overnight were anxious to emulate the lucky ones. And disgust at Rai Durlabh's bad faith fostered the notion that such Asiatics could never be trusted to run the country as the British would like.

The British had, after all, performed not unlike Cortés and his conquistadores. Scrafton, writing some three years after Plassey, still did not talk of further conquests. He dwelled on the gains for British trade. The EIC had received not only the £1,250,000 stipulated in its treaty with Mir Jafar, but also, in the *parganas*, land yielding revenue worth, Scrafton reckoned, £100,000 a year. The French were well-worsted while their fortunate rivals could now trade without the need to import bullion. But neo-Roman boasting was bound to creep in. ' ... What prospect,' Scrafton asked, regarding Plassey, 'was there that such a handful of men should overcome such numerous forces? ... No longer considered as mere merchants, we were now thought the umpires of Indostan ... '[114]

So important a happening as this battle calls for a summary verdict. This is hard to give. The actors evade stereotypes. They were complex human beings whose self-contradictions make moralising treacherous. Siraj was not quite the vicious despot of legend, nor a patriot merciful to a fault; he was an intelligent young ruler with bad habits and little experience and, perhaps, too much imagination for his own good. Holwell does not make a suitable martyr nor a doubled-dyed racist villain. Mir Jafar was not a traitor to India but a foreign adventurer taking one more chance. In the long perspective of history, everyone seems to be dwarfed by the crucial factor of British sea-power. After the previous exploits of Dupleix, Bussy and Clive, it was a matter of time before one or other European rival established ascendancy over the parts of the sub-continent where both traded. Even if the French had given Siraj more help and Plassey had gone the other way, British dominance of sea-lanes to India should have enabled the EIC to reassert itself in Bengal.

But the custom of debunking Clive has gone too far. In guerrilla warfare, personality matters. Clive's triumphs in the Carnatic had been much like those of a brilliant guerrilla. They had given him natural ascendancy over small forces of British troops, a reputation to impress Sepoys, and an aura to terrify Siraj-ud-daula. The morale of the British soldiers and sailors was high. Clive was swift to exploit the chances they brought him. Though common soldiers, not generals, win battles, direct personal leadership fires soldiers. Clive's won Plassey. Glory as well as loot lured him. The same was true of his forces. Every man was out for himself, yet all moved together without hesitation when he called them on. And his imagination was larger, it seems, than that of any other man in the field. It was not, of course, disinterested in the least, but there are less risky ways of making a fortune than leading 3,000 men against 50,000 in thunderous tropical heat very far from home.

When the news reached London, King George spoke warmly of Clive. Pitt in the Commons praised him, not quite backhandedly, as a 'heaven-born general who had never learned the art of war'. Yet Beckford sneered at him in the same House as a 'dirty writer' and Plassey made only a moderate impact at home.[115] War had been bringing more comprehensible triumphs.

IX

In 1758 Fort St Louis in Senegal was seized, with booty worth nearly a quarter of a million pounds. Gorée, the other main French West African settlement, followed it into the hands of the British, who now controlled a valuable commerce in gum as well as increasing their dominance in the slave trade.

The naval blockade of France tightened, and in April Admiral Hawke drove a relief expedition for Louisbourg ashore after finding it in the Basque roads. Pitt's American programme for 1758 was the by now habitual one – attacks aimed at Louisbourg, Fort Duquesne and Ticonderoga. Colonial legislatures responded to his call that they should furnish, clothe and pay 20,000 troops. The results must have enhanced their confidence in their own prowess while confirming their poor opinion of British regulars. Montcalm at Ticonderoga had only 3,500 French regulars with which to resist General Abercrombie who marched north with 6,000 regulars and 10,000 colonial troops. But he threw up an entrenchment, thickly defended by a log barricade eight feet high and, outside that, an 'almost impenetrable frieze of branches placed in layers with their points sharpened … ' Abercrombie absurdly hurled his men at the branches for four hours while the French fired from behind cover. Nearly 2,000 British troops were killed and the 42nd Highlanders, for all their hardy race, lost half their men. Then the French were reinforced, until 12,000 men opposed what was left of Abercrombie's army. But a mere colonial named Bradstreet, commanding 3,000 colonial troops, dashed to Lake Ontario and destroyed Fort Frontenac, and Brigadier Forbes with 4,000 colonials and only 1,600 regulars (mostly Highlanders like himself) hewed a new route across the Alleghenies to Fort Duquesne, which was renamed Pittsburgh.[116] No one had ever thought of calling such a significant place Pelhamton or Walpolesville.

Louisbourg had faced in July the assault of 13,000 soldiers and as many sailors, carried in 180 ships. The British general, Amherst, did not display much flair, but he got on well, unusually, with Admiral Boscawen, and his second-in-command, a young man named James Wolfe, displayed brilliant opportunism, leading his men in person up through the surf at the first difficult landing, and then, after Amherst had dawdled, cutting matters short by taking a detachment one foggy day to set up a battery in a commanding position, whence the fort was bombarded to ruins and surrender. The news lit bonfires in London and Boston, set off fireworks in Philadelphia, and prompted the residents of Halifax, Nova Scotia, to consume 60,000 gallons of rum. Plassey's reception was completely eclipsed. Pitt, not Clive, was hailed as the noblest Roman, on both sides of the Atlantic ocean. '*Your* America, *your* Lakes, *your* Mr. Amherst', George II grumbled at him as, grudgingly, he agreed to the despatch of yet more troops to America, where Wolfe, having caught Pitt's eye, would lead an attack on Quebec the next summer.[117]

With Louisbourg bagged at last, Pitt turned his attention to the West Indies. He was an unflinching friend of the West India lobby, though its members were now beginning to run into the same kind of public disfavour, partly idealistic, part snobbish, and partly jealous, as would confront Clive on his return. Yet Pitt himself created problems for his allies by his readiness to grab French sugar islands, despite Beckford's warnings that this would produce a glut.

An assault on Martinique failed in January 1759, but the expedition went on to capture Guadeloupe in the spring. This was joy for the Yankee rum-cobblers, whose ships now poured in to purchase molasses; joy for the Liverpool slavers who over the next four years shipped 12,500 Africans into the island; and joy, not least, for the Guadeloupe planters who made 'a sudden transition from misery to plenty'.[118] They had been starved of French shipping (their slaves had starved literally) and in debt, of course, to merchants at home. Now they began clean slates with new creditors, shipped their sugar away briskly, and enjoyed a uniquely favoured status under generous British rule, which permitted them to retain their old laws, yet gave them the same freedom of trade within the Empire as any of George II's subjects. It was not good news for Beckford and his compeers. The expected glut, and lower prices, resulted. But this pleased customers in Britain, some of whom began to perceive that mercantilism had had its drawbacks, and that general free trade might be a good thing.

The seizure of the so-called 'Neutral' islands in the Windward group soon followed. St Vincent and Dominica had been left to the Caribs. (On St Vincent there were 400 'Yellow' pure-breds and 1,100 'Black Caribs' of part-African parentage.) St Lucia and Tobago were 'neutral' in the sense that neither France nor Britain had established clear title. In practice, men of both nations frequented or lived on all four islands. The French had far more settlers in them, but drove less than half their trade.[119] Besides affording a mart for contraband slaves, the 'Neutrals' grew minor staples and supplied other islands with provisions and timber. They had military value. In the 1740s the French had annexed St Lucia and had for a time established a fort on Tobago. All four islands were now secured for Britain.

Since St Domingue remained in French possession, the problem of trade with the enemy persisted. The 'Flags of Truce' which ships carried when they were sent to exchange prisoners provided, as in previous wars, a camouflage. Yankee merchants purchased captured men. Frenchman were sometimes hired to serve as prisoners, then brought back to North America for further use. Governor Denny of Pennsylvania issued blank 'Flag of Truce' commissions with lists of imaginary French names, and sold them at £20 apiece in his own and other colonies. Many other high officials profited likewise. Though West Indian judges condemned them, North American courts usually acquitted people caught trading under Flags of Truce, and the 'Flour Act' of 1757 which forbade the export of colonial foodstuffs to foreign parts was for a time quite ineffectual.[120] Innumerable means of evasion were found, and avaricious naval officers, noting that under existing regulations they could only acquire the whole of a prize if they seized a returning vessel, blithely let Pennsylvania corn go through and seized ships when they came out with French sugar.

Despite complaints that only British North American corn was keeping the French troops in Canada alive, 'so that these People in their Marches to Destroy one English Province, are actually supported by the Bread raised in another', Pitt, to avoid annoying colonials, took no action against trade with the enemy until 1760. The 'Flag of Truce' trade was then suppressed. But not commerce with the French. Besides the old-established 'free ports' on Dutch and Danish islands, a new trade sprang up at a village named Monte Cristi, on the Spanish side of the border on Hispaniola. The Spanish authorities dubbed this a free port. As many as 130 North American vessels were found there at one time, and the lieutenant-governor of Monte Cristi and his nephew were happy, for a consideration, to certify that Yankee masters had dealt only with Spaniards and residents.[121]

The British government's hostility to illegal trade was causing grave political problems in Massachusetts. But in 1759, the 'year of victories', alarums and jubilation precluded due worry. David Garrick wrote 'Heart of Oak', a kind of anthem for sailors:

> Come, cheer up my lads! 'tis to glory we steer,
> To add something more to this wonderful year.

It began with news of the capture of Gorée. In the summer came word of Guadeloupe's surrender. On August 6, Londoners heard of triumph in Europe at last; the British and their allies had beaten a larger French force at Minden. But with 27,000 troops in America, 10,000 in Germany, 5,000 at Gibraltar, 4,000 in Africa, Britain was now short of soldiers for home defence.[122] Groundless rumours went about that the French had actually landed. The militia was called out and replaced regular troops on garrison duties. Garrick's 'lads' held the wooden-shoed papists off. In August, a fleet under the ubiquitous Admiral Boscawen caught up with a French fleet from Toulon which was trying to slip through the straits of Gibraltar, destroyed several ships in Lagos Bay, and closely blockaded the rest in Cadiz. The French still planned to invade, despite this disaster, and in November, when a westerly gale had blown British ships from their close watch of the Atlantic coast, a fleet locked in Brest tried to escape south-eastwards. Admiral Hawke, rushing back, chased it into Quiberon Bay, despite a rising hurricane, violent seas, and a lee shore horrid with rocks and shoals. Upon these, two British vessels went down, but as the inspired Hawke savaged it, the French fleet lost five ships, and 2,500 men with them. Its shreds were now trapped in ports from Dunkirk to Marseilles. The coastwise traffic of France was almost paralysed. Hawke's men worked islets on the Basque coast as vegetable gardens for their own refreshment. Pitt was free to send 20,000 more troops to Germany.

Great though such news was, the best had come before it. Besides word of new contests won in India, October had brought the tale, sublime, pathetic and highly neo-classical, of James Wolfe's death as his men won at Quebec. Bonfires had burned in every town and village. The North American campaign of 1758 had been intended to climax with the convergence of three victorious British armies to conquer Canada itself. Since Boscawen had refused to move from Louisbourg to Quebec, and Montcalm had checked the northward thrust at Ticonderoga, another three-point attack was required in 1759. In the west, Fort Niagara was captured. In the centre, Amherst took Ticonderoga, but was so slow that only at the end of the summer did his threat to Montreal divert troops from Quebec, the target of the main thrust, which was led by James Wolfe, only 32 years old, and specially promoted to major general.

Wolfe was a sickly, odd-looking little man with a turned-up nose, weak chin and receding forehead. The son of a soldier, he had been only 14 when he had been commissioned in his father's marine regiment, only 16 when he had served at the battle of Dettingen, only 18 when, Brevet-Major at Culloden, he had admired the fierce charge of the Camerons and the resolution with which his own regiment met it. Thereafter, he had worked mainly in Scotland, where he had helped to raise Highland troops. Remarks in his letters about Gaels — 'this itchy race' — display a mixture of grudging respect and especially nasty and callow contempt. To a friend serving in Nova Scotia, he wrote in 1751 that he thought that 'two or three independent Highland Companies' might be of use in that remote frontier province: 'they are hardy, intrepid, accustomed to a rough country, and no great mischief if they fall ... ' Three years later, to the same correspondent, he sketched ways in which fresh Highland revolt might be stifled before birth; for instance, 'Mr McPherson should have a couple of hundred men in his neighbourhood, with orders to massacre the whole clan if they shew the least symptom of rebellion.' He disliked still more, however, the Lowland Scots of Glasgow — 'civil, designing and treacherous, with their imme-diate interests always in view; they pursue trade with warmth and a necessary mercantile spirit, arising from the baseness of their other qualifications. The women, coarse, cold, and cunning, for ever enquiring after men's circumstances. They make that the standard of their good breeding.'

Matters of 'good breeding' worried Wolfe, whose father was comparatively poor, and who was painfully conscious of his own lack of education. ('When a man leaves his studies at fifteen', he once wrote, 'he will never be justly called a man of letters.') But he had an upstart professional disdain, almost Napoleonic in its intensity, for officers without merit except the money which had bought their commissions. He had written to his mother from Inverness, 'There are young men amongst us, that have great revenues and high military stations, that repine at 3 months service with their Regiments, if they go 50 miles from home: Soup, and Venaison and Turtle, is their supream delight and joy; an effeminate Race of Coxcombs; the future leaders of our Armies; the defenders and Pro-tectors of a great & free Nation!'

It will be clear that this priggish young man, fabricating his own personality, striving not quite with success for polish and poise, despised most sections of the human race. His tense temperament might have been at home wielding pike and bible in Cromwell's army. Now that God had withdrawn, Wolfe's aspiring mind found its expression in a heroic fatalism joined with a lofty and no doubt sincere patriotism. It was not merely snobbery which had made Wolfe so con-temptuous of Glasgow and its counting-house, bawbee-led ethos. 'What a wretch is he', Wolfe had written, 'who lives for himself alone! his only aim.' He idealised (before he had been there) his country's achievements in America. 'What a state of felicity' red men enjoyed under British rule. 'It is to the eternal honour of the English nation that we have helped to heal the wound given by the Spaniards to mankind by their cruelty pride and covetousness.' England was worth human sacrifice and for all his professionalism, Wolfe believed that risks must be taken. 'In war something must be allowed to chance and fortune,' he had declared. ' ... In particular circumstances and times the loss of 1,000 men is rather an advantage to a nation than otherwise, seeing that gallant attempts raise its reputation, and make it respectable.' His hypochondria brooded over the likely effects of the American climate on his gravel and on his rheumatism. He wanted to serve in Europe, wrongly believing that this was the only sphere where that 'chance' which had now displaced Cromwell's Providence might bestow immortal fame upon a soldier. But when Pitt gave him command, his reaction was characteristically sententious. To a brother officer, he reported, ' ... I have this day signified to Mr Pitt that he may dispose of my slight carcase as he pleases ... '[123]

Wolfe was efficient as well as neurotic. He had exactly the right experience. He had served as quartermaster general at the botched amphibious raid on Rochefort in 1757 and had learnt from that fiasco the dangers of what he called 'excessive' caution, before going on at Louisbourg to put his carcase just where his mouth had been. The common problem with combined operations had been jealousy between general and admirals. Wolfe now showed that he could co-operate well with Admiral Saunders, a fine sailor who was respected for his modesty as well as for the fortune which he had made from prizes. As in Bengal, the role of the navy would be decisive. While Hawke and Boscawen penned French fleets in home waters and made reinforcement of Quebec impossible, Saunders performed the astounding feat of conducting twenty-two sail of the line, together with frigates and sloops and about 200 troop transports through 300 miles of uncharted tidal waters without losing a single ship. Of course, it was not his achievement alone. In places, the canny, experienced skippers of transports piloted safely by observing the ripple and colour of the water. The generally high standards of British civilian seamanship would before long be epitomised famously by James Cook, former mate of a North Sea collier, who served on the St Lawrence as master of the *Pembroke*. On June 26 the whole fleet anchored safely off the south-east side of the island of Orleans, from which they could see, across two miles of water, the citadel of the Upper Town of Quebec, with 106 guns in its batteries, towering over the slate-roofed houses which ranged along the waterfront of the Lower Town.

An Irish lieutenant in Wolfe's army was much taken with the 'delightful country on every side; windmills, water-mills, churches, chapels, and compact farmhouses, all built with stone, and covered, some with wood, others with straw. The lands appear to be every-where well cultivated ... '[124] No European foe until now had accosted Quebec, and Canada's honour was still not weakly defended. Montcalm had 16,000 men under him. Wolfe had brought only 8,500 soldiers. But his men admired their brave little commander. A higher proportion of them were regulars – all but 3,500 of Montcalm's troops were militiamen and Indians whom their general (like Wolfe) considered inferior. In the previous winter Montcalm had sent Comte Louis de Bougainville, whose prowess in the South Sea would one day rival Cook's, to plead at the French court for 1,500 more troops for Canada. Only 360 had been sent, and these had been lucky to slip through the British blockades. By mid-July Montcalm's cannon would be short of powder. And the guns and sailors of the British navy meant that the French were effectively outnumbered. However Montcalm put most of his forces on the low-lying Beauport shore which seemed to offer the best chance of a landing, and confidently expected to hold out until the winter forced British withdrawal. Quebec on its heights was, as Champlain had recognised long ago, one of the best natural sites for defence in the world.

All the frustrated Wolfe could do was to get his troops ashore and make camp on the south bank of the river, where he found a point from which the Lower Town could be bombarded, with cruel effectiveness. His idealism concerning Indians had not survived experience of North America. Indian ambushes constantly hit his foraging parties, and his colonial 'Nova Scotia Rangers' had learnt to retort to Indian warfare in kind. Wolfe forbade 'the inhuman practice of scalping', except, he was careful to add, 'when the enemy are Indians, or Canadians dressed like Indians.'[125] But at first he ordered all respect for such *habitants* as stayed quietly in their farms, and he preserved the civilities of eighteenth-century European warfare in his dealings with Montcalm. These commanders conceived themselves to be lonely polite persons in a vastness of savagery, red and colonial. A French officer saved a wounded Briton from scalping. Wolfe sent him £20. Montcalm outpointed this vulgar gesture (poor Wolfe, the gaps in his polish still showed) by returning the money; his man, he said, had only performed his duty.

Meanwhile, the thrash of floggings on military backs was heard daily, though Wolfe was not harsh to his men by the standards of his time. Apart from the Rangers, whom he called 'the worst soldiers in the universe', Wolfe's troops were dressed as if for the formal set-piece battles still prevalent in the European arena where he had hoped to shine himself. Their uniforms were impressive but worse than useless (the British were mostly in red and white, the French in white and blue facings). Ruffles, gaiters, spatterdashes, pipe-clayed belt and tall headgear shaped like a bishop's mitre figured in an ensemble made, as one sergeant complained, 'so tight and braced so firm that we almost stood like automata of wood ... ' The 'Brown Bess' muskets weighed 50 lb. each, but were inaccurate above 50 paces, and could not be used when rain fell and damped the powder in the priming pans. They fired a maximum of about three volleys in a minute. Between each, the soldier had to pull a cartridge from his pouch, bite the top off it, shake powder into his priming pan, put ball and wadding into the barrel, press these down with a ramrod, return the ramrod to a loop on the musket, and fix the bayonet. The discipline required to keep doing such things to order under fire largely explains why battles in Europe were rule-bound, but also why Clive's regulars had made such impact. Unlike Clive, Wolfe was an innovator in tactics; he trained his men to reserve their fire until the enemy was thirty yards away, and then to discharge their muskets by platoons.[126]

The same practical enterprise characterised James Cook. French pilots denied that ships could use the channel between the St Lawrence north shore and the island of Orleans, but thanks to Cook's survey a frigate and a sloop were able to work their way into it to protect a landing by British troops to the east of the gorge which protected Montcalm's main force. Then there was a lull of three weeks, while transports and victuallers steadily came from New England with ammunition, supplies, and 400 more Rangers. On July 31 Wolfe ordered a full-scale attack aimed at seizing a redoubt at the top of a cliff on the extreme end of Montcalm's left flank. It proved abortive, with over 400 casualties. French confidence increased. Wolfe lost prestige with his troops. His officers despised his vacillations and resented his habit of keeping his ideas to himself. The troops were annoyed at his reprimand to the companies which had failed in the assault, and were depressed by outbreaks of fever, scurvy and dysentery. Wolfe himself was confined to bed with a mysterious 'slow fever', and began to seek solace in cruelty. He had not served under 'Butcher' Cumberland for nothing. He offered five guineas for every Indian scalp. He ordered his men to seize the *habitants* and their herds, to lay waste farms and to burn villages.[127] Summer was starting to ebb away. The French might be starved into surrender.

Soldiers under him were aware of the psychological element in Wolfe's illness. One shrewdly observed that this young man was laid low by the fiasco of his attack, 'fearing he should do nothing to plant a laurel on his brow ... which was what he thirsted so much after ... ' and further suggested that Wolfe was 'afraid he should be exposed to the contumelies of a harsh and unthinking populace ... ' (Admiral Byng had recently been shot.) A month after his defeat, Wolfe wrote to his mother, 'the enemy puts nothing to risk, & I cant in conscience put the whole army to risk ... I cant get at him, without spilling a torrent of blood ... '[128] Three days later he sent a despatch to Pitt in which he admitted himself at a loss. Dismay spread in London on its arrival.

Yet there was news that Amherst was advancing. A final bid must be made before ice froze the river. The sick commander for the first time condescended to discuss matters with his brigadiers. They rejected all Wolfe's ideas and gave him one of their own which he glumly accepted. British naval command of the river was now such that troops could strike upstream of the city and take its defences in reverse, while cutting its links with Montreal. For ten days, as the attack was prepared, a series of feints and raids kept the defenders dashing to and fro. The French thought the British aimed to land ten or twenty miles above Quebec. On September 10 a still-gloomy Wolfe, staring from the high ground across the river, saw that if the British could climb a precipitous path from a site named Anse de Foulon to the Heights of Abraham west of Quebec, they would find them weakly defended. His choice was made, but he kept it a secret, even from his brigadiers, until just before the moment of embarkation.

The first boatloads of soldiers for the assault began to move with the tide about 2 a.m. on the morning of September 13. The vanguard to scale the Heights first were eight Light Infantry men who had originally volunteered for the army, together with sixteen others whom these had chosen. Of the original eight, six were Highland Gaels, one bore the old Liddesdale reiving surname of Bell, and one the proud Irish title of Fitzgerald.[129] Hence historians write of the valour of 'English troops' at Quebec. A reprieved Jacobite, Donald Macdonald, who had picked up excellent French on the Continent, used it going down river to satisfy two challenges from enemy sentries. First on top, he spoke to the sentry watching the path, told him that he had been sent to relieve the post, and said that the other guards should be recalled. Most of the French soldiers here were fast asleep, and no match at all for the hardy race. The rest of Wolfe's men, learning that all was safe, scrambled up the 250-foot cliff in the dark, using stumps and boughs of trees to pull themselves forward. Thousands disembarked before dawn: Light Infantry, Fraser's Highlanders, then Grenadiers.

What now happened was almost exactly the species of battle for which Wolfe and his troops had been trained. He had sent the obnoxious Rangers away to burn the Canadian countryside, and British soldiery alone now found themselves on a bare plateau, like a blackboard on which to sketch perfect manoeuvres. There were nearly 5,000 of them making for Quebec when, at 6 a.m., they saw French troops approaching on their left. The British troops formed a line with the Highlanders in its centre. Wolfe ordered them to lie down, both to rest and to hide their numbers. Perhaps 4,500 French drew up opposite. Feints had ensured that the rest of Montcalm's force was elsewhere, but he rashly attacked before reinforcements could come up. Discipline settled the outcome. Montcalm's colonial troops confirmed his worst fears. Never drilled for formal battle, they pressed forward shouting and firing at random. Wolfe's men waited for his order and then won the battle with one fearsome unanimous volley at short range. When further British firing stopped after six or ten minutes, the French and Canadians were fleeing in rout before Highlanders hacking them down with broadswords, chasing them without mercy up to the walls of the city. Montcalm had been mortally hurt. The French had some 1,500 casualties in the short, fierce fight. Besides 600 men wounded, the British lost 58 dead, including their general.[130]

Wolfe, wearing a brilliant and distinctive uniform, might seem to have courted that death. He had twice been hit, in waist and groin, while turning the line before the battle began. The third, fatal bullet struck just after he gave the order to advance. Many persons, present or not, were eager to relay his dying words to mankind. Most agreed that, hearing the French were in flight, he said, 'I die contented', or something similar, and expired with a smile on his wan lips. One heretic was a surgeon, whose job perhaps gives his evidence some authority: he reported Wolfe's final bequest of speech as, 'Lay me down; I am suffocating.'[131]

Never mind. What suited the public would be accepted. Thus it was believed that Wolfe, moving up river to Anse de Foulon, had recited, in the stern of a leading boat, the famous passage from Thomas Gray's recent poem, 'Elegy in a Country Churchyard', about paths of glory which led only to the grave; this despite the fact that the general himself had ordered the rowlocks muffled and strict silence. However, Wolfe had admired Gray and had been attempting verse himself. A sample was found in his pocket after his death:

> But since ignoble age must come
> Disease and Death's inexorable Doom,
> That life which others pay let us bestow
> And give to Fame what we to Nature owe;
> Brave let us fall, or honor'd if we live,
> Or let us Glory gain, or glory give –
> Such men [alone] deserve a Sovereign State,
> Envied by those who dare not Imitate.[132]

The rather subversive suggestion that only men like himself deserved to be monarchs could be ignored in delight at this evidence of Wolfe's sense of heroic destiny. He had in fact conspired with that potent new factor in British life, the newspaper-reading middle-class public, in the creation of his own myth.

Smollett admired Wolfe's 'passion for glory' and reckoned that had he lived, 'he would, without doubt, have rivalled in reputation the most celebrated captains of antiquity.' Though this writer felt nevertheless that the praise heaped on the dead man was 'ridiculous', the cult infected even a young Deist named Thomas Paine who wrote, for the social club which he attended in Lewes, Sussex, an elegy on the death of General Wolfe. Horace Walpole would remark that in the late 1750s, 'there were no religious combustibles in the temper of the times. Popery and Protestantism seemed at a stand. The modes of Christianity were exhausted, and could not furnish novelty enough to fix attention.' He did not notice that patriotism had for many usurped the place of religion, perhaps because he was so patriotic himself. Of Pitt's valedictory speech upon Wolfe in the Commons, Walpole said scornfully that all the 'parallels which he drew from Greek and Roman story did but flatten the pathetic of the topic. Mr Pitt himself had done far more for Britain than any orator for Rome. Our three last campaigns had over-run more world than they conquered in a century – and for the Grecians, their story were a pretty theme if the town of St Albans were waging war with that of Brentford.'[133]

Christ and the classics alike could now be demoted below 'English' heroism. Several painters shortly broke from the theory that martial 'history' themes should be given classical robes, to present Wolfe's death in contemporary dress. Penny in 1763 borrowed for his composition a formula used by old masters to portray lamentation over the dead Saviour. A young Pennsylvanian artist, Benjamin West, went even further. He caused a sensation in 1771 with a canvas of the death scene which portrayed various persons as present who had not in fact been there (some had paid him 100 guineas for the compliment), and also an Indian stricken with grief in the foreground, though Wolfe had loathed red warriors and had never commanded any. Despite such anomalies, people swooned with emotion at the first exhibition. West, modelling his central figure on a well-known depiction of the dead Jesus by Van Dyck, 'transferred to Wolfe the emotions of awe, pride, gratitude and grief which the passion of Christ, the pattern of heroism, had inspired among Christian people for centuries.' Engraved for the popular market, West's picture was a bestseller in Britain and abroad, and remained a public favourite for many decades.[134]

It had little enough to do with the actual Canada, where the hardy race found much opportunity to display its distinguishing quality. After Quebec had surrendered on September 18, and the French troops had retired to Montreal, the British entered a city, wrecked by their own guns, where people were on the edge of starvation. A miserable winter set in. The Indians still lurked close; near the end of October, for instance, a missing soldier was found in a neighbouring coppice, 'killed and scalped; one of his arms was cut off; his bowels were taken out and cut into shreds almost innumerable, with a long skewer thrust through his upper lip, nostrils and the crown of his head; the blood-hounds carried away his heart.' It was colder than many men there had ever known. Nuns made trews for the kilted Highlanders, *'pauvres gens sans culottes'*. Frostbite and scurvy did their work. Brigadier Murray, now commanding, had over 7,000 men in September; by March more than a thousand had died and only 4,800 were fit for duty. When the French army came back near the end of April, the troops left to oppose them seemed 'a poor pitiful handful of starved, Scorbutic Skeletons; many of whom had laid by their Crutches on the occasion ... ' Outnumbered two to one now, the British contested a dreadful morning-long battle in the slush of melting snow on the Heights of Abraham till they retreated after suffering 1,100 casualties.[135] But officers had worked with men through the winter to strengthen Quebec's fortifications. The French were kept out.

The great question now was, which nation would get the first vessel up the unfreezing St Lawrence River. On May 9 a British relief ship appeared. Within a week, the French had been driven away, and British naval power had clinched yet another victory. In September 1760, three British armies at last realised the master plan and converged at Montreal, 17,000 strong, against 2,500 French. Canada was surrendered. Britain ruled from Hudson's Bay to the borders of Florida.

X

'The years after Plassey', Philip Mason has written regarding India, 'are in some ways among the most distasteful in English history.'[136] He seems to underestimate Scots rapacity; the East India Company service had long drawn disproportionately from 'North Britain'. The scale of Clive's personal proceeds was such that he could now turn down polite and corrupting offers from prominent Asiatic persons and profess himself careless about money. Others in Bengal, English, Scottish or Irish, found restraint less appealing.

Rumours had located £40 million in Siraj-ud-daula's treasury. It turned out that it held only £1½ million. Sums roughly equivalent to Bengal's revenues of an entire year eventually found their way into British pockets and before long were on their way out to purchase country estates in Britain. The new Nawab, having to fork out more than his coffers held, was forced to offer about half in the form of instalments from his own revenue. Several districts were handed over to direct British exploitation. Mir Jafar had to squeeze Hindu chiefs, who looked to the British for support against him. Short of resources, he himself had to depend on British military assistance – for which he would be called upon to pay. Any prospect of independent Asian rule in Bengal was swiftly under-mined. Yet noblemen coveting Mir Jafar's position would still be ready to offer fresh baits for British support, until the richest province in India was ruined. A vast and rapid decanting had begun. Scrafton, for instance, as Resident at Mir Jafar's court, engaged in revenue farming under two fictitious Indian names and lent money out at exorbitant rates.[137] EIC men, now entitled to trade free of duty, abused the *dustuck* system without inhibition and further impoverished the provincial revenues, in an exultant and merciless bonanza. The nest was full not merely of cuckoos, but of birds of prey.

Clive was anxious to get home with his own meat, but stayed because he seemed to be indispensable. The French still remained a problem. Coote was sent to pursue their small force, which passed through Bihar and escaped into Oudh. It might seem an epic march – the longest yet made by British soldiers in India, 400 miles to the border of Oudh in three weeks; but first Coote's white soldiers mutinied, then his Sepoys. The former were flogged, the latter were won back by argument. Then Clive had to pacify virtual mutiny among white officers angered by quarrels over prize money and over seniority.

When Clive entertained Mir Jafar in Calcutta, the show, which included twelve standing waxwork representations of Venus, cost nearly £8,000. Clive shortly acquired hookahs of blue and green lacquer, set with rubies and dia-monds. His wife kept a young tiger as her pet, along with a bear, two porcu-pines, and various birds. When Mir Jafar was confirmed as Nawab by the Mughal Emperor he asked that Clive should be given imperial rank as a com-mander, and the Englishman was duly awarded the title of 'Zadat-ul-Mulk, Nasir-ud Daula Colonel Clive Sabit Jang Bahadur.' He was no longer a foreigner. 'To the Nawab and his nobles, Clive was one of their sort, a soldier, and a nobleman', far above a mere merchant like Drake or Holwell; he was 'Flower of the Empire, Defender of the Country, the Brave, Firm in War.' Mir Jafar, indebted to him, seems also to have been personally fond of him. For a year and a half Clive had no official authority in Bengal even under the EIC – the directors at home thought he must have gone back to Madras after Plassey. Yet he was in practice the most powerful man in a country almost as large as France, though he spoke no Persian, let alone Bengali, never got to know the province's natives well and indeed prided himself on his mere

Englishness. 'I would leave all trickery to the Hindoos and Mussalmen to whom it is natural, being convinced that the reputation we have in this country is owing, among other causes, to the ingenity [*sic*] and plain dealing for which we are distinguished.'[138]

Room had always been found for foreign entrants into the Emperor's service. Mir Jafar and others believed that they were dealing with a military adventurer of their own kind. They would not easily have understood the thinking which he expressed, in December 1758, to Lawrence Sulivan, the new Chairman of the EIC's Court of Directors, which had just confirmed the appointment as governor of Bengal unofficially given to Clive a few months before by the shrewd and admiring Calcutta Council. Clive told Sulivan that a force of 2,000 Europeans could 'totally' subdue Bengal, and that the 'Great Mogul' would then confirm the EIC's possession if it paid the same rent as former nawabs. The terrain, being 'full of great and navigable rivers' and 'very woody, enclosed by mountains with narrow passes', was open to British ships and was such that infantry would be 'formidable' and cavalry, the main strength of Indian rulers, 'a meer bugbear'. The people were temperamentally ungrateful and had 'adopted a system of Politicks more peculiar to this Country than any other, viz.; to attempt every thing by treachery rather than force.' So the EIC could only maintain its position, or improve it, by 'such a force as leaves nothing to the power of Treachery or Ingratitude'.[139]

But the drive to direct rule which this implied would originate only in India itself; it would not be London policy. Meanwhile, Clive, in effect, proposed and disposed, arbitrating between local notables. The Seth bankers were amongst those elements, dissatisfied with Mir Jafar, which now invited the intervention of the Shahzada (cf. dauphin), the disaffected son of the Emperor, who was cruising as an adventurer, looking for a kingdom, and had picked up the support of the small band of French soldiers driven from Bengal. In February 1759, Clive took the field again in support of Mir Jafar. The Shahzada, besieging Patna, fled at his mere approach. This service won Clive another exorbitant reward. The Emperor had given him rank without the income, in rents from allotted land, which normally went with it. Clive had been pressing for his due. Mir Jafar now assigned him the *jaghir* which he desired, allotting to him the quitrent due to the Nawab from the twenty-four *parganas* presented to the EIC after Plassey. The Company, gathering revenues on these lands, would now pay nine-tenths of them over to Clive, who thus stood in relation to his employers on a footing somewhere between that of a landlord and that of a feudal superior. On top of his vast capital gain, he now had an annual income of £27,000 or so to spend on himself — since there was no question that he need actually use it to support troops for the Emperor as Mughal custom had laid down.[140]

With such prizes in view, it was hardly amazing that the Dutch, at Chinsura on the Hugli, should do their best to take over the British position. They had shown their pique at Mir Jafar's installation, and he retorted by actions against their trade. They were then outraged when he granted a saltpetre monopoly to the British, and raised the export duty on opium, which the Dutch took in great quantity to Indonesia. Three hundred European troops in the Dutch pay, together with 600 Malays, were despatched from Java. When this force arrived, in November 1759, it was easily crushed both on land and on water, and the Dutch were compelled to pay out about £100,000.

Clive was helped in this decisive defeat of the Bengal EIC's remaining white rivals by the opportune return of troops which he had sent off southwards a year before. By April 1758 2,000 French soldiers in two regiments had arrived in the Carnatic with a new plenipotentiary, Comte Lally de Tollendal, a man of Irish Gaelic extraction. Fort St David soon fell to him. He recalled Bussy from the Deccan at last – this marked the end of effective French control at Hyderabad – and then he besieged Madras. But besides French weakness at sea, which was as usual the major single factor, the British commanded, in Bengal, great supplies of produce, currency – and saltpetre. The French effort broke down for lack of these things. Clive had rubbed this advantage in by sending Colonel Forde with more than half the Bengal troops to oust the French from a coastal area known as the Northern Circars where Bussy had collected revenue. Thanks to Forde's flair and the bravery of the Sepoys under him, the French were decisively beaten and the British succeeded them as revenue farmers of the area. So Lally was cut off from another source of help.

By September 1759, when Admiral Pocock, Watson's successor, defeated a French fleet and drove the enemy out of Indian waters for the rest of the war, the initiative in the Carnatic lay with the British. Coote returned next month from England with new troops and the status of commander-in-chief. Clive's lordly contempt for small-scale go-getters was evidenced in his reaction to news of Coote's appointment over Forde's head – 'I tremble when I think of the fatal consequences of such a mercenary man as Coote commanding here.'[141] But the Irishman covered himself with belated glory. He captured a place called Wandewash and, though outnumbered, thoroughly whipped Lally's force, in January 1760, when the attempt was made to regain it. The French were unable to hold their native allies now they were penniless, shipless and on the run. In January 1761, after months of blockade, Pondicherry surrendered. The French had no ground in India left.

Some time before this, Pitt had received a disturbing letter from Clive, written behind the EIC's back. It pointed out that complete takeover in Bengal was possible, but suggested that 'so large a sovereignty' might 'possibly be an object too extensive for a mercantile company.' The British government must take it in hand.[142] Clive aimed to become the Crown's viceroy in India. This broached a political problem which would worry politicians in Britain for decades. How could a trading company, however opulent, be permitted to exercise independent powers of revenue collection, to make peace and war, to raise and break rulers, to assume rule? Pitt did not like Clive's prescient logic. He had no interest in Britain's ruling alien millions. He feared that rich revenues, coming to the Crown, would endanger 'English liberty'. He merely wished to cripple French trade – and that had been done.

Clive had come home, in 1760, to a mixed reception. The Duke of Newcastle busied himself to procure a peerage. 'Lord Clive of Plassey' was soon proclaimed, but this was only an Irish title. Real noblemen looked down on this upstart 'nabob', though his fortune was exaggerated to £1,200,000, and his wife was alleged to have brought back a casket of jewels worth £200,000.[143] He and his like would take the role of scapegoats in the phase of political seasickness in Britain which was foreshadowed by the succession, in 1760, of the young George III to the throne.

XI

Tories and independent gentry who had backed Pitt in 1757 now fell away as the Land Tax stayed up at 4s. in the £ and their erstwhile hero completely reneged on his one-time opposition to Continental involvements. By the end of 1760 there would be 200,000 troops under British government pay, amongst them scores of thousands of Germans.[144] Pitt, apparently converted to George II's 'Hanoverian' policy, would claim later with much justice that America had been won in Germany, and that the drain upon France of war in Europe permitted British conquests overseas. But while City interests wanted continued war, many other people were sick of it.

Pitt's megalomania, arrogance and theatricality had begun to exhaust his colleagues' patience. They had also alienated the young Prince of Wales, George II's grandson, and his tutor Lord Bute, a serious-minded, handsome and priggish Scot of refined taste who, as the boy's mother wished, had sheltered the prince from the experiences (such as debauchery) then normal for males of his class and age. George III came to the throne as a raw young man, readily flooded with righteous emotion, not very clever but, for a king, oddly intellectual – a studious patron of arts and sciences. From 1765, a mysterious disease would make him act for long periods as if he were mad.

' ... His policy, so far as he had one in 1760, was made up almost entirely of vindictive personal grudges against everything and everybody who had been connected with his despised grandfather.'[145] George II had had mistresses; George III after his death would be mocked by Lord Byron for having ' ... that household virtue, most uncommon, of constancy to a bad ugly woman.' George II had been seen on three occasions unable to use the most important of the surviving royal prerogatives, his right to choose his own minister; the new King was resolved to have none of that, and to take back royal patronage from the hands of Newcastle and his like. This earnest, stupid, uncompromising man would seem to domineer over his ministers and would lend credibility to the

x

charge that he was trying to undermine 'English liberties', to restore a Stuart-style despotism, though this would never be his intention.

At once he insisted that Bute must join the Cabinet, where Pitt was now beginning to face the nemesis of his own vainglory. With almost all France's colonies in British hands, further aggression seemed merely wanton. The Spaniards, neutral till now, were getting very angry over British highhanded-ness with their shipping and over that tough perennial, logwood cutting; but surely war with Spain was not desirable? Pitt began to negotiate with France. The key issue for both sides was the Newfoundland fisheries. Pitt insisted on a complete British monopoly; yet the New World brought French fishing ports £500,000 annually, and its cod were too valuable to be conceded. Pitt's colleagues growingly deplored his stubbornness. The crisis came in October 1761, when Pitt wanted war with Spain and the Cabinet outvoted him. He resigned. Bute took over, the first Scot ever to have such standing at West-minster, which was not lucky for him or his compatriots. The hardy race had not been forgiven the Stuarts, its accent, or the '45 – and Bute himself was not at all hardy.

Irony preyed upon Bute from the outset. Spain declared war anyway, early in 1762. Bute, like his royal master, was after peace; negotiations resumed a few weeks later. Yet he found himself presiding over a new land war in Iberia, and a sudden conquest of prime targets in the Spanish empire. British sea-power now made easy projects unfeasible even fifteen years before. In October 1762 an amphibious force sent from India captured Manila in the Philip-pines and took a Mexican galleon with some three million dollars on board. Just before this, Havana had been seized. A third of Spain's navy was destroyed there. The British admiral and general commanding took the princely, or Clively, sums of £122,697 each, while each common sailor received just £3 as his share of the loot. During the brief British occupation, Cuba's history was transformed. It had been a bucolic island of small plantations, its characteristic crop the world's best tobacco. Now British slavers rushed in 10,700 Africans in nine months. They were to grow sugar. Cuba was launched on its way towards becoming the largest and cruellest of island sugar economies.[146]

All the familiar moulds seemed to have been broken, including those of British politics. Within eight months of Pitt's going, Newcastle had been forced into resignation after forty years of continuous office and constant care over patronage. Now whiggery shattered into a chaos of factions. This made it easy for George III to assert himself, but impossible for him, over the next few years, to find the makings of a stable government.

In November 1762, 'preliminaries' of a treaty were signed at Fontainebleau in France. Britain had such a heap of counters for exchange that the outcome must be excessively in her favour. Only in India was the status quo of 1749 restored, and there the EIC had effectively made that provision nonsensical. In Europe, France returned Minorca and various gains from Britain's German allies. In

Africa, Britain handed back Gorée but kept Senegal. When news of Manila's capture came belatedly, that town was restored for a mere ransom, but in return for the restoration of Havana, the embarrassed British had had to demand Florida, and rights to cut logwood in Honduras were vaguely conceded. The most controversial exchanges involved French America. Canada and Cape Breton Island were ceded to Britain, along with the left bank of the Mississippi. But the French were to retain fishing rights round Newfoundland, with two small islands, St Pierre and Miquelon, as bases. Britain kept Grenada, Dominica, St Vincent and Tobago, but passed back to France the prime sugar islands of Martinique and Guadeloupe, and the fine harbour of St Lucia.

The terms were so good for Britain that they made fresh war sooner or later inevitable. Yet they provoked a well-orchestrated outcry. Bute was hissed, jeered and pelted by a mob in the streets; trying to reach home in a hired sedan chair, he was noticed and its glass windows were shattered. Pitt had in effect timed his resignation well. He could not have won the sweeping peace terms for which he had led his supporters to hope. Now he could gather easy new laurels as prophet. He arrived in the House deathly pale, dressed in black velvet, his legs swathed in rolls of flannel, thick gloves on his hands. His voice was feeble, and he was permitted to sit during parts of a speech which lasted for three and a half hours. He denounced virtually every concession. Havana, Guadeloupe, Martinique should have been kept, so should St Lucia, so should Gorée. France, having regained her 'nursery' in the fisheries, could now recover 'her prodigious losses' and became 'once more formidable to us at sea'. In exchange for Minorca, Britain was conceding 'the East Indies, the West Indies, and Africa'. Jobs, threats and direct cash bribes of £100, £200, £300 helped win the Ministry 319 votes. Only 65 M.P.s, including Beckford and Clive, voted with Pitt; but people cheered him in the streets outside.[147] A frightened and jaded Bute resigned office early next year, after the Treaty of Paris had confirmed the 'preliminaries'.

Pitt's prediction that France would become 'formidable' again was of the sort which is bound to be proved true. Any terms which made peace possible must offer a country with such resources the chance to recover. Tobias Smollett had observed that peace must deprive Britain of captured markets and give France the opportunity to undersell her again; 'it would be for the interest of Great Britain to be at continual variance with that restless neighbour, provided the contest could be limited to the operations of a sea war, in which England would be always invincible and victorious.'[148] An alternative to war, as it now struck some men, would be universal 'free trade'. But it was by no means clear yet that the advantage in such conditions would lie with Britain.

Within eight years of the peace, Bordeaux trade would be running at two and a half times its previous record figure. Recklessly shipping in slaves and developing plantations, the British had actually forwarded the development of several captured islands which they had since returned. By 1775 it could be said that of all imports to Europe from the West Indies, France received nearly half, Britain less than a third.[149]

The 'golden age' of the French islands after 1763 was therefore a somewhat uneasy time for British West Indian interests. The surge forward of British trade in the East and in Africa, let alone the expanding markets of North America, meant that the central importance of the Caribbean was now less self-evident than before. The power of the West India lobby, still great, was not so much stronger than that of other groups; it was a sign of growing embattlement that the Planters' Club leagued with the recently founded 'Society of West India Merchants' to form a common political front. While British grocers, distillers and refiners were calling for cheap sugar, slavers were willing to sell their cargoes wherever prices were highest, inside or outside the empire. The development of the 'ceded islands' also helped push up the cost of Africans; by 1774 a governor of the Leewards would be complaining that the price of slaves had more than doubled in thirty years.[150]

The three Virgin Islands owned by Denmark were flourishing now, largely thanks to emigrants from the British Leewards. Migrating British planters had also helped to build up Dutch Guiana. Now land on the 'ceded islands' — Grenada, the Grenadines, Dominica, St Vincent and Tobago — was offered for sale by commissioners in parcels of up to 500 acres only, with large tracts in each parish reserved for poor settlers. 'Small whites' flocked there from Barbados and other 'old' islands, where the militias were thus depleted.

The ceded islands had problems of their own. French settlers already present were allowed to remain. The part-African 'Black Caribs' of St Vincent struggled against incomers till 1772 when a brutal expeditionary force of North American troops brought them to recognise British control and accept by treaty a reservation of land in the north of the island. But smallholders on the new acquisitions could relish the benefits of growing most of their own food. Sugar gained ground only slowly as coffee, nutmeg and other minor staples prospered. Scots were to the fore in Grenada as it expanded to become a colony second in value only to Jamaica among the British islands, with 300,000 cocoa trees bearing by 1775.[151]

Development on the sub-tropical mainland was slower. Lands ceded by Spain and France were divided into two provinces, East and West Florida. The Spaniards pulled out almost unanimously, and eleven years after the Treaty of Paris, East Florida still had only 3,000 settlers despite the importation, assisted by government bounties, of some 1,400 Greek, Italian, and Minorcan servants. In West Florida, French settlers stayed on, and there was some spontaneous movement in from older British colonies and earlier frontiers, to occupy lands on the lower east bank of the Mississippi and along the coast of the Gulf of Mexico.[152]

Governor Johnstone called a representative assembly in West Florida as early as 1766. Heads of families holding houses were to vote. Here, as in the ceded islands, the empire faced a novel problem. In Britain and Ireland Catholics suffered political disabilities. To what extent did this apply overseas? Canada would be hardest of all to sort out.

The Canadians, native priests as well as farmers, had not wasted much love on metropolitan Frenchmen. Montcalm had noted with disdain that well-off peasants in Canada lived like minor noblemen in France. After the British conquest, almost no native thought of leaving. General Amherst was conciliatory. The clergy were permitted free exercise of the Catholic religion, and by 1762 were, in obedience to an order from their bishop, offering prayers for the British royal family. Alienation from France was deepened when Louis XV's ministers seized the chance, by reducing certain notes in face value, to offer less than 7,000,000 livres in repayment of a debt of 16,000,000 to their former subjects. Seventy-five thousand Canadians were now posing as grateful and loyal subjects to George III and were protected by the terms of the Treaty. A British proclamation of 1763 proposed an assembly which would have led to the introduction of English common law and the destruction of Canadian distinctiveness. But the time of its calling was left to the discretion of the governor, James Murray, a Scot full of sympathy for the hardy folk whom he found in Canada, 'perhaps', he remarked, 'the bravest and the best race upon the globe.'[153]

He shared their contempt for the British North American merchants now wending into Quebec and Montreal – 'adventurers', he called them, 'of mean education'.[154] Their aim was to take over the French alliance in trade with the 'Western Indians', at the expense of the Hudson's Bay Company (which responded to this renewed competition from Montreal by sending Samuel Hearne on a daring exploration of the Arctic coast (1769–72), and by building a new trade base, Cumberland House, on the route between the Saskatchewan and Churchill Rivers). The friction between the 'old subjects' and the British military prompted Murray to defend the Canadian 'new subjects' even more strongly.

He pointed out that the proposed assembly, in which Catholics would not sit, would make some five hundred Yankees, and the like, masters of many times their own number. The 'old subjects' clamoured for self-government and for Murray's recall. In 1765 law officers in London gave it as their opinion that Canadian Catholics were not subject to political disabilities, and four years later the Board of Trade recommended that the 'confusion' in the province should be ended by the admission of papists to an assembly. Meanwhile, Murray had been succeeded, in 1766, by Colonel Guy Carleton, a reactionary, self-important, authoritarian man who liked the military traditions and feudal trappings of old Canada, and argued that careers in office should be thrown open to natives of noble birth.

After most French 'Acadians' had been deported in mass, some hundreds had lingered on in the forests of Nova Scotia, operating, with Indian allies, as small-time pirates and guerrilla raiders. By 1761 they had been rounded up. After they had been used to repair their famous dykes, an attempt was made to deport them in turn, but New England would not have them, and they were brought back. Nor did the French colonies want them; the French authorities said they were now British subjects. Realising at length that they had been abandoned, numerous Acadians settled in Nova Scotia as loyal subjects. Compatriots came back to join them from other parts of the New World and even from France itself, and there were about 1,500 rooted again within a dozen years of the Treaty of Paris. By this time, however, they were greatly outnumbered by recent English-speaking incomers.

Nova Scotia remained scantily populated. It was virtually an island, attached to the mainland only at its far north-eastern corner and reached from other settled regions by sea; since its own farmed lands were disjoined by rough wooded mountains and there were no roads for wheeled vehicles, its villages also relied on the sea for communication with each other. Governor Lawrence, in 1758, had conducted a busy publicity campaign to attract settlers. He explicitly promised New Englanders that there would be no Anglican tithes and that they could maintain their town meeting system. For ten years Yankees came in spate, and by 1775 they formed approaching two-thirds of the colony's population of 17,000 or 20,000.[155] There was an orgy of land speculation, in which Benjamin Franklin involved himself. An Ulsterman named McNutt, by 1765, had secured temporary control of most of the ungranted arable lands in the province. Meanwhile a mainly Scottish consortium acquired most of the island of St John, later known as Prince Edward Island – over 2,000 square miles of fertile ground. The land boom collapsed in 1768 when territories in the Ohio valley were opened up and diverted attention.

However, it had helped to confirm Nova Scotia as a satellite of New England, with the important reservation that Halifax, isolated from the rest of the colony, was a centre for interests securely tied to Great Britain. Though parliamentary grants to the colony were reduced after 1760 and the naval and military establishment was withdrawn from Halifax to Boston in 1768, Britain still sent thousands of pounds every year to the strategically placed little town, and this was of great moment in the affairs of a colony of debtors. One Joshua Mauger, a Jersey sea-captain, had enriched himself as a victualler to the British navy and trader in contraband with the Louisbourg French. In the 1750s he had achieved monopoly in Halifax's chief industry, rum distillation. He eventually made enough to buy his way into the British Parliament, and his London connections came to exercise much financial control in Nova Scotia, beating off the challenge of Bostoners.

Though Halifax had some pretty Georgian houses, most life in Nova Scotia was rudimentary. Despite all the whaling which went on now in the Gulf of St Lawrence, women in this colony could not afford whalebone stays.[156] But like fish oil and furs, walrus ivory and sealskin, whalebone was an esteemed addendum to the comforts of the British middle classes, and Nova Scotia's other staple industries, which were lumber and naval stores, helped to strengthen the wooden walls of the home island, the new maritime Rome.

When the great Scottish architect Robert Adam remodelled Syon House, near London, for Sir Hugh Smithson in 1762, it contained in an anteroom off the entrance hall twelve columns and twelve pilasters of verd-antique dredged up from the bed of Rome's own River Tiber. This space was merely for the use of servants. The eclectic opulence of the rest of the house suggested how far Britain had overmatched Rome. Some walls were hung with fine London silk, others with paper imported from China. Ormolu, gilt and mahogany vied with marble. While foreigners gasped at the private wealth of such British citizens, the pleasure gardens at Vauxhall frequented by comfortably-off Londoners showed the passionate pride of the English in their own history. Besides scenes from the plays of Shakespeare, whose universal pre-eminence was now a national article of faith, paintings displayed there depicted the modern Augustans in action by land and sea. There was Vernon capturing Porto Bello 'with six ships only', Hawke's feat at Quiberon Bay in allegory, Montreal surrendering to Amherst, Britannia handing out laurels to Coote, Clive receiving 'the homage of the Nabob'.[157] What nation, some moralists were already asking, had reached such a summit of glory without retributory reverses succeeding? Edward Gibbon, seated amid the ruins of the Capitol, hearing barefooted friars sing Vespers in the temple of Jupiter, conceived about this time the idea of writing the story of Rome's decline and fall.

The British ruling class thought that retribution would be absurd and impertinent. Their empire, they supposed, was just, not cruel. It had no autocratic, caesarian ruler. Since Canada's acquisition four different creeds — Anglican, Presbyterian, Congregational, now Roman Catholic — were established by law in different parts of its reach, and other faiths were also permitted. Conscious of the unique virtues, as they conceived them, of their own constitution, the British were eager that every colony should enjoy representative home rule under Westminster's ultimate authority.

British military success meant that middle-class intellectuals and thoughtful aristocrats on the continent of Europe were drawn towards imitation of British indifference in religion and British representative institutions. British literature was coming into fashion from Lisbon to the Urals. Europeans wept over Richardson's bourgeois *Clarissa*. David Hume's writings stirred the great German philosopher Kant from his dogmatic slumbers. Now, from the hardy race, came James Macpherson's alleged translations of the Gaelic epic poet, Ossian. Jefferson, Goethe, Napoleon, would dote on these prose effusions which defied reason and 'enlightenment' in 'the compulsive telling over of defeat, darkness, despair, the eradication of clear outline and all degree, the world torn and scattered.'[158]

For they matched something in the times. Twenty-four years of war between

Britain and the Bourbon powers, had coincided with an earthquake in European consciousness, or, to change metaphors, with a watershed in social and cultural history. Whatever field one prospects, one finds momentous changes, tending to tear and scatter views of the world still distantly rooted in the Middle Ages. Voltaire detected 'a civil war in every soul'.[159] The period spawned complex novel sorts of men; conservative rebels, classicist proto-romantics, oligarchical democrats, patriot internationalists, despots adjusting their policies to 'enlightened' ideas.

George III was a mild and confused English counterpart of monarchs all over Europe now anxious to assert their authority over excessively powerful nobles. His assault on the whig élite thrust into opposition talented men, who felt that they had a right to rule. They could not, as in the reigns of two previous Georges, legitimise their opposition by flocking around a malcontent heir to the throne, who might soon succeed and hoist them back into office. They had to turn to the middle-class 'public'. They had to play with fire, to run the risk of inflaming a revolutionary conflagration. Even fussy old Newcastle now claimed it was his duty 'to relieve the publick and my friends from the haughtiness and power of an absolute Scotch Minister.'[160]

The opposition had advantages as they set about inciting paranoia, indignation and panic. Many City of London men were on their side. Industrialists in the Midlands and North were excluded from the franchise and were commonly religious dissenters. The expanding professional and commercial classes bought the newspapers now proliferating everywhere, which found opposition views easy to sell, and spread dangerous notions among clerks and artisans — men of the lower orders whose education had been rendered imperative by the needs of a complex and waxing economy, and who were gathered in larger and larger concentrations by the expansion of London and other cities. Thanks to improved communications, news from the capital could now reach Liverpool in two days. 'By 1768 there was a well established Conversation Club at Liverpool which met weekly and debated general, and specific, political questions. One week, they debated under what conditions was a man most free. Another week, whether political liberty could possibly be achieved in England without the introduction of the ballot box.'[161]

People in Boston and Philadelphia, and wherever prints from those places were read along the entire American seaboard, heard with dismay the howls of the whigs in England. These coincided with increasing strains within Britain's imperial commercial system. It had simply been too successful.

There had been a curious little pamphlet war during the negotiations towards the Treaty of Paris. It had no influence on events. The minds of the British ministers were made up. They were going to insist on retaining Canada. Britain had gone to war to defend her American colonies, and so much expense of blood and treasure must not be in vain. But some writers had argued in favour of keeping Guadeloupe and letting Canada go. Slave traders wanted another island to sell blacks in. The strongest pro-Guadeloupe arguments were: that an island could be defended by the navy, without the expense of a military establishment; and that its retention would improve the balance between the expanding North American colonies and the British West Indian islands. The weight of the Empire now seemed to have fallen too much into the temperate-zone, corn-and-lumber side of the scales, against sugar. To keep Canada would make this worse. As Samuel Martin, a leading Antiguan planter, remarked in a letter of 1762, ' … If our Sugar Colonies are not extended in proportion to our African trade, and the extension of our North American settlements, the French Colonies will have all the benefit of that extension … '[162] American vessels would have perforce to continue trading with his island's foreign-owned competitors.

British and British-colonial merchants could supply far more provisions, more slaves, more manufactures than the British West Indies could consume. The Spaniards now successfully tightened up their own colonial system against smugglers, but the French, needing British goods and buyers, opened successful 'free ports' on four of their islands between 1763 and 1767. The British government followed suit. The Free Ports Act of 1766 admitted foreign shipping, with certain reservations and precautions, to four ports in Jamaica and two in Dominica. The regulations had the effect of discriminating in favour of British-based traders as against North American merchants. While the home country, through the free ports, sold more manufactured goods, and drew in raw material needed for British industry and trade, the colonial ships found it hard to pick up satisfactory return cargoes.[163] It was one more heave in the longstanding tug of war between British interests and North American enterprise.

William Pitt the elder,
on a mug by Richard Chaffers

BOOK THREE:
1763–85

A pretence of Art to destroy Art; a pretence of Liberty
To destroy Liberty; a pretence of Religion to destroy Religion
Oshea and Caleb fight: they contend in the valleys of Peor,
In the terrible Family Contentions of those who love each other.
The Armies of Balaam weep – no women come to the field ...
The English are scatter'd over the face of the Nations: are these
Jerusalem's children? Hark! hear the Giants of Albion cry at night:
'We smell the blood of the English! we delight in their blood on our Altars.
The living & the dead shall be ground in our rumbling Mills
For bread of the Sons of Albion, of the Giants Hand & Scofield.
Scofeld and Kox are let loose upon my Saxons! they accumulate
A World in which Man is by his Nature the Enemy of Man,
In pride of Selfhood unwieldy stretching out into Non Entity
Generalising Art & Science till Art & Science is lost ...
Instead of Albion's lovely mountains & the curtains of Jerusalem,
I see a Cave, a Rock, a Tree deadly and poisonous, unimaginative.
Instead of the Mutual Forgiveness, the Minute Particulars, I see
Pits of bitumen ever burning, artificial Riches of the Canaanite
Like Lakes of liquid lead: instead of heavenly Chapels built
By our dear Lord, I see Worlds crusted with snows & ice.
I see a Wicker Idol woven round Jerusalem's children. I see
The Canaanite, the Amalekite, the Moabite, the Egyptian,
By Demonstrations the cruel Sons of Quality & Negation,
Driven on the Void, in incoherent despair into Non Entity.
I see America clos'd apart, & Jerusalem driven in terror
Away from Albion's mountains, far away from London's spires.

WILLIAM BLAKE, from *Jerusalem* (1804)

The Ruin of Liberty?

*The Gazette says 10000 people a year go from the North of
Ireland to America and 40000 in all. May they flourish and set up
in due time a glorious free government in the country which may
serve as a retreat to those Free men who may survive the final ruin
of Liberty in this Country; an event which I am afraid is at no
great distance. Mrs. Winnick says if she was young she would fly
from our oppressors and go to the banks of the Ohio.*

From the diary of SYLAS NEVILLE, February 1767[1]

I

From the late 1750s, Methodist preachers appeared on the Isle of Man. Wesley
himself went there. ' ... A more loving simple-hearted people than this I never
saw. And no wonder; for they have but six papists, and no dissenters in the
island. It is supposed to contain near thirty thousand people, remarkably
courteous and humane.' Yet he was outraged when one of his preachers proposed to publish a hymn book in Manx Gaelic. 'On the contrary,' he wrote,
'we should do everything in our power to abolish it from the earth, and persuade every member of our Society to learn and talk English.' Such a volume
was published only after his death.[2]

Though for generations now the gentry and better-off people on Man had
used English and had lived very much like their counterparts in Lancashire, the
lower classes had clung to Manx. Until the second half of the eighteenth century,
there were no wheeled carriages on the island and sleds were employed instead.
Tenant farmers enjoyed effective ownership of their land, but this peasantry was
as archaic as any in Europe. Only the busy smuggling industry had linked Man
with the bounding economy of the new Rome across the water, from which it
remained politically distinct.

Lordship over the island had passed in the 1730s, at the death of the childless tenth Earl of Derby, to a distant relative, the Duke of Atholl. Under George III,
a new king with a keen sense of his own importance, the anachronism of Man
was at last tidied up. The British government was anxious to appoint customs
officers for the island. The third Duke of Atholl sold his sovereignty to the
Crown in 1765 for £70,000. The Union, consummated by arrogant legislation
at Westminster, was most unpopular with the Manx people. Customs duties
ended their highly profitable smuggling trade. The British Parliament taxed them

directly, though they had no representative in it. The island's own oligarchical little assembly, the 'House of Keys', continued to make laws for its inhabitants, but Britain paid the costs of administration and creamed off surplus revenues for its own treasury. Man woke into the modern world to find itself being cheated. The islanders learnt fast. In 1780, 800 of them signed a petition asking for the House of Keys to be replaced by a popularly elected body. Echoes of revolution were heard even here.[3]

II

The final quarter of the eighteenth century saw a sharp upward sweep in British overseas trade. So far as imperfect statistics can tell us, the annual level of imports rose from £7.3 million in the 1740s to £12.8 million in the early 1770s, and that of exports and re-exports together climbed from £10.1 million to £15.6. English-owned shipping, by tonnage, increased between 1751 and 1775 from 421,000 to 608,000.[4]

The non-European products generally known as 'groceries', including tea and sugar, coffee, rice, and pepper, had contributed a sixth of English imports in 1700; in 1772 they provided over a third. The East Indies, Africa and the New World were thus critical in the growth of commerce. The West Indian islands, which had provided in 1700 approximately a tenth of all foreign trade, now contributed between a sixth and a fifth. And the North American mainland was now an even more important market for exports (£1.8 million per year in 1766–70) than the Caribbean (£1.4 million). The New World colonies combined now sent Britain approaching half her imports, and their call for large quantities of cheap manufactures was having extremely important effects on Britain's western ports and the regions around them.[5]

Nantes, in France, depended heavily on the 'triangular trade' with Africa and the West Indies. But its industrial hinterland was inadequate. Its exports to Guinea were in fact mostly re-exports – oriental textiles brought in by the French East India Company, provisions originating in Ireland, firearms and cutlery and the like brought in from Northern Europe by Dutch merchants. Little except for brandy, of all that the slavers sent, was manufactured in France. Since African customers preferred English guns, and the import of these into France was banned, supplies had to be obtained via Holland.[6]

Contrast Glasgow. Imports of tobacco into that trim and pretty town multiplied six times in thirty years to the early 1770s, and Scots came to command more than half Britain's total tobacco trade. Most of the goods they shipped out to the New World originated in Scotland, and about nine-tenths of Scottish linen exports crossed the Atlantic to the colonies. Tobacco merchants were deeply involved in linen manufacture, and promoted and dominated new industries. Visiting Glasgow in 1772, an Englishman saw them at work: ' ... A great porter brewery, which supplies some part of less-industrious *Ireland* ...

manufactures of linnens, cambricks, lawns, fustians, tapes and striped linnens; sugar houses and glass houses; great roperies; vast manufactures of shoes, boots and saddles, and all sorts of horse furniture; also vast tanneries, carried on under a company who have £60,000 capital, chiefly for the use of the colonists, whose bark is found unfit for tanning. The magazine of saddles, and other works respecting that business, is an amazing sight: all these are destined for *America* ... ' Five hundred men were employed in Bell's Tannery. Five tobacco merchants were partners in it. James Dunlop, scion of a great tobacco dynasty, became probably the most powerful coalmaster in the west of Scotland, investing £10,000 over sixteen years in one field alone. Here trade stimulated industry which helped trade which in turn fostered new industries.

And over 98 per cent of all the tobacco which reached the Clyde was re-exported. France was the main market. The French Farmers General, who had a monopoly in the purchase of tobacco came to the Scots for cheapness and convenience. The factors of Glasgow houses bought their tobacco outright in Virginia, and could undercut their London rivals, who still sold for planters on commission and so were obliged to haggle for the highest possible price.[7]

The tiny élite of Glasgow 'tobacco lords' were almost as potent a symbol of the new era as Clive and his fellow 'nabobs'. Like the Byrds, Lees and Carters of Virginia itself, they intermarried to form a single, growing kinship group. One of their number, Andrew Buchanan, laid out 'Virginia St' and his own son sited in it a grand 'Virginia Mansion'. Other 'tobacco lords' built in this street or bought or erected mansions elsewhere. Only the town's churches rivalled these houses in size.

Liverpool was a less attractive place. The streets were narrow. The inns were poor. But beautiful thoroughfares would have been incongruous with its position as Europe's chief slaving town. In 1771, 107 ships cleared out of Liverpool for Guinea, and drew from that coast 29,250 slaves, not far off the population of their home port. London in the same year sent only 58, Bristol (quite eclipsed now) only 23; the small town of Lancaster chipped in with four. These 190 British ships took from Africa 47,146 people. Around this time, Britain could expect to profit from over half the slaves shipped to the New World, with France taking perhaps a quarter, the New Englanders some few thousand each year. Such dominance has rarely been won by any nation in any branch of commerce.[8]

So much depended on this trade. Gun-makers in the Midlands needed it almost as much as Jamaican planters. Indeed, the latter's island assembly actually passed three Bills between 1760 and 1774 aimed at restraining the importation of slaves; it was worried by the disparity between black and white numbers, and by a series of slave rebellions. The British government scotched these Acts. 'We cannot allow the colonies to check or discourage in any degree a traffic so beneficial to the nation.'[9]

By the 1760s, protests against slavery and the slave trade were ceasing to be merely literary or marginal. What has been called an 'intellectual revolution' was gathering momentum.[10]

The planters themselves were less easy nowadays in their brutality. Rising slave prices encouraged humanity – better treatment made economic sense. Science suggested sounder diets, improved medical care. John Pinney, absentee owner of a long-established planting family, ordered his manager to be 'mild', observing, 'a merciful Man is So, even to his Beast: How much more then is it incumbent upon us to exercise it upon those poor Creatures, who only want the light of revelation and Learning to be upon a Level with us.' In would-be patriarchal Virginia, an Anglican minister, unable to imagine how comfortable life might be possible without servile labour (when a white, free, 'bungling carpenter' charged 2s. a day for his work), yet convinced that slave-owning was 'the original sin and curse' of the colony, resorted to blaming the British government for forcing blacks on its American subjects.[11] This not very logical view would become pretty commonplace. Guilt, for most people, insists on a scapegoat.

But Lord! how the money rolled in, rolled in, rolled in. From the mid-1730s demand for sugar in Europe tended to run ahead of supply. Barbados muscovado, fetching only 17s. per cwt in 1733, took over 30s. 6d. throughout the third quarter of the century, with a high point of 45s. 9d. in 1759. Soil exhaustion limited the advantage which the older British islands could take of growing markets – production on Barbados was somehow increased by half between 1730 and 1765, but then fell back to a lower figure than before. The idyllic landscape of St Kitts was dominated by huge heaps of ordure, since even that very rich soil was flagging. Jamaicans, however, had plenty of virgin land for expansion, and that island, during its heyday of stench and elegance, brought the Empire, in 1774, a clear profit of over £1½ million, and provided a more attractive outlet for capital than Britain itself could easily offer. But whereas a Bristol merchant trading to Jamaica could expect 15 per cent profit, an island planter, after paying the interest on his debt and other charges would probably get no more than about 5 per cent. Hence small men were commonly hard pressed. The rich who flourished were chiefly absentees. Two-thirds of the annual income and profit of Jamaica went to people residing in the British Isles, with the London West Indies merchants the prime gainers. The wealth of the West Indies was sucked to Europe, like the proceeds of the rape of Bengal. ' ... One country', Richard Sheridan argues, 'had captured a large enough segment of the Atlantic trading area to launch the Industrial Revolution.'[12]

That revolution would involve a momentous shift in the balance of regions within Britain. For centuries London had dominated the island's economy. Its cultural and political pre-eminence within England were unassailable. But compared to Liverpool and Glasgow, London was stagnant. The shipping owned in the City, by 1775, was no greater than at the start of the century; that of the 'outports' had waxed two and a half times. Seen simply by figures of tonnage clearing outwards, Whitehaven in Cumberland, a coal port which had become the main English entrepôt for tobacco, was now a rather close second to London. The turbulence of London politics after 1763 may well have had much to do with the deceleration of the city's growth and the psychological effects of loss of unchallenged supremacy; as in Virginia, easeless men found the government a convenient scapegoat.[13] A similar reflex may help to explain equal, riotous insolence on the far side of the Atlantic, where Boston, once master of a seaboard, had likewise stagnated, and had fallen behind Philadelphia.

In an age of unsanctified prosperity based on slavery and the hard lives of the white poor, men searched with desperation for ideas which would give their lives dignity. The flatulent opulence of Augustan Rome could hardly appeal as a prototype to voteless manufacturers, breadless labourers, debt-laden planters, insecure Yankee smugglers. While some Englishmen revived the subversive levelling attitudes which had flourished in the 1640s, educated American colonists looked back to a different Rome, to that republic established by Junius Brutus who had ousted the Tarquin kings, and defended unavailingly by his descendant Marcus when he assassinated Julius Caesar. Austerity, public spirit, unflinching contempt for tyrants – the cult of such antique virtues had explosive contemporary potential.

III

In 1763, the British North American mainland colonies, excluding Canada, had at least 1,750,000 and perhaps two million inhabitants. The people of the British Isles outnumbered the North Americans by perhaps six to one. But even without the help of refined statistics, they could observe how fast the latter were increasing. Modern estimates suggest that white population grew by over 30 per cent in the 1760s, then by over a quarter again in the following decade, while slave imports, at nearly 6,000 a year, were unprecedentedly high. There was a new spate of voluntary immigration, perhaps 60,000 from Ireland, perhaps 25,000 from Scotland, maybe 15,000 from England and Wales, with untold legions of Germans and others making a total towards or around 150,000 between Bute's peace and 1776.[14]

To a growing number of thinkers, the portents seemed clear. Benjamin Franklin wrote to a Scottish philosopher, Lord Kames, in 1760: 'I have long been of opinion, that the foundations of the future grandeur and stability of the British Empire lie in America ... All the country from the St. Lawrence to the Mississippi will in another century be filled with British people.' To a British customs official, Comptroller Weare, present in North America in the same year, it seemed that the colonies were expanding at a rate dangerous to Britain's interests. Settlers would be lured from Europe by the 'property and independency' which they could enjoy in America, having learnt that 'under the forms of a democratical government, all mortifying distinctions of rank' could be 'lost in a common equality'. The colonists would probably think of independence. 'An event so fatal to the British empire, might the less be apprehended, did a single instance remain of any colony, that ever continued in subjection, after it could assert its liberty, or could the desire of independency be thought irradicable from the human heart; or that a thousand leagues distance from the eye and strength of government should never suggest to a people accustomed to more than British liberty, a thought of setting up for themselves.'[15]

Weare thought political factors more important than economic ones. For that sphere, in that period, he was in general right. Individual stresses and strains within the 'old colonial system' bore critically hard on individuals, on some groups, and the system could not have gone on for long without major revision. But the North American colonists were not hard done by.

They could, save in time of war, export freely to foreign markets most of the foodstuffs which they grew or reared and most of the products of their timber forests. By 1775, Pennsylvania alone was annually sending abroad about 350,000 barrels of flour, with other produce in proportion. Of course, some staples were 'enumerated' and could only be shipped to Britain – but of these, indigo, naval stores and ship's timber were awarded bounties by the government. While South Carolinan exports of rice had doubled in twenty years, indigo now brought in almost as much, though colonial dye was inferior to the French and Spanish types, and depended on British government assistance to find buyers in the home cloth industry. North Carolina's naval stores would likewise have stood a poor chance on an open market.[16]

The various Acts against colonial manufactures were scarcely enforced, and evoked little protest. Why should they, when labour costs in the colonies were high, and iron utensils could be imported from Britain as cheaply as made in the New World? New England could export its competitive manufactures to other colonies – candles and coaches, leather goods and rum – and a colonist could create all the hats or woollens he liked so long as they were not sold outside his own province. By 1775 the colonies were producing more bar and pig iron than Britain itself. They were beginning to compete in pottery, stoneware, even in glassware. About three-tenths of the ships engaged in the empire's commerce were American built, while three-quarters of all the trade of the mainland colonies was carried in ships belonging to colonists. The New England fishing fleet numbered over 1,000. New England vessels had already driven British fishermen out of Maine and Nova Scotia waters, and now there were fears that they would oust them from the Banks of Newfoundland.[17]

Ships built and owned in America traded between the West Indies and Britain itself in such numbers as to annoy London shipping interests. The Navigation Acts had in fact encouraged the growth of a large colonial merchant marine – and the extent to which this was devoted to smuggling could be deduced from the fact that in 1760-1, when other colonies, with the war virtually won, expressed their pent-up demand for manufactures in greatly increased imports from Britain, legal importations into New York and New England dropped by approaching half, into Pennsylvania by five-sevenths. Even the role of the mainland *vis-à-vis* the West Indies could give rise to irritation. British sugar planters could fairly complain that North American trade with the French and Dutch colonies raised the price of provisions to themselves, and that Yankees who could get cheaper molasses from foreigners therefore insisted on cash, always in short supply, rather than produce, from fellow subjects of George III; the governor of Jamaica, in 1752, had protested that over £70,000 in specie annually was drawn from his colony into their hands in this way.[18]

Yet the islands could not have been fed otherwise. On balance, the system must still seem mutually advantageous. 'The American is apparelled from head to foot in our manufactures ... ', a writer in the *London Magazine* smugly observed in 1766; 'he scarcely drinks, sits, moves, labours or recreates himself, without contributing to the emolument of the mother country.' And the colonists themselves had the good fortune to be tied to a nation whose manufactures were generally declining in price and improving in quality.[19]

They were prosperous. They were dependent. They seemed to be thriving because they were dependent. New England's vital need of West Indian markets was emphasised in the use of rum and molasses in every kind of barter transaction. When the Browns, famous Rhode Island merchants, had a sloop built in 1764, they paid in merchantable molasses at 1s. 8½d. lawful money per gallon. Obadiah Brown managed to pay an insurance premium in molasses; and one of the family tipped people with molasses for minor services. Credit from Britain provided the main operating capital of American planters and merchants; in 1760, when the value of British exports to the colonists was estimated to total over £2 million per year, British merchants carried over £4 million of American debts on their ledgers. And the late 1760s and early 1770s saw a new peak of colonial prosperity. By 1768, the balance of trade between Massachusetts and Britain was actually in the colony's favour, while the sale of provincial lands provided a fund which obviated the need for taxation.[20]

The British themselves were at this time the most heavily taxed people in Europe, apart from the Dutch. About 1765, they paid an average of 26 shillings per head per year. The burden was visibly rising. An excise duty of 4s. on every hogshead of cider (1763) provoked riots in the apple-growing counties. The average tax burden in Ireland was 6s. 8d. per head. For Pennsylvania and Maryland the figure was 1s.; for New York 8d., for Virginia only 5d. In all Europe, only the Poles were as lightly taxed as Britain's American colonists. Georgia, though its trade was now booming, was still assisted by an annual parliamentary grant of several thousand pounds. Connecticut, which had had the best record of any colony in supporting the Seven Years War, had been more than reimbursed for its expenses by a series of parliamentary grants, and between 1764 and 1770 found it unnecessary to levy any taxes, though this was concealed from the authorities in Whitehall. When taxation thereafter returned, it was only at the rate of 7d. *per capita*. South Carolina levied no taxes in 1764 or 1765, and after 1769 made do with no more than port duties. In North Carolina, such small sums as were collected were largely embezzled by the sheriffs. And so on. New World colonists under other powers were also more lightly taxed than their European fellow subjects; but, even omitting customs duties, New Spain, through various impositions, would send about £1,000,000 every year to Old Spain in the 1780s, while Brazil, more populous and far richer than Portugal, quite cheerfully, in the mid-eighteenth century, supported its mother country to the tune of about £900,000 annually. French planters in the West Indies were lightly taxed but this was because the Crown preferred to subsidise its colonies rather than call representative assemblies to vote money.[21]

All European powers acted according to the mercantilist view that colonies must benefit the mother country. All restricted colonial trade – Britain's rules were, in this matter as in others, the most generous. All faced, in the aftermath of the Treaty of Paris, two problems of epochal significance. The rising cost of colonial defence seemed to make it essential to tighten control of New World possessions in the interests of obtaining more revenue – this the Spanish Crown, notably, did with great short-term success. But fresh assertions of power from Europe ran up against growing, distinctive self-consciousness of 'American' or 'creole' identity on the part of important classes in the colonies. Canadian resentment of Montcalm was typical. From about the 1750s, whites in Spain's vast New World territories started calling themselves '*Americanos*', and people at home began to refer to them as '*criollos*'.[22] After Charles III (an 'enlightened despot') ascended the Spanish throne in 1759, administrative reforms alienated *criollo* magnates, merchants and even priests, as they found themselves blocked, supplanted or challenged by Iberian-born intruders.

As the ideas of Montesquieu and Rousseau began to find hearers in Rio, Port au Prince and Caracas, 'enlightened' men all over the New World envied the freedoms enjoyed by British subjects. 'In no colonial empire then or since had the metropolitan state less direct power.'[23]

Rhode Island and Connecticut, retaining their seventeenth-century charters, were virtually independent states except in matters of defence. Governors, treasurers, secretaries and Council members were all elected, and in Rhode Island the Assembly made its annual choice of about 300 lesser executive and judicial officers, including the judges. No places in the world were more 'democratical'. Deputies to the Assembly were elected annually in Connecticut, twice a year in Rhode Island. In the three proprietory provinces (Maryland, Pennsylvania and Delaware) governors were still appointed by the proprietors, and would on their behalf withhold consent to annoying Bills. Though the remaining colonies were all under royal government, Massachusetts had certain exceptional privileges, such as a Council indirectly elected. Any royal governor had in theory great powers. But in practice assemblies controlled the purse strings. Most governors depended on salaries voted only for a year at a time. And Whitehall rarely meddled much with colonial legislation; of all the more than 8,500 laws submitted by mainland colonies to the Privy Council before 1775, only one in twenty or so was disallowed.[24] Assemblies directed when and where the militia might be employed. They had usurped power to appoint various provincial office-holders. They preened themselves on having similar form and status to the Westminster Parliament, and their members showed no enthusiasm for the notion that the colonies might send representatives to that body—such M.P.s would have no great vote-power, would be expensive to send, and would be out of touch with their electorates.

A British traveller in Virginia during the Seven Years War reported the people there to be 'haughty and jealous of their liberties, impatient of restraint' and scarcely able to 'bear the thought of being controlled by any superior power.' Many of them thought of the colonies as 'independent states, not connected with Great Britain, otherwise than by having the same common king, and being bound to her by natural affection.'[25] Many colonists, here and elsewhere, believed devoutly that Parliament had no right to tax them. Followers of the whig tradition and students of Enlightenment thought readily argued that the laws of nature prohibited taxation by Parliament of persons not represented within it.

Some colonies, of course, were far more 'democratical' than others. If a 40s. freehold entitled a man to vote in Connecticut, the qualification was £40 in New York.[26] But even the most conservative native Americans shared assumptions about the world which ran counter to those prevalent in the Westminster Parliament elected in 1761, where over half the members were related to baronets and peers, where bought holders of sinecures sat rejoicing in such titles as 'Clerk of the Venison Warrants' and 'Master of the Hanaper' and even able and honourable men, if not aristocratic by birth, depended on aristocratic patronage. (Edmund Burke, over fifteen years, was paid about £30,000 by his leader, the second Marquis of Rockingham.) George III was not a despot. While most of his ministers came from aristocratic families, and even Pitt ultimately accepted a peerage, these men were not altogether like Spanish grandees. Nevertheless, the challenge now made from America in the name of 'English liberty' harbingered the coming conflict throughout the Atlantic world between aristocratical' and 'democratical' tendencies.

In most parts of Europe at this time, monarchs attacked the privileges of fortunate groups. The colonists whose blessed position George III and his ministers now sought to modify reacted, like French and Swedish noblemen, to defend what they saw as their rights, so their stand was deeply conservative and yet it was also revolutionary. The assembly of Massachusetts, R. R. Palmer points out, ' ... was actually elected, and elected by a population of small and relatively equal independent farmers. In this respect it was as different as possible from the Diet of Hungary, the Estates of Brabant or Brittany, the *Parlement* of Paris, or, for that matter, the Parliament of Great Britain. What was conservative or customary in America was radical innovation for Europe.'[27]

In Britain, the theory was that all people, even those living in rising towns like Birmingham and Manchester which sent no M.P.s to Parliament, were 'virtually represented' at Westminster. In Burke's words, Parliament was 'a deliberative assembly of *one* nation, with *one* interest, that of the whole, where, not local purposes, not local prejudices ought to guide, but the general good ... '[28] But in the colonies, assembly members were generally residents of the localities which they represented and were closely responsible to their constituents. People thought in terms of government 'by' the people as well as 'for' it. In Britain the idea of universal suffrage was cherished only by a few eccentrics, but many in America would have agreed with James Otis of Massachusetts when he argued that Manchester ought to have an M.P. – 'Right reason and the spirit of a free constitution require that the representation of the whole people should be as equal as possible' – and that every male of sound mind should have a vote. 'If a man has but little property to protect and defend, yet his life and liberty are things of some importance.'[29]

England and Wales had perhaps a hundred and twenty people to the square mile while Virginia had roughly seven. Less cramped, free to cut wood and shoot game, free to move on, men living in that colony, if they were not servants or slaves, had a practical experience of 'liberty', and of 'independence' of limiting ties and bonds. This made their psychology sharply different. Cossacks in the Siberian Wild East shared the same advantages, but they did not belong to a culture which emphasised the word 'liberty'. 'If we are made in some degree for others,' Thomas Jefferson would proclaim, 'yet, in a greater, are we made for ourselves.' The American remained, in most cases, an 'Englishman', but one who had grown up in a society where feudalism had never been an effective presence, who gave free rather than obligatory respect to the local equivalents of squire and parson, and had scope to express the 'democratical' tendencies latent in the thinking of his Stuart forbears. In Britain, deference, sacred social forms, beloved hypocrisies, institutional cosmetics, all masked the processes of politics. In America, Jefferson could plausibly write, 'The whole art of government consists in the art of being honest.'[30]

George III was in fact an honest man. His policy was perfectly straightforward. J. H. Plumb sums it up: ' ... the colonists must be reduced to absolute obedience, if need be, by the ruthless use of force.'[31] The King did not understand that coercion could not succeed in a land with an almost limitless frontier where people were accustomed to use arms. The colonists themselves, for some dozen years, did not grasp that the gulf between British and American views of the world had been growing so wide as to be unbridgeable; even then, those many who would be called 'Loyalists' failed to realise until it was too late that they belonged to a novel species of mankind.

Winckelmann, German prophet of Europe's latest artistic creed, extolled, in

1755, the American Indian and Homer in successive sentences. The still more potent Jean Jacques Rousseau was identified in the eyes of his growing number of admirers with the cults of the 'noble savage', of uninhibited, frank display of feeling, and of rapture over unspoilt nature, and when Frederick the Great of Prussia, a staunch classicist, declared that Shakespeare's plays were 'ridiculous farces, worthy of Canadian savages', he was paying the latter a back-handed compliment. A Frenchman named Crèvecoeur in his *Letters from an American Farmer* (1782) would set the 'broad lap' of American nature, open to a 'perpetual accession of new comers', against 'the musty ruins of Rome', and establish a stereotype of the 'farmer of feelings'. Meanwhile, Voltaire himself extolled the Pennsylvanians, and the 'Good Quaker' became a symbol of intellectual opposition in monarchical, priest-ridden France.[32]

The colonists themselves expressed their growing self-confidence in a cult of simplicity which employed different symbols. To James Otis, as for many others, in Britain as well as in the New World, it seemed that the Anglo-Saxon ancestors of the English had enjoyed a government 'founded upon principles of the most perfect liberty', with every freeholder entitled to vote, but that the Norman Conquest had brought 'the rage of despotism'. The liberties now possessed by Englishmen had been secured by militant struggle against medieval kings and against the 'execrable race of Stuarts'.[33] For 'King John' and 'Charles I' read 'Tarquin' and 'Caesar', and then the drama is transferred to Rome and the agonies of its republic. It was easy for men of that day to compare George Wythe, who taught Thomas Jefferson law, to the virtuous Cato, and Richard Henry Lee, the Virginian politician, to the great Roman orator Cicero, and such comparisons tugged imaginations towards a republican ideal.

If frugal Romans and rude Anglo-Saxons had held sounder political notions than the courts of eighteenth-century Europe, the same might apply to an unlettered frontiersman. 'State a moral case to a plowman and a professor', Jefferson would remark to his nephew. 'The former will decide it as well, and often better than the latter, because he has not been led astray by artificial rules.' Such egalitarian theorising might cross over into denunciation of colour prejudice. Philadelphia Quakers, in 1758, gave a practical lead to world opinion when their Yearly Meeting recorded its hope that Friends would free their slaves and ruled that any Friend buying or selling slaves should be excluded from the Society's business affairs. The publication, in 1773, of a volume of poems, uninspired but competent, by a Boston black girl, Phyllis Wheatley, would be hailed as proving that racial stereotypes were invalid. Benjamin Rush, a leading colonial intellectual, summed up the view of generous contemporaries: 'Human Nature is the same in all Ages and Countries ... '[34]

This was in tune with the vaguely benevolent credo of the lodges of Freemasons. The world's 'mother' Grand Lodge, established in London in 1717, had presided over the very swift and significant spread of Masonry throughout Europe and its colonial settlements. It provided a freely chosen bond between individuals irrespective of class or nationality. All Masons were equal. While Walpole and Newcastle had been Masons, and lodges in the English-speaking countries were highly respectable institutions, they were also secure centres for the dissemination of ideas, within and across political frontiers. 'Benevolence, fraternity, utility, morality: these were what freemasonry was about for anybody who took it seriously, and there is much evidence that many did.'[35] Washington, Franklin and John Adams were Freemasons; so was their French admirer Lafayette. These men, and scores of thousands of others all over the world, were identified with an optimistic view of human nature, tiptoe on the brink of revolution, alert to notions of 'natural rights' which were as subversive as anything propounded beforehand by Calvinists or in our own time by Marxists.

In America visions of idealised past and ideal future could combine explosively in a chemistry which left natural conservatives heading revolt alongside demagogic or democratical hotheads. Everywhere in the colonies, leading men were likely to venerate an inheritance, the English Common Law, which had been preserved for them by the actions of seventeenth-century revolutionaries; every justice of the peace had to have some knowledge of it. To dote as Jefferson and Otis did on the famous primer *Coke Upon Littleton* was to look backwards; the consistent appeal to precedent might seem at odds with Enlightenment rationalism; yet because the law had to be seen to be universal in application, its cult might be subversive, the rhetoric lavished upon it might hide a radical critique. 'From the "liberties of Englishmen" it was an easy step to the universalist assertion that all men had a right to be free.'[36]

Jefferson seized, as his personal motto, upon a statement attributed to one of the men who had cut off King Charles I's head – 'Rebellion to tyrants is obedience to God.'[37] Looking backward to the seventeenth century meant recognising the views of such radical thinkers as John Milton. But the writings of the anti-Walpolian opposition in England, which had been read and re-read in the colonies, were a wider and more immediate influence. Their prime ideas were currently being developed by a new generation of British intellectuals – such people as the Welsh savant Richard Price, the great chemist Joseph Priestley, and Major Cartwright, the parliamentary reformer. Propagandists of this school saw government itself as inherently hostile to human liberty, and as properly existing only by sufferance of the people whose needs it served. They commonly shared in the fervent faith in the magical liberty-making properties of the unique British constitution, which found its classic expositor in Sir William Blackstone, whose *Commentaries on the Laws of England* were published in the late 1760s, selling as many copies in the colonies as in Britain itself. Blackstone extolled the checks and balances found in British government, thanks to the roles played by King, Lords and Commons. The people checked the nobility, noblemen checked the people, the King checked both. But opposition writers stirred up the fear that, first Walpole and his 'Robinarchical' corruption, now

George III with his Stuart-like lust for despotic rule, threatened liberty throughout the empire. A mercenary army raised by means of taxes wrung from the people might revive the Norman Yoke and reverse the Glorious Revolution of 1689.

Paranoia prevailed on both sides of the Atlantic. Colonists would not have credited that George III himself sincerely believed the British constitution to be 'the most beautiful combination ever framed'. Virtually no evidence exists that any American, except John Adams, thought before 1763 of breaking away, yet agents of Whitehall were reporting back that the Americans craved separation and were only waiting their chance. Some fatalists at home thought like Lord Camden: 'It is impossible that this petty island can continue in dependence that mighty continent, increasing daily in numbers and in strength. To protract the time of separation to a distant day is all that can be hoped.' But how to 'protract' it, save by strong legislation and, if necessary, sheer military force? Meanwhile, colonists were believing the wildest allegations of a 'conspiracy against liberty' in high circles in England. Liberty, precious, was also precarious. All over the world, it seemed, tyranny prevailed, save in the English-speaking countries. In Venice, in Sweden, liberty had been overridden in quite recent times. The eighteenth-century mind favoured static or cyclical views of how history worked. So the struggle for liberty must be resumed again and again. That the time was at hand might be inferred not only from the shrieks and wails of the English opposition, but also from certain recent behaviour by Britons in North America. When the British commander-in-chief kept colonial troops against their will in Nova Scotia over the winter of 1759–60, a New England soldier wrote in his journal, 'Although we be Englishmen born yet we are debarred Englishmens liberty, therefore we now see what it is to be under martial law and to be with the regulars who are but little better than slaves to their officers ... '38

Of course, British politics really were corrupt. A young Pennsylvanian, John Dickinson, in London as a law student during the election year of 1754, reported in letters home to his father, 'If a man cannot be brought to vote as he is desired, he is made dead drunk and kept in that state, never heard of by his family or friends till all is over and he can do no harm. The oath of their not being bribed is as strict and solemn as language can form it, but is so little regarded that few people can refrain from laughing while they take it.'39 Other colonial visitors suffered similar shock. Their own eyes seemed to confirm that Walpolian corruption and the sycophancy of ambitious men were leaving Englishmen with little more than the shadow of their famous liberty.

Benjamin Franklin, it is true, was extremely happy to live in London from 1757 to 1762 as agent for the Pennsylvanian Assembly. His son, aged only 31, was given the governorship of New Jersey. After the pleasures of hobnobbing with the great and the flattering interest of leading intellectuals, Franklin was sorry when he had to go home. The strength of the forces making for irreversible rupture is illustrated by the fact that this Anglophile imperialist, cool and elderly, was moved by the 1770s into support for American independence. He craved high political office in Britain itself. But brilliant plebeians, clear-eyed exponents of middle-class ethics, did not belong in British politics. If the government had been prepared to lavish peerages and other honours upon out-standing colonials at this time, revolution might have been averted. But few Americans were very rich, not many were Anglicans, almost none could shove their way into the queue of aspirants. Colonials did not look like aristocrats. They did not think like aristocrats. Only a handful ever received titles.

Franklin dressed like a Dissenter, and he was most at ease with Dissenting intellectuals. One of these, Richard Price, would write in 1776 that 'the meanest person among us is disposed to look upon himself as having a body of subjects in *America* ... ' Britons commonly saw the colonists as riff-raff, not a patch on your true beef-eating islanders. They were represented as descendants of con-victs, as near-Indians tainted with savagery – apart from which many were Irish or German. Yet the colonies were fast maturing a range of institutions to match those of the mother country. On their coasts, if not on their frontiers, the days of amateur justice were ending. Maryland, rather ahead of some colonies, had developed an indigenous class of professional lawyers, highly esteemed in their own community and concerned to enforce and improve their own standards. Though such men had to have wider knowledge than lawyers in England, where specialisation was general, they were conscious of being viewed with contempt by professionals in the mother country. Why should men of high local standing and great proficiency meekly accept insolent slights? George Washington, in 1774, broke off relations with an English firm with which he had traded for twenty years when it questioned one of his bills of exchange.[40]

Of course, money was involved there as well as pride. A cynical twentieth-century mind perceives comfortably-off parcels of men in the colonies ridden by fear, greed, ambition and pique, who took leadership upon themselves and worked successfully on the resentments of sections of the masses to provoke an unnecessary breach with the most generous of imperial powers. But such a view misses the context of action, the relativities which make history. The masses were not so easily bemused. From the vantage point of late eighteenth-century Paris or Warsaw or Amsterdam, events in the New World suggested a new war of faith to young men who found them deeply exciting. Washington, Franklin, Jefferson seemed epic heroes, noble in intellect, fortitude, daring and self-denial, leading a people permeated by the pristine Roman virtues of high moral sense and plain living. And some American leaders were in fact, by the standards of their age (and of ours), notably high-minded men who did indeed live modestly by comparison with debauched English milords and foppish French *noblesse*. They believed devoutly in their own virtue, which often has the effect of making men act somewhat less badly than otherwise. They gave themselves ideals worth living up to, and Europe the vision of democratic revolution.

THE RUIN OF LIBERTY? 643

Revolution began in the consciousness of the generation which included John Adams (born in 1735), Patrick Henry (1736), Ethan Allen (1737) and Jefferson (1743). Our knowledge that such men died old and revered, should not blind us to the fact that they were, in the 1760s, young and rash. They were affected not only by the major shift of European ideas and sensibility which was proceeding during their formative years, but also by what they saw happening around them. British military performance, except at Quebec, was feeble. The Great Awakening had set off psychic ferment. Moulds were being broken, or seemed fit to be broken.

The rapidly growing American population was – this is too rarely mentioned – a young population. Young Otis and Henry, with their intoxicating oratory, pointed their coevals vaguely past traditional sources of political power and mystique and mobilised them in the name of 'patriotism'. This generation had grown up with the sense of manifest destiny aroused by the opening of the trans-Appalachian frontier. It could handle, and could be formed by, the periodical press, that relatively new medium which passed controversial ideas and worrying news from colony to colony, making a common response possible. There were thirty-eight newspapers publishing in the mainland provinces by 1775, besides, in the quarter century before that, some four hundred pamphlets bearing on the Anglo-American quarrel and written, for the most part, not by professional scribblers, but by lawyers, ministers, planters and merchants who were spurred by events into public-spirited blasts and affirmations.[41]

The sheer numbers of rising, able young men meant that the imperial authorities could not buy over all the natural local leaders. Thus, Richard Henry Lee, a Virginian anxious to provide for his growing family, repeatedly asked his brother Arthur, who was in England, to secure him a 'place', but Arthur had to reply that 'real merit or virtue' were not justly rewarded within the British Empire. The European middle class, in an age of population explosion, would confront a like shortage of opportunity – but American numbers exploded earlier and ran ahead faster. As they spilled over the mountains westward, the idea that a new land-based, home-made polity would make better sense than adherence to a British system which was in emphasis maritime, came to seem natural to young people. 'The Almighty,' a South Carolinan would announce in 1776, ' ... has made choice of the present generation to erect the American Empire.'[42]

South of New England, half the population was now non-English in origin. The renewed flood of immigrants after 1763 brought in preponderantly Germans, Scotch-Irish and Irish with no ancestral affection for royal rule from London. But this jeopardised chances of united action. There was no love lost in Pennsylvania between Indian-slaying Ulstermen on the frontier and fat Quakers in Philadelphia. The Virginian ruling class was skilful enough to avert tension between 'Tidewater' and 'Piedmont' settlers, but in the Carolinas, groups of so-called 'Regulators' expressed the furious discontent of pioneers. A flood of immigration into the South Carolina back-country after the so-called 'Great Cherokee War' of 1759–61 brought many settlers into areas where governmental institutions were almost entirely absent, and the nearest courts were in Charles Town at least a week's journey away. Outlaws dominated whole communities, and respectable persons accordingly banded together to take vigilante action. The irresponsible Charles Town ruling class were very fond of talking about 'liberty', but in the words of one indignant back-country clergyman, they looked 'on the poor White People in a Meaner light than their Black Slaves', and they failed promptly to respond to the movement's demands.[43] The 'Regulators' went into open rebellion, seizing officials and refusing to pay taxes. But the trouble abated when the provincial government at last set up six new circuit courts in 1769. Meanwhile, some North Carolina settlers had borrowed the 'Regulator' nickname. They rose violently against the clique which dominated the colony, till in 1771 they were defeated by a better-armed force of militia. In this province, the back-country people were greatly under-represented in the colonial Assembly; in South Carolina, until the 1770s, they were not represented at all. So for some Americans the struggle for 'Rights' must initially be directed against fellow-colonials.

IV

Sooner or later, America must have asserted independence of Britain. But why did the break come in the two decades after 1763, not in 1830 or 1919?

In brief, because New France had been conquered. As Colonel Murray, commanding at Quebec, had observed just after Wolfe's triumph, the flourishing existence of that (remarkably beautiful) town had been 'a guarantee for the good behaviour of its neighbouring colonies'.[44] So long as the French enemy prowled to the west, self-interest, even self-preservation, tied the mainland colonies securely to Britain, which bore almost the whole cost of the necessary wars. The victory of 1760 simultaneously withdrew this motive for obedience, and gave English-speaking colonials the clear chance of expansion at least as far as the Mississippi.

Coinciding with growing strains within the 'old colonial system' and with the ideological onrush of a revolutionary generation, the defeat of the French licensed men to react with violence to measures of British ministers which were ill-judged and infirm, and were taken against a background of political turmoil in London which both excited and frightened the colonists.

Much of the rhetoric in their cause, and eventually much of the practical leadership, came from Virginia. This fact was connected with the peculiarities of the Chesapeake region. Whereas most American farmers borrowed from merchants in colonial towns (who themselves depended on credit from people in Britain) the wealthier tobacco planters were directly in debt to British creditors, and grandly so: in the mid-1770s, Virginia and Maryland, with some three-tenths of the mainland colonial population, owned nearly 60 per cent of debts due from the colonies to the mother country. (The London firm of John Norton and Sons, for instance, was creditor to Virginians for £11,000 in February 1769. By July 1773, sums owing had soared to £41,000 and it was virtually impossible for the firm to continue extending new credit.)[45] From 1749, the Virginia Assembly shamelessly legislated on several occasions in favour of local debtors as against their British creditors. The so-called 'Two-penny Act' of 1758 was disallowed by the home government, which prompted indignation in the colony and also a series of lawsuits brought by clergymen. The Act had laid down that parsons should be paid in the rapidly depreciating colonial currency. They pointed out that they had been paid in tobacco when the price had been low, but now that it had been fixed high, at 2d. a lb., they were being cheated. Some tried to recover their back pay through the colony's law courts. Not one was successful. A lawyer named Patrick Henry was hired to defend collectors of parish rates against a suit brought in 1763 by the Reverend James Maury, and famously broadened the issue. Hawk-nosed, hollow of cheek, incandescent in rhetoric, Henry talked of the compact between King and people, and urged that a monarch annulling a good Act 'from being the Father to his people degenerated into a Tyrant', so forfeiting 'all right to his subjects' Obedience'. The jury awarded Maury derisory damages of one penny. Henry was carried shoulder high from the courtroom.[46]

The benefits of the 'old colonial system' were not self-evident to Virginia planters, for whom, arguably, they did not exist. Of an average of 96,000 hogs-heads of tobacco sent from the Chesapeake to Britain every year, 82,000 were re-exported. Because colonial supply so much exceeded metropolitan demand, tariff preference had little effect. The price of tobacco in Britain was in effect determined by the world price, and so, of course, was that of re-exports. But extra cost to the planters was imposed by the need to ship tobacco to Europe via the mother country, where it had to be unloaded, reloaded, and reshipped, paying double freight, insurance, commission and handling charges. Daniel Dulany of Maryland reckoned that planters would have got £3 more per hogs-head had they been allowed to send their crop direct to the continent of Europe. Meanwhile planters deeply resented their British creditors, 'whom they blamed bitterly for having loaned them money', and accused these merchants of cheating over weights and measures, and of dumping inferior manufactures on them. The Scots were especially unpopular. In 1766, Colonel Chiswell of Virginia called one Robert Routledge, merchant, a 'fugitive rebel, a villain who came to Virginia to cheat and defraud men of their property, and a Presbyterian fellow.' Then he ran him through with his sword, crying, 'He deserves his fate, damn him ... '[47]

By the 1760s, though the Piedmont planters were prospering, large numbers of planters in the traditional Tidewater areas faced bankruptcy. The more sen-sible plantocrats drove for self-sufficiency in an effort to free themselves from debt and from dependence on British goods. They switched to general farming and to wheat-growing. George Washington was one of the pioneers of advanced methods of husbandry like those used in England. His wife Martha superintended a large establishment, staffed with black labour, which manufactured woollen, linen and cotton cloth. To liberate oneself from tobacco culture was to cut at the reins which harnessed one to Britain's commercial system. It was to opt in one's mind for independence.

But the American Revolution belongs to Boston, as the French belongs to Paris, the Russian to St Petersburg. Though the New England provinces were most 'English' in stock of all the colonies, it was here that dislike of the British navigation laws was oldest and most pervasive. Direct competitors of Britain in the fisheries, and now in the slave trade, New England merchants, by the mid-1770s, carried on over 60 per cent of the trade between the various colonies and out from them overseas.[48] John Adams could claim that 'the child Independence was born' in Massachusetts in 1761, with the speech of a young lawyer, James Otis, in a case arising over 'Writs of Assistance'.

A customs officer in Salem had asked for such a writ to entitle him to search for goods which he had reason to think had been smuggled. 'Writs of Assistance' had been issued before that to eight customs officers in this colony, and employed without controversy. But Massachusetts had just acquired a new Chief Justice, Thomas Hutchinson, who was also lieutenant-governor. The job had been promised to James Otis's father by two former governors, but Governor Bernard chose instead to insert his own ally. Otis accordingly helped to stir up trouble over the writs. He argued in the Superior Court that Acts of Parliament could not justify them. An Act against the constitution was void, an Act against natural equity was void. According to John Adams, who was present, Otis 'asserted that every man, merely natural, was an independent sovereign, subject to no law, but the law written on his heart, and revealed to him by his Maker, in the constitution of his nature, and the inspiration of his understanding and his conscience', and he spoke like a 'flame of fire'. The effective use of such writs was thereafter impossible in Massachusetts.[49] Otis had given direction and inspiration to many men in an uneasy colony.

Smuggling was of prime importance to New England. 'Faced with the charge that Boston whigs smuggled, John Adams's rather lame reply was that tories did it too.' When word came of a new Westminster Act which ordered absentee customs officers to their posts and baited them with an increased share – half instead of a third – of any prizes they seized, the news was said to cause 'greater alarm' in Massachusetts than Montcalm's capture of Fort William Henry had done five years before.[50] The Sugar Act of 1733 had never been seriously enforced in peacetime. The trade in foreign molasses which it taxed was vital to New England's prime industry, rum manufacture. New England fishermen depended on exchanging their lowest-grade fish for molasses. Even 'fair traders' who frowned on the smuggling of European and East Indian goods regarded the twilight molasses trade as respectable. Now tightening up of customs brought visions of ruin.

While the smuggling issue mattered in all Yankee ports, Boston was especially inflammable. People were troubled as their town slipped gradually further and further from the pre-eminence which it had once enjoyed. Assemblies in other colonies had deliberately passed quasi-mercantilist legislation so as to keep their own export and import trades to themselves. Jealousy of Rhode Island, where law officers and magistrates were elected and customs men remained impotent, has been seen as 'the main factor' behind the angry fight of Boston merchants against the 'Writs of Assistance'.[51] Post-war commercial depression now compounded insecurity.

There were vivid traditions of defiance. The very origins of Massachusetts derived from resistance to royal authority. In 1689, Boston had overthrown Andros, the tool of a would-be despot. The suppression by Parliament of the Massachusetts Land Bank set up in 1740 in response to the needs of ordinary people had raised the prospect of new revolution, and though Governor Shirley had been astute enough to ensure that no one suffered too much, the affairs of the scheme dragged bitterly on till 1770. There was an abiding worry that the British government would grow impatient again with this troublesome colony and would move once more to deprive it of its cherished charter, even of its characteristic organ of grass roots self-government, the town meeting. In the early 1760s, this fear flickered high again, along with concern over church matters. Thomas Secker, Archbishop of Canterbury, began to revive hereditary fears of his see dating back to the days of Laud. He secured the disallowance of a Massachusetts Act to incorporate a new Congregationalist Missionary Society for work among the Indians. He took up the horrifying idea that there should be colonial bishops, fully equipped with ecclesiastical courts.

'The town of Boston,' Thomas Hutchinson lamented in 1767, 'is an absolute democracy and I am mistaken if some of the inhabitants don't wish for an independence upon province authority as much as they wish to see the province independent of the authority of Parliament.' The richest man in Northampton, Massachusetts, was a blacksmith.[52] Since workmen could engage in the politics of Boston, and the General Court was dominated by the votes of mere artisans and farmers, the methods of oligarchical rule which prevailed at this time in most other parts of the Empire worked only on sufferance here. A huff and a puff, and the house must come down.

In his sixteen years in office (1741–57) Governor Shirley had built up a 'court party' of wealthy merchants, landowners and officials. His successor, Pownall, for the sake of the war effort, had given favour to members of the 'out' faction. But now Bernard had clumsily alienated them again. Thomas Hutchinson, arch opponent of the Land Bank, had been able to allot most of the choice administrative and legal posts to friends, relatives and political followers, while holding some half-dozen positions himself. To men like that rising young lawyer John

Adams, it seemed that liberty was direly imperilled by the concentration of legislative, executive and judicial power in the hands of a small cabal. Great-great-grandson of the exiled heretic Anne, Thomas Hutchinson was to taste, at the end of a long career of public service, equally bitter hatred and rejection.

Born in 1711 into a prosperous Boston mercantile clan, Hutchinson had become the prime representative of his class, jealous on its behalf in defence of the colony's economic interests and of the sacred Massachusetts Charter. Though he sought wealth and power through politics, the shameless flaunting of Robert Walpole or Charles Price was utterly alien to his Yankee spirit. While he despised Puritan fanaticism, and often attended an Anglican church, he remained a Congregationalist and, in British terms, a Dissenter. The house which he built near Boston showed simple, modest good taste such as non-conformist bankers and brewers followed in England. Persistent but never rapacious in his quest for profit, he measured himself by the highest standards of public spirit. He embodied many characteristic American traits, virtues, and astigmatisms, but tragically for himself, he could not understand, let alone share in, the heroic idealism which was now coming into fashion. The oratory of a Pitt or a Patrick Henry could not stir him to 'patriotic' fervour. The Great Awakening had, so to speak, found him asleep, and had left him so. Utterly humourless, frail in his health, an obsessional worker, he presented to his fellow colonials a mask circumspect, temperate and restrained. He was insulated by his age, by his caution, and by the members of his own inbred Hutchinson-Sanford-Oliver clan who came to surround him in the colony's highest offices. He was not and could not be a man of the people. But as his family scooped most of the jam and left none for Otis or Adams bread, the 'outs' turned to the people to give them their revenge.

Governor Bernard, an inexperienced and undistinguished figure, owed his appointment to the patronage of one of the King's ministers who happened to be his wife's uncle. He proved to be no match in political skills for the extremely artful 'patriot' leaders. James Otis was the outstanding demagogue. John Hancock was 'Milch Cow to the Faction', a fashionable, conceited, not very clever young man whose smuggler uncle in 1764 bequeathed him most of his £70,000 fortune. Since he was a leading employer – a thousand New England families were said to depend for support on his enterprises – Hancock's influence could deliver many votes.[53] But the most dangerous opposition leader was without doubt Sam Adams, John's older cousin.

A shabbily dressed man who took a pride in his poverty (though it did not prevent him from owning a black slave girl), Sam Adams seemed an old-fashioned Puritan by the standards of his Boston – a scrupulous observer of the Lord's Day whose household was famed for its strictness in religious matters, and who sincerely wished to revive the manners and morals of the seventeenth-century founders. He was 40 years old in 1762. The son of a prosperous Boston brewer and merchant, he did not partake of his parent's business sense. After he

59, 60 and 61 A well-dressed colonial lady (Mrs Mary Pickman) by John Singleton Copley contrasts with the rugged frontiersman Daniel Boone (by Chester Harding) and the revolutionary Congressman Roger Sherman (by Ralph Earl, *below right*), a severe figure in the Puritan tradition

62 A propagandist tea-pot

63 Joseph Brandt, Chief of the Mohawks, by Romney

64 Colonel Benedict Arnold — revolutionary hero and traitor

65 American troops under Washington's command

66 Portrait of a British Artillery Officer, by Thomas Gainsborough

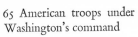

had wasted his inheritance, he had little more than the meagre income brought in by a job as tax collector in Boston; in 1767 it would be found, from his records, that he owed nearly £4,000 to town and province, but eventually he was permitted, thanks to his popularity, to repay only a small part.[54] In politics, however, he was an apt pupil of his father, who had been a director of the Land Bank and leader of the popular party in the General Court. Like him, he was a member of the 'Boston Caucus', a club of small shopkeepers, mechanics and shipyard workers which met in the Green Dragon Tavern and controlled appointments to all Boston offices by manipulating the town meeting.

When Otis in the early 1760s revived the Massachusetts 'Country Party', Adams stood behind him as organiser, agitator, and newspaper propagandist, master of hugger-mugger intrigue in smoke-filled rooms, always ready to snip up letters which might give the game away, or to throw them by handfuls into the fire. Puritan though, in some senses, he might be, he kept abreast of the times. In his writings, he equated the spirit of old Congregationalist Massachusetts with the republican ethos of Ancient Rome, and he did not object to leaguing with Otis's fellow Freemasons. While his piety gave Adams influence amongst church people, the 'mob' was his most efficacious instrument. This was the great age of 'mob' politics, but Adams was a master with nothing to learn from that momentous rouser, John Wilkes. He was popular in the taverns, admired by wharfingers and weavers, bricklayers, shipwrights and tanners. The gulf in income between Boston workers and the likes of Hutchinson was steadily widening, and they responded to Otis's denunciations of wealthy merchants grinding the faces of the poor, eating the bread of oppression without fear and waxing fat upon the spoils of the people.

There was no police force in Britain or America. To create one would have seemed a monstrous threat to 'liberty'. A 'mob' could rule a town for days. The use of troops against it would inflame feeling further ('standing army' ... 'Turkish despotism'). So when a government decided to employ armed force against English-speakers, it was bound to put itself in the wrong, and was likely to be defeated. The British government rashly imagined that it could tame Boston by sending a large body of troops there. That was the proximate cause of revolution. Boston was small. But Boston was far away, and Boston was proud of traditions of rebellion. The government made the fatal mistake of supposing that it could bully Bostonians though it could not crush John Wilkes.

V

Wilkes had an Irish forerunner, Dr Charles Lucas, an energetic tribune sprung from the Dublin middle classes, who began in 1747 to publish a weekly *Citizen's Journal*. The American colonists paid much attention to Lucas. He revived Molyneux's argument that Ireland was a distinct kingdom whose parliament could acknowledge no superior, he denounced British restrictions on Irish

Y

trade, and inveighed against corruption in elections. In 1749 an angry viceroy secured from the Irish House of Commons a series of resolutions declaring Lucas a public enemy and ordering his immediate arrest. The public-spirited (but anti-papist) apothecary was forced into exile for some years.

However, another factor arose towards mid-century to complicate the lives of the Irish ruling class. The Irish treasury, thanks to rising trade, was showing a surplus. The question arose, whose was it? The Dublin Parliament claimed the right to dispose of it; the British government declared that the money was the King's, so that his consent must be given before it could be appropriated for use in Ireland. The Ponsonby family faction was out to supplant Speaker Boyle from his pre-eminence. Boyle, aiming to show that the majority of the Commons was still his, picked a quarrel over the financial issue, knowing that public feeling would be aroused by it. In 1753 the Dublin Commons rejected a money Bill which, sent to England for approval as Poynings' Law required, had been adorned by the Privy Council there with a clause acknowledging the necessity for royal consent to disposal of the surplus. Dublin whoopeed. 'The ladies made balls, the mobs bonfires ... '⁵⁵ The viceroy prorogued Parliament. Boyle and other defiant office-holders were purged. But government could not go on without their support. Irish politicians discovered how profitable opposition could be as a new viceroy doled out peerages to win back the defectors. Boyle was restored to office and became Earl of Shannon. Before long, his faction and Ponsonby's had composed their differences and were combining to dominate the viceroy.

'Patriotism' was coming into vogue. Irish M.P.s outside the golden circle of patronage could draw attention to themselves by talk of national independence. The entire reign of George II had seen only one parliament. His death compelled the first election for thirty-three years. Associations of voters aired popular issues. But the electoral system offered no scope for transformation. Out of a population of some two million, less than a quarter were Protestants, and of these only the 300,000 or so episcopalians were free to take any part in government, though Presbyterians were not wholly impotent, and Catholic landowners could sometimes influence elections by telling Protestant tenants how to vote. However, only the thirty-two counties and some of the larger boroughs commonly saw elections at all. Dublin's electorate was quite broad, and liked to return anti-Establishment members. (In 1768, it would elect Lucas.) But most of the 109 boroughs, which, with two members each, returned a majority of the 300 M.P.s, were 'rotten', wholly under their patrons' control; a man wishing to be an M.P. might have to pay around £2,000 for a borough seat, about the same price as in England.⁵⁶ Henry Flood, heir to great estates in Kilkenny, could well afford it. Allied with Lucas, now back from exile, he emerged as the 'patriot' leader in the new parliament.

'Patriots' called for the limitation of the life of parliaments to seven years each, for a reduction in the notorious Irish pension list, for a habeas corpus Act, and for security of tenure for judges. Men like Lucas or Flood seemed to represent the tide of the age which we can now see was revolutionary – the growth of the middle classes and of the newspaper press with them; their call for wider and truer representation in government. But much of the Irish middle class was Catholic. The aim of well-to-do Catholics now was to prove their loyalty. When, in 1760, a French commander, Thurot, had raided Belfast Lough and briefly captured Carrickfergus, local Catholics had given no sign of sympathy; and when war had broken out with Spain, their bishops had ordered Irish papists to pray for a British victory. The Catholic middle class sought peaceful redress of its grievances, and its spokesmen minimised the claims of the Pope and protested (too much?) their fidelity to the Hanoverian Succession. Their restraint, together with some abatement of Protestant intolerance, meant that religious issues had withdrawn from the forefront of Irish thinking and it was possible for Flood and his allies to focus attention on political questions. However, the Catholic masses were still 'fanatical', still poor, and still dangerous. Protestant politicians could, and did, debate issue after issue without acknowledging the existence of their papist labour force at all. Yet ultimately, the orators knew that the very survival of their class depended on the link with Britain. Flood brought dignity to the 'Patriot' cause with his declamation. He had studied with care and effect the orators of ancient Greece and Rome. He was experienced in the amateur theatre. He produced fine political histrionics. But he and his fellow 'Patriots' would in the end flinch from the realisation of their rhetoric.

In a sense, Edmund Burke was more 'revolutionary'. The most distinguished Irishman of his day, Burke was emotional to the point of imbalance, 'foaming like Niagra' in the Commons, a prophet of the Romantic era, perhaps the most sincere politician at Westminster, certainly one of the most violent in his language, 'the most eloquent madman I ever knew', according to the great historian, Gibbon.[57] It is amusing that such a man should be hailed as the founder of modern conservativism. But Ireland, of course, is irony's chosen country.

Burke was the son of a Dublin lawyer. His mother was a Roman Catholic. His sisters were brought up as Catholics. He spent some five years of his childhood with Catholic relatives in County Cork. In his student days at Trinity College, Dublin he was a patriotic enthusiast for Irish art, Irish literature, Irish manufactures, much moved by Irish poverty and its injustice. He himself married a Catholic, and throughout his political life his opponents smeared him as crypto-papist. Yet he became a devoted British imperialist. He went to England aged 21, in 1750, and made his career in that country as writer and politician. By his early thirties, he was beginning to think of himself as English. He entered the Commons in 1765, and 'The fact that he, an obscure middle class Irishman, could sit in the British parliament never failed to impress him or to fill him with a truly reverential awe and appreciation for the imperial system which made such a thing possible.'[58]

With the whig front now in splinters, Burke hitched his career to the faction grouped round the second Marquis of Rockingham, which found it useful to have an orator who could whip himself into strong and noble-sounding feeling even over a case, such as the tax on absentee owners of Irish lands which was proposed in 1773, where his leader's personal interests were sordidly involved. Rockingham, who made Burke his private secretary, was a pre-eminent specimen of the whig aristocracy, pushed into political life neither by fervour nor by aptitude but by 'a sense of what he owed to his position ... '[59] His faction, like Pitt's small following, found themselves in a queasy position as cries rose from the City of London and elsewhere for annual parliaments, for equal representation, for legislation against corruption. They abhorred what Burke called 'vulgar opinion'. Yet anyone who declaimed against their successful rivals, the 'King's Friends', might for a moment seem a useful ally. The British 'outs' shamelessly made capital out of anything which could trouble George III and the men he favoured with office, and their lurid accusations deeply alarmed far-away colonials.

In the 1760s, the vaunted British Parliament found its character and its actions questioned, its credibility, even at home, tottering. King and Parliament hastened ideological crisis forward by the mistake of persecuting John Wilkes, a man with exactly the knacks required to spotlight the unrepresentative nature of British government.

This squinting satyr, hardly sincere, but a publicist of genius, was the son of a well-to-do Dissenting distiller. He bought the Commons seat of Aylesbury, in 1757, for some £7,000, but lost his hopes of office under the Crown when Pitt left the government four years later. He became co-editor, with the poet Charles Churchill, of an anti-Bute journal, the *North Briton*. The cheap jibe against the Scots made by its title was characteristic of its tone. In April 1763, its 45th and last number appeared, with a hard, sly attack on the King's Speech to Parliament regarding the peace with France. It insinuated that George III was a liar.

The government retorted by using a procedure developed in the despotic days of Charles II. Massachusetts patriots, fresh from the struggle against 'Writs of Assistance', were interested and dismayed to learn that a 'general warrant' had been issued in London for the arrest of the author, printers and publishers of the *North Briton*. The charge was 'seditious libel'. Wilkes was sent to the Tower. Opposition leaders flocked to visit him there. His patron, Earl Temple, moved for a writ of habeas corpus in the Court of Common Pleas, where Lord Chief Justice Pratt discharged him on the specialised grounds that as an M.P. his person was 'sacred'. Wilkes played to the gallery, with his speech in court. 'My Lords, the liberty of all peers and gentlemen, and, what touches me more sensibly, that of all the middling and inferior set of people, who stand most in need of protection, is in my case this day to be finally decided upon a question of such importance as to determine at once whether English Liberty shall be a reality or a shadow.' As thousands of supporters escorted him home, the slogan 'Wilkes and Liberty' was born.[60]

'General warrants' were soon found to be illegal. But the beaten government struck back. In November 1763 the House of Commons carried, by 273 votes to 111, a motion that No. 45 of the *North Briton* was likely to excite people to treachery. Liable to fresh prosecution, Wilkes slipped across to the Continent and exile, and the House expelled him in his absence. The Commons' rejection of a popular hero seemed to confirm that they had been corrupted into servility.

Wilkes's bravado captivated a very mixed support—among the 20,000 or so 'liverymen' and 'freemen' who dominated the politics of the City of London, among the swelling middle class of professionals, merchants and prosperous craftsmen who lived in the spreading suburbs; and also among the capital's masses of journeymen, apprentices and 'servants', skilled or semi-skilled, drunken or sober—watchmakers, tailors and hatters, Spitalfields silk weavers, Bermondsey tanners, Shadwell coal heavers. Working hours were long—from six in the morning till six or nine at night. Labourers got 9s. or 12s. a week, journeymen in the worse paid trades between 12s. and 15s. Even in good times, a man might spend quarter of his income on bread, of which the average Londoner then consumed over 1 lb. a day. The period from 1756 to 1773 was one of high bread prices, which provoked riots all over Britain.[61] These were commonly well-disciplined, purposefully directed towards achieving fair prices. But 'mobs' could also be whipped out by gentry, politicians or city leaders, for purposes only indirectly of interest to the poor, or utterly useless to them.

When he returned from exile, Wilkes would show that, although he was no orator, had no political programme, had no original ideas, and had perhaps no principles stronger than self-esteem and a delight in mischief, he could rally besides Londoners, worried country gentry, angry cider producers, rural freeholders threatened by enclosures, merchants in the provincial ports, all manner of 'outs'. Such a vast, diverse constituency could not have been united by any slogan less vague than 'liberty'. Another great binding force was xenophobia. The English reacted to their domestic problems by pouring contempt on alien scapegoats. In 1736, London had seen riots against Irish labourers. Some years later, Jews had been the target. Now the Scots were the great bugbear. Wilkes used the Scots.

A Scot was identified, presumably, by his accent. There were various Scottish accents; their differences seem to have gone unmarked. Gallovidians and Aberdonians, Gaels and Sassenachs, were all identified as Jacobites at heart. In fact, thanks to English prejudice, some Lowland and whig Scots did forget their hatred of Gaels and Stuarts and acquired fellow feeling for bare-legged Jacobite clansmen. Young James Boswell went to Covent Garden to hear a new opera one night late in 1762 when Bute was Prime Minister and his unpopular peace was being made. Just before the overture, two Highland officers came in: 'The mob in the upper gallery roared out, "No Scots! No Scots! Out with them!", hissed and pelted them with apples. My heart warmed to my countrymen, my Scotch blood boiled with indignation ... I hated the English; I wished from my soul that the Union was broke and that we might give them another battle of Bannockburn.' Here, Boswell observed, was their famous 'English liberty' – 'the liberty of bullying and being abusive with their blackguard tongues.'[62]

Whig peers were as prejudiced as the 'vulgar'. Lord Shelburne thought that most Scots 'had no regard to truth whatever'. Lord Holland claimed that the Scots inflamed resentment by their own 'excessive' national feeling. Wilkes and Churchill in the *North Briton* crystallised a myth that was to exercise great influence on events over fifteen or twenty years. In the wake of their leader Bute, it was alleged, Scotchmen had swarmed down from their barren home-land, where 'half starved spiders prey'd on half-starved flies', to rob the English of their fruits of their toil, of their trade, of their fat harvests.

> Into our places, states, and beds they creep;
> They've sense to get what we want sense to keep.

The use of Scots soldiers against Wilkesite rioters would produce gleeful furies of indignation. The myth was confirmed! Although Bute (whose family name was, horrifically, Stewart) had ostensibly resigned from office, he was held to be still behind the throne, exercising what Pitt called 'the secret influence of an invisible power'.[63]

If noble English statesmen believed such nonsense, American colonists can perhaps be excused for their devout faith in the myth. They could see ravenous Scots flocking into their own country. Pitt's army had eventually included a dozen or more 'hardy' Highland regiments. Scots traders following in its wake came to dominate the trade of the conquered area round the Great Lakes. Else-where, Virginians nurtured fear, not baseless, that this clannish brood would take over their whole colony. 'A North Briton', William Lee wrote, 'is some-thing like the stinking and troublesome weed we call in Virginia wild onion. Whenever one is permitted to fix the number soon increases so fast, that it is extremely difficult to eradicate them, and they can poison the ground so, that no wholesome plant can thrive.' The 'Jacobitical', 'lying' Scots seemed to Americans natural proponents of feudal chains, ingrained enemies of all 'liberty'. (Further, as John Adams would soon imply, the Westminster Parliament, which now included Scots, had no obvious right to govern colonists whose orbears had left England before the 1707 Treaty of Union.)[64]

So Wilkes was a hero for Americans, who hearkened also to the paranoid rhetoric of the ailing, ageing Pitt, and to the Rockingham faction's talk of the sinister corps of 'placemen' whom they called 'the King's Friends'. So far from being malignant conspirators, these unattractive persons, it has been argued, were in effect a civil service in embryo, men whose interest in efficient adminis-tration made them ready to identify with the State, which for practical purposes still meant the Crown, rather than with some gang of whig aristocrats.[65] But the votes in the Commons given by these budding *apparatchiks* (if such they were) maintained policies towards America which failed as comprehensively as might be. If George III and his ministers were not wicked men, they were, in truth, extremely silly.

VI

In theory, the entire British Empire was ruled by a single, absolute sovereign power. Through the struggles of the seventeenth century, Parliament, seen as the aggregate body of King, Lords and Commons, had taken over the arbitrary authority previously claimed by the Crown alone. In the view of all good English 'whigs' Parliament was absolute.

There were virtually no self-proclaimed 'tories' in America. The word was a term of abuse. The people who called themselves 'whigs' there actually corresponded to the 'radicals' now emerging in small numbers in Britain. And parliamentary power had, over generations, flicked them little. The function of the Acts of Trade had been, not to raise a revenue, but to direct commerce. During the late war, Newcastle had resisted strong calls from British officials and military in America that Parliament should tax the colonies.

Many colonists suggested that a federation of self-governing polities each owing allegiance to the British King might be a good solution for the anomalous situation. But the concepts of the 'dominion' and the 'commonwealth' would not be practicable until the Crown was completely removed from politics. George III was still the 'mainspring of the executive', not only in England, but in Ireland, where on occasion he made decisions on petty details of administration. By his own logic, his role in America could not be different from his position in Ireland.[66]

From Bute's resignation till mid-1765, George's chosen Prime Minister was George Grenville — aristocratic and unimaginative. He was by prevailing standards hard-working, but the Wilkes affair took up a lot of his time. In any case, his options regarding America were narrow, and a bolder, more independent mind might have hit upon similar measures. Prominent colleagues favoured stronger control of the Empire, but no new credo, no drastic shift in ideas was involved in their attitudes. The government's thinking was in the mercantilist tradition. It had to act, in the early 1760s, because of the pressure of the times.

The Empire was now too large, its problems too diverse and pressing, for Newcastle's style of 'salutory neglect' to be feasible. Its lands, and the interests involved in them, must be defended. But the costs of defence were rising almost intolerably. The British landed classes bewailed their burden of taxes, and loathed as always the very idea of a standing army in peacetime. All considerations pointed one way. An army stationed largely in North America, and paid for by the colonists there, could not only protect the mainland provinces, but could 'stand', well away from Britain itself, at the ready for future wars. The wish to increase central control of what one future proconsul, George Macartney, called in 1773 'this vast empire on which the sun never sets, and whose bounds nature has not yet ascertained', matched all too neatly the growing desire that colonists should pay for the soldiers who guarded them.[67] This could have been called a 'plot' against American 'liberty', if the ministers concerned had been capable of understanding what that word meant to the colonists themselves.

One alternative to the line now taken would have been to eschew colonies altogether. A few thinkers in Britain were ready to argue this way. Military costs could be saved. Bounties on colonial produce need not be paid. 'Little Englandism', compounding idealism and meanness, was starting upon its long history. But its prophets were still scant. To most people it still seemed self-evident that the colonies must be kept, and defended.

The need for extra defences was made plainer by the so-called 'Pontiac Rising' which began in May 1763 and bloodied the frontiers of the Middle Colonies for nearly a year, killing over 2,000 settlers. The destruction of French power had weakened the position of every Indian tribe. No longer could one white nation be played off against the other. Besides the establishment of new British military posts, and the cheating, bullying ways of British traders, the Indians had been confronted with rumours of projected white colonies. Amherst, the commander-in-chief, loathed red men, and toyed with the notion of genocide, even of spreading smallpox among disaffected tribes. He withheld from allies even the customary presents of shot and gunpowder. The revolt began when Indian bands seized outlying British posts south of the Great Lakes. By June it threatened Virginia, Maryland and Pennsylvania. As in the case of a Cherokee rising further south, which had been put down in 1761, British regulars proved essential. The provincial legislatures were as reluctant as ever to help. Virginia refused to vote troops for any offensive war. New York, asked for 1,400 troops, provided only 300. Even the frontiersmen themselves failed to join in the British campaign. Yet they were brave enough, it seemed, against harmless, friendly red men. In December 1763 a group of fifty-seven men from Donegal and Paxton townships in frontier Pennsylvania cold-bloodedly massacred a score of Christian Indians, then, when the Assembly ordered their arrest, marched east with hundreds of others vociferating their grievances and slaughtering more converts as they proceeded. Benjamin Franklin, whose persuasions stopped these 'Paxton Boys' short just before they entered Philadelphia, called them 'Christian white savages'. But frontiersmen were not keen to fight red 'savages' – they held out for bounties on Indian scalps, and would serve only as packhorse and wagon drivers.[68]

Meanwhile, plans for the government of the conquered territories were being completed. Colonists would see some ominous precedents. The new province of West Florida, for instance, would be plagued by feuds between governor and legislature, while a quarter of laws passed there would be disallowed by the Crown.[69] In Quebec, Governor Murray did not hide his prejudice against 'old subjects' who came in from the British mainland colonies. Papist Canadians were allowed to serve on juries. Murray refused to call an assembly.

The largest problem was that of the western wilderness. The lands between the seaboard colonies and the Mississippi were roamed, or cultivated in pockets, by perhaps 70,000 red men, of whom about 20,000 – Shawnee and Delaware, Wyandot and Miami, Potawatomi, Kickapoo and Cherokee – had claims on the huge area later known as the 'Old North-West' where there were about three red people to thirty-six square miles. Between Louisiana and Canada there were only about 2,000 European people in widely scattered settlements, with a few hundred traders in season around the forts and posts.[70]

Old colonies, under their charters, made competing claims to enormous territories. The colonial love of speculation in land rose to the level of mania after Bute's peace, and British army officers joined in the scramble. A barrage of schemes fell on Whitehall, and ministers there were themselves infected. By 1773, even Mansfield, the Lord Chief Justice, a staid, shrewd Scot, would be buying tracts in the 'Illinois Country'.[71] And British manufacturers must welcome the prospect of fresh captive settler markets in the areas later designated Tennessee, Kentucky, Ohio, Indiana, Michigan, Wisconsin and Illinois. But what about the valuable fur trade, ultimately controlled by great merchants in London? This thriving commerce was already in being, whereas new colonies would involve massive outlay by the British treasury, and a succession of costly wars with the Indians. Besides which, some influential people argued that colonies far inland would be out of reach not only of British jurisdiction, but also of British trade. With carriage costs so high, might they not set up their own manufactures?

In its perplexity, the government settled for what seemed the cheapest short-term recourses. Its officials on the spot were already checking westward advance of settlement as well as they could, and were trying to control trade with the Indians. 'Justice' for the red men could be advanced as a reason, *ad hoc* and *pro tem.*, for extending this policy. British interests currently required that movement of settlers out of the old colonies should flow into Nova Scotia, Quebec and the Floridas, where there was plenty of land to be taken up, papist inhabitants must be outnumbered, and strength would be needed if war began again. The drive over the Appalachians must be slowed to a pace at which it might be possible to sustain peace with the Indians, with firm agreement arrived at over the transfer of each parcel of land.

Hence the 'Proclamation' of 1763. No purchases of land beyond the Appalachian watershed would be authorised for the time being. The west was to be ruled by the commander-in-chief of the British army. The wartime improvisation under which Sir William Johnson in the north and John Stuart in the south had acted as 'superintendents' of relations with the Indians was confirmed; the aim was to enforce licensing of all British traders and make them deal only at recognised centres.

The 'Proclamation' was both ineffectual and resented. Free lands were offered to British soldiers disbanding in North America, and while more than a dozen regiments of colonial and Highland troops were accommodated in Nova Scotia, others were actually moved by the government into the vast new Indian 'reservation'. Yet Virginian speculators in 'Ohio' and 'Loyal' companies met frustration by government veto; not an acre of land was now legally theirs, despite grants approved almost a generation before. Yet the progress of settlement was not really impeded. Anyone willing to risk Indian anger could go ahead. Speculation went on undeterred. George Washington, baulked as a member of the Ohio Company, nevertheless obtained 24,000 acres in Ohio under the promise made to ex-soldiers.

New Hampshire and the area known as Vermont were opened up by squatters and land jobbers, amongst whom Ethan Allen and his three brothers took the lead. Elsewhere, 'long hunters' and traders who found tracks across the 'Proclamation Line', broke down Indian resistance in advance of the frontier. The southern superintendent, John Stuart, strove honourably for justice for the Indians. He oversaw deals which transferred, with the natives' consent, huge areas to the colonies, yet governors and legislatures repudiated or sabotaged his further dealings, and Georgia, for instance, contrived to cheat the Creeks and Cherokees of more than two million acres of land.[72]

Stuart's northern counterpart was Sir William Johnson, Irish born, who held a great tract in the Mohawk Valley, and lived in high feudal style there in a stockaded mansion, Johnson Hall, with a large retinue which included a dwarf as jester. He openly cohabited with the sister of a christianised Mohawk chief, often wore Iroquois dress, and entertained Indians in his house. His deputy, George Croghan, was another notable man. A semi-literate letter which he sent to his chief from London, where, in 1764, he was representing the interests of certain fur traders, makes him appear a noble enough savage: ' ... I blive itt is hard to Say wh party is ye honistist was I to Spake My Mind I wold Say they are all R-g-e-s- aLicke I am Nott Sorry I Came hear as it will Larn Me to be Contented on a Litle farm in amerrica if I Can gett one when I go back ... '[73] But 'Colonel' Croghan in fact lived in frontier luxury, and played his part in great speculations.

Johnson never had patience with the 'Proclamation Line'. He controlled the Six Nations of Iroquois and through them, it was reckoned, the Shawnee and Delaware. Departing from his instructions, he used his power to negotiate a new settlement line, running down the Ohio River to the mouth of the Tennessee, and this was formalised, with Whitehall approval, at the Treaty of Fort Stanwix in 1768, whereby the Iroquois ceded a territory thence known as 'Indiana'. Stuart was then prodded into adjusting the southern 'line' accordingly. The sole inspiration of this change of policy was the pressure from speculators,

who sensibly enlisted prominent collaborators in Britain. Ministers, civil ser-
vants, M.P.s, peers, bankers and merchants joined them in the so-called 'Walpole
Association' of 1769, which also included Benjamin Franklin, now resident in
London again, and extremely active in speculative schemes.

While the 'Proclamation' did not prevent many millions of acres passing into
private hands, regulation of trade with the Indians merely annoyed the traders
without achieving its object, and in 1768 its management was returned to the
colonial governments. Nor, although that had been a prime aim, did the 'Proclamation' policy seem to save money.

The government now found itself maintaining some twenty-nine remote,
exposed and expensive military posts, sixteen of which were directly guarding
the frontiers of the old mainland colonies.[74] The value of these was doubtful. If
the Indians rose, such forts might provide refuge for settlers, and the regulars
there would beat the red men at last, but they could not 'protect' lives directly.
The Indians were adept at surprise attack. So what was the point of spreading
such a large proportion of the 8,000 British troops now in America out over
difficult country in puny parcels?

'Dishonist' politicians, as Croghan thought them, must surely have ulterior
motives? Edmund Burke would sum up one colonial suspicion; in 1763, so he
later alleged, 'the necessity was established of keeping up no less than twenty
new regiments, with twenty colonels capable of seats in this house.' Added to
the new offices now created in Quebec and the Floridas, it seemed that this
access of patronage pushed America some way down the road where Ireland
trudged ahead – that the colonies were to be loaded with lucrative sinecures for
absentees. But the troops were real enough, and some believed that, as one
Connecticut man wrote, they were not there to defend the colonists 'but rather
designd as a rod and Check over us'.[75]

And Grenville was clear that the colonists must pay for them. Taking over
the treasury, he had found an estimate for defence in mainland North America
pitched at £200,000 a year. The British were about to 'groan' under the hated
Cider Tax. Surely their luckier fellow subjects could not fairly object to paying
a little?

So two lines were energetically followed. One was administrative. The
existing Acts of Trade were to be strictly enforced, as wartime regulations had
been. The second line required fresh legislation. For the first time, an Act of
Trade was to be introduced with the avowed object of 'applying the produce
of such duties ... towards defraying the expenses of defending, protecting, and
securing the said colonies and plantations.'[76] This was the so-called 'Sugar Act'
of 1764. Its provisions in fact covered wine and various other goods beside
sugar. But the most important trade affected was that in molasses. While the
duty on foreign refined sugar stayed prohibitive, and the entry of foreign rum
was simply forbidden, the duty on foreign molasses imported into North
America was lowered from 6d. to 3d. per gallon. This in itself might seem

generous; but there were also administrative provisions for the enforcement of this Act and earlier ones, and a hint of a new, single Vice-Admiralty Court, to cover the whole of America but to be sited at Halifax, Nova Scotia.

The aim was to please as well as to chasten. The North American distillers were given a complete monopoly on their home patch; Grenville gave new bounties for production of hemp and flax; South Carolina was licensed to ship its rice to any part of Latin America; and so on. But Virginians 'groaned' in time-honoured plantation style because the duty on their favourite tipple, Madeira wine, had now been raised. More importantly, the rum men proclaimed that they would be ruined because, though the duty on molasses was halved, the intention was clearly now to collect every 3*d*. In fact, rum sold at 16*s*. a gallon in Maryland taverns at this time, and so the profits could bear a little trimming, while in practice most of the duty could have been passed on to French sugar planters, who could hardly dispose of their molasses save to North American skippers.[77] But the new administrative provisions were genuinely vexatious. A squadron of warships arrived in American waters. Coastal traffic between the colonies was seriously impeded by zealous naval officers questing for prizes. Merchants required clearance papers merely to cross open sea more than seven miles from the shore in passing between two ports within the same colony. Halifax had been chosen for the new Vice-Admiralty Court partly to boost the Nova Scotian economy with the prizes which would be condemned there, partly because it was remote from the mobs and local pressures which swayed juries in more southerly ports. To trek there from Charles Town or even from Boston was an immense inconvenience to shipowners.

Another Westminster statute of the same year aggravated colonial merchants further. The issue of paper money, illegal in New England since 1751, was now outlawed in other colonies also. Men in the seaboard towns were so angry with Grenville that stirrings of a boycott began, with a movement to encourage colonial manufactures. In Maryland thread stockings were produced with AMERICA worked into the pattern. Everything which this government did from now on would be suspect. An Act of 1765 which imposed on colonists, as under English common law, certain obligations to provide troops with accommodation and supplies, ran into furious opposition in New York, where the legislature refused for two years to acknowledge it until extreme pressure was applied by Parliament. Meanwhile, Virginian Anglican vestrymen, who were accustomed to pick their own clergy, were almost as worried as Yankee Congregationalists by continuing rumours that a bishop was to be sent to the colonies. It could be said that 'the sight of lawn sleeves in this country would be more terrible to us than 10,000 Mohawks.'[78] (The British government, in fact, had no interest at all in appointing a bishop – there was no revenue to be gained from that.)

Uncomprehendingly, Grenville went ahead with a new Bill far more obnoxious than the 'Sugar Act'. It commonly took two or three months for a letter to cross the Atlantic. The effects of one decision might not be known before another had to be taken. The Stamp Act was fathered by irreproachable logic out of arrogant ignorance. Geography favoured rupture so strongly that even Benjamin Franklin had lost touch.

VII

Grenville decided that, for the first time, Parliament should directly tax the colonies. He did not act in completely cavalier fashion. He took the trouble to persuade the colonies' London agents of the rightness of his logic and they accepted it, though seven colonial assemblies, hearing of his proposals, petitioned against them, and though such a respected official as Chief Justice Thomas Hutchinson showed his disapproval plainly, pointing out that the Scots in 1707 had received a guarantee that taxes imposed on them would not exceed a certain proportion of Britain's total, but the Americans had no such assurance.

Hutchinson saw no real distinction between 'external' taxation, as in the Sugar Act, and 'internal' taxation such as Grenville now proposed. To others, including the British ministers, the novelty of the Stamp Act seemed clear. Yet when it was voted through in March 1765 by a bored House of Commons, only 50 M.P.s opposed it. Americans were going to have to pay certain duties already imposed in Britain, though the colonial rates would be generally lighter. The Act taxed many sorts of bits and pieces of paper — among them legal documents, pamphlets and newspapers. It meant that a colonist could not acquire land, send a ship out of port, buy playing cards, or sell liquor without purchasing stamped paper. Though British merchants would probably pay out £1 for every £3 disbursed by colonists, the revenue of about £60,000 a year which the measure was expected to yield would be employed solely in America.[79]

Benjamin Franklin, now back in London again as agent for Pennsylvania, sent home a letter full of folksy wisdom urging his fellow countrymen to accept the Act philosophically. 'Idleness and pride tax with a heavier hand than kings and parliaments; if we can get rid of the former, we may easily bear the latter.' He nominated one friend as distributor of stamped paper in Pennsylvania, and advised another to take the post in Connecticut. Meanwhile, Richard Henry Lee, for all his 'patriotic' proclivities, sought unsuccessfully for the Virginian post.[80] He was lucky not to get it.

The sudden explosion of feeling in almost all the mainland seaboard colonies expressed every pent-up fear and resentment of the last five years. Even the Act's moderation intensified suspicion. The smaller the taxes, the worse, argued John Dickinson; they would the more readily be accepted by gullible colonists, and precedents would be set. Perhaps, some wondered, the aim was to force the colonies into rebellion and then reduce them to servitude? John Adams spied still more subtle wiles at work; he detected a British design to impose canon and feudal law on America, and saw the Stamp Tax, loaded on the press and the colleges, as a device to reduce that high level of literacy and education which characterised the colonies. 'A native of America who cannot read and write is as rare an appearance as a Jacobite or a Roman Catholic, that is, as rare as a comet or an earthquake.' Taxes on knowledge would help to make the people fitter for a papistical sort of servitude.[81]

The Act bore directly on every leading group. Merchants and gamblers, planters and land speculators, the lawyers and printers who led public opinion, all would be constantly paying out for stamped paper. But money was not the real issue. The Stamp Act was seen as the start of a long process by which the British Parliament, now corrupted by evil men, would shift more and more of the burden of empire from Britain to colonists unrepresented in Parliament, and use illegal taxation in America to pay for judges, admiralty courts, customs collectors, army officers, who between them would destroy liberty. It all seemed clear. The Stamp Act made everything plain. In this revolution of consciousness, all restrictions came to seem irksome and ominous. Very few colonists had been remotely bothered by the various ineffectual Acts prohibiting colonial manufactures. But now a Bostonian could be heard complaining, 'A colonist cannot make a button, horse-shoe, nor a hob-nail, but some sooty ironmonger or respectable button-maker of Britain shall bawl and squal that his honors worship is most egregiously maltreated, injured, cheated and robb'd by the rascally American republicans.'[82] Opinion swept one way through all the colonies. The somewhat ignoble 'groans' of Virginian debtors and New England smugglers over recent laws were magically dignified by a touch from the threatened goddess, Liberty.

The celestial consort of Liberty was Rhetoric. One patriot urged Rhode Islanders to awaken 'all that is Roman in Providence'.[83] (No one heard the shade of Roger Williams keening.) Now Patrick Henry's oratory helped tighten the novel unity of American leaders.

Henry had learnt much from the revivalist preaching of the 'Great Awakening'. His slouching, indolent frame would be transformed as his message seemed to grip him — 'he had the actor's trick, in his oratory, of lifting his whole body up towards climaxes, along with his voice, as if he *could* add cubits by wanting to.' His role in the so-called 'Parson's Cause' had given him a following in the back-country where he lived. Ambitious for power in Virginia, he rejected the usual method of fawning upon the successful and chose instead to put himself at the head of popular feeling over the Stamp Act, allied with the disappointed Richard Henry Lee. In May 1765, when only a third of the members of the Virginia House of Burgesses were present, Henry proposed a string of resolutions denouncing the British government. To Thomas Jefferson, still a law student, who stood at the door of the House's lobby to hear the debate, Henry seemed 'to speak as Homer wrote'. Five resolutions were passed by narrow majorities (for example, 22 to 17, 20 to 19). Two days later, the Burgesses withdrew their support for the fifth one and refused to accept two additional motions, one of which argued that colonists need obey no British laws, 'designed to impose any Taxation upon them'. A thin House, bombast rejected – nothing of moment had happened. And yet it had. Because the conservative editor of the *Virginia Gazette* refused to print even the four milder resolutions which had been passed, no correct report was published. Newspapers in other colonies, however, printed every resolution as if the House of Burgesses had accepted them all. Lower Houses in eight other provinces followed Virginia's apparent 'lead', sometimes using the same language. Governor Bernard of Massachusetts, who had been optimistic that 'murmurs' over the Stamp Act would die away, regarded the publication of Henry's resolutions as an 'Alarm Bell'.[84]

Who heard it? Even before the news from Virginia, the Massachusetts House of Representatives had proposed a congress to represent the elected assemblies of the continental colonies. There were sixteen of these, and also nearly that number in the islands – Bermuda, the Bahamas and the Antilles. Out of some thirty separate colonies in the new World, only eight were represented when the 'Stamp Act Congress' assembled at New York in October 1765.

Jamaica, of all colonies, had led the way in the assertion of provincial rights. For the last dozen years, its politics had been far more dramatic and bitter than those of any other colony, Massachusetts not excepted. Admiral Knowles, a quarrelsome sailor of humble origins, who became governor in 1752, had found that Charles Price's 'Jamaica Association' was in effect usurping the position of the Council. Against Price's planters stood the Kingston merchants, with whom Knowles duly allied himself. Battle was joined over his proposal to switch the island's capital from Spanish Town to Kingston. In 1755, a new election gave Knowles control of the Assembly, but after he imprisoned Price and fifteen more of the latter's party, the colony became ungovernable. Knowles was recalled. The Act for removing the seat of government was disallowed in Whitehall, but the House of Commons upheld Knowles, asserting its supremacy over the Jamaica Assembly and all uppity bodies like that. It huffed and puffed to no avail. When William Lyttelton arrived in Jamaica late in 1761, the Price faction was still triumphant.

Lyttelton had been most successful as governor of South Carolina. He found Jamaica a far tougher habitat. Grenville's stricter line with the colonies prompted furious resistance here. After the Board of Trade had disallowed one of its Acts, which tampered with the Acts of Trade, the Jamaica Assembly passed a resolution that they would not bow to 'their Lordships' at home, nor would 'ever at any time suffer them in any Respect to direct or influence their Proceedings by any Proposition or Decision whatever.' Otis or Henry could not have gone further. The home government wisely refrained from comment, but in 1764 Lyttelton could not duck a conflict with the Assembly over the issue of 'parliamentary' privilege. One of the members had a coach and horses seized for debt. John Wilkes had been heard of. The House ordered the plaintiff into gaol, along with the officer who had made the seizure. Then its members decided, in face of royal disapproval, that their privileges did not flow from the grace of the King, but were rights inherent in all assemblies. Lyttelton dissolved no fewer than three assemblies in less than a year. But this meant he could not get money voted, and could only pay his soldiers by drawing, with Whitehall consent, on extra-ordinary funds. Charles Price and his gang were too many for him, and he shortly retreated from his post. The home government now conceded that an assemblyman's goods and chattels, like his person, were free from arrest. Joyful illuminations and decorations signalled the climb down when word of it reached the island. But there was another ruling that the Assembly must refund to the British government the extraordinary money drawn by Lyttelton. This the heroic planters refused to do. They won complete victory. The matter was dropped.[85]

There was no organised protest on Jamaica against the Stamp Tax, because there was no assembly sitting. But there were riots against the Act in the Lee-wards, where feeling ran so high that the Distributor of Stamps declared, 'I dare not go to St. Kitts ... as I have been advised by my Friends there that I shall certainly be assassinated if I attempt it.'[86] Why did the blusterous Caribbean planters henceforward play almost no part in the colonial struggle against Westminster?

The power of Price, as we have seen, depended on political connections in Britain such as even a Hutchinson never enjoyed. The West Indians were still, in sentiment, wholly 'British'. Success would carry them back to a plump estate in the home island. Meanwhile, their need for Britain was overwhelming. Economically, they depended on the captive British consumers. In a free market, St Domingue competition would crush them. Local manufactures, besides, were far more exiguous than on the mainland. These were islands – the British navy could swiftly make them starve. And they needed the wilting garrisons of the British army. Jamaica in 1760 had seen its most dangerous insurrection yet. 'Tacky', with a hundred slave followers, massacred settlers in St Mary's Parish, and inspired revolt in several other places. About sixty whites (besides hundreds of blacks) were killed. 1766 saw smaller, but still bloody, risings. The postures and declamations of Price and his gang were flimsier even than those of Flood's Irish 'patriots'.[87]

Nova Scotia is a more puzzling instance. Nearly two-thirds of its settlers had originally come from New England, and might have been expected to sym-pathise heartily with James Otis and Sam Adams. But pockets of settlement were dispersed. The largest, Halifax, was very directly dependent on Britain. A local newspaper editor ran a campaign for a while against the Stamp Act, but gained little or no active support.

Georgia was a partly similar case, since Parliament still gave it generous grants. It proved to be the only continental colony south of Maine (and bar the Floridas) where stamped paper could for a while be distributed. Elsewhere, active resistance had begun before the paper arrived. Non-payment of debts was effective: as early as August, a Bristol merchant reported that he and his fellows were at their 'Witts End for Want of Money ... '[88] But more violent action began the business of revolution, separating the cautious from the extreme.

Dawn on August 14 in Boston disclosed an effigy of Andrew Oliver, brother-in-law of Thomas Hutchinson, and newly-appointed Stamp Distributor, hanged from a tree in the High Street. Later that day a 'mob' attacked and levelled a new building which was reputed to be the intended Stamp Office, beheaded the effigy outside Oliver's house (like Charles I) and finally burnt it on a bonfire (like Guy Fawkes). Then it returned to Oliver's house and broke in. Warned that his life would be in 'Continual Danger' unless he resigned, Oliver quit his Distributor's post.

On the 26th, 'mobs' were out again. One invaded the home of the register of the Vice-Admiralty Court and burnt all the records. Another wrecked the home of the Comptroller of Customs and drank his wine. With the Acts of Trade thus symbolically eschewed, the two groups combined in a fearsome gesture. As Thomas Hutchinson supped there with his family, his town mansion was attacked. He had opposed the Stamp Act. But he had urged caution upon his fellow colonists. He was rich. The times demanded a scapegoat whose person could be refurnished to represent all the graft of Walpole, the hauteur of George III's ministers, all the threats detected against 'liberty'. The day before, a minister, Jonathan Mayhew, had preached to the text, 'I would they were even cut off which trouble you.' Now Hutchinson's cash, plate and clothes were stolen, his furniture was splintered, his cellar drunk dry, all his books and papers strewn in the mud, his garden ravaged. Only annihilation could bring satisfaction. The inner walls of the house were smashed. Men worked for three hours to bring down a cupola, and tried to destroy even the outer walls.

Other cautious men, in every colony, were appalled to hear of such an attack on property. The time for choice had arrived. One must decide to resist, at great risk, or to keep quiet, or to side with the passions which had found vent. In Boston, not one rioter could be punished, and even leading merchants and 'men of property' rallied to prevent action against the shoemaker, Ebenezer Mackintosh, who had led the attack on Hutchinson's house. Some half-dozen lesser rioters were committed, but a crowd released them from gaol before their trial. The methods of the Boston 'Sons of Liberty' were copied in other colonies, and every Distributor was soon forced to resign, like Oliver, or to flee.

Yet the tone of the 'Stamp Act Congress' which met in October was relatively moderate. Virginia could send no representatives because Governor Fauquier had refused to convene the Burgesses and so had prevented their accepting the invitation. New Hampshire, North Carolina and Georgia also sent no spokesmen. But though South Carolina was clearly a beneficiary of the Acts of Trade, its delegation was amongst the most vocal. John Dickinson of Pennsylvania was the chief penman at work in the production of a declaration of 'rights and grievances'. Agreement was easily reached on the main colonial argument, which could be expressed in a slogan: 'NO TAXATION WITHOUT REPRESENTATION'. None the less, the petition sent to Britain was respectful, admitting the colonies' 'due subordination' to Parliament, though it denied that body's right to tax them, and announcing that Americans still 'gloried' in being subjects of 'the best of Kings'.[89]

November 1, when the Act came into force, was generally observed as a day of mourning. The Boston 'Sons of Liberty' hanged Grenville in effigy. Their counterparts in New York demonstrated violently in their thousands. In Georgia, where the Distributor arrived only in January 1766, he was able to sell some stamped paper, but soon quit his post for 'parts unknown', after which a crowd advanced upon Savannah and the governor sent the paper aboard a British sloop for safety. Elsewhere, no such paper was brought at all. Journals bravely appeared without it. Customs officials soon were perforce authorised to permit cargoes to clear the ports without it. Many colonial courts proceeded without it. Gamblers made do with old packs of cards. People married without stamped licences. Life was not too abnormal, except for British merchants, who did not get paid, and royal officials, who were quite helpless. They could not call out the militia – its members abhorred the Stamp Act. Government had been set aside. 'Sons of Liberty' ruled, and whereas in Virginia one 'mob' was described as 'chiefly' composed of 'gentlemen of property', in Massachusetts the leaders were two distillers, two braziers, a painter, a printer and the master of a vessel.[90]

Grenville had quarrelled with George III and had left office before the effects of his Act were seen. Rockingham had succeeded him. His Ministry had no clear American policy of its own, but at least could abandon Grenville's line without loss of face. The clamour from British merchants made this almost imperative. Orders worth over £700,000 had been countermanded. Debts of £4 million could not be collected.[91] Trading towns big and small were petitioning Parliament for mitigation or repeal of the recent obnoxious legislation.

Americans soon heard that the Stamp Act was dead. They had killed it. And the methods, including the violent ones, which they had used, now seemed amply justified by success. The Massachusetts elections of 1766 purged the legislature of cautious elements. The House of Representatives elected Otis as Speaker, Sam Adams as Clerk, picked a new Council from which supporters of Governor Bernard were excluded, and saw to it that the rioters of the previous year remained immune to prosecution. Disobedience was de facto legitimised.

Elsewhere also new leaders had come to the fore, while established leaders had called the populace into play much in the manner of the sorcerer's apprentice. Thus in New York, the wealthy De Lancey and Livingston factions had competed for the honour of leading the Assembly against British tyranny. James De Lancey had openly hobnobbed with 'Sons of Liberty' (led by such persons as John Lamb, a liquor dealer; Isaac Sears, who had been both sailor and petty merchant; and Alexander MacDougall, son of a milkman, owner of a slop shop) till, shocked by what he heard at their meetings, he withdrew and organised some genteel 'Sons' on his own account. The newspaper press was virtually all in the hands of the 'whigs' and, from the seaports, mobilised rustic opinion by wild exaggerations and baseless assertions – a scare was set up, for instance, that cattle would be taxed. Sam Adams, besides his gifts as a master of subversive pageantry – parades, fireworks, bonfires, songs, celebratory dinners – knew how to use a good smear of 'Popery' so as to terrify Congregationalist farmers.[92] Conservative elements in the colonies had lost the initiative, and would not fully regain it.

Members of Parliament were not accustomed to thinking hard about America. But they sensed that the troubles there somehow related to their own problems with Wilkes and to the foolish behaviour of certain politicians and rustics in Ireland. Methodism and worse were at some dire work. 'Liberty'? For colonial wharfingers? Stands must be taken. Colonials, like Irish helots and London coal-heavers, must be kept in their proper place. Towards what was all this talk about 'representation' leading, when only one Englishman in thirty could vote? As for these 'laws of nature' invoked by fanatical persons, surely their implication was that any man could rise up against any law which did not suit his fancy. Anarchy must be averted. Degree must be acknowledged. If the dignity of Parliament were neglected, why, fat country gentlemen might yet find themselves touching their forelocks to ploughmen and weavers.

With members feeling this way, a reassertion of parliamentary supremacy must be the price of pushing through repeal of the Stamp Act. A 'Declaratory Act' had been passed in 1719 regarding Ireland, though Parliament had not in fact used since then its clearly proclaimed right to tax that country. Pitt was firm that a declaration must be made, but favoured one which would accept the colonists' main principle – that Britain might bind their trade, confine their manufactures, and exercise every power whatsoever, 'except that of taking their money out of their pockets without their consent.'[93] The Rockinghams could not accept this principle. Their Declaratory Bill seemed to meet the views of the obdurate Grenville, Bedford and Bute factions. Whereas the repeal of the Stamp Act was bitterly debated and passed only by quite small majorities, the Declaratory Bill went through the Commons without a division. But it did not explicitly mention the power to tax, and could be misread as excluding it.

This ingenious ministry also revised the laws of trade. The Sugar Act's $3d.$ duty on foreign molasses was replaced with a flat rate of $1d.$ on all molasses. Though the colonists did not object this time, the fact was that the removal of imperial preference made the duty clearly a revenue measure and nothing more; taxation, in fact, without representation. However, the specious Benjamin Franklin, giving evidence to the House of Commons, had spread the wholly erroneous notion that the colonists saw as fundamental the hair-splitting distinction between 'external' and 'internal' taxation. So it was thought that revenue might yet be raised from American trade without protest. The prevailing temper at Westminster combined complacency, apathy, irritation and delusion.

Three months after the Stamp Act was repealed, the fragile Rockingham ministry fell. George III, now wholly weaned from Bute's influence, picked Pitt as his new Prime Minister. The 'great commoner' permitted himself to be translated to the House of Lords as Earl of Chatham, cutting himself off from his Commons base — 'Samson without his hair', the French minister, Choiseul, now called him[94] — and losing much of his popularity. Then nervous disease laid him low. He pleaded to be permitted to quit, but it was two years before George III released him. The Duke of Grafton meanwhile became the true head of a ministry which bungled over the East India Company, created a new crisis over John Wilkes, and behaved absurdly towards America.

The Chancellor of the Exchequer was now Charles Townshend, much admired for his ability to make a brilliant speech in the Commons when drunk. The British people were mutinous over heavy taxation. Bread riots were pandemic. The land tax kept up the price of wheat, and Townshend was defeated when he proposed to maintain it at the war level of 4s. in the £. He had to seek other sources of revenue. It emerged in 1767 that garrisons in North America were costing about £700,000 a year, far more than had been estimated. So Townshend insisted on the withdrawal of costly posts from the American west, where British control now completely collapsed. He also brought in new proposals to tax the colonies.

His 1767 Revenue Act was a sillier measure than the Stamp Act. At most, it could have produced less than one-tenth of the revenue now lost through reduction of the British land tax. Believing that the colonists had no objection to 'external' taxation, Townshend put duties on glass, paints, lead and paper, which they did not import in large quantities, as well as on tea which they swilled with British fervour. The fund thus raised was to be devoted only secondarily to defence — the first call upon it was 'defraying the Charge of the Administration of Justice, and the Support of Civil Government ... '[95] Townshend wanted to make colonial governors and officials financially independent of local assemblies. Recent happenings in Jamaica, as well as in Massachusetts, re-emphasised the advantages of this. But no project was better calculated to inflame North American fears of 'tyranny'. The aim, as colonial whigs could insist, was to make America another Ireland.

When the text of the new Revenue Act became known, John Dickinson began to write a series of 'Letters from a Farmer in Pennsylvania' which were reprinted in newspapers up and down the seaboard and focused opposition in all provinces. Dickinson's firm denial that 'external' taxation was legal made him a popular hero; his image was placed in the waxworks at Boston alongside those of George Whitefield and of the Prodigal Son. The Boston town meeting, chaired by Otis, had swiftly called for a boycott of 'foreign' (that is, British) manufactures, and early next year the Massachusetts House of Representatives addressed to the other colonial assemblies a 'Circular Letter', drafted by Sam Adams, calling for united action. An order came from Whitehall that this must be rescinded. The House refused, and in June 1768 Governor Bernard dissolved it. But Boston was now under the rule of rioters, brought out by the seizure of John Hancock's sloop *Liberty* on a charge of smuggling. The customs commissioners were forced to flee for safety to Castle William on an island in the harbour. The people seemed to Hutchinson to be 'in a state of absolute dementation'.[96]

Feelings did not run so high elsewhere. The movement for 'non-consumption' of British goods was resumed. Home-grown New England balm was alleged to 'far' surpass the 'Teas of India', patriots dressed in homespun clothes, vineyards were planted in Virginia. Colonial manufacturing proved a disappointment to its proponents. 'Non-importation' by merchants did not work so well as it had with the Stamp Act. Though Boston merchants entered a 'non-importation' agreement in March 1768, and New York merchants followed in August, Philadelphians came in only after months of hesitation. But a joint committee of planters, merchants and 'mechanics' in Charles Town was eventually set up to secure that, as with other British goods, no slaves should be brought in during 1770.[97] New York and Philadelphia merchants openly imported Dutch tea in great quantities. As colonists found they could ignore the Acts of Trade with impunity, all imperial authority seemed on the verge of collapse. Boston, the storm centre, was still wholly out of control.

Sam Adams, for one, was now privately thinking in terms of complete freedom from parliamentary authority. His faction called for, and got, a 'convention' of delegates from ninety Massachusetts towns which was in effect an assembly summoned by colonists without due authority. On September 28, the day before it broke up, about a thousand troops arrived in Boston from Halifax. Two more regiments shortly followed, from Ireland. To the home government, this seemed the only way to restore order. To the colonists, it was confirmation that Stuart tyranny had revived. They had heard of the 'massacre' by guardsmen of Wilkesite demonstrators in London in May. The cause of liberty had its martyrs already. One Bostonian around this time gave his two children the names of 'Oliver Cromwell' and 'John Wilkes'.[98]

Wilkes returned to England in January 1768. He had picked a good moment. A bitter winter, coupled with high bread prices, helped trigger a wave of strikes and demonstrations. Sailors struck, and every ship on the Thames was immobilised. A body of 15,000 seamen marched on Parliament with a petition. The Hudson's Bay Company was forced to pay 'the exorbitant wages of 40s per month' for the privilege of getting their ships off.[99]

Wilkes promptly secured election as M.P. for the county of Middlesex, where the broad franchise permitted lower-middling men to assert their predilection for 'Liberty'. A joyful mob then roamed the London streets for two days, smashing the windows of many fine houses, including Bute's. Disturbances went on for several weeks, before Wilkes was tried, fined £1,000 and sentenced to twenty-two months' imprisonment on the old charge of 'seditious libel'. When the doors of the King's Bench prison closed upon him at the end of April, continuous riots ensued for a fortnight. In May, watermen, hatters and coal-heavers struck in London, while sawyers attacked and partly destroyed a mechanical sawmill which threatened their livelihoods and the journeymen silk weavers were fighting a cut in wages with acts of industrial sabotage. Reports of food riots and other unrest came in from the provinces.

The situation was growing nightmarish for the rich. Lord Weymouth, Secretary of State, instructed the Middlesex magistrates to employ troops in cases of civil disorder. On May 10, the day when Parliament opened, 15,000 or 20,000 (even as many as 40,000) demonstrators gathered on St George's Fields in Southwark. After they had refused to disperse, troops fired, killing or wounding a score of people.[100]

To that still conservative old man, Franklin, who was actually present in London, the strike wave, the 'Mobs patrolling the streets at noonday', suggested 'a great black cloud coming on, ready to burst in a general tempest'. The English people, it seemed to him, were 'ungratefully abusing the best constitution and the best king any nation was ever blessed with ... ' But many back in his homeland saw matters quite otherwise. Wilkes's fate seemed to be closely involved with their own. Colonists shuddered and thrilled when Wilkes published the text of Weymouth's letter with his own comments, alleging a deep-laid government plot against liberty. They were appalled to hear that he had again been expelled from the Commons. Three times the defiant Middlesex voters chose Wilkes again; then after the fourth, his opponent Luttrell was declared the victor, although he had been beaten by nearly four votes to one. Amid all this rioters shouted 'Wilkes and No King' outside St James's Palace itself. Though Wilkes himself never considered crossing the ocean in any lesser capacity than that of governor of Canada, many colonists hoped that their hero would flee Bute's tyranny and settle among them. Virginian 'patriots' shipped him forty-five hogsheads of tobacco. Alexander McDougall of New York, gaoled after denouncing his colony's Assembly for providing British troops with supplies, set himself up as an American Wilkes; on the 45th day of the year, forty-five gentlemen went to dine with him in prison 'on Forty-five Pounds of Beef Stakes, cut from a Bullock of Forty-five Months old.' On another occasion, forty-five virgins arrived to sing to him forty-five songs.[101]

In February 1769, a 'Society of the Supporters of the Bill of Rights' was formed in the London Tavern, with M.P.s and other wealthy persons among its members. Its prime object was to buy off Wilkes's creditors, to whom he owed about £30,000, but it was also the first organisation in Britain to use modern methods of agitation. The Society sent paid agents around the land to make speeches. It used the press cleverly. It organised 'public opinion'. The petitions which rushed towards Parliament after the Commons' recognition of Luttrell as M.P. for Middlesex were signed by 55,000 people, more than a quarter of England's total voting population.[102] The Society began to look rather like a modern 'political party'. The Wilkesites called for reform of Parliament and appealed to a wide range of other grievances. They sought for a while to build up a nationwide network of 'corresponding societies'. The Society 'instructed' sympathetic M.P.s on their conduct in Parliament, and invented the 'election pledge' by persuading parliamentary candidates to promise their support, if successful, for a listed number of causes.

The idea of 'party' had not appealed to political thinkers; it had seemed merely another name for faction. But in 1770 Edmund Burke published *Thoughts on the Cause of the Present Discontents* which announced that a 'party' was a good thing if it was a body of men united, not by connections and 'interest', but by attachment to shared principles. This foreshadowed a tendency in English public life by which naked material 'interest' would be well-clothed to hide its shame, now felt. Class reflexes, sordid considerations, would still sway the ruling élite; but from now on it would take more care over its dignity and some politicians would begin to believe the fine words which they recited.

Wilkes himself was hardly an ideologist. Released in April 1770, he turned his attention to consolidating a strong position for himself in the City of London, which had elected him an Alderman while he was in prison. In 1774, he became Lord Mayor and, re-elected for Middlesex, was allowed to take his seat in the Commons. But he did little there. Reform was for him a war-cry, not a commitment. His Society had split in 1770 after the South Carolina Assembly, defying the governor, had made it a grant of £1,500, and Wilkes had quarrelled over the money with his chief helper, Horne Tooke.

Wilkes had mobilised support outside the 'political nation' as men had understood it, rousing unenfranchised craftsmen and journeymen and acting as midwife for interest in reform among the labouring classes. A mass radical movement had come into being; but this, paradoxically, weakened the Westminster opposition. Aristocratic grandees and hangers-on such as Burke were frightened of being too closely identified with this dangerous new sort of thinking 'mob', and in any case disdained the 'democratical' concepts now being voiced. Hence the Rockingham and Chatham groups would be enfeebled by their own caution as drastic events unfolded across the Atlantic. The revision of the Townshend Duties was the last occasion on which politicians and merchants in Britain acted in consort to modify policy in the colonials' favour. Early in 1770, all the duties were abolished except for that on tea, which was retained as a symbol of Parliament's right to tax the colonies.

In Boston hardly a man could be found to vote against Otis, Adams or Hancock in the 1769 elections. The Massachusetts lower house voted 109 to 0 for a motion demanding Governor Bernard's recall, and though he had long been anxious to leave his post, his actual departure was hailed as a 'patriot' victory. Thomas Hutchinson was appointed to succeed him, and his weakness was soon exposed.

After numerous minor clashes between Bostonians and the hated soldiers, a guard sent to the custom house to protect a sentry there was provoked into firing on a hostile crowd. Five people were killed, others wounded. The 'Boston Massacre' of 5 March 1770 gave Sam Adams what he wanted; an American counterpart to St George's Fields. The patriot leaders demanded that the guards stand trial for murder and that all troops be withdrawn from Boston. Hutchinson and the military commander could only submit to the 'faction's' demands.

But the 'Liberal Party' were soon crestfallen. The soldiers involved in the Massacre, given a fair trial, were all at last acquitted of murder. And the London government's concession over the Townshend Duties seemed to have worked. At first, merchants in the three leading American ports resolved to continue 'non-importation', but in July New Yorkers resumed normal trading, Philadelphians soon followed suit, and Boston itself gave way in October. Merchants had for some time been accusing each other of unfair competition (Rhode Island men, for instance, had brought in British goods and sold them to former customers of Boston), and they were irked and worried by signs that control of the 'non-importation' agreement was passing out of their own hands into those of the mob. The 'patriotic' movement fell into apathy and recrimination, just as the Wilkesite turbulence died down in England.

But paranoiac fears persisted, and Chatham, now somewhat recovered, enhanced them by his speeches in the Lords. Was it true that the 'riches of Asia' were subverting the constitution? It was certainly the case that the 1768 election had seen an apparently sinister influx of 'nabobs', buying seats with their spoils, into the Commons, and Massachusetts had been shocked by a rumour that Thomas Hutchinson had received 'a trunk of rich silks, a present from Lord Clive of £500 value' (though in fact he had merely acquired for sale a consignment of ordinary cloth bandannas). Chatham harped on the 'Secret Influence' of Bute, 'dangerous, base, unconstitutional and wicked', which had 'undermined and overturned every administration, however constituted or supported.'[103] The colonists believed him. Sam Adams would not have to wait very long before fresh chance was given him to make trouble.

VIII

What another Townshend had been doing in Ireland gave ample fuel to notions of conspiracy, while pamphlets concerned with the American crisis crossed the Atlantic and were reprinted in Dublin in ceaseless spate. Irish opinion mostly sided with the colonists. Irishmen were prepared to learn from them.

Ireland had seen 'mobs' as well. A rumour, spread in 1759, of parliamentary union with Britain had brought out a 'mob' which invaded the Dublin House of Commons and compelled M.P.s to swear that they would vote against it. In the handsome rotunda of their chamber, where Tuscan pillars supported a great gallery in which nearly 700 people could sit to hear an important debate, landowner members now quaked before the 'public opinion' of the Protestant middling classes, as well as considering angrily and fearfully the dangers they now faced from rural 'mobs'.

In 1759, restrictions upon the import of Irish cattle into England were lifted. Landlords increased the acreage under pasture. Commons were enclosed. Whole villages disappeared. Though graziers paid no tithes for their pasture land, cottiers and small farmers, whether or not they were Anglican, still had to disburse to maintain the 'Church of Ireland'. Half a century of quiet ended. In 1761, the first 'Whiteboys' came out. Wesley, in Ireland soon after, described this beginning. ' ... A few men met by night near Nenagh, in the county of Limerick, and threw down the fences of some commons which had been lately inclosed. Near the same time, others met in the counties of Tipperary, Waterford and Cork. As no one offered to suppress or hinder them, they increased in numbers continually, calling themselves Whiteboys, wearing white cockades and white linen frocks. In February there were five or six parties of them, 200 to 300 men in each, who moved up and down chiefly in the night ... levelled a few fences, dug up some grounds, and hamstrung some cattle, perhaps fifty or sixty in all. One body of them came into Clogheen, of about 500 foot, and 200 horse. They moved as exactly as regular troops, and appeared to be thoroughly disciplined.'[104]

The movement soon spread over Munster and parts of Leinster and Connacht. Whiteboys tried to settle the rate at which tithes should be levied, as well as attacking the livestock and buildings of unpopular landlords and tenants. On occasions, they moved in great force in the light of day, braving garrisons, releasing imprisoned comrades and overawing whole towns. Exports of grain and flour were sometimes obstructed, blackmail was levied from farmers to pay for the legal defence of Whiteboys on trial. There were few murders, but many displays of outlaw justice. 'One of the mildest punishments was to drag a man at midnight from his bed, often in mid-winter, beat him, and leave him bound and naked in a ditch ... '[105] But the followers of 'Captain Right', as the Whiteboys called their fictitious, symbolic leader, were as well disciplined, by their own code, as the city 'mobs' of the day. They eschewed highway robbery and took no action except against oppressors and their agents, or people who co-operated with the enemy. Over large areas, no tithes were paid, and evidence against Whiteboys was impossible to procure.

The Irish Parliament retorted brutally. Whiteboy offences were made capital. The power of magistrates was extended. In many areas, landlords armed their more reliable tenants and formed troops of horse to exact revenge. Edmund Burke was aghast at their 'unfeeling Tyranny'. He wrote that, 'An old acquaintance of mine at the Temple, a man formerly of integrity & good nature, had by living some years in Corke contracted such horrible habits, that I think whilst he talked on these late disturbances, none but hangmen could have had any pleasure in his company.' The landed classes invented a 'popish plot' at the bottom of it all, and in 1766 a popular Tipperary priest named Father Sheehy was hanged and quartered after conviction by Protestant magistrates for allegedly 'inciting to riot and rebellion'. Burke inspired an official enquiry which showed that there were Protestant as well as Catholic Whiteboys, that talk of a popish plot was baseless, and that bad agrarian conditions were the cause of the disturbances. But the landed classes persisted in what Burke called 'unmeaning Senseless Malice'.[106]

A similar movement emerged in Ulster, as 'Hearts of Oak' or 'Oakboys' acted against tithes and tyrannous landlords. An unpopular law enabled landlords to force householders to build and repair roads of little use to people at large but of benefit to the great estates. When this was modified, turbulence abated. But then, in 1770, Lord Donegall, absentee owner of great tracts, demanded heavy fines for renewing the leases on his County Antrim lands, and dispossessed the many who could not pay, then brought in as tenants two or three wealthy Belfast merchants. Rents in some other parts of Ulster were trebled. The 'Hearts of Steel' or 'Steelboys' rose up. 'Betwixt landlord and rectors', one of their proclamations asserted, 'the very marrow is screwed out of our bones ... They have reduced us to such a deplorable state by such grievious oppressions that the poor is turned black in the face, and the skin parched on their back ... ' In this area, the effect of rackrents, high food prices, and of a slump in the linen trade, was to spur on the existing movement of emigration. In four years some 37,000 people quit Ulster for America, and the Hearts of Steel, losing both leaders and followers, were extinct by 1773.[107]

However, from now on agrarian unrest, in 'Whiteboy' and other forms, would be a perennial feature of Irish life. The labourer's condition was commonly deteriorating. In some parts, everyone could still obtain land and, as population soared, subdivision into smaller and smaller plots brought more and more cottiers and their families into dependence on a diet of milk and potatoes. In others, where commercial farming was well developed, a farmer would be reluctant to grant plots except to such men as he required as labourers, so that landlessness was a goad to class hatred and constant unrest.[108]

The landlord, ensconced in the handsome country house which rising rents had enabled him to build, was often, in these days of the 'Ossian' cult, to be found collecting Celtic manuscripts, speculating about ancient ruins, listening to old Irish music, or even studying the Gaelic language. One such enthusiast even compared the Tailteann sports of the Irish aborigines to the Olympic games of Classical Greece.[109] But even a good-hearted, cultivated man would see the resentments of present-day peasants rearing up dangerously around him, while from another direction, his pride was assaulted by the demeanour of the British government. Compound insecurity nurtured political passion.

British policy towards Ireland took a turn closely related to Grenville's decisions over America. With imperial defence so much of a problem, Ireland offered the delectable prospect of raising troops with money voted by the Dublin Parliament, which would nevertheless have no control over their disposition since it was not permitted to pass its own Mutiny Act. The 'Irish' army (which was exclusively Protestant) already stood at 12,000 men. In 1767, Lord Townshend, elder brother of clever Charles, was sent over to get it raised to about 15,200.

The viceroyalty of Ireland was one of the richest offices at the disposal of the British Cabinet. The salary stood at £16,000, later £20,000 a year. This was ample, so long as the fortunate holder did not reside in Dublin but left government there in the hands of the leading 'undertakers'. But the view was now taken in government circles that the viceroy should actually live in Ireland. Townshend, a bluff cheerful soldier, who had served under Wolfe at Quebec, resided in Dublin for over five years, nobly disbursing his salary on the liberal hospitality which was expected of a man in his position, and which of course helped to soften, or anyway fuddle, the native political class.

Townshend was ready to make concessions to local feeling. Despite his public support for a measure introducing habeas corpus, the British government refused to let the Irish Parliament pass it – the rights of freeborn subjects of George III must be curtailed in a land with a violent alien peasantry, or Whiteboys and such like might find them useful. But a new Act swiftly went through, limiting parliaments to eight years. This was perhaps more agreeable, in truth, to absentee landowners residing in England, whose authority over their tenantry gave them great influence over elections, than to native politicians who now had to face more frequent, expensive contests. However, awed by the public, the latter had asked for it, and, whether they liked it or not, they were given it.

Townshend at first tried to make a deal with the leading undertakers – the second Lord Shannon, Speaker Ponsonby and John Hely Hutchinson, an able careerist whose avarice was so inordinate that it was said, 'If you gave him Great Britain and Ireland for a demesne, he would ask for the Isle of Man as a potato garden.'[110] But Whitehall would not accept their terms, and they went into opposition. The British government nevertheless insisted that Townshend must quickly get them more troops from Ireland. The proposal was put to the Dublin Commons in April 1768. They rejected it.

Poynings' Law, so much resented by Irish Protestants, had promoted a regular pantomime of defiance. Bills which the Parliament wanted to pass were sent across to England to be doctored. When they came back, Irish politicians looked them over to see what alterations had been made, and if these were considered excessive or insulting, the Bill was rejected. But commonly the Irish Parliament itself, having satisfied its honour, would then present the rejected Bill as one of its own and, after all, would calmly pass it. Such antics were harmless enough, but in 1769 a novel, more serious, drama was staged. The Commons rejected a government finance Bill on the grounds that it had not taken its rise in their House, then went ahead to pass a money Bill of their own. Faced with this impudence, Townshend prorogued Parliament. Then he shocked the borough-mongers horribly.

They must have expected that, as in the past, the Viceroy would buy back their necessary support. But now they, with their tails of followers, were swept out of all lucrative offices. The nightmare of the American patriots was really enacted in Dublin, with Townshend creating new places and pensions as bribes for those prepared to support his line. When Parliament reassembled early in 1771, he was firmly in control of the Commons. His chief secretary now manipulated the House, buying votes as required from men who were never slow to sell themselves. Townshend resigned in 1772, but his system ticked over smoothly under his successor, and in 1775 the exalted Flood himself deserted the 'patriot' ranks and accepted the Cabinet post of Vice-Treasurer. That great god Hercules, his eloquence, deserted him on the government benches – Irish politicians were never good at making constructive and positive orations. Their Parliament, childish in its pride and its sulks, seemed for a blink of five years to be happy sucking its candy.

But these men, whose selfishness was so blatant, whose business was so irregularly conducted, still trembled before 'public opinion'. The effect of dispensing with the 'undertakers' was that, when discontent mounted high, the Viceroy at Dublin Castle would have no buffer, there must be direct confrontation between the public and the British government. British control now depended on visible corruption. Thirty-four Irish politicians were given peerages between 1767 and 1785. The Commons seemed more manageable than Britain's; whereas it was reckoned that 5,723 people controlled half the seats in the Westminster House, a mere hundred or so disposed of two-thirds in the Dublin one. But the Viceroy must still win the support of one or two of the great borough-mongering families, and though most of the House were pensioners and placemen, many of whom had no other profession and depended wholly on the pickings of politics, even these could not always be safely relied upon. As in Britain, there were 'independent' gentlemen representing county constituencies where they were under direct pressure from quite a wide electorate, and as at Westminster such men could be swayed by oratory. Though each had his price, the Castle could not control all of them. Over forty lawyers sat in the House, and while most had been given minor legal places, they were frustrated by the intrusion of Englishmen into the highest positions in the judiciary, and the eloquence which their profession exacted might be unleashed in a frenzy of opposition.[111]

How inconvenient that the rotunda existed! Edinburgh, where the 'Parliament House' was now given merely to routine legal business, was, unlike Dublin, a city of model docility.

IX

A rising Scottish politician named Wedderburn observed smugly in 1768 that while the south of England was 'a great Bedlam under the dominion of a beggarly, idle and intoxicated mob without keepers, actuated solely by the word *Wilkes*', the north was frugal, sober and loyal. As to the Scots, another 'North British' politician could report that they detested Wilkes with 'the greatest unanimity'.[112] The old picture was now stood on its head. London and the Home Counties could hardly be governed; Scotland gave no serious trouble at all.

This was true even of the Highlands. Culloden had swept away the last chiefs who had tried to preserve the old ways. Not only arms, but also the Highland dress, were forbidden for a generation. Within a dozen years cattle rustling had been suppressed with amazing completeness. The military spirit of the clan system remained ingrained in the population. Over nine-tenths of the people, still, spoke only Gaelic.[113] Smuggling continued to employ an even larger proportion of Highlanders than of people in Galloway or Ayrshire. Gaels still farmed on the run-rig, 'open', system, using primitive ploughs and the 'cascrome', a sort of crooked wooden spade with an iron tip. Localised famines were commonplace. But the Highlands were at last safe for travellers, and had come within the grasp of 'civilisation'.

The chiefs were now anxious to prove their loyalty, and happy, also, to make cash out of purveying their faithful 'children' to the government. Between 1740 and 1815, some fifty or so Scottish battalions were raised, mostly in the Highlands. The army provided scope for Gaelic military traditions. Soldiers could wear the tartan while that was still barred to civilians. Young men could always find employment. All the mutinies provoked over the years by the lies told to Gaelic soldiers by officers whom they trusted and by bullying and floggings such as the Gaelic view of the world made intolerable, would not destroy the army's value, to the authorities, as a safety valve. Emigration helped to keep the peace as well, and though industry in the Lowlands was not quite ready yet to absorb hordes of dark Gaelic-speaking people, America was taking many off.

In the late 1760s and 1770s, a fervour for emigration emerged both in the Lowlands and in the Highlands, but especially in the latter. Over 20,000 people left Scotland in eight years. The Lowlanders were commonly skilled men seeking to better their lot, especially after an economic crisis in 1772 which threw thousands of artisans out of work. They generally saw themselves as temporary exiles; when they had made their fortunes, they planned to go home.[114]

In the Highlands, by contrast, the initiative came from the higher levels of society. The growing invasion of the area by the values and practices of an up-to-date money economy bereft the tacksmen of their traditional role. Too proud to be mere commercial farmers, some of these minor gentry struck out west, taking bodies of their clan followers with them, and hoping to recreate a life-style where, as one observer reported, 'a tacksman of fifty pounds a year often keeps twenty servants ... ' Other substantial Gaels and Lowlanders, seeing a chance of profit, urged on the movement. Crop failures and cattle blights and overpopulation gave ample spur. On Skye, in 1773, James Boswell, travelling with Dr Johnson, saw testimony of emigration fever in a new dance performed at Macdonald of Sleat's house. 'They call it "America". A brisk reel is played. The first couple begin, and each sets to one—then each to another—then as they set to the next couple, the second and third couples are setting; and so it goes on till all are set a-going, setting and wheeling round each other, while each is making the tour of all in the dance. It shows how emigration catches till all are set afloat. Mrs. Mackinnon told me that last year when the ship sailed from Portree for America, the people on shore were almost distracted when they saw their relations go off; they lay down on the ground and tumbled, and tore the grass with their teeth. This year there was not a tear shed. The people on shore seemed to think that they would soon follow.'[115]

Highland emigrants tended to cluster together in certain districts, clinging to their characteristic dress and to their Gaelic language (which was still spoken in North Carolina in the nineteenth century, in Nova Scotia even in the twentieth). The Highland tradition of rearing cattle flourished on virgin American acres, where the Gaels remained a race apart, continuing to give obedience to their leaders, who, whatever their views at the time of the '45, were now firm supporters of the Hanoverian Crown.

In spite of all this, Highland population rose by nearly one-third between 1755 and 1801. The abatement of violence was not an important reason. The spread of the potato through Scotland was critical. It reached Uist and Benbecula in 1743, Lewis and Sutherland in the 1750s. By 1770 it was a common crop on the holdings of the poor throughout the Lowlands and was on its way to becoming the staple food of the Highlands. It helped to balance the diet and check scurvy in a country traditionally short of vegetables, it provided a safeguard against the failure of the oat crop, which still happened quite frequently, and, as in Ireland, it proved the means whereby an expanding population could be fed from the same, or even reduced, acreage of ground.[116]

In 1747, no fewer than forty-one estates, most of them in the Highlands, were declared forfeited by Jacobite 'traitors'. Five years later, thirteen of these were annexed inalienably to the Crown by an Act providing that their rent and profits were to go towards civilising the Gaels and promoting among them 'the Protestant Religion', and 'the Principles of Duty and Loyalty to his Majesty'. The Commissioners put in charge came to manage about one Highland parish in seven. They consciously imitated the Roman idea of planting *coloniae* of veterans. Though the soldiers themselves were mostly Highlanders, only a couple of these artificial new villages succeeded. Other devices worked better. The Commissioners built schools where all instruction was given in English. They enforced new agricultural habits upon their tenants, encouraged them to plant trees, and to build better houses. The making of linen cloth was promoted. New roads and bridges were built.[117]

Though the aim in the first place was to obliterate Jacobitism, the Commissioners, doubtless, sincerely thought that they were bringing a better way of life to the impoverished and 'idle' Gaels. 'There are Crowds of little Girls here', their factor at Crieff once observed, 'that stroll about the Streets, playing at hand Ball and other such Employments and diversions, who might be usefully employed in Spinning.'[118] The Gospel of Work was preached by Lowland incomers, energising but joyless and utterly alien to the traditions of Gaelic society. Scots who had made fortunes by diligence in Jamaica, by commerce or hard soldiering in Bengal, now bought up estates in the Highlands. Their competition raised the price of lands. Rents increased as they tried to recoup their outlay. More 'efficient' use of the soil was essential. Those who could not pay or adapt must now go to the wall, or to America.

For the moment, the prospects seemed good. The terms of trade were moving strongly in the region's favour; between the 1740s and 1790s the price of cattle, the Highlands' main export to the Lowlands, rose 300 per cent, while that of oats, which the Highlands imported, did not quite double.[119] New villages did spring into existence and some — Ullapool, Grantown and Oban amongst them — became important centres of population, industry and 'civility'. In various places the Lowland social pattern was introduced with success (for those who succeeded) and capitalist farmers employed landless labourers. In others, the expulsion of the tacksmen, or their convenient exodus to America, assisted landlords to subdivide lands formerly farmed jointly. The peasants then split them into still smaller units among themselves, but the rents came in somehow.

Kelp was a godsend to landlords on the remote and sterile western coasts. This was the ash of burnt seaweed, sold to serve as a low-grade alkali in the manufacture of soap, alum, glass and other goods. It was the easiest thing in the world to make it. Your people need do no more than cut the weed from the rocks at low tide, dry it, then roast it to ashes in simple kilns. But it implied the disruption of old ways. Hands and legs, as many as could be found, must be concentrated on the coast, where the traditional cattle economy lapsed and potatoes from small plots became the staff of life.

Another departure from tradition evident by the 1770s was the widespread distillation of whisky. The common drink of the Highlands had been strong ale. But now the landlord was asking such rents, in cash, whisky might seem the best way to pay him. The pattern of taxes in force encouraged illegal production. Over 6,000 illegal stills were seized in the Highlands in the 1780s, though at the end of that decade there were only about 350 legal ones. The delicious peaty flavours of Highland malts commonly reached Lowland palates by bootlegging.[120]

None of this meant that Highlanders were essentially better off. The old customs of the region had been well adapted to its geography. As Rosalind

Mitchison observes, 'Great numbers of underfed ponies were more use than a few good Clydesdales when there were no roads, and they could winter out on the hills.' Lowlanders misread what they saw. The Gaelic character seemed to them to be the cause of the region's crude living standards. Hence the English-man Thomas Pennant's self-contradictory verdict on Sutherland in the 1770s. The people, he wrote, were 'almost torpid with idleness, and most wretched.' Yet he added, 'they are content with little at present, and are thoughtless of futurity ... '[121] If they were thoughtless, why did they emigrate, voluntarily, as he claimed they did, in response to the pressure of population on grain supplies? If they were 'content' with their own way of life, what was the point of vainly striving to make Sutherland as prosperous as the Lothians?

The truth would only enforce itself slowly against the obstinate optimism of government and 'improvers' that geography, in the Highlands, made high prosperity impossible. It was true that the potato would flourish in soil which had previously been heathery moorland; Lachlan MacIntosh brought home his fortune from India, purchased hundreds of acres of waste near Inverness in 1776, and proceeded to make fertile fields of them.[122] But even at maximum there was scant arable land, while a remote glen, however adept its people, could not compete in textile manufacture with towns and villages close to the great ports. Weavers in Yorkshire and elsewhere cried out for wool. The price was rising. Some men were already glimpsing that sheep might be the best source of profit in the Highlands.

This would be the sharpest break with tradition of all. 'Here are no sheep,' Thomas Pennant reported from Skye, 'but what are kept for home consump-tion, or for the wool for the cloathing of the inhabitants.'[123] The animals were thin and dark, coarse of fleece. But by the 1760s, new breeds were invading the glens, as Border country men leased lands and introduced large flocks, first in the southern Highlands, then up the west coast, and into the Spey Valley and the Great Glen. The discovery that fine-woolled sheep could live, all year round out in the open, north of the Highland line had, over several decades, famous effects. Sheep-walks disrupted the balance of plant and animal life. Eagles were slaughtered in their interests. Vast sheep-walks, employing few men, ousted people. And the lonely life of the shepherd, tending hundreds of sheep on his own, seemed horrible to Gaels whose way of life had been intimately communal.

Sheep symbolised the delight in the values of capitalism now taken by Low-landers who were themselves far from sheep-like. Scottish Lowland society was better educated, and more disputatious than that of southern England. Everyone knew a good deal, or thought he did. The *Encyclopaedia Britannica* was first published in Edinburgh in 1771 thanks to the energy of obscure young men, and at once sold widely at home and in the colonies. It represented the versatile intellect now almost commonplace in Scotland. The middling and lower ranks of society seemed an inexhaustible reservoir of inventive talent. A tenant farmer's son, Robert Burns, would become the most famous poet of his day. Thomas

67 A Virginian landscape near Yorktown, from the 1780s

68 Paul Revere's picture of the 'Bloody Massacre', Boston, 1770

69 William Murray, Lord Mansfield, by J. B. Van Loo

70 Lord Shelburne, after Joshua Reynolds

71 A press-gang in London in the 1780s

Telford, from a shepherd's cottage, would rise as 'The Colossus of Roads', the greatest civil engineer of his time. Opportunity seemed open to all.

A constellation of pioneering Scottish scientists found an eager audience among practical engineers and industrialists. Dr Joseph Black, who discovered both carbon dioxide and latent heat, attracted crowds of non-students to his lectures at Edinburgh University, opening minds to the excitement of science, while Dr William Cullen of the Edinburgh medical faculty broke radically with the past in his 1776 catalogue of *Materia Medica* which swept out such loathsome and useless simples as ants' eggs, millipedes, frogspawn, peacock dung, dog dung, and powder of Egyptian mummy.[124]

Yet a young English radical, Sylas Neville, who went in the 1770s to become Cullen's student, was shocked by the political conservatism of otherwise daring and open-minded men like these. A great geologist, Dr James Hutton, remarked one day to Neville over dinner that he was 'for having all laws against bribery & corruption abolished' so that every man could sell his vote as he did anything else. Joseph Black, who was present, concurred with Hutton in thinking that the British enjoyed 'perfect liberty' and had 'no political evils to complain of'.[125]

Principal William Robertson of Edinburgh University, a historian matched in fame only by Gibbon (whom he greatly influenced), led the party of so-called 'Moderates' which now dominated the General Assembly of the Kirk, men who condoned the *status quo* in politics, disdained the old theocratic ideals, and accepted lay patronage over the ministry, which gave Anglicised lairds the chance to put in polite clergymen. Dissenting religion obsessed many lively minds in the artisan class which might otherwise have been drawn towards 'democratical' notions. Instead of crying out for 'Liberty', weavers jawed over theological niceties and purchased books on church history. There were virtually no agrarian 'outrages' — enclosures were pushed through by lairds who kept unquestioned control, cordially accepted by their tenantry. Self-colonisation of Scotland proceeded peacefully. 'So absolute was the control of the lairds', writes Christopher Harvie, 'that even the serfs of Russia — who could at least elect their head-men — seem to have had more freedom than the countrymen of Burns.'[126]

This was an easy country to govern. There were no turbulent 'popular' constituencies corresponding to Middlesex, Westminster or Dublin. The fifteen M.P.s who sat for the Scottish burghs would be elected in 1790 by a total of 1,301 town councillors, most of them under the thumbs of powerful patrons. In Glasgow, thirty-two people had the vote. The thirty-three electors of Edinburgh were entitled to choose their own successors. Since the county franchise depended not exactly upon a 'property' qualification but on immediate vassalage to the King, or its equivalent, great magnates could increase their control by creating 'faggot' voters — men given title deeds or superiorities of nominal portions of land, whose electoral choices were then controlled absolutely. By 1788, 1,370 out of 2,662 county electors in Scotland would be 'parchment

z

barons' of this species. A few score people only had any effective say over Scotland's representation at Westminster. By contrast, in Wales, though that country was very much under the thumbs of thirty or forty leading families who controlled and contested elections — Williams-Wynns and Bulkeleys in North Wales, Morgans of Tredegar, Philipps of Picton Castle — roughly one adult male in eight had the vote.[127]

Scotland was the dreamland of eighteenth-century political 'management'. The 3rd Duke of Argyll who had controlled things so well died in 1761. For a time, no strong personality took his place, but in 1766, Henry Dundas, a man in his early twenties from a not very lofty landed family which had sought fortune through the law, was given the ministerial post of Solicitor-General for Scotland. In 1775, he reached the grander office of Lord Advocate. 'King Harry the Ninth' would soon be more widely known.

Thanks to the complexities of the Scottish legal system, even the wealthiest Englishmen could not in practice buy up Scottish county seats, though Scots of the landed classes were often elected in England. Englishmen did not practise Scottish law, but Scots rose to the highest legal positions in England. This disparity worried James Boswell, a Scottish lawyer, who wished that Englishmen might become Scottish judges. 'Such interchange,' he wrote, 'would make a beneficial mixture of manners, and render our union more complete.'[128]

Boswell's self-division was typical of his class and time. Men with deep feeling for Scotland, true pride in their country, wanted to make themselves more like the English. 'Elocution' was all the rage. Gentility was craved. To be genteel was to be Anglicised. Hence the 'New Town' of Edinburgh was rising. In the 'Old Town', rich and poor had, literally, lived on top of each other. No wonder that few people of rank had resided there. In 1767, James Craig's plan was accepted for the first stage of the 'New Town' to the north of the city. A fine Register House by Robert and James Adam was soon going up at one end of the new development. Elegant, regular streets, circuses and crescents, handsome new bridges and public buildings, followed continuously, matching the growth of the well-to-do population, the city's success in attracting men of rank, and its due pride in its own pre-eminence as a centre of literature, science and scholarship.

The Scottish philosophers, lawyers and students debated ideas and ideals of potentially revolutionary nature, but stood politically aloof while other men, in England and in America, actually struggled and fought for tangible changes.

X

'Moderate' though he was, William Robertson denounced slavery in his historical works. But this was hardly daring. No important philosopher of the day would have defended it. Dr Johnson, 'tory' at a time when the word was coming to mean 'foe of democracy', nevertheless shocked Boswell by proposing 'in company with some very grave men at Oxford', a toast to the next slave rebellion in the West Indies.[129]

Anti-slavery opinion had been crystallised in a famous ironical attack by Montesquieu in 1748. It appeared in the same work, *The Spirit of the Laws*, in which he extolled the British constitution. 'It is impossible for us to suppose these creatures to be men, because allowing them to be men, a suspicion would follow that we ourselves are not Christians.' Writer after subsequent writer quoted such passages. But Scottish philosophers made the intellectual pikes wielded by those who followed through the breach. Francis Hutcheson's *System of Moral Philosophy* (1755) spoke out for 'benevolence' and denied absolute authority in every sphere. A man must not tyrannise over his wife or children. His rights over a servant were limited. Slavery was not 'natural', though men since Aristotle's day had argued as if it were.

The first volume of George Wallace's *System of the Principles of the Law of Scotland*, appearing in 1760, contained a systematic attack on the legal basis of slavery. The human right to liberty was, he argued, inalienable, since only a madman or someone coerced would give it up. Plagiarised by the famous French *Encyclopédie*, Wallace's view attained comprehensive influence. In the social and debating clubs which proliferated in the Scottish university towns at this time, the subject of slavery was discussed time and again. But there was as yet no interest in practical reform. 'Enlightened' Scots studied the question, not quite in the abstract only, but chiefly for the light which it might throw on their own society. How much subjection could the Scots themselves take without being harmed? The Dalzel brothers, Andrew and Archibald, sons of a carpenter, illustrate the absence of practical application. Andrew, Professor of Greek at Edinburgh, attacked the 'abominable institution' of slavery in his lectures, yet remained on friendly terms with Archibald, who became a free-lance slave trader, governor of Cape Coast Castle, and author of a history of Dahomey which offered important help to the pro-slavery case.[130]

The first efforts to bring bold new ideas into conformity with reality came from the Quakers, in England and America. They were deeply upset by the Seven Years War. Their opposition to it ensured that weaker brethren fell away, and its impotence meant that those who remained were anxious to prove that Friends could achieve something. No fewer than eighty-eight Quakers, probably slave traders, had been members in 1756 of the London 'Company of Merchants trading to Africa'. But in 1758 the London Yearly Meeting, the most influential Quaker body in the world, came out with a strong injunction that Friends must avoid the 'iniquitous practice' of slaving, and three years later it threatened with disownment all Friends who continued to participate.[131] Quakers had moved with the times. Though their prime case was, of course, that slavery violated Christian truth and Christian love, talk of 'liberty' and 'natural rights' figured more and more in Quaker campaigning. The fact that many Friends were now drawn into sympathy with the new evangelical effervescence which was at work in other Churches meant that they could co-operate cordially with Christians of other denominations, as they began to lobby against the slave trade, though without Quaker energy, and Quaker wealth, it is hard to see how an effective movement could have come into being.

Quaker pacifism and egalitarianism marched parallel with a new, 'progressive' school of Christian thought. The great chemist, Joseph Priestley, told his students in the famous Dissenting academy at Warrington that things were 'in a progress towards a state of greater perfection' not only in arts, science, religion and commerce, but even in human happiness.[132] However, many serious Christians continued to hold vivid belief in sin. Slavery had been justified as a natural concomitant of the slave's sin, while sin had been seen as itself a sort of enslavement. But now a mental somersault brought growing numbers of Christians into assent with a contrary argument. Slaveholding was a sin. The planter, with bloody whip in one hand, glass of rum in the other, was agent of Antichrist or of the devil. Slavery was the root of all corruption. To root it out would realise, through secular politics, millenarian goals. Sin would be defeated.

And if Britons achieved this, it would validate their rule over so much of the world's surface and seas. The most effective polemicists against slavery were mostly men who harped on the theme of 'national' retribution and 'national' salvation. At times saving the slave would seem almost incidental to the task of saving the British Empire from God's wrath. The first, and greatest, of British pamphleteers in this cause was also the most insistent upon this theme. Granville Sharp wrote in 1776 that the encouragement of the slave trade by Parliament, the toleration of slavery by the colonial assemblies, meant that the 'horrible Guilt' incurred was 'no longer confined to the few hardened *Individuals*, that are immediately concerned in these baneful Practices, but alas! the WHOLE BRITISH EMPIRE is involved. By the unhappy Concurrence of *National Authority*, the GUILT is rendered *National*; and *National* GUILT must inevitably draw down from GOD some tremendous *National* Punishment ... '[133]

Sharp, as his capitalisations suggest, was fervent to the point of eccentricity. David Brion Davis suggests that 'the role of eccentric allowed him to expose the moral compromises of his society without being branded as a rebel.' He was lucky in his background. The grandson of an archbishop, the son of an archdeacon, he had wealthy and philanthropic elder brothers who loved and supported him despite the perversity which made him content to work first as a linen-draper's apprentice, then as a petty clerk in the civil service. He shared his family's devotion to music. 'Singing and playing at sight were his favourite recreations. He had a good bass voice; and played on the common English flute, clarionet, oboe, and double flute ... At the Sunday evening concerts, which were held alternately at the houses of his brothers James and William, he beat the kettle drums. Those concerts consisted wholly of performances of sacred music ... '[134]

Though the Sharp brothers entertained ambassadors, ministers, even the

King and Queen, to concerts on a barge which they kept on the Thames, Granville's vision was unclouded with any considerations of interest, cash or political expediency. Every morning when he rose from bed, he began the day either by reading in the Bible or by chanting Hebrew Psalms to the accompaniment of the 'traverse harp', which he had invented. He campaigned against indecency in the theatre, sought to convert Jews to Christianity, and agitated for the creation of American bishoprics. But, unlike many evangelical Christians, he was a genuine political radical. He took up the cause of seamen seized by press-gangs. He grew very angry indeed over the plight of the 'black Caribs' on St Vincent, whose land had been stolen from them and whose extirpation was now talked of in high government circles in Britain. He sympathised warmly with the American colonists in their conflict with the British ministry. He backed the demand for annual parliaments in England. While he (correctly) denied that the case of black slaves was the same as that of English labourers, he was dismayed by the 'scanty pittance of wages' grudgingly given by employers. 'The misery of our own poor will not be any excuse for the oppression of the poor elsewhere!'[135]

When the plight of black people in Britain came to his notice in the 1760s, he began to think the destruction of slavery essential to the redemption of the honour of the Church of England. He did not see 'Negroes'. He saw people. The ranking of men as 'mere Chattels' appalled him.

In 1756, a Westminster goldsmith had advertised that he made 'silver padlocks for Blacks or Dogs.' In London, Bristol and Liverpool seamen openly sold blacks, now a regular bonus-in-kind for those who served on slaving vessels. Other slaves came in as the property of colonial planters or 'nabobs' returning home to enjoy their spoils. Aristocratic ladies liked to have black boys for servants. When young they resembled pets or exotic ornaments (fine in the background of a portrait by Reynolds or Zoffany, the glister of teeth and of highlights on smiling chocolate skin). When older, their famed sexual prowess would provide welcome experimental relief from the embraces of wine-sodden English noblemen. The Duchess of Queensberry's infatuation with a slave named Soubise was only one of many similar scandals. She educated him as a gentleman and he ran through the upper classes 'as general a lover as Don Juan'. Blacks found other careers within the scope of their supposed innate attributes. Many black seamen clustered in the ports. Black musicians were commonly used in army regiments. Blacks were quite frequently seen on the stage or exhibited as curiosities at fairs. Black heavyweight boxers were champions of England. There may have been 15,000 or 20,000 black people in Britain in the 1760s.[136]

Some found esteem. Dr Johnson employed a black servant for over thirty years, and eventually left him a generous annuity. But one of the two blacks brought by Benjamin Franklin to London ran away from him after a year. Such fugitive slaves and servants were the basis of the free black community which grew up in London. One reads of a gathering in a Fleet Street tavern in 1764, for drinking and music, attended by three score blacks, from which all whites were excluded. A few blacks prospered as small businessmen. A handful attracted upper-class patronage. Ignacius Sancho rose from the status of servant to that of small grocer through the interest of the Duchess of Montagu. He was befriended by literary men, acquired fame from his writing (after his death), and used his prominent contacts to help other blacks. Most blacks needed help. They mixed in the London underworld with equally poor whites, who by custom gave shelter to runaway slaves and, at this time, displayed little prejudice. Most blacks in Britain were male, but poor white women would marry them. White servants and sailors accepted their black co-workers. But life was hard, at this level, for both colours, and many blacks became thieves or beggars.[137]

In 1765 a black boy who had been savagely beaten by his master went to Dr William Sharp's surgery. Granville, the doctor's brother, saw him there. After four months' treatment, the boy was found work as a chemist's messenger. But his former master noticed him, had him imprisoned, and sold him to a Jamaican planter. Sharp, learning of this, had found what would be his main cause for the rest of his life. He now studied law books as well as the Bible. The English Common Law, he concluded, left no place for slavery. Inferior law must give way to superior. Man's law must bow to God's law. He amassed such weight of legal opinion and scholarly citation that the Jamaican planter dropped the case and relinquished his purchase. Other black people brought their problems to Sharp and he soon succeeded in freeing two more slaves. Meanwhile, as Sharp was well aware, in Scotland colliers and salters were commonly called slaves.

'Serfdom' more exactly fitted their position. Coal-owners, during the seventeenth century, had found it necessary to compel people to such dirty and arduous toil. Now most colliers' children were regarded as serfs from birth. In 1701, colliers and salters, alone in the population, had been excluded from the Scottish equivalent of habeas corpus; in 1708 it had been established that runaways might be brought back even after eight years; in 1762 it transpired that an owner could freely shift his ascripted colliers to any mine where he wanted them. Attainment of freedom was almost impossible, and since miners were caste apart, to break into some other calling would be hard; most runaways fled to other mines. Since coal dust was hard to shift, the sense of apartness extended even to skin colour, as an eighteenth-century ballad illustrates:

> The collier had a dochter, and O she's wonder bonie;
> A laird he was that socht her, rich in lands and money;
> She wadna hae a laird, she wadna be a leddy,
> But she wad hae a collier lad, the colour o' her deddie.

They were not quite slaves. They could not be sold as chattels. They might own property. They were paid wages – and since their servile position deterred new recruits, they were actually paid higher rates than miners in England or farm servants in Scotland. Even so, some wanted freedom. In 1770 a black slave was brought to Fife by a returning planter. Local colliers, salters and farm workers raised funds so that he could apply to the Court of Session for his liberty, but his master died before a decision was reached.[138]

Sharp now also sought a test case. The legal position in England was thoroughly confused. The law was strong in defence of property. Slaves were property. Nevertheless, under the Habeas Corpus Act of 1679, used by John Wilkes, coveted by Irish 'patriots', the shipping of human beings to the colonies against their wish was clearly illegal. Were slaves human beings? This was the fundamental issue which Sharp raised before, or rather against, Mansfield.

Mansfield, a conservative Scot from Perthshire, Lord Chief Justice from 1756–88, was anxious to sit on the fence as long as possible. He was guardian over English commercial law, and to decide that slavery was not legal would deprive owners resident in England of property worth hundreds of thousands of pounds. Hence what Sharp himself described as his 'long contest with Lord Mansfield'.[139] Sharp thought that slaves were not property but people.

James Somerset seemed to provide a cause which would settle the matter. He was a black slave whose Scottish master, Charles Stewart, had been a crown official in Boston. He had been brought to England, had escaped, had been recaptured and put aboard ship for sale in Jamaica, but then released on a writ of habeas corpus. His case came before Mansfield in eight separate hearings between December 1771 and June 1772. Sharp organised Somerset's side. Three counsel were found to appear for Somerset, all of whom refused to accept any payment. One of them pleaded powerfully that if Stewart's right were admitted, slavery with its 'horrid train of evils' would invade England from every part of the world where it was practised — from 'Poland, Russia, Spain, and Turkey, and from the coast of Barbary' — and Britain, 'so famous for public liberty', would 'become the chief seat of private tyranny.' Mansfield showed his bias plainly; though Stewart was the defendant, it was Somerset who was called on to provide sureties for his appearance in court. He spun the case out as long as he could, hoping that the two sides would arrive at a private compromise. But at last he gave his judgment, enforced upon him, that the claim of a master to exercise power over a slave was 'not known to the laws of England', and therefore Somerset must go free.[140]

This was soon followed by clarifications in Scotland. The more enterprising coal-owners there were now irked by serfdom, which deterred fresh labour from entering their fast-expanding industry. They themselves put a Bill through Parliament in 1774 making new recruits to the mines automatically free, though current serfs would have to institute legal proceedings to emancipate themselves and even then might have to wait ten years for liberty. In practice, serfdom continued till a new Act in 1799 at last swept it completely away.

Regarding black slavery, however, the Scottish courts were swiftly decisive. In 1778 the case of a black runaway, Knight v. Wedderburn, came up to the Court of Session which ruled that slavery, 'being unjust, could not be supported in this country ... '141

In reactionary Scotland all black slaves were now automatically free. But though humane persons in liberty-loving England had rejoiced over Mansfield's judgment for Somerset, and though Sharp, using the press, had won an important propaganda victory — dazzling enough to blind historians down to very recent times — the truth was that nothing south of the Border had truly changed. The case had turned on a legal technicality. Mansfield had not said that all slaves in England were free, merely that they might not be compelled to go abroad; even so, within a year there were fresh instances of forcible removal. In a ruling of 1785, Mansfield himself confirmed that a slave was still a slave on English soil. Slave-owners in the colonies settled matters by making slaves before they left for Britain sign an indenture promising to work for their masters under certain conditions. This was valid under English law, and a court would decide in 1799 that no master was obliged to pay wages to such an 'indentured' black unless a clause specifically exacted them. For sixty years after the Somerset case, there were slaves in England, people were sold, runaways were captured.142

Racialism, long latent, was beginning to focus its arguments in opposition to those of Sharp and the Quakers. Each side was abetted in its zeal by the fact that there was still very little up-to-date information to be had concerning the African cultures from which the slaves came. Forward scientific minds were concerned to learn more about the continent; thus, in 1771, Sir Joseph Banks, a wealthy amateur natural historian, sent Henry Smeathman to live in the Banana Islands off Sierra Leone, where, over several years, he made the first substantial collection of West African plants and insects. Cultures, however, could not be collected and brought home for inspection. The few first-hand accounts in print were mainly written by traders who had little prejudice against Africans in mass, but were unenthusiastic about life on the Guinea Coast, knew little or nothing of the interior, tended to see all African cultures as much the same, and, so as to titillate their readers, emphasised the more picturesque and outlandish festivals and customs.

Such details were bad on the whole for the mental images formed of Africa. So, in some of their implications, were certain characteristic currents of new thought, in this age of the revolutionary middle class. Thus the Glasgow philosopher John Millar, in 1771, proposed a four-stage model of human development which would have wide and long-enduring influence. From hunting and gathering, mankind had moved on to pastoralism, then to farming, and then to commerce. Africa, which seemed to lack much commerce, would seem from this model to be more 'backward' than Europe. Why, then, were its people less advanced? Montesquieu had produced another enduring theory, of the effect of the climate upon the human psyche. Northerners were more active in mind and body, southerners more sensitive in soul and spirit. Crudely applied, this produced the stereotypes of the fierce Sicilian and the sexy Levantine – and the concept that Africans were and must be 'timid, lazy, oversensitive, and over-sexed'.[143] Meanwhile, reaction had set in against the elegant, but austere and disappointingly rational Newtonian model of the universe. Poets and dilettantes now found chemistry more exciting than physics; its elements were more colourful and diverse than the unvarying laws of gravity and thermodynamics. Unity was unfashionable, diversity was the rage. Many people quested for differences, averting their eyes from blatant similarities. 'Polygenetic' theories of human origins increased their appeal as against 'monogenetic' ones. The great Linnaeus in 1735 had identified four races, white, yellow, red and black (not at all the obvious division which it now appears to be) and then, in 1758, had divided the genus *Homo* into two species to make room for the orang outangs and for supposed wild men who could not speak. In 1775 a German, J. F. Blumenbach, created a fivefold system by naming three primary races, 'Cauca-sian', 'Ethiopian' and 'Mongolian', and making Amerindians a mixture of Caucasian and Mongolian and Malays a mixture of Mongolian and Ethiopian. As so often in the late eighteenth century, we spy a modern convention of thought at its source; Blumenbach's classifications have been used by the U.S. Immigration service in our own day.

Blumenbach himself spoke out nobly for the equality of blacks and whites. But even he described 'Ethiopian' physiognomy in unattractive terms. All biologists using any sort of classification felt compelled to decide which order the races stood in, and all, unhesitatingly, put Europeans on top of their scales. As Africans were at the other extreme of colour, they would naturally gravitate to the bottom. Blacks seemed immune to certain diseases affecting whites, and vice versa. Here was a basis seized on by polygeneticists to found a 'scientific' racism.

The spokesmen for the West Indian planters were thus well armed to counter the cock-a-hoop cries of humanitarians over the Somerset case. Samuel Estwick weighed in at once with a pamphlet, stoutly reasserting that black slaves were *commercial property*, so that all commerce would be threatened by their libera-tion, and cleverly arguing that the whippings they suffered were merely com-parable to the 'hundreds of stripes' commonly given to British soldiers. He proposed that Negroes were a separate species, utterly lacking that innate 'moral sense' which Hutcheson attributed to human nature.[144]

Edward Long's *History of Jamaica*, published two years after Mansfield's judgment, is the first classic of modern racialist thought. After all, many readers concluded, Long was a brilliant man who knew blacks well at first hand. What he said must be true; even though he asserted that mulattoes were infertile hybrids who could only breed successfully through intercourse with one or other of the 'pure' races; even though he alleged that, when not eating human flesh, Africans consumed by choice meat 'almost raw', putrid and full of maggots; even though he averred that not one black could draw a straight line. These wretches were far better off in Jamaica than in their homeland – domestic slaves in the West Indies lived better than the 'poorer class' in England itself, though not one black ever did half so much work. As for the white Jamaican, he was a model of 'disinterested charity, philanthropy, and clemency'. Despite the unbalanced grossness of Long's physical loathing of blacks ('bestial fleece' of woolly hair, 'bestial and fetid smell'), the success of his book made him one of the most important harbingers of the Darwinian theory of biological evolution.[145]

His praise for the planters was easily countered by direct observation; a young visitor to Barbados fresh out of England, in the very year when Long's book was published, watched with horror as men were flogged to insensibility 'for the most trifling faults, sometimes for mere whims ... '[146] Long's more absurd remarks on black intelligence were abashed, if not silenced, as abolitionists brought forward such literate, polished and talented blacks as the author, Olaudah Equiano. However, well-meaning Christians, as Christians, were inevitably prejudiced themselves. They had no real knowledge of African religions and customs which, in any case, they must have rejected, however gently, as inferior to their own. Their counter-stereotype married Hutcheson's theory of innate moral sense with notions derived from the cult of the noble savage, to produce a view of the African as a charming, perhaps rather childlike creature who would make an apt and easy Christian convert if only the devilish planter would assent to his conversion. John Wesley wrote a tract against the slave trade in 1774 which swung his Methodist followers quite swiftly into the Sharp camp, and painted a most attractive picture of life in the West African interior, about which he knew as little as anyone else.

The strongest force in the abolitionists' favour was not that of their arguments, good though they sometimes were. It was the shift of feeling which made each successive generation of young people in Britain on the whole more sensitive to cruelty. This surely had much to do with growing standards of comfort and hygiene among the middle classes, who were growingly screened from the sordor and brutality which mere survival might entail for the less comfortable. Thus young Sylas Neville not only shuddered at cock-fighting (which nevertheless remained in favour for generations longer among those whom he characterised as 'dead to all benevolent and tender sensations') but actually, catching two mice in his town house, went to the fields to set them at liberty. Literary fashion continued its work. One of the more important well-springs of cliché in an epoch well served by such sources was the fiction of Henry Mackenzie, follower of Sterne in the school of 'sentiment'. The young Scot, in this characteristic of his countrymen, somehow found himself able to write pro-slavery pamphlets while loading his lachrymose novels with emotion against the trade. And also against what the British were doing in India.

Mackenzie's *Man of Feeling* swept all before it in 1771. The novel's fainting hero talks to a soldier back from that far land and deplores the rapacity of the East India Company. A neo-classical disdain for riches allies with the new humanitarianism. ' ... What title have the subjects of another kingdom to establish an empire in India?'[147]

XI

From India in the 1760s had come news of revolution upon revolution, each engineered in turn by East India Company servants who pocketed large presents and then, it seemed, set about scheming for the next. Before Plassey, trading in the East had been a respectable middle-class occupation offering special prospects of early death but, except for occasional bouncers like Thomas Pitt, little hope of great wealth. Now, as Richard Barwell wrote home from Bengal, India seemed to give 'a sure path to competency. A moderate share of attention and your being not quite an idiot' were 'ample qualities for the attainment of riches.' He exaggerated. A vastly successful minority sought in Calcutta and elsewhere to match the opulent ways of Mughal princelings, and raised the social stakes so high that many young men could only retain respect by borrowing heavily from native 'banyans' until they acquired burdens which they could never shake off, ending their hopes in the Calcutta gaol.[148] The rush for wealth largely destroyed, for a generation of Company personnel, the balance between their private interests and those of the shareholders at home. Finding themselves rulers, they ceased to think like 'servants'. A prime case was John Zephaniah Holwell.

Temporarily in charge in Calcutta after the departure of Clive and of other senior servants hasting home to spend their fortunes, Holwell sought to depose Mir Jafar in favour of Mir Qasim, who was a relative of the Nawab by marriage, and probably far the abler man. Clive's successor as governor, Henry Vansittart, arrived to take over from Holwell in July 1760, but three months later the coup was executed. The price which Mir Qasim had to pay was the cession of three districts for the maintenance of EIC troops and donations worth over £200,000 to the obliging 'English gentlemen', amongst whom Holwell was promised over £20,000 personally. Relations were soon uneasy. Mir Qasim refused to be a puppet. He reorganised his army on European lines, with uniforms, with regular, drilled battalions, and with muskets, manufactured in India, which were actually better than those used by the EIC troops. But he had relinquished to the Company about a third of all his revenue from land. He was short of money to support his own power. His attempts to collect his legitimate duties from commerce ran him slap against the private interests of the Company's employees, who claimed the right to trade everywhere duty free.[149]

A characteristic figure of this phase was one William Bolts, Dutch in origin, who arrived in Bengal as a factor in 1760 and made £90,000 in six years. He entered partnership with two members of the Calcutta Council, both Scots, John Johnstone and William Hay, and they pushed their trade ruthlessly, avoiding customs, and forcing native merchants and shopkeepers to take their goods at 30 or even 50 per cent above market price. Mir Qasim was soon complaining bitterly of EIC 'gentlemen' such as these who were establishing new 'factories' everywhere and robbing the peasant by paying ridiculously low prices for produce. London policy was to strengthen the Nawab's authority in Bengal as an alternative to direct involvement in government. Vansittart, aware of this, and conciliatory, made a treaty with Mir Qasim. This was grossly advantageous to the Company – in future English merchants were to pay 9 per cent on all goods in transit, Indian merchants 30 to 40 per cent – and, in honour of his diplomacy, Vansittart accepted from the Nawab a present of £70,000. He and his one supporter in 'moderate' policies, a young man named Warren Hastings, were denounced as the Nawab's 'hired solicitors' by other members of the Calcutta Council, which refused to accept the deal. EIC men, it declared, would henceforward pay only 2½ per cent on one commodity only, salt.[150]

Mir Qasim retorted by freeing all trade from duty, depriving the EIC of special advantage. The Council, in July 1763, decided on war. It found that victories now cost more than in Clive's day. The British and their Sepoys defeated Mir Qasim but only by hard fighting in four pitched battles. The Nawab fled to the province of Oudh and allied himself with the ruler there, and with the new titular Emperor Shah Alam (the former Shahzada). The EIC now reinstalled Mir Jafar, who agreed to all their bullying demands, including a limitation of his army. But the threat from Oudh remained, and the Company's own army seemed on the verge of dissolution because the soldiers, like their employers, saw a generous rake-off as their right. First European troops mutinied because they had not received their share of the money promised by Mir Jafar, then the Sepoys revolted in turn when they found out that each of them was to get only six rupees compared to forty rupees for each white private, returning to duty only on promise that the ratio would be adjusted to one to two.[151]

After months of inconclusive campaigning, a fresh commander, Major Hector Munro, found the Sepoys mutinous once more, and restored order by having twenty-four ringleaders blown from the mouths of guns – a spectacular punishment, copied from the Mughals, which scattered blood, bones and brains over a wide radius. Then he moved against Mir Qasim and defeated him at Baksar, in Oudh, on October 23, 1764. This victory was far more costly than Plassey. The EIC suffered 847 casualties out of about 7,000 men.[152] But their ablest opponent, well backed, had been decisively defeated. Mir Qasim vanished into obscurity. The Emperor came to terms with the EIC.

Mir Jafar's restoration cost his treasury (and ultimately the people of Bengal) £375,000 due to the EIC's armed forces, £300,000 in compensation for the

Company's losses, or supposed losses, in the war with Mir Qasim, and up to £530,000 for 'losses' by individuals, including Vansittart and his councillors. The directors in London now got round at last to banning acceptance of presents from native rulers. But when Mir Jafar died early in 1765, the opportunity was irresistible. In full knowledge of the new ruling, the Council recognised Mir Jafar's son Najm-ud-daula as Nawab, insisted on his appointing Muhammad Reza Khan as his chief minister, and creamed off over £100,000 in donations from both these parties and from others involved. The rapacious Johnstone got about £36,000. It was the last grand haul of its sort. In the political changes since 1757, perhaps £2,500,000 had fallen as 'presents' into British hands.[153] From now on the nawabship mattered less and less. It would pass, through deaths, from Najm to a second son of Mir Jafar's, then, in 1769, to a third son aged only 12. The resources granted to the incumbent by the EIC would be halved, and then soon halved again. That rupee tree could bear no more shaking. Meanwhile Lord Clive was sent as plenipotentiary to Bengal with instructions to check EIC rapacity.

Clive had returned to England in 1760 to find the EIC in the throes of transformation. Since the reorganisation of Queen Anne's day, there had been very little drama in its internal politics. Under the constitution then established, the Court of Directors, consisting of twenty-four persons, each holding over £2,000 in EIC stock, summoned a General Court at least once every quarter, or whenever one was demanded by nine or more of the shareholders who were entitled to vote – those with over £500 stock. The EIC had been a safe, even 'dull' investment, attracting money from the landed classes, from charities, from trusts, and from hard-headed Dutchmen. Every year the outgoing directors had submitted their own list of nominees to the General Court, which, thanks to the mechanics of patronage, had obligingly voted for it. The Company and the ministries led by Walpole and the Pelhams had found each other mutually useful. The EIC had given successive governments leverage in the politics of the City of London, and a modest reservoir of patronage which could help them buy Commons votes.

The virtual acquisition of Bengal transformed the scene from calm to tempest. Directorships now seemed worth hard struggle to get, since their holders shared between themselves the appointments of new Writers and factors, and more and more people wanted to send their sons East. Even Lord Bute, like other aristocrats, now sought and got a Writership for his son. Under pressure from people whose support they sought in Company politics, the directors raised the total of covenanted 'civil' servants in Bengal from 70-odd to 250 in some sixteen years after 1760, while the increase in officers in the Company's army was even more rapid and sudden. In 1772, it would cost a young Scot named Charles Grant no less than £5,000 to acquire a Writership on the black market which was opened by certain directors, though £2,000 or £3,000 would be a commoner figure.[154] Other directors preferred to serve their own families, or their political supporters.

Each lucky young sprig sent out needed further help from home once he reached India, so that he could leapfrog swiftly into the senior posts where most money was to be made. Control of the Court was therefore sharply contested. And the government could not stand aloof; it wanted its own share of the spoils.

In the spring of 1758, a fiercely contested election produced a new Court of Directors which elected Laurence Sulivan Chairman. He held this post for the next six years. He was an Irishman, sprung from a County Cork family which had produced many outlaws and soldiers of fortune. He had tried his own luck in Bombay and had risen in the EIC through sheer competence. Though he had brought back a modest fortune he would boast that he had never accepted a present worth more than £20. Bombay had not been a lush pasture. He had seen an India very different from Clive's, one of cautious commerce awed by native power. Sulivan used his position in the Company to send East his only son and three other young Sulivan kinsmen, but by prevailing standards he was not corrupt. A contemporary said that his 'ruling passion' was the 'vanity of being supposed the head of the India Company and the power of giving protection to his friends in the Company's service.'[155] Towards that end, he was coldly unscrupulous.

Clive had begun to build up his own small family party in the Commons, seeking political power at home. But the need to defend Mir Jafar's great gift of the *jaghir* diverted him into sordid EIC feuding. Many Company men envied him. The source of his huge annual income from the *jaghir* was revenues which the Nawab might otherwise have used to make good his debts to the Company. Clive could thus be accused of virtually pilfering from his own employers. Sulivan seems to have blackmailed Clive with threats of confiscation. Clive threw in his lot with other 'nabobs' who had returned from the East with grievances against Sulivan and who now formed a clear party, the 'Bengal Squad', in Company politics. In 1763 the contest with Sulivan for control was joined.

Politicians involved themselves. Henry Fox, the Paymaster-General, put the government's weight, and his own department's funds, behind Sulivan. Rockingham and other opposition whigs took up voting qualifications in the EIC. Both sides went in for 'vote-splitting', whereby a large holder of stock nominally divided it among friends and supporters so as to create new voters. The price of shares soared. Sulivan triumphed in the elections. The Bengal Council was ordered to stop the payment to Clive of his *jaghir*.

Clive now offered his Commons votes to the government if it would get his *jaghir* back for him. Though Ministry money was switched to his side in the 1764 elections, there was hardly enough of it this time to sway the result. What saved Clive was news of the war against Mir Qasim. At the General Court in March, worried proprietors clamoured that the heaven-born general should be sent back to Bengal. He told them that he would return only if the directors shared their enthusiasm, and this influenced the elections next month.

Though there was a dead heat, Sulivan could not secure re-election as chairman, and backed out defeated, leaving Clive's party in command. A ballot followed in which, by nearly three to two, the shareholders agreed that Clive should enjoy his *jaghir* for ten more years.

Clive arrived in Madras, after a voyage of nearly a year, to find that the military work had been done for him. Munro's victory at Baksar left him with no great military role, only the prospect of further political glory. This he was perfectly ready to grasp. He swiftly concluded that the EIC must become the Nawabs of Bengal themselves, 'in Fact, if not in Name'. Even so, he disapproved of Munro's having advanced so far towards Delhi. 'I mean absolutely to bound our Possessions, Assistance and Conquests to Bengal ... '156

The position in North India was now such that the EIC might have taken control of all Hindustan. In 1761, the Afghans had decisively beaten the Marathas at Panipat to the north of Delhi. Then they had gone home with their plunder. Delhi and the Punjab were left without government. Only three powers had survived; the Rohilla Afghans to the north-east of Delhi, Shuja-ud-daula of Oudh, and the Emperor Shah Alam. At Baksar, two of these had been defeated. Clive might have led the Company's troops to Lahore. But that would have been to flout the Company's interests, which were also, substantially, his own. What the shareholders who had acclaimed him had wanted was peaceful commerce only. More fighting might bankrupt the EIC.

Clive came swiftly to terms with the beaten powers. Though the EIC troops had overrun all Oudh, Shuja was given back his dominions. Shah Alam accepted the districts of Kora and Allahabad, and an offer of tribute from the EIC. In return, he gave, in August 1765, the *diwani* of Bengal, without limit in time – complete control of all the province's finances. The EIC now became a direct vassal of the Mughal, and this convenient fiction would be maintained for decades, with each coin which the Company struck bearing the Emperor's image.

Neither in the short nor the long run did this arrangement work as Clive had intended. Though Shah Alam and Shuja did form a buffer of allied states against the menace from Afghans and Marathas, the EIC would soon be at war again. To defend a frontier, it transpired, meant conquest, defence of a new frontier, then fresh conquest. Clive underrated the expense, civil as well as military, which the *diwani* would entail, and grossly overestimated the likely revenue. It swiftly transpired that rule in Bengal could only be paid for by pitiless extortion and the ruination of the rich province. Clive was still a guerrilla, not a sage staff officer; he saw a problem before him, improvised, and then left before the consequences were plain.

Outwardly, though, this was a new Clive. He had promised to cleanse the 'Augoean [sic] Stables'. He avowed that he was 'determined' to return without having acquired 'one Farthing Addition' to his fortune. (Though in fact he sent home some £165,000 to add to his pile.) He aimed to convince the shareholders

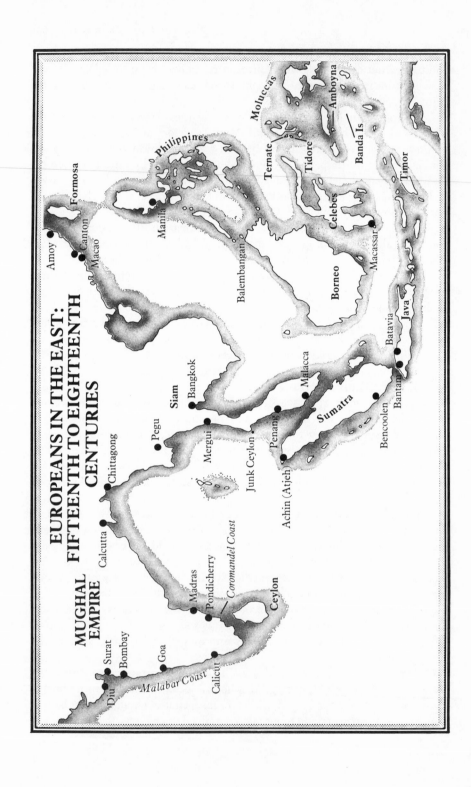

EUROPEANS IN THE EAST:
FIFTEENTH TO EIGHTEENTH
CENTURIES

MUGHAL EMPIRE

Amoy
Formosa
Macao
Canton
Manila
Philippines
Moluccas
Ternate
Tidore
Amboyna
Banda Is
Celebes
Macassar
Timor
Borneo
Balembangan
Batavia
Java
Bantam
Sumatra
Bencoolen
Malacca
Penang
Junk Ceylon
Achin (Atjeh)
Bangkok
Siam
Pegu
Mergui
Chittagong
Calcutta
Madras
Pondicherry
Coromandel Coast
Ceylon
Surat
Bombay
Goa
Diu
Calicut
Malabar Coast

of his 'disinterestedness'. While he lived in even greater state than six years before, and rewarded his personal staff more than lavishly, by his own accounting his governorship, this time, would leave him several thousand pounds out of pocket.[157]

Almost his first action in Bengal was to make Company servants sign covenants binding them not to take presents. They might keep up to about £100 without permission, and up to about £400 if governor and council consented – but anything larger must be handed over to the EIC. Men used to thinking in terms of tens of thousands were outraged by these restrictions, not least because they were pressed by someone with Clive's record. But he saw that rapacity could only be checked if the EIC paid its servants more; while a councillor's official salary was only £300 a year, one could hardly keep up appearances here for less than £3,000. So he put the lucrative salt, betel nut and tobacco trades under a new trading company closely controlled by the council in which all the Company's principal civil and military servants were given shares. This secured them a general annual income, at the expense of Bengal's inhabitants, who paid outrageous prices for their salt. Though the directors soon quashed this scheme, Clive had clarified the principle which would make British rule in the East exorbitantly expensive to the natives; men must be paid so that they could live not only in comfort but in splendour.

Clive's reform of the Bengal army provoked yet another mutiny. Discipline was tightened. The officer cadre was increased. Clive insisted on officers staying with their regiments, learning the language of the Sepoys, and studying the habits of their men. And he hit them in their pockets. By custom, officers in India claimed batta, an allowance intended to make good the extra cost of living in the field rather than in a garrison. After Plassey, Mir Jafar had paid it as well as the EIC and 'double batta' had become normal. Clive now aimed to reduce Bengal batta to the Madras level. Though a Maratha advance was expected, officers in all the three main garrisons tried to resist by simultaneous resignation. Clive worsted them by characteristically swift and courageous action. Loyal Sepoys were used to frighten white officers into submission with their muskets. Seven officers were cashiered, but the rest, chastened, returned to their duties.

Having charged so hard and so fast at so many problems, Clive suffered one of his nervous and physical collapses. Though the Court of Directors implored him to stay, he sailed home from Calcutta early in 1767. His brusque moves in Bengal had made many enemies for him there, and the aftermath of his second governorship, gave their abuse much scope. News of the diwani, which he imagined would be so profitable, had sparked off a boom in EIC stock, which rose in a year or so from 164 to 273. Speculators sought to manipulate Company affairs in their own interests and acquired great leverage through another round of 'vote splitting'. Their sordid manipulation coincided with chaos and suffering in Bengal itself; both raised acutely the question of whether a private trading company should be allowed to control a distant alien province. Clive wrote to an EIC friend in 1769: 'Our wide and extended possessions are become too great for the mother country, or for our abilities, to manage. America is making great strides towards independency; so is Ireland. The East Indies also, I think, cannot remain long to us, if our present constitution be not altered.'[158]

Some of the 'King's Friends' were already thinking in terms of parliamentary control of India. The looters of Bengal, like the smugglers of Massachusetts, must be brought under sovereign power. The EIC was technically no more, even now, than a *diwan* of the Mughal Empire. The age shrank back from interference with Property above all things, and the ousting of India House from control could be represented as a vicious invasion of private rights, but it seemed clear enough that the administration, so pressed for funds that it had to tax American tea, must lay hands on some part at least of the fabled profits from the *diwani*. Chatham called it a 'gift from heaven'. And meanwhile something had to be done to regulate the internal affairs of a company which, twice in eight months, raised its dividends to satisfy speculators. So in 1767 five separate reforming Acts were passed. Dividends were regulated. The EIC was obliged to pay £400,000 a year to the national exchequer for the privilege of retaining its territorial acquisitions.

In the 1769 election of directors, Laurence Sulivan clawed his way back to the top after a furore of vote creation which had more than doubled the number of electors in a year. Then a sudden fall in the price of stock brought many investors to the brink of ruin, and put Sulivan and his allies in the awkward position of having stock still 'split' in the hands of people to whom they were pledged to pay the old, top price. The cause of this disaster was the victory of Hydar Ali over the EIC in the Carnatic.

This region was naturally less rich than Bengal and offered less temptation to unscrupulous traders. EIC personnel therefore enriched themselves by usury. At the fall of Pondicherry in 1761, their puppet Nawab, Muhammad Ali, had owed the EIC vast sums for the help of their soldiers. Over the years, some was paid back, but the Nawab's position worsened continually, as virtually every Company man in Madras obligingly lent him money at very high local rates of interest, ranging up to 45 per cent, till his debts to them exceeded his original obligation to their employers. John Call, an engineer officer, found his dealings with the Nawab so profitable that he was able, on his return, to set up a banking house in London and buy a seat in the Commons; John Macpherson, son of a Skye clergyman, kinsman to the author of *Ossian*, advanced himself towards his eventual governor-generalship of British India; but the manager of all, king spider, was Paul Benfield, another engineer, whose money-lending made him personal paymaster to the Nawab and put him beyond the control of any Company governor.

Since the Nawab met his creditors' claims by assigning to them revenues from his land, the seizure of fresh territories for him – eyes fell again on the Kingdom of Tanjore – became a prime aim for EIC personnel. They met their match in Hydar Ali, a brave, able, ambitious and unscrupulous adventurer who had usurped power in Mysore, westward of the Carnatic, and now menaced every neighbouring state. His bribes winkled native allies away and left the EIC facing alone Hydar's powerful army joined with that of the Nizam of Hyderabad. He ravaged the Carnatic up to the very outskirts of Madras, where the doors and window frames of the 'garden houses' erected for recreation by EIC men made camp fires for his scarlet-clad lancers.

So, in 1769, peace was made on Hydar Ali's terms, which included a defensive alliance, but could not stabilise the situation. Hydar remained a natural rival of the Nizam and of the Marathas. Prudence, and its shareholders' interests, should have kept the EIC aloof from entanglements. But the interests of the Nawab's creditors overrode sagacity in Madras. In 1773, the Benfield gang had its way. The Madras Council helped the Nawab annex Tanjore, and his creditors gratefully guzzled that kingdom's revenues.

The situation in Bengal had been even more scandalous. Clive's *diwani* had meant that the EIC had to act as revenue collector over the whole province. It had insufficient European personnel, and in any case its men were ignorant of the customs of Indian rural society. Hence the so-called 'dual system' was adopted, whereby Muhammad Reza Khan acted as deputy (*naib diwan*). This man was himself an outsider, Persian by birth, but deeply devoted to Mughal traditions of government and to the interests, as he saw them, of the Nawab, to whom he was chief minister. He was also a firm upholder of the rights of the *zemindars*. These were the rural landholders whose role under Mughal rule was that of subordinate revenue gatherers, but who could with some stretch of the imagination be compared to the English nobility and squirearchy; Reza Khan himself insisted that they were 'masters of their own lands' whom their ruler might punish but not dispossess.[159] Ironically, he provided the Company's servants with a mask and a scapegoat as they attacked Bengal's social structure, shoving *zemindars* aside and ruining numerous native traders.

Since Plassey, and as a result of that victory, British involvement in Bengal's internal trade had vastly increased. The salt pans, for instance, had largely been taken over by Europeans. Whites had set up trading posts everywhere whence their *gumashtas* (native agents) used armed terror, if need be, to exercise independent authority over the natives, to drive out rivals, to regulate prices. Hitherto remote frontier districts had been invaded by ruthless adventurers, and from 1765 such men also moved into Oudh. Some Indians, collaborating with the British, were able to thrive handsomely, but other formerly prosperous merchants and bankers were hard hit, and the cultivators and artisans were helpless before the crudest British exploitation. Salt prices soared while the rewards of those who made salt remained stationary. Bihar poppy-growers received lower prices than before Plassey. Weavers' incomes, it seems, were driven down. The rewards for Britons were commonly enormous. John Johnstone, after his sordid adventures, went home to Scotland worth £300,000, a fortune probably second only to Clive's. While many junior servants died hopelessly in debt, others rapidly made fortunes, like another Scot, Alexander Campbell, a former journalist who arrived in 1763 and left Bengal four years later with £30,000 and 'a contented mind'. Altogether, at least £15 million seem to have been sent home from Bengal by British individuals between Plassey and 1784 – compared with only about £3 million over the previous half century.[160]

Francis Sykes, who said once that his actions regarding money were guided by a simple question – 'It was this, whether it should go into a blackman's pocket or my own' – used his position as resident at the Nawab's court and Company watchdog over Reza Khan to further his private interests as against those of other EIC men. Under cover of Reza Khan's name, for instance, he ousted Richard Barwell, no mean pocketer himself, from the timber trade. Barwell virtuously wrote home that the country had 'absolutely been plundered' by those appointed to collect taxes. Reza Khan himself protested that looting adventurers interfered with collection through their native agents, who seized revenue at source on the pretext of debts due to them, and were terrorising the peasants into flight.[161]

A very serious trade recession set in by early 1768. Reza Khan was soon announcing that every branch of Bengal's foreign commerce had been wrecked and that business was 'almost to a total stand'. The revenues were 'extorted rather than collected.' Harry Verelst, Clive's successor as governor, had enough sense to point out to his masters at home that they could not 'act on the level of mere merchants' now that they ruled Bengal directly. To gather a huge revenue without 'possessing an adequate protective power over the people who pay it' would be 'highly injurious to our national character.'[162] The sanctimonious principle of 'trusteeship', by which the British would later excuse their rule over coloured races, was thus adumbrated in Bengal by a man who could see before his eyes the evidence that, if labouring taxpayers were ruined, the goose which laid the golden eggs would be killed. No 'protection', no profit. Verelst decided to put British 'supervisors' into the rural districts. Naturally, Company servants scrambled to get these posts, seeing yet further chances for graft and extortionate trade.

Nemesis came. Two sparse crops of rice were followed by the failure of grain and pulse crops. An epidemic ensued. Estimates of mortality range up to half of the rural population. Ten million people may have perished in 1769 and 1770. The EIC had not caused the drought and did not itself spread germs, but its conduct had helped to ensure low morale and low resistance – and its employees, not implausibly, were accused of heartless profiteering in rice. Whole tracts of Bengal were abandoned to waste, and desperate survivors took to armed robbery. The trading recession deepened, and its effects were still felt in the mid-1770s.[163]

Remorseless squeezing meant that the value of goods shipped home from the EIC to Britain, which had stood at £437,000 in 1765–6, was up to £633,000 during the famine year, and to £904,000 in 1770–1. One contemporary calculated that Bengal was losing £1½ million annually through her trade with Europe and that specie was draining out at the rate of £500,000 a year. Yet the Company at home was soon in a desperate situation.

Administration in the East was costing more, partly thanks to fears of French resurgence and consequent mounting military expenses, but also because of escalating EIC payrolls. The number of Company servants in the East tripled, as we have seen, in some sixteen years. And pay and allowances had been increased, so that the average given per man was three times as high in 1774 as in 1757; £455 as compared with under £150. Yet between 1767 and 1771, collections of revenue fell by £400,000. Staff in Bengal financed increased purchases by raising money on bills of exchange drawn on the EIC in London. The EIC's weakness was exposed in that general credit crisis of 1772–3 which sent Scottish craftsmen and Ulster weavers migrating in such numbers to America (where the Company's affairs would have momentous side-effects, as a vastly increased surplus of tea in its London warehouses coincided with a drop in sales largely due to smuggling on both sides of the Atlantic). Books and pamphlets broadcast indignation through Britain at the horrors heard of from Bengal. Sulivan had been trying to get through the Company's own Bill for reorganising its affairs. The Commons would not have it. Instead, General Burgoyne, denouncing 'the most atrocious abuses that ever stained the name of civil government', carried a motion for a select committee to investigate matters. Though the EIC had kept its dividends up at 12½ per cent, it found itself compelled, in August 1772, to ask the government for a loan of £1 million. Now something simply had to be done.[164]

In 1770, George III had at last acquired a prime minister whom he liked. Chatham's resignation in 1768 had left power in the hands of the Duke of Grafton, who was pushed to resign in turn by a brief unification of the opposition. Lord North replaced him. He suited the King because he was pliable, and remained in office for twelve years because, whenever he wished to resign, George would not permit it. A lazy man with no strong views of his own, let alone any original ones, North, generous, affable and amusing, was very popular and effective in the Commons (where he sat despite his courtesy title).

When North moved successfully for the appointment of a 'committee of secrecy' to consider India, this meant that there were two parliamentary committees in existence. The eighteen reports which they produced between them all damned the EIC. 'India,' Chatham concluded, 'teems with iniquities so rank, as to smell to earth and heaven.' By March 1773, the Company was again petitioning for support, this time for £1½ million. The Commons resolved that all territorial acquisitions abroad did 'of right belong to the State.' In June, two Acts were passed. One gave the EIC a loan, on certain conditions. The other, 'North's Regulating Act', struck at vote-splitting by raising the qualification for voters in the EIC Court to £1,000 in stock, held for at least twelve months; it ruled that the directors should be elected for four-year stints, with a quarter resigning each year, to remain at least one year out of office; and it remodelled government in India. Military rationalisation was a prime consideration. A governor-general in Calcutta, assisted by a council of four, was to have power to superintend all three presidencies in the making of war and peace, though in civilian matters he would rule only in Bengal. Salaries were to be generous beyond precedent – £25,000 to the governor-general, £10,000 to each of his councillors, £8,000 to the chief justice in the new Supreme Court which was to be founded. The directors of the EIC were to lay open to the government all their correspondence with India.

Before its passage, the measure was fiercely attacked by the Rockingham faction. Edmund Burke had been for several years a stern opponent of State intervention (a position not unconnected with the fact that he and his relatives had been part of an important group of speculators in EIC stock) and he denounced North's Bill fiercely as an 'infringement of national right, national faith and national justice.' But the Bill passed the Commons with only twenty-one dissentients, the Lords with only seventeen. It remained in force for eleven critical years.[165]

It probably went as far as could have been gone. The government, which was failing so badly to keep America under control, could hardly have extended its own administrative machinery to India as well. As it was, the Treasury 'managed' the EIC and bribed its directors with contracts and other lollipops, while the government now had disposal of a fixed proportion of the posts in the Company's service.

But fresh storms were inevitable. One reason was the unsatisfactory nature of the provisions laid down in 1773 for government under the EIC in India. Another was the strong feeling in Britain against 'nabobs'.

Clive, the chief scapegoat, emerged from several bitter attacks in the Commons free from the threat of prosecution but politically thwarted; public odium blocked his way to high office. Plagued by bad health, late in 1774, the victor of Plassey obliged his execrators by cutting his throat with a penknife during one of his fits of depression. Of course the rumour went round that a guilty conscience had killed him, and even the sage Dr Johnson was glad to believe it.[166]

On the question of India, men otherwise opposed might find themselves in perverse agreement. While the great slave-owner William Beckford bellowed in the Commons against 'rapine and oppression', humanitarian feeling shuddered over Bengal as it did over the capture and sale of Africans. The idea that national guilt must bring God's vengeance was played on when Burgoyne, moving for his select committee, pictured both India and Great Britain 'sunk and overwhelmed never to rise again.'[167] The Clives, for all their wealth, were snubbed in polite society and had to fall back on the company of other 'nabobs'.

The word, a corruption of 'nawab', carried with it, besides connotations of ill-got wealth and social climbing, the reek of 'Asiatic' despotism and cruelty. It fitted, for instance, such an absurd yet disturbing figure as General Richard Smith of the EIC army, the son of a cheesemonger who comported himself with haughty insolence. People in Britain beheld with disgust a spate of such upstarts buying their way into fine country estates and Commons seats. William Sumner, who received about £25,000 after Mir Qasim's succession to the nawabship, eventually became sheriff of Surrey. William Watts's daughter by a Eurasian woman married Charles Jenkinson, a leading 'King's Friend', who later made her Countess of Liverpool and the mother of a future prime minister. Just as gentlefolk were horrified to hear that some nine families out of ten were now drinking tea twice a day and so aping their betters, they flinched from the 'nabobs' as from agents of social upheaval, insurrectionists. They could rational-ise their reaction as pious horror at unchristian habits – these men of vulgar birth slept in the East with Muslim mistresses and returned with livers diseased by excessive drinking. More to the point, the 'nabobs' had grown used to inordinate opulence and pomp such as great noblemen scarce afforded at home. A wealthy squire in the Home Counties might have a dozen or so servants. In Bengal, a mere advocate would maintain more than three score. Bombay was a far poorer place than Calcutta, yet a Scottish footman who went there with his master in 1771–2 noted that a commandant of artillery 'had as many atten-dants about him as a royal or a noble prince in England.'[168]

Napoleon's upstart aristocracy springs to mind. Revolutions can create such classes. But the nabobs inserted themselves into the British social structure with much friction yet no violence. A nineteenth-century author would neatly call the East India Company's service a 'great Monarchy of the Middle Classes.' Writers for the commercial side, cadets for the army, were drawn overwhelm-ingly from the very strata which elsewhere in Europe made revolution. Mer-chants, traders and professional people found opportunities there for sons who might otherwise in frustration have shouted 'Wilkes and Liberty' or, later, more dangerous slogans. Warren Hastings, named as governor-general in the text of North's Regulating Act, was in no doubt that India could be a useful vent. Proposing, in 1777, a grand scheme for consolidating British power there, he argued, 'It will afford employment and support to the middle class of the subjects of Great Britain, whose services are less required at home than those of the lower rank of life.'[169]

While other EIC servants mimicked in turn the Mughal rulers of the East and the aristocratic grandees of Britain, Hastings went in for negative ostentation. He flaunted his middle-classness. If his adored wife wore gorgeous plumage, well, that was the case in many hard-working bourgeois families. His secretary, returning home with Hastings's portrait, remarked that he feared that people would not believe that the great governor of whom they had heard so much was 'but a plain looking man like any of us, with a brown coat'. He drank wine only if necessary, and then mixed it with water, ate no supper and went to bed at ten. Shy and reserved, dry in his humour, rather pompous, he must nowadays infallibly have become the paragon of university Vice-Chancellors. His curiosity, in the academic manner, was both eager and dispassionate. In his eighties he would take great (if perhaps amused) interest in the ideas of Robert Owen. Politically, he was always a man of the new age, though touched with a some-what romantic feeling for 'ancient nobility'.[170] He had something in common with Jefferson, John Adams, and other American revolutionaries.

But India gave him a very different direction. He gained immense power without having to force his way up through the compact indignant ranks of the governing classes, though at last he fell foul of the rage which the 'democratical' raree-show of a man in a plain brown coat sending armies hither and thither, commanding in war against the French, making treaties, exerting power without majesty, must evoke in the bosoms of whig aristocrats.

He came from a ruined West Country landowning family. His mother was merely the daughter of a farmer. She died giving him birth, in 1732. His father a clergyman, then abandoned his children and went off to Barbados. As a boy, Hastings resolved that one day he would buy back the family manor, Dayles-ford, which had been sold in 1715. An uncle's charity sent him to Westminster School. When Hastings was fifteen, this uncle died, and the more distant relative to whose care he now fell, having some influence in the EIC, found him the Writership which took him to Calcutta in 1750. Organising a sub-factory in a rural district, Hastings developed an unusual gift for understanding and getting on with Indians. He became fluent in Bengali, learnt some Persian, and acquired a good knowledge of Urdu. He was still only 25 when he succeeded Luke Scrafton as representative at the Nawab's court. The dirty work had been done. Hastings soon thought that enough was enough, and made himself very unpopular by his support for the Nawab, Mir Qasim. In 1764, he went home with a fortune modest by 'nabob' standards. Whereas the rapacious John John-stone returned next year worth £300,000, Hastings had £30,000, and of this only £5,000 came with him to Britain. In 1767, he heard that the rest, unwisely invested, had all been lost. The notorious Sykes interceded for him with Clive, remarking that Hastings's finances were 'more to the credit of his moderation than knowledge of the world. He is almost literally worth nothing, and must return to India or want bread.'[171] The EIC sent Hastings to Fort St George as Second in the Council, with the prospect of succeeding to the presidency. On the voyage out he fell in love with Baroness Imhoff, the wife of a German portrait painter. Hastings was later able to marry her, and remained devoted to her for fifty years.

Hastings alone, among EIC men in Madras, took no part in the custom of profiteering from the Nawab of the Carnatic's debts. But his motivations were not of unmixed purity. He had no skill in book-keeping and his private finances were always in confusion. However, he wanted to make money. The wish to keep Mrs Hastings in appropriate style joined his old desire to buy back

Daylesford. The East had taught him to judge his fellow men, not by the exalted standards of a Jefferson, but in terms of subtle shades of distinction. He had never lamented, he once remarked drily, 'that all men were not as virtuous and disinterested as myself.' He helped allies who had made vast pickings to send them home, then to cover their tracks. When governor-general he told an intimate, 'as to my friends, I shall be glad to serve them', though he added, 'as to my friends' friends I neither can nor will serve them.' He wished to serve Britain as well. He was loyal to the EIC and to its interests as he conceived them. Such spurs were fiercer with him than with most men. So was an interest in administration. The arts of government delighted him. 'I have catched the desire of applause in public life', he once informed the EIC directors. An enemy's verdict perhaps gets close to his centre – 'fond of power but despises wealth.'[172]

In other historical contexts, such men have striven to reshape whole societies. This the East of his day would not permit. Hastings's inconsistencies, his elusiveness, reflect the enormity of India, where the EIC, now the strongest single power, could not, however, control the situation. Shifting and unpredictable realities encouraged him to make opportunistic responses. Now one motive, now another, would seem to predominate. His genuine liking for some Indians, and his respect for native institutions, could be overridden by real political pressures. The British around him were untameable. So many men had political ties at home and might use them to undo his work or unseat him. Support had to be bought by posts and contracts. Friends of Sulivan ruined in the financial disasters of 1769 and 1772–3 had to be set on their feet by his patronage. All this made his government of Bengal costly and burdensome to its people.

He was confident of his own integrity. 'I do not know a man,' he told Sulivan, 'who may be more safely entrusted with extraordinary powers than myself.' His favourite maxims from the Hindu *Gita* – 'Let the Motive be in the Deed, and not in the Event. Be not one whose motive for Action is the Hope of Reward. Perform thy Duty. Abandon all thought of the consequence' – provided, in practice, a recipe for antinomianism.[173] Whatever he thought he must do was right. Whoever stood in his way – European, Muslim, Hindu – was wrong and might be attacked and pursued vindictively.

His task was to maintain British power in India. He did not believe that this could be liked by the natives. He did not think that it could endure for long: 'The dominion exercised by the British Empire in India is fraught with many radical and incurable defects, besides those to which all human institutions are liable, arising from the distance of its scene of operations, the impossibility of furnishing it at all times with those aids which it requires from home, and the difficulty of reconciling its primary exigencies with those which in all States ought to take place of every other concern, the interests of the people who are subjected to its authority. All that the wisest institutions can effect in such a system can only be to improve the advantages of a temporary possession, and to protract that decay, which sooner or later must end it.' Yet the work of 'dominion' must go firmly on. ' ... The sword which gave us the dominion of Bengal must be the instrument of its preservation.'[174] Hastings worked from day to day, improvising. India was not America, not a New World fit for first principles to act in. It was very old, and its ruling goddess was decay. Hastings's brilliant mind lavished itself upon shifts, manoeuvres and expediencies.

At the end of 1771, the EIC transferred him from Madras to Calcutta as governor. It was trying to put its own house in order, and Hastings was told to enact certain reforms. Though actually in control, the EIC in Bengal nominally governed only a 'curious conglomeration of territories held by a curious variety of titles.' Burdwan, Midnapur and Chittagong, acquired in 1760, were held free of all tribute. In Calcutta and the '24 Parganas', the EIC was *zemindar*, handing an annual revenue to the Nawab. Over the rest of Bengal, Bihar and Orissa the EIC held the *diwani*, paying at this time twenty-six lakhs of rupees annually to the Emperor, thirty-two lakhs to the Nawab, and retaining the rest. The actual administration of all territories was in the hands of two *naib diwans*, Muhammad Reza Khan in Bengal, Shitab Rai in Bihar. The aim now was to make government pay its own way.[175]

Executing orders from home, Hastings abolished the use of 'dustucks' (free passes), suppressed all but five of the custom houses as impediments to the free circulation of merchandise, and lowered the duty on almost all goods to 2½ per cent, payable by Europeans as well as Asians. The purpose of these liberal reforms was to revive the trade of the province. Hastings was also charged with sweeping away the 'dual system' so that the EIC itself took full responsibility for the whole civil administration. Sacrificial victims were necessary. Though Hastings believed Shitab Rai to be innocent, he had both *naib diwans* arrested and tried for peculation, and employed a notorious forger and intriguer named Nandakumar to find evidence and witnesses against Reza Khan. Both men were eventually acquitted by the Council on all charges.

Tax collecting had in fact, since Plassey, been a grand source of iniquitous gain for whites. The cultivators of Bengal and Bihar, over all of whom the EIC stood as *diwan*, paid over £2 million every year. Such rapacious men as Johnstone and Bolts had obtained tax-farms under the native *zemindars* and had creamed off enormous sums at the expense both of peasants and EIC. Then the white Collectors sent in by Verelst had commonly seized with glee opportunities for straightforward embezzlement, for the levying of extra cesses for their own personal profit, and for the receipt of *nazrs* (cf. protection money) from *zemindars*, from tax-farmers, and from their own native subordinates. Furthermore, *zemindars* had always borrowed money in advance of their receipts, and whites in the nascent Revenue Department now operated as creditors, charging interest at rates up to 180 per cent. Hastings believed that Collectorships had become 'more lucrative than any posts in the service.'

The game was not quite over, though Hastings replaced Verelst's district

'Supervisors' with Provincial Revenue Councils and though, under the Regulating Act, all EIC servants concerned in revenue collection were prohibited from all trade. Profiteering from tax-gathering went on, as did gross and blatant frauds in the 'Commercial Department', to which Hastings turned a blind eye. His principle, like Clive's, was that servants should be given official emoluments so large that the temptation to cheat would weaken. After the Regulating Act, he himself was much higher paid than any British public official save the Lord Lieutenant of Ireland, and when, in 1781, he remodelled tax collection, setting up a Committee of Revenue, its members, rewarded by commission, would legitimately take about £10,000 a year. Under his rule, average earnings in the Bengal 'civil' service would more than triple in seven years, to £2,261 in 1783 – far higher than salaries in the British Treasury, where a Chief Clerk took home £800. Steady income from work done for the Company would begin to replace, for men coming to India, the gambling impulse which had done so much damage. Great swift fortunes were now hard to make. As the true resources of Bengal's various districts became better known to the Company, it would be more difficult for Collectors to take a large cut without being noticed. Trade depression and famine had withered the profits from private trade. Various lucrative traffics – in salt, betel nuts, rice, tobacco, opium – were now barred to all Europeans or became EIC monopolies. And the flow of presents had dried up.[176]

The boy Nawab's allowance was halved yet again. But neither public opinion at home nor Hastings's own understanding of India permitted him to destroy all show of native rule. Though he would later confess to having usurped the Nawab's powers over criminal law, he would claim that he had preserved the 'spirit' of the Bengal 'Constitution'. Courts of Justice had to be set up. In each district civil courts and criminal courts were presided over by Verelst's white Collectors, but Hindu experts helped in the civil courts and Muhammadan law governed the second entirely. The Collectorships were soon abolished on orders from home, so that native *diwans* took charge of local justice. The governor and two members of the Council sat as judges in the Civil Court of Appeal at Calcutta, but an Indian presided in the Criminal Court of Appeal, assisted by Muhammadan law officers. The basic principle, as Hastings saw it, was that existing laws should prevail. Muhammadan law was already codified. Hastings now invited ten of the most learned pundits in Bengal to prepare a digest of Hindu law for use in the civil courts. He had this translated and sent extracts to the directors so as to convince them that, as he said, 'the people of this country do not require our aid to furnish them with a rule for their conduct, or a stand for their property.'[177] But, 'Perform thy Duty.' Brigandage must be repressed. Hastings thought Muhammadan law ineffectual, since it permitted sentence of death only if robbery was accompanied by murder, and decided that every convicted *dacoit* should be hanged in his own village, his family made state slaves and his neighbours fined, whatever the court sentences laid down.

In external relations, Hastings's great problem was the position in Oudh. Shuja-ud-daula, the ruler, had prohibited commerce with Bengal for fear that his own province might go the same way, overrun by grasping whites. Hastings's aim was a 'free trade' with Oudh. Events seemed to help him to open the country up. In 1771 the Marathas had reoccupied Delhi and Shah Alam let them install him as Emperor there. They forced him to make over Kora and Allahabad, given to him by Clive in 1765. The EIC promptly discontinued its tribute to him and granted these places to Oudh for fifty lakhs of rupees. Hastings noted with gratification that this deal would make the Vizier of Oudh 'more dependent upon us, as he is more exposed to the hostilities of the Marathas ... '[178] Since the latter claimed Kora and Allahabad, Shuja could not ally with them, and thus should provide Bengal with a permanent buffer. But such hopes of peace did not allow for the machinations of the British military who still squatted in Shuja's domain. The commander-in-chief in Bengal, Sir Robert Barker, was a prime specimen of a military 'nabob'; having grown wealthy trading in saltpetre, diamonds and opium, he made a second fortune out of clothing Shuja's army. He intervened, against Hastings's wishes, in the matter of Rohilkand. This small state, governed by a loose confederacy of Rohilla Afghan chiefs, was invaded by the Marathas in 1772. Prompted by Barker, Shuja agreed to help the Rohillas in return for forty lakhs of rupees. (More cash for British commanders.) As Oudh and EIC forces came in, the Marathas fled. Then the Rohillas refused to pay up on the grounds that there had been no fighting. The EIC directors disliked offensive wars, as Hastings well knew; but Shuja, an ally, must be backed up. There was easy money to be made for the Company. The EIC, in return for forty lakhs, gave Shuja a brigade to help conquer Rohilkand. In April 1774, this was done. Shuja took most of the country, and the small rump state remaining entered into treaty with the EIC.

The proprietors in London were shocked by Hastings's involvement in the Rohilla War. The directors condemned him, but mildly, and they were still pleased that this paragon of (relative) virtue had been named governor-general in India. Hastings would be, as it turned out, the only man to serve as governor-general during the span of North's Act.

XII

In his first year as governor of Bengal, Warren Hastings shipped fifty chests of opium, on his private account, to China. Critical and dramatic though events in India had been, their effect, by making the EIC there primarily a political institution, receiving produce in return for government, was to emphasise the fact that the subcontinent was only a link in the system of trade between Britain and China. The chief value of India was that it produced commodities useful for barter in China and in the Eastern seas. By the end of the Seven Years War Britain had brought home more from Canton than all other European nations combined. Now competition had stiffened again, especially from the Dutch, Danish and Swedish India Companies.

There were serious problems over payment. Bengal opium, like Bombay cotton and Cornish tin, was invaluable. But the main recourse must still be silver, and this must come chiefly from Spanish America, via the sale of British manufactures, directly through Spain, indirectly through the West Indies, or still more indirectly through Spanish purchases from other European customers of Britain. Or through Manila in the Philippines. Mexican silver could be had there in exchange for British goods brought by merchants trading under the colours of some Eastern prince. Taken back to Madras, it could then be sent to Canton. The British conquest of Manila in 1762 had upset this. Though the place was soon handed back, the flow of silver was dammed. In 1768, the government of Madras was complaining, 'our intercourse with the Spaniards no longer subsists', and was crying out for silver from London. Silver was found somehow; an average of £700,000 a year was sent to China by the EIC in the 1780s.[179]

The bullion problem emphasised the importance of opening up trade in Malaya, the East Indies and Indo-China, where British manufactures and Indian piece goods, opium and saltpetre could be exchanged for gold, sago and drugs, for spices, for sugar and for tin, which in turn would command good prices in China. The 1760s saw government, merchants and opportunists aiming towards the Far East, both from India and by way of the Pacific.

In 1760, the governor and council of Madras approved an idea worked out by a Scot named Alexander Dalrymple. Why not set up a mart off Borneo, in the area claimed by the Sultanate of Sulu? Chinese merchants, who were almost all forbidden to deal with foreigners at home, might send their junks to such an entrepôt, and Chinese immigrants might be brought in to work pepper, cinnamon and sugar plantations. In 1763, having made a deal with the Sultan, Dalrymple took possession of the island of Balembangan, and started to introduce Indian and Chinese colonists. Meanwhile, through his diplomatic skill, he was able to gain for the EIC full sovereignty over the whole of the northern tip of Borneo and the adjacent islands, some 20,000 square miles, with the Sultan's son installed to rule as its vassal. But Dalrymple went home to propose even grander schemes. His successor as Chief Resident, John Herbert, settled Balembangan with an expedition from England, built warehouses and wharves, organised a chain of trading posts, and meanwhile, with his colleagues, turned to fraud and speculation. For instance, he sold large quantities of opium to the EIC at 600 dollars a chest, and then on behalf of the Company re-sold it, on long credit, to natives of Sulu at 550 dollars a chest. After little more than a year, in February 1775, the colony was wiped out by a Suluan nobleman, probably anxious to liquidate creditors who were growing too powerful. The whole Borneo venture had lost the EIC £170,000.[180]

A similar scheme had failed in the Strait of Malacca. A private syndicate of

Madras merchants established in 1766 a factory at Achin in North Sumatra where Indian goods were exchanged for Malay goods saleable in China. Malaya was already well known as a source of tin. When a new syndicate took over the Achin factory in 1770, it acquired the chance of a foothold in the Peninsula through Francis Light, one of the factors. The Raja of Kedah, hard pressed by his enemies, offered Light a strip of coast in return for military support. Light pleaded for Sepoys. The Danes, he pointed out, were at hand, and would clinch with the Raja if the British did not. 'Had I authority to act, neither Danes, Dutch, French or any else should drive me out.'[181] The Madras government offered defensive help to Kedah and Achin in return for trading privileges, but the Raja of Kedah wanted to use EIC troops in offensive operations, and when Madras absolutely refused permission, he withdrew his grant to Light. The Sultan of Achin, who had been happy enough with British private traders, did not want to see the great Company established in his territory. By the end of 1772, the Madras authorities had decided to pull out.

Meanwhile, the idea of trade across the Pacific, dormant since Elizabeth's day, was resumed. Besides giving scope to the greatest of all British navigators, it yielded rich farce over the Falkland Islands. These lay east of the Straits of Magellan, two largish pieces of land which, together with islets and rocks, totalled some 4,600 square miles, remote and sun-starved. Westerly winds, often of gale force, brought rain and drizzle for almost nine months of the year. Their moorland and marshland would prove suitable for very little except sheep-farming. Few spots on earth were less attractive to settlement. But they offered large and secure harbours for first rate ships of war. Though Spain claimed both 'Malvinas', Bougainville, for the French, put a settlement on the eastern 'Malouine' in 1764. In the same year the British government sent out Captain Byron to discover unknown lands in southern latitudes, and to search for a North West Passage up the Pacific Coast. He failed to carry out his orders, but he did circumnavigate the globe and did claim a harbour, which he named Port Egmont, on 'West Falkland'.

At first, no government was quite sure that the islands claimed were the same. Were Malvinas, Malouines and Falklands not perhaps different groups?[182] It emerged that they were identical. In 1766 Captain McBride arrived to found a colony at Port Egmont and warned off the French next door for trespassing. The French went next year but out of politeness to Spain. The Spaniards now took over East Falkland and, in 1770, expelled the British colony. The opposition in Britain, in fact delighted, hypocritically shrieked that they were appalled. Chatham, on his most high-fantastical form, revived the old Bourbon bogey, and called for war with Spain, no doubt expecting that if it came the public would hubbub him back into office. For a moment war seemed certain. But France urged concessions on the Spaniards, and Lord North's ministry settled all with a curious deal whereby the Spaniards restored Port Egmont on the understanding that the British would shortly withdraw. In 1771 the British reoccupied the place, in 1774 they quit again, but they left behind them an inscription in lead as a token of British possession, so sustaining a legal wrangle which would recur, off and on, for over two hundred years.

The Pacific Ocean covers more than a third of the earth's entire surface. Since Magellan, voyager after voyager from Europe had crossed it, yet people were sure that somewhere, in temperate latitudes, there must be a great undiscovered southern continent, *Terra Australis*, a new New World. Ancient geographers had insisted that such a landmass was essential to the equilibrium of a spherical earth, and when Marco Polo had written of the riches of the Malayan Peninsula, the text of his *Travels* had wrongly placed it 1,200 miles between south and west of Java. A Frenchman, de Brosses, in 1756, had speculated that while Europeans might have much to learn from the civilised peoples found living on *Terra Australis*, there would be wide open spaces where colonies might be planted without any injury to dispossessed natives, and, rather more prophetically, foresaw a better France rising in the Antipodes, where criminal elements from the old country would be purified. In the 1760s his ideas were published in English by a Scottish plagiarist named Callender.[183]

While the Danish explorer Bering, serving the Russian Tsar, had made sense of the ocean's far north and Russian trappers and seal hunters were already at work in Alaska, such land as had been found in the central and southern Pacific had almost all been lost again. The Solomon Islands, discovered by Mendaña in the 1560s, had never since been revisited. Small specks in a vast ocean could not be accurately charted until secure measurement of longitude at sea was possible. In 1714, the British government had set up a Board of Longitude to adjudicate proposals, and to award, if satisfied, a prize of £20,000. There were now two workable British solutions. One used astronomy, the 'lunar distance' method propounded by Neville Maskelyne in 1763. Another involved a more accurate measure of time on shipboard; in 1764 John Harrison's chronometer passed its first test, a voyage to Barbados.

Some 10,000 islands, very few glimpsed even once by Europeans, lay scattered across some 750,000 square miles of sea. Three different groups of peoples had evolved here, virtually all speaking languages of the 'Austronesian' type. 'Micronesians' lived on west-central Pacific islands. Darker 'Melanesians', some of them almost black, with frizzy hair and broad noses, were ranged in the south-west centre from New Guinea to Fiji. 'Polynesians' inhabited a triangle with its peak in Hawaii, its base on a line between Easter Island and New Zealand, and its western side running between Fiji and Samoa, and of all peoples in the world, they were the greatest masters of basic seafaring. Using stone, coral or shell tools they created huge double canoes a hundred to a hundred and fifty feet in length out of small wooden components fitted and lashed together, and these could voyage for distances vaster than that between London and Boston. In some places they erected impressive stone monuments, such as the mysterious, huge, carved heads of Easter Island. These fair-skinned people were comely by

European standards. Those Europeans who cherished advanced and 'Enlightened' concepts, when they encountered or read about Polynesians, thought at first that their visions of the ideal had been realised.

Captain Samuel Wallis was sent out by the British government to look again for *Terra Australis*. Forced north by the winds west of Chile, he examined only a tiny fraction of the unexplored area where the new continent might still be found. But in 1767 he did reach Tahiti, which he named after King George III and where he and his crew made an idyllic recovery from their hardships. Here were 'noble savages' in the flesh – untouched by the rage for possession, unspoilt by class divisions. Theorisers, enraptured, completely misread Polynesian society. Whereas the Melanesians, far less attractive to European eyes, did live in more or less classless societies, the handsome Polynesians fought cruel inter-tribal wars and had chiefs whose punishments involved ritual sacrifice and cannibalism. On some Polynesian islands, if a commoner touched a chief's shadow he would be killed, and elaborate codes of *tapu* (taboo) were often thus protected by capital punishment. However, this was veiled from intellectuals, in Europe and America, whose idealism was touched by what seemed proof of man's inherent goodness – the charm and friendliness of these 'natural' people. The great French explorer Bougainville, sent out to hand East Falkland over to Spain, was told also to search for the 'Great Southern Continent'. He struck Tahiti nearly a year after Wallis and, using 'lunar distance', Veron, the astronomer with him, established the first accurate longitude for the Philippines, thus showing how wide the ocean really was.

Alexander Dalrymple, quitting his beach-head in Borneo, had returned to Britain in 1765, and stood forth as an enthusiast for the theory of a 'Great Southern Continent' in the most extreme form then possible. New Zealand he averred, was its west coast. Its eastern coast had been sighted many times. It probably had more than fifty million people and covered a greater area than all civilised Asia. The mere 'scraps from this table would be sufficient to maintain the power, dominion, and sovereignty of Britain, by employing all its manufactures and ships.'[184] His notion was that he would discover the Continent himself, and match the achievements of Christopher Columbus.

The transit of the planet Venus across the sun, a rare event, was expected in 1769. It would not recur for a century. If it were accurately observed at widely different points, astronomers might be able to establish the distance of the earth from the sun. The Royal Society of London appealed to George III for help in sending a team to the central Pacific, one of the best posts for observation, and the King, early in 1768, promised £4,000 and a naval ship. Dalrymple, a member of the Royal Society, also a sailor, also a geographer, also an astronomer, saw his chance. The Admiralty, like him, wanted to combine scientific aims with the search for *Terra Australis*. But it could not stomach a civilian, let alone such an opinionated one. Captain James Cook was met by destiny.

Before Cook was appointed, the Admiralty had chosen a Whitby collier as the expedition's ship. This was precisely the kind of vessel on which the captain had learnt the arts of seamanship. His father had migrated from Scotland to Yorkshire, where he had risen from labourer to farm-manager, and where Cook was born in 1728. He attended school long enough to learn reading and writing, worked on the farm under his father, and then in a grocer's shop. He had gone to sea later than most sailors, apprenticed in the coal trade at eighteen. But the ships which plied between the North and London gave an exceptionally good training. They were big (300 to 500 tons), and very strong in construction. Their moderate draught enabled them to make the best use of the shallow harbours and shallow waters along the coast. Every voyage involved pilotage among sands which stretched far into the cold and dangerous North Sea. Cook studied mathematics and navigation in his spare time, developed a self-taught mastery of coastal surveying and in 1755 decided to 'take his future', as he put it, in the Navy.[185] He joined as mere able seaman, but soon won promotion, and his outstanding work in the charting of the St Lawrence for Wolfe's expedition of 1759 led to fruitful employment over the next eight years. After completing a survey of the St Lawrence, he was sent to work off Newfoundland where, in 1766, he made observations of an eclipse of the sun, which greatly impressed the Royal Society, and gave him the chance to command in the South Seas.

Cook's limitations were obvious enough. He seems to have had no religion, and no politics. Like his skill in navigation, his stubbornness and coolness in adversity at sea belonged to the North Sea coal trade, in which disasters and drownings were common enough. Sloppy work by sailors could bring out the heat of his temper. Like other commanders he flogged his men on occasions, but, probably, less than most. He retained sympathy for the common sailor, seeing that when food was short, captain got no more than ship's boy. Achieving deserved fame, he remained sincerely modest. James Boswell found him 'a plain, sensible man with an uncommon attention to veracity. My metaphor was that he had a ballance in his mind for truth as nice as scales for weighing a guinea.' It was not original scientific theories but a devotion to exactitude which would bring him a Fellowship of the Royal Society. He could use the best instruments of his day, and exploit to the full the recent work bearing on longitude. The internationalist idealism of the mid-eighteenth-century intellect touched him and gave him added nobility; he would tell an admirer, a French naval officer, that he worked not for Britain alone but for Europe, and would give him excellent advice on where future discoveries might be made. He was scrupulous and, until his last days, humane in his dealings with coloured natives. As J. C. Beaglehole puts it, 'Geography provided him with the imaginative, Navigation with morals.'[186] One day Joseph Conrad would extol his type as the anchor of values in a diseased world.

His ship, the Endeavour, had the virtues of her own type. Very broad for her length, she could not sail so fast nor so close to the wind as the frigate which Bougainville used, but she could carry enough food to feed her crew for eighteen

2A

months and was ideal for work near uncharted coasts. Otherwise, she was much adapted. She was equipped as a floating laboratory, with a library containing every available text on the Pacific. Cook was one of two astronomers appointed to observe the transit. The other was Joseph Banks, F.R.S., a wealthy young landowner with a passion for botany, who brought on board a personal suite consisting of two artists, a secretary, and four servants, two of them black. Cook's first instruction was to sail to Tahiti. Observation completed, he was to go south in search of *Terra Australis*. The great aim was to find a vent for British trade.

The ship sailed, in August 1768, with seventy-one seamen on board, twelve marines and eleven landsmen. Cook's patient common sense at first bore hard on his sailors. He had no novel ideas about diet or hygiene. The virtues of lemon juice against scurvy had been repeatedly glimpsed and forgotten since Elizabethan days. The value of hygiene against disease was almost self-evident. But Cook, unlike other commanders, took Admiralty instructions on food and cleanliness seriously, and applied them with rigorous method. He insisted on fresh food at every possible opportunity. 'Scarcly any thing Came wrong to him that was Green.' He was always gathering wild stuff on shore himself, and praised his men if he saw them doing likewise. He fined sailors in rum if he noticed their hands were dirty. Eventually, they saw his point.[187] Cook, navigating by 'lunar distance', arrived in Tahiti with not a single sick man aboard.

The party stayed three months on the island. Scientifically, they failed; both here and at other posts of observation at the North Cape and in Hudson's Bay, there was optical distortion of the readings. But both Cook and Banks observed the Tahitians with objective honesty and humane feeling. This was not quite a paradise. 'Yaws' (a contagious skin disease) was endemic, producing symptoms similar to those of syphilis, besides which Bougainville's sailors (if not Wallis's) had introduced gonorrhoea, which affected about a third of Cook's crew. There was also the sort of incessant pilfering to be expected when island customs were so different from European ones. Cook's stockings were stolen from under his head while he lay asleep or (as he claimed) awake. Cook displayed that prodigious catholicity of appetite which not only permitted him to claim that Tahitian dog, baked for four hours in an earth oven, was the sweetest meat ever tasted, but later to swallow good-humouredly shags, kangaroos, and walrus.

He judged correctly that there were social divisions in Tahiti. Upper-class women were physically larger than those in the lower classes. While the people were very clean, bathing three times a day, they generally carried a 'pretty good stock' of lice and wore rancid coconut oil in their hair. 'Both sexes', he observed, as a middle-class man of his time, 'express the most indecent ideas in conversation without the least emotion ... Chastity indeed is but little valued ... ' He watched with interest as 'a young fellow above 6 feet high lay with a little Girl about 10 or 12 years of age publickly before several of our people and a number of the Natives. What makes me mention this, is because, it appear'd to be done more from Custom than Lewdness ... ' An elder woman stood by, it seemed, to instruct the girl on 'how she should act her part'.[188] Shrewd, uncensorious, and generous, Cook established essentially good relations with the Tahitians, before he sailed onward in mid-July 1769 to explore the 'Society' group of islands to the north-west, and then to strike south for *Terra Australis*.

He proceeded, as his instructions enjoined, as far as 40°S. There was no sign of a continent. The huge swell rolling from southward showed there was no land at all close in that direction. So, on to New Zealand, discovered by Tasman thirteen decades before. He sighted the unknown east coast in October, just in time, as a Frenchman, de Surville, reached North Island only a couple of months later. The Maoris would prove a disappointment to panegyrists of the Southern Continent. No other Polynesian people erected, as they did, large fortified villages. They warred amongst themselves and ate enemies killed in battle; their cannibalism revolted the Tahitians who had sailed here with Cook. Four or five Maoris were shot within a couple of days in three separate quarrels. Cook was deeply upset and found it hard to justify his own conduct to himself in his Journal. Banks in his wrote of 'the most disagreeable day My life has yet seen ... ' But Cook learnt to get on with Maoris, and even to admire them as a 'brave warlike people with sentiments voide of treachery ...'[189] Having sailed round North Island anti-clockwise, he steered clockwise about South Island, charting 2,400 miles of coastline in less than three months, largely in difficult weather.

Had he now felt able to pass eastwards back to Cape Horn, he could have disposed of the Southern Continent finally. But there were only four months' provisions left and the ship would not stand it. He headed for Java. On the way, he encountered Australia and followed its unknown south-eastern coastline up to a deep indentation, reached in April 1770, first called 'Stingray Harbour' but later, in tribute to so many new plants found there, renamed 'Botany Bay'. The British landing was opposed by two brave aborigines; three discharges of small shot were needed to budge them. Cook admired these people also; straight-bodied, slender limbed, soft in voice.[190] Nevertheless, without their permission, he took possession of the whole coastline for George III. He was overimpressed with the soil round Botany Bay, but as his expedition moved northward, the shore grew distinctly barren and unpleasant. He found himself, off Queensland, between coastal shoals and the Great Barrier Reef. On June 11, passing over steep submerged hills of coral, the *Endeavour* struck a ledge and stuck fast. Cook was seen at his best. Panic was averted, as water, stores, ballast and guns were thrown overboard till next night the ship floated free on the tide. Water now poured in through a great breach, but makeshifts, and the shallow draught of his ship, enabled Cook to attain the safety of a river mouth, where things were patched up as well as possible. Through the Torres Strait, he at last reached Batavia in October. At this point just eight sailors had died, mostly through accidents, an astonishing rate; but now tropical diseases took their toll, and only fifty-six out of ninety-four men reached Britain again, after nearly three years' absence.

Cook was modestly apologetic. The discoveries made, he admitted, were 'not great'. New Zealand had struck everyone as a good place for colonisation – all sorts of European plants would grow there. Australia naturally produced 'hardly any thing fit for a man to eat' (and coming from Cook, this was quite a statement) but here too most plants would flourish if 'cultivated by the hand of Industry' and the potential for cattle struck him as vast.[191]

Banks was awarded an honorary doctorate by Oxford University. The great Linnaeus suggested that New South Wales should be named 'Banksia'. Cook, who had been to neither Eton nor Oxford, was merely promoted to commander and told that he was to work on correcting existing charts of the English coast. But the crisis over the Falklands had helped ensure the continued interest of Britain, France and Spain in southern latitudes and in the Pacific. Various French expeditions were finding islands. The Spaniards formally annexed Easter Island and Tahiti, and in 1775-6 they would settle San Francisco. The British government planned a second, larger expedition, for Cook. This time, two Whitby colliers were remodelled at great cost, and called *Resolution* and *Adventure*.

Banks, confused by his fame, now made a fool of himself. He proposed to take a personal party of seventeen, including two horn-players for his amusement. To accommodate all his expensive ideas, he put an extra upper deck on the *Resolution* which made it top heavy and unseaworthy. When the First Lord of the Admiralty ordered the work undone, Banks withdrew in a huff. But scientific purpose was maintained. Various specifics against disease were to be tested, including Dr James's 'Fever Powders' and a marmalade of yellow carrots invented by Baron Storsch of Berlin. And John Harrison's chronometer was to be pitted against another device made by John Arnold. It won. While Arnold's chronometers proved useless, Harrison's pleased Cook by accumulating an error of less than twenty minutes in nearly a year. The expedition might aptly be compared to a twentieth-century moonshot. The glory of its purpose was signified when a Birmingham manufacturer, Matthew Boulton, struck a medal for distribution throughout the Pacific which duly found its way to such unlikely spots as Easter Island and the New Hebrides.

The major objective was such as Cook would have chosen himself. He was instructed to settle the question of the Southern Continent by sailing at high latitudes right round the globe. The two crews of picked men were given special warm clothing. Starting from Plymouth in July, Cook crossed the Antarctic circle the following January, the first known commander ever to do so. As he sailed east into the Indian Ocean, conditions were so extreme that even Cook found them 'curious and romantick'.[192] Scores of icebergs might be seen in one day. The ropes were like wires, the sails like boards, the sheaves were frozen fast in the blocks. Sailing at an average latitude of about 60°, Cook sighted not so much as one island, all the way from the meridian of Greenwich to that of New South Wales. With the southern winter coming, he sought the milder clime of New Zealand. He sailed east from there between 41° and 46° till near the meridian of Pitcairn's Island. Again, the ocean proved empty. He turned to Tahiti to stamp out an outbreak of scurvy, with the concept of a great Southern Continent almost destroyed.

Patient observation, which had achieved this, now convinced Cook that he had been wrong about Tahitian morals. ' ... The favours of Married women and also the unmarried of the better sort, are as difficult to obtain here as in any other Country whatever ... ' Some girls were loose, but 'On the whole, a stranger who visits England might with equal justice draw the Characters of the women there, from those which he might meet with on board the Ships in one of the Naval Ports, or in the Purlieus of Covent Garden & Dury Lane.'[193]

Late in November 1773, having lost touch with the *Adventure*, he pressed again from New Zealand eastward, through empty seas and great ocean swells, determined to go as far south as it was possible for a man to go. The ship was soon directly opposite to London, with an astronomer on board wryly noting that people there, contrary to Dalrymple and other theorists, had 'no Antipodes besides Pengwins and Peteralls [petrels], unless Seals can be admitted as such ... '[194] In January 1774, Cook reached latitude 71° 10'. No sailing ship, in that longitude, would ever get there again. Cook found a solid and limitless ice barrier.

Rather than go home at once, he explored northward once more. The Marquesan Islands enraptured him. Surely the Polynesians there were 'as fine a race of people as any in this sea or perhaps any other.' In a great sweep round the Pacific back to New Zealand, he called at the New Hebrides and New Caledonia. Meeting hostility at the first group, he wrote of the Melanesians calmly, 'One cannot blame them ... in what other light can they at first look upon us but as invaders of their Country ... '[195] Few explorers have been so little prejudiced.

In November 1774, he sailed east again through the mid-50°s, surveyed Tierra del Fuego, and crossed the South Atlantic, calling on South Georgia, where the message of his whole voyage was confirmed. Though the latitude was no higher than that of York, on this bleak island not a tree or shrub could be seen 'no not even big enough to make a tooth-pick'; there were snow and ice at the height of summer, and glaciers could be seen spawning icebergs.[196] He reached home again in July 1775.

Captain Tobias Furneaux, commanding the *Adventure*, had meanwhile completed his own circumnavigation, bringing to London a fine curiosity, its first Tahitian, Omai, who became the rage of society. Introduced to George III, so gossip related, he greeted him 'How do King Tosh'. Literary London adored Omai. The young novelist Fanny Burney declared that he seemed 'to shame Education'. Dr Johnson, who dined with him, joked that when he and a certain peer sat together with backs to the light, 'there was so little of the savage in Omai, that I was afraid to speak to either, lest I should mistake one for the other.' Granville Sharp, characteristically, made earnest attempts to convert Omai to Christianity.[197]

The goodness of human nature, regardless of colour and creed, seemed vindicated as Omai went to the opera and learned to skate. Other deductions from Cook's second expedition would prove more enduring. Though he had explored the east coast of the island of continental size which was later named 'Australia', the old concept of *Terra Australis* was as dead as that huge flightless pigeon, the dodo, latterly extinct on Ile de France. By losing only four men from 112, only one of these through disease, and that not scurvy, Cook had shown what care and science could do. However, he had carried so many real or reputed anti-scorbutics that it was not yet clear to him or others that citrus fruits, though simple, were best of all. The Royal Navy did not make its first regular issue of lemon juice until 1795, but after that scurvy was almost wiped out in five years.[198]

For all his great work, the Navy did no more than promote Cook to post captain, but the Royal Society decently made him a Fellow. The epic tale of his voyages gave British readers some pride and relief in these sad new times of war with America.

Revolutions

Birmingham, where we got to breakfast – a very irregular town &
to me by no means agreable – the old part is very mean – some large
handsome new streets – but in my opinion somewhat disagreable in
all. They boast only one square & that is the Church Yard. Dopo
colazione *took a chaise & went to Soho, the name Mr Bolton has*
given his great manufactory, where every thing done at Birmingham
may be seen at one house. That house however is larger than some
towns ...

Saw the various operations of button making. It is really surprising
how many persons are employed to make a single button – one
makes one part, another another &c, not one of these could make a
whole button ...

From the diary of SYLAS NEVILLE, October 1781[1]

I

From 1770, for a couple of years, 'patriot' opposition in America lost its
momentum. Correspondence between leaders in various colonies almost ceased.
British merchandise poured in and local traders throve; New Yorkers had
owned 477 vessels in 1762; the city had 709 ten years later.[2] Lord North's
ministry thought it could relax. The colonies seemed for a blink less interested
in arguments with Whitehall than with quarrels between themselves over
frontier lands.

Governor Benning Wentworth of New Hampshire profited exceedingly
from fees in respect of grants which he made in land claimed by New York.
The New York authorities fought back. In the 'New Hampshire Grants', later
Vermont, they met fierce resistance from the 'Green Mountain Boys', an irregular corps with Ethan Allen as its colonel; one of the archetypal Americans of his
age, who could throttle a bear with his naked hands, but who also wrote and
published an earnest expression of frontier Enlightenment, *Reason the Only*
Oracle of Man. As 'reason', presumably, insisted, the Green Mountain Boys
waged a thuggish campaign of terror against settlers submitting to New York
jurisdiction. Virtual civil war broke out also further south. The Susquehanna
Company based on Connecticut shovelled settlers into land claimed by Pennsylvania and both sides recruited bands of violent men. Virginian speculators

struggled with Philadelphia merchants for control of the area round Pittsburgh.

The 'Wild West' celebrated in our own time was here prefigured. Already, along the frontier of the southern colonies, cowboys, both black and white, rounded up every year thousands of branded cattle which ran on open ranges, and drove them down to the coast for shipment to Europe or to the Caribbean. After Daniel Boone and others had explored the Kentucky country, 1769–71 had seen the famous incursion there of James Knox's 'long hunters' – men in caps of otter or beaver, with heavy buckskin leggings, hunting shirts of soft leather, hatchets in their belts, and big black rifles. At the site of the future Nashville, moving down the Cumberland River, they came upon such vast numbers of buffalo that they hesitated to disembark for fear of being trampled to death. But the beasts were easy to kill at the saltlicks which they frequented, and their humps were said to make 'the finest steaks in the world'.[3] Another species was following the beaver towards extermination, as Judge Richard Henderson of North Carolina bribed some elderly Cherokee chiefs to sell him the Kentucky and Cumberland basins – land claimed by Virginia, by the Shawnees and by the Chickasaws – and sent Daniel Boone, with a band of axemen, to blaze a trail through the Cumberland Gap. By 1775, Boonesborough, in Kentucky, had been established, despite a bitter war with the Shawnees which had been deliberately provoked by Lord Dunmore, the Scottish governor of Virginia.

So it would not have been inappropriate if Benjamin Franklin and his colleagues in the so-called 'Walpole Association' had had their way and fathered a new colony named 'Vandalia', though the reason they themselves gave for their choice of cognomen was that the Queen was descended from the Vandals. Though the proposed colony would have overlapped quite a lot of Pennsylvania and straddled Virginia's westward claims, after fierce lobbying the Privy Council approved the 'Vandalia' scheme in 1772. Then the crown law officers refused to pass it.[4] One special reason was their objection to the Crown's conferring favours on the egregious Franklin, now London agent not only for Pennsylvania, Georgia and New Jersey but also for the Assembly of truculent Massachusetts.

There were still British troops in Massachusetts. The redcoats were called 'bloodybacks' by Yankees in bitter allusion to the horrific floggings practised upon these agents of 'Turkish' despotism. Sam Adams still had his knife out for Governor Hutchinson and his clan: 'Andrew Oliver, lieutenant governor; Peter Oliver and Foster Hutchinson, chief justice and associate justice of the superior court, respectively; a nephew, Nathaniel Rogers, nominated province secretary in succession to Andrew Oliver – all of this within the same years in which three intermarriages took place between the Oliver and Hutchinson families.'[5]

Turkishly, it was decided that Hutchinson and other crown officials were to be paid from England, out of the Royal Exchequer. The news arriving in 1772, that there would be judges supported by imperial funds sent shivers of dread down the spine of every liberty-loving slave-owner, and every self-respecting smuggler. In that year, the *Gaspee*, a vessel employed on customs enforcement, was boarded at night in Narragansett Bay. The commander was shot in the arm and groin and the rioters, organised by prominent Rhode Island merchants, burnt his ship to the water's edge. The British government appointed a Commission of Inquiry. But though no one had been disguised, and everyone knew who had done it, evidence could not be obtained against a single rioter. The Virginian House of Burgesses expressed its horror at Britain's Turkish proceedings in this matter — suspects were to be sent to England for trial — by setting up a new Committee of Correspondence to uphold the common interests of all the colonies.

Then came news which seemed to justify colonial paranoia. In June 1773, a closed session of the Massachusetts Assembly had read to it 'letters of an extraordinary nature ... ' which had been forwarded by Benjamin Franklin. Two weeks later, thirteen samples of the correspondence of Hutchinson and others of his clique with a British civil servant named Thomas Whately were broadcast to the world in a pamphlet published by Sam Adams's Boston Committee of Correspondence. Whately was now dead. Who gave Franklin the letters is not exactly known. Franklin's motive was still to preserve the Empire. Out of touch with colonial opinion, he thought that if his fellow Americans saw proof that Hutchinson had instigated the objectionable trend of British government policy, they would become peaceable subjects once the detested governor and his cronies had been driven 'like the scapegoats of old ... into the wilderness', carrying with them 'all the offenses which have arisen between the two countries.' Written in January 1769, one sentence above all seemed to prove Hutchinson's villainy, suggesting that, in the colonies, 'there must be an abridgement of what are called English liberties.' Carefully edited by Sam Adams, who had adjusted the punctuation cunningly, the letters appeared to establish beyond doubt that the 'conspiracy' against liberty had existed on both sides of the Atlantic.[6] Hutchinson was damned. But the British government was not, as Franklin had foolishly hoped, exonerated.

The Massachusetts Assembly petitioned for Hutchinson's removal from his post. The official hearing by the Privy Council in January 1774 turned into a public tongue-whipping of Franklin before thirty-six of the great men of Britain and a crowd of other eminent persons. Wedderburn, the Solicitor-General, Scot, compatriot of the arch-'conspirator' Bute, declaimed that Franklin had 'forfeited all the respect of societies and of men', and accused him of 'the coolest and most deliberate malevolence' in the publication of Hutchinson's letters.[7] Franklin was shortly dismissed from his post of deputy Postmaster-General of the American colonies. Wedderburn's arrogance helped turn a would-be friend of Britain into a very dangerous enemy.

Just before this, word had reached London of a shocking event which marked the intersection of the crisis in Massachusetts with that in the affairs of the East India Company. With the Company's warehouses choked with 17 million lb. of surplus leaf, an Act had gone through, in May 1773, by which all duties charged on re-exported tea were to be remitted and the EIC was authorised to set up its own retail agencies in the colonies. The main aim was to help it offload its stock. But Americans would now get cheaper tea. All the propaganda of 'patriots' since the Townshend duty had come into force had failed to wean colonists from that delicious beverage; James Otis complained that they would 'part with all their liberties, and religion too, rather than renounce it.'[8] Smuggled tea from Holland had provided a patriotic source of refreshment. The government hoped that the smugglers would now be beaten out of the market and that colonists, sipping their cheap Bohea, would be reconciled to the one tax still imposed on them. This was naïve. As the *Gaspee* incident should have shown, smugglers had wide support, and to drive them out of business would mean trouble. And legitimate merchants in the American ports would not be pleased by the new EIC monopoly.

Merchants allied themselves again with 'Sons of Liberty'. Intimidation forced the resignations of the men appointed EIC agents, in every port except in Boston where, as it unsurprisingly happened, two sons of Hutchinson and certain relatives of his were the principal consignees. (The governor himself, though he kept this secret, had nearly £4,000, most of his liquid capital, invested in East India stock.)[9] Sam Adams now urged on his fellow Bostonians that they must stop the tea landing, or face the scorn of Sons of Liberty elsewhere.

In late November, the first consignments arrived in three vessels, each with over a hundred chests. Other goods were unloaded. The tea stayed aboard. British naval vessels blocked the harbour. Neither Hutchinson nor the patriots could back down from confrontation. The governor would not let the ships leave with the tea. The patriots kept watch lest it should be landed surreptitiously. Under the law, customs officers could have seized the tea to collect the duty upon it after twenty days. On the nineteenth day, Sam Adams produced his most brilliant stroke – a gigantic act of purposeful vandalism which he successfully presented, to his colonial contemporaries and posterity, as a mild, even witty, riposte to oppression.

> Rally, Mohawks! bring out your axes,
> And tell King George we'll pay no taxes
>   On his foreign tea;
> His threats are vain, and vain to think
> To force our girls and wives to drink
>   His vile Bohea!
> Then rally, boys, and hasten on
> To meet our chiefs at the Green Dragon.

Some two hundred men — artisans, shipyard workers, sailors — mustered in the evening. They were 'cloathed in blankets with the heads muffled, and copper-colored countenances, being each armed with a hatchet or axe, and pair pistols.' The three vessels were boarded. The 'Indians' showed the discipline of a good eighteenth-century 'mob'. Nothing but tea was touched. In three hours of sweaty effort, every chest was 'knocked to pieces and flung over the sides.' Choice leaf from Canton worth about £9,000 was shoved into the dark, chill waters of the harbour, where the morning light showed it islanded in windrows, so that boats had to be sent out to carve a passage for larger vessels through it.[10]

Nine days later a ship reached the Delaware with nearly 700 chests of tea. Faced with a huge crowd, the captain was easily persuaded to take it back to England at once. In April next year, the 'Boston Tea Party' was repeated in New York, and the bells of the town's churches pealed for joy. Tea was permitted to land in Charles Town alone — and there it remained unsold for three years.

A new word, 'revolutionary', was first used in 1774. 'Revolution' now cracked what Franklin called 'that fine and noble China Vase, the British Empire.'[11]

The British government decided that Boston must be punished. Four Bills were presented to the Commons. The port of Boston was to be closed to commerce until the inhabitants compensated the EIC. The custom house and the seat of provincial government were to be moved to Salem. A second Bill remodelled the constitution of Massachusetts. A nominated Council replaced the elective one. The Assembly was deprived of its powers to appoint and direct local officials, the freeholders of their right to elect jurymen. Town meetings were to be limited to one per year and restricted to purely local matters. A third Bill, prompted by the 'Boston massacre', provided that people accused of capital offences for carrying out their duties might be sent for trial to Britain or some other colony. A fourth increased the governor's power to quarter troops in private homes.

The parliamentary opposition was weak, and divided. Rockingham, whose loose confederation of supporters numbered probably less than forty M.P.s, believed in Britain's absolute supremacy over the colonies; Chatham, with at most a dozen followers, believed that supremacy was qualified by natural rights. Several followers of both groups supported the Boston Port Bill, and apart from Burke almost no one spoke against it. British merchants were far less inclined than before to side with the Americans. They had survived the previous non-importation agreement, and the threat no longer worried them so much. While exports to America had been running recently at less than a quarter of the average level of the late 1760s, British trade with Russia had increased three times, to Africa, Sweden and Flanders by over 100 per cent, and by over 30 per cent to various other European countries.[12]

One M.P. said that Boston was a 'nest of locusts' which should be 'knocked about their ears and destroyed'. Another likewise exposed the sneering contempt which was common: ''Tis said that America will be exasperated. Will she then take arms? 'Tis not as yet, thank God, the strength of America which we dread when put in competition with this country. She has neither army, navy, money, or men ... 'Tis an absurd supposition that the various colonies in America, separated from one another at such a distance, differing so much in the nature of their governments, in many respects in their interests, enjoying at present the benefit of the most perfect system of civil liberty, and the protection of the greatest naval power the world ever knew, should at once unite through pique.'[13]

The 'Coercive Acts' went through by huge majorities. General Gage, commander-in-chief in America, was now given the extra commission of governor in Massachusetts. More troops were sent to Boston. The limited British electorate thought all this well done.

The 'Quebec Act' also went through at this time — most likely precipitated by the crisis, but not directly connected with the Coercive Acts. It stabbed at problems long overdue for solution. Something had to be done about the western lands, where Indians were fighting settlers who fought each other. Now jurisdiction over the land north and west of a line running along Pennsylvania's western edge to the Ohio, and then along the Ohio to the Mississippi, was given to the governor of Quebec. With the old British North-American colonies so troublesome, it seemed important to give the Quebec constitution more firmness and to appease the French Canadians. Regarding Quebec itself the Act regularised, in great part, *ad hoc* arrangements already worked out on the spot. Rule was to be by governor and nominated council — the alternatives, both unacceptable, would have been to give Roman Catholics a full political role, or to set up a farcical system for English-speakers only. Now Catholics would at least be admitted to public office. Full recognition was given to the Catholic Church establishment, and this advanced toleration was regarded as permanent. Other provisions were temporary. Canadian civil law and seigneurial law were for the moment to go on co-existing with British criminal law.

Horrific though the 'Coercive Acts' against Massachusetts seemed to people in all the colonies, the Quebec Act was perhaps a still greater force in unifying a large sector of American opinion against Britain. In the debates preceding it, that detested Scot, Wedderburn, declared flatly: 'I would not say, "cross the Ohio, you will find the Utopia of some great and mighty empire." I would say, "This is the border, beyond which, for the advantage of your whole empire, You shall not extend Yourselves." '[14] Every land speculator in the colonies would find these words, and the Act's provisions, disturbing. Furthermore, the creation of a nominated legislature in Quebec seemed clear evidence that Bute's 'conspiracy' was proceeding. Few assemblymen could feel easy about that. The Canadians, furthermore, were hereditary enemies; could not the government use its papist 'slaves', in standing armies, to 'enslave' Britons and Americans in their turn? Above all the toleration extended to papistry shocked zealous

Protestants of all shades and species. The Act was a gift to Sam Adams. See! Massive papist migration from Europe was now planned to encircle the colonists. See! The Inquisition would function in Philadelphia.

Gage, arriving in Boston to take up his duties in May 1774, found that he had no control outwith the range of the guns of his warships, which closed the port so effectively that its wharves were deserted, but were of no use in extracting compensation for the drowned tea. The General Court defiantly voted, before Gage closed it, a call for a 'continental' congress to defend American rights. When Gage, in August, received the list of thirty-six councillors nominated under the Act, a howl of popular fury forced most of these men to resign, or to take refuge with Gage himself, who now clamoured for still more troops. In October, the townships sent representatives to an unauthorised provincial congress. This body effectively governed Massachusetts.

Support had burgeoned in other colonies. George Washington wrote that Americans must now assert their rights, lest 'custom and use' should make them as 'tame and abject' as the blacks whom they ruled over 'with such arbitrary sway'.[15] The guilt felt by white Virginians over slavery helped propel them towards revolt nearly unanimously. To Boston, deprived of its trade, gifts of food flowed from all parts. Even the small Quebec merchant community sent 1,000 bushels of wheat. Illegal meetings everywhere took up Boston's call for a Continental Congress.

It met at Philadelphia in September. The emergent Yankee twang and the prototype Southern drawl were heard together; of the seaboard colonies, only Georgia and Nova Scotia were unrepresented. It might have aborted in inter-necine quarrels. The sea, which was the main means of communication between colonies jealous of each others' trade and embattled over control of frontier lands, linked each at least as directly with London. The Congregationalist Yankee lamb must lie down with the Anglican lion from Virginia. Everyone present was meeting most of the others for the first time, and each of these strangers was a potential informer or spy. But Sam Adams plotted and planned; and the alchemy of shared grievance, and shared risk, worked a miracle.

John Adams, representing Massachusetts, wrote home to his wife that the delegates debated from nine to three, then adjourned, feasted 'upon ten thousand delicacies' and sat drinking madeira, claret and burgundy till six or seven. Con-viviality cemented common purpose. Patrick Henry was soon on his feet pro-claiming, 'Government is dissolved. Where are your landmarks, your boun-daries of Colonies? We are in a state of Nature, sir ... The distinctions between Virginians, Pennsylvanians, New Yorkers and New Englanders are no more. I am not a Virginian, but an American.'[16] His oratory was admired; so was the military bearing of that magnificent horseman George Washington, who sat mostly silent through the debates wearing his British uniform, and his sword. The most radical person present, by the sound of him, was Christopher Gadsden of South Carolina, who proclaimed himself ready to take up his musket and march direct to Boston. But of course, many said wild things when the burgundy had flowed and the toasts had gone round damning Bute and Mansfield, applauding Chatham and Doctor Franklin.

No delegate could imagine that things could ever again be as they had been. British rule died as these men discovered that they were all splendid fellows, and all Americans. On October 14 they unanimously agreed on a statement of 'Declarations and Resolves' which referred to the British government as a 'foreign power'. On the 20th, Congress voted to boycott trade with Britain, and from now on rule in America passed into the hands of extralegal 'Committees of Association' erected to enforce non-importation, non-exportation and non-consumption. They encouraged drilling, seized government military stores, set up gunpowder factories, bought arms abroad. Gage reported that Massachusetts was in 'a state of actual open rebellion; there is not a man from sixteen to sixty, nay, to a hundred years old, who is not armed and obliged to attend at stated times to train.'[17]

A young Englishman from Derbyshire, Nicholas Cresswell, who had just come to the Chesapeake to seek his fortune, noted in February 1775, 'The Committees act as Justices. If any person is found to be inimical to the liberties of America, they give them over to the mobility to punish as they think proper ... The people are arming and training in every place. They are all liberty mad.'[18]

The term 'Lynch law' is said to have derived from the eagerness with which one Captain Lynch of Virginia pursued anyone who was friendly to the British government or disrespectful to Congress. Such persons were now branded tories'. Tarring and feathering was the classic punishment. 'First strip a Person naked, then heat the Tar until it is thin, and pour it upon the naked Flesh, or rub it over with a Tar Brush, *quantum sufficit*. After which, sprinkle decently upon the Tar, whilst it is as yet warm, as many Feathers as will stick to it. Then hold a lighted Candle to the Feathers, and try to set it all on Fire; if it will burn so much the better. But as the Experiment is often made in cold Weather; it will not then succeed — take also an Halter and put it round the Person's Neck, and then cart him the Rounds.' Another favourite was 'riding on a rail', where the victim was jogged roughly along on a sharp rail between his legs. Drenching in dung and simple assault and battery were also efficacious supports of 'whig' rule. One tory lawyer was plundered and stripped of everything by whigs at four different places, before he removed to 'loyal' Nova Scotia, where, melancholy mad, he cut his own throat.[19] Even milder coercion — sending to Coventry, loss of clients or custom — was enough to break a man's heart.

Very few people in America had supported the Stamp Act. But the once solid front against the British government was now fractured. Many men who had led the opposition to Grenville, who had written eloquent pamphlets against Townshend, who had helped to organise boycotts and extralegal congresses, were not prepared to move into revolt, and were denounced by the 'patriots' and subjected to treatment which embittered them permanently. The final sorting of sheep from goats had not yet been done; Congress had not yet deposed the King in America. But George III himself was in no mood to make life easy for waverers. He was as clear on the value of *force majeure* as any revolutionary in the colonies. On November 19, 1774, he told Lord North, ' ... We must either master them, or totally leave them to themselves and treat them as Aliens.' He was not prepared to recommend the second course. Hard blows would bring them to reason, and to submission.[20]

This polarisation within the Empire presented West Indian planters with a dismal predicament. Sugar planters were as shocked as tobacco men by Parliament's assertion of a sovereignty which seemed to threaten all rights of property. In December 1774, the Jamaica Assembly passed an address to George III which viewed 'with amazement, a plan almost carried into execution for enslaving the colonies', attacked the Coercive Acts and the Quebec Act, and greatly annoyed the government in Whitehall. But the address had assured the King of loyalty. ' ... Weak and feeble as this colony is, from its very small number of white inhabitants and its peculiar situation, from the encumbrance of more than 200,000 slaves, it cannot be supposed that we intend, or ever could have intended resistance to Great Britain.'[21] The Assembly, after its protest, slumped into quiescence, though the dire effects of American boycott were soon plain. Early in 1775, West Indian interests in Britain met in London and petitioned the new Parliament, contending that North American supplies were vital to the islands. But that body was in no mood to respond.

In February 1775, it declared Massachusetts to be in a state of rebellion. In March it barred all the New England colonies from trade outside the Empire and from the Newfoundland fisheries. The ban was extended to most of the other colonies as each in turn made its sympathy for the Yankees known. Huge majorities backed these actions. The Earl of Sandwich, First Lord of the Admiralty, sneered at the colonists as 'raw, undisciplined, cowardly men',[22] though Gage, from his close-up position, kept warning that they would fight well and would take much conquering. Lord North indicated the limit of British readiness to concede. If the colonists would make sufficient and permanent provision for the support of civil government, justice and defence – if, that is, they agreed to deprive themselves of control over royal governors – then, Parliament would not tax them.

Chatham unsuccessfully moved in the Lords a 'Conciliation Bill' which reaffirmed parliamentary sovereignty, but proposed the recognition of Congress and its erection into a permanent institution. He had praised the sagacity of that body. ' ... All attempts to impose servitude upon such men, to establish despotism over such a mighty continental *nation*, must be vain, must be fatal.' All thought of 'internal' taxation must be abandoned. 'Property is private, individual, absolute ... I recognise to the Americans their supreme unalienable right in their property; a right which they are justified in the defence of to the last extremity.'[23] There was one true God, and Locke was His prophet. Burke, who moved somewhat beyond the platitudes of old-time whiggery, produced a resolution a few weeks later urging, on purely practical grounds, the concession of virtually everything which Congress had demanded. But not many well-to-do people in Britain thought that their empire faced dissolution. A Glasgow 'tobacco lord', William Cunninghame, summed up the complacency of most of his class: ' ... What madmen the Virginians are. How can they live or keep their negroes alive without coarse linens and cloth?'[24]

Like certain modern economic historians, he failed to understand that man does not live by coarse linens, or bread, alone. Virginians, as we have seen, had many causes to grumble over their connection with Britain, but they were in the habit of referring, as they grumbled, to splendid political principles. Their economic interests were multifarious, diverse and equivocal. For revolution to happen, principles, hopes, had to sweep men past calculation into actions which might have ruined them utterly. Patrick Henry might seem at a distance only a vainglorious rhetorician, but his fellow-countrymen found his eloquence uplifting, his voice musical. The extralegal Virginian Convention, in March 1775, heard him call on them to set up and to arm a rebel militia. ' ... Give me liberty or give me death!'[25] By sixty-five votes to sixty they settled for liberty, perhaps, or death. 'Freeborn Englishmen' had become, in their own minds, 'Freeborn Americans'.

Gage received orders to arrest the leaders of the Massachusetts provincial congress. Promptly, on the night of 18 April, he sent a force of around 700 light infantry, grenadiers and marines up towards Concord, some sixteen miles from Boston, where the rebels had a dump of arms. The movement was not kept secret. A Boston silversmith and engraver, Paul Revere, set off to warn the patriot leaders, was taken by a British patrol and, with a pistol against his head, told everything he knew. But word that the British were coming got through anyway. It reached Lexington, where Sam Adams and Hancock were spending the night with the minister, and they were able to flee in good time. The Massachusetts militia had agreed to turn out at a minute's warning.

The British troops had to pass through Lexington on their way to Concord. Arriving at daybreak, the advance party, hungry and tired after a bad march in the dark, found some seventy 'minute men' lined up on the green to confront them.

Major Pitcairn, commanding, shouted, 'ye rebels, disperse!' What happened then is disputed. The Americans may have been 'dispersing' when the British troops fired. Or they may have been filing off towards a stone wall on the right flank of the British column, from behind which some of them may have shot their muskets as the royal troops moved to surround and disarm them. In any case, pistol or musket, redcoat or minute man, somebody fired. Suddenly, martyrs and heroes were made. Eight Americans were killed, ten were wounded. One British soldier was slightly injured.

Joined by the main British body, the royal troops proceeded to Concord and destroyed what military supplies were still there. But the countryside had risen, every village. The march back to Boston became a near rout. A British soldier wrote, with due respect, 'We were fired on from houses and behind trees, and before we had gone ½ mile we were fired on from all sides, but mostly from the rear, where people had hid themselves in houses till we had passed, and then fired. The country was an amazing strong one, full of hills, woods, stone walls, etc., which the Rebels did not fail to take advantage of, for they were all lined with people who kept an incessant fire upon us, as we did too upon them, but not with the same advantage, for they were so concealed there was hardly any seeing them. In this way we marched between 9 and 10 miles, their numbers increasing from all parts, while ours was reduced by deaths, wounds and fatigue ... '

Another British account shows how the galled and goaded redcoats retaliated. 'Even weamin had firelocks. One was seen to fire a blunder bus between her father and husband, from their windows; there they three with an infant child soon suffered the fury of the day. In another house which was long defended by 8 resolute fellows the Grenadiers at last got possession when, after having run their bayonets into 7, the 8th continued to abuse them with all the moat-like rage of a true Cromwellian, and but a moment before he quitted this world applyed such epethets as I must leave unmentioned.'

Gage had to send up a relieving force of 1,200 men to get his troops back to Boston. The total British casualties were 273; the rebels lost some 95. The moral effect was enormous. Yankee guerrillas had bested British regulars – who knew very well that they had been bested. The Massachusetts rebels hastened to print and circulate their own account of the affair: the British had fired at Lexington without provocation, and had then burned and raped their way through the countryside, spitting infants and women in childbed with their bayonets. This version went as far as England, even before the British one. Gage's men were up against a protean foe which might fire skilfully from behind any tree and which used their own language to swifter effect than they did.[26]

Word of Lexington took over a month to reach London. But it raced up and down the American coast at the speed of the fastest horseman. As Massachusetts militiamen swarmed around Boston, a contingent from New Hampshire came in to join them by dawn on April 21, having marched fifty-five miles in eighteen hours. Rhode Islanders and Connecticut men followed. Gage was besieged in Boston.

On May 10, the Captain commanding the British garrison at Ticonderoga on Lake Champlain, was startled from sleep in the gray of the morning by a command that he must come forth at once or his men would be slaughtered. Holding his trousers in his hand, he opened the door to confront Ethan Allen, who demanded that the fort must be surrendered, 'In the name of the great Jehovah, and the Continental Congress.'[27] Allen's 'Green Mountain Boys' took about a hundred cannon and moved on to acquire a similar number again by capturing Crown Point, then seized the British sloop of war which cruised on the lake. Rebels commanded the crucial New York–Montreal corridor.

The Second Continental Congress, now meeting in Philadelphia, found Allen's success a momentary embarrassment. This was clearly aggression by their own supporters, and to sustain the role of injured loyal subjects, the delegates came up with the accusation that the Ministry had been planning a 'cruel invasion' from Quebec. After despatching one last loyal petition, begging the King to protect their rights against Parliament, they boldly declared their 'Causes of Taking up Arms'. Congress took on the burden of a sovereign power. It set up its own postal service under Benjamin Franklin, present as a Pennsylvanian delegate, it voted to issue several million dollars of its own paper currency, and it adopted the army besieging Boston. Individual colonies were required to raise specified numbers of troops. They would choose officers of ranks up to colonel, but Congress itself would appoint the higher commanders. Washington was the unanimous choice as chief. With other 'Continental' officers, he shortly left for Boston.

He found there not an army, but a revolutionary movement in arms. The Massachusetts militiamen, who had elected their own officers, saw their service as temporary, three months at the most, and slipped off home for brief visits to attend to pressing business. The Connecticut men who had joined them were under officers appointed by the colony's Assembly, but were enlisted to serve only till the new year, and were just as ignorant of drill as the rest. This 'people's army' had no tents. Men slept on straw under shelters improvised from sailcloth, sacking and boards. There was no notion of sanitation, and no supply system. There were few horses, almost no carts or wagons, and not enough balls for the rare cannon. Men dressed in their usual clothes. Several 'majors' were tavern-keepers in private life. Blacksmiths, even, were captains. These men would not order their friends and neighbours distastefully, let alone flog their backs to a mass of raw flesh.

'I dare say,' Washington wrote, with the values of his class shaping his sentence, 'the men would fight very well (if properly Officered) although they are an exceeding dirty and nasty people ... '[28] He started a spate of court martials. Three colonels were cashiered. Floggings began.

Let us pause to inspect certain ironies and complexities. As the preachers with Washington's army called down the curses of heaven on Bute and Mansfield, Gage's soldiers in Boston were on the verge of mutiny against their Scots officers, and had to be threatened with exemplary punishment 'for swearing they ought to be commanded by Englishmen, and that they would not sacrifice their lives in an attempt to butcher their friends and fellow-subjects for any interested North Briton upon earth.'[29]

Washington's fellow-Virginian, Thomas Jefferson, had recently sent a present of several dozen bottles of old madeira to his favourite teacher, William Small, a Scot, who now lived in the English Midlands where he had become physician, adviser and friend to an entrepreneur named Matthew Boulton.[30]

The Glasgow factors, awake at last to the danger, were buying up every leaf of tobacco which they could find in the Chesapeake colonies, so that their seniors made spectacular windfall profits as, with war, the price in some eighteen months soared from below 2*d*. a lb. towards 2*s*.[31] The Scots traders in Virginia were, almost to a man, against the political views of their planter clients.

But authorities in Britain still mistrusted all Scots. They reckoned that those who were not still Jacobite rebels at heart were, as Presbyterians, much like New Englanders, surely? Since Charles I's day no attempt had been made to prevent emigration from any British port. In September 1775, emigration from Scotland would be blocked, lest it should swell the ranks of rebellion.[32]

While the American commander before Boston despised the democratical views of New Englanders and imposed on some of the latter such degrading 'Turkish' floggings as, given to redcoats, had seemed to these same Yankees unmistakeable tokens of despotism, the British troops confronting them shared their excessive dislike of Scots and, out of the army, at home, might well have joined 'mobs' in the streets for Wilkes.

Do we say then that the confused relationships between Lowland Scotland and Highland Gaeldom, and between England and Scotland since 1707, were in some complicated way a major cause in the breakdown of mutual understanding between the American colonists and Britain? Perhaps historians should think hard about this. But they will not demonstrate that this one factor 'caused' revolution, any more than devoted mythologists can show that George Washington's leadership won independence; narrative conventions may also mislead us.

Washington, as it proved, would never beat a British army in pitched battle, but the New Englanders whom he thought so 'dirty' had virtually managed that very difficult feat, a few days before his appointment as commander. Gage had been joined in May by three new generals from Britain: Howe, Clinton and that 'Gentleman Johnny' Burgoyne who had hectored against the nabobs in the Commons. They urged Gage to take the offensive. He aimed to strengthen the British position by occupying the heights on the Dorchester and Charles-town peninsulas flanking Boston. The rebels got wind of this. Their amateur general Artemas Ward and his council decided that the hills overlooking Charlestown must be pre-emptively occupied. For some reason, the force they sent intrenched itself not on Bunker Hill, but on the lower Breed's Hill. Gage accepted a typically slow and orthodox plan for straightforward frontal assault proposed by Howe, who therefore, with his redcoats, marched, on June 17, 1775, slowly uphill in melting summer heat, stopping every few yards to dress ranks. The Yankees watched them shimmering closer and then, when time was ripe, released three shattering volleys in ninety seconds. The redcoats went downhill again. They came up a second time. Again they were hurled into retreat. Howe called for reinforcements. At last, a third assault succeeded.

Over 1,000 redcoats — four out of ten — had been killed or wounded. American casualties had been lighter. Technically, 'Bunker Hill' was a British 'victory', but in fact it was a mortifying setback. Gage drew the moral. 'These people shew a spirit and conduct against us they never shewed against the French, and every body has judged of them from their formed appearance and behaviour when joyned with the King's forces in the last war; which has led many into great mistakes.' He added, 'The loss we have sustained is greater than we can bear.'[33]

In November, Lord North brought in a Bill which tried to establish a complete naval blockade of America, authorising seizure of the colonials' goods wherever they were found at sea. Meanwhile recruitment went ahead. The government had already planned to gather new regiments of Highlanders and to enlist more marines in Ireland, but these would not be enough. Unsuccessful efforts were made to hire troops from that notorious despot, Catherine of Russia. Agreements were entered into with rulers of six petty German states, who eventually provided almost 30,000 soldiers for Britain. The Landgrave of Hesse Kassel was the chief supplier, and so they would be known across the Atlantic as 'Hessians'. News of their purchase shocked Americans. These were men reared outwith traditions of 'English liberty' and sold by grasping rulers who had swept them out of gaols. Their use seemed to close all hope of reconciliation.

An Englishman, Thomas Paine, was on hand to help Americans make the decisive break from their former loyalty. The son of a Quaker master-stay-maker, he had worked in his father's trade himself, but had failed, and had entered the Crown's service as an exciseman. His first writing had been a pamphlet urging higher salaries for revenue officers. In 1774 disaster pushed him into emigration. His tobacconist's business collapsed. His marriage broke up. The Excise dismissed him. He met Benjamin Franklin, who encouraged him to go to America. Arriving in Philadelphia in November 1774, he soon became editor of the *Pennsylvania Magazine*.

Paine like Franklin (and like James Cook) represented the versatile, self-teaching, practical intellect of the English-speaking middle classes which would help transform the world. He invented, amongst other things, a smokeless candle and an iron bridge. But it was his gifts as a journalist and polemicist, suddenly bearing fruit in his late thirties, which gave him his place in world history.

On January 10, 1776, Paine published, at Philadelphia, a fifty-page pamphlet called *Common Sense*. Its clear and forceful prose made seem perfectly obvious certain ideas which men had shrunk from expressing. Paine sharply denied the vaunted perfection of the 'constitution of England', and hurled sarcasm at the hitherto sacred institutions of kingship and hereditary succession. 'Of more worth is one honest man to society, and in the sight of God, than all the crowned ruffians that ever lived.'

The time for debate was over, Paine said. 'Arms as the last resource decide the contest ... The sun never shone on a cause of greater worth ... Now is the seed-time of continental union, faith and honour.' He refused to credit any special relationship between the colonies and Britain. 'This new world hath been the asylum for the persecuted lovers of civil and religious liberty from *every part* of Europe.' How stupid it was, 'To be always running three or four thousand miles with a tale or a petition, waiting four or five months for an answer ... There is something absurd, in supposing a Continent to be perpetually governed by an island.' There was no point in trying to patch up a relationship already ruptured by bloodshed. The cause of America was the cause of Man. 'Every spot of the old world is overrun with oppression. Freedom hath been hunted round the globe ... O! receive the fugitive, and prepare in time an asylum for mankind.' Paine called for an 'open and determined DECLARATION FOR INDEPENDENCE'.[34]

In three months, 120,000 copies of his pamphlet were printed. By 19 January, Nicholas Cresswell was noting in Virginia, 'A pamphlet called "Commonsense" makes a great noise.' Three days later, 'Nothing but Independence talked.' On the 26th, 'Nothing but Independence will go down. The Devil is in the people.' Governor Dunmore, who had retreated to the safety of a Royal Naval vessel, abetted Paine's propaganda mightily with his raids on the colony's coast, his attempts to bring Indians down on the western frontier, and, most shocking of all, his promise of freedom to slaves who would join the British. Virginia was now directly at war. Its slave-owning revolutionary militia wore hunting-shirts, and some of them printed 'Liberty or Death' upon them.[35]

North Carolina, in February 1776, saw the first, poignant, loyalist counter-rising. From the 1730s, Scottish Gaels had settled on the upper reaches of the Cape Fear River. By this time there were perhaps as many as 12,000 Highlanders in the area, rather outnumbered, it seems, by their slaves. They spoke Gaelic and so did their blacks. Many were from Argyllshire, a Campbell stronghold, Presbyterians with traditional Hanoverian loyalties, but among the wealthiest people in the region were Flora Macdonald, once Bonnie Prince Charlie's saviour during his wanderings after Culloden, and her husband Allan, who owned a plantation of 475 acres. A high proportion of the Highlanders were Macdonalds or MacLeods who had favoured the Jacobite cause. Gage gave them a chance to prove their new loyalty. He sent Brigadier General Donald Macdonald and Colonel Donald MacLeod to create a Highland army. Flora Macdonald's husband was especially prominent in urging full support for the King. Some 1,300 tartan-clad men mustered to the sound of the pibroch. They marched to join other units at the river mouth. Eighteen miles from the coast, they were opposed by patriot militia. The battle was brief. The Gaels panicked. About 50 were killed and 880 captured. The patriots lost only two of their men.[36]

At Boston, Howe had succeeded Gage in command. Over the winter, Washington had brought up fifty-nine guns captured at Ticonderoga. Then he moved on to the commanding Dorchester Heights which Howe had unaccountably failed to occupy. Facing bombardment, Howe evacuated on March 17, taking his troops and 1,100 loyalist refugees off to Halifax, Nova Scotia.

In April, Congress declared American ports open to ships of all countries excepting Britain, and in effect, declared itself independent of Parliament. Colonies from Massachusetts to Georgia were now setting up elected 'state' assemblies outwith British law. Men who had usurped power, and had begun to treat with French agents, risked as much if they went back on their 'treason' as if they moved forward to independence. Only victory could safeguard them from reprisals. To break from England was painful. But England, it seemed, had been taken over by liberty-hating Scots. Ezra Stiles of Connecticut wrote in his diary, 'Let us boldly say, for History will say it, that the whole of this War is so far chargeable to the Scotch councils, & to the Scotch as a Nation ... '[37]

On June 7, 1776, Richard Henry Lee proposed to Congress a resolution calling for a declaration of independence and an American confederation. By July 2, twelve out of thirteen delegations, with that of New York abstaining but approving, declared the bond between the new 'states' and Britain to be 'totally dissolved'. Two days later the great Declaration was adopted.

The committee of five appointed to produce it had included such choice penmen as Franklin and John Adams, but Thomas Jefferson was in effect the author. He epitomised most of what was best in the thought and temper of eighteenth-century 'enlightenment', as well as many common self-contradictions. Six foot two and a half inches tall, lounging, gangling, large boned, with freckles and red hair, he was not a very good speaker and his manner was shy and scholarly. He had been born in frontier country, thickly forested, where wolves still howled. In a comfortable house, however – his father, a land surveyor and speculator eventually owned more than sixty slaves. Jefferson had grown up in touch with the latest currents of Scottish and European thought. His versatility now seems astounding, though there were others in his time who could match it. His interest in scientific and technological matters was deep and fruitful. Had he never meddled in politics, we would still remember him as a great self-taught architect, designer of his own beautiful house at Monticello.

He was very much a Virginian of his class. He had hardly travelled outside his colony. Virginia was still predominantly 'Anglo-Saxon' in stock, and Jefferson was opposed to mass immigration from European countries where people had been indoctrinated in the perverse ways of absolute monarchy. He disliked manufacturing industry, and wanted to keep it out. 'Those who labour in the earth are the chosen people of God, if ever He had a chosen people ... ' But the scepticism implicit in that remark shows how he transcended conventional thought. Traditional theology did not impress him. Original sin was not for him a reality. He believed that 'goodness lay at the heart of things.' Hence he was a generous radical, far in advance of most Americans. Politically, he sought to further the interests of frontier squatters and small settlers. He opposed capital punishment, save for treason and murder, and favoured complete religious toleration, besides free schooling for all (white) children. In 1826, near the end of his long life, he would reaffirm his belief in the 'palpable truth, that the mass of mankind has not been born with saddles on their backs, nor a favoured few booted and spurred, ready to ride them legitimately, by the grace of God.'[38]

Yet he was a devoted holder of individual property rights. As much as Adam Smith's great *Wealth of Nations*, published in this same remarkable year, the Declaration which Jefferson drafted was a refinement of middle-class individualism. 'Liberty' was the twin of 'Property'.

Congress tidied his draft somewhat. It put in some remarks about God, whom Jefferson had almost ignored. Unconvinced by his dubious logic, it struck out one passage which referred to the slave trade as 'cruel war against human nature itself', but which coupled the accusation that the British had forced colonists to buy slaves with the complaint that they were now inciting these very slaves to rise against their rebel masters. It also removed an abusive remark about the use of 'Scotch & foreign mercenaries'. But the resounding prose was still mostly his. 'We hold these truths to be self-evident: that all men are created equal; that they are endowed by their creator with certain inalienable Rights; that among these are life, liberty & the pursuit of happiness: that to secure these rights, governments are instituted among men, deriving their just powers from the consent of the governed; that whenever any form of government becomes destructive of these ends, it is the right of the people to alter or to abolish it ... ' The Declaration shifted blame at last from Parliament to George III himself, who was personally charged with an immense list of 'injuries & usurpations' and with the aim of establishing 'an absolute tyranny over these states'. The 'United colonies' were now 'free and independent', and the signatories pledged lives, fortunes and 'sacred honour' in support of this Declaration.[39]

The delegates stood in suitable awe of their own conduct. In their letters home they frequently invoked the 'generations yet unborn' whose lives and liberties depended on their decisions. But the Declaration, which bound and thrilled some, shocked or excluded others.

'Tories' or 'loyalists' had been declared traitors. All states eventually amerced, taxed or confiscated loyalist property. Some royalists were gaoled, many, most harshly, in cells forty yards below the surface in copper mines at Simsbury, Connecticut. Others arrived as refugees in Nova Scotia.

This seaboard colony might have seemed an obvious candidate for a fourteenth state. Its Yankee settlers were deeply resentful of the clique of Halifax merchants which ran the colony's government. The authorities expected these 'bitter bad subjects' to flock to the American standard. However, there was very little indigenous revolutionary activity. Congress showed almost no interest in liberating the province, and Washington calculated, probably rightly, that British naval strength made it impossible. Though American privateers plundered almost every coastal settlement, Nova Scotian Yankees remained reluctant to fight for the British. They sat on the fence, effectively neutral. Some traded with New England illicitly, others profited richly by selling their provisions to the British base at Halifax. They had not shared in the intellectual transformations which had taken place in New England and further south over the last ten years. Bewildered as to which side they should support, the Nova Scotians consoled and uplifted themselves through a belated 'Great Awakening'. Henry Alline, a young revivalist preacher, went everywhere telling them that old England was corrupt. New England had missed its way, and that they, simple, high-minded men and women, were now God's chosen people.[40]

Congress paid far more attention to Quebec, and had made a sustained effort to bring that colony into the fold. The Quebec Act came partially into force from May 1775. On the new Council, seven members were French-speaking Catholics, but all these were drawn from the seigneurial class, and small farmers viewed their elevation coldly. For the next dozen years a 'French Party', so-called, although its leaders were British, dominated Quebec's government. English-speaking merchants and traders remained 'out'. But their class was small and as yet hardly rooted. The great mass of Canadian peasants, however fearful they were that the British would tax them hard and that their landlords would raise rents, did not speak Jefferson's mother tongue and were wholly unused to discussing constitutional questions.

An Ulsterman, Guy Carleton, hesitant, plodding and unimaginative, was commander-in-chief as well as governor. He had few soldiers at his disposal, and much of his small force must be deployed to defend the Great Lakes country. It was vital, until reinforcements arrived from Britain, that he should create a Canadian militia. It was equally important to Congress that the Canadians should not arm against them. An energetic propaganda campaign took American agents through the Canadian villages, assuring farmers of the virtues of elective assemblies and prompting the first talk amongst them of the Rights of Man. People wavered and havered. When Ethan Allen tried to seize Montreal with a small force in September 1775, he was swiftly forced to surrender by Canadian townspeople who rallied with a few British merchants. Richard Montgomery, Irish born, made more progress later that month. Despite pressure from priests and seigneurs, the militia did not much help Carleton. The British were able to hold Fort St John on the Richelieu against Montgomery for eight critical weeks. Yet after they withdrew from there in November, the Montreal people, contemptuous of British weakness, opened the gates of their town to Montgomery.

During his flight, Carleton passed an American force led by Benedict Arnold, on its way up river to join Montgomery, after an epic march from the Maine coast through 320 miles of virgin forest. His men had pressed on with soaked feet, on short rations, through rain and snow, to receive at last, after five wasting weeks, a cordial welcome from the Canadians. But Arnold had reached Quebec just too late. Lieutenant-Colonel Allan Maclean had had time to rally a motley force – fellow-Highlanders, Canadians, British seamen, British civilians – which was sufficient to make Arnold head away. Eleven hundred men had set out with him. Six hundred and seventy-five were still on hand.

The Canadians now tasted American military occupation, and did not like it. Montgomery found only a few score natives willing to serve with his force. Besieging Quebec, he decided to risk an attack before the engagements of his American troops expired at the end of the year. On the night of December 30, in darkness and driving snow, he was killed as he led his advance party into the Lower Town. The rash assault then ended, though Arnold kept up the siege.

In February 1776, Congress decided to send a commission of four, including Benjamin Franklin, to woo the Canadian *habitants*. They could achieve nothing. With the help of the priests, offering no reward, Carleton raised 2,000 Canadian volunteers. Arnold, who paid, could attract only 500. The country people had turned against the Americans, who gave them paper money, if any at all, and arrested Catholic priests for preaching loyalty. In May, British reinforcements arrived at last. They sortied immediately, and the Americans fled. The Americans looted as they fell back, and they left unpaid debts and bitter memories. The *habitants*, still reluctant to serve the British, now recalled that history gave them little reason to like Americans. Two days before Congress declared independence, Carleton shooed the last American soldier out of Canada.

II

In 1776, the first regular coach service was instituted between Chester and Holyhead, in Anglesey, bringing the depths of Welsh-speaking North Wales into rapid communication with England. The 'picturesque' and remote Welsh landscapes were beginning to draw sophisticated tourists. In tune with movements in Scotland and Ireland a literary revival in the Welsh language went on. Three brothers called Morris from Anglesey, all civil servants, had gathered around them a circle of poets and scholars who wrote verse in traditional metres and rescued old texts from oblivion's dust. One of this group, Evan Evans, had published in 1764 his *Specimens of the Poetry of the Antient Welsh Bards*. But not all Welshmen were obsessed with the past. Methodism had brought many of them into a movement belonging to the new age. The American War now added political awareness. The first publication in Welsh purely concerned with politics was also launched in 1776, a translation of a pamphlet on the American quarrel.[41]

The same year brought to print *On Civil Liberty* by the leading Welsh Dissenter, Richard Price, which sold 60,000 copies immediately, then double that number in a cheap edition.[42] Like the great Joseph Priestley and other English Dissenting intellectuals, Price was a whole-hearted supporter of the American revolutionaries. A campaign for parliamentary reform was gathering momentum – Major Cartwright's *Take Your Choice*, demanding universal male suffrage, also came out in 1776 – and its supporters naturally identified with the demo-cratical persons now causing trouble in Massachusetts.

Granville Sharp, though no Dissenter, resigned his post in the Ordnance Board on the outbreak of war with America – 'that unnatural business' – and relied on the kindness of his brothers for support till eventually 'an accidental acquaintance with General Oglethorpe' (who was also a pro-American) '... restored him to independence'.[43] As well as kindly philanthropists, advanced economic thinkers were questioning the point of the conflict, and the greatest of all British works in economics was yet another new publication this year: Adam Smith's *Wealth of Nations*, a bestseller, attacked both 'mercantilism' and war.

Chatham appealed in the Lords for an end to the war, saying over and over again in his last speeches, 'You CANNOT conquer America'. His rhetoric was madder than ever, as he elaborated the quaint notion that the Americans if conciliated, would, like the Highlanders after the '45, gladly serve the British on their battlefields. He could not bear the thought of his empire's dissolution. In April 1778 he vehemently denied that American independence should ever be admitted: 'Shall we tarnish the lustre of this nation by an ignominious surrender of its rights and fairest possessions?' Then he collapsed in the chamber, to die a month later.[44]

To the rather less crazy voice of Burke was added in opposition in the Commons the eloquence of a rising star, Charles James Fox, son of the most corrupt politician of all, himself a rake, gambler and womaniser, but an ardent supporter of the Americans, whom he saw as proponents of true whig principles. However, the regular opposition could never muster more than a fifth of the House. And recognised 'interests' outside Parliament were not applying much pressure against the war. Bristol merchants ceased to oppose it as valuable government contracts offered themselves, and by the end of 1776, the town's leadership was firmly committed to support of the Ministry. Liverpool might have been expected to show truculence. A general embargo on the export of arms, lest these might reach the rebels, had hit the slave trade hard, since guns were still an essential item of barter in Guinea. A Liverpool news-paper lamented, 'Our once extensive trade to Africa is at a stand ... ' The town's merchants reacted characteristically by slashing their seamen's wages, provoking a riotous strike in which sailors firing small arms and cannon attacked the Exchange and dragoons were called in from Manchester. The war hurt poor Liverpool people – by its end 10,000 were depending on public relief or private charity. However, rich shipowners turned with gusto to privateering, launching, in 1778–9, some 120 private men-of-war in nine months. And from 1780 their slave trade revived.[45]

Glasgow merchants would never again lead Europe in dispensing tobacco, but the war brought no drastic disruption of their prosperity, and trade with the thirteen colonies continued, not only directly through ports still in British hands, but deviously through Quebec, Nova Scotia, and the Dutch and Danish West Indian islands. Upper- and middle-class opinion in Scotland was over-whelmingly pro-government over the war. As in England, it is hard to know what the poor thought or felt, though it is clear that the Edinburgh townsfolk encouraged mutinous Highland regiments.[46]

Eleven new Highland regiments were raised during the war, through what John Prebble calls a 'market in human cattle'. But it was soon difficult to raise troops in the Gaelic areas, and regiments wearing the government's dark tartan had to be brought up to strength with Lowlanders and Irishmen. There were four mutinies in and around Edinburgh in thirteen months, during 1778–9. In one brutal case, some sixty soldiers of Fraser's Regiment and the Black Watch fought a bloody battle at Leith Harbour with Border troops sent in to tame them, and half the Highlanders were killed or wounded. Their grievance had been that they were being drafted into a Lowland regiment. So far from being in tune with democratical Yankees, these Gaels were more feudalist than their own chiefs, who enticed them into uniform with pledges that they would serve only under officers of their own name or race and in the clothing they liked best to wear. Highland self-respect was outraged by army floggings and punishment in the Black Hole. In a gesture which prefigured a later and greater Mutiny far away, Argyll Fencibles flung aside with scorn the untraditional cartridge pouches and the goatskin sporrans forced on them by their officers.[47]

However, such Gaelic soldiers as read English may have begun at this time to appreciate the point of Tom Paine's contempt for hereditary succession by nobles and monarchs. What example could have served Paine's arguments better than Alexander, Lord Macdonald of Macdonald and Sleat, descendant of High Kings of Ireland and of Lords of the Isles, whose effete Anglicised bearing had infuriated Dr Johnson and whose clansmen, raised for his own regi-ment, rose up against him beside the Forth, on their way to fight the American rebels? Amongst poor people in England, as war began, John Wesley found bitterness everywhere. He reported that 'The bulk of the people in every city, town and village' were alienated from George III. 'They heartily despise his Majesty and hate him with a perfect hatred. They wish to imbrue their hands in his blood; they are full of the spirit of murder and rebellion.'[48] This reaction was prompted by a slump in commerce bringing temporary high unemploy-ment. But even as the economy picked itself up, we must suppose that few ordinary Englishmen had much heart for the conflict.

III

If most British people were not eager supporters of North and the King, only a minority of Americans were ardent, committed 'patriots'. The thirteen colonies were an arena of bitter civil war, in which both sides enlisted Red Indian auxiliaries and went in for summary execution of their opponents.

With Britain's world-conquering power behind them, few loyalists can have dreamt at the outset that they might lose. Nowhere did they take the initiative. Patriots acted; loyalists reacted. Patriots found inspiration in hope – they aimed to create the best nation in the world – and where families divided, the younger generation generally tended to be whig. The overwhelming majority of members of lower houses of assembly were whigs, but about half or two-thirds of upper house members were loyalists. Though there were tens of thousands of loyalists who were not wealthy, 'the richer segments of society contributed proportionately more heavily, especially to the activists.' Rich men were loyalists from fear, lest 'New England principles' might triumph everywhere. James Allen of Philadelphia was a hot supporter of Congress as late as the summer of 1775. But by October, drilling with the militia, he was complaining, ' ... The most insignificant now lord it with impunity and without discretion over the most respectable characters.' Fear of social revolution soon pulled him into the loyalist camp.[49]

Patriots, full of passionate intensity, made more effective polemicists and speakers. It was easy for them to dramatise the issues. They were against the King. They wanted an independent republic. Anyone could understand what they meant. Loyalists were rarely so sure what they wanted. Most loyalist leaders had been sharply critical of the British government. Few would have liked a simple return to the situation of 1763. Hence their voices were diverse and blurred. Their writings commonly offered vague, dull, legalistic proposals. Their staple scorn for the patriot leaders took on the sneering accents of aristocratic hauteur, as they derided the lowly origins of Congressmen and patriot colonels. They could not easily appeal to these whom they dismissed as the 'mob', the 'populace' and the 'frenzied multitude'.

Even so, loyalists were very numerous. Perhaps 30,000, perhaps more, actually fought for George III. In 1780, when Washington's army numbered only about 9,000, 8,000 American loyalists were aiding the British. During and after the war, maybe 60,000, perhaps 100,000 loyalists left the colonies as exiles. Perhaps a tenth even of New Englanders, a third or a quarter of southerners, and a half of the people of the middle colonies, could have been described as loyalists.[50]

They came in all shapes and sizes. Even among the Virginian ruling class, where loyalists were exceptionally scanty, men with such great plantocrat names as Byrd and Randolph were found among them. Most Scotch-Irish were patriots, but not all. Natives of Scotland, Gael and Lowlander, rich and poor alike, were generally on George III's side (though two Scots signed the Declaration of Independence, and of thirteen known Scottish parsons in Virginia, eight sided with the patriots). Germans were commonly passive in the south, but those in New York State were largely patriots – in a region where there were many 'tory' small farmers. While smugglers, of course, were patriots, merchants depending on licit trade with Britain tended, despite all the Acts of Trade, to be loyalist.[51]

No documentary evidence can give us a sure estimate of the proportion of colonials who would have welcomed, or accepted, a British victory. Many must have been apathetic. Many loyalists lay low. 'We are at present all Whigs', one wrote in 1775, 'until the arrival of the King's troops.'[52]

When they did raise their heads, loyalists proved, as soldiers, no whit inferior to their patriot enemies. Some led Indian allies against frontier settlements. Thus, the Cherokees attacked in the south with the help of a few back-country loyalists (though patriot militia beat them so thoroughly that they were never a military threat again). Later, the British made some use of the Creeks, while Iroquois assisted them in the north. The Indians, of course, were quite right to think that a British victory would be better for them than the triumph of patriot land speculators.

Pro-British Indian raids, however, might kill or alienate potential friends as well as convinced foes. And while every loyalist success strengthened whig determination by the hatred which it evoked, each British failure disillusioned colonials not deeply hostile to the 'mother country'. That section, perhaps the largest of the three, who prudently backed whichever side was currently winning in the locality, selling produce to either army impartially, gradually shifted towards the patriot side as the British showed how vincible they were. George III's forces could never control more than a few scattered strips of land on the coast.

Where should the main British thrust be made? There was no single city in America, comparable to London or Paris, whose loss must bring the patriots to terms. The war might be won if the Hudson–Lake Champlain line could be recaptured and held, so cutting New England off from its allies, while the middle colonies were brought firmly under control. Alternatively, the southern-most colonies, where loyalism seemed strong, could perhaps be conquered as the base for a northward push. These two strategies were tried in turn. Neither, however, even if it succeeded, would bring all thirteen colonies automatically to their knees. The hope must be that most Americans were at heart loyal, and that at some point the rebel leaders would be disavowed, or would give up the struggle.

Tight blockade might have brought the rebels to terms. But British naval strength was now inadequate. In the critical first year of war, the rebels got plenty of gunpowder from Europe. The British fleet, in 1776, captured numerous American vessels, but could not lock the Americans in. The success of rebel privateers rubbed home the truth of Chatham's assertion that America had been 'the nerve of our strength, the nursery and basis of our naval power.' Though Lord Sandwich at the Admiralty worked well, and, by 1779, the Royal Navy had a battle fleet comparable in strength to its best in the Seven Years War, achieving this had been beyond the royal shipyards. Every available private yard had been used, but the shortage of skilled shipwrights could not be easily made up. American craftsmen, yards, masts, and timber, had been essential to Britain's naval pre-eminence.

An oak tree took a hundred years to mature. Nearly 2,000 trees must be felled to produce a 74-gun third-rater. Former wars had stripped England's southern counties almost bare, and only increased use of oak and softwoods from America had kept Britain ahead of her rivals. And American seamen had been very useful. In their absence, the pressing service in Britain itself had to work on a larger and more unpopular scale than ever before. By 1779 it employed over 1,000 men. In the whole course of the war, no fewer than 171,000 sailors were found, but perhaps nearly half of these were 'landsmen', unskilled in their new tasks and raked out of slums and gaols. Thanks in part to the diseases which these brought on board with them, 18,500 men, over one in ten, died of sickness. A quarter, 42,000, deserted. By contrast, only 1,240 perished in action.[53]

The Navy, in any case, could not be used to great, offensive effect when so many troops had to be shipped across, then supplied once they reached America. The logistical feats essayed by North's ministry had no parallel till our own century. The British never controlled enough territory to feed their army. Apart from hay and some fresh provisions, everything had to come by sea. 'Every year a third of a ton of food was needed for each man in America, besides the weight of the casks in which it was packed.' And besides arms and other equipment. There simply could not be enough ships, enough sailors.[54]

The British now put far more men into America than had beaten the French out of Canada. Then, they had had help from the thirteen colonies. Now, British losses had to be replaced by shipping new men across the Atlantic. Washington's men were of course, home-grown; hence, each British casualty cost more. Their home terrain gave the patriots huge advantages. A Frenchman who served on their side remarked, 'though the people of America might be conquered by well-disciplined European troops, the country of America was unconquerable.' The land was vast. The British army was always short of transport. Its communications were always vulnerable. It could not pursue the rebels far from the navigable rivers. Its men, in any case, were enfeebled by a climate to which their foes were contentedly adjusted. The winters were much colder than in Britain, and the summers were hotter. British soldiers commonly collapsed in the heat, and on more than one occasion, sheer exhaustion prevented them from pressing home an advantage.[55]

The character of the whole war was epitomised in its earliest stages. As they had promised at Bunker Hill, disciplined British troops would always possess the field in a formal battle, but accurate American shooting could make the cost excessive. Regulars were at a loss against the guerrilla spirit first encountered on the march back from Concord. Anywhere in the colonies, some guerrilla body might come from nowhere to hit the British hard on the nose. The British learnt from their enemies. Before long, they too were using special units of fast mounted infantry. British foot soldiers were superb at close order drill. They were extremely brave under fire. But they fought for their pay, not out of love for their cause. Their virtue was that they obeyed orders. The virtue of the American soldier was that he questioned them. Baron von Steuben, a German serving with Washington, wrote home to a military friend, 'You say to your soldier, "Do this", and he does it; but I am obliged to say "This is the reason why you ought to do that"; and then he does it.'[56] British generals were not inept by European standards. But the very fact that they were professionals was against them. If they followed the 'rules' safely, they would be paid. Patriot commanders were fighting for their lives, and their property. In revolutions, it is not cautious men who come to the fore. Though they wrangled with each other, fumbled and bungled, the better patriot commanders, technically beaten, were not going to accept defeat tamely. They would come back, and back again.

Internally, the American revolution was drastic in its immediate effects. Perhaps twenty-four people in a thousand were driven into exile, as compared with only five in a thousand expelled in the French revolution a few years later. Great quantities of loyalist-owned land passed into others' hands. Sometimes the effect was to spread property more widely; in New York State, James de Lancey's acres came under the ownership of 275 different people.[57] But more commonly, unto those who had it was given, with merchants, army contractors and revolutionary leaders acquiring large properties.

Until 1781, the Second Continental Congress continued to govern, or rather misgovern, the 'United States'. Articles of confederation, completed four years before, were not ratified until then because of disputes between states over western lands. Near chaos prevailed. The country was desperately short of the manufactured goods formerly acquired from Britain, and as English and Scots found ways of getting them in, 'long before the war ended control had begun to slip back into the hands of British merchant firms.'[58] But inflation raged upwards, worsened by the spate of paper currency put out by Congress and the states, and by gleeful profiteering on the part of merchants, contractors and commissaries. Most of the states lacked the nerve to impose taxes so as to curb inflation and finance the war. In 1780, when the paper Continental dollar was almost worthless, Congress resorted to repudiation, wiping out almost 200 million dollars of debts.

Connecticut, Rhode Island, and, at first, Massachusetts, simply proceeded under their charters, slightly amended to exclude the Crown. Ten other states swiftly produced new constitutions. Pennsylvania's was the most dramatic. Existing leaders were loyalist or timid. In the summer of 1776, Paine and his radical friends supplanted the Assembly with their own provincial conference of delegates, which in turn arranged an elected Constitutional Convention to settle a new form of government for the colony. The new constitution for which this voted, and which operated till 1789, provided for a unicameral legislature, to be elected by all free male taxpayers; for the local election of J.P.s and sheriffs; and for an enlightened penal code. But this time, a reaction against Paineite ideas was setting in among propertied men. John Adams had led it with a riposte to *Common Sense* in which he argued the case for elected upper houses. His views had great weight with those making constitutions in other states, who mostly found Pennsylvanian 'mobocracy' deeply distasteful.

The dominance of existing élites was confirmed. Jefferson could not persuade his fellow Virginians to widen the franchise beyond its colonial limits. Though North Carolina's new constitution gave all taxpayers (but not blacks or mulattoes) the right to vote, only men of considerable property were entitled to sit in the Assembly. And so on.

However, in all thirteen colonies, governors were now elected. In Europe, this spectacle seemed either outrageous or inspiring. The new states confirmed in law the peculiarities of American life as they already existed in practice. Manorial rights, quitrents, primogeniture, entail — vestiges of feudal Europe — were swept aside. Though the Congregational churches in New England held on to most of their privileges, the Anglican Church was disestablished in New York and in the states south of Maryland, and by 1786 Virginia had accepted Jefferson's proposals for full religious freedom, a 'natural right'. The new nation's leaders all accepted the principle of 'popular government', though they saw 'democracy' as an unworkable or detestable form of it. John Adams exulted that 'aristocracy' was made impossible in America: 'the dons, the bashaws, the grandees, the patricians, the sachems, the nabobs, call them by what name you please, sigh, and groan, and fret, and sometimes stamp, and foam, and curse, but all in vain. The decree is gone forth, and cannot be recalled, that a more equal liberty than has prevailed in other parts of the earth, must be established in America.'[59]

Amidst all this, black slaves could hardly be forgotten. 'With what face, Sir,' an Englishman, Thomas Day, asked in an argument addressed to Henry Laurens, South Carolina's leading slave trader and leading patriot, 'can he who has never respected the rights of nature in another, pretend to claim them in his own favour?' When the Declaration of Independence was voted, talking of natural rights for 'all men', colonial anti-slavery campaigners were swift to point out that if Africans were men, they must be included.[60]

Rhode Island had prohibited slave importation in 1774, and proceeded to raise a (separate) battalion of black troops during the war. The shortage of men willing to fight for Washington meant that slaves and free blacks were drawn in elsewhere, though South Carolina and Georgia held out against enlisting them to the end. During or immediately after the war, all states except these same two passed laws against fresh imports. A Pennsylvania law of 1780 provided for gradual emancipation in that state. Massachusetts had outlawed slavery by 1783. Rhode Island and Connecticut followed in 1784. In the north, slavery thus withered away, and even in the south, few at this time actually endorsed it in public. A Virginian law of 1782 made manumission easier.[61]

The 'right' wing in American politics, once loyalists had been extruded, would have seemed 'centre' or 'left' wing anywhere else in the Atlantic world. The

72 Captain James Cook — a non-idealised portrait by J. Webber, who sailed with him

73 Dr Joseph Black, James Watt's scientific mentor

74 Matthew Boulton, suitably 'princely' in an engraving after W. Beachey

75 John Wilkinson, iron-master extraordinary

76 Webber's portrait of a Tahitian 'princess'

77 A Nootka Sound Indian, also portrayed by Cook's last expedition

78 The Parys Copper Mine on Anglesey, by J. C. Ibbetson

new leaders in the states had pushed their way to the top, had become governors, senators, holders of office, by such revolutionary means as extralegal Associations, illegal militias and constitutional conventions. Their legitimacy succeeded upon 'mob' violence, expropriation and guerrilla war. Americans had displayed the power of the 'people' to seize their own destiny from the hands of anointed rulers and their hirelings. For another hundred years, élitists in Britain would view the new nation with deep disdain and dismay, as a bad example to their own poor. Anti-slavery agitation by otherwise conservative British people would be heated at least in part by a wish to recapture the moral leadership of the English-speaking world from the likes of Thomas Jefferson.

Culturally, Americans would remain 'provincial' for a long time yet. The hymns of Watts and Wesley would be sung in the wilderness; the way of life of the English gentry would be copied, by those who could afford it, even west of the mountains; the first famous American novelist would be a heavy-handed imitator of a very great Scottish writer. But political severance, with all its important consequences, had happened.

Independency, in 1776, was already a fact. We now see that it was irreversible. However, the war lasted five more years. Neither side won 'great victories' like Blenheim, though several generals on both sides, including Washington, showed unprecedented talent for handing their own men over into captivity in thousands. Washington, by surviving in command, secured his status as the most overrated soldier of all time and eventual translation into presidency and long-nosed marble. Carleton, by doing virtually nothing, acquired for later historians the aura of having been the best royal general in America, if only he had got round to doing something. Lord North, failing to resign or madly to cut his throat, as Chatham would clearly have had the sense to do, joined, with 'Gentleman Johnny' Burgoyne, the cast of the textbooks' puppet theatre, where the buffoons of the past are endlessly jeered at by schoolchildren for their misfortunes. Redcoats died. Their comrades sang sadly of lasses at home. American soldiers died. Their comrades sang the same songs. Slaves were still whipped here and there. Glasgow merchants, deprived of their property in Virginia, made up for it by selling the rebels linen and so forth via St Eustatius, etc. etc. American farmers prospered, offering produce to either side.

Shortly before the Declaration of Independence, General Howe landed near New York with a powerful force from Halifax. Soon after, Admiral Lord Howe (his brother) arrived with the battle fleet from Britain. Washington vied with General Howe in indecisiveness. While Howe, having captured the town, wasted a month throwing up defences against a weak and retreating enemy, Washington needlessly left behind nearly 3,000 soldiers to fall into British hands. He passed through New Jersey with a dispirited, dwindling band. But Howe was sluggish in pursuit. While the British were in winter quarters, Washington scored an important point. At dawn on December 26, he attacked Trenton, garrisoned by 3,000 Hessians, somnolent after their Christmas celebrations. A third of them had to surrender. The place was recaptured by the British soon after, but the Americans' guerrilla dash had had vital psychological effect. Nicholas Cresswell was still in Virginia when news of Trenton came. 'The minds of the people,' he noted, 'are much altered. A few days ago they had given up the cause for lost. Their late successes have turned the scale and now they are all liberty mad again. Their Recruiting parties could not get a man (except he bought him from his master) no longer since than last week, and now the men are coming in by companies.'[62] Washington shortly achieved another little victory at Princeton. Frederick the Great himself hailed his prowess, and a cautious, moderate slave-owner became the hero of a revolutionary people.

In 1777, Congress was able to raise 34,000 troops, and thanks to secret help from France and Spain these were well armed and quite well clothed. Benjamin Franklin had gone to Paris as ambassador from Congress. His reputation as scientist and *philosophe* preceded him, as did the cult, in French intellectual circles, of the 'good Quaker'. Dissident young Frenchmen already identified his country with principles of civil and religious liberty which were eschewed by their own royal government. New England and Pennsylvania were in fashion; South Carolina had to be forgotten. The Comte de Ségur remarked, at Spa in the summer of 1776, how, among international high society, 'The serious English card game whist was suddenly replaced in all the salons by a no less sober game which was christened "Boston." ' Franklin found that the fur cap which he wore to hide his eczema was hailed as the badge of the honest frontiersman. All classes were clamouring his praises. His benign, shrewd features now found their way into numberless prints, on to 'medallions, snuff boxes, rings, watches, vases, clocks, dishes, handkerchiefs, and even pocket knives.'[63] He dressed in Quaker fashion, in public, lived in private luxury, and flirted, despite his advanced age, with pretty noblewomen. The art of American public relations was coeval with the infant republic.

While the French government saw a chance of revenge against Pitt's conquests, young officers rushed to volunteer for Washington's army. They were commonly disillusioned by their reception across the Atlantic. The Americans who had too few commissions available for all of them, were, furthermore, still very 'English'. Sam Adams was heartily surprised to hear a young Frenchman talk of republican principles. 'Where did you learn all that?' 'In France.' 'In France! That's impossible.' Then, after thinking a moment, 'Well,' said Adams, 'because a man was born in a stable, it is no reason why he should be a horse.' This young Frenchman soon learned 'that an Englishman could beat three Frenchmen; that the French were a poor, meagre, puny, little, dark-coloured and almost dwarfish nation; that they fed on *soupe maigre* and frogs; that they wore wooden shoes and ruffles without shirts, to which popery and slavery being added the French nation was represented as sufficiently contemptible ... I was often complimented with the observation that I did not look like a Frenchman.'⁶⁴ However, French gunpowder came in very handy during the campaigns of 1777.

In that year the British commanders came up with two good ideas. One was General Howe's, that he should strike at Philadelphia via the Chesapeake. The other was Burgoyne's, a push southward from Canada towards New York, isolating rebarbative New England. The trouble was that these notions were not co-ordinated. Howe sailed off in July, beat Washington thoroughly at Brandy-wine Creek, and occupied Philadelphia. Meanwhile, Burgoyne had led nearly ten thousand troops southward from Canada. Two companies of Canadian militia went with him; their members deserted in mass on the way, refusing to serve outside their homeland. Burgoyne's Indian allies also proved unreliable. Nevertheless, full of bounce, he recaptured Ticonderoga. After that he made slow, painful progress. The Americans felled trees across his path. When he sent off a strong force to forage in Vermont, it was defeated by local militia, with heavy losses. By September, General Gates, opposing him, actually had more men. Burgoyne rashly attacked a strong American position at Bemis Heights; British casualties outweighed the value of the ground he took; then a reconnaissance in force was badly mauled. Burgoyne, completely surrounded, soon knew he had had it. Clinton, commanding at New York, was sending up help, but too few men, and too late. Howe, of course, was hundreds of miles away. On October 17, at Saratoga, Burgoyne surrendered. His 5,000 remaining men passed into captivity.

The British government had been taught a lesson in geography. No quick success would be possible in that wild country. Frantic recruiting followed; in three years, thirty-one new regiments were created. 'To find the men the bounty was raised, and raised again. Physical requirements were lowered, and age limits widened.'⁶⁵ North and Parliament now made enormous concessions. The Tea Act and the Massachusetts Charter Act were repealed. Parliament renounced its power to tax the colonies. Five peace commissioners, led by the Earl of Carlisle, were empowered to offer the rebels even more than the first Continental Congress had demanded, though not the independence which the second had actually seized.

It was too late. News of Saratoga prompted immediate French recognition of the new republic. Treaties between the two countries were ratified by Congress in May next year. Carlisle's commission, arriving soon after, could do nothing. There was no French army in the United States until 1780, but the naval effects of the alliance were felt at once.

Spain shortly entered the war against Britain, aiming to get back Gibraltar at last. Britain itself declared war, pre-emptively, on the Dutch, after the Nether-lands had entered a 'League of Armed Neutrality' launched by Russian and joined, over two years, by half a dozen other European powers. Even Portugal joined. The dog bit its master. Every navy of consequence, by 1782, was resisting Britain's. What doubters had told Pitt in 1760 had come true – the very magnitude of Britain's success must unite Europe against her. This time, there was no land war in Europe to give Britain allies and distract France.

France and Spain between them had half as many ships again as the Royal Navy, which faced now an exorbitant range of tasks. The homeland must be defended against French invasion. The French must be coped with in the Indian Ocean. The army in the New World must be supplied, and British merchantmen must be convoyed. Inevitably, the British lost control, from time to time, of American waters, where patriot privateers swarmed in hundreds, recalling in spirit the guerrilla war at sea waged by Elizabeth's people for England and for profit. Before the end, Britain lost about 2,000 ships, and 12,000 captured sailors, to these marauders.[66]

To launch another effort in America as large as that which had failed in 1777 would mean almost certain loss of the British West Indies to France. The islands must have priority. Most prominent persons, including George III, believed that Britain would be ruined without them. In March 1778, the Cabinet decided that Admiral Lord Howe must not only send home twenty ships to make good the shortage of cruisers in British waters, but also despatch a strong naval force to the Leewards. General Howe had resigned after Saratoga. Clinton, his successor, was to send 3,000 troops to reinforce the Floridas and 5,000 to the West Indies. The rest of his army was to quit Philadelphia for New York, and thence send yet another detachment to strengthen Halifax. This left only two points in the thirteen colonies, New York and Rhode Island, in British hands.

The West Indian colonies were indeed in a serious plight. They had utterly depended on North American provisions, and imports from Britain and Ireland could not now avert food shortage. Slaves starved. About 3,000 deaths from malnutrition were reported from the Leewards alone by March 1778. Maize cost three times as much on Jamaica during the war as before it. Credit collapsed. Insurance and freight rates soared. For the first time, the British islands felt commercial strangulation such as had formerly been the lot of the French. Natural disasters deepened despondency. A long drought affected Antigua. Bridgetown, Barbados, was almost wholly destroyed in a storm.[67]

In the autumn of 1778, the French seized Dominica. To balance this, Clinton's reinforcements captured St Lucia in December. It was quite a fierce little struggle, but the French were, as one British officer noted, 'remarkably polite. Their chief surgeon was sent in to offer General Medows his assistance. The General's horse strayed out; they sent him back ... Their sentries often, when they saw our soldiers passing near, would point to their arms, shake their heads, and laugh, but never fired, — a very different style of war,' he remarked pointedly, 'from that which we had been used to in America.' In the rainy season, discomfort drew Europeans together. 'Their officers agreed with us most feelingly, that the climate was most villainous; that if we stayed much longer here, both armies would perish; and that the island was not worth the fighting for.'[68]

Sure enough, disease did its worst again. Of 5,000 British rank and file arriving fit for duty in December, 1,800 were sick or dead by May.[69] The French regained control of the sea. St Vincent and Grenada fell to them in 1779. Three years later they would add St Kitts, Nevis and Montserrat.

Britain itself was in danger. The exploits of one sea-guerrilla in home waters shook government supporters. He was a Scot, the son of a gardener, born John Paul, to which he added, on his own account, 'Jones'. The first lieutenant commissioned in the infant 'Continental Navy', he went to raid commerce off Ireland, then suddenly hit Whitehaven in Cumbria one night in the spring of 1778. He did little damage, but this was the first time an English seaport had been so raided for over a hundred years. Jones sailed across to his homeland, Galloway, and stole the Countess of Selkirk's silver from her mansion before her eyes. He was shortly given command of a converted French East Indiaman which he renamed the *Bonhomme Richard*. In it, he cruised right round Britain with a small squadron, capturing prizes and causing consternation. Off Flamborough Head, in September 1779, he ran into a convoy from the Baltic escorted by two British ships of war. He grappled the frigate *Serapis*, a better ship than his own. The *Bonhomme Richard* was shot to splinters and on the verge of sinking, but Jones desperately fought on, the British captain lost his nerve, and both Royal Navy vessels were captured. As British ships scoured the seas in vain for him, Jones became a folk-hero in England and Scotland. Ballads were printed in his honour.

One aim of the *Bonhomme Richard*'s cruise had been to divert British vessels from opposing a planned Franco-Spanish Armada. Thirty thousand troops were due to invade from France. Britain could muster only 21,000 regulars on home soil, though 30,000 militiamen also stood ready. The winds were Protestant once again. The attack failed.

For the British, America was now a sideshow, where impotence confronted impotence. The Continental army dwindled in numbers—service was hard, food and clothing were still bad, pay was worth little more than the paper on which it was printed. There were dangerous mutinies, and in the autumn of 1780, the best American general, Benedict Arnold, unmasked as a traitor, went over to the British. A fresh American invasion of Canada had been planned after Saratoga. It was to be led by the 20-year-old Marquis de la Fayette, the most notable of the French volunteers. But he turned up at Albany to find only half the troops promised to him, and these half-clad. Congress soon stopped the adventure.

The Canadian position was paradoxical. French-speaking Canadians hoped and believed that a French fleet would soon arrive but the alliance between Congress and France secretly stipulated that if the province were recaptured it would become part of the United States, and France would renounce it forever. The French government really desired that Canada should remain British; it correctly foresaw that this would be a perpetual source of animosity between Britain and the States. Yet Washington scotched a new invasion plan because he thought that the French, if they co-operated, would be tempted to hang on to Canada and through it have the chance of 'awing and controlling' the United States. The Americans made no further military effort, though their agents wormed everywhere in Canada making disaffection.[70]

The British were now too weak to attack Washington's weak army. They could do much damage with raids on the coastline and on the frontier. Some major New York landowners, John and Walter Butler and Guy Johnson (son of Sir William, who was now dead), had retreated into Canada, where they organised loyalists into military corps. Many Iroquois joined them, though two of the Six Nations, Oneidas and Tuscaroras, sided with the States. Loyalist raids along the northern frontier sent panic-stricken settlers fleeing east for their lives. General John Sullivan led a successful American counter-attack. More than forty Iroquois towns and 160,000 bushels of corn were destroyed, and in the severe winter of 1779–80, while many Indians died of starvation, thousands flocked to Niagara to the food and protection of the British. The Six Nations were never a force again, though Sullivan's cruelty for the time being gave Iroquois-loyalist raids extra bitterness, and the Americans soon stood on the defensive once more. Even the northern frontier, then, saw stalemate.[71]

The new British strategy was to attempt the piecemeal reduction of the separate states with the help of loyalist militia. The belief that most of the former colonists were still loyalists was encouraged by leading exiles in London.

'Tories' washed up in Britain, in straitened financial circumstances, had had enforced upon them a dismal recognition of what it meant to be 'colonial' and 'American' in an arrogant, wealthy society. Thomas Hutchinson, the most distinguished of them, died, heartbroken, in 1780, having missed his native land painfully. ' … I should prefer even my humble cottage upon Milton Hill to the lofty palaces upon Richmond Hill, so that upon the whole I am more of a New England man than ever … ' He was shocked by British political corruption. The morals of the mother country appalled him. How could rich women ignore a child killed by their carriage? How could fashionable Londoners enjoy the 'trifling, puerile, insipid' amusements to which they gave so much of their time and money? He preferred Bristol, a smaller, more mercantile place. 'The manners and customs of the people are very like those of the people of New England, and you might pick out a set of Boston selectmen from any of their churches.'[72]

Lesser loyalists mostly reacted likewise, mingling as much as possible with people from their own colonies, and gradually migrating from expensive London to Bristol and other provincial towns. But after Saratoga, the influence of their spokesmen grew markedly. They presented the government with an argument which was most reassuring, and perfectly circular. The colonies had been enjoying a virtual Golden Age of prosperity under benevolent rule. Somehow, as one prominent exile put it, they had 'run Mad with too much Happiness'.[73] A small clique, setting their sights on independence, had 'deluded' the ignorant 'populace'. Their puny minority could be disarmed by the loyal and grateful majority. This notion lured North's ministry as a rope appeals to a drowning man. There was no way that massive reinforcements could now be sent to America. M.P.s knew that, and only by persuading them that the loyalists could be depended upon for heavy support was North able to keep a majority in favour of continuing the war.

The southern states seemed the best bet. The first strokes there had worked well. A British force of 3,000 easily recaptured Savannah at the end of 1778, and within a month Georgia was under control. A royal governor ruled there for three years. In December 1779, Clinton came down with 8,000 troops to attack South Carolina. Charles Town fell next May, and General Benjamin Lincoln, with over 5,000 men, made another massive surrender. General Lord Cornwallis was left in charge as Clinton sailed off again to deal with a successful French attack on Rhode Island. The position in South Carolina seemed excellent. Cornwallis had 8,000 men. Loyalists were flocking to join him. Hundreds of repentant patriots were taking oaths of allegiance to the King. Washington sent General Gates with a sizeable army, but Cornwallis beat this decisively at Camden.

Next year Cornwallis despatched an army under Benedict Arnold to conquer Virginia. Jefferson was governor of that state, but his term of office had been far from successful, and now the British reduced him to impotence. British troops captured Richmond. The legislature fled. Cornwallis defeated another American army in North Carolina and moved off to join Arnold at Yorktown, on the Chesapeake. American armies had been beaten in four states in quick succession. This run of victories would have meant triumph in any European theatre of war. It meant nothing of the kind in this steamy near-wilderness. Cornwallis left behind him about 8,000 troops, most of them loyalists, to defend South Carolina and Georgia. Now General Nathanael Greene, defeated in the open field, could rally enough guerrillas in the creeks and on the hills and in the woods to inflict losses which forced the royal force on to the defensive. It controlled nothing more than a few square miles around Savannah and Charles Town. Southern back-countrymen changed sides with the tide of war, and as British troops gave way, loyalist militiamen prudently slipped over to join the whigs.

Cornwallis fancied Yorktown as a base, and set about establishing himself there. A French army which had wintered at Newport, well disciplined and well supplied with money, was now ready for offensive operations. Its commander persuaded Washington that the British must be caught in Virginia. A French fleet was in American waters, and Admiral de Grasse agreed to come to the Chesapeake in August, bringing 3,000 French regular troops with him.

Washington brought down 12,000 men. Facing superior forces on the land side, Cornwallis found that de Grasse had cut his seaward communications. He surrendered, with 7,000 troops, on October 19. Lord North, hearing of this in late November, flung his arms wide and cried 'Oh God! it is all over.' The British still had 30,000 effectives in America. But Yorktown was final because of the juncture at which the news struck. There had been defeats in India, West Florida had been lost, Minorca had been invaded, French and Spanish fleets were menacing in the Channel again, and that squad of independent country gentleman M.P.s who figure in histories of this period rather like a confused and timorous chorus in some tragedy by Euripides, were 'groaning' under the weight of taxation. The British government gave America up.[74]

IV

Many country gentlemen, however, seemed to have caught bad habits from the rebels. Calls for cheaper government mingled with protests against corruption and aims to make Parliament more representative, in a spontaneous movement which welled up among the electors after Saratoga.

The freeholders of Yorkshire, led by the Reverend Christopher Wyvill, agreed, at a mass meeting of electors, on a petition against waste of public money and set up a committee to carry on correspondence. In 1780, the 'petitioning movement' spread quite widely through the country, infecting even the Isle of Man. Wyvill planned an association on a national base. The American patriots had shown how such things might be created, and how powerful they might prove. One aim was to add to the House of Commons a hundred more representatives of the counties, elected on the broad freeholder franchise. It was decided to hold a meeting in London of deputies elected by local committees. The proponents of this assembly had the virtually revolutionary hope that it might take over effective control of the country from North's corrupt Parliament. Only twelve counties and eight boroughs were represented when it convened in March 1780, but the parliamentary opposition was stirred into action. Next month, the Commons passed a resolution moved by one Dunning which stated: ' ... The influence of the Crown has increased, is increasing, and ought to be diminished.'[75]

It seemed for a moment that North must fall. But the passage of Dunning's resolution paradoxically helped to head off crisis, since it showed that the Commons were not wholly subservient and did something to restore their prestige. The opposition, inside and outside Parliament, was anyway deeply divided over prescriptions. The Rockingham faction, including Burke, favoured aristocratic domination, and accordingly wished to curtail royal influence. But Charles James Fox, who had become chairman of the Westminster Committee of Correspondence, was now flirting with the radical movement for franchise reform. Westminster constituency's reforming hotheads agreed on proposals which went as far as universal suffrage.

Dr Johnson had remarked a couple of years before: 'Subordination is sadly broken down in this age. No man, now, has the same authority which his father had, — except a gaoler ... There is a general relaxation of reverence.'[76] This was not just the grumbling of an old man dismayed by change. It was true that the authority of the King in the country, the lord over the villager, the master over his worker, the father over his son, all seemed to be collapsing together. Dunning's resolution epitomised the trend, which must have owed much to the inspiration of America, since even those who did not support the rebels could see that their methods had succeeded. More profoundly, it had to do with the vaulting rise of British population and British trade, preceding a change in the character of the whole economy. There was now a big, prosperous, largely Dissenting, largely voteless middle class. Manufacturers in particular had a new self-confidence which jarred against the political system. Growing population implied growing social distance – one landlord, one master, could not know five hundred inferiors as well as his father had known a hundred – and increased the sense amongst middle and lower orders of the potential power of sheer numbers. Unthinking deference prevailed less and less. A generation of anti-radical thinkers, including Burke, Henry Dundas and such rising men as the younger Pitt and Wilberforce – had to find new and plausible arguments to justify upper-class rule, the hereditary principle. They would win. But it would be a close-run race. It was not, or did not seem, preordained that Burke and Wilberforce would be held up as heroes for twentieth-century schoolchildren, while a deprecating sneer ('idealist, extremist') still put the dreaded Tom Paine down.

The labouring classes of England seemed at times to require more military attention than the American rebels, or the French. Machine-breaking – sabotage – was one of their weapons. Miners had used it in the 1760s to win the freedom to choose their employers annually. Stocking-makers in the Midlands also adopted this tactic, and between 1776 and 1778, they combined with Londoners in the same trade to petition Parliament as one body for a Bill to regulate wages.

Would angry middle-class persons join with their workmen in a revolutionary movement embracing, before it destroyed them, the 'groaning' squires, and led by such rebel aristocrats as Fox and such ideologues as Price, Paine and Priestley? Or would the division of interest between all propertied men and the unpropertied act to secure the existing élite? 1780, in retrospect, seems to have been a critical year.

Two years before, both Houses of Parliament had comfortably passed legislation, inspired by Edmund Burke, which restored civil, though not political, rights to Roman Catholics in England. Men in governing circles had now grown impatient, as the Quebec Act had shown, with religious intolerance. However, precisely such bitter, hereditary prejudice as had loaded the muskets of New England farmers still flourished in Presbyterian Scotland. The suggestion of similar changes in Scottish law provoked riots in Glasgow and Edinburgh and the formation of a 'Protestant Association'. Lord George Gordon M.P. appeared at its head. This charming, ambitious young man somehow had equal appeal for Gaelic highlanders and for Lowland heirs of the Covenanting tradition. He wore tartan trews in the House of Commons, spoke in favour of the American rebels, and kept open house for Scots of all ranks and both races. His movement prevented relief for Scottish Catholics. A similar Protestant Association arose in England, and Gordon was asked to become its president.

On June 2, 1780, sixty thousand people marched on Westminster where Gordon presented a petition for the repeal of the Act in favour of English Catholics. A week of astonishing violence, matched in few revolutions, now followed. Gordon's supporters attacked the chapels, homes and businesses of Catholics. They sacked Newgate Prison and freed all the inmates, assailed the Fleet Prison and the Bank of England, and burnt Lord Mansfield's fine house down. Troops regained control of the metropolis. Gordon was gaoled in the Tower. But religious unreason had saved the existing order. Every propertied man in the country could see what fate might await him if rash political challenge handed initiative over to the 'populace'. The election later that year gave North another House which he could control.

Though Yorktown broke North, it did not break the system. George III had to turn again to Rockingham and his supporters, who were very happy to end the war for him, but had no intention of drastic reform at home. They made a token attack on royal patronage. Burke's 'Economical Reform' Bills pruned the king's household of some of its sinecures. Revenue officers were disfranchised, government contractors were excluded from the House of Commons. But deeper 'reform' would not come for half a century. Great changes occurred only in Ireland.

V

One Protestant gentleman claimed, in 1782, 'it was on the plains of America that Ireland obtained her freedom.' To break free from British commercial restrictions and to assert the independence of their parliament, his people had consciously copied American methods. They had observed, to the west, the emergence for the first time of something which we may sensibly call 'nationalism'. Though John Paul Jones had informed the Countess of Selkirk that he was a 'Citizen of the World, totally unfettered by the little mean distinctions of Climate or of Country, which diminish the benevolence of the Heart and set bounds to Philanthropy', American patriots had set the world a portentous example. They were creating a new 'nation'. Their success was not lost on Irish patriots, though as Protestants they flinched from the full realisation of 'nationhood', and wished, as the modern scholar Harlow put it, 'to remain independent both of the native Irish and of Westminster.'[77]

Their favourite orator was now a little hatchet-faced barrister named Grattan. A contemporary described his delivery as 'thin, sharp and far from powerful.' He lacked the fine voice of Patrick Henry, the masterly elocution of Chatham. His style belonged with the dawning Romantic period. He was warm.

He was lively. He seemed sincere. He was sincere. The strange mowing action of his arms as he spoke, the very difficulty of hearing him, as another observer reported, 'only excited a more anxious attention to his language.' What fine language that was, too, 'now a wide spreading conflagration, and anon a concentred fire … ' The man was unbribeable. He seemed to live only for Ireland. Under the impulse of his orations, the influence of 'place, pension, and peerage' had for a moment 'but an enfeebled hold.'[78]

However, his views were well to the 'right' of Thomas Jefferson's. He was an aristocratical whig, who approved of the 'people' – the 'property of the nation' – but distinguished them sharply from the 'populace' – the 'poverty of the kingdom'.[79] In practice, such views had cruel, repressive results. Grattan avoided the taint of consequences. He never held office. He made it a virtue not to hold office. So what went well and inspiringly, what bathed all feeling men in warm emotion, could be attributed to the fire of his speeches. Whatever was bungled, sordid, cruel and self-interested, had nothing to do with him. His oratory was a brilliant fencing weapon. Middle-class Protestantism carried real guns.

During the American war, the Irish middle class was awakened politically. It discovered its own power. Ireland had new leverage. North needed all the troops the country could give him. Throughout the war his ministry recruited new soldiers heavily from Ireland, including Roman Catholics whose enlistment outraged local Protestant opinion. Furthermore, with American markets partly blocked, British merchants and manufacturers looked to the Irish market for compensation. And no one in Britain wanted another province of empire to revolt. In October 1775 large majorities in the Irish Parliament denounced the rebellion in America. But the Irish middle class was not so complaisant and gave strength to the pro-American 'patriots', led by Grattan.

Protestant opinion was overwhelmingly on the rebels' side. Besides blood-ties created by emigration, there were obvious parallels between the States and Ireland. If North's gang bullied America into submission, would they not freely tax Ireland in turn? Irish newspapers gave ample space to the rebels' case. The citizens of Dublin, Belfast and Cork made their sympathy clear from the outset, while in the small town of Tandragee, for instance, a society of Protestant gentlemen toasted 'The memory of the saints and martyrs that fell at Lexington … '[80] No corps of middle-class Irishmen rushed to die under Washington's command. But the state of the island's economy ensured that rebellious views had some real bitterness.

In February 1776, fearing that the French would join in the war and that Irish provisions might reach them through neutral shippers, the government imposed an embargo on trade in food except to Britain and colonies still loyal. This outraged Irish opinion. The patriots called it unconstitutional. One, Hussey Burgh, raved in the Commons that this kind of exercise of the royal prerogative had 'struck the Crown off one king, and Head off another'. The reaction was rhetorically excessive. The British army and navy were willing to pay soaring prices for Irish provisions. But merchants could not unload the low-grade beef which they had been supplying to the French colonies. The war hampered Ireland in her illegal commerce with France, and in that valuable smuggling trade with North America which had consoled merchants for the commercial restrictions imposed by Britain. Wartime depression in England hit sales and prices of Irish linen exported there, and 1778 was a disastrous year for the linen industry.[81] For generations, the answer in hard times had been to emigrate to America. Now that was blocked. Angry men stayed at home.

The attitude of Irish Catholics was the greatest source of relief to the authorities. No one knew, or knows, what the majority thought. But the community's leaders, as war broke out, expressed their 'abhorrence of the unnatural rebellion' and offered 'two millions of loyal, faithful, and affectionate hearts and hands' to the British government. Prominent Catholic individuals gave bounties in support of recruiting drives. Without elementary civil rights themselves, such men were unlikely to be much impressed with Yankee grievances. Government propaganda cleverly stressed certain parallels. Americans owned slaves. They wanted a freer hand against Red Indians. Were they not rather like the Ascendancy blatherers who ground down the Catholic poor of Ireland? Lord Shelburne, a great absentee landlord, visited Kerry in 1779 and found the poor peasants there 'under a degree of oppression scarce conceivable'. As he noticed, 'In every Protestant or Dissenters' house the established toast is success to the Americans. Among the Roman Catholics they not only talk but act very freely on the other side.'[82]

Catholics, however, did not elect Irish M.P.s. The viceroy, Lord Harcourt, finding Parliament hard to control, dissolved it and lavished money and honours, creating seventeen new peers in one day, so as to get a favourable result.[83] The Duke of Buckinghamshire took over from him late in 1776. His chief secretary was a much less able manager of Parliament than Harcourt's had been, and the Irish administration was now on the verge of bankruptcy. He pleaded with Whitehall to lift the obnoxious export embargo, and it did so at last during 1778. Patriots now had a new slogan, 'free trade'. Lord North, after Saratoga, was offering the Americans virtual independence within the Empire, with restraints upon commerce abated. Why not Ireland? Let all restrictions be lifted. Let the Dublin Parliament regulate Irish trade.

The army in Ireland, weakened by withdrawals for service overseas, was now inadequate to defend the country against French invasion, or to protect landlords against Whiteboys, manufacturers against their workmen. Government credit had collapsed. Dublin Castle could not raise loans from the banks or from the public. Buckinghamshire had to suspend payment of all salaries and pensions. Only loans from the Bank of England shored up his rule. In July 1778 an Act went through authorising, for the first time, the mustering of an Irish militia. But this would cost approaching £40,000 a year. It could not be afforded.

How were rents to be gathered? How were strikes to be broken? In Dublin,

Cork and Belfast, spontaneous moves had been made towards creating a Protestant vigilante force. In the autumn of 1778, the 'Dublin Volunteers' were organised under the command of the Duke of Leinster. Similar corps sprang up elsewhere, some raised by great aristocrats, others, later, by county meetings. With the invasion scare continuing, Dublin Castle could not refuse them the arms allocated for the militia. Spectators in the Commons gallery cheered as Hussey Burgh, quitting the government side, declaimed, 'Talk not to me of peace – it is not peace, but smothered war. England has sown her laws in dragon's teeth, and they have sprung up armed men.'[84]

It looks like a classic revolutionary situation. The regime was hard pressed on the defensive. Most of the ruling class were partially disaffected. And now the people armed. There was just one factor askew. Protestants armed. The Catholic masses were armed, if at all, as soldiers in royal regiments.

Volunteering was great fun. The uniforms, patriotically fashioned from Irish cloth, were brightly coloured and gorgeously faced. After their drilling, performed with great pleasure and pride, the Volunteers drank bumper upon bumper, toasting the Glorious Revolution, the siege of Derry, the battles of the Boyne, Aughrim and Culloden. They saw themselves as true 'Whigs' opposing a 'Tory' court. Since invasion did not occur, their only function was to act as a police force, conducting prisoners to gaol, helping collect tithes, quelling disturbances among the Catholic masses. Yet, to show they were loyally anti-French, some Catholics subscribed to Volunteer funds. A few Catholics were allowed to join the force, despite the laws prohibiting papists from bearing arms. The Volunteers, in their high excitement, showed a novel generosity of spirit. As their movement took on the character of a chain of debating societies, the patriot calls for free trade and Irish independence were echoed and discussed. But how could the vision be realised if Catholics preferred rule from Britain to that of a home-grown Protestant assembly?

Grattan proclaimed that 'the Irish protestant could never be free till the Irish Catholic had ceased to be a slave.' Some Dublin M.P.s had been finding reasons to change their minds about the Penal Code. Ascendancy landowners were less notable, on the whole, for business capacity than for their stomach for liquor. Rum shrub was 'universally drunk in quantities nearly incredible, generally from supper time till morning, by all country gentlemen, as they said, to keep down their claret.' Calling the ailments which resulted 'gout', they then used Drogheda whiskey, 'the hottest-distilled drinkable liquor ever invented', as a specific against that versatile disease. Their relatives in Britain were building fine houses. To match such splendour, they threw up mansions beyond their means, and commonly found they had (as Maria Edgeworth would put it) to 'sell an estate to pay for a house'. Those who were not falling into the power of Catholic moneylenders were commonly looking for rich Catholic tenants.[85]

From 1762 there had been a movement in Parliament to enable landowners to mortgage estates to Catholics. Seven Bills failed in a dozen years, as did others designed to permit longer leases for papists. However, in 1778 the influence of rich Catholic merchants combined with pressure from Westminster to force 'relief' upon the Irish Parliament, even though Grattan himself still opposed it, along with most of the other patriots. An Act was passed under which Catholics might take leases up to 999 years; the reason for denying them outright ownership was that possession of certain lands involved the right to elect M.P.s.

Opposition politicians at Westminster were pointing to the analogies between Ireland and America. North's ministry itself saw the need for concessions. But when Parliament passed, *nem. con.*, four resolutions intended to lift restrictions on Ireland's commerce, a howl of petitioning came from British trading and manufacturing interests. Parliament nevertheless made some concessions. The Irish might now export most goods to the colonies. They were given equality in the Newfoundland fisheries. But despite North's support, and a plea from Edmund Burke, the most valuable trophy of all was denied; the Commons refused to permit Ireland to import goods direct from the plantations. The Bristol electors threw Burke out at the next opportunity. They did not mind his support for America, but favouritism to Ireland was insupportable.

Irish traders retorted by adopting the Yankee notion of 'non-importation'. In April 1779, an 'Aggregate Body of the Citizens' of Dublin passed a vehement motion and soon began to incite 'mob' action against importers of goods from Britain. Other counties and towns also took up non-importation, though Ulster held aloof for fear of a counter-boycott of Irish linen.

Buckinghamshire was as helpless as Governor Hutchinson had been. It was middle-class interests which stood to benefit from free trade; the 'middling ranks of society', swelling the Volunteer movement, were gaining a sense of their corporate power. In face of this power, within three years, the laws disabling dissenters, the laws restricting trade and the laws which denied free scope to the Irish Parliament crashed as if in a political earthquake.

When the Irish Parliament met in mid-October 1779, the streets were full of armed men. On November 4, Volunteers demonstrated around William III's statue. Inscriptions were hung round the pedestal calling for 'A Free Trade – Or Else' and indicating that Volunteers were prepared to die for their country. Twenty counties and many cities and towns saw meetings of electors which instructed or more politely 'desired' their Members of Parliament to vote supplies only for six months, rather than the usual two years, until a free trade was granted. Unlike Wyvill's movement, this gained immediate success. M.P.s were frightened. On November 15, a 'mob' of 3,000 or 4,000 in Dublin intimidated M.P.s trying to enter the Commons, while Volunteers stood aloof, permitting, for once, the lower orders to get out of hand.[86]

It seemed that another province would soon go the way of Massachusetts. Lord North rushed to announce, on November 25, that Ireland would be freed from unequal commercial restriction.

Adam Smith's *Wealth of Nations* had already made a deep impression. Some

British politicians now talked as if 'free trade' for Ireland should mean an absence of any restrictions at all. But North's Cabinet decided merely to put Irish subjects on the same footing as British ones, who traded, of course, under many regulations. This went through the English Parliament almost without opposition and received the royal assent before Christmas. Within six weeks, the Dublin 'mob' and its instigators had won a handsome victory. Their triumph was completed by a second Act in February which conceded Ireland's right to import direct from the colonies.

Buckinghamshire bought support in the Dublin Commons by lavish promises and a notable step was made to placate the Presbyterians, through the repeal of the clause in the 1704 Test Act which barred them from full political participation. But the patriots, having tasted the power of public opinion, now determined to use it to free the Irish Parliament from British control. Many corps of Volunteers passed resolutions against 'enslaving statutes'. Meetings in most counties called for the repeal of Poynings' Law. Grattan, in April 1780, moved in the Commons that only the Irish Parliament was competent to make laws for Ireland. Now was the time to claim independence. Britain stood alone in the world, Ireland was 'the only nation in Europe' which was not her foe. 'I never will be satisfied so long as the meanest cottager in Ireland has a link of the British chain clanking to his rags ... ' But he failed, by ninety-seven votes to a hundred and thirty-seven.[87]

Even many of the professed 'patriot' M.P.s were as frightened of a head-on clash with Britain as they were of public opinion in Ireland. It soon became clear that the Viceroy had regained control of Parliament and that even direct threats of violence from Grattan could not shake it. The union of mob with Volunteers had been ruptured. In June 1780, a week after the Gordon Riots had raged through London, Dublin Volunteers turned out with real alacrity to disperse a large assembly of unarmed journeymen. When the Earl of Carlisle took over as Viceroy, he noted with satisfaction that the upper classes were anxious now for stability and resentful of pressure from middling people.[88] His first year in office was deceptively quiet.

Radicals in the Volunteer Movement now called louder and louder for the reform of Parliament. The two principal boroughmongers were the Duke of Leinster and the Earl of Shannon, controlling ten and eighteen seats respectively. Both were leaders in the Volunteer movement. Both were strongly criticised in the ranks, and though Napper Tandy, a Dublin lawyer who served under Leinster, failed in a move to have the Duke expelled, the various Dublin corps voted seven to three that not Leinster, but Lord Charlemont should review their November 4 parade.[89]

Charlemont, the most consistent aristocratic patriot, now became the effective leader of the Volunteers. Hypersensitive, cultured, and humourless, he disliked speaking in public and suffered from chronic ill health. He claimed that toleration was for him a 'predominant principle', and though he opposed giving political rights to papists, he was anxious to conciliate the majority. Catholics were now being admitted in increasing numbers as Volunteers. It seemed that, among the middle classes, real 'national' unity might be emerging. As the Volunteer movement grew, so did its earnestness. One-day reviews gave way to manoeuvres and parades over two or three. A display given in Belfast in the summer of 1781 was hailed as a 'scene of military grandeur beyond all powers of description.' The self-confidence of the middling people was soaring. A writer in one of the Dublin papers extolled this in menacing terms. 'Every Volunteer at this instant feels and exults in his own consequence: Did he feel this ardour for liberty, this independence upon rank and wealth before he became a Volunteer?'[90]

On 15 February 1782 delegates from the Volunteers of Ulster met in a Convention at Dungannon which passed a resolution calling for legislative independence for Ireland. It also, momentously, agreed that it held 'the right of private judgement in matters of Religion to be equally sacred in others as in ourselves', and rejoiced 'in the relaxation of the Penal Laws against our Roman Catholic fellow-subjects ... ' The implication of this motion seconded by a Presbyterian minister, passed with only two dissentient voices, was that the British government could no longer rely on religious disunity to maintain its grip on Ireland. The Convention openly threatened revolution. 'We know our duty to ourselves, and are resolved to be free.'[91]

How serious the threat was is hard to judge. Jonah Barrington, then a young Volunteer, would claim years later, 'We were very sincere, and, really I think, determined to perish, if necessary, in the cause – at least, I am sure, I was so.' But there was an element of bluff. As one writer put it, 'all the powers of oratory will not gain the people one additional vote in the next session of parliament unless ... you occasionally display before the spies of the castle, some rhetorical flourishes of the firelock, or some pathetic touches from a park of artillery.'[92]

In the two months following the Dungannon Convention, countless Volunteer corps, counties, towns and grand juries held meetings in support of some or all of its resolutions. Carlisle realised that he had been living in a fool's paradise. It was no good having a parliamentary majority, in face of 'thirty thousand men actually in arms'. North's fall relieved him from a dangerous position. The Rockingham faction were old friends of the Irish patriots. They sent over the Duke of Portland as viceroy. By April, Grattan was on his feet proposing independence for the third time and on this occasion, as he knew, no one would dare vote against it. 'I am now to address a free people ... I found Ireland on her knees, I watched over her with an eternal solicitude; I have traced her progress from injuries to arms, and from arms to liberty. Spirit of Swift! Spirit of Molyneux! your genius has prevailed! Ireland is now a nation!'[93]

Portland saw no alternative to immediate independence. The British Parliament swiftly repealed its Declaratory Act of 1719, its formal assertion of its right to legislate for Ireland.

Grattan was presented with £50,000 by the madly enthusiastic Dublin Commons, but his blink of supreme popularity was soon over. Henry Flood, dismissed from office towards the end of 1781 and now fully returned to the patriot camp, was busy outflanking him on the left. His more muscular oratory suited rank and file Volunteers rather better than Grattan's high-flying cadences. Flood loudly averred that repeal of the Declaratory Act meant nothing – had Britain not legislated for Ireland before 1719? – and he won the leadership of public opinion. Much against its will, the British government bowed, and in January 1783 the Westminster Parliament passed a 'Renunciation Act' establishing Ireland's complete legislative and judicial independence 'for ever'.

Division between Flood and Grattan was soon open. Grattan had made his view clear at his hour of triumph; the Volunteers, having 'given a parliament to the people', should now 'leave the people to Parliament'.[94] That is, pressure on Parliament should cease. Only Parliament should reform Parliament. Flood now appealed to the 'middling and lower sort' who were impatient with aristocratic dominance.

In March 1783, delegates of the Munster Volunteers called for the reform of rotten boroughs. Ulster Volunteers followed this up with another fiery session at Dungannon, which summoned a National Convention of Volunteer delegates, to meet in Dublin in November and to deliberate how Ireland might be saved from 'an absolute monarchy, or, that still more odious government, a tyrannical aristocracy.' It would be, as R. R. Palmer points out, 'the first body calling itself a national convention in a world that was to know many such in the next fifteen years.' The Volunteers were in touch with advanced English reformers like Cartwright and Price. Their Convention seemed a revolutionary challenge. Grattan, though nominated, refused to sit in it, and was duly expelled by his own corps of Volunteers. The delegates, who wore arms, agreed on demands for triennial elections, and for the enfranchisement of Protestant freeholders and leaseholders, but decided against the enfranchisement of Catholics. Flood, in uniform, carried their plan down to the House of Commons and moved there for leave to bring in a Bill for the 'more equal representation of the People in Parliament.' The House voted two to one against receiving it and then passed a resolution expressing 'perfect satisfaction' with Ireland's 'present happy constitution'.[95]

The Convention received this news quietly. Charlemont had packed it with moderate friends of his own. Peace, returning prosperity, independence, defused the issue. Flood's Bill was voted down when he introduced it again in the spring of 1784. Dublin reformers, later that year, called a 'Congress' – fateful, American term. Numerous counties and towns responded. But again, the weight of cautious gentility was felt. It had three sessions, amid decreasing interest, then quietly put itself to sleep. Flood, now a Westminster M.P., had turned his attention elsewhere. More sincere reformers still in Ireland began to think in terms of plots and insurrections. The question of votes for Catholics was divisive, and Dublin Castle hoped that it would stay so. Whereas Grattan was almost romantic now on the subject of Catholics, Flood was implacably opposed to giving them any share in the choice of M.P.s. Charlemont agreed with him. An Act of 1782 which allowed papists to buy estates as freely as Protestants had specifically excluded land situated in parliamentary boroughs.

The results of all the commotion were deeply ironic. Now that Catholics could spend like gentlemen, they proceeded to make gentlemen of their sons, sending them into professions instead of business, and so draining money and talent from commerce and industry. Meanwhile, members of the glorious Irish Parliament enjoyed immense privilege and took little responsibility. In the 1783 elections, 72 owners of rotten boroughs, half of them peers, returned 178 M.P.s between them.[96] The Protestant landowning class was fulsomely loyal now that 'independence' had been granted, and there was, save in two instances, no need for ministries in England to use their ultimate power to recommend the King to suppress Irish Bills. Administration remained in the hands of a viceroy who was a member of the British government. The group of high officials whom he appointed, though sometimes called the 'Irish Cabinet', had no independent basis of authority. 'Representing' a small privileged group within a minority, the Dublin House of Commons was still dependent on Britain. Its most prominent M.P. had far less authority than Warren Hastings, the servant of a trading company.

VI

Hastings, however, depended on the support of shareholders at home. The rapacious Sykes wrote from Britain pressing the fact on him brutally. ' ... There is a general complaint, that all letters of recommendation from those you have experienced real favors from in this country have been totally neglected ... We live in an age that, without some reciprocal return, the wheels of the machine will not move.'[97] Since the Board of Trade, from 1774, controlled promotion and preferment in the commercial branch, and since promotion by seniority was the rule in other branches, Hastings was hard put to find lucrative positions for the failures, incompetents and ruined men sent out to him by the Sulivan party. The British position in Oudh was of great consequence to him, since the Nawab-Vizier there could be surrounded by parasitical British aides and advisers. Elsewhere, official contracts also gave Hastings scope.

The opium monopoly which he established, while it brought the East India Company £1,277,000 profit in its first seventeen years, provided enormous pickings for those who contracted to find the drug. Its main source was in Bihar. It was also made in Oudh, in Benares and in some of the northern parts of Bengal. The seed was planted in October or November by cultivators given advances by a contractor, who received in return the moist opium from the poppy seeds in May. After drying for half a year, it was sent to Calcutta to be auctioned, and the fuddling of the Chinese emperor's subjects provided bohea for ladies in England's home counties. In 1781, Hastings awarded the contract to Laurence Sulivan's son, for four years. Stephen Sulivan and his associates arranged that the EIC contracted for too little opium at too high a price, sold surplus chests at a premium to the Company, and also traded on their own account against the EIC monopoly. Hastings knew what was going on, but ignored it. He made similar use of army contracts. The agency for feeding the Calcutta garrison was bestowed on his private secretary, who made a profit of over £15,000 from it in three years.[98]

He could not have retained authority without using such methods to gratify friends and buy allies. His powers under the 1773 Act were limited. The subordinate presidencies in Madras and Bombay had latitude to make war and treaties where immediate necessity seemed to arise, or on receipt of orders direct from home. And the governor-general could not override his council.

His new councillors arrived in October 1774. The nominal second to himself was General Sir John Clavering, the commandre-in-chief. Colonel Monson was rash and greedy. Richard Barwell was a prime instance of the 'nabob', who would be loathed for his arrogance in rural Sussex when he bought an estate there on his retirement. According to Philip Francis, he was 'rapacious without industry, and ambitious without an exertion of his faculties or steady application to affairs.'[99]

Francis, the remaining member of the Council, was probably seen at his best in his relationships with women rather than with other men, though he attracted and influenced several youngsters in the Bengal service – John Shore, Charles Grant, Charles Rouse – who would have important careers in India. His 'enlightened' views were close to those of Hastings. His capacity was perhaps no less. Like Hastings, he had risen by merit, without parliamentary influence or obvious patrons. Francis prided himself upon having 'one or two qualities at least to which this infamous climate cannot reach.' He wanted only enough profit from India to enable him to live at home in comfort, and meanwhile found himself forced, as he saw it, to pass his life 'in one eternal combat with villainy, folly, and prostitution of every species.' He believed that Company rule in Bengal was in principle a bad thing. Hastings was now committed to the reality of EIC rule. The British could not, he said, 'redescend to the humble and undreaded character of trading adventurers.'[100]

Francis's own humourless arrogance ran up against the relish for power which Hastings had acquired. Hastings was convinced that only decisive, confident action could work in India. 'Self-distrust will never fail to create a distrust in others, and make them become your enemies; for in no part of the world is the principle of supporting a rising interest and depressing a falling one more prevalent than in India.' The governor-general, in Hastings's view, 'should possess a power absolute and complete within himself, and independent of actual controul', even though this might seem to contravene the British constitution. In a land of despots one must be a despot. If he could have done so, Hastings would have gaoled Francis for opposing him. The fact that Francis was clever increased his obnoxiousness. Barwell observed that Hastings, temperamentally, could not 'yield to another the least share of reputation that might be derived in the conduct of his Government.'[101]

For two years, however, Hastings was steadily outvoted and overruled. Only Barwell allied with him. The quarrel was sometimes farcical, sometimes murderous — Clavering fought a duel with Barwell after accusing him, quite justly, of profiteering corruptly in the salt department. The sordid issue of patronage was dominant. Hastings's people were pushed out of their places. But the climate helped him defeat his enemies. 'My two colleagues,' Francis wrote wryly, 'are in a woeful condition — Colonel Monson obliged to go to sea to save his life, and General Clavering on his back covered with boils...As for Hastings, I promise you he is much more tough than any of us, and will never die a natural death.'[102] With Monson giving up the ghost in September 1776 and Clavering dying a year later, Hastings could sweep his adversaries' supporters out of office in their turn, and could 'reform' the revenue service so as to gratify his own people.

In Calcutta, a tiny parcel of quarrelsome Europeans lived in a style well adapted to smother human fellow-feeling. Calcutta was a 'City of Palaces'. Its fine houses, in classical style, were literally dazzling, since they were finished in a brilliant white plaster, made out of sea-shells and lime, which blinded the eye. In striking and not too pleasant contrast, they were surrounded by the grimy, thatched mud huts of the servant quarters. Well-to-do whites also owned elegant one-storey 'garden houses' in the countryside close to Calcutta, whither they sent their families to escape pestilence during the hot and rainy months.

Despite the humidity, ladies followed European fashion and heaped their hair up in fantastic extravaganzas of gauze, powder, feathers and pomade. They wore great hooped petticoats under fine gowns imported from Europe, and drenched themselves in the diamonds and pearls of India. The entertainments of polite society involved a similar grandiose blend of British custom with local opportunity. There were expeditions on the river in magnificent private budgerows and pinnaces, with bands playing on board, oars keeping time to their notes, and umbrella boys in white linen trousers and jackets, brilliant red or green turbans on their heads, holding sunshades over perspiring faces. In the early evenings, ladies went driving in carriages imported from England, Indian grooms running alongside. The winter 'season' was lavish with its diversions. Whenever ladies arrived from Britain, they were socially displayed at once for two, three or four nights in succession, during which 'sittings up' even plain spinsters could hope to find husbands. Public suppers on festival days were accompanied by balls where the female minority were danced till they nearly melted. There were also subscription balls once a fortnight from November through to February, and such exotic occasions as the *nautch* given by a rich

Hindu for the reigning belle, Miss Emma Wrangham, the 'Chinsura Beauty'.

Gambling, as in England, was an obsession; Francis was said to have creamed £40,000 off the less quick-witted Barwell. Cricket, played here at least as early as 1780, provided further scope for betting, as did the horse races also becoming popular. English country life could not provide such chances as Bengal gave for the slaughter of wild creatures. Hogs, leopards, buffalo, even rhinoceros, were eagerly despatched, and in one tiger shoot no fewer than thirty elephants were employed.[103]

From 1775, Calcutta had a theatre. The parts, at first, were all taken by gentleman amateurs, who characteristically squabbled over the best roles, so that several duels resulted before professionals were imported from Britain. As well as current London comedies, Shakespeare was played, it would seem well. There must have been some intelligent conversation. The very numerous Scots now employed in Bengal had received superior education. The inventory of the effects of one Scot about this time listed the works of Shakespeare, Milton and Swift, as well as a backgammon table, a hookah, four empty gin cases and '2 Malay slave girls'. (African slaves cost a lot and were symbols of high status — Asian slaves were cheaper and commoner.)[104]

White men still sensibly adopted Indian dress for informal wear. They had not yet realised that the ground floors of their houses, currently used for store-houses, were in fact much cooler than the upper floors. But, against the heat, two devices were now coming in: 'tatties' — screens fixed to open doors and windows and kept constantly wet so that the air blowing through them was cooled; and the 'punkah', a heavy cloth fixed to a wooden beam and hung from the ceiling; the man who pulled this to and fro with a rope to stir the air was yet another addition to the vast roster of indispensable servants.

The day of a typical Englishman in Bengal at this time, as a contemporary described it, began at eight o'clock when his mistress left him and disappeared via a private staircase. His servants had been foregathering outside. 'The moment the master throws his legs out of bed, the whole posse in waiting rush into his room, each making three salams ... In about half an hour after undoing and taking off his long drawers, a clean shirt, breeches, stockings, and slippers are put upon his body, thighs, legs and feet, without any greater exertion on his own part, than if he was a statue. The barber enters, shaves him, cuts his nails, and cleans his ears. The chillumjee and ewer are brought by a servant, whose duty it is, who pours water upon his hands and face, and presents a towel.' When the master went out, eight bearers, relieving each other at intervals, carried him in his palanquin, which was preceded by a further eight or dozen servants in livery. By two o'clock, he was eating his dinner. This great task encompassed, he took a siesta at four, like every other European in town, getting up at seven or eight to be dressed and preened as before by his retinue.[105]

Not all Europeans would be quite so idle. William Hickey, an Irish lawyer who prospered rapidly, always propelled himself to his desk before seven in the morning; but even he never took pen in hand after the early afternoon dinner. This meal reflected the cheapness of food locally. A sheep, in 1780, could be bought in Calcutta for two rupees – say six British shillings. Six good fowls could be had for a single rupee. Even pretty girls were described as wolfing some two pounds of mutton chops each at a sitting. A housewife in Calcutta in Hastings's day gave as an ordinary day's bill of fare for dinner: soup, a roast fowl, curry and rice, a mutton pie, a forequarter of lamb, a rice pudding, tarts, cheese, bread and butter, Madeira. Supper, taken late in the evening, might present itself as 'great joints of roasted goat, with endless dishes of cold fish.' Over this collation, the custom in Bengal was for ladies and gentlemen to hurl pellets of bread at each other. Perhaps this mild exercise helped to mitigate the disastrous effects of so much eating and drinking: while a lady would drink a bottle of wine every day, a gentleman was expected to put away three or four. The Calcutta British may have been learning to restrain themselves at table just a little more than in former days – certainly, the death-rate had dropped markedly, and only 44 per cent of the Writers appointed to Bengal between 1767 and 1775 would eventually leave their bones in India.[106] But the context of the incessant quarrelling, over cards, over matters of etiquette, and at Hastings's Council table, was that almost everyone suffered from stomach trouble almost all the time.

From the ordinary EIC servant relying on the business sense of his banyan, to the great men on the governor-general's Council, every EIC person was deeply involved with Asian intermediaries – with such people as the Hindu Naba Krishna ('Nobkissen') from whom Hastings took a present of three lakhs of rupees when he made him *zemindar* of Burdwan, and the unsavoury Nanda-kumar, whom Hastings had used to gather information against Muhammad Reza Khan. Snubbed later by Hastings, Nandakumar allied with an Englishman named Fowke who also nurtured a grievance. They brought the charge against Hastings that he had received a large bribe from the Munni Begam whom he had appointed guardian to the young Nawab-Vizier of Oudh.

Shuja-ud-daula had died in 1775. The succession of the young prince Asaf-ud-daula, high-spirited, incompetent and spendthrift, had given the British the chance to screw Oudh harder. They forced the new Nawab-Vizier to pay a heavier subsidy for the use of British troops, and to cede to the EIC sovereignty over the region of Benares. Hastings had certainly taken the 150,000 rupees 'entertainment allowance' offered him by the Munni Begam, Asaf's aunt. (Though Hastings was covenanted with the EIC not to pocket such tempting items, this was far from being the only such gift which he quietly held on to.) The Council insisted that he must give the money back. Hastings was not pre-pared to lose face. He prosecuted Nandakumar and certain others on a charge of conspiring to coerce someone to accuse the governor-general of having taken other bribes. Meanwhile Nandakumar was committed for trial on charges of forgery brought against him by an Indian, whom Hastings, or at least his friends, had encouraged to come forward. He was found guilty in the court presided over by Hastings's old school-friend Impey, and, in August 1775, was executed.[107]

His death shocked Hindu opinion. Nandakumar, however unpleasant, had been an important figure. He was executed under English law for a crime regarded by Indians as only a misdemeanour. People in England saw the anomaly. If the Supreme Court in Calcutta applied the whole of English criminal law, would polygamists be hanged? Hastings himself had encouraged the view that it was unjust to make men liable for punishments not sanctioned by their own custom. But Hastings, it would seem, had decided to show that no one could monkey with the governor-general and get away with it.

To succeed Clavering, General Sir Eyre Coote arrived in 1779 as commander-in-chief, tetchy and grasping as ever. Hastings bought him. Matters were so arranged that he had an incentive of over £18,000 a year to stay away from the Council and draw his field allowances by serving outside Bengal. When the directors from London insisted on an end to these allowances, Hastings ordered them to be charged to the Nawab-Vizier of Oudh, upon whom Coote became a burden whether he was in Oudh or not. All this was merely sufficient to secure, not Coote's full support, but neutrality as between Hastings and Francis. Hatred at last reached the point, in August 1780, where Hastings precipitated a duel. He was not an experienced marksman, but Francis had never fired a pistol before. Hastings wounded his adversary quite severely. Francis had had enough. Before the new year, he was gone, predicting that 'desolation' would strike Bengal after his departure. Hastings exulted: 'I shall have no competitor to oppose my designs; to encourage disobedience to my authority ... to excite and foment popular odium against me ... In a word, I have power ... ' Barwell had also left. Hastings's only colleague on the Council, when Coote was away, was a newcomer named Wheler. He was easily bought. 'I have made it a rule,' Hastings wrote to an ally, 'to give him the first option in most vacant appointments, and have provided handsomely for all his friends ... His judgement has literally accompanied mine in every measure.'[108]

Calcutta, from 1780, had its first newspaper. The editor was a 'Wild Irishman' named J. A. Hicky who fancied himself as Bengal's Wilkes. Now that Hastings was omnipotent, the *Gazette* dubbed him 'the Grand Turk' and raked up the scandal over Nandakumar. Hicky was arrested, tried before Impey and a packed jury for libel, and gaoled. The *Bengal Gazette* bravely continued to satirise the governor-general until Hicky's types were seized. His temerity cost him two years in prison.

The middle-class despot used no guillotine. After Nandakumar, his enemies were not murdered. Apologists for British rule in India, anxious to dignify its earliest stages, would later argue that Hastings's ability to act as an autocrat saved the British position in the new war with France. It is hard to evaluate this view. The British in Bengal were no longer directly threatened. Hastings, hard-working, highly intelligent, acted as a successful opportunist, helping to rescue the Bombay and Madras presidencies from the trouble into which they had pitched themselves.

Bombay was the poorest and unhealthiest of the main British settlements in India. Its white inhabitants, whose houses mingled with those of Indians, Portuguese, Armenians and Parsees, were themselves rather ashamed of their island city. Merchants had once been courted to come there, and an attitude of respect for native businessmen persisted. In 1736, a Parsi shipbuilder had been persuaded to take charge of the infant Bombay dockyard, which thereafter turned out many excellent vessels, and reconciled the directors at home to the presidency's disappointing returns. The wealthy Parsi community came to dominate the city. They did not practise purdah. They ate pork and beef and drank wine without inhibition. They had no caste distinctions. They took readily to European clothes and manners. While Calcutta and Madras made middle-class Europeans insolent towards natives and poor whites alike, Bombay had retained an antique middle-class character.

But now this settlement too was drawn into military adventures. In 1775, the Bombay Council made a deal with Raghunath Rao, an ambitious intriguer within the Maratha ruling class. In return for their military support he promised them certain useful territories – as well as a share of the revenues from the Broach and Surat districts. The Bombay navy destroyed the Maratha fleet, and its army advanced successfully against Raghunath's enemies. Hastings and the Council in Calcutta were shocked to hear of all this. They ordered immediate withdrawal, and sent their own embassy to the Marathas, who finally in 1776 conceded some, but not all, of what Bombay had asked for. Annoyed, the Bombay Council broke the treaty and gave asylum to Raghunath Rao.

A French agent arriving at Poona, the Maratha capital, was given a good reception there. In 1778 Hastings sent six battalions under Colonel Leslie off on an unprecedented march across India from Kalpi to Surat, and when news of the French declaration of war reached Bengal the governor gave full backing to the Bombay Council, which despatched a force of nearly 4,000, to put Raghunath Rao on the throne. But confronted by a large Maratha force, this army broke and had to surrender.

Leslie died as his force dawdled across the subcontinent. The abler Colonel Goddard succeeded him, and brought his men into Surat soon after the Bombay army's reverse. His remarkable march restored British prestige. Raghunath Rao, having served his turn, was duly abandoned as a lost cause, and the British pursued the war on their own account. In 1782, the Marathas agreed to the Treaty of Salbai with Hastings's emissary. This procured, as it turned out, twenty years of peace with the Marathas. The Bombay government had to hand back various conquests. The British had to be reasonable. They needed Maratha support, or at least neutrality, in their renewed struggle with Haidar Ali, now made doubly dangerous by French intervention.

Madras had pursued its course of epic corruption. Hastings and his Council accepted, de facto, the coup by which Governor Pigot, in 1776, attempting to clean up the mess created by the Nawab's debts, was imprisoned by Paul Benfield and his gang of profiteers, and died, still in confinement, the next year. Pigot's successor, Sir Thomas Rumbold, picked a quarrel with the Nizam of Hyderabad over a district called the Sarkar of Guntoor.

Grateful to see the British at odds with the Nizam, Hydar Ali, in July 1780, launched a new attack on Madras, and again mastered the whole Carnatic. The Madras government whined for help from Hastings, who was glad enough to give them Sir Eyre Coote, even with the cream of the Bengal army. Coote floundered about the Carnatic, never able to command more territory than the range of his guns covered.

A French squadron appeared off the Coromandel Coast in 1782. Only nine British ships were at hand to oppose the twelve under Admiral Suffren, and they were worsted in four actions. But, with the Marathas at peace, troops from all the three presidencies under Hastings could now be deployed against Hydar Ali. A force from Bombay seized Mysore, Hydar's capital. Hydar himself had died. His son, Tipu, succeeding him, had to take most of his troops back home, and a large body of French troops, arriving at the Coromandel coast in April 1783, found their expected allies elsewhere. Even so, the British were immensely relieved when word came in June that peace had been made in Europe. War with Tipu continued for some months more, before the Madras government came to terms. These infuriated Hastings, chiefly because it was Lord Macartney who had negotiated them.

Whitehall was taking India seriously. Macartney, who had recently come out as governor of Madras, had been a member of both Irish and British Houses of Commons, chief secretary in Ireland, a diplomat in Russia, a governor in the Caribbean. He could not get on with the upstart Hastings, whom he clearly hoped to succeed, nor with his fellow-Irishman Coote (who shortly died, in character, of apoplexy). He opposed the Benfield gang. Benfield had votes in Britain which he used in Hastings's favour. So Hastings sided with the Nawab's creditors. A new breed – the lordly and virtuous outsider – had now appeared in India, ardent to confront the squalid profiteering 'nabobs' of whom Hastings, not quite fairly, could be represented as the ringleader.

In 1781, before Macartney's arrival, the Nawab of the Carnatic had agreed with Hastings to assign his revenues to the EIC for the duration of the war, so long as appointments of collectors were approved by him. Macartney would not wear this. He put in collectors over the Nawab's head. Hastings ordered him to restore administration to the Nawab. Macartney refused to obey until the EIC itself overruled him, and he went home.

Though Hastings had little control over the other presidencies, he had effectively orchestrated campaigns over a vast area against three dangerous enemies, and had shown great prowess as a diplomat. It had all cost a great deal of

INDIA IN THE MID– AND
LATE EIGHTEENTH CENTURY

AFGHANS

Rohillas

Panipat ●
Delhi ●

R. Ganges

Oudh

Benares ●

Bihar

Sindhia

MARATHA

Murshidabad ●
Plassey ●
Chandernagore ●
Calcutta ●

Bengal

Holkar
CONFEDERACY

Gaekwar

Surat ●

Bhonsla

Bombay

Peshwa

**NIZAM'S
TERRITORIES**

Northern Circars

Goa ●

Mysore

Carnatic

Madras ●
Arcot ●
Pondicherry ●
Ft St David ●
Tanjore

Rough extent of Maratha power in the time of Warren Hastings money. So far as he could, he made the Bengali cultivators pay for it. He increased the assessments of revenue payable by the large *zemindars*, and had screwed further cash out by dubious, furtive means.[109] But not enough. He turned to strongarm methods. He left Wheler in charge in July 1781 and went up river with a bodyguard of some five hundred troops.

Hastings did not want to see British rule in India extended beyond its present bounds. Excessive expansion, he thought, must dilute and weaken British civil and military power. The EIC should secure its present holdings by fair and moderate alliances with native princes, and if such persons wished to come under British protection, their adherence was to be welcomed. The aim should be, he once wrote, 'to extend the influence of the British nation to every part of India not too remote from their possessions, without enlarging the circle of their defence or involving them in hazardous or indefinite engagements ... '[110]

Hastings could clearly see the evils which had befallen Oudh through its ruler's attachment to the British. The alliance with Oudh, he wrote, 'was in the beginning an unprofitable charge to the Company. It was placed on a footing of mutual advantage to both. It is now become an oppressive burthen on that province, which must soon fall with increased weight on the Company. The late Vizier paid to the Company a tribute of 25,20,00 rupees, and cheerfully paid it. It was optional, because he was at liberty to dismiss the brigade when the exigency of his affairs no longer required it; and he could safely dispense with it.' But the boy Asaf-ud-daula had now 'yielded up a revenue of twenty three lacs in the cession of Benares; he pays, or rather ought to pay, 31,20,000 rupees a year for the subsidy; and we have added to his expenses an extravagant military establishment which, at its estimated amount, is an annual charge of above forty lacs. So that we are in fact the distributors of a crore of rupees drawn from his treasury, which is already exhausted, and that part of his army which still remains under his own direction is rendered a useless and even a dangerous incumbrance, because he cannot pay it. Our brigade, therefore, must continue a fixture to that province, which would be prey to the meanest invader the instant that it was deprived of its support.'[111]

However, the *Gita* said, 'Abandon all thought of the consequence.' Willy-nilly, the war must be fought. The Company must show a profit. Hastings's first target was the Raja of Benares, Chait Singh, installed by the EIC as its *zemindar*. Rightly or wrongly, Hastings saw this man as a dangerous rebel, 'culpable in a very high degree ... ' Pressed for troops to defend Bengal, he had called on him to provide the EIC with at least 1,000 cavalry. Chait Singh had offered only 500, with 500 infantry. Hastings now proposed to fine him £500,000 for this impertinence.

He refused to hear Chait Singh's own explanations, and ordered his arrest. The Raja's armed retainers rose up and massacred the British-hired Sepoys who were guarding him. Chait Singh escaped. For a while, Hastings himself was in great danger. But he kept his nerve and repressed the rebellion. Since his troops had partitioned Chait Singh's treasury among themselves Hastings had incurred the cost of another campaign without getting any loot for the Company. So he decided to suck Benares dry. The area was given to Chait Singh's nephew. Its rent was raised from twenty-two lakhs of rupees a year to forty. This was extortionate, and could only be paid by extortion. The region was swiftly reduced to ruin.[112]

Amongst the native princes who had rallied to Hastings's support, the Nawab of Oudh himself had been pleasantly forward. Asaf-ud-daula was in effect a puppet. His capital, Lucknow, seemed to Hastings himself a 'Sink of Iniquity'. The governor-general maintained a fastidious distaste for the behaviour of the very white men whom he had sent in to batten on Oudh – 'beardless Boys rejecting with indignation the offer of monthly Gratuities of 3000 and 5000 Rupees ... Men receiving the Wages of Service from the nabob, and disclaiming his Right to command it ... a City filled with as many independant and absolute Sovereignities as there are Englishmen in it.'[113]

Asaf's finances recalled those of the Nawab of the Carnatic. British soldiers had lent him money at huge rates of interest, creaming off pensions and *jaghirs* in return. Meanwhile he owed the EIC large sums. Hastings now persuaded him to reduce his army, to fix a set sum for his private disbursements, and to put his public expenditures in the hands of ministers who would co-operate with the British Resident. In return, Hastings would reduce the EIC military contingent in Oudh to one brigade, and order all British subjects to leave within three months. He encouraged Asaf to get his hands on the *jaghirs* and treasure held by his mother and grandmother, the later-famous Begams of Oudh, though the EIC itself was party to agreements which bound him to respect their possession of them. The EIC's shortage of cash drove Hastings to endorse naked bullying. It was clear that otherwise Asaf could not repay the forty-four lakhs of rupees which he owed the Company.

Accompanied by the British Resident and by EIC troops, Asaf captured the Begams' fortress. Fifty-five lakhs of rupees were extracted from their treasury. But even by the Machiavellian test, Hastings's strongarm methods failed, as they had done with Chait Singh. Asaf's debts were too large. Fifty-five lakhs disappeared 'almost without trace'.[114]

In 1784, Hastings returned to Lucknow, trying again to sort out Asaf's affairs. The Nawab-Vizier's debt to the EIC now stood at seventy-three lakhs. Hastings recovered about half of this, and arranged a retrenchment in Asaf's expenses. He appeased Asaf by removing the EIC Resident, but left an agent of the governor-general in his place, at a salary of £22,000, who cost the people of Oudh nearly twice as much. Whatever Hastings had wished, and partly because of his own actions, Oudh was now in effect British territory. Hastings's successor would find Oudh 'desolated' by years of British despoliation.[115]

Hastings's term of office had expired in 1779, but Lord North, pressed upon by so many problems, had been happy enough to let him stay in Calcutta.

However, Philip Francis had returned to England – 'pale yellow, and a look of diabolic purpose.' He sold his own EIC stock at a loss, allied himself with the parliamentary opposition, and made as much trouble as he could. News of Hastings's fiasco at Benares came opportunely. After Lord North fell, in May 1782, Dundas proposed, and the House of Commons carried, a motion censuring Hastings for having 'acted in a manner repugnant to the honour and policy of this nation ... '[116] Hastings early in 1783 announced his own intention to resign. The bitterness, though, with which EIC affairs were again debated in Britain meant that no successor was swiftly appointed, and he lingered on for two more years. He finally quit India in February 1785. His first reception at home was flattering. But a week after his arrival Edmund Burke gave notice to the Commons that he would make a motion against him.

In the vehement debates which had taken place in Parliament, the Rockingham faction had agreed with supporters of Lord North that government intervention in India was necessary. Both sides had spoken of British responsibility for the orderly, just and humane government of Indian peoples. Political and moral reformers in England had begun to see India as a sphere where virtuous 'trusteeship' over native peoples could be accompanied by experiments in disinterested administration. While the wealth of India, properly exploited, would compensate for lost New World colonies, the honour recently forfeited at Yorktown could be regained by enlightened rule in Calcutta. Whereas Hastings had reacted on the defensive, his more aggressive successors would seize province after province, but would talk about God and the interests of native peoples as they did so.

Under Hastings, the British in Bengal had still greatly enjoyed 'nautches' – displays of Indian dancing, given by native noblemen as standard entertainment for European guests, then adopted among white people themselves as a favourite diversion. Though the dancers were female, and nubile, there were cheaper and nastier ways of exploiting Indian flesh. Like the custom of hookah-smoking, to which most white men were addicted, and also some ladies, it showed that some good was seen in Asian ways.

Hastings himself had thought, and written, that attempts to convert Hindus to Christianity would be presumptuous. He aimed at 'reconciling the people of England to the natives of Hindostan.' He wrote to Dr Johnson in 1775, 'It has been one of my first wishes to be able to free the inhabitants of this country from the reproach of ignorance and barbarism, which has been undeservedly cast upon them ... ' He patronised Charles Wilkins, the first European ever to translate at length from Sanskrit, who published in 1785 a translation of the *Bhagavad-gita*, and in his own introduction to this work, implied that the *Mahabharata* was as fine an epic as Milton's. The great Hindu writings, Hastings said, would 'survive when the British dominion in India shall have long ceased to exist ...'[117]

He welcomed the famous scholar Sir William Jones when he arrived as a

High Court Judge in Calcutta in 1783, and with him founded the Asiatic Society of Bengal. Jones's pioneering researches displayed the similarities between Sanskrit, Latin and Greek and publicised the existence of an 'Indo-European' family of languages. He studied Indian law, history, religion, literature, music, philosophy and science, and his work had considerable impact on the Romantic poets and philosophers of Europe. It also had the effect, unfortunately, of setting the minds of Christians at rest upon a dangerous doubt which had been raised.

Europeans had been growing aware of Hindu belief in a religious entity whom they presumed to be a god like their own. Some writers, furthermore, had found Hindu ethical teaching admirable. Now, if Deists and Masons could show that these features had existed before the birth of Christ, this would indicate that Christianity had developed from some earlier religion. John Zephaniah Holwell, 'hero' of the Black Hole, had bluntly stated that Christ's teaching was merely a restatement of truths received by the Hindus earlier. Other writers suggested that Hindu chronology stretched back beyond the presumed date of the biblical Flood, set by scholars at about 2500 B.C. Jones pacified worried minds by dating the Buddha no earlier than 1000 B.C. and arguing that the earliest Indian writings were later than those attributed to Moses.[118]

But Hinduism appealed greatly to many British thinkers. Burke always 'spoke of the piety of the Hindoos with admiration, and of their holy religion and sacred functions with an awe bordering on devotion', and thought them the most benevolent of all people. Holwell extolled Hindu vegetarianism, and abstention from alcohol, as relics of a 'primitive age' of innocence. Of course, there were beef-eating Englishman a-plenty who saw Hindu eating and drinking habits as signs of ingrained effeteness. The Hindu, Robert Orme said, had 'no chance of opposing with success the onset of an inhabitant of more northern regions.' But he excepted the gallant Rajputs from these generalisations.[119] The cult of the 'martial races' was beginning, whereby coloured peoples would be divided, usefully, into idle weaklings fit only to be ruled, and handsome bullies well suited to keeping the first sort in order.

Lieut.-Col. Alexander Dow, in his *History of Hindostan* (1768–72), praised the Marathas very highly, as a 'great and rising people'. Dow admired Hindu literature as warmly as Hastings. But his generalisation was that the 'Hindoos' were 'of all nations on earth the most easily conquered and governed.' They had no public spirit, no loyalty. 'The people permit themselves to be transferred from one tyrant to another, without murmuring ... ' Dow suggested that this was the ideal religion for Britain's purposes; 'it prepares mankind for the government of foreign lords.'[120]

Luckily, these enfeebled persons were also (somehow) creators of great wealth. Adam Smith, who had never been East, affirmed in his *Wealth of Nations* what would become a received idea. ' ... In manufacturing art and industry, China and Indostan, though inferior, seem not to be much inferior to any part of Europe.' It so happened that, in this very period, Europeans for the first time were beginning to gain a clear technological lead over Asians. A surgeon who served with Clive could thus note casually that Indian craftsmen, while very good, were committed to an 'old way of working' and 'dull at invention'.[121] Hence it was coming to seem that the natural role of the mild Hindu was to work to orders from Europeans.

But could the bullying of Hindu labour be justified when these were such inoffensive and good natured people? Christianity offered the necessary argument. The Hindu, like the African, must be found to be wicked, in need of tutelage. The fact that his penal code was much less savage than Britain's must be ignored, and attention focused upon such customs as that of *sati*, whereby widows consigned themselves to their husbands' funeral pyres. Holwell excused the custom warmly. He had seen it many times. The action of the women seemed to him both voluntary and heroic. A Scottish footman, who also had seen *sati*, observed more drily and with forceful irony, ' ... They are as glad to burn as two women in England would be to get an estate.'[122] Relative to the world of Fanny Burney and Jane Austen, where heiresses were bought and sold on the British marriage market, the horror expressed at the custom must seem excessive. So, in view of the conduct of EIC personnel, must the odium frequently heaped on the 'trickery', cunning, 'treachery' of the Indians. But the Hindu must be made to seem a ripe subject for conversion. Then extracting the fruits of his labour would be a bounden duty for all good people.

The switch from 'enlightened' appreciation of the Hindu's virtues was beginning by the 1780s under Evangelical direction. Evangelicalism had attracted more and more respectable, well-to-do members of the Church of England. The days when Methodism had seemed subversive were now greatly distant. Evangelicals in India wrote harshly about Hinduism. Charles Grant, on the spot, wrote to inform Thomas Coke, a pioneering Methodist missionary, 'It is hardly possible to conceive any people more completely enchained than they are by their superstition.' He and certain others drafted, in 1787, a proposal for launching missions which stated that the people of India were 'universally and wholly corrupt, they are as depraved as they are blind, and as wretched as they are depraved.' Such Evangelicals were turning the coloured races of the world into the basis of a moral bank, from which Britain would draw more and more heavily. Every Hindu widow saved from the flames, every dark convert lisping his Saviour's name, swelled the funds of righteousness at the disposal of God's chosen Protestant nation for investment in further profitable 'trusteeship' overseas. As Burke prepared his attack on Warren Hastings, the British anti-slavery movement gathered itself formidably together. Its young hero, Wilberforce, showed equal if not more fervour for the cause of intruding missionaries into India, where the natives were sunk, as he put it, 'into the most abject ignorance and vice'.[123]

VII

In 1773, Humphrey Marten, Hudson's Bay Company chief at York Fort, put one of his men in irons and gave him eighteen strokes of the cat for trading, privately, one skin. In the same year, the brig *Nancy* left Dornoch, in northern Scotland, with two hundred emigrants. Of fifty children aboard below the age of four, only one survived the voyage. Altogether, only one hundred people reached New York. The captain of the vessel, in violation of his contract, had issued foul and inadequate food.[124]

Neither episode made a great stir. Floggings of soldiers continued in the British army. Men, women and children were still hanged in Britain for petty offences against property. Why was it, then, that the first national campaign on a humanitarian issue was directed against the slave trade with Africa?

Partly, of course, because that trade was consistently cruel, systematically iniquitous. But partly also because of the American war, which coincided with the publication of two enormously influential books. An English translation of the Abbé Raynal's *History of the Two Indies* and Adam Smith's *Wealth of Nations* were both published in 1776. Each went through fifteen editions by 1804. Raynal summed up the objections to slavery of advanced European thinkers, and proposed a scheme for gradual emancipation. Smith seemed to show that slavery was not only offensive to man's innate sense of fellow feeling, but was also economically stupid. It seemed 'from the experience of all ages and nations' that work done by freemen came 'cheaper in the end than that performed by slaves.' The cost of 'repairing' the 'wear and tear of the slave' fell upon the neglectful master or careless overseer. The free man repaired himself.[125] Hence, in Smith's view, as commerce rose in the cities, as agriculture progressed, slavery must be eliminated by the owners themselves, from regard to self-interest; they could get more from free workers and thus have more to exchange for urban manufactures.

Smith was a prophet for class-conscious persons in the middle ranks of society who were likely to identify idle, 'negligent' West Indian planters with the 'landed interest' which monopolised British politics. Every year, such elements grew stronger, and anti-slavery opinion with them, while the interests arrayed against it were weakened. While official British propagandists had animadverted with moral disgust upon the American rebels' ownership of human beings, the sugar islands had been severely hit by the loss of American provisions. American independence removed most English-speaking slave-owners from the Empire. By 1783, some planters detected an ominous buzz in the air. An absentee wrote from England to a friend in Nevis, 'The people here seem devoted to our destruction – they entertain the most horrid ideas of our cruelties – it now pervades all ranks of people – they think Slavery ought not to be permitted in any part of the British dominions ... '[126]

With slavery now outlawed in the northern states of the U.S.A., British

79 View from Point Venus, Tahiti, by William Hodges

80 Cyfartha Ironworks, Merthyr Tydfil, Wales, by J. C. Ibbetson

81 A Loyalist encampment on the banks of the St Lawrence River, by James Peachey

82 Arkwright's Cotton Mill, Cromford, by moonlight (Joseph Wright)

Quakers, in constant touch still with Friends across the Atlantic, had to act to save their self-esteem. Such bankers as Samuel Hoare and John Lloyd, amongst the richest men in Britain, were leaders in the Quaker campaign which petitioned Parliament, in 1783, for total abolition of the slave trade. Thousands of copies of a pamphlet by Benezet were distributed through Britain. To do this a network of scores of correspondents was established in the provinces – 'an embryonic national organisation'.[127]

VIII

Perversely, much middle-class revulsion against slavery may have drawn strength from middle-class guilt over the epochal transformations which, in the 1780s, were obviously occurring in British industry. Britain's exports quadrupled in volume between 1780 and 1800. ' ... Almost every available statistical series of industrial output reveals a sharp upward turn.' The most spectacular climb was in the production of cotton textiles. In the first half of the eighteenth century Britain's consumption of raw cotton wool had risen slowly to about 2 million lb. per year. In the 1760s it had been over $3\frac{1}{4}$ million, in the 1770s over 5 million. Then, apocalyptically, it soared to 22 million in 1787. The chief centre of cotton textile production was Lancashire. By 1801, Manchester–Salford (84,000 people) and Liverpool (78,000) were the largest English provincial cities.[128]

But far more than increases of scale were involved. Since the origins of human industry, the main material used in making machines had been wood. 1784 saw the world's first large-scale all-iron plant, the Albion Flour Mill at Southwark, in London. The motive power here was steam. The great magician who had tamed steam was James Watt. His fellow countryman, Walter Scott, would hail him as ' ... The man whose genius discovered the means of multiplying our national resources to a degree perhaps even beyond his own stupendous powers of calculation and combination; bringing the treasures of the abyss to the summit of the earth – giving the feeble arm of man the momentum of an Afrite – commanding manufactures to arise, as the rod of the prophet produced water in the desert, affording the means of dispensing with that time and tide which wait for no man, and of sailing without that wind which defied the commands and threats of Xerxes himself.'[129]

The implications of steam power were world-changing. For the first time industry itself was set to become a giant consumer of the products of industry. Flowing water remained the chief source of motive power until well into the nineteenth century, but the tendency swiftly emerged for areas where coal was cheaply available to attract manufacturing. Coal drove steam engines. Coal made iron. Iron made engines. A complex of mining, engineering and mass-production of consumer goods began to establish itself on the coalfields. And the astonishing success of the steam engine suggested that further inventions could and should be made. Invention itself, as it were, had been invented.

'Industrialists', a new species of mankind, had invested in large and expensive machinery, thus incurring high overheads. They had a rising incentive to keep plant running as close to full capacity as might be. So they poured out goods in unprecedented quantities. Markets had to be found for them. Prices, cut for the home consumer, increased demand, and again prompted increased production. But where the home market was insufficient, consumers must be found overseas. As overseas markets grew, this likewise triggered increased production at home. As profit margins dwindled, new inventions were sought and found as a way to cut costs. The engineering industry was called on to provide more and more new machines. Coal was ripped at a faster and faster rate from the seams. By 1850, more British people would live in towns than in the countryside. Man's life on earth was being transformed.

At the time of the 1707 Treaty of Union, Britain, for all its commercial prowess, had been what we would now call an 'underdeveloped country'. Perhaps half its arable land had still been cultivated under the system where the strips owned by individuals were mixed together and communal thinking prevailed.[130] With a few exceptions – shipbuilding and textiles were the most important – the country's industries had either produced primary products or had made goods for sale in local markets. Small masters had served local needs for chairs and pans as country folk amongst other country folk, though the size of London, with its market draining coal and beef, grain and fruit from distant areas, had already portended transformation.

The shortage of wood had begun to press. Britain had abundant coal. In 1709, Abraham Darby, a Quaker ironmaster, began to smelt with coke at Coalbrookdale in Shropshire, so releasing himself from the need for charcoal. Three years later, a steam engine, designed by a gentleman named Savery and a blacksmith named Newcomen, was put to work on a coalfield in the Midlands. It met the practical problem that as demand for coal and tin sent miners deeper and deeper, some way must be found, cheaper than horse power, of pumping water out of the workings. 'Newcomen' engines were slow, unimpressive creations, but they did their job, and spread: by 1775, there were about forty at work in Cornwall, about sixty on the Northumberland coalfield.[131]

Meanwhile, the potential of factory organisation had begun to catch the eyes of some Englishmen. The Royal Arsenal at Chatham, racing out armaments for the wars of William III and Marlborough, had shown how large-scale demand might impel large-scale organisation. And the West Indian slave plantation had revealed the practical efficacity of holding large numbers of workers together under strict discipline. There was an abundance of helpless poor people in England. From the late seventeenth century, the idea of the 'workhouse' evolved as a way of relieving the well-to-do of the need to provide for them through the parish rates. Parishes combined to maintain workhouses where wool was spun, hosiery made, and so forth. The death-rate amongst those employed was horrific.

Administered as ineptly and corruptly as other public institutions of the period, these places did not pay. But individual entrepreneurs saw the potential of pauper children. By the 1750s, in cotton-processing Lancashire, such men were in effect buying 'parish apprentices' on a grand scale. 'The poor Children,' one spokesman for Manchester weavers exclaimed, had been 'sold into worse Slavery, and harder Bondage, than the Negroes in our *English* plantations in *America*.' Their treatment, he said, crippled them in mind and body before they were returned to the streets to beg. The analogy with plantation slavery also struck an economist, Josiah Tucker, observing about the same time the woollen industry in the hinterland of slave-trading Bristol. He saw south-western clothiers bringing adult weavers together in 'great numbers' in the 'same shop', and remarked that the new social distance created, with 'the master ... placed so high above the condition of the journeyman', was more like that between planter and black 'than might be expected in such a country as England.'[132]

The dependence of hundreds, even thousands, of workers on a single capitalist clothier was an old fact in the textile industries. The bringing together of many machines in one place, where before spinners and weavers had worked at home, was a straightforward logical development. In 1719, Thomas Lombe put up a building 500 feet long and six storeys high where he employed 300 people to prepare silk yarn for weaving. He chose the wrong industry, at the wrong time. The market for silks was narrow, supplies of raw material were inelastic. As with Darby's coke-smelting, imitators were slow to come forward.

Then in 1765 Matthew Boulton built his Soho factory outside Birmingham. Josiah Wedgwood, the great potter, established 'Etruria' in Staffordshire four years later. In 1771 Richard Arkwright created a cotton-spinning mill, at Cromford, where he was soon employing about 600 workers, most of them children.

For some two generations, men concerned with the cotton industry had been devising new machines. The ideas involved had been familiar enough to anyone expert with machines in the Middle Ages. The new inventions could have been perfected at any time in the intervening centuries. What had been missing was incentive, and this was given by a sudden doubling of the rate of growth of the British cotton industry in the 1740s.[133]

The first famous inventions, Kay's 'flying shuttle' of 1733, Hargreaves's 'spinning jenny' of 1766, were still compatible with cottage industry – a man and his family could work them by hand together. But in 1768 Arkwright, a Lancashire barber and wig-maker, took up someone else's 30-year-old idea for the use of rollers in spinning, in his own 'water frame'. Eleven years later Samuel Crompton, a Bolton weaver, combined features from 'jenny' and 'water frame' in a machine therefore called the 'mule', which produced at last a yarn with which Lancashire could match the fine muslins of India.

The 'frame' and the 'mule' demanded power greater than that of human muscles. Water power had long been used to mill flour and to full cloth. So the early cotton mills sprang up by streams in the countryside, till James Watt's invention made revolution possible.

Watt was a man of the lower middle classes, a mathematical instrument maker with a shop within the precincts of Glasgow University, where the great scientist Joseph Black was lecturing on his own discovery, latent heat. Another professor used a model Newcomen steam engine in his classes. Watt was asked to repair it, and saw that it was wasteful of energy. He discussed its defects with Black and other scientists. Then, in 1765, in his thirtieth year, this sober Lowland Scot, walking on Glasgow Green, hit upon 'conceptually much the most difficult invention of the century.' His separate condenser quadrupled the steam engine's efficiency. John Roebuck, an Englishman who controlled the great Carron ironworks near Falkirk, financed Watt's experiments. But it was the drive and imagination of another Englishman, Matthew Boulton, which eventually proved crucial. Watt was introduced, in 1767–8, first to the famous Soho works, then to the great manufacturer himself, by the latter's close friend and adviser, Dr William Small, who had not long before been Thomas Jefferson's teacher, had been introduced to Boulton by Benjamin Franklin, and thus provides an intimate personal link between two world-transforming revolutions. For Watt found in Birmingham, where he became Boulton's partner, the engineering skills, still lacking in Scotland, which would make his invention commercially viable. A Midlands ironmaster, John Wilkinson, had recently patented a way of boring cannon which could be used to bore cylinders with hitherto impossible accuracy. In the last quarter of the eighteenth century, Watt and Boulton sold nearly five hundred steam engines. Boulton spurred Watt on to further and still more potent inventions. 'The people in London Manchester and Birmingham are *steam mill mad*,' he wrote to him in 1781. 'I don't mean to hurry you but ... ' In that year, Watt converted his engine for rotary motion. By a series of further devices he soon achieved a smoothness and regularity of movement irresistibly useful to industrialists.[134]

The early 1780s were the years of 'industrial revolution' (though the term itself would not be coined for half a century). In 1783, another Scot, Thomas Bell, came up with a method of printing calico by power. In 1783–4, Henry Cort devised a superior new 'puddling' process for coke smelting, and finally released the iron industry from bondage to water power by his invention of the rolling mill, which meant that a steam engine could be applied to making bar iron and rolled iron. The next year Arkwright bought a machine from Boulton and Watt and the marriage of steam and cotton was consummated. Mills now sprang up in coalfield towns. In 1782 there had been only two cotton mills in and around Manchester. Within twenty years there were fifty more.[135]

Except for Watt and the scientists, mostly Scottish, who were revolutionising bleaching and thus pioneering the modern chemical industry, the famous inventors were men who, like Captain James Cook, 'discovered' what was there waiting for them, and did not concern themselves with theory. Public educational provision in England was far inferior to that in Scotland, New England or Prussia. The famous Dissenting academies did something to compensate. So, as in the case of Cook, did 'self help'. England was not badly off for craftsmen who could read and write and manage arithmetic. The Midlands, home of many small masters in the metal industries, were especially prolific in invention. Self-help was in the atmosphere here. William Hutton remembered how Birmingham had seemed to him when he first visited it in the 1740s, as a young working man: 'I had been among dreamers, but now I saw men awake: Their very step along the street shewed alacrity: Every man seemed to know and prosecute his own affairs ... '[136]

But Philadelphians, equally wakeful, did not at this time make 'industrial revolution'. And in England, even rudimentary education was not always necessary for a technological pioneer – the great canal engineer James Brindley never learnt to spell and was nearly illiterate. Invention bred itself bacterially under the sun of opportunity, which shone for people in Britain hot and high. Watt wrote of Boulton: 'His conception of the nature of any invention was quick & he was not less quick in perceiving the uses to which it might be applied & the profits which might accrue from it.'[137] Arkwright, Wilkinson, Watt himself, joined Boulton in the first capitalist class in history which was committed to technical change. Such men were great organisers. They seized absolute control over production, oversaw all its processes, and yearned beyond that to have equally total control over buying and merchanting.

Lord Shelburne, most thoughtful nobleman of his day, was struck, in 1766, by the portent of Boulton's Birmingham button. ' ... Instead of employing the same hand to finish a button or any other thing, they subdivide it into as many different hands as possible ... Thus a button passes through fifty hands, and each hand perhaps passes a thousand in a day ... By this means, the work becomes so simple that, five times in six, children of six or eight years old do it as well as men, and earn from ten pence to eight shillings a week.'[138] The craftsman who cared for the quality of a product which he finished himself, which reflected his personal prowess, gave way to the child, brain detached from handiwork, limbs moving in alien regular rhythm.

In other times and places regulations existed to govern the employment of children and the quality of goods. In Britain few were in operation. The Elizabethan Statute of Apprentices applied only to trades practised in Tudor days and so had no purchase on the industrialists of Birmingham and Manchester. But such restrictions as did survive excited indignation amongst manufacturers. A prophet had arisen to express their discontent. 'In Sheffield', he acidly observed, 'no master cutler can have more than one apprentice at a time, by a bye-law of the corporation.' Thus, Adam Smith, in his *Wealth of Nations*.[139]

Like other revolutions, this one had its ideologists, limping after reality. Scotland, unsurprisingly, fathered most of them. Smith is regarded as founder of the 'science' of economics. Extending and partially humanising the insights of such bleak thinkers as William Petty, he systematised the subject magisterially.

Many readers responded avidly to his defence of 'self-love'. 'It is not from the benevolence of the butcher, the brewer, or the baker that we expect our dinner, but from their regard to their own interest.'[140] Each man was the best judge of his 'own interest'. He should be free to pursue it as he saw fit. If he did so, everyone would benefit. This assertion, detached from Smith's own refinements, cheered (as it still cheers) self-making businessmen. They did not so easily digest Smith's view that amongst the motives from which human behaviour sprung could be found not only self-love, a desire to be free, a habit of labour and a propensity to trade, but also sympathy and a sense of propriety. But they were delighted by the simpler concept, which his great work seemed to support, of a world moving inexorably from the primitive state of the hunter to the present flowering of commerce. Division of labour brought the substitution of cash incentives for feudal ties, making each individual more free. From being the plaything of potentates and magnates, man graduated to dependence on the more generous forces of the market. 'Natural' laws of supply and demand ruled, or should rule, everything.

Commerce, as Smith saw it, should be the 'bond of union and friendship' between men. Why then was Europe torn by wars? 'Mercantilism' was the culprit. Governments presumed to interfere with the naturally beneficent system, in the interests of their own power. The State, in Smith's view, should be responsible only for defence, for justice, and for certain public works – roads, canal-building, water supply – where the profit motive might be too weak to secure necessary social amenities. Attempts to do down competitors with protective tariffs were iniquitous. If foreign goods were cheaper, they should be imported. Plenty should be the aim, not power. Britain prospered in spite of its rulers' mistakes only because 'The uniform, constant, and uninterrupted effort of every man to better his condition ... is frequently powerful enough to maintain the natural progress of things towards improvement in spite both of the extravagance of government and of the greatest errors of administration.'[141]

Thrift and hard work, the middle-class virtues, were those on which plenty depended. 'The expense of a great lord feeds generally more idle than industrious people ... Every prodigal appears to be a public enemy, and every frugal man a public benefactor.'[142] Smith developed importantly the theory that labour was the source of all value. He saw man as an active being always disposed to improve the material conditions of his life. Work was 'natural' and therefore good. Labour and 'civilisation' were virtually the same thing.

His view of human nature made much sense in terms of Scotland itself, where thrift had become ingrained by relative poverty and hard work was transforming a barren country. Another Scots economist, James Steuart, was arguing in the 1770s that a stern environment where men had to struggle to win food from the soil was preferable to those delicious conditions, which were supposed to exist in the tropics, where the earth gave of her bounty and made the inhabitants 'lazy'.[143] The gospel of work, as such Scots proclaimed it, gave bumptious personages a new test for establishing that they were more virtuous than those whom they wished to exploit. People who did not wear trousers, kilted Gaels included, were clearly lazy. People who were poor, British poor included, were evidently the victims of their own indolence. To bully them to work for one's own profit was therefore to do them a good turn.

Smith himself was a moralist, incapable of the crassness of many of his followers. He recognised that advancing materialism might erode human virtues. He saw that great cities could be dehumanising and that 'mental mutilation' might result from excessive division of labour. But what he witnessed around him in Scotland gave his study an effervescence of optimism. There had recently been a 'considerable rise in the demand for labour' around Glasgow, around Carron, elsewhere in the Lowlands. Smith saw cheaper grain, cheaper potatoes, cheaper 'turnips, carrots, cabbages; things which were never formerly raised but by the spade, but which are now commonly raised by the plough.' Clothes were cheaper. Tools were cheaper. He was glad to see that real wages in Scotland were rising, and with them the expectations of the labouring classes.[144]

His optimism delighted contemporaries who took from his work what it suited them to take and ignored his qualms, his warnings, his reservations. Not all his views were adopted. Not all his views matched the facts which others saw.

Thus he foolishly denounced 'great fleets and armies, who in time of peace produce nothing, and in time of war acquire nothing which can compensate the expense of maintaining them, even while the war lasts.' To decry the long series of conflicts with France was naïve, as most contemporaries realised. The only defence against mercantilist France was, as they correctly reckoned, attack. War favoured many industries greatly. While some British products were relieved of hot foreign competition in the home market, the iron industry progressed under the stimulus of military demand. The great Carron ironworks owed its beginnings in the late 1750s to the Seven Years War, faltered thereafter, then throve as naval demand resumed in the 1770s, turning out the famous light guns called 'carronades'. Wilkinson's amazing career was likewise advanced, as was that of a Manxman named Anthony Bacon who reaped great rewards from victualling troops in the West Indies and in Africa, founded an important ironworks in South Wales, and was one of the largest suppliers of munitions during the War of American Independence.[145]

It was equally misguided for Smith to suggest that protective tariffs and bounties were deleterious. In the years preceding Britain's industrial revolution, protection for home manufactures had actually increased markedly. The Welsh tin-plate industry grew behind the shelter of Acts of 1703 and 1704 increasing duty on foreign plate. Paper-making was a similar story. The Scottish and Irish linen industries benefited greatly from public money. Most critically, the cotton industry was protected, after the relevant Act of 1721, against East Indian competition.[146]

Above all, it was naïve of Smith to decry the economic value of slavery. R. B. Sheridan now contends that 'the economic growth of Great Britain was chiefly from without inwards, that the Atlantic was the most dynamic trading area, and that, outside the metropolis, the most important element in the growth of this area in the century or more prior to 1776 was the slave plantation ... ' It seems that if all the profits from the slave trade itself, without exception, had been invested in British industry, they would have made little more than one-seventieth of total national investment. If only an average proportion had been reinvested, this would have been no more than one-ninehundredth. But such calculations do little to weaken the argument that slavery was crucial to the take-off of British industrial capitalism. Capital investment itself does not produce industrial revolution. In the 1790s, the Scottish cotton industry had less invested in it than the Scottish fishing industry. The latter, however, had no epochal consequences. Factories, ironworks and steam engines were expensive to set up. The entrepreneur must find banks ready to lend him money till his firm's profits themselves floated him forward. Here the wealth of merchants trading with slave economies, was, beyond doubt, vitally important. The business of West India merchants with planters had always involved lending, holding and reinvestment of money. Many veered into full-time banking and such famous banks as Barclays and William Deacons began in this way. At one stage, the whole future of Boulton and Watt depended on the arrival of a West India fleet in which their London bankers were deeply committed.[147]

Anthony Bacon developed his South Wales ironworks with a West Indian planter as partner. Bacon himself had been a slave trader. So had Samuel Touchet, of Manchester, who in 1747 personally bought over one-fifth of the total import of raw cotton into England, and who financed Lewis Paul's experimental spinning machine. When innovating men required quantities of capital large by the standards of their time, they looked for wealthy partners. In south-west Scotland, merchants trading with the New World were the obvious candidates. Around Glasgow, 'entire industries were dominated by the capital of tobacco lords and West India merchant princes.' Bristol merchants largely financed the Coalbrookdale ironworks, and slave traders from that port were active by the late 1730s in promoting the Welsh copper industry, to which the commerce in people was very important; there was demand on the Guinea Coast for wrought copper 'manillas', rods and copper wire.[148]

Trade with other continents grew faster than trade with Europe. In 1700, Europe took over 75 per cent of British exports; in 1800 only 45 per cent. And even within Europe, trade with Portugal and Spain 'reflected, at one stage removed, the increasing importance of the transatlantic commerce to their colonies.' During the eighteenth century, while industries looking almost entirely to home markets increased production by some 50 per cent, those to which exports were important waxed five and a half times. Cloth was still the most important export industry, but by the end of the century cottons were clearly overtaking woollens, accounting already for a quarter of all textiles exported: 'The strategic industry in the British industrial revolution was undoubtedly cotton, even if its contribution to the national income was at first small.'[149]

And the rise of cotton depended on the tropics. In the mid-1760s, more than a quarter of all ships owned in the port of Liverpool were 'Guineamen'. Black slaves were sometimes sold in the auction rooms of the Exchange, which was decorated with reliefs of blackamoors and elephants. Raw cotton was brought home by the slavers, along with other West Indian produce. Though the Levant provided a quarter or a third of British imports of raw cotton, the West Indies were still the chief source of supply. As demand soared, in the 1780s, beyond the potential of the British and French islands, Brazil became essential to Manchester. New World cotton, however, was poorer than that grown in the East Indies. Lancashire in the eighteenth century was consciously imitating superior Indian products. The Board of Trade asked in 1787, was it the quality of Indian raw material, or better ways of spinning and weaving, which gave Indian textiles their edge? British manufacturers asserted confidently that the Indians did not weave better. They spun a better yarn. 'But we are coming near them very fast.'[150] Within a few years, India would be supplying Britain with increasingly large amounts of raw cotton, and British piece goods would be invading Indian markets.

Cotton textiles were still increasing their popularity at home. 'As for the ladies', a pamphlet of 1782 asserted, 'they wear scarcely anything now but cotton, calicoes, muslin, or silks, and think no more of woollen stuffs than we think of an old almanac. We have scarcely any woollens now about our beds but blankets, and they would most likely be thrown aside, could we keep our bodies warm without them.' But this was amusing exaggeration and, anyway, the British market alone could not have fuelled cotton textiles' exceptional growth. Their natural market was in warmer climes. Of British exports, in 1739, over three-quarters went to tropical and American markets, in 1769 a similar proportion (£165,412 out of £211,606). They competed with linens for the orders of New World planters, but the African coast came to provide their biggest vent. The disorganisation of East India Company trade by war and revolution in the 1750s and 1760s gave Manchester its opportunity in Africa. African customers had been loath to accept inferior British imitations. One governor at Cape Coast in 1720 had said they were 'of no other service than to put away to the Castle working slaves.' But with Indian competition diminished, the Lancashire men pushed their wares in successfully. By 1769 nearly half the money earned, if that is the word, by British cotton piece goods came from sales in Africa.[151] As Indian cottons reappeared in sufficient quantities, African customers returned to them gladly, but meanwhile Lancashire had enjoyed three critical decades of industrial acceleration towards take-off.

Yorkshire woollens lagged behind Lancashire cotton in moving towards factory production largely because markets overseas were harder to capture for such heavy products, but the fact that by 1770 they had outstripped their English rivals partly reflected the success of Halifax 'says' on the Guinea coast. Noting how the Canadian fur trade tended 'to the encouragement of British manufactory', the great explorer Alexander Mackenzie listed, amongst goods which Red Indians favoured, not only Manchester cotton wares, but also arms and ammunition, hardware, cutlery and ironmongery. Birmingham manufacturers during wars supplied guns to the British army. But in peacetime, they were kept going by the demands of the fur trade, by the needs of the East India Company, and by the Guinea slave trade, to which the town supplied 100,000 to 150,000 flint muskets annually. The Midlands nail trade also leant heavily on colonial markets. The growth of both industries stimulated the revolutionary iron industry.[152]

The home market was large and growing. The British middle class was achieving increasing standards of comfort, and most of the labouring poor had now been sucked from peasant subsistence into dependence upon bought goods. A fast-growing population ensured rapid expansion of demand. Yet it was colonial trades, calling for large quantities of identical, cheap items, which directed manufacturers in Birmingham, Manchester and Glasgow to the transforming reorganisation of industry. It was foreign, above all colonial, trade which provided the chance of expanding production far beyond the growth of the home market. Colonial war had won British businessmen markets overseas, while news of victories in far places, speculation about a Pacific continent, had expanded entrepreneurial imaginations. Empire brought industrial revolution. Without the Bight of Biafra, no Cottonopolis. Without war for trade, no breakthrough in ironmaking, no Watt steam engine. Without Plassey, smaller markets in India.

Had Bengal not come into British hands when it did, France might have achieved superiority in India during the American War, when her rival was momentarily weakened everywhere. But Britain's industrial revolution by then was beginning anyway. Granted that the tropics had made this possible, why was it Britain which had achieved such pre-eminence in the tropics? Why, to ask the same question another way, did France not have a prior, or simultaneous revolution in industry?

In 1789, France's total industrial production was greater than Britain's, French foreign trade was as large, and had been growing faster. French production of pig iron was greater. France had had its own cotton industry since the sixteenth century. Rouen, Manchester's French rival, had kept up with the latest technical developments in Britain, and had forged ahead in techniques of dyeing. It had its own entry, through Le Havre, into the slave-cotton triangle. French West

Indian raw cotton was better than British. Though British seamanship was unsurpassed, the French had led in naval construction and in cartography, and their activity in the Pacific matched Britain's.[153]

Such factors as had helped Britain fight and win three great wars for trade earlier in the century must also explain why Britain could now enter a new industrial league of its own. A medium-sized island had great advantages. Transport of goods was intrinsically easier. No point in Britain was very far from the sea. Cook's home port of Whitby at one time had five shipyards, and, with upwards of 10,000 inhabitants, owned, in the mid-eighteenth century, over 200 ships. Its coastal coal trade reflected Britain's greatest luck, the natural abundance of this mineral. While France still mined and used very little, British production had tripled during the century down to the 1780s.[154] Coal was available in the hinterland of all three great western ports. The shortage of timber and the turn to coal were important preconditions for industrial revolution.

Arising from geographical conditions, there were all-important cultural ones. French industry largely concerned itself with the production of luxuries, fine things for élite markets. The French class structure was more rigid, the middle class was less powerful, the agriculturalists were poorer. Compared to the United States, Britain was thoroughly 'European' in its emphatic social hierarchy and the arrogance of its aristocratic élite. Compared to France, Britain was almost 'American', a land of quite widely diffused wealth and quite flexible social relationships. In the absence of legal barriers between classes, Britain differed from other European countries. Most noblemen married outside the peerage. The younger son of a baron was plain 'Mr'.[155] A vulgarian absentee planter like Beckford, an overweening 'nabob' like Barwell, might encounter sharp snobbish prejudice, but the very sensitivity of the English over matters of class reflected fluidity and uncertainty.

Bankers, for instance, were highly regarded men, socially indistinguishable from their customers. The British banking system was better than that of France. By 1784 there were a hundred and twenty banks in England outside London.[156] 'Country banks' mobilised the wealth of landowners for possible use in industrial development. The landowning classes themselves threw up men who adventured in industry, like the Duke of Bridgewater, the Earl of Dundonald, and the first Robert Peel of calico-printing fame, while manufacturers such as Arkwright ended their lives as 'improving' landlords. Set beside hard-working Virginian planters, British landowners might seem idle and wasteful. Contrasted with their European counterparts, they were besottedly practical commercialists. There was no 'agricultural revolution', in England as distinct from Scotland, because there was no need for one. The 'improved' methods introduced in some areas in the seventeenth century had gradually been adapted and extended in most parts of the country. The showplace of English agriculture was Thomas Coke's estate in Norfolk. Coke's mansion was designed by William

Kent with a great hall of Roman magnificence, but it was his technical prowess which brought experts in their hundreds from all over Europe to witness his sheep shearings. The English gentleman's passion for foxhunting and horse racing gave the island pre-eminence in the breeding of showy bloodstock, those glossy and elegant animals captured so finely by the cold, clear artisan's eye of George Stubbs in his paintings. But this hobby related to, even encouraged, a craze for 'improving' strains of useful livestock. 'Improvement' was the fashion. George III led it, establishing model farms on the royal estate at Windsor and writing for agricultural journals under the pseudonym of 'Mr. Robinson'.

The British landscape had been tamed and smoothed to a unique extent. Wolves were extinct. Wild deer were now rare. The gentry themselves were growingly civil and hard headed. Squire Western was on his way out, Mr Knightley was coming in. In Bere Regis, Dorset (to evoke a third novelist), the ancient Norman family of Turbervilles gave way early in the eighteenth century to Draxes whose ancestors had pioneered sugar production in Barbados. The former died out, the latter took over one of their largest farms and expanded from there to dominate the whole area, which they made into a notable fox-hunting district. 'See,' called a voice from Manchester in 1756, 'as the Owners of old Family Estates in your Neighbourhood, are selling off their Patrimonies, how your Townsmen are constantly purchasing, and thereby laying the Foundation of a new Race of Gentry. Not adorned, it's true, with Coats of Arms and a long Parchment Pedigree of useless Members of Society, but deck'd with Virtue and Frugality ... '[157] As so often later, Manchester's middle-class spleen exaggerated. While merchants moving into the country did bring commercial instincts to bear on estate management, older-established families now showed sharp money sense.

As cities grew, their call for food brought opportunity. During the long agricultural depression between 1730 and 1750, large landowners could afford to adjust their costs to lower prices and their production to the needs of the market, but the small landowner and copyholder suffered. Wars hit such lesser people hard, making it harder to get credit and raising the taxes they had to pay. As they fell away, the new profile of English country life emerged; a relatively small number of landlords, a middling number of tenant farmers, and a mass of labourers working for money.

The tenant farmer was the beneficiary of enclosures of common lands, which were the great mainsprings of 'improvement'. In Tudor days, enclosures had been for pasture. Now the aim was commercial production of cereals, profiting from rising prices as the growth of population accelerated and manufacturing industry increased its sway.

Enclosure enabled landlords to raise rents. After 1760, the new device of the private Enclosure Act meant that it was no longer necessary for a great landlord to secure the agreement of small landowners in the area. He could now force them to comply, and the whole weight of sovereign king-in-parliament was behind him. Perhaps half of England had been enclosed already, while over large areas of the south-west, west, north and south-east open fields had either never existed or had been outmoded for centuries; but change in the Midland heart-land of English agriculture was drastic. Before 1760, there had been only 130 parliamentary enclosure awards. In the next fifty-five years over 1,800 more went through, concerning 7 million acres. Besides these, there were 'drainage Acts' for the Fens. For a century after Cromwell, most of this area had been left in peace. Now piecemeal drainage recommenced.[158]

Thanks to expanding acreage and 'improving' agriculture, Britain could industrialise swiftly without needing to import much food. Corn output nearly doubled between 1700 and 1820.[159] Technical change did not yet produce rural depopulation. Numbers employed on the land continued to rise. But it was no longer the case that everyone born in the countryside had automatic access to the land. As more and more children were born, young people had to look for work elsewhere. In this way, change in agriculture provided one necessary condition for industrial revolution – a mobile labour force willing to gravitate to the new centres of innovating industry.

Population of England and Wales seems to have risen from about 6½ million in 1750 to 9 million at the end of the century. Over the same period, Scotland's increased from about 1¼ million to 1,608,000. There is no reason to suppose that this sharp rise had much to do with increasing prosperity. Growth was swift in the most backward regions – the Highlands, rural Wales, Ireland. There were comparable increases elsewhere in Europe – the Continent's population rose from 120 to 210 million in the century after 1750.[160] The upsurge was world wide. Chinese population also increased enormously. Food crops from the New World (potatoes in Britain and Europe, sweet potatoes, maize and peanuts in China) had spread gradually since Columbus's day and everywhere brought an improvement in diet. But like the opening up of frontier lands in China, in Russia, and in America, the adoption of new crops seems as likely to have been a consequence as a cause of rising population. An explanation in terms of disease seems more likely. Western medicine, despite the limited successes of inocula-tion against smallpox, was still more likely to kill than cure. But it may be that for reasons not yet known epidemic and pandemic diseases abated in virulence during the eighteenth century. A shift in weather, altering climates, is another possible factor.

Population explosion occurred at just the right time for British industry. In Britain guild regulations and other medieval restrictions on the mobility of labour were moribund. New workers could move wherever pay was available. In other European countries, rulers interfered, on 'mercantilist' grounds, with economic organisation. The British State let revolution in industry happen, hardly intervening at all. Such State action as there was tended to favour take-off. Protective tariffs aided industry. The tax system helped rich individuals grow richer, transferring money to them from the poor. The money needed to fight war after war was chiefly raised by indirect taxes on commodities used by everyone – alcoholic drinks, bricks, salt, glass, tea and sugar and tobacco. It was handed over to holders of government bonds, to contractors, to shipbuilders and to ironmasters. The profits and capital of business were virtually untaxed.

Under Britain's parliamentary system, rich men could transform the country-side much as they wished. Since the days of the Saxons, hardly any new roads had been made in Britain. The innovations in transport which opened up Britain's little local markets and fused them in a single great one were eased by land-owners through an assembly of landowners. From the first decade of the eighteenth century, private Turnpike Acts gave powers to self-appointed boards of local trustees to borrow money with which to improve and keep up certain stretches of road, and then to recoup by levying tolls on passing vehicles and animals. Two thousand road Acts passed through Parliament in the eighteenth century, three-quarters of these in the last fifty years.[161] In the 1780s the Earl of Dundonald extracted tar from coal, and two other Scots, Telford and McAdam, applied new techniques which enabled mail coaches to halve the speed of travel on the long trunk routes. 'Tarmacadam', a by-product of coke, sped forward the wheels of the new coal-based economy.

Canals were the most captivating harbingers of revolution. In 1757, the first industrial canal was fashioned, joining the river Mersey with St Helens to bring Cheshire salt to Lancashire coal. Four years later the Duke of Bridgewater opened the famous waterway from his colliery at Worsley towards Manchester. Trunk canals soon connected river systems from east to west and from north to south. By 1790, London was linked by inland waterway with Hull and Liverpool, Bristol and Birmingham. Sleepy villages became thriving landports. Josiah Wedgwood's fine pottery slipped safely down still waters to its markets. Coal moved in bulk from mine to distant town.

Rural England was studded with wonders. To Arthur Young, the view of the Bridgewater Canal crossing the river Irwell at Barton Aqueduct seemed 'some-what like enchantment'. Over one river, another river 'hung in the air, with barges sailing upon it'. The Romans long ago had built mighty aqueducts, but never anything like the great iron bridges, the first of which, in 1779, crossed the Severn at Coalbrookdale with a span of 100 feet. One versifier sang the prodi-gious coal-mine, that 'City of Subterraneous Streets', and the new factories, set at first beside country streams, evoked for the genteel delicious awe rather than menace. 'These cotton mills, seven storeys high, and fill'd with inhabitants, remind me of a first rate man of war,' an aristocrat wrote in the 1780s, 'and when they are lighted up, on a dark night, look most luminously beautiful.'[162] Yet even as new awareness of man's inventive potential grasped delighted imaginations, the maiming and twisting effects of this revolution were plain.

Agricultural change was destroying ancient communality in the countryside, weakening authority, sifting inert tradition, but also fracturing closeness and ease. Common lands were enclosed which had given grazing, firewood, berries, nuts and play room to the meanest, and many villagers were forced into greater dependence on the poor law, with its dismal workhouses. Enclosure transformed familiar landscapes. ' ... The open fields, with their complex pattern of narrow strips, their winding green balks or cart roads, their headlands and grassy foot-paths,' gave way to 'the modern chequer-board pattern of small, squarish fields, enclosed by hedgerows of hawthorn, with new roads running more or less straight and wide across the parish in all directions.'[163] The need for timber for fencing meant that thinly wooded areas lost many trees. Before hedgerows grew and fresh associations began to be homelike, the first effect of enclosure was one of nakedness, rawness, life scraped off.

Isolated new farmhouses rose, where portly wives of port-drinking tenants pestered their consorts to buy pianofortes, and to despatch the girls to boarding schools so that they might be worthy of more genteel husbands. The old villages grew more squalid. Some became towns within a generation. Oldham in Lancashire, in the 1750s, was a 'handful of scattered hamlets set in unimproved moorland.' By 1800 it was one of the largest towns in England.[164]

St Helens already portended urban horrors to come, with its glass works and copper works fouling every stream and blighting every plant and tree. Water power was intrinsically clean. But as the use of steam spread, so did soot and filth. Midland and northern towns soon acquired layers of grime which they have not shed even today.

In the 1780s, most were still free of soot. But the moral environment created by the industrialists was already alien and shocking. Under the old conditions of domestic industry, the worker had had some control over his own rate of labour. He could take a free day for sport or sleep. The rites of 'St Monday' were reli-giously followed. The new-style entrepreneur would have none of that. He had lavished money on building and plant. Every machine was geared to the regular beat of the engine. Every worker must bow his will to the factory's metal disposition. The owner himself was enserfed psychologically by the genie he had released to work for him. The problem of disciplining men unused to regularity obsessed him. The public clock in the medieval town had given Western man his sense of 'time'. Now the clock set up prominently in the fac-tory made Time tyrannise the natural rhythms of dawn, noon and sundown, gave Time a new character, bullying, racing, dawdling, as the machine and exhaustion between them, pushing and pulling, exacted.

The entrepreneur built houses for his imported workers. He also erected churches, where parsons or ministers preached the virtues of obedience, regular habits, sobriety. Evangelical Christianity found a new role. Having wakened men, it was used to put them to sleep. 'I have left most of my works in Lanca-shire under the management of Methodists,' the first Robert Peel wrote in 1787, 'and they serve me exceedingly well.' With its rows of mean identical houses, with its shops where workers exchanged credit slips given them by their employer for goods which he sold them himself, with its blackening monitory chapel, 'The industrial unit,' T. S. Ashton observes, 'was often not a single establishment but something approaching a colonial settlement.'[165] It was colonialist, too, in its bid to reshape and control the minds of people.

Adults, in this generation, reacted much like slaves new fetched from Africa. So industrialists preferred child labour, which could be trained to factory ways, from infancy. At Arkwright's three mills in Derbyshire in 1789, about two-thirds of the 1,150 workers were children. Children commonly laboured at this time up to fifteen hours a day, six days a week. If not children, women at least were more malleable than men. The wholesale employment of children and wives thrust fathers away, humiliating them, deforming family relationships. ('Wholesale' it was. 'TO LETT', an advertisement called in a Manchester news-paper, 1784, 'THE LABOUR OF 260 CHILDREN. With Rooms and every Convenience for carrying on the Cotton Business.')[166]

The labour force was emasculated. The factory owner usurped the place of the father, reminding his children meanwhile of a still greater Father in Heaven whose practice, concerning rewards and punishments, was far more drastic than mere fines for drunkenness, sloth and gambling, bonuses for subservient behaviour. Paternalism in the countryside had found its legitimacy in tradition. God had set squire and poor man in their places. It had always been so. Now just as its co-worker, Evangelicalism, had replaced merely habitual faith with ener-getic spiritual masturbation, so paternalism in the new order based its claim of respect upon active benevolence. The new authority, not innately felt right, was *made* 'right' by the character of its possessor. Look, he would say, like empire-builders after him, at what *I* have done for *you*.

The surest defence of his rule, in these early days, was the wages he managed to pay. Mechanisation gave the chance of higher wages with lower prices. The new industry not only paid its workers more money but also drove up the wages of agricultural labour in the vicinity. However, it brought periods of high cyclical unemployment. Cash was then an overweening tyrant. Things which people had grown, reared or made for themselves in the older life-style now had to be paid, paid, paid for.

The manufacturer might be genuinely kind and well meaning, in so far as his business would let him. Or he might, mouthing slogans from Adam Smith, excuse hard behaviour by saying that what suited his interest must, however obscurely, be for the good of the victims of *laissez faire*. These new masters came from diverse backgrounds. Some were aristocrats, like Lord Dundonald in Fife, who gladly freed his collier serfs, but forced on one of his chemical workers a contract for twenty-five years. Some were former helots themselves, like David Dale, a herd boy, then weaver, then small pedlar, who began to import cotton yarn and started in 1786 the famous model paternalist mill at New Lanark. Most, however, came from the middling ranks, sons of landowners, sons of merchants or traders. The antinomian arrogation of nabobs had its counterpart in the amazing John Wilkinson, accused of smuggling arms to the

enemy during the American war, who came to be mine-owner and coal merchant as well as smelter and founder, and who paid his workmen in his own
personal coinage, where his own head stood in place of the king's, with one of
his own tilt forges featured on the reverse. He insisted that when he died his
body must go underground in an iron coffin, and his awed people spread the
story that he would rise from it and visit his blast furnaces seven years after
his death. Richard Arkwright, a less engaging upstart, rode into Derby in 1787
in a style which would have impressed Calcutta, with a tail of gentlemen, thirty
javelin men in rich liveries, and trumpeters dressed in scarlet and gold.[167]

Yet a very large proportion of manufacturers were sober-sided persons.
Nonconformist Protestantism came into its own. Ironmasters were commonly
Quakers, cotton spinners commonly Unitarians. Boulton, Roebuck and
Wilkinson had all been educated in Dissenting academies. Dissenters were
blocked from civil and military office. They ganged closely, and lent each other
money readily. Denied upper-class status, they spurned upper-class prodigality.
Clustering in business, they saved, invested, and helped each other forward, the
Panzer division of the middle class.

Aggressive middle-class consciousness emerged. Adam Smith, as a Scot of
his time and station, had respect for aristocracy, but even his writings took on
a somewhat Paineite flavour as, drawing his distinction between productive and
unproductive labour, he coolly listed churchmen and members of the armed
forces together with 'menial servants' and 'buffoons', and added the King himself for good measure. The 'princely Boulton', as Watt called him, was ready to
express contempt for the landed gentry. 'Early in life', he told one correspondent, 'Fortune gave me the option of assuming the character of an idle man
commonly called a Gent^n, but I rather chose to be of the class wch Le Baron
Montesque [sic] describes as the constant contributors to the purse of the commonwealth rather than of another class which he says are always taking out of it
without contributing anything towards it.' This usage of 'class' was new.[168]

Middle-class consciousness was commonly just as bitter against the labouring
classes. As early as 1755, we find a spokesman for the Manchester employers
attributing to the character of the poor the existence of poverty in this thriving
town. 'The Poor refuse or neglect to help themselves, and thereby disable their
Betters from effectually helping them. They have an abject Mind, which entails
their Miseries upon them; a mean sordid Spirit, which prevents all Attempts of
bettering their Condition. They are so familiarised to Filth and Rags, as renders
them in a manner, natural ... ' Only low wages and harsh poor laws could goad
such undermen to work hard. If they got too much money, they would labour
only four days a week, then flock to alehouses and cockfights. A magistrate
near Bolton, Lancashire, noticed with horror in the summer of 1783 that 'there
was so little appearance of want ... that one evening I met a very large procession
of young men and women with fiddles, garlands and other ostentation of
rural finery, dancing morris dances in the highway merely to celebrate an idle

anniversary, or, what they had been pleased to call for a year or two, a fair at a paltry thatched alehouse upon the neighbouring common.' Finery ... dancing ... fair ... alehouse ... common – all the preferred resorts and amusements of the poor could be summed up and dismissed with that one word 'idle'.[169]

In Gloucestershire, where the woollen clothiers did not bring in water wheels, let alone steam power, where they did not resort to employment of women and children, where they merely concentrated looms and jennies in their own shops and abolished apprenticeship, a weaver would cry that the capitalists looked on his own class as 'an army defeated and taken prisoner', and had 'driven us away from our houses and gardens to work as prisoners in their factories and their seminaries of vice.' Nostalgia for a past of fresher air, idealised in receding retrospect, would persist among industrial workers for generations, and would be a main force propelling immigrants to other continents, where a man might stand tall and free on his own land. But meanwhile, people could not be persuaded to take what employers gave them without complaint. 'Combinations' of workers emerged in the cotton industry as early as the 1750s. The Carron Company soon ran into serious labour troubles and called in troops to quell a riot in the 1760s. Soon, shortlived 'combinations' emerged among Scottish colliers also.[170] The faster transport of the new era made it easier for employers to get together and keep in touch, but as workers adjusted to their new situation and their understanding of it increased, they too could contemplate organisations embracing whole regions, or several regions.

IX

The balance of regions within Britain was shifting. The growth of Birmingham and Manchester would create what were almost rival capitals, dominated by the middle classes, where men in plain dress with broad provincial accents would sneer at the fopperies of London high society. The industrial revolution reached Scotland and Wales as quickly as it happened in England. Lairds and Welsh squirelings had been different sorts of men from the dominant English landed gentry. But industrialists behaved much the same anywhere.

'Scotland packed into about thirty years of crowded development between 1750 and 1780 the economic growth that in England had spread itself over two centuries.'[171] It could not have done so without direct help from English experts, or without the opportunities which the Empire had given to Scots themselves. Men came back from the East and West Indies laden with money, and set about running their estates so as to make more. Those lairds who had never left had to keep up with the nabobs. In the 1760s and 1770s 'improvement' began to sweep forward with Cossack velocity. By the end of the century, tenant farmers in south-east Scotland who had imitated English methods were teaching the English new tricks in their turn, and 'Lothian husbandry' was becoming the cynosure of progressive eyes everywhere in Europe. Small's improved plough of 1763, Meikle's power-driven threshing machine of 1786, were important Scottish inventions. The Scots pioneered modern field drainage. Demand for coal soared as farmers clamoured for is to burn limestone and so make fertiliser.

Innovation in industry was likewise seeded from England. Two Englishmen, John Roebuck and his partner, established the first Scottish chemical works, at Prestonpans in 1749, and the first great ironworks, Carron, ten years later. New ideas of colliery engineering and management came in from the south, and English workmen were brought north as supervisors. The new cotton technology rushed in when Lancashire yarn manufacturers found that they had a surplus, and disposed of it to the west of Scotland linen industry, which had run into hard times and underemployment. South-west Scotland had plenty of water power and wages were low. Lancashire spinners saw they could profit from both. As Glasgow and Paisley became great cotton towns, local men learnt fast. By the 1790s they were introducing their own innovations.

Scotland was well prepared to seize its hour of national glory. The labour force was adaptable and inventive. The system of poor relief through the churches was far more flexible than the English poor law, and made labour even more mobile than in England. Besides this, traditions of thrift had produced an exceptionally strong banking system, the assets of which, it is estimated, increased six times between 1750 and 1770, largely thanks to the proceeds of empire overseas.[172]

Linen output had risen thrice in volume and four times in value between 1736 and the slump in 1772. Textile working, therefore, was well known. While linen continued to grow, more than doubling its output in the next fifty years, cotton now outstripped it. Imports of raw cotton wool into the Clyde rose in value from £150,000 per year in the early 1770s to £2,000,000 by 1789, then to £7,500,000 in 1801. Textile production spread up remote braes and Highland glens. Cotton chiefly accounted for an increase of 270 per cent in shipments of British manufactures from Scottish ports between 1770 and the end of the century.[173]

Every middle-class group in Scotland, even authors, benefited from the bonanza. (William Robertson received £4,500 for his second work of history.) There was little or no tension here between 'aristocrats' and middle classes. Landowners, professional people, merchants, maunfacturers shared a common enthusiasm and rose alike in wealth. Scottish artisans, Watt in the lead, had an education which helped them see and seize the opportunities of the new age. Everyone in the Lowlands seemed to be climbing socially at the same time, uniquely combining clannish deference with American appetite for adventure. Sir John Sinclair, an earnest, unflagging, Quixotic agricultural improver, revelled in 'the spectacle' of a 'people naturally possessed but of few territorial resources, and living in a bleak and unpropitious climate, employing their activity, their constancy, and their genius in triumphing over a sterile soil –

directing their attention to the riches of the mind ... and making agriculture, manufacture and commerce, instruction, morality and liberty flourish together.'[174] The conquest by man of his own innate sin was somehow proved possible in this bare, windy country, where mind and hard work had triumphed over matter, and Covenanting arrogance was reborn as practical, hard-driving, censorious Scots took their new economic and technological gospels to the English and other unregenerate races.

The losses hardly seemed worth counting. When David Dale waylaid a party of Highlanders who were on their way to the New World and settled them down to make cotton for him at New Lanark, and then advertised that further intending emigrants from Argyllshire and the Isles should come to this model milltown likewise, it seemed that industry could solve Scotland's human problems. Yet certain losses were irreparable, and would seem tragic. Glasgow would be transformed from a notably clean and stately town to a smoky sprawl with the worst housing conditions in Europe. Social apartheid would divide Edinburgh. The Georgian New Town now going up would survive as a dignified symbol and product of success, but the Old Town, where as late as 1773 a dowager duchess was still found living sandwiched 'between a fishmonger and a crowd of tailors and milliners', was beginning its decay into a dangerous slum. While Burns was publishing his poetry, the almost miraculous culture from which he sprang, of peasants with barefooted wives and children who lived in low two-roomed houses ('but and ben') yet shared with servants and cottars a passion for reading, was being seen off by the march of enclosure. The friendly gudeman gave way to farmers who built tall stone houses to mark their social distance from their hired labourers.[175] That closeness of Scots well-to-do and poor to each other, which had made revolution possible, was fractured as industrialism advanced.

Wales could not make its own revolution. Towards the second half of the eighteenth century, Carmarthen, with some 5,000 people, was its largest town. Grass grew in the main streets of Swansea, the chief Welsh harbour. Coracles were still used on the River Taff at Cardiff. Bristol's September Fair was the pivot of economic life in South Wales. Wool from South Wales went to the clothiers of south-west England. The Drapers Company of Shrewsbury dominated and exploited from England the cottage woollen weavers of Denbigh, Merioneth and Montgomery, as they had done in Tudor days, and profited from the ready market which cheap Welsh cloth found in the slave-owning colonies. The main support of Wales was the trade in cattle and sheep which were driven across the border in thousands every year for fattening in the Home Counties. Without the returning drovers, rural Wales would have had little currency and no news. The gentry, some of whom still employed harpers, mostly lived in dwellings which hardly exceeded the size of a good farmhouse. Yet there was very little pauperism. Meagre self-sufficiency prevailed. Labourers and small farmers teetered always on the edge of poverty, but strong family feeling and fellow feeling ensured that very few toppled over. Nucleated villages of the English type were rarely found outside the richest lowlands, and these were the only areas which were much effected by enclosures. Welshmen with a head for business went to England. Their own country still looked economically much as it had done in the reign of Elizabeth. Some landowners exploited deposits of coal and lead. A little coal was sometimes exported abroad. The main novelty was the tin-plate industry established at Pontypool, which produced so-called 'Japan-ware' resembling eastern lacquered wood, and enjoyed modest prosperity.[176]

But then 'wave after wave of immigrant capitalists swept over the country'. Large parts of Wales were shaken suddenly from a quasi-feudal, near-tribal way of life to suffer under the dominance of alien entrepreneurs. Big monopolistically integrated concerns ruled where previously there had been few enough little ones. In these early stages, very few Welsh people profited much from their country's natural wealth.[177]

The temptation of Wales to capital was its profusion of minerals. Merchants from London and Bristol laid the basis of iron and coal industries. Progress was slow till the American war. The demand which that brought set a new pace. It gave John Wilkinson his chance to make great the iron furnace at Bersham, in North Wales, which he had inherited from his Lancashire father, and which he married with the coal mines he owned. It spurred the development of the vast acreage which Anthony Bacon had acquired in South Wales.[178] And then Cort's invention of the 'puddling' process made coal and iron a still more attractive combination.

From 1761, British warships were sheathed with copper bottoms to protect them in tropical waters. The discovery of copper in Anglesey shortly preceded the American war. Two landlords had a stake in the rich vein. Thomas Williams (a Welshman, for once) made himself partner to both of them. He built furnaces, wire mills, rolling mills. He sold sheathing and nails to the navies of Europe, and cheap brass ornaments to the British slave traders. The Parys Mine Company minted its own coinage. The Anglesey mines faltered and died in the nineteenth century, but at their peak of breakneck exploitation, Parys Mountain had dominated the world market for copper.[179]

In the 1780s cotton mills came to Flintshire, as they did to many country districts in Britain so long as water power was commonly used and steam engines were still rare. As Watt's invention and its successors ramped wider, proximity to coal would be decisive. This would be the misfortune of Ireland.

There was no human reason why Ireland should not have shared to the full in the integrating experience of simultaneous revolution shared by the three neighbour countries. It was less 'backward' than Wales. The Newry Canal and the Grand Canal had actually preceded the famous artificial navigations of England. The small coalfield in Leinster had had its first steam engine as early as 1740. After the Seven Years War, Ireland too saw the arrival of large-scale flour mills, breweries, grain mills, sugar refineries, glass factories. The climate was ideal for textile production. The cotton industry naturally spread from England, and very large mills sprang up – using water power.[180]

So much water, so little coal, meant a tragic distance opening up between Ireland's experience and that of Britain. In the 1780s, Ireland and Devon between them produced less than one-fourhundredth of the coal mined in the British Isles. And large-scale emigration had started from Ireland to industrial Lancashire. By the early years of the next century, perhaps one person in ten in Manchester would be Irish.[181]

X

After Rockingham's sudden death in July 1782 William Petty, Lord Shelburne, became Prime Minister. He too owned vast estates in Ireland, where he had been brought up. A haughty grandee, whose affected manners and obvious contempt for most other people made him extremely unpopular in Parliament, he nevertheless numbered among his friends many of the most brilliant plebeians of the day, Price, Priestley, and Benjamin Franklin among them.

Shelburne was a proponent of Smithite ideas, of 'burning all Tariffs and opening every Port Duty free ... ' He saw close connection between American and Irish problems, and hoped unavailingly that both countries might be sister states of Britain within an empire based on equality and reciprocal concession. His instructions for a new governor whom he sent out to Barbados were such as almost to concede self-government.[182] In negotiations to end the war with America, his attitude was as conciliatory as possible.

After Yorktown, all notions of further offensive against the United States were abandoned. The great aim was to save the West Indies. Good luck permitted this. Rodney found himself the first admiral during the war able to fight a major French fleet with a superior British one. In the 'Battle of the Saints' in April 1782, his thirty-six ships overmatched de Grasse's thirty-three and a planned French attack on Jamaica was thwarted. Britain's position in the negotiations was thus less disastrously weak than it might have been.

Hostilities were suspended early in 1783. The terms of the proposed treaties evoked a hypocritical chorus of horror from the followers of Fox and North, now strange bedfellows in opposition, and Shelburne was forced to resign. But basically everyone wanted peace. Shelburne's deal went through. France handed back six of the West Indian islands captured during the war, but Britain returned St Lucia, the French forts in Senegal and Gorée, and the French factories in India. Spain did well. Britain agreed to evacuate the Moskito Coast of Central America. The Floridas and Minorca were confirmed in Spanish possession, but Britain kept Gibraltar, and Spain guaranteed the British right to cut logwood in Honduras Bay.

The terms agreed with the United States were perhaps, thanks to Shelburne, unnecessarily generous. American fishermen were given great privileges in imperial waters. A geographically meaningless northern boundary for the U.S.A. was drawn through the drainage basin of the Great Lakes. The western limit of the new nation was set at the Mississippi. Beyond that, the Spanish claim still held. Shelburne aimed at free trade with the U.S., giving their subjects a right to participate equally in the trade of the Empire. This would have been greatly to the benefit of the British West Indies. But mercantilism still ruled most thinking in Britain, and even Adam Smith conceded that the Navigation Acts were necessary for purposes of defence. The Commons defeated Shelburne's proposal. It was hoped that those northern parts of America which Britain still held would replace the States as suppliers of fish, lumber and flour to the West Indies.

Shelburne was replaced by a coalition between Fox and North. This was deeply obnoxious to George III, and he soon seized the chance to bring this ministry down which was afforded by its problems over India.

It was clear that something had to be done. The failure of the British government to secure the recall of Hastings, in face of the support given him by the East India Company's shareholders, showed that in practice the Company was not under effective State restraint. Yet it owed the State, in 1780, more than £4 million. Two more parliamentary Committees of Enquiry were set up in 1781, one 'select', on the administration of justice in India, one 'secret', on the causes of the war in the Carnatic. One immediate outcome was a Bengal Judicature Act (1781) which meant that the British Crown clearly assumed responsibility for creating a new judicial system in India. But the chief importance of the Committees lay in the expertise acquired through them by the chairmen, Edmund Burke and Henry Dundas respectively.

Dundas's interest was opportunistic. It was a way of advancing his career, and incidentally, as it would turn out, the careers of countless fellow Scots. He was a very able man who argued hard for the changes which his judgment told him were necessary. Burke, by contrast, developed sincere passion. A kinsman and close friend, his namesake William Burke, had become agent in England for the Raja of Tanjore. The fact that Warren Hastings supported the Nawab of the Carnatic against the Raja was one important element in the suspicion which Burke came to feel of the governor-general. His committee was briefed to consider 'how the British possessions in the East Indies may be held and governed with the greatest security and advantage to this country, and by what means the happiness of the native inhabitants may be best promoted.' Report after report passed censure on Hastings's administration. What Philip Francis now told him persuaded Burke that Hastings was 'the greatest delinquent that India ever saw'.[183] Meanwhile Dundas presented the Commons with a string of resolutions condemning Hastings's foreign policy as one of aggrandisement damaging to British honour and interests. The Rockingham whigs had long defended the EIC on the grounds that private property was sacred. Now Burke, with a consensus of leading politicians, agreed that the Company must be thoroughly regulated.

Ruinous wars in India must be halted. Territorial expansion must stop. Lord John Cavendish more than once declared in the Commons that 'he wished to God every European could be extirpated from India and the country resorted to merely on the principles of commerce.' Prodigal conquests, calling for large armies, had lost Britain thirteen colonies. Britain itself had recently come close to explosion. Rulers henceforth must take care of their moral stature and must improve and tighten administration. What went for Britain went also for India. The younger Pitt spoke for others when he observed that if Britain hoped to draw commercial profit from India, she must prevent extortion there by her own subjects, and bring the inhabitants happiness and tranquillity.[184]

In March 1783 the EIC once again had to petition for financial assistance. Three Bills in succession now aimed to settle the problem. Dundas had decided that Lord Cornwallis, despite his surrender at Yorktown, was the man to restore propriety to British rule in India. The subcontinent had been plagued by grasping commoners. A nobleman must clear up the mess. 'Here,' Dundas said of Cornwallis, 'there was no broken fortune to be mended, here was no avarice to be gratified. Here was no beggarly mushroom kindred to be provided for – no crew of hungry followers gaping to be gorged.'[185] But Dundas's Bill was blocked and the Fox–North ministry then had a try itself. Burke, now having a brief taste of office, was largely responsible for its proposals. The political tradition in which whig ministers had been brought up, their instincts, also, as aristocrats or supporters of aristocracy, told them to fear a strong executive. Men such as Dundas and Pitt had broken with old whiggery in their readiness for a strong ›xecutive, but Fox and Burke shuddered at the idea of giving the Crown more power.

In November 1783, Fox introduced a Bill to remodel the EIC's constitution. The Court of Directors and the Court of Proprietors were to be swept away and replaced by seven commissioners. Fox argued that whereas Dundas would have set up a despotic government in India, his scheme lodged the government of the subcontinent in London. But in striving to avoid giving increased patronage to the Crown, his ministry took it into their own hands. Their seven nominees, even when Fox and North fell from office, would, for the duration of their own lives, wield immense powers of patronage. Young Pitt denounced it as 'one of the boldest, most unprecedented, most desperate and alarming attempts at the exercise of tyranny, that ever disgraced the annals of this or any other country.' Burke, defending the Bill, advanced his famous concept of trusteeship. Government must be seen as a trust, must act for the benefit of all subjects. The EIC's servants must be baulked from exploitation. ' ... Animated with all the avarice of age, and all the impetuosity of youth, they roll in one after another; wave after wave; and there is nothing before the eyes of the natives but an endless, hopeless, prospect of new flights of birds of prey and passage, with appetites continually renewing for a food that is continually wasting.' Rolling or flying, this Bill was not going to stop them. The King saw to that. It passed the Commons by a two to one majority, but was defeated in the Lords after George III had made it known that he would regard any peer who voted for it as 'not only not his friend, but his enemy.'[186] Fox and North were dismissed. Pitt, only 24, became Prime Minister. Dundas was his most powerful colleague. The Indian issue had served them well.

Widespread indignation over Fox's apparent attempt to supplant King and Parliament in favour of an aristocratic oligarchy, helped to ensure that over a hundred of his supporters were swept out in the general election that followed. Though no one could have guessed it at the time, Pitt would be Prime Minister for almost a generation. Behind and around his slender figure most of the wealthy rallied themselves. One might almost speak of a new, one must certainly speak of a restyled, ruling class. Except for his relatives the Grenvilles, Pitt lacked support among the great landed families who had dominated politics so long. Besides the backing of George III, he could look for support to reformers, now disillusioned with Fox, to merchants, shocked by the India Bill and affectionate to the memory of Pitt's father, and to such men as John Robinson and Charles Jenkinson, eager administrators, 'King's Friends'. Peerages and knighthoods were lavished on such persons, and on new rich upstarts, swamping the old whig aristocracy.

Pitt was tough, almost transparent, plastic. So young that he had no existence in politics predating the new élite which he fronted, he was the ideal chairman for an industrialising country which might have been torn apart by the contention of rival wealthy classes. This cool, calculating man, a disciple of Adam Smith, was at home in the new world of steam. Personally incorruptible, he was a 'reformer', but one without warmth of passion, quick to bow principle to exigency. He was what the times made him – priggish, shifty and competent. His only obvious failing, not endearing, was the drunkenness in which bluff Dundas instructed him.

In this new consolidated ruling class – moderately reforming and avid for expanded trade at first, reactionary, but still expansionist, as the years lined boy Pitt's face – Scots were included, perfectly at home. Ironically, Dundas did possess almost the influence once falsely attributed to Bute. His arrival epitomised social change. He was middle class, from the legal profession. Even more than Pitt, he was indifferent to high-sounding ideas. He was the great 'manager', the great fixer. He fixed in turn for North, Shelburne and Pitt. He had shown the stuff he was made of in 1780, when out of forty-five Scottish M.P.s thirteen were committed to Dundas personally, and, thanks to his powers of management, only twelve were opponents of North's ministry. His talents were obvious. His price was high. Pitt gladly paid it. Dundas went on from strength to strength. By 1790 he had absolute control of thirty-two of the Scottish M.P.s.

Even this did not satisfy him, and in 1796 he ensured that only one firm opponent sat among the Scots in the Commons.[187]

He was a genial man who never tried to lose his Scottish accent. His blunt, sensible speeches sounded candid. He was good at telling funny stories to children and talked charmingly to old ladies. He found jobs for young Scots who were not connected with important families and otherwise went out of his way to help quite humble fellow countrymen. Unlike the icy Pitt, he was popular wherever he went.

India gave him the patronage which he needed to rule Scotland. It was characteristic of his cheerful disdain for principle that he should actually seize much of the power which Pitt had accused Fox of aiming at. This was through the India Act of 1784.

It established six commissioners in a body commonly known as the 'Board of Control', comprising the Chancellor of the Exchequer (Pitt), a Secretary of State for India (Dundas) and four Privy Councillors appointed by the King. This had power to send secret orders to India through the EIC directors. The Court of Proprietors was deprived of any right to annul or suspend what the Board of Control had approved. Government in India itself was given to a governor-general, Cornwallis, with a council of three. The lesser presidencies were now definitely subjected to Calcutta. Pitt could claim that his Bill gave the British 'public' charge of the country's Eastern possessions without confiscating the EIC's property. The Board did not appoint or dismiss EIC servants in India. But Dundas made sure that any new directors were friends of his. Since no one whom he did not support could get elected director, he could send Scot upon Scot rolling or flying to India. However, the boys were well educated, and Dundas did not knowingly give jobs to incompetents.[188]

General Oglethorpe, born at the time of the Darien débâcle, died in 1785 soon after he had called to congratulate John Adams, the first U.S. Ambassador to London. During his long lifetime he had seen other extraordinary changes besides American independence and the thriving union between Scotland and England. In his childhood, few people had taken tea. Now labourers drank it. The sugar and tobacco colonies westwards had been Britain's overseas empire, which he had founded a colony to defend. Now the East Indies dominated the minds of statesmen, Georgia was part of a new and separate empire, and the West Indies, though still greatly valued, were starting to matter less than the coalfields of Wales.

The planter class of Jamaica was more dependent than ever on Britain, and knew it. It now faced a long and bitter defensive battle against the advancing anti-slavers. The island could have done without fresh slaves. It could have been self-sufficient in food. But its whites refused to adjust themselves to a new age. Typically, though their island had much timber, they moaned and petitioned that they could not make do without the red oak staves of the U.S.A. Though even Wales was covered with improving Agricultural Societies, Jamaican planters remained indifferent to experiment. The British government, alarmed by the problem of feeding the West Indies, sent warships to the Pacific to collect plants. Hence the famous story of Captain Bligh, sent to bring breadfruit from Tahiti, whose crew mutinied and founded, with Polynesian concubines, a macabre society on little Pitcairn Island. Bligh eventually reached the West Indies with breadfruit in 1793, but the slaves refused to eat it and it was fed to pigs.[189]

Jamaican white society had some reinforcement as rising 1,700 mainland loyalists, with more than 7,500 slaves, sought refuge after the evacuation of Savannah and Charles Town. The exodus from the former thirteen colonies had, however, less marked effect here than elsewhere. In the Bahamas and what is now Canada the presence of newcomers was transforming.

In the Treaty of Versailles, the undertaking was given that Congress would recommend the individual states to consider reparation to loyalists. The failure after that to make good loyalist losses became a pretext for Britain to retain its frontier posts in the ceded portion of Quebec. Despite the treaty, tories returning to the United States were tarred and feathered, harassed and abused, until some U.S. citizens gradually realised they and their money could be useful. Before long, active and even prominent loyalists, if they accepted republican citizenship, were tolerated well enough. Some served on state legislatures and in Congress. Some became Jeffersonian Democrats.

However, the vast majority did not go back. The British government gave over £3 million in compensation to its unlucky subjects. About half of the émigrés settled in parts of North America still British. Nova Scotia took perhaps 35,000, an influx outnumbering the previous population. They were given free land, arms, spades, clothing and so on. Human nature ensured that genteel loyalists were querulous rather than grateful. 'We have nothing', one wrote, 'but his Majesty's rotten pork and unbaked flour to subsist on ... It is the most inhospitable clime that ever mortal set foot in.'[190] The region offered little scope to professional men, and the clamour for jobs helped inspire the British government to divide the colony in 1784, creating New Brunswick and with it a second administration.

Some 6,000 to 10,000 loyalists went to 'Canada' proper. New York tories, mostly modest farmers, knowing of good lands above Montreal, settled along the St Lawrence and the Niagara rivers, chiefly to the west of the old French area, and gave what became known as 'Upper Canada' an English-American character distinct from that of French-speaking 'Lower Canada'.

Eight thousand people, mostly blacks, arrived in the Bahamas, and the proportion of slaves in the colony suddenly soared from half to three-quarters. By 1786, the incoming tories had largely penetrated the old ruling group. Their arrival prompted a new, harsher, slave code, and they showed their American upbringing by demanding increased power for the assembly, just as loyalists in Quebec pressed for habeas corpus and an elected legislature.[191]

The new political division between British and U.S. empires was natural and yet artificial. For all France's military support for the States, French merchants lost heavily trading with America after the war. They were not willing (or able?) to give the long terms of credit to which the Americans were accustomed; they would not modify their products to suit American taste. Preferring to stick with their old suppliers, the Americans, by 1790, were importing as much from Britain as ever, and nine-twentieths of American exports still went there. British merchants soon resumed control of the Chesapeake tobacco crop. Since the leaf now mostly went directly to Europe, Glasgow lost its pre-eminent entrepôt status, but dozens of Scottish stores soon flourished again on the Piedmont. And British slavers found markets on the mainland; in thirty years after the war, despite laws against it, the U.S. imported as many Africans as had come in during the previous one hundred and sixty.[192]

For a while, Southern states continued to relax their codes and make manumission of slaves easier, but this trend was reversed as a new crop tied them almost as tightly to Britain as in colonial days. A young New Englander named Eli Whitney, staying on the Georgia estate of the widow of the revolutionary General Greene, heard that upland cotton would be a suitable crop if the laborious process of picking out the seeds could be circumvented. In a few months, by April 1793, he had perfected a machine so efficient that one black could grind out 50 lb. of fibre in a day. Manchester soon reaped the benefit.

The British played on the diplomatic weakness of the thirteen loosely tied states, intriguing with Vermont settlers to try to wean them from the others, and maintaining seven fortified posts in the interior, where they still had Indian alliances. The Spanish, now holding the mouth of the Mississippi, had closed it to American shipping, and were encouraging frontiersmen in Kentucky and Tennessee to quit the Union. It looked as if the unity of revolutionary days had been a temporary miracle. With the British exporting freely to America but denying Americans access to the West Indies, self-interest might have brought the rebels back into the British political sphere. Instead, they agreed on a Federal Constitution in 1787, opting for nationhood and for the creation of a strong state, aiming at domination of a continent. As Washington, the first President, put it, the new republic was 'an infant empire'.[193]

A nation – identifying itself as such – had been created, through the active participation of all classes, mobilised by the printing press. As David Ramsay mythologised in 1789, 'In establishing American independence, the pen and the press had merit equal to that of the sword. As the war was the people's war, and was carried on without funds, the exertions of the army would have been insufficient to effect the revolution, unless the great body of the people had been prepared for it, and also kept in constant disposition to oppose Great Britain.'[194] Franklin, then Jefferson, as U.S. ambassadors in Paris, ensured that Europe heard the gospel of the future; democratical revolutionary nationalism. Eight-thousand common French soldiers had fought in America. Some must have digested, and carried home, the anti-feudalist message of people's war.

Congress firmly decided, in 1788, against the British government's suggestion that the U.S.A. might care to buy convicts, as in colonial days. So Whitehall turned its mind to the Pacific and what Captain Cook had discovered there.

XI

The Hudson's Bay Company faced strong competition, by the early 1770s, from British fur traders, based on Montreal, who had backing from London commercial interests and had allied themselves with the French Canadian experts in the trade. Both parties to the struggle pushed exploration westwards, so that while Cook sailed the Pacific, others were moving towards it overland.

In 1773, an ex-sailor named Hearne, in HBC employ, guided by a Chipewyan Indian, struck the Coppermine River and followed it to its mouth in the Northern Sea. Next year, he founded a new post in the interior, Cumberland House, at a point which gave his company the key to a whole system of waterways. But the Montreal 'pedlars' fought back, and by 1779 had coalesced into a formal 'North West Company', which with annual trade worth £100,000 a year, compared to the HBC's £30,000, was able to dictate prices on the London market.[195] The small Montreal concerns who had stayed outside it were digested in 1787, and under the leadership of a Scot named Simon McTavish, its brave and brilliant explorers continued to rout the Hudson's Bay men. Through it, the sons of Scottish lairds and ministers found, as Samuel Vetch had once prophesied, scope for success in the prairies.

Hearne's discovery rated, for a while, as the largest new contribution to geographical understanding. He had shown, at last, that there simply could not be a North West Passage out of Hudson's Bay. The spread of tea drinking had revived interest in the Passage – tea was a bulky commodity which reached Britain on the longest of all trade routes. Hearne's findings left just one chance Alaska might be an island, and it was thought that there might be an open sea Passage south of it, then round the north of Canada – there was a theory that sea water did not freeze.

So Cook was sent out by the government on a third voyage. He was to reach Francis Drake's 'New Albion', then coast north. If he failed to find a North West Passage, he might look for a North Eastern one around Siberia. He left in July 1776, before word of the U.S. Declaration of Independence had reached London, and before it could be fully appreciated that one effect of discoveries made by him might be to establish British claims to North America's west coast in opposition to those of a new American empire.

On his way, he discovered Hawaii and the Sandwich Islands. Reaching the North American mainland in March 1778, he visited Nootka Sound and traded with the Indians there. (These fishing people were so very greasy that the common sailors left the women alone, but some of the officers overcame their revulsion at the odour of fish, train oil and smoke, and found, by dint of hard scrubbing, as Cook's surgeon reported, 'some Jewels that rewarded our trouble, Namely two sparkling black Eyes accompanied with a beautiful face ... ')[196] Sailing along the barren rugged shores of Alaska, behind which great white peaks towered inland, Cook established that the Bering Strait was the only approach on this side to the Northern Sea. At last in $70\frac{1}{2}°$ N. he ran into an impenetrable wall of ice, and turned back. In the Aleutians he found Russian traders bullying a peaceful native people and exchanging tobacco, now a local addiction, for the very valuable skins of the sea otter. Then he returned for another look at Hawaii.

It may be that the scenario of so many subsequent stories and films had a real origin here; that the Polynesians on Hawaii were told by their priests that Cook was one of their gods who had long ago left by sea, promising to return in a great ship. Or perhaps not. In any case, Cook was mystified by the deep respect accorded him. The Hawaiians, at first, were very willing to feed the strangers. But they chafed as this costly visitation protracted itself. As Cook tried to leave, the *Resolution* was damaged in a gale. When it came back with its companion, the pilfering which Cook had encountered widely in the Pacific started up here as well. Cook's temper had worsened with age. Earlier on this voyage, in the Tonga Islands, he had shown signs that he was losing his sense of proportion over such things; he had flogged natives heavily and had had crosses slashed on men's arms with knives. When Hawaiians stole a cutter from the *Discovery*, he reacted with fatal fury.

He went ashore to take a hostage towards regaining the boat, loading his own double-barrelled shotgun and telling the nine marines who escorted him to put ball in their muskets. Nemesis came very quickly. A huge crowd pressed him back down the beach. When a native rushed at him Cook fired. If he thought that the unfamiliar crack of gunfire would deter these people, he was wrong. In the sudden affray, seventeen Hawaiians were killed, four of Cook's marines, and the captain himself, struck down with a club from behind as he waved for more men to come ashore.[197] Captain John Gore eventually brought the two ships home in October 1780.

The death of Cook was a blow to the myth of Pacific paradise, as were the pictures of human sacrifice witnessed on Tahiti which this expedition brought back. Perhaps Cook's fatal impatience had reflected his own growing disillusionment. But his voyages had helped ensure that Polynesian societies would grow less rather than more happy. 'The rise of pocket-Napoleons was implicit in the first sight of a musket on an island shore ... ' Tahiti had had high chiefs, a whole ruling class of them, but it was not till the British came that one Tu, treated by the visitors as 'king', though he was weak compared to other chiefs, got the notion of asserting supreme authority (which his son actually gained, with British help, in 1815). Cook's third visit to Tahiti was followed by an epidemic.

The island's population, perhaps 40,000 before its discovery, was halved by the end of the century.[198]

Europeans could not be blamed in respect of germs whose existence they did not yet recognise. But the traders who swarmed in Cook's wake, seeking sandal-wood, sea-otter skins and the dried sea-slugs and birds' nests which the Chinese loved to eat, brought with them the casual rapacity of their class and age, and the whalers who came again and again did not scruple to pay for supplies with cheap firearms and crude spirits. To complete the rape of Paradise, missionaries appeared; there were British ones on Tahiti by 1797, telling the people about original sin.

After Cook, it seemed that the British would go everywhere. Even in defeat the British government had conducted the War of American Independence with a strategic boldness such as the elder Pitt had never matched. In 1781 it had sent an expedition to conquer the Cape of Good Hope, an essential staging post on the way to the East – Cook had compared it to 'one great Inn fited up for the reception of all comers and goers.' St Helena was no longer adequate to the East India Company's requirements. Declaration of war on Holland gave Britain a chance to strike at the Dutch empire. A French expedition got to the Cape first, but from now on its conquest would be a prime British consideration. In the same year, the British had tried, but failed, to establish a base in Celebes from which to seize control of the East Indies. And the Cabinet had previously approved an idea, not, however, put into execution, for an invasion of South America from India.[199]

The products of revolutionary industry, pouring out faster and faster, must be sold. The younger Pitt and his colleagues, like the classes whose support they mobilised, believed that markets must be captured, and could be captured, all over the globe. Despite the loss of the North American colonies, Britain was stronger than ever before. Not far behind brave explorers and honest if foolish missionaries, Manchester cotton would follow, Birmingham guns.

References

My bibliography provides a key to the abbreviations used for most works.

In transcribing quotations, I have merely followed the sources cited here (a consistent principle producing apparent inconsistency), except in respect of old-fashioned 'u's for 'v's, 'f's for 's's, 'y's for 'th's and 'wch's for 'which's.

All books, unless otherwise identified, are published in London.

Introduction

1 Bailyn, OTH, viii–x
2 D. H. Lawrence, *The Rainbow* (Penguin edn, 1949), 11
3 Stone, CER, xi
4 W. B. Yeats, *Collected Poems* (Macmillan, 1950), 233
5 Ibid., 'Meditations in Time of Civil War', 230–1

Prologue: The World is the World's World

1 Dante, *Divine Comedy — I: Inferno*, ed. and trans. John D. Sinclair (Oxford University Press, 1971), 326–7
2 Needham, SCC 3, 557–8
3 Needham, SCC 4–iii, 487–8
4 Ibid., 515–16, 522
5 Reischauer and Fairbank, 290
6 Parry, ed., ER, 32–5
7 Reischauer and Fairbank, 319
8 Postan in CEHE 2, 216
9 Hale, RE, 29–30
10 M. Aston, 172
11 Koenigsberger and Mosse, 96
12 Kiernan, LHK, 5
13 H. Aubin in CEHE 1, 454
14 Elliott, ED, 44–9
15 D. B. Davis, PSWC, 57–9
16 E. Carus Wilson in CEHE 2, 419–21
17 Needham, SCC 4–iii, 520–1
18 A. R. Hall in CEHE 4, 98
19 Hale, RE, 51–3
20 Hay, EEI, 86–7
21 Columbus, 300; Koenigsberger and Mosse, 94
22 Boxer, PSE, 13

23 Parry, AR, 34
24 F. G. Cassidy in Hymes, 207–8
25 Tawney, RRC, 76
26 Morison, NV, 39–62
27 O Gorman, 113–15, 122–4
28 O Gorman, 86
29 Parry, ed., ER, 178
30 Parry, AR, 246
31 Boxer, PSE, 102
32 Parry, AR, 257–8
33 Elliott, OWN, 82
34 Morison, NV, 435
35 Ibid., 159
36 Ibid., 167–91; Cuming et al., 52
37 Morison, NV, 237–8; Cuming et al., 153

BOOK ONE

1 Hodgen, 364
2 M. Abrams et al., eds, *Norton Anthology of English Literature* (Norton, New York, 3rd edn, 1974), vol. 1, 1529–30

Cromwell the First

1 *Dean of Lismore*, 161
2 *See* Kinvig
3 Otway-Ruthven, 109
4 T. Jones Pierce in Roderick 1, 116
5 Otway-Ruthven, 125
6 Camoens, *Lusiads*, trans. W. C. Atkinson (Penguin, 1952), 149
7 Hay, FFC, 77; C. Hill, RIR, 20, 98, 115; Hale, RE, 281
8 Hoskins, MEL, 137
9 J. R. Hale in NCMH 1, 287
10 R. Davis, EOT, 12
11 Hay, FFC, 77
12 Koenigsberger and Mosse, 40
13 C. Hill, RIR, 51
14 Hilton, 55–6
15 Thirsk, AH, 255
16 Chinua Achebe, *Things Fall Apart* (Heinemann Educational Books, 1962), 160
17 Hoskins, MEL, 154
18 Thomas More, *Utopia*, trans. P. Turner (Penguin, 1965), 48–9
19 Hoskins, MEL, 177–8; E. Carus Wilson in CEHE 2, 427
20 C. Hill, RIR, 82–3; John Hales (?) 1549, quoted in Koenigsberger and Mosse, 38
21 Rowse, TC, 121–34
22 Thirsk, AH, 21–5

23 F. Child, *English and Scottish Popular Ballads* (Houghton Mifflin, Boston, 1888-9) vol. 4, 24-8

24 Rae, 10-11

25 G. M. Fraser, 65, 217

26 Child, loc. cit.

27 Scott, MSB 1, 215

28 Tough, 26-8

29 Bartley, 79

30 Smout, HSP, 43

31 Hume Brown, ET, 43

32 Hume Brown, SBS, 172

33 Smout, HSP, 95-6

34 Grant, SEDS, 525-7; Grant, M, 133-4

35 Grant, SEDS, 484; *Dean of Lismore*, 91-5

36 Maxwell, IH, 79-81

37 Nicholls, 92-102

38 O Clery, 1415-17

39 T. Jones Pierce in Thirsk, AH, 358

40 G. A. Williams in Roderick 1, 176 ff.; W. O. Williams, TG, 39 ff.

41 D. Williams, HMW, 20

42 P. Williams, WB, 19

43 Estyn Evans, 27

44 McNeill and Nicholson, 74

45 Sir Philip Sidney, *An Apologie for Poetry*, ed. Collins (Oxford University Press, 1907) 32

46 O Cuiv, 38-41

47 Hoskins, MEL, 163

48 Leland, 104

49 Hume Brown, SBS, 60-1

50 Mackenzie, HIS, 188

51 Quinn, EI, 56

52 Morley, 91

53 Quoted in Hurstfield, FCG, 23

54 Dickens, ER, 157-8

55 Hale, RE, 117

56 Elton, ET, 160-1

57 Stone, CER, 72-3; C. Hill, RIR, 64

58 Dickens, ER, 193, 264

59 Tawney, RRC, 109

60 P. Williams, CMW, 15-19; D. Williams, HMW, 31

61 Rees, UEW, 81 ff.

62 W. O. Williams in Roderick 2, 22

63 G. D. Owen, 93-4

64 Powel, 'To the Reader'

65 A. H. Dodd in Roderick 2, 54

66 Koebner, 62

67 Quinn in IHS (1947), 303-4

68 Quinn in IHS (1961), 322–8; Maxwell, IH, 89–91
69 Quinn in IHS (1947), 305
70 Maxwell, IH, 105–6
71 O Cuiv, 117–18
72 Bagwell, IT 1, 251–3
73 Scott, MSB 1, 407–13
74 Mackenzie, HIS, 142
75 Rowse, TC, 253–90
76 Elliott, ED, 70

The Age of Ralegh

1 Morison, NV, 128–9
2 Shakespeare, *Henry VIII*, Act V, sc. v
3 C. Hill, RIR, 44
4 Thirsk, AH, 74–5; Rowse, TC, 23–4
5 Nef 1, 36; J. E. Williams, DM, 15–18
6 Elton, ET, 253–5; C. Hill, RIR, 101–7; Ramsay, EOT, 174–99; Mathew, 294–306; G. D. Owen, 124–5, 131–47
7 Hurstfield, EI, 150–1
8 Elton, TE, 237
9 C. Hill, RIR, 83–4, 87
10 Jordan, WOB, 51; C. Hill, RIR, 58, 84
11 Dickens, ER, 425–7
12 Trilling, 22
13 Elton, TE, 317–18
14 Elliott, ED, 60–1, 256
15 Elton, TE, 298
16 Morley, 54
17 Maxwell, IH, 49
18 R. Dudley Edwards, CSTI, 177–90
19 Hayes-McCoy, 90–1
20 Falls, 94–8
21 Hayes-McCoy, 79
22 Quinn in HS (1958), 26–7
23 Canny, 66–76
24 Quinn, EI, 127–8
25 Falls, 138–41
26 Quinn, EI, 129; Canny, 124 (spelling adapted)
27 Quinn, EI, 46–7
28 Quinn in HS (1958), 27; Maxwell, IH, 254–5
29 Falls, 114–16
30 O Clery, 1715–17
31 G. Morton, 56; O Clery, 1731
32 G. Morton, 58
33 Bagwell, IT 3, 114

34 Quinn in HS (1958), 28
35 Quinn, RBE, 105
36 A. R. Hall in CEHE 4, 100; Cipolla, EC, 43-9
37 Ramsay, EOT, 25
38 C. Hill, RIR, 73-5, 94
39 Koenigsberger and Mosse, 196 fn.
40 R. Davis, EOT, 26
41 Morison, NV, 501; K. Andrews, DV, 58
42 Morison, NV, 132
43 Williamson, HP, 26-33
44 Blake, 138
45 Ibid., 140-3; Hakluyt 6, 148-51
46 Hakluyt 10, 25
47 Williamson, HP, 145-56
48 Walvin, BW, 109
49 E. Spenser, 'Colin Clout's Come Home Again' (1591), *Minor Poems*, ed. Osgood and Lotspeich (Johns Hopkins Press, Baltimore, 1943), vol. 1, 154
50 Hakluyt 1, xvii-viii
51 *See* French
52 Mathew, 323; Ramsay, EOT, 190
53 Hakluyt 1, xliii
54 K. Andrews, EP, 16
55 Rowse, RG, 54-5, 234-5, 256
56 Quinn, VG 1, 102
57 Ibid., 164
58 Rowse, RG, 90-3; *but see* K. Andrews, DV, 47-53
59 K. Andrews, DV, 67
60 Quinn, VG 1, 157, 160-1
61 Hakluyt 7, 228, 238
62 Quinn, VG 1, 173-80
63 Morison, NV, 566
64 Quinn, VG 1, 55
65 Ibid., 58-9, 74
66 Ibid., 59-62
67 Ibid., 82-4
68 Hakluyt 8, 10-11, 53-4
69 Ibid., 65-74
70 Aubrey, 255
71 Ibid., 254
72 Quinn, RBE, 118-19
73 E. Edwards, WR 2, 17
74 Rowse, RT, 327
75 Ralegh, *Poems*, ed. A. Latham (Routledge, 1951), 51-2
76 C. Hill, IOER, 145
77 Ibid., 167-8
78 Quinn, RV, 91-115
79 Taylor 2, 215, 234-6, 239, 247-9, 315

80 K. Andrews, EP, 163, 191
81 Quinn, RV, 116–17, 853–4
82 Ibid., 108
83 Ibid., 323
84 Ibid., 498, 541–2
85 Elliott, ED, 280
86 Mattingly, 191–2
87 Quinn, RV, 614–15
88 Morison, NV, 677–8; Quinn, EDA, 432–81
89 Quinn, RBE, 101
90 Ibid., 111–13
91 Morley, 192–3
92 Quinn, RBE, 118
93 Falls, 165–6
94 Ibid., 186
95 Ralegh, DG, 12, 15, 16, 40, 42, 44, 46–7
96 E. Edwards, WR 2, 107–11
97 Ralegh, DG, 73, 146
98 K. Andrews, EP, 32–4, 40–5, 73 etc.
99 Ibid., 41, 76–9, 209–12, 224–6 etc.
100 Ibid., 69–80
101 Ibid., 104–123
102 Ibid., 128, 228–32, 84–6, 172
103 'The Alchemist', Ben Jonson, ed. Herford and Simpson (Oxford University Press, 1937), vol. 5, 320
104 K. Andrews, EP, 207–8; Boxer, PSE, 104–5
105 K. Andrews, EP, 213–21; Foster, EQ, 144–7
106 Walvin, BW, 7–9
107 Elton, TE, 362–4
108 Ibid., 359–60
109 Falls, 45–7, 51
110 Maxwell, IH, 213
111 Falls, 72–6, Maxwell, IH, 191–2; Hayes-McCoy, 260–1, 271
112 Falls, 178–9, 248–9
113 Maxwell, IH, 187
114 Falls, 214–220
115 Maxwell, IH, 212
116 Falls, 232
117 Falls, 239
118 Maxwell, IH, 199–203
119 Maxwell, IH, 201
120 Falls, 292–308
121 Morley, 162–5, 193–205; Quinn in PRIA (1942), 157–8
122 Rae, 220–1; G. M. Fraser, 98
123 G. M. Fraser, 124
124 Carey, 154–64
125 Ibid., 171–90

126 Rowse, EEE, 28
127 Stowe, quoted in Scott, MSB 1, 175-6
128 G. M. Fraser, 366-78
129 Elliott, ED, 376
130 K. Andrews, EP, 226-7
131 'Eastward Ho', *Ben Jonson*, ed. Herford and Simpson (Oxford University Press, 1932), vol. 4, 569-70
132 Quoted in Cawley, 153

Thomas Smythe's Expansion

1 Tawney, RRC, 105
2 *Dean of Lismore*, 31
3 Donaldson, 231-2
4 Gordon, 248
5 Grant, SEDS, 536, 539
6 Hume Brown, SBS, 139, 153, 259-60, 276
7 Mackenzie, OH, 156, 185-6; Grant, M, 188-205
8 Mackenzie, OH, 228-9, 242-3 etc.
9 MacPhail, 277
10 Lythe, 59-60
11 Grant, M, 208-212
12 Ibid., 237
13 Smout, HSP, 132
14 Russell, 258-9
15 C. Hill, CR, 51; Davis, EOT, 53
16 E. J. Hobsbawm in T. Aston, 27
17 Wilson, EA, 39-40, 45
18 Davis, EOT, 20-5
19 Clark, TA, 16-17
20 Child, NDT, 4
21 Boxer, DSE, 61
22 Ibid., 95-9, 189
23 Thornton, 23
24 Wilson, EA, 41-2
25 Tawney, BP, 25
26 Davis, EOT, 38
27 Mun, 73-4, 78
28 Wilson, M, 11-13
29 Ibid., 26
30 Mun, 7
31 Ibid., 3-4, 10
32 Ibid., 1, 72-3
33 T. Hobbes, 'Behemoth', in F. Maseres, ed., *Select Tracts Relating to the Civil Wars ...* Vol. 2 (London, 1815), 576-7
34 Tawney, BP, 20

35 Rabb, 26–7, 93–5, 121, 127–8
36 Ibid., 50, 52–5, 66, 121
37 Ramsay, 68, 188–9
38 Tawney, BP, 75–81
39 Darby, 23–7
40 Ibid., 49–55
41 Ibid., 32, 38
42 Cullen, LI, 58
43 Beckett, 34–5, 37–8
44 Bossy, 155–69; MacCurtain, 140–2
45 Kearney, 10
46 Bagwell, IS 1, 160–1; Butler, 63–75
47 Butler, 82, 87–8, 90
48 O Clery, 2359
49 Butler, 45–6, 50–1
50 Bagwell IS 1, 78–9
51 Ibid., 72–3
52 Ibid., 75–6; G. Hill, PU, 535–7
53 G. Hill, PU, 573–4, 589
54 Moody, LP, 273, 279, 339
55 Perceval-Maxwell, 49–68, 229–51
56 Ibid., 104, 207–9, 286–9, 295–6, 311
57 Quinn, EDA, 450–1
58 Barbour, JS, 91–2
59 C. Andrews, CP, 87–8
60 Ibid., 98–100; Barbour, JS, 102–8
61 J. Smith, 361–2
62 J. Smith, cvi, cvxiv, 357–9, 363–8, 377–8
63 J. Smith, 369
64 Barbour, PW, 1–7; Quinn, EDA, 453 ff.
65 J. Smith, 350–1, 382
66 J. Smith, lxxii, lxxxix, 378–9
67 J. Smith, 399–401, 410, 453–5, 531–4; Barbour, PW, 23–35
68 J. Smith, 407
69 Ibid., 434–8
70 Ibid., 466, 472
71 Craven, SC, 83–4
72 Ibid., 96
73 Lefroy 1, 10–50
74 Barbour, PW, 62–6; C. Andrews, CP 1, 110
75 Craven, SC, 102–4; C. Andrews, CP 1, 106, 112
76 Wilkinson, 57–8, 75 etc.
77 Brooks, 82
78 Barbour, PW, 247–52
79 Rolfe, 33–41
80 J. Smith, 533–4
81 Craven, SC, 135

82 C. Andrews, CP 1, 221–2
83 Craven, SC, 138; A. E. Smith, 12–15
84 Craven, SC, 146–7; Pomfret, 42
85 Barbour, PW, 209–11; W. Washburn in J. M. Smith, 20–2
86 Cell, 21, 53
87 E. R. Williams, SS, 154–63; Cell, 81–6; Dodd, 33–5
88 Powys, 118
89 W. Morton, 32
90 Insh, SCS, 40–66; McGrail, 77–104
91 Willison, 20–1; Quinn, NAED, 469–72
92 Bradford, 33, 44–6
93 Miller, EW, 3–4
94 Bradford, 92–3
95 Willison, 62–5
96 Bradford, 106–7
97 Willison, 67–71
98 Bradford, 95–7
99 Willison, 88
100 Bradford, 111
101 Ibid., 121–4
102 Willison, 107; Langdon, 79; Pomfret, 121–2, 125–6
103 Langdon, 34; Willison, 115–16; Pomfret, 114
104 Willison, 163–7; Bradford, 236–43
105 Rabb, 58–66; Brenner, 65–6
106 K. Chaudhuri, 27–38; Rabb, 39–40
107 Foster, EQ, 153
108 Ibid., 160–1; K. Chaudhuri, 22
109 K. Chaudhuri, 14–19, 111–18
110 Spear, HI, 42
111 Ibid., 44–8
112 Foster, EQ, 238
113 Hunter 1, 320–6
114 Roe, 463–5
115 Foster, EQ, 198–207
116 D. Hall, SEA, 295–309; K. Chaudhuri, 61–2
117 Hunter 1, 387–405
118 Boxer, DSE, 196–7; W. Foster in CHBE 4, 93–4
119 K. Chaudhuri, 89–108; S. A. Khan, 15
120 Christy 2, 359
121 Jobson, 120
122 Rowse, RT, 318

Puritans

1 C. Hill, GE, 242
2 Burns, 179–80, 187–90; J. Smith, 898
3 Harlow, CE, 1–2

4 Harlow, HB, 338
5 Hirst, 105
6 Darby, 55
7 Darby, 59–61
8 Williamson, CI, 38–47
9 C. Andrews, CP 2, 276–8
10 C. C. Hall, 7
11 Ibid., 40
12 B. Bailyn in J. M. Smith, 95
13 Craven, SC, 173–4, 177; Pomfret, 50, 53–6
14 J. Smith, 615
15 Bruce, 1; 290, 300, 307–8, 323–4; Craven, SC, 238–9
16 Harlow, HB, 10–20
17 Ligon, 28
18 J. Smith, 909; Bridenbaugh, NP, 268–72
19 Bridenbaugh, NP, 121
20 Harlow, CE, 66
21 B. Edwards 1, 463
22 Ligon, 24
23 Bridenbaugh, NP, 52–61
24 Rabb, 61–2, 85–6
25 Insh, SCS, 83
26 Eccles, 42
27 Russell, 166
28 Hexter, 85
29 C. Andrews, CP 1, 386–7
30 Ibid., 395–6
31 Dunn, PY, 11
32 Bridenbaugh, VT, 395
33 Petty, EW 2, 389–90; Strauss, 18
34 Bridenbaugh, VT, 11; Leach, NCF, 32–3
35 Bridenbaugh, VT, 397
36 Ibid., 98–101, 141, 384
37 Ibid., 377
38 Ibid., 457
39 Morison, BBC, 45–6; Bridenbaugh, VT, 461–2
40 Bridenbaugh, VT, 465
41 Dunn, PY, 33–4
42 Langdon, 81–7
43 Willison, 194–8
44 Winthrop 1, 108
45 Dunn, PY, 23
46 Laslett, 62–5
47 Miller, EW, 72
48 Ibid., 46; Ziff, 14
49 Bradford, 261–2
50 Ziff, 56–7

51 C. Andrews, CP 2, 81
52 Pomfret, 238
53 C. Andrews, CP 2, 181
54 Miller, RW, 83, 147, 150-1 etc.; Ziff, 100
55 R. Williams 1, 153, 164 etc.
56 Bradford, 339
57 Winthrop 1, 282-3; and 2, 93; R. Thompson, 29, 84-98 etc.
58 Ziff, 48; Bailyn, NEM, 41-3
59 Battis, 39
60 E. Johnson, 127, 132
61 K. Chaudhuri, 91
62 Hunter 1, 272-4; and 2, 154-8
63 Hunter 2, 156 fn., 159; Boxer, DSE, 208-9
64 K. Chaudhuri, 77
65 W. Foster in CHBE, 4, 89
66 W. R. Scott 2, 109-10, 112-15
67 Lounsbury, 68-86; Cell, 108-17
68 Newton, CA, 95
69 Ibid., 148-51, 258-61
70 Ibid., 143
71 Ibid., 257-8, 298
72 Bagwell, IS 1, 204
73 Kearney, 33-4, 44 etc.
74 Moody, Martin and Byrne, 246; T. O. Ranger in T. Aston, 282-3, 286-9
75 Kearney, 171-84
76 Clarke, 87-8
77 Clarke, 93, 96-7 etc.
78 Kearney, 98-9
79 Bagwell, IS 1, 207-9
80 Kearney, 113-18; Bagwell, IS 1, 205-7
81 Russell, 323
82 Mitchison, HS, 195
83 Bagwell, IS 1, 242
84 Stone, CER, 95, 135-6
85 Bagwell, IS 1, 323-4
86 Ibid., 331, 338-41, 344-7; Coffey, 58-62
87 Bagwell, IS 1, 333-5
88 Brenner, 53-84; Stone, CER, 71
89 Stone, CER, 72
90 Burrell, 17
91 Clarke, 201-9; Bottigheimer, 40-5, 79-80
92 Turner, 19-21
93 Bagwell, IS 2, 35
94 C. Hill, MER, 279-81
95 Lamont and Oldfield, 103-4
96 A. Fraser, 24-8, 313, 363, 468
97 A. Fraser, 117

98 Burnet 1, 43
99 Mitchison, HS, 227–8
100 Bagwell, IS 2, 117–121
101 Ibid., 177
102 Quoted by Wedgwood in R. H. Parry, 56
103 Bagwell, IS 2, 192–6; C. Hill, GE, 112; A. Fraser, 389–97, 408–9
104 C. Hill, GE, 113; Bagwell, IS 2, 198–201; A. Fraser, 401–3
105 Donaldson, 341; Mitchison, HS, 230–1
106 Eric Williams, CS, 12; A. E. Smith, 92–3
107 A. E. Smith, 152–9; Jordan, 88–9
108 Donaldson, 356–7; Smout, ST, 175
109 Donaldson, 395
110 Smout, HSP, 79
111 Petty, PAI, 17–18; Cullen, EHI, 9–10
112 Dunlop, 6–9, 343–4
113 Barnard, 14
114 Ibid., 214–15, 229–37; Webster, 225–231, 428–44
115 Barnard, 27
116 Ibid., 124
117 Ibid., 178–9, 187–9
118 Dunlop, 496–7, 618, 432
119 Cullen, EHI, 19–20; Barnard, vii
120 Bottigheimer, 54–6, 64–75, 116–19
121 Butler, 121–39; Dunlop, 659
122 Butler, 143–59; Barnard, 61
123 Dunlop, 711–12
124 Butler, 159–64; Barnard, 53–7
125 Simms, JI, 4–5
126 Roderick 2, 62
127 Barnard, 179
128 Darby, 67–8
129 McInnes, EETT, 92–129
130 Wilson, EA, 61–4
131 Brenner, 97
132 Miller, RW, 248
133 Bradford, 356
134 Demos, 37–8
135 Dunn, PY, 87–96; Bailyn, NEM, 60–74; C. Andrews, CP 1, 513
136 Bailyn, NEM, 14, 78
137 Ibid., 83–4
138 Winthrop 2, 341; E. Johnson, 35
139 Dunn, PY, 52–3
140 Ibid., 37; C. Andrews, CP 1, 498–9
141 Marcus 1, 137
142 Ibid., 140 fn.
143 Craven, SC, 231–5
144 Ibid., 269–70

145 B. Bailyn in J. M. Smith, 98–100
146 Craven, SC, 240
147 Harlow, HB, 65, 72
148 Ibid., 108–9
149 Burns, 252–61; Bridenbaugh, NP, 202–4
150 Stone, CER, 91
151 Hecksher 2, 289
152 C. Hill, CR, 166
153 Williamson, NCH, 61
154 Barnard, 217–18; Roll, 98–112; Strauss, *passim*; Letwin, 114 ff.; Webster, 434–44
155 Letwin, 202
156 Petty, EW 2, 529–621
157 Petty, PAI, 21–2

BOOK TWO

1 Jonathan Swift, *The Examiner* [etc.] *1710–11*, ed. H. Davis (Blackwell, Oxford, 1940), 5
2 James Thomson, *Complete Poetical Works* (Oxford University Press, 1908), 422–3

King Sugar

1 Quoted in Bernard Semmel, *Rise of Free Trade Imperialism* (Cambridge University Press, 1970), 111
2 Parry and Sherlock, 63
3 E. Williams, CC, 122
4 Ligon, 22, 86, 108
5 Ligon, 34, 38–40; Bridenbaugh, NP, 127–8; Dunn, SS, 88, 92–3, 96
6 R. Davis, RAE, 251, 253; E. Williams, CC, 114; Bridenbaugh, NP, 94; Ligon, 35, 42
7 Bridenbaugh, NP, 303
8 Ibid., 269 fn.
9 Burns, 343–5; Higham, 124–36
10 Morgan, ASAF, 126–9; Dunn, SS, 52–3; Mannix and Cowley, 57–8
11 Bruce 1, 600–1; Picton, 82
12 A. E. Smith, 39
13 Ibid., 58–60
14 Ibid., 67–86; Bridenbaugh, VT, 419; Bruce 1, 612–14
15 Bridenbaugh, NP, 17; Burns, 338, 396; A. E. Smith, 172–4; Dunlop, 655–6
16 Pitman, 6; A. E. Smith, 142–3; E. Williams, CC, 98
17 Ligon, 37, 43–5
18 Bridenbaugh, NP, 366
19 Jeaffreson 1, 258–9; and 2, 195–8
20 Donnan 1, 125
21 Lyttelton, 7
22 Craven, CIT, 294
23 Lefroy 1, 308–9; Bruce 2, 23–4, 52–3, 75–6; Craven, SC, 218–19; Jordan, 64, 72–80
24 Jordan, 66–71; Donnan 3, 4–9, 108

25 Walvin, BW, 10–11, 38–9
26 Curtin, AST, 86–7, 268
27 K. Davies, 11
28 Ibid., 72–9
29 E. Williams, CC, 137; Bridenbaugh, NP, 257
30 R. Davis, RAE, 136
31 P. Curtin in Ajayi and Crowder, 252–7
32 K. Davies, 113–14; Donnan 1, 271
33 Charles Wilson, EA, 161, 171
34 Ibid., 271; C. Hill, CR, 186; R. Davis, EOT, 33–7; Minchinton, 21
35 Minchinton, 33–4; Pepys 9, 234
36 Ramsay, 141–51; Charles Wilson, EA, 274
37 Nef 1, 379; and 2, 139–40
38 R. Davis, RAE, 247–8
39 Charles Wilson, EA, 169, 238, 307–8
40 Wadsworth and Mann, 14–21, 97–108; Charles Wilson, EA, 193–4
41 Thirsk, R, 133–4
42 Lawrence Stone in Thirsk, R, 171–5
43 Plumb, GPSE, 11–13
44 Clark, LS, 63
45 Pepys 6, 255
46 John Bunyan, *Pilgrim's Progress* (Penguin, 1965 edn.), 129–34
47 Donaldson, SJJ, 401
48 Smout, ST, 144–6, 175–8
49 Donaldson, SJJ, 367
50 Prebble, G, 61
51 Cowan, 82–133
52 Mitchison, HS, 296
53 Walker 1, 229
54 Law, 143
55 Walker 1, 65–6
56 Butler, 165–205; Simms, JI, 4
57 Petty, PAI, 43
58 Kearney, 220; Petty, PAI, 7–8
59 Simms, JI, 9; Bagwell, IS 3, 139–40
60 MacLysaght, 92, 182, 288–91, 308–13, 320–2
61 Bagwell, IS 3, 142
62 Cullen, EH, 18–19, 24–5
63 Petty, PAI, 79–82
64 Cullen, AIT, 18, 37
65 Petty, PAI, 33; Cullen, AIT, 38
66 Simms, JI, 15–16
67 Letwin, 20–37, 44
68 Hecksher 2, 285
69 Petty, EW, 1, 68; Child, NDT, 56, 157, 169–73, 176, 179
70 Petty, EW, 1, 263
71 Hecksher 1, 172–4

72 Child, NDT, 155
73 S. A. Khan, 150; Hunter 2, 276-9
74 Dunn, PY, 213
75 Thornton, WIP, 7
76 Craven, CIT, 214
77 Child, NDT, 204
78 Thornton, WIP, 19
79 Craven, CIT, 62-3, 146
80 Coleman, 1953-4, 135-7
81 C. Lloyd, BS, 76
82 Ibid., 90-100, 106
83 Rogers, 82-5; Lounsbury, 111
84 Lounsbury, 196, 199-200
85 Rich 1, 42
86 Rich 1, 155, 238
87 Innis, FTC, 48
88 Ibid., 129; Mackay, 67; Rich 1, 82, 101
89 Bailyn, NEM, 88-91
90 Ibid., 96-8
91 Ibid., 98-9
92 Mumford Jones, 189-92
93 Craven, CIT, 108-10
94 Leach, NCF, 9
95 C. C. Hall, 44
96 Craven, SC, 132, 142-4; C. C. Hall, 124-40
97 C. Andrews, CP, 1, 369; Miller and Johnson 2, 503; Ziff, 44-5, 169-71; Miller, RW, 53
98 Kellaway, 83; Morison, BBC, 291-4; E. Johnson, 72
99 Kellaway, 17, 36
100 Ibid., 106, 116; Morison, BBC, 304-6
101 Willison, 243-4
102 E. Johnson, 72; Kellaway, 120
103 Knorr, 58
104 Leach, NCF, 91, 102
105 Craven, CIT, 116; Craven, SC, 364-7
106 Ziff, 92
107 Craven, CIT, 118-24; Josephy, PC, 41-62; Langdon, 164-187; Kellaway, 116-20; Winslow, RW, 280-5; Leach, FT, passim
108 Morison, BBC, 316-17
109 Dunn, PY, 147
110 Leach, FT, 244; Langdon, 181-2
111 Kellaway, 206-7; Miller and Johnson 2, 504-5; Ziff, 240
112 Craven, SC, 400-1
113 Bruce 1, 378
114 Craven, SC, 281-2
115 McInnes, 59, 68, 147-50. 177-81
116 Craven, SC, 222

117 C. Andrews, NI, 16
118 Washburn, GR, 31
119 C. Andrews, NI, 112–13; Craven, SC, 379
120 C. Andrews, NI, 110
121 Ibid., 28–30, 116–17
122 Ibid., 34; Morgan, ASAF, 267
123 N. O. Lurie in J. M. Smith, 56
124 Exquemelin, 145
125 Exquemelin, 134–40; Pope, 145–55
126 Thornton, WIP, 114
127 Exquemelin, 167–208; Pope, 230–47
128 Exquemelin, 81–2
129 Burns, 321
130 Hamshere, 90
131 Bridenbaugh, NP, 189–91; 314–16, 329, 366–7, 375–6
132 Bridenbaugh, NP, 167
133 Harlow, HB, 263–5; Burns, 288; Dunn, SS, 106
134 Bridenbaugh, NP, 336
135 Ibid., 338–42; Burns, 362–5; Thornton, WIP, 215–17; Exquemelin, 219–20; Burdon 1, 8
136 Bridenbaugh, NP, 341; Dunn, SS, 336; R. Davis, RAE, 262–3
137 Dalby Thomas, 349
138 Lyttelton, 28–9
139 Thornton, WIP, 237–52
140 Harlow, HB, 98–102, 123–6, 140
141 Ibid., 242–59; Thornton, WIP, 199
142 Long 1, 4; E. Williams, CC, 180; Harlow, CC, 177
143 Burns, 367
144 Burns, 345–6
145 Lyttelton, 18
146 Bridenbaugh, NP, 283
147 Ibid., 226–7
148 Harlow, HB, 340
149 Bridenbaugh, NP, 303
150 Dunn, SS, 96; Bridenbaugh, NP, 367–9
151 Bridenbaugh, NP, 381–2
152 Jeaffreson 1, 84; Bridenbaugh, NP, 406
153 Pares, WIF, 25
154 Ligon, 107
155 E. Williams, CC, 186; A. E. Smith, 90; Craton and Walvin, 47; Dunn, SS, 301
156 Lyttelton, 19–20
157 Ligon, 49–50
158 Harlow, HB, 325–6
159 Ibid., 326–7
160 Bridenbaugh, NP, 357–9, 386–93, 397–8; Dunn, SS, 103–6
161 Hansen, 35–6
162 Tolles, MC, 29–30, 38–40; MacCurtain, 168–9

163 Tolles, QAC, 57–8
164 Hansen, 35; Bridenbaugh, CW, 104; Tolles, QAC, 24
165 Craven, CIT, 185–8
166 Pepys 5, 255
167 Tolles, QAC, 71
168 Peare, 297
169 Comfort, 33–4
170 Tolles, QAC, 118
171 Ibid., 122–4
172 Tolles, MC, 109–11
173 Comfort, 44
174 Tolles, MC, 38–44
175 Peare, 271–3
176 C. Andrews, CP 3, 310

Parcels of Rogues

1 Ogg, ERJW, 149–54
2 Coleman in EHR (1953–4), 136
3 Simms, JI, 24–5
4 Ibid., 32–4
5 Ibid., 63–4
6 Ibid., 71; MacLysaght, 284
7 Simms, JI, 90–1
8 Ibid., 95–113; Bagwell IS 3, 239–50
9 Simms, JI, 127
10 Ibid., 136
11 Ibid., 157
12 Bagwell IS 3, 299
13 Simms, JI, 158
14 Ibid., 216–29
15 Ibid., 260
16 Simms, WC, 86–95, 160
17 MacLysaght, 341–7
18 Ibid., 226–7
19 K. Davies, 143, 206–9; Donnan 2, 13
20 Hopkins, 93
21 Barbot, 181
22 Hopkins, 81–3
23 R. A. Adeleye in Ajayi and Crowder, 525
24 Hopkins, 23–7; I. Wilks in Ajayi and Crowder, 454; Moore, 78
25 Curtin, IA, 71–83; Dunn, SS, 310
26 K. Davies, 236, 251
27 I. Wilks in Ajayi and Crowder, 344; Phillips, 232; Harlow, CC, 122
28 Phillips, 232–3, 244
29 K. Davies, 235–6; Bosman, 82–3; Barbot, 273–4; Hopkins, 111

30 Phillips, 218–19; K. Davies, 6, 240–4, 251–2
31 K. Davies, 259–64; 277–90; Daaku, 98–9
32 Phillips, 216, 231
33 Ibid., 220–1; K. Davies, 254
34 Phillips, 234–5
35 Ibid., 235; Parry and Sherlock, 106–8; Davidson, 191; Donnan 1, 272, 355; K. Davies, 292–3; Atkins, 71–3
36 Phillips, 246, 252–3
37 Barbot, 272
38 Phillips, 243; K. Davies, 179–81, 220–1; Daaku, 44–6
39 Dunn, SS, 48, 202–7
40 K. Davies, 170–9
41 K. Davies, 181
42 Chandler, 131–2
43 E. Williams, CC, 148–9
44 Gosse, 51
45 Hunter 2, 198, 225; Ovington, 86–7
46 Fryer, 68–9, 82–5
47 Love 1, 413–15
48 Woodruff 1, 64–6; Fryer 38
49 Master 2, 345–7; Hedges 2, 284, 290–2
50 Master 2, 11
51 W. Foster in CHBE 4, 106
52 Child, *Treatise*, 23; Hedges 2, 308
53 Krishna, 134
54 Forrest, TB, 22–32; Krishna, 151; Ovington, 181
55 Coleman, EE, 162; S. A. Khan, 155, 163; Ovington, 167
56 S. A. Khan, 154–60; Anon., 7–9
57 Hedges 2, 357
58 Letwin, 20–37; S. A. Khan 196; Hunter 2, 302
59 Child, *Honour*, 30; Child, NDT, 143–6; Child, *Treatise*, 41–3; Krishna, 136–7
60 Child, *Treatise, passim*
61 Fryer, 88
62 Bastin, xxii, 12
63 W. Foster in CHBE 4, 102
64 Hunter 2, 237; Love 1, 498, 503
65 Hunter 2, 303–4
66 Hedges 1, 123, 130; and 3, 10–11
67 C. R. Wilson, EB 1, 78–9
68 Hedges 1, 161, 165; Hunter 2, 238–45
69 Hunter 2, 247–8
70 Hamilton 2, 5; Hedges 1, 52, 78–82, 87, 121, 138–9, 144, 146; and 2, 48–9
71 Hedges 2, 87
72 Hunter 2, 268–9; Hedges 2, 92–3
73 Hunter 2, 271, 279–80
74 Ibid., 306–11
75 Dalton, 100, 110

76 Plumb, GPSE, 85–94
77 Ibid., 69
78 Ibid., 98–128
79 Steele, 10
80 Clapham, 270
81 Clark, LS, 174–8
82 Steele, 18
83 Prebble, G, 153, 178
84 Smout, ST, 28, 49, 54
85 Clerk, 188
86 Donaldson, SO, 39–41; Insh, SCS, 114, 179–80
87 Smout, ST, 24
88 *Darien Papers*, 3–4
89 Clerk, 190
90 Insh, C of S, 61–5
91 Ibid., 65–7; Smout, ST, 150–1, 252; *Darien Papers*, 371–417
92 Insh, C of S, 68–73
93 Letwin, 44
94 Steele, 37–8
95 Prebble, DD, *passim*
96 Smout, ST, 252; Defoe, 67–8
97 Bailyn, NEM, 155–7
98 Craven, CIT, 166–8
99 Dunn, SS, 133
100 Dunn, PY, 229
101 Ziff, 235–40; Clapham, 270
102 Ettinger, 41
103 Ziff, 242–3; *see also* Dunn, PY, 264–7; Miller, NEMCP, 191–208; Burr, *passim*
104 Haffenden, 15, 38–41, 56, 59
105 W. Morton, 60; Eccles, 75–7
106 Eccles, 71
107 Creighton, 83
108 Eccles, 37
109 Josephy, IH, 95
110 Craven, CIT, 286–9; Bridenbaugh, CW, 143; R. Thompson, 121–38
111 Leach, NCF, 32–3, 64–5
112 A. E. Smith, 27–8; Bruce 2, 53–4, 79
113 A. E. Smith, 96; Bruce 1, 606–7
114 R. Thompson, 73; A. E. Smith, 253–84; Hofstadter, 53–5
115 A. E. Smith, 285–306
116 Bruce 2, 108
117 Donnan 4, 67
118 Jordan, 79–80; Bruce 2, 110–11; Craven, CIT, 301
119 Bruce 2, 123–9
120 Bridenbaugh, CW, 49; Donnan 3, 17–26
121 Miller and Johnson 2, 437
122 Bridenbaugh, CW, 72; Demos, 52–8; Miller and Johnson 2, 391–5; Dunn, PY, 191–2

123 Hofstadter, 188
124 Bridenbaugh, CW, 99; Dunn, PY, 172–3
125 Dunn, SS, 265–6, 269–72
126 Craven, SC, 404
127 Wright, CL, 126–44; Miller and Johnson 2, 557 etc.
128 Craven, CIT, 266
129 B. Bailyn in J. M. Smith, 106
130 Comfort, 150–1
131 Ziff, 268–72
132 Miller, CP, 156–7
133 Steele, 57
134 Hamilton 1, 20–1
135 Dalton, 155
136 Hunter 2, 374–5
137 Love 1, 549–50; Dalton, 353
138 Hamilton 2, 6
139 Spear, N, 17–19; Dalton, 113–15; Marshall, EIF, 217–19
140 Marshall, EIF, 159
141 Ibid., 18–20, 88
142 Ovington, 89; Spear, N, 13; Dalton, 128
143 Ovington, 153
144 Dalton, 203; Hamilton 2, 8
145 Ovington, 57–64; Gosse, 129–33
146 Bastin, xxi–ii, 43
147 Love 2, 73–85
148 C. R. Wilson, EB 1, 189–216; Hamilton 2, 7
149 Barnett, 144, 148
150 Harlow, CC, 112–14
151 Ibid., 114–18
152 Ibid., 137
153 Ibid., 201
154 Ibid., 210–13
155 Ibid., 192; Burns, 417–19
156 Burns, 419–23; B. Edwards 1, 476–82; Cal. SP Col. 1710–11, 386–401, 458–61;
     Harlow, CC, 199–200
157 Dunn, SS, 206–7
158 Craven, CIT, 304–9
159 T. C. Smout in Holmes, 183–4; Lenman, 51–2
160 Lockhart, 24
161 Pryde, 9
162 Mackinnon, 84–8; Ferguson, SRE, 186–95
163 Lockhart, 69–70
164 Ibid., 68; Mackenzie, FS, 85–94, 199–205
165 Mackinnon, 105
166 Ibid., 115
167 Ferguson, SRE, 218
168 Defoe, 85

169 *Jerviswood*, 28
170 Mackinnon, 185–7
171 Ferguson, SRE, 235
172 Mackinnon, 233–5
173 Defoe, 229
174 *Jerviswood*, 145
175 Pryde, 29; Mackinnon, 316–17
176 Pryde, 105; Mackinnon, 334–5
177 Daiches, SU, 152–3
178 Ferguson, 1689TP, 49
179 Mackenzie, FS, 167
180 *Jerviswood*, 18–19, 138; Smout, ST, 255
181 Pryde, 26; Smout, ST, 73–5, 150, 270–3
182 Smout in Holmes, 176
183 Mackinnon, 242–3
184 Burns, 418
185 Cal. SP Col. 1708–9, 41–51
186 Sheridan, SS, 155–8, 197–200, 369–70
187 C. Andrews in CHBE I, 287
188 Beckett, MMI, 156; Johnston, IEC, 60–1
189 Johnston, IEC, 22
190 Lecky, 42; Beckett, MMI, 157–9
191 Lecky, 49–50, 81

Empire of the Oligarchs

1 E. P. Thompson, WH, 245
2 Defoe, xxvi
3 Sinclair-Stevenson, 113–14
4 Ibid., 141
5 Ibid., 165
6 Petrie, 266–78; Mitchison in Phillipson, 30–1, 35–6
7 H. T. Dickinson, 18
8 C. Hill, CR, 256–7
9 E. P. Thompson, WH, 198
10 H. T. Dickinson, 81
11 Plumb, GPSE, 188
12 Mingay, 19–28, 71
13 Charles Wilson, 357
14 Ogg, 30
15 Hay in Hay et al., 19
16 E. P. Thompson, WH, 206–7
17 Ibid., 21–3, 110–11, 142–6, 190–1
18 Gay, 43
19 Hay in Hay et al., 32–49
20 Minchinton, 15, 62; Boxer, PSE, 164–8, 173–5

21 H. T. Dickinson, 107
22 W. F. Reddaway in CHBE 1, 349; H. T. Dickinson, 94–5
23 R. Davis, RAE, 230
24 C. Winslow in Hay et al., 149–52
25 D. Forrest, TB, 53–5
26 Adam Smith, 188; D. Marshall, 153–4; C. Winslow in Hay et al., 124–5
27 Jarvis, xx–xxi, 68–71; C. Winslow in Hay et al., 124, 126–7, 133 etc.; *see also*
      W. A. Cole in Minchinton, 121–42 and Ramsay, 166–206
28 Minchinton, 30–1
29 Ibid., 22–6
30 Braudel, 337–44
31 Parry, TD, 81–5
32 Ibid., 87
33 D. Forrest, TB, 42
34 W. Foster in CHBE 4, 108–10; Krishna, 193–6, 198, 208–12, 215; Hickey 1, 197
35 Information from John Riddy; W. Foster in CHBE 4, 111–12; Love, 223–4, 247;
      P. Marshall, EIF, 7; Spear, HI, 77
36 K. Davies, 345–6
37 Ramsay, 152–60; Parkinson, 93–6
38 Parkinson, 96, 110, 134
39 Parry and Sherlock, 110–11; Eric Williams, CC, 148–9
40 Hodgen, 213–14, 389–90, 418–22; D. Grant, 6; Atkins, 34, 39
41 D. Grant, 61–118, 145–7
42 Atkins, 176–80; Sypher, 13
43 F. Moore, 29–30, 58–61
44 Hopkins, 103–5
45 Daaku, 30; Hopkins, 106–8
46 R. Oliver and Fage, 121–2; I. A. Akinjogbin in Ajayi and Crowder, 326–7; P. Cur-
      tin in ibid., 256; Daaku, 151–2
47 Akinjogbin in Ajayi and Crowder, 313, 323–38; Hopkins, 107
48 Atkins, 179
49 Curtin, AST, 150; Davidson, 188–90; E. J. Alagoa in Ajayi and Crowder, 273–301
50 R. A. Adeleye in ibid., 525–6; I. Wilks in ibid., 384–5; J. R. Willis in ibid., 468
51 D. Grant, 97–8; N. Owen, 71
52 P. Oliver, 67–75; Curtin, AST, 156–7; Long 2, 403–4
53 Eric Williams, CC, 104–5, 145–6; Deerr 2, 278–81
54 Fogel and Engerman, 155–6
55 Long 2, 432–8; Craton and Walvin, 126 ff.; Eric Williams, CS, 38
56 Craton and Walvin, 141–2; Sheridan, DP, 43; B. Edwards 1, 255
57 Burns, 460; Metcalf, 4–6
58 Long 2, 488
59 Ibid., 423–4; Patterson, 137–8, 153, 253–9; F. G. Cassidy and I. F. Hancock in Hymes,
      203–21; 287–91
60 Patterson, 236–48; Brathwaite, 228–32; Long 2, 420–5
61 Patterson, 224–30
62 Ibid., 174–81; Long 2, 426–7
63 Metcalf, 38–52

64 Dallas 1, 53–4
65 Ibid., 92–120
66 Patterson, 266–83; Long 2, 447–462
67 Cal. SP Col. 1737, 10–13, 50, 145–9, 171; Pitman, 60; Deerr 2, 322
68 Eric Williams, CC, 190; B. Edwards 2, 20–3
69 Jordan, 175–7; Long 2, 260–1, 321
70 Long 2, 337, 475–85
71 A. E. Smith, 295
72 Pitman, 50–5, 111–13, 118–23
73 Metcalf, 71–4; Long 1, 314–27
74 Craton, HB, 11, 56–64, 84–100
75 Sirmans, 124–5; R. L. Morton, 460–2
76 Craton, HB, 102–6
77 Ibid., 100–7
78 Burns, 461; Pitman, 105–7
79 Sheridan, DP, 32, 44–7
80 Pitman, 77–9
81 Pares, MP, 41–2; Sheridan, DP, 23, 37, 41–2; Eric Williams, CC, 126–7
82 R. Davis, RAE, 255–7; Eric Williams, CC, 133
83 Pares, MP, 38–50
84 Ibid., 36–7; Eric Williams, CS, 85–97; Mario Praz, 'Introductory Essay', *Three Gothic Novels* (Penguin, 1968), 24
85 R. Davis, RAE, 251; Eric Williams, CS, 53–5
86 Pitman, 133–4, 182–6, 263
87 Ibid., 35
88 Long 2, 286–8, 292
89 Patterson, 45–6, 48; Sheridan, SS, 174, 180
90 Pitman, 22; Metcalf, 16–27
91 Metcalf, 28–35
92 Ibid., 58–61, 82
93 Craton and Walvin, 76–82
94 Long 2, 76–7; 93–5; Craton and Walvin, 93
95 Metcalf, 12; Schaw, 95–100
96 Long 2, 281
97 Ibid., 102–22, 246; Pitman, 12, 24
98 Pitman, 25; Long 2, 278–9
99 Schaw, 113–15, 125
100 Ibid., 111–12; B. Edwards 2, 7–11
101 Eccles, 120–3
102 Ibid., 132, 134, 140–5, 158–71
103 Innis, 97
104 Rich 1, 486–91, 528–31; Mackay, 81
105 Innis, 130–5; Rich 1, 497
106 Isham, 66, 71–2, 116–17
107 Rich 1, 432–43; Mackay, 77
108 Rich 1, 645; Isham, 78–82
109 Isham, 85–7

110 Rich 1, 545
111 Isham, 144, 155–6; Rich 1, 541, 547
112 Rich 1, 589, 613
113 J. D. Rogers, 113–14, 116
114 Lounsbury, 254, 258–60, 302; Prowse, 218; J. D. Rogers, 116–19
115 Lounsbury, 311–15
116 C. M. Andrews in CHBE 1, 290–9; Clark, RBT, 15–20, 60–2; A. Hamilton, 157
117 C. M. Andrews in CHBE 1, 411
118 Ibid., 416
119 R. L. Morton, 475–6; Jones, 86–7
120 Wood, 110–13
121 Furnas, 30–3; Jones, 92
122 Gipson, CR, 15–16; Bridenbaugh, CW, 184; Deerr 2, 461–2; Gipson, BE 3, 16; Byrd, 205; Ziff, 289
123 R. L. Morton, 482–3, 528; Tolles, MC, 98–100; Bridenbaugh, CW, 339
124 Bridenbaugh, CW, 203–4; Furnas, 211–15
125 Bridenbaugh, CW, 359–61; Kammen, 48; R. Davis, RAE, 280–2; Tolles, MC, 100–6
126 Tolles, MC, 85–8
127 Bridenbaugh, CW, 303, 330–1; Ziff, 286–8
128 A. Hamilton, 18–30, 41–9, 88; Bridenbaugh, CW, 303
129 Tolles, MC, 91, 131, 137
130 A. Hamilton, 20
131 Bridenbaugh, CW, 159–60, 303, 318–19, 340
132 R. Davis, RAE, 264–8; Jones, 74; Hofstadter, 158
133 Jones, 9
134 Ibid., 8, 78, 86; Mullin, 3–12
135 Jones, 8; Byrd, 1–38
136 Bridenbaugh, MR, 14; Mullin, 8; L. Wright, CL, 7–12
137 Cresswell, 252; Jones, 93; Mingay, 32–5; B. Bailyn in J. M. Smith, 107–11
138 Jones, 81; Bridenbaugh, MR, 25; R. L. Morton, 482
139 Hofstadter, 167–9; Byrd, 204, 207
140 Sirmans, 114–16, 126–8
141 Ibid., 167
142 Wood, 61
143 Bridenbaugh, MR, 56
144 Ibid., 54–118; Rutman, 83–4
145 Sirmans, 245–6; Bridenbaugh, MR, 75
146 Wood, 145–8, 165; Bridenbaugh, MR, 100–3
147 Jordan, 102–3; Bridenbaugh, CW, 249
148 Hofstadter, 102–3; Furnas, 120–1
149 Hofstadter, 102–5; H. P. Thompson, 73–4; Jordan, 121, 125–6, 138
150 Jordan, 115–20; A. Hamilton, 88
151 Rice, 188, 193–203
152 Hofstadter, 72–5
153 Curtin, AST, 140; Hofstadter, 89–90
154 Mullin, 47–62; Hofstadter, 93–8
155 Jordan, 122–5, 139–47, 154–7

156 Fogel and Engerman, 22–9; Curtin, AST, 89–93
157 Donnan 4, 93, 127 etc.
158 Jordan, 111–12, 124, 127; R. L. Morton, 523–4; Donnan 4, 131–2
159 Jordan, 162–3; Byrd, 160–1, 221–2; Mullin, *passim*
160 Wood, 151, 160, 279
161 Ibid., 308–26
162 Bridenbaugh, CW, 343; Wood, 114–24, 135, 155–6, 166–91, 200–5
163 Jordan, 103; Hofstadter, 66–7
164 R. Davis, RAE, 126; Hofstadter, 3–6
165 Hofstadter, 6–8
166 Leach, 138–40
167 Gipson, BE 4, 53, 188–9
168 R. L. Morton, 556–8; Leach, 170–1, 177
169 R. L. Morton, 435
170 Jones, 59
171 H. P. Thompson, 27; Jones, 174–5
172 Kellaway, 259, 269–76; R. E. Brown, 40–2
173 A. Hamilton, 98, 172
174 Ettinger, 122; A. E. Smith, 23
175 Ettinger, 130, 134; Callaway, 10; Stephens 1, 370
176 Callaway, 18–20, 29–30
177 Ettinger, 141
178 Spalding, 87
179 Stephens 1, 12, 15, 19–20, 30–1, 40, 45–7, 211, 222
180 Callaway, 45–6
181 Dickson, 3, 61–4; I. C. C. Graham, 18–19; Leyburn, 180
182 A. E. Smith, 110–35
183 Ibid., 25, 27, 324; Hofstadter, 56–8
184 Labaree 4, 234
185 A. E. Smith, 20–1, 50; Hofstadter, 36; L. Wright, CL, 60–1
186 Dickson, 208–9, 213; Hofstadter, 37–42; A. E. Smith, 207–14, 223
187 Bridenbaugh, CW, 409; Hofstadter, 19; L. Wright, CL, 61–3
188 Dickson, 37
189 Ibid., 8–18
190 Ibid., 13, 86–7, 90, 94–7
191 Ibid., 109–10
192 Ibid., 21–3, 35; Hofstadter, 26
193 Dickson, 41–7, 58–9
194 Hofstadter, 27–9; Leyburn, 191–4; Dunaway, 58–9
195 Bridenbaugh, MR, 121
196 Ibid., 132–55; Dunaway, 165–75
197 Furnas, 38; Leyburn, 228
198 Woodmason, 24, 31–2, 36, 39, 53, 99–100
199 Bridenbaugh, MR, 136, 156–72; Hofstadter, 176–9
200 J. P. Greene in Billington, 170
201 Ibid., 173–5
202 R. L. Morton, 415–16; A. Hamilton, 31; Byrd, 207

203 J. P. Greene in Billington, 156–9; R. E. Brown, 21–52; Hofstadter, 137; A. Hamilton, 54–5
204 A. Hamilton, 13–14; Hofstadter, 138
205 Hofstadter, 131–3
206 Bridenbaugh, CW, 452–3, 455
207 E. Wright, BF, 30–4
208 Bridenbaugh, RG, 22–6, 35, 55–63, 70–99; Bridenbaugh, CW, 447
209 Bridenbaugh MR, 45–6; Furnas, 190, 197; Jones, 80
210 Mingay, 43–7
211 Maxwell, 21
212 Corkery, 27, 36
213 Lecky, 84; Salaman, 248–9
214 Young (Pt 2), 40–1
215 O. Ferguson, 49
216 Cullen, EH, 69; Corkery, 31
217 O. Ferguson, 47, 57–8; James, 106–9
218 Johnston, IEC, 71–2; O. Ferguson, 95
219 Swift, DL, 5, 8, 14; O. Ferguson, 38
220 Swift, IT, 9; O. Ferguson, 144
221 Swift, IT, 107–18, 171–8
222 Plumb, GPSE, 182–4; Charlemont, 23
223 Cullen, EH, 53
224 Johnston, IEC, 42; Beckett, MMI, 158–9; Lecky, 49
225 Maxwell, 349–61
226 Lecky, 78; Maxwell, 170–5, 204–5
227 Cullen, EH, 76–82
228 Connell, 25; Cullen, EH, 54, 82–4
229 Beckett, AIT, 79
230 A. Ferguson, 30
231 Walker 1, 11; W. C. Mackenzie, 187
232 D. Withrington in Phillipson, 179; Smout, HSP, 432
233 Burt 1, 77–8
234 J. Adam Smith in Phillipson, 108–9
235 N. T. Phillipson in Wolfe, 168; Plumb, GPSE, 125–6, 180–2; J. Simpson in Phillipson, 68–9
236 Clerk, 182; Campbell, 58–63
237 T. C. Smout in Phillipson, 82, 93
238 A. Ferguson, i, 19; Pollard, 71
239 Cassidy and Le Page, 18, 396; A. Hamilton, 69
240 I. C. C. Graham, 77–81; A. E. Smith, 198–200
241 I. C. C. Graham, 115–25; H. Hamilton, 256
242 H. P. Thompson, 100 etc.; I. C. C. Graham, 142; Metcalf, *passim*
243 Jefferson, 4

Romans and Hardy Races

1 Adam Ferguson, 24–5
2 Hofstadter, 183, 187
3 Hofstadter, 181, 206–7, 254–61; H. P. Thompson, 102
4 M. Williams, 514–16
5 M. Edwards in Davies and Rupp 1, 47
6 Ibid., 47–51
7 Ibid., 52–6; Briggs, 67–9
8 Hofstadter, 244–54; Bridenbaugh, MR, 96
9 D. Williams, 147
10 Nuttall, 3, 6, 15, 52–3, 56
11 Evans, 89–91, 95
12 Drummond and Bullock, 50 ff.
13 John and Charles Wesley, *Poetical Works* (Wesleyan–Methodist Conference Office, 1868–71), vol. 7, 149; Stephens 2, 269–70; M. Edwards in Davies and Rupp 1, 57, 74
14 Jordan, 212–15; R. L. Morton, 595; Washburn, 114
15 Nuttall, 46; Equiano, 92
16 Eccles, 172–3; Pares, WT, 60–4, 68–9; Namier, 47
17 Pares, WT, 11–28
18 Ayling, 60; Hertz, 30–4
19 Almon 1, 24–31
20 Ayling, 13, 18–19
21 Ibid., 102–12; B. Williams 1, 190–2
22 Robertson, 182
23 Tunstall, 9; Walpole, GII 1, 79–81
24 Plumb, C, 156–7; Pares, WT, 609
25 Hertz, 42–4, 49, 60-109; Mitchell, 27–8
26 P. Rogers, 281
27 Dobree, 3–19; Koebner, 84
28 Pares, WT, 64; DNB – Vernon; Malone 1, 28
29 Pares, WT, 258–61; Sheppard, 39
30 Almon 1, 96
31 Daiches, 107–8, 110
32 Evans, 58–63; D. Williams, 158–62
33 Burt 1, 248, and 2, 92
34 Burt 1, 5, 54; and 2, 183–6, 193
35 Burt 1, 40–1, 95–6
36 Smout, HSP, 432–7
37 Burt 2, 95–6, 219–20
38 Burt 1, 58; I. F. Grant, 352–3; Haldane, 14, 135–7
39 Burt 1, 54–5; I. F. Grant, 396–409, 484–98
40 E. Cregeen in Phillipson, 5–13
41 Daiches, 129–32
42 Hogg, 113–15
43 Daiches, 196–7; Mitchison, HS, 339–40; W. Ferguson, 151
44 Petrie, 469; A. E. Smith, 201–2

45 Hogg, 195–6
46 Daiches, 122–3; Prebble, C, 103
47 Almon 1, 426
48 Ayling, 94–101
49 Anson, 15–16
50 Marcus, 340; Lloyd, BS, 286–8
51 Boswell, *Johnson* 1, 348; Marcus, 382–3; Lloyd, BS, 229–66
52 Lloyd, BS, 143, 149, 166 etc.
53 Dorn, 108–21; E. Robson in NCMH 7, 187–90
54 Marcus, 379–81
55 Marcus, 275
56 Pares, WT, 351
57 Hall, 332–7; Boxer, DSE, 272–8
58 Orme 1, 81–2
59 Dodwell, DC, 20–1
60 P. Mason, 45
61 Chaudhuri, 64
62 Dodwell, DC, 28–30; G. Forrest, LC 1, 76; Orme 1, 105–6
63 Marcus, 271; Pares, WT, 390
64 R. E. Brown, 135–40; Smollett 3, 232
65 Orme 1, 111
66 G. Forrest, LC 1, 61–2
67 Dodwell, DC, 82–3
68 Orme 1, 187–200; G. Forrest, LC 1, 138–53; Chaudhuri, 83–5, 417–20
69 Walpole, SL, 348
70 Abernethy, 5–13; Sosin, RF, 31–3
71 E. Wright, WAR, 18
72 Ibid., 29
73 Van Alstyne, AE, 5–6; Koebner, 105–18
74 Van Alstyne, RAE, 23
75 Franklin, 223–4
76 A. G. Bradley in CMH 7, 123–5; Cresswell, 65
77 Franklin, 226; R. E. Brown, 152–4; Freeman 2, 132–68
78 Walpole, GII 1, 413; Marcus, 283–4; Smollett 3, 503; Tunstall, 156–7
79 Lloyd, CQ, 39
80 Tunstall, 165
81 Walpole, GII, 271; Almon 1, 426
82 D. Marshall, 279 fn.
83 Namier, 157
84 Tunstall, 188
85 Ibid., 168–9, 251–2; D. Marshall, 283
86 Christie, 32
87 Miller, OAR, 45, 47
88 Ibid., 49
89 Lloyd, BS, 258; Pares, WT, 273, 390–1; Marcus, 334–5; B. Williams 2, 124
90 Tunstall, 293–4; B. Williams 2, 53
91 Orme 2, 4–5

92 Spear, MB, 70
93 P. Marshall, EIF, 22, 24
94 Ibid., 35; Gupta, 15
95 Edwardes, 35–6
96 Macfarlane, 184–6, 198–200
97 Edwardes, 51–63; Chaudhuri, 161–2
98 Holwell, IT, 389
99 Gupta, 70–80, 146–57; Spear, MB, 74; G. Forrest, LC 2, 121; S. Hill 1, 61–119, 214–19, 248–301; and 3, 69, 88, 379–83
100 Holwell, IT, 391–404
101 Gupta, 80; S. Hill 3, 93; Holwell, IT, 400, 402–3
102 Smollett 3, 538–44; Orme 2, 73–7; Macaulay 1, 505–6
103 S. Hill 1, 214–19; Gupta, 80–1
104 Edwardes, 66–7
105 G. Forrest, LC 1, 275
106 Ives, 99–101; S. Hill 2, 97
107 G. Forrest, LC 1, 363
108 S. Hill 2, 273
109 Chaudhuri, 196, 216
110 Edwardes, ix, 130–43; Chaudhuri, 226–34; G. Forrest, LC 1, 435–60; H. Dodwell in CHBE 4, 149–50; Malcolm 1, 258–66; Orme 2, 163–78; Scrafton, 89–94; Spear, MB, 86–91; Pannikar, 78–9
111 Chaudhuri, 238
112 Ives, 176–8; Scrafton, 98; Chaudhuri, 243–4; Edwardes, 148
113 A. M. Khan, 22; G. Forrest, LC 2, 394
114 Scrafton, 101, 125–6
115 Bence Jones, 169
116 A. G. Bradley in CMH 7, 134–6
117 Tunstall, 212, 218
118 Pares, WT, 186–91
119 Ibid., 195–6
120 Ibid., 446–55
121 Gipson, CR, 28–32; Pares, WT, 445–6, 456–68
122 B. Williams 2, 1–5; Marcus, 305
123 Doughty 6, 1–3, 4, 9, 16, 22, 28, 30
124 Knox 1, 374–5
125 Doughty 2, 121
126 Lloyd, CQ, 65–7, 72
127 Doughty 2, 123, 223; and 5, 258
128 Doughty 5, 95; and 6, 37
129 Doughty 5, 187
130 Lloyd, CQ, 136; Doughty 3, 165–8
131 Doughty 3, 149–61, 201–25
132 Lloyd, CQ, 119–22
133 Smollett 5, 61, 64; Hawke, 15, 30; Walpole, GII 2, 282, 392–3
134 Mitchell, 20–33
135 Lloyd, CQ, 154–7; Doughty 5, 120–4; Knox 2, 248

136 P. Mason, 84
137 Spear, MB, 106–7; Bence Jones, 149, 156
138 Spear, MB, 97; A. M. Khan, 5; Bence Jones, 154–6, 172; Dodwell, DC, 149 fn.
139 G. Forrest 2, 119–22
140 P. Marshall, EIF, 235–6
141 Bence Jones, 183
142 G. Forrest, LC 2, 412–14
143 Bence Jones, 188–93
144 Ayling, 272
145 Pares, GIII, 61
146 Lloyd, BS, 253; Pares, WT, 594; Eric Williams, CS, 33
147 Ayling, 307–9; Almon 1, 356, 358
148 Smollett 5, 320–1
149 Pares, WT, 392; Sheridan, EWIP, 106
150 Ragatz, 130
151 Sheridan, EWIP, 94–5; Ragatz, 131
152 Sosin, RF, 61–5
153 Lanctot, 4–9; Reid et al., 52
154 Lanctot, 11
155 Brebner, 117
156 Brebner, 131
157 Sitwell, 244–5; Mitchell, 29
158 Trilling, 51
159 Rudé, 18C, 138
160 Ayling, 301
161 Plumb, EEC, 118–19
162 Sosin, WW, 8–10, 23–6; Pares, WT, 216–24; Sheridan, EWIP, 82
163 Goveia, 3–4

BOOK THREE

The Ruin of Liberty?

 1 Neville, 3–4
 2 Kinvig, 128–31
 3 Ibid., 114–16, 134–5
 4 Minchinton, 16, 62
 5 Ibid., 22–6, 30; Sheridan, SS, 309
 6 Ramsay, 163–5
 7 Smout, HSP, 227; Devine, 34–48, 62–8; Pennant, 131
 8 Pitman, 67; Sheridan, EWIP, 81
 9 Deerr 2, 290
10 Rice, 155
11 Sheridan, EWIP, 108–9; McInnes, 210–11; Donnan 4, 142–3
12 Sheridan, EWIP, 75, 84, 101, 102, 106, 111; Schaw, 127
13 Charles Wilson, 273–5; Minchinton, 35, 62

14 Gipson, CR, 10; Simmons, 320; Charles Wilson, 365; Smout, HSP, 241; Beckett, MMI, 244

15 Van Alstyne, RAE, 26; R. Brown, 169-75

16 Gipson, CR, 18; Alden, SR, 18-23

17 Miller, OAR, 20-1; Gipson, CR, 13-19, 120-1

18 Gipson, CR, 60-1; Metcalf, 112

19 Miller, OAR, 8, 11

20 Pares, YC, 121-2; Miller, OAR, 9; Gipson, CR, 125

21 Palmer 1, 154-8; Gipson, CR, 57-8; 128-9, 144-6, 149; Fieldhouse, 25-6, 32-3, 39-40

22 Parry, SSE, 334-5

23 Fieldhouse, 61

24 Christie, 14-22; Gipson, CR, 41

25 Alden, SR, 64

26 Gipson, CR, 129

27 R. R. Palmer in NCMH 8, 439

28 Bailyn, 10, 163

29 Miller, OAR, 212-15

30 Beloff, 16; Jefferson, 310, 364

31 Plumb, FFG, 117

32 Eitner 1, 6; Lentin; Crèvecoeur, 7-8, 24; Echeverria, 17-20

33 Bailyn, IOAR, 80-1

34 Jefferson, 431; Jordan, 287

35 Roberts, 67

36 Jordan, 289

37 Malone 1, 226

38 Briggs, 88; Knollenberg, 7-10; Miller, OAR, 209-10; R. Brown, 164

39 Bailyn, IOAR, 90

40 Miller, OAR, 203-7; Alan Day, 'Colonial Lawyers in Maryland', seminar given at Edinburgh University, 21.2.77; Wright, WAR, 80

41 Bailyn, IOAR, 1-2, 8, 13-14

42 Miller, OAR, 57-8; Van Alstyne, RAE, 1

43 Woodmason, 60

44 Knollenberg, 9

45 Devine, 59; F. Mason, xxiv-xxvi

46 Gipson, CR, 52-4; Knollenberg, 53-62

47 Miller, OAR, 14-18

48 Rutman, 57

49 Gipson, CR, 34-9; Bailyn, OTH, 54-6

50 Wills, 39; Gipson, CR, 62

51 Pares, YC, 24-9; Christie, 37

52 R. Brown, 16, 58

53 Miller, SA, 99-100

54 Ibid., 98

55 Beckett, MMI, 193-4

56 Johnston, GBI, 134, 149-51, 159 ff., 199

57 Kramnick, 180-1

58 Maloney, 57

59 D. Marshall, 350–1
60 Rudé, WL, 26–7
61 Ibid., 7–8
62 Boswell, *London Journal*, 71–2
63 Knollenberg, 31; Charles Churchill, *Poetical Works* (Bell, 1892), vol. 1, 107, 112; G. O. Trevelyan, AR, 224–30; Hickey, 1, 92–4
64 Sosin, RF, 30; Hook, 47–70; Devine, 60; Wills, 86–7
65 D. Marshall, 364–5
66 Donoughue, 43–4; Johnston, GBI, 12–13, 16
67 McDowell, 18
68 Sosin, RF, 6–10; Van Doren, 307–8; Rich 2, 2–4
69 Philbrick, 7–8
70 Ibid., 1, 21–4
71 Ibid., 42
72 Sosin, RF, 84
73 Abernethy, 24
74 Sosin, RF, 13–14
75 Harlow 1, 178 fn.; Knollenberg, 91
76 Clark, RBT, 117–18
77 Gipson, CR, 63
78 Miller, OAR, 189
79 Christie, 50–3
80 Van Doren, 320; Abernethy, 154
81 Bailyn, IOAR, 100–1; R. Brown, 216–20
82 Miller, OAR, 23
83 Ibid., 169
84 Wills, 8; Jefferson, 6; Alden, SR, 67–73; Morgan, SAC, 88–102; Gipson, CR, 88
85 Metcalf, 157–76
86 Goveia, 77
87 Metcalf, 150–2, 170
88 Gipson, CR, 106
89 Ibid., 100
90 Knollenberg, 230–7
91 Gipson, CR, 107; Wright, BF, 87
92 Miller, OAR, 299–303; Miller, SA, 112–13; J. T. Adams, 359–60
93 Almon 1, 430–1
94 Plumb, C, 113
95 Gipson, CR, 172–5
96 Bailyn, OTH, 122
97 Miller, OAR, 268–75; Alden, SR, 111
98 Miller, OAR, 322
99 Rudé, WL, 90–2
100 Ibid., 49–52
101 Van Doren, 379; Miller, OAR, 304–6, 322–5
102 Rudé, WL, 135
103 Almon 2, 126–7, 143; Namier, 170; Bailyn, OTH, 125
104 Lecky, 120

105 Ibid., 122–4
106 Beckett, MMI, 156–9; Maloney, 21–2, 34
107 Dickson, 58–81
108 Cullen, FIE, 16–18; Cullen in PP (1968), 73–82
109 Maxwell, 46; McDowell, 23
110 Beckett, MMI, 200
111 Johnston, GBI, 214–256, 257; Palmer 1, 288
112 Rudé, WL, 172–3
113 Youngson, 1
114 I. C. C. Graham, 188–9
115 Pennant, 309; I. C. C. Graham, 32–42; Youngson, 41–6; Boswell, JTH, 242–3
116 Smout, HSP, 250–2; Mitchison, HS, 376
117 Smout in Phillipson, 90–1; Youngson, 27–34
118 Youngson, 37
119 Smout, HSP, 323
120 Youngson, 111–17
121 Mitchison, ASJ, 104–5; Pennant, 315–16
122 Youngson, 165
123 Pennant, 310
124 H. G. Graham, 478–81
125 Neville, 145
126 Harvie, 77
127 Smout, HSP, 202–3; Furber, 175–88; P. D. G. Thomas in D. Moore, 19–20, 23
128 Boswell, JTH, 16
129 Boswell, *Johnson* 3, 200
130 Rice, 160–74; seminars by C. Duncan Rice at Edinburgh University, 20.1.75, 6.3.75
131 Anstey, 218–22
132 Ibid., 130–3
133 Sharp, LL, 49
134 D. B. Davis, 391; Hoare, 145
135 Sharp, JL, 36, 60
136 Walvin, BW, 46–8, 53, 70–1; Shyllon, 9
137 Walvin, BW, 49–50, 55–73, 84–9; Van Doren, 276
138 Duckham 1, 240–53, 256, 261–2, 280; Smout, HSP, 403–6
139 Hoare, 91
140 Walvin, BW, 120–4; Shyllon, 96
141 Walvin, BW, 132–3
142 Ibid., 124–41; Shyllon, 165–76
143 Curtin, IA, 66
144 Estwick, 30–1, 40–7, 59, 70–82
145 Long 2, 267–71, 351–83, 400 ff.
146 Cresswell, 39
147 Neville, 2–3, 25; Henry Mackenzie, *Man of Feeling*, in *Works* 1 (Edinburgh, 1808), i, 190
148 Ghosh, 12, 128–9
149 P. Marshall, EIF, 168–70; Spear, MB, 133–6; P. Mason, 97–8
150 Hallward, 3–18; Spear, MB, 136–7; Feiling, 49

151 P. Mason, 102–3
152 Spear, MB, 138
153 Ibid., 138–9; P. Marshall, EIF, 171–4, 179
154 Ghosh, 21; P. Marshall, EIF, 13–17
155 Sutherland, 59–74
156 G. Forrest, LC 2, 256–8
157 Ibid., 256–8; Chaudhuri, 356–7
158 Sutherland, 138–46; G. Forrest 2, 367
159 A. M. Khan, 15
160 P. Marshall, EIF, 113–24, 128, 236–9, 255, 267–70
161 A. M. Khan, 142–3, 160, 162
162 Ibid., 171–2; Moon, 79–80
163 Spear, MB, 185–6; P. Marshall, EIF, 147–8
164 Sutherland, 225–6; Dow 3, lxxvi–viii, lxxxiv–vi; P. Marshall, EIF, 180; D. Forrest,
     TB, 63–4; R. Roberts in CHBE 4, 186
165 R. Roberts in CHBE 4, 184–9
166 Chaudhuri, 405–11, 433–4
167 Sutherland, 148; R. Roberts in CHBE 4, 186
168 Hickey 1, 236–41; D. Marshall, 15; Spear, MB, 207–11; Ghosh, 108–11; Macdonald,
     132
169 Ghosh, 30–1, 53; Gleig 2, 147
170 Feiling, 158; Grier, 16–17; Hickey 3, 245; Moon, 175; Gleig 3, 427, 499–500, 503
171 Feiling, 56; Moon, 58–9; Chaudhuri, 340
172 Grier, 28–34; Feiling, 83, 104, 122–3, 161; Moon, 116; P. Marshall, IWH, 85
173 Feiling, 104, 238
174 Feiling, 116; Gleig 2, 149–50
175 R. Roberts in CHBE 4, 206
176 P. Marshall, EIF, 180–98, 243
177 Moon, 101–4
178 R. Roberts in CHBE 4, 216
179 Feiling, 87; Harlow 1, 63–7
180 Harlow 1, 70–97
181 Ibid., 2, 333–4
182 Goebel, 240
183 Beaglehole, 107–10, 118–20
184 Ibid., 121
185 Ibid., 15
186 Ibid., 451, 453, 713
187 Ibid., 703–6
188 Cook 1, 93–4, 96, 103, 118–39
189 Ibid., 171, 507
190 Ibid., 399
191 Beaglehole, 271; Cook 1, 276, 392–7
192 Cook 2, 98–9
193 Ibid., 238–9
194 Ibid., 302 fn.
195 Ibid., 371–6, 493, 539

196 Ibid., 621–2
197 Beaglehole, 447–9; Boswell, *Johnson* 3, 8; Hoare, 147–52
198 Parry, TD, 218

Revolutions

1 Neville, 279–80
2 Miller, OAR, 25
3 Abernethy, 82–4; Cresswell, 85
4 Sosin, WW, 181–210
5 Bailyn, OTH, 183–4
6 Ibid., 223, 227, 238, 246 etc.
7 Van Doren, 469–70
8 Miller, SA, 285
9 Bailyn, OTH, 259
10 Ibid., 260–2; Commager and Morris, 3–4; Wills, 26–9
11 V. G. Kiernan in Dudley Edwards, 31; Benjamin Franklin, *The Autobiography ...* [etc.], ed. C. Van Doren (Pocket Books, New York, 1940), 315
12 Donoughue, 127–42, 150–4
13 Ibid., 97–8; Commager and Morris, 12
14 Harlow 2, 698–9
15 Christie, 91
16 Griffith, 133–4; Commager and Morris, 49–50
17 Griffith, 140
18 Cresswell, 57
19 W. Brown, 135–6, 140–1
20 Griffith, 140–1
21 Metcalf, 187–9
22 Alden, AR, 17
23 Almon 2, 265–9
24 Devine, 104–5
25 Commager and Morris, 107–9
26 Griffith, 165–71; Commager and Morris, 66–97; Dorson, 20–9
27 Dorson, 36–9
28 Griffith, 197
29 Commager and Morris, 166–7
30 Malone 1, 55
31 Devine, 107–9
32 I. C. C. Graham, 99–100
33 Commager and Morris, 134–5
34 Paine 1, 16, 17, 19, 24, 30–1, 39
35 Cresswell, 136; Alden, AR, 77; Malone 1, 195
36 Meyer, 84–5, 108–9, 112–13, 117–19, 120–1, 147–60
37 I. C. C. Graham, 130
38 Jefferson, 279–80, 729–30

39 Wills, 65–75, 374–9
40 G. Rawlyk in Dudley Edwards, 104–10
41 Dodd, 97–8; A. Jarman in Roderick 2, 145–6; D. Williams, 168–9
42 Plumb, EEC, 135
43 Hoare, 123–7
44 Almon 2, 303, 323, 350–4
45 McInnes, 287–96; Parkinson, 124–37
46 T. Devine and D. Swinfen in Dudley Edwards, 61–74
47 Prebble, M, 91–259
48 Commager and Morris, 244–5
49 W. Brown, 72, 76–7, 242–3
50 Ibid., 97–9, 226–7; Simmons, 374–5
51 W. Brown, 44–58, 240–2; Sosin, RF, 93, 99; I. C. C. Graham, 149; C. H. Haws in
   Dudley Edwards, 54–5
52 W. Brown, 59; Sosin, RF, 94–5
53 Mackesy, 165–70, 175–7; Almon 2, 307; Marcus, 344–6
54 Mackesy, 65–7
55 Mackesy, 82, 266, 510; D. Marshall, 423–4; I. H. Adams in Dudley Edwards, 54–5
56 Echeverria, 86
57 Palmer 1, 188; Alden, AR, 168
58 Devine, 126–34
59 Hofstadter, PH, 257–9; Simmons, 370
60 Day, 33; Jordan, 289–92
61 Jordan, 291, 302–4, 345–7
62 Cresswell, 179–80
63 Echeverria, 39, 46
64 Ibid., 80–3
65 Mackesy, 368–9
66 Alden, AR, 205–6
67 Ragatz, 144–58
68 Lindsay, 3:350
69 Mackesy, 272
70 Lanctot, 168–210
71 Sosin, RF, 122
72 Bailyn, OTH, 299, 324, 326
73 Norton, 134
74 Mackesy, 435–6
75 D. Marshall, 461–9
76 Boswell, *Johnson* 3, 262
77 McDowell, 40; Morison, 149–50; Harlow 1, 509
78 Grattan 1, xxxvii–viii, xliii–iv; Lecky, 187
79 Lecky, 207
80 McDowell, 43
81 Cullen, EHI, 57–8, 75; O Connell, 44–5
82 O Connell, 32–3, 124; Harlow 1, 522
83 Beckett, MMI, 209
84 Lecky, 173

85 Beckett, MMI, 213–14; Barrington 1, 6–8; Johnston, IEC, 139–44; M. Wall in Cullen, FIE, 45–6

86 O Connell, 172–83

87 Ibid., 223–31; Grattan 1, 41, 53

88 O Connell, 262–3, 294–5

89 Ibid., 284–92

90 Charlemont, 47; O Connell, 92–3, 95

91 O Connell, 319–21; Lecky, 181–3

92 Barrington 1, 86–7; McDowell, 65

93 O Connell, 321–7; Grattan 1, 123

94 Grattan 1, 127

95 O Connell, 375–94; Palmer 1, 303; Beckett, MMI, 231–2

96 M. Wall in Cullen, FIE, 47–8; Johnston, GBI, 329

97 P. Marshall, IWH, 164

98 Ibid., 166–75

99 Busteed, 151–2

100 Ibid., 172–4; Hastings, M, 100–1

101 Moon, 215–16; Hastings, M, 157–60; R. Roberts in CHBE 4, 231

102 Busteed, 161

103 Ghosh, 130–44; Busteed, 195–200

104 Hickey 3, 206–9; Ghosh, 50–2, 114–15, 135–6, 182

105 Macintosh 2, 214–19

106 Hickey 2, 138; Ghosh, 119–26, 132; Busteed, 122–5; P. Marshall, EIF, 217–19

107 P. Marshall, IWH, 132–52

108 Ibid., 177–9; Gleig 2, 330–1, 383–8

109 P. Marshall, IWH, 161–2

110 Gleig 2, 136

111 Ibid., 141–2

112 P. Marshall, IWH, 88–108; Hastings, NI, 9

113 Hastings, LM, 106–7

114 P. Marshall, IWH, 109–29

115 R. Roberts in CHBE 4, 305–6

116 Feiling, 283; Sutherland, 384

117 Feiling, 236; Gleig 2, 17–20; P. Marshall, BDH, 184–91

118 P. Marshall, BDH, 20–38

119 Ibid., 37–9; Holwell, IH 3, 147–60; Orme 1, 5–7

120 Dow 1, xiii; and 3, xxxv–vii, cxxviii

121 Adam Smith, 311; Ives, 52–3

122 Holwell, IH 2, 87–100; Macdonald, 158

123 P. Marshall, BDH, 42–3

124 Rich, 2, 103; Meyer, 64–5

125 Rice, 178; Adam Smith, 39–40, 183–4

126 McInnes, 334

127 Anstey, 229–31

128 Briggs, 18; Wadsworth and Mann, 170; G. M. Trevelyan, ESH, 388

129 Sir Walter Scott, *The Monastery* (Edinburgh, 1820), 'Answer to the Introductory Epistle'

130 D. Marshall, 11
131 Mathias, 134–5
132 Wilson, 350–2; Wadsworth and Mann, 349, 385
133 S. Lilley in FEHE 3, 192–5
134 Ibid., 213; H. W. Dickinson, 38, 113, 202; Briggs, 26
135 Ashton, 60
136 Court, 245–7; Klingender, 12
137 H. W. Dickinson, 208
138 Court, 239–40
139 Adam Smith, 223
140 Ibid., 119
141 Ibid., 77–8, 443
142 Ibid., 433, 441
143 Curtin, IA, 61–2
144 Adam Smith, 79–81, 179–81, 268
145 Ibid., 442; Wilson, 276–87; Namier, 58
146 Wilson, 304–7; Wadsworth and Mann, 144
147 Sheridan, SS, 475; Anstey, 49–50; Craton, SE, 152–4
148 Wadsworth and Mann, 229, 233, 244–8; Devine, 34–48; Lythe and Butt, 163–8; Mathias, 105–6; John, 7–8, 110
149 Mathias, 100–5
150 Wadsworth and Mann, 183–92; Harlow 2, 284
151 G. M. Trevelyan, ESH, 389; Wadsworth and Mann, 146, 151, 157–61
152 A. Mackenzie, xxv; Court, 142–7, 206–10; Wilson, 294–6
153 F. Crouzet in M. Williams, 136–43; Wadsworth and Mann, 179–82, 193–208; Beaglehole, 85–6, 99–101, 117–18
154 Beaglehole, 6–8; Nef 1, 19–20
155 Laslett, 41, 49–50, 52
156 Mathias, 169
157 Kerr, 124, 128; Wadsworth and Mann, 242
158 Mathias, 73–5
159 Mathias, 71
160 Ashton, 2; Smout, HSP, 241; D. Williams in Roderick 2, 147–8; C. Cipolla in FEHE 3, 15
161 G. M. Trevelyan, ESH, 382
162 Klingender, 13, 14, 19, 49
163 Hoskins, 179
164 Briggs, 52–3
165 Ibid., 69; Ashton, 90
166 Ashton, 91–3; Wadsworth and Mann, 408
167 Ashton, 90; Smout, HSP, 361; Dodd, 133–42; Klingender, 71; Briggs, 23, 28, 38 fn.
168 Adam Smith, 429–31; H. W. Dickinson, 37, 197
169 Wadsworth and Mann, 386–92
170 Ibid., 361–83, 393; Duckham 1, 305–6
171 Mitchison, HS, 345
172 Smout, HSP, 228
173 Ibid., 227, 233

174 Ibid., 238–9, 340
175 Sinclair 15, 40; Smout, HSP, 282–94, 342–8
176 John, 1–21; Dodd, 1–30; H. Carter in D. Moore, 56–7
177 Dodd, 306–9; John, 23–4, 137
178 John, 24–5; Dodd, 136
179 Dodd, 152–60
180 Cullen, EH, 90–9
181 Nef 1, 19–20; Wadsworth and Mann, 311–13
182 Harlow 1, 226–34, 405; Manning, 20–2
183 P. Marshall, IWH, 2–20
184 Harlow 2, 139, 157
185 R. Roberts in CHBE 4, 194–5
186 Ibid., 195–200
187 Furber, 193–4, 228, 264–5
188 Ghosh, 14–26, 49–52
189 Brathwaite, 80–95; Parry and Sherlock, 149
190 W. Brown, 172–80, 204, 217–18
191 W. Brown, 191–221; Norton, 235–42; Craton, HB, 162–70
192 Harlow 1, 486 fn.; Fogel and Engerman, 24
193 Van Alstyne, RAE, 69
194 M. Jensen in Billington, 112
195 Rich 2, 119–20
196 Cook 3, 1100
197 Beaglehole, 542, 648–72, 674–5
198 Cook 1, clxxii, clxxiv–vii
199 Beaglehole, 266; Harlow 1, 104–45

Bibliography

Books directly cited, together with some titles used but not quoted, but minus certain 'literary' works of which details are given in the references, will be found listed in four sections: to 1603; 1603–60; 1660–1713; 1713–85. All titles are published in London unless it is otherwise stated; I have not indulged in the fussy pedantry of giving home towns for university presses.

I hope the lists will be useful, but they do not provide anything near to comprehensive 'select bibliographies'. The literature of empire is vast. I have used only a selection of secondary sources, a scattering of important published primary sources. However, many of the works listed themselves contain excellent bibliographies.

I will group at the outset certain titles of such wide scope that they would provide apt points of entry for a general reader or student beginning to follow up her or his own interests.

European Expansion in General

The excellent *Cambridge Economic History of Europe* can now be supplemented with the *Fontana Economic History of Europe* (ed. Carlo Cipolla, from 1972).

Richard Koebner's *Empire* (Cambridge, 1961) is the history of a concept. D. K. Fieldhouse's *The Colonial Empires ... from the Eighteenth Century* (1966) is a handy comparative survey. Three volumes in one series are invaluable: J. H. Parry's *Spanish Seaborne Empire* (1966); and *The Dutch Seaborne Empire 1600–1800* (1966) and *The Portuguese Seaborne Empire 1415–1825* (1969), both by the masterly C. R. Boxer. There is unfortunately no counterpart for French expansion, but W. J. Eccles's *France in America* (New York, 1972) takes one part of the way.

V. G. Kiernan's *The Lords of Humankind* (1969) is an acute and erudite survey of European attitudes towards other races. These can be further studied in Margaret T. Hodgen's *Early Anthropology in the Sixteenth and Seventeenth Centuries* (Philadelphia, 1964) and George L. Mosse's *Towards The Final Solution* (1978), which deals with racism since the eighteenth century.

The intellectual consequences of Columbus are brilliantly illuminated in J. H. Elliott's *The Old World and the New 1492–1650* (Cambridge, 1970). Maritime expansion is admirably overviewed in J. H. Parry's *The Age of Reconnaissance* (1963) and its sequel, *Trade and Dominion: The European Oversea Empires in the Eighteenth Century* (1971). These can be used in conjunction with Fernand

Braudel's *Capitalism and Material Life 1400–1800* (translated 1973) and Ralph Davis's *The Rise of the Atlantic Economies* (1973).

Mercantilism is the title of a compendious work by Eli F. Hecksher (second edition, 1955) and of a short and trenchant summary by Charles Wilson (1958). Eric Roll's standard *History of Economic Thought* (fourth edition, 1973) and William Letwin's *Origins of Scientific Economics ... 1660–1776* (1963) have much to say about British 'mercantilist' thought; see also Klaus E. Knorr's indispensable *British Colonial Theories 1570–1850* (Toronto, 1944).

British Expansion

The account of the 'Old Empire, from the Beginnings to 1783' in the first volume of the *Cambridge History of the British Empire* (1929) was the work of a skilful generation of scholars and remains valuable. I think the best treatment by a single writer is still J. A. Williamson's *Short History of British Expansion*, vol. 1 (originally published in 1922, most lately revised in 1945), reeking of old-school imperialism, yet solid in scholarship and masterly in concision. Williamson's *Notebook of Commonwealth History* (third edition, 1967) is extremely useful for quick reference. L. H. Gipson's monumental 15-volume survey of *The British Empire before the American Revolution* (Idaho and New York, 1936–74) is limited to the mid-eighteenth century, but is panoramic.

This book is vastly indebted to two suggestive surveys of economic history: Christopher Hill's *Reformation to Industrial Revolution* (1969) and Charles Wilson's *England's Apprenticeship 1603–1763* (1965). There are very useful studies of *English Overseas Trade During the Centuries of Emergence* by G. D. Ramsay (1957) and *English Overseas Trade 1500–1700* by Ralph Davis (1973). E. J. Hobsbawm's *Industry and Empire* (1968) gives an acute analysis of the role of expansion in helping promote 'industrial revolution'.

Corelli Barnett's *Britain and Her Army 1509–1970* (1970) is readable and well-informed. G. J. Marcus's *Naval History of England* (first volume, 1961) is a clear work of reference; see also Christopher Lloyd, *The British Seaman* (1968).

The hitherto overlooked black minority in Britain itself has been given some of its dues in James Walvin's *Black and White ... 1555–1945* (1973). The partly related question of English attitudes towards Celts is explored by J. O. Bartley in *Teague, Shenkin and Sawney* (Cork, 1954). Michael Hechter deserves much credit for initiative in his *Internal Colonialism: The Celtic Fringe in British National Development 1536–1966* (1975) – almost no recent historian has tried to see the British archipelago as a whole, or, rather, as a set of separate countries closely interacting. But though his book is suggestive, Hechter's historical judgments are rash.

Ireland

J. C. Beckett's *The Making of Modern Ireland 1603–1923* is a very reliable survey (new edition, 1979). The sixteenth and seventeenth centuries are covered succinctly in Margaret MacCurtain's *Tudor and Stuart Ireland* (Dublin, 1972) and in detail in volume 3 of *A New History of Ireland* (Oxford, 1976), edited by T. W. Moody, F. X. Martin and F. J. Byrne. Lecky's great study of the eighteenth century still exerts direct influence; there is a useful abridgment of it by L. P. Curtis Jr (Chicago, 1972). See Edith Mary Johnston's short *Ireland in the Eighteenth Century* (Dublin, 1974), Francis G. James's *Ireland in the Empire 1688–1770* (Cambridge, Mass., 1973) and Constantia Maxwell's valuable social history of *Country and Town in Ireland Under the Georges* (1940). L. M. Cullen has produced important revisionist studies of the *Economic History of Ireland Since 1600* (1972) and *Anglo-Irish Trade 1660–1800* (Manchester, 1968). *Seven Centuries of Irish Learning 1000–1700* (second edition, Cork, 1971) is an expert introduction to Gaelic culture edited by Brian O Cuiv. R. N. Salaman's pioneering *History and Social Influence of the Potato* (1949) contains much useful material, but should be used with caution.

Scotland

Rosalind Mitchison's *History of Scotland* (1970) is a splendidly readable introduction. Gordon Donaldson's *Scotland: James V to James VII* (Edinburgh, 1965) is followed in the same standard series by William Ferguson's *Scotland 1689 to the Present* (Edinburgh, 1968). These give the political history: social history is very well handled in T. C. Smout's *History of the Scottish People 1560–1830* (1969). Gordon Donaldson also provides, in *The Scots Overseas* (1966), a brief introduction to a vast subject. S. G. Lythe and John Butt offer a compact *Economic History of Scotland 1100–1939* (Glasgow, 1975) and R. H. Campbell a standard economic study of *Scotland Since 1707* (Oxford, 1965). W. C. Mackenzie, *The Highlands and Isles of Scotland* (revised edition, Edinburgh, 1949) remains a standard account, but should be used alongside I. F. Grant's sharper *The Macleods: The History of a Clan 1200–1956* (1959).

Wales

Many aspects of Welsh history seem sadly neglected. *Wales Through The Ages* (Llandybie, 1959–60) is a sprightly introduction edited by A. J. Roderick. David Williams's standard *History of Modern Wales* (second edition, 1977) can now be supplemented with two volumes in series: 1485–1660 by Hugh Thomas and 1660–1815 by E. D. Evans (Cardiff, 1972 and 1976 respectively).

The Isle of Man

This is the subject of a very interesting historical survey by R. O. Kinvig (second edition, Liverpool, 1975).

West Indies

Eric Williams's *From Columbus to Castro* (1970) is a racy account of the area – less sound but often more stimulating than J. H. Parry and Philip Sherlock's *Short History of the West Indies* (third edition, 1971). Sir Alan Burns's *History of the British West Indies* (revised edition, 1965) is a 'political' account but can be complemented with Cyril Hamshere's social history of *The British in the Caribbean* (1972) and Richard Sheridan's excellent *Sugar and Slavery: An Economic History of the British West Indies* (Barbados, 1974). Noel Deerr's *History of Sugar* (1949–50) has dated somewhat, but is still valuable. Richard Pares's *War and Trade in the West Indies* (1936) remains essential for the eighteenth century. Richard S. Dunn's penetrating account of the rise of the planter class, *Sugar and Slaves ... 1624–1713* (1973) is also outstanding. *A Jamaican Plantation ... 1670–1970* by Michael Craton and James Walvin (1970) is another case study to put beside Richard Pares's classic work on an individual planting family, *A West India Fortune* (1950). See also Michael Craton's *History of the Bahamas* (1962).

Present-day Canada

Ralph G. Lounsbury's *British Fishery at Newfoundland 1634–1763* (New Haven, 1934) is in part superseded by Gillian T. Cell's *English Enterprise at Newfoundland 1577–1660* (Toronto, 1969). The history of 'Canada' proper before British conquest is sympathetically handled in W. J. Eccles's *France in America* (New York, 1972). Readers can take their pick from several good standard histories of Canada within its present-day boundaries: Donald Creighton (new edition, 1958) for style; W. L. Morton (Toronto, 1963) for detail; A. R. M. Lower (revised edition, Don Mills, 1964); and J. B. Brebner (new edition, Ann Arbor, 1970). Harold A. Innis, *The Fur Trade in Canada* (revised edition, Toronto, 1956) is introductory and fundamental; there is a wealth of fascinating detail in E. E. Rich's *History of the Hudson's Bay Company 1670–1870* (1958–9).

The Thirteen Colonies

Books on the fur trade have much to say about America's aboriginal inhabitants. Wilcomb E. Washburn, *The Indian in America* (New York, 1975) and Alvin M. Josephy Jr's *The Indian Heritage of America* (British edition, 1972) are unprejudiced and informative.

The literature on the colonising whites is so vast that any short list must seem ludicrously partial. In any case, it will soon be out of date; thus, Edmund S. Morgan's important new study of seventeenth-century Virginia, *American Slavery American Freedom* (New York, 1975), appeared too late to enter R. G. Simmons's valiantly comprehensive bibliography in his useful new synthesis, *The American Colonies: From Settlement to Independence* (1976). For seventeenth-century foundations, Charles M. Andrews, *The Colonial Period of American History* (New Haven, 1934–8) remains a valuable source of detail. Also on early days, see Wesley Frank Craven, *The Southern Colonies ... 1607–1689* (Baton Rouge, 1949) – and Henry C. Wilkinson on *The Adventurers of Bermuda*, to 1684 (second edition, 1958). Richard S. Dunn's *Puritans and Yankees 1630–1717* (Princeton, 1962) gives a fine introduction to New England history through a study of the Winthrop dynasty. Larzer Ziff's *Puritanism in America* (1973) is stimulating reading for both seventeenth and eighteenth centuries. A start can be made on Pennsylvania with Frederick B. Tolles's *Meeting House and Counting House: The Quaker Merchants of Colonial Philadelphia* (New York, 1948).

Carl Bridenbaugh's valuable studies of colonial society are too numerous to list here; for instance, *Cities in the Wilderness ... 1625–1742* (New York, 1938) deals with the villages which became towns. Louis B. Wright's *The Cultural Life of the American Colonies* (New York, 1957) is a useful introduction to a field in which some scholars, notably Perry Miller, have made massive achievements. Roger Thompson's *Women in Stuart England and America* (1974) is a suggestive pioneering work.

Michael Kammen's *Empire and Interest* (Philadelphia, 1970) brings sharp if limited focus to politics from 1660 to 1783. The period from the Glorious Revolution of 1689 to the rupture with Britain is a historical mine-field, to be approached with caution through Simmons's bibliography; thus, even Richard Hofstadter's *America at 1750* (1971), a synthesis by a great historian and fine writer, does not satisfy advanced scholars, and Garry Wills's *Inventing America: Jefferson's Declaration of Independence* (New York, 1978) has recently made suspect all the previous books which have attributed much in the period to the influence of John Locke's political ideas, and has given joy to those who have been suggesting the paramountcy of Scottish thought. It must be stressed that the quantity and sophistication of American scholarship devoted to the colonial period vastly overmatches, relative to then population, what can be found for any other section of the empire. If only we had monographs on British towns to compare with those devoted to New England villages ...

Slavery

For instance, recent historiography of colonial America has been transforming our understanding of slavery, overlapping as it does so with researches in the Caribbean.

852   BIBLIOGRAPHY

The standard work on white servitude, in both areas, is still Abbot E. Smith's *Colonists in Bondage ... 1607–1776* (Chapel Hill, 1947). The modern debate over black servitude begins with Eric Williams's bold *Capitalism and Slavery* (Chapel Hill, 1944). His methods have their imperfections, but the work of Richard Sheridan (*see under* West Indies) gives much of his thesis new life. Meanwhile, David Brion Davis (Ithaca, 1966) has brought a new depth of understanding to the intellectual history of *The Problem of Slavery in Western Culture*.

Philip D. Curtin's masterly revision of the statistics of *The Atlantic Slave Trade* (Madison, 1969) is basic to all discussion. C. Duncan Rice, *The Rise and Fall of Black Slavery* (1975) is an invaluable recent synthesis. Winthrop D. Jordan, *White Over Black* (Chapel Hill, 1968) treats North American slavery comprehensively; see also Peter H. Wood, *Black Majority* (New York, 1974) on South Carolina. C. Northcote Parkinson, *The Rise of the Port of Liverpool* (Liverpool, 1952) and T. M. Devine, *The Tobacco Lords ... c. 1740–1790* (Edinburgh, 1975), on Glasgow, show something of the effects in Britain.

On the trade itself, see Michael Craton's *Sinews of Empire* (1974) and Roger Anstey, *The Atlantic Slave Trade and British Abolition 1760–1810* (1975). The fundamental study for the earlier period is K. G. Davies, *The Royal African Company* (1957), which is also important, of course, for African history.

Africa

The historiography of the whole continent is in an exciting state of flux. Volume 4 of the *Cambridge History of Africa* (ed. R. Gray, 1977) is relevant for the 'old colonial' period, as is volume 1 of the *History of West Africa* (ed. J. F. A. Ajayi and M. Crowder, 1971). But A. G. Hopkins's *Economic History of West Africa* 1973) is a dazzling example of the sort of revisionism which can make scores of books out of date overnight. K. Y. Daaku, *Trade and Politics on the Gold Coast 1600–1720* (Oxford, 1970) remains, however, an informative monograph.

India

By contrast, the early days of British involvement in India have received all too little attention since a devoted band of white apologists worked over them late in the last century and early in this. (See, for instance, the four captivating volumes of *Vestiges of Old Madras 1640–1800*, brought out by H. D. Love in 1913.) So the nostalgic first volume of Philip Woodruff's *Men Who Ruled India* (1953) is still an acceptable light introduction. Percival Spear is more objective in his second volume of the Penguin *History of India* (revised edition, 1978). But for standard narrative one must still go to the fourth volume of the *Cambridge History of the British Empire – British India 1497–1858*, published in 1929 and edited by the redoubtable H. H. Dodwell, and for seventeenth-century detail to Sir W. W. Hunter's incomplete *History of British India* (1899–1900).

Fortunately K. N. Chaudhuri's polished study of the first forty years of *The English East India Company* (1965) has been followed (too late for use here) by his huge investigation of *The Trading World of Asia and the English East India Company 1660–1760* (Cambridge, 1978). And P. J. Marshall's *East India Fortunes: The British in Bengal in the Eighteenth Century* (Oxford, 1976) is a refreshing example of the kind of new work which needs doing; it complements Lucy S. Sutherland's formidable *The EIC in Eighteenth Century Politics* (1952) and helps us flesh out Percival Spear's short social history of *The Nabobs* (1963).

British involvement in the Far East in the period covered by this book was very largely concerned with tea, and Denys Forrest's *Tea for the British* (1973) is a good popular introduction to this momentous subject.

I would think myself ungrateful if I ended here, having mentioned hardly or not at all so many scholars whose work sets daunting standards and has taught me a great deal but whose books lack the wide scope of those mentioned above. I think, for instance, how blank Tudor Ireland would have been for me, despite the usable studies I had found, without the offprints of articles by D. B. Quinn which Professor George Shepperson kindly lent to me. As this example shows, my debts to authors of historical works have often been involved with debts to historian friends who have pointed me towards studies I needed. One of these once remarked to me that he thought I would be the last person ever to attempt this kind of synthesis; over the last quarter-century, the literature has grown virtually unmanageable. Certainly, whoever tries it again will face an even longer task than mine, and will rely even more greatly on the judgment of expert friends.

To 1603

AJAYI, J. F. A. and CROWDER, M., eds, *History of West Africa*, vol. 1, Longman, 1971

ANDREWS, KENNETH R., *Drake's Voyages*, Weidenfeld & Nicolson, 1967

—— *Elizabethan Privateering*, Cambridge University Press, 1964

ASTON, MARGARET, *The Fifteenth Century: The Prospect of Europe*, Thames and Hudson, 1968

AUBREY, JOHN, *Brief Lives*, ed. O. L. Dick, Secker, 1958

BAGWELL, RICHARD, *Ireland under the Tudors*, Longman, 1885–90

BAILYN, BERNARD, *The Ordeal of Thomas Hutchinson*, Allen Lane, 1975

BARTLEY, J. O., *Teague, Shenkin and Sawney*, Cork University Press, 1954

BLAKE, JOHN W., *European Beginnings in West Africa 1454–1578*, Longman, 1937

BOXER, C. R., *The Portuguese Seaborne Empire 1415–1825*, Hutchinson, 1969

CEHE I, *Cambridge Economic History of Europe*. Vol. 1: *The Agrarian Life of the Middle Ages*, ed. M. M. Postan (second edition), Cambridge University Press, 1966

CEHE 2, Ibid. Vol. 2: *Trade and Industry in the Middle Ages*, ed. M. M. Postan and and E. E. Rich, Cambridge University Press, 1952

CEHE 3, Ibid. Vol. 3: *Economic Organisation and Policies in the Middle Ages*, ed. M. M. Postan, E. E. Rich and E. Miller, Cambridge University Press, 1963

CEHE 4, Ibid. Vol. 4: *The Economy of Expanding Europe in the Sixteenth and Seventeenth Centuries*, ed. E. E. Rich and C. H. Wilson, Cambridge University Press, 1967

CHBE I, *Cambridge History of the British Empire*. Vol. 1: *The Old Empire, from the Beginnings to 1783*, ed. J. Holland Rose, A. P. Newton and E. A. Benians, Cambridge University Press, 1960 (originally 1929)

CANNY, NICHOLAS P., *The Elizabethan Conquest of Ireland: A Pattern Established 1565-76*, Harvester Press (Hassocks), 1976

CAREY, ROBERT, *Memoirs* (second edition), London, 1759

CAWLEY, ROBERT R., *Unpathed Waters*, Princeton University Press, 1940

CELL, GILLIAN T., *English Enterprise in Newfoundland 1577-1660*, University of Toronto Press, 1969

CIPOLLA, CARLO M., *European Culture and Overseas Expansion*, Penguin, 1970

COHN, NORMAN, *The Pursuit of the Millennium; Revolutionary Messianism in the Middle Ages*, Secker, 1957

COLUMBUS, CHRISTOPHER, *The Four Voyages of Christopher Columbus*, ed. and trans. J. M. Cohen, Penguin, 1969

CUMMING, W. P., SKELTON, R. A., QUINN, D. B., *The Discovery of North America*, Elek, 1971

CURTIN, PHILIP D., *The Atlantic Slave Trade*, University of Wisconsin Press, 1969

DAVIS, DAVID BRION, *The Problem of Slavery in Western Culture*, Penguin, 1970 (originally 1966)

DAVIS, RALPH, *English Overseas Trade 1500-1700*, Macmillan, 1973

—— *The Rise of the Atlantic Economies*, Weidenfeld & Nicolson, 1973

(*Dean of Lismore*), *Scottish Verse from the Book of the Dean of Lismore*, ed. W. J. Watson, Oliver and Boyd (Edinburgh), 1937

DICKENS, A. G., *The English Reformation*, Fontana, 1967

DONALDSON, GORDON, *Scotland: James V to James VII*, Oliver and Boyd (Edinburgh), 1965

DOUGLAS, DAVID C., *The Norman Achievement*, Eyre and Spottiswoode, 1969

DUDLEY EDWARDS, ROBERT, *Church and State in Tudor Ireland*, Longman, 1935

—— *Ireland in the Age of the Tudors*, Croom Helm, 1977

EDWARDS, EDWARD, *Life of Sir Walter Ralegh*, Macmillan, 1868

ELLIOTT, J. H., *Europe Divided 1559-1598*, Fontana, 1968

—— *Imperial Spain 1469-1716*, Penguin, 1970

—— *The Old World and the New 1492-1650*, Cambridge University Press, 1970

ELTON, G. R., *England Under the Tudors* (revised edition), Methuen, 1962

—— *Reformation Europe 1517-1559*, Fontana, 1963

EVANS, E. ESTYN, *Irish Folkways*, Routledge, 1957

FEHE I, *Fontana Economic History of Europe*. Vol. 1: *The Middle Ages*, ed. C. M. Cipolla, Fontana, 1972

FALLS, CYRIL, *Elizabeth's Irish Wars*, Methuen, 1950

FOSTER, SIR WILLIAM, *England's Quest for Eastern Trade*, A. and C. Black, 1933

FRASER, GEORGE MACDONALD, *The Steel Bonnets: The Story of the Anglo-Scottish Border Reivers*, Barrie and Jenkins, 1971

FRENCH, PETER J., *John Dee*, Routledge & Kegan Paul, 1972

GRANT, I. F., *The Macleods: The History of a Clan 1200–1956*, Faber & Faber, 1959
—— *The Social and Economic Development of Scotland Before 1603*, Oliver and Boyd (Edinburgh), 1930

HAKLUYT, RICHARD (the Younger), *The Principal Navigations Voyages Traffiques and Discoveries of the English Nation*, Maclehose (Glasgow), 1903–5

HALE, J. R., *Renaissance Europe 1480–1520*, Fontana, 1971

HALL, D. G. E., *A History of South East Asia* (third edition), Macmillan, 1968

HAY, DENYS, *Europe: The Emergence of an Idea*, Edinburgh University Press, 1957
—— *Europe in the Fourteenth and Fifteenth Centuries*, Longman, 1966

HAYES-MCCOY, G. A., *Scots Mercenary Forces in Ireland*, Burns & Oates, 1937

HILL, CHRISTOPHER, *Intellectual Origins of the English Revolution*, Panther, 1972 (originally 1965)
—— *Reformation to Industrial Revolution*, Penguin, 1969

HILTON, R. H., *The Decline of Serfdom in Medieval England*, Macmillan, 1969

HINTON, EDWARD M., *Ireland Through Tudor Eyes*, University of Pennsylvania Press, 1935

HODGEN, MARGARET T., *Early Anthropology in the Sixteenth and Seventeenth Centuries*, University of Pennsylvania Press, 1964

HOSKINS, W. G., *The Making of the English Landscape*, Penguin, 1970

HUIZINGA, JOHAN, *The Waning of the Middle Ages*, Penguin, 1955 (originally 1924)

HUME BROWN, P., ed., *Early Travellers in Scotland*, David Douglas (Edinburgh), 1891
—— ed., *Scotland Before 1700 from Contemporary Documents*, David Douglas (Edinburgh), 1893

HURSTFIELD, JOEL, *Elizabeth I and the Unity of England*, Penguin, 1971 (originally 1960)
—— *Freedom, Corruption and Government in Elizabethan England*, Cape, 1973

HYMES, DELL, ed., *Pidginization and Creolization of Languages*, Cambridge University Press, 1971

JONES, GARETH, *A New History of Wales: The Gentry and the Elizabethan State*, Christopher Davies (Swansea), 1977

JORDAN, WINTHROP D., *White Over Black*, University of North Carolina Press, 1968

KIERNAN, V. G., *The Lords of Humankind*, Penguin, 1972 (originally 1969)

KINVIG, R. O., *The Isle of Man: A Social, Cultural and Political History* (second edition), Liverpool University Press, 1975

KOEBNER, RICHARD, *Empire*, Cambridge University Press, 1961

KOENIGSBERGER, H. G. and MOSSE, GEORGE L., *Europe in the Sixteenth Century* (third edition), Longman, 1971

LELAND, JOHN, *The Itinerary in Wales*, ed. L. Toulmin-Smith, Bell, 1906

LYTHE, S. G. E., *The Economy of Scotland in its European Setting 1550–1625*, Oliver and Boyd (Edinburgh), 1960

MacCURTAIN, MARGARET, *Tudor and Stuart Ireland*, Gill (Dublin), 1972

MACKENZIE, W. C., *The Highlands and Isles of Scotland* (revised edition), Moray Press (Edinburgh), 1949

MCNEILL, PETER and NICHOLSON, RANALD, *An Historical Atlas of Scotland c. 400–c. 1600*, Conference of Scottish Medievalists (St Andrews), 1975

MATHEW, DAVID, *The Celtic People and Renaissance Europe*, Sheed and Ward, 1933

MATTINGLY, GARRETT, *The Defeat of the Spanish Armada*, Cape, 1959

MAXWELL, CONSTANTIA, *Irish History from Contemporary Sources 1509–1610*, Allen and Unwin, 1923

MORISON, SAMUEL ELIOT, *The European Discovery of America: The Northern Voyages A.D. 500–1600*. Oxford University Press (New York), 1971

MORLEY, HENRY, ed., *Ireland Under Elizabeth and James the First*, Routledge, 1890

MORTON, GRENFELL, *Elizabethan Ireland*, Longman, 1971

NCMH 1, *New Cambridge Modern History*. Vol. 1: *The Renaissance 1493–1520*, ed. G. R. Potter, Cambridge University Press, 1957

NCMH 2, Ibid. Vol. 2: *The Reformation*, ed. G. R. Elton, Cambridge University Press, 1958

NEEDHAM, JOSEPH with WANG LING and LU GWEI-DJEN, *Science and Civilisation in China*, Cambridge University Press, 1954–71

NEF, J. U., *The Rise of the British Coal Industry*, Routledge, 1932

NICHOLLS, KENNETH, *Gaelic and Gaelicised Ireland in the Middle Ages*, Gill (Dublin), 1972

(O Clery), *Annals of the Kingdom of Ireland by the Four Masters*, ed. and trans. John O Donovan, Hodges and Smith (Dublin), 1848

O CUIV, BRIAN, *Seven Centuries of Irish Learning: 1000–1700*, Mercier Press (Cork), 1971

O FAOLAIN, SEAN, *The Great O Neill*, Mercier Press (Cork), 1970 (originally 1942)

O GORMAN, EDMUNDO, *The Invention of America*, Indiana University Press, 1961

OTWAY-RUTHVEN, A. J., *A History of Medieval Ireland*, Benn, 1968

OWEN, G. DYFFNALLT, *Elizabethan Wales: The Social Scene*, University of Wales Press (Cardiff), 1962

PARRY, J. H., *The Age of Reconnaissance*, Mentor (New York), 1964 (originally 1963)

—— ed., *The European Reconnaissance: Selected Documents*, Harper (New York), 1968

PENROSE, BOIES, *Travel and Discovery in the Renaissance 1420–1620*, Harvard University Press, 1952

POWEL, DAVID, ed., *The History of Cambria, now called Wales ... Translated into English by H. Lhoyd Gentleman ...* , London, 1584

QUINN, DAVID BEERS, *The Elizabethans and the Irish*, Cornell University Press, 1966

—— *England and the Discovery of America 1481–1620*, Allen and Unwin, 1974

—— *North America from Earliest Discovery to First Settlements: The Norse Voyages to 1612*, Harper and Row (New York), 1971

—— *Ralegh and the British Empire* (revised edition), Penguin, 1973

—— ' "A Discourse of Ireland" (circa 1599) ... ' in *Proceedings of the Royal Irish Academy*, vol. XLVII, Sect. C, No. 3, 1942

—— 'Edward Walshe's "Conjectures" ... (1552)', in *Irish Historical Studies*, vol. V, No. 20, 1947

—— 'Ireland and Sixteenth Century European Expansion', in *Historical Studies: I*, ed. T. Desmond Williams, London, 1958

—— 'Historical Revision XIII: Henry VIII and Ireland 1509–34', in *Irish Historical Studies*, vol. XII, No. 48, 1961

—— ed., *The Roanoke Voyages 1584–1590*, Hakluyt Society, 1955

—— ed., *The Voyages and Colonising Enterprises of Sir Humphrey Gilbert*, Hakluyt Society, 1940

RABB, THEODORE K., *Enterprise and Empire: Merchant and Gentry Investment in the Expansion of England 1575–1630*, Harvard University Press, 1967

RAE, THOMAS I., *The Administration of the Scottish Frontier 1513–1603*, Edinburgh University Press, 1966

RALEGH, SIR WALTER, *The Discoveries of the Large and Bewtiful Empire of Guiana*, ed. V. T. Harlow, Argonaut Press, 1928

RAMSAY, G. D., *English Overseas Trade During the Centuries of Emergence*, Macmillan, 1957

REES, WILLIAM, *The Union of England and Wales*, University of Wales, 1939

REISCHAUER, EDWIN O. and FAIRBANK, JOHN K., *East Asia: The Great Tradition*, Houghton Mifflin (Boston), 1960

RODERICK, A. J., ed., *Wales Through the Ages*, Christopher Davies (Llandybie), 1959–60

ROWSE, A. L., *The Expansion of Elizabethan England*, Macmillan, 1955

—— *The Elizabethans and America*, Macmillan, 1959

—— *Ralegh and the Throckmortons*, Macmillan, 1962

—— *Sir Richard Grenville*, Cape, 1937

—— *Tudor Cornwall*, Cape, 1941

RUSSELL, CONRAD, *The Crisis of Parliaments: English History 1509–1660*, Oxford University Press, 1971

SCOTT, SIR WALTER, *The Minstrelsy of the Scottish Border – Poetical Works*, vols. I–III, Cadell (Edinburgh), 1833

STONE, LAWRENCE, *The Causes of the English Revolution 1529–1642*, Routledge & Kegan Paul, 1972

TAWNEY, R. H., *Religion and the Rise of Capitalism*, Penguin, 1938 (originally 1926)

TAYLOR, E. G. R., ed., *The Original Writings and Correspondence of The Two Richard Hakluyts*, Hakluyt Society, 1935

THIRSK, JOAN, ed., *The Agrarian History of England and Wales*, vol. 4: 1500–1640, Cambridge University Press, 1967

TOUGH, D. W., *The Last Years of a Frontier*, Oxford University Press, 1928

TRILLING, LIONEL, *Sincerity and Authenticity*, Oxford University Press, 1974

WALVIN, JAMES, *Black and White: The Negro and English Society 1555–1945*, Allen Lane, 1973

WILLIAMS, DAVID, *A History of Modern Wales* (second edition), Murray, 1977

WILLIAMS, J. E., *The Derbyshire Miners*, Allen and Unwin, 1962

WILLIAMS, PENRY, *The Council in the Marches of Wales Under Elizabeth I*, University of Wales Press (Cardiff), 1958

—— 'The Welsh Borderlands under Queen Elizabeth', in *Welsh History Review* vol. 1, 1960–3

WILLIAMS, W. OGWEN, *Tudor Gwynedd*, Caernarvonshire Historical Society, 1958

WILLIAMSON, JAMES A., *The Age of Drake* (second edition), A. and C. Black, 1946

—— *Hawkins of Plymouth*, A. and C. Black, 1949

1603–60

ANDREWS, CHARLES M., *The Colonial Period in American History*, Yale University Press, 1934–8

ANDREWS, K. R., *Elizabethan Privateering*, Cambridge University Press, 1964

ASTON, TREVOR, ed., *Crisis in Europe 1560–1660*, Routledge & Kegan Paul, 1965

BAGWELL, RICHARD, *Ireland Under the Stuarts*, Holland Press, 1963 (originally 1909–16)

BAILYN, BERNARD, *The New England Merchants in the Seventeenth Century*, Harvard University Press, 1955

BARBOUR, PHILIP L., *Pocahontas and her World*, Robert Hale, 1971

—— *The Three Worlds of Captain John Smith*, Macmillan, 1964

BARNARD, T. C., *Cromwellian Ireland*, Oxford University Press, 1975

BATTIS, EMERY, *Saints and Sectaries: Anne Hutchinson and the Antinomian Controversy*, University of North Carolina Press, 1962

BECKETT, J. C., *The Making of Modern Ireland 1603–1923*, Faber & Faber, 1966

BOSSY, JOHN, 'The Counter-Reformation and the People of Catholic Ireland', in *Historical Studies: 8*, ed. T. D. Williams, Gill (Dublin), 1971

BOTTIGHEIMER, KARL S., *English Money and Irish Land: The 'Adventurers' in the Cromwellian Settlement of Ireland*, Oxford University Press, 1971

BOXER, C. R., *The Dutch Seaborne Empire 1600–1800*, Hutchinson, 1965

—— *The Portuguese Seaborne Empire 1415–1825*, Hutchinson, 1969

BRADFORD, WILLIAM, *History of Plymouth Plantation*, ed. W. T. Davis, Barnes and Noble (New York), 1959 (originally 1908)

BRENNER, ROBERT, 'The Civil War Politics of London's Merchant Community', in *Past and Present 58*, 1973

BRIDENBAUGH, CARL, *Vexed and Troubled Englishmen 1590–1642*, Oxford University Press, 1968

BRIDENBAUGH, CARL and ROBERTA, *No Peace Beyond the Line: The English in the Caribbean 1624–1690*, Oxford University Press (New York), 1972

BROOKS, JEROME E., *The Mighty Leaf: Tobacco Through the Centuries*, Redman, 1953

BRUCE, PHILIP A., *Economic History of Virginia in the Seventeenth Century*, Macmillan, 1896

BURNET, GILBERT, *History of His Own Time*, London, 1724–34

BURNS, SIR ALAN, *History of the British West Indies* (second edition), Allen and Unwin, 1965

BURRELL, S. H., 'The Apocalyptic Vision of the Early Covenanters', in *Scottish Historical Review 43: I*, 1964

BUTLER, W. F. T., *Confiscation in Irish History*, Talbot Press (Dublin), 1917

CHBE 1, *The Cambridge History of the British Empire*. Vol. 1: *The Old Empire, from the Beginnings to 1783*, ed. J. Holland Rose, A. P. Newton and E. A. Benians, Cambridge University Press, 1960 (originally 1929)

CHBE 4, *British India 1497–1858*, ed. H. H. Dodwell, Cambridge University Press, 1929

CELL, GILLIAN T., *English Enterprise in Newfoundland 1577–1660*, University of Toronto Press, 1969

CHAUDHURI, K. N., *The English East India Company ... 1600–1640*, Cass, 1965

CHILD, SIR JOSIAH, *A New Discourse of Trade*, London, 1693

CHRISTY, MILLER, ed., *The Voyages of Captain Luke Foxe ... and Captain Thomas James ... 1631–32*, Hakluyt Society, 1894

CLARK, SIR GEORGE, *Three Aspects of Stuart England*, Oxford University Press, 1960

CLARKE, AIDAN, *The Old English in Ireland 1625–42*, MacGibbon and Kee, 1966

COFFEY, DIARMID, *O Neill and Ormond*, Maunsel (Dublin), 1914

CRAVEN, WESLEY FRANK, *The Southern Colonies in the Seventeenth Century 1607–1689*, Louisiana State University Press, 1949

CULLEN, L. M., *An Economic History of Ireland Since 1660*, Batsford, 1972

—— *Life in Ireland*, Batsford, 1968

DARBY, H. C., *The Draining of the Fens*, (second edition), Cambridge University Press, 1956

DAVIES, K. G., *The Royal African Company*, Longman, 1957

DAVIS, RALPH, *English Overseas Trade 1500–1700*, Macmillan, 1973

(*Dean of Lismore*), *Scottish Verse from the Book of the Dean of Lismore*, ed. W. J. Watson, Oliver and Boyd (Edinburgh), 1937

DEMOS, JOHN, *A Little Commonwealth: Family Life in Plymouth Colony*, Oxford University Press (New York), 1970

DODD, A. H., *Studies in Stuart Wales* (second edition), University of Wales Press (Cardiff), 1971

DONALDSON, GORDON, *Scotland: James V to James VII*, Oliver and Boyd (Edinburgh), 1965

DUNLOP, ROBERT, *Ireland Under the Commonwealth*, Manchester University Press, 1913

DUNN, RICHARD S., *Puritans and Yankees: The Winthrop Dynasty of New England 1630–1717*, Princeton University Press, 1962

—— *Sugar and Slaves: The Rise of the Planter Class in the English West Indies, 1624–1713*, Cape, 1973

ECCLES, W. J., *France in America*, Harper and Row (New York), 1972

EDWARDS, BRYAN, *The History ... of the British West Indies* (fifth edition), London, 1819 (originally 1793)

FOSTER, SIR WILLIAM, *England's Quest of Eastern Trade*, A. and C. Black, 1933

FRASER, ANTONIA, *Cromwell*, Dell (New York), 1975 (originally Weidenfeld & Nicolson, 1973)

GORDON, SIR ROBERT, *A Genealogical History of the Earldom of Sutherland*, Constable (Edinburgh), 1813

GRANT, I. F., *The Macleods: The History of a Clan, 1200–1956*, Faber & Faber, 1959

—— *The Social and Economic Development of Scotland Before 1603*, Oliver and Boyd (Edinburgh), 1930

HALL, CLAYTON C., *Narratives of Early Maryland 1633–1684*, Barnes and Noble (New York), 1953

HALL, D. G. E., *A History of South-East Asia* (third edition), Macmillan, 1968

HAMSHERE, CYRIL, *The British in the Caribbean*, Weidenfeld & Nicolson, 1972

HARLOW, VINCENT T., *Colonising Expeditions to the West Indies and Guiana 1623–1667*, Hakluyt Society, 1925

—— *A History of Barbados 1625–1685*, Oxford University Press, 1926

HECKSHER, ELI F., *Mercantilism* (second edition), Allen and Unwin, 1955

HEXTER, J. H., *The Reign of King Pym*, Harvard University Press, 1941

HILL, CHRISTOPHER, *The Century of Revolution*, Sphere, 1969 (originally 1961)

—— *God's Englishman: Oliver Cromwell and The English Revolution*, Penguin, 1972 (originally 1970)

—— *Milton and the English Revolution*, Faber & Faber, 1977

—— *Reformation to Industrial Revolution*, Penguin, 1969

HILL, GEORGE, *... The Plantation in Ulster ... 1608–1620*, Irish University Press (Shannon), 1970 (originally 1877)

HIRST, DEREK, *The Representative of the People?: Voters and Voting in England Under the Early Stuarts*, Cambridge University Press, 1975

HUME BROWN, P., ed., *Early Travellers in Scotland*, David Douglas (Edinburgh), 1891

—— ed., *Scotland Before 1700 from Contemporary Documents*, David Douglas (Edinburgh), 1893

HUNTER, SIR W. W., *History of British India*, Longman, 1899–1900

INNIS, HAROLD A., *The Fur Trade in Canada* (revised edition), University of Toronto Press, 1956

INSH, GEORGE PRATT, *Scottish Colonial Schemes 1620–1686*, Maclehose (Glasgow), 1922

JOBSON, RICHARD, *The Golden Trade*, Penguin, 1932 (originally 1623)

JOHNSON, EDWARD, *Johnson's Wonder-Working Providence 1628–1651*, ed. J. F. Jamieson, Barnes and Noble (New York), 1959 (originally 1910)

JORDAN, WINTHROP D., *White Over Black*, University of North Carolina Press, 1968

KEARNEY, H. F., *Strafford in Ireland 1633–41*, Manchester University Press, 1959

KHAN, SHAFAAT AHMAD, *The East India Trade in the XVIIth Century*, Oxford University Press, 1923

KNORR, KLAUS E., *British Colonial Theories 1570–1850*, University of Toronto Press, 1944

KRISHNA, BAL, *Commercial Relations between India and England 1601–1757*, Routledge, 1924

LAMONT, WILLIAM and OLDFIELD, SYBIL, *Politics, Religion and Literature in the Seventeenth Century*, Dent, 1975

LANGDON, GEORGE D., Jr, *Pilgrim Colony: A History of New Plymouth 1620–1691*, Yale University Press, 1966

LASLETT, PETER, *The World We Have Lost* (second edition), Methuen, 1971

LEACH, DOUGLAS E., *The Northern Colonial Frontier 1607–1763*, Holt, Rinehart and Winston (New York), 1966

LEFROY, J. H., *Memorials of the Discovery and Early Settlement of the Bermudas or Somers Islands 1515–1685*, Longman, 1877

LETWIN, WILLIAM, *The Origins of Scientific Economics ... 1660–1776*, Methuen, 1963

LIGON, RICHARD, *A True and Exact History of the Island of Barbadoes*, London, 1673

LOUNSBURY, RALPH G., *The British Fishery at Newfoundland 1634–1763*, Yale University Press, 1934

LYTHE, S. G. E., *The Economy of Scotland in its European Setting 1550–1625*, Oliver and Boyd (Edinburgh), 1960

MacCURTAIN, MARGARET, *Tudor and Stuart Ireland*, Gill (Dublin), 1972

MCGRAIL, THOMAS H., *Sir William Alexander*, Oliver and Boyd (Edinburgh), 1940

MCINNES, C. M., *The Early English Tobacco Trade*, Kegan Paul, 1926

MACKENZIE, W. C., *The Highlands and Isles of Scotland* (revised edition), Moray Press (Edinburgh), 1949

—— *History of the Outer Hebrides*, Alexander Gardner (Paisley), 1903

MACPHAIL, J. R. N., ed., *Highland Papers*, vol. 2, Scottish History Society (Edinburgh), 1916

MARCUS, G. J., *A Naval History of England: (I) The Formative Centuries*, Longman. 1961

MILLER, PERRY, *Errand into the Wilderness*, Harvard University Press, 1956

—— *The New England Mind: The Seventeenth Century*, Harvard University Press, 1939

—— *Roger Williams*, Bobbs Merrill (Indianapolis and New York), 1953

MINCHINTON, W. E., ed., *The Growth of English Overseas Trade in the Seventeenth and Eighteenth Centuries*, Methuen, 1969

MITCHISON, ROSALIND, *A History of Scotland*, Methuen, 1970

MOODY, T. W., *The Londonderry Plantation 1609-41*, William Mullan (Belfast), 1939

MOODY, T. W., MARTIN, F. X., BYRNE, F. J., eds., *A New History of Ireland*, vol. 3: *Early Modern Ireland*, Oxford University Press, 1976

MORGAN, EDMUND S., *American Slavery American Freedom: The Ordeal of Colonial Virginia*, Norton (New York), 1975

MORISON, SAMUEL ELIOT, *Builders of the Bay Colony*, Oxford University Press, 1930

MORTON, W. L., *The Kingdom of Canada*, McClelland and Stewart (Toronto), 1963

MUMFORD JONES, HOWARD, *O Strange New World: American Culture: The Formative Years*, Chatto & Windus, 1965

MUN, THOMAS, *England's Treasure by Forraign Trade*, Blackwell (Oxford), 1928 (originally 1664)

NEWTON, A. P., *The Colonising Activities of the English Puritans*, Yale University Press, 1914

(O Clery), *Annals of the Kingdom of Ireland by the Four Masters*, ed. and trans. J. O Donovan, Hodges and Smith (Dublin), 1848

PARRY, R. H., ed., *The English Civil War and After, 1642-1658*, Macmillan, 1970

PERCEVAL-MAXWELL, M., *The Scottish Migration to Ulster in the Reign of James I*, Routledge and Kegan Paul, 1973

PETTY, SIR WILLIAM, *The Economic Writings ...* , ed. C. H. Hull, Cambridge University Press, 1899

—— *The Political Anatomy of Ireland 1672*, London, 1691

POMFRET, JOHN E. with SHUMWAY, FLOYD M., *Founding the American Colonies 1583-1660*, Harper and Row (New York), 1970

POWYS, LLEWELLYN, *Henry Hudson*, Bodley Head, 1927

QUINN, DAVID B., *England and the Discovery of America 1481-1620*, Allen and Unwin, 1974

—— *North America from Earliest Discovery to First Settlements: The Norse Voyages to 1612*, Harper and Row (New York), 1971

RABB, THEODORE K., *Enterprise and Empire: Merchant and Gentry Investment in the Expansion of England 1575-1630*, Harvard University Press, 1967

RAMSAY, G. D., *English Overseas Trade During the Centuries of Emergence*, Macmillan, 1957

RODERICK, A. J., ed., *Wales Through the Ages*, Christopher Davies (Llandybie), 1959-60

ROE, SIR THOMAS, *The Embassy of Sir Thomas Roe to India 1615-19*, ed. W. Foster, Oxford University Press, 1926

ROLFE, JOHN, *A True Relation of the State of Virginia Lefte by Sir Thomas Dale Knight in May Last 1616*, H. C. Taylor (New Haven), 1951

ROLL, ERIC, *A History of Economic Thought* (fourth edition), Faber & Faber, 1973

ROWSE, A. L., *Ralegh and the Throckmortons*, Macmillan, 1962

RUSSELL, CONRAD, *The Crisis of Parliaments: English History 1509–1660*, Oxford University Press, 1971

SCOTT, WILLIAM ROBERT, *The Constitution and Finance of English, Scottish and Irish Joint Stock Companies To 1720*, Cambridge University Press, 1910–12

SIMMONS, R. C., *The American Colonies: From Settlement to Independence*, Longman, 1976

SIMMS, J. G., *Jacobite Ireland 1685–91*, Routledge & Kegan Paul, 1969

SMITH, ABBOT EMERSON, *Colonists in Bondage: White Servitude and Convict Labour in America 1607–1776*, University of North Carolina Press, 1947

SMITH, JAMES M., ed., *Seventeenth Century America: Essays in Colonial History*, University of North Carolina Press, 1959

SMITH, CAPTAIN JOHN, *Works 1608–1631*, ed. E. Arber (Birmingham), 1884

SMOUT, T. C., *History of the Scottish People 1560–1830*, Collins, 1972 (originally 1969)

—— *Scottish Trade on the Eve of Union*, Oliver and Boyd (Edinburgh), 1963

SPEAR, PERCIVAL, *A History of India*, vol. 2 (second edition), Penguin, 1970

STEVENSON, DAVID, *The Scottish Revolution 1637–1644*, David and Charles (Newton Abbot), 1973

STONE, LAWRENCE, *The Causes of the English Revolution 1529–1642*, Routledge & Kegan Paul, 1972

STRAUSS, E., *Sir William Petty*, Bodley Head, 1954

TAWNEY, R. H., *Business and Politics Under James I*, Cambridge University Press, 1958

THOMPSON, ROGER, *Women in Stuart England and America*, Routledge & Kegan Paul, 1974

THORNTON, A. P., *West India Policy Under the Restoration*, Oxford University Press, 1956

TURNER, SIR JAMES, *Memoirs ... 1632–1670*, Bannatyne Club (Edinburgh), 1829

WASHBURN, WILCOMB E., *The Indian in America*, Harper and Row (New York), 1975

WEBSTER, CHARLES, *The Great Instauration: Science, Medicine and Reform*, Duckworth, 1975

WILKINSON, HENRY C., *The Adventurers of Bermuda* (second edition), Oxford University Press, 1958

WILLIAMS, E. ROLAND, *Some Studies in Elizabethan Wales*, Welsh Outlook Press (Newtown), 1924

WILLIAMS, ERIC, *Capitalism and Slavery*, Deutsch, 1964 (originally 1944)

WILLIAMS, ROGER, *Complete Writings*, Russell and Russell (New York), 1963

WILLIAMSON, JAMES A., *The Caribee Islands Under the Proprietary Patents*, Oxford University Press, 1926

—— *A Notebook of Commonwealth History* (third edition), ed. and rev. D. G. Southgate, Macmillan, 1967

WILLISON, GEORGE F., *Saints and Strangers* (revised edition), Heinemann, 1966

WILSON, CHARLES, *England's Apprenticeship 1603–1763*, Longman, 1971 (originally 1965)

—— *Mercantilism*, Historical Association, 1958

WINSLOW, OLA E., *Master Roger Williams*, Macmillan (New York), 1957

WINTHROP, JOHN, Sr, *Winthrop's Journal "History of New England" 1630–1649*, ed. J. K. Hosmer, Barnes and Noble (New York), 1959 (originally 1908)

ZIFF, LARZER, *Puritanism in America*, Oxford University Press, 1973

1660–1713

AJAYI, J. F. A. and CROWDER, M., eds, *History of West Africa*, vol. 1, Longman, 1971

ANDREWS, CHARLES M., *The Colonial Period of American History*, Yale University Press, 1934–8

—— ed., *Narratives of the Insurrections 1675–1690*, Barnes and Noble (New York), 1959 (originally 1915)

ANON., *Two Letters Concerning the East India Company*, London, 1676

ASTON, TREVOR, ed., *Crisis in Europe 1560–1660*, Routledge & Kegan Paul, 1965

ATKINS, JOHN, *A Voyage to Guinea, Brasil and the West Indies* (second edition) London, 1737

BAGWELL, RICHARD, *Ireland Under the Stuarts*, Holland Press, 1963 (originally 1909–16)

BAILYN, BERNARD, *The New England Merchants in the Seventeenth Century*, Harvard University Press, 1955

BARBOT, JOHN, *A Description of the Coasts of North and South Guinea and of ... Angola*, in *A Collection of Voyages and Travels*, ed. A. and J. Churchill, vol. 5, London, 1732

BARNETT, CORELLI, *Britain and Her Army 1509–1970*, Penguin, 1974

BASTIN, JOHN, ed., *The British in West Sumatra (1685–1825)*, University of Malaya Press, 1965

BECKETT, J. C., *The Making of Modern Ireland 1603–1923*, Faber & Faber, 1966

BOSMAN, WILLIAM, *A New and Accurate Description of the Coast of Guinea*, London, 1705

BRIDENBAUGH, CARL, *Cities in the Wilderness: The First Century of Urban Life in America 1625–1742*, Ronald (New York), 1938

—— *Vexed and Troubled Englishmen 1590–1642*, Oxford University Press, 1968

BRIDENBAUGH, CARL and ROBERTA, *No Peace Beyond the Line: The English in the Caribbean 1624–1690*, Oxford University Press (New York), 1972

BROOKS, JEROME E., *The Mighty Leaf: Tobacco Through the Centuries*, Redman, 1953

BRUCE, PHILIP A., *Economic History of Virginia in the Seventeenth Century*, Macmillan, 1896

BURDON, SIR J. A., *Archives of British Honduras*, Sifton Praed, 1931

BURNS, SIR ALAN, *History of the British West Indies* (second edition), Allen and Unwin, 1965

BURR, G. L., *Narratives of the Witchcraft Cases 1648–1706*, Barnes and Noble (New York), 1963 (originally 1914)

BUTLER, W. F. T., *Confiscation in Irish History*, Talbot Press (Dublin), 1917

BYRD, WILLIAM, *Prose Works* … , ed. Louis B. Wright, Harvard University Press, 1966

CAL. SP COL., *Calendar of State Papers, Colonial Series, America and West Indies, June 1708–1709*, ed. C. Headlam, HMSO, 1922, and *1710–June 1711*, ed. C. Headlam, HMSO, 1924

CHBE 1, *The Cambridge History of the British Empire*. Vol. 1: *The Old Empire* … , ed. J. Holland Rose, A. P. Newton and E. A. Benians, Cambridge University Press, 1960 (originally 1929)

CHBE 4, *British India 1497–1858*, ed. H. H. Dodwell, Cambridge University Press, 1929

CHANDLER, GEORGE, *Liverpool*, Batsford, 1957

CHILD, SIR JOSIAH, *The Great Honour and Advantage of the East-India Trade to the Kingdom, Asserted*, London, 1697

—— *A New Discourse of Trade*, London, 1693

—— *A Treatise … (Concerning The) East India Trade* … , London, 1681

CLAPHAM, SIR JOHN, *A Concise Economic History of Britain … To 1750* (revised edition), Cambridge University Press, 1957

CLARK, SIR GEORGE, *The Later Stuarts 1660–1714* (second edition), Oxford University Press, 1955

CLERK, SIR JOHN, 'Observations on the Present Circumstances of Scotland, 1730', ed. T. C. Smout, in *Miscellany X*, Scottish History Society (Edinburgh), 1965

COLEMAN, D. C., *The Economy of England 1450–1750*, Oxford University Press, 1977

—— 'Naval Dockyards Under the Later Stuarts', in *Economic History Review*, 2nd series, vol. VI, 1953–4

COMFORT, WILLIAM W., *William Penn 1644–1718*, University of Pennsylvania Press, 1944

COWAN, IAN B., *The Scottish Covenanters 1660–1688*, Gollancz, 1976

CRATON, MICHAEL, *Sinews of Europe: A Short History of British Slavery*, Temple Smith, 1974

CRATON, MICHAEL and WALVIN, JAMES, *A Jamaican Plantation: The History of Worthy Park 1670–1970*, W. H. Allen, 1970

CRAVEN, WESLEY F., *The Colonies in Transition 1660–1713*, Harper and Row (New York), 1968

—— *The Southern Colonies in the Seventeenth Century 1607–1689*, Louisiana State University Press, 1949

CREIGHTON, DONALD, *Dominion of the North* (new edition), Macmillan, 1958

CULLEN, L. M., *Anglo-Irish Trade 1660–1800*, Manchester University Press, 1968

—— *An Economic History of Ireland Since 1660*, Batsford, 1972

CURTIN, PHILIP D., *The Atlantic Slave Trade*, University of Wisconsin Press, 1969

—— *The Image of Africa: British Ideas and Action 1780–1850*, University of Wisconsin Press, 1964

DAAKU, K. Y., *Trade and Politics on the Gold Coast 1600–1720*, Oxford University Press, 1970

DAICHES, DAVID, *Scotland and the Union*, Murray, 1977

DALTON, SIR CORNELIUS N., *The Life of Thomas Pitt*, Cambridge University Press, 1915

(*Darien Papers*), *The Darien Papers ... 1695–1700*, ed. J. H. Burton, Bannatyne Club (Edinburgh), 1849

DAVIDSON, BASIL, *Black Mother*, Longman, 1970 (originally 1961)

DAVIES, K. G., *The Royal African Company*, Longman, 1957

DAVIS, RALPH, *English Overseas Trade 1500–1700*, Macmillan, 1973

—— *The Rise of the Atlantic Economies*, Weidenfeld & Nicolson, 1973

DEERR, NOEL, *The History of Sugar*, Chapman and Hall, 1949–50

DEFOE, DANIEL, *The History of the Union*, Stockdale, 1786 (originally 1709)

DEMOS, JOHN, *A Little Commonwealth: Family Life in Plymouth Colony*, Oxford University Press (New York), 1970

DONALDSON, GORDON, *Scotland: James V to James VII*, Oliver and Boyd (Edinburgh), 1965

—— *The Scots Overseas*, Robert Hale, 1966

DONNAN, ELIZABETH, ed., *Documents Illustrative of the History of the Slave Trade to America*, Octagon Books (New York), 1965 (originally 1930)

DUNLOP, ROBERT, *Ireland Under the Commonwealth*, Manchester University Press, 1913

DUNN, RICHARD S., *Puritans and Yankees: The Winthrop Dynasty of New England 1630–1717*, Princeton University Press, 1962

—— *Sugar and Slaves: The Rise of the Planter Class in the English West Indies 1624–1713*, Cape, 1973

ECCLES, W. J., *France in America*, Harper and Row (New York), 1972

EDWARDS, BRYAN, *History ... of the British West Indies* (fifth edition), London, 1819 (originally 1793)

ETTINGER, AMOS A., *James Edward Oglethorpe: Imperial Idealist*, Oxford University Press, 1936

EXQUEMELIN, ALEXANDER O., *The Buccaneers of America*, trans. A. Brown, Penguin, 1969 (originally 1678)

FERGUSON, WILLIAM, *Scotland's Relations with England: A Survey to 1607*, John Donald (Edinburgh), 1977

—— *Scotland 1689 to the Present*, Oliver and Boyd (Edinburgh), 1968

FORREST, DENYS, *Tea for the British*, Chatto & Windus, 1973

FRYER, JOHN, M.D., *A New Account of East India and Persia ... 1672 ... 1681*, London, 1698

GOSSE, PHILIP, *St Helena 1502–1938*, Cassell, 1938

HAFFENDEN, PHILIP S., *New England in the English Nation 1689–1713*, Oxford University Press, 1974

HALL, CLAYTON C., *Narratives of Early Maryland 1633–1684*, Barnes and Noble (New York), 1953

HALL, D. G. E., *A History of South-East Asia* (third edition), Macmillan, 1968

HAMILTON, ALEXANDER, *A New Account of the East Indies*, ed. Sir W. Foster, Argonaut Press, 1930 (originally 1727)

HAMSHERE, CYRIL, *The British in the Caribbean*, Weidenfeld & Nicolson, 1972

HANSEN, MARCUS L., *The Atlantic Migration 1607–1860*, Harvard University Press, 1945

HARING, C. H., *The Buccaneers in the West Indies in the 17th Century*, Archon (Hamden, Conn.), 1966 (originally 1910)

HARLOW, VINCENT T., *Christopher Codrington 1668–1710*, Oxford University Press, 1928

—— *A History of Barbados 1625–1685*, Oxford University Press, 1926

HECKSHER, ELI F., *Mercantilism* (revised edition), Allen and Unwin, 1955

HEDGES, WILLIAM, *The Diary of William Hedges ... (1681–1687)*, ed. R. Barlow and H. Yule, Hakluyt Society, 1887

HIGHAM, C. S. S., *The Development of the Leeward Islands Under The Restoration*, Cambridge University Press, 1921

HILL, CHRISTOPHER, *The Century of Revolution*, Sphere, 1969 (originally 1961)

—— *Reformation to Industrial Revolution*, Penguin, 1969

HOFSTADTER, RICHARD, *America at 1750: A Social Portrait*, Cape, 1972

HOLMES, GEOFFREY, ed., *Britain After the Glorious Revolution 1689–1714*, Macmillan, 1969

HOPKINS, A. G., *An Economic History of West Africa*, Longman, 1973

HUNTER, SIR W. W., *A History of British India*, Longman, 1899–1900

INNIS, HAROLD A., *The Fur Trade in Canada* (revised edition), University of Toronto Press, 1956

INSH, GEORGE PRATT, *The Company of Scotland*, Scribner's, 1932

—— *Scottish Colonial Schemes 1620–1686*, Maclehose (Glasgow), 1922

JEAFFRESON, JOHN CORDY, *A Young Squire of the Seventeenth Century*, Hurst and Blackett, 1878

(*Jerviswood*), *Correspondence of George Baillie of Jerviswood 1702–1708*, Bannatyne Club (Edinburgh), 1842

JOHNSON, EDWARD, *Johnson's Wonder-Working Providence 1628–1651*, ed. J. F. Jamieson, Barnes and Noble (New York), 1959 (originally 1910)

JOHNSTON, EDITH MARY, *Ireland in the Eighteenth Century*, Gill (Dublin), 1974

JONES, HOWARD MUMFORD, *O Strange New World: American Culture: The Formative Years*, Chatto & Windus, 1965

JORDAN, WINTHROP D., *White Over Black*, University of North Carolina Press, 1968

JOSEPHY, ALVIN M., Jr, *The Indian Heritage of America*, Cape, 1972

—— *The Patriot Chiefs*, Eyre and Spottiswoode, 1962

KEARNEY, HUGH, *Strafford in Ireland, 1633–41*, Manchester University Press, 1959

KELLAWAY, WILLIAM, *The New England Company 1649–1776*, Longman, 1961

KHAN, SHAFAAT AHMAD, *The East India Trade in the 17th Century*, Oxford University Press, 1923

KNORR, KLAUS E., *British Colonial Theories 1570–1850*, University of Toronto Press, 1944

KRISHNA, BAL, *Commercial Relations Between India and England 1601–1757*, Routledge, 1924

LANGDON, GEORGE D., Jr, *Pilgrim Colony: A History of New Plymouth 1620–1691*, Yale University Press, 1966

LAW, REV. ROBERT, *Memorialls ... 1638 to 1684*, ed. C. K. Sharpe, Constable (Edinburgh), 1818

LEACH, DOUGLAS E., *Flintlock and Tomahawk: New England in King Philip's War*, Macmillan (New York), 1958

—— *The Northern Colonial Frontier 1607–1763*, Holt, Rinehart and Winston (New York), 1966

LECKY, W. E. H., *A History of Ireland in the Eighteenth Century* (abridged by L. P. Curtis Jr), University of Chicago Press, 1972

LEFROY, J. H., *Memorials of the ... Bermudas ... 1515–1685*, Longman, 1877

LENMAN, BRUCE, *Economic History of Modern Scotland 1660–1976*, Batsford, 1977

LETWIN, WILLIAM, *The Origins of Scientific Economics ... 1660–1776*, Methuen, 1963

LIGON, RICHARD, *A True and Exact History of the Island of Barbadoes ...* , London, 1673

LLOYD, CHRISTOPHER, *The British Seaman*, Collins, 1968

LOCKHART, GEORGE, *Memoirs Concerning the Affairs of Scotland ... (1702–07)*, London, 1714

LONG, EDWARD, *History of Jamaica*, London, 1774

LOUNSBURY, RALPH G., *The British Fishery at Newfoundland 1634–1763*, Yale University Press, 1934

LOVE, HENRY DAVISON, *Vestiges of Old Madras 1640–1800*, Murray, 1913

LYTTELTON, EDWARD, *The Groans of the Plantations ...* , London, 1689

MacCURTAIN, MARGARET, *Tudor and Stuart Ireland*, Gill (Dublin), 1972

McINNES, C. M., *The Early English Tobacco Trade*, Kegan Paul, 1926

MACKAY, DOUGLAS, *The Honourable Company: A History of the Hudson's Bay Company*, McClelland and Stewart (Toronto), 1949 (originally 1937)

MACKENZIE, W. C., *Andrew Fletcher of Saltoun*, Porpoise Press (Edinburgh), 1935

MACKINNON, JAMES, *The Union of Scotland and England*, Longman, 1896

MacLYSAGHT, EDWARD, *Irish Life in the Seventeenth Century: After Cromwell*, Longman, 1939

MANNIX, DANIEL P. and COWLEY, MALCOLM, *Black Cargoes: A History of the Atlantic Slave Trade 1518–1865*, Longman, 1963

MARSHALL, P. J., *East India Fortunes: The British in Bengal in the Eighteenth Century*, Oxford University Press, 1976

MASTER, SIR STREYNSHAM, *The Diaries of Streynsham Master 1675–1680*, ed. Sir R. Temple, Murray, 1911

MILLER, PERRY, *Errand into the Wilderness*, Harvard University Press, 1956

—— *The New England Mind: From Colony to Province*, Harvard University Press, 1953

—— *Roger Williams*, Bobbs Merill (Indianapolis and New York), 1953

MILLER, PERRY and JOHNSON, THOMAS H., eds, *The Puritans*, Harper and Row (New York), 1963 (originally 1938)

MINCHINTON, W. E., ed., *The Growth of English Overseas Trade in the Seventeenth and Eighteenth Centuries*, Methuen, 1969

MITCHISON, ROSALIND, *A History of Scotland*, Methuen, 1970

MOORE, FRANCIS, *Travels into the Inland Parts of Africa* (second edition), London, 1738

MORGAN, EDMUND S., *American Slavery American Freedom: The Ordeal of Colonial Virginia*, Norton (New York), 1975

MORISON, SAMUEL ELIOT, *Builders of the Bay Colony*, Oxford University Press, 1930

MORTON, W. L., *The Kingdom of Canada*, McClelland and Stewart (Toronto), 1963

NEF, J. U., *The Rise of the British Coal Industry*, Routledge, 1932

OGG, DAVID, *England in the Reigns of James II and William III*, Oxford University Press, 1955

OVINGTON, JOHN, *A Voyage to Surat in the Year 1689*, ed. H. Rawlinson, Oxford University Press, 1929

PARES, RICHARD, *Merchants and Planters*, Cambridge University Press, 1960

—— *A West India Fortune*, Longman, 1950

PARRY, J. H. and SHERLOCK, PHILIP, *A Short History of the West Indies* (third edition), Macmillan, 1971

PEARE, CATHERINE O., *William Penn*, Dobson, 1959

PEPYS, SAMUEL, *Diary* ... , ed. R. Latham and W. Matthews, Bell, 1970–

PETTY, SIR WILLIAM, *The Economic Writings*, ed. C. H. Hull, Cambridge University Press, 1899

—— The Political Anatomy of Ireland 1672, London, 1691

PHILLIPS, THOMAS, A Journal of a Voyage ... 1693, 1694 ... To ... Africa ... and ... Barbadoes, in A Collection of Voyages and Travels, ed. A. and J. Churchill, vol. 6, London, 1752

PICTON, SIR JAMES, City of Liverpool: Municipal Archives and Records ... 1700 to ... 1835, Walmsley (Liverpool), 1886

PITMAN, FRANK WESLEY, The Development of the British West Indies 1700–1763, Yale University Press, 1917

PLUMB, J. H., The Growth of Political Stability in England 1675–1725, Macmillan, 1967

POPE, DUDLEY, Harry Morgan's Way: The Biography of Sir Henry Morgan 1635–1688, Secker & Warburg, 1977

PREBBLE, JOHN, The Darien Disaster, Penguin, 1970

—— Glencoe, Penguin, 1966

PRYDE, G. S., ed., The Treaty of Union of Scotland and England, Nelson, 1950

RAMSAY, G. D., English Overseas Trade During the Centuries of Emergence, Macmillan, 1957

RICE, C. DUNCAN, The Rise and Fall of Black Slavery, Macmillan, 1975

RICH, E. E., The History of the Hudson's Bay Company 1670–1870, Hudson's Bay Record Society, 1958–9

ROGERS, J. D., ... Newfoundland, Oxford University Press, 1911

SHERIDAN, RICHARD B., Sugar and Slavery: An Economic History of the British West Indies 1623–1775, Caribbean Universities Press, 1974

SIMMONS, R. C., The American Colonies: From Settlement to Independence, Longman, 1976

SIMMS, J. G., Jacobite Ireland 1685–91, Routledge & Kegan Paul, 1969

—— The Williamite Confiscations in Ireland 1690–1703, Faber & Faber, 1956

SMITH, ABBOT EMERSON, Colonists in Bondage: White Servitude and Convict Labour in America 1607–1776, University of North Carolina Press, 1947

SMITH, JAMES M., ed., Seventeenth Century America: Essays in Colonial History, University of North Carolina Press, 1959

SMOUT, T. C., A History of the Scottish People 1560–1830, Collins, 1972 (originally 1969)

—— Scottish Trade on the Eve of Union, Oliver and Boyd (Edinburgh), 1963

SPEAR, PERCIVAL, The Nabobs, Oxford University Press, 1963

STEELE, I. K., Politics of Colonial Policy: The Board of Trade in Colonial Administration 1696–1720, Oxford University Press, 1968

THIRSK, JOAN, ed., The Restoration, Longman, 1976

THOMAS, SIR DALBY, An Historical Account of the Rise and Growth of the West India Colonies ... (1690), in Harleian Miscellany ... vol. 2, London, 1744

THORNTON, A. P., West India Policy Under the Restoration, Oxford University Press, 1956

TOLLES, FREDERICK B., *Meeting House and Counting House: The Quaker Merchants of Colonial Philadelphia 1682–1763*, Norton (New York), 1963 (originally 1948)

—— *Quakers and the Atlantic Culture*, Macmillan (New York), 1960

WADSWORTH, ALFRED P. and MANN, JULIA, *The Cotton Trade and Industrial Lancashire 1600–1780*, Manchester University Press, 1931

WALKER, PATRICK, *Six Saints of the Covenant*, ed. D. H. Fleming, Hodder, 1901

WALLER, G. M., *Samuel Vetch: Colonial Enterpriser*, University of North Carolina Press, 1960

WALVIN, JAMES, *Black and White: The Negro and English Society 1555–1945*, Allen Lane, 1973

WASHBURN, WILCOMB E., *The Governor and the Rebel: ... Bacon's Rebellion ... ,* University of North Carolina Press, 1957

—— *The Indian in America*, Harper and Row (New York), 1975

WILKINSON, HENRY C., *Bermuda in the Old Empire ... 1684–1784*, Oxford University Press, 1950

WILLIAMS, ERIC, *Capitalism and Slavery*, Deutsch, 1964 (originally 1944)

—— *From Columbus to Castro: The History of the Caribbean 1492–1969*, Deutsch, 1970

WILLISON, GEORGE F., *Saints and Strangers* (revised edition), Heinemann, 1966

WILSON, CHARLES, *England's Apprenticeship 1603–1763*, Longman, 1971 (originally 1965)

WILSON, C. R., *The Early Annals of the English in Bengal*, Thacker, 1895

WINSLOW, OLA ELIZABETH, *Master Roger Williams*, Macmillan (New York), 1957

—— *Meetinghouse Hill: 1630–1783*, Macmillan (New York), 1952

WOODRUFF, PHILIP, *The Men Who Ruled India*, vol. 1: *The Founders*, Cape, 1953

WRIGHT, LOUIS B., *The Cultural Life of the American Colonies 1607–1763*, Harper and Row (New York), 1957

ZIFF, LARZER, *Puritanism in America*, Oxford University Press, 1973

1713–85

ABERNETHY, THOMAS P., *Western Lands and the American Revolution*, Appleton-Century (New York), 1937

ADAMS, JAMES T., *Revolutionary New England 1691–1776*, Little, Brown (Boston), 1941

AJAYI, J. F. A. and CROWDER, M., eds, *History of West Africa*, vol. 1, Longman, 1971

ALDEN, JOHN R., *The American Revolution 1775–1783*, Harper (New York), 1954

—— *The South in the Revolution 1763–1789*, Louisiana State University Press, 1957

ALMON, J., *Anecdotes of the Life of ... Chatham ... with his Speeches in Parliament* (seventh edition), Longman, 1810

ANSON, LORD, *A Voyage Round the World in the Years 1740–4* (written by Richard Walter), Dent, 1911 (originally 1748)

ANSTEY, ROGER, *The Atlantic Slave Trade and British Abolition 1760–1810*, Macmillan, 1975

ASHTON, T. S., *The Industrial Revolution 1760–1830*, Oxford University Press, 1968 (originally 1948)

ATKINS, JOHN, *A Voyage to Guinea, Brasil and the West Indies* (second edition), London, 1737

AYLING, STANLEY, *The Elder Pitt*, Collins, 1976

BAILYN, BERNARD, *The Ideological Origins of the American Revolution*, Harvard University Press, 1967

—— *The Ordeal of Thomas Hutchinson*, Allen Lane, 1975

BARRINGTON, SIR JONAH, *Personal Sketches of his Own Times*, Colburn, 1827–32

BASTIN, JOHN, ed., *The British in West Sumatra (1685–1825)*, University of Malaya Press, 1965

BEAGLEHOLE, J. C., *The Life of Captain James Cook*, A. and C. Black, 1974

BECKETT, J. C., *The Anglo-Irish Tradition*, Faber & Faber, 1976

—— *The Making of Modern Ireland 1603–1923*, Faber & Faber, 1966

—— *Protestant Dissent in Ireland 1687–1788*, Faber & Faber, 1948

BELOFF, MAX, *Thomas Jefferson and American Democracy*, English Universities Press, 1948

BENCE-JONES, M., *Clive of India*, Constable, 1974

BILLINGTON, RAY A., ed., *The Reinterpretation of Early American History*, Norton (New York), 1968

BOSWELL, JAMES, *Journal of a Tour to the Hebrides … 1773*, ed. F. A. Pottle and C. H. Bennett, Heinemann, 1963

—— *Life of Johnson*, ed. G. B. Hill, rev. L. F. Powell, Oxford University Press, 1934

—— *London Journal 1762–3*, ed. F. A. Pottle, Heinemann, 1950

BOXER, C. R., *The Dutch Seaborne Empire 1600–1800*, Hutchinson, 1965

—— *The Portuguese Seaborne Empire 1415–1825*, Hutchinson, 1969

BRATHWAITE, EDWARD, *The Development of Creole Society in Jamaica 1770–1820*, Oxford University Press, 1971

BRAUDEL, FERNAND, *Capitalism and Material Life 1400–1800*, trans. M. Kochan, Collins, 1974

BREBNER, JOHN B., *The Neutral Yankees of Nova Scotia*, Columbia University Press, 1937

BRIDENBAUGH, CARL, *Cities in the Wilderness: The First Century of Urban Life in America 1625–1742*, Ronald (New York), 1938

—— *Myths and Realities: Societies of the Colonial South*, Louisiana State University Press, 1952

BRIDENBAUGH, CARL and JESSICA, *Rebels and Gentlemen: Philadelphia in the Age of Franklin* (second edition), Oxford University Press (New York), 1962

BRIGGS, ASA, *The Age of Improvement 1783-1867*, Longman, 1959

BROWN, ROBERT E., *Middle Class Democracy and the Revolution in Massachusetts 1691-1780*, Cornell University Press, 1955

BROWN, WALLACE, *The Good Americans: The Loyalists in the American Revolution*, Morrow (New York), 1969

BURNS, SIR ALAN, *History of the British West Indies* (revised edition), Allen and Unwin, 1965

BURT, EDWARD, *Letters from a Gentleman in the North of Scotland* ... (second edition), London, 1759

BUSTEED, H. E., *Echoes from Old Calcutta* (fourth edition), Thacker, 1908

BYRD, WILLIAM, *Prose Works* ... , ed. L. B. Wright, Harvard University Press, 1966

CAL. SP COL. 1737, *Calendar of State Papers, Colonial Series, America and West Indies Vol. XLIII 1737*, ed. K. G. Davies, HMSO, 1963

CHBE 1, *The Cambridge History of the British Empire*. Vol. 1: *The Old Empire, from the beginnings to 1783*, ed. J. H. Rose, A. P. Newton and E. A. Benians, Cambridge University Press, 1960 (originally 1929)

CHBE 4, Ibid. Vol. 4: *British India 1497-1858*, ed. H. H. Dodwell, Cambridge University Press, 1929

CMH 7, *The Cambridge Modern History*. Vol. 7: *The United States*, ed. A. A. Ward, G. W. Prothero, and S. Leathes, Cambridge University Press, 1903

CALLAWAY, JAMES E., *The Early Settlement of Georgia*, University of Georgia Press, 1948

CAMPBELL, R. H., *Scotland since 1707*, Blackwell (Oxford), 1965

CASSIDY, F. G. and LE PAGE, R. B., *Dictionary of Jamaican English*, Cambridge University Press, 1967

CHARLEMONT, EARL OF, *Manuscripts and Correspondence* ... vol. 1, HMSO, 1891

CHAUDHURI, NIRAD C., *Clive of India*, Barrie and Jenkins, 1975

CHRISTIE, IAN R., *Crisis of Empire: Great Britain and The American Colonies 1754-1783*, Arnold, 1966

CLARK, DORA MAE, *British Opinion and the American Revolution*, Yale University Press, 1930

—— *The Rise of the British Treasury: Colonial Administration in the Eighteenth Century*, Yale University Press, 1960

CLERK, SIR JOHN, 'Observations on the Present Circumstances of Scotland, 1730', ed. T. C. Smout, in *Miscellany X*, Scottish History Society (Edinburgh), 1965

COBBAN, ALFRED, *Edmund Burke and the Revolt against the Eighteenth Century*, Allen and Unwin, 1960 (originally 1929)

COMMAGER, HENRY S. and MORRIS, RICHARD B., eds, *The Spirit of 'Seventy Six*, Harper and Row (New York), 1967

CONNELL, K. H., *The Population of Ireland 1750-1845*, Oxford University Press, 1950

2F

COOK, JAMES, *Journals* … , ed. J. C. Beaglehole, Hakluyt Society (Cambridge), 1955–69

CORKERY, DANIEL, *The Hidden Ireland: A Study of Gaelic Munster in the Eighteenth Century*, Gill (Dublin), 1967 (originally 1924)

COURT, W. H. B., *The Rise of the Midland Industries 1600–1838* (second edition), Oxford University Press, 1953

COWAN, HELEN I., *British Emigration to British North America: The First Hundred Years* (revised edition), University of Toronto Press, 1961

CRATON, MICHAEL, *A History of the Bahamas*, Collins, 1962

—— *Sinews of Empire: A Short History of British Slavery*, Temple Smith, 1974

CRATON, MICHAEL and WALVIN, JAMES, *A Jamaican Plantation: The History of Worthy Park 1670–1970*, W. H. Allen, 1970

CREIGHTON, DONALD, *Dominion of the North* (new edition), Macmillan, 1958

CRESSWELL, NICHOLAS, *Journal … 1774–1777*, Cape, 1925

[DE CRÈVECOEUR], J. HECTOR ST JOHN, *Letters from an American Farmer*, Thomas Davies, 1782

CULLEN, L. M., *Anglo-Irish Trade 1660–1800*, Manchester University Press, 1968

—— *An Economic History of Ireland Since 1660*, Batsford, 1972

—— ed., *The Formation of the Irish Economy*, Mercier Press (Cork), 1969

—— 'Irish History without the Potato', in *Past and Present* 40, 1968

CURTIN, PHILIP D., *The Atlantic Slave Trade*, University of Wisconsin Press, 1969

—— *The Image of Africa: British Ideas and Action 1780–1850*, University of Wisconsin Press, 1964

DAAKU, KWAME Y., *Trade and Politics on the Gold Coast 1600–1720*, Oxford University Press, 1970

DAICHES, DAVID, *Charles Edward Stuart*, Thames and Hudson, 1973

DALLAS, R. C., *History of the Maroons*, London, 1803

DAVIDSON, BASIL, *Black Mother*, Longman, 1970 (originally 1961)

DAVIES, K. G., *The Royal African Company*, Longman, 1957

DAVIES, RUPERT and RUPP, GORDON, eds., *A History of the Methodist Church in Great Britain*, vol. I, Epworth Press, 1965

DAVIS, DAVID BRION, *The Problem of Slavery in the Age of Revolution 1770–1823*, Cornell University Press, 1975

DAVIS, RALPH, *The Rise of the Atlantic Economies*, Weidenfeld & Nicolson, 1973

DAY, THOMAS, *Fragment of an Original Letter on the Slavery of the Negroes*, Stockdale, 1784

DEERR, NOEL, *The History of Sugar*, Chapman and Hall, 1949–50

DEFOE, DANIEL, *The History of the Union*, Stockdale, 1786 (originally 1709)

DEVINE, T. M., *The Tobacco Lords: A Study of the Tobacco Merchants of Glasgow and their Trading Activities c. 1740–90*, John Donald (Edinburgh), 1975

DICKINSON, H. T., *Walpole and the Whig Supremacy*, English Universities Press, 1973

DICKINSON, H. W., *Matthew Boulton*, Cambridge University Press, 1937

DICKSON, R. J., *Ulster Emigration to Colonial America 1718–1774*, Routledge & Kegan Paul, 1966

DOBRÉE, BONAMY, *The Theme of Patriotism in the Poetry of the Early Eighteenth Century*, British Academy, 1949

DODD, A. H., *The Industrial Revolution in North Wales* (second edition), University of Wales Press, 1951

DODWELL, H. H., *Dupleix and Clive: The Beginning of Empire*, Methuen, 1920

DONNAN, ELIZABETH, ed., *Documents Illustrative of the History of the Slave Trade to America*, Octagon Books (New York), 1965 (originally 1930)

DONOOGHUE, BERNARD, *British Politics and the American Revolution ... 1773–75*, Macmillan, 1964

DORN, WALTER L., *Competition for Empire 1740–1763*, Harper (New York), 1940

DORSON, RICHARD M., ed., *America Rebels: Personal Narratives of the American Revolution*, Pantheon (New York), 1953

DOUGHTY, A. G. with PARMELEE, G. W., *The Siege of Quebec and the Battle of The Plains of Abraham*, Dussault and Proux (Quebec), 1901

DOW, ALEXANDER, *The History of Hindostan*, Becket and De Hondt, 1768–72

DRUMMOND, ANDREW L. and BULLOCH, JAMES, *The Scottish Church 1688–1843*, St Andrew Press (Edinburgh), 1973

DUCKHAM, BARON F., *A History of the Scottish Coal Industry*. Vol. I, *1700–1815*, David and Charles (Newton Abbot), 1970

DUDLEY EDWARDS, OWEN and SHEPPERSON, GEORGE, eds, *Scotland, Europe and The American Revolution*, Edinburgh University Student Publications Board, 1976

DUNAWAY, WAYLAND F., *The Scotch-Irish of Colonial Pennsylvania*, Archon Books, 1962

ECCLES, W. J., *France in America*, Harper and Row (New York), 1972

ECHEVERRIA, DURAND, *Mirage in the West: A History of the French Image of American Society to 1815*, Princeton University Press, 1957

EDWARDES, MICHAEL, *Plassey: The Founding of an Empire*, Hamish Hamilton, 1969

EDWARDS, BRYAN, *The History ... of the British West Indies* (fifth edition), London, 1819 (originally 1793)

EITNER, LORENZ, ed., *Neoclassicism and Romanticism 1750–1850*. Vol. I, *Enlightenment/Revolution*, Prentice Hall, 1971

EQUIANO, OLAUDAH, *Equiano's Travels*, abridged and ed. P. Edwards, Heinemann Educational, 1967 (originally 1789)

ESTWICK, SAMUEL, *Considerations on the Negroe Cause ...* (third edition), Dodsley, 1788

ETTINGER, AMOS A., *James Edward Oglethorpe: Imperial Idealist*, Oxford University Press, 1936

EVANS, E. D., *A History of Wales 1660–1815*, University of Wales Press, 1976

FEHE 3, *Fontana Economic History of Europe*. Vol. 3, *The Industrial Revolution*, ed. C. Cipolla, Collins, 1973

FEILING, KEITH, *Warren Hastings*, Macmillan, 1954

FERGUSON, ADAM, *Essay on the History of Civil Society*, ed. D. Forbes, Edinburgh University Press, 1966 (originally 1767)

FERGUSON, OLIVER W., *Jonathan Swift and Ireland*, University of Illinois Press, 1962

FERGUSON, WILLIAM, *Scotland 1689 to the Present*, Oliver and Boyd (Edinburgh), 1968

FIELDHOUSE, D. K., *The Colonial Empires: A Comparative Survey from the Eighteenth Century*, Weidenfeld & Nicolson, 1966

FOGEL, R. W. and ENGERMAN, S. L., *Time on the Cross: The Economics of American Negro Slavery*, Wildwood House, 1974

FORREST, DENYS, *Tea for the British*, Chatto & Windus, 1973

FORREST, SIR GEORGE, *Life of Lord Clive*, Cassell, 1918

FRANKLIN, BENJAMIN, *Autobiography*, ed. L. W. Labaree et al., Yale University Press, 1964

FREEMAN, DOUGLAS, *George Washington*, vols 1–4, Eyre and Spottiswoode, 1948–51

FRY, HOWARD T., *Alexander Dalrymple (1737–1808) and the Expansion of British Trade*, Cass, 1970

FURBER, HOLDEN, *Henry Dundas First Viscount Melville*, Oxford University Press, 1931

FURNAS, J. C., *The Americans: A Social History of the United States 1587–1914*, Putnam, 1969

GAY, PETER, *Voltaire's Politics*, Princeton University Press, 1959

GHOSH, SURESH CHANDRA, *The Social Condition of the British Community in Bengal*, Brill (Leiden), 1970

GIPSON, L. H., *The British Empire Before the American Revolution*, Caxton (Caldwell, Ida.) then Knopf (New York), 1936–72

—— *The Coming of the Revolution 1763–75*, Harper (New York), 1954

GLEIG, G. R., *Memoirs of the Life of … Warren Hastings*, Bentley, 1841

GOEBEL, JULIUS, Jr, *The Struggle for the Falkland Islands*, Yale University Press, 1927

GOVEIA, ELSA V., *Slave Society in the British Leewards Islands at the End of the Eighteenth Century*, Yale University Press, 1965

GRAHAM, HENRY GRAY, *The Social Life of Scotland in the Eighteenth Century*, A. and C. Black, 1937 (originally 1899)

GRAHAM, IAN C. C., *Colonists from Scotland: Emigration to North America 1707–1783*, Cornell University Press, 1956

GRANT, DOUGLAS, *The Fortunate Slave*, Oxford University Press, 1968

GRANT, I. F., *The Macleods: The History of a Clan 1200–1956*, Faber & Faber, 1959

GRATTAN, HENRY, *The Speeches*, ed. H. Grattan Jr, Longman, 1822

GRIER, SYDNEY C., *The Letters of Warren Hastings to his Wife*, Blackwood (Edinburgh), 1905

GRIFFITH, SAMUEL B., *In Defence of the Public Liberty: Britain, America, and the Struggle for Independence 1760–1781*, Cape, 1977

GUPTA, BRIJEN K., *Sirajuddaulah and the East India Company, 1756–1757*, Brill (Leiden), 1962

GWYNN, STEPHEN, *Henry Grattan and his Times*, Harrap, 1939

HALDANE, A. R. B., *The Drove Roads of Scotland*, David and Charles (Newton Abbot), 1973 (originally 1952)

HALL, D. G. E., *A History of South-East Asia* (third edition), Macmillan, 1968

HALLWARD, N. L., *William Bolts*, Cambridge University Press, 1920

HAMILTON, ALEXANDER, *Gentleman's Progress ... 1744*, ed. and introd. C. Bridenbaugh, University of North Carolina Press, 1948

HAMILTON, HENRY, *An Economic History of Scotland in the Eighteenth Century*, Oxford University Press, 1963

HAMSHERE, CYRIL, *The British in the Caribbean*, Weidenfeld & Nicolson, 1972

HARLOW, VINCENT T., *The Founding of the Second British Empire 1763–1793*, Longman, 1952–64

HARVIE, CHRISTOPHER, *Scotland and Nationalism ... 1707–1977*, Allen and Unwin, 1977

HASTINGS, WARREN, *Letters to Sir John Macpherson*, ed. H. Dodwell, Faber, 1927

—— *Memoirs Relative to the State of India* (new edition), Murray, 1786

—— *Narrative of the Insurrection ... in ... Banaris ... 1781*, Calcutta, 1782

HAWKE, DAVID F., *Paine*, Harper and Row (New York), 1974

HAY, DOUGLAS, et al., *Albion's Fatal Tree: Crime and Society in Eighteenth Century England*, Allen Lane, 1975

HERTZ, GERALD B., *British Imperialism in the Eighteenth Century*, Constable, 1908

HICKEY, WILLIAM, *Memoirs 1749–1809*, ed. and bowdlerised A. Spencer, Hurst and Blackett, 1913

HILL, CHRISTOPHER, *The Century of Revolution*, Sphere, 1969

—— *Reformation to Industrial Revolution*, Penguin, 1969

HILL, S. C., *Bengal in 1756–1757: A Selection of Public and Private Papers*, Murray, 1905

HOARE, PRINCE, *Memoirs of Granville Sharp ...* , Colburn, 1820

HOBSBAWM, E. J., *Industry and Empire: An Economic History of Britain Since 1750*, Weidenfeld & Nicolson, 1968

HODGEN, MARGARET T., *Early Anthropology in the Sixteenth and Seventeenth Centuries*, University of Pennsylvania Press, 1964

HOFSTADTER, RICHARD, *America at 1750: A Social Portrait*, Cape, 1972

—— *The Progressive Historians: Turner, Beard Parrington*, Cape, 1969

HOGG, JAMES, *The Jacobite Relics of Scotland ... Second Series*, Blackwood (Edinburgh), 1821

HOLWELL, JOHN ZEPHANIAH, *India Tracts* (third edition), Becket, 1774 (originally 1758)

—— *Interesting Historical Events Relative to the Provinces of Bengal and the Empire of Indostan*, Becket and De Hondt, 1766–71

HOOK, ANDREW, *Scotland and America*, Blackie (Glasgow), 1975

HOPKINS, A. G., *An Economic History of West Africa*, Longman, 1973

HOSKINS, W. G., *The Making of the English Landscape*, Penguin, 1970

HYMES, DELL, ed., *Pidginization and Creolization of Languages*, Cambridge University Press, 1971

INNIS, HAROLD A., *The Fur Trade in Canada* (revised edition), University of Toronto Press, 1956

ISHAM, JAMES, *Observations on Hudsons Bay, 1743 ...* , ed. E. E. Rich and A. M. Johnson, Hudson's Bay Record Society, 1949

IVES, EDWARD, *A Voyage from England to India, in the Year 1754*, Dilly, 1773

JAMES, FRANCIS GODWIN, *Ireland in the Empire 1688–1770*, Harvard University Press, 1973

JARVIS, RUPERT C., *Customs Letter Book of the Port of Liverpool*, Chetham Society (Manchester), 1954

JEFFERSON, THOMAS, *The Life and Selected Writings ...* , ed. A. Koch and W. Peden, Random House (New York), 1944

JOHN, A. H., *The Industrial Development of South Wales 1750–1850*, University of Wales Press, 1950

JOHNSTON, EDITH MARY, *Great Britain and Ireland 1760–1800: A Study in Political Administration*, Oliver and Boyd (Edinburgh), 1963

—— *Ireland in the Eighteenth Century*, Gill (Dublin), 1974

JONES, HUGH, *The Present State of Virginia ...* , ed. R. L. Morton, University of North Carolina Press, 1956 (originally 1724)

JORDAN, WINTHROP D., *White Over Black*, University of North Carolina Press, 1968

KAMMEN, MICHAEL, *Empire and Interest* [1660–1783], Lippincott (Philadelphia), 1970

KELLAWAY, WILLIAM, *The New England Company 1649–1776*, Longman, 1961

KERR, BARBARA, *Bound to the Soil: A Social History of Dorset 1750–1918*, John Baker, 1968

KHAN, ABDUL MAJED, *The Transition in Bengal, 1756–1775: A Study of Saiyid Muhammad Reza Khan*, Cambridge University Press, 1969

KINVIG, R. O., *The Isle of Man: A Social, Cultural and Political History* (second edition), Liverpool University Press, 1975

KLINGENDER, FRANCIS D., *Art and the Industrial Revolution*, Paladin, 1972 (originally 1947)

KNOLLENBERG, BERNHARD, *Origin of the American Revolution 1759–1766*, Macmillan (New York), 1960

KNORR, KLAUS E., *British Colonial Theories 1570–1850*, University of Toronto Press, 1944

KNOX, JOHN, *Journal* ... , ed. A. G. Doughty, Champlain Society (Toronto)ˎ 1916 (originally 1769)

KOEBNER, RICHARD, *Empire*, Cambridge University Press, 1961

KRAMNICK, ISAAC, *The Rage of Edmund Burke*, Basic Books (New York), 1978

KRISHNA, BAL, *Commercial Relations Between India and England 1601–1757*, Routledge, 1924

LABAREE, LEONARD W., ed., followed by WILLCOX, WILLIAM B., *The Papers of Benjamin Franklin*, Yale University Press, 1959–

LANCTOT, GUSTAVE, *Canada and the American Revolution*, Harrap, 1967

LASLETT, PETER, *The World We Have Lost* (second edition), Methuen, 1971

LEACH, DOUGLAS E., *The Northern Colonial Frontier 1607–1763*, Holt, Rinehart and Winston (New York), 1966

LECKY, W. E. H., *A History of Ireland in the Eighteenth Century*, abridged L. P. Curtis Jr, University of Chicago Press, 1972

LENTIN, TONY, *Frederick the Great: Letters and Documents*, Open University Press, 1980

LEYBURN, JAMES G., *The Scotch-Irish: A Social History*, University of North Carolina Press, 1962

LINDSAY, LORD, *Lives of the Lindsays*, Murray, 1849

LLOYD, CHRISTOPHER, *The British Seaman*, Collins, 1968

—— *The Capture of Quebec*, Macmillan (New York), 1959

LONG, EDWARD, *History of Jamaica*, London, 1774

LOUNSBURY, RALPH G., *The British Fishery at Newfoundland 1634–1763*, Yale University Press, 1934

LOVE, HENRY DAVISON, *Vestiges of Old Madras 1640–1800*, Murray, 1913

LYTHE, S. G. and BUTT, J., *Economic History of Scotland 1100–1939*, Blackie (Glasgow), 1975

MACAULAY, THOMAS BABINGTON, *Critical and Historical Essays*, Dent [1907]

MACDONALD, JOHN, *Travels ... (1745–1779)*, Routledge, 1927 (originally 1790)

MCDOWELL, R. B., *Irish Public Opinion 1750–1800*, Faber & Faber, 1944

MACFARLANE, IRIS, *The Black Hole*, Allen and Unwin, 1975

MCINNES, C. M., *A Gateway of Empire* [Bristol], Arrowsmith (Bristol), 1939

[MACINTOSH, WILLIAM?], *Travels in Europe, Asia, and Africa ... 1777 ... 1781*, Murray, 1782

MACKAY, DOUGLAS, *The Honourable Company: A History of The Hudson's Bay Company*, Cassell, 1937

MACKENZIE, ALEXANDER, *Voyages from Montreal ... To the Frozen and Pacific Oceans in the Years 1789 and 1793 ...* , Cadell, 1801

MACKENZIE, W. C., *Andrew Fletcher of Saltoun*, Porpoise Press (Edinburgh), 1935

MACKESY, PIERS, *The War for America*, Longman, 1964

MALCOLM, SIR JOHN, *Life of Robert, Lord Clive*, Murray, 1836

MALONE, DUMAS, *Jefferson and His Time*. Vol. 1: *Jefferson the Virginian*, Eyre and Spottiswoode, 1948

MALONEY, THOMAS H. D., *Edmund Burke and Ireland*, Harvard University Press, 1960

MANNING, HELEN TAFT, *British Colonial Government After the American Revolution 1782–1820*, Yale University Press, 1933

MARCUS, G. J., *A Naval History of England*. Vol. 1, *The Formative Centuries*, Longman, 1961

MARSHALL, DOROTHY, *Eighteenth Century England* (second edition), Longman, 1974

MARSHALL, P. J., *East India Fortunes: The British in Bengal in the Eighteenth Century*, Oxford University Press, 1976

—— *The Impeachment of Warren Hastings*, Oxford University Press, 1965

—— ed., *The British Discovery of Hinduism in the Eighteenth Century*, Cambridge University Press, 1970

MASON, FRANCES N., *John Norton and Sons: Merchants of London and Virginia … 1750 to 1795*, David and Charles (Newton Abbot), 1968

MASON, PHILIP, *A Matter of Honour: An Account of the Indian Army, Its Officers and Men*, Penguin, 1976

MATHIAS, PETER, *The First Industrial Nation: An Economic History of Britain 1700–1914*, Methuen, 1969

MAXWELL, CONSTANTIA, *Country and Town in Ireland Under the Georges*, Harrap, 1940

METCALF, GEORGE, *Royal Government and Political Conflict in Jamaica 1729–1783*, Longman, 1965

MEYER, DUANE, *The Highland Scots of North Carolina 1732–1776*, University of North Carolina Press, 1961

MILLER, JOHN C., *Origins of the American Revolution* (revised edition), Stanford University Press, 1959

—— *Sam Adams: Pioneer in Propaganda*, Stanford University Press, 1936

MINCHINTON, W. E., ed., *The Growth of English Overseas Trade in the Seventeenth and Eighteenth Centuries*, Methuen, 1969

MINGAY, G. E., *English Landed Society in the Eighteenth Century*, Routledge & Kegan Paul, 1963

MITCHELL, CHARLES, 'Benjamin West's "Death of General Wolfe" and the Popular History Piece', in *Journal of the Warburg and Courtauld Institute*, vol. 7, 1944

MITCHISON, ROSALIND, *Agricultural Sir John: The Life of Sir John Sinclair of Ulbster 1745–1835*, Geoffrey Bles, 1962

—— *A History of Scotland*, Methuen, 1970

MOON, PENDEREL, *Warren Hastings and British India*, Hodder and Stoughton, 1947

MOORE, DONALD, ed., *Wales in the Eighteenth Century*, Christopher Davies (Swansea), 1976

MOORE, FRANCIS, *Travels into the Inland Parts of Africa* (second edition), London [1738]

MORGAN, EDMUND S. and MORGAN, HELEN M., *The Stamp Act Crisis*, University of North Carolina Press, 1953

MORISON, SAMUEL ELIOT, *John Paul Jones*, Faber & Faber, 1960

MORTON, RICHARD L., *Colonial Virginia*, University of North Carolina Press, 1960

MORTON, W. L., *The Kingdom of Canada*, McClelland and Stewart (Toronto), 1963

MULLIN, GERALD W., *Flight and Rebellion: Slave Resistance in Eighteenth Century Virginia*, Oxford University Press (New York), 1972

NCMH 7, *New Cambridge Modern History*. Vol. 7, *The Old Regime 1713–1763*, ed. J. O. Lindsay, Cambridge University Press, 1957

NCMH 8, Ibid. Vol. 8, *The American and French Revolutions 1763–1793*, ed. A. Goodwin, Cambridge University Press, 1965

NAMIER, SIR LEWIS, *The Structure of Politics at the Accession of George III* (second edition), Macmillan 1957

NEF, J. U., *The Rise of the British Coal Industry*, Routledge, 1932

NEVILLE, SYLAS, *Diary ... 1767–1788*, ed. B. Cozens-Hardy, Oxford University Press, 1950

NORTON, MARY BETH, *The British Americans: The Loyalist Exiles in England 1774–1789*, Constable, 1974

NUTTALL, GEOFFREY F., *Howell Harris 1714–1773*, University of Wales Press, 1965

O CONNELL, MAURICE R., *Irish Politics and Social Conflict in the Age of the American Revolution*, University of Pennsylvania Press, 1965

OGG, DAVID, *Europe of the Ancien Regime 1715–1783*, Fontana, 1965

OLIVER, PAUL, *Savannah Syncopators: African Retentions in the Blues*, Studio Vista, 1970

OLIVER, ROLAND and FAGE, J. A., *Short History of Africa*, Penguin, 1962

ORME, ROBERT, *A History of the Military Transactions of the British Nation in Indostan from the Year 1745*, Nourse, 1763–78

OWEN, NICOLAS, *Journal of a Slave Dealer [1746–1757]*, ed. E. Martin, Routledge, 1930

PAINE, THOMAS, *Complete Writings*, ed. P. Foner, Citadel Press (New York), 1945

PALMER, R. R., *The Age of the Democratic Revolution ... 1760–1800*, Princeton University Press, 1959–64

PANIKKAR, K. M., *Asia and Western Dominance* (second edition), Allen and Unwin, 1959

PARES, RICHARD, *King George III and the Politicians*, Oxford University Press, 1953

—— *Merchants and Planters*, Cambridge University Press, 1960

—— *War and Trade in the West Indies 1739–1763*, Oxford University Press, 1936

—— *A West India Fortune*, Longman, 1950

—— *Yankees and Creoles: The Trade Between North America and the West Indies Before the American Revolution*, Longman, 1956

PARKINSON, C. N., *The Rise of the Port of Liverpool*, Liverpool University Press, 1952

PARRY, J. H., *The Spanish Seaborne Empire*, Hutchinson, 1966

—— *Trade and Dominion: The European Oversea Empires in the Eighteenth Century*, Weidenfeld & Nicolson, 1971

—— and SHERLOCK, PHILIP, *A Short History of the West Indies* (third edition), Macmillan, 1971

PATTERSON, ORLANDO, *The Sociology of Slavery*, MacGibbon and Kee, 1967

PENNANT, THOMAS, *A Tour in Scotland and Voyage to the Hebrides 1772*, Monk (Chester), 1774

PETRIE, SIR CHARLES, *The Jacobite Movement* (third edition), Eyre and Spottiswoode, 1959

PHILBRICK, FRANCIS S., *The Rise of the West 1754–1830*, Harper (New York), 1965

PHILLIPSON, N. T. and MITCHISON, ROSALIND, ed., *Scotland in the Age of Improvement*, Edinburgh University Press, 1970

PITMAN, FRANK WESLEY, *The Development of the British West Indies 1700–1763*, Yale University Press, 1917

PLUMB, J. H., *Chatham*, Collins, 1965 (originally 1953)

—— *England in the Eighteenth Century*, Penguin, 1950

—— *The First Four Georges*, Fontana, 1966 (originally 1956)

—— *The Growth of Political Stability in England 1675–1725*, Macmillan, 1967

—— *Sir Robert Walpole*, Cresset Press, 1956–60

POLLARD, SIDNEY, *The Idea of Progress: History and Society*, Penguin, 1971

PREBBLE, JOHN, *Culloden*, Penguin, 1967

—— *Mutiny: Highland Regiments in Revolt 1743–1804*, Penguin, 1977

PROWSE, D. W., *History of Newfoundland*, Macmillan, 1895

RAGATZ, LOWELL JOSEPH, *The Fall of the Planter Class in the British Caribbean 1763–1833*, Century (New York), 1928

RAMSAY, G. D., *English Overseas Trade During the Centuries of Emergence*, Macmillan, 1957

REID, J. H. STEWART, et al., eds., *A Source-Book of Canadian History* (revised edition), Longman Canada (Toronto), 1964

REILLY, ROBIN, *Wolfe of Quebec*, White Lion, 1973 (originally 1960)

RICE, C. DUNCAN, *The Rise and Fall of Black Slavery*, Macmillan, 1975

RICH, E. E., *The History of the Hudson's Bay Company 1670–1870*, Hudson's Bay Record Society, 1958–9

ROBERTS, J. M., *The Mythology of the Secret Societies*, Secker & Warburg, 1972

ROBERTSON, SIR CHARLES GRANT, *Chatham and the British Empire*, Hodder and Stoughton, 1946

RODERICK, A. J., ed., *Wales Through the Ages*, Christopher Davies (Llandybie), 1959–60

ROGERS, J. D., ... *Newfoundland*, Oxford University Press, 1911

ROGERS, PAT, *Grub Street*, Methuen, 1972

ROLL, ERIC, *History of Economic Thought* (fourth edition), Faber & Faber, 1973

RUDÉ, GEORGE, *Europe in the Eighteenth Century*, Weidenfeld & Nicolson, 1972

—— *Wilkes and Liberty*, Oxford University Press, 1965

RUTMAN, DARRETT B., *The Morning of America, 1603–1789*, Houghton Mifflin (Boston), 1971

SALAMAN, REDCLIFFE N., *The History and Social Influence of the Potato*, Cambridge University Press, 1949

SCHAW, JANET, *Journal of a Lady of Quality ... 1774 to 1776*, ed. E. W. and C. M. Andrews, Yale University Press, 1921

SCRAFTON, LUKE, *Reflections on the Government, &c, of Indostan and a Short Sketch of the History of Bengal ... 1739 to 1756*, Edinburgh, 1761

SEMMEL, BERNARD, *The Rise of Free Trade Imperialism ... 1750–1850*, Cambridge University Press, 1970

SHARP, GRANVILLE, *The Just Limitation of Slavery ...* , London, 1776

—— *The Law of Liberty*, London, 1776

SHEPPARD, ERIC W., *A Short History of the British Army* (fourth edition), Constable, 1950

SHERIDAN, RICHARD B., *The Development of the Plantations to 1750 and An Era of West Indian Prosperity 1750–1775*, Caribbean University Press, 1970

—— *Sugar and Slavery: An Economic History of the British West Indies 1623–1775*, Caribbean University Press, 1974

SHYLLON, F. O., *Black Slaves in Britain*, Oxford University Press, 1974

SIMMONS, R. C., *The American Colonies: From Settlement to Independence*, Longman, 1976

SINCLAIR, SIR JOHN, *The Statistical Account of Scotland*, Edinburgh 1791–9

SINCLAIR-STEVENSON, CHRISTOPHER, *Inglorious Rebellion: The Jacobite Risings of 1708, 1715 and 1719*, Panther, 1973

SIRMANS, M. EUGENE, *Colonial South Carolina: A Political History 1663–1763*, University of North Carolina Press, 1966

SITWELL, SACHEVERELL, *British Architects and Craftsmen*, Pan, 1960

SMITH, ABBOT EMERSON, *Colonists in Bondage: White Servitude and Convict Labour in America 1607–1776*, University of North Carolina Press, 1947

SMITH, ADAM, *The Wealth of Nations Books 1–3*, introd. A. Skinner, Penguin, 1970 (originally 1776)

SMITH, JAMES M., ed., *Seventeenth Century America: Essays in Colonial History*, University of North Carolina Press, 1959

SMOLLETT, TOBIAS, *The History of England from the Revolution to the Death of George II*, Richardson, 1820 (originally 1757–61)

SMOUT, T. C., *A History of the Scottish People 1560–1630*, Collins, 1972 (originally 1969)

SOSIN, JACK M., *The Revolutionary Frontier 1763–1783*, Holt, Rinehart and Winston (New York), 1967

—— *Whitehall and the Wilderness: The Middle West in British Colonial Policy 1760–1775*, University of Nebraska Press, 1961

SPALDING, PHINIZY, *Oglethorpe in America*, University of Chicago Press, 1977

SPEAR, PERCIVAL, *A History of India*, vol. 2 (second edition), Penguin, 1970

—— *Master of Bengal: Clive and His India*, Thames and Hudson, 1975

—— *The Nabobs* (second edition), Oxford University Press, 1963

STEPHENS, WILLIAM, *A Journal of the Proceedings in Georgia* (facsimile of 1742 edition), University Microfilms (Ann Arbor), 1966

SUTHERLAND, LUCY S., *The East India Company in Eighteenth Century Politics*, Oxford University Press, 1952

SWIFT, JONATHAN, *The Drapier's Letters*, ed. H. Davis, Oxford University Press, 1965

—— *Irish Tracts 1728-1733*, ed. H. Davis, Blackwell (Oxford), 1955

SYPHER, WYLIE, *Guinea's Captive Kings: British Anti-Slavery Literature of the Eighteenth Century*, University of North Carolina Press, 1942

THOMPSON, E. P., *The Making of the English Working Class*, Gollancz, 1963

—— *Whigs and Hunters: The Origin of the Black Act*, Allen Lane, 1975

THOMPSON, H. P., *Into All Lands: The History of the Society for the Propagation of the Gospel in Foreign Parts*, SPCK, 1951

TOLLES, FREDERICK B., *Meeting House and Counting House: The Quaker Merchants of Colonial Philadelphia 1682-1763*, Norton (New York), 1963 (originally 1948)

TREVELYAN, G. M., *English Social History*, Longman, 1944

TREVELYAN, GEORGE OTTO, *The American Revolution*, ed. R. B. Morris, Longman, 1965 (originally 1899-1914)

TRILLING, LIONEL, *Sincerity and Authenticity*, Oxford University Press, 1974

TUNSTALL, BRIAN, *William Pitt, Earl of Chatham*, Hodder and Stoughton, 1938

VAN ALSTYNE, RICHARD W., *The American Empire*, Historical Association, 1960

—— *The Rising American Empire*, Blackwell (Oxford), 1960

VAN DOREN, CARL, *Benjamin Franklin*, Putnam, 1939

WADSWORTH, ALFRED P. and DE LACY MANN, JULIA, *The Cotton Trade and Industrial Lancashire 1600-1780*, Manchester University Press, 1931

WALKER, PATRICK, *Six Saints of the Covenant*, ed. D. Hay Fleming, Hodder and Stoughton, 1901

WALPOLE, HORACE, *Memoires of the Last Ten Years of the Reign of George II*, Murray, 1822

—— *Selected Letters*, Dent, 1959

WALVIN, JAMES, *Black and White: The Negro and English Society 1555-1945*, Allen Lane, 1973

WASHBURN, WILCOMB E., *The Indian in America*, Harper and Row (New York), 1975

WILLIAMS, BASIL, *The Life of William Pitt, Earl of Chatham*, Longman, 1913

WILLIAMS, DAVID, *A History of Modern Wales* (second edition), Murray, 1977

WILLIAMS, ERIC, *Capitalism and Slavery*, Deutsch, 1964 (originally 1944)

—— *From Columbus to Castro: The History of the Caribbean 1492-1969*, Deutsch, 1970

WILLIAMS, MERRYN, ed., *1775-1830: Revolutions*, Penguin, 1971

WILLIAMSON, JAMES A., *Cook and the Opening of the Pacific*, Hodder and Stoughton, 1946

WILLS, GARY, *Inventing America: Jefferson's Declaration of Independence*, Doubleday (New York), 1978

WILSON, CHARLES, *England's Apprenticeship 1603-1763*, Longman, 1971 (originally 1965)

WINCH, DONALD, *Classical Political Economy and Colonies*, Bell, 1965

WOLFE, J. N., ed., *Government and Nationalism in Scotland*, Edinburgh University Press, 1969

WOOD, PETER H., *Black Majority: Negroes in South Carolina from 1670 Through the Stono Rebellion*, Knopf (New York), 1974

WOODMASON, CHARLES, *The Carolina Backcountry on the Eve of Revolution*, ed. R. J. Hooker, University of North Carolina Press, 1953

WRIGHT, ESMOND, *Benjamin Franklin and American Independence*, English Universities Press, 1966

—— *Fabric of Freedom 1763-1800*, Macmillan, 1965

—— *Washington and the American Revolution*, Penguin, 1973

WRIGHT, LOUIS B., *The Cultural Life of the American Colonies 1607-1763*, Harper (New York), 1957

YOUNG, ARTHUR, *A Tour in Ireland ... [1776-9]*, Dublin, 1780

YOUNGSON, A. J., *After the Forty-Five*, Edinburgh University Press, 1973

ZIFF, LARZER, *Puritanism in America*, Oxford University Press, 1973

Index